Revenue Law: Text an

Revenue Law: Text and Materials

David Salter, LLB
Solicitor, Reader in Law, University of Warwick

Natalie Lee, LLB
Barrister, Professor of Taxation Law, University of Southampton

John Snape, MA
Solicitor, Associate Professor of Law, University of Warwick

Tottel publishing

Tottel Publishing, Maxwelton House, 41–43 Boltro Road, Haywards Heath, West Sussex, RH16 1BJ

A CIP Catalogue record for this book is available from the British Library.

ISBN 978 1 84766 084 8

Typeset by Phoenix Photosetting, Chatham, Kent
Printed and bound in Great Britain by William Clowes Limited, Beccles, Suffolk

Preface

In the early 1970s, the late Alex Easson wrote what might be described, generically, as the first sourcebook on the law of taxation, namely, *Cases and Materials on Revenue Law*. In the preface to that book, he said, 'what I have attempted to provide is a collection of materials to illustrate the basic principles, the nature of the more important problems and the application of the law to their attempted solution'; an objective that was reiterated when a second edition (written by David Salter and the late Julia Kerr) was published in 1990.

In this book, we have sought to build on and, hopefully, expand the horizons of that pathfinding book, and we have done so through a combination of commentary and materials that aims in an integrated narrative to blend aspects of tax policy and principles made manifest in diverse sources such as governmental and non-governmental reports, consultative documents and academic and extra-judicial writing with substantive law. We have concentrated on the major direct taxes in the United Kingdom, namely, income tax, corporation tax, capital gains tax and inheritance tax, and, where appropriate, we have highlighted the significance of EC law (see, particularly, Chapter 18) and the growing influence of the Convention rights identified in the Human Rights Act 1998 on tax law and practice (see, especially, Chapter 4).

This book is the product of a collective and collaborative effort and one to which each of us has made an important contribution. However, we decided that David Salter's name should be the first mentioned name in order, inter alia, to recognise his position as the initiator and leader of the project and to acknowledge the overall responsibility which he bore in shepherding the book from the early stages through to the proofreading of the final set of proofs.

We owe many debts of gratitude. We would, however, like to thank, in particular, our families for their constant and fortifying support throughout what must, at times, have seemed to them (as, indeed, it sometimes seemed to us!) to have been an interminable process. Our thanks are also extended to Juliet Doyle, our editor, who worked efficiently and unstintingly on the original manuscripts and various sets of proofs. Lastly, but by no means least, we are also indebted and extremely grateful to our publishers, Tottel Publishing (and, particularly, Sarah Blair) for their initial decision to commission this book and then for the most expeditious and professional manner in which the publication of the book was managed and overseen.

David Salter, Natalie Lee and John Snape
October 2007

Acknowledgments

We are most grateful to the following authors and publishers who gave permission for the various copyright materials to be published in this form:

Arden, The Right Honourable Lady Justice, DBE: 'The Interpretation of UK domestic legislation in the light of the European Convention on Human Rights jurisprudence' (2004) 25(3) *Statute Law Review* 165, 168–169, by permission of Oxford University Press.

Avery Jones, J F: 'Taxing Foreign Income from Pitt to the Tax Law Rewrite – the Decline of the Remittance Basis', in *Studies in the History of Tax Law* (ed Tiley, J) (Oxford: Hart Publishing, 2004). Reprinted with permission of Hart Publishing.

Bland, R: 'Hallmarks and the Direct Tax Disclosure Regime' (2006) *British Tax Review* 653, pp 653, 654–659, 659–660, 668. By permission of Sweet & Maxwell.

Bond, S: 'Taxation of Multinationals and the ECJ' in *The IFS Green Budget 2007* (eds Chote, R, Emmerson, C, Leicester, A, and Miles, D) (London: Institute for Fiscal Studies, 2007). © By permission of the Institute for Fiscal Studies.

Brewer, M, Clark, T, Myck, M: 'Credit Where It's Due' in *An Assessment of the New Tax Credits* (London: Institute for Fiscal Studies, 2001). © By permission of the Institute for Fiscal Studies.

Cnossen, S: 'What kind of Corporation Tax?' in *Key Issues in Tax Reform* (ed Sandford, C) (Bath: Fiscal Publications, 1993). Reprinted by permission of Fiscal Publications (http://www.fiscalpublications.com).

Collison, D: *Self-Assessment: Dealing with the New Income Tax Regime* (3rd edn, 1996). Reprinted by permission of CCH (a trading name of Wolters Kluwer (UK) Limited).

Daunton, M: *Trusting Leviathan: the Politics of Taxation in Britain, 1799–1914* (Cambridge: Cambridge University Press, 2001). © Martin Daunton, reproduced with permission from the author and Cambridge University Press.

Devereux, M, and Freeman, H: 'A General Neutral Profits Tax', (1991) 12(3) *Fiscal Studies*, pp 4–6. © By permission of the Institute for Fiscal Studies.

Dilnot, A, and Webb, S: 'Reforming National Insurance Contributions: A Progress Report', (1989) 10(2) *Fiscal Studies*, pp 38–47. © By permission of the Institute for Fiscal Studies.

Fabian Society: 'Paying for Progress: A New Politics of Tax for Public Spending', Fabian Commission (2000).

——: Patrick, R and Jacobs, M, 'Wealth's Fair Measure – The Reform of Inheritance Tax', Fabian Society (2003).

Freedman, J: 'Ordinary Principles of Commercial Accounting – Clear Guidance or a Mystery Tour?' (1993) *British Tax Review* 468, pp 477–478. By permission of Sweet & Maxwell.

——: *Employed or Self-employed? Tax Classification of Workers and the Changing Labour Market* (Tax Law Review Committee Discussion Paper No 1, the Institute for Fiscal Studies, 2001). © By permission of the Institute for Fiscal Studies.

——: 'Defining Taxpayer Responsibility: In Support of a General Anti-Avoidance Principle' (2004) *British Tax Review* 332, 353–356. By permission of Sweet & Maxwell.

——: 'Aligning Taxable Profits and Accounting Profits: Accounting Standards, Legislators and Judges' (2004) 2 *ejournal of Tax Research* 71. By permission of the author and the editors of the ejournal of Tax Research.

——: 'Treatment of capital gains and losses' in *The Notion of Income from Capital* (eds Essers, P and Rijkers, A) (Amsterdam: International Bureau of Fiscal Documentation , 2005). © International Bureau of Fiscal Documentation. By permission of the author and the International Bureau of Fiscal Documentation.

Gammie, M: 'Corporate Taxation in Europe – Paths to a Solution' (2001) *British Tax Review* 253, pp 244–246. By permission of Sweet & Maxwell.

Hoffmann, L: 'Tax Avoidance' (2005) *British Tax Review* 197, pp 197–198, 199–200, 201–204, 205, 206. By permission of Sweet & Maxwell.

Holmes, K: *The Concept of Income: A Multi-disciplinary Analysis,* International Bureau of Fiscal Documentation, 2001. © International Bureau of Fiscal Documentation. By permission of the author and the International Bureau of Fiscal Documentation.

Incorporated Council of Law Reporting for England and Wales: Weekly Law Reports; Appeal Cases; Chancery Reports, Kings Bench/Queens Bench Reports.

Kerridge, R: 'The Income Tax (Earnings and Pensions) Act 2003' (2003) *British Tax Review* 257, pp 257–258, 258–261, 262–264. By permission of Sweet & Maxwell.

——: 'The Rule in Sharkey v. Whernher – Time for a Reappraisal?' (2005) *British Tax Review* 287, pp 293–298. By permission of Sweet & Maxwell.

Laird, Lord Irvine of : 'The Impact of the Human Rights Act: Parliament, the Courts and the Executive' (2003) *Public Law* 308, pp 314–316, 318–319. By permission of Sweet & Maxwell.

Laws, Sir John: 'Law and Fact' (1999) *British Tax Review* 159, pp 159–162. By permission of Sweet & Maxwell.

MacDonald G, and Martin D: 'Taxing Corporate Capital Gains: Proposals for Reform' (2005) *British Tax Review* 628, pp 629. By permission of Sweet & Maxwell.

McCutcheon B, and Withers LLP: *Inheritance Tax* 4th edn (London: Sweet & Maxwell, 2005). By permission of Sweet & Maxwell.

Meade, JR: *The Structure and Reform of Direct Taxation* (London: Institute for Fiscal Studies, 1978). © By permission of the Institute for Fiscal Studies.

Moffat, M: *Trusts Law: Text and Materials* 4th edn (Cambridge: Cambridge University Press, 2005). © Graham Moffat, reproduced with permission from the author and Cambridge University Press.

Morse, G, and Williams, D: *Davies: Principles of Tax Law* 4th edn (London: Sweet & Maxwell, 2000). By permission of Sweet & Maxwell.

——: *Davies: Principles of Tax Law* 5th edn (London: Sweet & Maxwell, 2004). By permission of Sweet & Maxwell.

Office of Public Sector Information: Crown and Parliamentary copyright material reproduced under the terms of PSI and Parliamentary click-on licences respectively.

Olowofoyeku, A A: 'In the Performance of the Duties: Fact, Law or Both?' (1996) 28, pp 41–45. By permission of Sweet & Maxwell.

Park, Sir Andrew: 'A Judge's Tale: Corporation Tax and Community Law' (2006) *British Tax Review* 322, pp 323–325. By permission of Sweet & Maxwell.

Pearce-Crump, D: 'Paddocks Lodge Revisited (or Private Residence Relief Again)' (1993) *British Tax Review* 12, pp 13–17. By permission of Sweet & Maxwell.

Reed Elsevier (UK) Limited: All England Reports; Simon's Tax Cases; Simon's Weekly Tax Intelligence. Reproduced by permission of Reed Elsevier (UK) Limited trading as LexisNexis Butterworths.

Robertson, D: *Judicial Discretion in the House of Lords* (Oxford: Oxford University Press, 1998). © By permission of Oxford University Press.

Robson, M: 'Taxation and Household Survey: Reflections on the OECD Report' (1995) 16(1) *Fiscal Studies*, pp 55–56. © By permission of the Institute for Fiscal Studies.

Roxan, I: 'Imputed Income (including deductible costs)' in *The Notion of Income from Capital* (eds Essers, P and Rijkers, A) (Amsterdam: International Bureau of Fiscal Documentation, 2005). © International Bureau of Fiscal Documentation. By permission of the author and the International Bureau of Fiscal Documentation.

Royal Commission on Taxation (The Carter Commission Report) Year of publication: 1966. Reproduced with the permission of the Minister of Public Works and Government Services, Canada, 2007, and Courtesy of the Privy Council Office, Canada.

Soos, PE: 'Taxation at the Source and Withholding in England, 1512–1640' (1995) *British Tax Review* 49, p 49. By permission of Sweet & Maxwell.

Stebbings, C: 'The Revenue Adjudicator' (1993) *British Tax Review* 301, pp 302–304. By permission of Sweet & Maxwell.

Tax Law Review Committee: *Interim Report on the Tax Appeals System* (London: Institute for Fiscal Studies, 1996). © By permission of the Institute for Fiscal Studies.

: *Tax Avoidance* (London: Institute for Fiscal Studies, 1997). © By permission of the Institute for Fiscal Studies.

Tiley, J: *Revenue Law* 4th edn (Oxford: Hart Publishing, 2000). Reprinted with permission of Hart Publishing, Oxford.

——: 'Aspects of Schedule A' in *Studies in the History of Tax Law* (ed Tiley, J) (Oxford: Hart Publishing, 2004). Reprinted with permission of Hart Publishing, Oxford.

——: *Revenue Law* 5th edn (Oxford: Hart Publishing, 2005). Reprinted with permission of Hart Publishing, Oxford.

——: 'Barclays Mercantile and Scottish Provident: avoidance and highest courts; less chaos but more uncertainty' (2005) *British Tax Review* 273, pp 273, 277–278, 280. By permission of Sweet & Maxwell.

Whiting, J: 'Tax and Accounting' (2006) *British Tax Review* 267, p 272. By permission of Sweet & Maxwell.

Although care has been taken to establish and acknowledge copyright, and to contact copyright owners, the publishers tender their apologies for any accidental infringement. They would be pleased to negotiate a suitable arrangement with the rightful copyright owners in cases where such an accidental infringement may have occurred.

Contents

Table of statutes

Table of statutory instruments

Table of European and other legislation

Table of cases

PARA

A

PARA

Black-Clawson International Ltd v Papierwerke Waldhof-Aschaffenburg AG [1975] AC 591, [1975] 1 All ER 810, [1975] 2 WLR 513, [1975] 2 Lloyd's Rep 11, 119 Sol Jo 221 .... 3.28
Blackpool Marton Rotary Club v Martin (Inspector of Taxes) [1990] STC 1 .. 18.11
Blackwell (Inspector of Taxes) v Mills [1945] 2 All ER 655, 26 TC 468, 24 ATC 233, 174 LT 217 .... 8.66
Blakiston v Cooper (Surveyor of Taxes), *sub nom* Cooper (Surveyor of Taxes) v Blakiston [1909] AC 104, 5 TC 347, 78 LJKB 135, [1908-10] All ER Rep 682, 53 Sol Jo 149, 100 LT 51, 25 TLR 164 .... 7.26, 8.27, 8.29
Bloom v Kinder (Inspector of Taxes) (1958) 38 TC 77, 37 ATC 158, 51 R & IT 336, [1958] TR 91 .... 13.11
Bolam (Inspector of Taxes) v Barlow (1949) 31 TC 136, 28 ATC 10, 42 R & IT 107, [1949] TR 65, L(TC) 1479 .... 8.67
Bold v Brough, Nicholson and Hall Ltd [1963] 3 All ER 849, [1964] 1 WLR 201, 43 ATC 13, [1964] TR 17, 108 Sol Jo 177 .... 8.38
Bond v Barrow Haematite Steel Co [1902] 1 Ch 353, 71 LJ Ch 246, 9 Mans 69, 50 WR 295, [1900-3] All ER Rep 484, 46 Sol Jo 280, 86 LT 10, 18 TLR 249 .... 11.5
Bookey v Edwards (Inspector of Taxes) [1982] STC 135, 55 TC 486, [1981] TR 423 .... 3.21
Bouch v Sproule (1887) 12 App Cas 385, 56 LJ Ch 1037, 36 WR 193, [1886-90] All ER Rep 319, 57 LT 345 .... 6.19
BP Australia Ltd v Commonwealth of Australia Taxation Comr [1966] AC 224, [1965] 3 All ER 209, [1965] 3 WLR 60, 44 ATC 312, [1965] TR 317, [1966] ALR 274 .... 6.15, 10.29
Bracegirdle v Oxley [1947] KB 349, [1947] 1 All ER 126, 45 LGR 69, 111 JP 131, [1947] LJR 815, 91 Sol Jo 27, 176 LT 187, 63 TLR 98 .... 3.7
Bradbury (Inspector of Taxes) v Arnold (1957) 37 TC 665, 36 ATC 332, 51 R & IT 62, [1957] TR 333 .... 13.11
Bray (Inspector of Taxes) v Best [1989] 1 All ER 969, [1989] 1 WLR 167, [1989] STC 159, 61 TC 705, 133 Sol Jo 323, [1989] 17 LS Gaz R 43 .... 7.9, 8.36
Bridges (Inspector of Taxes) v Hewitt [1957] 2 All ER 281, [1957] 1 WLR 674, 37 TC 289, 36 ATC 87, 50 R & IT 397, [1957] TR 89, 101 Sol Jo 391 ..... 8.26
British Airways plc v Customs and Excise Comrs [1990] STC 643 .... 3.12
British Commonwealth International Newsfilm Agency Ltd v Mahany (Inspector of Taxes) [1963] 1 All ER 88, [1963] 1 WLR 69, 40 TC 550, 41 ATC 407, [1962] TR 383, 107 Sol Jo 14 .... 11.14
British Insulated and Helsby Cables Ltd v Atherton (Inspector of Taxes) [1926] AC 205, 10 TC 155, 4 ATC 47, 95 LJKB 336, [1925] All ER Rep 623, 134 LT 289, 42 TLR 187 .... 6.14, 10.21, 10.27, 10.29
British Launderers' Research Association v Hendon Borough Rating Authority [1949] 1 KB 434, 462, [1949] 1 All ER 21, 47 LGR 102, 113, 41 R & IT 564, 113 JP 72, [1949] LJR 416, 646, 93 Sol Jo 58, 117, 65 LR 103, 183 .... 3.7
British Olympic Association v Winter (Inspector of Taxes) [1995] STC (SCD) 85 .... 9.6
British Transport Commission v Gourley [1956] AC 185, [1955] 3 All ER 796, [1956] 2 WLR 41, [1955] 2 Lloyd's Rep 475, 34 ATC 305, 49 R & IT 11, [1955] TR 303, 100 Sol Jo 12 .... 8.38
Briton Ferry Steel Co Ltd v Barry (Inspector of Taxes) [1940] 1 KB 463, [1939] 4 All ER 541, 23 TC 414, 109 LJKB 250, 84 Sol Jo 59, 162 LT 202, 56 TLR 248 .... 10.37
Brocklesby v Merricks (1934) 18 TC 576 .... 13.11
Brodie's Will Trustees v IRC (1933) (1933) 17 TC 432, 12 ATC 140 .... 11.181, 6.26, 16.27
Brogan and others v United Kingdom (Applications 11209/84, 11234/84, 11266/84, 11386/85) (1988) 11 EHRR 117 .... 4.12
Brown (Surveyor of Taxes) v National Provident Institution, *sub nom* National Provident Institution v Brown (Surveyor of Taxes) [1921] 2 AC 222, 8 TC 57, 90 LJKB 1009, 125 LT 417, 37 TLR 804 .... 7.9, 7.11, 7 12

C

PARA

D

E

PARA

Helverling v Gregory (1934) 69 F 2d 809, affd (1935) 293 US 465 .... 5.12, 5.15
Henley v Murray (Inspector of Taxes) [1950] 1 All ER 908, 31 TC 351, 29 ATC 35, 43 R & IT 328, [1950] TR 25, L(TC) 1510 .... 8.36, 8.37
Henry (Inspector of Taxes) v Foster, sub nom Dewhurst v Hunter (Inspector of Taxes) (1932) 16 TC 605, 9 ATC 574, [1932] All ER Rep 753, 146 LT 510 .... 8.24, 8.37, 8 39, 8.41
Herald and Weekly Times Ltd v Federal Comr of Taxation (1932) 48 CLR 113 .... 10.34
Herbert Smith (a firm) v Honour (Inspector of Taxes) [1999] STC 173 ...... 3.18
Herbert v McQuade (Inspector of Taxes) [1902] 2 KB 631, 4 TC 489, 66 JP 692, 71 LJKB 884, 87 LT 349, 18 TLR 728 .... 8.30
Higgs (Inspector of Taxes) v Olivier [1952] Ch 311, 33 TC 136, 31 ATC 8, 45 R & IT 142, [1952] TR 57, 96 Sol Jo 90, [1952] 1 TLR 441, L(TC) 1583 .... 10.16
Hillerns and Fowler v Murray (Inspector of Taxes) (1932) 17 TC 77, 11 ATC 31, [1932] All ER Rep 814, 146 LT 474, 48 TLR 213 .... 9.3, 9.33
Hillyer v Leeke (Inspector of Taxes) [1976] STC 490, 51 TC 90, [1976] TR 215, 120 Sol Jo 571 .... 8.69, 8.76
Hinckes, Re, Dashwood v Hinckes [1921] 1 Ch 475, 90 LJ Ch 335, [1921] All ER Rep 558, 65 Sol Jo 291, 124 LT 681, 37 TLR 308 .... 5.2
Hobbs v Hussey (Inspector of Taxes) [1942] 1 KB 491, [1942] 1 All ER 445, 24 TC 153, 21 ATC 78, 111 LJKB 404, 167 LT 155 .... 13.8
Hobbs v United Kingdom (Applications 63469/00, 63475/00, 63484/00, 63684/00) (2006) Times, 28 November, [2006] ECHR 63684/00, [2006] SWTI 2506, [2006] All ER (D) 178 (Nov) 4.38
Hochstrasser (Inspector of Taxes) v Mayes [1960] AC 376, [1959] 3 All ER 817, [1960] 2 WLR 63, 38 TC 673, 38 ATC 360, 53 R & IT 12, [1959] TR 355, 104 Sol Jo 30, L(TC) 1920 .... 7.26, 8.20, 8 21, 8.23, 8 24, 8.27, 8.36, 8.39
Holland (Inspector of Taxes) v Geoghegan [1972] 3 All ER 333, [1972] 1 WLR 1473, 70 LGR 627, 48 TC 482, 51 ATC 153, [1972] TR 141, 116 Sol Jo 546 .... 8.41
Holland v IRC [2002] UKSC SPC00356, (2003) STI 62 .... 4.30
Honour (Inspector of Taxes) v Norris [1992] STC 304, 64 TC 599 .... 3.18
Hose v Warwick (Inspector of Taxes) (1946) 27 TC 459, 25 ATC 194 .... 8.32
Housden (Inspector of Taxes) v Marshall [1958] 3 All ER 639, [1959] 1 WLR 1, 38 TC 233, 37 ATC 337, 52 R & IT 60, [1958] TR 337, 103 Sol Jo 16, L(TC) 1887 .... 13.9
Household v Grimshaw (Inspector of Taxes) [1953] 2 All ER 12, [1953] 1 WLR 710, 34 TC 366, 32 ATC 133, 46 R & IT 347, [1953] TR 147, 97 Sol Jo 372, L(TC) 1644 .... 8.10
Howden Boiler and Armaments Co Ltd v Stewart (Inspector of Taxes) (1924) 9 TC 205 .... 9.10
Howe (Earl) v IRC [1919] 2 KB 336, 7 TC 289, 88 LJKB 821, [1918-19] All ER Rep 1088, 63 Sol Jo 516, 121 LT 161, 35 TLR 461 .... 11.16
Hudson v Wrightson (Inspector of Taxes) (1934) 26 TC 55 .... 9.28
Hudson's Bay Co v Stevens (Surveyor of Taxes), sub nom Stevens (Surveyor of Taxes) v Hudson's Bay Co (1909) 5 TC 424, 101 LT 96, 25 TLR 709 ..... 9.30
Humbles (Inspector of Taxes) v Brooks (1962) 40 TC 500, 41 ATC 309, [1962] TR 297 .... 8.66, 8.67
Hurlingham Estates Ltd v Wilde & Partners [1997] 1 Lloyd's Rep 525, [1997] STC 627, [1997] NLJR 453 .... 12.14

I

ICI v Colmer Case C-264/96 [1998] ECR I-4695, [1998] STC 874; [1996] STC 352; [1999] STC 1089 .... 8.15, 18.21, 18.22, 18.23
Ikimi v Ikimi [2001] EWCA Civ 873, [2002] Fam 72, [2001] 3 WLR 672, [2001] 2 FCR 385, [2001] 2 FLR 1288, [2001] Fam Law 660, [2001] 27 LS Gaz R 38, (2001) Times, 18 July, 145 Sol Jo LB 163, [2001] All ER (D) 107 (Jun) 19.12

PARA

IRC v John Lewis Properties plc [2002] EWCA Civ 1869, [2003] Ch 513, [2003] 2 WLR 1196, [2003] STC 117, 75 TC 131, [2003] 10 LS Gaz R 29, (2003) Times, 16 January, 147 Sol Jo LB 180, [2002] All ER (D) 352 (Dec) 20.3
IRC v Land Securities Investment Trust Ltd [1969] 2 All ER 430, [1969] 1 WLR 604, 45 TC 495, 48 ATC 185, [1969] TR 173, 113 Sol Jo 407, 211 Estates Gazette 405 .... 11.21
IRC v Lebus [1946] 1 All ER 476, 27 TC 136, 174 LT 358 .... 17.5
IRC v Livingston (1927) 11 TC 538, 1927 SC 251 .... 9.20, 9.29
IRC v Lysaght, sub nom Lysaght v IRC [1928] AC 234, 13 TC 526, 7 ATC 69, 97 LJKB 385, [1928] All ER Rep 575, 72 Sol Jo 270, 139 LT 6, 44 TLR 374 .... 3.14, 19.6, 19.10, 19.13
IRC v Mallaby-Deeley [1938] 4 All ER 818, 23 TC 153, 82 Sol Jo 1049, 55 TLR 293 .... 6.13, 11.19, 11.20
IRC v Mann, sub nom Re Crossman, Re Paulin [1937] AC 26, [1936] 1 All ER 762, 105 LJKB 540, 80 Sol Jo 485, 154 LT 570, 52 TLR 415 .... 20.18
IRC v Maxse [1919] 1 KB 647, 12 TC 41, 88 LJKB 752, 63 Sol Jo 429, 120 LT 680, 35 TLR 348 .... 9.12
IRC v McGuckian [1997] NI 157, [1997] 3 All ER 817, [1997] 1 WLR 991, [1997] STC 908, 69 TC 1, 94 LS Gaz R 23, 141 Sol Jo LB 153 ... 3.1, 3.24, 3.31, 3 33, 5.11, 5.12, 5 13, 5 15, 5 18
IRC v Miller [1930] AC 222, 15 TC 25, 99 LJPC 87, [1930] All ER Rep 713, 74 Sol Jo 138, 142 LT 497, 46 TLR 207
IRC v Montgomery [1975] Ch 266, [1975] 1 All ER 664, [1975] 2 WLR 326, [1975] STC 182, 49 TC 679, [1974] TR 377, 119 Sol Jo 152 .... 20.33
IRC v National Book League [1957] Ch 488, [1957] 2 All ER 644, [1957] 3 WLR 222, 37 TC 455, 36 ATC 130, 50 R & IT 603, [1957] TR 141, 101 Sol Jo 553 .... 11.17
IRC v Nelson (1939) 22 TC 716, 1939 SC 689 .... 9.33
IRC v Newcastle Breweries Ltd, sub nom Newcastle Breweries Ltd v IRC (1927) 12 TC 927, 95 LJKB 936, 96 LJKB 735, [1927] All ER Rep 287, 70 Sol Jo 734, 135 LT 618, 137 LT 426, 42 TLR 609, 43 TLR 476 .... 10.21
IRC v Northfleet Coal and Ballast Co Ltd (1927) 12 TC 1102 .... 10.21
IRC v Oban Distillery Co Ltd (Liquidator) (1933) 18 TC 33, 1933 SC 44 ..... 9.33
IRC v Old Bushmills Distillery Co Ltd [1928] NI 56, 12 TC 1148 .... 9.33
IRC v Payne (1940) 23 TC 610, 110 LJKB 323 .... 16.34
IRC v Plummer [1979] STC 793, [1980] AC 896 .... 3.31, 5.5, 5.6, 5 7, 5.12, 5 15, 16.32, 16.33, 16.34
IRC v Ramsay (1935) 20 TC 79, [1935] All ER Rep 847, 79 Sol Jo 987, 154 LT 141 .... 11.20
IRC v Reinhold (1953) 34 TC 389, 32 ATC 10, 46 R & IT 108, [1953] TR 11, L(TC) 1635, 1953 SC 49, 1953 SLT 94 .... 9.3
IRC v Scottish Provident Institution [2004] UKHL 52, [2005] 1 All ER 325, [2004] 1 WLR 3172, [2005] STC 15, 76 TC 538, (2004) Times, 26 November, [2004] All ER (D) 403 (Nov) 5.14, 5 16
IRC v Toll Property Co Ltd (1952) 34 TC 13, 31 ATC 322, 45 R & IT 574, [1952] TR 303, L(TC) 1608, 1952 SC 387, 1952 SLT 371 .... 9.33
IRC v Wattie [1999] 1 WLR 873, [1998] STC 1160 .... 5.15
IRC v Wemyss (1924) 8 TC 551 .... 16.23
IRC v Wesleyan and General Assurance Society 1948] 1 All ER 555, 30 TC 11, 27 ATC 75, 41 R & IT 182, [1948] TR 67, [1948] LJR 948, 92 Sol Jo 193, 64 TLR 173, L(TC) 1452; affd [1946] 2 All ER 749, 176 LT 84, CA 5.7, 11.6, 11.20
IRC v William Grant & Sons Distillers Ltd [2005] CSIH 63, [2006] STC 69, [2005] SWTI 1647 .... 3.1, 10.11
IRC v William Ransom & Son Ltd [1918] 2 KB 709, 12 TC 21, 88 LJKB 342, 199 LT 369, 34 TLR 533 .... 10.37
IRC v Williamson (1928) 14 TC 335 .... 17.4
IRC v Willoughby [1997] 4 All ER 65, [1997] 1 WLR 1071, [1997] STC 995, 70 TC 57, [1997] 29 LS Gaz R 28, [1997] NLJR 1062 .... 5.12, 5 18

T

1 The Characteristics of a Good Tax System

The raising of revenue through taxation is critical to the funding by government of public purposes. Over time, the policies and revenue requirements of government fluctuate as societal norms and structures change; fluctuations which may encourage the levying of new taxes and the abandonment of taxes whose utility is doubted. Any fiscal change must be examined objectively and critically. This involves not only the application to individual taxes of the principles made manifest in Adam Smith's Canons of Taxation[1] (and in subsequent refinements thereof), but also consideration of the workings and effect of the tax system as a whole, and of its interaction with the benefits system.[2] [1.1]

Adam Smith *An Inquiry into the Nature and Causes of the Wealth of Nations* (1776)

Book V Chapter II

Of taxes

The private revenue of individuals . . . arises ultimately from three different sources; rent, profit, and wages. Every tax must finally be paid from some one or other of those three different sorts of revenue, or from all of them indifferently. I shall endeavour to give the best account I can, first, of those taxes which, it is intended, should fall upon rent; secondly, of those which, it is intended, should fall upon profit; thirdly, of those which it is intended, should fall upon wages; and, fourthly, of those which, it is intended, should fall indifferently upon all those three different sources of private revenue.

. . . it is necessary to premise the four following maxims with regard to taxes in general.

1. The subjects of every state ought to contribute towards the support of the government, as nearly as possible, in proportion to their respective abilities; that is, in proportion to the revenue which they respectively enjoy under the protection of the state . . .
2. The tax which each individual is bound to pay, ought to be certain, and not arbitrary. The time of payment, the manner of payment, the quantity to be paid, ought all to be clear and plain to the contributor, and to every other person. Where it is otherwise, every person subject to the tax is put more or less in the power of the tax-gatherer, who can either aggravate the tax upon

1 Below.
2 In this respect, see, in particular, the consideration of tax credits in Chapter 15.

any obnoxious contributor, or extort, by the terror of such aggravation, some present or perquisite to himself. The uncertainty of taxation encourages the insolence, and favours the corruption, of an order of men who are naturally unpopular, even where they are neither insolent nor corrupt . . .

3. Every tax ought to be levied at the time, or in the manner, in which it is most likely to be convenient for the contributor to pay it. A tax upon the rent of land or of houses, payable at the same term at which such rents are usually paid, is levied at the time when it is most likely to be convenient for the contributor to pay; or, when he is most likely to have wherewithal to pay. Taxes upon such consumable goods as are articles of luxury, are all finally paid by the consumer, and generally in a manner that is very convenient for him. He pays them by little and little, as he has occasion to buy the goods. As he is at liberty, too, either to buy, or not to buy, as he pleases, it must be his own fault if he ever suffers any considerable inconveniency from such taxes.

4. Every tax ought to be so contrived, as both to take out and to keep out of the pockets of the people as little as possible, over and above what it brings into the public treasury of the state. A tax may either take out or keep out of the pockets of the people, a great deal more than it brings into the public treasury, in the four following ways. First, the levying of it may require a great number of officers, whose salaries may eat up the greater part of the produce of the tax, and whose perquisites may impose another additional tax upon the people. Secondly, it may obstruct the industry of the people, and discourage them from applying to certain branches of business which might give maintenance and employment to great multitudes. While it obliges the people to pay, it may thus diminish, or perhaps destroy, some of the funds which might enable them more easily to do so. Thirdly, by the forfeitures and other penalties which those unfortunate individuals incur, who attempt unsuccessfully to evade the tax, it may frequently ruin them, and thereby put an end to the benefit which the community might have received from the employment of their capitals. An injudicious tax offers a great temptation to smuggling. But the penalties for smuggling must rise in proportion to the temptation. The law, contrary to all the ordinary principles of justice, first creates the temptation, and then punishes those who yield to it; and it commonly enhances the punishment, too, in proportion to the very circumstance which ought certainly to alleviate it, the temptation to commit the crime. Fourthly, by subjecting the people to the frequent visits and the odious examination of the tax-gatherers, it may expose them to much unnecessary trouble, vexation, and oppression; and though vexation is not, strictly speaking, expense, it is certainly equivalent to the expense at which every man would be willing to redeem himself from it. It is in some one or other of these four different ways, that taxes are frequently so much more burdensome to the people than they are beneficial to the sovereign.

The evident justice and utility of the foregoing maxims have recommended them, more or less, to the attention of all nations. All nations have endeavoured, to the best of their judgment, to render their taxes as equal as they could contrive; as certain, as convenient to the contributor, both in the time and in the mode of payment, and in proportion to the revenue which they brought to the prince, as little burdensome to the people . . . **[1.1a]**

Latterly, it has been common for a fifth canon of taxation to be added to those identified by Adam Smith, namely neutrality. Broadly, neutrality requires that the tax system itself should influence as little as possible the manner in which economic activities are undertaken. Further, there is also recognition, as the following extract shows, of the need to take account of the effectiveness of tax laws in the international sphere especially in terms of their compatibility with EU law and their competitiveness with tax laws in other countries. **[1.2]**

The Structure and Reform of Direct Taxation. Report of a Committee chaired by Professor JE Meade (1978) pp 7–21

2 THE CHARACTERISTICS OF A GOOD TAX STRUCTURE

. . . As we interpret the phrase 'the structure of direct taxes in the United Kingdom' we are seeking answers to questions of the following kind: Do the various direct taxes make a coherent whole, or do they overlap and impinge on each other in an inconsistent and undesirable manner? Are there any ways in which, for example, the tax bases of the particular direct taxes and the rules relating one such tax to another could be modified so as to make the whole structure simpler, more effective and fairer in its operation?

In order to answer such questions one must have in mind what one would regard as the desirable characteristics of a tax structure. We consider the most important of these under the following six headings:

1. Incentives and economic efficiency
2. Distributional effects
3. International aspects
4. Simplicity and costs of administration and compliance
5. Flexibility and stability
6. Transitional problems

I INCENTIVES AND ECONOMIC EFFICIENCY

There are many channels through which a tax system may affect economic efficiency. It can have important effects on incentives and opportunities to work, to save, to invest in capital developments, to take risks and innovate, to use resources efficiently and to allocate them to uses which best serve the needs of society.

To a large extent these efficiency effects depend upon the total level of taxation. If the need for tax revenue to finance a large public sector is high, some tax rates will inevitably be high with inevitable effects upon some economic opportunities and incentives. We have not regarded it as part of our task to consider what is the proper balance between the public and private sectors of the economy and what, in consequence, is the proper target for total tax revenue. But there are different ways of raising a given tax revenue with differing effects upon economic opportunities and incentives; and this aspect of the matter we do regard as being at the heart of our inquiry.

The economist distinguishes between the *'income effect'* and the *'substitution effect'* of a tax burden. Thus heavier taxes on income will reduce the taxpayer's spendable income, and this consideration alone would probably make it desirable for him to work harder to restore in part his post-tax income (the 'income effect'); but at the same time a higher marginal tax rate will reduce the net spendable income which he can get from an extra hour's work, and this reduction in the extra goods which he can earn from an hour's work will tend to make him prefer leisure to work (the 'substitution effect').

'Income effects' are not a symptom of economic inefficiency and waste; they are merely the result of the most effective way of meeting the inevitable cost of given tax burdens. But 'substitution effects' are an indication of economic inefficiencies and wastes, even if they do no more than offset the influence of the 'income effects'. They may take many forms. The doctor may emigrate to substitute higher foreign earning for lower earnings at home, and some part of the differential may be due to differences in rates of tax. The wage earner may reduce his hours of work in order to substitute untaxed domestic leisure or do-it-yourself activity at home for taxed work. The housewife may substitute untaxed domestic work for taxed earnings outside the home. A business executive may refuse promotion and thus substitute his present occupation for the alternative more productive job, because the low post-tax increase in his earnings in the higher paid job would not compensate for the cost of movement to that job or for the additional strain or risk of possible failure in the higher paid and more responsible post which he is being offered. An active businessman may substitute an easy life for the energy and worry needed to improve the efficient use of his resources, because the post-tax increase in his profit makes the payoff unattractive. A saver may substitute present consumption for future consumption by himself or his heirs, because of the tax on the yield from his savings. . . .

Taxation may cause other kinds of distortion. Thus it may lead to the substitution of one form of business organisation for another. For example, differences in the tax treatment of unincorporated businesses and of incorporated businesses may lead to the choice of a form of business organisation which is not the most appropriate and efficient for the particular purpose in hand. Or taxation may lead to the substitution of a less profitable but steady business for a more profitable but fluctuating business, because with a progressive tax system the tax burden on a given average income is higher if the income fluctuates than if it is steady.

The importance to be attached to each of these possible forms of inefficiency depends upon the extent of each relevant substitution effect. Obtaining and interpreting the relevant information is difficult, and in fact little is known about the importance of these substitution effects.[3] But in principle it is a question of fact whether in any particular sector of economic activity these substitution effects are large or small . . .

2 DISTRIBUTIONAL EFFECTS

Any system of taxes is bound to have distributional effects even if it is only a matter of deciding who should bear the burden of the tax revenue needed to finance some particular level of budgetary expenditure. In some cases it is possible and appropriate to tax those particular members of society who will benefit from the particular budgetary expenditure. For example, social security has been regarded at least partly in this light, with the implication that the insured should pay contributions which are related to the benefits which they may expect to derive from the scheme. But in many cases, such as national defence, it is difficult or impossible to attribute different amounts of the benefits of the public expenditure to particular individuals or groups of individuals. Moreover, in modern society the distributional aspects of a fiscal system are often more pervasive and more purposive than the simple determination of who should bear the burden of an

3 In Appendix 2.1 we [the authors of the report] give a brief account of the existing studies which have been made of the effects of taxation on the amount of work done. The results of these studies are rather inconclusive, partly because it is difficult to distinguish between the income effects and the substitution effects of taxation. The case in which there appears to be the most marked disincentive effects of high rates of tax is in discouraging married women to seek paid work.

otherwise given level of government expenditure; progressive taxation combined with social security benefits and other elements of social expenditure (e.g. on education or health) are often expressly designed to improve the relative position of the poorer members of society.

In addition to the effect of a tax system on redistribution between rich and poor (the effects on *'vertical'* redistribution), the equity of a tax system must also be judged by the extent to which it treats fairly and equally those members of society who are equally rich or poor (the *'horizontal'* equity criterion).

The following points are clear:

1 A good tax system should be horizontally equitable, i.e. should treat like with like.

2 A modern tax system must be so constructed as to be capable of use for vertical redistribution between rich and poor.

3 There will almost inevitably be some clash between the criteria of economic efficiency (which require low *marginal* tax rates) and of vertical redistribution (which will require high *average* rates of tax on the rich); but a good tax system is one which minimises this clash and promotes a given redistribution with a minimum loss of efficiency.

4 The final choice of redistributional aims for a tax system involves basic value judgments about the nature of a good society, which are matters for political decision and are not the direct concern of the Committee; but a good tax structure is one which is sufficiently flexible to allow scope in a democratic society for different political choices (e.g. by variations in rates of tax).

Moreover, in considering the distributional effects of a fiscal system, account must be taken of certain elements of public expenditure. This is most obvious in the case of direct social transfer payments (sickness and unemployment benefits, old age pensions, child benefits, family income supplement, supplementary benefit, and so on). Indeed, the very fact that some schemes for the reform of this part of the UK fiscal and welfare arrangements are called *'negative income tax'* schemes makes the point unambiguously.[4] But other forms of public expenditure (such as the cost of rent and rate rebates or allowances, the subsidisation of the price of essential foodstuffs, the provision of free health and education) may be expressly designed in part or whole to influence distribution.

So much for general principles. Unfortunately, in considering the tax side of the budget equation neither 'horizontal equity' nor 'vertical' redistribution are in fact straightforward simple objectives, and in judging any particular tax structure it is necessary to consider in more detail how these ideas should be interpreted.

In the case of 'horizontal equity' it is often a matter of passing judgment on the effects of a change in a tax structure rather than on the nature of the tax structure itself. In this respect there is an element of truth in the adage that 'an old tax is a good tax'. If there were no existing special tax on the profits of corporate as contrasted with unincorporated business, it could be argued that a proposal to introduce such a tax with its consequential effects on share values was not horizontally equitable on the grounds that it was inequitable to tax one man who received a certain income from profits and to exempt from tax another man who received the same income from profits simply because the one arose from corporate business and the other from an unincorporated concern. But the situation is different if the tax has already been introduced and has been in operation for many years without any expectation of its removal. Businessmen will have made their choices between the corporate or unincorporated form of their concerns, and investors will have put their funds into various forms of property, on

4 [For the interaction between the tax and social security systems, see below, Chapter 14, especially para **[14.19]**.]

a comparison of expected post-tax rates of return. To remove the special tax on corporate profits would then give an unexpected advantage to the holders of ordinary shares in corporate enterprises, these shareholders being a quite different set of person (indeed possibly a totally different generation of persons) from those who owned the shares and were therefore hurt when the tax was first introduced. Everyone in the present generation will have made the same free choice between corporate and unincorporated concerns in the knowledge that the tax existed and on the assumption that it would continue. Its abolition would now favour one man more than another, though both have the same post-tax incomes . . .

. . . Horizontal equity implies that people who are equally well off should bear equal tax burdens. Vertical redistribution involves redistribution from those who are better off to those who are worse off. Thus any distributional principles involve some measurement of how well off a taxpayer is. But it is not always easy to determine what are the relevant aspects of welfare for tax purposes. One or two examples of this difficulty must suffice.

(1) Is it similarity of opportunity or similarity of outcome which is relevant? Messrs Smith and Jones both start with the same opportunities. Smith goes in for a risky career as a professional musician while Jones chooses a safe job as a civil servant. They both choose with their eyes open, taking into account the risks involved. If Smith succeeds he will be better off than Jones; if he fails he will be much worse off. If there is a highly progressive tax system, Smith will be heavily taxed if he succeeds and he may be somewhat subsidised if he is totally impoverished. This is to judge horizontal equity on the basis of outcome rather than opportunity, a result which is presumably inevitable if a tax system is simultaneously devised to promote vertical redistribution.

(2) Should differences in needs or tastes be considered in comparing taxable capacities?

There are some differences in needs which may well be considered relevant in the assessment of taxable capacity. An obvious case is the need for a larger income to provide a given standard of living for those persons who, because of incapacity of one kind or another, have greater needs for help and attention. But how should such needs be assessed? Should the deaf as well as the blind receive special tax treatment? . . .

Horizontal equity and taxable capacity raise the familiar but difficult problem of comparison of the taxable capacity of persons in different family conditions. Should family expenditure on children be regarded simply as a way in which the parents choose to enjoy the expenditure of their income, or as a measure of the increased needs of the family, or as partly one and partly the other?

(3) This leads to the closely connected question of the nature of the tax units which it is fair to employ for comparisons of taxable capacity. Is it the individual, the nuclear family, the extended family, the household or some other form of community? . . .

(4) Even when it has been decided whose welfare it is that is to be considered (e.g. the individual's or the family's), there remains the basic question what type of redistribution of welfare among tax units it is wished to promote. A frequent answer is 'less inequality'. But there is no simple single measurement of the degree of equality or inequality in any distribution. There is a very large number of types of change in a distributional pattern, and the relative importance which is attached to these different possibilities raises basic value judgments about the nature of the good society. One attitude is to be concerned primarily, even solely, with raising the standards of the poorest members of society. On this view little or no importance will be attached to the degree of inequality or equality between those in the middle and top ranges who are well above the minimum level. Others will regard it as offensive that there should be very large concentrations of riches at the top, and

would regard it as a matter of importance to reduce inequalities between the rich and the poor even if this involved no improvement in the standard of living of the poor. Indeed some persons might put such emphasis on the moral merits of the egalitarian society without distinctions of riches and poverty that they would advocate carrying the taxation of the rich to a point at which the effect on incentives might so reduce the national income that there was even some net reduction in material standards of living throughout the population . . .

3 INTERNATIONAL ASPECTS

The Committee has . . . conducted its survey of the UK tax structure on the assumption that the international order will continue to be relatively free and liberal. This itself sets certain constraints on the UK fiscal system. To some extent these constraints arise not so much from the form of the national tax structure, but rather as a result of the level and the distribution of national tax burdens. The more intimate and free are the international economic and financial relationships, the more important it becomes for the national governments concerned not to get too far out of step in their fiscal systems . . . Experience suggests that there can be quite marked differences in national tax burdens without these resulting in extensive movements of capital and of persons to low tax centres; but the fact remains that some loss will occur and that this loss will be the greater, the more freely persons and capital learn to move and the greater are the differences of tax burdens.

But the incentive for inefficient international movements of capital and persons may be due not only to the general level and distribution of national tax burdens but also to differences in the structure and form of national taxes . . .

. . . international constraints on a national tax structure may arise in more precise forms from specific international treaty or other obligations. Such obligations in the case of the United Kingdom can be enumerated under three headings:

1. There are the general obligations undertaken as a member of international organisations of broad scope, such as the International Monetary Fund and the General Agreement on Tariffs and Trade.
2. There are the more specific obligations and programmes for tax harmonisation of the European Economic Community.
3. There are a number of bilateral double taxation agreements with many other countries containing specific rules for the treatment of the taxes levied in the other . . .

For a country like the United Kingdom an extremely important criterion for a good tax structure is the ease with which it can be fitted into the existing system of international economic and financial relationships and obligations. Given the tax structures of other countries, would a given tax structure in the United Kingdom be likely to lead to serious distortions in the movement of goods, capital and persons? How difficult would it be to modify it in such a way as to avoid any such distortions? Is the tax structure so modified compatible with existing international obligations? If not, what prospect is there of obtaining some appropriate change in those obligations?

4 SIMPLICITY AND COSTS OF ADMINISTRATION AND COMPLIANCE

In addition to being efficient and just and compatible with the country's international position, a good tax system should also be coherent, simple and straightforward.

In a democratic society one of the most important aspects of a tax system is that the taxing authorities should be accountable to the electorate at large. This can be so only if the tax system is such that the man and woman in the street can comprehend clearly what is the nature of the taxpayer's liability. Tax burdens which are disguised by inflationary movements of prices, or by complexities in the devising or the administration of the tax, or by uncertainties in its application cannot properly meet this criterion of simplicity. There are many aspects to this quality.

In the first place, it should be clear to the taxpayer what is and what is not taxable. Different taxes score differently on this head. In the case of an income tax there are well-known difficulties in defining precisely what is an income, what is a capital gain and what is a simple capital receipt. In the case of a tax on consumption there would be the, perhaps somewhat easier, problem of defining precisely what items of expenditure were to be defined as items of current expenditure.

Closely allied to this question of the clear definition of what is to be taxed is the question of certainty as to the amount of tax which should be paid on each taxable object. On this head also different taxes score differently. Problems of valuation are particularly important in this connection ...

Moreover, precision of definition of the tax base and of the consequential tax liability is not the only element in ease of understanding. The taxpayer should, as far as possible, be able not only to see clearly what is to be taxed, but also to understand the purpose which it is intended to serve by choosing the particular form of tax. The principle on which the tax base is chosen should also itself be simple and easy to perceive ...

... A tax system cannot be simple and easy to understand unless it makes a coherent whole. This aspect of a good tax system lies at the heart of the matter for the Committee, since it is the main purpose of the Committee to examine the tax structure as a whole and to judge whether the different parts are consistent with each other ...

A tax system must be acceptable to the public, and simplicity of the system is necessary for acceptability. Moreover, a tax system based on one or two simple clear-cut principles will make unjustifiable concessions to special interests more obvious and therefore easier to resist.

Another aspect of the simplicity of a tax system is to be found in the case of its administration. Ease of understanding by the taxpayer and simplicity of administration may often be combined, but they are by no means always to be found together ...

In the case of ease of administration a distinction must be drawn between complexity of administration and costs of administration. Normally complexity leads to costs; but although these two things may often go together it is not necessarily always the case ...

The costs of application of a given system of taxation must be judged not only by their official administrative costs but also by the costs which the private taxpayers must incur in order to cope with their tax liabilities. There is evidence[5] that such private compliance costs are often heavy and in many cases much heavier than the official administrative costs themselves. Such costs of compliance may be reduced by ensuring that the tax system is simple, straightforward and precise – qualities which are desirable in themselves in order to make the tax system easy to understand; for the more straightforward are the taxpayer's obligations, the less time and trouble need be spent on the preparation of tax returns and appeals. Moreover, there is less scope for the expenditure of time and resources on the search for complicated ways to reduce legal liabilities of tax. But even in the case of a straightforward precise tax the private costs of compliance may be considerable when, as in the case of deduction of tax on wages at the source by the employer

5 See Appendix 22.1 [to the Meade Report].

through a pay-as-you-earn (PAYE) scheme, a private body or person is used to collect the tax revenue.

The total social cost of tax collection must include private compliance costs and official administrative costs. In some cases (e.g. PAYE) the cheapest method of collecting a tax may well be to make use of private individuals or businesses as agents for the collection of tax. Moreover, it is arguable that the imposition of some of the costs of tax gathering on private persons and companies may itself lead to a desirable insistence on simplicity for tax arrangements in the interests of reduction of collection costs, and that to leave to competing firms the task of tax collection may induce a healthy search for the most efficient methods of carrying out the operation.

On the other hand, other things being equal, there are at least three reasons for tipping the balance away from compliance costs on to official administrative costs where it is reasonably possible to make a choice of administrative arrangements which have this effect.

1 Administrative costs are themselves met from taxation which can itself be determined with reference to fairness of tax burden, whereas compliance costs fall on the private taxpayer and can be markedly regressive in their incidence.
2 Compliance costs are likely to be much resented by taxpayers, particularly where much time and trouble must be spent by small taxpayers only to show a very low or indeed a nil liability to tax.
3 Administrative costs are easier of ascertainment and more open to public scrutiny than are compliance costs.

5 FLEXIBILITY AND STABILITY

A good tax structure must be flexible for two rather distinct purposes, the first being primarily economic and the second primarily political.

In the former category there must be recognition of the need to be able to adjust total tax burdens reasonably rapidly and frequently in the interest of demand management. One of the tools of control in the hands of Western governments is to plan total taxation in part as a means for the stimulation or restriction of the total demand for goods and services by the private sector of the economy. Fashions change in the relative emphasis placed on monetary policy and on fiscal policy for this purpose; but unless and until there is general political agreement that fiscal policy should not be used for this purpose, one criterion for an acceptable tax structure is that it should contain important elements which can be varied flexibly for this purpose.

But in a democratic community flexibility in a tax system is needed for a more basically political reason. Different political parties represent in part different political, social and economic philosophies. In a healthy democratic society there must be broad political consensus – or at least willingness to compromise – over certain basic matters; but there must at the same time be the possibility of changes of emphasis in economic policy as one government succeeds another. Such changes of emphasis will show themselves in the trade-off which is preferred among the various objectives of a good tax system. How much adverse effect on incentives will one government accept in order to obtain a given decrease in inequalities of standards of living? How complicated is one government prepared to make the tax rules in order to achieve a given measure of horizontal equity in taxation? How far is one government ready to control international movements of goods, capital or persons in order to achieve a given domestic objective? . . .

But at the same time there is a clear need for a certain stability in taxation in order that persons may be in a position to make reasonably far-sighted plans.

Fundamental uncertainty breeds lack of confidence and is a serious impediment to production and prosperity . . .

CONCLUSIONS

The choice of tax structure must take into account many factors: the effects on economic incentives; its fairness as between persons of similar taxable capacity; its effects upon distribution between rich and poor; whether it is compatible with desirable international economic relations; and its simplicity, ease of understanding, and absence of excessive administrative costs. The transition from one tax structure to another inevitably takes time and involves costs which must be set against any gains expected from the new structure. Where these various characteristics conflict, it is an essential function of the political process to determine how much weight to give to each of them . . . **[1.3]**

Following an acknowledgment by the Chancellor of the Exchequer, the Right Honourable Kenneth Clarke MP, in his 1995 budget statement that tax law had become 'too long and too complicated', a project, the Tax Law Rewrite, was initiated in the following year with a view to rewriting in a clearer form and language most of the existing direct tax legislation.[6] The principal aim of the Tax Law Rewrite is to preserve the application of the legislation but not its language, whilst accepting that changes in language may lead in the search for clarity to some minor changes of substance. Initially, progress was slow, but, presently, four rewrite statutes have been enacted, namely the Capital Allowances Act 2001 (CAA 2001), the Income Tax (Earnings and Pensions) Act 2003 (ITEPA 2003), the Income Tax (Trading and Other Income) Act 2005 (ITTOIA 2005), and the Income Tax Act 2007 (ITA 2007),[7] each of which is referred to, where appropriate, in subsequent chapters. **[1.4]**

Roger Kerridge 'The Income Tax (Earnings and Pensions) Act 2003' [2003] BTR 257, 257–258; see also paras [1.7] and [8.2]

The Rewrite

The Tax Law Rewrite is an awesome undertaking. It sets out to rewrite the whole of United Kingdom direct tax legislation in clearer, simpler language. A project team has been given the task of rewriting almost all of the United Kingdom's primary direct tax legislation, the work is overseen by a Steering Committee, chaired by Lord Howe of Aberavon, and is also reviewed by a Consultative Committee, representing the accountancy and legal professions and the interests of taxpayers. There has been public consultation in the form of a series of Exposure Drafts which have published clauses in draft . . .

Rewrite bills are not consolidation bills, but neither should they, to any significant extent, represent new law: they aim to reproduce the effect of existing law. Because of this, Parliament has adopted a new streamlined procedure whereby, after a Rewrite bill has been introduced in the House of Commons, it is referred on Second

6 This includes the taxes which are covered in this book, namely income tax, corporation tax, capital gains tax and inheritance tax.

7 It is intended that the rewrite of corporation tax will be completed in the next three years; see Tax Law Rewrite – Report and Plans 2007/08.

Reading to a Joint Committee of both Houses of Parliament. This committee's task is to scrutinise the rewritten legislation, but not to debate fiscal policy matters.

When the Rewrite project began in, in 1996, it was suggested, with what now appears to have been surprising optimism, that the first Rewrite bill would be enacted by 1998 and it seems to have been assumed, at that stage, that the entire project, the rewriting of the whole of United Kingdom direct taxation, would be completed within five years, i.e. by about 2002 ... The whole process has proved much slower, more time consuming, and more expensive, than originally envisaged ...

What the Rewrite attempts to do is to set out the relevant legislation in such a way as to give it a new, more logical structure, to use modern language, shorter sentences, better use of definitions,[8] better signposting and a new format and layout to make it easier to read, but without changing the substance ... **[1.5]**

See also David Salter 'Pre-Parliamentary Procedure, Consultation and the Tax Law Rewrite' (1997) 16 CJQ 294 and 'Towards a Parliamentary Procedure for the Tax Law Rewrite' (1998) 19 Stat LR 65. **[1.5a]**

As seen above, the limited remit of the Tax Law Rewrite precludes substantial changes to the law through rewriting (although, it is open to the Steering Committee to draw to the attention of government matters unearthed during the rewriting process that may be considered for inclusion in subsequent legislation). As a result, it has been variously suggested, *inter alia*, that the Tax Law Rewrite could usefully be complemented by the establishment of a body charged specifically with reviewing tax legislation particularly from the perspective of simplifying the tax system. **[1.6]**

Roger Kerridge 'The Income Tax (Earnings and Pensions) Act 2003' [2003] BTR 257, 262–264; see also paras [1.5] and [8.2]

Simplifying the United Kingdom tax system

Simplification of the United Kingdom tax system could take various different forms. At its most radical it could involve scrapping all our existing taxes and replacing them with something completely different – something along the lines suggested in the 1970s by the Meade Committee. For all sorts of reasons, something this radical is very unlikely to occur. On a lower plane, it could involve purposive re-drafting of existing legislation, not the sort of re-drafting to be found in the Rewrite, but re-drafting in a completely different style. Some contributors to this journal have been in favour of purposive drafting. Whether existing legislation can be redrafted purposively depends on whether its purposes can be discerned. There seems to be disagreement about this.[9] The present writer believes that there would be no

8 Sch 1, Pt 2 of the Act is an index of expressions defined in the Act. Lord Brightman, during the course of the Meeting of the Joint Parliamentary Committee on January 14 2003, noted how helpful it was to have such an index, but thought that, when further Rewrite legislation is being planned, it would be better if the indices were put at the end, to make them easier to locate.

9 John Avery Jones [1996] BTR 580 and Leonard Beighton [1998] BTR 273 have both spoken in favour of purposive drafting, for the future at least; John Prebble, by contrast appears to believe that income tax legislation cannot be drafted purposively, because he believes that income tax legislation is an artificial construct, see [1994] BTR 380 and [1998] BTR 112.

problem, in principle, in drafting, or redrafting, income tax legislation purposively, but, again, it is too big a step to take at the present time. It would involve too much change and would take too long. Having said this, it is quite possible to aim for something somewhere between a purposive re-draft on the one hand and the present form of the Rewrite on the other. A purposive re-draft may be over-ambitious, but to think of the Rewrite, in its present form, as the culmination of some sort of simplification process is to be too easily satisfied. What is now needed is to set in train a process whereby the legislation is *first* rewritten and *then* simplified.

A turning point

We are now at a turning point. Any attempt at simplification of the United Kingdom tax system could stall here. If it does, it will be a wasted opportunity. The Rewrite has highlighted all sorts of oddities and inconsistencies and has cruelly exposed laws which are 'inconsistent, irrational and fundamentally complex.'[10] So, now is the time to begin the real simplification process. In areas where the basic rules have never been properly thought through, and where the failure to think them through has been disguised by layers, and then further layers, of detail,[11] they must be thought through. It is not good enough simply to set out the layers of the detail neatly . . .

What is needed is the creation of a body whose job it is to scrutinise the rewritten legislation and to simplify it. This means amending it. Such a body could, as a long term objective, move towards purposive redrafting, but it could only do this after it had given thought to purposes. In the shorter term, it would need to construct basic rules where they do not exist, or where they are not clear, and, at the same time, carry out a radical simplification of the existing structure. What is needed is a rolling reform programme overseen by some sort of Tax Law Reform Committee. This is certainly not a new idea. It was suggested in 1977 by Sir Geoffrey Howe,[12] as he then was, and goes back before that. It has come back on the agenda at regular intervals during the past quarter century.[13] But the need for such a body is now urgent. The recent report of the Budd Committee[14] concentrated on the enactment of new legislation,[15] but it noted that '[i]mprovements in the way in which Parliament fulfils its role of scrutinising the government's current tax proposals leave untouched the vast bulk of current tax measures'[16] and it went on to suggest that '[t]he solution lies in the creation of a parallel Tax Structure Review Project team ,which could select topics for review and to which the existing TLRP team could pass issues that it had identified for review.'[17]

There is no conflict between creating machinery for scrutinising new legislation and, at the same time, creating a body which will review current tax measures. But

10 Maurice Parry-Wingfields's words [in [2000] BTR 597, 598].

11 The fringe benefit rules [in relation to the taxation of employment income] are a good example.

12 [1977] BTR 97.

13 See, e.g., Adam Broke [2000] BTR 18 and Maurice Parry-Wingfield [2000] BTR 597.

14 *Making Tax Law*, Report of a Working Party on the Institutional Processes for the Parliamentary Scrutiny of Tax Proposals and for the Enactment of Tax Legislation, Chaired by Sir Alan Budd, TLRC Discussion Paper No 3.

15 This was in accordance with its terms of reference, which were: 'To review the institutional processes for the Parliamentary scrutiny of tax proposals and for the enactment of tax legislation and to consider whether changes to those processes would promote simplification and improve the quality of tax legislation and, if so, what the nature of those institutional changes should be.'

16 Para 7.1.

17 Para 7.6.

if priority has to be given to one project rather than to the other, it ought to be given to the review of current tax measures. However well thought through new legislation may be, enacting it on shaky foundations is a recipe for trouble. The foundations need to be stabilised first . . . **[1.6a]**

The importance of establishing the characteristics of a good tax system was reinforced, recently, when the Institute for Fiscal Studies launched a review which is intended to 'identify the characteristics of a good tax system for any open developed economy in the 21st century, to assess the extent to which the UK tax system conforms to these ideals, and to recommend how it might realistically be reformed in that direction'. The review will be conducted under the chairmanship of Sir James Mirrlees. The intention is to publish a report in 2008 to coincide with the 30th anniversary of the Meade Report (see http://www.ifs.org.uk/mirrleesreview/). **[1.7]**

2 Aspects of the Administration of the Tax System

Adam Smith regarded it as essential that any system of taxation should be efficient.[1] An efficient tax system is a product not only of fair and clearly stated legislation, but also of a well run administration. Such a system should ensure that taxpayers are treated fairly and with respect and that they can understand what their tax liability is and when the tax should be paid. Moreover, it is only fair to those who pay the tax for which they are liable that those who seek not to do so should be brought to book. The merging of the two former Revenue departments, namely, the Inland Revenue and Her Majesty's Customs and Excise, was a move towards a more efficient system and, as a first step towards the rationalisation of HMRC's 'heterogeneous powers',[2] a review of its powers, deterrents and safeguards is currently being undertaken.[3] **[2.1]**

1. Her Majesty's Revenue and Customs: the newly merged department

The recently integrated department of HM Revenue and Customs (HMRC), which has its legal basis in the Commissioners for Revenue and Customs Act 2005 (CRCA 2005), is responsible for all the functions previously exercised by the Inland Revenue and the Commissioners of Customs and Excise, apart from prosecutions. HMRC, together with the newly created Revenue and Customs Prosecutions Office (RCPO), which now has sole responsibility for prosecutions in relation to tax offences, is the product of a review carried out by Gus O'Donnell.[4] Since the former functions of the two former departments were very different, it is believed that despite the formal integration of the two departments, 'the actual integration of the two is anticipated to take a number of years'.[5]

HMRC comprises the Commissioners and officers of Revenue and Customs. The Commissioners are ultimately responsible for the collection and management of income tax, corporation tax, capital gains tax, inheritance tax, stamp duty land tax[6] and VAT, and for the payment and

1 See Chapter 1, above para **[1.2]**.
2 Natalie Lee (gen ed) *Revenue Law* (24th edn, 2006) at **[4.1]**.
3 See below, paras **[2.12]** and **[2.13]**.
4 *Financing Britain's Future: Review of the Revenue Departments*, Cm 6163, HM Treasury, 2004; see below, para **[2.3]**. At the time of the Review, Gus O'Donnell was Permanent Secretary to the Treasury; he was appointed Cabinet Secretary in 2005.
5 See n 2, above. FA 2007 has amended the Police and Criminal Evidence Act 1984, s 114 to eliminate the inconsistency in respect of the powers of the former Customs and Excise and Inland Revenue concerning criminal investigations.
6 This tax is not considered in this book. For a review of stamp taxes, see Natalie Lee (gen ed) *Revenue Law* (24th edn, 2006), ch 49.

management of tax credits.[7] The officers, made up of those who were previously known as inspectors and collectors, together with receivers and other authorised persons, carry out the routine work in respect of assessment and collection under the auspices of the Taxpayer Service Offices; they also staff the Taxpayer District Office, which deals with local companies and with technical and compliance issues.

The O'Donnell Review was underpinned by a desire to provide the best possible customer service and also, bearing in mind how essential information is to any system of taxation, to ensure the best possible use of information gathered. The ultimate goal was to make the life of honest taxpayers much simpler, using a 'lighter touch' approach for them, with time and resources thereby saved being expended upon the non-compliant. **[2.2]**

HM Treasury *Financing Britain's Future: Review of the Revenue Departments* Cm 6163 (2004)

A NEW TAX SERVICE

1.32 This review is about building upon the success of Customs and of the Revenue in order to provide a fair, modern and effective tax service, for its customers, and for society by ensuring that public services are well financed. This new service should build on the history and strengths of Customs and the Revenue, preserving values such as integrity, objectivity, and commitment to public service, and recognising the diversity of talents and cultures that will contribute towards success in the future.

1.33 The new service must also become something different from its predecessors, achieving a step change in the Government's approach to tax, providing benefits for companies, public services, and staff by:

- Using the discretion provided by the new accountability arrangements to create a first class service;
- Using information provided by taxpayers to develop a better understanding of customer needs so that policies and services can be best targeted. This means that the burden for compliant taxpayers should be reduced by simplifying interactions with the new service;
- Using information so that honest businesses in the UK are not subject to unfair competition from the non-compliant;
- Ensuring resources are allocated so as to minimise tax losses to the Exchequer and so ensure public services are well financed;
- Developing the skills and knowledge of existing staff and ensuring that Government tax careers are viewed as an attractive option;
- Building modern and professional transactional and support services where both quality of service and efficiency can be favourably compared to the best in the world;
- Maintaining the momentum in existing strategies and policy developments that are guarding the UK against tax fraud, modernising systems and processes, delivering key government objectives and securing the country's borders.

7 CRCA 2005, s 5.

...*A NEW SINGLE REVENUE DEPARTMENT*

3.114 The review has identified a strong case for change. *Status quo* plus is an option with low risk in the short term, but which cannot respond to the difficulties caused by rigidities imposed by the existing departmental structure. The review has shown that these are seriously affecting the ability of the two departments to perform to their maximum potential in supporting the economic and social well being of the country. This is not a reflection on the staff, who have performed to a high standard, but a result of sub-optimal organisational structures.

3.115 Strategic alignment, if successful, could provide the UK with some of the benefits of creating a new department with less risk. It would not, however, allow fast progress towards addressing the fundamental challenges of coherent services and crosscutting tax administration. Furthermore, many would be suspicious of an underlying 'hidden agenda' that this arrangement was simply a precursor to a full integration, and the resultant uncertainty and suspicion could be counter-productive. There are also doubts over the clarity of accountability in a regime in which responsibility for strategy rests with one body – the strategic board – and responsibility for implementation (including accounting officer responsibilities) rest with another. The potential for continued departmental conflict over how to optimise them would remain.

3.116 Creating a new department is the most radical option, opening the way to transformational change in the way the revenue departments conduct their business. It would be a major challenge to continue effective implementation, while developing plans consistent with the vision set out in this review. It carries substantial transitional risks and costs, but also potentially the greatest rewards in terms of effective tax collection, customer service and greater efficiency, and the review assesses that the benefits significantly outweigh the risks and costs. Because of the scale of the task, it is clear that creating the new department and managing existing work will be a considerable leadership challenge. As such, the new organisation should be headed by a full time Executive Chairman.

3.117 While the government has not in the past ruled out the integration of the revenue departments, it has in the past judged that other priorities, such as the introduction of tax credits, should take precedence. The review has also benefited from examining the success of the creation of DWP in 2001 as a customer focused delivery organisation, and of examining the benefits of organisational change to revenue departments in other countries. The review assesses that now is the time to embark on the challenge of integrating the revenue departments, to create a new and more efficient tax service for the benefit of its customers and the exchequer.

...*BETTER INFORMATION USE*

Summary and recommendations

Information is central to the revenue departments' business – information wasted is revenue lost or an opportunity to improve customer service or efficiency missed. The creation of a new department ... represents an opportunity to make better use and improve sharing of information across the tax system, to the benefit of the department and its customers, as:

- Compliance action is more effectively targeted, improving use of resources and fairness for honest customers by enabling a 'lighter touch' approach to compliant groups while focussing efforts on the non-compliant; and

- Understanding of customers is improved, moving towards a 'whole customer' view so that processes can be focussed most effectively and efficiently on meeting customers' needs coherently across the tax system.

Good quality data also underpin coherent and evidence-based policy making and implementation – and vice versa as policy design and implementation powerfully influence the content and form of information gathered, as well as the way it is used.

The use of information is a key theme of this review ... **[2.3]**

2. Self-Assessment

There are three main elements to the administration of the tax system: obtaining the necessary information about their tax affairs from the taxpayers themselves, or from third parties (see below, para **[2.9]**), assessment to tax, and the collection of tax. Prior to the tax year 1996–97, tax inspectors were responsible for making the assessment to tax, based mainly on the information provided by the taxpayer in his annual tax return. Special procedures existed, and continue to exist, where the taxpayer's earnings are taxed under the Income Tax (Earnings and Pensions) Act 2003 (ITEPA),[8] where the Pay As You Earn (PAYE) system[9] usually applies. As a result of legislation introduced by the Finance Acts 1994, 1995 and 1996, a new system for assessing personal taxation was introduced.[10] Under this 'self-assessment' system, 'the primary responsibility for making an assessment of the tax payable each year falls on the individual taxpayer, not HMRC.'[11] Taxpayers who are sent returns (ie, those who are self-employed or whose tax affairs are complicated[12]) must complete and deliver them to HMRC, and calculate and pay the tax by the 'filing date', which is 31 January following the end of the tax year.[13] To ensure that taxpayers comply with their self-assessment duties, HMRC may charge interest on late payments, make surcharges and impose penalties.[14] For a brief explanation of these enforcement tools, see Natalie Lee (gen ed) *Revenue Law* (24th edn, 2006), ch 4 (Hartley Foster), and John Tiley *Revenue Law* (5th edn, 2006) pp 79–83. There also exist provisions permitting HMRC to make enquiries into the accuracy of a tax return whether or not the return is incorrect,[15] and to make 'discovery assessments' where it has found that the taxpayer has either failed to assess income or gains that

8 See Chapter 8.

9 See ITEPA 2003, Part 11.

10 Corporation tax has also had a self-assessment system since 1 July 1999; see FA 1994, s 199 and the Finance Act 1994, Section 199 (Appointed Day) Order 1988, SI 1998/3173; FA 1998, Sch 18.

11 See n 2, above at **[4.22]**.

12 As John Tiley points out, there is no legislative reason why recipients are limited in this way; see *Revenue Law* (5th edn, 2005) at p 66.

13 Thus, for the tax year 2006–07, the filing date will be 31 January 2008. A taxpayer may request HMRC to calculate their tax liability for them; in this case, the return must be delivered to HMRC by 30 September after the year of assessment.

14 As part of the review, *Modernising Powers, Deterrents and Safeguards*, HMRC has published a consultative document, *A new approach to penalties for incorrect tax returns*, HM Revenue & Customs, December 2006.

15 TMA 1970, ss 9A and 19A. These enquiries may be random, or specific to a particular return.

should have been assessed, or claimed relief in excess of that which should have been allowed.[16]

Part of the rationale for the introduction of self-assessment was to free-up the time of tax inspectors and enable them to focus their attention on those whom they suspect of having undisclosed sources of income.[17] Due, in part, to the fact that large numbers of taxpayers are not required to submit an annual return, the black, or informal, economy was, and continues to be, a serious problem in the UK, and underpins the current review of HMRC's powers and deterrents (see below, para **[2.13]**). **[2.4]**

David Collison *Self-Assessment: Dealing with the New Income Tax Regime* (3rd edn, 1996), pp 1–2, 283 and 297–298

1.1 WHAT IS SELF-ASSESSMENT?

Self-assessment is the most fundamental reform of the administration of personal taxation since the introduction of PAYE in 1944. The responsibility for the management of an individual's tax affairs is placed firmly on that individual. No longer will the system be driven by an assessment raised by the Revenue. Instead, it is the individual who is to make his own assessment . . . If a market value is required, the taxpayer must supply it; if information will not be available until a later date, the taxpayer must supply an estimate and in both cases accept the consequences of the deficiency of the estimate. Reference is sometimes made to asking the Revenue to assess the tax liability, by submission of the return at an early date. This is misleading, the Revenue are prepared to transfer the taxpayer's own figures from one part of the form to the part of the form where the arithmetic calculation is performed, but this is still the taxpayer's own self-assessment. Nothing can be done by the taxpayer to change the date on which he is obliged to pay tax, nor to avoid interest accruing from that date if tax is found not to have been paid fully . . .

1.2 THE TAXPAYER ASSESSES HIMSELF

1.2.1 Basis of measure of income

. . . trading profits subject to tax in a fiscal year *[are]* those based on accounts drawn up for a period ending in that year . . .

All other income enjoyed by an individual is brought into the self-assessment calculation. There is, thus, a holistic approach, with a single payment on a single date of the total remaining liability to income tax of the taxpayer. (Payments will, of

16 TMA 1970, s 29, as amended by FA 1994, ss 191, 194. This power can only be exercised where the taxpayer's conduct has been fraudulent or negligent or where the 'officer could not have been reasonably expected, on the basis of the information made available to him' to be aware that additional tax was due (TMA 1970, s 29(5)). See *Langham v Veltema* [2004] STC 544, where the Court of Appeal held that this provision referred to the officer's objective awareness of an actual insufficiency arising from the information made available to him by the taxpayer, and not an objective awareness that he should do something to check whether there was such an insufficiency.

17 Another reason for the introduction of the self-assessment system was the saving of costs for the Inland Revenue.

course, continue to be made during the year under PAYE in respect of income from employment and by taxation at source in respect of many types of investment income. In addition, it *[is]* necessary to make interim payments of tax in respect of tax liabilities.

27.1 REVENUE POWERS

27.1.1 Power to make enquiries

In the year ended 31 March 1994, the Inland Revenue collected additional tax of £4,377,400,000 as a result of inspecting accounts and investigations. Of this, £3,082,000,000 arose from the review of accounts and other computations. Under self-assessment, there is no suggestion that the Inland Revenue is expecting to collect any less than this sum. However, the structure of the process by which returns are tested is substantially different.

... Statute[18] empowers an *[sic]* Revenue officer to enquire into any tax return ... It is not necessary for the *[officer]* to have a reason for commencing enquiries and it is not expected that a reason will be given. It is, however, required that a formal, written notice is given by the *[officer]* of the commencement of enquiries. Where a tax return has been submitted by the due filing date, the *[officer]* is only entitled to issue such a notice during the period up to one year after that filing date.

...

Records

28.1 STATUTORY REQUIREMENT

There is a statutory requirement for all taxpayers to retain certain documents until 31 January following the normal filing date.[19] If the return is delivered late, the requirement is to retain records until the expiry of 12 months after the end of the calendar quarter in which the return is submitted.[20]

Statute only gives a very general statement as to the records required. Section 12B(1)(a) TMA 1970 requires the retention of:

> 'all such records as may be requisite for the purpose of enabling him to make and deliver a correct and complete return.'

For trades and professions, the requirement for the retention of records is made more specific by s 12B(3) TMA 1970, as amended by s 105 FA 1995 ... The effect of *[the]* definition is that any person who has income assessable under [*Income Tax (Trading and Other Income) Act 2005, Pt 2*] must retain records for five years ten months after the end of the fiscal year, in respect of *all* of his income. Thus, an individual who is a partner in a trading etc partnership is required to retain statements of a personal bank deposit account (or other adequate record of interest credited to that account) for nearly six years, whereas an employee of that partnership is only required to retain such a bank statement for under two years.

... **[2.5]**

18 Taxes Management Act 1970, s. 9.
19 *Ibid*, s. 12B(2)(a).
20 *Ibid*, s. 12B(2)(b).

For a critique of the self-assessment system see Simon James 'Self-Assessment for Income Tax' [1994] BTR 204; Cedric Sandford 'Self-Assessment for Income Tax – Another View' [1994] BTR 674; David Williams, 'Self-Assessment: A Practitioner's View' [1999] BTR 229; Doug Smith 'Self-Assessment: An Inland Revenue Perspective' [1999] BTR 241; and Susan Thompson and Wilma Teviotdale 'Self-Assessment: Revenue Authorities v Taxpayer – A State of Conflict?' [1999] BTR 272. See also John Tiley *Revenue Law* (5th edn, 2006), p 72. **[2.6]**

Report of the Committee on Enforcement Powers of the Revenue Departments (Chairman: the Right Honourable The Lord Keith of Kinkel PC), 1983 (Cmnd 8822 and 9120)

The Black Economy

27.1. DEFINITIONS, TRENDS, IMPLICATIONS FOR TAX ENFORCEMENT

Definition. 27.1.1 ... We have followed the Departments[21] in selecting our own working definition of the black economy as 'all activities which are concealed from the revenue collecting authorities with the specific intention of evading tax.' Black economy activity is by definition illegal; the Departments note that it does not include tax avoidance which is within the law.[22] ... The black economy is subversive of the law at the base of the tax system in one of two ways: either the activities are not reported to the tax authorities at all, or the activities are known to the authorities but the amount of income or turnover is understated or otherwise misrepresented. The former category includes as its main component the individuals most instantly recognisable to the public at large as operators in the black economy: the "moonlighter" is someone who has, in addition to his main employment which is taxed under PAYE,[23] a secondary spare time paid occupation, either another job or a business activity. A "ghost" is someone with taxable income who does not make a return to any tax office ... In Inland Revenue terms the first category also includes those persons who are known to the authorities but who omit miscellaneous items from their tax returns such as interest, rents or occasional capital gains. The second category includes trading taxpayers, whether corporate or individual, who do not record all the takings or who overstate business expenses ... As regards employees, it includes those who understate part of their earnings, for example, tips, with or without the collusion of their employers, or who overstate their expenses when claiming a tax allowance for them.

Implications for tax enforcement. 27.1.3. The principal implication for tax enforcement is that when evasion is seen to succeed, erstwhile honest citizens may be tempted to try it. This can lead to a declining band of honest taxpayers coming increasingly to feel resentment at the burden they are left to bear. Witnesses left us in no doubt that in their view the principal deterrent to tax evasion is fear of

21 The Departments of Inland Revenue and Customs and Excise.
22 [Chapter 7 of the Report; see below, Chapter 5.]
23 As we note at 27.4.5., a self-employed person might equally well have a secondary spare time paid occupation.

detection and of the consequences. We share that robust and commonsense approach. To the extent that perusal of the results of the Inland Revenue's enforcement efforts suggests that the chances of 'getting away with it' are good, compliance can be expected to continue to decline. A constant theme of representations to us was of the perceived need for the Revenue Departments in combating evasion to display equivalent energy and effectiveness across all kinds and classes of taxpayers, otherwise the effort directed at any one group might well be resented as unfair and discriminatory by that group. **[2.7]**

HM Treasury, *The Informal Economy: A Report by Lord Grabiner QC* (2000)[24]

Size and Nature of the Informal Economy

DEFINITION

1.1 The hidden, or informal economy, is usually taken to mean any undeclared economic activity. It covers tax evasion of all kinds, ranging from casual moonlighting and work paid cash-in-hand through to organised crime. Some of the informal economy is truly 'hidden' (for example, firms that are not registered with any Government agency); much of it, though, consists of undeclared profits from known businesses.

1.2 This report concentrates on unregistered businesses – in particular, colluding employers – and on the self-employed people and employees who work in the hidden economy. In most cases, there will be a loss of income tax, National Insurance Contributions ("NICs") and, sometimes, Value Added Tax ("VAT") . . .

1.4 For the purpose of this report, being in the hidden economy means not complying with the basic legal requirements to declare and pay tax . . .

Unreported businesses

1.5 Historically, the profits from any kind of dealing in goods or providing services are taxable, whether from legitimate activities, such as repairing cars, gardening and building, or from criminal acts, such as trading in drugs or smuggled cigarettes. But the Government will not get to know of them unless it is told.

1.6 So, when business activity is commenced and there is liability for tax, there is a legal requirement[25] to notify the Inland Revenue[26] unless the person(s) involved in the business already completes an annual tax return. This notification is especially important because of the large number of people who are not asked to complete tax returns. These include not only those for whom the Revenue has no current records but also most of the 20 million people whose income is taxed at source. Businesses that do not make this report to the Revenue constitute part of the hidden economy.

. . .

24 This Report concerned not only abuse of the tax system, but also of the benefit system.
25 Taxes Management Act 1970, section 7.
26 [From April 6, 2005, HMRC.]

Collusive employers

1.12 Collusive employers are those who pay their workers partly in cash which does not go through the pay-roll records. As a result:

- the employer avoids paying secondary Class 1 NICs on the unrecorded pay . . .
- by avoiding NICs and income tax due under PAYE, it is cheaper for the employer to offer an employee a given amount of take-home pay;
- employees can claim more means-tested benefit[27] than they are entitled to, by concealing the unrecorded cash element of their earnings;
- the employer typically presents a false picture of the business's taxable income, since the cash part of employees' pay usually comes from cash sales that have not gone through the books[28] . . .

Scale of the hidden economy

1.14 By its nature, the size of the informal economy is hard to measure . . .

1.15 . . . For the purposes of this report, I have assumed that the hidden economy is a major problem, involving billions of pounds and . . . I am quite sure this assumption is a reasonable one.

1.16 Similarly, the number of tax-evaders is not known. A random investigation of Inland Revenue self-assessment tax returns might estimate how many tax payers under-declare their income; it could not measure those who are not registered at all.

Nature of the hidden economy

1.18 Again, there is little direct information about the nature of the hidden economy, but there is strong anecdotal evidence from investigations carried out by Departments.

1.19 Typically, businesses in the informal economy tend to be low-wage and labour-intensive, often with a seasonal or irregular element to their work. Examples include: domestic service, household building, taxis and mini-cabs, market trading, tourism, hotels and catering, agriculture and fishing, fashion and clothing manufacture.

. . .

1.22 Increasingly, people in the hidden economy are using modern technology to facilitate their frauds. Professional-looking false invoices can be created by computer, which enable a firm to exaggerate its tax-deductible expenses and withdraw cash from the business, for example to pay off-record wages. There are even businesses which exist solely to manufacture and trade in false invoices.

1.23 Another issue for the revenue Departments is the growing use of the Internet and e-commerce. Although the Internet brings many advantages (for example, the potential for improving customer service by accepting tax returns electronically), it increases the difficulty of enforcing tax compliance. It is already having an impact in the more traditional areas for the hidden

27 [And also tax credits; see Chapter 15.]

28 This may involve *overstating* taxable profits, since the wages and NICs that should have been paid would themselves be tax-deductible expenses. However, many employers who use the cash from unrecorded sales to pay wages will also take some to line their own pockets – which would not be tax-deductible.

economy. Many market traders and restaurants have their own web sites, which they use to receive payment for goods and services. If this payment goes into a bank account which has not been declared, it can be a way to conceal taxable income (though still not as convenient for them as the ability to withdraw cash).

The Damaging Effect of the Hidden Economy

. . .

A burden on the law-abiding and on the economy

2.8 The hidden economy is a burden on the taxpayer. Unpaid taxes . . . represent a huge opportunity cost that must be made up by higher taxes and lower public spending for the law-abiding. It is also unfair. Most taxpayers . . . are honest, even if equally short of money.

2.9 The hidden economy is a burden on the economy as a whole. People running their own businesses may be financially better off in the short term in the hidden economy, by evading taxes and perhaps claiming benefits. But if they want to expand their business, or experience temporary difficulties, they will be severely inhibited. Their ability to raise finance, gain access to advice and support, take on staff and acquire premises will be restricted in the informal economy.

Prevention: Cutting Off the Supply

- To prevent people joining the hidden economy, Departments must try to ensure that they are registered correctly and comply with tax . . . rules from the outset.
- I recommend that:
  - businesses should be required to register with the Inland Revenue as soon as they are set up, rather than after up to 18 months[29] . . .

Detection: Intelligence Gathering

- The Government's ability to investigate and detect people in the informal economy depends on using information effectively.
- I recommend that:
  - the Government should examine how to make use of information held by the private sector. This is a valuable source of data which has not yet been tapped; . . .
  - Departments should agree common guidelines for staff about what data sharing is legally permissible and how it should be carried out in practice. There should be a central point of contact to co-ordinate the exercise and monitor its effectiveness. **[2.8]**

29 [The existing rule: Taxes Management Act 1970, s 7.]

3. Powers of investigation: information gathering

Whilst the obligation is on taxpayers to notify HMRC of their liability to income tax or capital gains tax even though a tax return has not been issued to them,[30] HMRC have wide powers that enable them to gather further information from the taxpayers themselves, as well as from third parties. The investigatory powers of the former Inland Revenue and HM Customs and Excise were, in some cases, very different. On the merger of the two departments, these powers have continued to operate as though they were still distinct. Recognising that this situation could not continue in the long term, during the Second Reading of the Commissioners for Revenue and Customs Bill, the Paymaster General announced a major review and consultation in respect of the powers, deterrents and safeguards that would 'underpin' the newly merged HMRC. This review and consultation process is currently ongoing.[31]

John Tiley[32] groups the existing powers of the former Inland Revenue, which also apply for the purpose of a tax liability under the law of another member state of the European Community,[33] under four heads:

(a) Powers, with the consent of a General or Special Commissioner, to require a taxpayer to deliver documents[34] in that person's possession or power[35] or furnish other particulars[36] containing information relevant to the tax liability of that person, where the HMRC officer reasonably believes that those documents, or other information, are needed.[37]

(b) Power to require equivalent documents or information from any other person.[38] This power is exercisable only by the Board itself (as opposed to officers of HMRC), when it has reasonable grounds for believing that there has been a failure to comply with the Act and that, as a consequence, the proper assessment or collection of tax has been prejudiced.[39]

30 TMA 1970, s 7 (as substituted by FA 1994, s196 and Sch 19, Pt 1, para 1) requires 'every person who (a) is chargeable to income tax or capital gains tax for any year of assessment, and (b) has not received a notice under section 8 of this Act requiring a return for that year of his total income and chargeable gains' – subject to a number of exceptions – to notify HMRC that he is so chargeable no later than six months after the end of the year of assessment in question. The penalty for failing to do so is a maximum of the tax due on the undeclared income and gains. As far as employers who deduct tax under the PAYE scheme are concerned, see Income Tax (Pay As You Earn) Regulations 2003, SI 2003/2682, regs 73–75.

31 As of January, 2007 the Review comprises *HM Revenue and Customs and the Taxpayer: Modernising Powers, Deterrents and Safeguards*, Inland Revenue and HM Customs and Excise, March 2005, *Summary of Responses to the Consultation*, HM Revenue & Customs, July 2005, *A consultation on the developing programme of work*, HM Revenue & Customs, March 2006, *Criminal Investigation Powers: A Technical Consultation Document*, HM Revenue & Customs, August 2006 and *A new approach to penalties for incorrect returns*, HM Revenue & Customs, December 2006.

32 Note 12, above, p 87.

33 FA 1990, s 125; see also Directive 77/799/EEC.

34 TMA 1970, s 20(1). Documents include computer records.

35 *Ibid*, s 20(1)(a).

36 *Ibid*, s 20(1)(b).

37 See *R v IRC, ex p Rossminster Ltd* [1980] 1 All ER 80, where the court applied an objective test. A written summary of the officer's reasons for his reasonable belief must be given: TMA 1970, s 20(8E), although the person from whom the information is being elicited has no right to see this summary.

38 TMA 1970, s 20(2).

39 *Ibid*, s 20(7A)(a).

(c) Power requiring the person to make documents relating to another person available for inspection[40]; the conditions for the exercise of this power are the same as those in (a), above but, in this case, the notice under which the power is exercised must name the taxpayer unless a Special Commissioner has decided otherwise.[41]

(d) Power, authorised by a member of the Board of HMRC, to call for the papers[42] of a tax accountant who has been convicted of a tax-related offence.[43]

In cases where *serious* fraud is suspected, HMRC have two additional powers. The first enables an officer of HMRC, after obtaining a warrant from a circuit judge, to enter private premises, if necessary by force, to search for, and remove, documents that he reasonably believes to be evidence of such fraud,[44] unless those documents are subject to legal privilege.[45] The warrant does not need to specify any particular offence.[46] Secondly, a judge may issue an order requiring a third party (frequently firms of professional advisors) to hand over documents (not subject to legal privilege), which are evidence of an offence under investigation by HMRC;[47] failure to comply is a contempt of court.

Where, as a result of their enquiries into a taxpayer's affairs, for example, undisclosed income is discovered, HMRC may impose penalties as well as the tax due plus interest. In very serious cases, a criminal prosecution may be brought.[48] **[2.9]**

R v IRC, ex p Rossminster Ltd [1980] AC 952 (HL)

Pursuant to a number of warrants issued under TMA 1970, s 20C, officers of the Inland Revenue entered and searched the offices and homes of the managing director of Rossminster Ltd and one other person, seizing documents from all four locations. The respondents claimed that the Revenue were not entitled to remove

40 *Ibid*, s 20(3); personal medical records and journalistic materials are excluded.
41 *Ibid*, s 20(8B).
42 Excluding personal medical records and journalistic materials.
43 TMA 1970, s 20A.
44 *Ibid*, s 20C.
45 *Ibid*, s 20C(4A). See *R v IRC, ex p Tamosius and Partners* [2000] 1 WLR 453, below, para **[2.16]** and Chapter 4, below, para **[4.43]**.
46 This is discussed in *IRC v Rossminster* [1980] 1 All ER 80, below.
47 TMA 1970, s 20BA and Delivery of Documents (Procedure) Regulations 2000, SI 2000/2875. Although s 20BA does not require HMRC to apply for a search and seizure warrant to obtain documents from a third party, other procedural safeguards are similar to those in s 20C. Section 20BA was a result of the criticism that 'the execution of a s 20C warrant is intrusive, is resource intensive for the Revenue, and is ineffective where papers are stored at a location other than the premises specified in the warrant ...', TAXREP 5/00: *Serious Fraud*, Memorandum submitted in January 2000 to the Revenue by the Tax Faculty of the Institute of Chartered Accountants in England and Wales.
48 Prosecutions are brought against a person who is 'knowingly concerned in the fraudulent evasion of income tax by him or any other person' (FA 2000, s 144(1); see David Salter 'Some Thoughts on Fraudulent Evasion of Income Tax' [2003] BTR 489), for conspiracy to defraud the Crown of taxes due to it, for perjury (see *R v Hood-Barrs* [1943] 1 KB 455) and for the common law offence of cheating the public revenue (see *R v Hudson* [1956] 2 QB 252). In England and Wales proceedings may also be brought under the Theft Act 1968, s 16 (obtaining a pecuniary advantage by deception) and s 17 (false accounting). It is now quite common for professional tax advisors to be prosecuted for such offences; see *R v Charlton* [1996] STC 1418, where the Court of Appeal discussed the extent to which an ineffective tax avoidance scheme could give rise to a successful criminal prosecution for cheating the public revenue.

such documents where there was no reasonable cause for belief that they might be required as evidence in proceedings in respect of an offence involving tax fraud. The House of Lords found in favour of the Revenue, agreeing with the view taken by the Divisional Court.

LORD WILBERFORCE: ... The organised searches by officers of the Inland Revenue ... on the respondents' offices and private premises were carried out under powers claimed to be conferred by Act of Parliament—the Finance Act 1976, section 57, and Schedule 6, section 20C amending the Taxes Management Act 1970, section 20.

The integrity and privacy of a man's home, and of his place of business, an important human right has, since the second world war, been eroded by a number of statutes passed by Parliament in the belief, presumably, that this right of privacy ought in some cases to be over-ridden by the interest which the public has in preventing evasions of the law. Some of these powers of search are reflections of dirigisme and of heavy taxation, others of changes in mores....

The courts have the duty to supervise, I would say critically, even jealously, the legality of any purported exercise of these powers. They are the guardians of the citizens' right to privacy. But they must do this in the context of the times, i.e. of increasing Parliamentary intervention, and of the modern power of judicial review. In my respectful opinion appeals to 18th century precedents of arbitrary action by Secretaries of State and references to general warrants do nothing to throw light on the issue. Furthermore, while the courts may look critically at legislation which impairs the rights of citizens and should resolve any doubt in interpretation in their favour, it is no part of their duty, or power, to restrict or impede the working of legislation, even of unpopular legislation; to do so would be to weaken rather than to advance the democratic process.

It is necessary to be clear at once that Parliament, in conferring these wide powers, has introduced substantial safeguards. Those relevant to this case are three:

(1) No action can be taken under section 20C without the approval of the Board of Inland Revenue—viz., two members, at least, acting personally. The board consists of senior and responsible officials expert in the subject matter, who must be expected to weigh carefully the issues of public interest involved.

(2) No warrant to enter can be issued except by a circuit judge, not, as is usually the case, by a magistrate. There has to be laid before him information on oath, and on this he must be satisfied that there is reasonable ground for suspecting the commission of a "tax fraud"[49] and that evidence of it is to be found in the premises sought to be searched. If the judge does his duty (and we must assume that *[he]* did in the present case) he must carefully consider for himself the grounds put forward by the revenue officer and judicially satisfy himself, in relation to each of the premises concerned, that these amount to reasonable grounds for suspecting, etc. It would be quite wrong to suppose that he acts simply as a rubber stamp on the revenue's application.

(3) The courts retain their full power of supervision of judicial and executive action. There is nothing in section 20C which cuts these down: on the contrary, Parliament, by using such phrases as "is satisfied," "has reasonable cause to believe" must be taken to accept the restraints which courts in many cases have held to be inherent in them. The courts are concerned, in this case, only with two matters bearing upon legality.

First, were the warrants valid? Secondly, can the actual action taken under subsection (3) be challenged on the ground that the officers did not have, or could not have had, reasonable cause to believe that the documents they seized might be required as evidence for the purposes of proceedings in respect of a "tax fraud"? ...

... I have no doubt that the view taken by the Divisional Court on each was correct and I am willing to adopt their judgment. I add a few observations of my own.

1. I can understand very well the perplexity, and indeed indignation, of those present on the premises, when they were searched. Beyond knowing, as appears in the warrant, that the search is in connection with a "tax fraud," they were not told what the precise nature of the fraud was, when it was committed, or by whom it was committed. In the case of a concern with numerous clients, for example, a bank, without this knowledge the occupier of the premises is totally unable to protect his customers' confidential information from

49 [Now '*serious* tax fraud'; FA 1989, s 146(1), (2), (3), amending TMA 1970, s 20C(1).]

investigation and seizure. I cannot believe that this does not call for a fresh look by Parliament. But, on the plain words of the enactment, the officers are entitled if they can persuade the board and the judge, to enter and search *premises* regardless of whom they belong to: a warrant which confers this power is strictly and exactly within the parliamentary authority, and the occupier has no answer to it. I accept that some information as regards the person (so who are alleged to have committed an offence and possibly as to the approximate dates of the offences) must almost certainly have been laid before the board and the judge. But the occupier has no right to be told of this at this stage, nor has he the right to be informed of the "reasonable grounds" of which the judge was satisfied. Both courts agree to this: all this information is clearly protected by the public interest immunity which covers investigations into possible criminal offences. With reference to the police, Lord Reid stated this in these words:

> "The police are carrying on an unending war with criminals many of whom are today highly intelligent. So it is essential that there should be no disclosure of anything which might give any useful information to those who organise criminal activities. And it would generally be wrong to require disclosure in a civil case of anything which might be material in a pending prosecution: but after a verdict has been given or it has been decided to take no proceedings there is not the same need for secrecy." (*Conway v Rimmer* [1968] AC 910, 953–954).

The Court of Appeal took the view that the warrants were invalid because they did not sufficiently particularise the alleged offence(s). The court did not make clear exactly what particulars should have been given—and indeed I think that this cannot be done. The warrant followed the wording of the statute "fraud in connection with or in relation to tax": a portmanteau description which covers a number of common law (cheating) and statutory offences (under the Theft Act 1968 et al.). To require specification at this investigatory stage would be impracticable given the complexity of "tax frauds" and the different persons who may be involved (companies, officers of companies, accountants, tax consultants, taxpayers, wives of taxpayers etc.). Moreover, particularisation, if required, would no doubt take the form of a listing of one offence and/or another or others and so would be of little help to those concerned. Finally, there would clearly be power, on principles well accepted in the common law, after entry had been made in connection with one particular offence, to seize material bearing upon other offences within the portmanteau. So, particularisation, even if practicable, would not help the occupier.

I am unable, therefore, to escape the conclusion, that adherence to the statutory formula is sufficient.

... *[His Lordship then held that, on the second matter of the validity of the seizure and removal of documents, there was insufficient evidence for the grant of a final declaration that the Revenue could not have had reasonable cause to believe that the documents they seized might be required as evidence for the purposes of proceedings in respect of a tax fraud]*

... in conclusion ... I would wish to make it clear that the failure of the respondents at this stage is not necessarily the end of the matter. They can proceed with an action against the revenue for, in effect, excess of power and for trespass and any aggravation can be taken into account. At some stage, which cannot be particularised now with precision but which broadly would be when criminal proceedings are over, or, within a reasonable time, are not taken, the immunity which exists at the stage of initial investigation will lapse. Then the revenue will have to make good and specify the existence and cause of their belief that things removed might be required as evidence for the purpose of "tax fraud" proceedings and the issue will be tried in a normal manner. **[2.10]**

A similar decision was reached in *R v Middlesex Guildhall Crown Court, ex p Tamosius & Partners* [2000] 1 WLR 453 (see below, paras **[2.16]**–**[2.18]**), which case concerned the issue of documents protected by legal professional privilege.[50]

50 For a discussion of legal professional privilege, see below, paras **[2.15]**–**[2.19]**.

In spite of the wide powers of investigation vested in HMRC, serious tax, and tax credit, fraud continues to be a major problem. This was highlighted in a 2003 report,[51] which was discussed by David Salter and Monuhar Ullah in [2003] BTR 330. The principle emerging from the current review of HMRC's information powers is that the greater the degree of culpability in taxpayer non-compliance, the more rigorous investigatory powers and penalties should become, culminating in criminal investigation and prosecution for those who deliberately fail to comply with their tax obligations. Thus, taxpayer behaviour is divided into categories to reflect the spectrum of behaviour.[52] Mistakes or misinterpretations of fact or law where reasonable care has been taken would not be subject to a penalty. However, failure to take reasonable care, deliberate understatements or over-claims and deliberate understatements where the behaviour is aggravated by concealment (but is not to be investigated with a view to criminal prosecution) would all be subject to penalties at levels that would reflect the increasing seriousness of the behaviour. **[2.11]**

Inland Revenue and HM Customs and Excise *HM Revenue and Customs and the Taxpayer: Modernising Powers, Deterrents and Safeguards* (March, 2005)

The aim of the review will be to provide a framework of law and practice for HMRC that supports the Government's objectives of a tax system that is fair and better adapted to the needs of customers. It will consider the scope for aligning and rationalising existing powers so as to make it easier for individuals and businesses to comply with their tax obligations and receive the tax credits to which they are entitled. It will also consider how best to obtain the information needed for better risk assessment and for better-targeted compliance activities.

. . . In particular consultation will cover the law and practice that governs:

- the information that is provided on a routine basis, for example in registering with HMRC or in tax returns, and is used to calculate the amount due or payable, to assess risks of non-compliance and for other purposes such as forecasting tax receipts or providing targeted support;
- the powers to obtain additional information and to make assessments in the course of enquiries and inspections into the amounts of tax due, to obtain evidence where an offence is suspected and to settle the tax and any interest and penalties which is ultimately due;
- the financial and other sanctions that can be applied in cases where complete and accurate information is not provided, the appropriate amount of tax is not paid at the right time, there is a need to deter non-compliance or to ensure that those who break the rules do not obtain an unfair benefit;
- the restrictions and appeal rights that apply to the use of these powers and provide an essential safeguard for taxpayers.[53]

. . .

51 *Tackling Fraud against the Inland Revenue*, a report by the Comptroller and Auditor General, 28 February 2003.

52 Currently, penalties are not determined by the nature of the behaviour giving rise to the penalty but by the tax or duty regime within which the behaviour occurs. It is argued that this leads to inconsistencies in the treatment of similar non-compliant behaviours.

53 [For taxpayer safeguards, see below, paras **[2.14]–[2.24]**.]

Objectives

The creation of HMRC provides the opportunity to achieve a step change in the approach to tax. The aim will be to introduce better customer focus, greater effectiveness and greater efficiency into the system . . .

Improved use of information will be central to achieving all of these . . . underpinned by a legal framework with appropriate checks and balances. **[2.12]**

HM Revenue & Customs *HM Revenue and Customs and the Taxpayer: Modernising Powers, Deterrents and Safeguards*, A consultation on the developing programme of work (March 2006)

The principles underlying the design of powers, deterrents and safeguards

3.5 HMRC can achieve its compliance and customer service objectives only by treating taxpayers according to their needs, circumstances and behaviours and by understanding the perceptions, attitudes, incentives and opportunities that drive their behaviour. Numerous factors play into these attitudes and perceptions, for instance:

- the availability and quality of HMRC support;
- the extent to which, through the use of risk assessment, HMRC is able to reduce checking of the compliant;
- recognition of previously compliant behaviour; and
- public awareness that HMRC is actively promoting a level playing field by detecting and deterring non-compliance.

3.6 A balanced and effective framework of statutory powers and safeguards provides an infrastructure that should foster positive perceptions and attitudes, supporting good service to taxpayers and helping to promote compliance. However, if statutory powers are seen as onerous, unclear, ineffective in deterring non-compliance and lacking in adequate safeguards they are likely to promote behaviours that run counter to the Government's objectives and compliance will rely too heavily on sanctions and deterrence.

3.7 The work done by the Review has identified a series of principles which should underpin a balanced and effective framework for powers, deterrents and safeguards . . .

To be both effective and respected:

Powers and the statutory obligations they impose need to be

- set within a clear statutory framework,
- easily understood – by taxpayers, their agents and HMRC staff,
- straightforward to comply with,
- proportionate to what HMRC needs to discharge its responsibilities or to protect the Exchequer from the risk assessed,
- used consistently, and
- effective and deal with non-compliance.

Sanctions for non-compliance must be

- set in statute,
- clear and publicised,
- proportionate to the offence,

- used consistently, and
- effective in deterring non-compliance and returning the non-compliant to compliance.

Safeguards for citizens and businesses must be

- clear, publicised and accessible,
- effective, and
- responsive to the nature and purpose of particular powers and sanctions.

3.8 The Review is seeking to translate these principles into a design framework for powers, deterrents and safeguards that is built up in proportion to the identified risk.

- HMRC has an obligation to support and help taxpayers right across the compliance spectrum ... There also have to be some checks at random to validate the risk assessment criteria that underpin HMRC's approach to risk.
- Where the risk is that someone may have made a mistake, despite taking reasonable care to get it right, HMRC may need to check and, if there has been a mistake, help correct it and explain how to avoid it in future.
- When someone fails to take reasonable care to get their tax affairs right, HMRC may make more detailed enquiries to understand what has gone wrong and ensure the intention was not to understate or over-claim deliberately. HMRC will charge penalties where there has been a failure to take reasonable care.
- Where from the risk assessment it appears that there is a risk of deliberate non-compliance HMRC will often need to use additional powers, for example to access personal and third party documentation. In some cases HMRC will use criminal powers to investigate with a view to prosecution.

3.9 This can be represented diagrammatically:

Those who get it right	*Those who try to comply but make mistakes*	*Those who don't take reasonable care*	*Those who deliberately do not comply*	*Those whose deliberate non compliance merits criminal investigation*
SUPPORT	HELP	COLLECT		
		EDUCATE	CORRECT	
		INSPECT	ENQUIRE	PENALISE
			INVESTIGATE	
				PROSECUTE

3.10 As risk increases the range of powers and sanctions available to HMRC should increase proportionately. Routine powers that support interventions to collect tax and check returns are available across the spectrum. Additional powers, supported by appropriate safeguards, become available as the risks become more serious.[54] **[2.13]**

54 HMRC investigates some cases with a view to criminal prosecution where, for example, there have been previous serious offences, false statements have been made to HMRC or false documents created to facilitate the offence. Prosecutions are undertaken by and at the discretion of the independent Revenue and Customs Prosecution Office.

4. Taxpayers' safeguards

The powers exercisable by HMRC to obtain information are subject to rules that seek to give the taxpayer a measure of protection. Some of these are merely procedural,[55] whilst others are of a more substantive nature. These substantive measures are discussed below. Moreover, although taxpayers have access to the ordinary appeals process discussed in Chapter 3, they are provided with further protection in the guise of the Revenue Adjudicator and the Parliamentary Ombudsman in the event that they may have sustained damage by HMRC's actions and yet have no legal redress. **[2.14]**

A. Legal professional privilege

Barristers, advocates and solicitors are protected against having to produce documents in their possession, without the consent of their clients, to which a claim of professional privilege can be maintained.[56] **[2.15]**

R v Middlesex Guildhall Crown Court, ex p Tamosius & Partners [2000] 1 WLR 453 (Ch D); see below, para [4.43]

The Inland Revenue had reasonable grounds for suspecting that the applicant, a United States citizen engaged in legal practice in London, was involved in arrangements for evading tax on commissions paid by one of the firm's clients, by diverting payments offshore, and that he had assisted in concealing those arrangements from the Inland Revenue. On these grounds, it obtained a warrant to enter and search his offices under TMA 1970, s 20C. The applicant subsequently applied for judicial review on the basis that the search warrants were invalid. The High Court held that the prevention of removal of documents was limited to those in respect of which a claim to professional privilege could be 'maintained' and did not include documents 'claimed' by the taxpayer as being privileged.

> MOSES J:
> *The statutory framework*
>
> ...
>
> I should observe, at the outset, two significant features of the legislation.
>
> (1) The warrant provides authority to an officer of the board to enter the premises and search. This is to be contrasted with the power to seize and remove "any things whatsoever found there which he has reasonable cause to believe may be required as evidence." That power is conferred by the statute: see section 20C(3). Thus the power to seize and remove is conferred by statute and not by the warrant. Equally the prohibition on seizure and removal of documents in the possession of a solicitor "with respect to which a claim to professional privilege could be maintained" is imposed by the statute and not by the warrant.
>
> (2) There is an absolute prohibition in section 20C(4) against seizure and removal of documents in respect of which a claim for professional privilege could be maintained. That prohibition does not depend upon whether an officer of the board had reasonable grounds for believing that the documents are subject to legal professional privilege. This is to be contrasted with the provisions of section 8(1) of the Police and Criminal Evidence

55 For example, the powers to obtain information or documents cannot be used when that information or those documents relate to the conduct of an appeal (TMA 1970, s 20B).

56 TMA 1970, s 20B(8).

Act 1984 which require a magistrate to whom an application is made for a warrant to consider whether there are reasonable grounds for believing that the material in respect of which a warrant is sought consists of items subject to such privilege.

The first issue: were the warrants... invalid?

Mr. O'Connor on behalf of the applicant contended that the warrants are invalid because they fail properly to specify the nature and dates of the relevant offences under investigation ... Further, he contended that the *[earlier]* warrants ... ought to have identified the persons and entities relevant to the investigation, a defect cured by means of the schedule attached to the *[later]* warrant... He eschewed any proposition of general application. He did not contend that all warrants must always contain that information but, he said, in relation to these warrants, it was practicable and necessary to give that information, bearing in mind that the investigation had been in progress since at least 1996. If the warrants had been more specific they could not have prejudiced an investigation which had led to charges by the time of the first warrants ...

Underlying the applicant's contentions lies the emphasis Mr. O'Connor placed upon the importance of legal professional privilege. This case concerned a raid upon the offices of a legal adviser ...

It is ... as Lord Taylor of Gosforth C.J. said, a fundamental human right protected by the European Convention for the Protection of Human Rights and Fundamental Freedoms (1953) (Cmd. 8969).[57] As the European Court of Human Rights said in *Niemietz v Germany*,[58] "an encroachment on professional secrecy may have repercussions on the proper administration of justice and hence on the rights guaranteed by article 6 of the convention."[59]

Legal professional privilege, contended Mr. O'Connor, is fragile. It requires careful protection since in a matter of moments damage may be irredeemably caused to the relationship between lawyer and client.

Further, apart from the public interest in protection of the administration of justice there lies the public interest in protecting the security and integrity of a person's place of business and property.

These two aspects of public interest would be afforded, he contended, better protection by providing more specific information in these warrants. If the applicant's solicitor had been better informed as to the nature and scope of the investigation he would have been in a better position to ensure that the officers confined their seizure and removal to those documents relevant to the investigation and to those documents not subject to legal professional privilege. On the contrary, he said, the unspecific warrants in this case deprived the solicitor of making any sensible objection to an excessively wide search. Moreover, it hampered him in seeking a prompt and effective legal remedy. Had these warrants been more specific it would have been easier, so it was argued, for the applicant to demonstrate to a court that the documents seized were irrelevant or subject to legal professional privilege. In short, it was contended, that greater specificity within the warrants provides greater protection against excessive intrusion.

The importance of safeguarding the integrity of a person's property and of legal professional privilege cannot be gainsaid. But I reject the conclusion which the applicant invited me to draw. Under the statutory scheme of section 20C of the Taxes Management Act 1970, the validity of the warrant depends not upon its particularity but upon (1) there being reasonable ground for suspecting that an offence involving serious fraud (as identified by section 20C(1A), as inserted by section 46 of the Finance Act 1989) in connection with tax is being, has been or is about to be committed; (2) there being reasonable ground for suspecting that evidence of that offence is to be found on premises specified in the information (section 20C(1)(a)); and (3) the officer acting with the approval of the board in relation to the particular case (section 20C(1)(b)).

If the judicial authority is satisfied as to those conditions then it may issue a warrant authorising entry and search. Neither the judicial authority nor the warrant has anything

57 [See Chapter 4, below, paras **[4.40]**–**[4.46]**.]
58 (1992) 16 EHRR 97.
59 (1992) 16 EHRR 97 at 114.

to say as to the power to seize and remove and the prohibition against seizure and removal. There is nothing in the statute which requires the particularity for which the applicant contended.

...Apart from the principles to be discerned from the statutory regime itself, there is insuperable authority against the applicant's proposition. No one concerned at the revenue's powers of seizure could forget that in 1979, when searching for needles indicative of tax fraud the revenue took haystacks from the homes of Mr. Plummer and Mr. Tucker amongst others: see *R v Inland Revenue Commissioners, ex parte Rossminster Ltd*[60] rejected the contention that the warrants were invalid because they failed to identify the nature of the suspected offences and failed to provide sufficient particularity to identify what was being sought or whether the officers had reasonable grounds to believe that a document might be required as evidence. The House of Lords held that the occupier and owner of the documents had no right to be told of the grounds on which the judge had been satisfied before authorising the issue of the warrant. **[2.16]**

The taxpayer also contended that the process by which the material was sifted and seized was unlawful. **[2.17]**

The second issue: the legality of the seizure and removal

The applicant's next contention related to the wording of subsection 20C(4). Mr. O'Connor contended that in relation to all the documents retained by the legal adviser "a claim to professional privilege could be maintained."

This means that, when executing a warrant upon a solicitor's office, the officers must allow for a claim which is merely potentially valid.

Mr. O'Connor accepted that, if his construction of section 20C(4) is correct, it will prevent seizure and removal of nearly every document from any solicitor's office and emasculates any authority to search such offices. It would certainly prevent any considered investigation as to whether those items identified in section 10 of the Police and Criminal Evidence Act 1984 were not in fact the subject of legal professional privilege because they were "held with the intention of furthering a criminal purpose:" see section 10(2) of the Police and Criminal Evidence Act 1984.

He accepted that it will, in nearly every case, be impossible to discover whether documents, perhaps innocently held by a solicitor, were not in fact subject to legal privilege because they were designed to further a criminal purpose.

In my judgment the submission fails on the plain wording of section 20C(4). The word is "maintained" not "made." A claim may be made but it by no means follows that it can be maintained. It is clear to me that subsection (4) relates to documents which are properly the subject of professional privilege, in other words, in respect of which a claim could successfully be made. The word "maintained" carries with it the implication of a successful claim not a claim designed, perhaps, to defeat any investigation as to whether documents were held for a criminal purpose. **[2.18]**

R (on the application of Morgan Grenfell) v Special Commissioner of Income Tax [2003] 1 AC 563 (HL); see below, para [4.45]

The taxpayer had applied for judicial review to quash a notice under TMA 1970, s 20(1) requiring the production of documents relating to legal advice obtained in relation to a tax avoidance scheme. The House of Lords held that the scope of legal professional privilege was not restricted to particular powers referred to in the statute.

60 [1980] AC 952 [above, para **[2.10]**.]

LORD HOBHOUSE OF WOODBOROUGH:
43 The question is one of statutory construction. It is now accepted for the purposes of this litigation that the documents in respect of which the right to demand production remains in dispute contain or may contain information relevant to a tax liability to which Morgan Grenfell may be liable or its amount and that they are documents which are subject to legal professional privilege (advice privilege) which has not been waived. It is likewise accepted that the character of the privilege is that described in the speech of Lord Taylor of Gosforth CJ in your Lordships' House in *R v Derby Magistrates' Court, Ex p B*[61] its character is absolute and:

> "if a balancing exercise was ever required in the case of legal professional privilege, it was performed once and for all in the 16th century, and since then has applied across the board in every case, irrespective of the client's individual merits."

At the least, some and, more probably, all of these premises would benefit from further examination but they have not been the subject of argument on the present appeal. The question of construction is therefore whether the statute empowers the revenue to require the delivery up to them of documents notwithstanding that they are covered by legal professional privilege.

44 The next step in the legal analysis is also not disputed and was expressly adopted by the Court of Appeal. The principle of statutory construction is succinctly stated in a quotation from the speech of Lord Hoffmann in *R v Secretary of State for the Home Department, Ex p Simms*[62]:

> "Parliamentary sovereignty means that Parliament can, if it chooses, legislate contrary to fundamental principles of human rights ... The constraints upon its exercise by Parliament are ultimately political, not legal. But the principle of legality means that Parliament must squarely confront what it is doing and accept the political cost. Fundamental rights cannot be overridden by general or ambiguous words. This is because there is too great a risk that the full implications of their unqualified meaning may have passed unnoticed in the democratic process. In the absence of express language or necessary implication to the contrary, the courts therefore presume that even the most general words were intended to be subject to the basic rights of the individual. In this way the courts of the United Kingdom, though acknowledging the sovereignty of Parliament, apply principles of constitutionality little different from those which exist in countries where the power of the legislature is expressly limited by a constitutional document."

The context in which Lord Hoffmann was speaking was human rights but the principle of statutory construction is not new and has long been applied in relation to the question whether a statute is to be read as having overridden some basic tenet of the common law: Viscountess Rhondda's Claim[63]; *B (A Minor) v Director of Public Prosecutions.*[64] The protection given by the common law to those entitled to claim legal professional privilege is a basic tenet of the common law as has been reaffirmed by *B (A Minor) v Director of Public Prosecutions.*

45 It is accepted that the statute does not contain any express words that abrogate the taxpayer's common law right to rely upon legal professional privilege. The question therefore becomes whether there is a necessary implication to that effect. A necessary implication is not the same as a reasonable implication as was pointed out by Lord Hutton in *B (A Minor) v Director of Public Prosecutions.*[65] A necessary implication is one which necessarily follows from the express provisions of the statute construed in their context. It distinguishes between what it would have been sensible or reasonable for Parliament to have included or what Parliament would, if it had thought about it, probably have included

61 [1996] AC 487 at 508.
62 [2000] 2 AC 115 at 131.
63 [1922] 2 AC 339.
64 [2000] 2 AC 428.
65 [2000] 2 AC 428, 481.

and what it is clear that the express language of the statute shows that the statute must have included. A necessary implication is a matter of express language and logic not interpretation.

46 In the present case the statutory language falls a long way short of meeting this criterion. The arguments advanced by the revenue are fully discussed in the opinion of my noble and learned friend. I agree with his conclusion. At best from the point of view of the revenue the legislation is equivocal. Left to myself I would incline to the view that the implication, if any, is that the legislature was intending to preserve the legal professional privilege of the taxpayer rather than abrogate it; otherwise, why preserve it in respect of documents in the hands of the adviser when the client has not consented to waive the privilege? Further, the argument that a general public interest in collecting revenue for the executive suffices (in peace-time) implicitly to override the basic right and public interest represented by legal professional privilege is contrary to the authorities and the principles which the revenue accept that those authorities lay down.

47 The present appeal thus falls to be decided applying the well established principles of statutory construction to be found in English law. The appellants do not need the assistance of the Human Rights Act 1998 or the Convention for the Protection of Human Rights and Fundamental Freedoms. The judgments of the European Court of Human Rights in *Foxley v United Kingdom*,[66] and the European Court of Justice in *A M & S Europe Ltd v Commission of the European Communities*,[67] show a general recognition of the importance of legal professional privilege.

48 There were cited to your Lordships decisions of the courts of other common law jurisdictions which have also arrived at conclusions very similar to those of your Lordships in this case. I do not wish to add anything to what my noble and learned friend [Lord Hoffmann] has said in this connection nor to what he has said about the English authorities which will now have to be read with the judgment of this House. Attention has rightly been drawn by my noble and learned friend to what was said by Glidewell LJ in *R v Inland Revenue Comrs, Ex p Taylor* (No 2)[68] concerning the implicit restriction upon the use which may be made of documents which are obtained under a statutory power and its possible interaction with the question whether a client's privilege will be infringed by requiring the disclosure of documents by the professional adviser. It is a general principle that where a power is given for a particular purpose it is not permissible to use that power for a collateral purpose.

LORD HOFFMANN:

39 It is of course open to Parliament, if it considers that the revenue require such powers, to enact them in unambiguous terms. But there is also the Human Rights Act 1998 to be borne in mind. The appellants put forward an alternative submission that, if your Lordships agreed with the construction given to section 20(1) by the Court of Appeal, you should make a declaration that it was incompatible with the right to privacy under article 8 of the Convention for the Protection of Human Rights and Fundamental Freedoms (scheduled to the Human Rights Act 1998). In the circumstances it is unnecessary for your Lordships to pronounce upon the point. It is however the case, as I have mentioned, that the European Court of Human Rights has said that LPP is a fundamental human right which can be invaded only in exceptional circumstances: see *Foxley v United Kingdom*[69] Mr Brennan said that the public interest in the collection of the revenue could provide the necessary justification but I very much doubt whether this is right. Nor is it sufficient to say simply that the power is not used very often. That is no consolation to the person against whom it is used. If new legislation is passed, it will have to be seen whether it is limited to cases in which the interference with LPP can be shown to have a legitimate aim which is necessary in a democratic society. **[2.19]**

66 31 EHRR 637.
67 (Case 155/79) [1983] QB 878.
68 [1989] 3 All ER 353, 360.
69 (2000) 31 EHRR 637, 647, para 44.

B. Human rights

In *R (on the application of Morgan Grenfell) v Special Commissioner of Income Tax*, considered above, Lord Hoffmann referred to the fact that the Human Rights Act 1998 (HRA), which effectively incorporates into English law the fundamental human rights set out in the European Convention on Human Rights, should be borne in mind when consideration is given to the HMRC's exercise of its powers to obtain information. A breach of a Convention right had not been pleaded in the *Morgan Grenfell* case, so the HRA was not at issue, but it may well be in future cases. In particular, art 8, which provides that everyone is entitled 'to respect for his private and family life, his home and his correspondence', may prove to be of importance where questions concerning HMRC information-gathering powers are at issue. This is considered in Chapter 4, paras **[4.40]–[4.46]**, below. **[2.20]**

C. The Taxpayer's Charter, the Revenue Adjudicator and the Ombudsman

The Taxpayer's Charter was part of the Government's commitment to improving the standard of public services and making them 'more responsive to their users.'[70] For its part, the former Inland Revenue committed itself to a review of the complaints procedure 'to make sure that all taxpayers have access to an effective system for ensuring that the standards set out in the Taxpayer's Charter and its supporting codes of practice are met.'[71] One result of the review was the appointment in 1993 of a Revenue Adjudicator. The Adjudicator's remit was, and continues to be, to examine complaints about the handling of taxpayers' tax affairs. Since taxpayers have always been able to complain, through their MP, to the Parliamentary Ombudsman about matters concerning the conduct of the revenue authorities towards their tax affairs, it must be recognised that there exists an overlap between the functions of the Adjudicator and the Ombudsman. **[2.21]**

Natalie Lee (gen ed) *Revenue Law – Principles and Practice* (24th edn, 2006), para [4.92]

In August 1991, the Taxpayer's Charter was launched, setting out the standard of service to be expected of the Inland Revenue and Customs and Excise. Subsequently the Revenue introduced three new codes of practice in support of the Charter (dealing with the conduct of tax investigations, the conduct of inspections of employers' PAYE records and compensation for serious delays or mistakes) and a Code of Practice for the Provision of Information and Advice. The Taxpayer's Charter has now been replaced by a 'mission statement' ('Our Service Commitment To You') setting out what HMRC's customers can expect to receive by way of service. This is underpinned by two charters, one for taxpayers (IR 167) and one for NI[72] contributors.

70 The Citizen's Charter, First Report: 1992, Cm 2101.
71 Ibid, p 33.
72 [National Insurance.]

In addition there exists an independent Adjudicator. The Adjudicator's function is to examine complaints from taxpayers. They are not responsible for hearing appeals on matters of law; such appeals continue to rest with the Commissioners.[73] The Adjudicator is, instead, concerned with the manner in which HMRC conducts a taxpayer's affairs, eg whether there has been excessive delays, any error or any discourtesy. Unless the circumstances are exceptional, normally HMRC will accept the Adjudicator's decision. **[2.22]**

Chantal Stebbings 'The Revenue Adjudicator' [1993] BTR 301, 302–304

The Inland Revenue has described and promoted the Revenue Adjudicator as "independent." In making the announcement the Chancellor of the Exchequer referred to the Revenue Adjudicator as "impartial" and "independent,"[74] and the Inland Revenue Press Release of February 1993 stated that the Adjudicator "will be independent of the Inland Revenue."[75] The Inland Revenue literature repeatedly describes the Adjudicator as independent in the same way that it refers to the truly independent General and Special Commissioners and the Ombudsman. The Inland Revenue used such terms because it wished to settle as many complaints as possible using its internal procedures, and to do so it had to "convince the general public that [its] internal procedures are entirely dispassionate."[76]

It believed that such a person could be made to seem independent of the Revenue.[77] The Adjudicator certainly aspires to a degree of independence. It is true to say that the Adjudicator does not have to have a tax background, and indeed the first Adjudicator, Elizabeth Filkin, is a former chief executive of the National Association of Citizen's Advice Bureaux and former chief executive of London Docklands Corporation . . . It has been observed, however, that "inexperience is not the same as independence."[78] The Adjudicator will not be subject to any direction from the Inland Revenue in respect of any complaint under investigation, and doubtless will always be, in the words of the Chairman of the Board of Inland Revenue prior to the appointment, "someone of independent mind who will see their function as truly independent."[79]

To describe the Adjudicator as independent, however, is misleading. While any one individual holder of the office may well be quite independent in mind and function of the Inland Revenue, his or her connections with the Inland Revenue cannot be ignored. The Adjudicator is appointed and remunerated by contract with the Inland Revenue as an office-holder and will report annually to the Inland Revenue. His or her support staff, initially at least, will be seconded from the Inland Revenue, and, as the Chairman of the Select Committee on the Parliamentary Commissioner for Administration observed, "quite clearly, he will be guided by Revenue staff, by Revenue precedent and by the Revenue philosophy."[80]

73 [See Chapter 3, para **[3.14]**.]
74 (1993) STI 287.
75 *Ibid.*
76 Minutes of Evidence taken before the Select Committee on the Parliamentary Commissioner for Administration, H.C. 387 Sess. 1992–93, q. 137.
77 *Ibid*, q. 120.
78 Report of the Select Committee on the Parliamentary Commissioner for Administration, H.C. 387 Sess. 1992–93 p viii, hereafter cited as the *Report.*
79 Minutes of Evidence taken before the Select Committee on the Parliamentary Commissioner for Administration, H.C. 387 Sess. 1992–93, q. 126.
80 *Ibid*, q. 125.

Thus to say the Adjudicator is independent is, in the words of the Ombudsman himself, "getting towards a faulty description of goods."[81] The Adjudicator is nothing more nor indeed less than the top tier of the internal Inland Revenue complaints procedure.

On learning of the creation of the post of Revenue Adjudicator, and its description in the terms discussed above, the Select Committee on the Parliamentary Commissioner for Administration expressed concern that such an appointment would undermine the work of the Ombudsman. Not only was it misleading to describe the Adjudicator as independent, it also gave rise to the perception that the Adjudicator is directly challenging the Ombudsman.

The Ombudsman is one of the two existing independent bodies which hear complaints of different kinds from taxpayers. The General and Special Commissioners hear taxpayers' appeals, largely against assessments to tax, while the Ombudsman hears complaints against maladministration in tax affairs. The appointment of the Adjudicator will leave the former unaffected, for he or she does not have the authority to take appeals on matters subject to existing rights of appeal, namely matters involving tax law or liability.[82] The relationship between the Adjudicator and the Ombudsman is more problematic, for the remit of the Adjudicator runs in areas very similar to that of the Ombudsman, and the Ombudsman at present devotes a substantial amount of his time to investigating complaints of injustice suffered as a result of maladministration in tax matters.[83] Their inquisitorial methods and procedures are similar, with both having full access to the information necessary for an effective investigation, though of course their authority for so doing is different. Neither can compel the Inland Revenue to adopt his recommendations, though it is likely that in both instances they will be so adopted. This is because in the case of the Adjudicator the Revenue has agreed to do so in principle, and in the case of the Ombudsman past practice has shown that in the interests of good administration and to avoid adverse comment in Parliament recommendations are adopted. Whether a taxpayer takes his complaint to the Adjudicator or the Ombudsman, he will not incur costs.

The Adjudicator and the Ombudsman are, however, very different creatures. At the heart of the distinction lies the Adjudicator's inevitable lack of independence. It is essential that the Inland Revenue amends its literature to ensure that taxpayers are aware that if they refer their complaints to the Adjudicator, they are so doing within the internal framework of the Inland Revenue. Otherwise it is likely that they would be under the mistaken impression that their complaints were being investigated by a body distinct from the Inland Revenue and accordingly quite impartial. If this perception were to be allowed to develop among taxpayers, matters which should properly be investigated by the Ombudsman may well be directed by misguided taxpayers to the Adjudicator instead.[84] **[2.23]**

For a more detailed examination and critique of the Revenue Adjudicator's functions, see Barbara Mills QC[85] *Taxation*, Vol 145, No 3762, p 306. **[2.24]**

81 *Ibid*, q. 117.
82 (1993) S.T.I. at pp. 287–278.
83 *Report*, p vi. On the work of the Ombudsman in the field of tax, see generally R. T. Bartlett 'The Ombudsman in Taxation: A Tripartite Perspective' [1988] B.T.R. 164.
84 *Report*, p ix. . .
85 The current Revenue Adjudicator; the first was Elizabeth Filkin.

3 How Tax Cases are Decided

1. Introduction

Where there is an appeal from a decision of an officer of HMRC,[1] it will be heard, initially, by either the General or Special Commissioners, both of whom have jurisdiction over direct taxes,[2] and it is for the taxpayer to show that the decision is wrong, rather than for HMRC to show that it is correct.[3] The General Commissioners are similar to magistrates, being laypersons appointed locally for a district, whereas the Special Commissioners are tax specialists, comprising barristers, advocates or solicitors of at least ten years' standing.[4] Generally, the taxpayer is free to choose whether to appeal to the General Commissioners or to the Special Commissioners, but the choice may be disapplied by agreement, or by a direction from the General Commissioners.[5]

Appeals against decisions of the General Commissioners must be made by way of 'case stated' to the High Court;[6] those against Special Commissioners' decisions are by appeal,[7] either to the High Court,[8] or, in certain circumstances, direct to the Court of Appeal.[9] Further appeals lie to the House of Lords (either via the Court of Appeal)[10] or, in certain cases, direct from the High Court.[11] In all cases, appeals can only be made on questions of

1 This chapter does not cover judicial review of the actions of officers of HMRC or of the decisions of the General and Special Commissioners (see John Tiley *Revenue Law* (5th edn, 2005) pp 77–78). Judges have pointed out that judicial review should not be used as a way of sidestepping the appeals process: see eg *R v IRC, ex p Bishopp* [1999] STC 531 (Dyson J). For a recent example of the judicial review of a decision by General Commissioners, see *R (on the application of Browallia Cal Ltd) v General Commissioners of Income Tax* [2003] EWHC 2779 (Admin), [2004] STC 296.

2 Although the Special Commissioners have exclusive jurisdiction with respect to certain specific matters, such as issues concerning international tax.

3 TMA 1970, s 50(6); see below, para **[3.20]**.

4 *Ibid*, s 4.

5 *Ibid*, s 31D.

6 See TMA 1970, s 56(3). In Scotland, it is the Court of Session (see TMA, s 56(10)) and in Northern Ireland, to the Court of Appeal in Northern Ireland (see TMA 1970, s 58(2)).

7 See TMA 1970, s 56A.

8 Or the Court of Session in Scotland, or the Court of Appeal in Northern Ireland.

9 See TMA 1970, s 56A(2).

10 See TMA 1970, s 56(8) (General Commissioners); TMA, s 56A(5) (Special Commissioners).

11 See TMA 1970, s 56(8)(b) (General Commissioners); TMA, s 56A(5) (Special Commissioners). The consolidated appeals in *Small (Inspector of Taxes) v Mars UK Ltd* (High Court decision at [2005] EWHC 553, [2005] STC 958 and *Inland Revenue Commissioners v William Grant and Sons Distillers Ltd* (Court of Session decision at [2005] CSIH 63, [2006] STC 6) were direct appeals from the High Court/Court of Session to the House of Lords (see below, para **[10.11]**).

law,[12] not on questions of fact. There also exists the possibility, where relevant, of a reference to the European Court of Justice (ECJ)[13] and an appeal to the European Court of Human Rights. As far as the former is concerned, its role has been described as that of 'guardian of the 'constitution' and supreme interpreter of EU law'.[14] Although direct tax law has not been harmonised, the ECJ is concerned to see that the tax laws of member states do not infringe the non-discrimination principles,[15] which, as Tiley points out, are at the heart of the EC Treaty and the law.[16] As far as the European Court of Human Rights (ECHR) is concerned, it has always heard a large number of tax cases, even before the Human Rights Act 1998 came into force, some of which have been brought by UK taxpayers against the UK government.[17] Such taxpayers have experienced mixed success, and the ECHR has often placed reliance upon the principle of the margin of appreciation in those cases in which it has found in favour of the UK government.[18]

Exceptionally, proceedings in tax cases may be initiated in the High Court. This can occur where UK statutory provisions are challenged on the ground that they are inconsistent/incompatible with EC law; these cases fall outside the jurisdiction of the Commissioners (Special or General).[19] In this respect, there has been, in recent years, a spate of cases (relating to various aspects of UK corporation tax) in which claimants have pursued claims in the High Court that raise common or connected issues of fact and/or law.[20] The respective claims have been conducted within the framework of a group litigation order (GLO)[21] the general operation of which has been described by Sir Andrew Park as follows:[22]

> 'The basic idea of a GLO is that it regulates litigation in which there are a number of claimants whose claims all raise "common or related issues of fact or law": rule 19.10 [CPR]. There is a management court and a management judge. A register has to be kept of all the participants in the GLO. The order can, and in my experience does, direct that all claims which raise "GLO issues" have to be transferred to the management court, and are dealt with as part of the group litigation. One or more test cases are identified and proceed to trial. Meanwhile all the other cases are stayed pending the determination of the test cases. Any judgment or order in the test case is binding on all participants in the GLO.'

12 See TMA 1970, s 56(6), '. . . any question or questions of law arising on a case stated' (General Commissioners to High Court); TMA 1970, s 56A '. . . shall hear and determine any question of law arising on an appeal . . .' (Special Commissioners to High Court or Court of Appeal).

13 See art 234 (ex 177), EC Treaty.

14 Colin Manchester and David Salter *Exploring the Law: The Dynamics of Precedent and Statutory Interpretation* (3rd edn, 2006) p 101.

15 See Timothy Lyons 'Discrimination Against Individuals and Enterprises on Grounds of Nationality: Direct Taxation and the European Court of Justice' [1994] BTR 554.

16 John Tiley *Revenue Law* (5th edn, 2005) p 33.

17 Eg *National and Provincial Building Society v UK* (1998) 25 EHRR 127, [1997] STC 1466; *A, B, C & D v UK* (1981) 23 DR 203; *Nap Holdings UK Ltd v UK* (1996) 22 EHRR 114. Each of these cases concerned the issue of retrospective legislation.

18 See generally, Natalie Lee 'The Effect of the Human Rights Act 1998 on Taxation Policy and Administration', eJournal of Tax Research, vol 2, no 2, 2004.

19 However, the courts are keen to ensure that the usual progression of a tax case is followed wherever this is appropriate, and, in particular, to protect the jurisdiction of the Special and General Commissioners; see *Autologic Holdings plc and Others v IRC (re claimants under Loss Relief Group Litigation Order)* [2005] UKHL 54, [2005] STC 1357.

20 See further, Chapter 18, paras **[18.21]–[18.24]**.

21 GLOs are provided for by rr 19.10–19.15 of the Civil Procedure Rules which came into force on 2 May 2000.

22 'A Judge's Tale: Corporation Tax and Community Law' [2006] BTR 322 at 325. In this article, the author discusses, inter alia, his participation as a Chancery judge in a number of cases concerning the impact of EC law on aspects of UK corporation tax.

Sir Andrew Park, immediately prior to his recent retirement, was the management judge for the tax-related GLOs.

When dealing with appeals, the Commissioners and the courts are faced with detailed and complex legislation. Traditionally, and generally to the taxpayer's advantage, the view was taken that tax statutes should be given their literal meaning. More recently, however, there has been advanced an argument for a purposive approach, and whilst this has seemed to find favour in a certain number of tax avoidance cases,[23] it has enjoyed less success in other types of tax cases.[24] **[3.1]**

2. Reform of the General and Special Commissioners

Although proposals for reform of the tax appeals system were made as long ago as 1996,[25] reform has been slow to materialise.[26] However, change, as part of the reform of the tribunal system generally, is now imminent.[27] **[3.2]**

The Tax Law Review Committee *Interim Report on the Tax Appeals System* (IFS, 1996)

Introduction – the underlying principle

The appeals system is a crucial safeguard for the taxpayer. If the appeals system is ineffective or inaccessible, taxpayers are for practical purposes unable to challenge the revenue department's own interpretation of the law. Improving the appeals system should therefore be seen as a vital part of the initiative to improve the standards of customer service by the revenue departments at the most fundamental level – namely, the performance of their obligation to collect tax only in accordance with the law.

Of course, in the vast majority of cases, the taxpayer's affairs will be settled without any need for recourse to an independent body. Normally, no serious dispute will arise. Even where there is a genuine point of difference, often this will be resolved at an early stage by negotiations between the taxpayer and Customs or the revenue. Cases where there is a persisting disagreement are therefore the exception. But in such cases the taxpayer will believe that the revenue department has made a mistake about either the correct interpretation of the law, or its application to his circumstances. The obligation of the appeals system is to allow the parties to obtain a ruling on this from an independent tribunal or, on a point of law,

23 See eg *Ramsay (WT) Ltd v IRC* [1982] AC 300; *IRC v McGuckian* [1997] 3 All ER 817; see below, paras **[5.7]** and **[5.11]** respectively.

24 See eg *Frankland v IRC* [1997] STC 1450, below, para **[3.32]**.

25 See the Tax Law Review Committee *Interim Report on the Tax Appeals System* (below).

26 See John F Avery Jones 'The Reform of the Tax Tribunals: a Story of Uncompleted Business' [2006] BTR 282.

27 See Department for Constitutional Affairs *The draft Tribunals, Courts and Enforcement Bill* (Cm 6885) (London, 2006), Part 1 (available from www.dca.gov.uk); see Jane Moore 'The Tribunals, Courts and Enforcement Bill' The Tax Journal, 21 August 2006, pp 11–12, and below, para **[3.4]**.

the courts.[28] It is crucial therefore that the appeals system is fast, effective and affordable. We note in this context, the views of the Keith Committee:

> A point which we have made throughout this Report is the necessity for the Revenue Departments to have sufficient powers to make taxpayers comply with their obligations and to investigate those who do not. The counterpart of such powers is the right of the taxpayer to dispute cases in which he considers the exercise of those powers to be excessive . . . What is needed . . . is a proper disputes procedure under which the taxpayer can complain to an independent tribunal when he considers that powers have been misused. Accordingly we consider that this subject is central to the theme of providing the necessary balance between the taxpayer and the Revenue Departments.

We also note the general principles set out by the Deregulation Unit in its May 1995 Consultation Document on a Model Appeals Mechanism. These emphasised the importance of a fair and independent appeals process against enforcement action by government departments and agencies, and were confirmed in the introduction to the Model Appeals Mechanism published in March of this year. It was accepted that without more accessible and simpler appeals business may be deterred from challenging an enforcement decision they feel to be unfair. The uncertainty created by delays, it was considered, could adversely affect investment and enforcement was acknowledged. These points hold good in the tax content. It should also be noted that tax liabilities disputed by business, as a potential direct cost, will often be locked into tax provisions until the dispute is resolved.

. . . The appeals system is a key element in maintaining the balance of power between the revenue departments and taxpayer. It must provide an adequate and timely remedy where there is a dispute on a technical matter or where the taxpayer argues that the revenue departments have exceeded their powers. Conversely, it is essential that the goal of efficient tax administration is not prejudiced by poor quality decision-making within the appeals system, or by delays which may encourage opportunistic challenges by taxpayers trying to postpone payment of amounts legally due. This means that taxpayers and the revenue departments have in many key respects a common interest in the effective and efficient functioning of the appeals system.

However, there are also some significant differences in their perspectives. In particular, there is at present a potential conflict of interest in the role of the revenue departments as both the instigators of key appeal provisions and the defending party in all individual cases concerning the taxes which they administer. We believe that there needs to be a clear, publicly available policy as to the scope of appeal rights to underpin discussion of individual decisions in relation to the extent of appeal rights or the rules governing the exercise of these. Together with the restructuring of the direct tax appeals legislation . . . this should help to ensure that decisions about the scope of appeal rights are, and are seen to be, based on legitimate policy considerations rather than being haphazard. By increasing transparency, it would also reduce the scope for fears – however unfounded – that decisions about the extent of appeal rights may on occasion be tainted by the desire to protect administrative decisions from external scrutiny.

28 As with any other form of independent scrutiny, it may also influence the way decisions are taken or even, in some cases, the decisions actually reached, as the decision-maker takes into account the possibility he will be required to defend the decision to an independent adjudicator. (For decision-makers' own assessment of the influence of the appeal system on their decision making process in the context of social security see Baldwin, Wikeley and Young (1992) pp. 83–89. This study suggested that officers who had direct contact with the tribunal were also more likely to be influenced by the approach they expected the tribunal to take to a case than officers who would not personally be involved in tribunal hearings.)

We have also derived from our consideration of the functions of the appeals system six key objectives for the tax appeals system.

(i) **It must be adequate in scope, and all the key rules governing its operation (not merely the procedural rules for the tribunals) should be the subject of a coherent and publicly available policy.** This principle derives from the fact that the value of the appeals system to the taxpayer depends on the extent of his appeal rights and the way in which these can be exercised.

(ii) **It must ensure a high quality of decision-making. This entails:**
- that each case should be allocated to a suitable level within the appeal system, by reference to the nature and complexity of the issues involved; and
- that each case should be allocated to a suitable level within the appeal system, by reference to the nature and complexity of the issues involved; and

(iii) **It must be fair.** The system needs to be:
- even-handed as between the parties to an appeal, normally a taxpayer and the Inland Revenue or Customs;
- even-handed as between different taxpayers.

(iv) **It must be accessible.** This means it must be:
- affordable;
- as simple and easy to understand as possible, so that procedural formality and complexity are kept to a minimum consistent with the achievement of other objectives;
- physically accessible, offering sufficiently local hearings not to deter appellants or cause them unacceptable cost or inconvenience; and
- Make adequate provision for information and assistance for taxpayers about the way in which they should prepare an appeal and what will happen at an appeal hearing.

(v) **It must be flexible,** so that there is adequate provision for the full range of tax cases and for taxpayers of widely differing degrees of sophistication.

(vi) **It must resolve cases quickly and efficiently. This means that:**
- Successive tiers of appeal should be kept to the necessary minimum;
- Cases should be allocated to an appellate level suited to the determination of the issues at stake;
- Procedure should be streamlined, and procedural rules should not generally operate to prevent issues arising out of the same or closely related facts being dealt with as part of a single set of proceedings in a single forum. [3.3]

Natalie Lee (gen ed) *Revenue Law – Principles and Practice* (24th edn, 2006) para [4.58]

The Leggatt Inquiry (which examined the Tribunal system in general) was commenced almost simultaneously with the issue of a consultation document entitled *Tax Appeals* by the Lord Chancellor's Department in 2000. In his Report, a unified tax appeals system was proposed. In July 2004, the Government published a White Paper entitled 'Transforming Public Service: Complaints, Redress and Tribunals', its response to the Leggatt Report. The key proposal that is set out in the White Paper is a unified tribunal service organisation. This was intended to come into being in April 2006; it has yet to be implemented.

Under the White Paper, it is proposed that the current jurisdictions of the VAT and Duties Tribunal, the Special and the General Commissioners will be combined.

The High Court's role in tax appeals will be eliminated; and, instead, there will be a two-tier tax tribunal system, with a right of appeal from the second-tier tribunal to the Court of Appeal. The first tier will be responsible for hearing most direct and indirect tax appeals at first instance; the second-tier tax tribunal will be an appellate tier to which an appeal will lie with permission from the first tier on a point of law (it will also have a first-instance jurisdiction for cases that are of sufficient size and complexity to justify starting at that level). Decisions of the second tier (almost certainly) would be binding on the lower tier ... **[3.4]**

3. Issues of fact and issues of law

The appeals system relies on a fundamental distinction between matters of law and matters of fact because appeals against decisions of Commissioners can be made only on questions of law. This has led some judges to devise concepts such as 'mixed law and fact', in order that the higher courts can retain some measure of control. Others have adopted a 'hands off' approach and stuck to the apparently more straightforward distinction between law and fact. Although each group of distinctions is problematic, what is clear is that, subject to only one exception, if a finding is correctly characterised as one of fact only, then it is final. The exception is where 'the facts found are such that no person acting judicially and properly instructed as to the relevant law could have come to the determination under appeal',[29] ie that the case is 'one in which the true and only reasonable conclusion contradicts the determination'.[30] Although this exception gives the higher courts an opportunity to review decisions, it is not a licence to interfere, and the higher court's mere disagreement with the Commissioners' decision is not by itself enough to bring the exception into play. **[3.5]**

A. *The fact/law distinction*

Some questions, such as whether tax was paid on a particular day, are clearly questions of fact. Others, such as what the wording of a particular statute means, are clearly questions of law. Questions such as whether a particular situation fits a statutory definition can be more difficult.

Case law discloses a distinction between 'primary facts', on the one hand, and 'inferences' or 'conclusions' from those facts, on the other. The latter may, depending on a court's view of the case, be described as findings of 'mixed fact and law', 'findings of law', or 'findings of fact'.[31] **[3.6]**

British Launderers' Research Association v Borough of Hendon Rating Authority **[1949] 1 KB 462 (CA)**

DENNING LJ: ... Primary facts are facts which are observed by witnesses and proved by oral testimony or facts proved by the production of the thing itself, such as original documents. Their determination is essentially a question of fact for the tribunal of fact, and

29 See *Edwards (Inspector of Taxes) v Bairstow and Harrison* [1956] AC 14; below, para **[3.15]**.
30 Ibid.
31 See *Furniss v Dawson*, per Lord Brightman ([1984] STC 153 at 167): 'If they are inferences, they are nevertheless facts to be found by the commissioners.'

the only question of law that can arise on them is whether there was any evidence to support the finding. The conclusions from primary facts are, however, inferences deduced by a process of reasoning from them. If, and in so far as, those conclusions can as well be drawn by a layman (properly instructed on the law) as by a lawyer, they are conclusions of fact for the tribunal of fact: and the only questions of law which can arise on them are whether there was a proper direction in point of law; and whether the conclusion is one which could reasonably be drawn from the primary facts: see *Bracegirdle v. Oxley.*[32] If, and in so far, however, as the correct conclusion to be drawn from primary facts requires, for its correctness, determination by a trained lawyer – as, for instance, because it involves the interpretation of documents or because the law and the facts cannot be separated, or because the law on the point cannot properly be understood or applied except by a trained lawyer – the conclusion is a conclusion of law on which an appellate tribunal is as competent to form an opinion as the tribunal of first instance . . . **[3.7]**

Griffiths (Inspector of Taxes) v JP Harrison (Watford) Ltd [1963] AC 1 (HL)

The question to be decided was whether the taxpayers' 'dividend-stripping' activity[33] was an 'adventure in the nature of trade'.[34]

LORD DENNING *(dissenting)*: . . . Now the powers of the High Court on an appeal are very limited. The judge cannot reverse the commissioners on their findings of fact. He can only reverse their decision if it is "erroneous in point of law." Now here the primary facts were all found by the commissioners. They were stated in the case. They cannot be disputed. What is disputed is their conclusion from them. And it is now settled,[35] as well as anything can be, that their conclusion cannot be challenged unless it was unreasonable, so unreasonable that it can be dismissed as one which could not reasonably be entertained by them. It is not sufficient that the judge would himself have come to a different conclusion . . .

LORD REID: . . . In some exceptional cases the question whether a particular word or phrase in an Act applies to particular facts has come to be regarded, for reasons that I do not fully understand, as a question of fact. A line of authorities culminating in *Edwards v. Bairstow*[36] has decided that this is so as regards the word 'trade' in the Income Tax Act. But I can find no reason for supposing that the nature of the judicial process is different when the question is said to be one of fact from what it is when the question is said to be one of law. I do not know what novel method the Commissioners could adopt in determining whether the word 'trade' applies to particular facts. Like any court or other tribunal, they must defer to authority which is binding on them and pay heed to what has been said in authorities which are not directly in point. But, having done so, I cannot think that they must proceed in some way different from the way in which a court proceeds or the way in which they themselves must proceed when deciding, as a question of law, the application of some other words in the Act. . . . **[3.8]**

The decision of the House of Lords in the consolidated cases of *Smith (Inspector of Taxes) v Abbott and related appeals* and *Fitzpatrick v IRC (No 2) and related appeals*[37] is instructive in relation to the above distinctions. There were

32 [1947] KB 349.

33 This kind of transaction has been described as being 'the easiest way I can recall of getting money out of the Revenue' (see [2005] BTR 29–39, 30) and by Lord Denning, in *Griffiths . Harrison* itself, as 'a way of getting money out of the Revenue authorities . . . [requiring] a good deal of skill . . .' on the part of people he described as 'prospectors' (see [1963] AC 1 at 17).

34 See below, para **[9.5]**.

35 [See *Edwards (Inspector of Taxes) v Bairstow and Harrison* [1956] AC 14 (HL); below, para **[3.15]**.]

36 [Ibid.]

37 [1994] 1 All ER 673; see below, para **[8.66]**.

two sets of appeals. *Abbott* and others were 'English appeals'; *Fitzpatrick* and others were Scottish appeals.

In each of these appeals, journalists claimed to be entitled to deduct the cost of daily newspapers, magazines, etc, in calculating their employment income.[38] They claimed that it was a 'condition' of their employment to do so and 'an integral part of . . . [their] duties'. The Special Commissioners who heard the Scottish appeals rejected the taxpayers' claims and held that the costs of the magazines and newspapers was preparatory to, and not 'in the performance of' their duties.[39] By contrast, the General Commissioners, who heard the English appeals, 'upheld the claims of each journalist . . . on the grounds that the journalist was reading 'in the performance' of his duties'.[40]

The House of Lords (Lord Browne-Wilkinson dissenting) dismissed the taxpayers' appeals in the Scottish appeals and upheld the Crown's appeals in the English appeals. Lord Templeman opined that the '[q]uestions involved in the present cases are mixed questions of law and fact'.[41] By contrast, Lord Browne-Wilkinson in his dissenting opinion said:[42]

> 'Your Lordships' only function is to decide whether or not on the facts found in each case the decision of the commissioners in that case was in law correct. If, as in these cases, on the evidence before them the commissioners in the two cases have made differing findings of fact, your Lordships may be required to hold that their conclusions in each set of appeals (though conflicting) are right in law. It is not legitimate for this House, in seeking to reach a common sense outcome, to disregard or alter the findings of fact made by the commissioners or to characterise as a question of law what is in reality a question of fact.'

These appeals reveal a clear inconsistency in the judicial approach to questions of fact and law, and highlight the opportunity for an appellate court to reverse the Commissioners' decision by holding inferences from the primary facts to be mixed fact and law. **[3.9]**

Abimbola A Olowofoyeku 'In the Performance of the Duties: Fact, Law or Both?' [1996] BTR 28, 41–45

Fact, law, or both?

Four of the five speeches [*in Smith (Inspector of Taxes) v Abbott; Fitzpatrick v. IRC (No. 2)*] raised the perennial "fact, law, or both" question. Indeed, it is evident from the speeches that this question was regarded as more or less decisive. For example, Lord Mustill would have considered that the court was not entitled to intervene if the matter had been one of fact only. This is also apparent in the speech of Lord Jauncey. It is important to appreciate here that the real matter around which the question is raised is whether the reading of the newspapers was in the performance of the duties of the journalists. This itself can be negatively decisive, in the sense that if this activity is not part of the duties of the journalists, then expenses thereon could not have been incurred "in the performance of the duties" of the journalists,

38 Under ICTA 1988, s 198(1); see now Income Tax (Earnings and Pensions) Act 2003, s 336(1)(b); see also below, para **[8.65]**.
39 See [1994] 1 All ER 673 at 677.
40 *Ibid.*, 677.
41 *Ibid.*, 684; see also Tiley, n 1 above, p 76.
42 *Ibid.*, 686.

and none of the other questions as to deductibility (*i.e.* whether the expenses on the activity were incurred wholly, exclusively, and necessarily) would arise at all. It therefore follows that in a case on Schedule E expenses,[43] two matters fall to be decided in the first instance – what the duties of the particular office or employment are, and whether the expenses sought to be deducted were incurred while performing those duties (or alternatively whether the relevant activity fell within those duties).

In the opinion of Lord Browne-Wilkinson, these questions would be questions of fact to be established by evidence. In his view, there were sufficient primary facts to justify the conclusions of fact made by the English commissioners. Lords Jauncey and Mustill claimed that the question involved questions of law and fact , but omitted to specify which was which, and so very little assistance can be derived from their speeches. Lord Templeman claimed that they were questions of law – "... the question of law which is whether the reading was in the performance of the duties".[44] It is interesting to note his formulation of how this was a matter of law: "In all the cases there was but one question of law, namely, whether on the facts and on the true construction of [Taxes Act 1988, s 198(1)] the journalist incurred expense in the performance of his duties when he selected, purchased and read newspapers and periodicals in his own time."[45] It is obvious that some questions of law may be involved here. For example, the *meaning* of "necessarily", or "in the performance of" are possibly questions of law. Whether a particular activity *can be* a duty of the employment is also possibly a question of law. There was no suggestion that the English commissioners answered any of these questions wrongly. The question which they are said to have answered wrongly is whether the relevant activity was a duty of the employment or office. With all respect, it is hard to see how the question whether a particular activity *is* a duty of the employment can be a question of law. It seems that the words "in fact" could easily (and correctly) be interposed between "journalist" and "incurred" in the above quotation, and that the words "on the true construction of [the relevant statute]" do not add anything to the statement (since it is only stating the obvious). This seems to be what Lord Browne-Wilkinson described as characterising "as a question of law what is in reality a question of fact".[46] It seems insufficient to state that a matter involves questions of law and fact without stating which questions are questions of law and which ones are questions of fact, and neither does it seem enough to merely state that it is a matter of law without explaining how or why this is so. In the *Smith v. Abbott* appeals, whether the reading of competing newspapers can in any circumstances be *a* duty of the employment of *a* journalist is possibly a question of law. This question was obviously not of great concern in *Smith v. Abbott* because it was hardly raised at all. The proceedings were apparently conducted on the basis that it was possible for reading to be part of the duties of the employments of the journalists. The real question was whether for these particular journalists, reading newspapers was indeed part of the duties of their employment (and, perhaps, whether while they were so reading, they were actually performing the duties of their employment).

The possible conclusions on this question are finite – either they are only reading for pleasure, in a manner totally unconnected with their employments as journalists, or they are reading as part of an endeavour to remain qualified to perform their duties (*i.e.* reading was only generally preparatory), or they are reading as part of the

43 [Now referred to as expenses of an employment; see Chapter 8, below, paras **[8.64]**–**[8.76]**.]
44 At p. 685.
45 *Ibid.*
46 At p. 686. According to Lord Templeman (at p. 685) Lord Browne-Wilkinson's suggestions as to the proper resolution of the matter "demonstrates a confusion of facts, opinion and law . . ."

daily performance of duties of their employments. It is hard to see how this question can be answered at all, except by evidence. It is not a matter for legal argument, for the lawyers will only be able to speculate. Some of Lord Templeman's own statements are rather indicative of this . . .

What Lord Templeman seems to have done is to treat findings of secondary fact as questions of law. That this is not a correct approach is well established. It was Lord Brightman who said in *Furniss v. Dawson*:[47] "They may be primary facts, or more probably, inferences to be drawn from the primary facts. If they are inferences, they are nevertheless facts to be found by the commissioners. Such inferences cannot be disturbed by the court save on the principles of *Edwards (Inspector of Taxes) v. Bairstow* [1956] AC 14." . . .

. . . [This is] . . . an accurate representation of the true position . . ., which in *Smith v. Abbott* was forcefully reiterated by Lord Browne-Wilkinson, but which was (rather weakly, it is submitted) undermined by the majority. There is no rule that says that two sets of commissioners have to reach identical conclusions in identical situations. By rejecting the findings of the English commissioners on the basis that the question was a question of law or of mixed law and fact (in which the question of law that the English commissioners answered wrongly was not clearly shown) in order to reach a consistent result, the majority in *Smith v. Abbott* seems to have sacrificed accuracy for consistency.[48] It is not clear what precedent is being sought thereby to be established, and it is submitted that the majority, in overruling the Court of Appeal, arrived at a decision which is incorrect. It is also submitted that the approach of Lord Browne-Wilkinson is to be preferred, *i.e.* if the commissioners have on the evidence before them made differing findings of fact, the court may be required to hold that their conclusions in each set of appeals, though conflicting, are right in law. **[3.10]**

The tenability of the concept of 'mixed law and fact', which entitles the court to review the Commissioners' decision, was considered by Sir John Laws extra-judicially. **[3.11]**

Sir John Laws[49] 'Law and Fact' [1999] BTR 159, 159–162

The expression "a mixed question of law and fact" is a familiar member of the law's vocabulary. It appears, I suppose, in countless judgments. It arises especially when the question for the court is whether a particular set of facts falls within the meaning of statutory words where that meaning is itself loose or even vague. The law of VAT is very familiar with this. Take the case where the Tribunal has to decide whether work at a site constitutes works of "the conversion, reconstruction, alteration, or enlargement of any existing building" for the purpose of zero-rating. In other areas of the law the court may have to decide whether a particular business relationship amounts to "a contract for services" or "a contract of service", there being different legal results, in relation to such various fields as tax, social security, and tortious liability to third parties, according to which analysis is right.

The distinction between law and fact is far from academic. Where a case has been decided by a statutory tribunal from which appeal lies to the High Court under the

47 [1984] S.T.C. 153 at 166–167.

48 Perhaps for the purpose of preventing the floodgates from being opened (see p 683).

49 Lord Justice of Appeal. This is the text of a talk delivered recently to a conference of VAT and Duties Tribunal chairmen and is reproduced with kind permission.

Tribunals and Inquiries Act or other legislation on law only, it will be critical to decide whether the point put in issue in the appeal is really one of fact or of law, since in the former case the High Court will lack jurisdiction, and in the latter case possess it. And the distinction marks one of the de facto boundaries of the judicial review jurisdiction: if the complaint is only as to the factual merits of the decision, the judicial review court will decline to interfere.

In this paper I propose to advance two propositions.

(1) There is no such thing as a mixed question of law and fact – the concept is actually self-contradictory, but
(2) the boundary between the very ideas of law and fact is not fixed; it largely depends on the answer to a question which transcends the internal rules of any legal system, namely what are the characteristics of a decision which ought to expose it to control by the courts?

The first proposition, that there is no such thing as a mixed question of law and fact, is really self-evident. Facts are ascertained by evidence or judicial notice; law is ascertained from statute and judicial decisions. There is no cross-over, but the unravelling of law and fact has often caused difficulty. Sometimes it is blithely ignored altogether. Why should this be so? Why should the courts resort to the intellectually incoherent notion of a mixed question of law and fact? The answers to these questions really belong to my second proposition, that the boundary between law and fact is not fixed.

It is useful to give some examples, to show where this difficulty of classification has arisen.... In *British Airways plc v. Customs & Excise Comrs*[50] the court held that the question whether in-flight meals on domestic flights were, for the purposes of the Value Added Tax Act 1983, part of a single supply of transport services or a separate supply was a question of law, although it seems they accepted that this turned on the further question whether (as Otton J. at first instance put it) "in substance and reality was the in-flight catering an integral part of the transport?" But how can this latter question be categorised as a question of law?

A supposedly mixed question of fact and law generally arises where the court or tribunal's task is to decide whether a particular set of circumstances falls within a concept or definition given usually by statute. If it does, certain consequences which the law prescribes will flow; if it does not, they will not. There will as a matter of analysis always be three questions:

(1) What are the relevant facts?
(2) What is the relevant legal concept?
(3) Do the facts as found bring the case within the concept?

Generally there is no difficulty when the legal concept or definition is tight and unambiguous. ... But what if the legal concept or definition is not tight and unambiguous? Save in the rare case where the law prescribes something in the nature of a mathematical formula having legal consequences (as happened in some areas of local government finance in the 1980s), the relevant legal definition will of course be expressed in ordinary, if sometimes convoluted, English. The words used may be capable of a range of meanings. Now, the meaning of an ordinary English word, unless the statute provides a special interpretation, is generally taken to be a matter of fact: so the House of Lords held in *Brutus v. Cozens*.[51] Are we driven to conclude, in such a case, that the meaning of the legal definition under scrutiny is after all a question of fact, although it arises under my question (2) above – what is the relevant legal concept: what, in other words, is the relevant law?

50 [1990] S.T.C. 643.
51 [1973] A.C. 854.

The tension here is between the notion that ordinary English words are a matter of fact, and the elementary principle that the construction of statute is a matter of law. I think it is usually to be resolved by a two-stage process. First, in interpreting the definition or concept given by the statute, the court will look at the context in which it appears: that will often demonstrate that the legislature intended to accord this or that sense to the expression in question, so as to narrow the options of interpretation which seem to be available upon the words used to express the concept taken in isolation. So far, this is a purely legal exercise – an exercise in construction. It may, and perhaps often will, reduce the available options to one. In that case the result is the same as where the concept or definition is on its face tight and unambiguous. A single meaning is attributed to the statutory words; the court will proceed to decide whether the facts it finds fall within the definition so ascertained; law and fact are satisfactorily divided.

But it is not always so simple. There are cases where an appeal to the definition's statutory context will not yield a single or unitary result. The court may in such a case find that the statutory words are capable of more than one meaning. But that is not quite right; where the statutory definition is not tight, even after the court has applied the test of statutory context, the real result is not that it is ambiguous, but that it may cover a range of factual situations. The court will then proceed to decide whether the instant facts fall within the range. In this sort of case, the court's determination of the available range of situations becomes, I think, a *Wednesbury* question. The appeal court has to decide whether the range of meanings allowed by the first instance tribunal was reasonably arrived at, given the statutory context and the specific language used in the statute.

This brings me at once to the second proposition: the boundary between law and fact is not fixed.

Where there are reasonable choices to be made between one interpretation and another of a defining phrase in legislation – where there is a range of available interpretations – the higher courts will adopt a strict, or a loose, approach according to the subject-matter. If they perceive that fundamental rights are involved, they are more likely to insist on a particular interpretation, supporting the fundamental right, even though other meanings might perfectly well be available as a matter of language. Or they might not: it depends on the culture of the times, the Zeitgeist. It depends on what the higher courts think ought to be a matter of law: or, more pointedly, what they think should be subject to judicial control.

I do not think this is a bad thing. Even if I did, there would be no use protesting it, for the tension between the judges' power and the legislature's power is necessarily variable in a free society. The question at the end of all the argument is, what is to be regarded as law, and thus in the province of the judges; and what is to be regarded as fact, and thus in the province of the Executive and the Executive's administrators. **[3.12]**

B. *Conclusiveness of findings of fact*

Levene v Commissioners of Inland Revenue [1928] AC 217 (HL)[52]

VISCOUNT SUMNER: . . . In substance persons are chargeable or exempt, as the case may be, according as they are deemed by this body of Commissioners or that to be resident

52 See also Chapter 19, below, para [**19.18**].

or the reverse, whatever resident may mean in the particular circumstances of each case. The tribunal thus provided is neither bound by the findings of other similar tribunals in other cases nor is it open to review, so long as it commits no palpable error of law, and the Legislature practically transfers to it the function of imposing taxes on individuals, since it empowers them in terms so general, that no one can be certainly advised in advance, whether he must pay or can escape payment. The way of taxpayers is hard and the Legislature does not go out of its way to make it any easier. If it had been possible in this case to apply the principle that a taxing statute must impose a charge in clear terms or fail, since it is to be construed contra proferentem, our duty would have been plain, but since the words are plain and it is only their application that is haphazard and beyond all forecast, Mr. Levene has no remedy in your Lordships' House . . . **[3.13]**

C. Appeals from the conclusions of the Commissioners

***Commissioners of Inland Revenue v Lysaght* [1928] AC 234 (HL)**

The House of Lords had to decide whether there was evidence upon which the Commissioners could properly arrive at the conclusion that the taxpayer, who lived in Ireland but retained a post as a company director in England and who came to England for meetings every month, staying in hotels here, was resident in England for income tax purposes.

VISCOUNT SUMNER: . . . It is well settled that, when the Commissioners have thus ascertained the facts of the case and then have found the conclusion of fact which the facts prove, their decision is not open to review, provided (a) that they have had before them evidence, from which such a conclusion could properly be drawn, and (b) that they did not misdirect themselves in law in any of the forms of legal error, which amount to misdirection . . . **[3.14]**

(1) 'The true and only reasonable conclusion contradicts the determination'

***Edwards (Inspector of Taxes) v Bairstow and Harrison* [1956] AC 14 (HL); below, para [9.19]**

LORD RADCLIFFE: . . . If a party to a hearing before commissioners expresses dissatisfaction with their determination as being erroneous in point in law, it is for them to state a case and in the body of it to set out the facts that they have found as well as their determination. I do not think that inferences drawn from other facts are incapable of being themselves findings of fact, although there is value in the distinction between primary facts and inferences drawn from them. When the case comes before the court it is its duty to examine the determination having regard to its knowledge of the relevant law. If the case contains anything ex facie which is bad law and which bears upon the determination, it is, obviously, erroneous in point of law. But, without any such misconception appearing ex facie, it may be that the facts found are such that no person acting judicially and properly instructed as to the relevant law could have come to the determination under appeal. In those circumstances, too, the court must intervene. It has no option but to assume that there has been some misconception of the law and that this has been responsible for the determination. So there, too, there has been an error in point of law. I do not think that it much matters whether this state of affairs is described as one in which there is no evidence to support the determination or as one in which the evidence is inconsistent with and contradictory of the determination, or as one in which the true and only reasonable conclusion contradicts the determination. Rightly understood, each phrase propounds the same test. For my part, I prefer the last of the three, since I think that it is rather misleading to speak of there being no evidence to support a conclusion when in cases such as these many of the facts are likely to be neutral in themselves, and only to take their colour from the combination of circumstances in which they are found to occur ... **[3.15]**

(2) There can be no substitution of a court's conclusion if no error of law has been made by the Commissioners and their decision is supportable on the facts

Lucy and Sutherland Ltd v Hunt [1962] 1 WLR 7 (Ch D)

CROSS J. ... When a judge thinks – as I certainly do – that he himself would not have arrived at the conclusion that the commissioners have arrived at, there is a temptation for him also to think that the conclusion at which the commissioners have arrived must be an unreasonable one. I must guard myself against that. But, while bearing that in mind I have come to the conclusion that here there was no evidence upon which the commissioners could have properly reached the conclusion that they did reach.... **[3.16]**

Pilkington v Randall (1966) 42 TC 662 (CA)

SALMON LJ: ... Now, as was restated by the House of Lords in *Edwards v Bairstow and Harrison*,[53] the decision of the Commissioners on any question of this sort must be accepted and cannot be overruled unless it is plain from the primary facts found that "no person acting judicially and properly instructed as to the relevant law could have come to the determination under appeal," or unless one comes to the conclusion that no reasonable person could have arrived at the same conclusion as the Commissioners. I agree that this case is very close to the borderline, and I am by no means certain that if I had been sitting as a Commissioner and had had to draw inferences of fact, I should have come to the same conclusion as the Commissioners. But it is important to guard oneself against the temptation, to which I suppose we are all prone, and which is happily put by Cross J., in *Lucy & Sutherland v. Hunt*.[54] When we think a conclusion of fact is one at which we would not have arrived ourselves, we are tempted to say that it follows that no reasonable person could have come to that conclusion. I think the facts here were evenly balanced. On the whole I think I would have come down the other way, but I cannot say that the view at which the Commissioners arrived is not a possible view for a reasonable man to take ... **[3.17]**

Where the court upholds the finding of the Commissioners, its decision has little value as a precedent (see, eg, *Iswera v Commissioner of Inland Revenue* [1965] 1 WLR 663 (PC)). If, however, courts overturn the Commissioners' decision, the value of the case as a precedent tends to be high: see, eg, *Lewis v Lady Rook* [1992] 1 WLR 662;[55] *Honour v Norris* [1992] STC 304;[56] and *Herbert Smith (a firm) v Honour (Inspector of Taxes)* [1999] STC 173.[57] **[3.18]**

53 [1956] AC 14; [see above, para **[3.15]**.]
54 (1961) 40 TC 132 at 138.
55 See below, para **[20.54]**.
56 But see William Norris 'Capital Gains Tax – More about Residences' [1993] BTR 24, 40.
57 See below, para **[10.57]**.

Usetech Ltd v Young (Inspector of Taxes) [2004] EWHC 2248 (Ch), [2004] STC 1671 (Ch D)

This was an appeal against the Special Commissioner's conclusion that the main shareholder, director and sole employee of a company was an 'employed earner' of the company, for the purposes of the relevant income tax and national insurance rules on 'personal service companies'.[58] The company's appeal was dismissed.

PARK J: . . . I would like to repeat the point, implicit if not explicit in earlier parts of this judgment . . . , that my decision does not necessarily mean that the Special Commissioner was bound to reach the decision which he did. He looked at the entire circumstances in the round (as I believe that both the Inspector and the advocate for Usetech invited him to do), and he came to the conclusion that, if there had been no Usetech, a direct contract between Mr Hood and ABB would have been a contract of employment. Suppose that he had looked at the case in a similar way (perhaps also taking account of Mr Hood's earlier history of being a specialist in his particular field), and had reached the opposite conclusion: that a contract between Mr Hood and ABB would not have been a contract of employment but rather would have been an ingredient in a self-employed profession. My present decision should not be understood as meaning that such a decision by the Special Commissioner would have been wrong in law. It might or might not have been, and I have heard no argument on the question. However, given that decisions of Commissioners are generally final on questions of fact rather than law, the grounds on which I could now reach a decision in favour of Usetech are much narrower than those on which the Special Commissioner could have reached such a decision.

Mr Devonshire [counsel for the taxpayer] has appropriately limited his submissions to me to grounds on which it can be said that the Commissioner made a clear error of law, rather than that he came to one conclusion rather than another on a question of fact and degree which arguably might have gone either way. **[3.19]**

D. Burden of proof

Evidence may be adduced by either side at the hearing before the Commissioners.[59] According to Tiley, the onus is on the taxpayer to disprove the assessment,[60] a rule which may be rationalised on the basis that he knows all the facts and, therefore, should have to prove them.[61] **[3.20]**

Bookey v Edwards [1982] STC 135 (Ch D)

WALTON J: . . . I have a very uncomfortable feeling that it is possible that something may have gone wrong in this case for which the Appellant himself, Mr. Bookey, is not at any rate entirely to blame, but so far as the law is concerned the matter is in fact crystal clear. Mr. Bookey is a person who is a motor delivery agent employed apparently by one firm and one firm only, the firm of Daniel Hustings Ltd., and he does a certain amount of work for them. I say he does a certain amount of work for them because in the recent years with which we are concerned – that is to say, the tax years 1976–77 to 1979–80 inclusive – he apparently earned fees from the firm of really very small amounts indeed, ranging from £1,175 for the year ended 30 November 1975, to £1,606 for the year ended 30

58 Ie 'the IR 35 rules' (see now ITEPA 2003, ss 48–61, in so far as these relate to income tax); see below, paras **[8.13]–[8.18]**.
59 See TMA 1970,ss 56B and 56C. See Special Commissioners (Jurisdiction and Procedure) Regulations 1994, SI 1994/1811 and General Commissioners (Jurisdiction and Procedure) Regulations 1994, SI 1994/1812.
60 *Norman v Golder* [1945] 1 All ER 352, 26 TC 293.
61 See Tiley, n 1 above, p 75.

November 1978. He did not, as he should have done, give notice of his liability to pay tax for the years 1976–77, 1977–78, 1978–79 and 1979–80 pursuant to the Taxes Management Act 1970. There is no doubt that he was in fact subject to tax, and when the tax inspector found that out he made assessments for the first three years in the sum of £5,000 and for the last year in the sum of £6,000. Those assessments were made upon Mr. Bookey in respect of the profits from his trade, described in the notices of assessment as a 'cab driver' . . .

The matter went to appeal against those assessments to the General Commissioners . . . Now the unfortunate fact is that Mr. Bookey did not appreciate how the matter would go in front of the Commissioners. He felt that he had given his accountants all the information which was in his possession and power, that they had communicated that to the Inspector of Taxes and that therefore that information would be, as it were, common ground and would be in front of the General Commissioners. But that, of course, is not the position at all. There is no doubt, pursuant to s 50(6) of the Taxes management Act 1970, that the onus is very much upon an appellant to convince the Commissioners of Income Tax as to the accuracy of his case. That subsection reads:

> "If, on an appeal, it appears to the majority of the Commissioners present at the hearing, by examination of the appellant on oath or affirmation, or by other lawful evidence, that the appellant is overcharged by any assessment, the assessment shall be reduced accordingly, but otherwise every assessment shall stand good."

So the onus was very much upon Mr. Bookey.

There were two matters which led the Inspector of Taxes not to accept the figures which were put forward by Mr. Bookey and his accountants as being the sums which he had had from Daniel Hustings Ltd. by way of remuneration in the relevant years . . . first of all, whether (I dare say in part having regard to those figures) Mr. Bookey was not also employed by some other firm as well. The Inspector submitted that he was, but on that point the Commissioners found in Mr. Bookey's favour and accepted that he did not in fact work for any other company than Daniel Hustings Ltd. The second matter – and this is where I am afraid that Mr. Bookey's case was not, as it should have been, properly presented to the Commissioners – was that the company that I have already named, in various accounting years, paid sums to Mr. Bookey described as 'Reimbursement of expenses.' Now the law as to the extent to which the reimbursement of expenses can be added properly to the profits arising from any trade or profession is a matter of some difficulty in a good many cases; but here was Mr. Bookey saying that he had received these sums (which were roughly in each case about double the sums which were paid to him by way of fees) by way of reimbursement of expenses. Of course, that is perfectly possible . . . But – and this is where I think the matter went completely wrong – the onus being upon Mr. Bookey to convince the General Commissioners of the truth of his story that those sums were the reimbursement of expenses not containing any hidden element of profit, he failed to produce any evidence in front of the Commissioners as to exactly and precisely to what it was that each of the sums making up those various payments referred . . . So the situation was that in front of the General Commissioners there really was no evidence at all on the part of Mr. Bookey as to the nature of the reimbursements of the expenses which he claimed.

. . . What were the General Commissioners to do in the circumstances? It seems to me that they have done what most people faced with that sort of totally unsatisfactory position would do; that is to say, they have made the best estimate they can, coming down somewhere in the middle. I say 'somewhere in the middle' because there is no consistent pattern which emerges from the figures in which they have confirmed the assessments, but what they say in their findings is: 'In the absence of submission by the Appellant of any satisfactory written evidence of records of his expenses we determined the appeals as follows,' and then they set out the figures. They are, for 1976–77 and 1977–78, £2,500 each in place of the Inspector's £5,000; and for 1979–80, £2,700 in place of the Inspector's £6,000. So this is not a case where the Commissioners did not pay a great deal of attention to what was told to them by Mr. Bookey; but, although it does not matter whether if I had been in their shoes I would have come to precisely the same conclusion as that to which they came, I think that in that totally unsatisfactory state of affairs I would have been obliged to come to more or less the conclusion to which in fact they came.

> Immediately after the determination of the appeal by the Commissioners dissatisfaction therewith as being erroneous (and I must stress these words) in point of law was expressed by Mr. Bookey – because it is only in point of law that I am entitled to overrule the Commissioners. ... But I am afraid that the facts before them were so wholly unsatisfactory that they were bound, as it were, to grope to some extent in the dark, and I cannot possibly say that in so groping on such insufficient material they have in any way gone wrong in law, that being the only ground upon which I could overrule them.
>
> So, unsatisfactory as it is, I am obliged to dismiss this appeal. I say 'unsatisfactory' because I think that if Mr. Bookey had been better advised the matter would have proceeded before the Commissioners in an entirely different manner ... **[3.21]**

See also *Owton Fens Properties Ltd v Redden* [1984] STC 618; *Barnes-Sherrocks v McIntosh* [1989] STC 674; *Auckland v PAVH (International) Ltd* [1992] STC 712; and *MacEachern v Carr* [1996] STC 282. **[3.22]**

4. Statutory interpretation[62]

A. *Introduction*

Natalie Lee 'A Purposive Approach to the Interpretation of Tax Statutes?' (1999) 20 Stat LR 124

It is the basic function of the court to give a meaning to the particular words in the statute under consideration, the "rules" of, or approaches to, interpretation are merely the tools which are used to fulfil that function. These traditional "tools" comprise the literal rule, the golden rule and the mischief rule. The literal rule requires the judge to look at the actual words used, and to attribute to them their ordinary meaning within the context of the statute. The golden rule allows a judge to depart from the literal rule when the application of the ordinary meaning of words would lead to inconsistency, absurdity or inconvenience. In applying the golden rule, the court will be at liberty to find another meaning either by ignoring the words used, or by reading in words to the existing statute. This operation requires a consideration of whether the inconsistency, absurdity or inconvenience is so great that Parliament could not have intended that the words should be given their ordinary meaning. The mischief rule will apply when, having had regard to the whole of the enacting part of the statute, the court has found that the words are manifestly obscure or ambiguous. In such a case, the court must construe the statute in such a way that avoids the mischief which the statute sought to remedy.

Until relatively recent times, judges insisted upon a strict approach to the interpretation of taxing statutes.[63] The reason commonly offered for this was that taxing statutes operated in a similar way to penal statutes, and that if a taxpayer is to be charged to tax, this can only be achieved by the giving of very clear authority. ... it is the very perception of the nature of taxing statutes that has caused the

62 See, for example, Colin Manchester and David Salter *Exploring the Law: The Dynamics of Precedent and Statutory Interpretation*, (3rd edn, 2006), ch 2; Michael Zander *The Law-Making Process* (6th edn, 2004), ch 3.

63 For an interesting historical review of judicial attitudes towards tax statutes, see D. Williams, *Taxing Statutes are Taxing Statutes* [1978] MLR 404 at 408–12.

rejection, in many cases, of both the golden and the mischief rules. Taxing statutes are commonly believed to be about revenue collection and nothing else; what, precisely, can be said to be the "mischief" in such a statute? **[3.23]**

Although a number of tax avoidance cases, and *IRC v McGuckian*[64] in particular, have led to the suggestion that the 'literal' approach to the interpretation of tax statutes has given way to a 'purposive' approach, it is far from clear that this is the case, and there undoubtedly exists a tension between the two approaches. On the one hand, there are claims that '*McGuckian* is therefore as sure a confirmation as we are likely to get that the literal approach to statutory interpretation is now dead and buried',[65] and, on the other, the view that:

> 'What we must look for is the intention of Parliament . . . But we can only take the intention of Parliament from the words they have used in the Act, and therefore the question is whether these words are capable of a more limited construction. If not, then we must apply them as they stand, however unreasonable or unjust the consequences, and however strongly we may suspect that this was not the real intention of Parliament.'[66]

The purposive approach is similar to, though wider than, the mischief rule, and its use may involve recourse to parliamentary materials. **[3.24]**

B. The literal approach

This approach was summarised by Lord Donovan in the following case, in which his Lordship also alluded to several key earlier authorities. **[3.25]**

Owen Thomas Mangin v Inland Revenue Commissioner [1971] AC 739 (PC)

> LORD DONOVAN: . . . it may be useful to recall at the outset some of the rules of interpretation which fall to be applied.
>
> First, the words are to be given their ordinary meaning. They are not to be given some other meaning simply because their object is to frustrate legitimate tax avoidance devices. As Turner J. says in his (albeit dissenting) judgment in *Marx v. Inland Revenue Commissioner* [1970] N.Z.L.R. 182, 208, moral precepts are not applicable to the interpretation of revenue statutes.
>
> Secondly, ' . . . one has to look merely at what is clearly said. There is no room for any intendment. There is no equity about a tax. There is no presumption as to tax. Nothing is to be read in, nothing is to be implied. One can only look fairly at the language used.': *per* Rowlatt J. in *Cape Brandy Syndicate v Inland Revenue Commissioners* [1921] 1 K.B. 64, 71, approved by Viscount Simons L.C. in *Canadian Eagle Oil Co Ltd v. The King* [1946] A.C. 119, 140.
>
> Thirdly, the object of the construction of a statute being to ascertain the will of the legislature it may be presumed that neither injustice nor absurdity was intended. If therefore a literal interpretation would produce such a result, and the language admits of an interpretation which would avoid it, then such an interpretation may be adopted.
>
> Fourthly, the history of an enactment and the reasons which led to its being passed may be used as an aid to its construction. **[3.26]**

64 [1997] 1 WLR 991; see below, para **[3.31]**.
65 R Goodman, *Taxation Practitioner* January 1998, p 9.
66 *IRC v Hinchey* [1960] AC 748 at 767 (Lord Reid).

C. *The purposive approach*

As seen above, the courts, in some instances, have purported to adopt a purposive approach in tax cases which seeks to give effect to the purpose of legislation. The difficulty with this approach is that the statutory purpose is not always discernible from the words used. Hence, the House of Lords in *Pepper v Hart*[67] departed from the previous 'exclusionary' rule of disallowing references to parliamentary material as an aid to construction, and held that subject to certain conditions,[68] reference to *Hansard* could be made. It has been suggested, however, that 'the permitted use of parliamentary material should provide the defining limit of the purposive approach, and that to go further and impute an intention to Parliament would be pure conjecture and a clear usurpation by the courts of the function of Parliament'.[69] **[3.27]**

Pepper (Inspector of Taxes) v Hart [1993] AC 593 (HL)

For the facts of this case and its relevance to the taxation of employment income, see below, para **[8.61]**.

> LORD BROWNE-WILKINSON: ... Thus the reasons put forward for the present rule *[the exclusionary rule]* are: first, that it preserves the constitutional proprieties, leaving Parliament to legislate in words and the courts (not parliamentary speakers) to construe the meaning of the words finally enacted; second, the practical difficulty of the expense of researching parliamentary material which would arise if the material could be looked at; third, the need for the citizen to have access to a known defined text which regulates his legal rights; fourth, the improbability of finding helpful guidance from Hansard.
>
> The Law Commissions of England and Scotland in their joint report on *The Interpretation of Statutes* ((1969) Law Com no 21) (Scot Law Com no 11) and the Renton Committee on *The Preparation of Legislation* ((1975) Cmnd 6053) both recognised that there was much to be said in principle for relaxing the rule but advised against a relaxation at present on the same practical grounds as are reflected in the authorities. However, both bodies recommended changes in the form of legislation which would, if implemented, have assisted the court in its search for the true parliamentary intention in using the statutory words.
>
> Mr Lester *[counsel for the taxpayers]* submitted that the time has come to relax the rule ... He points out that the courts have departed from the old literal approach of statutory construction and now adopt a purposive approach, seeking to discover the parliamentary intention lying behind the words used and construing the legislation so as to give effect to, rather than thwart, the intentions of Parliament. Where the words used by Parliament are obscure or ambiguous, the parliamentary material may throw considerable light not only on the mischief which the Act was designed to remedy but also on the purpose of the legislation and its anticipated effect. If there are statements by the minister or other promoter of the Bill, these may throw as much light on the "mischief" which the Bill seeks to remedy as do the white papers, reports of official committees and Law Commission reports to which the courts already have regard for that purpose. If a minister clearly states the effect of a provision and there is no subsequent relevant amendment to the Bill or withdrawal of the statement it is reasonable to assume that Parliament passed the Bill on the basis that the provision would have the effect stated. There is no logical distinction

67 [1993] AC 593; see below.

68 These conditions are: (i) the legislation in question must be ambiguous or obscure or would lead to an absurdity; (ii) the material relied on should consist of statements, for example, by a Minister together with such other parliamentary material as is necessary to understand such statements and their effect; and (iii) the statements relied on are clear; see below, para **[3.28]**.

69 Natalie Lee 'Frankland v IRC' [1998] BTR 262, 267.

between the use of ministerial statements introducing subordinate legislation (to which recourse was had in the *Pickstone case* [1989] AC 66 and such statements made in relation to other statutory provisions which are not in fact subsequently amended. Other common law jurisdictions have abandoned the rule without adverse consequences. Although the practical reasons for the rule (difficulty in getting access to parliamentary materials and the cost and delay in researching it) are not without substance, they can be greatly exaggerated: experience in Commonwealth countries which have abandoned the rule does not suggest that the drawbacks are substantial, provided that the court keeps a tight control on the circumstances in which references to parliamentary material are allowed.

On the other side, the Attorney General submitted that the existing rule had a sound constitutional and practical basis. If statements by ministers as to the intent or effect of an Act were allowed to prevail, this would contravene the constitutional rule that Parliament is "sovereign only in respect of what it expresses by the words used in the legislation it has passed" (see *Black-Clawson* [1975] AC 591 at 638 per Lord Diplock). It is for the courts alone to construe such legislation. It may be unwise to attach importance to ministerial explanations which are made to satisfy the political requirements of persuasion and debate, often under pressure of time and business. Moreover, in order to establish the significance to be attached to any particular statement, it is necessary both to consider and to understand the context in which it was made. For the courts to have regard to parliamentary material might necessitate changes in parliamentary procedures to ensure that ministerial statements are sufficiently detailed to be taken into account. In addition, there are all the practical difficulties as to the accessibility of parliamentary material, the cost of researching it and the use of court time in analysing it, which are good reasons for maintaining the rule. Finally, to use what is said in Parliament for the purpose of construing legislation would be a breach of art 9 of the Bill of Rights (1688) as being an impeachment or questioning of the freedom of speech in debates in proceedings in Parliament.

My Lords, I have come to the conclusion that, as a matter of law, there are sound reasons for making a limited modification to the existing rule (subject to strict safeguards) unless there are constitutional or practical reasons which outweigh them. In my judgment, subject to the questions of the privileges of the House of Commons, reference to parliamentary material should be permitted as an aid to the construction of legislation which is ambiguous or obscure or the literal meaning of which leads to an absurdity. Even in such cases references in court to parliamentary material should only be permitted where such material clearly discloses the mischief aimed at or the legislative intention lying behind the ambiguous or obscure words. In the case of statements made in Parliament, as at present advised I cannot foresee that any statement other than the statement of the minister or other promoter of the Bill is likely to meet these criteria.

I accept Mr Lester's submissions, but my main reason for reaching this conclusion is based on principle. Statute law consists of the words that Parliament has enacted. It is for the courts to construe those words and it is the court's duty in so doing to give effect to the intention of Parliament in using those words. It is an inescapable fact that, despite all the care taken in passing legislation, some statutory provisions when applied to the circumstances under consideration in any specific case are found to be ambiguous. One of the reasons for such ambiguity is that the members of the legislature in enacting the statutory provision may have been told what result those words are intended to achieve. Faced with a given set of words which are capable of conveying that meaning it is not surprising if the words are accepted as having that meaning. Parliament never intends to enact an ambiguity. Contrast with that the position of the courts. The courts are faced simply with a set of words which are in fact capable of bearing two meanings. The courts are ignorant of the underlying parliamentary purpose. Unless something in other parts of the legislation discloses such purpose, the courts are forced to adopt one of the two possible meanings using highly technical rules of construction. In many, I suspect most, cases references to parliamentary materials will not throw any light on the matter. But in a few cases it may emerge that the very question was considered by Parliament in passing the legislation. Why in such a case should the courts blind themselves to a clear indication of what Parliament intended in using those words? The court cannot attach a meaning to words which they cannot bear, but if the words are capable of bearing more than one meaning why should not Parliament's true intention be enforced rather than thwarted?

A number of other factors support this view. As I have said, the courts can now look at white papers and official reports for the purpose of finding the "mischief" sought to be corrected, although not at draft clauses or proposals for the remedying of such mischief. A ministerial statement made in Parliament is an equally authoritative source of such information; why should the courts be cut off from this source of information as to the mischief aimed at? In any event, the distinction between looking at reports to identify the mischief aimed at but not to find the intention of Parliament in enacting the legislation is highly artificial. Take the normal Law Commission report which analyses the problem and then annexes a draft Bill to remedy it. It is now permissible to look at the report to find the mischief and at the draft Bill to see that a provision in the draft was *not* included in the legislation enacted (see *Ex p Factortame* [1990] 2 AC 85). There can be no logical distinction between that case and looking at the draft Bill to see that the statute as enacted reproduced, often in the same words, the provision in the Law Commission's draft. Given the purposive approach to construction now adopted by the courts in order to give effect to the true intentions of the legislature, the fine distinctions between looking for the mischief and looking for the intention in using words to provide the remedy are technical and inappropriate. Clear and unambiguous statements made by ministers in Parliament are as much the background to the enactment of legislation as white papers and parliamentary reports.

... I therefore reach the conclusion, subject to any question of parliamentary privilege, that the exclusionary rule should be relaxed so as to permit reference to parliamentary materials where: (a) legislation is ambiguous or obscure, or leads to an absurdity; (b) the material relied on consists of one or more statements by a minister or other promoter of the Bill together if necessary with such other parliamentary material as is necessary to understand such statements and their effect; (c) the statements relied on are clear. Further than this, I would not at present go. **[3.28]**

David Robertson *Judicial Discretion in the House of Lords* (1998) pp 160–164

[In *Pepper v Hart*] Browne-Wilkinson reviews quickly the arguments for the taxpayer's interpretation which rest on supposed anomalies likely to be produced by the Revenue's construction, but finds as many and as good arising from their preferred version. He described very well the main problem about interpreting this statute, which is that there is an odd absence of something one would expect to be there:

> What is taxable is the benefit to the employee and *one would have expected the quantum of that benefit to be assessed by reference to the value of that benefit to the employee* [*our emphasis*]. But the statutory formula does not seek to value the benefit to the employee as such, but requires the quantum of the benefit to be fixed by reference to the cost to the employer of providing it.

Because there is therefore no guidance to parliamentary intention, he argues, it is necessary to interpret the statute literally, and the Revenue must win. One might well ask why the statute has such an odd form. Now we can look at *Hansard*, this becomes clear. But what becomes clear is that, in a fundamental way, the literal interpretation is actually the correct guess at the core meaning of the statute, but that Parliament cannot, indeed, be said to have intended to give effect to its core meaning. It is useful quickly to note that the main arguments given, by Griffiths, for interpreting in favour of the taxpayers without looking at the legislative history are classical parliamentary intent arguments of the form which involve deducing an unpleasant consequence of the Revenue's interpretation and then asserting that Parliament could not possibly have wanted to do any such thing. Much of the force of Griffiths' argument comes from an analogy with the way in which the Government slowly phased in taxation of company cars, the most common "perk", rather than hitting the beneficiaries immediately, the suggestion being that this shows what Parliament can be expected to intend such [*sic*] policies. Griffiths, it must be remembered, is the only one of the original committee who does claim to have derived a pro-taxpayer stance before looking at *Hansard*. It is fairly well known that Lord Griffiths, after working out this answer and his justification, then privately read the debates and brought them to the attention of his brethren as a clear example of where the Lords would give the wrong answer if they did not relax the exclusionary rule. Lord Griffiths, along with Lord Templeman, had long sought to have the rule changed. Indeed he admits in the course of his opinion:

> I have to confess that on many occasions I have had recourse to Hansard, of course only to check if my interpretation had conflicted with an express parliamentary intention . . .[70]

Griffiths does not, alas, tell us how often his interpretations have turned out to conflict, and even more interestingly, he does not tell us what he did when there was conflict.

2. The parliamentary record

The parliamentary record is fascinating – but more as an example of lobbying at work than anything else. For those whose only knowledge of the case is that *Hansard* was consulted, and what was found therein forced several law Lords to change their mind about the meaning of the Act, exactly what they found and relied on may come as somewhat of a surprise. Because they did not find a speech by a minister which said: "Oh, by the way, the word 'cost' in section 63 means marginal not average cost."

In the draft legislation the original plan was to distinguish between two sorts of benefit in kind. One was a benefit which the employer would himself have to purchase or subsidise, which would be taxed on the basis of the cost to the employer. The second were in-house benefits, the provision to an employee of the services the institution was in business to provide for fees to the general public. These, covered by clause 54(4) of the Bill, were to be taxed on the price to the public. The overall aim was fairly clear – where someone gained from his employment a service or benefit he would have to buy for himself otherwise, this was to be treated, as indeed it is, as a direct increase in his consumption capacity. As such he would be taxed for the benefit worth £*x* as though his salary was increased by £*x*. However, the Financial Secretary to the Treasury was obviously lobbied intensely – his phrases were "Representation has been made . . ." and "I have had many interviews, discussions and meetings on this matter . . .".[71] These representations and so forth seem to have been mainly concerned with concessionary travel for workers in the rail and airline industry. They were effective, because the Treasury withdrew clause 54(4), and the rest of clause 54 became the section 63 of the Act which caused the problems.

The reasons the Financial Secretary gave for withdrawing clause 54(4) were interesting, because they did not begin to relate to what must have been the original thinking – instead the clause was to be removed because: (1) the cost to the employer was trivial compared with the taxable value of the benefit, (2) the high cost of the benefit would depress use of the benefit and therefore no one, including the Revenue, would gain, and (3) there would be administrative and enforcement difficulties. No replacement clause was written, however. Various rather muddy statements were made in response to questions from MPs, which implied that taxation of such benefits would continue on the past basis. The past basis in fact was

70 *Pepper* at [[1993] 1 All ER 42,] 50.
71 Taken from Browne-Wilkinson's account, *Pepper* at [[1993] 1 All ER 42,] 58.

largely the result of non-legislative agreements between the Revenue and various bodies, and was certainly not the result of any clear judicial pronouncement. Furthermore, there was no past basis for schoolteachers, as they had previously been exempted, as employees of charitable bodies, from any taxation on benefits. What happened, therefore, was that the machinery for taxing the out-of-house benefits was left in place and allowed to become the machinery for taxing all benefits. All of the examples raised by MPs related to aspects of travel services, including free use of empty rooms for hotel workers and free steamship trips for merchant seamen's families. It was taxation of such benefits that had been the original concern in the Select Committee; this was the area in which there was a past experience of Revenue and beneficiaries colliding; and this was the area about which the "representations" had been made. In other words, the problems were seen as arising in connection with minor, attractive, but "extra" perks of working in rather specialised industries. Furthermore, because of particular problems in subsidised travel industries, there were (and continued to be even on the basis of the rest of clause 54) seriously logical problems of costing. Nothing in the committee's discussions or the Government's justifications dealt with the very different situation covered by the appeal. Except that one MP did ask the crucial question in committee:

> the . . . matter applies particularly to private sector, fee-paying schools where, as the Financial Secretary knows, there is often an arrangement for the children of staff in these schools to be taught at less than the commercial fee in other schools. I take it that because of the deletion of clause 54(4) that is now not caught . . .

The Financial Secretary responded:

> He mentioned the children of teachers. The removal of clause 54(4) will affect the position of a child of one of the teachers at the child's school, because now the benefit will be assessed on the cost to the employer, which would be very small indeed in this case.

Are these preliminary quotations a clear guide to the meaning of the Act? In one sense they certainly are – the Financial Secretary to the Treasury specifically promised that a specific category of worker whose case was brought up would pay very little, if any, tax on their special benefit. Once their Lordships took judicial notice of such a highly particularistic promise, the resolution of this case was ordained. Lord Bridge puts it clearly – "I should find it very difficult, in conscience, to reach a conclusion adverse to the taxpayers on the basis of a technical rule of construction . . .".[72] But there is, after all, a good reason why we have the general conception of judicial notice, and the position their Lordships put themselves in by reading *Hansard* may be one that should be avoided. Because there is something very unsatisfactory about the equation of Parliament's intention with such *ad hocery*. Bridge's sentence goes on to read ". . . requiring me to ignore the very material which in this case indicates unequivocally which of the two possible interpretations . . . was intended by Parliament". There is a huge leap of reasoning, or perhaps of faith, to conjure up anything that could valuably be called an intent of Parliament from this material.

Suppose that particular question had not been asked but some other, non-travel industry group had a champion in the House? Let us imagine that nurses in private sector hospitals are entitled to hospital care at no charge except the surgeon's fee and the cost of drugs, on the grounds that all the beds, theatres, and machinery have to be provided anyway. Had the question been asked about them, rather than teachers, and received the equivalent answer, would recourse to *Hansard* have

72 *Pepper* at [[1993] 1 All ER 42,] 49.

solved *Pepper*? If the answer is yes, it is so by a process of induction, not because the minister made any general interpretative statement.

What we know from the legislative history is:

1. all benefits are to be taxed under the same regime.
2. The regime, section 63(1) and (2), was designed to cover cases where the basis, the cost to the provider, was more or less the market price, because it was to cover bought-in benefits.
3. In several cases the minister estimated that the tax would be low because the costs would be low.

It is point (3) which is doing the work, in that it is being treated as a general answer to the original question of whether costs, in the legislation, are to be average or marginal costs. They have to be taken as marginal costs in order to make the minister's *ad hoc* promises come true. But is this the sort of general "intent" of Parliament that in principle should underlie the making of general rules in a political system hallowing the democratic value of 'rule by laws and not by men'? The Revenue, cast throughout this case as villains, were pressing for an interpretation of the Act which was in keeping with the original plan, which had been to tax benefits at something like the value to the recipient, a policy which still applies to any benefit which is not "in-house". That is why, after all, there is no statement of intent. The Act as envisioned did not need such a statement because equality between recipients of different sorts of benefits on the basis of taxation at rough market value followed automatically. The irony is that if the exclusionary rule, first established in 1769, had not been abandoned, the judges would have reimposed the original plan of the Act. Indeed clause 54(4) was never needed to carry out this plan because the effect of treating costs as equal to average costs is to set in–house benefits at the same costs as bought-in benefits. The reason there was never a general statement after clause 54(4) was withdrawn could well be that it would have forced the Financial Secretary to justify a glaring inequality in treatment where there appears to have been no thought-out rationale at all. It was no less a judicial personage than the first Presiding Judge of the European Court of Justice who insisted that Parliamentary debate had, as a major role, not the explicating but the hiding of legislative intentions. It may be apposite that the Act in question is a Finance Act. Such legislation by its very nature is unlike most of what Parliament does – it is not really an example of Parliament carrying out the political rule-making function of the classic division of powers. Passing the Finance Acts is, instead, an exercise in the "power of the purse", an equally vital but constitutionally rather different function. It could be argued with some force either that recourse to *Hansard* is especially inappropriate in cases like *Pepper*, or, in the alternative, that it is only when considering Parliament's exercise of this power that legislative history should be noted. And it may be relevant here that when Browne-Wilkinson tries to deal with arguments against the new relaxation he leaps on a rare comment by Lord Wilberforce, a major supporter of the exclusionary rule, in favour of using *Hansard*. The comment, made in his extrajudicial capacity in a seminar, specifically refers to another occasion where a minister, during passage of a Finance Bill, expressly stated that it was not intended to tax a particular class of beneficiaries.[73] But depending on which of these two arguments were made, a very different theory of the constitution would be implied. **[3.29]**

For further criticism of *Pepper v Hart*, see Michael Zander *The Law Making Process* (6th edn, 2004), pp 176–179. **[3.30]**

73 Browne-Wilkinson in *Pepper* at 65.

IRC v McGuckian [1997] STC 908 (HL); below, para [5.11]

A tax avoidance scheme sought to avoid income tax under what are now ICTA 1988, ss 739–746 ('Transfer of Assets Abroad')[74] The essence of the scheme was to characterise certain sums received by trustees as capital rather than income receipts. The House of Lords used the *Ramsay* principle (see below, paras **[5.7]–[5.9]**) to cancel the sought-for tax advantage, and regarded the receipts as income.

LORD STEYN: My Lords, it matters how a court should approach the construction and application of a tax statute, notably in respect of the impact of the legislation on schemes for tax avoidance. In this case the approach to be adopted may well be determinative of the appeal. In his excellent speech Mr Nugee QC, for the taxpayer, referred to the often quoted observations of Lord Tomlin in *IRC v Duke of Westminster* [1936] AC 1, 19 TC 490. Lord Tomlin said that every man is entitled if he can to order his affairs so that the tax under a tax statute is less than it would otherwise be. The case was authority for the proposition that whatever the substance of the arrangements may have been, their fiscal effect had to be in accordance with the legal rights and obligations they created. Mr Nugee, for the taxpayer, invited your Lordships to approach the appeal in this way. He said that the principle first laid down in *WT Ramsay Ltd v IRC* [1981] STC 174, [1982] AC 300, and developed in later House of Lords decisions, amounted to "an extreme form of statutory interpretation". It was implicit in this argument that the foundation of the principle is somewhat suspect. Mr Nugee said that while the actual decisions of the House of Lords must be respected the scope of the underlying principle should not be extended beyond those decisions. I understood his argument to be a plea for damage limitation. I would reject this approach as a false foundation for the consideration of this appeal.

It is necessary to distinguish between two separate questions of law. The first is whether there is a special rule applicable to the construction of fiscal legislation. The second question is whether there is a rule precluding the court from examining the substance of a composite tax avoidance scheme. I consider first the construction of tax statutes. [*Considering the first question of law, Lord Steyn continued . . .*]

Towards the end of the last century Pollock characterised the approach of judges to statutory construction as follows ". . . Parliament generally changes the law for the worse, and that the business of the judges is to keep the mischief of its interference within the narrowest possible bounds" (see Pollock *Essays in Jurisprudence and Ethics* (1882) p 85). Whatever the merits of this observation may have been when it was made, or even earlier in this century, it is demonstrably no longer true. During the last 30 years there has been a shift away from literalist to purposive methods of construction. Where there is no obvious meaning of a statutory provision the modern emphasis is on a contextual approach designed to identify the purpose of a statute and to give effect to it. But under the influence of the narrow *Duke of Westminster* doctrine, tax law remained remarkably resistant to the new non-formalist methods of interpretation. It was said that the taxpayer was entitled to stand on a literal construction of the words used regardless of the purpose of the statute (see *Pryce v Monmouthshire Canal and Railway Cos* (1879) 4 App Cas 197 at 202–203; *Cape Brandy Syndicate v IRC* [1921] 2 KB 64 at 71, 12 TC 358 at 366; *IRC v Plummer* [1979] STC 793, [1980] AC 896). Tax law was by and large left behind as some island of literal interpretation. The second problem was that in regard to tax avoidance schemes the courts regarded themselves as compelled to adopt a step by step analysis of such schemes, treating each step as a distinct transaction producing its own tax consequences. It was thought that if the steps were genuine, ie not sham or simulated documents or arrangements, the court was not entitled to go behind the form of the individual transactions. In combination those two features - literal interpretation of tax statutes and the formalistic insistence on examining steps in a composite scheme separately – allowed tax avoidance schemes to flourish to the detriment of the general body of taxpayers. The

74 The case was decided on the basis of the predecessor provisions to ss 739–746, namely the Income and Corporation Taxes Act 1970, ss 478–481. See now, ITA 2007, Pt 13 (Tax Avoidance), ch 2 (Transfer of Assets Abroad).

result was that the court appeared to be relegated to the role of a spectator concentrating on the individual moves in a highly skilled game: the court was mesmerised by the moves in the game and paid no regard to the strategy of the participants or the end result. The courts became habituated to this narrow view of their role.

On both fronts the intellectual breakthrough came in 1981 in the *Ramsay* case, and notably in Lord Wilberforce's seminal speech which carried the agreement of Lord Russell of Killowen, Lord Roskill and Lord Bridge of Harwich. Lord Wilberforce restated the principle of statutory construction that a subject is only to be taxed upon clear words ([1981] STC 174 at 179, [1982] AC 300 at 323). To the question "What are 'clear words'?" he gave the answer that the court is not confined to a literal interpretation. He added "There may, indeed should, be considered the context and scheme of the relevant Act as a whole, and its purpose may, indeed should, be regarded". This sentence was critical. It marked the rejection by the House of pure literalism in the interpretation of tax statutes. [3.31]

Frankland v IRC [1997] STC 1450 (CA)

A post-mortem tax planning scheme failed due to an alleged ambiguity in the Inheritance Tax Act 1984. The taxpayer argued unsuccessfully that Parliament could not have intended the legislation to have this effect, and that words should be read into the relevant provisions to prevent the ambiguity from arising.

> PETER GIBSON LJ: I fully accept that in construing a fiscal statute, no less than any other type of statute, one must read the statutory words in their context, and where the statutory purpose of the provision is discernible one should attempt to give effect to that purpose rather than to frustrate it, so far as the words allow. But there are limits to what can legitimately be done as a matter of statutory construction. The court's function is to interpret the legislation and not to legislate under the guise of interpretation. [3.32]

Natalie Lee 'A Purposive Approach to the Interpretation of Tax Statutes?' (1999) 20 Stat LR 124; above, para [3.23]

. . . The Law Commissions[75] believed that the purposive approach and the mischief rule had much in common, but disapproved of the term "mischief". It was considered that the term suggested that legislation was designed only to deal with an evil rather than furthering a positive social purpose. Moreover, it was believed to be too restrictive to look merely at the "mischief" of a particular statute, when the general legislative purpose underlying a provision may emerge from a series of statutes. These criticisms would suggest, then, that the purposive approach is wider than the mischief rule. The words of Mr Justice Vinelott would appear to echo that view:

> . . . if the words of a particular provision literally construed lead to a result which is unjust to the taxpayer or at odds with the scope of the scheme of taxation to be inferred from the legislation as a whole, then the courts can mould even clear language of the particular provision to produce a more harmonious and fair result.[76]

And yet, Lord Reid, who had appeared to espouse the purposive approach, expressed the view that:

75 See Law Commissions of England and Scotland *The Interpretation of Statutes* (1969) (Law Com. No. 21) (Scot Law Com. No. 11).

76 Vinelott J. 'Interpretation of Fiscal Statutes' [1982] Stat. LR 78 at 85.

> What we must look for is the intention of Parliament ... But we can only take the intention of parliament from the words they have used in the Act, and therefore the question is whether these words are capable of a more limited construction. If not, then we must apply them as they stand, however unreasonable or unjust the consequences, and however strongly we may suspect that this was not the real intention of Parliament.[77]

These two contrasting views demonstrate quite clearly the point made earlier that the "purposive approach" holds a different meaning for different people.

... the basis of the purposive approach is the intention of Parliament, but how does an interpreter know what the intention of Parliament is? The concern is that it may be a purely "conjectural intention". This question raises difficulties at two levels. First, and on the higher and more theoretical level, it must be asked whether a thing such as "parliamentary intention" can exist, particularly in relation to taxing statutes.... In some cases it may be artificial to ascribe to the legislature a particular intent, but that it is possible to theorise about parliamentary intention. This can be achieved by distinguishing between the subjective intentions of individual legislators not expressed in the text on the one hand and, on the other, the objective intention of Parliament, which can be attributed to the words used in the statute and in any other admissible materials.

The second, and more practical, difficulty arises when adopting the latter approach to "parliamentary intention". It may well be that the words used in a statute and, it has to be admitted, particularly in tax legislation, simply do not enable an interpreter to discern *any* purpose.

... This article has sought to determine the meaning of the term "purposive interpretation" and to discuss whether this approach is now being used as a matter of course in tax cases. What has been revealed is the difficulty of ascribing to "purposive interpretation" any one single meaning. Because of that very fact, some view the approach with extreme caution, if not dislike, whilst others applaud its use.[78] Moreover, even if a simple meaning based upon the intention of parliament could be found, a further difficulty arises in determining exactly what that intention was.

Perhaps it is because of the existence of these difficulties that in only relatively few cases have judges championed the use of the purposive approach in interpreting a tax statute. Two of those cases, most notably *Pepper v. Hart*[79] and *IRC v. McGuckian*,[80] were high profile cases. The publicity surrounding each of them had the effect of catapulting various *dicta* of eminent members of the House of Lords to a level that perhaps they did not deserve. *IRC v. McGuckian* was not directly concerned with the interpretation of any particular statutory provision but, rather, how composite transactions should be recharacterised for the purpose of applying the statutory provision. This, of course, was not the case with *Pepper v. Hart*, which did concern the meaning of an ambiguous statutory provision. And yet, despite the stark words of Lord Griffiths in that case,[81] the ultimate decision was surely that, whilst the court should seek to give effect to the true purpose of the legislation, it

77 *IRC v. Hinchy* [1960] AC 748 at 767.

78 [As witness the following exchange between Lord Goodhart, QC, and John Morris, Team Leader, the Tax Law Rewrite Project, in evidence given by the latter to the Joint Committee on Tax Law Rewrite Bills, 1 February 2005: ' ... *Lord Goodhart:* I think the problem with tax avoidance legislation is that it is virtually incomprehensible unless you know what the scheme was that it was intended to stop? *Mr Morris:* It helps to understand the background and the intent, yes, but I think your comments can apply to a lot more of the current legislation than just the tax avoidance legislation.' [*Emphasis added.*] (see House of Lords and House of Commons Joint Committee on Tax Law Rewrite Bills, *First Report. Income Tax (Trading and Other Income) Bill* (HL and HC Papers, Session 2004–05, HL Paper 37 and HC Paper 285), p. Ev 25).]

79 [[1993] AC 593; see above, para **[3.28]**.]

80 [[1997] STC 918; see above para **[3.31]**.]

81 [ie "The courts now adopt a purposive approach which seeks to give effect to the true purpose of the legislation." ([1993] AC 593 at 617).]

could only do so if the purpose could be discerned from the permitted use of parliamentary material rather than through conjecture as to what Parliament might have intended . . . **[3.33]**

A further issue raised in the above article relates to the impact which the methodology of the Tax Law Rewrite project may have on the purposive approach: (see (1999) 20 Stat LR 124, 141):

It is submitted that . . . [*the special procedure for Tax Law Rewrite Bills*][82] will not make purposive interpretation any easier; rather, the legislation will have been considered only in its narrowest form. Technicalities will have been discussed exhaustively, but it must be a matter of some concern that the overriding purpose of the original enactment will have been overlooked in the mass of detail confronting the relevant committee.[83] **[3.33a]**

D. The impact of the Human Rights Act 1998[84]

One of the main principles upon which the Human Rights Act (HRA) 1998 operates is that courts and tribunals are required to construe, in so far as that is possible, both primary and secondary legislation in a way that is compatible with the rights guaranteed by the European Convention on Human Rights and Fundamental Freedoms.[85] In doing this, there is a fine line between the courts' interpretative duty and the rewriting of law.[86] **[3.34]**

R (on the application of Wilkinson) v IRC [2005] UKHL 30, [2006] 1 All ER 529 (HL)

For the facts of this case, see below, para **[4.26]**.

> LORD HOFFMANN: The important change in the process of interpretation which was made by section 3 was to deem the Convention to form a significant part of the background against which all statutes, whether passed before or after the 1998 Act came into force, had to be interpreted. Just as the "principle of legality" meant that statutes were construed against the background of human rights subsisting at common law . . . so now, section 3 requires them to be construed against the background of Convention rights. There is a strong presumption, arising from the fundamental nature of Convention rights, that Parliament did not intend a statute to mean something which would be incompatible with those rights. This, of course, goes far beyond the old-fashioned notion of using background to "resolve ambiguities" in a text which had notionally been read without raising one's eyes to look beyond it. The Convention, like the rest of the admissible background, forms part of the primary materials for the process of interpretation. But, with the addition of the Convention as background, the question is still one of *interpretation*, i.e. the ascertainment of what, taking into account the presumption created by section 3, Parliament would reasonably be understood to have meant by using the actual language of the statute. **[3.36]**

82 See Chapter 1, above, para **[1.4]**.
83 (1999) 20 Stat LR 124 at 141.
84 This is discussed fully in Chapter 4.
85 Human Rights Act 1998, s 3.
86 See, generally, Colin Manchester and David Salter *Exploring the Law: The Dynamics of Precedent and Statutory Interpretation* (3rd edn, 2006).

Seminar Wk 5.
- 114

4 Taxation and Human Rights

1. Introduction

In October 2000, the Human Rights Act 1998 incorporated into English law[1] the European Convention on Human Rights and Fundamental Freedoms (the Convention). The Convention is a treaty of the Council of Europe, which was itself established on 5 May 1949 by ten founding western European states.[2] The Council also established the European Commission of Human Rights[3] and the European Court of Human Rights, both in Strasbourg, to which people from countries that had signed up to the Convention could take their complaints and have them judicially determined.

The effect of the Convention is to guarantee a number of basic human rights by allowing *individuals* to complain about the behaviour of their *own* government.[4] Prior to October 2000,[5] any person within the jurisdiction of the UK could submit a petition to the European Commission of Human Rights if they felt aggrieved about the effect of an existing law or an action of the executive, provided they had exhausted all the possible means of challenge within the UK system. If a friendly settlement between the Commission and the applicant could not be secured, then the Commission would send to the Committee of Ministers of the Council of Europe a report, including its opinion on whether or not there had been a violation of a Convention right. The Committee itself could make a decision, thereby concluding the matter, or the case could have been referred to the European Court of Human Rights for consideration. Then, as now, if the Court found that there had been a violation, it could either make a simple formal finding to that effect, or it could make an award of damages or of costs and expenses to the injured party. For its part, the country concerned would be expected to amend the relevant law or procedure so as to bring it into line with the Convention.

At the time of ratification by the UK, it was believed that the rights guaranteed by the Convention were already protected by British law, and that there was no pressing need for their actual incorporation. In practice, the Convention had very limited effect upon UK law since, apart from changes

1 The devolution provisions brought the Convention into domestic law in Northern Ireland, Scotland and Wales before the Human Rights Act came into force; see respectively the Northern Ireland Act 1998, s 6, the Scotland Act 1998, ss 29,57 and the Government of Wales Act 1998, s 107.
2 Including the UK and France.
3 Abolished in November 1998.
4 Before the adoption of the Convention in 1953 by the UK, individuals enjoyed few opportunities to assert rights under international law.
5 Although the Human Rights Act received the Royal Assent in 1998, most of its provisions did not come into effect until October 2000.

made to domestic law through public and political pressure following a Strasbourg decision, it was used only as an aid to interpretation of statute or common law. And even here, the Convention could only be considered where it was necessary to resolve an ambiguity in a statute or there was some uncertainty in the common law.[6]

By 1997 it had become clear that non-incorporation had serious repercussions, not least the fact that the cost of taking a case to Strasbourg was enormous, and the time involved too great. Thus it was resolved that these problems should be overcome by 'bringing home' fundamental rights and freedoms. Accordingly, since October 2000, individuals in the UK have been able to bring human rights issues directly before the British courts, whilst remaining entitled to petition Strasbourg after all possible domestic remedies have been exhausted. **[4.1]**

'Rights Brought Home: The Human Rights Bill' Cm 3782 (1997)

The case for incorporation

1.14 The effect of non-incorporation on the British people is a very practical one. The rights, originally developed with major help from the United Kingdom Government, are no longer actually seen as British rights. And enforcing them takes too long and costs too much. It takes on average five years to get an action into the European Court of Human Rights once all domestic remedies have been exhausted; and it costs an average of £30,000. Bringing these rights home will mean that British people will be able to argue for their rights in the British courts – without this inordinate delay and cost. It will also mean that the rights will be brought much more fully into the jurisprudence of the courts throughout the United Kingdom, and their interpretation will thus be far more subtly and powerfully woven into our law. And there will be another distinct benefit. British judges will be enabled to make a distinctively British contribution to the development of the jurisprudence of human rights in Europe.

Bringing Rights Home

1.18 We therefore believe that the time has come to enable people to enforce their Convention rights against the State in the British courts, rather than having to incur the delays and expense which are involved in taking the case to the European Human Rights Commission and Court in Strasbourg and which may altogether deter some people from pursuing their rights. Enabling courts in the United Kingdom to rule on the application of the Convention will also help to influence the development of case law on the Convention by the European Court of Human Rights on the basis of familiarity with our laws and customs and of sensitivity to practices and procedures in the United Kingdom. Our courts' decisions will provide the European Court with a useful source of information and reasoning for its own decisions. United Kingdom judges have a very high reputation internationally, but the fact that they do not deal in the same concepts as the European Court of Human Rights limits the extent to which their judgments can be drawn upon and followed.

6 *Derbyshire County Council v Times Newspapers* [1993] 1 All ER 1011.

Enabling the Convention rights to be judged by British courts will also lead to closer scrutiny of the human rights implications of new legislation and new policies. If legislation is enacted which is incompatible with the Convention, a ruling by the domestic courts to that effect will be much more direct and immediate than a ruling from the European Court of Human Rights. The Government of the day, and Parliament, will want to minimise the risk of that happening. **[4.2]**

2. The main principles of the Human Rights Act 1998

Convention rights have been incorporated into UK law by the Human Rights Act 1998 only insofar as this is consistent with parliamentary sovereignty. So, the Act, which itself can be repealed, does not give the courts power to strike down primary legislation that is inconsistent with Convention rights, and Parliament may, if it chooses, maintain in force such legislation. Moreover, whilst the Act makes it unlawful for a 'public authority' to act incompatibly with convention rights,[7] Parliament is excluded from the definition of 'public authority'[8] for these purposes. Subject to that overriding caveat, the Act operates on three main principles. **[4.3]**

A. Legislation is to be interpreted compatibly with Convention rights

Courts and tribunals are required to construe both primary and secondary legislation in a way that is, as far as possible, compatible with Convention rights.[9] In practical terms, this section introduces a new and different approach to statutory interpretation by UK courts, going beyond the common law rules. Thus, rather than searching for the true meaning of words or phrases in the traditional manner, courts will now seek to find a meaning that will prevent legislation from being incompatible with Convention rights.[10] The main question is where to draw the constitutional boundary between the courts' interpretative duty on the one hand, and the rewriting of law on the other.[11] **[4.4]**

7 Human Rights Act 1998 s 6(1).
8 *Ibid.*, s 6(3).
9 Human Rights Act 1998, s 3(1).
10 Lord Cooke of Thorndon, Hansard, HL, vol 582, cols 1272–1273, 3 November 1997; see also below, paras **[4.5]**–**[4.7]**.
11 Writing extra-judicially prior to the enactment of the Human Rights Act 1998, the then Lord Chancellor, Lord Irvine of Lairg wrote:

> 'The Act will require the courts to read and give effect to the legislation in a way compatible with the Convention rights 'so far as it is possible to do so'. This ... goes far beyond the present rule. It will not be necessary to find an ambiguity. On the contrary the courts will be required to interpret legislation so as to uphold the Convention rights unless the legislation itself is so clearly incompatible with the Convention that it is impossible to do so..... Whilst this particular approach is innovative, there are some precedents which will assist the courts. In cases involving European Community law, decisions of our courts already show that interpretative techniques may be used to make the domestic legislation comply with the community law, even where this requires straining the meaning of words or reading in words which are not there.' 'The Development of Human Rights in Britain under an Incorporated Convention on Human Rights' [1998] PL 221.

The Right Honourable Lady Justice Arden DBE 'The Interpretation of UK Domestic Legislation in the Light of the European Convention on Human Rights Jurisprudence' [2004] Stat LR 165, 168–169

The interpretative obligation imposed on the courts by section 3 (1) of the 1998 Act has a very respectable genealogy. In *Garland v. British Rail Engineering Ltd,*[12] where the issue was whether domestic legislation was incompatible with European Community legislation, Lord Diplock stated that:

> . . . it is a principle of construction of United Kingdom statutes, now too well established to call for citation of authority, that the words of a statute passed after the Treaty has been signed and dealing with the subject matter of an international obligation of the United Kingdom, are to be construed, if they are reasonably capable of bearing such a meaning, as intended to carry out the obligation and not to be inconsistent with it.

This observation was made with respect to international treaties generally. The words in section 3(1) of the 1998 Act 'so far as it is possible to do so' are just a simpler way of saying 'if they are reasonably capable of bearing such a meaning' (the words used by Lord Diplock).

It is all well established that in relation to constitutional instruments, the court should adopt generous and purposive construction. Thus, for example, in *Ministry of Health v. Fisher*[13] Lord Wilberforce said that constitutional instruments:

> . . . call for a generous interpretation of wording avoiding what has been called 'the austerity of tabulated legalism', suitable to give individuals the full measure of the fundamental rights and freedoms referred to.

Similarly, the Strasbourg Court construes the Convention in a purposive way. It chooses the interpretation which best reflects the democratic purpose of the Convention. As the Strasbourg Court put it in *Soering v. UK*:

> . . . any interpretation of the rights and freedoms guaranteed has to be consistent with the general spirit of the Convention, an instrument designed to maintain and promote the ideals and values of a democratic society.[14]

The Strasbourg Court also adopts the principle known as the principle of dynamic or evolutive interpretation. The Convention uses concepts linked to societal values and these change from time to time. The object of interpretation is to seek the current, not the historic, meaning. As one judge put it: 'The Convention is written in the present tense'. Thus, while birching was considered acceptable in the 1950s, matters had changed when the Strasbourg Court came to consider the matter in 1978. Similarly, the Strasbourg Court's attitude to illegitimate children and transsexuals has changed over the course of time. In relation to transsexuals, the Strasbourg Court at one time held that no violation was involved in a failure to change the birth certificate of a transsexual because there was no generalized approach in the member states of the Council of Europe to the treatment of transsexuals in certain circumstances. However, in the recent case of *Goodwin v. United Kingdom,*[15] the Strasbourg Court held that there was no justification for barring a transsexual from enjoying the right to marry under any circumstances, and that the treatment of transsexuals for legal purposes was no longer within this

12 [1983] 2 AC 751,771.
13 [1980] AC 319, 323
14 [1989] 11 EHRR 439, 467 para. 87.
15 [2002] 35 EHRR 447.

country's margin of appreciation. In reaching this conclusion, the Strasbourg Court took into account the evidence of a continuing international trend in favour of the increased social acceptance and legal recognition of transsexuals.

Because the interpretation of Convention rights is dynamic and changes from time to time, special problems may arise for the statute law of member states. A statute may be passed in 2000 which may fully respect all Convention rights as they are then understood. However, 10 years later, Convention jurisprudence may have moved on so that conclusion is no longer correct. Section 3 of the 1998 Act will require the court to construe the Act not against the context of Convention rights as they stood when the legislation was enacted but against the context of Convention rights as they stand at the time of the judgment. Accordingly, the meaning of statutes may change as the Convention rights which it touches change with the course of time. **[4.5]**

Ghaidan v Godin-Mendoza [2004] UKHL 30, [2004] 2 AC 557 (HL); see also para [4.9]

The respondent claimed that he should become a statutory tenant by succession on the death of his partner, the protected tenant of a residential flat in London, with whom he had lived in a stable and monogamous homosexual relationship. The relevant legislation[16] provided that both a spouse *and* a person who was living with the original tenant 'as his or her wife or husband' could succeed to a statutory tenancy. The appellant, the landlord who sought possession of the property, argued that the survivor of a same sex relationship did not, by definition, fall within the terms of the legislation, and could not become a statutory tenant by succession. The respondent claimed that the right to respect for a person's home, guaranteed by Article 8[17] of the Convention, had not been secured in his case without discrimination, thereby infringing Article 14.[18]

LORD NICHOLLS OF BIRKENHEAD:

26. Section 3 is a key section in the Human Rights Act 1998. It is one of the primary means by which Convention rights are brought into the law of this country. Parliament has decreed that all legislation, existing and future, shall be interpreted in a particular way. All legislation must be read and given effect to in a way which is compatible with the Convention rights 'so far as it is possible to do so'. This is the intention of Parliament, expressed in section 3, and the courts must give effect to this intention.

27. Unfortunately, in making this provision for the interpretation of legislation, section 3 itself is not free from ambiguity. Section 3 is open to more than one interpretation. The difficulty lies in the word 'possible'. Section 3(1), read in conjunction with section 3(2) and section 4, makes one matter clear: Parliament expressly envisaged that not all legislation would be capable of being made Convention-compliant by application of section 3. Sometimes it would be possible, sometimes not. What is not clear is the test to be applied in separating the sheep from the goats. What is the standard, or the criterion, by which 'possibility' is to be judged? A comprehensive answer to this question is proving elusive. The courts, including your Lordships' House, are still cautiously feeling their way forward as experience in the application of section 3 gradually accumulates.

28. One tenable interpretation of the word 'possible' would be that section 3 is confined to requiring courts to resolve ambiguities. Where the words under

16 Rent Act 1977, s 2(1)(b) and Schedule 1, para 2(2). This provision has since been amended to include civil partners by the Civil Partnership Act, s 81 and Schedule 8, para 13.
17 See below, para **[4.40]**.
18 See below, para **[4.25]**.

consideration fairly admit of more than one meaning the Convention-compliant meaning is to prevail. Words should be given the meaning which best accords with the Convention rights.

29. This interpretation of section 3 would give the section a comparatively narrow scope. This is not the view which has prevailed. It is now generally accepted that the application of section 3 does not depend upon the presence of ambiguity in the legislation being interpreted. Even if, construed according to the ordinary principles of interpretation, the meaning of the legislation admits of no doubt, section 3 may nonetheless require the legislation to be given a different meaning. The decision of your Lordships' House in *R v A (No 2)* [2002] 1 AC 45 is an instance of this. The House read words into section 41 of the Youth Justice and Criminal Evidence Act 1999 so as to make that section compliant with an accused's right to a fair trial under article 6. The House did so even though the statutory language was not ambiguous.

30. From this it follows that the interpretative obligation decreed by section 3 is of an unusually far-reaching character. Section 3 may require a court to depart from the unambiguous meaning the legislation would otherwise bear. In the ordinary course the interpretation of legislation involves seeking the intention reasonably to be attributed to Parliament in using the language in question. Section 3 may require the court to depart from this legislative intention, that is, depart from the intention of the Parliament which enacted the legislation. The question of difficulty is how far, and in what circumstances, section 3 requires a court to depart from the intention of the enacting Parliament. The answer to this question depends upon the intention reasonably to be attributed to Parliament in enacting section 3.

31. On this first point to be considered is how far, when enacting section 3, Parliament intended that the actual language of a statute, as distinct from the concept expressed in that language, should be determinative. Since section 3 relates to the 'interpretation' of legislation, it is natural to focus attention initially on the language used in the legislative provision being considered. But once it is accepted that section 3 may require legislation to bear a meaning which departs from the unambiguous meaning the legislation would otherwise bear, it becomes impossible to suppose Parliament intended that the operation of section 3 should depend critically upon the particular form of words adopted by the parliamentary draftsman in the statutory provision under consideration. That would make the application of section 3 something of a semantic lottery. If the draftsman chose to express the concept being enacted in one form of words, section 3 would be available to achieve Convention-compliance. If he chose a different form of words, section 3 would be impotent.

32. From this the conclusion which seems inescapable is that the mere fact the language under consideration is inconsistent with a Convention-compliant meaning does not of itself make a Convention-compliant interpretation under section 3 impossible. Section 3 enables language to be interpreted restrictively or expansively. But section 3 goes further than this. It is also apt to require a court to read in words which change the meaning of the enacted legislation, so as to make it Convention-compliant. In other words, the intention of Parliament in enacting section 3 was that, to an extent bounded only by what is 'possible', a court can modify the meaning, and hence the effect, of primary and secondary legislation.

33. Parliament, however, cannot have intended that in the discharge of this extended interpretative function the courts should adopt a meaning inconsistent with a fundamental feature of legislation. That would be to cross the constitutional boundary section 3 seeks to demarcate and preserve. Parliament has retained the right to enact legislation in terms which are not Convention-compliant. The meaning imported by application of section 3 must be compatible with the underlying thrust of the legislation being construed. Words implied must, in the phrase of my noble and learned friend Lord Rodger of Earlsferry, 'go with the grain of the legislation'. Nor can Parliament have intended that section 3 should require courts to make decisions for which they are not equipped. There may be several ways of making a provision Convention-compliant, and the choice may involve issues calling for legislative deliberation.

34. Both these features were present in *In re S (Minors)(Care Order: Implementation of Care Plan)* [2002] 2 AC 291. There the proposed 'starring system' was inconsistent in an important respect with the scheme of the Children Act 1989, and the proposed system had far-reaching practical ramifications for local authorities. Again, in *R (Anderson) v Secretary of State for the Home Department* [2003] 1 AC 837 section 29 of the Crime (Sentences) Act 1997 could not be read in a Convention-compliant way without giving the section a meaning inconsistent with an important feature expressed clearly in the legislation. In *Bellinger v Bellinger* [2003] 2 AC 467 recognition of Mrs Bellinger as female for the purposes of section 11 (c) of the Matrimonial Causes Act 1973 would have had exceedingly wide ramifications, raising issues ill-suited for determination by the courts or court procedures.

35. In some cases difficult problems may arise. No difficulty arises in the present case. Paragraph 2 of Schedule 1 to the Rent Act 1977 is unambiguous. But the social policy underlying the 1988 extension of security of tenure under paragraph 2 to the survivor of couples living together as husband and wife is equally applicable to the survivor of homosexual couples living together in a close and stable relationship. In this circumstance I see no reason to doubt that application of section 3 to paragraph 2 has the effect that paragraph 2 should be read and given effect to as though the survivor of such a homosexual couple were the surviving spouse of the original tenant. Reading paragraph 2 in this way would have the result that cohabiting heterosexual couples and cohabiting homosexual couples would be treated alike for the purposes of succession as a statutory tenant. This would eliminate the discriminatory effect of paragraph 2 and would do so consistently with the social policy underlying paragraph 2. The precise form of words read in for this purpose is of no significance. It is their substantive effect which matters.

This approach, however, must be viewed with caution. **[4.6]**

R v Lambert [2001] UKHL 37, [2001] 3 WLR 206 (HL)

LORD HOPE OF CRAIGHEAD:

78. Section 3(1) of the 1998 Act provides that, so far as it is possible to do so, primary and secondary legislation must be read and given effect in a way which is compatible with the Convention rights. I should now like to explain how, as I see it, this important and far-reaching new approach to the construction of statutes should be employed consistently with the need (a) to respect the will of the legislature so far as this remains appropriate and (b) to preserve the integrity of our statute law so far as this is possible.

79. The first point, as I said in paragraph 108 of my speech in *R v A* [2001] UKHL 25, is that the effect of section 3(1) is that the interpretation which it requires is to be achieved only so far as this is possible. The word "must", which section 3(1) uses, is qualified by the phrase "so far as it is possible to do so". The obligation, powerful though it is, is not to be performed without regard to its limitations. Resort to it will not be possible if the legislation contains provisions, either in the words or phrases which are under scrutiny or elsewhere, which expressly contradict the meaning which the enactment would have to be given to make it compatible. The same consequence will follow if legislation contains provisions which have this effect by necessary implication. Further justification for giving this qualified meaning to section 3(1) is to be found in the words "read and give effect." As the side note indicates, the obligation is one which applies to the interpretation of legislation. This function belongs, as it has always done, to the judges. But it is not for them to legislate. Section 3(1) preserves the sovereignty of Parliament. It does not give power to the judges to overrule decisions which the language of the statute shows have been taken on the very point at issue by the legislator.

80. The second point, as I said in paragraph 110 of my speech in *R v A*, is that great care must be taken, in cases where a different meaning has to be given to the legislation from the ordinary meaning of the words used by the legislator, to identify precisely the word or

phrase which, if given its ordinary meaning, would otherwise be incompatible. Just as much care must then be taken to say how the word or phrase is to be construed if it is to be made compatible. The justification for this approach to the use of section 3(1) is to be found in the nature of legislation itself. Its primary characteristic, for present purposes, is its ability to achieve certainty by the use of clear and precise language. It provides a set of rules by which, according to the ordinary meaning of the words used, the conduct of affairs may be regulated. So far as possible judges should seek to achieve the same attention to detail in their use of language to express the effect of applying section 3(1) as the parliamentary draftsman would have done if he had been amending the statute. It ought to be possible for any words that need to be substituted to be fitted in to the statute as if they had been inserted there by amendment. If this cannot be done without doing such violence to the statute as to make it unintelligible or unworkable, the use of this technique will not be possible. It will then be necessary to leave it to Parliament to amend the statute and to resort instead to the making of a declaration of incompatibility.

81. As to the techniques that may be used, it is clear that the courts are not bound by previous authority as to what the statute means. It has been suggested that a strained or non-literal construction may be adopted, that words may be read in by way of addition to those used by the legislator and that the words may be "read down" to give them a narrower construction than their ordinary meaning would bear: Clayton and Tomlinson, The Law of Human Rights, para 4.28, p 168 (Oxford, 2000). It may be enough simply to say what the effect of the provision is without altering the ordinary meaning of the words used: see *Brown v Stott* 2000 JC 328, 355B-C, per Lord Justice General Rodger. In other cases, as in *Vasquez v The Queen* [1994] 1 WLR 1304, the words used will require to be expressed in different language in order to explain how they are to be read in a way that is compatible. The exercise in these cases is one of translation into compatible language from language that is incompatible. In other cases, as in *R v A*, it may be necessary for words to be read in to explain the meaning that must be given to the provision if it is to be compatible. But the interpretation of a statute by reading words in to give effect to the presumed intention must always be distinguished carefully from amendment. Amendment is a legislative act. It is an exercise which must be reserved to Parliament. **[4.7]**

B. *Declaration of incompatibility*

Although no court is able to strike down or disregard legislation that conflicts with Convention rights, the High Court and above[19] may make a 'declaration of incompatibility',[20] which may be viewed as a first step towards correcting the primary or secondary legislation. Legislation subject to such a declaration will continue in force until the relevant Minister chooses to exercise his power to amend it by way of remedial order, which can have retrospective effect.[21] Moreover, a Minister responsible for the introduction of a Bill in either the House of Commons or the House of Lords must now make a written statement prior to the Second Reading of such Bill to the effect that either it is compatible with Convention rights or, if this cannot be done, that the Government has nonetheless decided to proceed with the Bill.[22] This ensures that every new piece of legislation must be considered in the light of the Human Rights Act 1998 and, although the Government is still able to proceed with legislation that does not necessarily have the 'stamp of approval', the force of public opinion may make such an attempt very difficult. The main issue is the interrelationship between ss 3 and 4 of the Act, and whether the courts should strive to interpret a provision compatibly with Convention rights at all costs, or use s 4 in order to engage both the executive and Parliament in an exercise in defining and furthering human rights. **[4.8]**

19 But not tribunals.
20 Human Rights Act 1998, s 4(2).
21 *Ibid*, s 10(2), (3).
22 *Ibid*, s 19.

Ghaidan v Godin-Mendoza

(The case is cited with its facts at para **[4.6]** above.)

LORD STEYN:

40. My impression is that two factors are contributing to a misunderstanding of the remedial scheme of the 1998 Act. First, there is the constant refrain that a judicial reading down, or reading in, under section 3 would flout the will of Parliament as expressed in the statute under examination. This question cannot sensibly be considered without giving full weight to the countervailing will of Parliament as expressed in the 1998 Act.

41. The second factor may be an excessive concentration on linguistic features of the particular statute. Nowhere in our legal system is a literalistic approach more inappropriate than when considering whether a breach of a Convention right may be removed by interpretation under section 3. Section 3 requires a broad approach concentrating, amongst other things, in a purposive way on the importance of the fundamental right involved.

42. In enacting the 1998 Act Parliament legislated "to bring rights home" from the European Court of Human Rights to be determined in the courts of the United Kingdom. That is what the White Paper said: see Rights Brought Home: The Human Rights Bill (1997) (cm 3782), para 2.7. That is what Parliament was told. The mischief to be addressed was the fact that Convention rights as set out in the ECHR, which Britain ratified in 1951, could not be vindicated in our courts. Critical to this purpose was the enactment of effective remedial provisions.

43. The provisions adopted read as follows:

'3. Interpretation of legislation

(1) So far as it is possible to do so, primary legislation and subordinate legislation must be read and given effect in a way which is compatible with the Convention rights.

(2) This section –

(a) applies to primary legislation and subordinate legislation whenever enacted;

(b) does not affect the validity, continuing operation or enforcement of any incompatible primary legislation; and

(c) does not affect the validity, continuing operation or enforcement of any incompatible subordinate legislation if (disregarding any possibility of revocation) primary legislation prevents removal of the incompatibility.

4. Declaration of incompatibility

(1) Subsection (2) applies in any proceedings in which a court determines whether a provision of primary legislation is compatible with a Convention right.

(2) If the court is satisfied that the provision is incompatible with a Convention right, it may make a declaration of that incompatibility.'

If Parliament disagrees with an interpretation by the courts under section 3(1), it is free to override it by amending the legislation and expressly reinstating the incompatibility.

44. It is necessary to state what section 3(1), and in particular the word "possible" does not mean. First, section 3(1) applies even if there is no ambiguity in the language in the sense of it being capable of bearing two possible meanings. The word "possible" in section 3(1) is used in a different and much stronger sense. Secondly, section 3(1) imposes a stronger and more radical obligation than to adopt a purposive interpretation in the light of the ECHR. Thirdly, the draftsman of the Act had before him the model of the New Zealand Bill of Rights Act which imposes a requirement that the interpretation to be adopted must be reasonable. Parliament specifically rejected the legislative model of requiring a reasonable interpretation.

45. Instead the draftsman had resort to the analogy of the obligation under the EEC Treaty on national courts, as far as possible, to interpret national legislation in the light of the wording and purpose of directives. In *Marleasing SA v La Comercial Internacional de Alimentacion SA* (Case C-106/89) [1990] ECR I-4135, 4159 the European Court of Justice defined this obligation as follows:

> "It follows that, in applying national law, whether the provisions in question were adopted before or after the directive, the national court called upon to interpret it is required to do so, as far as possible, in light of the wording and the purpose of the directive in order to achieve the result pursued by the latter and thereby comply with the third paragraph of Article 189 of the Treaty."

Given the undoubted strength of this interpretative obligation under EEC law, this is a significant signpost to the meaning of section 3(1) in the 1998 Act.

46. Parliament had before it the mischief and objective sought to be addressed, viz the need "to bring rights home". The linch-pin of the legislative scheme to achieve this purpose was section 3(1). Rights could only be effectively brought home if section 3(1) was the prime remedial measure, and section 4 a measure of last resort. How the system modelled on the EEC interpretative obligation would work was graphically illustrated for Parliament during the progress of the Bill through both Houses. The Lord Chancellor observed that "in 99% of the cases that will arise, there will be no need for judicial declarations of incompatibility" and the Home Secretary said "We expect that, in almost all cases, the courts will be able to interpret the legislation compatibly with the Convention": Hansard (HL Debates), 5 February 1998, col 840 (3rd reading) and Hansard (HC Debates,) 16 February 1998, col 778 (2nd reading). It was envisaged that the duty of the court would be to strive to find (if possible) a meaning which would best accord with Convention rights. This is the remedial scheme which Parliament adopted. **[4.9]**

In *R (on the application of Wilkinson) v IRC*,[23] despite protestations from counsel for the Crown that it would be pointless to do so, Moses J made a declaration of incompatibility in respect of ICTA 1988, s 262 (widow's bereavement allowance), which allowance had been abolished prospectively by the time the Human Rights Act 1998 had come into force. **[4.10]**

C. Public authorities must act in accordance with Convention rights

The requirement that all public authorities (and this would include Her Majesty's Commissioners of Revenue & Customs) must act in accordance with Convention rights,[24] is subject to the all-important doctrine of the 'margin of appreciation', which refers to the ability of public authorities to make discretionary decisions with which courts should not unduly interfere, and requires the court to consider not only whether the relevant authority acted reasonably, carefully and in good faith but, in addition, whether the authority's action was proportionate to the aim pursued. Certain of the

23 [2002] STC 347. This issue was not the subject of later appeals to the Court of Appeal and House of Lords.

24 Human Rights Act 1998, s 6(1). Public authorities include courts and tribunals, but not the Houses of Parliament or any individual person (such as a Minister) exercising functions in connection with proceedings in Parliament. In holding that a parochial church council was not a 'public authority' for these purposes, the House of Lords in *Aston Cantlow & Wilmcote with Billesley PCC v WallBank & Wallbank* [2003] UKHL 37, [2003] 3 WLR 283 drew a distinction between persons who, in Convention terms, are governmental organisations on the one hand, and those who are non-governmental on the other. Section 6(2) provides:
'Subsection (1) does not apply to an act if –
(a) as the result of one or more provisions of primary legislation, the authority could not have acted differently; or
(b) in the case of one or more provisions of, or made under, primary legislation which cannot be read or given effect in a way which is compatible with the Convention rights, the authority was acting so as to give effect to or enforce those provisions.'

Convention rights are specifically subject to what may loosely be called restrictions. Thus, for example, the right in art 8 to respect for private and family life is subject to the caveat that there may be interference in accordance with the law to achieve a legitimate aim in light of a pressing social need. So also is art 1 of the First Protocol, the peaceful enjoyment of possessions by a person, limited by the right of a state to enforce laws that it deems to be necessary for the control of the use of property or 'to secure the payment of taxes or other contributions or penalties' in 'accordance with the general interest'. Whilst the words of the Convention itself provide for the purposes for which these restrictions may be made, thereby giving an indication of the width of a discretionary area of judgment enjoyed by public authorities in actually deciding whether to introduce measures restrictive of fundamental rights, they do not spell out a doctrine of proportionality. Rather, the question of whether the action of a public body, which has the effect of restricting fundamental rights, is proportionate to the needs of a democratic society (which had, in the past, been left to the Strasbourg Court to decide) is now 'at the heart of the HRA case law'[25]: incorporation of Convention rights by the HRA has 'brought the concept of proportionality directly into force in the law of the United Kingdom'.[26] What this actually means in practice is that, rather than questioning whether a public authority reasonably believed that their decision was proportionate and not therefore irrational, it has to be asked whether the decision was *in fact* proportionate. **[4.11]**

Lord Irvine of Laird 'The Impact of the Human Rights Act: Parliament, The Courts And The Executive' [2003] PL 308, 314–316 and 318–319

[W]e have seen the development of a domestic version of the "margin of appreciation", long recognised in Strasbourg. The concept reflects the willingness of the European Court, when assessing whether a restriction on a Convention right is justified under the Convention, to extend leeway to domestic authorities, on the basis that they are, generally speaking, in a better position to make that assessment. As the court recognised in *Handyside v UK*:

> By reason of their direct and continuous contact with the vital forces of their countries, State authorities are in principle in a better position than the international judge to give an opinion on the ... "necessity" of a "restriction" or "penalty" ... it is for the national authorities to make the initial assessment of the reality of the pressing social need implied by the notion of "necessity" in this context.[27]

The domestic version addresses when, why, and the degree to which, the domestic courts defer to the decisions of Parliament and the executive, rather than seek to weigh up the merits of those decisions themselves. 'Judicial deference', as it is also known, does not mean that the courts are subordinate partners in the tripartite relationship, but that they recognise that, in certain areas, the government or Parliament are better placed to make judgements because of the knowledge and experience available to them.

25 Nicholas Blake, 'Importing Proportionality: Clarification or Confusion' (2002) EHLR 1, 19.
26 *Ibid*, p 20.
27 *Handyside v. UK* (1979–80) 1 EHRR 737 at 753.

Nor does deference represent an abdication of the responsibility, given by Parliament to the courts, to scrutinise executive conduct and guard against unjustified interference with Convention rights. Certainly the government would not want that. The Human Rights Act constitutes a promise to citizens that public bodies will, subject to parliamentary sovereignty, act compatibly with their rights.[28] And the guarantee backing that promise is that citizens can take the government to court if they believe government has failed.[29]

The courts have not been slow to utilise the enhanced form of scrutiny provided for by the Human Rights Act, and called for by the European Court in Strasbourg. In *Smith and Grady v UK*—decided by the European Court after the passing of the Human Rights Act, but before it came into force—the court examined the treatment of a group of servicemen and women.[30] It found that the Ministry of Defence's policy of excluding homosexuals from the armed forces had violated their Art. 8 rights to respect for private and family life. But the court also held that there had been a violation of Art. 13, since challenging the MoD policy in the domestic courts could not provide an effective remedy, given the limitations of judicial review. The domestic courts could only interfere with the exercise of administrative discretion on substantive grounds where a decision was unreasonable in the sense that it was beyond the range of responses open to a reasonable decision-maker. They were precluded, therefore, from considering whether the interference with the applicants' rights answered a pressing social need or was proportionate to the national security and public order aims pursued. Now the Act did not incorporate Art. 13 because the Act itself provided the effective remedy that was previously lacking. But what *Smith and Grady* illustrated was that the courts would need to use the Act to extend the traditional parameters of judicial review to enable greater scrutiny of the proportionality of decisions being challenged. . . .

It is all about balance. The balance between intense judicial scrutiny and reasonable deference to elected decision-makers is a delicate one to strike. But the judiciary have struck it well; and I welcome that. Whilst scrutiny is undoubtedly an important aid to better governance, there are areas in which decisions are best taken by the decision-makers entrusted by Parliament to make them. This may be for reasons of democratic accountability, expertise or complexity. But we recognise that we cannot simply recite the need for "deference" or "self-restraint". Rather, we must, where appropriate, argue the case for it carefully and persuasively. This often involves "policy advocacy"—the equivalent of 'Brandeis briefs' in the US Supreme Court—by which government counsel gives the court a thorough analysis of the policy behind legislation.

Our judges have been receptive to this approach. Lord Bingham demonstrated that in the Scottish case of *Brown v Stott*.[31] The case was about drink driving, and the rule in s. 172 of the Road Traffic Act 1988 requiring a suspect to declare who had been driving a car at the material time. The defendant argued that the rule infringed her right to a fair trial, and in particular her privilege against self-incrimination. In the Privy Council, Lord Bingham accepted evidence of the social menace presented by drink driving, and was persuaded that the Road Traffic Act was a fair way of countering and punishing that behaviour. The case ceased to be a legalistic debate about self-incrimination. Instead, it showed an astute awareness by our judges of the needs of the community and the responsibilities of government. . . .

28 Human Rights Act 1998, s 6(1).
29 *Ibid.* s. 7(1).
30 (2000) 29 EHRR 493.
31 [2001] 2 WLR 817. Note, the ECHR point in this case was considered under the Scotland Act 1998, rather than the Human Rights Act 1998.

Balancing individual rights with the wider public interest

. . . the jurisprudence of the European Court . . . has often said that it is inherent in the Convention that a fair balance must be struck between the general interest of the community and the protection of the individual's fundamental rights.[32] This is also an important express requirement of Arts 8, 9, 10 and 11 of the Convention, each of which is subject to limitation or restriction clauses which enable the general public interest to be taken into account. The leading cases show, contrary to views expressed in sections of the press, that the courts have not sacrificed the wider public interest in favour of the rights of individuals. Rather, they have applied a principled approach and have sought to strike a fair balance between the two. So, in the case of *Roth* a German road transport carrier challenged the civil penalty scheme under the Immigration and Asylum Act 1999.[33] The scheme imposed a fixed penalty on carriers who brought in illegal immigrants unless they could show, not only that they had no knowledge of having carried the entrants, but that they had an effective system for preventing this, which was operated properly on the occasion in question. A majority of the Court of Appeal held that the scheme was incompatible with Art. 6 because the fixed nature of the penalties offended the right to have a penalty determined by an independent tribunal. In addition, the scale and inflexibility of the penalty constituted an interference with an individual's property **rights** under Art. 1, Protocol 1, that was disproportionate to the public interest objectives it sought to achieve.

But in *Farrakhan* the balance struck by the court was in favour of the wider public interest.[34] The case involved an American national who was refused entry to the United Kingdom, by the Home Secretary, on the grounds that his presence in the country might provide a catalyst for public disorder, given his publicly pronounced views, which could be seen to be racially divisive. The Court of Appeal found against Farrakhan because, although Art. 10 was engaged, the Home Secretary had struck a proportionate balance between the public interest aim of preventing disorder and Mr Farrakhan's freedom of expression. **[4.12]**

3. The courts and human rights

The findings of the European Court of Human Rights have to be applied in over forty different States, all having different cultures and politics. Consequently, domestic courts and tribunals will take into consideration the jurisprudence of the Strasbourg Court, indeed they are obliged to do so by s 2(1) of the Human Rights Act 1998 but, like the Strasbourg Court itself, they are not bound by any of its decisions. **[4.13]**

32 See, e.g., *Klass v Germany* (1978) 2 EHRR 214; *Brogan v UK* (1988) 11 EHRR 117; *Goodwin v UK* (2002) 35 EHRR 447. See also *R (on the application of McCann) v Crown Court at Manchester* [2002] UKHL 39; [2002] 2 WLR 1313, in which Lord Hope said at 1330, that it is a theme running right through the Convention that the exercise of freedoms carries with it duties and responsibilities.

33 *International Transport Roth GmbH v Secretary of State for the Home Department* [2002] EWCA Civ 158; [2002] 3 WLR 344.

34 [2002] 3 WLR 481.

Han v Customs and Excise Commissioners [2001] EWCA Civ 1040, [2001] 1 WLR 2253 (CA)

(See below, para **[4.54]** for the facts of this case.)

POTTER LJ:

25. Since s. 2(1) of the HRA requires the court or tribunal to take into account the Strasbourg case law of the European Court of Human Rights (the Strasbourg Court) when determining a question which has arisen in connection with a Convention right, the case law provides the starting point for the domestic court or tribunal's deliberations and the court or tribunal has a duty to consider such case law for the purpose of making its adjudication. It is not bound to follow such case law (which itself has no doctrine of precedent) but, if study reveals some clear principle, test or autonomous meaning consistently applied by the Strasbourg Court and applicable to a convention question arising before the English courts, then the court should not depart from it without strong reason. **[4.14]**

4. Taxation and the Convention

Since the Preamble to the Convention talks of the 'fundamental freedoms which are the foundation of justice and peace in the world ....', it is questionable whether human rights apply, or were ever meant to apply, to taxpayers, bearing in mind particularly that a number of them are corporate bodies whose property interests could not have been uppermost in the minds of those who drafted the Convention.[35] In maintaining that Convention rights should apply to taxpayers, it has been argued that they have as much right to protection as do criminals whose right, for example, to a fair trial is guaranteed by art 6, and that the 'system of human rights is, after all, a matter of protecting the individual human being and not especially protecting governments'.[36]

Taxation was mentioned for the first time in the Convention only when Protocol No 1 was adopted a few years after the original Convention, and only then to permit contracting states to limit the right of an individual's enjoyment to property in order to secure the payment of taxes. However, even before incorporation, a number of tax cases were heard before the European Court of Human Rights, a few of these being by UK taxpayers against the Government,[37] and the Court has explained fully the principles that it, in its supervisory role, should apply with respect to taxation. The result is that, whilst individuals cannot maintain that an ordinary assessment to tax or the imposition of very high rates of tax is a breach of art 1 of Protocol No 1, cases can be brought on the basis that a certain tax measure was not proportionate to society's needs. Nonetheless, the Strasbourg Court

35 In arguing that they do, see Nicholas Jordan 'The Implications for Commercial Lawyers in Practice' in Basil S Markesinis (ed) *The Impact of the Human Rights Bill on English Law* (Oxford University Press: New York, 1998), where he wrote: 'Until now, this was a jurisdiction mainly developed by men whose motives were ethical or political or urgently personal, but the potential for applying many of the Convention rights to business life has been dawning upon lawyers in the UK for some years now.'

36 Isi Foighel, 'Do human rights apply to taxpayers?' in *Protecting Human Rights: The European Perspective* (Koln: Heymanns, 2000) 535, 543.

37 For example, *National and Provincial Building Society and Others v United Kingdom* (1998) 25 EHRR 127, [1997] STC 1466; *A, B, C & D v UK* (1981) 23 DR 203; *Nap Holdings UK Ltd v UK* (1996) 22 EHRR 114. All of these cases concerned the issue of retrospective legislation.

has shown reluctance to reach a finding that a particular piece of tax legislation, even retrospective legislation,[38] is in breach of Convention rights, and probably for political reasons.[39] Domestic courts may well follow suit, their unexpressed view being that it should not be left to the courts to arbitrate on matters of tax policy, and an expressed conclusion being reached on the ground of securing the payment of tax in the public interest and the wide margin of appreciation. **[4.15]**

Wasa Liv Omsesidigt v Sweden (1988) 58 DR 163

An application by certain life insurance companies to the European Commission of Human Rights concerned the introduction in Sweden of a windfall property tax on life insurance companies, certain friendly societies and pension foundations.

> EUROPEAN COMMISSION OF HUMAN RIGHTS: . . . though it is certain that no general prohibition of taxes payable exclusively out of the taxpayer's capital can be derived from Article 1, a financial liability arising out of the raising of taxes or contributions may adversely affect the guarantee secured under this provision if it places an excessive burden on the person or entity concerned or fundamentally interferes with his or its financial position. However, it is in the first place for the national authorities to decide what kind of taxes or contributions are to be collected. Furthermore the decisions in this area will commonly involve the appreciation of political, economic and social questions which the Convention leaves within the competence of the Contracting States. The power of appreciation of Contracting States is therefore a wide one . . . .
>
> Considering the case in this light the Commission notes the applicants' contention that, whilst the redistribution of wealth from more favoured to less favoured groups in society is a legal aim, the arbitrary and discriminatory taking of wealth from particular sections of the public, in circumstances where there is no "fair balance", constitutes an aim which is "manifestly without reasonable foundation". They contend that the respondent State seeks by the levying of the tax to increase its revenues by approximately one third of the revenue normally obtained through income tax. Furthermore, there is no reasonable proportionality between the operation of the Act and the State's aim of reducing the national debt and thus it amounts to a taking of property which is manifestly not in the public interest or within the scope of the second paragraph of Article 1 of Protocol No. 1.
>
> The Commission also recalls that the main reason for introducing the one-off tax were considerations concerning a continuing low inflation, essential in the Government's view for any favourable economic development, combined with the necessity of a further limitation of the national budget deficit. It is undoubtedly within the sovereign power of a State to enact legislation of this nature and the Commission finds that this is clearly a measure introduced with a public purpose and considered by the State to be in the general interest. This aim was pursued by levying the one-off tax on *inter alia* the applicants amounting to 7% of their assets exceeding 10 million Swedish crowns due, in particular, to the fact that the situation in the entire life insurance sector was unique at the time and because of the favourable treatment afforded to this sector as regards taxation in general, a treatment which is still maintained. In such circumstances the Commission cannot find that the one-off tax affected the applicants' right of ownership of its assets, be it monetary or other assets, or interfered with their financial situation to such an extent that this could be considered disproportionate or an abuse of the State's right under Article 1 of Protocol No. 1 to levy taxes. **[4.16]**

38 As in *National and Provincial Building Society v UK*.

39 The findings of the Strasbourg Court have to be applied in over forty states, all having very different cultures and politics and, accordingly, it would not be surprising for it to act in a conservative fashion and apply a particularly wide margin of appreciation under Article 1 of Protocol No 1 in favour of the Government.

Gasus Dosier-Und Fördertechnik GmbH v Netherlands (1995) 20 EHRR 403 (ECHR)

The applicant company had sold a concrete mixer to a Dutch company on the condition that title to it would not pass until the full price had been paid. The machine was seized to cover the Dutch company's tax debts. The applicant company argued, *inter alia,* that it had been deprived of its possession in violation of Article 1 of Protocol No. 1. The European Court of Human Rights held, by a majority, that there had been no such violation.

EUROPEAN COURT OF HUMAN RIGHTS:

60. the present case concerns the rights of States to enact such laws as they deem necessary for the purpose of "securing the payment of taxes".

In the present case the Court is not called upon to ascertain whether this right, as the wording of the provision may suggest, is limited to procedural tax laws[40] or whether it also covers substantive tax laws[41]; the 1855 Act, which is at issue in the present case, was plainly a procedural tax law. In passing such laws the legislature must be allowed a wide margin of appreciation, especially with regard to the question whether – and if so, to what extent – the tax authorities should be put in a better position to enforce tax debts than ordinary creditors are in to enforce commercial debts. The Court will respect the legislature's assessment in such matters unless it is devoid of reasonable foundation. . . .

61. Section 16(3) of the 1845 Act gave the tax authorities the power to recover tax debts against certain goods which, although in fact in the possession of their debtor . . . were owned, as a matter of law, by a third party. It thus dispensed the tax authorities from having to consider whether these goods were actually the property of the debtor. The purpose of this provision was obviously to facilitate the enforcement of tax debts, which in itself is clearly in the general interest . . .

62. According to the Court's well-established case law . . . an interference must achieve a "fair balance" between the demands of the general interest of the community and the requirements of the protection of the individual's fundamental rights. The concern to achieve this balance is reflected in the structure of Article 1 as a whole, including the second paragraph: there must therefore be a reasonable relationship of proportionality between the means employed and the aim pursued. **[4.17]**

National and Provincial Building Society and Others v United Kingdom [1997] STC 1466 (ECHR)

Three building societies challenged retrospective legislation introduced by the Government to prevent a windfall benefit to the applicants that would otherwise have occurred due to technical defects in the regulations governing the taxation of interest paid to investors, and to frustrate any attempts to challenge the validity of the regulations. For their part, the applicants claimed that the legislation would result in double taxation, that it was invalid and that it sought specifically to limit their access to justice. The European Court of Human Rights rejected the argument that there had been double taxation, and concluded that, despite the fact that the legislation did constitute an interference with the applicants' rights of possession to property under Article 1 of Protocol No. 1, the interference was justified in the public interest in that it secured the payment of taxes. The Court rejected the

40 That is to say: laws which regulate the formalities of taxation, including the enforcement of tax debts.

41 That is to say: laws which lay down the circumstances under which tax is due and the amount payable.

applicants' further claim that the retrospective legislation restricted their right of access to a court and that there was therefore a breach of Article 6(1),[42] on the grounds that it was in the public interest that legislation should intervene to prevent litigation that was aimed at frustrating the intention of Parliament and, in any event, the dispute concerned matters of taxation, where recourse to retrospective legislation is not confined to the UK.

> EUROPEAN COURT OF HUMAN RIGHTS:
>
> 80. According to the court's well-established case-law (see, among many other authorities, the *Gasus Dosier- und Fördertechnik GmbH v the Netherlands* judgment of 23 February 1995, p. 49, 62), an interference, including one resulting from a measure to secure the payment of taxes, must strike a "fair balance" between the demands of the general interest of the community and the requirements of the protection of the individual's fundamental rights. The concern to achieve this balance is reflected in the structure of art. 1 as a whole, including the second paragraph: there must therefore be a reasonable relationship of proportionality between the means employed and the aims pursued. Furthermore, in determining whether this requirement has been met, it is recognised that a contracting state, not least when framing and implementing policies in the area of taxation, enjoys a wide margin of appreciation and the court will respect the legislature's assessment in such matters unless it is devoid of reasonable foundation (see the *Gasus Dosier- und Fördertechnic GmbH v the Netherlands* judgment, pp. 48–49, 60).
>
> 81. Against that background, the court notes that in enacting s. 53 of the 1991 Act with retroactive effect Parliament was concerned to restore and reassert its original intention which had been stymied by the finding of the House of Lords in the Woolwich litigation that the 1986 regulations were ultra vires on technical grounds. . . . it does not appear to the court that the ultimate aim of the measure was without reasonable foundation having regards to the public interest considerations which underpinned the proposal to legislate with retroactive effect and Parliament's endorsement of that proposal.
>
> There is in fact an obvious and compelling public interest to ensure that private entities do not enjoy the benefit of a windfall in a changeover to a new tax payment regime and do not deny the Exchequer revenue simply on account of inadvertent defects in the enabling tax legislation, the more so when such entities have followed the debates on the original proposal in Parliament and, while disagreeing with that proposal, have clearly understood that it was Parliament's firm intention to incorporate it in legislation. **[4.18]**

Whilst this latter case demonstrates the hurdles faced by all applicants, it should not be thought that the decision places doubt on whether applicants in tax matters will ever be successful. It has been argued that the case was lost on its merits;[43] the court took the view that there was no double taxation in any real sense, and that all the retrospective legislation was intended to do was to cure technical defects in earlier legislation. The suggestion is that where there are issues of real double taxation, or cases where legislation is introduced with the sole aim of depriving taxpayers of the fruits of successful litigation, then such actions may well be open to a successful challenge. **[4.19]**

42 Right to a fair trial.

43 Michael Smyth, 'The United Kingdom's Incorporation of the European Convention and its implications for business' (1998) EHRLR 3 273, 285.

5. Convention articles and Protocols that are of relevance to taxation

The precise circumstances in which Convention rights might be invoked in tax will remain a matter of speculation for some time to come, although the cases to date show that challenges in respect of tax administration are more likely to be successful than challenges to tax policy.[44] **[4.20]**

A. Article 1 of Protocol No 1

Article 1 of Protocol No 1 to the European Convention guarantees, in effect, the right to property, with an express reservation for contracting states to pass such laws as they deem necessary to secure the payment of taxes. Theoretically, this provision could be invoked in respect of the levying of a so-called 'windfall tax',[45] the imposition of retrospective legislation,[46] as a challenge to the restrictions preventing recovery of overpaid tax[47] and in respect of the seizure of goods and documents.[48] **[4.21]**

National and Provincial Building Society and Others v UK

(The case is cited with its facts at para **[4.18]** above.)

EUROPEAN COURT OF HUMAN RIGHTS:

78. ... art. 1 of Protocol No. 1 guarantees in substance the right to property. It comprises three distinct rules. The first, which is expressed in the first sentence of the

44 Compare the unsuccessful challenge to the application of the widow's bereavement allowance by Mr Wilkinson (*R (on the application of Wilkinson) v IRC* [2003] EWCA Civ 814, [2003] 1 WLR 2683, with *Han v Customs & Excise Commissioners* [2001] STC 1188, in which case the Court of Appeal held that appeals against civil evasion penalties constituted criminal proceedings for the purpose of the Convention, thereby guaranteeing the taxpayer the more generous rights afforded by art 6, such as the presumption of innocence, a right to be informed of the nature and cause of the charges (and to have the assistance of an interpreter if necessary), adequate time to prepare a defence and the right to secure the attendance of witnesses.

45 The claim that such a tax was in breach of art 1 of Protocol No 1was dismissed in *Wasa Liv v Sweden* (1988) 58 DR 163 (above, para **[4.16]**), and, although counsel's opinion was sought on the matter, no action was brought against the Government when, in 1997, it imposed a windfall tax on the newly privatised utilities.

46 Although such legislation does not automatically infringe the European Convention, it would seem that there may be the possibility of a challenge under art 1 of Protocol No 1, since it undermines the rule of law and legal certainty. A claimant would have to show that the legislation in question was not objectively justifiable and that it was disproportionate to the aims behind its implementation.

47 A taxpayer who has overpaid income tax or corporation tax by reason of an error or mistake in a return, has a statutory right to make a claim for repayment (TMA 1970, s 33). Relief is restricted by the fact that: (a) the Revenue is entitled to give only such relief as is 'reasonable and just'; (b) where a return is made in accordance with the 'prevailing practice' at the time, recovery is prevented; and (c) any claim is subject to time limits. The statutory right to the recovery of overpaid VAT is also restricted if the claimant would thereby be unjustly enriched (VATA 1994, s 80).

48 Seizure may be justified depending on the facts of each particular case. In deciding whether provisions allowing for the seizure are necessary and proportionate, the claimant's case will largely depend upon whether the exercise of such powers is subject to effective judicial supervision and a right of appeal: see *AGOSI v United Kingdom* (1987) 9 EHRR 1, and also *Lindsay v C & E Comrs* [2002] EWCA Civ 267; [2002] 3 All ER 118; [2002] 1 WLR 1766; [2002] STC 588 and *R (on the application of Hoverspeed) v C & E Comrs* [2002] EWCA Civ 1804, [2003] 2 All ER 553, [2003] 2 WLR 950, the last two cases concerning the seizure of vehicles following allegations of illegal importation of goods. Search and seizure may also infringe Article 8.

first paragraph and is of a general nature, lays down the principle of the peaceful enjoyment of possessions. The second, in the second sentence of the same paragraph, covers deprivation of possessions and makes it subject to certain conditions. The third, contained in the second paragraph, recognises that the contracting states are entitled to control the use of property in accordance with the general interest or to secure the payment of taxes or other contributions or penalties.

However, the three rules are not 'distinct' in the sense of being unconnected: the second and the third rules are concerned with particular interferences with the right to peaceful enjoyment of property and should therefore be construed in the light of the general principle enunciated in the first rule (see, among many other authorities, the *Gasus Dosier-und Fördertechnic GmbH v the Netherlands* judgment of 23 February 1995 (Series A No. 306–B, pp. 46–47 55)).

79. Having regard to the fact that the background to the alleged deprivation of the applicant societies' rights is constituted by the first unsuccessful steps taken by Parliament to ensure that interest paid in the gap period was charged to tax, it would appear to the court to be the most natural approach to examine their complaints from the angle of a control of the use of property in the general interest 'to secure the payment of tax', which falls within the rule in the second paragraph of art. 1. In so proceeding it recalls that it has already found that the transitional arrangements contained in the 1986 regulations did not, contrary to the assertions of the applicant societies, impose double taxation on the interest paid to their investors in the gap period or amount to a wrongful expropriation of their assets . . .

On that factual understanding, the efforts to secure a firm legal basis firstly, and unsuccessfully, in s. 47 of the *Finance Act* 1986 . . . and secondly in s. 53 of the 1991 Act . . . to give effect to Parliament's legitimate aim when adopting the defective regulations . . . could be considered equally to be measures to secure payment of tax. It is to be recalled in this regard that irrespective of the move to the actual year system the interest at issue would always have been liable to be brought into account for tax purposes . . . **[4.22]**

R (on the application of Professional Contractors Group Ltd) v IRC [2001] EWHC Admin 236, [2001] STC 629 (QBD)

The Professional Contractors' Group represent the owners of 'personal service' companies. These are primarily one-man companies, which charge out the services of the owner (the 'service contractor') to a client for fees paid to the service company in circumstances where the service contractor would be an employee of the client if he had provided his services directly to it. Out of this remuneration, the service contractor is paid a small salary, from which income tax and employees' national insurance contributions (NICs) are deducted, and the service company pays employers NICs. From the balance will be deducted allowable expenses, and a substantial dividend out of the profit may eventually be paid to the service contractor which will not attract NICs, and in respect of which income tax will only be payable as and when the dividend is declared. Any retained profit will suffer corporation tax, generally at the special low rate applicable to small companies. Following the imposition of the IR 35 legislation that aimed to treat the fees as income from employment, with income tax and employees' NICs being deductible on the whole amount, the claimants argued that a right to enjoy the benefit of a shareholding in a service company is a right of property, and the effect of the IR35 legislation was to cause an interference with the enjoyment of that right contrary to Article 1 of Protocol No 1 because the imposition of income tax and NICs on the notional remuneration together with the way in which expenses are treated meant that the 'right' was rendered more expensive. The claim was dismissed on the basis that even if the full amount of a service company's earnings (without any allowance for expenses) in a given year were treated as the remuneration of the service contractor, this would not amount to a confiscation of property, nor to a fundamental interference with the claimants' financial position, and nor would it amount to an abuse of the UK's rights to levy taxes.[49]

BURTON J:

41. The question then is whether the impact of IR35 is sufficient to amount to a breach of art. 1 of the First Protocol. The two material authorities to which I have been referred by Mr Barling QC[50] are neither of them helpful to him. In *X v France* (1983) 32 DR 266, the Commission rejected the application of a French national seeking to challenge a provision of the general tax code which stipulated that, in cases of obvious personal expenditure exceeding the declared income, tax would be assessed on the basis of that expenditure, without the taxpayer being able to counter that assessment by alleging that he had drawn on capital, or received gifts from a third party. The applicant complained that this amounted to a 'de facto confiscation of his property'. The commission concluded, in rejecting that application, as 'manifestly ill-founded', at pp. 272–273 that:

> 'The legislation of most of the States Parties to the Convention provides that the authorities should, when assessing income tax, take account in some cases of certain other factors distinct from income in the strict sense. ... Regulations of this kind should not generally speaking be considered incompatible with Article 1 of the First protocol, except in cases where, by taxing a straightforward investment – apart from measures to counter tax avoidance or fraud – it amounted to a de facto confiscation of some part of the taxpayer's possessions.'

42. In *Svenska Managementgruppen AB v Sweden* (1985) 45 DR 211, the applicant complained of the imposition of a new profit-sharing tax together with a supplementary pension charge. The Commission concluded (at pp. 222–223) that:

> 'A financial liability arising out of the raising of taxes or contributions may adversely affect the guarantee of ownership if it places an excessive burden on the person concerned or fundamentally interferes with his financial position. However, it is in the first place for the national authorities to decide what kind of taxes or contributions are to be collected.
>
> Furthermore the decisions in this area will commonly involve the appreciation of political, economic and social questions which the Convention leaves within the competence of the Contracting States. The power of appreciation of the Contracting States is therefore a wide one ... The Commission cannot find that these obligations affect the applicant's guarantee of ownership or interfere with its financial situation to such an extent that this could be considered disproportionate or an abuse of the Contracting Parties' rights ... to levy taxes.' **[4.23]**

Bearing in mind the amount of publicity given to the IR35 legislation, and the furore with which it was met, the decision of Burton J, coupled with the fact that the claimants' chose not to appeal on the human rights issue,

49 The claimants also argued that they had suffered an interference with their right of property because the IR35 legislation had rendered it uncertain as to whether a particular service contractor would be classified as an employee, and this would result either in a loss of enjoyment of the shareholding, or it put the very existence of the service companies in jeopardy. This claim was also rejected. Burton J concluded that the effect of IR35 was to submit service companies to the same common law test of employment with respect to each engagement to which they would have been subject but for the interposition of the service company, and thus it could not offend against the concept of certainty for the common law of employment to apply to a service contractor.

50 [Counsel for the claimants.]

demonstrates quite clearly how difficult it is likely to be to challenge successfully any particular aspect of tax policy, with the exception, perhaps, of legislation that could be said to be discriminatory. **[4.24]**

B. Article 14: the enjoyment of Convention rights without discrimination

(1) General principles and the scope of article 14

Whilst there is no general prohibition on discrimination in the Convention, art 14 requires that the enjoyment of Convention rights is to be secured without discrimination. In practice, this means that a claimant must plead a substantive right alongside discrimination. In the area of taxation, the substantive right that will most often be alleged to have been violated is art 1 of Protocol No 1, although the connection between some substantive rights and art 14 may be somewhat tenuous. Challenges under art 14 have been made where legislation has resulted in discrimination on the grounds of gender or of marital status, discrimination between similarly situated taxpayers, discrimination between employees and self-employed persons and discrimination as to prosecution. All but one of the challenges have so far been unsuccessful, either because no similarity could be found between the claimant and the comparator, or because of the wide margin of appreciation. Thus, UK legislation that provided for allowances discriminating between single and married people[51] has been held not to be an infringement of the Convention on the grounds that it was within the discretion allowed to contracting states and that the distinction was objectively justifiable.[52] And, since the recent decision of the European Court of Human Rights that legislation restricting income tax relief for qualifying maintenance payments to parents who had previously been *married* was discriminatory[53] (see below, para **[4.29]**) was based on grounds of the comparability of married and unmarried *parents*, generally the ability to legislate on the basis of a distinction between married and unmarried persons continues to be within a government's competence, although whether this distinction will remain justifiable with the changing attitudes of society to marriage remains to be seen. **[4.25]**

R (on the application of Wilkinson) v IRC [2002] EWHC Admin 182, [2002] STC 347 (QBD)

A provision[54] (now abolished with respect to deaths occurring after 5 April 2000[55]) that allowed for a widow, but not a widower, to claim a bereavement

51 Of less significance in current times because, since 2000–01, the only remaining allowance in favour of a married couple is the married couple's allowance, available only where one of the spouses (and, since December 2005, this term includes civil partners) has attained the age of 65 on or before 5 April 2000.

52 *Lindsay v UK* (11089/84) 11 November 1986.

53 *PM v United Kingdom* (2006) 42 EHRR 45, [2005] STC 1566.

54 Section ICTA 1988, 262(1).

55 FA 1999, s 34 . The Welfare Reform and Pensions Act 1999 now provides for social security benefits which are available to both widows and widowers alike.

allowance, had been the subject of a previous challenge under the Convention. In order to avoid setting a precedent, the UK Government had reached a 'friendly settlement' with the claimant widower, whereby the same amount was paid to him as would have been given to a widow.[56] The second challenge, and the subject of this case, arose in the wake of the Revenue's refusal to provide the same treatment for other widowers in the same position as the claimant in the first challenge.

> MOSES J:
>
> 10. . . . in order to establish a breach of art. 14, a claimant must establish that the facts of the case come within the ambit of other provisions of the convention. Article 1 of the First protocol provides:
>
> > 'Every natural or legal person is entitled to the peaceful enjoyment of his possessions. No one shall be deprived of his possessions except in the public interest and subject to the conditions provided for by law and by the general principles of international law. The preceding provision shall not, however, in any way impair the right of a State to enforce such laws as it deems necessary . . . . to secure the payment of taxes or other contributions or penalties.'
>
> 11. Although Mr Brennan QC on behalf of the Inland Revenue argued faintly to the contrary, it seems clear to me that this case falls within the ambit of art. 1 of the First Protocol. It concerns the payment of taxes. Dr Darby claimed repayment of tax he had paid as a result of discriminatory church tax imposed in *Darby v Sweden* (1991) 13 EHRR 774. The court observed that the second paragraph of art. 1 of the First Protocol establishes that the duty to pay tax falls within its field of application (see para. 30, at p. 781).
>
> 12. It is clear that the refusal to grant an income tax reduction to men in a similar situation to women, is in breach of art. 14 read with art. 1 of the First Protocol in the absence of any objective justification advanced for such discrimination. **[4.26]**

In the Court of Appeal, the Revenue conceded that the discrimination alleged fell within the ambit of art 1 of Protocol No. 1 and was thus not in issue. Further, both the Court of Appeal and the House of Lords agreed with Moses J that there was no precedent in either the Strasbourg or domestic jurisprudence to form the basis for a principle whereby a friendly settlement of a claim in Strasbourg requires a State to treat all others in the same position as the claimant in the same way. A taxpayer bringing proceedings in Strasbourg is not in the same situation as a taxpayer seeking an extra-statutory allowance in the UK. **[4.27]**

56 *Crossland v United Kingdom*, 9 November 1999 (unreported). A similar set of events occurred in *Fielding v United Kingdom* (36940/97) (2002) Times, 25 February. Historically, this provision was introduced to compensate for the fact that if a husband died early in the tax year, his widow would only be entitled to a single person's allowance, whereas a husband would continue to receive the higher married man's allowance in the year of his wife's death. Moreover, it was extended in 1983 to the year of assessment following the year of death because, if a husband died towards the end of a tax year, a wife would often not have sufficient income in the remainder of the year to use the allowance in full.

R (on the application of Hooper and others) v Secretary of State for Work and Pensions [2003] EWCA Civ 813, [2003] 1 WLR 2623 (CA)[57]

A number of male claimants contended that they were victims of sex discrimination in breach of article 14 (read together with article 8) of the Convention because their claim to be paid the equivalent of (amongst other benefits) the widow's pension for a period of years prior to its abolition had been denied.

LORD PHILLIPS:

82. Article 14 forbids discrimination in securing Convention rights and obligations. This Article makes plain the grounds of discrimination against which it is primarily addressed, namely 'any ground such as sex, race, colour, language, religion, political or other opinion, national or social origin, association with a national minority, property, birth or other status'. Thus, typically, the Article addresses the situation where a State discriminates against a readily identifiable class in the manner in which it respects, or fails to respect, Convention rights. The discrimination need not go so far as infringing the Convention rights of the party discriminated against – were that the case Article 14 would be superfluous. More generous treatment in securing the enjoyment of a Convention right by one class rather than the other can suffice to engage Article 14, in conjunction with the right in question. We repeat the principle stated by the Strasbourg Court in *Abdulaziz*[58]:

> 'The victim of discrimination within the meaning of Article 14 includes, in general, cases where a person or group is treated, without proper justification, less favourably than another, even though the more favourable treatment is not called for by the Convention.'

The nature of the nexus between Article 14 and some other Convention right is usually described, not very helpfully, by the proposition that the facts must fall 'within the ambit' of substantive Convention right.

83. Where it is alleged that Article 14 has been infringed it is first necessary to consider whether the claimant has been treated less favourably in relation to the enjoyment of a Convention right than others. If he has, the next task is to identify why this is – on what grounds has he suffered discrimination? If there is no rational explanation for the discrimination, Article 14 will not be engaged. Equally, if the discrimination has been for some idiosyncratic reason, such as personal dislike of the claimant on the part of the state official, Article 14 will not be engaged. The terms of Article 14 suggest that what has to be demonstrated is that the claimant is one of a class or group who share a distinguishing characteristic and that this characteristic is the ground upon which the State distinguishes against the members of the class or group. Racial discrimination is the paradigm example.

84. It follows that the reason for the discrimination will be the touchstone of the identification of the class. The identification of a common factor which results in discrimination will at the same time result in the identification of the class or group discriminated against. Care has to be taken to make sure that the common factor is, indeed, the ground for discrimination. This will not be so if there are other factors which explain treating the claimants differently from others. Thus it is necessary to be sure that, apart from the alleged ground for discrimination, the claimants are in an analogous situation to those who are more favourably treated. Consideration of an Article 14 claim usually involves comparing the class into which the claimant falls with a comparator class that is treated more favourably. An issue can arise, and does arise in this case, as to whether the distinction between the two classes has to be a personal characteristic or status, such as one of the examples listed in Article 14.

57 The conclusion of the Court of Appeal in this case that there was no 'objective justification' for continuing the payment of pensions to widows in the six-year period prior to its abolition in April 2001, was overturned by the House of Lords: see [2005] UKHL 29.
58 *Abdulaziz Cabales and Balkandali v UK* [1985] 7 EHRR 471.

85. In the leading judgment in *Michalak v London Borough of Wandsworth* [2002] EWCA Civ 271; [2002] 39 HLR 721; [2002] 4 All ER 1136, Brooke LJ recommended the following structured approach in consideration of an Article 14 claim. The court should ask, sequentially, four questions. If any one is answered in the negative it will normally follow that the claim is ill-founded. The questions are:

'(i) Do the facts fall within the ambit of one or more of the substantive Convention provisions (for the relevant Convention rights see *Human Rights Act 1998, section 1(1)*)?

(ii) If so, was there different treatment as respects that right between the complainant on the one hand and the other persons put forward for comparison ('the chosen comparators') on the other?

(iii) Were the chosen comparators in an analogous situation to the complainant's situation?

(iv) If so, did the difference in treatment have an objective and reasonable justification: in other words, did it pursue a legitimate aim and did the differential treatment bear a reasonable relationship of proportionality to the aim sought to be achieved?' **[4.28]**

PM v United Kingdom (2006) 42 EHRR 45, [2005] STC 1566 (ECHR)

Following the separation of an unmarried couple who had previously lived and had a daughter together, it was agreed under the terms of a Deed of Separation that the applicant, the father, would pay weekly maintenance for his daughter. He was granted tax relief for the maintenance payments made during the tax year in which they began, but it was later claimed by the UK Government that this was an error on the part of the Revenue. The applicant was refused relief for later years on the basis that he had never been married to his daughter's mother and, accordingly, his payments could not be qualifying maintenance payments within TA 1988, s 347(B).[59] The applicant argued that there had been a violation of Article 14 in conjunction with Article 1 of Protocol No 1 on the basis that he was being treated differently from a married (or previously married) father, and that there was no objective or reasonable justification for the difference in treatment. For its part, the Government submitted that, for the purpose of s 347B, paternity was not relevant in determining whether a payment was a qualifying maintenance payment; rather, it 'was the relationship of marriage that was at the core of the legislation', and that *Lindsay v UK*[60] precluded any argument denying the right of a government to distinguish between married and unmarried persons. Moreover, the Government argued, there was an objective and reasonable justification for the difference in treatment, based on a policy of promoting the institution of marriage, even after the break-down of the marriage. The applicant's claim was successful.

EUROPEAN COURT OF HUMAN RIGHTS:

26 For the purposes of Art. 14 a difference in treatment between persons in analogous or relevantly similar positions is discriminatory if it has no objective and reasonable justification, that is if it does not pursue a legitimate aim or if there is not a reasonable relationship of proportionality between the means employed and the aim sought to be realised. Moreover, the Contracting States enjoy a margin of appreciation in assessing whether and to what extent differences in otherwise similar situations justify a different treatment.[61]

59 The relief claimed by the applicant is no longer available, unless one of the parties to the marriage or former marriage was aged 65 or over on the 5 April 2000; see Chapter 14, below, para **[14.32]**.

60 App. No. 11089/84, November 11, 1986.

61 See *Camp and Bourimi v Netherlands* (2002) 34 EHRR 59.

27 The Court notes the Government's arguments that this case is not about paternity/maternity but the married status of the parents. It is true that any person, not married to the mother of the child concerned, would not qualify for tax deductions for maintenance payments made. That said however, it is nonetheless the case that the applicant may claim to be treated differently as an unmarried father from a married father, though both are parents of the child to be maintained and under obligations to pay maintenance. This is not a situation where the applicant seeks to compare himself to a couple living in a subsisting marriage,[62] but one where the married father has separated or divorced and is also living apart from the child of the family. Other persons, not parents, are not covered by the child support provisions and are generally in a different situation. This applicant differs from a married father only as regards the issue of marital status and may, for the purposes of this application, claim to be in a relevantly similar position.

28 The justification for the difference in treatment relied on by the Government is the special regime of marriage which confers specific rights and obligations on those who choose to join it. The Court recalls that it has in some cases found that differences in treatment on the basis of marital status has had objective and reasonable justification.[63] It may be noted however that as a general rule unmarried fathers, who have established family life with their children, can claim equal rights of contact and custody with married fathers.[64] In the present case, the applicant has been acknowledged as the father and has acted in that role. Given that he has financial obligations towards his daughter, which he has duly fulfilled, the Court perceives no reason for treating him differently from a married father, now divorced and separated from the mother, as regards the tax deductibility of those payments. The purpose of the tax deductions was purportedly to render it easier for married fathers to support a new family; it is not readily apparent why unmarried fathers, who undertook similar new relationships, would not have similar financial commitments equally requiring relief.

29 The Court concludes therefore that there has been a violation of Art. 14 of the Convention in conjunction with Art. 1 of Protocol No. 1 in this case. **[4.29]**

Holland v IRC [2002] UKSC SPC00356, (2003) STI 62 (SCD); see below, para [14.10]

The claimant in this case argued that although she and her deceased partner had not been legally married, they had lived together as husband and wife for thirty-one years before his death, and accordingly she should be treated as his spouse for Inheritance Tax purposes, thus enabling her to claim the inter-spouse exemption.[65] The Revenue accepted that marriage was a question of status within Article 14, and that the facts of the case fell within both Article 1 of Protocol No. 1 and Article 8 (right to respect for family and private life), but the Special Commissioners dismissed the claimant's argument.

THE SPECIAL COMMISSIONERS (STEPHEN OLIVER QC and DR NUALA BRICE):

90. ... in our view it is permissible for Parliament to legislate so that different tax provisions apply to married persons. This reflects the fact that married persons have mutual rights and obligations relating to maintenance during their lives and after their deaths. For example, Parliament has given spouse-specific rights to married persons in the intestacy

62 See, e.g., *Lindsay v United Kingdom* (11089/84) November 11, 1986, where married and unmarried couples, taxed differently, were not found to be in a comparable position.

63 See, e.g., *McMichael v United Kingdom* (1995) 20 EHRR 205, concerning legislation which did not grant automatic parental responsibility to unmarried fathers who inevitably varied in their commitment and interest in, or even knowledge of, their children.

64 See *Sahin v Germany* (2003) 36 EHRR 43.

65 Inheritance Tax Act 1984, s 18.

> rules. These interlocking property rights and obligations are a justification for a different tax treatment. The difference in treatment does not raise matters of high constitutional importance. And, finally, the steps taken by Parliament to implement its policy of recognising in the tax laws the mutual obligations of married persons are reasonable and proportionate and logically explicable as forwarding that policy. **[4.30]**

The Special Commissioners' findings were necessarily *obiter dicta* since the Human Rights Act 1998 was not in force at the time of death. Note also that, as from 5 December 2005, single sex couples who have registered a civil partnership under the Civil Partnerships Act 2004 are treated in the same way as married couples for tax and tax credit purposes.[66] **[4.31]**

Carney v Nathan [2002] UKSC SPC00350, (2003) STI 33 (SCD)

The taxpayer, a self-employed person, argued unsuccessfully that, whilst (subject to conditions) employees are not taxed on the benefit of childcare expenses for which employers have obtained a deduction,[67] self-employed persons can make no deduction for expenses incurred in respect of childcare,[68] and that the disallowance of such expenditure constituted discrimination within Article 14 in relation to Article 1 of Protocol No. 1.

> THE SPECIAL COMMISSIONER (DR JOHN AVERY JONES CBE):
>
> 14. I was not referred to any authority where different treatment between an employer and a self-employed person was held to be within article 14. Mr Mitchell pointed out that the Commission on Human Rights declared a claim inadmissible and accepted a distinction in taxing rules between employed and self-employed persons in *X v Austria*, Application No 6163/73. In that case employed persons paid tax at fixed rates and self-employed at progressive rates and employees receiving special payments obtained preferential tax treatment. The Commission found that different tax treatment was justified and not discriminatory. I am aware of other cases to the same effect in relation to national insurance contributions: *National Federation of the Self-Employed v UK*, Application No. 7995/77 and *Juby v UK* No. 11592/85. The same must apply to childcare expenses. An employer obtains a deduction for childcare expenses for employees as the provision of a benefit to its employees; the employee is not taxed on that benefit, perhaps because it is difficult to value the benefit to a single employee, but the employee cannot deduct the expense if he or she incurs it. The Appellant as a self-employed person paying childcare expenses for herself is not in a similar situation to an employer paying for an employee. There is no discrimination within article 14 to which article 1 of Protocol 1 can apply. **[4.32]**

Given that the UK rules allowing for deduction of expenditure are generally more generous to the self-employed than to the employed (see below, paras **[10.23–10.35]** and **[8.64–8.76]** respectively), this decision must be seen as a pragmatic one. **[4.33]**

(2) Objective justification and deference to Parliament

In striking a balance between, on the one hand, the principle of equality between the sexes from which there should be departure only when there

66 FA 2005, s 103; Civil Partnership Act 2004, Sch 24, Pt 14.
67 Income Tax (Earning and Pensions) Act 2003, s 318.
68 Income Tax (Trading and Other Income) Act 2005, s 34 (formerly ICTA 1988, s 74(1)(a)).

exist compelling reasons and the adoption of alternative measures that cause minimum interference to the right to non-discrimination and, on the other, the need to defer to Parliament in matters of social and economic policy, the weight of authority seems clearly to favour deference to Parliament. **[4.34]**

R (on the application of Hooper and others) v Secretary of State for Work and Pensions [2002] EWHC (Admin) 191 (QBD)

(The facts of this case can be found at para **[4.28]** above)

MOSES J:

97. The resolution of the issue whether the undoubted discrimination was objectively justified requires consideration of the extent to which the court should defer, on democratic grounds, to the considered opinion of Parliament. Is it a wide margin or a narrow edge? . . . . . .The well known dicta of Lord Hope in *R v DPP ex parte Kebilene* [2002] 2 AC 326 at 375 reveals a signpost which points in opposite directions in relation to cases which involve both social and economic policy and rights of high constitutional importance:-

> 'It will be easier for such an area of judgment [within which the judiciary will defer] to be recognised where the Convention itself requires a balance to be struck, much less so where the right is stated in terms which are unqualified. It will be easier for it to be recognised where the issues involved questions of social or economic policy, much less so where the rights are of high constitutional importance of the kind where the courts are especially well placed to assess the need for protection'.

98. There can be no doubt that the principle of equality between the sexes is fundamental to democracy, see e.g. Lord Hoffmann in *Matadeen v Pointou* [1999] 1 AC 98 at 109. It is for that reason . . . that compelling reasons are required to justify any departure from the principle of equality between the sexes. . . . .

99. Further, . . . a Government which derogates from the principle of equality of the sexes must adopt measures which cause the minimum interference to the right to non-discrimination. The wide acceptance by member states of the Council of Europe and of the European Union provides further support for intrusive scrutiny (see e.g. *The Sunday Times v United Kingdom* [1979] 2 EHRR 245 at 276).

100. Yet, in a democracy it is the democratic institutions which have the responsibility for deciding how public funds should be spent. Both domestic and Convention jurisprudence recognise that it is primarily for Parliament to strike the balance between equitable treatment and efficient use of resources which are necessarily limited. Traditionally, in assessing the legitimacy of the balance to be struck in relation to issues involving social policy and the allocation of resources, considerable deference has been paid to the judgment of the legislature. In *Steele Ford and Newton v CPS (No. 2)* the House of Lords considered the court's jurisdiction to award costs out of central funds. Whilst part of the reasoning of Lord Bridge in relation to statutory construction is of no application in the instant case his second basis for concluding that there was no power to award costs out of central funds in that case is of relevance:-

> 'But still more important, in the present context, is the special constitutional convention which jealously safeguards the exclusive control exercised by Parliament over both the levying and expenditure of the public revenue. It is trite law that nothing less than clear, express and unambiguous language is effective to levy a tax. Scarcely less stringent is the requirement of clear statutory authority for public expenditure.'

101. In *R v Chief Constable of Sussex ex parte International Traders Ferry Ltd* [1999] 2 AC 418, Lord Slynn emphasised the impossibility of an enquiry undertaken by the court as to how competing claims for money should be resolved (see in particular page 439A-E).

102. The ECtHR has itself acknowledged the need to afford a wide margin of appreciation to the High Contracting Parties in cases concerning social policy. Affording a wide margin of appreciation has the consequence that the court will not itself decide whether the measures adopted represented the best solution for dealing with the problem, nor whether the legislature could have adopted an alternative solution. In the context of housing policy, the court said in *Mellacher v Austria* [1989] 12 EHRR 391:-

> 'Such laws [controlling the use of property] are especially called for and usual in the field of housing, which in our modern society is a central concern of social and economic policies.
>
> In order to implement such policies, the legislature must have a wide margin of appreciation both with regard to the existence of a problem of public concern warranting measures of control and as to the choice of the detailed rules for the implementation of such measures. The court will respect the legislator's judgment as to what is in the general interest unless that judgment be manifestly without reasonable foundation'.

Later it said:-

> 'The possible existence of alternative solutions does not in itself render the contested legislation unjustified. Provided that the legislature remains within the bounds of its margin of appreciation, it is not for the Court to say whether the legislation represented the best solution for dealing with the problem or whether the legislative discretion should have been exercised in another way.'

103. Similarly in *Stubbings v United Kingdom* [1996] 23 EHRR 213, in the context of the limitation period for civil action in respect of child abuse, the Court would not substitute its own view for that of the State as to what would be the most appropriate policy (see paragraph 54).

104. Now that domestic courts are bound to take account the jurisprudence of the ECtHR, a degree of deference, which marches in step with a wide margin of appreciation, has been paid to the judgment of the legislature in the field of social policy and the allocation of resources. In relation to housing policy, Lord Woolf stated in *Poplar Housing and Regeneration Community Association Ltd v Donoghue* [2001] 3 WLR 183, paragraph 69, page 202:-

> 'The economic and other implications of any policy in this area are extremely complex and far-reaching. This is an area where, in our judgment, the courts must treat the decisions of Parliament as to what is in the public interest with particular deference .... The correctness of this decision is more appropriate for Parliament than the courts and the Human Rights Act 1998 does not require the courts to disregard the decisions of Parliament in relation to situations of this sort when deciding whether there has been a breach of the Convention.'

105. Nevertheless, despite the broad degree of deference afforded to Governments in the field of social and economic policy, the significance of the general recognition by members of the Council of Europe and the European Union cannot be overlooked. As the Court pointed out in *Petrovich v Austria* [1998] 4 BHRC 232 (paragraph 38, page 238), one of the factors relevant to the scope of the margin of appreciation is the existence of common ground between the laws of the Contracting States (see also *The Sunday Times* case at page 276). In *Petrovitch* the great disparity between the legal systems of the Contracting States in relation to entitlement to parental leave is to be contrasted with the non-discriminatory survivors benefits for which members of the Council of Europe and of the European Union, but not the United Kingdom, make provision. The fact that the court was concerned with issues of social and economic policy provided no bar to its dismissal of The Netherlands attempted justification of its discriminatory policy in relation to exemption for unmarried childless women as opposed to men in the absence of compelling reasons (*Van Raalte* ...[69]).

69 *Van Raalte v Netherlands* [1997] 24 EHRR 503.

CONCLUSION AS TO OBJECTIVE JUSTIFICATION

106. I suspect that it is neither possible nor productive to determine with any precision the degree of deference to be paid to the legislature when the issues concern social and economic policy and the constitutionally important right not to be discriminated against on the grounds of gender. It seems to me that the court can have regard to both these features by, on the one hand, subjecting the reasons advanced by the Government to a degree of scrutiny commensurate with the importance of the right. In so doing the court is merely exercising judicial techniques with which it is familiar. Whatever expression is used ("*are the reasons compelling? Do they stack up?*") a court is unlikely to find justification where the reasons advanced do not support the conclusion. It is true that, for example, statistics require skilled evaluation, but if, in the course of a lengthy affidavit the expert . . . does not persuade the court then I can see no reason why the court should be inhibited from saying so. If the reasons advanced by the Defendant are insubstantial or, even if they are substantial, they do not persuade me, I shall decline to find any objective justification.

107. On the other hand, in relation to the issue as to whether an alternative could have been adopted, it seems to me that the court should adopt a restrained approach. That question directly engages questions of social and economic policy with which the court is ill-equipped to deal. It concerns the appropriate allocation of resources. In so far as the justification is attacked on the basis that the solution was not the best which could have been devised, I shall adopt an approach derived from *Mellacher*. I shall not substitute my view for that of the Government in relation to alternative solutions. **[4.35]**

This view was also adopted by the House of Lords in the same case: **[4.36]**

R (on the application of Hooper and others) v Secretary of State for Work and Pensions [2005] UKHL 29, [2005] 1 WLR 1681

LORD HOFFMANN:

32. . . . in making decisions about social and economic policy, particularly those concerned with the equitable distribution of public resources, the Strasbourg court allows member states a generous margin of appreciation . . . . In a domestic system which (unlike the Strasbourg court) is concerned with the separation of powers, such decisions are ordinarily recognized by the courts to be matters for the judgment of the elected representatives of the people. The fact that the complaint concerns discrimination on grounds of sex is not in itself a reason for a court to impose its own judgment. Once it is accepted that older widows were historically an economically disadvantaged class which merited special treatment but were gradually becoming less disadvantaged, the question of the precise moment at which such special treatment is no longer justified becomes a social and political question within the competence of Parliament. **[4.37]**

In *R (on the application of Wilkinson) v IRC*, Moses J could find no objective justification for the discrimination resulting from the widow's bereavement allowance, and made a declaration of incompatibility, seemingly ignoring the fact that the legislation concerned could be justified on an historical basis[70] and, moreover, had already been repealed. The point was not at issue in the Court of Appeal or House of Lords, where it was common ground that the offending provision was discriminatory, and the Revenue conceded that this discrimination fell within the ambit of art 1 of Protocol No.1. Despite this

70 See note 51 above.

finding, the taxpayer failed in his claim to be paid a sum of money equivalent to the allowance, on the basis that the Revenue had no power to make such a payment. The taxpayer had argued that the Revenue had the authority to afford to the taxpayer an extra-statutory concession by way of an income tax deduction equivalent to the allowance in question. The House of Lords rejected this argument. Lord Hoffmann said that whilst the Taxes Management Act 1970, s 1 gave the Revenue a wide managerial discretion which enabled the commissioners to formulate policy in the interstices of the tax legislation, dealing pragmatically with minor or transitory anomalies, cases of hardship at the margins or cases in which a statutory rule is difficult to formulate, this power was not wide enough to enable the commissioners to concede, by extra-statutory concession, an allowance which Parliament could have granted but, in fact, did not, and on grounds not of pragmatism in the collection of tax, but of general equity between men and women.[71] **[4.38]**

Burden and Burden v United Kingdom (2007) 44 EHRR 51 (ECHR)

Two elderly sisters who had lived together all their lives and, for the last 30 years, in a house owned by them jointly and built upon land inherited from their parents, complained to the ECtHR under art 1 of Protocol No 1 in conjunction with art 14 (the enjoyment of Convention rights without discrimination; see above, para **[4.25]**), arguing that they should be regarded as being in a similar situation to a married or civil partnership couple, entitling them to the spouse/civil partner exemption on the first death for inheritance tax purposes (see below, para **[21.1]**). The majority of the court rejected their claim.

EUROPEAN COURT OF HUMAN RIGHTS: MAJORITY JUDGMENT

54 It is for the national authorities to make the initial assessment, in the field of taxation, of the aims to be followed and the means to be used. The State enjoys a wide margin of appreciation in this field, as is usual when it comes to general measures of economic or social strategy. A government may often have to strike a balance between the need to raise revenue and the need to reflect other social objectives in its taxation policies. Because of their direct knowledge of their society and its needs, the national authorities are in principle better placed than the international judge to appreciate what is in the public interest on social or economic grounds. The Court will generally respect the legislature's policy choice in this field unless it is "manifestly without reasonable foundation" and subject to the proviso that, in creating and implementing a scheme of taxation, the State must not discriminate between taxpayers in a manner which is inconsistent with Art. 14 of the Convention.

DISSENTING OPINION (Judges Bonello and Garlicki)

We do agree that there must be a wide margin of appreciation offered to the national authorities in tax matters. We further agree that any system of taxation, to be workable, has to use broad categorizations to distinguish between different groups of taxpayers. We would also be prepared to agree that, with regard to tax matters, there may be some kind of presumption that the solutions adopted by the national legislature remain within this margin of appreciation. Such presumption would mean that it is, in principle, the applicant who must demonstrate that the application of the tax legislation in his or her case

71 This case re-emerged before the European Court of Human Rights as *Hobbs and others v UK* (2007) 44 EHRR 54, where a claim for an award of pecuniary damage was dismissed because, although the existence of the widow's bereavement allowance had been discriminatory during a particular period of time, its existence had been an anomaly, and to give widower's the equivalent of the benefit would be to perpetuate that anomaly.

exceeded the State's margin of appreciation and led to unreasonable and unjustified effects.

However, this "burden of proof" is not unlimited . . .

The national legislature is, generally speaking, free to adopt any reasonable policy of inheritance tax exemptions. As long as the United Kingdom confined the exemptions to married couples, such categorisation might have been justified under Art.12[72] of the Convention. However, once the UK legislature decided to extend the exemption to permanently cohabiting same-sex couples, the problem left the specific sphere of Art.12. Thus, any further categorisation in the area of inheritance tax exemptions has to satisfy general standards of reasonableness and non-arbitrariness resulting from Art.14. Of course, we do not want to cast doubt upon the reasonableness of extending exemptions to those same-sex couples choosing to form a civil partnership and denying such exemption to mixed-sex couples preferring not to enter into any form of official union. But once the legislature decides that a permanent union of two persons could or should enjoy tax privileges, it must be able to justify why such a possibility has been offered to some unions while continuing to be denied to others. The problem of siblings living together permanently did not escape the attention of the UK legislators and an appropriate amendment was proposed by the House of Lords. It was, however, rejected in the House of Commons on the basis of widespread agreement that the Civil Partnership Bill "is not the appropriate legislative base on which to deal with [the problem]". Such an approach may have been correct from the perspective of parliamentary technique, but it could not absolve the legislature from providing an equitable solution to the problem at a later stage. **[4.39]**

C. Article 8: respect for privacy

In the context of taxation, art 8 tends to be raised in connection with compliance issues rather than substantive issues,[73] and much of the case law concerns challenges against revenue authorities in respect of oppressive demands for information[74] and searches without warrant.[75] The primary protection in art 8 is that everyone is entitled to respect for his private and family life, his home and his correspondence. This does not provide a comprehensive privacy provision, and the right that is granted is subject to the strict limitations that any interference must be in accordance with the law, and necessary in a democratic society in the interests of national security, public safety, the economic well-being of the country, the prevention of crime, the protection of health and morals and the protection of the rights and freedoms of others. Accordingly, legislation that gives authority to the Revenue, within limits, to secure information necessary for investigations into taxpayers' affairs, will generally, although not necessarily always, be held inviolable on the ground of being in the interests of the economic well-being of the country. **[4.40]**

72 [Article 12 provides that men and women of marriageable age have the right to marry and to found a family, according to the national laws governing the exercise of this right.]

73 Cases concerning a challenge to a substantive provision of tax law have also been combined with complaints under other provisions, eg art 1 of Protocol No 1 or art 14. Cases include *Lindsay v United Kingdom* (11089/84) 11 November 1986 (involving the systems for taxing husband and wives) and *Fielding v United Kingdom* (36940/97) (2002) Times, 25 February (concerning the widows' bereavement allowance, and which was dealt with primarily under art 14). In none of the cases was a substantive tax rule held to infringe the right to respect for private and family life.

74 See *X v Belgium* (9804/82) (unreported); *Tamosius v UK* [2002] STC 1307.

75 See *Funke v France* [1993] 1 CMLR 897, 16 EHRR 297.

X v Belgium Application No 9804/82 (unreported)

The applicant was requested by the relevant tax authorities to supply information concerning how he had used the proceeds from the sale of a number of properties. Having found the information supplied inadequate, the tax authorities asked the applicant for a detailed explanation of his private expenditure. The applicant contended that an obligation to give further details would compel him to reveal personal and intimate details of his private life. The Strasbourg court, whilst accepting that the acts in question interfered with the applicant's privacy, rejected his claim.

> EUROPEAN COMMISSION OF HUMAN RIGHTS: ... The Commission considers without hesitation that the fact that a tax authority is entitled to require the applicant to produce a list of his private expenditure, subject to the risk of a tax assessment measure, constitutes an interference with his private life.
>
> It must now examine the question whether this interference complies with paragraph 2 of Article 8.
>
> In this respect ... the Commission will seek to establish whether the interference was 'in accordance with the law', based on the legitimate objectives under Article 2 and was 'necessary in a democratic society' for the achievement of such objectives. **[4.41]**

A similar conclusion was reached in *Gould (t/a Garry's Private Hire) v Revenue and Customs Commrs*,[76] in which case, the Special Commissioner (Dr John Avery Jones CBE) said that:

> 'while an investigation into *[the taxpayers']* private expenditure is an interference with their private life, it is in accordance with the law and is necessary in a democratic society for the economic well-being of the country that such investigation should be permitted for the purpose of establishing the true taxable profit.' **[4.42]**

Tamosius v United Kingdom [2002] STC 1307 (ECHR); see above, para [2.16]

The Revenue obtained from the Crown Court ex parte search warrants in order to search the premises of the applicant, a US lawyer and partner of a firm of solicitors based in offices in London, for documents evidencing offences of serious tax fraud. This was pursuant to the committal for tax evasion of one of the applicant's clients, and a belief that further serious tax fraud had been perpetrated by one or more of the applicant's clients, together with the applicant himself. No prior resolution had been reached upon issues of legal professional privilege, and thus documents seized following two searches were examined by an independent counsel, instructed by the Revenue, to adjudge whether any of them were subject to legal professional privilege. The applicant complained under art 8 of the Convention that the issue and execution of the warrants were in breach of the applicant's right to respect for his private life, and his correspondence, in particular that the scope of the search warrant was not restricted to information relating to named persons only, that the statutory definition of legal privilege was too narrow and that supervising counsel was not genuinely independent.

> EUROPEAN COURT OF HUMAN RIGHTS: ...The Court observes that it is not disputed that the search of the applicant's offices constituted an interference with his rights under Article 8 of the Convention ...

76 [2007] UKSPC SPC00604.

It is not disputed that the search was carried out "in accordance with the law" and that it pursued the aims of the prevention of crime and disorder, as well as the economic well-being of the country. The main dispute between the parties is whether the measure can be regarded as "necessary in a democratic society" in pursuit of those aims, in particular whether it was proportionate to those aims and whether there were sufficient procedural safeguards attaching to the procedure to prevent any abuse or arbitrariness. In that context, it must be noted that the search of a lawyer's office impinges, or threatens to impinge, on professional secrecy and may have repercussions on the proper administration of justice, and hence on the rights guaranteed by Article 6 of the Convention . . .

In the present case, the Court notes that the search was carried out under a warrant issued by a judge, who was required by law to be satisfied that there was reasonable ground for suspecting that the commission of a tax fraud had occurred and that evidence might be found at the premises to be searched. While the applicant complains that the granting of the warrant was obtained in an *ex parte* procedure, whereas in other statutory contexts *inter partes* procedures are provided for, the Court would note that there may be good reason not to give forewarning of a proposed search. The scrutiny given by a judge, even in an ex parte procedure, is nonetheless an important safeguard against abuse (see, e.g. *Funke v. France* (1993) 16 E.H.R.R. 297, para. 57; see also *Chappell v. United Kingdom* (1990) 12 E.H.R.R. 1, paras 59–61), concerning the grant *ex parte* of an *Anton Piller* order). It does not consider any strong objection arises from the fact that it was a circuit judge in this case, rather than a more senior judge. It would note that in domestic law it is often a magistrate who provides the police with warrants for criminal investigations.

The applicant has also complained about the breadth of the warrant granted, in particular that it did not give specific detail of the articles or persons which were the subject of the search. The Court recalls that the first warrant related to any items relating to serious tax fraud. However, a second warrant was issued, which included a schedule of 35 companies and individuals listed as being under investigation. It was this warrant that was executed, although the domestic courts gave the opinion that both were equally lawful. The Court is not persuaded that in these circumstances the applicant was denied sufficient indication of the purpose of the search to enable him to assess whether the investigation team acted unlawfully or exceeded their powers.

The Court also recalls that the search was carried out under the supervision of counsel, whose task was to identify which documents were covered by legal professional privilege and should not be removed. Though the applicant has denied that this provided any substantial safeguard, the Court notes that the counsel, nominated by the Attorney General, was under instructions to act independently from the investigation team and to give independent advice. The applicant has not claimed, in any domestic proceedings, that the counsel erred in the exercise of his judgment. The Court sees nothing sinister in the inclusion in counsel's instructions of a reference to consulting the investigation team where necessary to clarify the alleged relevance of an item to the investigation. It would appear only logical that the investigation team be required to justify why they wish to remove certain items.

Nor does the Court consider that the approach taken to legal professional privilege provides too narrow a protection as alleged by the applicant. Having regard to the definition of privilege in domestic law, a prohibition on removing documents in respect of which such privilege can be maintained provides a concrete safeguard against interference with professional secrecy and the administration of justice, bearing in mind in addition that the removal of any documents to which privilege in fact attached would have rendered the Inland Revenue liable to legal challenge and, potentially, to pay damages. The Court is not persuaded that it can be required, in order to prevent any possibility of error, that all documents to which privilege could prima facie attach should be covered.

The Court concludes that the search as carried out in this case was not disproportionate to the legitimate aims pursued and that adequate safeguards attached to the procedure. The interference can accordingly be regarded as "necessary in a democratic society" within the meaning of Article 8(2) of the Convention. **[4.43]**

Funcke v France [1993] 1 CMLR 897 (ECHR)

The European Court of Human Rights had to consider searches of premises, and the seizure of documents found therein, by French Customs officers.

EUROPEAN COURT OF HUMAN RIGHTS:

56. Undoubtedly, in the field under consideration – the prevention of capital outflows and tax evasion – States encounter serious difficulties owing to the scale and complexity of banking systems and financial channels and to the immense scope for international investment, made all the easier by the relative porousness of national borders. The Court therefore recognises that they may consider it necessary to have recourse to measures such as house searches and seizures in order to obtain physical evidence of exchange-control offences and, where appropriate, to prosecute those responsible. Nevertheless, the relevant legislation and practice must afford adequate and effective safeguards against abuse.

57. This was not so in the instant case ... **[4.44]**

R (on the application of Morgan Grenfell & Co Ltd) v Special Commissioners of Income Tax [2002] UKHL 21, [2003] 1 AC 563 (HL); see above, para [2.19]

The issue in this case was whether the taxpayer was protected against a notice under s 20(1) of the Taxes Management Act 1970 requiring production of documents covered by legal professional privilege. The appeal to the House of Lords was concerned solely with the construction of the Act. However, in the event that the court should reach a finding unfavourable to the appellants, they put forward an alternative submission that the provision should be declared incompatible with art 8. This proved unnecessary, but a pronouncement on the human rights issue was made in any event.

LORD HOFFMANN:

39. ... The appellants put forward an alternative submission that, if your Lordships agreed with the construction given to section 20(1) by the Court of Appeal, you should make a declaration that it was incompatible with the right to privacy under article 8 of the Convention for the Protection of Human Rights and Fundamental Freedoms (1953) (Cmd 8969). In the circumstances it is unnecessary for your Lordships to pronounce upon the point. It is however the case, as I have mentioned, that the European Court of Human Rights has said that LPP is a fundamental human right which can be invaded only in exceptional circumstances: see *Foxley v United Kingdom* (2001) 31 EHRR 25 p 647, para 44. Mr Brennan said that the public interest in the collection of the revenue could provide the necessary justification but I very much doubt whether this is right. Nor is it sufficient to say simply that the power is not used very often. That is no consolation to the person against whom it is used. If new legislation is passed, it will have to be seen whether it is limited to cases in which the interference with LPP can be shown to have a legitimate aim which is necessary in a democratic society. **[4.45]**

Lord Hoffmann's words of caution are limited to an 'interference with privilege' and, as vitally important as that may be, would not have a more general effect of curtailing Revenue powers in the future. **[4.46]**

D. *Article 6: the right to a fair hearing*

One of the cornerstones of the Convention, art 6(1) entitles everyone in both civil and criminal cases to a 'fair and public hearing within a reasonable time by an independent and impartial tribunal established by law'. **[4.47]**

(1) The obligations of the taxpayer and art 6(1)

Article 6(1) requires either that a claimant is the subject of a criminal charge, or that his 'civil rights and obligations' must have been affected. **[4.48]**

(a) Civil rights and obligations

Strasbourg jurisprudence indicates that a taxpayer's obligations are outside the scope of art 6(1) because they are public in nature. Thus it would appear that public law rights and obligations are not civil rights and obligations, whereas private law rights and obligations are. So, the obligations to make social security payments and to pay taxes are 'public' obligations since they derive from the citizen's normal civic duties in a democratic society[77] and any procedural dispute, for example, concerning the restriction of a right of appeal[78] in respect of the payment of such taxes, will not fall within the scope of art 6(1). In contrast, restitution proceedings for tax paid under regulations later declared invalid do involve the determination of the applicant's civil rights because the action concerns a private law claim against the Revenue based on unjust enrichment.[79] In such a case, where a taxpayer is given no right of appeal against a particular decision, or the right of appeal is so restricted that it is impossible to exercise, then art 6(1) may be invoked. **[4.49]**

Ferrazzini v Italy **[2001] STC 1314 (ECHR)**

The claimant alleged a violation of art 6 due to the length of tax proceedings to which he was a party. The majority of the European Court of Human Rights (sitting as the Grand Chamber of 17 judges, thus giving an indication of the importance of the issue) rejected the notion that the pecuniary nature of the claim was in itself sufficient to attract the applicability of art 6(1) under the 'civil' head.

EUROPEAN COURT OF HUMAN RIGHTS: MAJORITY JUDGMENT:

24. According to the Court's case-law, the concept of "civil rights and obligations" cannot be interpreted solely by reference to the domestic law of the respondent State. The Court has on several occasions affirmed the principle that this concept is "autonomous", within the meaning of Article 6 § 1 of the Convention (see, among other authorities, the *König v. Federal Republic of Germany* judgment of 28 June 1978, Series A no. 27, pp 29–30, §§ 88–89, and the *Baraona v. Portugal* judgment of 8 July 1987, Series A no. 122, pp17–18, § 42). The Court confirms this case-law in the instant case. It considers that any other solution is liable to lead to results that are incompatible with the object and purpose of the Convention (see, *mutatis mutandis*, the *König* judgment cited above, § 88, and *Maaouia v France* [GC], no. 39652/98, § 34, ECHR 2000–X).

77 *Schouten and Meldrum v Netherlands* (1994) 19 EHRR 432.
78 *Eagerpath v Edwards* [2001] STC 26.
79 *National and Provincial Building Society v United Kingdom* (1998) 25 EHRR 127, [1997] STC 1466 at 1490.

25. Pecuniary interests are clearly at stake in tax proceedings, but merely showing that a dispute is "pecuniary" in nature is not in itself sufficient to attract the applicability of Article 6 § 1 under its "civil" head (see the *Pierre-Bloch v. France* judgment of 21 October 1997, *Reports of Judgments and Decisions 1997–VI*, p 2223, § 51, and *Pellegrin v. France* [GC], no. 28541/95, § 60, ECHR 1999–VIII, cf. the *Editions Périscope v. France* judgment of 26 March 1992, Series A no. 234–B, p 66, § 40). In particular, according to the traditional case-law of the Convention institutions,

> 'There may exist 'pecuniary' obligations *vis-à-vis* the State or its subordinate authorities which, for the purpose of Article 6 § 1 are to be considered as belonging exclusively to the realm of public law and are accordingly not covered by the notion of 'civil rights and obligations'. Apart from fines imposed by way of 'criminal sanction', this will be the case, in particular, where an obligation which is pecuniary in nature derives from tax legislation or is otherwise part of normal civic duties in a democratic society (see, among other authorities, the *Schouten and Meldrum v. the Netherlands* judgment of 9 December 1994, Series A no. 304, p. 21, § 50; application no. 11189/84, Commission decision of 11 December 1986, Decisions and Reports (DR) 50, p. 121, at p. 140; and application no. 20471/92, Commission decision of 15 April 1996, DR 85, p. 29, at p. 46).'

26. The Convention is, however, a living instrument to be interpreted in the light of present-day conditions (see, among other authorities, *Johnston and Others v. Ireland*, judgment of 18 December 1986, Series A no. 112, pp. 24–25, § 53), and it is incumbent on the Court to review whether, in the light of changed attitudes in society as to the legal protection that falls to be accorded to individuals in their relations with the State, the scope of Article 6 § 1 should not be extended to cover disputes between citizens and public authorities as to the lawfulness under domestic law of the tax authorities' decisions.

27. Relations between the individual and the State have clearly evolved in many spheres during the fifty years which have elapsed since the Convention was adopted, with State regulation increasingly intervening in private-law relations. This has led the Court to find that procedures classified under national law as being part of "public law" could come within the purview of Article 6 under its "civil" head if the outcome was decisive for private rights and obligations, in regard to such matters as, to give some examples, the sale of land, the running of a private clinic, property interests, the granting of administrative authorisations relating to the conditions of professional practice or of a licence to serve alcoholic beverages (see, among other authorities, *Ringeisen v. Austria*, judgment of 16 July 1971, Series A no. 13, p. 39, § 94; *König*, cited above, p. 32, §§ 94–95; *Sporrong and Lönnroth v. Sweden*, judgment of 23 September 1982, Series A no. 52, p. 29, § 79; *Allan Jacobsson v. Sweden (no. 1)*, judgment of 25 October 1989, Series A no. 163, pp. 20–21, § 73; *Benthem v. the Netherlands*, judgment of 23 October 1985, Series A no. 97, p. 16, § 36; and *Tre Traktörer AB v. Sweden*, judgment of 7 July 1989, Series A no. 159, p. 19, § 43). Moreover, the State's increasing intervention in the individual's day-to-day life, in terms of welfare protection for example, has required the Court to evaluate features of public law and private law before concluding that the asserted right could be classified as "civil" (see, among other authorities, *Feldbrugge v. the Netherlands*, judgment of 29 May 1986, Series A no. 99, p. 16, § 40; *Deumeland v. Germany*, judgment of 29 May 1986, Series A no. 100, p. 25, § 74; *Salesi v. Italy*, judgment of 26 February 1993, Series A no. 257–E, pp. 59–60, § 19; and *Schouten and Meldrum*, cited above, p. 24, § 60).

28. However, rights and obligations existing for an individual are not necessarily civil in nature. Thus, political rights and obligations, such as the right to stand for election to the National Assembly (see *Pierre-Bloch*, cited above, p. 2223, § 50), even though in those proceedings the applicant's pecuniary interests were at stake (ibid., § 51), are not civil in nature, with the consequence that Article 6 § 1 does not apply. Neither does that provision apply to disputes between administrative authorities and those of their employees who occupy posts involving participation in the exercise of powers conferred by public law (see *Pellegrin*, cited above, §§ 66–67). Similarly, the expulsion of aliens does not give rise to disputes (*contestations*) over civil rights for the purposes of Article 6 § 1 of the Convention, which accordingly does not apply (see *Maaouia*, cited above, §§ 37–38).

29. In the tax field, developments which might have occurred in democratic societies do not, however, affect the fundamental nature of the obligation on individuals or companies to pay tax. In comparison with the position when the Convention was adopted, those developments have not entailed a further intervention by the State into the "civil" sphere of the individual's life. The Court considers that tax matters still form part of the hard core of public-authority prerogatives, with the public nature of the relationship between the taxpayer and the community remaining predominant. Bearing in mind that the Convention and its Protocols must be interpreted as a whole, the Court also observes that Article 1 of Protocol No. 1, which concerns the protection of property, reserves the right of States to enact such laws as they deem necessary for the purpose of securing the payment of taxes (see, *mutatis mutandis*, *Gasus Dosier- und Fördertechnik GmbH v. the Netherlands*, judgment of 23 February 1995, Series A no. 306–B, pp. 48–49, § 60). Although the Court does not attach decisive importance to that factor, it does take it into account. It considers that tax disputes fall outside the scope of civil rights and obligations, despite the pecuniary effects which they necessarily produce for the taxpayer.

30. The principle according to which the autonomous concepts contained in the Convention must be interpreted in the light of present-day conditions in democratic societies does not give the Court power to interpret Article 6 § 1 as though the adjective "civil" (with the restriction that that adjective necessarily places on the category of "rights and obligations" to which that Article applies) were not present in the text.

DISSENTING OPINION (Judges Lorenzen, Rozakis, Bonello, Strážnická, Bîrsan and Fischbach):

8. The majority considers that in the field of taxation there have been no major developments concerning the nature of the obligations of individuals and companies compared with the situation at the time of the drafting of the Convention. Accordingly, the majority is of the opinion that taxation still belongs to the "hard core of public-authority prerogatives, with the public nature of the relationship between the taxpayer and the community remaining predominant". The majority also takes into account that Article 1 of Protocol No. 1 reserves the right of States to enact such laws as they deem necessary for the purpose of securing the payment of taxes.

I am not convinced by that reasoning.

The finding that Article 6 § 1 of the Convention under its civil head is applicable to tax cases does not in any way restrict the States' power to place whatever fiscal obligations they wish on individuals and companies. Nor does such a finding restrict the States' freedom to enforce any such laws as they deem necessary in order to secure the payment of taxes (see Article 1 of Protocol No. 1). Article 6 of the Convention is a procedural guarantee that grants primarily the right of access to a court and the right to have court proceedings determined fairly within a reasonable time. In that respect there have in fact been important developments in the field of taxation since the drafting of the Convention. Whereas at that time it was doubtful in some legal systems to what extent administrative decisions in fiscal matters could be reviewed by a court – if at all – it is now recognised, at least in the vast majority of the Contracting Parties, that disputes in fiscal matters can be decided in ordinary proceedings by a court or a tribunal. It is therefore difficult to see why it is still necessary to grant the States a special prerogative under the Convention in this field and thus deny litigants in tax proceedings the elementary procedural guarantees of Article 6 § 1. As demonstrated, *inter alia*, in the concurring opinion of Judge Ress, there is a clear need to grant such protection – not least against lengthy proceedings combined with an obligation to pay taxes before a dispute concerning the legality of the tax decision is finally settled. In my opinion there is no basis in Article 1 of Protocol No. 1 for the assumption that the intention was to grant States the right to deny individuals any procedural protection in disputes on tax matters. How might it be justifiable to exempt from the Court's scrutiny the procedural rights guaranteed by Article 6 § 1 in respect of a dispute whose substance is directly linked to a civil right (in this case the right to peaceful enjoyment of possessions)? Such an interpretation would also be contrary to the constantly developing case-law of the Court according to which substantive Articles of the Convention, such as Articles 2, 3 and 8, must be interpreted as also implying procedural obligations on States.

> Furthermore, it is difficult to justify that an extended application of Article 6 § 1 under its civil head is not possible on grounds of the need to preserve a prerogative for States in fiscal matters, when the Court has gone sufficiently far in its case-law to include tax disputes under its criminal head. Since *Bendenoun v. France* (judgment of 24 February 1994, Series A no. 284), the Court has consistently considered proceedings relating to tax disputes to be "criminal" if tax fines, surcharges, etc., with a deterrent and punitive purpose are imposed or even if there is a risk that they may be imposed (see, most recently, *J.B. v. Switzerland*, no. 31827/96, ECHR 2001–III). The result is no different if the proceedings also concern the tax assessment as such (see the admissibility decision of 16 May 2000 in *Georgiou v. the United Kingdom*, no. 40042/98, unreported). This implies that the level of protection under Article 6 § 1 of the Convention varies depending on how the legal framework for tax proceedings is organised in the different legal systems; and even within one legal system it may be purely a matter of coincidence whether penalty proceedings and tax assessment proceedings are joined or not. An interpretation of the Convention that leads to such random results is far from satisfactory. **[4.50]**

Despite the strong and well reasoned dissenting minority opinion in *Ferrazzini* that suggested a possible shift in direction, the European Court of Human Rights has more recently followed the majority opinion in the case and held, without further discussion, that the assessment of tax and the imposition of surcharges fall outside the scope of art 6 under its civil head.[80] Nevertheless, *Ferrazzini* has been rejected in one case by the UK VAT and Duties Tribunal. In *N Ali & S Begum and others v Customs & Excise Commissioners*,[81] the tribunal had to consider the preliminary issue of the extent of the human rights of a taxable or potentially taxable person under art 6, prior to deciding whether the tribunal and its procedures afforded that person a fair and independent hearing by an independent tribunal. Recognising that it was required to take into account decisions of the Strasbourg Court, but that it was not bound by them, the tribunal held that the majority decision in *Ferrazzini* was not applicable since 'there is no place in the laws of any part of the United Kingdom for a "public law" relationship, distinct from civil law rights and obligations, between taxpayer [sic] and the tax authorities'.[82] Preferring the view of the minority in that case, the tribunal held that the obligations imposed by the VAT assessments, default surcharge assessments, misdeclaration, late registration and civil penalty notices and notices of requirement for security were within the scope of art 6(1) although, in the event, it was decided that the tribunal was sufficiently independent and impartial to satisfy the requirement set out therein. Although this decision should be hailed as representing a sea change in approach since the Human Rights Act 1998, whether it will be followed in cases before the Special Commissioners remains questionable, bearing in mind that the decision was emphatically limited to VAT. As the tribunal pointed out: 'The rights and obligations under the VAT code, a product of EC law, were not within the contemplation of those who drafted the Convention.'[83] **[4.51]**

80 *Jussila v Finland* (Application 73053/01) (judgment delivered on 23 November 2006, 9 ITL Rep 662).
81 (2002) VAT Trib 176851, (2002) Simons Tax Intelligence 1675.
82 (2002) STC 1675 at 1676.
83 Ibid.

(b) A criminal charge

In addition to the right to a fair trial enshrined in art 6(1), art 6(2) confirms the principle of innocence until proven guilty, and art 6(3) guarantees certain minimum rights, to everyone charged with a criminal offence. These include a right to be informed of the nature and cause of the charges (and to have the assistance of an interpreter if necessary), adequate time to prepare a defence and the right to secure the attendance of witnesses. Accordingly, the all-important question is whether certain tax, and seemingly civil, penalties give rise to criminal charges within the meaning of art 6(1).[84] **[4.52]**

Georgiou v United Kingdom 40042/98 [2001] STC 80 (ECHR)

At issue in this case was whether penalty assessments in respect of VAT and the hearing of appeals from these were 'criminal'. The European Court of Human Rights held that they were.

> EUROPEAN COURT OF HUMAN RIGHTS: ...In the present case, the applicants argue that the penalty proceedings under s 13 of the 1985 Act determined a "criminal charge". The criteria for establishing whether a "criminal charge" has been determined are the domestic classification of the "offence" and the nature and degree of severity of the potential and actual penalty ...The court notes that the penalty proceedings in the present case were classified as civil, rather than criminal, in domestic law. However, as in *Bendenoun v France* (1994) 18 EHRR 54 at para. 44–48, the penalty was intended as a punishment to deter re-offending, its purpose was both deterrent and punitive and the penalty itself was substantial. These factors taken together indicate that the penalty imposed in the present case was a "criminal charge" within the meaning of art.6(1). **[4.53]**

Han and Yau and others v Customs and Excise Commissioners [2001] EWCA Civ 1040, [2001] 1 WLR 2253 (CA); see below, paras [4.56 and 4.59]

The respondents, who operated a food take-away business, were issued with a notice of assessment of unpaid tax plus interest pursuant to s 73(1) of the Value Added Tax Act 1994, and were further assessed to a penalty pursuant to s 60(1) of the same Act in the sum of £67,095, which represented 90% of the assessed sum. The 10% reduction was stated to be made for the respondents' 'partial assistance'. The respondents argued successfully that Article 6 should apply and, in that event, the interviews which took place were unfair, contending in particular that no account was taken of their linguistic limitations and, whilst denying any dishonesty on their part, that if there was any liability to a penalty, they were not afforded any adequate inducement or opportunity to co-operate with a view to mitigation of the penalty.

> POTTER LJ:
>
> 26. It is not in dispute between the parties that the Strasbourg case law makes clear that the concept of a "criminal charge" under Article 6 has an "autonomous" Convention meaning: *Engel v Netherlands* [1979–80] EHRR 647 para 81. There are effectively three

84 Whilst it is clear that a charge under FA 2000, s 144 (evading income tax) is a criminal charge, certain other provisions relating to, for example, the fraudulent or negligent delivery of an incorrect tax return, leave room for doubt.

criteria applied by the Strasbourg Court in order to determine whether a criminal charge has been imposed: see *Engel* and more recently *AP, MP & TP v Switzerland* [1998] 26 EHRR 541 para 39.[85] They are:

(a) the classification of the proceedings in domestic law;
(b) the nature of the offence; and
(c) the nature and degree of severity of the penalty that the person concerned risked incurring.

The Strasbourg Court does not in practice treat these three requirements as analytically distinct or as a "three stage test", but as factors together to be weighed in seeking to decide whether, taken cumulatively, the relevant measure should be treated as "criminal". When coming to such decision in the course of the court's "autonomous" approach, factors (b) and (c) carry substantially greater weight than factor (a).....

65. ... in considering the three criteria routinely applied by the Strasbourg Court for the purpose of determining whether the applicant is the subject of a "criminal charge", the first criterion, namely the categorisation of the allegation in domestic law, is no more than a starting point for the classification, and is not decisive of the nature of the allegation. If the offence the subject of the allegation is not criminalised by the national law, the court determines whether it is nonetheless criminal in character for the purposes of Article 6 by proceeding to the second and third criteria, namely the nature of the offence and the severity of the penalty which it invokes. As stated in *Lauko*,[86] the second and third criteria are alternative rather than cumulative. However, that is not an approach which appears to have been adopted in practice and, as also stated in *Lauko*, a cumulative approach may be adopted where the analysis of each criterion does not lead to a clear conclusion; see *Bendenoun*.[87]

66. Under the second criterion, the court considers whether or not, under the law concerned, the "offence" is one which applies generally to the public at large or is restricted to a specific group. If the former, then despite its "de-criminalisation" by the national law, it is apt to be regarded as criminal. Further, if a punitive and deterrent penalty is attached, it is likely to be regarded as criminal in character, even in cases where the penalty is in the nature of a fine rather than imprisonment. On the other hand, where the offence is limited to a restricted group, as is generally the case in relation to disciplinary offences, the court is unlikely to classify a charge under the applicable disciplinary or regulatory code as criminal, at least unless it involves or may lead to loss of liberty.

67. In the context of disciplinary proceedings, the Strasbourg court has placed great emphasis on the seriousness of the penalty or imprisonment attached to the offence as the touchstone for holding the proceedings criminal rather than disciplinary: see *Engel* and see *Campbell and Fell v United Kingdom* (1984) 7 EHRR 165, a case concerning a serious prison disciplinary offence resulting in an award of 570 days' loss of remission. The latter case was distinguished by the Divisional Court in the recent decision of *Greenfield v The Secretary of State for the Home Department* (Case No: CO/248/2001), 22nd February 2001, in a case where the maximum penalty which could be awarded for the prison disciplinary offence in question was 42 additional days, and was wholly different in kind from the penalty which might have been imposed for an equivalent criminal charge. It is plain that the imposition of a substantial fine in disciplinary proceedings will not in itself render charges criminal in nature: see *Brown v United Kingdom* (1998) 28 EHRR CD 233, in which it was held that the fact that a £10,000 fine was imposed by the Solicitors' Complaints Tribunal did not attract the provisions of Article 6. However, outside the context of disciplinary proceedings, and in particular, in the field of tax evasion, it appears that a substantial financial penalty which is imposed by way of punishment and deterrence will suffice: see *Bendenoun* and *Georgiou*.

85 [This approach has more recently been confirmed in *Ezeh and Connors v UK* (2004) 39 EHRR 1, a case concerning prison disciplinary offences.]
86 *Lauko v Slovakia* Reports of Judgments and Decisions 1998–VI, p. 2492.
87 (1994) 18 EHRR 54.

68. Finally, it is to be observed that the treatment of the categorisation of the allegation in domestic law merely as a starting point marginalises, and indeed largely renders irrelevant, the rationale underlying a national law which seeks to de-criminalise conduct which would otherwise be treated, or generally regarded, as criminal in nature. The trend of the Strasbourg decisions, exemplified in *Bendenoun* and *Georgiou* has been to fasten upon and emphasise the applicability of the second and third criteria, despite the view reflected in the opinions of the dissenting judges in *Ozturk* to the effect that de-criminalisation, at least of "minor offences", may work in the general interests of individuals by elimination of the moral judgment and the drawbacks customarily connected with criminal proceedings: see in particular the dissenting opinion of Judge Bernhardt, with which Judge Thor Vilhjalmsson also agreed. Equally the Strasbourg court has ignored the observations of Judge Matscher that differences in the conceptions which underlie criminal and "regulatory" offences and, in particular, differences in their legal effects whether of substance or procedure, affect their very nature and that excessively broad interpretation of the concept of "criminal" and "civil" for the purpose of extending the guarantees included in Article 6 is not an appropriate solution. . . .

75. So far as the first criterion is concerned, it is plain that the classification of the penalties provided for as "civil", albeit coupled with a procedure appropriate to civil rather than criminal proceedings, cannot be regarded as more than the starting point where the levying and enforcement of the penalty concerned is designed to punish and deter members of the public at large in respect of dishonest conduct. Furthermore, the classification does not represent a decision on the part of the legislature to de-criminalise dishonest evasion of VAT, given the parallel provision under s.72(1) for the criminal prosecution of any person knowingly concerned in the fraudulent evasion of VAT and, under 72(3), of any person acting fraudulently in the respects therein set out. This, rather, creates alternative regimes in respect of which the Customs and Excise may nonetheless decide in the course of an investigation, to change from one to the other. The provisions of Article 6 however are concerned to protect a potential defendant to criminal proceedings from an early stage, and the nature and consequences of the 'charge' may affect the degree of co-operation which he is prepared to afford in the course of an investigation.

76. So far as the second criterion is concerned, the nature of the offence suspected and sanctioned by the application of civil penalties is fraud/dishonesty in respect of the tax payable or actually payable, whether under s.60 or s.72 VATA, and the Customs and Excise enjoy a discretion as to whether, on a particular set of facts to apply a civil penalty or to prosecute. As observed by the Chairman at paragraph 7 of his judgment below (p.315):

> 'Cases where section 60 penalties are in issue usually involve allegations of dishonest and systemic suppressions of sales or use of fictitious invoices over a number of accounting periods . . . to those of us with judicial experience of criminal proceedings, the level of criminality alleged against the appellant does not appear significantly different from that involved in Crown Court fraud trials.'

He went on to observe:

> 'The essential contrasts are these. The appeal before the Tribunal is quicker and less demanding on the Commissioners' resources. The standard of proof is lower. Criminal proceedings do not apply. Instead the procedure is regulated by the VAT Tribunal Rules 1986. In particular, the Tribunal has a broad discretion in respect of the evidence it may admit under Rule 28. The imposition of a penalty does not give rise to a criminal record and loss of liberty is not a possibility.' . . .

78. So far as the third criterion, the nature and degree of the penalty, is concerned, again the weight of Strasbourg authority is in favour of the respondents in the sense that, in the area of tax evasion at least, such authority does not require that, for the purposes of a 'criminal' charge, it is necessary to demonstrate that the penalty to which the taxpayer is subject involves, or may involve, imprisonment. It is sufficient that it is substantial and its' purpose is punitive and deterrent. It seems to me that those requirements are made out in the case of these respondents. **[4.54]**

Potter LJ reached his decision in the light of what he regarded to be the 'clear state of the Strasbourg case law in relation to a case of this kind', but only with some reluctance. The 'Civil Penalty Scheme,' which replaced the former VAT Offence code that had provided solely for criminal offences, was introduced as a result of the *Report of the Committee on Enforcement of Powers of the Revenue Departments, 1983* ('The Keith Report'). In the view of Potter LJ, the rationale for the new scheme was 'convincingly propounded in the Keith Report as a just balance between the legitimate interests of the Customs and Excise in improving the collection of a tax in relation to which widespread evasion was prevalent, and the interests of the taxpayer in avoiding the travails of a criminal prosecution and the stigma of conviction of a criminal offence of dishonesty in cases of deliberate evasion.' He also noted that the decision of Jacob J in *King v Walden*,[88] which held that the system for imposition of penalties for fraudulent or negligent delivery of incorrect tax returns or statements was 'criminal' for the purposes of art 6(2), went further than the conclusions that he himself had expressed, but that they were not inconsistent with them.

It has already been noted that the importance of the question at issue in cases such as *Han* lies in the protection afforded to taxpayers by the various minimum rights provided for by art 6(2) and (3). It is critical, then, to have some certainty on the matter, and yet there is none. In *N Ali and S Begum and others v Customs and Excise*[89] the VAT Tribunal concluded that serious misdeclaration penalties, default surcharges and late registration penalties were not criminal for the purposes of art 6, a decision seemingly at odds with both the Strasbourg jurisprudence and the Court of Appeal. The Tribunal said that the penalties and surcharges in question had none of the characteristics of a criminal penalty, despite the fact that the 15% default surcharge appeared severe where the delay on payment was small,[90] and that the operation of the penalty regime under UK law adequately protected the rights of alleged defaulters, with no need for further safeguards.[91] What is not clear is whether the decision rests on the fact that the penalty was lower than in other cases, or on the fact that the Tribunal considered that the VAT system had inbuilt safeguards. If it is the former, then there needs to be spelt out with some precision how severe a penalty has to be before it metamorphosises into a 'criminal charge;' if it is the latter, then it is questionable whether such an approach will withstand a review by the Court of Appeal. The Strasbourg Court has taken the view that so-called 'civil' surcharges amounting to 20% and 40% of the increased tax liability were criminal for the purposes of art 6,[92] although the Grand Chamber of the Court has more recently stressed the

88 *King v Walden* [2001] STC 822.

89 (2002) VAT Trib 176851, (2002) Simons Tax Intelligence 1675.

90 See also *Bancroft and another v Crutchfield* (2002) Sp C 322, [2002] STC (SCD) 347, where the late payment surcharge of 5% of unpaid tax under the Taxes Management Act 1970, s 59C was thought not to be sufficiently severe to constitute a criminal charge.

91 See n 89 above at p 1677.

92 See *Vastberga Taxi AB v Sweden* (36985/97) 5 ITL Rep 65 and *Janosevic v Sweden* (34619/97) (2004) 38 EHRR 22. In spite of all the uncertainty, when considering how any future cases concerning penalties for misdeclaration, belated VAT registration, default surcharges, demand for security and refusal to restore seized excise, together with any future cases involving direct tax civil penalties were likely to be decided, both Potter LJ and Mance LJ made it clear in *Han v Customs & Excise Commissioners* that there is unlikely to be any great change in existing procedures, provided all the necessary steps are taken to explain to the taxpayer his rights under the Convention and he is afforded his minimum rights under art 6(3).

need to consider *all* the criteria, and approved the approach in *Janosevic v Sweden*[93] in deciding that there was no established or authoritative basis for holding that the minor nature of the penalty in taxation proceedings or otherwise was decisive in removing an offence, otherwise criminal by nature, from the scope of art 6.[94] **[4.55]**

(2) The burden of proof

Han and Yau and others v Customs and Excise Commissioners [2001] EWCA Civ 1040, [2001] 1 WLR 2253 (CA); see above, para [4.54] and below, para [4.59]

MANCE LJ:

88. The classification of a case as criminal for the purpose of Article 6(3) of the Convention on Human Rights ... is a classification for the purposes of the Convention only. It entitles the defendant to the safeguards provided expressly or by implication by that Article. It does not make the case criminal for all domestic purposes. In particular, it does not, necessarily, engage protections such as those provided by the Police and Criminal Evidence Act 1984.... **[4.56]**

A slightly different view was expressed by the VAT tribunal in *Ajay Chandubhai Kumar Patel v Customs & Excise Commissioners*.[95] Citing the House of Lords decision in *Khawaja v Secretary of State for the Home Department*,[96] it considered that the 'standard is the civil standard of the balance of probabilities; however, under art 6(2) the appellant is innocent until proved guilty. In any event, clear evidence is needed for a finding of dishonesty; the more serious the allegation, the more cogent the evidence must be.' **[4.57]**

(3) The right to silence and the privilege against self-incrimination

The invitation to a taxpayer to co-operate with HMRC, and the subsequent disclosure of information, are at the heart of HMRC's civil investigation of fraud procedures. For investigations that began prior to 1 September 2005, the relevant procedures (the *Hansard* procedure in relation to direct taxes, and the civil evasion procedures operated by HM Customs & Excise for indirect taxes), permitted the Revenue/HM Customs & Excise to accept a money settlement in lieu of instituting criminal proceedings in respect of alleged fraud. The case of *R v Allen*, below, and the Human Rights Act 1998 highlighted the concern that a breach of art 6 could arise where information was obtained under these procedures and then subsequently used in criminal proceedings against the taxpayer. It was thought that in these circumstances, the taxpayer could argue that his right to a fair trial had been breached because, by providing sensitive information under threat of penalty, he had

93 Application 34619/97 (2004) 38 EHRR 22.
94 *Jussila v Finland* (Application 73053/01) (judgment delivered on 23 November 2006, 9 ITL Rep. 662). The penalty in this case amounted to 10% of the increased tax liability.
95 (2001) VAT Trib 17248.
96 [1984] AC 74, [1983] 1 All ER 765, [1982] Imm AR 139.

been forced to incriminate himself. To prevent a possible breach of art 6, the procedures were amended to ensure that a taxpayer who made a full confession would be assured that a criminal prosecution would not be pursued.[97] Moreover, as a direct response to the decision in *R v Gill and Gill*,[98] and contrary to the view of Potter LJ in *Han and Yau and others v Customs and Excise Commissioners*, below, *Hansard* interviews began to be conducted under caution and taped according to the Police and Criminal Evidence Act 1984 (PACE).

HMRC introduced a new combined code – Code of Practice 9 (COP 9) – to deal with the civil investigation of fraud, which governs investigations starting on or after 1 September 2005. Although COP 9 reproduces many of the features of the old *Hansard* procedure, it no longer includes the PACE requirements. This means that a taxpayer will not be cautioned as to his rights, nor will meetings be tape-recorded, a situation that reflects the view of Potter LJ in *Han and Yau and others v Customs and Excise Commissioners*, that these are civil matters and should not be dealt with according to the tenets of the criminal law. **[4.58]**

Han and Yau and others v Customs and Excise Commissioners [2001] EWCA Civ 1040, [2001] 1 WLR 2253 (CA); see above, paras [4.54] and [4.56]

POTTER LJ:

82. We have been informed that, whereas a variety of points await disposal, the Commissioners' principal concern relates to their desire to make continued use of the 'inducement' procedure as a method of obtaining the co-operation of the taxpayer for the purpose of establishing the amount of tax evaded and imposing a civil penalty discounted upon the basis of the degree of co-operation received. It is envisaged that the Customs and Excise may be vulnerable to the Tribunal excluding as inadmissible evidence obtained during an interview, or subsequently, as a result of supplying to the taxpayer the Statement of Practice in VAT Notice 730. If such rulings were to become widespread it would significantly affect the ability of Customs and Excise successfully to defend appeals and would threaten the basis of the whole of the civil evasion penalty regime. Arguments have apparently already been 'flagged' to the effect that the inducement procedure may amount to a breach of the right to silence and the right against self-incrimination. Whether this is correct has not been argued before us. However, I would only observe that the fears of the Commissioners seem to me likely to prove unfounded in this respect.

83. It appears that the inducement procedure, at least as refined in December 2000, makes explicit to the taxpayer, in addition to the information supplied in VAT Notice 730, that the civil evasion investigation is not being conducted with a view to prosecuting the trader for VAT evasion, that the trader is not obliged to co-operate in the Customs investigation, and it is entirely a decision for the trader to decide whether or not to speak to the investigating officer or assist generally in the Customs investigation. It must be remembered that the requirements of Article 6(1) in relation to a fair trial, together with what has been held to be the implicit recognition of a right to silence and a privilege against self-incrimination, are of a general nature and are not prescriptive of the precise means or procedural rules by which domestic law recognises and protects such rights.

It by no means follows from a conclusion that Article 6 applies that civil penalty proceedings are, for other domestic purposes, to be regarded as criminal and, therefore,

97 See Jonathan Hilliard, 'The *Hansard* procedure and the rights against self-incrimination: recent developments' [2003] 1 BTR 6.

98 [2003] EWCA Crim 2256, [2004] 1 WLR 469.

subject to those provisions of PACE and/or the Codes produced thereunder, which relate to the investigation of crime and the conduct of criminal proceedings *as defined by English law*. Any argument as to whether and how far that Act and the Codes apply is one which will have to be separately considered if and when it is advanced. In this context, however, the specific provisions of s.60(4) VATA are plainly of considerable importance. I would merely add my view that, if matters are made clear to the taxpayer on the lines indicated in paragraph 77 above at the time when the nature and effect of the inducement procedure are also made clear to him (whether by VAT Notice 730 or otherwise), it is difficult to see that there would be any breach of Article 6. It also seems to me that, even if PACE were applicable, it is most unlikely that a court or tribunal would rule inadmissible under s.76 or s.78 any statements made or documents produced as a result, at any rate in the absence of exceptional circumstances. On the other hand, it follows from this decision that a person made subject to a civil penalty under s.60(1) will be entitled to the minimum rights specifically provided for in Article 6(3). **[4.59]**

R v Allen [2002] 1 AC 509, [2001] 4 All ER 768 (HL)

The taxpayer, who was being investigated for tax fraud, had failed to comply with a notice requiring him to furnish the Revenue with certain information. The *Hansard* procedure was adopted, and the taxpayer answered the Revenue's questions, albeit giving false information. He was subsequently charged with the criminal offence of cheating the public revenue, and he argued that the demands made upon him by both the provision under which he was required to impart information and the *Hansard* procedure had caused the information to be given involuntary and was a breach of his right not to incriminate himself.

LORD HUTTON:

29. My Lords, the present case is one which relates to the obligation of a citizen to pay taxes and to his duty not to cheat the Revenue. It is self-evident that the payment of taxes, fixed by the legislature, is essential for the functioning of any democratic State. It is also self-evident that to ensure the due payment of taxes the State must have power to require its citizens to inform it of the amount of their annual income, and to have sanctions available to enforce the provision of that information. In the United Kingdom this power is contained in the provisions of the Taxes Management Act 1970. . . .

It is clearly permissible for a State to enact such provisions and there could be no substance in an argument that there is a violation of article 6(1) if the revenue prosecuted a citizen for cheating the revenue by furnishing a standard tax return containing false information. Similarly in the present case, viewed against the background that the State, for the purpose of collecting tax, is entitled to require a citizen to inform it of his income and to enforce penalties for failure to do so, the section 20(1) notice requiring information cannot constitute a violation of the right against self-incrimination. The present case is therefore clearly distinguishable from *Saunders* on that ground.

As Lord Bingham of Cornhill stated in *Brown v Stott (Procurator Fiscal, Dunfermline)* [2001] 2 WLR 817, 836:

> 'The jurisprudence of the European Court very clearly establishes that while the overall fairness of a criminal trial cannot be compromised, the constituent rights comprised, whether expressly or implicitly, within article 6 are not themselves absolute. Limited qualification of these rights is acceptable if reasonably directed by national authorities towards a clear and proper public objective and if representing no greater qualification than the situation calls for . . . . The Court has also recognised the need for a fair balance between the general interest of the community and the personal rights of the individual, the search for which balance has been described as inherent in the whole of the Convention: see *Sporrong and Lönnroth v Sweden* (1982) 5 EHRR 35, 52, para 69; *Sheffield and Horsham v United Kingdom* (1998) 27 EHRR 163, 191, para 52.' . . .

31. In respect of his argument that there had been a breach of article 6(1) because the delivery of the schedule of assets had been "involuntary" having been induced by a promise implicit in the Hansard statement that the appellant would not be prosecuted if he furnished the required information . . .

35. . . . the appellant's argument is . . . . invalid. If, in response to the Hansard statement, the appellant had given true and accurate information which disclosed that he had earlier cheated the revenue and had then been prosecuted for that earlier dishonesty, he would have had a strong argument that the criminal proceedings were unfair and an even stronger argument that the Crown should not rely on evidence of his admission, but that is the reverse of what actually occurred. **[4.60]**

Although the taxpayer's appeal was heard after the relevant sections of the Human Rights Act 1998 had come into force on 2 October 2000, the trial and conviction took place before that date. The House of Lords held that the Act did not operate retrospectively to make unsafe by reason of a breach of art 6 a conviction that was safe under English law at the time the conviction took place. Accordingly, Lord Hutton's comments must be viewed as *obiter*. The question of whether evidence obtained during interview or by way of disclosure breached the taxpayer's right to silence and the right of self-incrimination was not resolved in the *Han* case, which the Court of Appeal recognised could only be dealt with by individual rulings by the VAT and Duties Tribunal in the light of the decision in *Han*. **[4.61]**

Code of Practice 9, HMRC (2005)

Civil investigation of fraud statement

The practice of HM Revenue & Customs (HMRC) in cases of suspected serious tax fraud is as follows.

- The Commissioners reserve complete discretion to pursue a criminal investigation with a view to prosecution where they consider it necessary and appropriate.
- Where a criminal investigation is not considered necessary or appropriate, the Commissioners may decide to investigate using the Civil Investigation of Fraud procedure.
- Where the Commissioners decide to investigate using the Civil Investigation of Fraud procedure they will not seek a prosecution for the tax fraud which is the subject of that investigation. The taxpayer will be given an opportunity to make a full and complete disclosure of all irregularities in their tax affairs.
- However, where materially false statements are made or materially false documents are provided with intent to deceive in the course of a civil investigation, the Commissioners may conduct a criminal investigation with a view to a prosecution of that conduct.
- If the Commissioners decide to investigate using the Civil Investigation of Fraud procedure the taxpayer will be given a copy of this statement by an authorised officer. **[4.62]**

For a critical discussion on how to reconcile art 6 with a system of tax administration that relies greatly on the provision of information from the taxpayer, see Jonathan Hilliard, 'Article 6 and the Scope of the Right not to Incriminate Oneself in the Tax Field' [2002] 6 BTR 470. **[4.63]**

5 Tax Avoidance

1. Introduction

A taxpayer who acts with a view to avoiding tax is not acting unlawfully.[1] Indeed, in some instances, a taxpayer may be encouraged to organise his affairs in one way rather than another, eg where tax incentives are provided for a taxpayer who opts to set up business in an area where Government wishes to promote economic development[2], whilst in others a taxpayer may be dissuaded from a particular course of action because Parliament has made it clear that such action will not be effective for tax purposes, eg through the enactment of targeted or specific anti-avoidance legislation.[3] In some jurisdictions, but not, as will be seen,[4] presently in the UK, the latter may be accompanied by a statutory general anti-avoidance rule (a GAAR) that sets out the parameters within which, generally, acts purporting to avoid tax may be regarded as ineffective for tax purposes.[5]

Thus, the critical issue in any case concerning purported tax avoidance relates not to the legality of the taxpayer's actions but as to whether those actions achieve the anticipated tax result, ie whether those actions are fiscally effective. In recent cases, it has been stressed that in resolving this issue, judges should have regard to the outcome of a time honoured, specific and simply framed question that may be pertinent to any tax case, namely does the relevant statutory provision, upon its true construction, apply to the facts as found? It may be felt that this is self-evident and incontrovertible, but the

1 Tax avoidance should be distinguished from tax evasion which is unlawful. In the words of the Royal Commission on the Taxation of Profits and Income in its Final Report: '[Tax evasion] denotes all those activities which are responsible for a person not paying the tax that the existing law charges upon his income. *Ex hypothesi* he is in the wrong . . .' (Cmd 9474 (1955), para 1016). The existence of that 'wrong' may lead to a criminal prosecution founded on the alleged commission of such offences as cheating the public revenue (see, for example, *R v Charlton* [1996] STC 1418, where the Inland Revenue successfully prosecuted several individuals for cheating the public revenue against the backdrop of what was purportedly a tax avoidance scheme).

2 See, for example, the initial capital allowances given for qualifying enterprise zone expenditure (CAA 2001, ss 305–308).

3 See, for example, the legislation relating to settlements in ITTOIA 2005, Pt 5, ch 5 and Chapter 16, below paras **[16.32]–[16.36]**.

4 See below, paras **[5.15]–[5.23]**.

5 Further, some jurisdictions (usually with a civil law tradition) may have recourse to the abuse of rights (*abus de droit*) doctrine/principle whereby (in the sphere of taxation) a taxpayer may have the right to arrange his affairs with a view to avoiding tax but may be deemed to have abused that right if his purpose was solely to avoid tax. See also *Halifax plc v C & E Commissioners* [2006] 2 WLR 905, in which the ECJ affirmed that the abuse of rights doctrine, as a principle of EC law, could apply to value added tax.

assertion is significant, because, as the next section of this chapter shows, there was a commonly held perception following the decisions of the House of Lords in *W T Ramsay v IRC; Eilbeck v Rawling* [1982] AC 300 (*Ramsay*) and in *Furniss v Dawson* [1984] AC 474 (*Furniss*) that a new approach to the resolution of tax avoidance cases had been established.

Subsequent sections of the chapter deal, respectively, with the consideration given in the late 1990s to the enactment of a GAAR in the UK and to the recently introduced disclosure rules relating to direct tax avoidance schemes which, as will be seen,[6] provide HMRC with an opportunity at an early stage to detect and act upon schemes that it may regard as fiscally ineffective, and, further, that may, in time, result in fewer cases reaching the courts. **[5.1]**

2. The judicial approach to tax avoidance

As intimated above, this section is concerned, principally, with tracing the path which led to the recent affirmation of the judicial role in tax avoidance cases and, incidentally, to the repudiation of the view that *Ramsay* was indicative of a new approach. For ease of understanding, it is divided into the four sequential parts which follow. **[5.2]**

A. *The starting point*

IRC v Duke of Westminster [1936] AC 1 (HL)

The Duke executed a series of deeds in which he covenanted to pay certain of his employees weekly sums for a period of seven years or for the joint lives of the parties. The covenantees continued in their employment and continued to receive such sums as, together with the payments under the covenants, made up the amount of their wages before the deeds were executed.

The employees could have left their employment and still enforced the covenants; however, there was an 'understanding' that an employee would not sue for full remuneration so long as he continued to receive the covenanted sums.

The Crown contended that the payments were, in reality, remuneration for services and could not be deducted from the Duke's total income for surtax purposes (the employees were not employed in any business by the Duke); the Duke contended that they were deductible as annual payments.[7]

> LORD ATKIN: . . . It was not, I think, denied – at any rate it is incontrovertible – that the deeds were brought into existence as a device by which the respondent might avoid some of the burden of surtax. I do not use the word device in any sinister sense, for it has to be recognised that the subject, whether poor and humble or wealthy and noble, has the right so to dispose of his capital and income as to attract upon himself the least amount of tax. The only function of a Court of law is to determine the legal result of his dispositions so far as they affect tax . . .
>
> LORD TOMLIN: . . . it is said that in revenue cases there is a doctrine that the Court may ignore the legal position and regard what is called "the substance of the matter," and that

6 See below, paras **[5.24]**–**[5.25]**.

7 For the present treatment of annual payments, see ITA 2007, Pt 15 (deduction of income tax at source). See also Chapter 11, below, para **[11.9]**.

here the substance of the matter is that the annuitant was serving the Duke for something equal to his former salary or wages, and that therefore, while he is so serving, the annuity must be treated as salary or wages. This supposed doctrine (upon which the Commissioners apparently acted) seems to rest for its support upon a misunderstanding of language used in some earlier cases. The sooner this misunderstanding is dispelled, and the supposed doctrine given its quietus, the better it will be for all concerned, for the doctrine seems to involve substituting "the incertain and crooked cord of discretion" for "the golden and streight metwand of the law."[8] Every man is entitled if he can to order his affairs so as that the tax attaching under the appropriate Acts is less than it otherwise would be. If he succeeds in ordering them so as to secure this result, then, however unappreciative the Commissioners of Inland Revenue or his fellow taxpayers may be of his ingenuity, he cannot be compelled to pay an increased tax. This so-called doctrine of "the substance" seems to me to be nothing more than an attempt to make a man pay notwithstanding that he has so ordered his affairs that the amount of tax sought from him is not legally claimable.

The principal passages relied upon are from opinions of Lord Herschell and Lord Halsbury in your Lordships' House. Lord Herschell L.C. in *Helby v. Matthews*[9] observed: "It is said that the substance of the transaction evidenced by the agreement must be looked at, and not its mere words." I quite agree; but he went on to explain that the substance must be ascertained by a consideration of the rights and obligations of the parties to be derived from a consideration of the whole of the agreement. In short Lord Herschell was saying that the substance of a transaction embodied in a written instrument is to be found by construing the document as a whole.

Support has also been sought by the appellants from the language of Lord Halsbury L.C. in *Secretary of State in Council of India v. Scoble.*[10] There Lord Halsbury said: "Still, looking at the whole nature and substance of the transaction (and it is agreed on all sides that we must look at the nature of the transaction and not be bound by the mere use of the words), this is not the case of a purchase of an annuity." Here again Lord Halsbury is only giving utterance to the indisputable rule that the surrounding circumstances must be regarded in construing a document.

Neither of these passages in my opinion affords the appellants any support or has any application to the present case. The matter was put accurately by my noble and learned friend Lord Warrington of Clyffe when as Warrington L.J. in *In re Hinckes, Dashwood v. Hinckes*[11] he used these words: "It is said we must go behind the form and look at the substance ... but, in order to ascertain the substance, I must look at the legal effort of the bargain which the parties have entered into." So here the substance is that which results from the legal rights and obligations of the parties ascertained upon ordinary legal principles, and, having regard to what I have already said, the conclusion must be that each annuitant is entitled to an annuity which as between himself and the payer is liable to deduction of income tax by the payer and which the payer is entitled to treat as a deduction from his total income for surtax purposes.

There may, of course, be cases where documents are not bona fide nor intended to be acted upon, but are only used as a cloak to conceal a different transaction.[12] No such case

8 4 Inst. 41.
9 [1895] A.C. 471 at 475.
10 [1903] A.C. 299 at 302.
11 [1921] 1 Ch. 475 at 489.
12 [Such instances (ie where transactions are intended to give the appearance of having a legal effect different from the legal effect intended by the parties) are referred to as shams. In an oft cited passage, Diplock LJ in *Snook v London and West Riding Investments Ltd* [1967] 2 QB 786, 802 described a sham as follows:

> "I apprehend that, if it has any meaning in law, it means acts done or documents executed by the parties to the 'sham' which are intended by them to give to third parties or the court the appearance of creating between the parties legal rights and obligations different from the actual legal rights and obligations (if any) which the parties intended to create."

See also the observations of Mustill LJ in *Hadjiloucas v Crean* [1987] 3 All ER 1008, 1019 about the situations in which a sham may arise.]

is made or even suggested here. The deeds of covenant are admittedly bona fide and have been given their proper legal operation. They cannot be ignored or treated as operating in some different way because as a result less duty is payable than would have been the case if some other arrangement (called for the purpose of the appellants' argument "the substance") had been made . . . **[5.3]**

B. Signs of change

Floor v Davis (Inspector of Taxes) [1978] Ch 295 (CA)[13]

The taxpayer wished to dispose of shares in a company to an American Company (KDI). A direct sale to KDI would have given rise to a liability to capital gains tax.

The taxpayer sought to avoid that liability by a scheme which involved, inter alia, the incorporation of another company, FNW, to which the taxpayer transferred the shares in consideration of the issue of shares in FNW and the transfer of the shares by FNW to KDI. FNW was subsequently placed in liquidation and its assets distributed.

The Crown argued that there was a disposal for capital gains tax purposes of the shares by the taxpayer to KDI.

SIR JOHN PENNYCUICK: . . . It was contended by Mr. Millett on behalf of the Crown that, even apart from any contractual or equitable obligation on the part of FNW to pass on the shares in IDM to KDI transactions (a) and (b)[14] looked at together, as they must be, should be regarded as simply a disposal by the taxpayer and the sons-in-law of their shares in IDM and KDI. It was pointed out that the Finance Act 1965 contains no definition of disposal and it was stressed that the combined effect, or end result, of the two transactions was indeed to pass the shares in IDM from the taxpayer and his sons-in-law to KDI, FNW being no more than a conduit pipe through which this passage was achieved. It seems to me that this contention disregards the legal effect of what were admittedly genuine transactions and really seeks to resurrect the conception of substance which was buried by the House of Lords in *Inland Revenue Commissioners v. Duke of Westminster*[15]: see for a recent affirmation of the principle laid down in the *Duke of Westminster's* case the statement by Lord Wilberforce in *Inland Revenue Commissioner v. Europa Oil (N.Z.) Ltd.*[16] In my judgment it is impossible, upon the plain legal effect of transactions (a) and (b), to maintain that the taxpayers and the sons-in-law sold their shares in IDM to anyone other than FNW or that KDI purchased those shares from anyone other than FNW. That is not a disposal by the taxpayer and the sons-in-law to KDI . . .

EVELEIGH L J (dissenting): . . . I take the view that the shares with which we are concerned were disposed of by the taxpayer to KDI. On all other points I agree with the judgment just delivered.

It is clear that right from the beginning KDI indicated that it would purchase the shares. The only reason for avoiding a direct sale to them was the prospect of capital gains tax. In an attempt to avoid paying this, as it frankly accepted, the initial transfer to FNW took place. There was however no real possibility at any time that the shares would not reach KDI. By virtue of their control of FNW the shareholders guaranteed from the moment they parted with the legal ownership that the shares would become the property of KDI.

13 The House of Lords decided the case on grounds other than the ground considered below. The relevance of the extracts from the judgments delivered in the Court of Appeal will become apparent later in this chapter.
14 [Ie the exchange and sale of the shares respectively.]
15 [1936] A.C. 1; [above, para **[5.3]**].
16 [1971] A.C. 760 at 771.

No one could prevent this against their wishes. By virtue of the arrangement initially made between them each was under an obligation to the other to do nothing to stop the shares arriving in the hands of KDI. They controlled the destiny of the shares from beginning to end in pursuance of a continuing intention on their part that the shares should be transferred to KDI.

This court is concerned to decide whether any capital gains accruing as a result of the transaction can be said to be gains accruing to a person on the disposal of assets within the meaning of section 19(1) of the Finance Act 1965.[17] There is no legal definition of the word "disposal" and I can see no reason to define it as "the first legal transfer in the ownership of property." Indeed I do not understand counsel for the taxpayer to contend that the meaning should be so limited. Property could be disposed of to C by transferring it to B in trust for C. If in the present case FNW had contracted to transfer the shares to KDI and had acquired them on those terms it seemed to me, as this case was argued before the court, that it would have been very difficult for counsel to contend that there was not a disposal by the taxpayer to KDI. However, what he said was that there was no such contract and consequently the only transaction by the respondent was a transfer (or disposal) of the shares to FNW. Thereafter he said the transfer to KDI was entirely separate. Emphasis was placed upon the fact that it was conceded that the transfer to FNW was a genuine one. I understand "genuine" in this context to mean that it was what it purported to be, namely, the transfer of the ownership to FNW. The court often meets the contention that a transaction is specious in the sense that it is not the legal transaction it appears to be. Hire-purchase agreements masquerading as bills of sale, and so-called furnished tenancies under the Rent Acts, are examples of this. Without the concession I would have treated the transfer to FNW as genuine, but it was only part of a larger transaction. The question that the court has to determine is whether that transaction was a disposal to KDI . . .

I see this case as one in which the court is not required to consider each step taken in isolation. It is a question of whether or not the shares were disposed of to KDI by the taxpayer. I believe that they were. Furthermore, they were in reality at the disposal of the original shareholders until the moment they reached the hand of KDI, although the legal ownership was in FNW. I do not think that this conclusion is any way vitiated by *Inland Revenue Commissioners v. Duke of Westminster*.[18] In that case it was sought to say that the payments under covenant were not such but were payments of wages. I do not seek to say that the transfer to FNW was not a transfer. The important feature of the present case is that the destiny of the shares was at all times under the control of the taxpayer who was arranging for them to be transferred to KDI. The transfer to FNW was but a step in that process. In the *Westminster* case the legal position was that there existed a covenant imposing upon the Duke a liability to make payments thereunder. The Crown was not permitted to say that those payments were anything else. Effect had to be given to the legal position. Lord Russell of Killowen said[19]:

> "I confess that I view with disfavour the doctrine that in taxation cases a subject is to be taxed if in accordance with a court's view of what it considers the substance of the transaction, the court thinks that the case falls within the contemplation or spirit of the statute. The subject is not taxable by inference or by analogy but only by the plain words of a statute applicable to the facts and circumstances of his case."

In deciding that there was a disposal within the plain words of the statute to KDI, I in no way deny the legal effect of the transfer to FNW . . . **[5.4]**

The legitimacy of an approach (such as that adopted by Eveleigh LJ in *Floor*) which enabled a court, where appropriate, to consider a series or combination of transactions as a whole rather than as separate transactions

17 [See now TCGA 1992, s 1(1).]
18 [1936] A.C. 1; [above, para **[5.3]**].
19 *Ibid*, at 24.

was endorsed, subsequently, by the House of Lords in *IRC v Plummer* [1980] AC 896 and *Chinn v Collins; Chinn v Hochstrasser* [1981] AC 533. **[5.5]**

IRC v Plummer [1980] AC 896 (HL); see below, para [16.33]

LORD WILBERFORCE: . . . this case arises out of a "tax saving scheme" devised by a firm of insurance and investment brokers. They sent out to a number of persons thought likely to be interested, under the heading "Most confidential", details of what they called a "capital income plan". The general nature of this was to enable taxpayers paying income tax at a high marginal rate to turn some of this income into capital, while, conversely, enabling a non income-taxpayer (viz. a charity) to convert some capital into income. Operations of this general description are quite common, and legal; indeed many investors in annuities or in insurance policies do just this in the normal course of prudent investment. This particular operation is perhaps an extreme case.

The plan involved was explained by the brokers in great detail, and its intended accomplishment set out, with timetables in almost military precision. This (as I ventured to suggest in *Inland Revenue Commissioners v. Church Commissioners for England*[20]) entitles and requires us to look at the plan as a whole. It does not entitle us to disregard the legal form and the nature of the transactions carried out. It was not suggested that any part of the plan was a sham – indeed the special commissioners found to the contrary. It is entitled to a fair, if not particularly, benevolent analysis . . . **[5.6]**

C. A new approach?

W T Ramsay Ltd v IRC; Eilbeck v Rawling [1982] AC 300 (HL)

LORD WILBERFORCE: . . . The first of these appeals is an appeal by W.T. Ramsay Ltd., a farming company. In its accounting period ending May 31, 1973, it made a "chargeable gain" for the purposes of corporation tax by a sale-leaseback transaction. This gain it desired to counteract, so as to avoid the tax, by establishing an allowable loss. The method chosen was to purchase from a company specialising in such matters a ready-made scheme. The general nature of this was to create out of a neutral situation two assets one of which would decrease in value for the benefit of the other. The decreasing asset would be sold, so as to create the desired loss; the increasing asset would be sold, yielding a gain which it was hoped would be exempt from tax.

In the courts below, attention was concentrated upon the question whether the gain just referred to was in truth exempt from tax or not. The Court of Appeal,[21] reversing the decision of Goulding J.[22] decided that it was not. In this House, the Crown, while supporting this decision of the Court of Appeal, mounted a fundamental attack upon the whole of the scheme acquired and used by the appellant. It contended that it should simply be disregarded as artificial and fiscally ineffective.

Immediately after this appeal there was heard another taxpayer's appeal – *Eilbeck v. Rawling*. This involved a scheme of a different character altogether, but one also designed to create a loss allowable for purposes of capital gains tax, together with a non-taxable gain, by a scheme acquired for this purpose. Similarly, this case was decided, against the taxpayer, in the Court of Appeal[23] upon consideration of a particular aspect of the scheme:

20 [1977] A.C. 329.
21 [1979] 1 W.L.R. 974.
22 [1978] 1 W.L.R. 1313.
23 [1980] 2 All E.R. 12.

and similarly, the Crown in this House advanced a fundamental argument against the scheme as a whole.

I propose to consider first the fundamental issue, which raises arguments common to both cases. This is obviously of great importance both in principle and in scope . . .

I will first state the general features of the schemes which are relevant to the wider argument.

In each case, we have a taxpayer who has realised an ascertained and quantified gain: in *Ramsay* £187,977, in *Rawling* £355,094. He is then advised to consult specialists willing to provide, for a fee, a preconceived and ready made plan designed to produce an equivalent allowable loss. The taxpayer merely has to state the figure involved, *i.e.* the amount of the gain he desires to counteract, and the necessary particulars are inserted into the scheme.

The scheme consists, as do others which have come to the notice of the courts, of a number of steps to be carried out, documents to be executed, payments to be made, according to a timetable, in each case rapid: see the attractive description by Buckley L.J. in *Rawling*.[24] In each case the two assets appear, like "particles" in a gas chamber with opposite charges, one of which is used to create the loss, the other of which gives rise to an equivalent gain which prevents the taxpayer from supporting any real loss, and which gain is intended not to be taxable. Like the particles, these assets have a very short life. Having served their purpose they cancel each other out and disappear. At the end of the series of operations, the taxpayer's financial position is precisely as it was at the beginning, except that he has paid a fee, and certain expenses, to the promoter of the scheme.

There are other significant features which are normally found in schemes of this character. First, it is the clear and stated intention that once started each scheme shall proceed through the various steps to the end – they are not intended to be arrested half-way: see *Chinn v. Hochstrasser*.[25] This intention may be expressed either as a firm contractual obligation (it was so in *Rawling*) or as in *Ramsay* as an expectation without contractual force.

Secondly, although sums of money, sometimes considerable, are supposed to be involved in individual transactions, the taxpayer does not have to put his hand in his pocket: see *Inland Revenue Commissioners v. Plummer*[26] and *Chinn v. Hochstrasser*. The money is provided by means of a loan from a finance house which is firmly secured by a charge on any asset the taxpayer may appear to have, and which is automatically repaid at the end of the operation. In some cases one may doubt whether, in any real sense, any money existed at all. It seems very doubtful whether any real money was involved in *Rawling*: but facts as to this matter are for the commissioners to find. I will assume that in some sense money did pass as expressed in respect of each transaction in each of the instant cases. Finally, in each of the present cases it is candidly, if inevitably, admitted that the whole and only purpose of each scheme was the avoidance of tax.

In these circumstances, your Lordships are invited to take, with regard to schemes of the character I have described, what may appear to be a new approach. We are asked, in fact, to treat them as fiscally, a nullity, not producing either a gain or a loss. Mr. Potter Q.C. described this as revolutionary, so I think it opportune to restate some familiar principles and some of the leading decisions so as to show the position we are now in.

1 A subject is only to be taxed upon clear words, not upon "intendment" or upon the "equity" of an Act. Any taxing Act of Parliament is to be construed in accordance with this principle. What are "clear words" is to be ascertained upon normal principles: these do not confine the courts to literal interpretation. There may, indeed should, be considered the context and scheme of the relevant Act as a whole, and its purpose may, indeed should, be regarded: see *Inland Revenue Commissioners v. Wesleyan and General Assurance Society per* Lord Greene M.R.[27] and *Mangin v. Inland Revenue Commisioner per* Lord Donovan.[28] The relevant Act in these cases is the Finance Act

24 *Ibid.* at 16.
25 [1981] A.C. 533.
26 [1980] A.C. 896; [above, para **[5.6]**].
27 (1946) 30 T.C. 11 at 16.
28 [1971] A.C. 739 at 746.

1965, the purpose of which is to impose a tax on gains less allowable losses, arising from disposals.

2 A subject is entitled to arrange his affairs so as to reduce his liability to tax. The fact that the motive for a transaction may be to avoid tax does not invalidate it unless a particular enactment so provides. It must be considered according to its legal effect.

3 It is for the fact-finding commissioners to find whether a document, or a transaction, is genuine or a sham. In this context to say that a document or transaction is a "sham" means that while professing to be one thing, it is in fact something different. To say that a document or transaction is genuine, means that, in law, it is what it professes to be, and it does not mean anything more than that. I shall return to this point.

Each of these three principles would be fully respected by the decision we are invited to make. Something more must be said as to the next principle.

4 Given that a document or transaction is genuine, the court cannot go behind it to some supposed underlying substance. This is the well-known principle of *Inland Revenue Commissioners v. Duke of Westminster.*[29] This is a cardinal principle but it must not be overstated or overextended. While obliging the court to accept documents or transactions, found to be genuine, as such, it does not compel the court to look at a document or a transaction in blinkers, isolated from any context to which it properly belongs. If it can be seen that a document or transaction was intended to have effect as part of a nexus or series of transactions, or as an ingredient of a wider transaction intended as a whole, there is nothing in the doctrine to prevent it being so regarded: to do so is not to prefer form to substance, or substance to form. It is the task of the court to ascertain the legal nature of any transaction to which it is sought to attach a tax or a tax consequence and if that emerges from a series or combination of transactions, intended to operate as such, it is that series or combination which may be regarded. For this there is authority in the law relating to income tax and capital gains tax: see *Chinn v. Hochstrasser*[30] and *Inland Revenue Commissioners v. Plummer.*[31]

For the commissioners considering a particular case it is wrong, and an unnecessary self limitation, to regard themselves as precluded by their own finding that documents or transactions are not "shams," from considering what, as evidenced by the documents themselves or by the manifested intentions of the parties, the relevant transaction is. They are not, under the *Westminster* doctrine or any other authority, bound to consider individually each separate step in the composite transaction intended to be carried through as a whole. This is particularly the case where (as in *Rawling*) it is proved that there was an accepted obligation once a scheme is set in motion, to carry it through its successive steps. It may be so where (as in *Ramsay* or in *Black Nominees Ltd. v. Nicol*[32]) there is an expectation that it will be so carried through, and no likelihood in practice that it will not. In such cases (which may vary in emphasis) the commissioners should find the facts and then decide as a matter (reviewable) of law whether what is in issue is a composite transaction, or a number of independent transactions.

I will now refer to some recent cases which show the limitations of the *Westminster* doctrine and illustrate the present situation in the law.

1 *Floor v. Davis.*[33] The key transaction to this scheme was a sale of shares in a company called IDM to one company (FNW) and a resale by that company to a further company (KDI). The majority of the Court of Appeal thought it right to look at each of the sales separately and rejected an argument by the Crown that they could be considered as an integrated transaction. But Eveleigh L.J. upheld that argument. He held that the fact that each sale was genuine did not prevent him from regarding each as part of a whole, or oblige him to consider each step in isolation. Nor was he so prevented by *Inland Revenue Commissioners v. Duke of Westminster.*[34] Looking at the

29 [1936] A.C. 1; [above, para **[5.3]**].
30 [1981] A.C. 533.
31 [1980] A.C. 896; [above, para **[5.6]**].
32 (1975) 50 T.C. 229.
33 [1978] Ch. 295; [above, para **[5.4]**].
34 [1936] A.C. 1; [above, para **[5.3]**].

scheme as a whole, and finding that the taxpayer and his sons-in-law had complete control of the IDM shares until they reached KDI, he was entitled to find that there was a disposal to KDI. When the case reached this House it was decided on a limited argument, and the wider point was not considered. This same approach has commended itself to Templeman L.J. and has been expressed by him in impressive reasoning in the Court of Appeal's judgment in *Rawling*.[35] It will be seen from what follows that these judgments, and their emerging principle, commend themselves to me.

2 *Inland Revenue Commissioners v. Plummer*.[36] This was a pre-arranged scheme, claimed by the revenue to be "circular" – in the sense that its aim and effect was to pass a capital sum round through various hands back to its starting point. There was a finding by the special commissioners that the transaction was a bona fide commercial transaction, but in this House their Lordships agreed that it was legitimate to have regard to all the arrangements as a whole. The majority upheld the taxpayer's case on the ground that there was commercial reality in them: as I described them,[37] they amounted to "a covenant, for a capital sum, to make annual payments, coupled with security arrangements for the payments" and I attempted to analyse the nature of the bargain with its advantages and risks to either side.

The case is no authority that the court may not in other cases and with different findings of fact reach a conclusion that, viewed as a whole, a composite transaction may produce an effect which brings it within a fiscal provision.

3 *Chinn v. Hochstrasser*.[38] This again was a pre-arranged scheme, described by the special commissioners as a single scheme. There was no express finding that the parties concerned were obliged to carry through each successive step: but the commissioners found that there was never any possibility that the appellant taxpayers and another party would not proceed from one critical stage to another. I reached the conclusion, on this finding and on the documents, that the machinery, once started, would follow out its instructions without further initiative and the same point was made graphically by Lord Russell of Killowen.[39] This case shows, in my opinion, that although separate steps were "genuine" and had to be accepted under the *Westminster* doctrine, the court could, on the basis of the findings made and of its own analysis in law, consider the scheme as a whole and was not confined to a step by step examination.

To hold, in relation to such schemes as those with which we are concerned, that the court is not confined to a single step approach, is thus a logical development from existing authorities, and a generalisation of particular decisions.

Before I come to examination of the particular scheme in these cases, there is one argument of a general character which needs serious consideration. For the taxpayers it was said that to accept the revenue's wide contention involved a rejection of accepted and established canons and that, if so general an attack upon schemes for tax avoidance as the revenue suggests is to be validated, that is a matter for Parliament. The function of the courts is to apply strictly and correctly the legislation which Parliament has enacted: if the taxpayer escapes the charge, it is for Parliament, if it disapproves of the result, to close the gap. General principles against tax avoidance are, it was claimed, for Parliament to lay down.

I have a full respect for the principles which have been stated but I do not consider that they should exclude the approach for which the Crown contends. That does not introduce a new principle: it would be to apply to new and sophisticated legal devices the undoubted power and duty of the courts to determine their nature in law and to relate them to existing legislation. While the techniques of tax avoidance progress and are technically improved, the courts are not obliged to stand still. Such immobility must result either in loss of tax, to the prejudice of other taxpayers, or to a Parliamentary congestion

35 [1980] 2 All E.R. 12 at 21–23.
36 [1980] A.C. 896; [above, para **[5.6]**.
37 *Ibid.* at 909.
38 [1981] A.C. 533.
39 *Ibid.* at 550.

or (most likely) to both. To force the courts to adopt, in relation to closely integrated situations, a step by step, dissecting approach which the parties themselves may have negated, would be a denial rather than an affirmation of the true judicial process. In each case the facts must be established, and a legal analysis made: legislation cannot be required or even be desirable, to enable the courts to arrive at a conclusion which corresponds with the parties' own intentions.

The capital gains tax was created to operate in the real world, not that of make-belief. As I said in *Aberdeen Construction Group Ltd. v. Inland Revenue Commissioners*,[40] it is a tax on gains (or I might have added gains less losses), it is not a tax on arithmetical differences. To say that a loss (or gain) which appears to arise at one stage in an indivisible process, and which is intended to be and is cancelled out by a later stage, so that at the end of what was bought as and planned as, a single continuous operation, there is not such a loss (or gain) as the legislation is dealing with, is in my opinion well and indeed essentially within the judicial function.

We were referred, on this point, to a number of cases in the United States of America in which the courts have denied efficacy to schemes or transactions designed only to avoid tax and lacking otherwise in economic or commercial reality. I venture to quote two key passages, not as authority, but as examples, expressed in vigorous and apt language, of a process of thought which seem to me not inappropriate for the courts in this country to follow. In *Knetsch v. United States*[41] the Supreme Court found that a transaction was a sham because it –

> 'did not appreciably affect the [taxpayer's] beneficial interest . . . there was nothing of substance to be realised by [him] from his transaction beyond a tax deduction . . . the difference between the two sums was in reality the fee for providing the façade of "loans".'

In *Gilbert v. Commissioner of Internal Revenue*[42] Judge Learned Hand (dissenting on the facts) said:

> 'The Income Tax Act imposes liability upon the taxpayers based upon their financial transaction . . . If, however, the taxpayer enters into a transaction that does not appreciably affect his beneficial interest except to reduce his tax, the law will disregard it.'

It is probable that the United States courts do not draw the line precisely where we with our different system, allowing less legislative power to the courts than they claim to exercise, would draw it, but the decisions do at least confirm me in the belief that it would be an excess of judicial abstinence to withdraw from the field now before us . . . **[5.7]**

IRC v Burmah Oil Co Ltd [1982] STC 30 (HL)

LORD DIPLOCK: . . . It would be disingenuous to suggest, and dangerous on the part of those who advise on elaborate tax-avoidance schemes to assume, that *Ramsay's* case did not mark a significant change in the approach adopted by this House in its judicial role to a pre-ordained series of transactions (whether or not they include the achievement of a legitimate commercial end) into which there are inserted steps that have no commercial purpose apart from the avoidance of a liability to tax which in the absence of those particular steps would have been payable. The difference is in approach. It does not necessitate the over-ruling of any earlier decisions of this House; but it does involve recognising that Lord Tomlin's oft-quoted dictum in *IRC v. Duke of Westminster*,[43] 'Every man is entitled if he can to order his affairs so as that the tax attaching under the appropriate Acts is less than it otherwise would be', tells us little or nothing as to what methods of

40 [1978] A.C. 885; [below, para **[20.50]**].
41 (1960) 364 US 361.
42 (1957) 248 F 2d 399.
43 ([1936] AC 1 at 19; [above, para **[5.3]**].

ordering one's affairs will be recognised by the courts as effective to lessen the tax that would attach to them if business transactions were conducted in a straight-forward way. The *Duke of Westminster*'s case was about a simple transaction entered into between two real persons each with a mind of his own, the Duke and his gardener, even though in the nineteen-thirties and at a time of high unemployment there might be reason to expect that the mind of the gardener would manifest some degree of subservience to that of the Duke. The kinds of tax-avoidance schemes that have occupied the attention of the courts in recent years, however, involve inter-connected transactions between artificial persons, limited companies, without minds of their own but directed by a single master-mind. In *Ramsay* the master-mind was the deviser and vendor of the tax-avoidance scheme; in the instant case it was Burmah, the parent company of the wholly-owned subsidiary companies between which the pre-ordained series of transactions took place. Burmah was acting in accordance with advice obtained from advisers of the highest integrity who, in reliance on Lord Tomlin's dictum, did not foresee the difference in approach to tax avoidance schemes involving inter-company transactions that would have been adopted by this House by the time some nine years later when the particular scheme that they had devised in 1972 was eventually to come before it . . .

LORD SCARMAN: . . . it is of the utmost importance that the business community (and others, including their advisers) should appreciate, as my noble and learned friend Lord Diplock has emphasised, that Ramsay's case marks 'a significant change in the approach adopted by this House in its judicial role' towards tax avoidance schemes. **[5.8]**

Furniss (Inspector of Taxes) v Dawson [1984] AC 474 (HL)

The taxpayers wanted to sell some shares to Wood Bastow Holdings Ltd for £152,000. Such a sale would have given rise to a liability to capital gains tax.

A plan was devised by virtue of which the taxpayers sought, *inter alia*, to defer liability to capital gains tax. Under the plan, the taxpayers transferred the shares to a newly incorporated company, Greenjacket Investments Ltd, in exchange for the issue to the taxpayers of shares in that company. Greenjacket Investments Ltd then sold the shares it had acquired from the taxpayers to Wood Bastow Holdings Ltd for £152,000.

The Crown argued that there was a disposal for capital gains tax purposes of the shares by the taxpayers to Wood Bastow Holdings Ltd.

LORD BRIGHTMAN: . . . Following the decision of this House in *Ramsay*, the revenue early in July 1981 gave notice to the respondents under R.S.S., Ord.91, r.4 that it would if necessary contend that the Dawsons had disposed of their shares in the operating companies to Wood Bastow and were liable to capital gains tax accordingly. The appeal came before Vinelott J. in mid-July and judgment was reserved. However, before judgment was delivered *Inland Revenue Commissioners v. Burmah Oil Co. Ltd.*[44] was argued and decided in this House. Vinelott J. therefore deferred giving judgment until the parties had had an opportunity to consider that case.

[*After referring to passages from the judgments of Lord Diplock and Lord Scarman in Burmah, his Lordship continued*]

That then was the state of judicial precedent when Vinelott J. came to give judgment in the instant case.[45] He said that the question which he had to decide was how far the new approach justified or required the proposition for which the Crown contended, that is to say, the proposition set out in the Order 91 notice. The gist of his long and careful

44 [1982] S.T.C. 30; [above, para **[5.8]**].
45 [1982] S.T.C. 267.

judgment is that the principle does not apply, and a transaction cannot be disregarded and treated as fiscally a nullity, if it has "enduring legal consequences," a phrase which he repeated several times in his judgment. He identified "the enduring legal consequences" in the instant case as (i) the fact that Greenjacket owned beneficially the proceeds of sale of the shares in the operating companies, which were brought into Greenjacket's accounts and upon the income of which Greenjacket was liable to tax, and (ii) the fact that Wood Bastow's rights under the second sale agreement were rights against Greenjacket, whereas it would have had no such rights if the sale had been by the Dawsons to Wood Bastow. The effect of his judgment was to change Lord Diplock's formulation from "a pre-ordinated series of transactions ... into which there are inserted steps that have no commercial purpose apart from the avoidance of a liability to tax" to "a pre-ordained series of transactions ... into which there are inserted steps that have no enduring legal consequences." That would confine the *Ramsay* principle to so-called self-cancelling transactions.

The learned judge's re-statement of Lord Diplock's formulation enabled him, as he thought, to escape from the difficulty imposed by this House's approval by the dissenting judgment in *Floor v. Davis*.[46] FNW was placed in liquidation and its assets distributed; consequently its existence had no enduring effect on the rights and obligations of the parties after the completion of the scheme.

It is difficult to escape the impression that the High Court and the Court of Appeal were determined to confine the *Ramsay* principle to the sort of self-cancelling arrangement which existed in that case, and to resist any inroad into the principles of *Inland Revenue Commissioners v. Duke of Westminster*.[47]

My Lords, in my opinion the rationale of the new approach is this. In a pre-planned tax-saving scheme, no distinction is to be drawn for fiscal purposes, because none exists in reality, between (i) a series of steps which are followed through by virtue of any arrangement which falls short of a binding contract, and (ii) a like series of steps which are followed through because the participants are contractually bound to take each step seriatim. In a contractual case the fiscal consequences will naturally fall to be assessed in the light of the contractually agreed results. For example, equitable interests may pass when the contract for sale is signed. In many cases equity will regard that as done which is contracted to be done. *Ramsay* says that the fiscal result is to be no different if the several steps are pre-ordained rather than pre-contracted. For example, in the instant case tax will, on the *Ramsay* principle, fall to be assessed on the basis that there was a tripartite contract between the Dawsons, Greenjacket and Wood Bastow under which the Dawsons contracted to transfer their shares in the operating companies to Greenjacket in return for allotment of shares in Greenjacket, and under which Greenjacket simultaneously contracted to transfer the same shares to Wood Bastow for a sum in cash. Under such a tripartite contract the Dawsons would clearly have disposed of the shares in the operating companies in favour of Wood Bastow in consideration of a sum of money paid by Wood Bastow with the concurrence of the Dawsons to Greenjacket. Tax would be assessed, and the base value of the Greenjacket shares calculated, accordingly. *Ramsay* says that this fiscal result cannot be avoided because the pre-ordained series of steps are to be found in an informal arrangement instead of in a binding contract. The day is not saved for the taxpayer because the arrangement is unsigned or contains the words "this is not a binding contract."

The formulation by Lord Diplock in *Inland Revenue Commissioners v. Burmah Oil Co. Ltd.*[48] expresses the limitations of the *Ramsay* principle. First, there must be a pre-ordained series of transactions; or, if one likes, one single composite transaction. This composite transaction may or may not include the achievement of a legitimate commercial, (*i.e.* business) end. The composite transaction does, in the instant case; it achieved a sale of the shares in the operating companies by the Dawsons to Wood Bastow. It did not in *Ramsay*. Secondly, there must be steps inserted which have no commercial (business) *purpose* apart from the avoidance of a liability to tax – not "no business *effect*." If those two ingredients

46 [1978] Ch. 295; [above, para **[5.4]**].
47 [1936] A.C. 1 [above, para **[5.3]**].
48 [1982] S.T.C. 30 at 33; [above, para **[5.8]**].

exist, the inserted steps are to be disregarded for fiscal purposes. The court must then look at the end result. Precisely how the end result will be taxed will depend on the terms of the taxing statute sought to be applied.

In the instant case the inserted step was the introduction of Greenjacket as a buyer from the Dawsons and as a seller to Wood Bastow. That inserted step had no business purpose apart from the deferment of tax, although it had a business effect. If the sale had taken place in 1964 before capital gains tax was introduced, there would have been no Greenjacket . . .

LORD BRIDGE OF HARWICH: . . . When one moves, however, from a single transaction to a series of interdependent transactions designed to produce a given result, it is, in my opinion, perfectly legitimate to draw a distinction between the substance and the form of the composite transaction without in any way suggesting that any of the single transactions which make up the whole are other than genuine. This has been the approach of the United States federal courts enabling them to develop a doctrine whereby the tax consequences of the composite transaction are dependent on its substance, not its form. I shall not attempt to review the American authorities, nor do I propose a wholesale importation of the American doctrine in all its ramifications into English law. But I do suggest that the distinction between form and substance is one which can usefully be drawn in determining the tax consequences of composite transactions . . .

I shall attempt no exhaustive exposition of all the criteria by which, for the purpose I suggest, form and substance are to be distinguished. Once a basic doctrine of form and substance is accepted, the drawing of precise boundaries will need to be worked out on a case by case basis. But I venture to point out what a simple and readily applicable test a distinction between form and substance would have provided to arrive at the conclusions already reached in some of the cases of composite transactions decided by your Lordships' House. It would need no more than a cursory exposition of the avoidance schemes in *Ramsay* and *Eilbeck v. Rawling*[49] to lead any intelligent layman to the conclusion that neither scheme was designed to achieve any substantial effect in the real world and that the elaborate steps designed to manufacture a tax deductible loss in each case were purely formal in character. If special or general commissioners had been directed to approach either case on the basis that the tax consequences of the interlocking, interdependent and predetermined transactions were to be judged by reference to the substance, not the form, of the composite transaction, I cannot think they would have had any difficulty in arriving at the right answer . . . **[5.9]**

For the applicability of the *Ramsay* approach to taxes concerned other than with the taxation of capital gains, see, for example, *Cairns v MacDiarmid* [1983] STC 178 (income tax), *Ingram v IRC* [1986] 2 WLR 598 (stamp duty), *IRC v Bowater Property Developments Ltd* [1986] STC 476 (development land tax), *C & E Commrs v Faith Construction Ltd* [1988] 3 WLR 500 (value added tax), and *Fitzwilliam (Countess) v IRC* [1993] STC 502 (inheritance tax). **[5.10]**

IRC v McGuckian [1997] STC 908 (HL)

For an outline of the facts, see above, para **[3.31]**.

LORD STEYN: . . . While Lord Tomlin's observations in the *Duke of Westminster* case still point to a material consideration, namely the general liberty of the citizen to arrange his financial affairs as he thinks fit, they have ceased to be canonical as to the consequence of a tax avoidance scheme. Indeed, as Lord Diplock observed, Lord Tomlin's observations tell us little or nothing as to what method of ordering one's affairs will be recognised by the courts as effective to lessen the tax that would otherwise be payable (see *IRC v Burmah Oil Co Ltd* [1982] STC 30 at 32–33).

49 [1982] A.C. 300; [above, para **[5.7]**].

The new *Ramsay* principle was not invented on a juristic basis independent of statute. That would have been indefensible since a court has no power to amend a tax statute. The principle was developed as a matter of statutory construction. That was made clear by Lord Wilberforce in the *Ramsay* case and is also made clear in subsequent decisions in this line of authority (see the review in the dissenting speech of Lord Goff in *Craven (Inspector of Taxes) v White* [1988] STC 476 at 511, [1989] AC 398 at 520–521). The new development was not based on a linguistic analysis of the meaning of particular words in a statute. It was founded on a broad purposive interpretation, giving effect to the intention of Parliament. The principle enunciated in the *Ramsay* case was therefore based on an orthodox form of statutory interpretation. And in asserting the power to examine the substance of a composite transaction the House of Lords was simply rejecting formalism in fiscal matters and choosing a more realistic legal analysis. Given the reasoning underlying the new approach it is wrong to regard the decision of the House of Lords in *Ramsay* as necessarily marking the limit of the law on tax avoidance schemes . . .

LORD COOKE OF THORNDON: . . . The principle which your Lordships have been developing in *WT Ramsay Ltd v IRC* [1981] STC 174, [1982] AC 300, *IRC v Burmah Oil Co Ltd* [1982] STC 30, and *Furniss (Inspector of Taxes) v Dawson* [1984] STC 153, [1984] AC 474, is not uncommonly seen as special to the construction of taxing Acts. Perhaps, more helpfully, however, it may be recognised as an application to taxing Acts of the general approach to statutory interpretation whereby, in determining the natural meaning of particular expressions in their context, weight is given to the purpose and spirit of the legislation. So, in the *Ramsay* case, Lord Wilberforce said ([1981] STC 174 at 182, [1982] AC 300 at 326) that it was well established and indeed essentially within the judicial function to determine whether there was such a loss (or gain) as the legislation was dealing with. In the *Burmah* case ([1982] STC 30 at 38), Lord Fraser of Tullybelton echoed those words in saying that there was no real loss and no loss in the sense contemplated by the legislation. In the *Furniss* case Lord Brightman said ([1984] STC 153 at 166, [1984] AC 474, 527) that in conditions which he defined the court must look at the end result; precisely how it would be taxed depended on the terms of the taxing statute . . .

In the *Furniss* case ([1984] STC 153 at 156, [1984] AC 474 at 527), Lord Brightman spoke of certain limitations (a preordained series of transactions including steps with no commercial purpose apart from the avoidance of a liability to tax). The present case does fall within those limitations, but it may be as well to add that, if the ultimate question is always the true bearing of a particular taxing provision on a particular set of facts, the limitations cannot be universals. Always one must go back to the discernible intent of the taxing Act. I suspect that advisers of those bent on tax avoidance, which in the end tends to involve an attempt to cast on other taxpayers more than their fair share of sustaining the national tax base, do not always pay sufficient heed to the themes of the speeches in the *Furniss* case, especially those of Lord Scarman, Lord Roskill and Lord Bridge of Harwich, to the effect that the journey's end may not yet have been found. **[5.11]**

D. *Reassessment*

Macniven (Inspector of Taxes) v Westmoreland Investments Ltd [2001] 2 WLR 377 (HL)

LORD NICHOLLS OF BIRKENHEAD: . . .

1 On this appeal the Inland Revenue Commissioners pray in aid what is loosely called the *Ramsay* principle. This is a reference to the decision in *WT Ramsay Ltd v Inland Revenue Comrs* [1982] AC 300. So it is necessary first to remind oneself what the House decided in that case. An initial point to note is that the very phrase "the *Ramsay* principle" is potentially misleading. In the *Ramsay* case the House did not enunciate any new legal principle. What the House did was to highlight that, confronted with the new and sophisticated tax avoidance devices, the courts' duty is to determine the legal

nature of the transactions in question and then relate them to the fiscal legislation: see Lord Wilberforce, at p 326.

2 The *Ramsay* case brought out three points in particular. First, when it is sought to attach a tax consequence to a transaction, the task of the courts is to ascertain the legal nature of the transaction. If that emerges from a series or combination of transactions, intended to operate as such, it is that series or combination which may be regarded. Courts are entitled to look at a pre-arranged tax avoidance scheme as a whole. It matters not whether the parties' intention to proceed with a scheme through all its stages takes the form of a contractual obligation or is expressed only as an expectation without a contractual force.

3 This development had already been foreshadowed in the dissenting judgment of Eveleigh LJ in *Floor v Davis* [1978] Ch 295 and in decisions of the House in *Inland Revenue Comrs v Plummer* [1980] AC 896 and *Chinn v Hochstrasser* [1981] AC 533. In *Furniss v Dawson* [1984] AC 474, 526, Lord Brightman set out his understanding of the rationale of this approach in these terms:

> "In a pre-planned tax-saving scheme, no distinction is to be drawn for fiscal purposes, because none exists in reality, between (i) a series of steps which are followed through by virtue of an arrangement which falls short of a binding contract, and (ii) a like series of steps which are followed through because the participants are contractually bound to take each step seriatim. In a contractual case the fiscal consequences will naturally fall to be assessed in the light of the contractually agreed results . . . *Ramsay* says that the fiscal result is to be no different if the several steps are pre-ordained rather than pre-contracted."

4 Second, this is not to treat a transaction, or any step in a transaction as though it were a "sham", meaning thereby, that it was intended to give the appearance of having a legal effect different from the actual legal effect intended by the parties: see the classic definition of Diplock LJ in *Snook v London and West Riding Investments Ltd* [1967] 2 QB 786, 802.[50] Nor is this to go behind a transaction for some supposed underlying substance. What this does is to enable the court to look at a document or transaction in the context to which it properly belongs.

5 Third, having identified the legal nature of the transaction, the courts must then relate this to the language of the statute. For instance, if the scheme has the apparently magical result of creating a loss without the taxpayer suffering any financial detriment, is this artificial loss a loss *within the meaning of the relevant statutory provision?* Thus, in *Ramsay* the taxpayer company sought to create an allowable loss to offset against a chargeable gain it had made on a sale-leaseback transaction. It sought to do so without suffering any financial detriment, by embarking on and carrying through a scheme which created both a loss which was allowable for tax purposes and a matching gain which was not chargeable. In rejecting the efficacy of this contrived "loss-creating" scheme, Lord Wilberforce [1982] AC 300, 326, observed that a loss which comes and goes as part of a pre-planned, single continuous operation "is not such a loss (or gain) as the legislation is dealing with". In *Inland Revenue Comrs v Burmah Oil Co Ltd* [1982] STC 30, 37 Lord Fraser of Tullybelton described this passage as the ratio of the decision in the *Ramsay* case.

6 As noted by Lord Steyn in *Inland Revenue Comrs v McGuckian* [1997] WLR 991, 1000, this is an exemplification of the established purposive approach to the interpretation of statutes. When searching for the meaning with which Parliament has used the statutory language in question, courts have regard to the underlying purpose that the statutory language is seeking to achieve. Likewise, Lord Cooke of Thorndon regarded the *Ramsay* case as an application to Taxing Acts of the general approach to statutory interpretation whereby, in determining the natural meaning of particular expressions in their context, weight is given to the purpose and spirit of the legislation: see [1997] 1 WLR 991, 1005.

50 [See above, n 12. See also M Gammie 'Sham and Reality: The Taxation of Composite Transactions' [2006] BTR 294, in which it is considered whether the *Ramsay* principle might be 'better seen as an evolution of "sham" designed to meet the particular issues of that concept in the tax avoidance context'.]

7 The *Ramsay* principle or, as I prefer to say, the *Ramsay* approach to ascertaining the legal nature of the transactions and to interpreting taxing statutes, has been the subject of observations in several later decisions. These observations should be read in the context of the particular statutory provisions and sets of facts under consideration. In particular, they cannot be understood as laying down factual pre-requisites which must exist before the court may apply the purposive, *Ramsay* approach to the interpretation of a taxing statute. That would be to misunderstand the nature of the decision in the *Ramsay* case. Failure to recognise this can all too easily lead into error. In particular, the much-quoted observation of Lord Brightman in *Furniss v Dawson* [1984] AC 474, 527 seems to have suffered in this way. Lord Brightman described, as the "limitations of the *Ramsay* principle", that there must be a pre-ordained series of transactions, or a single composite transaction, containing steps inserted which have no business purpose apart from the avoidance of a liability to tax. Where those two ingredients exist, the inserted steps are to be disregarded for fiscal purposes.

8 My Lords, I readily accept that the factual situation described by Lord Brightman is one where, typically, the *Ramsay* approach will be a valuable aid. In such a situation, when ascertaining the legal nature of the transaction and then relating this to the statute, application of the *Ramsay* approach may well have the effect stated by Lord Brightman. But, as I am sure Lord Brightman would be the first to acknowledge, the *Ramsay* approach is no more than a useful aid. This is not an area for absolutes. The paramount question always is one of interpretation of the particular statutory provisions and its application to the facts of the case. Further, as I have sought to explain, the *Ramsay* case did not introduce a new legal principle. It would be wrong, therefore, to set bounds to the circumstances in which the *Ramsay* approach may be appropriate and helpful. The need to consider a document or transaction in its proper context, and the need to adopt a purposive approach when construing taxation legislation, are principles of general application. Where this leads depends upon the particular set of facts and the particular statute. I have already mentioned where this led in the *Ramsay* case. In *Furniss v Dawson* [1984] AC 474 it led to the conclusion that, within the meaning of the Finance Act 1965, the disposal of shares was in favour of Wood Bastow and not, as the taxpayer contended, in favour of Greenjacket ...

LORD HOFFMANN:...

Ramsay: a principle of construction?

28 Everyone agrees that *Ramsay* is a principle of construction. The House of Lords said so in *Inland Revenue Comrs v McGuckian* [1997] 1 WLR 991. But what is that principle? Mr McCall formulated it as follows in his printed case.

> "When a court is asked (i) to apply a statutory provision on which a taxpayer relies for the sake of establishing some tax advantage (ii) in circumstances where the transaction said to give rise to the tax advantage is, or forms part of, some pre-ordained, circular, self-cancelling transaction (iii) which transaction though accepted as perfectly genuine (ie not impeached as a sham) was undertaken for no commercial purpose other than the obtaining of the tax advantage in question then (unless there is something in the statutory provisions concerned to indicate that this rule should not be applied) there is a rule of construction that the condition laid down in the statute for the obtaining of the tax advantage has not been satisfied."

29 My Lords, I am bound to say that this does not look to me like a principle of construction at all. There is ultimately only one principle of construction, namely to ascertain what Parliament meant by using the language of the statute. All other "principles of construction" can be no more than guides which past judges have put forward, some more helpful or insightful than others, to assist in the task of interpretation. But Mr McCall's formulation looks like an overriding legal principle, superimposed upon the whole of revenue law without regard to the language or purpose of any particular provision, save for the possibility of rebuttal by language which can be brought within his final parenthesis. This cannot be called a principle of construction except in the sense of some paramount provision subject to which everything else must be read, like section 2(2) of the European Communities Act 1972. But the courts have no constitutional

authority to impose such an overlay upon the tax legislation and, as I hope to demonstrate, they have not attempted to do so.

Ramsay: the fountainhead

30 As is well known, the *Ramsay* case [1982] AC 300 was concerned with a tax avoidance scheme designed to manufacture a capital loss to set off against a capital gain. The question before the House was whether a transaction by which the taxpayer company acquired certain shares for £185,034 and almost immediately sold them for £9,387, gave rise to "loss accruing on a disposal of an asset" within the meaning of section 23 (1) of the Finance Act 1965. Both the acquisitions and sale of the shares formed part of a pre-planned series of transactions by which the alleged loss was exactly balanced by a gain which was alleged to fall within an exemption from the charge. The aggregate effect was that the taxpayer suffered no loss except the payment of a fee to the promoters of the scheme.

31 It was not disputed that the transaction included a genuine purchase of the shares for £185,034 and a genuine sale of the same shares for £9,387. The taxpayer said that was the end of the matter. To look at the transaction as a whole would be to commit the heresy condemned by Lord Tomlin in *Inland Revenue Comrs v Duke of Westminster* [1936] AC 1, 19 as the "doctrine that the court may ignore the legal position and regard what is called 'the substance of the matter'." At first, the revenue agreed. Its attack on the scheme concentrated on whether the counterbalancing gain really was outside the charge to tax. In the House of Lords, however, Mr Millett QC argued that no loss within the meaning of the Act had accrued at all. The House accepted the argument. Lord Wilberforce said, at p 323, that while Lord Tomlin's statement was a "cardinal principle", it did not require a court to "look at a document or a transaction in blinkers". The capital gains tax was, see p 326:

> "a tax on gains (or I might have added gains less losses), it is not a tax on arithmetical differences. To say that a loss (or gain) which appears to arise at one stage in an indivisible process, and which is intended to be and is cancelled out by a later stage, so that at the end of what was brought as, and planned as, a single continuous operation, *there is not such a loss (or gain) as the legislation is dealing with*, is in my opinion well and essentially within the judicial function." (My emphasis.)

32 My Lords, it is worth pausing at this point to examine the characteristically compressed reasoning in a little more detail. A loss which arises at one stage of an indivisible process and cancelled out at a later stage of the same process is "not such a loss as the legislation is dealing with". The tax was not imposed "on arithmetical differences". In that case, what kind of loss was the legislation dealing with? The contrast being made throughout Lord Wilberforce's speech is between juristic or arithmetical realities on the one hand and commercial realities on the other. He is construing the words "disposal" and "loss" to refer to commercial concepts which are not necessarily confined by the categories of juristic analysis. In the *Ramsay* case [1982] AC 300, a director, or an accountant concerned to present a true and fair view of the taxpayer's dealings, would not have said that the company had entered into a transaction giving rise to a loss which happened to have been offset by a corresponding gain. There had never been any commercial possibility that the transactions would not have cancelled each other out. Therefore, notwithstanding the juristic independence of each of the stages of the circular transaction, the commercial view would have been to lump them all together, as the parties themselves intended, and describe them as a composite transaction which had no financial consequences. The innovation in the *Ramsay* case was to give the statutory concepts of "disposal" and "loss" a commercial meaning. The new principle of construction was a recognition that the statutory language was intended to refer to commercial concepts, so that in the case of a concept such as a "disposal", the court was required to take a view of the facts which transcended the juristic individuality of the various parts of a preplanned series of transactions.

Commercial concepts in tax legislation

33 There is nothing new about terms used in tax legislation (or, for that matter, any legislation) being construed as referring to business or commercial concepts which may

not be capable of being held within the confines of purely juristic analysis. A good example is the term "profits or gains of the year of assessment" which forms the basis of the charge to tax under Case I of Schedule D: see section 60 of the Income and Corporation Taxes Act 1988. In *Sun Insurance Office v Clark* [1912] AC 443, 455, Viscount Haldane said: "It is plain that the question of what is or is not profit or gain must primarily be one of fact, and of fact to be ascertained by the tests applied in ordinary business."

34 It is thus the statute itself which applies the tests of ordinary business. And for present purposes, the significant feature of applying a test of ordinary business is that it may require an aggregation of transactions which transcends their juristic individuality . . .

35 My Lords, it seems to me that what Lord Wilberforce was doing in the *Ramsay* case [1982] AC 300 was no more (but certainly no less) than to treat the statutory words "loss" and "disposal" as referring to commercial concepts to which a juristic analysis of the transaction, treating each step as autonomous and independent, might not be determinative. What was fresh and new about *Ramsay* was the realisation that such an approach need not be confined to well recognised accounting concepts such as profit and loss but could be the appropriate construction of other taxation concepts as well.

The American doctrine

36 Lord Wilberforce, while cautioning against a facile transposition of American decisions on different statutes, approved the approach of Judge Learned Hand in one of his many judgments dealing with tax avoidance schemes: *Gilbert v Comr of Internal Revenue* (1957) 248 F 2d 399.[51] Perhaps, the seminal judgment was in *Helverling v Gregory* (1934) 69 F 2d 809, affirmed (1935) 293 US 465, which concerned a scheme of great simplicity. The taxpayer was a stockholder in a corporation which held some shares which she wished to realise without paying tax on the gains. Instead of having the corporation sell the shares directly to the buyer, she caused it to incorporate a subsidiary and exchange the shares for an allotment of shares in the subsidiary. The subsidiary was put into liquidation and distributed the shares to the stockholder as a dividend. She then sold them to the buyer. She claimed that the exchange of shares fell within the tax exemption for "reorganisation" of capital. On the other hand, the exchange was real enough to constitute a realisation of the gain, so that no further gain was realised on the distribution to her. In the Court of Appeals (Second Circuit) Judge Learned Hand said, at p 811, that the transfer to the subsidiary did not fall within the terms of the statutory exemption:

> "we cannot treat as inoperative the transfer . . . shares by [A] [or] the issues of shares by [B] of its own shares . . . [B] had a juristic personality . . . All these steps were real, and *their only defect was that they were not what the statute means . . .*" (My emphasis.)

37 What, in that case, did the statute mean? The Supreme Court of the United States affirmed the decision in a single judgment delivered by Sutherland J "Reorganisation", he said, meant a reorganisation of the business of a corporation, having some business purpose. An exemption from tax could not be construed as applicable to a transaction with no business purpose except to obtain the exemption from tax.

The Duke of Westminster's case

38 In the *Ramsay* case [1982] AC 300 both Lord Wilberforce and Lord Fraser of Tullybelton, who gave the other principal speech, were careful to stress that the House was not departing from the principle in the *Duke of Westminster's* case [1936] AC 1. There has nevertheless been a good deal of discussion about how the two cases are to be reconciled. How, if the various juristically discrete acquisitions and disposals which made up the scheme were genuine, could the House collapse them into a composite self-cancelling transaction without being guilty of ignoring the legal position and looking at the substance of the matter?

39 My Lords, I venture to suggest that some of the difficulty which may have been felt in reconciling the *Ramsay* case with the *Duke of Westminster's* case arises out of an ambiguity

51 [See above, para **[5.7]**.]

in Lord Tomlin's statement that the courts cannot ignore "the legal position" and have regard to "the substance of the matter". If "the legal position" is that the tax is imposed by reference to a legally defined concept, such as stamp duty payable on a document which constitutes a conveyance on sale, the court cannot tax a transaction which uses no such document on the ground that it achieves the same economic effect. On the other hand, if the legal position is that tax is imposed by reference to a commercial concept, then to have regard to the business "substance" of the matter is not to ignore the legal position but to give effect to it.

The real world

40 The speeches in the *Ramsay* case [1982] AC 300 and subsequent cases contain numerous references to the "real" nature of the transaction and to what happens in "the real world". These expressions are illuminating in their context, but you have to be careful about the sense in which they are being used. Otherwise you land in all kinds of unnecessary philosophical difficulties about the nature of reality and, in particular, about how a transaction can be said not to be a "sham" and yet be "disregarded" for the purpose of deciding what happened in "the real world". The point to hold on to is that something may be real for one purpose but not for another. When people speak of something being a "real" something, they mean that it falls within some concept which they have in mind, by contrast with something else which might have been thought to do so, but does not. When an economist says that real incomes have fallen, he is not intending to contrast real incomes with imaginary incomes. The contrast is specifically between incomes which have been adjusted for inflation and those which have not. In order to know what he means by "real", one must first identify the concept (inflation adjustment) by reference to which he is using the word.

41 Thus in saying that the transactions in the *Ramsay* case were not sham transactions, one is accepting the juristic categorisation of the transactions as individual and discrete and saying that each of them involved no pretence. They were intended to do precisely what they purported to do. They had a legal reality. But in saying that they did not constitute a "real" disposal giving rise to a "real" loss, one is rejecting the juristic categorisation as not being necessarily determinative for the purposes of the statutory concepts of "disposal" and "loss" as properly interpreted. The contrast here is with a commercial meaning of these concepts. And in saying that the income tax legislation was intended to operate "in the real world", one is again referring to the commercial context which should influence the construction of the concepts used by Parliament.

The Burmah case

42 There is no doubt that the *Ramsay* case [1982] AC 300 was widely regarded as some form of judicial legislation and the concerns of taxpayers about its true scope of and its relationship with the *Duke of Westminster's* case [1936] AC 1 were not set at rest by what some regarded as the proclamation of a revolutionary credo by Lord Diplock in *Inland Revenue Comrs v Burmah Oil Co Ltd* [1982] STC 30, 32–33 . . .

[*His Lordship cited Lord Diplock's statement about the judicial approach to tax avoidance after the decision in Ramsay (see above,* para **[5.8]**) *and continued*]

43 The *Burmah* case also concerned the question of whether the company has suffered a loss for the purposes of capital gains tax. As in the *Ramsay* case, it had produced a loss by a circular series of transactions which had no business purpose. A subsidiary owed it a substantial sum which it could not repay. As a bad debt on capital account, this would not have been an allowable loss. Burmah therefore invested the same amount in shares in the subsidiary, which used the money to repay the debt and then went into liquidation. Burmah recovered nothing on its share investment and claimed that it had thereby suffered a loss. The House of Lords held that this was not a loss caused by a disposal within the meaning of the Act. The transaction left Burmah no worse off than it had been before and merely purported to convert a bad debt into an allowable loss.

44 My Lords, in retrospect the *Burmah* case is an entirely straightforward application of the construction which the *Ramsay* case gave to the concept of a disposal giving rise to a loss in the capital gains tax legislation, namely that it meant a loss in commercial terms and

not a series of preplanned transactions which had no business purpose. From this construction it followed that, as Lord Diplock said, the House would "ignore the intermediate circular book entries and ... look at the end result". Lord Diplock would have been the first to acknowledge that his remarks should be read in context. To "ignore" the intermediate stages of the transaction and look at the end result in something which follows logically from the decision to construe "disposal" and "loss" in a commercial sense which transcends the individuality of the "book entries". It is that decision, to give the statutory language such a construction, which I would regard as "the *Ramsay* principle". But I think that there may have been a tendency to construe Lord Diplock's statement of the consequences of applying the *Ramsay* principle to the particular provisions with which the House was concerned as if it were itself a general principle, applicable to all tax legislation. Of course such a construction could also be applied to other provisions of the taxing Acts, but this would depend upon their language and purpose. At any rate, the generalising tendency which I have described seems to be the most likely explanation of the proposition which Mr McCall has claimed to be the *Ramsay* principle in this appeal.

Furniss v Dawson

45 My Lords, in *Furniss v Dawson* [1984] AC 474 the *Ramsay* construction, which in the *Ramsay* case itself and the *Burmah* case had been used to interpret the concept of a disposal giving rise to a loss, was deployed for a different purpose. The difference is occasionally described by saying that whereas *Ramsay* was a circular transaction, *Furniss* was a linear transaction. The difference can conveniently be encapsulated in these metaphors, but I think it is more illuminating to concentrate on the question which the legislation required the House to answer ...

46 ... while the question in the *Ramsay* case [1982] AC 300 had been whether there was a disposal giving rise to a loss, the question in the *Furniss* case was whether the disposal had been to one person rather than another. But the House decided that the *Ramsay* construction, involving as I have said, a commercial characterisation of the relevant concept, could be equally applied to the latter question. Greenjacket was merely an artificially introduced intermediate party which was never intended to own the shares for more than an instant. Commercially, therefore, the transaction was a transfer by the Dawsons to Wood Bastow in exchange for a payment to Greenjacket. In answering the statutory question: "To whom was the disposal made?" the fact that the shares were routed through Greenjacket was irrelevant.

47 The consequence of adopting this construction was spelled out by Lord Brightman [1984] AC 474, 527 in a passage which paraphrased what Lord Diplock had said in the *Burmah* case [1982] STC 30 and has since been quoted many times. He stated the conditions under which the commercial nature of the transaction as a whole would transcend the juristic individuality of its parts:

> "First, there must be a pre-ordained series of transactions; or, if one likes, one single composite transaction. This composite transaction may or may not include the achievement of a legitimate commercial (ie business) end. The composite transaction does, in the instant case; it achieved a sale of the shares in the operating companies by the Dawsons to Wood Bastow. It did not in *Ramsay*. Secondly, there must be steps inserted which have no commercial (business) *purpose* apart from the avoidance of a liability to tax – not 'no business *effect*'. If those two ingredients exist, the inserted steps are to be disregarded for fiscal purposes. The court must then look at the end result. Precisely how the end result will be taxed will depend on the terms of the taxing statute sought to be applied."[52]

48 My Lords, this statement is a careful and accurate summary of the effect which the *Ramsay* construction of a statutory concept has upon the way the courts will decide whether a transaction falls within that concept or not. If the statutory language is construed as referring to a commercial concept, then it follows that steps which have no

52 [See above, para **[5.9]**.]

commercial purpose but which have been artificially inserted for tax purposes into a composite transaction will not affect the answer to the statutory question. When Lord Brightman said that the inserted steps are to be "disregarded for fiscal purposes", I think that he meant that they should be disregarded for the purpose of applying the relevant fiscal concept. In the *Furniss* case, this was the concept of a disposal by one person to another. For that purpose, and for that purpose only, the disposal to Greenjacket was disregarded. But that does not mean that it was treated, even for tax purposes, as if it had never happened. The payment by Wood Bastow was undoubtedly to Greenjacket and so far as might be relevant for tax or any other purposes, it could not be disregarded.

49 For present purposes, however, the point I wish to emphasise is that Lord Brightman's formulation in the *Furniss* case, like Lord Diplock's formulation in the *Burmah* case, is not a principle of construction. It is a statement of the consequences of giving a commercial construction to a fiscal concept. Before one can apply Lord Brightman's words, it is first necessary to construe the statutory language and decide that it refers to a concept which Parliament intended to be given a commercial meaning capable of transcending the juristic individuality of its component parts. But there are many terms in tax legislation which cannot be construed in this way. They refer to purely legal concepts which have no broader commercial meaning. In such cases, the *Ramsay* principle can have no application. It is necessary to make this point because, in the first flush of victory after the *Ramsay*, *Burmah* and *Furniss* cases, there was a tendency on the part of the Inland Revenue to treat Lord Brightman's words as if they were a broad spectrum antibiotic which killed off all tax avoidance schemes, whatever the tax and whatever the relevant statutory provisions . . .

Inland Revenue Comrs v McGuckian

51 In the *McGuckian* case [1997] 1 WLR 991 a Republic of Ireland company called Ballinamore had substantial distributable reserves. The shareholders, Mr and Mrs McGuckian, wanted to receive this money but not to pay income tax on the dividend. So they entered into a scheme by which they first transferred their shares to an offshore trustee called Shurltrust. By a series of preplanned transactions, it then assigned the right to receive the dividend to a UK company called Mallardchoice in consideration of the payment of a sum equal to 99% of the expected dividend. Ballinamore then declared the dividend and paid it to Mallardchoice, which immediately paid 99% to Shurltrust.

52 The statutory question was whether Shurltrust had received income or capital. If it was income, the effect of various tax avoidance provisions concerning this transfer of assets abroad was that the payment would be deemed to be income of the McGuckians. If it was capital, the McGuckians would not be liable for tax. The McGuckians said that if Shurltrust had simply received the dividend, it would of course have been income. But Shurltrust did not receive the dividend. It received a payment from Mallardchoice which was a capital payment for an assignment of its right to income.

53 The Inland Revenue's argument, relying upon the formulation in the *Furniss* case [1984] AC 474 was that the assignment should be disregarded. The Northern Ireland Court of Appeal said (not, if I may respectfully say so, without justification) that one could not simply "disregard" the assignment. The payment of the money by Mallardchoice to Shurltrust was the consideration for the assignment and an integral part of that transaction. If the assignment had to be disregarded, one could not explain how Shurltrust had received any money at all.

54 It seems to me that the Crown caused unnecessary difficulties for itself in the *McGuckian* case by failing to notice that the question was different from that in *Furniss v Dawson* and therefore did not necessarily respond to precisely the same analysis. In the *Furniss* case the question was the identity of the disponee. In the *McGuckian* case it was the nature of the payment received by Shurltrust – capital or income? In the former case, it is reasonable to speak of the middle stage of a chain of disposals being "disregarded". In the latter case, it makes much less sense. The question was not whether the assignment should be disregarded but whether, from a commercial point of view, it amounted to an exchange of income for capital. Such exchanges usually have a commercial reality; the purchase or sale of an annuity, for example, is an exchange of capital for an income stream,

involving a transfer of risk. But the transaction in the *McGuckian* case was nothing more than an attempt to relabel a sum of money. The fact that the assignment had no commercial purpose did not mean that it had to be disregarded. But it failed to perform the alchemy of transforming the receipt of a dividend from the company into the receipt of a capital sum from someone else. For the purpose of the fiscal concept at stake, namely the character of the receipt as income derived from the company, it made no difference.

55 My Lords, I think that it was for these reasons that their Lordships in the *McGuckian* case went back to Lord Wilberforce's analysis in the *Ramsay* case [1982] AC 300 and tried to identify the principle of construction in play. Lord Steyn said that the decision marked a shift away from literalism to a "broad purposive interpretation" and from "formalistic insistence on examining steps in a composite scheme separately" to "a more realistic legal analysis": [1997] 1 WLR 991, 999–1000. Lord Cooke of Thorndon suggested, at p 1005, that it was:

> "an application to taxing Acts of the general approach to statutory interpretation whereby, in determining the natural meaning of particular expressions in their context, weight is given to the purpose and spirit of the legislation."[53]

56 My Lords, these are valuable insights and I respectfully suggest that particular attention should be paid to the way Lord Cooke of Thorndon dealt with the criteria stated by Lord Brightman in *Furniss v Dawson*:

> "Lord Brightman spoke of certain limitations (a pre-ordained series of transactions including steps with no commercial or business purpose apart from the avoidance of a liability to tax). The present case does fall within these limitations, but it may be as well to add that, if the ultimate question is always the true bearing of a particular taxing provision on a particular set of facts, the limitations cannot be universals. Always one must go back to the discernible intent of the taxing Act. I suspect that the advisers of those bent on tax avoidance . . . do not always pay sufficient heed to the theme in the speeches in the *Furniss* case . . . to the effect that the journey's end may not yet have been found."[54]

57 I would only add that it is not only tax avoiders who may not pay sufficient heed to the necessity of concentrating on the application of the particular taxing provision to the particular facts. The Inland Revenue sometimes also fails to do so. The journey's end may be different because the journey itself is not the same.

The limits of Ramsay

58 The limitations of the *Ramsay* principle therefore arise out of the paramount necessity of giving effect to the statutory language. One cannot elide the first and fundamental step in the process of construction, namely to identify the concept to which the statute refers. I readily accept that many expressions used in tax legislation (and not only in tax legislation) can be construed as referring to commercial concepts and that the courts are today readier to give them such a construction than they were before the *Ramsay* case. But that is not always the case. Taxing statutes often refer to purely legal concepts. They use expressions of which a commercial man asked what they meant, would say "You had better ask a lawyer" . . .

59 Even if a statutory expression refers to a business or economic concept, one cannot disregard a transaction which comes within the statutory language, construed in the correct commercial sense, simply on the ground that it was entered into solely for tax reasons. Business concepts have their boundaries no less than legal ones. Thus in two of the cases considered in *Craven v White (Stephen)* [1989] AC 398 the House was unanimously of the view that although there had been an initial disposal with no commercial purpose, except to lay the ground for an avoidance of tax if and when there should be a further disposal to a third party, the transactions were so separate in fact as

53 [See above, para **[5.11]**.]
54 [*Ibid.*]

well as in law as to make it impossible to treat them, even in a commercial sense, as a single disposal to the third party. The lapse of time between the two transactions, the lack of contemplation of any specific later disposal at the time of the first transaction, were commercial realities. The division of opinion in the House over how the third transaction should be categorised did not detract from the agreement that it had to fall within the statutory language.

60 Likewise the use of business concepts like "income" and "capital" may give the taxpayer a choice of structuring a commercial transaction so as to come within one concept or the other . . .

61 It follows that a transaction which, for the avoidance of tax, has been structured to produce, say, capital, and does produce capital in the ordinary commercial sense of that concept (unlike the payment in *Inland Revenue Comrs v McGuckian* [1997] 1 WLR 991) cannot be "recharacterised" as producing income: see *Comr of Inland Revenue v Wattie* [1999] 1 WLR 873.

Tax mitigation and tax avoidance

62 My Lords, it has occasionally been said that the boundary of the *Ramsay* principle can be defined by asking whether the taxpayer's actions constituted (acceptable) tax mitigation or (unacceptable) tax avoidance. In *Inland Revenue Comrs v Willoughby* [1997] 1 WLR 1071, 1079 Lord Nolan described the concept of tax avoidance as "elusive". In that case, the House had to grapple with what it meant, or at any rate what its "hallmark" was because the statute expressly provided that certain provisions should not apply if the taxpayer could show that he had not acted with "the purpose of avoiding liability to taxation". The same question arises on the interpretation of the anti-avoidance provisions to which Lord Cooke of Thorndon referred in *Inland Revenue Comrs v McGuckian* [1997] 1 WLR 991, 1005. But when the statutory provisions do not contain words like "avoidance" or "mitigation", I do not think that it helps to introduce them. The fact that steps taken for the avoidance of tax are acceptable or unacceptable is the conclusion at which one arrives by applying the statutory language to the facts of the case. It is not a test for deciding whether it applies or not. If I may be allowed to repeat what I said in *Norglen Ltd v Reeds Rains Prudential Ltd* [1999] 2 AC 1, 13–14:

> "If the question is whether a given transaction is such as to attract a statutory benefit, such as a grant or assistance like legal aid, or a statutory burden, such as income tax, I do not think that it promotes clarity of thought to use terms like stratagem or device. The question is simply whether upon its true construction, the statute applies to the transaction. Tax avoidance schemes are perhaps the best example. They either work (*Inland Revenue Comrs v Duke of Westminster* [1936] AC 1) or they do not (*Furniss v Dawson* [1984] AC 474). If they do not work, the reason, as my noble and learned friend, Lord Steyn, pointed out in *Inland Revenue Comrs v McGuckian* [1997] 1 WLR 991, 1000, is simply that upon the true construction of the statute, the transaction which was designed to avoid the charge to tax actually comes within it. It is not that the statute has a penumbral spirit which strikes down devices or stratagems designed to avoid its terms or exploit its loopholes." **[5.12]**

Barclays Mercantile Finance Ltd v Mawson (Inspector of Taxes) [2004] 3 WLR 1383 (HL)

LORD NICHOLLS OF BIRKENHEAD: . . .

The Ramsay principle

26 . . . the Special Commissioners and Park J said that they were applying the principles of construction first applied by this House in *W T Ramsay Ltd v Inland Revenue Comrs* [1982] AC 300. These principles have since been discussed and explained in numerous cases both in lower courts and in your Lordships' House. But these attempts at clarification appear only to have raised fresh doubts and further appeals . . .

27 It is no doubt too much to expect that any exposition will remove all difficulties in the application of the principles because it is in the nature of questions of construction that there will be borderline cases about which people will have different views. It should be possible to achieve some clarity about basic principles.

28 As Lord Steyn explained in *Inland Revenue Comrs v McGuckian* [1977] 1 WLR 991, 999, the modern approach to statutory construction is to have regard to the purpose of a particular provision and interpret its language, so far as possible, in a way which best gives effect to that purpose. Until the *Ramsay* case, however, revenue statutes were "remarkably resistant to the new non-formalist methods of interpretation". The particular vice of formalism in this area of the law was the insistence of the courts on treating every transaction which had an individual legal identity (such as a payment of money, transfer of property, creation of a debt, etc) as having its own separate tax consequences, whatever might be the terms of the statute. As Lord Steyn said, it was "those two features – literal interpretation of tax statutes and the formalistic insistence on examining steps in a composite scheme separately – [which] allowed tax avoidance schemes to flourish".

29 The *Ramsay* case [1982] AC 300 liberated the construction of revenue statutes from being both literal and blinkered. It is worth quoting two passages from the influential speech of Lord Wilberforce. First, at p.323, on the general approach to construction:

> "What are 'clear words' is to be ascertained upon normal principles: these do not confine the courts to literal interpretation. There may, indeed should, be considered the context and scheme of the relevant Act as a whole, and its purpose may, indeed should, be regarded."[55]

30 Secondly, at pp. 323–324, on the application of a statutory provision so construed to a composite transaction:

> "It is the task of the court to ascertain the legal nature of any transaction to which it is sought to attach a tax or a tax consequence and if that emerges from a series or combination of transactions, intended to operate as such, it is that series or combination which may be regarded."[56]

31 The application of these two principles led to the conclusion, as a matter of construction, that the statutory provision with which the court was concerned, namely that imposing capital gains tax on chargeable gains less allowable losses was referring to gains and losses having a commercial reality ("The capital gains tax was created to operate in the real world, not that of make-belief") and that therefore:

> "To say that a loss (or gain) which appears to arise at one stage in an indivisible process, and which is intended to be and is cancelled out by a later stage, so that at the end of what was brought as, and planned as, a single continuous operation, there is not such a loss (or gain) as the legislation is dealing with, is in my opinion well and indeed essentially within the judicial function." (p326)[57]

32 The essence of the new approach was to give the statutory provision a purposive construction in order to determine the nature of the transaction to which it was intended to apply and then to decide whether the actual transaction (which might involve considering the overall effect of a number of elements intended to operate together) answered to the statutory description. Of course this does not mean that the courts have to put their reasoning into the straitjacket of first construing the statute in the abstract and then looking at the facts. It might be more convenient to analyse the facts and then ask whether they satisfy the requirements of the statute. But however one approaches the matter, the question is always whether the relevant provision of the statute, upon its true construction, applies to the facts as found. As Lord Nicholls of Birkenhead said in *MacNiven v Westmorland Investments Ltd* [2003] 1 AC 311, 320, para 8: "The paramount

55 [See above, para **[5.7]**.]
56 [*Ibid.*]
57 [*Ibid.*]

question always is one of interpretation of the particular statutory provision and its application to the facts of the case."

33 The simplicity of this question, however difficult it might be to answer on the facts of a particular case, shows that the *Ramsay* case did not introduce a new doctrine operating within the special field of revenue statutes. On the contrary, as Lord Steyn observed in *McGuckian* [1997] 1 WLR 991, 999 it rescued tax law from being "some island of literal interpretation" and brought it within generally applicable principles.

34 Unfortunately, the novelty for tax lawyers of this exposure to ordinary principles of statutory construction produced a tendency to regard *Ramsay* as establishing a new jurisprudence governed by special rules of its own. This tendency has been encouraged by two features characteristic of tax law, although by no means exclusively so. The first is that tax is generally imposed by reference to economic activities or transactions which exist, as Lord Wilberforce said, "in the real world". The second is that a good deal of intellectual effort is devoted to structuring transactions in a form which will have the same or nearly the same economic effect as a taxable transaction but which it is hoped will fall outside the terms of the taxing statute. It is characteristic of these composite transactions that they will include elements which have been inserted without any business or commercial purpose but are intended to have the effect of removing the transaction from the scope of the charge.

35 There have been a number of cases, such as *Inland Revenue v Burmah Oil Co Ltd* 1982 SC (HL) 114, *Furniss v Dawson* [1984] AC 474 and *Carreras Group Ltd v Stamp Comr* [2004] STC 1377 in which it has been decided that elements which have been inserted into a transaction without any business or commercial purpose did not, as the case might be, prevent the composite transaction from falling within a charge to tax or bring it within an exemption from tax. Thus in the *Burmah* case, a series of circular payments which left the taxpayer company in exactly the same financial position as before was not regarded as giving rise to a "loss" within the meaning of the legislation. In *Furniss*, the transfer of shares to a subsidiary as part of a planned scheme immediately to transfer them to an outside purchaser was regarded as a taxable disposition to the outside purchaser rather than an exempt transfer to a group company. In *Carreras* the transfer of shares in exchange for a debenture with a view to its redemption a fortnight later was not regarded as an exempt transfer in exchange for the debenture but rather as an exchange for money. In each case the court looked at the overall effect of the composite transactions by which the taxpayer company in *Burmah* suffered no loss, the shares in *Furniss* passed into the hands of the outside purchaser and the vendors in *Carreras* received cash. On the true construction of the relevant provisions of the statute, the elements inserted into the transactions without any commercial purpose were treated as having no significance.

36 Cases such as these gave rise to a view that, in the application of *any* taxing statute, transactions or elements of transactions which had no commercial purpose were to be disregarded. But that is going too far. It elides the two steps which are necessary in the application of any statutory provision: first, to decide, on a purposive construction, exactly what transaction will answer to the statutory description and secondly, to decide whether the transaction in question does so. As Ribeiro PJ said in *Collector of Stamp Revenue v Arrowtown Assets Ltd* [2003] HKCFA 46, para 35:

> "the driving principle in the *Ramsay* line of cases continues to involve a general rule of statutory construction and an unblinkered approach to the analysis of the facts. The ultimate question is whether the relevant statutory provisions, construed purposively, were intended to apply to the transaction, viewed realistically."

37 The need to avoid sweeping generalisations about disregarding transactions undertaken for the purpose of tax avoidance was shown by *MacNiven v Westmorland Investments Ltd* [2003] 1 AC 311 in which the question was whether a payment of interest by a debtor who had borrowed the money for that purpose from the creditor himself and which had been made solely to reduce liability to tax, was a "payment" of interest within the meaning of the statute which entitled him to a deduction or repayment of tax. The House decided that the purpose of requiring the interest to have been "paid" was to

produce symmetry by giving a right of deduction in respect of any payment which gave rise to a liability to tax in the hands of the recipient (or would have given rise to such a liability if the recipient had been a taxable entity.) As the payment was accepted to have had this effect, it answered the statutory description notwithstanding the circular nature of the payment and its tax avoidance purpose.

38 *MacNiven* shows the need to focus carefully upon the particular statutory provision and to identify its requirements before one can decide whether circular payments or elements inserted for the purpose of tax avoidance should be disregarded or treated as irrelevant for the purposes of the statute. In the speech of Lord Hoffmann in *MacNiven* it was said that if a statute laid down requirements by reference to some commercial concept such as gain or loss, it would usually follow that elements inserted into a composite transaction without any commercial purpose could be disregarded, whereas if the requirements of the statute were purely by reference to its nature (in *MacNiven*, the discharge of a debt) then an act having that legal effect would suffice, whatever its commercial purpose may have been. This is not an unreasonable generalisation, indeed perhaps something of a truism, but we do not think that it was intended to provide a substitute for a close analysis of what the statute means. It certainly does not justify the assumption that an answer can be obtained by classifying all concepts a priori as either "commercial" or "legal". That would be the very negation of purposive construction: see Ribeiro PJ in *Arrowtown*, at paras 37 and 39 and the perceptive judgment of the special commissioners (Theodore Wallace and Julian Ghosh) in *Campbell v Inland Revenue Comrs* [2004] STC (SCD) 396.

39 The present case, like *MacNiven*, illustrates the need for a close analysis of what, on a purposive construction, the statute actually requires. The object of granting the allowance is, as we have said, to provide a tax equivalent to the normal accounting deduction from profits for the depreciation of machinery and plant used for the purposes of a trade. Consistently with this purpose, section 24(1) [Capital Allowances Act 1990] requires that a trader should have incurred capital expenditure on the provision of machinery or plant for the purposes of his trade. When the trade is finance leasing, this means that the capital expenditure should have been incurred to acquire the machinery or plant for the purpose of leasing it in the course of the trade. In such a case, it is the lessor as owner who suffers the depreciation in the value of the plant and is therefore entitled to an allowance against the profits of his trade.

40 These statutory requirements, as it seems to us, are in the case of a finance lease concerned entirely with the acts and purposes of the lessor. The Act says nothing about what the lessee should do with the purchase price, how he should find the money to pay the rent or how he should use the plant. As Carnwath LJ said in the Court of Appeal [2003] STC 66, 89, para 54:

> "There is nothing in the statute to suggest that 'up-front finance' for the lessee is an essential feature of the right to allowances. The test is based on the purpose of the lessor's expenditure, not the benefits of the finance to the lessee."

41 So far as the lessor is concerned, all the requirements of section 24(1) were satisfied. Mr Boobyer, a director of BMBF, gave unchallenged evidence that from its point of view the purchase and leaseback was part of its ordinary trade of finance leasing. Indeed, if one examines the acts and purposes of BMBF, it would be very difficult to come to any other conclusion. The finding of the special commissioners that the transaction "had no commercial reality" depends entirely upon an examination of what happened to the purchase price after BMBF paid it to BGE. But these matters do not affect the reality of the expenditure by BMBF and its acquisition of the pipeline for the purposes of its finance leasing trade.

42 If the lessee chooses to make arrangements, even as a preordained part of the transaction for the sale and leaseback, which result in the bulk of the purchase price being irrevocably committed to paying the rent, that is no concern of the lessor. From his point of view, the transaction is exactly the same. No one disputes that BMBF had acquired ownership of the pipeline or that it generated income for BMBF in the course of its trade in the form of rent chargeable to corporation tax. In return it paid £91m. The circularity

of payments which so impressed Park J and the special commissioners arose because BMBF, in the ordinary course of its business, borrowed the money to buy the pipeline from Barclays Bank and Barclays happened to be the bank which provided the cash collateralised guarantee to BMBF for the payment of the rent. But these were happenstances. None of these transactions, whether circular or not, were necessary elements in creating the entitlement to the capital allowances.

43 For these reasons, which are substantially the same as those of the Court of Appeal, we would dismiss this appeal. **[5.13]**

Thus, in *Barclays*, the principal fact, which was pertinent to the statutory provision (Capital Allowances Act 1990, s 24(1)) as interpreted by their Lordships, was that the plant (the pipeline) was purchased for the purpose of the purchaser's (BMBF's) finance leasing business. It was immaterial that the associated arrangements made by the lessee (BGE) for the sale and leaseback of the plant meant that most of the purchase price would be irrecoverable. By way of contrast, in *IRC v Scottish Provident Institution* [2004] 1 WLR 3172, where a taxpayer entered into an artificial scheme in order to exploit a pending change in the taxation of gains on options to buy or sell bonds and gilts, the House of Lords (comprising the same members of the Appellate Committee who heard the appeal in *Barclays*) determined in the light of the relevant statutory provisions (FA 1994, ss 147A and 150A), that they should have regard to the scheme (which was a single composite transaction) in deciding whether the taxpayer was entitled to the tax advantage sought. **[5.14]**

Leonard Hoffmann[58] 'Tax Avoidance' [2005] BTR 197

The interpretation of taxing statutes, especially for the purpose of deciding whether they apply to transactions designed to avoid tax, has, for too long, been regarded as a specialised craft, to which experience of the interpretation of language used for other purposes has nothing to contribute. Recent cases have attempted to counter this tendency by emphasising that tax statutes are statutes and should be interpreted according to the same principles as other legislation . . .

In *Helvering v Gregory*[59] the question was whether shares issued to Mrs Gregory by the subsidiary of a company which she controlled were exempt from tax as a dividend because they had been issued "in pursuance of a plan of reorganisation". Ordinarily, the issue of shares in a subsidiary directly to the controlling shareholder would count as a reorganisation because economically it makes no difference. It gives him a direct interest in a company in which he previously had an indirect interest. In Mrs Gregory's case, however, the shares had been issued to her as part of a scheme under which the subsidiary had acquired an asset pregnant with capital gain and Mrs Gregory wanted to obtain the benefit of that gain without paying tax. Immediately after the share issue, the company went into liquidation and distributed the asset to Mrs Gregory, who sold it. Had the shares been issued to her pursuant to a plan or reorganisation? Learned Hand J. thought not. I quote from his reasons:

> "If what was done here was what was intended by [the statute], it is of no consequence that it was all an elaborate scheme to get rid of income tax, as it certainly

58 A Lord of Appeal in Ordinary. This article is based on the text of a lecture delivered at the Centre of Commercial Law Studies on 1 December 2004, commemorating the founding of the Centre by Prof. Sir Roy Goode in 1980. The lecture will also be published by LexisNexis in a volume of essays to mark the 25th anniversary of the Centre.

59 69 F 2nd 809 (1934).

> was . . . [But] the purpose of the section is plain enough: men engaged in enterprises . . . might wish to consolidate, or divide, to add to, or subtract from, their holdings. Such transactions were not to be considered as realizing any profit, because the collective interests still remain in solution. But the underlying presupposition is plain that the readjustment shall be undertaken for reasons germane to the conduct of the venture in hand, not as an ephemeral incident, egregious to its prosecution . . . We cannot treat as inoperative the transfer of shares . . . The transfer passed title . . . and the taxpayer became a shareholder in the transferee. All these steps were real and their only defect was that they were not what the statute means by a 'reorganisation'."[60]

Learned Hand J. makes it clear that he regards the matter as one of statutory construction. If it falls within the language of the Act, it does not matter that it was done solely to avoid tax. But in his opinion the concept of a "plan of reorganisation" involves doing something for a business purpose and not solely to avoid tax. The judgment was affirmed by the Supreme Court, which observed that Mrs Gregory had no "business or corporate purpose". I shall come back in a moment to the interpretation which has been put upon this decision. To an English lawyer, it looks as plain a case as one could wish to find of what Lord Diplock would have called "purposive construction". One looks at the purpose of the exemption from tax and sees that it is to allow people to readjust their shareholdings when it is commercially expedient to do so. One then construes that language as not applying to a case in which the adjustment has been solely to use the tax exemption. The judge is not applying any rule which steps outside the meaning of the statute . . .

Despite the fact that Hand J.'s judgment in *Gregory v Helvering* was based purely upon purposive construction, it and the Supreme Court judgment which affirmed it, have frequently been taken to mean that, whatever may be the terms of the statute, a transaction which has no business purpose cannot have any effect on liability for tax. It purports to be an all-purpose anti-tax avoidance remedy which dissolves the effect of tax avoidance schemes . . .

. . . The American background is of interest because in *WT Ramsay Ltd v IRC*,[61] Mr Peter Millett Q.C. for the Revenue referred the House to some of the American cases on the business purpose rule, Lord Wilberforce handled them gingerly:

> "It is probable that the United States courts do not draw the line precisely where we do with our different system, allowing less legislative power to the courts than they claim to exercise, would draw it."

To Lord Wilberforce in *Ramsay*, the question was very much a matter of construction:

> "To say that a loss (or gain) which appears to arise at one stage in an indivisible process, and which is intended to be and is cancelled out by a later stage, so that at the end of what was bought as, and planned as, a single continuous operation, there is not such a loss (or gain) as the legislation is dealing with, is in my opinion well and indeed essentially within the judicial function."[62]

Mr Millett Q.C. had more success three years later, when he dangled *Helvering v Gregory*[63] before the House of Lords in *Furniss v Dawson*,[64] and indeed, the facts of the two cases bore a striking resemblance. This time the fly was taken, because Lord Brightman, in the famous passage that every tax lawyer knows, stated the principle in general terms which contain no mention of the statutory language. The American cases are not cited in his speech, but the reference to disregarding inserted steps having no business purpose has a distinctly transatlantic accent. After *Furniss v Dawson* it appeared that the full-blooded American doctrine had been imported into the UK . . .

In tax avoidance, . . . the courts had stepped outside the meaning of the statute and

60 69 F 2nd 809 (1934).
61 [1982] AC 300.
62 [1982] AC 300 at 326; [see above, para **[5.7]**].
63 69 F 2nd 809 (1934).
64 [1984] AC 474.

developed a general anti-avoidance doctrine based upon whether the transaction or parts of the transaction had a business purpose or not . . .

Furniss v Dawson was in reaction to the *Duke of Westminster*[65] and some of the more extraordinary cases of literalism which followed, of which *IRC v Plummer*,[66] to which Lord Wilberforce subscribed less than three years before *Ramsay*, is a good example. As Lord Steyn afterwards said in *IRC v McGuckian*,[67] tax law had remained "some island of literal interpretation", despite the changing attitude of the courts to statutory interpretation and indeed to the interpretation of language generally. In *Ramsay* itself, Lord Wilberforce has been content to take a new approach to construction, but in *Furniss v Dawson* the law moved into territory which was previously uncharted except, and that rather inadequately, in the US.

There followed a period during which the limits of Lord Brightman's formula were tested. In *Craven v White*[68] there was a dispute over how seriously one took the requirement that there must have been a preordained scheme. Lord Templeman, who had been in the Court of Appeal for *Ramsay* and did not participate in *Furniss v Dawson*, wanted to concentrate on the business purpose rule. If steps had been taken for no business purpose but solely to secure a tax advantage at a later stage when the opportunity for a further transaction presented itself, then the tax-avoiding elements in the history of the taxpayer's dealings should be disregarded. Lord Oliver, who had been reversed by the House of Lords in *Furniss v Dawson* (with the comment that he seemed determined to confine *Ramsay* as narrowly as possible), insisted upon the whole scheme being preordained and said that Lord Brightman's principle applied: there must be "no practical likelihood" that the whole scheme will not work as planned. Neither side seemed to think that the answer might be different depending upon the language and purpose of the particular taxing provision which was being applied. The matter was treated as a general extra-statutory rule.

After *Craven v White* a good deal of learning began to cluster around Lord Brightman's formula: a good example of the complexity it could involve is the judgment of Hart J. in *DTE Financial Services Ltd v Wilson (HM Inspector of Taxes)*.[69] It was in *IRC v McGuckian*,[70] and in particular in the speech of Lord Steyn, that the primacy of the statutory language began to reassert itself. He went back to Lord Wilberforce in *Ramsay* and asserted that the construction which the House there gave to the Capital Gains Tax Act:

> "was not invented on a juristic basis independent of statute. That would have been indefensible since a court has no power to amend a tax statute. The principle was developed as a matter of statutory construction."[71]

Since the House in *McGuckian* did not explain how the *Furniss v Dawson* formula could be reconciled with pure purposive construction, the full implications of *McGuckian* took a while to sink in. It was only *MacNiven v Westmorland Investments Ltd*[72] that the House was faced with a clear conflict between a purposive interpretation of the statute and an extra-statutory application of the *Furniss v Dawson* formula. The question, you may remember, was whether a company could deduct interest for the purposes of corporation tax. In order to deduct, it had to have paid the interest. It had no money, so the lender, which happened to be its parent company, made it a loan which it paid back in discharge of the interest liability. This was a circular transaction, undertaken purely to save tax because the lender happened to be exempt from tax on the interest which it received and the payment generated a tax loss in the insolvent borrower which gave it some value in the market. The transaction satisfied the *Furniss v Dawson* formula, to say nothing of the more general business purpose rule supported by Lord Templeman: it was preordained and the

65 [1936] AC 1.
66 [1980] AC 896.
67 [1997] STC 908 at 915; [1997] 1 WLR 991 at 999.
68 [1989] 1 AC 398.
69 (2001) 74 TC 14.
70 [1997] STC 908; [1997] 1 WLR 991.
71 [1997] STC 908 at 916; [1997] 1 WLR 991 at 1000; [above, para **[5.11]**].
72 [2002] 1 AC 311.

payment was solely for the purpose of securing a tax deduction. But the House considered that the statute, on its true construction, required no more than that the interest liability should have been discharged by a payment which was taxable in the hands of the lender, or would have been taxable if it had not been exempt. The purpose of the payment was irrelevant.

In choosing the constructional approach rather than the *Furniss v Dawson* formula, the House had to rewrite history in a way which struck some people as a little disingenuous. We said that the formula was not a freestanding principle but rather the effect of construing a taxing provision in a particular way. If the statute required a transaction which had a business purpose, like the plan of reconstruction in *Gregory v Helvering*, why then, steps which had no business purpose would not satisfy the statute. If the statute required something which had a real commercial existence, like a profit or loss, then a series of preordained transactions which taken together produced no profit or loss would not satisfy the statute. On the other hand, if all that the statute required was something which had a particular legal effect, like discharging a debt or passing title to property, then a transaction which had that effect satisfied the statute even if it had no business purpose.

The sleight of hand which covered this retreat to constitutional propriety did not deceive Lord Templeman, who wrote a brilliant article for the *Law Quarterly Review*[73] accusing the House of Lords of having deserted the true faith and opened the door to tax avoidance. I shall come back to this question in a moment. Lord Templeman said, correctly, that *MacNiven* satisfied the *Furniss v Dawson* formula and was therefore in his opinion wrongly decided. Lord Millett, who has been a supporter of the American business purpose rule since he successfully sold it to the House of Lords in *Furniss v Dawson*, was more equivocal. As a judge of the Court of Final Appeal of Hong Kong, he made his own analysis of the authorities in *Collector of Stamp Revenue v Arrowtown Assets Ltd.*[74] He said that *IRC v Burmah Oil Co Ltd*,[75] decided shortly after *Ramsay*, where Lord Diplock had said that in deciding whether a composite circular transaction had caused *Burmah* to suffer a loss for capital gains tax, one could ignore "inserted steps that have no commercial purpose" was an explicit application of the "no business purpose" test. The case, he said: "did not depend upon an analysis of the meaning of the word 'loss' or the nature of the concept which that word involves."[76]

On the other hand, later in his judgment he says that the basis of *MacNiven* was that:

> "even if the payment in question was undertaken solely for the purpose of obtaining tax relief, the granting of such relief in such circumstances was nevertheless within the intendment of the statute."[77]

It would seem to follow that the reason why the transaction in *Burmah* did not produce an allowable loss was that such a transaction did *not* produce a loss within the intendment of the statute. If this does not involve an interpretation of the word "loss" or the concept which that word denotes, I find it hard to see what other question of construction can be involved.

The primacy of the construction of the particular taxing provision and the illegitimacy of rules of general application has been reaffirmed by the recent decision of the House in *Barclays Mercantile Business Finance Ltd v Mawson*.[78] Indeed it may be said that this case has killed off the *Ramsay* doctrine as a special theory of revenue law and subsumed it within the general theory of the interpretation of statutes, perhaps the interpretation of utterances of any kind . . . But I think that Lord Templeman's criticisms must be taken seriously and that the author should address the question of whether one should have a general theory of tax avoidance rather than a case-by-case analysis of the statutory requirements.

73 (2001) 117 LQR 575.
74 [2003] HK CFA 46.
75 [1982] STC 30.
76 [2003] HK CFA 46 at 118.
77 [2003] HK CFA 46 at 143.
78 [2003] STC 66; [2002] EWCA Civ 66.

The first question is what you mean by tax avoidance. Whole conferences and seminars have been held to discuss this question. At one of these, in 1997, Lord Templeman said: "Tax avoidance reduces the incidence of tax borne by an individual taxpayer contrary to the intentions of Parliament."[79] Others have said much the same in various different ways: the central idea is that you have arranged your affairs so as not to pay the tax which you ought to have paid. But this raises a logical difficulty. Why ought you to have paid tax? Presumably, because Parliament intended you to pay it. So Lord Templeman says that it reduced your tax "contrary to the intention of Parliament". But how do we know the intention of Parliament? There is only one way to know the intention of Parliament and that is to read the statute. So avoidance of tax assumes that you are not paying tax which, on a fair reading of the statute, you ought to have paid. But why in that case are you not liable to pay it? How can the courts give the statute a construction which means that people do not pay the tax which the statute shows that Parliament intended them to pay?

The first answer to this question is that there was a time, evidenced by cases like *IRC v Plummer*,[80] to say nothing of the *Duke of Westminster*,[81] when the courts did construe taxing statutes so literally and so blinkered that they did not give effect to the plain intention of Parliament. It was that approach which drove the Revenue to despair and inspired the legislatures in countries like Australia and New Zealand to enact general anti-avoidance provisions which they hoped, not always with success, would fill the gaps left by literal construction. But this peculiar technique for construing revenue statutes was, as Lord Steyn pointed out in *McGuckian*, abandoned by the House of Lords in *Ramsay*. Since then we have been able to say that employees who are paid in platinum sponge which is held at a bank where it can be instantly converted into money are, for PAYE purposes, being paid in money, or that a seller of shares who received an interest-free debenture redeemable a fortnight later is, for stamp duty purposes, being paid in money. We need no superimposed anti-avoidance doctrine: the employees are not receiving payments in kind and the share vendor is not entering into a rearrangement of securities within the meaning of a taxing statute . . .

There is however another dimension. It is not only literalism on the part of the judges which leads to what the Revenue regard as tax avoidance. There is also the way in which taxing statutes are often drafted. Judges sometimes draw a distinction between acceptable tax avoidance, like giving up smoking, and unacceptable tax avoidance, like schemes with platinum sponge. The difference, said Lord Templeman in *IRC v Challenge Corp Ltd*,[82] lies in the fact that in one case the taxpayer actually reorders his affairs: he stops buying the taxed commodity, or he receives less income or incurs more expense. In the other case, the taxpayer still buys the taxed commodity or receives the same income, but structures the transaction to fall outside the taxing statute. This distinction is, if I may say so, based upon sound instinct, but it depends upon the assumption that Parliament imposes taxation by reference to economic and other events in the real world. If only this were true. But Parliament, for various reasons, sometimes leaves the taxpayer a choice of achieving the same economic result by two different methods, one of which may attract tax and the other not.[83] Worse still, Parliament may not be content to describe the economic event which should attract tax because it does not trust the courts to understand such a concept and apply it in a practical way. Instead, it enacts a mass of detailed rules which it is hoped will tie up the taxpayer in a net from which he cannot escape. But sometimes there are holes in the net and the courts find that they cannot plug them by appealing to the economic event which, at a higher level of generality, it appears that Parliament wished to tax. It is one thing to give the statute a purposive construction. It is another to rectify the terms of highly prescriptive legislation in order to include provisions which might have been included but are not actually there . . .

The lesson, in my opinion, is that tax avoidance in the sense of transactions successfully structured to avoid a tax which Parliament intended to impose should be a contradiction

79 *Tax Avoidance and the Law,* (Adrian Shipwright (ed), Key Haven, London, 1997) at 1.
80 [1980] AC 896.
81 [1936] AC 1.
82 [1987] 1 AC 155.
83 See for example *IRC v Wattie* [1998] STC 1160.

in terms. The only way in which Parliament can express an intention to impose a tax is by a statute which means that such a tax is to be imposed. If that is what Parliament means, the courts should be trusted to give effect to its intention. Any other approach will lead us into dangerous and unpredictable territory. **[5.15]**

JT (John Tiley) 'Barclays Mercantile and Scottish Provident: avoidance and highest courts; less chaos but more uncertainty' [2005] BTR 273, 277–278 and 280

What emerges from the two UK cases [*Barclays Mercantile and Scottish Provident*] is a process of cleansing in which excresences (or even errors) already revealed in cases such as *MacNiven v Westmoreland Investments Ltd*[84] are removed and we are left with the simple fact that tax law is about interpreting statutes and that statutes should be interpreted purposively. There is less intellectual chaos since there is agreement on basic principles. The full mantra is that the words must be interpreted purposively and in their context. However this does not produce certainty since it is in the nature of questions of construction that there will be borderline cases about which people will have different views.[85] *MacNiven* showed that there was no general overriding judicial anti-avoidance rule of law (or doctrine) to be applied like a principle of EC law. *Barclays Mercantile* shows that there is no general overriding judicial anti-avoidance approach to construction. *Scottish Provident* shows that the House of Lords are not going to use their new approach to take us back to the 1960s and 1970s. The major case law beginning with *Ramsay* and ending earlier in 2004 is all upheld; in early 2005 we have also had a Revenue win in *West v Trennery*[86] where the House reversed the Court of Appeal on a "flip flop" scheme. The new era is not a haven for tax planners . . .

The cases beginning with *Ramsay* are now mere examples of points of construction on which people may, presumably, have different views. However, in *Barclays Mercantile*[87] the Committee do approve of the results of several key decisions: *IRC v Burmah Oil Co Ltd*, *Furniss v Dawson* and *Carreras Group Ltd v Stamp Comr*. They also[88] expressly mention, with approval, the approach of the Special Commissioners to Lord Hoffmann's commercial/legal distinction in *MacNiven* in *Campbell v IRC*.[89] The reader needs to be encouraged to go to *Campbell* where the Special Commissioners . . . looked at what the courts had actually done with the *Ramsay* principle rather than be beguiled by the rhetoric in the individual cases. The Commissioners found that the *Ramsay* doctrine had been applied in at least four different contexts[90]:

(a) to ascertain whether a series of self-cancelling, pre-ordained transactions, effected solely to generate an allowable loss for capital gains tax purposes, were to be respected for the purposes of capital gains tax legislation or not (*Ramsay*);

(b) to ascertain the true parties and the true dealing in a transaction (*Furniss v Dawson* and *Craven v White*);

84 [2001] UKHL 6; [2001] STC 237.
85 [2005] STC 1 at para 27.
86 [2005] STC 214.
87 [2005] STC 1 at para 35.
88 See at para 38.
89 [2004] SpC 421; [2004] STC (SCD) 396.
90 See at paras 70 *et seq.*

(c) to ascertain the true nature of a receipt in the hands of a taxpayer (*IRC v McGuckian*);
(d) to ascertain the true nature of instruments issued solely for tax avoidance purposes (*Arrowtown*).

The Special Commissioners made the important point that in (d) the notion of a preordained series of transactions was irrelevant.

There are various reasons for preferring this approach to simply looking at the words of the judges. The simplest is that in our common law system judges seem to remain barristers at heart; their judgments are written to persuade, even to persuade each other, and not to declaim, as in the usual practice in civil law counties. They also show a desire painstakingly to grope for the right principle, to display a proper appreciation for the facts of the case and to convince litigants and their advisors that they have been listened to.[91] Working out what the law is, is a different matter . . .

In the new world of construction it must be open to the taxpayer to argue cases on the overall effect of a series of transactions . . . For the same reason it must be possible to avoid being trapped in the very constricted world of a preordained transaction as promulgated by the House of Lords in *Craven v White*. The judicial need to rein in *Furniss v Dawson* may have gone too far. This is part of the importance of *Scottish Provident* but one must recall that in *Campbell* the Special Commissioners noted that some of the *Ramsay* cases did not require the notion of the preordained transaction at all. The third small point is to wonder whether, now that *Ramsay* in its more extreme forms has been brought to heel, it makes sense actually to talk about cases being avoidance cases. The clue here may be in the observation of Park J., before going on to apply the *Ramsay* doctrine to the facts before him, that *Barclays Mercantile* was not a tax avoidance scheme . . .[92]

Thus the judges have recovered control of the whole process. Whether this will lead back to those eras in which judges are seen particularly inclined towards a hostile, neutral or benevolent view of avoidance remains to be seen. We shall all have much to talk about. And some, not least in the Revenue, may wonder whether GAAR, applied properly and not as in the *Peterson* case[93], is to be preferred. Those not in the Revenue may pause to take a look at what has been happening by a process of stealth and wonder whether we now have, in many areas of law, all the disadvantages of the uncertainty of a GAAR without the protection of an advance rulings system, the one thing that makes a GAAR for some workable. Striking down a transaction for a non-allowable (avoidance) purpose has been part of the rules on loan relationships since 1996. Such a provision also forms part of the rules on derivatives (2002), intellectual property (2002), manufactured overseas dividends (2004) and management expenses (2004). None of these have a statutory advance clearing system. **[5.16]**

3. A statutory general anti-avoidance rule (GAAR) for the UK?

The possibility of enacting a GAAR in the UK, as alluded to by John Tiley in the above extract, was, in fact, considered in the late 1990s in circumstances in which there was some uncertainty about the way in which the judicial

91 See Munday [[2002] CLJ 621] . . .
92 [2002] STC 1068 at para 38.
93 [*Peterson v IRC* [2005] UKPC 5.]

approach to tax avoidance might develop and a growing awareness that often complex specific anti-avoidance provisions alone might not keep pace with taxpayers' attempts to avoid tax. In 1997, the Tax Law Review Committee (TLRC), in its report *Tax Avoidance* favoured the enactment of a GAAR for the reasons set out in the following extract. **[5.17]**

Tax Law Review Committee *Tax Avoidance*, (IFS, 1997)

EXECUTIVE SUMMARY

Overview

1. The question the Committee has addressed is whether current methods of dealing with tax avoidance are adequate and satisfactory and what, if any, other measures might be taken. The Committee's main conclusions are these-
    - Specific anti-avoidance provisions should continue to be in the forefront of the battle against tax avoidance. There remains, however, the question of whether specific provisions should be supported by the deterrent effect of the developing judicial general anti-avoidance doctrines or a statutory general anti-avoidance provision.
    - We prefer a sensibly targeted statutory general anti-avoidance provision, with a considered framework and appropriate safeguards for taxpayers (including a clearance procedure), to the continued development of judicial anti-avoidance doctrines.
    - We believe that such a statutory provision could make a contribution to the effort to deter and counter-act tax avoidance and may offer some opportunities for simplifying existing legislation.
    - A statutory provision that fails to address satisfactorily the issues to which we draw attention or to meet the criteria we identify (in particular for safeguarding taxpayers' rights), will inhibit the conduct of ordinary commercial and personnel affairs and prove an administrative nightmare for the Revenue authorities. The Committee would vehemently oppose such a provision.

Background

2. In our two reports on tax legislation we considered how such legislation could be made more intelligible.[94] Our conclusions were widely supported as sensible and useful. We are pleased to note that the Inland Revenue proposes to implement our main recommendations through its Tax Law Rewrite programme.[95]
3. In tackling that initial topic, we started from a position of virtual consensus within the Committee (and, we believe, the tax-aware world at large) that something ought to be done to improve tax legislation. The subject of tax avoidance, however, is very different and highly controversial. Totally opposed

94 [See *Interim Report on Tax Legislation* (IFS, November 1995) and *Final Report on Tax Legislation* (IFS, June 1996).]

95 [See Chapter 1, paras **[1.4]**–**[1.7]**.]

views are expressed as to the nature and extent of the problem, or indeed whether tax avoidance is a 'problem' at all.

4. So why did we decide to tackle this issue? Initially, we recognised that if you wish to improve tax legislation, you must reach a view on how to deal with tax avoidance. Tax avoidance legislation accounts for some of the more complicated parts of the tax code . . .

5. . . . as the discussions progressed, a common position started to emerge, and the conclusions set out in this report represent the consensus view of the Committee. This is particularly significant, given that the members of the Committee have widely differing tax backgrounds and perspectives.

What is tax avoidance?

6. We are concerned in this Report only with the issues of legal tax avoidance. We have not addressed the prevention and control of the illegal evasion of taxes.

7. We think it impossible to define the expression 'tax avoidance' in any truly satisfactory manner. People routinely alter their behaviour to reduce or defer their taxation liabilities. In doing so, commentators regard some actions as legitimate tax planning and categorise others as tax avoidance. No two commentators may agree on the categorisation of certain behaviour. So far as we have needed some broad framework within which to conduct our discussion of tax avoidance activity, we have regarded tax avoidance (in contra-distinction to legitimate tax mitigation or planning) as action taken to reduce or defer tax liabilities in a way that Parliament plainly did not intend or could not possibly have intended had the matter been put to it.

8. This is similar to the formulation used by the Law Lords in the recent *Willoughby* case that it is "a course of action designed to conflict with or defeat the evident intention of Parliament."[96] As tax avoidance is a legal activity, however, we appreciate that any definition or description is bound to raise issues of who should say what Parliament's intention was and what materials may be used to that end.

The extent of tax avoidance

9. We have not sought to quantify the extent of tax avoidance, either in terms of the proportion of taxpayers who seek to avoid tax or in the amount of tax lost to the Exchequer. Sometimes the Revenue departments, Treasury ministers or commentators put a figure on the sums which they say a currently fashionable tax avoidance scheme is costing the Exchequer but it will frequently be the case that the accuracy of these figures is difficult to establish and, in any event, one cannot predict how taxpayers will alter their behaviour in the face of new anti-avoidance measures.

10. But quantifiable or not, and whether very large or relatively small, we recognise that tax avoidance represents a distortion in taxpayers' behaviour. No country allows unfettered attacks on the integrity of its tax system. Every country adopts measures to curb avoidance.

Does more need to be done to reduce tax avoidance?

11. Some structures for levying taxation are more prone to avoidance than others. Complex legislation, imposing special tax penalties or conferring

96 *IRC v Willoughby* [1997] STC 995, 1004c.

special tax privileges, on selected kinds of economic activity, may prove a standing invitation to avoidance. The proper and satisfactory response to avoidance may therefore be to change the structure of the system or elements within it. The question the Committee has addressed is whether current methods of protecting the government's chosen tax structure are adequate and satisfactory and what, if any, other measures might be taken.

12. In our view the combined effect of three factors will curtail future opportunities for taxpayers to exploit tax legislation in ways not intended by Parliament. These factors are:-
    i. The abandonment by the Courts of an excessively literalist interpretation of tax legislation. This was confirmed recently in the House of Lords in the *McGuckian* decision,[97]
    ii. The development of the *Ramsay* and *Furniss* decisions, which enable the Inland Revenue to tax a pre-ordained series of transactions in accordance with their overall effect rather than in accordance with each individual legal step. This again has received new emphasis in the recent *McGuckian* decision; and
    iii. The Government's decision (accepting the conclusions of our own report on tax legislation) to rewrite tax legislation in more accessible language, and to accompany new legislation with a published memorandum explaining the legislation's purpose in non-statutory terms. In the long run this, combined with the more purposive interpretation adopted by the Courts, will in our view have a considerable impact in reducing the scope for tax avoidance.

13. We are concerned that the current political desire to "tackle avoidance" should not lead to the introduction of new measures that, given the factors we have listed, are not required and which unnecessarily extend the scope of Revenue powers in this field or that unduly fetter ordinary commercial or personal transactions. Nevertheless, we have considered in relation to paragraph 12(ii) whether we prefer a statutory general anti-avoidance provision to the continued development of judicial anti-avoidance doctrines.

The further development of the judicial anti-avoidance doctrine

14. The judicial doctrine exemplified by the *Ramsay* and *McGuckian* decisions has played an important role in counteracting some of the most uncommercial tax avoidance operations. The refinement of this doctrine in future cases may work to keep in check the ingenuity of those intent on adopting any legal means to limit their tax liabilities.

15. Nevertheless, we have concluded that innovative judicial anti-avoidance techniques are unsatisfactory, for two main reasons:
    i. A judicial doctrine fashioned on a case by case basis through the hierarchy of the Courts produces considerable uncertainty. Uncertainty is a matter of degree. The tax effect of an arrangement may be certain if it need only satisfy an excessively literalist interpretation. The tax effect may be less certain if it must be demonstrated to the court that arrangement is consistent with the intentions of Parliament in passing the legislation in question. The language of a statutory general anti-avoidance provision will not be certain and remains subject to interpretation by the courts. However, we think that undue uncertainty as to the direction a judicial anti-avoidance doctrine may follow is undesirable in taxpayers'

97 *IRC v McGuckian* [1997] STC 908 in particular in the speech of Lord Steyn at 915j.

and commercial affairs and unsatisfactory also for the Government, which must respond to avoidance activity long before the Courts are able to express their view of particular arrangements.

ii. A developing judicial doctrine – however radical – operates retrospectively and offers no clear framework within which it shall operate or not, which we consider unsatisfactory especially with the adoption of self-assessment for direct taxes.

We prefer a solution that avoids these problems.

16. We consider that tax avoidance should be countered principally by legislation rather than by the further development of the current judicial anti-avoidance doctrine. A statutory rule can attempt to make good some of the limitations inherent in a judicial rule and provide a proper framework for the application of a general anti-avoidance rule.

New legislation to curb tax avoidance

17. We have considered the two basic types of anti-avoidance legislation that Governments can adopt, namely: (i) specific provisions and (ii) general provisions. It is implicit in what we have said regarding a judicial anti-avoidance doctrine that we believe that legislative provisions, of either nature, should operate prospectively and not retrospectively.

(i) Specific anti-avoidance provisions

18. Specific anti-tax avoidance provisions are a familiar part of tax legislation. They contribute significantly to the complexity of the legislation in many areas but they do offer the very considerable advantage of being targeted at specific areas of the tax code and the avoidance issues that arise in those areas. We believe that the willingness of the judges to look at the underlying purpose of the legislation, and the publication of memoranda explaining the purpose of the legislation, will make it easier to target specific provisions more accurately in the future. Specific provisions (in the absence of more fundamental structural change) should be the first lines of defence against avoidance.

19. There remains, however, the question of whether specific provisions should be supported by the deterrent effect of judicial anti-avoidance doctrines or a statutory general anti-avoidance provision to deal with continuing tax avoidance in areas which, ex hypothesi, the specific provisions do not cover.

(ii) A statutory general anti-avoidance provision

20. We have not in recent years had a general anti-avoidance provision as part of the UK tax code. Experience in other Common Law countries that have adopted this type of provision suggests the limitations of such provisions. They remain subject to judicial interpretation and we consider that it would be wrong to attempt to exclude the jurisdiction of the courts. Australia, however, provides a notorious example of a general anti-avoidance provision that was perceived as inappropriate and, as a result, was emasculated by the courts.

21. Australia has re-enacted its general anti-avoidance rule and Canada and Ireland are among other Common Law countries that have introduced such provisions in recent years. The Revenue authorities in Australia and Canada have now had some success in the courts with their provisions but there have been relatively few cases. Meanwhile, tax avoidance remains an issue in those countries and each has continued to introduce and to rely upon specific tax avoidance provisions.

22. The experience of other common law countries underlines that a statutory general anti-avoidance provision is not a panacea. In principle, however, it can offer a number of advantages over judicial anti-avoidance doctrines-

- It can operate by reference to carefully considered and expressed criteria. In particular, it can describe the nature of the arrangements that fall within its scope of operation and – equally important – it can explicitly specify the arrangements that remain outside its scope.
- It can explicitly state the consequences of its application – which may sensibly require a transaction to be 'reconstructed' in the way that would go beyond what the Courts can adopt through a judicially developed anti-avoidance doctrine.
- The effect of a statutory rule would be prospective – i.e. it would only operate on transactions entered into after the rules were enacted (again, contrasting with a judicially developed doctrine which would necessarily apply to transactions entered into before the doctrine was pronounced).
- A general anti-avoidance provision could ensure greater consistency of application and replace the uncertainty produced by a developing judicial doctrine with a clear statutory framework within which the statutory rule would operate and be interpreted by the judges.
- Most important of all, in our opinion, a statutory general anti-avoidance provision could (and would need to) include an effective administrative clearance system under which taxpayers could quickly ascertain whether proposed transactions would be regarded by the Revenue authorities as falling within the scope of the provisions.

23. A general anti-avoidance rule inevitably requires the Revenue authorities to form their opinion in the first instance whether transactions that have the effect of reducing tax liabilities fall within the Parliamentary intent or not. The critical balance, therefore, between the public interest in seeing that taxes are not unduly avoided and the legitimate interests of taxpayers in their commercial and private affairs, lies in ensuring that (a) the rule is sensibly targeted, (b) there are sensible procedures for invoking the rule and (c) there is proper oversight of its exercise.
24. We believe that a statutory general anti-avoidance provision, if adopted, should be directed to deterring or counteracting courses of action that are designed to conflict with or defeat the evident intention of Parliament as appearing from the legislation. We would not intend to deter legitimate tax planning or mitigation in taxpayers' ordinary commercial or personal affairs.
25. To that end, we consider that, if a general anti-avoidance rule were adopted, it should incorporate the following features –
    i. Its scope of operation should be limited to transactions which, judged as a whole, have tax avoidance as a main purpose or, in the case of multi-step transactions, when a particular step in the transaction has tax avoidance as its sole purpose.
    ii. It should exclude transactions that are inconsistent with the intention of Parliament, as appears from the legislation taken as a whole.
    iii. The provision should at its introduction be evoked centrally by the Head Office of the Revenue authority concerned (ie. local or regional officers should not be able to invoke the rule or offer clearances in respect of the rule).
    iv. An administrative clearance system should be established so that taxpayers can ascertain whether the Revenue authorities would regard a proposed transaction as falling within the scope of the new provision. A clearance application necessarily implies some delay but this should be kept to the minimum.
    v. There should be a single stage appeal to an independent tribunal against a refusal of a clearance, based on the papers submitted to the Revenue authority.

vi. When invoking the rule against a completed transaction, the onus in the first instance should be on the Revenue authority to show why the transaction is of a nature that the general anti-avoidance rule ought to apply.

vii. As part of the procedure for invoking the rule, the Revenue authority would be required to state the alternative transaction that it considers should be substituted for the actual transaction as the basis for assessing tax. If there were more than one permitted alternative transaction, that which attracts the least tax should be adopted.

26. We wish to emphasise the importance of points ii and iv above. We recognise that many taxpayers and their professional advisers may be cautious in the face of a new general anti-avoidance provision. As a result, the Revenue authorities could be asked to give clearance on just about every case that might be thought to come within the ambit of the provision. If the scope of a general anti-avoidance provision is too widely drawn, this would create a serious impediment to commercial and personal transactions, and the Revenue authorities would need to devote very substantial resources to operate the clearance procedure satisfactorily.

27. We do not envisage, however, that the Government can produce a satisfactory general anti-avoidance rule at no administrative cost. The provision must strike the right balance and must be capable of practical application. We believe that the Government can only achieve this if it accepts whatever cost is involved in providing the proper administrative framework and safeguards for taxpayers. If it were not prepared to incur this cost, it should not propose a statutory rule.

28. A statutory provision would be designed to give effect to the Parliamentary intent and policy of the legislation. We think it important, as regards point iii, to secure a consistent application of the provision and to avoid any perception that the provision is a bargaining tool that the Revenue authorities can use in auditing ordinary tax liabilities. We think it appropriate also that the Revenue authorities be required to report annually to Parliament on the operation of the provision.

Conclusion

We have concluded that a sensibly targeted general anti-avoidance provision, with an appropriate clearance procedure, could make a contribution to the effort to deter and counteract tax avoidance; and we would prefer this to the development of some new judicial anti-avoidance doctrine. But, adopting a general anti-avoidance provision that fails to satisfy the criteria (in particular with respect to safeguards for taxpayers' rights) which we have set out or that fails to meet the requirements that we mention in paragraph 27, could well be a recipe for disaster, in the disruption that it could create for ordinary commercial and personal affairs, and in the administrative problems it posed for the Revenue authorities. It would certainly be vehemently opposed by most, if not all, of the members of this Committee. **[5.18]**

In 1998, the Inland Revenue, published a consultative document, *A General Anti-avoidance rule for Direct Taxes* (the reasons for which are set out in the following extract from that document) that purported to build on the work of the TLRC in its report, and which, similarly, favoured the enactment of a statutory general anti-avoidance rule but applicable, in the first instance, only to the 'corporate sector'. **[5.19]**

Inland Revenue, *A General Anti-avoidance Rule for Direct Taxes: Consultative Document* (1998)

4. Why a GAAR is under consideration

4.1 In the last 20 years or so, much legislation has been enacted to counter tax avoidance. At the same time, the courts have developed a doctrine, following the *Ramsay* case[98], which has put some limits on the scope for avoidance. However, new devices for avoiding tax continue to be developed.

4.2 For example, a company with a cash surplus available for a short-term investment purchases a newly-incorporated company from a bank. The purchase is arranged so that at the end of a set period, the acquired company will have liquid assets (provided by the bank) worth more than the purchase price. The margin is broadly equivalent to the interest which would have been paid if the company had placed its cash on deposit with the bank. Such interest would have been subject to income tax. This arrangement creates a potential chargeable gain but there is no need to sell the company straightaway. The "*Ramsay*" approach or arguments over the meaning of "discount" may be in point.

4.3 The United Kingdom is unusual among developed countries in having neither a statute nor an established legal principle to counter tax avoidance in general. Many other countries in the developed world have found such a rule or principle to be a very useful remedy for countering tax avoidance, although not a universal cure.

4.4 The aim of a GAAR would be to reduce tax avoidance. It should not unduly harm the level of certainty of tax treatment enjoyed by businesses that are not engaged in avoidance.

4.5 A GAAR, applying at first only to the corporate sector, would aim to put a stop to many of the complex avoidance schemes which currently cost the Exchequer large sums. In addition, it would be expected to discourage people from devising contrived avoidance schemes in the future.

4.6 Taxpayers using avoidance schemes stand to gain a lot while risking little. The sole or main purpose of the arrangements, or of one or more of the steps in them, is to gain a tax advantage.

4.7 The traditional way in the UK of countering such schemes has been to litigate or to introduce specific anti-avoidance legislation to stop them.

4.8 Litigation has its benefits and – with or without GAAR – there will always be cases at the borders of statute or case law where the courts will have to decide on the correct interpretation. But litigation in complex avoidance cases can take a long time to resolve and the uncertainty of the outcome can be prolonged considerably.

4.9 Legislation targeted at specific avoidance schemes or arrangements stops them for the future. But, short of retrospective legislation, the Government cannot recoup the tax lost to early users of the schemes. Consequently it has little or no deterrent effect. This type of legislation is vulnerable to yet further avoidance schemes, constructed to find a way around the letter of the law.

4.10 One possible approach would be to introduce "mini-GAARs" – general rules to stop avoidance in a particular area of the tax system ... But it seems unlikely that this would be as effective as a single, all-embracing

98 *W.T. Ramsay Ltd v CIR.*, 54 TC 101; [see above, para **[5.7]**].

GAAR for countering avoidance of corporate direct taxes. This is because of the complexity of the direct tax system and the scope for interaction within its provisions.

4.11 An important criterion of the success of a GAAR would be that it should not unduly harm the levels of certainty which companies currently have about the tax treatment of a transaction. The Tax Law Review Committee (TLRC) report on Tax Avoidance expressed concern about the uncertainty created by what it saw as "innovative judicial anti-avoidance techniques" operating retrospectively. To that extent, the introduction of a statutory GAAR would be a positive step in this area.

4.12 Although a GAAR should reduce avoidance and maintain certainty, it must be accepted that neither aim can be absolute. The need for targeted anti-avoidance legislation will remain, for instance where avoidance centres on the interaction between the tax systems of the UK and other countries, and there will always be some areas where the application of the law has to be resolved through the courts. **[5.20]**

The Inland Revenue's proposals in relation to a GAAR, as set out in the consultative document, were unfavourably received by business and tax professionals, and also, notably, by the TLRC in its *Response to Inland Revenue* (IFS, 1999). Broadly, the TLRC indicated in that document that the Inland Revenue's proposals, especially as to the form a GAAR might take and as to the nature of the related extra-statutory guidance provided by a clearance procedure, did not give effect to the TLRC's objectives in proposing a GAAR and did not produce a satisfactory balance between the Inland Revenue and taxpayers. In his foreword to the *Response*, the Right Honourable Lord Howe of Aberavon CH QC stated:[99]

> 'In 1997 [in the foreword to the TLRC's 1997 report] I warned against the unintended consequences of ill-judged change. And the Committee cautioned that a statutory provision which failed the Committee's standards – especially as to the framework and resources for its administration and the safeguards for taxpayers would be a recipe for disastrous disruption of ordinary commercial and personal affairs, as well as an administrative nightmare for the Revenue authorities.
>
> Those practical standards remain the yardstick today – and it is by those standards that the Committee concludes that the proposals set out in the Inland Revenue's Consultative Document are not well-judged.'

In these circumstances, it is not surprising, perhaps, that the proposals contained in the consultative document have not been implemented. Moreover, it may be, as the following extract suggests, that the focus should be not on devising a statutory general anti-avoidance *rule* but on the enactment of a general anti-avoidance *principle* (GANTIP). **[5.21]**

99 TLRC *Response to Inland Revenue* (IFS, 1999) p ii.

Judith Freedman, 'Defining Taxpayer Responsibility: In Support of a General Anti-Avoidance Principle' [2004] BTR 332, 353–356

The need for a statutory anti-avoidance principle

Rules and Principles

Some would suggest that the only way forward is more specific anti-avoidance legislation. The arguments for this are legitimacy and certainty. Yet certainty will not be achieved in this way. It is self-evident that increased specific provision results in complexity – what the US literature calls *hyperlexis*[100] – and the problem of creative compliance.[101] This produces more litigation and more uncertainty. These observations result in the conclusion that what we need is not more precise and detailed avoidance provisions but a principles or standards approach. Variants of this idea have been suggested by Surrey, Avery Jones, Braithwaite, Weisbach and others.[102] Some of these writers claim that this approach would result in greater certainty as well as reduced complexity but the claim here is only that the volume of legislation could be reduced and that a more sensible framework for managing tax avoidance could be produced by this route.

There is much jurisprudence on the meaning of principles as opposed to rules and some legal philosophers would deny that there is any logical difference between the two.[103] For our purposes here the distinction has a valuable role to play provided it is not made to carry too great a weight of meaning. In particular, the concept of principles is not used here to connote any notion of moral content since it has already been explained that it is not possible for the courts to decide issues of taxation on the basis of morality, without the morality being given legal content.[104] In addition, the principle argued for here is a statutory principle, not one derived from case law, although some principles may be derived from case law.[105] Braithwaite, looking for the common ground between the various writers rather than the distinctions, defines rules as specific prescriptions, whilst principles are unspecific or vague prescriptions.[106] There is debate over whether this is a

100 B.Manning, "Hyperlexis: Our National Disease" (1977) 71 *Northwestern University Law Review* 767; W. Schwidetzky, "Hyperlexis and the Loophole" (1996) 49 *Oklahoma Law Review* 403.

101 McBarnet [D McBarnet and C Whelan 'The Elusive Spirit of the Law: Formalism and the Struggle for Legal Control' (1991) 54 MLR 848].

102 S. Surrey, "Complexity and the Internal Revenue Code: The Problem of the Management of Tax Detail" (1969) 34 *Law and Contemporary Problems* 673; cited in Weisbach [D Weisbach 'Formalism in the Tax Law' (1999) 66 University of Chicago Law Review 860]; Braithwaite [J Braithwaite 'Making Tax Law More Certain: A Theory' (2003) 31 Australian Business Law Review 72]; J. Braithwaite, "Rules and Principles: A Theory of Legal Certainty" (2002) *Australian Journal of Legal Philosophy* 47; J. Avery Jones [J F Avery Jones 'Tax Law: Rules or Principles?' [1996] BTR 580].

103 The distinction drawn by R. Dworkin, initially in "The Model of Rules" (1967) 35 *University of Chicago Law Review* 25, has in any event changed over the years. There is not space to cite even a small proportion of the literature but a key debate has taken place between Dworkin and J. Raz [J Raz 'Legal Principles and the Limits of Law' (1971–1972) 81 Yale Law Review 823]. For a comprehensive rejection of principles as defined by Dworkin see A. Marmor, *Positive Law and Objective Values* (OUP, Oxford, 2001).

104 This is not, therefore, a true Dworkonian view of principles but is closer to that taken by Raz [J Raz 'Legal Principles and the Limits of Law' (1971–1972) 81 Yale Law Journal 823, 849].

105 Raz, *ibid.* 852.

106 Braithwaite (2002) [J Braithwaite 'Rules and Principles: A Theory of Legal Certainty' (2002) Australian Journal of Legal Philosophy 47] 47–52.

qualitative difference, or just one of degree. A Dworkonian principle is qualitatively different from a rule: rules are all or nothing, but principles can be weighed against each other. Others have pointed out, however, that rules too may have weight in that one rule may form an exception from another. The term principle is used here, as by Braithwaite, to indicate a provision which is broader than a detailed rule and thus can be used as a guide to interpret the rule.[107] In this context, the legislative principle would be a method of signposting; a Parliamentary indication that it was its intention that certain types of gap in its rule making should be filled by judicial decision based on the principles set out.

Ideally, any such general anti-avoidance principle or GANTIP would be accompanied by other gap-filling principles, as suggested by Avery Jones[108] and found in other European tax systems.[109] In addition, as in those other systems, more liberal use of explanatory memoranda or other descriptive material would be permitted than is the case now in the UK to back up this new approach to tax legislation.[110] Expressing the general intention of the legislature in the case of tax legislation is not going to be easy. Prebble has argued that income tax is not based in *a priori* principle but is a compromise.[111] In many cases the aim is simply to raise revenue. But just because the whole of tax law could not be based on high-level principles does not mean that some such principles could not be agreed and it might be an exceptionally good exercise for Parliament and its advisers to at least contemplate whether this was the case. A requirement for a preamble which could be used by judges for the purpose of interpretation might go a long way to clarify parliamentary intention, for example where tax law is being used to provide incentives, as we have seen in connection with the *Barclays* case.[112] Such a requirement might induce more governmental and Parliamentary reflection on the harmful culture of artificiality ...

Certainty the wrong test

A general anti-avoidance principle in tax in the UK has not so far been accepted. A major objection has been that such a principle would undermine certainty. Some of the authors discussed here have responded, not unconvincingly, that a system of rules interpreted in accordance with principles could increase certainty. It may be, however, in any event, that certainty is not the right test at the successful/unsuccessful avoidance boundary as opposed to the avoidance/evasion boundary, at least if criminal penalties are not involved at the former boundary.[113] What should take priority is producing a practical system with a fair test which is workable for

107 Raz [J Raz 'Legal Principles and the Limits of Law' (1971–1972) 81 Yale Law Journal 823] 839.

108 Avery Jones [J F Avery Jones 'Tax Law: Rules or Principles?' [1996] BTR 580.] See also L. Beighton 'Simplification of Tax Legislation' [1996] BTR 601.

109 For example in Spain, see Soler Roch [M T Soler Roch 'The Reform of a Tax Code: The Experience of the Spanish General Tax Act' [2004] BTR 234].

110 Going beyond the limited extension of such use in *Pepper v Hart* [1993] BTR 112.

111 J. Prebble, "Principles and Purpose or Precise and Detailed" [1998] BTR 112.

112 [Ie *Barclays Mercantile Finance Ltd v Mawson (Inspector of Taxes)*. For the House of Lords opinion in this case, see [2004] 3 WLR 1383, and above, para **[5.13]**.]

113 See the discussion of certainty above and contrast New Zealand where the *Tax Administration Act* 1994 imposes penalties for taking an abusive tax position (one which is based on an unacceptable interpretation of the law) or an unacceptable interpretation (one which, if viewed objectively, fails to meet the standard of being about as likely as not to be correct). Whilst it is understandable that the authorities wish to create a downside and deterrent to tax avoidance activity, here the fuzziness around these concepts may represent a deficit in the law. There is extensive revenue guidance available – whether this is an adequate substitute for clear legislative guidance in these circumstances is for discussion. (Thanks to Shelley Griffiths of University of Otago for this information.)

the compliant majority but not as susceptible to manipulation as would be an entirely certain test, even assuming such a test could be devised.

The Inland Revenue's proposal for a general anti-avoidance rule (GAAR) in 1998,[114] which built on a proposal from the Tax Law Review Committee (TLRC) in 1997,[115] was rejected in some degree for lack of certainty. The TRLC produced a draft clause based on the "evident intention" of Parliament and containing a purpose test as any GAAR or GANTIP would need to do. It also argued that a statutory GAAR would provide a framework in which sensible consequences of the application of the GAAR could be specified in a way that cannot happen with a judicial rule and that proper administrative procedures, such as a clearance mechanism, could be put in place to protect taxpayers. The Inland Revenue's own proposal tipped the balance away from the careful one constructed by the TLRC, both by redefining the GAAR and by expressing scepticism about clearances. The proposal was abandoned after negative responses from the tax community and when the TLRC could not support the Revenue's proposal.[116]

Commenting on the proposals, Philip Gillett, Taxation Controller of ICI, whilst keen to stop the "extreme scheme merchants" thought that unacceptable avoidance was a matter for the courts to determine, "in accordance with the social and political mores of the time".[117] Once again, this raises difficult jurisprudential questions of where these mores are to be found. At a practical level, the immediate problem is that the UK courts have not shown themselves willing to evolve a general anti-avoidance principle in a coherent and linear fashion. The majority of the judges do not accept that they may do so legitimately and certainly not on the basis of social and political mores. The place for a sensible debate about acceptability and social norms, and how to incorporate them into law, is not in the courts but in Parliament.

Troup, by contrast, objected to the proposed GARR as shifting responsibility for determination of tax liability away from Parliament and in practice to the Revenue, since it required a body other than Parliament to consider what Parliament would have intended had it considered an issue, which by definition it had not done. In his view a GAAR can never achieve certainty so must always be wrong in principle.[118] It is for this reason that it may be preferable to talk about a GANTIP, to make clear that certainty is not the claim.

A GANTIP would be drawn up in wide terms and not attempt to define the type of transaction that would be struck down in a detailed way. One of the problems with the TLRC illustrative provision and the Inland Revenue's own version was that they became too detailed and the debate quickly focused on the precise wording rather than deciding on the object of the exercise. The TLRC provision attempted to replicate the *Ramsay* rule in some respects with a concept of steps that was unnecessarily complex. It is notable that the Australian GAAR does not attempt this level of detail or precision and has met with some success.[119] It contains a purpose

114 Inland Revenue, *A General Anti-avoidance Rule for Direct Taxes: Consultative Document* (London, 1998); [see above, para **[5.20]**].

115 [See Tax Law Review Committee *Tax Avoidance* (IFS, 1997); above, para **[5.18]**.] The author was a member of the TLRC which agreed this report, although she did not work directly on this project as a researcher or writer.

116 TLRC , *Response to Inland Revenue* (IFS, London, 1999).

117 P. Gillett [1999] BTR 1.

118 E. Troup [1999] BTR 5. He accepted, though, that principles must be subject to pragmatism.

119 See Tiley [John Tiley 'Tax Avoidance Jurisprudence as Normal Law' [2004] BTR 304.] . . . The legislation has been extensively criticised in Australia and see Orow [Nabil Orow, "Structured Finance and the Operation of General Anti-Avoidance Rules [2004] BTR 410] but it would be a reasonable starting point for a feasibility study as it does appear to have altered the mindset of practitioners in that jurisdiction.

test and *indicia* of purpose are listed.[120] As Orow explains, one suggestion for an improvement of the Australian GAAR coming from the Ralph Committee was to propose a clause clarifying that the rule should be exercised in a manner consistent with and supportive of the tax policy principles embodied in other provisions of tax law, such as the availability of an election.[121] A UK GANTIP might contain a purpose test and a direction to consider what Parliament would have intended within the scheme of the legislation had it considered the scheme before it. This, coupled with the use of background papers and improved preambles and statements from Parliament about the rationale of legislation would give guidance to the courts in going beyond the wording of the legislation but always within the rationale of the legislation. Troup says that to look beyond what Parliament actually intended raises constitutional issues but this is the very point of the GANTIP. If we are currently facing a crisis of legitimacy and if the courts cannot or will not counteract the literal meaning of a statute by reference to an overriding legal principle they have created themselves, only a statutory GANTIP could remove this constitutional objection. Under a GANTIP, Parliament gives express permission for its intention to be constructed (within the overall scheme of the legislation) where there is a scheme which is carried out for the purpose of obtaining a tax benefit. This is not removing responsibility from Parliament but ensures that Parliamentary will can be carried forward in a practical way and without undue delay. The GANTIP would not permit the Revenue or courts to go beyond what could be justifiably discerned or established *would have been* the intention of Parliament[122] but would provide a legitimate framework in which the courts could operate to work out what Parliament would have intended ... **[5.22]**

For further consideration of the approach advocated in the above extract, see Judith Freedman 'Interpreting Tax Statutes: Tax Avoidance and the Intention of Parliament' (2007) 123 LQR 53, in which it is submitted, inter alia, that the judicial approach to tax avoidance requires a proper framework which could be provided by legislation including a principles-based GAAR, and that 'a properly drafted GAAR, referring to principles that included, but were not limited to, economic substance, could give the judiciary the powers it needed to give full effect to parliamentary intention and prevent the frustration of specific legislation'. **[5.23]**

4. A new development – disclosure of direct tax avoidance schemes

Recently, the ability of HMRC to manage the risk to tax revenues from the avoidance of tax has been enhanced by the introduction of disclosure rules the principal purposes of which are to enable HMRC to identify direct tax avoidance schemes earlier than was previously the case, to find out about schemes the existence of which it may otherwise have been unaware, and, thereafter, to take, if necessary, appropriate action to curb those schemes which it perceives not to be in conformity with what the tax system allows. The

120 For the provisions, see TLRC [*Tax Avoidance* (IFS, London, 1997)], Appendix 1 (Pt IVA).
121 Orow [n 119] at p. 420.
122 This is the formulation of the TLRC but with the words in italics added by the author: TLRC [*Tax Avoidance* (IFS, 1997)] para. 5.12.

rationale for these rules, which were introduced in 2004, is reflected in the following statement of the Paymaster General, the Right Honourable Dawn Primarolo MP, made during the Standing Committee debates on the Finance Bill 2004:[123]

> 'The dividing line between acceptable tax planning and unacceptable tax avoidance is very difficult to draw with precision.[124] Therefore, the Government are approaching the matter on the basis that the disclosure rules are designed to reflect that. They will operate entirely in a non-judgmental way and they are aimed at those types of transactions where, in the Inland Revenue's experience, there is a risk of unacceptably high avoidance.'

The following extract examines the direct tax disclosure rules following their amendment in 2006, and, in particular, the duty to disclose which is founded on the existence of factors known as 'hallmarks'.[125] **[5.24]**

Rebecca Bland 'Hallmarks and the Direct Tax Disclosure Regime' [2006] BTR 653

... One of the significant features of the disclosure regime is that it does not incorporate a definition of a tax avoidance transaction. Rather its scope is delineated by the use of "hallmarks" which are intended to encapsulate features which the Government perceives are common to arrangements it considers to be illegitimate ...

Notifiable arrangements

The primary legislation introducing the disclosure regime establishes the broad parameters of its scope. It provides that arrangements fall within the regime if they:
(i) enable, or might be expected to enable, the obtaining of a prescribed tax advantage (the "threshold requirement");
(ii) are such that the main benefit, or one of the main benefits, that might be expected to arise from the arrangements is the obtaining of that advantage (the "main benefit requirement"); and
(iii) fall within any description prescribed by regulations.[126]

The legislation does impose some limits on the scope of the regime. In particular, although "arrangements" and "tax advantage" are widely defined, the main benefit requirement has the potential to restrict the scope of the regime significantly. However further restrictions are introduced in regulations.

When the regime first came into force, regulations (the 2004 Regulations) limited the scope of the regime to arrangements "connected with employment" and those "in relation to financial products".[127] In the December 2005 Pre-Budget Report it was announced that the original regulations would be repealed and new regulations (the 2006 Regulations) have now been enacted.[128] These prescribe arrangements

123 HC Standing Committee Debates, 20th sitting, col. 714, 22 June 2004.
124 [Ie fiscally effective and fiscally ineffective respectively.]
125 For the disclosure regimes relating to value added tax and stamp duty land tax, see, Value Added Tax Act 1994, Sch 11A and the Stamp Duty Land Tax Avoidance Schemes (Prescribed Descriptions of Arrangements) Regulations (SI 2005/1868) respectively.
126 FA 2004, s.306.
127 The Tax Avoidance Schemes (Prescribed Description of Arrangements) Regulations 2004 (SI 2004 No. 1863).
128 The Tax Avoidance Schemes (Prescribed Description of Arrangements) Regulations 2006 (SI 2006 No. 1543).

that contain any of a list of hallmarks; which hallmarks are applicable depends on whether or not a promoter is involved in the arrangements.

The hallmarks applicable whether or not a promoter is involved in the arrangements are:

(1) confidentiality: if a promoter is involved then the hallmark looks to whether a (hypothetical) promoter might reasonably be expected to wish to keep the arrangements confidential from other promoters or the (actual) promoter would wish to keep the arrangements confidential from HMRC. If there is no promoter, the hallmark looks to whether the user of the arrangements wishes to keep the arrangements confidential from HMRC;

(2) premium fee: this hallmark looks to whether a (hypothetical) promoter might reasonably be expected to be able to charge a premium fee for the provision of tax services in relation to the arrangements; and

(3) leasing arrangements: this hallmark applies to leasing arrangements which satisfy certain detailed conditions.

The hallmarks which are only applicable if a promoter is involved in the arrangements are:

(4) off-market terms: this hallmark looks to whether the arrangements include one of a list of financial products, the tax advantage arising from the arrangements derives from the inclusion of the financial product, the promoter is party to the financial product and the price of the financial product is off-market. The Government has suggested that the purpose of this hallmark is to catch arrangements where the promoter is remunerated through the terms of a financial product rather than by charging a premium fee;[129]

(5) standardised tax products: this hallmark applies to arrangements with standardised documentation if it would be reasonable for an informed observer to conclude that the main purpose of the arrangements was to enable a client to obtain a tax advantage and the arrangements are not exempted by a white list set out in the regulations; and

(6) loss schemes: this hallmark applies where an informed observer could reasonably conclude that the main benefit of the arrangements is the provision of losses to individuals and the promoter expects more than one individual to implement the arrangements.

The function of the regulations

In introducing the disclosure regime following the 2004 Budget, the Government stated that its intention was to "focus on areas of high risk and to construct the disclosure requirements narrowly by targeting particular types of avoidance".[130] Limiting the scope of those arrangements subject to disclosure is essential both for the Government (to ensure that HMRC are not swamped with disclosures) and for taxpayers, to ensure they are not subject to undue compliance costs. The Government's decision to revise the 2004 Regulations amounts to a decision to refine the focus of the regime.

129 HMRC Guidance, Disclosure of Tax Avoidance Schemes – Income Tax, Corporation Tax, Capital Gains Tax and Stamp Duty Land Tax (July 2006), para.6.5.2 currently available at: www.hmrc.gov.uk/ria.disclosure-guidance.pdf.

130 HMRC Explanatory Notes, Regulatory Impact Assessment: Tackling Tax Avoidance – Disclosure Requirements April 6, 2004 (2004 RIA) at para.13 currently available at www.hmrc.gov.uk/ria/tackling-tax-avoidance.pdf.

While the content of the regulations gives a good idea of which areas the Government considers to be of "high risk", the regulations do not make explicit what the Government considers to constitute "tax avoidance". However the materials produced when the disclosure regime was introduced suggest that the Government considers that arrangements involve illegitimate tax avoidance when they "seek to defeat the Government's tax policy objectives".[131] This message was re-iterated when the 2006 Regulations were introduced.[132] The concept of "tax avoidance" is a notoriously difficult one and there is a vast academic literature attempting to define the term. It is not clear whether, for the purposes of the disclosure regime, the Government has formed the view that the essence of a tax avoidance transaction is one which is inconsistent with Government tax policy; though, if this is the Government's understanding of the term, it is submitted that it is a very controversial definition.

What is clear is that although the legislation and the regulations describe the disclosure regime as addressing "tax avoidance", the Government's goal has been to devise a scheme under which only arrangements that are contrary to its tax policy are disclosable. To achieve this goal, the Government has not sought to devise a definition of the types of transactions it considers to be illegitimate. Rather, the scope of the regime is determined through the use of features which the Government perceives to be common to those transactions.

The primary legislation

At first glance, the primary legislation might appear to provide a definition of the types of scheme which the Government considers to be illegitimate. The threshold requirement is a feature common to statutory anti-avoidance provisions; in particular it is very similar to the formulation used in section 709 of the Income and Corporation Taxes Act 1988. Similarly the main benefit requirement could be viewed as going to the essence of whether the arrangements are illegitimate. However it is submitted that these requirements are better viewed as features common to transactions which the Government perceives are illegitimate, rather than going to the essence of those transactions.

It is hard to imagine how the disclosure regime could have been drafted without utilising a threshold requirement. The existence of "arrangements" provides a framework within which the other limits on the scope of the disclosure regime can be considered. Further, unless the arrangements confer a "tax advantage", they are extremely unlikely to be of interest to the Government. However although the threshold requirement may be a pre-requisite to determine whether arrangements could be perceived by the Government as illegitimate, it is not a sufficient condition to determine whether this is the case. A very wide range of arrangements that produce a tax advantage would be perceived as constituting tax avoidance. The threshold requirement could have been used as the foundation for a definition of what the Government considers to be illegitimate tax avoidance, however an analysis of the other conditions in the disclosure regime demonstrates that it has not been used in this way.

Whether or not the main benefit that might be expected to arise from the arrangements is the obtaining of a tax advantage, could be perceived as a question going to the essence of whether the arrangements are inconsistent with the Government's tax policy. However this is not necessarily the case. The Government

131 2004 RIA [HMRC Explanatory Notes, Regulatory Impact Assessment: Tackling Tax Avoidance – Disclosure Requirements 6 April 2004], at paras 6–7.

132 2006 RIA [HMRC Regulatory Impact Assessment – The Tax Avoidance Schemes (Prescribed Description of Arrangements) Regulations 2006 (SI 2006/1543)] at para. 2.

uses tax law to achieve a variety of social and economic objectives including promoting enterprise, protecting the environment and encouraging saving and investment.[133] Consequently, the Government's tax policy reflects a variety of fiscal and non-fiscal goals. If they are consistent with a non-fiscal objective, arrangements which give rise to a very significant fiscal benefit will not necessarily be inconsistent with the Government's tax policy. Further, where there are very limited benefits to the participants from entering into given arrangements, it is possible that the main benefit expected to arise from those arrangements will be the obtaining of a tax advantage, even though the tax advantage in question is marginal. Such arrangement may not be inconsistent with the fiscal aspects of the Government's tax policy. For example, in *Crown Bedding v Commissioners of Inland Revenue*, the Commissioners concluded that the main benefit to the taxpayer company of removing a minority shareholder was a tax advantage which arose because the financial fortunes of the company changed significantly after the shareholder was removed. The Commissioners noted that the difficulty which arose in the case was "not the comparative greatness of the benefits . . . but their comparative smallness".[134]

It was noted above that, if the Government does consider that a transaction constitutes illegitimate tax avoidance if it is inconsistent with its tax policy, this is a controversial interpretation. One alternative theory of tax avoidance suggests that whether a tax-reducing activity is legitimate turns on the taxpayer's state of mind in participating in it.[135] Even if the main benefit filter does not go to the essence of tax avoidance as the term is used by the Government, it could be argued that it goes to the essence of tax avoidance for the purposes of this theory. However this theory looks to the taxpayer's actual, subjective state of mind. By contrast there is case law considering the meaning of the term "main benefit" when it has been used in other legislation provisions, which concludes that the term has an objective meaning.[136]

The regulations

Although there may be ambiguity as to the functions of the threshold and main benefit requirements, it is clear that the filters included in the 2004 Regulations did not, and the hallmarks included in the 2006 Regulations do not, aim to go to the essence of whether arrangements constitute illegitimate tax avoidance. What the Government perceived as objectionable about the arrangements that fell within the 2004 Regulations was not that they were "connected with employment" or "in relation to financial products". Similarly, the fact that arrangements fall within one of the hallmarks prescribed by the 2006 Regulations is not of itself objectionable to the Government. Rather the Government perceives that arrangements that it views as objectionable are frequently "connected with employment", "in relation to financial products" or fall within one of the prescribed hallmarks.

133 HM Treasury, Financing Britain's Future – Review of the Revenue Departments (Cm. 6163) at para. 5.8–5.10.

134 34 TC 107 at 111; this case considered the application of FA 1944, s.33.

135 There is a vast literature on this topic; see, for example, G.S.A. Wheatcroft, "The Attitude of the Legislature and the Courts to Tax Avoidance" 18 MLR 209; M.C. Flesch, "Tax Avoidance: the Attitude of the Courts and the Legislature" (1968) 21 Current Legal Problems 215 at 216–17; M. Gammie, "Tax Avoidance and the Rule of Law: A Perspective from the United Kingdom" in G.S.C. Cooper ed., Tax Avoidance and the Rule of Law (IBFD Publications BV, Amsterdam, 1997) 181 at 199–200.

136 See for example, (considering FA 1944, s.33) *Crown Bedding v IRC* 34 TC 107 at 117–118 and *Marshall Castings v IRC* 34 TC 122 at 135–136; (considering FA 1951, s.32(3)) *Ackland & Pratten Ltd v IRC* 39 TC 649 at 662 and *Jarvis Robinson Transport v IRC* 41 TC 410 at 415; (considering FA 1971, Sched.8 para.3(1)(c)) *Barclays Mercantile Industrial Finance v Melluish* [1990] STC 314 at 342–343.

This approach is clearly reflected in the Government's adoption of the term "hallmark" (meaning, broadly, distinctive feature) in connection with the 2006 Regulations.[137] Although the term was not employed in connection with the 2004 Regulations, the conditions that were required to be satisfied before arrangements fell to be considered as "connected with employment" or "in relation to financial products", effectively operated as hallmarks.

Significance of using hallmarks

Devising a legislative definition of what the Government appears to understand by the term "tax avoidance" would be extremely difficult and the resulting definition would almost certainly be complex and difficult to apply. This is not a problem exclusive to the Government's understanding of the term "tax avoidance", any other definition would be similarly challenging to devise. Accordingly the decision that the disclosure regime should not include a definition of the types of illegitimate arrangements it is intended to apply to, was a sensible one.

Using hallmarks may avoid the complexity that would arise if the regime incorporated a formal definition, but it is important to note that this approach may limit the accuracy of the regime's scope. No list of the typical features of a set of arrangements will ever be exactly right; consequently some arrangements that the Government would view as legitimate may be disclosable and some that it might view as illegitimate may not. This possibility has been recognised by the Government and HMRC's Guidance to the disclosure regime notes both that arrangements may need to be disclosed even if they are not considered to be illegitimate and that the fact arrangements are not disclosable does not mean that they are necessarily acceptable to HMRC.[138] The inaccuracies of a system based on hallmarks, rather than a formal definition, should not be overstated, given the difficulties of devising and applying any such definition. However the use of hallmarks means that some degree of accuracy has been sacrificed . . .

Selecting the hallmarks

Selecting the hallmarks to be used in the disclosure regime presents a paradox. For the Government to devise hallmarks encapsulating characteristics typical of arrangements it considers to be illegitimate, it needs to be aware of the arrangements that are being devised and their constituent elements. However the purpose of the disclosure regime is to remedy the Government's lack of knowledge about what transactions taxpayers are entering into. This was why, although the Government stated that it was pleased with the operation of the disclosure regime when it was first introduced, it was natural that the Government would wish to keep the scope of the regime under review and perhaps inevitable that the 2004 Regulations would be amended. The disclosures made while those regulations were in force, provided the Government with information which it could use to refine the scope of the regime.

There are further reasons why the hallmarks need to be kept under review. Even if the hallmarks in the 2004 Regulations did encapsulate the core features of arrangements in the market when the regulations came into force, the core features of such arrangements were always likely to change. Such changes could be caused by

137 The term "hallmark" is not used in the 2006 Regulations themselves; the term "description" is used.

138 HMRC Guidance, [HMRC Guidance, Disclosure of Tax Avoidance Schemes – Income Tax, Corporation Tax, Capital Gains Tax and Stamp Duty Land Tax (July 2006)], para. 2.3.2 and 6.1.

developments in the Government's tax policy which change the type of arrangements it considers to be illegitimate. They will also occur as new arrangements are devised, either organically or possibly in direct response to the hallmarks themselves . . .

The Government has been ambiguous about whether it is concerned that promoters in the UK have adopted this approach. In introducing the 2006 Regulations the Government explicitly stated that it did not believe that promoters had responded to the disclosure regime by creating "ever more complex schemes intended to avoid anti-avoidance measures themselves".[139] In the same document, however, the Government went on to note that the market had changed since the introduction of the 2004 Regulations and that the filters it contained no longer fully captured the way that promoters engage clients and earn fees.[140] This could be because the market had changed organically, but the Government observed that the effect of this was that certain areas of avoidance were outside the regime. In surveying its possible responses to this issue the Government concluded that leaving the 2004 Regulations unamended was not an option as "it would encourage the use of avoidance schemes outside the area covered by the disclosure regime".[141] This suggests that the Government may be concerned about promoters' willingness to exploit the scope of the regime.

Whether or not promoters are adopting this approach, it is likely that the characteristics of the transactions which the Government is interested in will change over time. Accordingly, the hallmarks will need to be subject to continuous review and the 2006 Regulations may need to be revised in due course. Whilst this is perhaps an inevitable feature of the hallmarks, it is an inconvenient one for both the Government and taxpayers, whose compliance costs will be increased every time new regulations are introduced.

Certainty in the hallmarks

Revision of the hallmarks imposes a compliance cost on taxpayers. The use of hallmarks, however, also provides an opportunity to reduce taxpayers' compliance costs as hallmarks provide a method of limiting the scope of the disclosure regime in a way that gives the regime clear and certain parameters. It is, therefore, important that the hallmarks are clearly drafted and easy to apply. This is especially important in light of the fact that the use of hallmarks may make the scope of the disclosure regime less accurate. To justify the lack of accuracy caused by the use of hallmarks, it is crucial that they enhance the regime's certainty. If the hallmarks are complex and difficult to apply then the disclosure regime will have assumed the disadvantages of a system based on hallmarks (namely, the lack of accuracy) and none of the potential advantages (namely, the opportunity to ensure that its scope is certain).

The Government has shown itself to be sympathetic to the need to ensure that conditions regulating the scope of the disclosure regime are easy to apply. In response to taxpayers' concerns that they were unworkable, the Government amended the initial draft regulations applicable to arrangements in relation to financial products, and produced the 2004 Regulations in close consultation with taxpayers and their advisers.[142] Similarly the Government consulted widely prior to the enactment of the 2006 Regulations.

139 2006 RIA, [n 132], para.16.
140 2006 RIA, [n 132], para.22.
141 2006 RIA, [n.132], para.30.
142 The initial draft regulations are discussed in Granwell and McGonigle ['US Tax Shelters: a UK Reprise?' [2006] 170], at 197–198.

Whether the hallmarks introduced under the 2006 Regulations are clear and easy to apply has been the subject of considerable debate and concern remains that they contain ambiguities.[143] It is submitted that the doubts raised are well-founded and that certain features of the hallmarks may give rise to difficulties in practice . . .

Conclusion

. . . The decision to use hallmarks to delineate the scope of the disclosure regime was a sensible one; it was a decision, however, that has implications for the way in which the regime needs to be administered. The introduction of the 2006 Regulations demonstrates the Government's awareness that one implication is that the hallmarks will need to be subject to continual review. However the content of the 2006 Regulations suggests that the second implication of using hallmarks, namely the need to ensure that they are clear and easy to apply, has not been fully appreciated. Whether the ramifications of the use of hallmarks on the way in which information collected under the disclosure regime is used will be reflected in the way the regime is administered, remains to be seen.[144] **[5.25]**

The direct tax disclosure rules have been amended further by FA 2007 which incorporates into FA 2004 (with retroactive effect) provisions that enable HMRC to challenge individuals *suspected* of promoting notifiable schemes but who deny doing so.[145] Previously, HMRC could not act against such individuals in the absence of definitive proof of non-compliance with the disclosure rules.

Finally, notwithstanding the introduction of the direct tax disclosure regime, it may be observed that it is not inconceivable, in view of evidence recently submitted by a Director General (D Hartnett) of HMRC to the House of Lords Select Committee on Economic Affairs to the effect that HMRC was undertaking a study of GAARs 'around the world' and their efficacy, that the prospect of the enactment of a GAAR in the UK may again be mooted.[146] **[5.26]**

143 See, for example, K.M. Gordon, "Descriptive Hallmarks" Taxation 20/7/2006 and R. Collier-Keywood, "Widening the Disclosure Regime" Tax Journal, May 15, 2006.

144 [The number of direct tax disclosures to 31 March 2007 can be found on the HMRC website (http://www.hmrc.gov.uk).]

145 See FA 2007, s 107.

146 See HL Select Committee on Economic Affairs, Minutes of Evidence, Examination of Witnesses (Question 281), 22 May 2006.

6 Income

1. Introduction

The concept of income is of the greatest importance in revenue law since it forms the base of income tax and also of part of corporation tax.[1] The reason why income was chosen is, in part, historical and based upon the Victorian view that it was anti-social to live on one's capital. But, as one commentator has pointed out, there is also the very good reason that 'the tax collector requires his money next year as well as this one. He does not want to kill the goose that lays the golden egg'.[2] However, economists are not in agreement as to what the concept of income involves. The definition of 'income' which is used for income tax purposes, and identified in the second part of this chapter, is much more restrictive than the various possibilities that economists have advanced over the years, and which are considered in the first part. The result is that not all receipts of what would normally be regarded as income are necessarily taxable; income tax is a tax on particular types of income,[3] and certain other types of income may therefore fall outside the tax net. **[6.1]**

2. The 'foundation concept of income'

The study by Holmes, from which the following extract is taken, draws together the various concepts of income in the economic literature, so as to arrive at what Holmes calls the 'foundation concept of income'. By this term, he means simply that an individual's income over a period of time consists of the total of his 'net increase in wealth' over that period, plus his 'consumption expenditure' over the same period. This also involves the concept of 'imputed income'. **[6.2]**

Kevin Holmes *The Concept of Income: A Multi-Disciplinary Analysis* (2001) pp 563–566

The Underlying Premise

Rational people live to enhance their material and non-material well-being. The ranking of people's well-beings determines who in society is in a better position to

1 'Profits', for corporation tax purposes, comprise income and chargeable gains (see below, para **[18.11]**).
2 G S A Wheatcroft 'What is Taxable Income?' [1957] BTR 310.
3 See Chapter 7.

contribute to the improvement of the well-being of less well-off people. Conversely, ranked well-being indicates which people are in need of social welfare support.

In terms of optimal tax theory, a person's well-being and therefore his ability to pay tax, is gauged by his individual characteristics, endowments, preferences and tastes. Unfortunately, well-being itself and individuals' traits, are not measurable in a way that makes them useful as a practical tax base. A surrogate indicator of those features of well-being must be found. Tax policy makers must therefore seek a tax base as close as possible to the real targets. But the chosen tax base must be capable of practical application. In most societies, income is the chosen surrogate indicator of an individual's characteristics, endowments, preference and tastes, and therefore her well-being.

The breadth of the taxation target (ultimately well-being) means that the surrogate indicator must be as all-encompassing as possible. The narrower the surrogate indicator, the less accurate it is as a representative of the target.

Horizontal equity is a well established principle of taxation: taxpayers in the same position should be taxed the same amount.[4] One aspect of achieving horizontal equity in an income tax system is to determine which factors are taken into account and which factors are excluded in ascertaining individuals' relative positions. Income is an imperfect but workable surrogate indicator of an individual's many characteristics, endowments, attributes and features, which reflect her ability to pay tax. Horizontal equity dictates that the notion of income is as broad as practicable: in other words, all types of income (including realised and unrealised gains) that are derived by a person from all sources should fall within income so far as the different types of income are practically measurable.

The Foundation Concept of Income

Economists like Fisher[5] posited that true income equates to psychological experiences. This approach is theoretically appealing because it integrates well with the fundamental notion of well-being as a basis for inter-personal transfers to increase welfare [*sic*] of society as a whole. However, like well-being, psychic income is unable to be measured in an objective and practical manner. In the search for that objective and practical measure, economists have turned to approximations of the inchoate ideal, which have concentrated on the measurable material or physical aspects of well-being, and have eliminated the non-material intangible aspects. The market value of goods and services consumed was adopted as a first approximation to the component of psychic income that arises from the materialism. In their move away from subjective interpretations in the search for objectivity, economists arrived at the Schanz-Haig-Simons notion of income.[6] As early as 1896, Schanz contended that income was a "net influx of wealth over a period of time".[7] Similarly, Haig later formulated income as "the money value of the net accretion to one's economic power between two points of time."[8] Schanz and Haig measured income

4 [See Chapter 1, above, para **[1.2]**.]

5 [See Kevin Holmes, *The Concept of Income: A Multi-Disciplinary Analysis* (2001), at pp 38–42, summarising Irving Fisher, *The Nature of Capital and Income* (1912).]

6 [Usually referred to simply as the 'Haig-Simons model' (see John Tiley *Revenue Law* (5th edn, 2005) p 20.]

7 [See Holmes, n 5 above, p 58, quoting G von Schanz 'Der Einkommensbegriff und die Einkommensteuergesetze' (1896) *Finanz-Archiv*, translated in P H Wueller 'Concepts of Taxable Income I – The German Contribution' (1938) 53(1) *Political Science Quarterly* 83, 103, 104.]

8 [See Holmes, n 5 above, p 60, quoting Robert M Haig 'The Concept of Income – Economic and Legal Aspects' in Robert M Haig (ed.), *The Federal Income Tax* (1921) p 2, 7.]

as an increase in economic power *before* expenditure was incurred on consumption.

Simons breaks down income into the sum of an individual's consumption expenditure during a period and her net increase in wealth during the period (that is, after she incurred the consumption expenditure).[9]

The focus of all three approaches is that income is represented by the increase in a person's economic power. The essential difference between the Schanz-Haig and Simons approaches is that Schanz and Haig measure income at an earlier time than Simons. For ease of practical measurement, Simons's formulation is preferred over that of Schanz and Haig. The foundation concept of income is then taken to be Simons's formulation where consumption includes imputed income.[10] Algebraically, the foundation concept of income is expressed as:

$$Y = \Delta W + C$$

where $Y \equiv$ income;
$\Delta W \equiv$ net change in wealth over a measurement period; and
$C \equiv$ consumption expenditure plus imputed income.

The foundation concept of income is the expression of income that is most susceptible to practical application and that most closely aligns to the underlying taxation targets (which represent a person's well-being) that are identified by optimal tax analysis.

Tax can neatly be imposed on the two components of the foundation concept of income by way of income tax levied on the ΔW element of the $Y = \Delta W + C$ formula, and goods and services tax levies on the C element. Ideally, the rates of tax on each variable would be equal to ensure that wealth accumulation is not favoured over consumption expenditure and vice versa.[11] Imputed income is an anomaly in that, administratively, it must be subject to income tax although it actually reflects the taxpayer's consumption activities. However, this consistency is of no moment if income and consumption tax rates are equal.

The foundation concept of income also readily conforms with the horizontal equity feature of well designed tax systems. Uniform application of the concept ensures that people with identical changes in wealth and with identical consumption patterns carry identical tax burdens. No differentiation is made between the nature and the source of a person's income. No-one can manipulate his tax base because wealth accretion is applied in a particular way. No form of income or expenditure is favoured over another. Therefore, the foundation concept of income can be used as a conceptually superior practical benchmark or standard against which to assess other concepts of income in the context of taxpayer equity.

The factors that comprise a person's physic [*sic*] income and well-being cannot be directly measured. However, Schanz's and Haig's concept of income broadly encompasses the satisfactions based notion of income, if one assumes that psychic income arises at the point where a person becomes aware that her increase in wealth (or savings in a general sense) provides her with the means to consume goods or services from which she can later derive favourable sensations from consumption. The individual's knowledge that she has the means or wealth now to consume later provides satisfactions or utility. These satisfactions constitute

9 [See Holmes, n 5 above, p 66, quoting Henry C Simons *Personal Income Taxation – The Definition of Income as a Problem of Fiscal Policy* (1938) pp 49–50.]

10 [For 'imputed income', see Tiley, n 6 above, pp 20–22 and Roxan, extracted below, see para **[6.5]**.]

11 An analysis of the appropriate tax rate and the relative economic merits of wealth accumulation and consumption is beyond the scope of this book.

income. Economists and tax policymakers who advocate taxation of consumption only ignore the conceptual link between satisfactions theory and the increase in economic power that wealth accrual (or savings) offers.

Measurement of income under the foundation concept depends on valuation of rights and expectations. Legally enforceable claims are more valuable than unenforceable rights or entitlements, which in turn are more valuable than mere expectations. The value of an expectation is calculated by reference to the probability associated with the outcome that is expected to occur. Although expectations are capable of valuation, they are generally excluded from the foundation concept of income because of the subjectivity of assessing the probability of occurrence and the vulnerability of the valuation to manipulation. **[6.3]**

The notion of 'imputed income' is encapsulated in the following extract:[12] **[6.4]**

Ian Roxan 'Imputed Income (Including Deductible Costs)' in Peter Essers and Arie Rijkers (eds) *The Notion of Income from Capital* (2005) p 249

The comprehensive income tax base (*Simons-Haig-Schanz* (SHS) base) comprises the net increase in wealth plus the value of consumption of goods and services in the tax period. Certain assets in effect provide consumption value over time. Examples are housing, durable goods (such as a washing machine), comparable intangible rights (e.g. licensed software for home use) and artwork. These assets in effect provide the owner with consumption 'services' from year to year. The problem is that other individuals may purchase comparable services directly (e.g. rented housing, laundry services, annual software licence, rented artwork or entrance to exhibitions/performances), leaving them with less net wealth to spend on other consumption. To ensure that the incomes of both individuals are measured on the same basis it is necessary to 'impute' to the asset owner as income the value of the consumption services that she has implicitly received.

Even where the comprehensive base is not used, it may be thought appropriate to tax such imputed income, if income from providing the comparable direct services would be taxed. Imputed income should also be taxed under a direct consumption tax with progressive rates (Meade Committee, 1978: 221).[13] **[6.5]**

In the light of the foregoing, how might income be defined along similar, though not identical, lines, so as to arrive at a fairer type of income tax? These issues were considered in the 1978 Meade Committee Report, which, in turn, referred to the findings of the 1966 Carter Commission. **[6.6]**

12 John Tiley examines the argument for an 'imputed income' element in the taxation of income from land in *Studies in the History of Tax Law* (2004), see Chapter 12, below, para **[12.2]**.

13 [The Institute for Fiscal Studies *The Structure and Reform of Direct Taxation: Report of a Committee chaired by Professor J E Meade* (1978) p 221.]

The Structure and Reform of Direct Taxation: Report of a Committee chaired by Professor J E Meade (1978) pp 30–32 and 127–128

Chapter 3 The Tax Base

INCOME AS THE TAX BASE

A taxpayer's *income* is an obvious candidate to serve as the base for his tax liability; but there are unfortunately difficulties in establishing what in principle is meant by a taxpayer's income, quite irrespective of any practical difficulties of ascertaining and measuring his income when it has been defined. A natural and commonsensical approach is to draw a distinction between a man's capital and his income by regarding his *capital* as the stock of resources from which the flow of income proceeds; in terms of the familiar analogy, the tree is the capital from which the annual income of the fruit crop is derived.[14]

But on examination this distinction is found to involve many difficulties. Should the whole of the fruit crop be counted as taxable income if the fruit trees are ageing and depreciating in value, so that part of the proceeds of the crop must be used to maintain the productive power of the orchard? Or to take an example at the other extreme, if a forester is growing trees from which there is no annual crop but which are ultimately cut down and sold for timber, does he have no income at any time but only a realisation of the gain in the capital value of his trees when he cuts them down and sells them? Or consider two Government bonds both of which are issued at a price of £100, the difference being that on bond A the government undertakes to pay no interest but to redeem the bond at a price of £110 in a year's time, whereas on bond B the government undertakes to redeem the bond at its issue price of £100 in a year's time but meanwhile to pay £10 in interest on its borrowing. Is there no income but only gain in capital value on bond A, while there is income but no capital gain on bond B?

The above are only some extremely simple and obvious examples of the relationships between gains and losses in capital values on the one hand and net income on the other. As rates of income tax have risen to their present high levels,[15] the distinction between income and capital gains has become more and more important; more and more sophisticated ways have been devised by taxpayers to turn highly taxable income into less highly taxable capital gains;[16] and the importance of finding, if it is possible, a definition of income which does not permit these uncertain and often irrelevant distinctions to continue has correspondingly increased. Two such definitions of income are in principle possible, which we shall call definition A and definition B.

14 [See Adam Smith [1776] *The Wealth of Nations* (1986), Book II, Chapter I; see below, para **[6.10]**.]

15 [This was written at a time when income tax rates were very high, relative to those in force today. As recently as the 1987/1988 tax year, there was a complicated structure of income tax rates, with a maximum rate of 60%.]

16 [Capital gains tax is now charged at income tax rates, so as to avoid the arbitrage possibilities implied here: see Chapter 20, below, para **[20.46]**.]

DEFINITION A OF TAXABLE INCOME

In the first of these two definitions it is argued that the proper measure of a taxpayer's income in any one year is the value of what he could have consumed during the year without living on and so diminishing his capital wealth in the process. This comprehensive measure would take account of any new capital gains or losses which had accrued in the course of the year and would include any other windfall receipts in addition to more narrowly defined income receipts from wages, dividends, rents, profits, etc. This measure, it may be argued, is the fairest one for tax purposes, because whatever the taxpayer may choose to do with these resources they constitute a true measure of the total economic opportunity accruing to him in the year in question.

We call this definition A . . .

DEFINITION B OF TAXABLE INCOME

There is, however, an alternative principle upon which income may be defined for fiscal purposes . . . This is to define an individual's income not as the amount which he could consume in any one year without diminishing his capital wealth in the course of that year, but as the amount which he could consume in any one year and yet be left with the resources and expectations at the end of that year which would enable him to maintain that same level of consumption indefinitely in the future. Let us call this definition B of income as a tax base . . .

Unfortunately this definition of income would be a quite impracticable criterion for tax purposes, because it depends essentially upon future expectations. The level of consumption expenditure which any individual can enjoy this year and expect to enjoy indefinitely for the future depends upon what his future earnings will in fact turn out to be, upon what will happen to the rate of interest in the future, and upon all such things as may affect what he should save this year in order to maintain his future spending power. It is not easy to envisage the tax inspector agreeing with each taxpayer upon what may reasonably be expected to constitute a maintainable level of consumption.

For this reason when it is suggested that comprehensive income should be chosen for the tax base, this is usually taken to imply the use of definition A, which – difficult as it may be to make the necessary valuations – does in principle rest on hard historic facts about what happened in the year in question, rather than definition B, which involves choosing between different expectations about the future. . .

CONSUMPTION AS A TAX BASE[17]

An alternative to taking income . . . is to take expenditure on consumption as the essential base for personal taxation. A strong case can be made for this base in that it levies a tax on the claims which a taxpayer makes at any one time on the community's resources which he uses up for his own consumption purposes. If he saves his income instead of consuming it, he is putting resources back into the productive pool; if he dissaves, he is taking resources out of the productive pool in addition to this other income. His relative low consumption in the case of savings and his relatively high consumption in the case of dissavings are measures of what he is appropriating at any one time for his own personal use.

17 [The Meade Report considers expenditure tax in further detail in Chapters 7 to 10. See also Kay and King *The British Tax System* (1990) ch 6, and Prest [1978] BTR 1.]

This expresses what is normally regarded as the essential case for the choice of expenditure on consumption as the base for progressive personal taxation. A *progressive expenditure tax* (as it is usually called) falls more heavily than progressive income tax on the wealthy who are financing high levels of consumption out of capital resources, but at the same time it gives much greater opportunity than does a progressive income tax for the finance of the development and growth of private enterprises out of private savings . . .

WEALTH AS A TAX BASE[18]

. . . apart from providing a source of income which is compatible with a life of leisure, wealth gives opportunity, security, social power, influence and independence. For this reason it may be argued that, however well a system of taxation of income or of consumption may be devised, equity requires that wealth itself should be included in the base for progressive taxation. On these grounds a surcharge on investment income may be justified as a proxy for a tax on the wealth which produces the investment income. But in order not to favour those who hold large wealth in forms which yield little or no income, it may be argued that it is wealth itself rather than investment income from wealth that should form the tax base.

THE TREATMENT OF GIFTS AND INHERITANCES[19]

So far we have said nothing about the treatment of transfers of wealth or spending power from one taxpayer to another by way of gifts *inter vivos* or of inheritances on the occasion of death.

We consider the matter first in terms of a comprehensive income base for taxation. Smith gives some money to Jones. In an obvious sense this can be regarded as increasing Jones's economic opportunities and thus his taxable capacity. But does it reduce Smith's taxable capacity? There are two quite reasonable ways of answering this question: one is to regard the gift simply as a transfer of economic opportunities from Smith to Jones, in which case total taxable income has not changed, since while Jones's has risen, Smith's has fallen; the other is to regard Smith's gift as one way in which he chose to use his economic opportunities (*i.e.* his income) and at the same time to recognise that Jones's opportunities have thereby also been increased, in which case there are two personal incomes to be taxed.

With consumption as the tax base exactly the same issue arises. When Smith gives money to Jones to spend, is this merely a transfer of consumption from Smith to Jones or is the gift by Smith one of the ways in which Smith decides to enjoy and consume his resources, so that the transfer should be included in Smith's consumption base as well as in Jones's consumption base if and when Jones uses the funds for his own consumption?. . .

Chapter 7 A Comprehensive Income Tax

In this chapter we shall describe the tax structure which would be needed if a truly comprehensive income tax (CIT) were to be introduced into the United Kingdom.

18 [See further, The Meade Report, ch 16. See also C T Sandford, J R M Willis and D J Ironside *An Annual Wealth Tax* (1975) and the Reports of the Select Committee on a Wealth Tax (HC 696 Vols I-IV, January 1977.]
19 [See Chapter 21, below, para **[21.1]**.]

THE CANADIAN CARTER COMMISSION

The problems of such a CIT have been analysed in great detail in the six volumes of the Report of the Canadian Carter Commission.[20]

The Carter Commission presented a masterly analysis of these problems, with one exception. They recognised the existence of inflation, but they stated that they were "opposed to automatic adjustments tied to price indices, for this would impair the power of the tax system to stabilise the economy".... [W]e take the view that adjustment for inflation is an essential feature for the UK tax structure unless we are ready to accept inflation as an extremely powerful but inefficient and unjust revenue raiser. If it were only a question of moderate rates of inflation or deflation, the argument of the Carter Commission would be acceptable. ... [I]nflationary price rises cause an unintended increase in the proportion of income taken in tax and impose an unintended tax on some forms of capital in the guise of a tax on income; this damps down private spending, restrains the inflationary demand and thus helps to stabilise the economy. But with the great and continuous rates of inflation which have been recently experienced the disturbing structural effects of an unadjusted income tax system are in our opinion so serious that they cannot be neglected.

The administration of a CIT becomes incomparably more complicated if a system of automatic adjustments for inflation must be introduced into it. In this chapter we shall consider rather briefly many of the points which have been so exhaustively and effectively analysed by the Carter Commission; but we shall put much stress on the problem involved in indexing such a structure for inflation. The resulting system, while it might conceivably be feasible, would impose such a strain on administration by the authorities and compliance by the taxpayer that, for that reason alone, we consider it to be ruled out in present circumstances.

THE NATURE AND PURPOSE OF A CIT

The basic idea of a CIT is to tax opportunities (the "accretion of economic spending power") rather than the actual use of such opportunities, which may be better measured by consumption expenditure. There are a number of ways in which income may be defined. The existing UK system draws a distinction between income and capital gains. But any definition of income which purports to measure "accretion of purchasing power" must bring income and capital gains under the same umbrella. For this purpose . . . there are at least two main ways of defining income. To measure income as the level of consumption which the recipient could maintain indefinitely (what we have called definition B), however desirable in principle, is in practice not an operative measure, since it depends upon subjective views about future developments. The measurement of income as current consumption plus the current addition to the taxpayer's net capital worth (what we have called definition A) is a feasible operative criterion, provided there are enough markets in which the most important assets can be valued. It is this definition of income which, probably for this reason, normally lies behind the concept of "*comprehensive income*" as a tax base; and it is this concept which we accordingly adopt in this chapter, although we would stress that there is plenty of room for disagreement as to whether it is in fact the best criterion of what actually constitutes "income".

One of the aims of a CIT is to promote what is sometimes termed "horizontal equity" by taxing all kinds of income under a single schedule. In this way, so it is argued, individuals with a given level of income would be treated in the same way

20 Report of the Royal Commission on Taxation (Ottawa: Queen's Printer, 1966).

regardless of the form in which their income accrued. This would also help to prevent resources from being wasted by attempts to convert one kind of income into another in circumstances where different kinds of income were taxed at different rates (e.g. dividends and capital gains). In addition, if the tax base of a CIT were larger than the current tax base, then a change to a CIT might enable a reduction in marginal tax rates to be made, which would reduce the disincentive effects on work decisions. And since, in its pure form, receipts of windfalls and inheritances would be included in the tax base, the CIT would make it possible to do without any separate system of tax on capital transfers and yet at the same time to tailor the rate of tax on gifts and inheritances received to the income of the recipient. But this would be at the expense of abandoning the cumulative principle.

The major differences between the current income tax and the CIT are that the latter would include in the tax base real capital gains (net of losses), and gifts and inheritances received, and that there would be no special tax reliefs on savings and investment. In addition, to be theoretically consistent, an annual CIT should include in its tax base the change each year in the present value of all assets owned by an individual. Severe problems arise where these assets cannot be marketed. Three cases which deserve particular mention are (i) the change in the current value of pension rights, (ii) the change in the value of the assets of closely owned businesses, and (iii) the change in the present discounted value of future earnings. There are no current markets to provide a valuation for these items, and, although in the case of (i) and (ii) values might be established by pragmatic methods, we are of the opinion that items (i) and (iii) should not be included in the tax base ... **[6.7]**

For an assessment of the Carter Report, see Cedric Sandford 'Carter Twenty Years On' [1987] BTR 148–165. **[6.8]**

3. The revenue law definition of 'income'

A. *The importance of the distinction between income and capital*

The concept of 'income' in revenue law cases has been influenced by the distinction between capital and income drawn by Adam Smith in the eighteenth century. Although this distinction is less important than it used to be because capital gains are now taxed as if they were the top slice of an individual's income,[21] it remains significant, not least because a number of tax avoidance schemes depend upon the successful conversion of income into capital or vice versa. **[6.9]**

Adam Smith *An Inquiry into the Nature and Causes of the Wealth of Nations (1776)*

Book II Chapter I

Of Division of Stock

When the stock which a man possesses is no more than sufficient to maintain him for a few days or a few weeks, he seldom thinks of deriving any revenue from it. He consumes it as sparingly as he can, and endeavours by his labour to acquire

21 See Chapter 20, below, para **[20.46]**.

something which may supply its place before it be consumed altogether. His revenue is, in this case, derived from his labour only. This is the state of the greater part of the labouring poor in all countries.

But when he possesses stock sufficient to maintain him for months or years, he naturally endeavours to derive a revenue from the greater part of it; reserving only so much for his immediate consumption as may maintain him till his revenue begins to come in. His whole stock, therefore, is distinguished into two parts. That part which, he expects, is to afford him this revenue, is called his capital. The other is that which supplies his immediate consumption; and which consists either, first, in that portion of his whole stock which was originally reserved for this purpose; or, secondly, in his revenue, from whatever source derived, as it gradually comes in; or, thirdly, in such things as had been purchased by either of these in former years, and which are not yet entirely consumed; such as a stock of clothes, household furniture, and the like. In one, or other, or all of these three articles, consists the stock which men commonly reserve for their own immediate consumption.

There are two different ways in which a capital may be employed so as to yield a revenue or profit to its employer.

First, it may be employed in raising, manufacturing, or purchasing goods, and selling them again with a profit. The capital employed in this manner yields no revenue or profit to its employer, while it either remains in his possession, or continues in the same shape. The goods of the merchant yield him no revenue or profit till he sells them for money, and the money yields him as little till it is again exchanged for goods. His capital is continuously going from him in one shape, and returning to him in another, and it is only by means of such circulation, or successive exchanges, that it can yield him any profit. Such capitals, therefore, may very properly be called circulating capitals.

Secondly, it may be employed in the improvement of land, in the purchase of useful machines and instruments of trade, or in such-like things as yield a revenue or profit without changing masters, or circulating any further. Such capitals, therefore, may very properly be called fixed capitals.

Different occupations require very different proportions between the fixed and circulating capitals employed in them.

The capital of a merchant, for example, is altogether a circulating capital. He has occasion for no machines or instruments of trade, unless his shop, or warehouse, be considered as such.

Some part of the capital of every master artificer or manufacturer must be fixed in the instruments of his trade. This part, however, is very small in some, and very great in others. A master tailor requires no other instruments of trade but a parcel of needles. Those of the master shoemaker are a little, though but a very little, more expensive. Those of the weaver rise a good deal above those of the shoemaker. The far greater part of the capital of all such master artificers, however, is circulated, either in the wages of their workmen, or in the price of their materials, and repaid with a profit by the price of the work.

In other works a much greater fixed capital is required. In a great iron-work, for example, the furnace for melting the ore, the forge, the slitt-mill, are instruments of trade which cannot be erected without a very great expense. In coal-works, and mines of every kind, the machinery necessary both for drawing out the water and for other purposes is frequently still more expensive ... **[6.10]**

John Smith & Son v Moore [1921] 2 AC 13 (HL)

A son purchased a colliery business, which included the benefit of a number of forward contracts, from the trustees of his father's will trust. The House of Lords held that the cost of purchasing the business was not deductible in calculating the son's own trading profits, since it was expenditure on fixed capital.

> VISCOUNT HALDANE: My Lords, profit may be produced in two ways. It may result from purchases on income account, the cost of which is debited to that account, and the prices realised therefrom are credited, or it may result from realisation at a profit of assets forming part of the concern. In such a case a prudent man of business will no doubt debit to profit and loss the value of capital assets realised, and take credit only for the balance. But what was the nature of what the appellant here had to deal with? He had bought as part of the capital of the business his father's contracts. These enabled him to purchase coal from the colliery owners at what we were told was a very advantageous price, about fourteen shillings per ton. He was able to buy at this price because the right to do so was part of the assets of the business. Was it circulating capital?
>
> My Lords, it is not necessary to draw an exact line of demarcation between fixed and circulating capital. Since Adam Smith drew the distinction in the Second Book of his Wealth of Nations, which appears in the chapter on the Division of Stock, a distinction which has since become classical, economists have never been able to define much more precisely what the line of demarcation is. Adam Smith described fixed capital as what the owner turns to profit by keeping it in his own possession, circulating capital as what he makes profit of by parting with it and letting it change masters. The latter capital circulates in this sense.
>
> My Lords, in the case before us the appellant, of course, made profit with circulating capital by buying coal under the contracts he had acquired from his father's estate at the stipulated price of fourteen shillings and reselling it for more, but he was able to do this simply because he had acquired, among other assets of his business, including the goodwill, the contracts in question. It was not by selling these contracts, of limited duration though they were, it was not by parting with them to other masters, but by retaining them, that he was able to employ his circulating capital in buying under them. I am accordingly of opinion that, although they may have been of short duration, they were none the less part of his fixed capital. That he had paid a price for them makes no difference. Indeed the description of their value by the accountants ... as of doubtful validity in the hands of outsiders, emphasises this conclusion. The £30,000 paid for the contracts or its equivalent, therefore, became part of the appellant's fixed capital and could not properly appear in his revenue account. If that be so, then it was a sum employed as capital in his trade, and has to be excluded as a deduction from the profits on which he is assessed. **[6.11]**

Golden Horse Shoe (New) Ltd v Thurgood [1934] 1 KB 548 (CA)

The Court of Appeal accepted a company's argument that the purchase price of dumps of 'tailings' from gold mines was deductible in calculating its trading profits on the basis that the dumps were part of its stock-in-trade, rather than capital assets.

> ROMER LJ: ... The question to be decided in this case is whether the dumps are to be regarded as fixed capital or as circulating capital. If they are the former, it is conceded by the appellants that the assessment made on them is correct. If, on the other hand, they are floating or circulating capital, it is conceded that the cost of them to the appellants must be debited in the profit and loss account, the account being credited with the cost price of what was left of the dumps at the end of the year of assessment. The dumps, in other words, must be dealt with in the profit and loss account as stock in hand has to be dealt with in the profit and loss account of any other trader. The reason for this distinction being drawn between fixed and floating or circulating capital is not far to seek. In assessing a trader to income tax under Schedule D, Case I, the revenue authorities are only concerned with his annual gains and profits; that is, gains and profits in the year of assessment or whatever may be the other material interval of time. They are not in the least concerned with his financial position as a whole at the end of the time as compared with his financial position at the beginning. Changes in the value of his fixed capital are

therefore disregarded except where it is otherwise expressly provided in the Act. On the other hand, changes in his floating or circulating capital must be taken into consideration in ascertaining his annual gains and profits. For the profits or losses in a year of trading cannot be ascertained unless a comparison be made of the circulating capital as it existed at the beginning of the year with the circulating capital as it exists at the end of the year. It is, indeed, by causing the floating capital to change in value that a loss or profit is made.

Unfortunately, however, it is not always easy to determine whether a particular asset belongs to the one category or the other. It depends in no way upon what may be the nature of the asset in fact or in law. Land may in certain circumstances be circulating capital. The determining factor must be the nature of the trade in which the asset is employed. The land upon which the manufacturer carries on his business is part of his fixed capital. The land with which a dealer in real estate carries on his business is part of his circulating capital. The machinery with which a manufacturer makes the articles that he sells is part of his fixed capital. The machinery that a dealer in machinery buys and sells is part of his circulating capital, as is the coal that a coal merchant buys and sells in the course of his trade.

... It seems to me to follow from these considerations that the question to be decided in the present case resolves itself into this: Are the dumps the raw material of the appellant's business or do they merely provide the means of obtaining the raw material? In my opinion they are that raw material itself ... **[6.12]**

IRC v Mallaby-Deeley [1938] 4 All ER 818 (CA)

The Court of Appeal held that, where payments were made to a publisher under a seven-year deed of covenant, in place of an earlier undertaking to pay a lump sum, the payments were capital, rather than revenue, in nature.

SIR WILFRID GREENE MR: ... The distinction which is to be drawn for the purposes of the Income Tax Acts between payments of an income character and payments of a capital nature is sometimes a very fine and rather artificial one. It may – in fact it does – depend upon the precise character of the transaction. To take a simple case, if the true bargain is that a capital sum shall be paid, the fact that the method of payment which is adopted in the document is a payment by instalments will not have the effect of giving to those instalments the character of income. Their nature is finally determined by the circumstances that the obligation is to pay a capital sum, and instalments are merely a method of effecting that payment. On the other hand, to take another simple case, where there is no undertaking to pay a capital sum and no capital obligation in existence, and all that exists is an undertaking to pay annual sums, those may, in the absence of other considerations, be annual payments of an income nature for the purposes of the Income Tax Acts. The operation of that distinction in individual cases may present some appearance of unreality. Nevertheless, it is a distinction which is now well-founded ... **[6.13]**

British Insulated and Helsby Cables Ltd v Atherton [1926] AC 205 (HL); below, para [10.27]

A company set up a pension fund trust for its technical and clerical staff. The trust deed provided for contributions from the company and the employees, with the company contributing £31,784 'to form the nucleus of the fund'. A majority of the House of Lords (Viscount Cave LC, Lord Buckmaster and Lord Atkinson (Lord Blanesburgh and Lord Carson dissenting)) held that the contribution of £31,784 was not deductible in calculating the company's trading profits, since it was capital expenditure.

VISCOUNT CAVE, LC: ... But when an expenditure is made, not only once and for all, but with a view to bringing into existence an asset or an advantage for the enduring benefit of a trade, I think that there is very good reason (in the absence of special circumstances leading to an opposite conclusion) for treating such an expenditure as properly attributable not to revenue but to capital . . . **[6.14]**

Whitehead v Tubbs (Elastics) Ltd [1984] STC 1

OLIVER LJ: . . . [*referring to the distinction to be made between revenue payments and capital ones*] Perhaps the most helpful introductory approach is that of Dixon J. (as he then was) in *Sun Newspapers Ltd.* v. *Federal Comr of Taxation*,[22] an approach adopted and approved by Lord Pearce in delivering the judgment of the Board in *BP Australia Ltd.* v. *Comr of Taxation of Commonwealth of Australia*[23]:

> "'There are, I think,' he said, 'three matters to be considered, *(a)* the character of the advantage sought, and in this its lasting qualities may play a part, *(b)* the manner in which it is to be used, relied upon or enjoyed, and in this and under the former head recurrence may play its part, and *(c)* the means adopted to obtain it; that is, by providing a periodical reward or outlay to cover its use or enjoyment for periods commensurate with the payment or by making a final provision or payment so as to secure future use or enjoyment.'"

The solution to the problem, Lord Pearce observed[24]:

> " . . . has to be derived from many aspects of the whole set of circumstances some of which may point in one direction, some in the other . . . It is a commonsense appreciation of all the guiding features which must provide the ultimate answer . . . That answer 'depends on what the expenditure is calculated to effect from a practical and business point of view rather than upon the juristic classification of the legal rights, if any, secured employed or exhausted in the process': per Dixon J., in *Hallstroms Pty. Ltd.* v. *Federal Comr of Taxation*."[25] **[6.15]**

This reasoning throughout all of these cases concerned with the deductibility of a payment, is mirrored in the following cases involving *receipts*. **[6.16]**

Commissioners of Inland Revenue v Blott [1921] 2 AC 171 (HL)

The respondent, a company shareholder, was assessed to super-tax[26] on a bonus issue to him of shares in the company. The House of Lords held that the shares were not part of his total income for the year but an accretion to his capital.

VISCOUNT FINLAY: . . . The case appears to stand exactly as Rowlatt J. put it:[27] "Now I do not think that there is a payment of a dividend to a shareholder unless a part of the profits of the company is thereby liberated to him in the sense that the company parts with it, and he takes it. If, in this case, the company could have found means to capitalise their

22 (1938) 61 CLR 337, 363.
23 [1966] AC 224, 261.
24 [1966] AC 224, 264.
25 (1947) 72 CLR 634, 648. [See, further, *RTZ Oil and Gas Ltd v Ellis* [1987] STC 512 at 541.]
26 See, eg, G S A Wheatcroft *The Law of Income Tax, Surtax and Profits Tax* (1962) para 1–014: 'The famous Lloyd George Budget of 1909 introduced a number of Radical reforms, including a new tax on individuals called "super-tax"; the rate was 6d. in the £ on incomes exceeding £3,000 with an exemption for incomes under £5,000. That Budget finally became law in the Finance (1909–10) Act, 1910, and by the outbreak of war in 1914 the top rate of super-tax was 1s 3d. When the war ended the top rate was 4s. 6d.; a tax structure, which in 1914 had maintained a maximum rate of income tax plus super-tax at 12½ per cent. was dealing in 1918 with a maximum combined rate of 52½ per cent'.
27 [1920] 1 KB 114, 133.

profits and divide them as capital without adopting the machinery of declaring a bonus and allotting shares by agreement (not, be it observed, a voluntary agreement) in satisfaction of such bonus, I do not think the case would have been arguable. I am asked to decide that there was a 'payment' of this bonus upon the strength of what I consider bare machinery. I cannot do so. The fact is simply that the shareholder was given shares instead of a bonus." There can be no super-tax upon income unless it has been received by the taxpayer. I may be permitted to quote in this connection what was said by Pitney J. in *Eisner v. Macomber*,[28] a case decided in the Supreme Court of the United States in March last year. In dealing with the definition of 'income' Pitney J., in delivering the opinion of the majority of the members of the Court in that case, said: 'Here we have the essential matter: not a gain accruing to capital, not a growth or increment of value in the investment; but a gain, a profit, something of exchangeable value proceeding from the property, severed from the capital however invested or employed, and coming in, being "derived", that is, received or drawn by the recipient (the taxpayer) for his separate use, benefit and disposal; that is income derived from property. Nothing else answers the description.' In the present case the bonus or so-called dividend was not severed from the capital; on the contrary, it was added to it. **[6.17]**

Ryall v Hoare [1923] 2 KB 447 (KBD)

A company director received a one-off commission as consideration for standing guarantor for the company's bank overdraft. The judge held that the commission was assessable under Case VI of Schedule D.

ROWLATT J.: . . . Two kinds of emolument may be excluded from Case 6. First, anything in the nature of capital accretion is excluded as being outside the scope and meaning of these Acts confirmed by the usage of a century. For this reason, a casual profit made on an isolated purchase and sale, unless merged with similar transactions in the carrying on of a trade or business is not liable to tax. "Profits or gains" in Case 6 refer to the interest or fruit as opposed to the principal or root of the tree. The second class of cases to be excluded consists of gifts and receipts, whether the emolument is from a gift *inter vivos*, or by will, or from finding an article of value, or from winning a bet. All these cases must be ruled out because they are not profits or gains at all . . . **[6.18]**

B. *Shortcomings of the legal meaning of income*

Kevin Holmes *The Concept of Income*, above, pp 571–576

Inadequacies of the legal concept of income

The legal meaning of income in English based law is not founded on the theoretically sound basis of the foundation concept of income. The legal meaning emerged from judges' interpretations in the nineteenth century of particular words in the United Kingdom Schedular income tax legislation.[29] Like some economists, judges developed selective criteria that a receipt of gain was required to exhibit before it would be treated as income. Considerable emphasis was placed on the idea of a periodic flow of receipts that "come in" as cash or in a form convertible into cash. But there were also other requirements. The receipt needed to be the reward of employment or vocation, or the produce of property, separated from its source, or the gain had to arise from a profit making purpose or motive. Thus, the legal

28 [252 US 189 (1919) (Supreme Court of the United States).]
29 [See Chapter 7, below, para **[7.1]**.]

approach was to distinguish between receipts that were income and those that were not income. A variety of receipts and gains could fall within the non-income category, including capital gains. The features of income that judges insisted upon created a chasm between the legal concept of income and the economic concept of a gain: a person's well-being could be enhanced by an economic gain, but that gain might not be levied taxation because it was not income in the legal sense. The taxation tenet of horizontal equity was breached.

The legal distinction between capital and income originated in the agricultural harvest cycle: annual income arose from the capital that produced it. This notion found its way into nineteenth century English trust law.[30] The House of Lords transposed the distinction in trust law into income tax law in 1921.[31] However, prior to 1921, judges distinguished between taxable income and non-taxable receipts on the basis of their interpretation of statutes. Trust law principles may have influenced judges [*sic*] interpretations, but prior to 1921 the judges' interpretations did not formerly embrace trust law principles. Thus, the income and capital distinction transferred from trust law was only one factor in the development of the concept of income for tax law purposes.

The legal concept of income is based on judges' progressive imposition of particular features of income. The creation of artificial distinctions about the nature of receipts means that the legal concept of income is narrower than, and lacks the theoretical and objective rigour of, the foundation concept of income. Furthermore, the law has been concerned with income determination in terms of the legal form of arrangements that people enter into, rather then [*sic*] appraising the overall economic effect of the arrangement. Consequently, the English based legal concept of income is not compatible with the public policy objective of an equitably distributed neutral tax impost.

Income concepts can be viewed as a pyramid. As one moves from the broad notion of psychic income (which corresponds with an individual's well-being)[32] through the foundation and accounting concepts to the legal concept, the interpretation of income continually narrows. More and more items are excluded from income as one progresses from one discipline to the next and in doing so one moves further away from the ideal taxation target. Taxation is based on the legal concept of income – the concept farthest removed from the ideal in the income pyramid.

Unfortunately, legislative reforms that have been designed to enlarge the legal concept of income have been piecemeal. Selected real economic gains have been grafted onto the traditional legal interpretation of income. The result is not a comprehensive concept of income that is founded on coherent income tax policy principles or objectives.

In the business context, the courts' interpretation of income has blurred the distinction between capital gains and ordinary business income. To determine whether a gain on the disposal of an asset is income, judges distinguish between a taxpayer's business operation and investments. To make the distinction, judges attempt to assess the taxpayer's purpose at the time that an asset is acquired. Different judges come to different conclusions about such imprecise gauges.

Variations in judicial opinion can be avoided by applying the foundation concept of income which offers as income an objective and observable economic result. Sometimes the legal concept treats a receipt as income when in fact there is no corresponding economic gain at all. Such income is illusory. To tax such income is illogical and inequitable.

30 [See *Bouch v Sproule* (1887) 12 App Cas 385.]
31 [See Holmes, n 5 above, pp 185–193, discussing *Commissioners of Inland Revenue v Blott* [1921] 2 AC 171; see above, para **[6.17]**.]
32 [See above, para **[6.3]**.]

The legal concept of income does not recognise inflation nor does it recognise a real decline in the value of an asset as the asset produces a cash flow. The legal concept concentrates on the cash flow only; the foundation concept assesses both the movement in the asset value and the cash flow together. Thus, the foundation concept of income recognises as income only real economic gains. Nominal and illusory gains are ignored.

Where the foundation and legal concepts of income agree that an amount of a gain is taxable income, each concept may recognise the income at different times; that is, the legal concept may recognise income in a period before the real economic gain is derived (as in the *Myer Emporium* case in Australia)[33] or, more commonly, the legal concept of income treats a receipt as income in a period after the real economic gain arises. Here, the legal concept waits until the gain has been realised. In each case a mismatch occurs between the accrual of the gain and its treatment as taxable income.

The foundation concept of income is concerned with identifying wealth accrual, which represents a benefit. Consequently, the foundation concept captures inflation adjusted unrealised capital gains. By contrast, New Zealand tax legislation brings within taxable income only selected, nominal and realised capital gains.[34] The legislation, which targets certain personal and real property transactions rather than all asset transactions, is neither equitable nor neutral. There is no conceptual justification on the grounds of tax equity and neutrality to treat as taxable income gains on some asset transactions but not gains on other asset transactions. The distinction, like the traditional legal distinction between taxable income and other non-taxable receipts invites taxpayers to apply strategies that convert otherwise taxable income into non-taxable capital gains.

The taxing statute often uses vague words and phrases to describe the border between income and capital. Judges must interpret those words and phrases, often using non-objective qualitative standards such as "questions of degree". Again, different judges take different views, which undermines the basic canons of taxation, particularly equity and certainty.

Although most capital gains that are subject to taxation in New Zealand must be realised, the legislation is inconsistent in that unrealised gains constitute taxable income; specifically, gains from financial arrangements and from foreign investment funds.

The receipt of gifts and windfall gains enhances a recipient's economic power by conferring property rights on the recipient. Therefore, gifts and windfall gains generally fall within the foundation concept of income. However, if an apparent gift carries with it customary obligations on the recipient to provide a gift to the donor in return, the recipient will not enjoy an increase in wealth equal to the value of the gift received (if she enjoys any increase in wealth at all). To determine a person's income, the foundation concept of income takes account of countervailing obligations to give gifs in return for those that the person receives.

English based law excludes gifts from income altogether on the grounds of exceptionality or the donee's lack of entitlement. But, once more, these criteria do not exhibit a solid theoretical underpinning. Ultimately, exceptionality is a subjective question of degree on which judicial opinion inevitably varies.

Benefits in kind are clearly income in terms of the foundation concept of income. They represent an increase in the recipient's net wealth. However, the feature of

33 [See *Federal Commissioner of Taxation v Myer Emporium Ltd* (1987) 18 ATR 693.]

34 Except for gains from financial arrangements and foreign investment funds, which are taxed on a nominal and unrealised basis.

legal income that requires a receipt (viewed in its strict legal form) to be convertible into cash excludes many benefits in kind from the legal concept of income.[35] This somewhat irrational approach to income determination has been the impetus for people to structure their rewards (particularly for services) in the form of a non-convertible benefit in kind. Consequently, legislative changes have been necessary to broaden the traditional narrow legal interpretation of income. In New Zealand, benefits in kind are brought within the tax net principally by way of fringe benefit tax, which is confined to employee-employer relationships.[36] The legislation does not extend to non-convertible benefits in kind that are derived by people who are not employees. The horizontal equity tenet is again eroded because the income tax legislation discriminates against employees who derive benefits in kind.

Imputed income is one type of benefit in kind that is generally excluded from the legal concept of income. Yet, imputed income is a form of consumption which logically falls within the foundation concept of income. However, income imputed to a person from self-performed services and leisure cannot be readily measured. Therefore, the foundation concept of income must exclude those forms of imputed income to be capable of practical application.

On the other hand, imputed income from owner use of assets (particularly owner occupied housing) is more amenable to practical measurement. Modern technology and the development of sophisticated property valuation methodology have facilitated up-to-date electronic databases of market values of various classes of property. Further, international experience demonstrates the feasibility of including imputed income from owner occupied housing in the legal concept of income to achieve tax equity and neutrality. **[6.19]**

Final Report of the Royal Commission on the Taxation of Profits and Income (Cmd 9474 (1955))

WHAT CONSTITUTES TAXABLE INCOME

28. The tax code contains no general definition of income. It is often said that it is impracticable or undesirable that it should. We do not feel it necessary to subscribe to either of those epithets. The codes of other countries have achieved the work of definition without any known ill-effects. What seems to us more important is that no real advantage could possibly result from the introduction of a general definition that had to cover so multifarious a subject as taxable income. If it were expressed in very general terms the work of deciding how to apply it to particular instances would have to be done by deductions drawn from other parts of the code's framework or with the help of general principles imported from without. To a large extent the United Kingdom system itself has proceeded by this method of interpretation. On the other hand, the more particular the definition, the more it tends to become a mere list of different classes of receipt, and the anxiety not to exclude some class by inadvertence or omission leads to the addition of a comprehensive "sweeping up" clause at the end which, in effect, raises over again the problem of interpreting the general phrase in the light of a particular instance. The United Kingdom code has in fact established the limits of what it will regard as

35 [See Holmes, n 5 above, pp 476–482, discussing *Tennant v Smith* [1892] AC 150. This 'common law' principle is altered, however, by extensive legislative measures on benefits in kind. See below, paras **[8.43]**–**[8.51]**.]

36 [See Holmes, n 5 above, pp 501–505.]

taxable income by formulating a list of different classes of income grouped under five Schedules:[37] and the interpretation of the wording and significance of these lists has been the subject of copious decisions of the Courts of law during the course of some three generations. Their interpretation has been governed by the principle, in itself unexceptionable, that income tax is a tax on income. We have not looked to refine upon this principle by producing a more precise definition. What we have looked for in the course of our review is to see whether the rules that determine the existing classifications and their application to all the varied forms of possible receipt fall short of or exceed a true conception of income for the purposes of a widely distributed annual tax.

Ibid. Memorandum of dissent by Mr. G. Woodcock, Mr. H.L. Bullock and Mr. N. Kaldor

10. The circularity inherent in ... [the legal concept of income] is well illustrated by the juxtaposition of two well-known judicial interpretations of the statute. "Income tax", according to Lord Macnaghten's famous dictum,[38] "is a tax on income". But "as regards the word income" said Lord Wrenbury,[39] "it means such income as is within the Act taxable under the Act". The law faces the same dilemma as the medieval Schoolmen who were forced to deny to exotic birds and beasts, captured by travellers in strange lands, the status of birds and beasts, since they relied for their definition on an exhaustive list of birds and beasts reported by tradition to have entered the Ark with Noah.

11. The inclusion or exclusion of particular types of receipts assumed an entirely different significance as income tax was gradually transformed from a small flat-rate impost to a steeply graduated tax calculated with reference to an individual's total income from all sources. Yet the trend towards the comprehensive tax base implied in the very notion of progressive taxation has been checked at various points, mainly on the basis of two distinct considerations. First, as the Majority point out[40] there has been a tendency to avoid the special problem of the heavy incidence of a steeply graduated tax on receipts which by their very nature are realised irregularly, instead of being spread evenly over the years in which they may be regarded as accruing, by the simple expedient of excluding such receipts altogether from the tax charge. Secondly, the ancient constricted conception of income as something which recurrently emerges and is separated off from its perpetual source, like the harvest from the soil, has lingered in the tax code from times when, by and large, income was the harvest from the soil. It has only been abandoned gradually, through the piecemeal adoption of basically inconsistent provisions, and without the consequences of its abandonment ever having been systematically taken into account. Thus the old view of the rigid separation between the income flow and its permanent source has been blurred by the allowances introduced for capital wastage and even losses, as permissible deductions in the calculation of income. The old boundary line afforded by the regularity or recurrence criterion has been discarded in judicial decisions which have established that casual or isolated gains are taxable provided that they are not of the character of "capital profits". **[6.20]**

37 [See Chapter 7.]

38 *Attorney-General v London County Council* (1900), 4 T.C. at p. 293. [See Chapter 7, below, para **[7.13]**.]

39 *Whitney v. C.I.R.*, (1925), 10 T.C. at p. 113.

40 Para. 32.

For a discussion of why, despite the inconsistencies referred to above, income tax has nonetheless proved to be a broadly acceptable fiscal solution, see Assaf Likhovski 'A Map of Society: Defining Income in British, British Colonial and American Tax Legislation' [2005] BTR 158. See also Martin Daunton 'What is Income?' in John Tiley (ed) *Studies in the History of Tax Law* (2004) pp 3–14. **[6.21]**

7 Categories of Income

1. Introduction

The structure of UK income tax means that it is important to categorise income according to its source.[1] One of the reasons for such categorisation is that different rules apply to the computation of income in each category. Thus, for instance, it is crucial to distinguish between income receipts from the carrying on of a trade and those from some kind of investment.

Income used to be categorised according to different Schedules for both income tax and corporation tax purposes. As a result of the Tax Law Rewrite project[2] and the resulting legislative changes, the Schedules have been eliminated for income tax purposes, with income now categorised by description. Schedule E, which covered employment income, was the first to be abandoned in favour of the Income Tax (Employment and Pensions) Act (ITEPA) 2003[3]; Schs A,[4] D,[5] and F[6] were later replaced by the Income Tax (Trading and Other Income) Act (ITTOIA) 2005. Significantly, however, the Schedules remain for corporation tax purposes.[7] **[7.1]**

The Parliamentary Under-Secretary of State, Department for Culture, Media and Sport (Lord McIntosh of Haringey) *Hansard*, HL, vol 671, col 325, 23 March 2005

The Bill [Income Tax (Trading and Other Income)] applies for income tax only. The project consulted at an early stage on whether to aim for a greater separation of the income tax code from corporation tax. Users of the legislation are in favour of making this split; so where the legislation written in this Bill applies at present to both codes, the current provisions will be repealed for income tax purposes, but will

1 See John Tiley, *Revenue Law* (5th edn, 2005) p 138.
2 The authors would like to thank Basil Rajamanie and Hazel Colclough, both of Her Majesty's Revenue and Customs ('HMRC's') Tax Law Rewrite project team, for assistance in clarifying a number of technical points arising from the Rewrite process. For consideration of the Tax Law Rewrite, see Chapter 1, para **[1.4]**.
3 See ITEPA 2003, Sch 6, para 6, and Sch 8, Pt 1; also Chapter 8, para **[8.1]**.
4 Income from land.
5 Income from trades, professions and vocations and various other types of income.
6 Dividend income. Schedule F did not apply to corporation tax (see ICTA 1988, s 208).
7 See ICTA 1988, ss 15 and 18. The use of the expression 'Schedules' often seems counter-intuitive to non-tax lawyers, since they are used to seeing 'Schedules' at the end of legislation. For historical reasons, the provisions called 'the Schedules' appear in the body of ICTA 1988 itself.

continue to apply for corporation tax. The Joint Committee heard that the Bill is the first step in the separation of the income and corporation tax codes. The project will consult further on how this aspect of the work should be taken forward. **[7.2]**

It is important to note that, for categorisation purposes, it is in form only, rather than in substance, that the difference between income tax and corporation tax exists. ITTOIA 2005 provides for the taxation of five categories of income: 'trading income'; 'property income'; 'savings and investment income'; 'miscellaneous income' (which includes items such as 'receipts from intellectual property', etc.); and 'exempt income'. For corporation tax purposes,[8] however, the division is between 'Schedule A', which, in corresponding very broadly to Part 3 of ITTOIA 2005, provides for the taxation of property income, and 'Schedule D', with its various 'Cases', which charges to corporation tax all the other types of income now covered, for income tax purposes, by ITTOIA 2005.

This chapter, which is divided into three main parts, illustrates the historical background to the Schedules, considers some key concepts in income tax and discusses the effect of the newly rewritten legislation on a Schedular system that has existed since 1803. **[7.2a]**

2. Historical background

Although income tax was first introduced in 1799 by William Pitt, the Schedular system only emerged with its successor, Addington's income tax of 1803. The difference between the two was evidently rather more subtle than has often been implied. An important aspect of the Schedular system was to enhance the efficiency with which the tax was administered. When corporation tax was introduced in 1965, the Schedular system was applied to that tax as well.[9] Despite being adjusted and, in a number of cases abolished,[10] the Schedules remained a feature of income tax law until 2005, when they were removed by ITTOIA 2005. The Schedular system has been temporarily retained for corporation tax purposes, but the likelihood is that it will be replaced once the Tax Law Rewrite is complete. **[7.3]**

Kevin Holmes *The Concept of Income: A Multi-Disciplinary Analysis* (2001) pp 154–158

William Pitt first introduced income tax in Great Britain in 1799.[11] The tax, called "duty", which was founded on the "gross-global" approach,[12] was to be a temporary impost to fund the Napoleonic War with France. The 1799 Act specified four general categories of income, which were divided into 19 "cases". Income under each case was aggregated. Specific deductions were also aggregated and subtracted

8 See ICTA 1988, s. 9; ITTOIA 2005, s. 9(2B).
9 See Chapter 18, para **[18.12]**.
10 Schedule B, by FA 1988, s. 148, and Sch 14, Pt V; Schedule C, by FA 1996, s 79, and Sch 7 and 41; and Schedule E, by ITEPA 2003, Sch 8, Pt 1. The abolition of Schedule C took effect in 1996 for *both* income tax and corporation tax.
11 (1799) 38 Geo. 3, c. 22.
12 The gross-global approach to calculation of income subject to tax requires aggregation of all income, regardless of source; aggregation of all allowable deductions; and subtracting total deductions from total income.

from the total amount of income to give a net amount of income chargeable with income tax.[13] The cases of income were very comprehensive for the time. In general terms, the four categories were made up as follows:

1. Income arising from lands, tenements and hereditaments, including:
   - Imputed income of owner occupied land, houses and buildings;
   - Rents and fines payable by tenants of land, tenements, hereditaments and houses;
   - Tithes; and
   - Profits of manors, timbers and woods that are "usually cut periodically",[14] mines, fire insurance and other "Profits of uncertain Annual Amount".[15]
2. Income arising from personal property and from trades, professions, offices, pensions, allowances, stipends, employments and vocations;
3. Income arising out of Great Britain from foreign possessions and foreign securities; and
4. Income not falling under any of the foregoing rules.

At the conclusion of the war in 1802, the income tax was repealed. It was reintroduced in more detail in 1803[16] with the resumption of war, but now on a schedular basis, rather than a global basis. The introduction of schedules, together with deduction of tax at source, was designed to overcome two difficulties with the global approach of the 1799 Act: (a) widespread evasion, which arose from dependence on taxpayers to declare all of their income in an unsophisticated enforcement environment; and (b) a widely held view that the requirement to disclose total income to the state was a gross infringement of a taxpayer's liberty.[17] Using schedules, taxpayers made separate declarations of income under each schedule[18] to different assessors in the Office for Taxes.

Unlike the earlier gross-global income tax regime, the schedular tax system did not impose tax on income *per se*. The system imposed tax on particular (net) receipts, which fell into predetermined categories.[19] However, the items subject to tax under the 1803 Act were not markedly different from those assessed under the 1799 Act. There were five schedules, which contained their own individual tax rates and deductions' code, again set out in the form of "cases", but now with the addition of "rules" for charging the duty.

Income tax remained in force until 1816 when it was abandoned.[20] Robert Peel reintroduced income tax in 1842,[21] again on the same schedular basis as the 1803 Act, and income tax has remained in force in Great Britain ever since. To a large extent, the 1842 Act was a tinkered version of the 1803 Act. The tenor of the

13 See *Schedule of Income* . . . footnote [11], 84–85.
14 Schedule A, Case 10.
15 *Idem.*
16 (1803) 43 Geo. 3, c. 122.
17 [See the account set out by M Emory in 'The Early English Income Tax: A Heritage for the Contemporary' (1965) 9 *American Journal of Legal History* 286.]
18 See Schedule G, *ibid.*, 1062–1067.
19 The English approach is fundamentally different from the global income tax models subsequently adopted in the United States, New Zealand and Australia. Like the United States, Australia's first federal income tax was motivated by the revenue requirements of war. The first Income Tax Assessment Act was passed in 1915. Unlike the United Kingdom and New Zealand legislation, the Australian Act incorporated from the outset the global, rather than schedular, approach to taxing income.
20 [See J E Cookson *Lord Liverpool's Administration* (Edinburgh, 1975), pp 36–69.]
21 [See Travis L Crosby *Sir Robert Peel's Administration, 1841–1846* (Newton Abbott, 1976) ch 2; Norman Gash, *Peel* (London, 1976) ch 16.]

schedules and rules were the same, but some of the language and organisation of the 1803 Act was changed.

The Income Tax Act 1853[22] was passed primarily to bring Ireland within the United Kingdom income tax regime. The 1853 Act specified the five schedules in essentially the same manner as the 1842 Act. The 1853 Act repeatedly cross-referenced to the 1842 Act on matters of calculation and administration of income tax . . . **[7.4]**

A R Ilersic (ed) *Stephen Dowell's History of Taxation and Taxes in England from the Earliest Times to the Present Day* (3rd edn, 6 vols, 1965) vol II pp 226–231

The provisions necessary for the regulation of the system of direct taxation thus introduced were embodied in an Act consisting of 124 lengthy sections, with several schedules. Great care had been taken in drafting the Bill ; but the government, deeming it not improbable that the legislation on the subject might appear somewhat formidable, caused it to be abstracted and explained in "A PLAIN, SHORT, AND EASY DESCRIPTION OF THE DIFFERENT CLAUSES OF THE INCOME TAX, SO AS TO RENDER IT FAMILIAR TO THE MEANEST CAPACITY," subsequently published. This forms the subject of one of Gillray's caricatures, where John Bull is represented at his studies, attended by his guardian angel, with a harp in hand, who sings –

Cease, rude Boreas, blustering railer;
Trust thy fortune's care to me.

This tax Pitt estimated would produce no less than 7,500,000*l*. a year.

. . . After the peace of Amiens, in May 1802, Addington repealed the income tax, stating that he considered it a tax to be reserved for war purposes. . .

When the war recommenced, Addington reimposed the income tax, but only at 5 per cent., estimated to yield 4,500,000*l*. And, as the principal cause of the unpopularity of the tax had been the necessity of giving a general declaration of income from all sources, the tax was now split up and parcelled out in schedules, so as to form, as regards the returns required, so many separate taxes. Schedule A contained the tax on owners of land, including houses, in respect of the ownership ; schedule B, the tax on farmers in respect of land and houses attached to farms, and included the additional benefit to persons in occupation of lands of their own; schedule C, the tax on dividends and annuities from public revenue; schedule D, the tax on income derived by residents in Great Britain from property or business abroad, and the tax on professions, trades, employments, or callings exercised in Great Britain; while schedule E contained the charge on public offices or employments of profit, including the army, navy, and civil service. Incomes under 60*l*. were exempted, and an abatement of tax was allowed for incomes between 60*l*. and 150*l*.[23]. . . **[7.5]**

22 16 & 17 Vic., c. 34.
23 43 Geo. III. C. 122. Aug. 11, 1803.

Martin Daunton *Trusting Leviathan: the Politics of Taxation in* Britain, 1799–1914 (2001) pp 184–187

The income tax introduced by Pitt in 1799 required taxpayers to divulge their entire income, which was then taxed as a whole. When Henry Addington* reintroduced the tax in 1803, after the short-lived peace of 1802–3, he abandoned the attempt to assess total income and the tax was divided into separate schedules or types of income (see table 7.1). The benefits of schedular taxation were obvious in the great improvement in yields: a rate of 2s in the £ produced £5,628,813 in 1801; a rate of 1s in the £ produced £5,341,907 in 1803.[24] In 1842, Peel re-enacted Addington's approach as codified in the Income Tax Act, 1806. Collection at source on particular types of income was preferred to direct assessment of total income which was "much more inquisitorial, more vexatious and more difficult".[25] Taxes from different categories of income could be levied in different ways. Tax was collected at source from rents and dividends in schedules A and C, and from official salaries in schedule E. This procedure was seen by many as the key to the success of the British tax system after the reintroduction of the income tax in 1842, allowing it to be "levied with a minimum of friction and a maximum of result", and allowing collection "to the utmost farthing which is due" from dividends, salaries and rent, without any disclosure to the tax authorities. Of course, there were attempts at evasion. In 1843, a Welsh landowner was found to have asked his tenants to under-report their rent so reducing his tax liability under Schedule A and their own under Schedule B. Indeed, one culprit was himself an assessor, who returned his rent as £60 rather than £64. But such cases of collusion did not cause much concern to the Inland Revenue which stressed the virtues of ease of collection at source.

Table 7.1 Income Tax schedules

Schedule A: rents of real estate and houses

Tax was paid at source by deduction from the rent, so that the owner of property received the income net of tax. The tax was on the gross rent, without an allowance for repairs or improvements. In 1894, when the death duties were reformed, a concession was granted to schedule A: a deduction of 10 per cent was allowed from the income of land and 15 per cent from the income of houses. The income tax rate was effectively reduced as a compensation for the graduated taxation of real property at death.

Schedule B: profits from the occupation of land, i.e. farming

The tax could not be paid at source, for the profits depended upon a large number of transactions as crops were sold and seeds, implements and animals purchased. In order to remove the need for farmers to produce complicated returns, it was assumed that profits amounted to three-quarters of rent in England and a half in Scotland. In 1842, the proportions were reduced to half and a third; and in 1851, farmers were permitted to pay tax on their actual profits when these were lower.

* Henry Addington (1757–1844) was the son of a physician; he was educated at Winchester and Brasenose College, Oxford. He entered Parliament in 1783 and was speaker from 1789 to 1801, when he became chancellor and prime minister. He quarrelled with Pitt, a childhood friend, in 1803 and resigned in 1804. He served as president of the council for a short time in 1805 and again in 1812; he was home secretary in Liverpool's government from 1812 to 1821, with a reputation for repression. He remained in the Cabinet until 1824, and opposed Catholic emancipation and the reform bill. (*DNB*, vol. I, ed. Stephen, pp. 117–21.)

24 PP [Parliamentary Papers] 1852 IX, *First Report from the Select Committee on the Income and Property Tax*, C. Pressly of Inland Revenue, Q. 367.

25 PP [Parliamentary Papers] 1852 IX, *First Report from the Select Committee on Income and Property Tax*, Q. 373.

Table 7.1 Income Tax schedules – contd

Schedule C: profits from government stock and dividends
The tax was deducted at source when the Bank of England paid the interest on stock.

Schedule D: profits from trade, commerce and the professions
It was not possible to collect the tax at source, for the profits rested upon a large number of transactions; neither was it possible to take rent (or any other simple measure) as an indicator of profits. The assessment of the tax therefore rested upon an assessment of the profits of the individual trader or professional. Tax was paid on the basis of average income of the previous three years in order to smooth out fluctuations of trade, unlike other schedules which paid on the basis of the preceding year. The procedure adopted for government stock was extended to companies which were treated as withholding agents in the payment of dividends. Income tax was paid at the standard rate on profits, and when dividends on shares and interest on stock were distributed, they were paid net of tax. Anyone who was exempt from tax, or paid a lower rate, claimed repayment of the tax from the authorities.

Schedule E: salaries and pensions from office
In the case of employment from office, income tax was deducted from the salary or pension at source, which was paid net of tax. When the income tax was introduced, payment of a regular annual salary was not common outside the government service. Employers made a return of their staff to the tax officials, who claimed payment of tax from the employees, but with the growth of larger, bureaucratic, organisations such as railway companies or joint-stock banks, the payment of salaries net of tax was extended to them.

Source: A. Hope-Jones, *Income Tax in the Napoleonic Wars* (Cambridge, 1939), pp. 20–1; PP1870 XX, *Report of the Commissioners of Inland Revenue on the duties under their management for the years 1856 to 1869 inclusive*, vol. I, pp. 326, 328.

E.W. Hamilton expressed a common view that the ease of collection of the income tax "is one of the wonders of the world. It is the envy of other nations."[26] An American commentator in 1910 agreed, arguing that "it obviat[es] the necessity for inquisitorial proceedings upon the one hand, while removing the opportunity for fraud and evasion upon the other".[27] The schedular system meant that it was no longer necessary to establish the entire income of an individual taxpayer, so reducing the scope for clashes between taxpayers and officials of the Inland Revenue; and collection at source limited the opportunity for under-assessment and evasion. It was repeatedly argued that such an arrangement meant that the relations between taxpayer and tax collector were trouble-free, and collection at source was considered to be "at the very root of the British income tax system ... Without deduction of tax at source the revenue is wholly dependent upon the care and accuracy with which the taxpayer makes up his Income Tax return; evasion is simple."[28] The entire tax receipt under schedules A, C and E was collected at source, and formed 63.5 per cent of the net revenue from the income tax in 1855/6. The proportion fell to 36.0 per cent in 1910/11, but an increasing proportion of income under schedule D from dividends on shares in public companies was deducted at source, as well as regular salaries under schedule E (see table 7.2). In 1905, 70 to 80

26 PP [Parliamentary Papers] 1905 XLIV, *Report of the Departmental Committee on Income Tax*, p. 221; Public Records Office, T168/68, miscellaneous memorandum by E. W. Hamilton, volume XIII, "Graduation of income tax', Hamilton to chancellor of the Exchequer, 6 June 1906; administration is outlined in PP 1870 XX, *Report of the Commissioners of Inland Revenue*, vol. I, pp. 307–13. Public Records Office, IR40/308, Thomas Kite, assistant inspector, Hereford, 11 Feb. 1843, and J. Timm, solicitor to Inland Revenue, 17 Feb. 1843.

27 K. K. Kennan, *Income Taxation: Methods and Results in Various Countries* (Milwaukee, 1910), pp. 58, 73–4.

28 PRO [Public Records Office], T176/18, undated and unsigned paper, ff. 17–18.

per cent of tax was collected either at source, or on income which could be verified in some way.[29]

Collection at source was not possible for incomes from unincorporated businesses in schedule D, that is the profits of professions or family firms and partnerships. Here, tax liability was determined by lay commissioners and assessors so that the income tax was less intrusive and the relationship between the state and civil society was not threatened. It was argued that taxpayers were protected against an over-powerful bureaucracy and a grasping state by relying on members of the taxpaying class to assess and collect taxes, and to arbitrate in disputes. Of course, an administrative system operated by taxpayers was susceptible to under-assessment of incomes, and a fine line needed to be drawn between the benefits of consent and the dangers of evasion. Permanent officials had powers to monitor the

Table 7.2 Net receipt from income tax by schedule, United Kingdom, 1855/6 and 1910/11 (per cent)

	1855/6	1910/11
Schedule A (rent)	47.2	25.3
Schedule B (farming)	5.6	0.5
Schedule C (dividends)	10.4	4.0
Schedule D (trades and professions)		
Public companies and foreign dividends		38.7
Trades and professions		20.1
Total	30.9	58.8
Schedule E (employment)	5.9	6.7
Supertax		4.6

Source: PP [Parliamentary Papers] 1857 (1st session) IV, *First Report of the Commissioners of the Inland Revenue*, pp. 251–2; PP 1911 XLV, *Return showing for the year ended 31 March 1911 (1) the amount contributed by England, Scotland and Ireland respectively to the revenue collected by imperial officers (2) the expenditure of English, Scottish and Irish services met out of such revenue; and (3) the balances of revenue contributed by England, Scotland and Ireland respectively, which are available for imperial expenditure* ..., p. 415.

system and prevent obvious cases of fraud and evasion, which would threaten mutual trust between taxpayers. Compliance would break down if one taxpayer thought that another was evading proper payment; commitment to taxation rested upon the belief that fellow taxpayers were at least as reliable and trustworthy as oneself. But care had to be taken that bureaucratic powers were not increased too far, for this would be interpreted as an act of "despotism" by the government which would undermine the relationship between the taxpayer and the state, and threaten consent to taxation. A careful balance needed to be struck between incorporating taxpayers into the administrative system in order to secure a high level of acceptance of taxation at the cost of a certain degree of avoidance; and the creation of a more bureaucratic system which would remove anomalies and abuses at the expense of tension or unrest. Of course, this line shifted as the structure of the taxpaying class altered: when miners came within reach of the income tax in the First World War, they were suspicious of a tax system which incorporated mineowners into assessment and collection. There was always a danger that the Inland Revenue would become more concerned to maintain tried and tested administrative procedures than to respond to the changing social relations of extraction. **[7.6]**

29 PRO [Public Records Office], T176/18; PP 1905 XLIV, *Report of the Departmental Committee on Income Tax*, p. 223.

3. Some fundamental concepts

As mentioned above, income tax contains some key ideas which, although developed two centuries ago, continue to be important as informing concepts, given the avowed purpose of ITEPA 2003 and ITTOIA 2005 as being only to make the former legislation 'clearer' and 'simpler'. Three of these key concepts are the doctrine of source, the unitary nature of income tax and the mutual exclusivity of the Schedules. **[7.7]**

A. The doctrine of source

The doctrine of source encompasses the idea that unless income has a source in a year of assessment (a tax year), it is not liable to tax. Prior to the enactment of ITEPA 2003 and ITTOIA 2005, this entailed a determination that particular income fell within one of the Schedules. **[7.8]**

***Brown (Surveyor of Taxes) v National Provident Institution* [1921] 2 AC 222 (HL)**[30]

The appellants, who had derived profits from discounts on Treasury Bills, were assessed to income tax under Schedule D, Case III. Since the 'preceding year' basis applied under the legislation then in force (the Income Tax Act 1853) the assessment for the 1917–1918 tax year was based on the profits of an earlier period. The appellants had ceased to hold the Treasury Bills in question before the beginning of the 1917–1918 tax year. The House of Lords[31] held that a person must possess a particular source of income in a tax year in order to be assessed to income tax for that year on the income in question.

> VISCOUNT HALDANE: . . . The remaining question is one of considerable difficulty. It is that of the chargeability by assessment for the year 1917–18, in which there were no transactions in bills, of the transactions during the previous year. The Court of Appeal, differing from Rowlatt J., thought that profits on discounts could only be charged under the Third Case of Sch. D in a year when the source of such profits still continued to exist, and that in consequence the profits on discounts of a previous year escaped taxation under that case if in the succeeding year no such profits had been made. My Lords, this question, the most important in the appeal brought before us, can only, I think, be answered if the principle on which the income-tax legislation is based has been first defined, and to this principle I therefore turn. The case is governed, not by the general Income Tax Act of 1918, an Act which has superseded the older legislation, but by the Income Tax Act of 1853, and the provisions of the Act of 1842, which it kept alive. The Finance Acts of 1916, 1917, and 1918 rendered those the governing statutes for the purposes of the question before us. My Lords, in *London County Council v. Attorney-General*[32] it was decided by this House that the Income Tax Acts of 1842 and 1853, as modified by the Customs and Inland Revenue Act 1882, do no more than impose a single tax on profits and gains brought into charge by the Income Tax Acts. There is no special or peculiar tax under each case of Sch. D and the other schedules or their branches, whatever be the idiosyncrasies of the methods prescribed for collection. The expression "income tax," as used by the Legislature, was a generic description of the tax which was levied under all the

30 See also *Grainger v Maxwell* [1926] 1 KB 430 (CA); *Leeming v Jones* [1930] 1 KB 279, 297 (Lord Hanworth MR) and *Bray v Best* [1989] 1 WLR 167, 173 (Lord Oliver).

31 Unusually, only four law Lords are recorded as having been present when the decision was handed down, namely Viscount Haldane, Viscount Cave, Lord Atkinson and Lord Sumner.

32 [1901] AC 26.

schedules alike, and it was not meant to be anything but a tax on income. There was imposed under the schedules no collection of taxes distinct from each other, but simply one tax, with standards for assessment, which varied according to the sources from which the taxable income was derived.

... It is to be observed that, speaking broadly at all events, the general principle of the Acts is to make the tax apply only to a source of income existing in the year of assessment.

... If a man carries on business by buying and discounting bills, this is, I think, as much a source of profit as any other for the purposes of the words employed. As in the case before us it is agreed that there was no such source, I think that we have to assume that there was no income on which to base the tax. Reading the Income Tax Acts as a whole it appears to me that the tax is one of a single kind based, speaking broadly, on a single principle. It is imposed on existing income, however the amount to be levied is to be computed in particular instances ... **[7.9]**

The 'purity' of the notion of source has been modified over the years by statute with, for example, the inclusion of exemptions in both ITEPA 2003 and ITTOIA 2005. Further, Lord Hoffmann has also emphasised in *Walker (Inspector of Taxes) v Centaur Clothes Group Ltd* [2000] STC 324[33] (and see below) that both income tax and corporation tax have now become too complex for it to be 'true to say that income ... [cannot] be within the charge to tax unless there ... [is] a source within the charge' or that 'a person ... [cannot] be within the charge unless he had a source of income within the charge'. Examples of when this may be the case are ITEPA 2003, s 17, which taxes earnings from an employment received even after the employment has finished,[34] and 'post-cessation receipts arising from a trade' that are usually taxed under ITTOIA 2005, s 242.[35] **[7.10]**

Walker (Inspector of Taxes) v Centaur Clothes Group Ltd [2000] STC 324 (HL)

LORD HOFFMANN: ... It is true that by s 9(3),[36] the computation of income for the purposes of corporation tax is to be computed according to income tax principles and under the same Schedules and Cases. Income tax is traditionally a source-based annual tax, liability depending upon the existence of a source of income falling under one of the Schedules during the year of assessment (see *Brown (Surveyor of Taxes) v National Provident Institution* [1921] 2 AC 222, 8 TC 57). If the income tax had retained that ancient simplicity, it would be true to say that income could not be within the charge to tax unless there was a source within the charge and a person could not be within the charge unless he had a source of income within the charge. But that would be because of the nature of the income tax and not anything in the language of the definition.

It is, however, no longer true to say that liability to income tax depends upon the existence during the year of assessment of a source within the charge. There are cases (such as post-cessation receipts) when liability depends upon the existence of income defined by reference to a source which does not exist within the year of assessment. Or

33 Although a corporation tax, rather than an income tax case, the fact does not affect the point being made here.

34 i.e. when 'the employee does not hold the employment'. This provision was originally introduced in 1989, 'in the course of changing the charge to tax [under the then Schedule E] from the arisings basis to the receipts basis' (see Natalie Lee *(gen ed.) Revenue Law – Principles and Practice* (24th edn, 2006), para **[6.42]**).

35 For further background details, see Tiley, n 1 above, pp 455–456.

36 [ie ICTA 1988; see Chapter 18, para **[18.12]**.]

liability may depend upon an event, such as a balancing charge on the sale of an asset which has attracted a capital allowance,[37] or the receipt of a capital sum from a particular kind of transaction, which is deemed to be taxable income received in that year of assessment[38] or sometimes spread over several years of assessment. In the case of corporation tax, liability is also imposed upon chargeable gains.[39] So there is no longer any basis for assuming that income, or a person, can only be within the charge to corporation tax in a given year of assessment if the income is from or the person has a source of income within the charge to that tax. **[7.11]**

B. Several Schedules but a single tax

The existence of the Schedules for income tax purposes did not mean that income tax was a series of separate taxes. This point, which was referred to by Viscount Haldane in the extract from *Brown (Surveyor of Taxes) v. National Provident Institution*, above, is elaborated in the following extract from *London County Council v. Attorney-General* [1901] AC 26, in which Lord Macnaghten reviews the provisions of the 1799 and 1803 Acts and, in doing so, alludes to Dowell's work extracted above. **[7.12]**

***London County Council v Attorney General* [1901] AC 26 (HL)**

LORD MACNAGHTEN: ... Income tax, if I may be pardoned for saying so, is a tax on income. It is not meant to be a tax on anything else. It is one tax, not a collection of taxes essentially distinct...

It is interesting and, I think, instructive to trace the development of income tax legislation. A very clear account of it is to be found in Mr. Stephen Dowell's excellent work. I turn at once to the original Act of 1799, 39 Geo. 3, c. 13, as amended by 39 Geo. 3, c. 22. For the purposes of the tax the income for the current year of persons to be assessed was ranged under four divisions: "I. Income arising from lands, tenements, and hereditaments. II. Income arising from personal property and from trades, professions, offices, pensions, stipends, employments, and vocations. III. Income arising out of Great Britain. IV. Income not falling under any of the foregoing rules." In the form of return required from the taxpayer, which is given in a schedule, these four heads of income were represented by nineteen "cases", of which the first fourteen fell under Division I. The taxpayer had to return his total income under each and all of these cases. From this total income the taxpayer was allowed to make a great many deductions under various heads also specified in the schedule. There were deductions for rents of all sorts. There was a deduction for "annual interest for debts," whether "personal" or charged on property enumerated in the several "cases," a deduction for "allowance to children or other relations," and a deduction for "annuities." The total amount of deductions was subtracted from the total amount of income, and the difference was the "income chargeable." That general return, as Mr. Dowell observes, was regarded as the most objectionable feature in the income tax. By the Act of 1803, in lieu of a general return, particular returns of income from particular sources were required. That was the origin of the five schedules of charge with which we are now so familiar. It was not that there was any difference in kind between the income arising from the different sources. The alteration was made in order to avoid disclosure of the taxpayer's circumstances. This new method was found to work so well that it has been continued in every Income Tax Act ever since. The Act of 1853,

37 [There may be a balancing charge when an asset in relation to which capital allowances have been claimed is disposed of; see Chapter 10, para **[10.65]**.]

38 [See, eg, ITA 2007, ss 752–772 ('Transactions in land').

39 [See ICTA 1988, ss 6(3) and 6(4)(a);[see Chapter 18, para **[18.11]**.]

after imposing the duties of income tax by s. 1, distributes those duties in s. 2 among the different Scheds. A, B, C, D, and E, on the ground, as there stated, of convenience of classification and facility of collection . . . **[7.13]**

C. Mutual exclusivity

The concept of 'mutual exclusivity', which meant that, where income was clearly chargeable under one of the Schedules, the Inland Revenue[40] had no power to tax it under one of the other Schedules instead, continues to be relevant only to corporation tax. For income tax purposes, it has been superseded by the priority rules (see below, para **[7.23]**). However, the priority rules are only explicable by reference to the mutual exclusivity principle. **[7.14]**

***Fry v Salisbury House Estate Ltd* [1930] AC 432 (HL)**

A company was the owner of a building ('Salisbury House'), which it rented out as unfurnished offices. In addition to the rent, the company levied a service charge for cleaning, heating, etc. In accordance with the legislation then in force, the company was assessed under Schedule A on the 'annual value' of the building.[41] This assessment was, however, less than the company's actual income from the rents. The Inland Revenue accordingly assessed the company to tax under Schedule D, Case I, both on the rents and on the income from the service charge, although making an allowance for the tax charged under Schedule A. The House of Lords held that, since the Schedules were mutually exclusive, the Schedule A assessment precluded a charge under Schedule D, Case I.

VISCOUNT DUNEDIN: . . . Now, the cardinal consideration in my judgment is that the income tax is only one tax, a tax on the income of the person whom it is sought to assess, and that the different Schedules are the modes in which the statute directs this to be levied. In other words, there are not five taxes which you might call income tax A, B, C, D and E, but only one tax. That tax is to be levied on the income of the individual whom it is proposed to assess, but then you have to consider the nature, the constituent parts, of his income to see which Schedule you are to apply. Now, if the income of the assessee consists in part of real property you are, under the statute, bound to apply Schedule A.

. . . Of course that does not mean that the assessee may not be liable in respect of other income under other Schedules.

. . . But he might be liable under any of the other Schedules if he has income to which they apply, and in particular he might be liable under Schedule D. It is a mere commonplace to remark that a man who possesses real property and is assessed under Schedule A, may also have investments and other forms of property which will be assessed under Schedule D.

Now, turning to this case. The income of the respondents, as represented by rents, is admittedly assessed and properly assessed under Schedule A. "But then," says the appellant, "you are carrying on a business, and a business falls to be assessed under Schedule D." To which the respondent replies, "Quite so; and I am willing to pay on the profits which I make on the cleaning and other services." To this the appellant replies, "No; that is not enough. Your business is one business not congeries of businesses, and if I estimate your profits from your own profit and loss account, I will get the higher figure which I ask." The answer to that is: "You cannot bring out that balance of profit without taking the rents I receive in computo. Now, these rents are also part of my income or property, and the statute says that any income which represents the value of real property

40 Now HMRC.

41 The operation of Schedule A on this basis is considered in Chapter 12, para **[12.2]**.

> is to be assessed in the manner directed under Schedule A." My Lords, I think the final answer is good. The rents, having been assessed under Schedule A, are, so to speak, exhausted as a source of income, and the so-called concession made by the appellant that there should not be double taxation, and that therefore he would be willing to allow deduction of the sum paid under Schedule A, is a concession which is beside the mark. It is a concession to avoid double taxation, but the concession cannot come into being where double taxation does not exist, because, it being imperative to deal with rents under Schedule A, there is no possibility of subsequently dealing with them under Schedule D . . . **[7.15]**

The mutual exclusivity concept did not, however, apply to the Cases within Schedules. **[7.16]**

4. The Schedules and the new heads of charge

A. *General approach of the Tax Law Rewrite project*

Although the Rewrite project has replaced Schedule E by ITEPA 2003, and Schedules A, D, and F by ITTOIA 2005, emphasis will be placed in this section on ITTOIA 2005 since the debates on the Income Tax (Trading and Other Income) Bill, which became ITTOIA 2005, covered, among other things, the reasons for keeping the Schedular system for corporation tax, while removing it for income tax.

The nature and purpose of the Tax Law Rewrite project have already been considered in Chapter 1. It is sufficient to note here several points of particular relevance to ITTOIA 2005.

(1) Most importantly, ITTOIA 2005 does not, except in specific cases,[42] change the pre-existing law. Although those specific cases total 159 altogether, the heading to Annex 1 to the EN to ITTOIA 2005 describes them as 'Minor changes in the law made by the Act'.[43]
(2) ITTOIA 2005 uses 'descriptive labels' instead of Schedules, but does not – given its purpose as 'Rewrite' legislation only – abandon the notion of the source as formerly embodied in the Schedules. This is also true of ITEPA 2003.
(3) ITTOIA 2005 does not apply to corporation tax.[44]

Further, whereas formerly, there were separate charges for UK-source and foreign-source income,[45] income now generally falls within a particular Part of ITTOIA 2005, irrespective of whether its source is in the UK or abroad.[46] **[7.17]**

42 See ITTOIA 2005, EN III, pp 52–179.
43 See below.
44 See ICTA 1988, s 9(2A).
45 Schedule D, Case IV charged to income tax 'income arising from securities out of the United Kingdom'. Trades carried on outside the UK were charged to income tax under Schedule D, Case V (unless the trade was carried on at least in part in the UK – see *Colquhoun v Brooks* (1889) 14 App Cas 493). Schedule D, Case V, also subjected to income tax income from land.
46 See ITTOIA 2005, s 6 ('Trading Income'); ITTOIA 2005, ss 269 ('Property Income'); ITTOIA 2005, s 368 ('Savings and Investment Income'); ITTOIA 2005, s 577 ('Miscellaneous Income'). See also ITEPA 2003, s 15 (earnings).

John F Avery Jones 'Taxing Foreign Income from Pitt to the Tax Law Rewrite – the Decline of the Remittance Basis' in John Tiley (ed), *Studies in the History of Tax Law* (2004) pp 54–55

The first and second features of the system of taxing foreign income with which we started[47] will change with the Tax Law Rewrite. Pitt's wording will be dropped as will any remaining distinctions between Cases IV and V, and foreign income will no longer be a type of income in itself.[48] This is sad from the historical point of view but it is amazing that the wording lasted so long and the courts were able to continue to make it fit all current types of foreign income. In the Rewrite where a type of income is considered, this includes the same type of foreign income so that, for example, there is no longer any distinction between UK and foreign source interest; the charge is on "all interest."[49] After enactment of the Rewrite's third Income Tax Bill in the 2004/2005 session of Parliament[50] there will be very few separate rules for foreign income, an example of an exception being dividends from non-resident companies.[51] It is only necessary to define foreign income for the remittance basis and rules for unremittable income. For this purpose "foreign income" is defined to mean "income arising from a source[52] outside the United Kingdom which is chargeable under or by virtue of" a list of provisions, such as trading income, property income, interest, etc, all of which deal with both UK and foreign income together.[53] Foreign source has the same meaning as foreign possession and so one could say that Pitt's single category of foreign income lives on under another name . . . **[7.18]**

The Parliamentary Under-Secretary of State, Department for Culture, Media and Sport (Lord McIntosh of Haringey) *Hansard*, HL, vol 671, col 324, 23 March 2005

I turn to the content and approach of the legislation. The charge to income tax is currently broken down into a number of schedules. Over the years, schedules have come and gone. I am old enough to remember the schedule that taxed imputed income on owner occupation, but that has been gone for some 40 years now.[54] The Bill tackles income tax charged under those schedules. It brings the charging and calculation rules for the different sorts of income together in updated

47 [ie, first, the use of eighteenth century expressions in tax legislation; and, secondly, the fact 'that Pitts' two categories of foreign income [ie 'interest arising from foreign securities' and 'income from foreign possessions'] treat foreign income as a separate type of income unrelated to the categories of domestic income, such as trading profits, interest etc ...'].

48 ED 13 [Exposure Draft No 13 *Foreign Income and Property Income*, March 2002], para. 65.

49 Draft Income Tax Bill in ED 13 . . . cl. 298. similarly with all other types of income, see the list in cl. 616.

50 This date is given in the Rewrite's Plans for 2002/03, July 2002.

51 Because the definition of distribution in part denies a deduction for various payments and so cannot be applied to non-resident companies: ED 13 . . . para. 883, and accompanying Draft Income Tax Bill cl. 322. The charge is on 'dividends', an undefined expression both here and as a component to distributions of UK resident companies.

52 ED 13 . . . para. 1158.

53 Draft Income Tax Bill in ED 13 . . . cl. 616.

54 [See Chapter 12, below, para **[12.2]**.]

classifications, such as trading income, savings and investment income and property income. Under the current legislation, it integrates foreign income in the same parts as equivalent United Kingdom income, confining any special rules that apply to foreign income to a different part. **[7.19]**

B. Separation of the income tax and corporation tax codes

One of the most controversial aspects of ITTOIA 2005 has been its application to income tax only. This issue was addressed when key witnesses were questioned by the House of Lords and House of Commons Joint Committee on Tax Law Rewrite Bills in February 2005, and discussed in a HMRC memorandum which was annexed to the report of the Committee's proceedings. **[7.20]**

House of Lords and House of Commons Joint Committee on Tax Law Rewrite Bills, *First Report. Income Tax (Trading and Other Income) Bill*, HL and HC Papers, Session 2004–2005, HL Paper 37 and HC Paper 285, London, 2005, pp Ev 24–25 (Examination of Witnesses on 1 February 2005)

Q1 Chairman [the Right Honourable Kenneth Clarke QC MP]: . . . May I begin by asking . . . that it seems to me the first decision of major principle taken in the course of creating this Bill was to produce an income tax bill as opposed to a corporation tax bill and it was decided as part of the Rewrite Project that it would make sense to separate out the income tax provisions—leaving open future decisions as to whether corporation tax should be totally taken out and dealt with separately. From reading the evidence, that decision has not actually given rise to any controversy or opposition from any of the practitioners involved. Would you just like to remind the Committee as to why that seems to be the one basic decision in principle which was taken?

Mr Morris: . . . [*Tax Law Rewrite Project, Inland Revenue, Team Leader*] the background starts in 1799 when we first had income tax; we did not have corporation tax until relatively recently in the Finance Act 1965. When corporation tax was brought in, it was sensible not to reinvent the wheel entirely at that stage and the aim was to piggyback on to income tax and use the income tax calculation rules. That was achieved through what is now section 9 of ICTA [Income and Corporation Tax 1988], which says that income for corporation tax purposes is calculated in accordance with income tax law and practice using the income tax schedules and cases. There is a legal fiction that is saying you have two codes but corporation tax is working through section 9 and picking up the income tax rules. Since 1965 the rules have diverged markedly. We have special corporation tax legislation and much of the income tax legislation applies for income tax purposes only. I suspect that the effect of section 9 has been overlooked on occasion because when you come to the legislation in ICTA and elsewhere it is not always clear whether or not it applies for income tax or corporation tax or both codes. It was obviously a question we had to confront fairly early on in the life of the Project and we did consult on this at an early stage. As you will have seen from the memorandum, none of the representative bodies we consulted were in favour of retaining this integrated approach which is so confusing in practice; and all were in favour of wanting to move to two separate Acts for the two codes (or neutral) and that is what we have started here. We have a Bill that is income tax only. The provisions we have rewritten (which apply also to corporation tax) at the moment are left freestanding in ICTA. Still working through section 9, so not entirely freestanding, we still have this working through section 9 for corporation tax and income tax; but we now have the start of two codes separate in different Acts. What we have not decided yet is the extent to which we will entirely separate them; that will need decisions when we come on to rewriting corporation tax in due course and we will again be consulting on the extent to which we will cross-refer or make it entirely freestanding. [7.21]

House of Lords and House of Commons Joint Committee on Tax Law Rewrite Bills, *First Report. Income Tax (Trading and Other Income) Bill*, above, p Ev 2 (Memorandum by the Inland Revenue)

12. Considerable time and effort has been spent on the issue of splitting income tax from corporation tax. The Bill rewrites provisions that in the source legislation apply for both income and corporation tax purposes. But it does so only for income tax purposes. Consequential amendments have been made to ensure that these provisions continue to operate as before for corporation tax.
13. The Project consulted at an early stage on whether we should aim for greater separation of the Income Tax and Corporation Tax codes.
14. None of the representative bodies favoured retaining ICTA in its present mammoth form and all but one either advocated splitting income tax and corporation tax or were neutral. The near-unanimous view in the consultation was that the combination of income tax and corporation tax in a single Act, with some rules applying for one tax alone, and some for both, makes the legislation difficult to understand because the logical flow for both taxes is fractured.
15. Moreover, since corporation tax was first enacted as an extension of income tax in 1965, the rules for the two taxes have diverged and continue to do so. For example:
    — the 1996 loan relationship legislation creates a regime for corporation tax completely different from that for income tax; and
    — large parts of Schedule D now apply only to income tax.
16. The general view in consultation was that the differences between income tax and corporation tax are now so significant that it makes sense to put each code into separate Acts. Most were willing to accept repetition of rules and a resulting increase in the length of legislation if that led to greater clarity. More than one remarked that what matters is not how many pages the rules take up but how long it takes to understand them.
17. Splitting ICTA is a substantial step. The main advantages are:
    — IT and CT users will not be diverted by provisions that do not apply to them;
    — each code can be given the structure best suited to its own provisions; and
    — future legislation can be made to apply more clearly to, and with suitable wording in, each of the codes.
18. The potential disadvantages are:
    — different legal interpretations of identically-worded provisions (this cannot be ruled out, although we doubt that it would arise frequently, if at all);

— unintentional divergence of the codes caused by the failure to pick up, say, the corporation tax consequential of an income tax change; and
— duplication of effort because a provision which requires amendment is in two Acts (but we do not expect that this would generally involve two Parliamentary debates).

19. A decision was taken to give effect to the income tax/corporation tax split in relation to the content of this Bill. And it is our intention to approach the rewrite of the balance of income tax legislation in the same way. This does not mean that we will necessarily rewrite corporation tax as a fully stand alone code. It provides the opportunity to take such a decision in the future. But it leaves open the possibility of utilising in full or in part the rewritten income tax code if or where it appears sensible to do so. A final decision on the approach to corporation tax will be made after full consultation when the project turns to this aspect of its task. **[7.22]**

C. *Priority rules*

The former Schedule D comprised a number of different Cases. In the event of income falling within more than one of those Cases, it was long accepted that the Revenue had the option to choose under which Case the income should be taxed. This practice, known as the 'Crown Option', was eventually given statutory authority.[55] ITTOIA 2005 attempts to deal with the issue by systematising the order in which its taxing provisions are invoked.[56] **[7.23]**

Explanatory Notes: Income Tax (Trading and Other Income) Act 2005, vol. I (London, 2005) pp 96–98

Change 66: Priority of the charge on trade profits: the "Crown Option" and sections 261, 366 and 575 . . .

This Act deals with the Crown Option by providing for an order of priority between the Parts if income is capable of being taxed under more than one Part.

Section 261 provides that if income is capable of being taxed under Part 3 of this Act in respect of an overseas property business and under Chapter 2 of Part 2 of this Act it is taxed under Part 2. ICTA taxes the profits arising from an overseas property business under Schedule D Case V so section 261 gives effect to the Crown Option in respect of trades carried on wholly or partly in the United Kingdom (and to section 65A(1)(b) of ICTA in respect of trades carried on wholly abroad).

Section 366(1) gives priority to Chapter 2 of Part 2 of this Act if income falls within both Part 2 and Part 4 of this Act. This gives effect to the Crown Option in respect of income within Part 4 of this Act that is taxed in ICTA under Schedule D Cases III, IV or V. It goes beyond the Crown Option in that it gives Part 2 of this Act

55 See TMA 1970, s 28A(7B).

56 See the Explanatory Notes ('EN') to ITTOIA 2005, on ss 4, 261, 366, 367, 575 and 576. See also Tiley, n 1 above, p 134.

priority over income that would be taxed under Schedule F or as a non-schedular charge. It applies the same approach to trades carried on wholly abroad as is applied to trades carried on wholly or partly in the United Kingdom. This is consistent with the law (see section 65(3) of ICTA) and practice that the profits of both types of trade should be calculated on the same basis as far as possible.

In the case of income taxed under Schedule F the statutory authority for this approach is given by section 95(1) of ICTA (applied to trades carried on wholly abroad by section 65(3) of ICTA) .

In the case of non-schedular charges it is unlikely that there would be any overlap for income tax payers. But in theory it is possible that, for example, stock dividends (Chapter 5 of Part 4 of this Act) and gains from contracts for life assurance (Chapter 10 of Part 4 of this Act) may rank as trade receipts. Taxing such income under Part 2 of this Act accords with the policy and practice of taking trade receipts into account in calculating trade profits and not otherwise.

Part 2 of this Act provides for a charge on the profits of professions and vocations as well as a charge on the profits of trades. So section 366(1) goes beyond the ambit of ICTA by giving priority to Part 2 of this Act if the source legislation gives priority to income taxed as a trade receipt or under Schedule D Case I. For example, section 56(2) of ICTA (rewritten as section 551 (transactions in deposits)) excludes income taxed as a trade receipt from the charge under Schedule D Case VI. Paragraph 1(2)(a) of Schedule 5AA to ICTA (rewritten as section 555 (disposals of futures and options involving guaranteed returns)) excludes income taxed under Schedule D Case I or V from the charge under Schedule D Case VI. Taxing such income under Part 2 of this Act accords with the policy of taking receipts into account in calculating Schedule D Case I or II profits, although the point is most unlikely to arise in practice in relation to a profession.

Section 575 gives priority to Part 2 of this Act if income falls both within Chapter 2 of Part 2 (trade receipts) of this Act and Part 5 of this Act. In this case the only possible overlap is with income that could be taxed under Schedule D Cases III and V. So the order of priority gives effect to the Crown Option. **[7.24]**

D. Employment income

'Employment income' comprises the income of employees, directors and office-holders.[57] Prior to 2003, employment income fell under the various Cases of Schedule E. The Income Tax (Earnings and Pensions) Act 2003 abolished Schedule E and replaced it with income tax rules on 'earnings'. The following extracts are from successive editions of Tiley's *Revenue Law*.[58] Both offer an overview of employee income taxation. Under sub-heading (i) is an extract from the edition describing Schedule E; under (ii) is an extract describing the law as rewritten in ITEPA 2003.

The older provisions are of more than historical interest in that an appreciation of the general features of Schedule E is necessary to understand the issues raised in the case law found in Chapter 8. **[7.25]**

57 See Chapter 8.
58 See Tiley, n 1 above.

(1) The former Schedule E

John Tiley *Revenue Law* (4th edn, 2000) pp 199–200

Income tax is charged under Schedule E on the emoluments from any office or employment[59] and certain pensions.[60] Liability arises under three Cases. The basic charging provision (TA 1988, s. 19(1)) taxes "emoluments from any office or employment." A payment from an employer to an employee for some other reason than the employment will escape tax. Conversely, and less obviously, a payment from a non-employer may be taxable – if it is for services rendered under a contract of employment.[61] The test in these cases is one of causation; an emolument is a payment in return for acting as or being an employee.[62] A running issue is the extent to which these are matters of form as opposed to substance, i.e. the question are [*sic*] to be answered by reference to what the parties said in their arrangements.[63] Income taxable under Schedule E is earned income.[64]

13.1.1 Scope

The term "emoluments" is defined to include "all salaries, fees, wages, perquisites and profits whatsoever.".[*sic*][65] This was enough to tax many benefits in kind under the general rule in s. 19. However, a payment in kind is taxable under s. 19 only if, in addition to being an emolument, it is convertible into money. For this reason a wider test (TA 1988, s. 154) applies to most employees (i.e. those earning £8,500 a year or more) and to directors. There are other special rules where either s. 19 or s. 154 are insufficient.

13.1.2 Expenses

By TA 1988, s. 198 expenses are deductible under Schedule E if they are incurred wholly, exclusively and necessarily in the performance of the duties of the office or

59 TA 1988, s. 19(1) as recast, for 1989–1990 and later years by FA 1989, s. 36(2). Until 1922, Schedule E was confined to income from a public office (including the director of a company) or public employment; other employments were in Schedule D. In 1922 employments were moved to Schedule E unless they came with [*sic*] Schedule D, Case V; overseas remuneration from non-public office or employment remained in Schedule D, Case V until FA 1956, s. 101 when the present three-Case structure was introduced. . . .

60 Certain public or foreign pensions are taxable under s. 19 paras 2, 3 and 4 ; voluntary pensions are taxable under TA 1988, s. 133; occupational pensions under TA 1988, s. 597; state retirement pensions under s. 617; and personal pensions schemes under s. 648A. Pensions arising under retirement annuity contracts are taxed under Schedule D, Case III but as earned income. A pension is a taxable subject matter distinct from the office or employment (*Tilley* v. *Wales* [1943] AC 386, 392, 25 TC 136, 149, *per* Viscount Simon LC). Pensions in respect of other overseas service will come within Case IV or V if the source is foreign . . . A reduction of 10% is applied to pensions within s. 19, para. 4 (TA 1988, s. 196).

61 *Blakiston* v. *Cooper* [1901] AC 104, 5 TC 347, HL; however, the fact that the payment is not by the employer may be a factor in helping a court conclude that such a payment is not an emolument (*Pritchard* v. *Arundale* [1972] Ch 229, 47 TC 680).

62 *Shilton v. Wilmshurst* [1991] STC 88, 64 TC 78; see also Lord Radcliffe in *Hochstrasser* v. *Mayes* [1960] AC 376, 389, 392 who said that the test goes beyond one of simple reward for services but must still be referable to the performance of duties under the contract.

63 See Ward [1992] *BTR* 139.

64 TA 1988, s. 833(4).

65 Ibid., s. 131. A perquisite is merely a casual emolument additional to regular salary or wages (*Owen v. Pook* [1970] AC 244, 225, [1969] 2 All ER 1, 5, *per* Lord Guest).

employment. Travelling expenses have their own rule – they must be "qualifying travelling expenses". These are either (i) "necessarily incurred in the performance of the duties of" the office or employment, a long-established and increasingly litigated expression, or (ii) come within a new category established in 1998 relating to travel to or from a temporary workplace. The holder of the office or employment must, in either case, have been obliged to incur and have defrayed the expenses "out of" the emoluments; these words mean, in the Revenue view, that no claim for loss relief can arise under Schedule E.

Capital allowances may be claimed by the employee in respect of machinery and plant if incurred necessarily.[66]

Most emoluments paid by the employer are subject to a system of deduction of tax at source – the PAYE system.[67] Whether or not subject to that system, income is assessed on a current year basis. It is taxed on when it is received or become due for payment, whichever is the earlier; the old case-law rule which backdated payments to the year in which the service was performed was abolished in 1989.[68] **[7.26]**

(2) ITEPA 2003

John Tiley *Revenue Law* (5th edn, 2005) pp 210–211

Income tax is now charged on employment income, ie the earnings from an employment or office.[69] The basic definition of earnings in chapter 3, Part 1 (ITEPA s. 62), having referred to salaries, wages, fees, certain gratuities and benefits in kind, then uses the old and continuing words "emoluments of the employment". Since ITEPA rewrites, but does not generally reform, the law, all the old case law built on the word "emolument" still applies ...

Unlike the old Schedule E, ITEPA expressly provides guidance as to how one moves from the various items of income – and allowable expenditure – to sums which are to be taxed. Where general earnings are concerned the amount charged is the net taxable earnings from the employment in that year. These are taxable earnings less allowable deductions; only very rarely can a loss arise.[70] The amount of the taxable earnings can be governed by international factors.[71] Where what the Act calls "specific income" is concerned, ie income within Parts 5 and 6, one has to calculate the "net taxable specific" income which again depends on amounts of specific income and relevant deductions; no loss relief is possible.[72] ITEPA goes on to define the person liable for tax or "taxable person" which is largely a function of what had gone before though it adds that the person's personal representatives are liable in respect of sums received after the death – as a debt from the estate.[73] One may say that the effort made by ITEPA is unmemorably phrased.[74]

The term "earnings" is defined by ITEPA s. 62(2) to include not only gratuities and incidental benefits but also "emoluments" a term defined under the previous

66 CAA 1990, s. 27.
67 TA 1988, s. 203.
68 FA 1989, s. 36.
69 Previously TA 1988, s 19(1).
70 ITEPA ss 9(2), (3) and (6) and 11.
71 ITEPA s 10(2) referring to Chapters 4 and 5 of Part 1.
72 ITEPA ss 9(4)-(6) and 12.
73 ITEPA s 13.
74 For explanation see ITEPA Technical Notes 4–7.

legislation as including "all salaries, fees, wages, perquisites and profits whatsoever".[75] This was enough to tax many benefits in kind. However, as s. 62 makes clear, a payment in kind is taxable as earnings only if, in addition to being an emolument, it is convertible into money. For this reason a wider test (now to be found in Part 3 Chapter 10, previously TA 1988, s. 154 ...) applies for many benefits in kind paid to employees earning £8,500 a year and to directors. Yet further specific rules apply to tax certain non-convertible benefits in kind whether or not this earnings threshold is reached. Unfortunately, these benefit in kind rules are lumped together in Chapters 3–11 of Part 3 to make the "benefits code". Great care is needed to know when the threshold applies and when it does not. Another regrettable feature of the 2003 Act is that certain limits on the application of these individual rules are treated as exemptions from liability and so are to be found not in part 3 but, many pages away, in Part 4.

13.1.2 Expenses

The rules on expenses are found in Part 5 of the Act. By ITEPA s. 336 (TA 1988, s. 198) expenses are deductible in calculating taxable earnings if they are incurred wholly, exclusively and necessarily in the performance of the duties of the office or employment. Travelling expenses have their own rules (ss 337 and 338) – they must be either (i) "necessarily incurred in the performance of the duties of" the office or employment, a long-established and interestingly-litigated expression, or (ii) come within a relatively new category, first established in 1998, relating to travel for necessary attendance at a temporary workplace. The holder of the office or employment must, for ss 336–338, have been obliged to incur and pay the expense as holder of the employment. Normally the amount of a deduction under Part 5 may not exceed the earnings from which it is deductible; consequently no claim for loss relief can arise under ITEPA E [*sic*].

Capital allowances may be claimed by the employee in respect of machinery and plant if incurred necessarily[76]... **[7.27]**

E. Trading income

Trading income is covered by ITTOIA 2005, Pt 2. In essence, it comprises the income of the self-employed. The detail of trading income is covered in Chapters 9 and 10. Whilst there is much case-law on the exact meaning of the expression 'trade', general guidance was provided by Lord Wilberforce in *Ransom v Higgs* [1974] 1 WLR 1594 (below, para **[9.6]**), where his Lordship said:

> 'Trade involves, normally, the exchange of goods, or of services, for reward . . . there must be something which the trade offers to provide by way of business.'

So a trade is a business, but not all businesses are trades. Originally, the basic rules relating to trading income were contained in Schedule D, Cases I (trade) and II (profession or vocation), ICTA 1988.[77] The Income Tax (Trading and Other Income) Act 2005 rewrote them for income tax only.

As with the section on employment income, the old law is outlined. This is followed by an extract from the EN to ITTOIA 2005. **[7.28]**

75 ITEPA s 62(2), ex TA 1988, s 131.
76 CAA 2001 s 15 but not for cars, *ibid*, s 36.
77 See ICTA 1988, s 18.

(1) Schedule D, Cases I and II

Geoffrey Morse and David Williams (eds) *Davies: Principles of Tax Law* (4th edn, 2000) pp 68–70

The basic section is section 18(1) of the Taxes Act. Section 18 sets out the broad provisions of Schedule D as a whole. So far as concerns trades and professions it provides that: "Tax under this Schedule shall be charged in respect of – (a) the annual profits or gains arising or accruing – . . . to any person residing in the United Kingdom from any trade, profession or vocation, whether carried on in the United Kingdom or elsewhere . . ." Section 18(3) sets out the various Cases of Schedule D and says that "The Cases are – Case I – tax in respect of any trade carried on in the United Kingdom or elsewhere; Case II – tax in respect of any profession or vocation not contained in any other Schedule . . ."

. . . "profits" and "gains" (in this context) mean the same thing. It is legislative tautology. And the word "annual" carries very little weight. It only means that profits, to be taxable, must be of an income nature;[78] it does not mean that they must be recurrent.

What we must define are the words "trade" in Case I and "profession or vocation" in Case II. Each of these definitions, and Cases, presents in practice a major problem requiring considerable thought in drawing the lines around activities caught within the words. Apart from these problems, the principles of the two Cases are broadly the same, although we will note a few differences. We will therefore follow the Tax Law Rewrite in assuming trading income includes professional income unless stated otherwise.

The Case I problem is this: Is a given sum a trading profit or a capital gain? In the good old days a capital gain was entirely free of tax; since 1965 it has been subject to capital gains tax.[79] Capital gains tax is distinct from income tax (this is unaffected by the unification of the rates of capital gains tax and income tax). Each tax has its own regime for the computation of gains/losses, and the characterisation of a particular gain/loss can have important repercussions for a taxpayer.

The Case II problem is this: Is a given person's exercise of a profession (or vocation) carried on within an office or employment, in which case he is to be taxed under Schedule E or is it carried on outside any office or employment, in which case he is to be taxed under Schedule D? Remember that section 18(3) in reference to Case II says "tax in respect of any profession or vocation not contained in any other Schedule". The issue is between Schedule D and Schedule E. It is nowadays accepted that the distinction falls to be made on the same principles as in the law of tort, and also employment law. In tort the distinction is important in connection with vicarious liability, and it is generally described as the distinction between a servant (or employee) and an independent contractor. **[7.29]**

78 [See Chapter 6, above, para **[6.9]**.]
79 [See Chapter 20, below, para **[20.4]**.]

(2) ITTOIA 2005, Part 2

Explanatory Notes: Income Tax (Trading and Other Income) Act 2005, vol I (London, 2005) pp 15–16

Part 2: Trading income

Overview

32. This Part contains the rules applying to trading income. The Part charges:
    - the profits of a trade, profession or vocation (charged in the source legislation under Schedule D Cases I, II or V);
    - amounts treated as income on a change of accounting basis (charged in the source legislation under Schedule D Case VI).
33. The structure of the Part is to:
    - identify the income taxed as profits of a trade (Chapter 2);
    - calculate the profits of the trade (Chapters 3 to 7);
    - apply the rules for particular trades (Chapters 8 to 11);
    - apply other rules affecting the calculation of profits of the trade (Chapters 12 to 14);
    - identify basis periods (Chapter 15);
    - apply averaging (Chapter 16);
    - identify other components of trading income (Chapters 17 and 18); and
    - provide supplementary material (Chapter 19).
34. The rules in Chapters 3 to 14, dealing with profits of the trade, determine the profit of the period of account. Once the profit for tax purposes of the period of account has been calculated:
    - the basis period rules convert the profit of the period of account to the profit for the tax year; and
    - the averaging rules, if applicable, adjust the profits of tax years.
35. Two particular changes are located in Chapters 17 and 18.
36. References to "profits or gains" in the source legislation which relate only to income are rewritten in this Part omitting the reference to "gains". This continues the tidying up of such references started in section 46(3) of and Schedule 7 to FA 1998. **[7.30]**

F. Property income

This is basically, although as the extracts below demonstrate, much more than just rent. **[7.31]**

(1) Schedule A

Revenue Law – Principles and Practice (22nd edn, 2004) paras [8.1]–[8.40]

Ambit of Schedule A

Schedule A charges *profits of a business of letting property* which include isolated or casual lettings, income from furnished lettings and certain lease premiums. TA 1988, s 15(1) provides:

> 'Tax is charged under this Schedule on the annual profits arising from a business carried on for the exploitation, as a source of rents or other receipts, of any estate, interest or rights in or over any land in the United Kingdom.'

The following matters should be noted.

First, the tax is not levied by reference to income produced from individual properties but instead looks at *all* properties owned by the individual under the umbrella of a "Schedule A business".

Secondly, that business includes isolated transactions provided that they are entered into "for the exploitation of a right in or over land". (Insofar as the term "a business" implies continuous activities, it is therefore something of a misnomer.) As a result a sum paid on the sale of a lease originally granted at an undervalue and which formerly fell within the income tax charge under Schedule D Case VI ... is now caught by these rules.

Thirdly, rents from furnished lettings which were formerly taxed under Case VI are also now within the Schedule A net.

Finally, "other receipts", not just rent, are caught by the Schedule although given that the charge is on *annual* profits or gains, it is only receipts of an *income* nature that are caught (subject to the special rules in TA 1988, ss 34–36 governing lease premiums ...

Exclusions from the Schedule A charge

Section 15(2) expressly excludes certain income from the Schedule A charge: namely, profits from the occupation of land; profits and gains arising from mines, quarries and certain other concerns such as markets, tolls, bridges and ferries (which by TA 1988 s 55 are taxed under Schedule D Case I); mineral rent and royalties (taxed half as income under Schedule D and half as capital) and miscellaneous receipts such as income from wayleaves or tolls, which is received after basic rate income tax has been deducted at source by the payer under TA 1988 s 119 (and see TA 1988 s 120 in relation to payment for wayleaves for electricity cables, telephone lines, etc).

Rental income from land outside the UK continues to be chargeable under Schedule D Case V. The basis of the charge is found in s 65A (income tax) and s 70A (corporation tax). Letting property abroad is treated as a separate trade with the same rules for computing receipts and expenses. The lease premium rules also apply to property outside the UK ...

Profits from the occupation of land such as farming are taxed as a trade under Schedule D Case I (TA 1988 s 53). There is a specific exemption from this charge in the case of "the occupation of land which comprises woodlands or is being prepared for use for forestry purposes" (s 53(4)) but in *Jaggers (t/a Shide Trees) v Ellis* (1997)[80] this was held not to cover the planting and cultivating of conifers for Christmas. This activity was taxable as a trade. **[7.32]**

80 [[1997] STC 1417.]

(2) ITTOIA 2005, Part 3

Explanatory Notes: Income Tax (Trading and Other Income) Act 2005, vol I (London, 2005), p 13

Part 3: Property income

Overview

1029. This Part charges "property income". That is, income from land.

1030. This Part taxes income that is taxed under different Schedules and Cases in the source legislation. So it covers, for example, income from land in the United Kingdom and abroad as well as post-cessation receipts and certain charges arising from changes in the basis on which a taxpayer calculates property business profits.

1031. This reflects the rewrite approach of grouping charges which are logically part of the same "family". In Part 3 the unifying factor is that all the charges are on amounts that are, ultimately, attributable to exploiting an interest in land.

1032. But although the charges that are, in the source legislation, distinct, are here grouped in one Part, they do not lose their identity for all purposes. Loss relief for example (not dealt with in this Act) requires them to be kept apart. For this reason the charge on "property income" has specific components . . .

1033. References to "profits or gains" in the source legislation which relate only to income are rewritten in this Part omitting the reference to "gains". This continues the tidying up of such references started in section 46(3) of and Schedule 7 to FA 1998. **[7.33]**

G. Savings and investment income

With savings and investment income, which is covered in Pt 4 of ITTOIA 2005, the comparison of the old and new income tax provisions is a little more complex. This is because, although the Rewrite drew together the old provisions under the generic heading of 'Savings and investment income', the 'source provisions' were located in a variety of Schedules and Cases.

Exemption provisions relating to the types of income covered by ITTOIA 2005, Pt 4 have been gathered together into Pt 6 (see below, para **[7.42]**). **[7.34]**

(i) Parts of Schedule D, Cases III; Schedule D, Case V and Schedule D, Case VI, plus Schedule F and certain 'non-schedular charges'

ITTOIA 2005, Pt 4 rewrites a range of rather disparate provisions, ie parts of Cases III to VI of Schedule D, plus the former Schedule F and certain 'non-Schedular' charges. From Case III of Schedule D came, inter alia: interest[81] (which has no statutory definition, but it was once described by Rowlatt J, as

81 ICTA 1988, s 18(1), (3); FA 1996, Sch 7, para 4(1) (see now ITTOIA 2005, Pt 4, Ch 2).

'payment by time for the use of money'),[82] 'purchased life annuity payments'[83] and distributions from unauthorised unit trusts.[84] From Schedule D, Case V, came an exception to the general principle that foreign source income be assimilated to its domestic equivalent. This exception consists of foreign income dividends, ie 'dividends from non-UK resident companies', which now appear in Pt 4, Ch 4.[85] From Schedule F came 'dividends etc. from UK resident companies etc'.[86] Finally, among the 'non-schedular charges'[87] which became part of ITTOIA 2005, Pt 4, were 'gains from contracts for life assurance'[88] and profits from 'transactions in deposits'.[89] **[7.35]**

(2) ITTOIA 2005, Part 4

Explanatory Notes: Income Tax (Trading and Other Income) Act 2005, vol II (London, 2005) p 7

Part 4: Savings and investment income

Overview

1. This Part contains the rules relating to savings and investment income. It consists of income that is charged under Schedule D Cases III, IV, V and VI; Schedule F and non-schedular charges in the source legislation.
2. There is a separate Chapter for each category of income arranged as follows:
   - interest (Chapter 2);
   - dividends and other distributions from UK resident companies (Chapter 3);
   - dividends from non-UK resident companies (Chapter 4);
   - stock dividends from UK resident companies (Chapter 5);
   - release of loan to participator in close company (Chapter 6);
   - purchased life annuity payments (Chapter 7);
   - profits from deeply discounted securities (Chapter 8);
   - gains from contracts for life insurance etc. (Chapter 9);
   - distributions from unauthorised unit trusts (Chapter 10);
   - transactions in deposits (Chapter 11);

82 See *Bennett v Ogston* (1930) 15 TC 374, 379; see also *Riches v Westminster Bank Ltd* [1947] 1 All ER 469: '[T]he essence of interest is that it is a payment which becomes due because the creditor has not had his money at the due date. It may be regarded either as representing the profit he might have made if he had had the use of the money, or, conversely, the loss he suffered because he had not that use. The general idea is that he is entitled to compensation for the deprivation. From that point of view, it would seem immaterial whether the money was due to him under a contract, express or implied, or a statute, or whether the money was due for any other reason in law . . . ' (Lord Wright).

83 ICTA 1988, s 18; FA 1996, Sch 7, para 4(1) (see now ITTOIA 2005, Pt 4, Ch 7).

84 ICTA 1988, ss. 18(1), (3), 469(3) and 469(4) (see now ITTOIA 2005, Pt 4, Ch 10).

85 ICTA 1988, ss 18 and 68B, and FA 1996, Sch 7, para 4(2).

86 ICTA 1988, s 20 (now, like Schedule E, completely repealed); see now ITTOIA 2005, Pt 4, Ch 3.

87 See the extract from *Walker (Inspector of Taxes) v Centaur Clothes Group Ltd*, above, para **[7.11]**.

88 ICTA 1988, ss 541(1), 543(1), 545(3), 547(1), 547(6) and 553(6) (see now ITTOIA 2005, Pt 4, Ch 9).

89 ICTA 1988, ss 56(2), 56A(2) and F(No 2)A 1992, Sch 8, para 1 (see now ITTOIA 2005, Pt 4, Ch 11).

- disposals of futures and options involving guaranteed returns (Chapter 12); and
- sales of foreign dividend coupons (Chapter 13).

Structure of Chapters

3. The basic structure of each Chapter is:
   - charge to tax on income;
   - the amount to be charged to tax;
   - the person liable for the tax charged; and
   - rules specific to that income.
4. This Part does not contain exemption provisions. Signposts to the exemptions most likely to be relevant have been placed in the charge to tax provisions. **[7.36]**

H. 'Miscellaneous income'

ITTOIA 2005, Pt 5 is a list of different types of income that formerly fell within Cases III and VI of Schedule D, but it also includes various anti-avoidance provisions. Notable among these are income which is regarded as the settlor's income under various attempts to avoid income tax through trusts.[90] Equally important, however, is the 'pure sweep up provision' in ITTOIA 2005, Pt 5, Ch 8.[91] Chapter 8, which consists of only two sections (ITTOIA 2005, ss 687 and 688) is considered in Chapter 13. **[7.37]**

(1) Parts of Schedule D, Cases III and VI

The interests that formerly fell within Schedule D, Cases III and VI include royalties from intellectual property (such as patents, copyrights, etc.),[92] as well as income from estates in administration[93] and certain 'annual payments'.[94] **[7.38]**

(2) ITTOIA 2005, Part 5

Explanatory Notes: Income Tax (Trading and Other Income) Act 2005, vol II (London, 2005) pp 91–92

Part 5: Miscellaneous income

Overview

790. This Part contains the rules relating to miscellaneous income. It consists of income that is charged under Schedules D Cases III, IV, V and VI and non-schedular charges in the source legislation.

90 From ICTA 1988, ss 660C(1), (1A), 677(7), FA 1995, Sch 17, para 1 and F(No 2)A 1997, Sch 4, para 14 (see now ITTOIA 2005, Pt 5, Ch 5).

91 From ICTA 1988, s 18, 20(2), FA 1996, Sch 7, paras 4(1) and (2), and ITEPA 2003, Sch 6, paras 5(2) and 5(3).

92 ICTA 1988, ss.18(1) and 18(3) (see now ITTOIA 2005, Pt 5, Ch 2, with 'intellectual property' being defined at ITTOIA 2005, s 579).

93 See ITTOIA 2005, Pt 5, Ch 6.

94 See ITTOIA 2005, Pt 5, Ch 7. For a discussion of the former use of annual payments in personal tax planning, see below, para **[11.11]**.

791. There is a separate Chapter for each category of income arranged as follows:
- receipts from intellectual property (Chapter 2);
- films and sound recordings: non-trade businesses (Chapter 3);
- certain telecommunication rights: non-trading income (Chapter 4);
- settlements: amounts treated as income of settlor (Chapter 5);
- beneficiaries' income from estates in administration (Chapter 6);
- annual payments not otherwise charged (Chapter 7); and
- income not otherwise charged (Chapter 8).

Structure of Chapters

792. The basic structure of each Chapter is:
- charge to tax on income;
- the amount to be charged to tax;
- the person liable for the tax charged; and
- rules specific to that income.

793. This Part does not contain exemption provisions. Signposts to the exemptions most likely to be relevant have been placed in the charge to tax provisions. **[7.39]**

I. Tax credits, pension income and social security income

In Chapter 15, there is a detailed consideration of these matters, which have grown in importance, both as a result of considerable social and economic changes over the last 25 years or so, and of Governmental policy responses thereto. The statutory provisions are contained in ITEPA 2003 and in the Tax Credits Act 2002. They are summarised, together with their context, in the following extract from *Davies.* **[7.40]**

Geoffrey Morse and David Williams (eds) Davies: Principles of Tax Law (5th edn, 2004) p 161

Huge changes have taken place in our social security systems and their interactions with personal taxation since ... [1980]. These changes reflect major demographic shifts in the British population. Put at its simplest, many more of us are living much longer, so there are many more pensioners. At the same time, the number of children joining us is dropping (from an average of 2.4 children a family to approaching half that). Each year there are fewer new members of our society and more old ones. That means that each year there are fewer people of working age to pay for the growing number of pensioners. That also means that it is increasingly important to get as many people of working age as reasonably possible to work. And we need more children to pay our pensions in the future. So it is regarded as responsible government for measures to be taken both to cut the public cost of pensions and to encourage us all to work and also to have children. Those social imperatives lie behind the tax and credit measures ...

... ITEPA was used to separate the taxation of earnings from the taxation of pensions and of social security income for the first time. At the same time – April 2003 – the government launched a major change in the provisions helping lower-paid workers and those responsible for children. These are in the Tax Credits Act 2002, administered by the Inland Revenue. It also transferred the administration of one of our major social security benefits – child benefit – to the Inland Revenue. This is because child benefit is closely allied to the child tax credit. The Revenue also acquired responsibility for supervising national minimum wage legislation, a necessary parallel measure to tax credits for the lower-paid...We start with the most important – pensions.

PENSION INCOME

"Pension income" is defined in ITEPA section 566 as pensions, annuities and income of other types listed in the section. There are 15 in the list, including voluntary annual payments. But the Act carefully avoids defining "pension" beyond saying that it includes pensions paid voluntarily or capable of being discontinued (section 570). The key for income tax purposes is in the reference to annuities and annual payments. This reminds us of Schedule D, Case III, which uses the same phrases to capture the tax on period payments that are, under that Case, regarded as savings and investment income. The practical difference in the case of a pension is that it is normally payable to those who have stopped work either permanently or on a long-term basis because of age, illness, disability or following the death of the husband or wife. In such a case it is a form of deferred earnings from work, or work-linked insurance against loss of earnings.

In this definition there is an obvious overlap between pensions, social security and other payments to those who are out of work but normally work. The approach of ITEPA is to treat as pension income those payments made to the retired (or widows and other survivors of deceased earners) and to treat as social security income those payments made to those whom, it is assumed will return to work. So the state retirement pension – which is a social security pension – is treated as pension income and not as social security income. The main practical application of that divide is to treat as pensions those payments to claimants of 60 or over, and as social security income payments to those under 60. This reflects the state pension age of women, which is 60. From 2010 this divide will shift upwards to 65.

There are three main forms of pension provision in the United Kingdom – often referred to as the three pillars of the retirement benefit system. The first pillar is the universal pension provided in the form of state basic flat-rate retirement pension, supplemented from October 2003 by the income-related state pension credit payable under the State Pension Credit Act 2002. The second pillar is the employment-based pension that most earners build up. In Britain there are three forms of this pension: the earnings–related occupational pension schemes run by employers and payable to employees when they finish work, the state second pension (previously known as the state earnings-related pension scheme or SERPS) which is available to those who do not have an occupational or personal pension, and personal pensions taken out by individual employees and the self-employed (to which employers may contribute). The third pillar is that of personal savings and investments, which need not be linked to retirement at all. This therefore does not give rise to "pension income", although it cannot be ignored in considering the overall tax treatment of retirement income...

SOCIAL SECURITY INCOME

Part 10 of ITEPA imposes tax, in principle, on all UK social security income. This principle is, however, subject to a list of exemptions that is considerably longer than the list of social security benefits that are taxable. Aside from retirement and survivor pensions (taxable as pension income) and statutory payments such as statutory sick pay (taxable as employment income), the only benefits subject to tax are some parts of incapacity benefit (payable to those of working age who are incapable of work), some forms of jobseeker's allowance (payable to those of working age who are unemployed but actively seeking employment), and some forms of income support (the state benefit for those with no other income and who do not need to look for work). But housing benefit and council tax benefit are not taxable even if payable to people receiving these taxable benefits.

Two forms of benefit are never taxable. First, the benefits to the disabled such as disabled living allowance. Second, benefits payable for children, of which child benefit is the most important...

TAX CREDITS

Two forms of tax credit were introduced from April 2003 under the Tax Credits Act 2002... [child tax credit and working tax credit]

... Child tax credit is in reality an earnings-related addition to child benefit whether or not the recipients are working and is very probably a social security payment. Nonetheless, besides replacing previous social security benefits it also replaces an income tax allowance (children's tax credit). So it has a tax element too. Working tax credit is altogether more confusing. This is because part at least of the entitlement to working tax credit may not have much to do with income tax, but it also has little to do with other social security either. It is (to borrow from a name of a former special tax) a negative selective employment tax for the lower-paid, designed to boost the pay packet of those with low earnings by using the extended form of PAYE system ... **[7.41]**

J. Exempt income

ITEPA 2003, Pt 4 together with ITTOIA 2005, Pt 6 comprise a range of different types of income which are exempt from income tax (eg national savings income, in the case of ITTOIA 2005,[95] and 'green' benefits in kind, designed to promote environmentally-friendly commuting, in the case of ITEPA 2003).[96] In the following extract, Tiley relates them to various categories of exempt person. **[7.42]**

John Tiley *Revenue Law* (5th edn, 2005) pp 142–143

Certain types of payment or persons are specifically exempt from liability to income tax by legislation or concession. The legislation and concessions are gathered together in statutory form in ITEPA Part 4 insofar as they relate to ITEPA income .... and in ITTOIA Part 6 insofar as the [*sic*] relate to other types of income. On effects of being exempt under ITTOIA see Part 6 Chapter 10 of that Act. The following list is not exhaustive, but indicates the type of exemption made.

(1) *Welfare payments:* ITEPA Part 10 Chapters 4 and 5 excluded certain social security benefits, eg, invalidity benefit and analogous payments by foreign countries to UK residents. On housing grants paid by local authorities, see s. 644. Exemptions apply to adoption allowances (ITTOIA s 744) and certain pensions for disabled employees. Interest on damages payable for personal injuries and annuities (including the assignment of such annuities) payable under structured settlements of claims for such injuries are exempt under

95 See ITTOIA 2005, Pt 6, Ch 2.

96 See, eg, ITEPA 2003, ss 242 ('Works transport services') and 244 ('Cycles and cyclist's safety equipment').

ITTOIA ss 731 and 751. Also exempt are New Deal payments to the over–50s, etc (ITTOIA s 781).

(2) *Employment-related payments*. ITEPA exempts many payments under this category eg, redundancy payments (s. 309), the first £30,000 of compensation for loss of employment (s. 403), long service awards, luncheon vouchers, and miners coal [*sic*] See, principally, ITEPA Part 4 . . .

(3) *State service*. ITEPA exempts from income tax war widows, pensions, wounds and disability pensions, allowances, bounties and gratuities paid for additional service in the armed forces and annuities and additional pensions to holders of gallantry awards ss 638–41. Other state service exemptions include Foreign Service allowances for civil servants (s. 299), certain payments for Ministers and MPs, etc (ss 291 and 294).

(4) *Savings*. The tax system grants special tax privileges to savings, see Part V but see also compensation for mis-sold pensions (FA 1996, s. 148), annuities under certain policies (ITTOIA Part 8 Chapter 8 ex TA 1988 ss 580A, 580B) and certain bonds when held by non-residents (FA 1996 s. 154, ITTOIA Part 8 Chapter 6).

(5) *Education and Training*. Scholarship income arising from a scholarship held by a person receiving full-time instruction at a university, college, school or other educational establishment is exempt from tax, s. 776 (see also SP 4/86, revised in 1992 on sandwich courses, the need for revision arising as a result of *Walters v Tickner* [1992] STC 343). Interest attached to certain repayments of student loans to the student attracts a special rule (ITTOIA s. 787 added by FA 1999).

(6) *Exempt Persons*. TA 1988 ss 505–14, not yet rewritten,[97] provide reliefs for, among others, charities, the British Museum and Natural History Museums, scientific research organisations, agricultural societies and the Atomic Energy Authority.

(7) *Exempt People – International*. There are exemptions for various Commonwealth and foreign representatives (ITEPA ss 300–2 and ITTOIA s. 771),[98] various payments to members of visiting forces (ITEPA s. 303), the international Maritime Satellite Organisation (TA 1988 s. 515)[99] and certain other international organisations (s. 582A).[100] Special rules also apply to government securities held by non-resident central banks (s. 516)[101] and the issue departments of the Reserve Bank of India and the State bank of Pakistan (s. 517).[102]

(8) *Government*. There are also exemptions for local authorities and health service bodies (TA 1988 ss. 519, 519A).[103] The Crown is not liable to tax unless statute otherwise provides[104]; therefore, the private estates of the Crown are subject to tax.[105] **[7.43]**

The EN to ITTOIA 2005 include the following observations about the exemptions in Pt 6:

97 [But see now ITA 2007, Part 10.]
98 See Morris [1991] *BTR* 207 and exchange of views by Adderley and Morris on a stamp duty point at [1992] *BTR* 122. The Government must be recognised by the UK: *Caglar v Billingham* [1996] STC (SCD) 150.
99 [Now repealed as obsolete by ITA 2007, s 1031, Sch 3, Pt 1.]
100 [See now ITA 2007, s 979.]
101 [See now ITA 2007, s 840.]
102 [See now ITA 2007, s 839.]
103 [See now ITA 2007, ss 838, 1000.]
104 TA 1988, s 829 [see now ITA 2007, s 978]; on royal taxation see Pearce and Crump [1994] *BTR* 635; and Bartlett [1983] *BTR* 99.
105 Crown Private Estates Act 1862. There is much background material in Hall, *Royal Fortune* (London, Bloomsbury, 1992), summarised in *The Economist*, 25 January 1992, 35.

Explanatory Notes: Income Tax (Trading and Other Income) Act 2005, vol II (London, 2005) p 138

Part 6: Exempt income

Overview

1200. This Part groups all of the sections which provide exemption for income otherwise charged to income tax by this Act. A signpost in each charging section points the user to the main exemptions from that particular charge contained in this Part.

1201. For the most part each Chapter in this Part relates to a particular type of income but there are also Chapters that deal with exemptions relevant to certain types of annual payment and to miscellaneous other income.

1202. The exemptions, where relevant, apply to both United Kingdom and foreign income unless one of these kinds of income is expressly excluded in the section.

Chapter 1: Introduction

Section 690: Overview of Part 6

1204. This section lists the Chapters in this Part. These provide exemption from income tax for:

- National savings income (Chapter 2);
- income from individual investment plans (Chapter 3);
- SAYE interest (Chapter 4);
- Venture capital trust dividends (Chapter 5);
- Income from FOTRA securities (Chapter 6);
- Purchased life annuity payments (Chapter 7);
- Other annual payments (Chapter 8); and
- Other income (Chapter 9).

1205. *Subsection (3)* explains the purpose of Chapter 10 (general). This Chapter provides that any exemption in this Part, unless there is specific provision to the contrary, is disregarded for all income tax purposes.

1206. *Subsection (4)* indicates that there are exemptions in other Acts relating to particular categories of person which could be relevant to the charges in this Act. For example see section 505 of ICTA which provides a general exemption for charities.

1207. *Subsection (5)* explains that the exemptions in this Act may apply, where relevant, to charges outside this Act. [7.44]

5. Summary

The Schedular system, together with the new categories of income in each of ITEPA 2003 and ITTOIA 2005, are conveniently summarised in diagrammatic form in the following extracts. The first table shows the position prior to 6 April 2005; the latter one shows the position after that date.

The tables also refer to the basis of assessment for each type of income. This is shown in the right hand column of the first table, and the inner right hand column of the second table. Thus, for example, looking at the first table, it can be seen that, if it was necessary to calculate the profits of a business of letting land for a particular tax year (say 2004/2005), those profits would be the profits of that tax year, ie 6 April 2004 to 5 April 2005. ('Tax year' is an abbreviation for 'year of assessment'.) **[7.45]**

Natalie Lee (gen ed) *Revenue Law – Principles and Practice* (24th edn, 2006) para [6.41]

Before 6 April 2005 the schedular system applied to income tax and charged income and profits as set out below – a system which continues to apply for the purposes of corporation tax.

The Schedules

Schedule	*Source*	*Basis of Assessment*
A	Profits from a business of letting land in UK	Income of the current year of assessment
D		
Case I	Profits of a trade in UK	The income of the accounting period ending in the tax year or income of the current year of assessment
Case II	Profits of a profession or vocation in UK	
Case III	Interest, annuities and other annual payments	
Case IV	Securities out of the UK	
Case V	Possessions out of the UK (but excluding foreign employment)	
Case VI	Annual profits or gains not falling under Cases I-V and not charged by virtue of any other Schedule; and certain income directed to be so charged	Income of the current year of assessment
F	Dividends and certain other distributions by companies	Income of the current year of assessment
ITEPA 2003	Offices, employments, pensions and chargeable benefits under the social security legislation	Income of the current year of assessment

The abolition of the schedules [ie for the purposes of income tax] means that the various types of income are charged as follows

Income category	*Income charged*	*Basis of assessment*	*Legislation*
Employment	Employment, pension and social security income	Current year	ITEPA 2003
Trading	Profits of a trade, profession or vocation	[Period of account ending in] current year	ITTOIA 2005 Part 2
Property	Rents and income from land	Current year	ITTOIA 2005 Part 3
Savings and investment income	Interest, dividends, distributions, securities, deposits, purchased life annuities, life insurance gains, futures and options	Current year	ITTOIA 2005 Part 4
Miscellaneous	Intellectual property, non-trade film recordings, telecommunication rights, settlements, income from estates in administration, annual payments and income not otherwise charged	Current year	ITTOIA 2005 Part 5
Exempt income	National savings, individual investment plans, FOTRA securities, life annuities, annual payments and other income	N/A	ITTOIA 2005 Part 6

[7.46]

8 Employment Income

Earnings from an office or employment are taxable under the Income Tax (Earnings and Pensions) Act 2003 (ITEPA).[1] The object of this piece of legislation, which forms part of the Tax Law Rewrite Project,[2] was to rewrite existing tax legislation relating to income from employment,[3] pensions and social security in order to make it clearer and simpler to use by taxpayers themselves, as well as by those upon whom the law imposes specific obligations (such as employers, professional tax advisers), those who apply, enforce and interpret tax law (from staff of HMRC to judges) and those in Parliament who are concerned with changes to tax law. Views are mixed on whether the outcome has been a success. Although rewritten legislation is not permitted to change the law, the Project team made it clear from the outset that it would be its policy to include within the rewritten legislation certain non-statutory material. This encompassed extra-statutory concessions, unless there were good reasons not to, and case law where it dealt with difficult statutory provisions or where it would help to fill gaps.[4] The result of this is that, while the legislation in this area is new, the principles behind it are old, and most of the case law, which still applies, was decided under the old provisions in ICTA 1988.

Discussion in this chapter is limited to the charge to income tax, and does not cover matters such as employee share schemes, the tax avoidance scheme disclosure obligation,[5] national insurance contributions[6] and pensions. It is further limited to the tax position of employees and officeholders who are resident, ordinarily resident and domiciled in the UK.[7] **[8.1]**

1 ITEPA 2003, ss 7(3)(a), 9(2)(4).

2 For the background to the Tax Law Rewrite and its aims, see Chapter 1, para **[1.4]**, above.

3 Found in the former Schedule E. ICTA 1988, s 19 imposed a charge to tax 'in respect of any office or employment on emoluments therefrom'. The demise of Schedule E also saw an end to the use of the term 'emoluments' as the generic term for income from employment, which has been replaced by the word 'earnings'.

4 *Tax Law Rewrite: Plans for 1988/99* (Inland Revenue, May 1998).

5 Introduced by FA 2004, with details found in SI 2004/1863 as amended. One of the types of Schemes that is required to be disclosed relates to certain arrangements in connection with employment; see para **[5.24]**, above.

6 See Chapter 14, para **[14.6]**.

7 For a discussion of the international aspects, see J Freedman and E Chamberlain 'Horizontal equity and the taxation of employed and self-employed workers' (1997) 18(1) Fiscal Studies 87 and Freedman, IFS Tax Law Review Committee Discussion Paper No 1, 2001, below, para **[8.8]** and para **[8.14]**.

Roger Kerridge 'The Income Tax (Earnings and Pensions) Act 2003' [2003] BTR 257, 258–261; see also above, paras [1.5] and [1.7]

The Act is not short. It consists of 725 sections plus a further 8 schedules. The sections are arranged in 13 parts and all but 4 of these parts are sub-divided into chapters. The layout is relatively easy to follow and a huge improvement on what it replaces. Having said this, the suggestion, made in the Joint Parliamentary Committee, that someone new to the subject, who wanted to understand his or her tax liability, would only have to buy a copy of the Act and read it, to obtain straightforward enlightenment, seems a bit optimistic. The layout is clear, the sentences are short, the English is modern, but the obvious disincentive, for the would-be-reader new to the subject, is the enormity of it all. He or she would probably not have too much difficulty in working out where to begin, and might then be able to work out where to go next, but after that? When there are 725 sections plus a further eight Schedules (to cover what is, essentially, only income from employment) it is not hard to see how the novice reader might feel ever-so-slightly deterred.

Those who really will welcome this rewritten legislation will not be novice readers; they will be those who had a reasonable acquaintance with what went before. For them, this is a clear improvement. But someone new to the subject, someone who did not know what things were like before, would be surprised to be told that this is "a simplification". If this rewritten legislation is looked at, not through the eyes of someone who is acquainted with what went before, but through those of someone coming from another world, or, less exotically, from another country, what would almost certainly strike him or her would be two things, (i) the enormous amount of pettifogging detail and (ii) the apparent lack of any underlying logic. This is not a criticism of the Rewrite in its terms, because it was not supposed to change the law (at least not to any significant extent). But the effect of rewriting tax legislation without changing the substance is to highlight all sorts of oddities and inconsistencies.

John Tiley, in his book on Revenue Law, describes United Kingdom tax legislation as "a shambles",[8] and in so far as it is possible to explain United Kingdom income tax law rationally it is usually best to begin with its history. One of the problems with the Rewrite is that it actually makes it more, rather than less, difficult to follow the history of particular provisions. The rules have been taken out of, or taken further out of, their historical context and have been assembled, or reassembled, neatly. But if an outsider were now to attempt to guess why particular rules had been enacted in the first place, he or she would generally have no clue.

There is insufficient space, in this Note, to go through much of the Act; but a part which illustrates particularly well its strengths and weaknesses is Part III, which deals with fringe benefits. Part III is divided into 12 chapters.

The division is neat, and in so far as it could ever be possible to set out the current fringe benefit rules in a way which could be described as logical, this has been achieved. But what must astound any outsider, anyone who has not spent his or her adult life engrossed in United Kingdom income tax law, is, first of all, the staggering (and seemingly unnecessary) detail. Section 89 of the Act, a section in Part III, Chapter 4 "Vouchers and Credit Tokens", reduces by 15p for each working day the total cash equivalent of the benefit of any non-transferable meal voucher provided to a worker in lower-paid employment, where such vouchers are provided

8 John Tiley, *Revenue Law* (4th ed., 2000) Hart Publishing, p. 45. [See now *Revenue Law* (5th edn, 2005), p 49.]

to all employees (if any) employed by the same employer in lower-paid employment. That was a précis, the section itself takes up half a page. The section derives from an extra-statutory concession (ESC A2 "luncheon vouchers"). The Rewrite incorporates not only the provisions which used to be found in primary legislation, but it also incorporates some provisions which used to be found in extra-statutory concessions[9] and it is also designed to incorporate some case law. The incorporation of extra-statutory concessions is to be welcomed. If rules exist they should be set out in the primary legislation, not hidden away somewhere. Treating them as "concessions" makes them difficult to locate and also raises constitutional questions in relation to the power to tax, and to relieve taxpayers from the burdens of taxation.[10] But that still leaves the question, is it really necessary to have a rule which reduces, *by 15 pence*, the cash equivalent of a luncheon voucher? The figure (15 pence) is historic. It was actually set in the far-off days before decimalisation and was originally three shillings. There was a time when it would cover lunch for an articled clerk,[11] but inflation means that the 15 pence reduction is not now worth administering.

So, what about all the other fringe benefit rules? They have been rearranged so that the rules which originally applied to taxpayers in "higher-paid employment"[12] have now become the standard rules, while what used to be the standard rules are now applied to a class described as taxpayers in "lower-paid employment". This is neat, but it lacks any kind of logical underpinning. Why, the outsider will ask, are taxpayers to be divided up, arbitrarily, into those earning more than, or less than, £8,500 p.a.?[13] And why, when dealing with living accommodation provided for an employee, are there different rules depending on whether the cost of providing the accommodation was greater or less than £75,000? The answers to these questions are, of course, to be found in the history of the tax, but the rewriting makes it harder to trace it.

The law relating to the taxation of employment income is full of rules which appear to make no sense. Some of them made sense, once upon a time, but circumstances, rates of pay and other rules have changed, while they have not. Some need to be revised, others need to be scrapped. Income tax is still a shambles. What used to be the Schedule E rules have been tidied up, but they have not been simplified. In some ways the tidying up operation has disguised the underlying incoherence, in other ways it has highlighted it.[14]

Incorporation of case law

There has been a tendency, over the years, for judges to put the blame for problems with the tax system on those who have drafted tax legislation. Lord Wrenbury did it eighty years ago in the *Bater* case where he criticised the draftsmen of the Income Tax Acts of 1842 and 1853.[15] At least three judges did it much more recently in the *Fitzpatrick* case.[16] This is not completely fair to the draftsmen. The problem with

9 Not all ESCs have been incorporated–some remain as "concessions".
10 Annex 3 to the Explanatory Notes to the Act . . . contains a table of destinations for the 19 ESCs to which the Act gives statutory effect.
11 An "articled clerk" was (in the olden days) a trainee solicitor, or accountant.
12 See, *e.g.* FA 1976.
13 With a series of complicated sub-rules for deciding on which side of the line those close to it fall.
14 Or, as Maurice Parry-Wingfield put it in [2000] BTR 597 at 598: "we now find that the rewrite cruelly exposes tax laws that are inconsistent, irrational or fundamentally complex."
15 *G.W.R. v Bater* (1922) 8 TC 231 at 255.
16 *Fitzpatrick v IRC* [1994] 1 WLR 306. Warner J. criticised the wording of the relevant section, he was then quoted with approval in the Court of Appeal and in the House of Lords.

much of United Kingdom tax legislation is not only that it has been densely drafted, in old-fashioned language and that it has been scattered about. It has been that many fundamental rules of the tax system have not been thought through when the legislation was enacted in the first place and the original draftsmen were often left to disguise this fact. So it was not necessarily their fault if they drafted sections which appear confusing or self-contradictory – it was not necessarily their fault that they failed to express clearly the applicable rules. If truth were told, nobody had decided what the applicable rules should be, and the judges were often left to invent them. On the whole, the judges have done a good job. In interpreting income tax legislation they have filled more gaps, been more inventive, than they have admitted. They have shown no apparent bias either towards, or against, the Revenue.[17] They have engaged in an intuitive process in which they have pretended to interpret sections, but have often fleshed them out. On the whole, they are to be congratulated.

But there is a danger in incorporating case law into the Rewrite. Statute law and case law are different. The words in a statute are designed to be of wide application. What a judge says in a case applies to the facts in front of him and needs to be read in the context of those facts. There are many occasions in income tax law when there may be general agreement that a particular case has been correctly decided, but much less agreement as to whether something said by a judge in the case can be exported and applied, out of context, to different sets of facts.

An example of what may be a doubtful incorporation of case law into the Rewrite is section 5(3) of the 2003 Act which incorporates (so say the Act's Explanatory Notes) the case of *Edwards v Clinch*.[18] *Edwards v Clinch* is treated as a case which deals with the meaning of the word "office" and, looked at from a narrow perspective, that is correct. But looked at in a wider perspective, it deals with the much bigger question of the overlap between Schedule D[19] and (what used to be) Schedule E. Treating it as simply a case on the meaning of the word "office" will suit the Revenue; it may not suit taxpayers who find themselves on the fault line between the two schedules.[20]

Income from employment and income from self-employment

This leads to the question whether it was a good idea to separate the rewriting of the two schedules. Obviously it is convenient. Had the two schedules been rewritten together, that would have taken (much) longer, but dealing with them

17 In relation to income tax.

18 (1981) 56 TC 367.

19 [Schedule D Cases I and II covered trading income (ie self-employment income), now dealt with by ITTOIA 2005. For a discussion of the overlap between employed and self-employed income see paras **[8.7]–[8.12]**, below.]

20 *Edwards v Clinch* was a case concerning a civil engineer who, from time to time, acted as an inspector at public local enquiries. The Revenue originally treated him as a Schedule D taxpayer for all purposes, but then there was "a change in Revenue practice" and they claimed that, when he acted as an inspector, he was the holder of an office and taxable under Schedule E. The taxpayer claimed that he was not the holder of an office. He succeeded before the General Commissioners, lost at first instance, succeeded in the Court of Appeal and, by a bare majority, succeeded in the House of Lords. It was a close run thing. The result (that the taxpayer should continue to be taxed under Schedule D) is correct, but the reasoning (that he was not the holder of an office) appears strained. A simpler way of getting to the same result would be to say that the taxpayer was the holder of an office but that the office was part of his profession. He would then fall under both schedules and should be taxed under D, because D comes before E. The Revenue will not be enthusiastic about this approach, they prefer to suggest that all borderline cases fall within Schedule E. See discussion in [1980] BTR 233.

together would have allowed those in the rewrite team to get more of a feeling for the underlying themes. The Revenue like to portray employment income and self-employed income as fundamentally distinct and to argue that, when there are cases of overlap (rare, they will say), income should be treated as employment income. It can, however, be suggested that the distinction between the two types of income is now less clear than it once was, and that it is becoming less and less significant.

Re-examining the original legislation

Something which remains to be seen, in relation to the Rewrite, is the degree to which disagreements about the interpretation of sections will entail the examination, or re-examination, of the original legislation. Suppose that there is a dispute over the interpretation of the section dealing with the deduction of expenses – the "wholly, exclusively and necessarily" rule – now section 336 of the 2003 Act, will it be permissible to look back at the section as it was immediately before the Rewrite? John Avery Jones raised this question in 1996[21] but it does not seem to have been answered. A recent example of a reference back from a consolidation Act[22] can be seen in *Strand Options and Futures Ltd. v Vojak.*[23] There was a real and substantial difficulty in interpreting a section in the 1988 consolidation by reference merely to its language and so Etherton J. considered it appropriate to refer to the original enactment.[24] It seems likely that references back will be relatively more frequent in the case of the Rewrite than they have been in relation to consolidation acts, and they may well raise difficulties which could not arise in the case of consolidated legislation. **[8.2]**

1. Introduction

ITEPA 2003, s 9 imposes a charge to tax on employment income, which encompasses 'general earnings'[25] and 'specific employment income'[26] arising from an office or employment. In the case of both general earnings and specific income, the amount charged under s 9 is the net amount, allowing for deductions and, in the case of general earnings, losses as well.[27]

The basic issues to be considered in relation to employment income are:

(a) the meaning of 'office' or 'employment';
(b) the meaning of 'earnings'; and
(c) those items of expenditure which are deductible in determining the net general earnings. **[8.3]**

21 [1996] BTR 580 at 582.
22 TA 1988.
23 [2003] STC 331.
24 FA 1965.
25 This equates to emoluments or income treated as emoluments formerly charged under ICTA 1988, s 19(1), para 1.
26 This is income that was previously charged to tax under ICTA 1988, s 19(1), para 5, and relates to income that is directed by another provision of the Tax Acts to be charged under ITEPA. Whether or not such income is taxable, depends upon the terms of that relevant provision rather than on the particular test for earnings.
27 ITEPA 2003, ss 9(2), (3), (6) and 11.

2. 'Office' or 'employment'

Prior to ITEPA 2003, neither the term 'office' or 'employment' was statutorily defined, and resort had to be made to the common law to provide the guidance needed. It will be seen that the new statutory provisions[28] provide only a non-exhaustive definition of the two terms, with the result that reliance upon the existing case law must continue.

Because of the inexactitude of the definition of the term employment, and because of the differences in liability to pay income tax that exist between the employed and the self-employed despite a similarity in income,[29] it has been possible for taxpayers to seek to avoid taxation as an employee, with benefits to both the would-be employer as well as the would-be employee. Legislation designed to catch such schemes was introduced, with the effect of ensuring that those within its remit are taxed as employees.[30] **[8.4]**

A. *Office*

By virtue of ITEPA 2003, s 5, the term 'office' is said to *include*

> 'in particular any position which has an existence independent of the person who holds it and may be filled by successive holders.'

Historically, the term 'office' was described as 'a subsisting, permanent, substantive position which had an existence independent of the person who filled it, which went on and was filled in succession by successive holders'.[31] However, in *Edwards* v *Clinch*,[32] upon which case the statutory provision is said to be based,[33] greater emphasis was placed on the requirement of some degree of continuance and of a position with an existence independent of the individual holding it.[34] An individual may hold more than one office at any one time, and be employed by more than one person at the same time as holding the office or offices. Equally, somebody may be self-employed, and taxable under ITTOIA 2005,[35] and hold an office at the same time.[36] Whether the position is an office is a matter of fact. **[8.5]**

28 ITEPA 203, ss 4,5.
29 The 'widespread perception of unfairness about the relative treatment of the employed and self-employed, current over many years and expressed by many committees and other bodies' was referred to by Judith Freedman in *Employed or Self-Employed? Tax Classification of Workers and the Changing Labour Market*, Tax Law Review Committee Discussion Paper No 1, (2001, Institute for Fiscal Studies); see below, paras **[8.8]**. This difference in treatment stems not only from income tax provisions, but also from the National Insurance legislation.
30 This legislation, known as IR 35 because its provisions were first announced in 1999 in Budget Press Release IR 35, is now found in ITEPA 2003, Pt 2, Ch 8, and see below, para **[8.13]**.
31 *Great Western Railway v Bater* [1920] 3KB 266, 274, per Rowlatt J.
32 [1982] AC 845 and see below, para **[8.6]**.
33 See Explanatory Notes to the Act, Annex 2, Note 2.
34 Examples of office-holders are auditors, company secretaries, trustees and personal representatives. A director, who is not also an employee because, for example, he is a non-executive director receiving fees for the work that he performs, is generally considered to be an office-holder, even in circumstances where the directorship is created for a particular individual: see *Taylor v Provan* [1975] AC 194, below, para **[8.74]**.
35 See Chapter 9, para **[9.1]**.
36 See Roger Kerridge 'Income from Offices which are parts of Professions: Schedule D or Schedule E?' [1980] BTR 233 and John Ward 'What can it matter? Why should it matter? The Taxation of Offices and Employments' [1989] BTR 281. Note that the references to Schedule D and Schedule E refer to what is now ITTOIA 2005, Pt 2 and ITEPA 2003 respectively.

Edwards v Clinch [1982] AC 845 (HL)

The taxpayer, who was a civil engineer, was from time to time appointed by the Department of the Environment[37] to act as an inspector at public local enquiries. Neither the Secretary of State nor any subordinate or representative of his could hold an enquiry himself, but issued the taxpayer with separate written authority to hold each inquiry, after which, the taxpayer submitted a factual report, with recommendations, to the Secretary of State, and rendered fee notes. He was duly paid fees which reflected the time spent on discharging the duties required of an inspector. The General Commissioners found that the income from the inquiries arose from his profession, but Walton J held that the fees arose from an office and, as such, were taxable under Schedule E.[38] The Court of Appeal allowed the taxpayer's appeal from Walton J and, by a majority of 3-2, the House of Lords agreed with the Court of Appeal and held that the taxpayer was not an office-holder.

LORD WILBERFORCE: . . . The word "office" has been in the income tax legislation all along: the Act of 1842 referred to "Every public office". Since 1922 the qualification "public" has disappeared so all offices are now taxed under Sch. E.[39] At no time has any definition of "office" been provided, so the judges have been left to work out what the word included.

In performing this task, they naturally looked for a context. They found one in rule 1 of Sch. E in the Act of 1842 (quoted by my noble and learned friend Lord *Bridge of Harwich*) which contemplated that the tax would be levied on the office as such over a whole year.

This it was, I think, which led to the well known *Rowlatt* definition of office, or, as it has later been called, a generally sufficient statement of the meaning of the word as used in the 1842 Act. An office was something "which was a subsisting, permanent, substantive position, which had an existence independent of the person who filled it and which went on and was filled in succession by successive holders" (*Great Western Railway Co. v. Bater*[40] – a definition or statement, which was, I dare to say, bred into the bones of every practitioner in income tax matters, and more importantly, was known to the legislature, and its drafting agents, on the many occasions when revisions of the Schedules were made or considered.

Because this was the origin of the income tax meaning of "office", I have doubts as to the value, or indeed legitimacy, of now resorting to a dictionary for a definition. Of course it would be desirable in an ideal world for expressions in tax legislation to bear ordinary meanings, such as the citizen could find out by consulting the *Oxford English Dictionary*. But it is a fact that many words of ordinary meaning acquire a signification coloured over the years by legal construction in a technical context such that return to the pure source of common parlance is no longer possible. I think that "office" is such a word.

My noble and learned friend, Lord Bridge of Harwich, has rendered us a service by designating as the critical question whether the *Rowlatt* definition should be considered as still retaining all its ingredients through successive legislative changes . . . . I would agree that in the natural course of development, it is open to the courts, and right, to consider whether the ingredients of the *Rowlatt* definition are still appropriate, at least in their full force. It would seem to me that the legislature, by continuing to use the word in the taxing words of Sch. E without any corrective definition, showed a general intention to adopt the judicial interpretation of it which, though uncritically, has been consistent and continuous. For myself I would accept that a rigid requirement of permanence is no longer appropriate, nor is vouched by any decided case and continuity need not be regarded as an absolute qualification. But still, if any meaning is to be given to "office" in this legislation,

37 Now the Department for Environment Food and Rural Affairs.
38 See now ITEPA 2003, s 9(2).
39 [See now ITEPA 2003, s 5(1) which provides that the 'provisions of the employment income Parts that are expressed to apply to employments apply equally to offices, unless otherwise indicated'.]
40 [1920] 3 KB 266 at p. 274.

as distinguished from "employment" or "profession" or "trade" or "vocation" (these are the various words used in order to tax people on their earnings), the word must involve a degree of continuance (not necessarily continuity) and of independent existence: it must connote a post to which a person can be appointed, which he can vacate and to which a successor can be appointed. This is the concept which was accepted by all three of the members of the Court of Appeal, who all desired, in my opinion rightly, to combine some degree of consistency with what had become accepted notions in the law of income tax, with practical common sense requirements, and without "treating as authoritative decisions which were reached for reasons which may no longer be appropriate", per Buckley L.J.[41] Thus the Lord Justice accepted that to constitute an office a post need not be capable of permanent or prolonged or indefinite existence – a development of the law with which I agree.

Acceptance of the admittedly somewhat indefinite guidelines suggested above does not, of course, solve the instant, or any similar, problem. It is necessary to appraise the characteristics of the respondent's "appointment". There is in this task an element of common sense evaluation of fact: a task which is committed in the first place to the general commissioners. Their finding was for the respondent, and though this is far from sacrosanct, indeed I think that they applied the *Rowlatt* definition too literally, nevertheless it is not in my opinion, wholly to be disregarded. They described it as "merely a transient, indeterminate, once-only execution of a task for which [the respondent] was peculiarly qualified" – adding an analogy which I do not find appropriate.

The Revenue does not contend that the respondent, who was a member of a panel, and was called on to conduct a number of inquiries, held one office. Their contention, which would seem an odd one to an ordinary man, is that he held a series of offices – so did, I suppose, each of the other 60 members of the panel who were called on to act. So each "appointment" has to be judged separately.

The relevant facts concerning a typical appointment are detailed in other opinions. I am happy to take those presented by Lord Bridge. But with very great hesitation, I have formed the opposite view, on this matter of impression, to his. I agree, on the other hand, with the conclusions of the members of the Court of Appeal:

> "...each appointment was personal to the taxpayer; it lacked the characteristic of independent existence and continuance which, in my judgement, is one of the essential characteristics of an 'office'", per Buckley L.J.[42]

> "It was a temporary, ad hoc, appointment confined to the taxpayer. He was not appointed to a position which had an existence of his own. It had no quality of permanency about it.", per Ackner L.J.[43]

> "There is no office of inquirer or inspector created by the Act, but merely a provision authorising the Minister to 'cause to be held' the appropriate enquiries.", per Oliver L.J.[44] (surely an effective point).

and again:

> "This [the concept of continuance apart from the individual holder] ... is something entirely lacking in the instant case. The duty of making the enquiry is one which is offered to and accepted by the individual ad hoc. If he is unable to complete it and to make his report for any reason, there is no question of appointing a successor to the office of conducting that inquiry. There has to be a new inquiry by another individual equally appointed ad hoc, and on terms which fall to be separately negotiated with him", per Oliver L.J.[45]

There is no doubt that the factual ingredients detected by their Lordships are correctly stated: I agree with their estimation of their weight. **[8.6]**

41 [1981] Ch 1 at p. 5.
42 *Ibid.*, at p. 12.
43 *Ibid.*, at p. 17.
44 *Ibid.*, at p. 19.
45 *Ibid.*, at p. 23.

B. Employment

Prior to ITEPA 2003, 'employment' had never been statutorily defined, and guidance hailed from the cases. As with the term 'office', the statute now gives some indication of the meaning of the term 'employment', although the brevity of the provision and the actual words used show this to be non-exhaustive. Thus, it is defined in ITEPA 2003, s 4 as including, in particular, any employment under a contract of service or apprenticeship and any employment in the service of the Crown. However, in respect of the all-important 'contract of service', there appears to be no attempt to define *when* such a contract exists and, while it may be very clear in the majority of cases to discern whether an individual is an employee or is self-employed, there may well be great difficulty in a number of borderline cases. And it matters, for there are differences in both the income tax and national insurance treatment between the employed and the self-employed, generally in favour of the self-employed. Problems may arise, in particular, where a taxpayer works for more than one person, either concurrently or consecutively; in such a case, is the taxpayer to be treated as holding a number of separate employments, or making a series of engagements carried out as part of a trade, profession or vocation? The basic distinction appears to be between a contract *of* service, the earnings from which would be liable to tax under ITEPA 2003, and a contract *for* services, the income therefrom falling within ITTOIA 2005.

A person may be employed, and thus assessable under ITEPA 2003, and carry on a trade, profession or vocation, and assessable under ITTOIA 2005, at the same time.[46] **[8.7]**

Judith Freedman *Employed or Self-Employed? Tax Classification of Workers and the Changing Labour Market* Tax Law Reform Committee Discussion Paper No 1 (IFS, 2001); below, para [8.14]

0.1 In *Reforming the Personal Tax System*,[47] the Committee responsible for that Report commented:

> 'In any reform it might be sensible to think about reducing the distinction in tax treatment between employment and self-employment, on simple equity grounds as much as for any other reason. Why should individuals carrying on essentially the same activity and deriving similar income from it, exhibit large differences in liability to pay income tax just because one does so as a self-employed person while the other is employed?'

0.3 The statement quoted in 0.1 needs to be submitted to thorough examination. First, the comment presupposes that individuals who are employed *can be* carrying on a 'similar activity' to those who are self-employed. Some would argue that, even where an employed and a self-employed person seem to be undertaking similar *tasks*, there is a fundamental difference in the nature of the *activities*. In other words,

46 In *Walls* v *Sinnett* (1986) 60 TC 150, a professional singer with an ongoing singing career obtained a part-time post as a lecturer in music at a University. He was liable to tax under what is now ITTOIA 2005 Part 2 in respect of income arising from his performances as a professional singer, and under what is now ITEPA 2003 with respect to his University income.

47 (1993) Commentary no. 35, Institute for Fiscal Studies, London.

the classification of the person as either employed or self-employed arises from a genuine and fundamental difference, so that describing them as carrying on similar activities is inaccurate. This view, of course, assumes that the legal classifications are always based on real differences. Others would disagree, taking the view that whilst frequently the activities of the employed and self-employed may be very different, it is possible for them to be carrying on similar activities. This is because, at the margins, the legal classification as employed or self-employed may not mark a fundamental distinction of substance. The extent to which the classification system really does mark some difference of substance between types of activity requires further consideration of the classification of 'employed' and 'self-employed' and the way in which they are applied.

0.4 Second, the statement in paragraph 0.1 assumes that horizontal equity should be the guiding policy objective – that is, that individuals with similar levels of income should bear similar tax burdens. This supposes that it is possible to find comparable measure of income for employed and self-employed. Even assuming that this is so, horizontal equity is likely to be only one policy consideration. Some, including government, might say that other policy objectives (for example, correcting market failures or providing incentives for certain activities) or practical considerations have to override horizontal equity in some situations. The statement therefore raises more complex questions than might at first appear.

0.5 The TLRC[48] decided in 1996 to examine this topic in greater detail. The terms of reference that it set out for this project were

> 'To consider the differences in tax treatment between the employed and the self-employed and the extent to which tax liabilities of similarly placed individuals differed as a result.'

0.6 The tax differences that are the primary focus of discontent in this area in the UK are well known and centre mainly on the rules on deduction of expenses and taxation of benefits and on timing and method of collection of tax. The general view is that the differences in the rules favour the self-employed, and this is broadly true, though there are circumstances in which the rules operate to the advantage of employees.[49] . . .

0.11 One starting point that has sometimes been suggested for reform would be to align all or some aspects of the tax treatment of the employed and self-employed. The argument is that reducing such differences would make determining whether someone is self-employed or employed – 'the classification issue' – less significant and therefore less problematic.

0.12 Reducing these differences is not simple. Major structural reform extending beyond the immediate issues being considered by the TLRC could be required. Change could bring with it new administrative difficulties and even new inequities, as well as solutions to existing problems.

0.21 One reason for these practical and other difficulties of alignment is that there is often, but not always, a fundamental structural and organisational difference between the self-employed and the employed. They may play different roles in the labour market, and risk allocation between them and the firm to which they are supplying services differs depending on their relationship.

0.22 Where these economic and social differences exist, arguably the employed and self-employed are *not* in comparable positions. They may be doing similar work and receiving similar financial benefits, but they are playing a different role in the

48 [The Tax Law Reform Committee.]

49 For a more detailed discussion of these differences, see J. Freedman and E. Chamberlain, 'Horizontal equity and the taxation of employed and self-employed workers', (1997) *Fiscal Studies*, vol. 18, no. 1, pp. 87-118 . . . .

labour market because of risk allocation and positioning in relation to the firm. This different role might make direct comparisons of their tax treatments inappropriate, even if superficially they seem to be in similar financial positions. At the very least, the tax comparison has to take account of these different economic roles, even if the conclusion is that the differences are insufficient to warrant different tax treatment.

0.23 To the extent that there are fundamental structural and economic differences between the self-employed and the employed, which are reflected in the method of classification for tax purposes, there may be no inequity in the different tax treatments accorded to each group. If, however, there can be differences in tax classification without any serious substantive difference existing in fact between some who are categorised as self-employed and some who are employees, then different tax treatments might well be inequitable and comparisons need to be made.

0.24 A sensible starting-point, therefore, is to examine whether the current method of classification between the self-employed and the employed for tax purposes is consistent and fair and to what extent it does indeed reflect real structural and economic differences in their positions. The current test is based primarily on case law drawn from many areas of law, though there are some statutory adjustments. Some would suggest further statutory intervention, whilst others consider the flexibility of case law to be helpful in changing circumstances. These issues are considered further in this paper.

0.25 Conditions and the nature of work are undergoing changes. At the margins, the distinction between the employed and self-employed was never entirely clear-cut, and now there are a growing number of workers occupying intermediate positions (or 'grey areas') between the two clear ends of the employed/self-employed spectrum. This has had consequences for employment law as well as for taxation, both of which are adapting in their own ways to meet the problem. Whether tax law is adapting sensibly is one of the questions discussed further in this paper. The question of the relationship between tax law and employment law and whether they can and should develop in tandem also requires discussion. There may be different policy objectives and practical considerations in the tax and employment fields. On the other hand, differences between classifications for these two purposes can cause cost and confusion for workers and employers and are particularly problematic in relation to NICs [National Insurance Contributions]. Although NICs need to follow the tax classification for collection purposes, the payment of these NICs also relates to benefits in some cases, and in this sense NICs might be thought to be more closely related to employment status for labour law purposes. NICs straddle the two areas of tax and employment law, making divergence between the two problematic.

0.26 Employment legislation is moving away from the traditional methods of classification between the self-employed and the employed. In a research report published by the European Commission,[50] it is suggested that the nature of work is changing, away from the job whose prototype was manufacturing, to a new type of work, where the prototype is the service relationship. This new type of work requires new institutional forms and new ways of protecting workers.

0.27 This changing nature of work is leading to labour law developments throughout Europe and elsewhere. In the UK, recent legislation has given non-standard workers (not defined as employees under the case law) some of the same

50 European Commission D-G V, *Transformation of Labour and Future of Labour Law in Europe: Final Report*, (1999) CE-19-98-302-EN-C EUR-OP, Luxembourg.

rights as employees in some circumstances.[51] The Employment Relations Act 1999 contains a wide power for government to extend existing employment rights to other workers.[52] In doing so, it follows the recommendations of a research report published by the DTI, which suggested that a move away from the employed/self-employed divide could both extend basic rights to persons requiring protection and reduce uncertainty in the operation of employment law.[53]

0.28 On the tax front, there have been fundamental changes in classification and collection in the construction industry, recognising that traditional case law tests of employment and self-employment are no longer sufficient to recognise the economic complexities. The structure and operation of these might give some guidance on how effective similar changes for other groups would be.[54] The tax system might attempt to identify each non-standard example and specify special treatment for such groups. Such multi-classification must be balanced, however, with administrative feasibility. On the other hand, multi-classification may be necessary if the tax system is to deal fairly with the complexities that exist as a matter of economic reality.

0.29 The legislation in the Finance Act 2000 dealing with personal service companies and other intermediaries, colloquially known as IR35, is another example of an attempt to adapt the tax system to meet changing work practices.[55] This legislation *deems* certain workers to receive Schedule E payments, even though the services of those workers are supplied through an intermediary company or partnership and payments are made to the worker by the intermediary in a way not subject to Schedule E taxation under normal rules.[56]

0.33 One of the difficulties of the current tax system is that it is attempting to deal with a spectrum of workers. It is inevitable that the focus both of the Inland Revenue and of taxpayers will be on 'hard cases': those workers at the borderline of the employee/self-employed classification – the 'grey area'. The vast majority of the working population, however, will fall clearly within one category or another. Any proposals for reform should not unsettle the position of the many for the sake of the few, nor should the classification rules be distorted in an attempt to deal with more fundamental structural problems of the tax system. **[8.8]**

Davies v Braithwaite [1931] 2 KB 628 (KBD)

Miss Braithwaite was a well-known actress who, in the year of assessment in question, appeared on stage, film and radio in the United Kingdom and in the US.

> ROWLATT J:. . .The question of principle in this case is whether the respondent ought to be assessed under Schedule D of the Income Tax Act 1918, as following her profession of an actress,[57] or whether she ought to be assessed under Schedule E[58] as exercising certain employments under the particular engagements which she makes.[59] The question is a

51 For examples, see Chapter 4. . .[of the Discussion Paper.]

52 Section 23.

53 B. Birchill, S. Deakin and S. Honey, *The Employment Status of Individuals in Non-Standard Employment,* (1999) URN 98/943 no.6, EMAR Employment Relations Research Series, DTI, London (hereafter the DTI employment status report).

54 See Chapter 4. . .[of the Discussion Paper.]

55 For more detail, see Chapter 4 . . . [of the Discussion Paper].

56 [See below, para **[8.13]**.]

57 [See now ITTOIA 2005, Pt 2.]

58 [See now ITEPA 2003.]

59 [The point of the case was that if Schedule E applied to each engagement, the taxpayer's earnings abroad would only be taxable if remitted to this country. On the other hand, if she was carrying on one profession and Schedule D applied, then, as the profession was being carried on in this country, *all* the profits of the profession would be assessed.]

difficult one, mainly because of the want of precision in the meaning of the term "employment" as it comes into this controversy.

The scheme of the Income Tax Acts used to be to include under Schedule D "profession, employment, or vocation." That was held to be a fairly comprehensive definition of the persons who carried on business on their own account. Under Schedule E were public offices. It was recognised that where a person was in a permanent situation it was much better to assess his salary as the salary of the situation than to go to him personally, and assess him in respect of his earnings. There were persons, like railway clerks, who were hired for an indefinite period. For the purposes of assessment to income tax they were treated as holders of offices. That was a very convenient method of assessment to income tax. Then a case arose (*Great Western Ry. Co. v. Bater*[60]), in which I pointed out that these railway clerks were not holders of offices at all. I said that my own view was that Parliament in using this language in 1842 meant by an office a substantive thing that existed apart from its holder. It was something which had an existence independent of the person who filled it. It was something which was held by tenure and title rather than by contract and which continued to exist, though the holders of it might change and it was filled in succession by successive holders. The House of Lords decided that my view was right. It was, therefore, found convenient to put "employment" expressly in Schedule E.

When the word "employment" is used in connection with a profession or vocation in Schedule D it means the way in which a man employs himself. But "employment" in Schedule E means something different. In that Schedule it means something analogous to an office and which is conveniently amenable to the scheme of taxation which is applied to offices as opposed to the earnings of a man who follows a profession or vocation.

That unhappy word "employment" has now to be construed with reference to this case. The respondent is an actress, and, of course, the contract which an actor or actress, or any person whose livelihood is earned in that sort of way, has, is rather different from other contracts, as has been pointed out, because it involves that the employer under the contract is bound to let the actor or actress appear. But what is the criterion? The Solicitor-General has said a good deal with regard to the degree of skill and attainment which is required of a lady who is in a position to enter into agreements of this kind. I do not think that the question turns on the degree of skill at all. It seems to me that the most skilful and distinguished persons, whose qualifications are very rare in art or medicine, or any other profession where distinction is difficult to obtain, may well enter an "employment, and if they take a situation for years and made it their life occupation, it would be no answer to a claim to assess them under Schedule E to say that they are very skilled and distinguished persons, because such very skilled and distinguished persons would be exercising an "employment" in the sense of Schedule E as much as anybody else who holds an office. On the other hand, if a very humble person takes a series of jobs for an hour or so each, he would be carrying on a trade. Nor is the mere duration of the engagement the criterion. An actress may make a contract for the run of a play, which might be a considerable time, but it would not necessarily thereby become "employment" within Schedule E.

It seems to be quite clear that a man can have both an employment and a profession at the same time, in different categories. A man may have the steadiest employment in the world by day and he may do something quite different in the evening and make some more money by the exercise of a profession or vocation. I cannot doubt that that would be so, and even if it were in the same sphere, I do not see why he should not have both an employment as well as a profession. For instance, a musician who holds an office or employment under a permanent engagement can at the same time follow his profession privately.

I have to formulate some line of cleavage and it seems to me that what I must glean my inspiration from is the purpose of the change from Schedule D to Schedule E in the Finance Act 1922, s.18. I have to consider the effect of the change which was made in the different methods of raising income tax. It seems to me that when the Legislature took

60 [[1920] 3 KB 266.]

"employment" out of Schedule D, and put it into Schedule E, alongside "Offices," the Legislature had in mind employments which were something like offices, and I thought of the expression "posts" as conveying the idea required. When a person occupies a post resting on a contract, and if then that is employment as opposed to a mere engagement in the course of carrying out a profession, I do not think that is a very difficult term of distinction, though perhaps a little difficult to apply to all cases. But I would go further than that and say that it seems to me that where one finds a method of earning a livelihood which does not consist of the obtaining of a post and staying in it, but consists of a series of engagements and moving from one to the other – and in the case of an actor's or actress's life it certainly involves going from one to the other and not going on playing one part for the rest of his or her life, but in obtaining first one engagement, then another, and a whole series of them – then each of those engagements cannot be considered an employment, but is a mere engagement in the course of exercising a profession and every profession and every trade does involve the making of successive engagements and successive contracts and, in one sense of the word, employments.

In this case I think it is quite clear that the respondent must be assessed to income tax under Schedule D, because here she does not make a contract with a producer for a post. She makes a contract with a producer for the next thing that she is going to do, and then with another producer, and then a third producer, and at any time she may make a record for a gramophone company or act for a film. I think that whatever she does and whatever contracts she makes are nothing but incidents in the conduct of her professional career. Therefore, I think she is taxable under Schedule D.

With regard to the question whether the respondent's American earnings ought to be included in the assessment, I am not in a position to decide that, because I have no decision on it from the Commissioners. But the point was raised because it was contended on her behalf on the appeal to the General Commissioners against the Schedule D assessments that, as no remittances had been made to this country, she could not be assessed under Case V of Schedule D. I shall allow this appeal, but I shall send the case back to the Commissioners, at Miss Braithwaite's option, to have a decision by them on the question whether her American earnings ought to be included in the assessment under Schedule D.[61] **[8.9]**

Fall v Hitchen [1973] Ch 66 (Ch D)

The taxpayer was a professional dancer employed by Sadler's Wells Trust Ltd. under a standard form of contract. He was assessed under Schedule E[62] in respect of his earnings under the contract, and appealed to the General Commissioners, who decided that these sums were assessable under Schedule D.[63] The Inland Revenue appealed.

PENNYCUICK VC: . . . The first matter which falls to be considered is whether the relation created by the contract was that of a contract of service or a contract for services. I was taken by Counsel for the Crown through a number of authorities dealing with this point . . . . It will be sufficient for the present purpose to quote one paragraph from a very illuminating judgment of Cooke J. in *Market Investigations Ltd v. Minister of Social Security.*[64]

The question was whether a given individual was or was not engaged under a contract of service. Cooke J. analysed some of the earlier law, and said this:[65]

"The observations of Lord Wright, of Denning L.J. and of the judges of the Supreme Court suggest that the fundamental test to be applied is this: 'Is the person who has engaged himself to perform these services performing them as a person in business on

61 [In a supplemental case, Finlay J held that the American profits must be included.]
62 See now ITEPA 2003.
63 See now ITTOIA 2005, Pt 2.
64 [1969] 2 QB 173.
65 [At p 184.]

his own account?' If the answer to that question is 'yes,' then the contract is a contract for services. If the answer is 'no,' then the contract is a contract of service. No exhaustive list has been compiled and perhaps no exhaustive list can be compiled of the considerations which are relevant to determining that question, nor can strict rules be laid down as to the relative weight which the various considerations should carry in particular cases. The most that can be said is that control will no doubt always have to be considered, although it can no longer be regarded as the sole determining factor; and that factors which may be of importance are such matters as whether the man performing the services provides his own equipment, whether he hires his own helpers, what degree of financial risk he takes, what degree of responsibility for investment and management he has, and whether and how far he has an opportunity of profiting from sound management in the performance of his task."

That judgement was quoted with approval by Lord Widgery C.J. in the recent case of *Global Plant Ltd v. Secretary of State for Social Services*.[66]

In the present case, it seems to me that virtually all the relevant factors point to this being a contract of service. Mr Hitchen is engaged to work for a minimum period of rehearsals plus 22 weeks, and thereafter until the contract is determined by a fortnight's notice on either side; he is engaged to work full-time during specified hours for a regular salary; the manager has the final call upon his services, and indeed the exclusive call subject only to this, that his consent to Mr. Hitchen performing elsewhere shall not be unreasonably withheld; and then again the manager provides and owns the gear used by Mr. Hitchen, with one exception. All these *indicia* point to the conclusion that he is not a person who is performing those services in business on his own account; and there are really no *indicia* to the contrary. I do not enlarge further on this point because at the outset of his argument Mr. Pinson[67] very candidly accepted that if this were a case under the National Insurance Act he would have found it difficult to maintain a different contention. However, I would observe at this point that the expressions "contract of service" and "contract for services" are of general application, and, unless one finds in the context some limitation upon the meaning of the words, those words must have the same meaning in any other context as they do under the National Insurance Act. I conclude, therefore, that this agreement is a contract of service within the ordinary meaning of the words.

Once it is accepted that this is a contract of service, it seems to me to follow that it must equally represent an employment within the terms of Schedule E. Indeed, unless some special limitation is to be put upon the word "employment" in any given context, the expression "contract of service" appears to be coterminous with the expression "employment." I can find no such context in relation to Schedule E. I do not see how it could be said that emoluments arising from a contract of service are not emoluments arising from an employment within the meaning of the charging words in Schedule E. The authorities in this connection are concerned with the particular facts of the cases before the Court. I have not been referred to any general statement equating a contract of service with employment. It may be that this is too obvious to state: but there is certainly no authority to the contrary. I shall refer in a moment to the case on which Mr. Pinson primarily relied. And once it is accepted that Mr. Hitchen's employment, being under a contract of service, represents an employment within the meaning of Schedule E, then it follows conclusively upon authority that the emoluments arising under that contract are chargeable under Schedule E, and not under Schedule D.

Mr. Pinson relied on *Davies v. Braithwaite*.[68] Indeed, he based his argument almost entirely on it. Broadly, his contention was that the word "employment" in Schedule E does not include engagements entered into by an actor as "incident" to the carrying on of his profession, and he explained that by "incident" he meant that which formed part of the fabric of the profession. That observation is derived from *Davies v. Braithwaite*...

66 [1972] 1 QB 139 at 150. [See also *Midland Sinfonia Concert Society Ltd. v Secretary of State for Social Services* [1981] ICR 454; *Ready Mixed Concrete (South East) Ltd. v Minister of Pensions and National Insurance* [1968] 2 QB 497.]

67 [For the taxpayer.]

68 [See above, para **[8.9]**.]

. . .In that judgement Rowlatt J. holds that the word "employment" means a post, and distinguishes it from a succession of engagements made in the course of carrying on a profession. He then goes on to hold that, on the particular facts of that case, Miss Braithwaite did not hold any post and that none of her particular engagements could be treated as a post, but that on the contrary all her successive engagements must be treated as incidents in the conduct of her profession. The learned Judge nowhere says that, if an actor enters into a contract in such terms as to amount to what he calls a post, then that actor is not chargeable under Schedule E but under Schedule D. On the contrary, it is implicit in the whole of his judgement, it seems to me, that if a professional person, whether an actor or anybody else, enters into a contract involving what the learned Judge calls a post, then that person will be chargeable in respect of the income arising from the post under Schedule E notwithstanding that he is at the same time carrying on his profession, the income of which will be chargeable under Schedule D. The instance of a musician puts that point very neatly. I do not think most people today would use the word "post," which does not seem very apt to cover the countless instances of employment in the sense of a contract of service; but every word of that judgment is applicable as between the carrying on of a profession and an engagement in the course of carrying on that profession, on the one hand, and a contract of employment, on the other hand. The fact that an actor normally undertakes a succession of engagements in the course of carrying on that profession in no way involves the result that, if an actor enters an acting employment in the nature of a post, then he is not assessable under Schedule E in respect of the income arising from that employment.

I think I need refer at any length to only one other decision, and that is *Mitchell v. Ross*. . . .[69]

I think I should read a short passage from the judgement of Upjohn J.[70] At page 34[71] he refers to the history of the matter[72] which is the same, really, as was recited by Rowlatt J. in *Davies v. Braithwaite*.[73] He then cites authorities on the meaning of the word "office," and on page 35 he goes on:

> "On the question of employment a large number of authorities were cited to me. Many tests have been laid down to determine whether the relation of master and servant exists, such as the degree of control exercised by the master, and so on. The relationship between a specialist and a board is so very special, however, that many of these cases, dealing either with entirely different types of engagements, to use a neutral word, or with the pre-Act relationship between hospitals and specialists, form no safe guide. The real question to be answered is this. Does a specialist who holds a part-time National Health appointment (a) occupy an office, or (b) undertake an employment, or (c) does he merely render services in the course of the exercise or practice of his profession?"

He then goes on to hold that alternative (a) is correct; i.e., that the specialist occupies an office. Having so held, obviously it was not necessary for him to decide whether he undertook an employment.[74]

The only other cases to which I think I can usefully refer are, first, *Household v. Grimshaw*[75] in which Upjohn J. upheld upon the particular facts of that case a conclusion by the Special Commissioners that an author who bound himself to a film company for a minimum period of 12 weeks in each year was assessable in respect of the profits from that engagement under Schedule D, and not as the holder of an office or employment under Schedule E; and, second, *Commissioners of Inland Revenue v. Brander & Cruickshank*[76]

69 [1962] AC 813; 40 TC 11.
70 The judge at first instance.
71 40 TC 11 at 34.
72 [The emergence of Schedule E.]
73 [See above, paras **[8.9]**.]
74 [In the Court of Appeal in *Mitchell v Ross* [1960] Ch 498, Lord Evershed MR, at 521, distinguished *Davies v Braithwaite* on its facts, in ruling against the taxpayer's argument that his engagement by the hospital was merely an incident of his professional activity as a doctor.]
75 [1953] 1 WLR 710; 34 TC 366.
76 [1971] 1 WLR 212; 46 TC 574.

in which the House of Lords held, in one case with manifest reluctance, that a firm of lawyers who had entered into an engagement as professional registrars and had derived profits therefrom were assessable in respect of those profits under Schedule E by reason of the fact that each of those engagements represented an office or employment within the meaning of Schedule E. I say "with manifest reluctance" because Lord Donovan considered that the distinction between Schedule E and Schedule D in this respect was an artificial one.

To return to the present case, it seems to me, as I have said, that the relation between Sadler's Wells Trust Ltd. and Mr. Hitchen under their contract was that of a contract of service; that that contract of service represented an employment for the purpose of Schedule E; and that Mr. Hitchen is assessable under Schedule E in respect of the income derived from that contract – and that none the less so by reason that at the same time he was carrying on, as found by the Commissioners, the profession of an actor and would have been assessable under Schedule D in respect of the profits of that profession if there had been any. I cannot see any reason why an actor should be in a different position in principle in this respect from that of any other professional man. It must depend on the particular facts whether or not he holds an employment within the meaning of Schedule E. **[8.10]**

Hall v Lorimer [1994] I WLR 209 (CA)

The taxpayer, who was a vision mixer, became freelance at the end of 1985, having left an employment where he had been trained. He then built up a client list to some twenty two production companies in the first fourteen months, and this number remained substantially the same until 1989, when all but five of the original clients were replaced by new ones. His engagements usually lasted one or two days, the annual number of engagements being between 120 and 150. The equipment required was provided by the production company, although the taxpayer's advice on the particular equipment needed was occasionally sought. A lump sum was paid for each engagement, and bookings were made by telephone from the taxpayer's office at his home. He was assessed to tax under Schedule E (earnings from an employment), and he appealed to the Special Commissioners, claiming that he should have been assessed under the then Schedule D, Case I (profits of a trade). The Special Commissioner found in the taxpayer's favour, on the basis that, although he provided no equipment or work place, he exploited his abilities in the market place, bearing a financial risk greater than that of an employee, accepting the risk of bad debts and outstanding invoices and of an insufficient number of engagements. The Court of Appeal agreed with the Commissioner.

NOLAN LJ: . . . the commissioner. . . said:

"[The taxpayer] provides no equipment (i.e. he has no tools) he provides no ' work place' or 'workshop' where the contract is to be performed, he provides no capital for the production, he hires no staff for it. No; he does not. But that is not his business. He has his office, he exploits his abilities in the market place, he bears his own financial risk which is greater than that of one who is an employee, accepting the risk of bad debts and outstanding invoices and of no or an insufficient number of engagements. He has the opportunity of profiting from being good at being a vision mixer. According to his reputation so there will be a demand for his services for which he will be able to charge accordingly. The more efficient he is at running the business of providing his services the greater is his prospect of profit."

Mr. Goldsmith *[counsel for the Revenue]* submitted that the commissioner was not entitled to attach significance to the taxpayer's risk of having no engagements because as was pointed out by Lord Griffiths in the *Lee Ting Sang*[77] case, this is a risk faced by casual

77 [1990] 2 AC 374.

employees who move from one job to another. That is so, but the risk of bad debts and outstanding invoices is certainly not one which is normally associated with employment. Moreover, the income and expenditure accounts annexed to the case stated reveal that the taxpayer incurred very substantial expenditure in the course of obtaining and organising his engagements and as an incident of carrying them out. . . . All of those expenses, as Mr. Allcock representing the taxpayer, told us, without contradiction, were considered to be deductible if the taxpayer were assessed under Schedule D.[78] In any event they would seem to me to be quite different in nature and scale from those likely to be incurred by an employee.

Mr. Goldsmith submitted that the fundamental distinction between a contract of employment and a contract for service is that in the former the contracting party sells his skill or labour; in the latter he sells the product of his labour. In one case the employer buys the man; in the other he buys the job. . . . I find the distinction very hard to apply in the case of a professional man. Surely the self-employed barrister advising in his chambers or the doctor advising in his surgery is selling his skill and labour and not its product. If the scene shifts to the court or to the operating theatre can the client or patient really be said to be buying the product which may be disastrous in spite of the best efforts of the advocate or the surgeon in the litigation or operation?

Again the question, whether the individual is in business on his own account, though often helpful, may be of little assistance in the case of one carrying on a profession or vocation. A self-employed author working from home or an actor or a singer may earn his living without any of the normal trappings of a business. For my part I would suggest there is much to be said in these cases for bearing in mind the traditional contrast between a servant and an independent contractor. The extent to which the individual is dependent upon or independent of a particular paymaster for the financial exploitation of his talents may well be significant. **[8.11]**

McManus v Griffiths [1997] STC 1089 (Ch D)

Under the terms of her contract of employment, the taxpayer,[79] who was employed by a golf club as stewardess, provided a catering service, giving her responsibility for the purchase of all the required food and ingredients, and for the menu and prices to be charged, although the club provided the necessary equipment and services. She was entitled to the proceeds of all the catering receipts. Evidence was given by the club's secretary and treasurer that they had no details of her income from the catering and considered that they were not entitled to such information. She was also responsible for the engagement and remuneration of any extra staff. Prior to this contract, the taxpayer, along with her husband (who was employed as the club's steward and managed the bar on behalf of the club), had responsibility for cleaning duties, and the contractual salary was paid to them jointly; they were also entitled to a fixed term annual holiday. Subsequently, responsibility for cleaning fell on, and the contractual salary was payable to, the husband alone and, while her husband continued to be subject to a fixed holiday period, although the taxpayer was required to provide the catering service at specified times, she could take her holiday by arrangement provided that she was able to provide the necessary cover. The taxpayer contended that she was employed under a contract of employment and that the profits of the catering business constituted earnings from that employment. The General Commissioners and the High Court disagreed.

LIGHTMAN J: . . . There are a number of indicia of holding her to be an employee. I have regard to the provisions in the contractual documents regulating her vacation: the thrust

78 [ie, on the profits of a trade, profession or vocation.]

79 In respect of the tax years prior to 1990–91 and independent taxation, the appeal against assessments was in the name of the taxpayer's husband.

of these provisions, as it seems to me, is that until the 1987 contract the club was insisting on Mrs McManus personally (and not by a substitute) providing the service save during suitable holiday periods. I take account of the fact that the club provides the premises, the equipment and services. This is explained by the fact that the club had the means to provide the service itself and recognised the need that such a service be available to its members, but decided that Mrs McManus rather than itself should have this responsibility. I have in mind the terminology, the language of employment which permeates the contractual documents. This can carry little weight in the case of documents such as the present drafted by laymen. It is suggested on behalf of Mr and Mrs McManus that the three month notice period is indicative of a contract for service rather than for services. I do not think that it is indicative of either. I regard the provision as neutral.

On the other hand, the indicia in favour of holding Mrs McManus self employed appear to me to be overwhelming. The critical factors . . . are that Mrs McManus is in business on her own account (a factor of importance, though not decisive: see *Hall (HMIT) v Lorimer*)[80]; that she is not subject to the control of the club in respect of the menu or the prices or indeed (save to hours and the character of the catering service) how the business is to be conducted; and that (as is common ground) she has a free hand in the employment of staff engaged in the provision of the service and is the employer and paymaster of such staff. In short, she is her own boss. The overwhelming balance comes down in favour of holding that Mrs McManus was to provide the catering service in a self-employed capacity. Indeed, the scenario painted by the contractual documents in my view is scarcely compatible with that of an employer/employee relationship in regard to the provision of catering and the label of employee attached generally to her by the contractual documents is inept. She has in effect a catering concession at the club. It is not as if the club agreed to remunerate her for the provision of the catering service by paying her a share of the profits, a sum equal to the profits or indeed all the profits. The club have agreed to pay nothing, for the business is hers, and the profits are hers, and not the club's. It is true that the emoluments of an employee may include authorised receipts from a third party (e.g. tips: see *Calvert (HMIT) v Wainwright* (1947) 27 TC 475). But that is a scenario far removed from the present, where Mrs McManus alone contracts with and receives and retains for herself all payments from the customers of her business.

I do not think that any status which Mrs McManus may have as an employee in respect of the cleaning duties can have the exclusionary effect on the applicability of Sch. D[81] in respect of the profits of the catering service. It is totally unreal to treat the profits as an emolument of her employment: her employment gave her the opportunity and indeed required her to trade on her own account (and accordingly was the *causa sine qua non* of her earning the profits made); but the profits were the profits of her trading, trading (and not employment) was the *causa causans* of these receipts, and accordingly the profits fall within Sch. D and are not an emolument of her employment. **[8.12]**

A useful discussion can be found on the distinction between a contract for services and a contract of service in a series of employment law cases, in particular, *Ready Mixed Concrete (South East) Ltd v Minister of Pensions and National Insurance*.[82] In that case, MacKenna J said that, for a contact of service to exist, three conditions must be satisfied: *first*, there must be a wage or other remuneration, in return for which the worker is obliged to provide his own work and skill. However, in considering the issue of personal service, the court was of the view that a limited right of delegation or substitution was not inconsistent with a contract of service. The importance of personal service was stressed by

80 [1994] 1 WLR 209 at 218.
81 [The profits of such a trade are now assessable to tax under ITTOIA 2005, Pt 2; see Chapter 9, para **[9.1]**.]
82 [1968] 2 QB 497. Other cases include *Young & Woods Ltd v West* [1980] IRLR 201; *Addison v London Philarmonic Orchestra Ltd* [1981] ICR 261; *Midland Sinfonia Concert Society Ltd v Secretary of State for Social Services* [1981] ICR 454.

Peter Gibson LJ in *Express and Echo Publications Limited v Ernest Tanton*,[83] saying that 'it is, in my judgment, established on the authorities that where, as here, a person who works for another is not required to perform his services personally, then as a matter of law the relationship between the worker and the person for whom he works is not that of employee and employer,'[84] adding that a provision enabling a worker not to perform services personally 'is a provision wholly inconsistent with the contract of service'[85]; *secondly*, the worker is subject to a right of control by his master, although this is not necessarily a determining factor; and *thirdly*, the other provisions of the contract are consistent with it being a contract of service. These include the ownership of significant assets and the financial risk borne by the worker, and his opportunity to profit. In reviewing the *Ready Mixed Concrete* case, Cooke J in *Market Investigations Ltd v Minister of Social Security*[86] was of the view that control was no longer a decisive factor, and that the fundamental issue was whether the worker is performing the services as a person in business on his own account; if he is, then the contract is a contract *for services* and, if he is not, then it is a contract *of service*. Significantly, the question of substitution was not discussed, even though, on the facts of the case, a substitute could not have been sent without the prior approval of the 'employing' company. Finally, in *O'Kelly v Trusthouse Forte*[87], the Court of Appeal stated that whether a contract is a contract of service or for services is a question of law involving questions of degree and fact, to which the principle in *Edwards v Bairstow and Harrison*[88] applied.[89] **[8.12a]**

C. *IR35 and personal service companies*

The Revenue's IR35 policy, introduced to restrict the tax avoidance opportunities for claiming to be self-employed, was brought into effect by the FA 2000, and is now to be found in ITEPA 2003, Pt 2, Ch 8. Put simply, this legislation is designed to counteract the situation where there are three parties: the worker, the intermediary and the client. The worker personally performs, or is under an obligation to perform, services for the purpose of a business carried on by the client. Rather than being performed under a contract between the worker and the client, those services arise under 'arrangements' involving the intermediary. The circumstances of the arrangement are such that, were there a direct contract between the client and the worker, based upon the principles discussed above, the worker would be regarded for tax purposes as an employee of the client. Typically the engagement the legislation has in mind is where an individual, the worker, hires out his services through the medium of a company, the sole business of which is to hire out the individual's services. But for the IR35 legislation, the client would not have to deduct PAYE, nor be liable to account for national insurance contributions, and the worker would take the bulk of his money out of the personal service company as dividends, which are not subject to national insurance contributions. Under IR35, where payment is made by the client to the intermediary for the worker's

83 [1999] ICR 693.
84 *Ibid.*, 699–700.
85 *Ibid.*, 700. The approach being taken by the Special Commissioners in a recent series of IR 35 cases is consistent with that principle; see paras **[8.16–8.18]**.
86 [1969] 2 QB 173.
87 [1984] QB 90.
88 [1956] AC 14, and see above, para **[3.15]**.
89 See also *Express and Echo Publications Limited v Ernest Tanton* [1998] UKEAT 1261_97_3001, Appeal No EAT/1261/97.

services, rather than to the worker himself, the difference between the receipts of the intermediary and those of the worker is deemed to be employment income.[90] Accordingly, the effect of the legislation is to treat the worker as a direct employee of the client. Believing the legislation to be ill-conceived, the Professional Contractors' Group brought an action for judicial review on behalf of its considerable membership. This proved to be unsuccessful, and the Revenue continue to use IR35 rigorously, although not all cases have been decided in their favour.[91] **[8.13]**

Judith Freedman *Employed or Self-Employed? Tax Classification of Workers and the Changing Labour Market* Tax Law Reform Committee Discussion Paper No 1 (IFS, 2001); above, para [8.8]

0.30 In effect, the IR35 legislation seeks to 'look through' the intermediary arrangement in cases where the 'real' relationship is one of employment by the client, although the compliance burden and cost of PAYE and NICS payments is put onto the intermediary and not the client. Only tax law and NICS are affected: the legislation is careful not to deem the individual to be an employee and employment law remains unchanged. The critical test of the relationship used for IR35 tax purposes is the case law test for employment or self-employment. The original proposal was for a special statutory test based on control, but this was quickly rejected as inadequate. The contentious IR35 legislation therefore places a new burden on the case law on classification and has highlighted the problems of uncertainty created by this test based on the facts of each case.

0.31 The IR35 approach assumes that the 'real relationship' can be captured by a set of criteria that can be set out in case law and legislation. Although the original motivation for the change in law was to tackle the use of intermediaries set up purely for tax and NICs purposes, the resulting legislation risks going wider and covering arrangements that exist as a result of the economics and market practices of an industry and not purely for tax reasons. Due to the difficulty of distinguishing employees from the self-employed ..., the legislation may catch workers who are attempting to create their own business but are at an early stage of this process. This has the curious result that the legislation could deter the very entrepreneurs the government seeks to encourage in other contexts.

0.32 The IR35 legislation has caused considerable disquiet amongst certain sectors of business (particularly the IT sector), industry and the tax professions. The reaction to it and the difficulty the Inland Revenue has encountered in producing sensible rules highlight the worker classification problem as well as other structural problems relating to the integration of corporate and personal taxation. IR35 is discussed further in the chapters below in the context of the classification test, although a full critique of the legislation is beyond the scope of this paper.[92] **[8.14]**

90 ITEPA 2003, s 50. For detailed rules for calculating the amount of the deemed employment payment, see s 54.

91 See *Tilbury Consulting Ltd v HM Inspector of Taxes* [2003] UKSC SPC 00390, and para **[8.16]**, below; *Ansell Computer Services Ltd v HM Inspector of Taxes* [2004] UKSC SPC 00425, and below, para **[8.18]**, and *Lime-IT Ltd v HM Inspector of Taxes* [2003] STC (SCD) 15 (Special Commissioners). In addition to these cases won by the taxpayer, the Revenue have conceded in a number of others. Cases won by the Revenue include *Synaptek v Young* [2003] EWHC 645 and *Usetech Ltd v HM Inspector of Taxes* [2004] STC 1671 (see above, para **[3.19]**).

92 The Professional Contractors Group *[was]* granted leave to proceed with a judicial review on the basis that the personal intermediary provisions in the Welfare Reform and Pensions Act 1999 and the Finance Act 2000 are incompatible with EC law and the Human Rights Act 1998: decision of High Court 10/10/2000 (*Evening Standard*, 10/10/2000).

R (on the application of the Professional Contractors Group Ltd) v IRC [2001] STC 629 (CA)

In opposition to the introduction of the IR35 legislation, a group representing the body of independent contractors, brought an action for judicial review of the legislation on two grounds; *first* that it infringed EC law on state aid and freedom of establishment;[93] and *secondly* it was contrary to the first Article of Protocol No.1 of the European Convention of Human Rights[94] in that it interfered with the right of the group's members to enjoy the benefit of a shareholding in a service company. The High Court found against the Group on both grounds, and its appeal, on the first ground only, was unsuccessful. Having reached the conclusion that there was no infringement of EC law, it was not necessary for the Court of Appeal to discuss the question of justification of the legislation and the issue of proportionality, but it did so nevertheless.

ROBERT WALKER LJ:

Justification: tax avoidance

80. On the view which I take this issue does not arise, but I will state my views on it briefly, since the court has heard full argument. The main focus of the argument has been as to whether the prevention of tax avoidance (as opposed to fiscal supervision and fiscal cohesion, two other expressions which recur in Community jurisprudence) can be a proper ground of justification.
81. The issue about tax avoidance resolved itself, in the course of argument, into whether the Court of Justice was in Case 270/83 *Commission v France*[95] and in *ICI v Colmer*[96] holding that *all* measures against tax avoidance, or only *discriminatory* measures against tax avoidance, were inadmissible by way of justification. The crucial texts are paragraphs 24 and 25 of the former judgment and paragraphs 24 to 29 of the latter. In my view it is clear that the Court was referring only to discriminatory measures. I note also that in paragraph 26 of *ICI v Colmer* the suggestion that the more artificial the tax avoidance which has to be countered the easier it may be to find justification. IR 35 is aimed at relatively artificial avoidance since it counters only activities which are the provision, in the guise of self-employment (normally through a corporate vehicle), of employee-like services.
82. There is a general principle (mentioned in *Syndesmos*[97]) that economic aims cannot be a justification for measures which offend fundamental principles of Community law. That principle is in a sense obvious, since a member state cannot rely on its own economic interests to flout the principles on which the common market is founded. But the principle must be understood in its context. It cannot be used to undermine the principle that direct taxation is at present, and unless and until harmonisation takes place, a matter for the legislatures of member states. Diminution of tax revenue cannot be a justification for unequal treatment (*ICI v Colmer*, paragraph 28) but the general prohibition on economic aims does not seem to take the argument any further.

Proportionality

83. If the IR 35 legislation had to be justified an essential part of the process of justification would be for the Revenue to show that its terms were appropriate and necessary to achieve its objectives; that whenever there was a choice between different measures which might be appropriate the least onerous had been chosen; and that the burdens imposed by the measures were not disproportionate to the aims pursued.

93 Article 87 of the EC Treaty.
94 See above, paras **[4.21]–[4.24]**.
95 [1986] ECR 273.
96 [1998] ECR I-4695.
97 [1997] ECR I-3091.

84. The judge found that the Revenue had discharged that burden. In particular he dismissed what he called the 'sledgehammer' argument to the effect that the only real problem was the extreme 'Friday to Mondays' and that that abuse could have been dealt with by simpler and less far-reaching measures. The judge saw the objectives of IR 35 as preventing not only tax evasion but also (and more importantly) widespread tax avoidance by persons who saw themselves as legitimately exploiting a gap in the law. The judge also rejected various suggestions (made in the course of argument before him) as to how the Revenue's objectives might have been achieved in other ways. The suggestions which he referred to were changing the method of taxing dividends, increasing the rate of corporation tax, increasing capital allowances and abolishing NIC. He said that in any event he was satisfied

> " . . . that for me as a judge to canvass other possible methods of fiscal reform is wholly inappropriate."

On that point he referred to the observations of Lord Slynn in *Queen v Chief Constable of Sussex ex parte International Trader's Ferry Ltd.*[98]

85. Mr Barling has criticised the judge's approach as failing to discharge his function when an issue of proportionality is raised. He cited the judgment of this court in *Queen v Secretary of State for Health ex parte Eastside Cheese.*[99]

> "In principle the decision on proportionality has to be taken by the national court which is seised of an issue on Article [30] EC, subject of course to any possible reference to the Court of Justice. But in the case of a legislative measure the national court *must not simply accept the view of the national legislature* or confine itself to deciding whether what the legislature has enacted is reasonable . . .
>
> The judge's task was . . . to see whether the exercise of the Secretary of State's power . . . had been objectively justified and had been shown not to be disproportionate. The test is more demanding than that of 'manifest error' and is also more demanding than that of *Wednesbury* unreasonableness."

86. That approach has been confirmed, he submitted, by the House of Lords in *Queen (Daly) v Secretary of State for the Home Department.*[100] Contrasting the principle of proportionality with the traditional grounds of judicial review, Lord Steyn said:

> "Most cases would be decided in the same way whichever approach is adopted. But the intensity of review is somewhat greater under the proportionality approach. Making due allowance for important structural differences between various convention rights, which I do not propose to discuss, a few generalisations are perhaps permissible. I would mention three concrete differences without suggesting that my statement is exhaustive. First, the doctrine of proportionality may require the reviewing court to assess the balance which the decision maker has struck, not merely whether it is within the range of rational or reasonable decisions. Secondly, the proportionality test may go further than the traditional grounds of review inasmuch as it may require attention to be directed to the relative weight accorded to interests and considerations. Thirdly, even the heightened scrutiny test developed in *R v Ministry of Defence, Ex p Smith*[101] is not necessarily appropriate to the protection of human rights."

87. I have to say that I see some validity in these criticisms. If proportionality were an issue in this appeal I would be inclined to think that the judge did not go far enough in asking himself whether the IR 35 measures were the least onerous which could be adopted in order to achieve their objective. In expressing that tentative view I am well aware of the difficulty of the task, and I sympathise with the judge's view that it was not for him to enter the political arena.

88. But tax legislation raises technical as well as political issues. The technical difficulties of finding fair and practical tests for distinguishing between employment and self-employment for tax purposes go back to the nineteenth century. But recent

98 [1999] 2 AC 418 at 439.
99 [1999] 3 CMLR 123 at 143, 146.
100 [2001] 2 WLR 1622 at 1635.
101 [1996] QB 517, at 554.

developments have intensified the problem. In the knowledge-based sectors from which PCG draws most of its members, the dividing line is often debatable. Moreover the ever-increasing responsibilities of employers for their employees have led to downsizing, outsourcing, 'bodyshopping' and similar practices. Many redundant employees, having found that employed status does not guarantee long-term job security, wish to explore the possibilities of self-employment.

89. All these considerations have led me to wonder whether it might not have been possible to bring forward measures which accorded some recognition to the existence of a sort of no-man's land between Schedule D and Schedule E, rather than insisting on the gulf which exists in theory (but not, always, in practice) between them. Such measures might still have contained robust sanctions against unacceptable tax avoidance. However it is not necessary or appropriate to express any final view, since in my judgment the appeal has fallen at an earlier hurdle. PCG and its members may continue to work through democratic means for amendment of IR 35 so as to meet their complaints, but they have in my judgment failed to strike it down under Community law. **[8.15]**

Tilbury Consulting Ltd v Margaret Gittens (HM Inspector of Taxes) [2003] UKSC SPC 00390 (SC)

The Ford Motor Company (the client) entered into a contract with Compuware (CW) to set up, service and staff an IT project (the AMC project). CW engaged Tilbury Consulting Ltd (TCL, the intermediary) to provide services and, in particular, to make available to CW the services of Roger Tilbury (the worker and taxpayer), who was a controlling shareholder and director of TCL. He worked on the project for some nine years, spending a substantial amount of time at the client's premises. The agreement between CW and TCL gave TCL the right, subject to conditions, to provide a replacement worker. The issue before the Special Commissioners was whether the taxpayer would have been regarded as an employee of Ford had the arrangements taken the form of a contract between the taxpayer and Ford.

STEPHEN OLIVER QC:

26. The legislation calls for a two stage exercise. The first is to find the facts as they existed during the period covered by the decision. The facts to be found are those that serve to identify the "arrangements" involving the intermediary and the circumstances in which those arrangements existed and the nature of the services performed by the "worker". The second is to assume that the worker ... was contracted to perform services to the client ... and to determine whether in the light of the facts as found *[the worker]* would be regarded as *[the client's]* employee....

27. The findings of fact set out above, which identify the arrangements involving the intermediary (TCL), the circumstances in the context of which the arrangements were made and the nature of the services performed by Mr Tilbury, show that Mr Tilbury would not have been regarded as Ford's employee (making the statutory assumption that he was contracted to perform services to Ford). The facts show that CW and not Ford had operational control of the AMC project. Ford had engaged CW to provide its IT services and to set up and operate the AMC project. CW was engaged as principal and acted personally in the project. It equipped itself with its own specialized personnel to discharge its own obligation to Ford, either by employing them directly or by engaging outside subcontractors, such as TCL which in turn provided Mr Tilbury. Ford did not exercise control over the manner in which the CW personnel carried out their duties. To the extent that control was exercisable over the performance of Mr Tilbury's services, that lay with CW. Ford accepted suitable substitutes from CW and CW was obliged to accept from TCL a suitable substitute to Mr Tilbury. At no time was Mr Tilbury a part of Ford's business or undertaking. Those facts are inconsistent with an employer/employee relationship between Ford and Mr Tilbury. **[8.16]**

Whilst the critical factor in this case was the right of substitution and not the length of time of the contract, other factors also militated against the worker being an employee. These included that Roger Tilbury had a different coloured pass from Ford employees which did not entitle him to the use of the gym, that he was paid by the hour and that some of the project work, although only a small amount, was undertaken on the premises of TCL. **[8.17]**

Ansell Computer Services Ltd v David Richardson (HM Inspector of Taxes) [2004] UKSC SPC 00425 (SC)

Michael Ansell (the worker and taxpayer), who was a director and shareholder in Ansell Computer Services Limited (ACSL, the intermediary), was a highly-regarded and experienced computer software engineer, with particular expertise in the defence sector. For several years he had been working on the software elements of weapons and other defence systems, acting as part of a large team of specialists given the overall task of designing, developing and testing the relevant electronic systems. During the relevant periods, he worked at the premises of two different companies working in the defence sector. The first was Alenia Marconi Systems Limited (Marconi) and the second was BAe Systems Avionics Limited (BAe). The issue before the Special Commissioner was whether the taxpayer would have been employed under a contract of service if, contrary to the actual contractual arrangements, he had worked for the client companies under a direct contract between him and them.

GRAHAM AARANSON QC:

53. I shall start with a very recent decision on the IR35 legislation, and the first (so far as I am aware) that has reached the High Court. This is the case of *Synaptek v Young*[102], a decision of Hart J. The case concerned the provision of computer software services through an intermediary company. The General Commissioners had decided that, on balance, under the hypothetical contract between the worker and the client the worker would have been an employee. Hart J held that the Commissioners' conclusion was clearly a possible one, and that they had not misdirected themselves in law, and accordingly he dismissed the appeal against their decision.
54. Hart J's judgment is a convenient place to recall the basic principles that have been developed over the years by the courts to differentiate between a contract of employment and a contract for the provision of services. At paragraph 16 he referred to the test propounded by MacKenna J in *Readymixed Concrete (South East) Limited v Minister of Pensions and National Insurance*[103]. This test has been cited on countless occasions. MacKenna J expressed the test in the following terms:-

"A contract of service exists if these three conditions are fulfilled.

(i) The servant agrees that, in consideration of a wage or other remuneration, he will provide his own work and skill in the performance of some service for his master.

(ii) He agrees, expressly or impliedly, that in the performance of that service he will be subject to the other's control in a sufficient degree to make that other master.

(iii) The other provisions of the contract are consistent with its being a contract of service."

102 [2003] EWHC 645 (Ch Div).

103 [1968] 2 QB 497 at 515.

55. This is clearly an important authority, although I would respectfully comment that I do not find this test to be invariably helpful. Expressions such as "for his master" and "control in a sufficient degree" can in some situations raise questions as to how one can tell whether those words are applicable to the case in hand; and the third requirement, to the effect that the other provisions of the contract have to be consistent with its being a contract of service, involves, as it seems to me, an element of circularity.

56. In paragraph 7 of his judgment Hart J refers to the judgment of Nolan LJ in *Hall v Lorimer*[104], where he said –

> "In cases of this sort there is no single path to a correct decision. An approach which suits the facts and arguments of one case may be unhelpful in another."

57. At paragraph 18 of his judgment Hart J referred to the judgment of Cooke J in *Market Investigations Limited v Minister of Social Security*[105]. Cooke J said that –

> "... The fundamental test to be applied is this: 'Is the person who has engaged himself to perform these services performing them as a person in business on his own account?' If the answer to that question is 'Yes', then the contract is a contract for services. If the answer is 'No', then the contract is a contract of service. No exhaustive list has been compiled and perhaps no exhaustive list can be compiled of the considerations which are relevant in determining that question, nor can strict rules be laid down as to the relative weight which the various considerations should carry in particular cases. The most that can be said is that control will no doubt always have to be considered, although it can no longer be regarded as the sole determining factor; and that factors which may be of importance are such matters as whether the man performing the service provides his own equipment, whether he hires his own helpers, what degree of financial risk he takes, what degree of responsibility for investment and management he has, and whether and how far he has an opportunity of profiting from sound management in the performance of his task."

58. I accept that, on the facts of the present case, Mr Ansell did little of the particular things which Cooke J enumerated as factors which may be of importance. Mr Ansell did not hire his own helpers; he provided his own equipment only for a few hours a week at home; he did not take on any great financial risk (although he was dependent for his remuneration upon payment by CDL to ADSL); and he did not have any significant opportunity to profit from sound management in the performance of his task, whether with Marconi or with BAe. Indeed, Mr Gleig emphasised these very points in urging me to conclude that Mr Ansell should be regarded, on the hypothetical contractual arrangement between himself and Marconi/BAe, as an employee.

59. However, as Cooke J made clear, those particular factors *may* be of importance; but, on the facts of any particular case, they may not. In the present case I consider that they are not of sufficient importance. This is because the very nature of Mr Ansell's work, shrouded as it has to be in secrecy and performed in isolation from anyone apart from other individuals with similar levels of security clearance, does not permit him to exercise his profession in the entrepreneurial way that would be available to someone working in less sensitive areas of activity (whether in the I.T. field or elsewhere).

60. In this situation it seems to me appropriate to look more to other factors to help decide on which side of the line the hypothetical contractual arrangement would fall. The factors which appear to me to be of greater significance in the present case are:-
    (i) the absence of any obligation on Marconi or BAe to keep Mr Ansell in work throughout the 3 months/6 months period of his respective engagements;
    (ii) the absence of any obligation by Mr Ansell to put in a particular amount of work, whether each day or each week or in aggregate during his period of engagement;

104 [1994] STC 23 at 28-29.
105 [1969] 2 QB 173 at 184-185.

(iii) the ability which Mr Ansell had to take time off at his own choosing, without seeking permission from the team leaders at Marconi or BAe; and
(iv) the ability to withdraw and suggest a substitute individual (which both Mr Ansell and Marconi/BAe regarded as genuine, even though it was very unlikely that the situation would in fact arise); and
(v) the various other practical matters (no company car, sick pay, holiday pay, social club etc.) which differentiated contractors from employees at a daily practical level. . . . .

66. Having considered the evidence I have concluded that the circumstances of the arrangements between Mr Ansell and Marconi/BAe are such that, had they taken the form of a contract between Mr Ansell and those companies, that contract would have been one for the provision of services and not of employment. **[8.18]**

3. Earnings

The term 'earnings' is defined to include any salary, wages, fees, gratuities or other incidental benefits and 'anything else that constitutes an emolument of the employment'.[106] Emoluments are defined under the previous legislation to include 'all salaries, fees, wages perquisites and profits whatsoever.'[107] Prior to ITEPA, that definition embraced benefits in kind; under s 62(3), it is made clear that benefits in kind are taxable as earnings only if they are convertible into money.[108] Accordingly, for those many 'perks' which are not so convertible, there exists a special benefits code that brings them within the tax net.[109] It will be seen that not every payment made by an employer to an employee[110] is taxable as earnings; equally, merely because a payment is made by someone other than the employer does not mean that the payment will not be taxable as earnings. Further, although a payment may appear on its face to be taxable, it may escape tax as an exempt payment.[111] **[8.19]**

A. *The earnings must derive from the office or employment*

Under ITEPA 2003, s 9, tax is charged on the 'net taxable earnings from an employment' in respect of general earnings,[112] and on the net taxable specific income from an employment' in respect of specific earnings.[113] In considering whether a payment received by an employee has arisen *from an employment* and is thus taxable, it has been said that 'it must be something in the nature of a

106 ITEPA 2003, s 62(2).
107 ICTA 1988, s 131. The term 'emoluments' was used in ICTA 1988, s 19, the basic charging provision for employment income, and thus it is this term, rather than 'earnings', which appears in the case extracts below.
108 This provision was incorporated in the legislation as a result of the interpretation by the courts of the term 'emoluments' under the previous provisions.
109 ITEPA 2003, s 63. The code is based on previous provisions introduced to prevent valuable benefits from escaping tax altogether, or being taxed on a low value.
110 ITEPA 2003, s 5 specifies that references to the terms 'employment', 'employee' and 'employer' apply equally to an 'office', 'office-holder' and 'the person under whom the office-holder holds office' respectively.
111 See ITEPA 2003, s 8 and Pt 4.
112 ITEPA 2003, s 9(2).
113 Ibid., s 9(4).

reward for services past, present or future,'[114] and that it must have 'been paid to him in return for acting as or being an employee'.[115] This principle was further elaborated by Lord Templeman who said:

> 'an emolument "from employment" means an emolument "from being or becoming an employee. The authorities are consistent with this analysis and are concerned to distinguish in each case between an emolument which is derived "from being or becoming an employee" on the one hand and an emolument which is attributable to something else on the other hand, for example, to a desire on the part of the provider of the emolument to relieve distress or to provide assistance to a home buyer.'[116]

Although some cases have cast doubt on that principle,[117] it has recently been reasserted by the Court of Appeal in *Wilson v Clayton*.[118] The case concerned a payment made to the taxpayer under a consent order settling unfair dismissal proceedings. In holding that it was not an emolument, Peter Gibson LJ asked:[119]

> 'is the payment an emolument (within the extended meaning of s. 131(1)[120] from the employment? The answer I give unhesitatingly is that it is not. It is not enough that Mr. Clayton would not have received it but for having been an employee. It is not a payment in return or as a reward for past services. It is not a payment in return for acting as or being an employee. It is not a payment as an inducement to enter into employment – he already was employed – or to provide future services. If one looks for what reason it was paid, the answer is obvious from para. 1 (b) of the consent order: it was to compensate Mr. Clayton for the unfair dismissal. As it was paid, and paid by way of settlement of his claim, it is irrelevant that objection might have been taken to the agreement evidenced by the consent order or to the order itself.'[121]

In any event, it remains the case that, to be taxable as employment income, a payment or benefit received by an employee, whether from the employer or some other person, must derive *from* the employment and not from any other source.[122] **[8.20]**

114 Per Upjohn J, *Hochstrasser v Mayes* [1958] 1 All ER 369 at 375.
115 Per Lord Radcliffe, *Hochstrasser v Mayes* [1960] AC 376 at 392, and below, para **[8.21]**.
116 *Shilton v Wilmshurst* [1991] AC 684 at 689.
117 See, in particular, *Hamblett v Godfrey* [1987] 1 All ER 916, and below, para **[8.22]**; *EMI Group Electronics Ltd v Coldicott* [1999] STC 803, and below, para **[8.24]**.
118 [2005] STC 157 (CA).
119 [2005] STC 157 at 167.
120 ICTA 1988, s 131(1) provided that the term 'emoluments' included 'all salaries, fees, wages, perquisites and profits whatsoever'.
121 It was held that the payment, having been made in connection with the termination of the taxpayer's employment, fell within ICTA 1988, s 148, and was free of tax because it did not exceed £30,000. For a discussion of the successor to this provision, see below, para **[8.36]**.
122 Similar language was used under the former legislation in ICTA 1988, s 19(1), which charged tax 'in respect of any office or employment *on emoluments therefrom*' (emphasis added). See *Hamblett v Godfrey* [1986] STC 213, where a civil servant was paid £1,000 in recognition of the loss of her previously enjoyed right to join a trade union. In deciding that the payment was an emolument, Knox J stated (at 226) '... the words in (what became ICTA 1988, s 19(1)) "emoluments therefrom" and in particular the preposition "from", in my judgment indicate that the employment must be the source of the emolument, but that too is quite capable of casting a wider net than mere remuneration.' The decision was confirmed by the Court of Appeal, [1987] 1 All ER 916, and see below, para **[8.22]**. See also *Pritchard v Arundale* [1972] 1 Ch 229.

Hochstrasser v Mayes [1960] AC 376 (HL)[123]

The employer operated a scheme to assist employees to purchase a house. If an employee was transferred within the company, he had the option to sell his house to the company at a fair valuation and, in addition, the company guaranteed him against any capital loss on the sale provided the house had been kept in good repair. The taxpayer, M., bought a house in 1951 for £1,850. In 1954 he was transferred to another factory and was only able to sell the house for £1,500. The company paid him £350 under the guarantee. M. was assessed on this amount under Schedule E.[124]

VISCOUNT SIMONDS: . . . My Lords, if in such cases as these the issue turns, as I think it does, upon whether the fact of employment is the *causa causans*, or only the *sine qua non*,[125] of benefit, which perhaps is only to give the natural meaning to the word "therefrom" in the statute, it must often be difficult to draw the line and say on which side of it a particular case falls. But I think that the approach should not be exactly that of Parker L.J. It is for the Crown, seeking to tax the subject, to prove that the tax is exigible, not for the subject to prove that his case falls within exceptions which are not expressed in the statute but arbitrarily inferred from it. Thus, in the present case it is for the Crown to establish that a payment made under the housing agreement is a reward for the employee's services...

There is nothing express or implicit in the agreement which suggests that the payment is a reward for services except the single fact of the relationship of the parties, and it is clear enough from *Inland Revenue Commissioners v. Duke of Westminster*[126] that that fact alone will not justify such a conclusion. On the other hand, there is the significant fact that the salary earned by the employee compares favourably with salaries paid by other employers not operating a housing scheme, and is the same whether or not he takes advantage of the housing scheme. This at once suggests that there is some other reason for the payment than services rendered or to be rendered...

LORD RADCLIFFE: . . . The test to be applied is the same for all. It is contained in the statutory requirement that the payment, if it is to be the subject of assessment, must arise "from" the office or employment. In the past several explanations have been offered by judges of eminence as to the significance of the word "from" in this context. It has been said that the payment must have been made to the employee "as such." It has been said that it must have been made to him "in his capacity of employee." It has been said that it is assessable if paid "by the way of remuneration for his services," and said further that this is what is meant by payment to him "as such." These are all glosses, and they are all of value as illustrating the idea which is expressed by the words of the statute. But it is perhaps worth observing that they do not displace those words. For my part, I think that their meaning is adequately conveyed by saying that, while it is not sufficient to render a payment assessable that an employee would not have received it unless he has been an employee, it is assessable if it has been paid to him in return for acting as or being an employee. It is just because I do not think that the £350 which are in question here were paid to the respondent for acting as or being an employee that I regard them as not being profits from his employment.

The money was not paid to him as wages. The wages of employees are calculated independently of anything which they get under the housing scheme, and the I.C.I. salaries compare favourably with salaries paid by other employers in the chemical industry who do not operate a housing scheme. We are bound to say on the facts found for us that the source of the £350 was the housing agreement into which the respondent had entered on June 1, 1951, and that the circumstance that brought about his entitlement to the money

123 See Roger Kerridge, 'Emoluments and Causation – Hochstrasser Investigated' [1982] BTR 272.

124 See now ITEPA 2003.

125 Cf. Oliver LJ in *Wicks v. Firth* [1982] Ch. 355.

126 [1936] AC 1; see above, para **[5.3]**.

> was not any services given by him but his personal embarrassment in having sold his house for a smaller sum than he had given for it.
>
> ...The essential point is that what was paid to him was paid to him in respect of his personal situation as a house-owner, who had taken advantage of the housing scheme and had obtained a claim to indemnity accordingly. In my opinion, such payment is no more taxable as a profit from his employment than would be a payment out of a provident or distress fund set up by an employer for the benefit of employees whose personal circumstances might justify assistance...

If similar facts were to arise today, it must be asked whether ITEPA 2003, ss 401, 403 might apply to payments of this type.[127] It is also possible that even though a payment might not be *earnings from an employment*, it might yet be held taxable under the category of 'residual' charge to tax on benefits in kind.[128] This was a view expressed by Lord Denning in *Laidler v Perry*.[129] Note that where an employer offers a guaranteed selling price scheme,[130] any incidental expenses incurred by the employer are exempt.[131] **[8.21]**

Hamblett v Godfrey [1987] 1 All ER 916 (CA)

The right to belong to a Trade Union and certain other rights under the employment protection legislation were withdrawn from civil servants working at GCHQ. A payment of £1,000 was made to those employees, including the taxpayer, who wished to continue to be employed at GCHQ, in recognition of the withdrawal of those rights. The taxpayer appealed against an assessment under Schedule E[132] made on the sum, contending that it was neither an emolument,[133] nor chargeable under what is now ITEPA 2003, s. 201,[134] but a solatium. The Court of Appeal held that the payment was earnings within what is now ITEPA 2003, ss 9(2),62, and consequently there was no need for the Court of Appeal to consider whether it fell within ITEPA 2003, s 201 (as had been done by the Special Commissioners).[135]

> PURCHAS LJ: ... So, in my judgement, the approach that the court should take, and, indeed, that Knox J. did in fact take, is to consider the status of the payment and the context in which it was made. The payment was made to recognise the loss of rights. I am now going to paraphrase, I hope accurately, from the findings of the Special Commissioners and the employers' letter and other records.
>
> The rights, the loss of which was being recognised, were rights under the employment protection legislation, and the right to join a union or other trade protection association. Both those rights, in my judgement, are directly connected with the fact of the taxpayer's employment. If the employment did not exist, there would be no need for the rights in the particular context in which the taxpayer found herself. So, I start from the position that

127 In addition to termination payments, s 401(1) provides that the payment must be in connection with a change in either the duties of a person's employment or the earnings from a person's employment. See para **[8.41]**, below.
128 ITEPA 2003, Part 3 Chapter 10, and see below, para **[8.56]**.
129 [1965] Ch 192, and see below, para **[8.27]**. The view was expressed *obiter* since the Court of Appeal upheld the decision of the Commissioners that the vouchers received by the employee at Christmas were in return for services rather than a gift. On the facts of this particular case, there is no longer any doubt, since vouchers are now taxable within the benefits code in ITEPA 2003, Part 3 Chapter 4.
130 Under such a scheme, the employer, or a relocation company, usually buys the employer's house from him at a guaranteed price.
131 ITEPA 2003, s 326.
132 See now ITEPA 2003.
133 Now referred to as 'earnings' in ITEPA 2003.
134 See below, para **[8.56]**.
135 See *Hamblett v Godfrey* [1986] STC 213 at 223 (Ch Div) on the priority in applying ICTA 1970, s 181 and FA 1976, s 61 (now ITEPA 2003, ss 6(1) and ICTA. 1988, ss 19(1) and 20(1).

those are rights directly connected with employment. Purely by way of contrast, to underline that approach, if for instance the employers had for some reason or other best known to themselves objected to some social or other activity which their employees or some of them enjoyed, such as joining a golf club or something of that sort (I think Lord Diplock mentioned payments in the hunting field), but whatever it is, activities not connected with the employment, then a payment by an employer to recognise the voluntary or, indeed, the compulsory withdrawal if the employer had sufficient influence with the committee of the golf club concerned, then that I can readily acknowledge would be a payment made to a person who was an employee but was not made in the circumstances which would satisfy the order of s.181; that is that the payment must arise "therefrom." I only mentioned that analogy to emphasise the point which I seek to make.

There is no doubt in this case that the employment protection legislation goes directly to the employment of the taxpayer with the employee. The right to join a union, in my judgement, also falls directly to be considered as in connection with that employment, because without the employment there is no purpose in joining the union except for esoteric or personal reasons which are not relevant in this case. But I can again see a situation in which persons involved in particularly sensitive areas of government service might be required to abandon their right of freedom of speech. In such a case, it would clearly have to be considered on the facts involved in the individual case to see whether the abandonment of that fundamental right was in fact connected and arose on the employment or not, and it would clearly differ from case to case.

I hope that I have said sufficient in this short judgement to confirm that, in my judgement, the judge was correct in holding that the Special Commissioners erred in law in the passages which I have cited at the beginning of this judgement. In my judgement, he was correct to intervene, and that having intervened, he did so correctly. This payment is rightly to be assessed under Sch.E and the provisions of s.181 of the 1970 Act.[136] **[8.22]**

Mairs v Haughey [1994] 1 AC 303 (HL); see below, para [8.39]

Payments were made to employees as compensation for giving up their contingent rights under a non-statutory redundancy scheme. Although the specific issue before the House of Lords was whether such payments were taxable as emoluments from the employment, their Lordships also considered whether the redundancy payments themselves would have been taxable.

LORD WOOLF: ... Redundancy, whether statutory or non-statutory, involves an employee finding himself without a job through circumstances over which he has no control. It is also a quality of redundancy that it does not give rise to a right to compensation unless the employee has been employed for a minimum period and that the right when it accrues increases, initially, with the period of employment and then subsequently reduces until eventually the employee loses any right of payment upon his reaching normal retirement age. These qualities were fully reflected in the enhanced redundancy payment scheme operated by H & W I. A redundancy payment has therefore a real element of compensating or relieving an employee for the consequences of his not being able to continue to earn a living in his former employment. The redundancy legislation reflects an appreciation that an employee who has remained in employment for the minimum time has a stake in his employment which justifies his receiving compensation if he loses that stake. It is distinct from the damages to which he would be entitled if his employment were terminated unlawfully. It is also unlike a deferred payment of wages in that the entitlement to a redundancy payment is never more than a contingent entitlement, which no doubt both the employer and employee normally hope will never accrue.

Having identified the nature of a redundancy payment it is now necessary to determine whether it falls within the description contained in limited statutory provisions which I

136 [Now ITEPA 2003, s 9(2).]

have already cited. Giving full effect to the wide statutory definition of emoluments in sec. 131(1) of the Act,[137] in the absence of authority I would have regarded a payment having the qualities which I have identified as not falling within the statutory definition of an emolument from employment. Instead of being an emolument from employment, it is a payment to compensate the employee for not being able to receive emoluments from his employment. However, this is an area in which there is an abundance of authority. It is not always easy to reconcile these authorities since as is to be expected they are frequently concerned with situations close to the borderline between payments which fall within and payments that fall without the statutory provision. It is possible to have almost an infinite variety of situations which, although they have common characteristics, as a matter of fact and degree fall one side of the border or the other. In each case ultimately it is a matter of applying the statutory language to the facts. However, general assistance is provided by the speeches in *Hochstrasser* v. *Mayes*[138] and *Shilton* v. *Wilmshurst*[139]. In the former case I find the passage in the speech of Lord Radcliffe at pp.391–392 of help where he said to the statutory language:

> "For my part, I think that their meaning is adequately conveyed by saying that, while it is not sufficient to render a payment assessable that an employee would not have received it unless he had been an employee, it is assessable if it has been paid to him in return for acting as or being an employee." **[8.23]**

EMI Group Electronics Ltd v Coldicott [1999] STC 803 (CA)

Exercising a right reserved to it under the contracts of employment of certain employees, the employer gave payment in lieu of notice on the termination by them of the employment. The Court of Appeal concluded that the payments were emoluments arising from the employment.

CHADWICK LJ: . . . The question, therefore, is whether a payment in lieu of notice made in pursuance of a contractual provision, agreed at the outset of the employment, which enables the employer to terminate the employment on making that payment is properly to be regarded as an emolument *from* that employment. In the absence of authority which compels a contrary conclusion, I would have no doubt that that question must be answered in the affirmative. It seems to me to fall squarely within the tests posed by Lord Radcliffe in *Hochstrasser v Mayes* [1960] AC 376, at pages 391-392 – "paid to him in return for acting as or being an employee" – and by Lord Templeman in *Shilton v Wilmshurst* [1991] 1 AC 684, at page 689 – "an emolument 'from being or becoming an employee'" – which Lord Woolf approved in *Mairs v Haughey* [1994] 1 AC 303, at pages 320-321.

The point can, I think, be illuminated by considering the related question "why is the employee entitled to six months' notice of the employer's intention to terminate his employment?". The answer must be " because that was the security, or continuity, of employment which the employee required as an inducement to enter into the contract of employment". The answer to the question "why is the employee entitled to a payment equal to his salary for the remainder of the six month period if his employment is terminated by less than six months' notice?" must be the same: "that was the security, or continuity, of salary which he required as an inducement to enter the employment". It is necessary to keep in mind that (save, perhaps, in exceptional circumstances) the real reason why an employee requires a period of notice is not because he wants to continue working while he finds alternative employment; it is because he wants to continue being paid while he finds alternative employment.

I turn, therefore, to consider whether there is authority which compels a contrary conclusion. In *Henry v Foster* (1932) 16 TC 605 the taxpayers, who had resigned from their office as directors of a limited company, received compensation, to which they were

137 [See now ITEPA 2003, s 62.]
138 [1960] AC 376; [see above, para **[8.21]**.]
139 [1991] 1 AC 684; [see above, para **[8.20]**.]

entitled under the provisions of article 109 in the articles of association, equivalent to the total remuneration which they had received in the previous five years. It was held, by the Court of Appeal, that the payments were emoluments from the office; and so taxable under Schedule E. Lord Justice Lawrence explained why he reached that conclusion, at page 632:

> "In my judgment, the determining factor in the present case is that the payment to the Respondent whatever the parties may have chosen to call it was a payment which the company had contracted to make to him as part of his remuneration for his services as a director. It is true that payment of this part of his remuneration was deferred until his death or retirement or cesser of office, and that in the articles it is called "compensation for loss of office". It is, however, a sum agreed to be paid in consideration of the Respondent accepting and serving in the office of director, and consequently is a sum paid by way of remuneration for his services as a director." **[8.24]**

It can be seen that *Hamblett v Godfrey*[140] casts some doubt on the principle that, to be taxable, a payment must be a reward for services, although in the Northern Ireland Court of Appeal in *Mairs v Haughey*,[141] Lord Hutton CJ construed the payment in *Hamblett* as being in return for the taxpayer continuing to be an employee. Of particular interest, and of concern to taxpayers, is the fact that the approach taken by the Court of Appeal in *EMI Group Electronics v Coldicott* suggests 'that the courts should be willing to assume that all contractual benefits act as an inducement and are taxable under ITEPA 2003, s. 9 (unless they are not earnings . . .).'[142] However, 'in his judgment in *Mairs v Haughey* (1993)[143] in the House of Lords, Lord Woolf thought otherwise'.[144] For a critique of some of the leading cases, see [1998] BTR 364.

Examples of payments that are problematic include:

(a) gifts;
(b) inducement payments; and
(c) payments made in relation to the termination or variation of employment, which is not made in consideration of past services or under the terms of a service agreement, but is, for example, gratuitous or paid as compensation or in respect of damages for wrongful termination of the contract of service.[145]

(1) Gifts

Whether or not the payment is made by the employer or a third party, the distinction to be made here is between, on the one hand, a reward for services and, on the other, an appreciation of the recipient's personal qualities. **[8.25]**

140 [1987] 1 All ER 916; see above, para **[8.22]**. This approach was also adopted in *Wilcock v Eve* [1995] STC 18 and *EMI Group Electronics v Coldicott* [1999] STC 803.
141 [1992] STC 495. The decision on the facts of the case was upheld by the House of Lords, [1994] 1 AC 303, and see paras **[8.23** and **8.39]**.
142 *Revenue Law: Principles and Practice* (24th edn, 2006) [8.42].
143 [1994] 1 AC 303; see paras **[8.23** and **8.39]**.
144 Ibid.
145 Certain payments made on retirement or removal from office or employment are not strictly 'earnings', but may nevertheless 'count' as employment income, and be taxable as such, by virtue of ITEPA 2003, ss 401, 403. Note that ss 405–414 provide for exceptions to the charge. For termination payments generally, see below, para **[8.36]**.

Moore v Griffiths [1972] 1 WLR 1024 (Ch D)

The late Bobby Moore captained the English football team which won the World Cup in 1966. As a result of this, Moore received a bonus of £1,000 from the Football Association, and 'best player' prizes of £500 and £250 from the manufacturers of certain bath products. The Crown contended that these payments were assessable to income tax.

BRIGHTMAN J:. . . The problem before me, therefore, is to decide whether the payments in question were "emoluments therefrom"; that is to say, emoluments from the employment of Mr. Moore. . . .

Moorhouse v. *Dooland*[146] was the case of a cricketer. I read from the headnote:

"The Respondent was employed as professional to a cricket club. The terms of his employment were governed by a written agreement which provided, *inter alia*, that 'collections shall be made for any meritorious performance by the Professional with bat or ball. . .in accordance with the Rules for the time being of the Lancashire Cricket League.' One of these rules directed that a collection was to be taken from spectators for any player scoring 50 runs or more in any one innings and in certain other circumstances. Allowing an appeal against an assessment to Income Tax under Schedule E for the year 1951-52 in an amount which included sums from collections for meritorious performances, the General Commissioners held that the collections were given as testimonials to the Respondent's abilities and were not profits arising from his employment. The Crown demanded a Case. *Held*, that the collections were part of the earnings of the Respondent's employment and not mere personal presents distinct from his earnings."

Jenkins L.J.[147] reviewed the earlier authorities and then said this:

"From these citations I deduce the following principles:-(i) The test of liability to tax on a voluntary payment made to the holder of an office or employment is whether, from the standpoint of the person who receives it, it accrues to him by virtue of his office or employment, or in other words, by way of remuneration for his services. (ii) If the recipient's contract of employment entitles him to receive the voluntary payment, whatever it may amount to, that is a ground, and I should say a strong ground, for holding that from the standpoint of the recipient it does accrue to him by virtue of his employment, or in other words by way of remuneration for his services. (iii) The fact that the voluntary payment is of a periodic or recurrent character affords a further, but I should say a less cogent, ground for the same conclusion. (iv) On the other hand, a voluntary payment may be made in circumstances which show that it is given by way of a present or testimonial on grounds personal to the recipient, as for example a collection made for a particular individual who is at the time a vicar of a given parish because he is in straitened circumstances, or a benefit held for a professional cricketer in recognition of his long and successful career in first-class cricket. In such cases the proper conclusion is likely to be that the voluntary payment is not a profit accruing to the recipient by virtue of his office or employment but a gift to him as an individual paid and received by reason of his personal needs in the former example and by reason of his personal qualities or attainments in the latter example."

From early days a distinction has been drawn between a payment which is a reward for services, and is therefore taxable under Schedule E, and a payment which is a testimonial, and is not so taxable.

. . . in *Mudd* v. *Collins*[148] Rowlatt J. said this[149]:

"I ventured to throw out during the argument that there was a distinction between a testimonial and a remuneration for services of this kind. When a man is given a

146 (1954) 36 TC 1.
147 (1954) 36 TC 1 at 12.
148 (1925) 9 TC 297.
149 (1925) 9 TC 297 at 300.

testimonial because of his work in the past, not directly remunerating him for that work, but recognising how high a regard has been held for him in the association of people with him arising out of the performance of those services, and people recognise the good qualities he has and how zealous and kind he has been and how eager to advance the interests of his employers or his parishioners or his constituents, or whatever they may be, and they say 'We would like to give you something as a mark of our esteem and regard,' that is a testimonial."

Perhaps the most striking case which applied the testimonial principle was *Reed* v. *Seymour.*[150] The taxpayer was a professional cricketer who for many years had been under contract to the Kent County Cricket Club. The staff regulations of the club empowered the committee to grant a professional player a benefit match. A benefit match was held for the taxpayer, and gate money and subscriptions were received. They were held not to be taxable. Viscount Cave L.C. said this[151]:

"... I do not doubt that in the present case the net proceeds of the benefit match should be regarded as a personal gift and not as income from the Appellant's employment. The terms of his employment did not entitle him to a benefit, though they provided that if a benefit were granted the Committee of the Club should have a voice in the application of the proceeds. A benefit is not usually given early in a cricketer's career, but rather towards its close, and in order to provide an endowment for him on retirement; and, except in a very special case, it is not granted more than once. Its purpose is not to encourage the cricketer to further exertions, but to express the gratitude of his employers and of the cricket-loving public for what he has already done and their appreciation of his personal qualities. It is usually associated, as in this case, with a public subscription; and, just as those subscriptions, which are the spontaneous gift of members of the public, are plainly not income or taxable as such, so the gate moneys taken at the benefit match, which may be regarded as the contribution of the Club to the subscription list, are (I think) in the same category. If the benefit had taken place after Seymour's retirement, no one would have sought to tax the proceeds as income; and the circumstance that it was given before, but in contemplation of, retirement does not alter its quality. The whole sum – gate money and subscriptions alike – is a testimonial and not a perquisite. In the end, that is to say, when all the facts have been considered, it is not remuneration for services, but a personal gift."

Before leaving these authorities I think it may be useful to read a passage spoken by Sir Raymond Evershed M.R. in the *Dooland* case,[152] which marks the distinction between a gift to an employee as a reward for services and a gift to an employee to mark an occasion. The Master of the Rolls said, referring first to a passage spoken by Lord Cave in the *Seymour* case[153]:

"And Lord Cave L.C., in the same case, immediately before his reference to Rowlatt J., already quoted,[154] had said that taxable payments under Schedule E 'include all payments made to the holder of an office or employment as such – that is to say, by way of remuneration for his services, even though such payments may be voluntary – but ... they do not include a mere gift or present (such as a testimonial) which is made to him on personal grounds and not by way of payment for his services.' It follows, in my view, that a gift or present made either upon some special occasion as a wedding, a century at cricket, a birthday or at a season of the year when it is customary to make presents, does not necessarily cease to be non-taxable merely because the ties that link the recipient and the giver are or are substantially those of service and are not or not exclusively those of blood or friendship; and this may still be so although the present is (for example, whenever another century is made or according to custom at Christmas) repeated."

150 (1927) 11 TC 625; [1927] AC 554 (*sub nom. Seymour* v. *Reed*).
151 (1927) 11 TC 625 at 646.
152 TC 1 at 18.
153 11 TC 625 at 646.
154 *Ibid.* at 630.

Lastly, I accept, with respect, the approach of Megarry J. in *Pritchard* v. *Arundale*.[155] The facts are unimportant for present purposes. I read from page 236[156]:

> "Either the emoluments are within the statutory word 'therefrom,' as explained by the cases, or they are not. At one stage in the argument, in commenting on *Bridges* v. *Hewitt*[157]...Mr. Heyworth Talbot said that the question there was whether the employees in the case got the shares as remuneration for services or as personal gifts. In the *Hochstrasser* case,[158] in the Court of Appeal, Parker L.J. had expressed himself in terms of any benefit in money or money's worth received by an employee during the course of his employment from his employer as being a taxable profit of his employment, with two exceptions, one of which was a gift to him in his personal capacity....In the House of Lords, Viscount Simonds deprecated this approach, saying that it was not for the subject to prove that his case fell within exceptions arbitrarily inferred from the Statute, but the Crown to prove that the tax was exigible....After a little discussion, I think that Mr. Heyworth Talbot accepted that the true issue was not the twofold question whether the benefit fell within the taxable category of remuneration for services (as it may briefly be described) or within the non-taxable category of personal gift, but a single question, namely, whether or not it fell within the taxable category of remuneration for services. 'Personal gift' is thus not a category which has to be defined or explained, but merely an example of a transaction which will not fall within the taxable category of remuneration for services. In other words, the question is not one of which of two strait-jackets the transaction best fits, but whether it comes within the statutory language, or else, failing to do so, falls into the undefined residuary class of cases not taught by the Statute."...

Before I express my conclusion as to the proper application of the law to the facts of this case, I wish to say one word on the status of Mr. Moore *vis-à-vis* the Association....Mr. Moore was for practical purposes in the employment of, or under the control or orders of, the Association in relation to the World Cup championship. On the other hand, that particular relationship of Mr. Moore to the Association, as it seems to me, terminated before Mr. Moore received or was aware of the possibility of receiving the £1,000 bonus. If, therefore, as I think, the payment made to Mr. Moore partook of the nature of a payment made by an employer to an employee, that particular employment had ceased before the payment was offered or made.

In my judgment, the taxpayer's submission is correct. I think it would be wrong to regard the payment to Mr. Moore as being something in the nature of a reward or remuneration for services. The true purpose of the payment was to mark his participation in an exceptional event, namely, the winning of the World Cup championship – exceptional because the Cup is open for competition only every four years and has never before been won by this country. In other words, the payment had the quality of a testimonial or accolade rather than the quality of remuneration for services rendered.

The following factors, taken as a whole, to my mind point to that conclusion. I do not seek to set out these factors in the order of their importance. (1) The payment had no foreseeable element of recurrence. Recurrence, or the possibility of recurrence, is not of course essential to tax liability in this type of case, but is a relevant factor and a not uncommon factor in the reported cases where the decision has favoured the Crown. (2) There was no expectation of reward. The employee was totally unaware of the prospect of the payment prior to the services which he performed. The terms of his contract with his club did not contemplate that gratuitous payments of that or any type would be made. (3) The payment was not made or even announced by the Association until after the World Cup had been won; that is to say, until after the Association had already dispensed with the services of Mr. Moore. (4) In the present case, I think it is relevant to take into account the nature of the donor in assessing the quality of its actions. The principal function of the Association is to promote the sport of football, and not to derive a benefit from the services of footballers. When, therefore, one finds the Association displaying

155 [1972] Ch 229; 47 TC 680.
156 47 TC 680 at 686.
157 [1957] 1 WLR 674; 37 TC 289.
158 38 TC 673; [above, para **[8.21]**].

financial benevolence upon the occasion of a great event such as this country's World Cup victory, it seems to me more sensible and more consistent with the character and functions of the Association to construe its action as applause for that victory and as a mark of the Association's esteem rather than as a reward for services rendered by employees. (5) As the question is whether the Association was as a matter of fact rewarding the services of Mr. Moore, it must be at least relevant, though not decisive, to consider what the Association said when it made the payment. I have already read the Association's letter of August 1, 1966, and I do not propose to quote from it again. Its terms indicate to me that the payment was intended by the Association to mark its pride in a great achievement rather than to remunerate the meritorious execution of the employee's services. (6) It is I think material to observe that by agreement with the Association each member of the team, regardless of the number of times that he played or whether he was a player or a reserve, received precisely the same sum of £1,000. The sum therefore was not in any way linked with the quantum of any services rendered.

In my judgment, the circumstances in which this payment of £1,000 was made, considered as a whole, lead away from the conclusion that the payment made by the Association to Mr. Moore was of the nature of a reward for services rendered by him to the Football Association or to West Ham United or anyone else. I do not think that the facts support the contrary conclusion reached by the Commissioners.

So far as the payments by Nicholas Products Ltd. are concerned, I find some difficulty in appreciating the basis on which they are said to be taxable under Schedule E. Mr. Moore performed no services whatever for that company. The company was wholly disinterested, in any realistic sense, in the quality of the services performed by Mr. Moore or by any other player. It did not matter to the company how well or how ill the members of the team played. The prizes were plainly offered in order to publicise the company's products. I do not see how it can reasonably be suggested that the payments were in the nature of a reward for services rendered by Mr. Moore to the Association or to the club, or indeed to anyone else.

In the result, in my judgment the Commissioners were wrong in finding that the £1,000 received from the Association was taxable, but were correct in finding that the sums of £500 and £250 received from Nicholas Products Ltd. were not taxable. **[8.26]**

Laidler v Perry [1965] Ch 192 (CA); affirmed [1966] AC 16 (HL)

To engender good will at Christmas, the employer company gave each of its 2,300 employees a voucher worth £10 which could be exchanged at the shop of the employee's choice. Only employees who had worked for the company for a year or more received a full £10 voucher; new employees received a voucher for less, the amount depending on the length of their service. Before this scheme was introduced, employees had, during the Second World War, received National Savings Certificates and, before the War, turkeys.

LORD DENNING MR: ... The question arises whether each individual member of the staff is chargeable with tax under Schedule E in respect of his £10. We have two cases before us. Dr. Laidler, who is on the research side and who earns more than £2,000 a year; and Morgan, who earns less than £2,000 a year. The question in each case is whether this money's worth of £10 a year can properly be said to be emoluments from the employment. "Emoluments therefrom" are the words of section 156 of the Income Tax Act 1952.[159] Emoluments includes "all salaries, fees, wages, perquisites and profits whatsoever," see Schedule 2, 1(1) of the Finance Act 1956.[160]

...As I read the cases, however, including *Hochstrasser v. Mayes*[161], the one question is all these cases is this: Was the payment made, or the money's worth given, to the employee

159 [See now ITEPA 2003, s 9(2), which refers to 'earnings from employment'.]
160 [See now ITEPA 2003, s 62(2).]
161 [1960] AC 376; [see above, para **[8.21]**].

as a reward or remuneration or in return for his services? If it was, it is taxable in his hands. That test explains the case of the Easter offerings[162] (which are by custom a return for the services of the parson), and the cricketer's benefit[163] (where a collection would be made for his benefit if he had scored more than fifty runs), and the case of the huntsman's tips (where money was collected for the huntsman on Boxing Day), see *Wright* v. *Boyce*.[164]

In this case the commissioners made this finding: "The first question for decision is whether the appellant is assessable under Schedule E in respect of vouchers given to him annually at Christmas. As we understand the authorities the value of the vouchers is so assessable only if they represent 'money's worth' which was made available to the appellant in return for acting as or being an employee, *i.e.* as a reward for his services"–a test which they took from the very words of Lord Radcliffe's judgment in *Hochstrasser* v. *Mayes*. Having asked themselves that question, they said: "After reviewing all the evidence and the arguments based on the many authorities cited to us we hold that the vouchers were made available in return for services rather than as gifts not constituting a reward for services."

That finding of the commissioners can only be upset by this court if it is a finding to which they could not have reasonably come. So I ask myself the question whether this finding was unreasonable. I put this case in the course of argument: Suppose it had been £100 a year which had been given to all the staff of these companies each year at Christmas. In that case it would clearly be open to the commissioners to find that it was a reward, a remuneration or a return for services rendered. But now suppose that, instead of £100, it was a box of chocolates or a bottle of whisky or £2, it might be merely a gesture of goodwill at Christmas without regard to services at all. So it is a question of degree. It seems to me that in this case when one finds that £10 a year was paid to each of the staff year after year, each of them must have come to expect the £10 as a regular payment, which went with their services. It was, I think, open to the commissioners to find that it was made in return for services. It is, therefore, taxable in the hands of the recipient. That is sufficient to decide both cases.

I would only add in regard to Dr. Laidler (who was paid over £2,000), that if there was any doubt on this point it is clear to me that this gift would be a "benefit" within section 161 of the Income Tax Act 1952,[165] which would be chargeable in his hands under the terms of that section.

For these reasons I think the judgment of Pennycuick J. was right and I would dismiss the appeals. **[8.27]**

In *Ball v Johnson*,[166] the taxpayer's employer, a Bank, paid him a sum of £130 as a prize for passing the Institute of Bankers' examinations. This was held not to be assessable as earnings from an employment, in spite of the fact that the Bank required the employee to take the examinations. **[8.28]**

Calvert v Wainwright [1947] KB 526 (KBD)

ATKINSON J: . . . This case raises the comparatively simple point: Are tips which are received by taxi drivers in the ordinary way assessable to income tax? . . . In *Blakiston v. Cooper*,[167] which was the Easter offerings case, the principle was stated by the Lord

162 [*Blakiston v Cooper* [1909] AC 104.]
163 [*Moorhouse v Dooland* [1955] Ch 284.]
164 [1958] 1 WLR 832 (CA). [For an interesting discussion of this and other cases, see H H Munroe, 'Fees, Wages, Perquisites and Profits Whatsoever' [1959] BTR 25.]
165 [See now ITEPA 2003, Part 3 Chapters 2-11 and below, paras **[8.56]**.]
166 (1971) 47 TC 155.
167 [1909] AC 104. [The Easter offerings were given by the parishioners (and were not part of the stipend paid to the Vicar by his diocese). They were therefore a payment from persons other than his employer.]

> Chancellor in this way: "In my opinion, where a sum of money is given to an incumbent substantially in respect of his services as incumbent, it accrues to him by reason of his office. Here the sum of money was given in respect of those services. Had it been a gift of an exceptional amount, such as a testimonial, or a contribution for a specific purpose, as to provide for a holiday, or a subscription peculiarly due to the personal qualities of the particular clergyman, it might not have been a voluntary payment for services, but a mere present." To my mind, that puts the principle very clearly. The distinction would apply to a taxi driver in this way, to give an illustration. Suppose somebody who has the same taxi every day, which comes in the morning as a matter of course, to take him to his work, and then takes him home at night. The ordinary tip given in those circumstances would be something which would be assessable, but supposing at Christmas, or, when the man is going for holiday, the hirer says "You have been very attentive to me, here is a £10 note," he would be making a present, and I should say it would not be assessable because it has been given to the man because of his qualities, his faithfulness, and the way he has stuck to the passenger. In those circumstances, it would, in my opinion, be a payment of an exceptional kind. But a tip given in the ordinary way as remuneration for services rendered is well within the principles defined in that case ... **[8.29]**

In *Channel 5 TV Group Ltd v Morehead,*[168] a case concerning the question of whether certain payments were 'gratuities' and therefore free of NICs, the Special Commissioners concluded that 'a gratuity means a voluntary payment given in return for services rendered where the amount of the payment depends on the donor and where there is no obligation on the part of the donor to make the payment. That meaning of the word gratuity includes, but is not restricted to, a tip.'

See also *Archbishop of Thyateira v Hubert,*[169] where voluntary contributions from churches in Britain and abroad and from the Greek Government to the Metropolitan of the Orthodox Church, resident in England, were held to be assessable under the then Schedule E, and *Herbert v McQuade,*[170] where Stirling LJ said that 'a profit accrues by reason of an office when it comes to the holder of an office as such – in that capacity – and without the fulfilment of any further condition on his part'.[171] Other examples can be found in *Moorhouse v Dooland,*[172] discussed by Brightman J in *Moore v Griffiths*[173] and *Seymour v Reed,*[174] (referred to by Brightman J in *Moore v Griffiths,* sub nom *Reed v Seymour),* where the gifts were made by persons other than the cricketer's employer, but where he had a contractual right to have the collections made; cf *Jarrold v Boustead,*[175] discussed in *Glantre Engineering Ltd v Goodhand.*[176]

Note also the provisions of ITEPA 2003, Pt 4, which exempt from charge, inter alia, gifts not exceeding £250 to employees from third parties.[177] **[8.30]**

(2) Inducement payments

It is important to distinguish between a payment made in respect of being or becoming an employee, even if they are made by a third party (as in *Shilton v*

168 [2003] UKSC SPC 00369.
169 (1942) 25 TC 249.
170 [1902] 2 KB 631.
171 *Ibid.*, 650.
172 [1955] Ch 284 .
173 Above, para **[8.26]**.
174 [1927] AC 554.
175 [1964] 1 WLR 1357.
176 [1983] 1 All ER 542, and below, para **[8.32]**.
177 ITEPA 2003, s 324.

Wilmhurst[178]), and a payment made to compensate the employee for having given up something he values in taking up the employment. By definition, the latter payment is not a reward for services. **[8.31]**

Glantre Engineering v Goodhand [1983] 1 All ER 542 (Ch D)

The taxpayer company offered a lump sum payment of £10,000 to Wells, as an inducement to him to leave the firm for which he was then working and take up employment with the taxpayer company. Wells accepted this offer, and was paid the £10,000 on taking up employment with the company.

> WARNER J:...The emoluments, in order to be chargeable, have to fall under one or more of the Cases of Sch. E, but it is not in dispute here that the sum of £10,000, if it constituted emoluments from Mr. Wells's office or employment with the company, fell under Case 1. The definition of "emoluments" in s.183(1)[179] is:
>
> > "... the expression 'emoluments' shall include all salaries, fees, wages, perquisites and profits whatsoever."
>
> Thus the question in this case is not, strictly speaking, whether the sum of £10,000 was paid to Mr. Wells as a reward for services to be rendered by him to the company but whether that sum constituted an emolument, in the wide sense indicated by s.183(1), from his full-time employment by the company.
>
> The weft of counsel's argument was derived from the three authorities that I referred to earlier, namely *Hose v. Warwick*,[180] *Jarrold v. Boustead*[181] and *Pritchard v. Arundale*.[182] Counsel submitted that those authorities established that, where at the inception of a person's employment a payment was made to him to compensate him for an identifiable loss that he would incur as a result of taking up the employment, that payment was not an emolument from the employment. Counsel for the company went so far as to say that that proposition would apply if a lump sum were paid to the person in question in order to induce him to move his residence from an attractive area to a less attractive one so as to enable him to take up the employment, though the proposition would not apply if the inducement to him to do that took the form of a larger salary. In my judgement, the authorities do not support so general a proposition...
>
> *Jarrold v. Boustead* is, I think, best understood if one contrasts the judgment of Pennycuick J. at first instance with the judgments in the Court of Appeal, particularly that of Lord Denning M.R. Pennycuick J. held that it was not permissible, in ascertaining the consideration for which the signing-on fee of £3,000 that was in question there had been paid, to look outside the terms of the agreement under which it was paid. On that footing there was no escape from the conclusion that the consideration for the signing-on fee was the obligation undertaken by Mr. Boustead to play Rugby football for the Hull Football Club. The Court of Appeal, however, held that, to ascertain the nature of the signing-on fee, it was necessary to look also at the byelaws of the Rugby League. When that was done, it became clear that the signing-on fee was compensation to Mr. Boustead for relinquishing for ever his amateur status and the advantages that flowed from that. Byelaw 24 of the Rugby League provided:
>
> > "A player who relinquishes his amateur status is permitted to receive a signing-on fee from the club which he first registers as a professional player. No club shall pay, or offer to pay a signing-on fee to a player who has previously been registered as a professional player with the League."
>
> Thus it was open to the commissioners who heard that case to hold, as they did hold, that the £3,000 was not an emolument of Mr. Boustead from his employment by the Hull

178 [1991] AC 684, and see below, para **[8.34]**.
179 [See now ITEPA 2003, s 62.]
180 (1946) 27 TC 459.
181 [1964] 1 WLR 1357 (Court of Appeal).
182 [1972] Ch 229.

Football Club. It was a once-for-all inducement to him to give up a status that precluded him from being employed by any club in the league.[183]

In his judgement, Lord Denning M.R. mentioned a hypothetical case that had been discussed during the argument. He said[184]

> "Suppose there was a man who was an expert organist but was very fond of playing golf on Sundays. He is asked to become the organist of the parish church for the ensuing seven months at a salary of £10 a month. It is expressly stipulated by this strange parish council that, if he takes up the post, he is to give up Sunday golf for the rest of his life. Thereupon he says that, if he is to give up golf, he wants an extra £500; and they agree to pay it. In such a case the £500 is not a payment for his services as an organist for seven months. It is a payment for relinquishing what he considered to be an advantage to him."

That is why, of course, counsel for the company placed so much emphasis on the fact that, in the present case, Mr. Wells was giving up irrevocably, or so at all events he thought, the status of a chartered accountant in private practice. But, as I have already indicated, the Special Commissioners appear to have taken the view that that was a less important factor than the loss of security that Mr. Wells would suffer as a result of leaving the employment of Whinney Murray Ernst & Ernst.

So I come to *Pritchard v. Arundale*,[185] with which counsel for the company submitted that the present case was "on all fours." That, certainly, is not so. In the first place, as I have already mentioned, *Pritchard v. Arundale* was a case not of a payment by the employer but of a transfer of shares by a third party. Second, Mr. Arundale was not merely changing from one employment to another. He was exchanging the status of a partner, indeed a senior partner, in a firm of chartered accountants for that of joint managing director of, and shareholder in, a company. Third, as Megarry J. pointed out, the tripartite agreement under which Mr. Arundale entered the service of the company and received the shares was so framed that he was entitled to the transfer of the shares 'forthwith' after the execution of the agreement but was not to enter into the service of the company until some months later. He might therefore have died after receiving the shares but before entering on his office or employment with the company. That explains, I think, a passage towards the end of judgment of Megarry J., by which I was at one time troubled, in which he drew a distinction between a payment made for undertaking an office or employment and a payment flowing from the office or employment, the latter being within Sch. E but the former not.

Indeed, perceiving that feature of *Pritchard v. Arundale*, counsel for the company boldly submitted that in the present case Mr. Wells would have been entitled, under the agreement between him and the taxpayer company, to receive the £10,000 even though he never entered the service of the company, provided that he left the employment of Whinney Murray Ernst & Ernst. That, it seems to me, cannot be right. If Mr. Wells had left the employment of Whinney Murray Ernst & Ernst, taken the £10,000 and then gone to work, say, for another firm of chartered accountants, I do not doubt that any court before which subsequent litigation between him and the company came would have held him to be in breach of the agreement.

It seems to me that the ratio decidendi of *Jarrold v. Boustead* and of *Pritchard v. Arundale* is that the quality of a payment made to an employee at the inception of his employment, that is to say whether or not it constitutes an emolument from his employment, is essentially a question of fact to be decided by the appellate commissioners on a consideration of all the evidence before them, and that, on the familiar principles laid down in *Edwards (Inspector of Taxes) v. Bairstow*,[186] their determination is not to be set aside by the court unless it is inconsistent with the only reasonable conclusion to be drawn from that evidence. I cannot hold that, in the present case, the only reasonable conclusion to be drawn from the evidence before the Special Commissioners was, as contended by counsel for the company, that the payment of £10,000 to Mr. Wells was severable from the

183 [Cf. *Shilton v Wilmshurst*, below, para **[8.34]**.]
184 [1964] 3 All ER 76 at 80; [1964] 1 WLR 1357 at 1365.
185 [1972] Ch 229.
186 [1956] AC 14; [1955] 3 All ER 48; [above, para **[3.15]**].

> other benefits to which he became entitled under the agreement between himself and the company, and was other than an added inducement to him to change his job and enter the full-time employment of the company. If it was the latter, it was, so it seems to me, an emolument from that employment within the meaning of Sch. E. **[8.32]**

The case of *Jarrold v Boustead*[187] should be compared with *Riley v Coglan*[188] where, in slightly different circumstances, a Rugby League signing-on fee was held to be taxable earnings. In that case, part of the £500 fee was repayable if the player failed to serve the stipulated period. In the opinion of Ungoed-Thomas J 'the £500 was to be a running payment for his making himself available to serve the club when required to do so'. **[8.33]**

Shilton v Wilmshurst [1991] AC 684 (HL)

Peter Shilton, sometime England goalkeeper, was transferred to Southampton Football Club one year before his contract with Nottingham Forest was due to expire. In a tripartite agreement between Shilton, Nottingham Forest and Southampton, Nottingham Forest paid Shilton a lump sum of £75,000 on his agreement to join Southampton, who paid a transfer fee of £325,000 to Nottingham Forest and a lump sum of £80,000[189] to Shilton. At issue was the sum of £75,000 paid by Nottingham Forest, upon which Shilton was assessed to tax as an emolument of his employment with Southampton. The House of Lords upheld this assessment.

> LORD TEMPLEMAN: . . . In the instant case Mr Thornhill, who appeared on behalf of Mr Shilton, argued in the first place that for the purposes of sec. 181 [*ICTA 1970*], an emolument must be "for" employment and not merely "from" that employment. If the argument were correct, no emolument provided by a third party would be taxable under sec. 181. The argument substitutes the words "emolument from the employer" for the words "emolument from the employment." The courts below shrank from this conclusion and accepted that an emolument provided by a third party in the employ of another could be an emolument from the employment in some circumstances. The courts below said that the third party must have an interest in the performance of the contract. . .
>
> There is nothing in sec. 181 or the authorities to justify the inference that an "emolument from employment" only applies to an emolument provided by a person who has an interest in the performance by the employee of the services which he becomes bound to perform when he enters into the contract of employment.
>
> If sec. 181 applies only to an emolument provided by an employer or by a third party who has an interest in the performance by the employee of this contract of service with the employer, there are difficulties in defining the "interest" which makes the employee liable to pay tax on the emoluments under sec. 181. Mr Thornhill suggested that if the £75,000 had been paid by a shareholder in Southampton Football Club Ltd interested in the dividends and capital value of his shares or if the £75,000 had been paid by a sponsor of the Southampton football team interested in obtaining valuable publicity or if the £75,000 had been a philanthropic millionaire supporter of Southampton sentimentally interested in the fortunes of the club, then the £75,000 would or might have been an emolument from the employment of Mr Shilton by Southampton. But, he said, as the £75,000 was provided by Nottingham Forest, who were only interested in the £325,000 payable if Mr Shilton agreed to play football for Southampton, sec. 181 does not apply. I prefer the simpler view that an emolument arises from employment if it is provided as a

187 Discussed in *Glantre Engineering Ltd v Goodhand* [1983] 1 All ER 542, and see above, para **[8.32]**.

188 [1967] 1 WLR 1300.

189 There was no dispute over this amount. The sum represented a clear inducement from Shilton's future employer and, as such, represented a reward for the future services Shilton would give Southampton.

reward or inducement for the employee to remain or become an employee and not for something else.

I can find nothing in the 1970 Act which suggests the gloss which the courts below have put on the statute. In the present case both Southampton and Nottingham Forest were interested in Mr Shilton becoming an employee of Southampton. Both Southampton and Nottingham Forest provided emoluments to induce Mr Shilton to become an employee of Southampton. So far as Mr Shilton, the taxpayer, is concerned, both the emoluments of £80,000 from Southampton and £75,000 from Nottingham Forest were paid to him for the same purpose and had the same effect, namely as an inducement to him to agree to become an employee of Southampton. The actual performance of the terms of his contract of employment did not depend on either or both the emoluments. Mr Shilton kept goal for Southampton because he had contracted to do so, not because he had received emoluments. Mr Shilton made miraculous saves for Southampton because he was an hourourable man and a professional footballer and was contractually bound to do his best for Southampton. Emoluments amounting to £155,000 may be expected to inspire a goal-keeper to great achievements but that inspiration came as much from the £75,000 provided by Nottingham Forest as it came from the £80,000 provided by Southampton. Indirectly, the whole of the £155,000 can be said to have been provided by Southampton. On the transfer of Mr Shilton there will be shown in the accounts of Nottingham Forest the receipt of the net sum of £250,000 from the transfer. Nottingham Forest received £325,000 from Southampton and were enabled to pay £75,000 to Mr Shilton leaving them with £250,000. **[8.34]**

Any payment made by an employer to an employee in consideration for the employee giving a restrictive undertaking in connection with his current, future or past employment is taxable under ITEPA 2003, ss 225, 226. The legislation, first introduced in 1988, was designed to defeat schemes that proliferated following the case of *Beak v Robson*,[190] which held that a sum paid by a company to an employee in return for a covenant not to compete with the employer for a certain period, was not earnings from the employment but, rather, a separate consideration which was to pass after the termination of the employment. For a discussion of whether a payment is in fulfilment of any undertaking within the section,[191] see *Vaughan-Neil v IRC*.[192] **[8.35]**

(3) Payments made on or after the termination or variation of employment

(a) Payments made on or after termination of employment

Payments made after the termination of employment will be taxable either (i) as earnings within ITEPA 2003, s 62, under s 394 (which provide for assessment in full of any relevant benefit[193] received under a non-approved retirement benefit scheme) or ss. 580, 581 (which provide for taxation in full

190 [1943] AC 352.

191 The former terminology referred to 'an undertaking' in connection with an office or employment, 'the tenor or effect of which is to restrict [*the office holder or employee*] as to his conduct or activities'.

192 [1979] STC 644.

193 ITEPA 2003, s 393B (inserted by FA 2004, s 249, with effect from 6 April, 2006) defines relevant benefits as 'any lump sum, gratuity or other benefit (including a non-cash benefit)' provided, inter alia, 'on or in anticipation of the retirement of an employee or former employee' and 'after the retirement or death of an employee or former employee in connection with past service'.

of any pension received from an approved retirement benefit scheme); or (ii) as 'specific employment income' under ITEPA 2003, s 403. In this context, specific employment income are amounts that are not caught by any other income tax provision and which are treated as earnings. The main difficulty is in determining whether a certain payment is within ITEPA 2003, s 62.

Generally, a payment made after the termination of employment is not taxable within s 62 because it is not earnings from that employment. However, it would appear that if the payment is made under the terms of the contract of employment, for example, where an employee receives payment after working out a period of notice, it will be taxable in full.[194] Similarly, a payment made by an employer in exercise of a contractual term providing for payment in lieu of notice will also be taxable.[195] However, and despite the view to the contrary taken by the Revenue,[196] a payment made by the employer as compensation for the wrongful termination of the contract of employment does not appear to fall within s 62, since it amounts to damages for breach of contract and would thus escape tax.[197] Less clear is where a non-contractual payment is made in consideration of past services; it may be taxed in full,[198] but Lord Templeman's view that, to be taxable, it would also have to act as an inducement to continue to perform services,[199] suggests that, when the payment is made after termination, it will, by definition, escape tax under s 62.[200] Finally, a non-statutory redundancy payment, and compensation for the loss of the right to such a payment, is not taxable.[201]

Where payments received on retirement or removal from office or employment are not otherwise chargeable to income tax, they are charged under ITEPA 2003, s 403[202] if, and to the extent that, they exceed £30,000. Such payments include statutory redundancy payments,[203] payments under non-statutory redundancy schemes[204] provided that they are made on a genuine redundancy and *ex gratia* payments.[205] **[8.36]**

Williams v Simmonds [1981] STC 715 (Ch D)

The taxpayer, Simmonds, a joint managing director of the employer company, negotiated a service agreement for himself, under clause 12 of which he was entitled to compensation for loss of office on the happening of any of certain specified events. However, if any of these events occurred, the taxpayer was entitled by the

194 See *Dale v. De Soissons* (1950) 32 TC 118 and *Williams v Simmonds* [1981] STC 715, and para **[8.37]**, below.
195 *EMI Group Electronics v Coldicott* [1999] STC 803.
196 See *Employment Income Manual*, paras 12976–12979, Her Majesty's Revenue and Customs.
197 *Henley v Murray* [1950] 1 All ER 908.
198 *Per* Upjohn J, *Hochstrasser v Mayes* [1958] 1 All ER 369. Payments made to former employees on the winding up of an employer trust were held by the House of Lords to be taxable in *Bray v Best* [1989] 1 All ER 969.
199 *Shilton v Wilmhurst* [1991] 1 AC 684.
200 Also see *Cowan v Seymour* [1920] 1 KB 500.
201 *Mairs v Haughey* [1994] 1 AC 303; see above, para **[8.23]**.
202 For exceptions to the charge, see ITEPA 2003, ss. 405-414.
203 ITEPA 2003, s 309(3).
204 *Mairs v Haughey* [1994] 1 AC 303.
205 Note, however, SP13/91, which could subject lump sum payments on a termination of office or employment to the same rules as those governing payments under retirement benefits schemes. This would mean that payments from an unapproved *ex gratia* scheme could be taxable in full under ITEPA 2003, s 394, without the benefit of the £30,000 threshold, whereas lump sum payments, by way of commutation, from an approved *ex gratia* scheme would be entirely tax free.

agreement to serve notice on the company electing not to treat his office as terminated. One of the events specified did occur, but the taxpayer did not so elect; his office was terminated, and the company paid him the sum stipulated in his service agreement.

VINELOTT J: . . . The dispute arises because, if chargeable under s.181,[206] the whole sum paid to the taxpayer attracted tax as part of his emoluments in 1976-77, whereas if it was chargeable under s.187,[207] the first £5,000 escaped tax and the taxpayer was entitled to spread the balance over a period of years for the purpose of ascertaining the rate of tax payable.[208]

Section 187,[209] and its related sections, and schedules reproduces elaborate provisions first embodied in the Finance Act 1960, the purpose of which was to bring into charge to tax, amongst other payments a payment made at the end of an employment which escaped a charge to tax as an emolument of the employment. The distinction between payments made at the end of an employment, which before 1960 attracted tax as emoluments and those which escaped tax altogether, is explained by Lord Wilberforce in a short passage in *Comptroller General of Inland Revenue v. Knight*,[210] which reads as follows:

> "Questions as to the taxability of payments received by employed persons at the end of their employment have frequently come before the courts; they have often been described as difficult, borderline and depending on narrow distinctions. Two propositions are accepted as common ground in the present case. First, where a sum of money is paid under a contract of employment, it is taxable, even though it is received at or after the termination of the employment: see for example *Henry v. Foster*.[211] Secondly, where a sum of money is paid as consideration for the abrogation of a contract of employment, or as damages for the breach of it, that sum is not taxable: see for example *Henley v. Murray*."[212]

The first of those two categories extends to a sum payable under a contract, even though it is and is expressed as compensation for loss of future earnings under the contract. The reason is explained by Lawrence L.J. in *Henry v. Foster*. In that case the articles of the company provided that a director who had held office for a term of not less than five years on ceasing to hold office for any cause, other than misconduct, bankruptcy, lunacy or incompetence, should be entitled, by way of compensation for loss of office, to a sum equal to the total remuneration he had received in the preceding five years. He said[213]:

> "In my judgment, the determining factor in the present case is that the payment to the Respondent whatever the parties may have chosen to call it was a payment which the company had contracted to make to him as part of his remuneration for his services as a director. It is true that payment of this part of his remuneration was deferred until his death or retirement or cessor of office, and that in the articles it is called 'compensation for loss of office.' It is, however, a sum agreed to be paid in consideration of the Respondent accepting and serving in the office of director, and consequently is a sum paid by way of remuneration for his services as director . . ."

Vinelott J. stated the facts, and then concluded:

It is, in my judgment, clear beyond question that the taxpayer accepted that, in the events which had happened, his employment had been terminated and he elected to accept compensation under the terms of his service agreement instead of serving notice under cl. 12(c). The result is unfortunate, in that, if the taxpayer had served notice under cl. 12(c) and, like the director in *Henley v. Murray*, had subsequently bowed to the pressure which was being exerted on him and had resigned his employment and

206 [See now ITEPA 2003, s 9(1).]
207 [See now ITEPA 2003, s 403. Under this provision, the first £30,000 escapes tax.]
208 [This provision was replaced by ICTA 1988, s 188(4), which was repealed by FA 1998, s 165.]
209 [ICTA 1970.]
210 [1973] AC 428 at 433.
211 (1932) 16 TC 605.
212 [1950] 1 All ER 908; 31 TC 351.
213 (1932) 16 TC 605 at 632.

had then agreed to accept, as compensation for the abrogation of his rights under the service agreement, a sum equal to the compensation which would have been payable under cl. 12 if he had not served notice, the sum so payable might well not have attracted tax as an emolument, but only under s.187.[214] However, the legal effect of the course actually taken by the taxpayer is, in my judgement, clear and I have no alternative but to allow this appeal. **[8.37]**

For the taxation of damages awarded by a court to an employee as compensation for loss of office, see *British Transport Commission v Gourley*;[215] *Parsons v BNM Laboratories*;[216] *Bold v Brough Nicholson and Hall Ltd*;[217] *London and Thames Haven Oil Wharves Ltd v Attwool*;[218] *Lyndale Fashion Manufacturers v Rich*[219] and *Shove v Downs Surgical plc.*[220] See also Roger Kerridge 'Dismissing Employees – Golden Handshakes and the Gourley Confusion' [1982] BTR 87 and W Bishop and J Kay 'Taxation and Damages' (1987) 103 LQR 211. **[8.38]**

Mairs v Haughey (see above, para [8.23])

LORD WOOLF: ... When these two short citations[221] of the highest authority are examined it is significant that they treat as being outside the charge payments which are either from a distress fund or to relieve distress. As I indicated earlier a characteristic of a redundancy payment is that it is to compensate or relieve an employee for what can be the unfortunate consequences of becoming unemployed.

The other significant characteristic of a redundancy payment is that it is payable after the employment has come to an end. Prima facie a payment made after the termination of employment is not an emolument from that employment. It can be, however, an emolument from the employment if for example it is a lump sum payment in the nature of deferred remuneration. As Lord Hanworth MR indicated in *Henry v. Foster*,[222] in order to determine whether this is the situation it is necessary to look at the substance of the matter. If a payment relates to the services rendered then the fact that the payment is made after employment comes to an end does not mean that it is divorced from the employment. The distinction between the deferred payment of wages or salary and a redundancy payment may be narrow but it is nonetheless real. In the case of a deferred payment once the employment comes to an end the right to payment will inevitably accrue. In the case of a redundancy payment, the sum is only payable in limited circumstances and there will be no entitlement if for example the employee leaves the employment on his own accord. **[8.39]**

For a critical appraisal of this judgment see John Ward [1994] BTR 77. See also the extract from the judgment of Chadwick LJ in *EMI Group Electronics Ltd v Coldicott*; [223] see above, para **[8.24]**. **[8.40]**

214 [ICTA 1970. See now ITEPA 2003, s 403.]
215 [1956] AC 185.
216 [1964] 1 QB 95.
217 [1963] 3 All ER 849.
218 (1966) 43 TC 491.
219 [1973] 1 WLR 73.
220 [1984] 1 All ER 7.
221 [Reference is being made to extracts from the judgments of Lord Radcliffe in *Hochstrasser v Mayes* [1960] AC 376 at 392, and of Lord Templeman in *Shilton v Wilmshurst* [1991] 1 AC 684 at 689-690.]
222 (1930) 16 TC 605 at 629–630.
223 [1999] STC 803.

(b) Payments on the variation of a contract of employment

A payment made to an employee on the withdrawal of some benefit will be taxable if it amounts to compensation for breach of contract (where the employer has withdrawn a contractual right from the employee) and where it is viewed as a payment for the continued services of the employee. Thus, in *Cameron v Prendergast*,[224] by virtue of an agreement between an employer company, who wanted to retain the services of one of its directors, and the director concerned, the director received a lump sum payment in return for taking a reduction in his annual salary. The House of Lords rejected the taxpayer's argument that the only consideration for the payment was his agreement not to resign, and held that the sum represented 'profits' from his directorship and was, accordingly taxable under what was then Schedule E, Viscount Caldecote LC saying that he could see no difference between a promise not to resign and a promise to continue to serve as a director.[225] See also *Tilley v Wales*,[226] *Bird v Maitland*,[227] *McGregor v Randall* [228] and *Holland v Geoghogan*,[229] where refuse collectors, striking after having their "totting" rights terminated, were paid a lump sum. This was held to be a taxable inducement to return to work rather than compensation for the loss of their "totting" rights. See further, *Hamblett v Godfrey*.[230] A different conclusion was reached in the case of *Hunter v Dewhurst*.[231] In that case, a taxpayer director agreed with his employer company to forego the right to the payment of a lump sum when he died, resigned or otherwise ceased to hold his office for reasons other than his own bad conduct, and to take a reduced salary, in return for an immediate payment of £10,000. The House of Lords held that this sum did not represent remuneration under the taxpayer's contract of employment but, rather, was paid by the company to obtain its release from a contingent liability. It is difficult to justify this decision, and most of the later cases have merely distinguished it on its own particular facts.[232] Indeed, in *Cameron v Prendergast*,[233] Viscount Maugham called it a 'curious case' which turned on unusual circumstances.[234] However, in *Mairs v Haughey*,[235] Lord Woolf refused to express an opinion on the decision. **[8.41]**

224 [1940] AC 549.
225 *Ibid* at 554.
226 [1943] AC 386. In this case, although the taxpayer had received a lump sum of £40,000, the House of Lords divided the sum into two parts, one part representing payment for foregoing a pension payable by the employer under a previous agreement. This was held not to be taxable; it amounted to the capitalisation of a pension, and since the pension itself would not have amounted to earnings, neither could the capital sum. However, the other part amounted to compensation for an agreement by the taxpayer to take a reduced salary and, following *Cameron v Prendergast*, was taxable as earnings.
227 [1982] STC 603.
228 [1984] STC 223.
229 [1972] 3 All ER 333.
230 [1987] 1 All ER 916, and above, paras **[8.22]**.
231 (1932) 16 TC 605.
232 It was applied in *Tilley v Wales* [1943] AC 386 in respect of the capitalised pension, and in *Duff v Barlow* (1941) 23 TC 633.
233 [1940] AC 549.
234 *Ibid* at 559. In the same case, Viscount Caldecote LC referred to the facts as being 'very special' (at 555).
235 [1994] 1 AC 303.

B. *What constitutes earnings?*

It is very common for some employees to receive not only a stated 'wage' or 'salary' as part of their remuneration package, but also a benefit in a form other than cash and, perhaps, an expenses allowance. The growth in the use of benefits stemmed from the decision in *Tennant v Smith*,[236] where the House of Lords held that the value of the benefit for income tax purposes was its second-hand value. It followed logically from this that a benefit could be taxable only if it could be converted into cash, thus paving the way for large-scale tax avoidance. Because of this, rules developed over the years to prevent benefits from escaping tax altogether, and also from being inadequately taxed. When first introduced in 1948, the statutory rules applied only to those employees and office-holders earning in excess of a stated figure (along with certain directors), thus drawing a distinction between 'higher-paid employees'[237] and others. Although this distinction has been maintained to the present day, it has become rather an artificial one, since the benefits code applies to anyone with earnings in excess of £8,500[238] and certain directors. Moreover, since 1976, when the benefits legislation was reviewed and the rules were tightened,[239] it became the case that *all* employees, including directors, should be taxable in respect of certain benefits.[240] Prior to ITEPA 2003, those who did not fall within the statutory rules were taxable according to the common law which, as stated earlier, required the benefit to be convertible into cash. These rules now have statutory force.

Under ITEPA 2003, all employees and office-holders are taxed on benefits in kind if they are convertible to cash,[241] since they are part of their earnings. If they earn over £8,500 or fall within the definition of 'director',[242] they may be subject to further tax under the benefits code,[243] the benefits giving rise to an amount treated as earnings.[244] In that event, to the extent that the amount treated as earnings under the benefits code exceeds the convertible value of the benefit, the excess is treated as earnings under the benefits code.[245] Further, all employees will be taxable in respect of certain stated benefits in kind, namely, vouchers and credit tokens,[246] and living accommodation[247] (subject to certain exceptions).[248] **[8.42]**

236 [1892] AC 150.
237 The term actually used in the legislation until 1989. FA 1989, s 53(2)(a) substituted the term 'employees earning £8,500 or more'.
238 This figure has remained constant since 1979 (FA 1978, s 23).
239 See 1976 Budget statement by the then Chancellor of the Exchequer, Mr Denis Healey MP, Hansard HC Debates vol 909, col 262, 6 April 1976.
240 In particular, see the charge introduced by FA 1976, s 61(2), now, ITEPA 2003, s 97, under which *any* employee is chargeable where living accommodation is provided for him, his family or household.
241 ITEPA 2003, ss 9(2), 62(2),(3).
242 *Ibid*, ss 67, 68.
243 *Ibid*, Pt 3, Ch 11, which excludes from parts of the benefits code those who earn less than £8,500 and who are not directors for these purposes.
244 *Ibid*, s 7(2)(5).
245 *Ibid*, s 64.
246 *Ibid*, Pt 3, Ch 4.
247 *Ibid*, Pt 3, Ch 5.
248 *Ibid*, s 99.

(1) Benefits in kind – earnings

ITEPA 2003, s 9 taxes 'general earnings' from an employment, which are made up of earnings and amounts treated as earnings.[249] The term 'earnings' is defined to include 'any gratuity or other profit or incidental benefit of any kind obtained by the employee if it is money or money's worth',[250] and 'money's worth' means something that is 'of direct monetary value to the employee'[251] or is 'capable of being converted into money or something of direct monetary value to the employee'.[252] This provision reflects the old authorities on what amounted to an emolument and how convertible benefits should be valued. **[8.43]**

Final Report of The Royal Commission on the Taxation of Profits and Income Cmd 9474 (1955)

208. We have already noted that the law includes in its conception of income a benefit having money's worth even though it is only received in kind. We found it necessary to give our full attention to this subject, since a period of high taxation gives it an importance that it would not otherwise possess. If advantage can be taken of any weakness in the tax treatment of such benefits, there is an obvious temptation to resort to them as a means of part remuneration. And the harm that results is not merely the absolute loss of revenue: it is unfairness in the distribution of tax as between one taxpayer and another.[253]

209. A benefit in kind may be convertible or inconvertible. It is convertible if it is of such a nature that the recipient can turn it into money: for instance, employees of many factories which produce consumer goods are allowed a free or reduced rate issue of such goods; the coal miner was, traditionally, allowed a free issue of coal. A benefit is inconvertible if it is of such a nature that it can only be enjoyed by the recipient: for instance the domestic servant's board and lodging, an employee's free meals, a railwayman's free travel, a bank manager's living accommodation at the bank, a teacher's free education for his children. Subject to certain special legislation in 1948,[254] the inconvertible benefit is not treated as taxable income apparently because it is not regarded as being equivalent to money's worth.[255] At any rate there is no ready means of assigning to it a monetary equivalent; and, whatever administrative expedients might be adopted, the task of assessing the annual value of every such benefit and collecting tax upon it strikes us as a singularly formidable and laborious one. This is the fundamental difficulty in any treatment of the matter that seeks to be consistent. And the fact that non-convertible benefits are not taxed has led, not unnaturally, to a relaxation of the rule about convertible benefits. Where the volume of goods allowed to an employee by way of perquisite does not exceed

249 ITEPA 2003, s 9(3). For amounts treated as earnings, see paras **[8.56]**, below.
250 *Ibid*, s 62(2)(b).
251 *Ibid*, s 62(3)(a).
252 *Ibid*, s 62(3)(b).
253 [See Chapter 1.]
254 [Formerly contained in ICTA 1970, ss. 195-203 which were repealed by FA 1976 Sched 9 and Sched 15, with effect from the year 1977-78, and replaced by ICTA 1988, ss 135-146 and ss 153-168G. The present special statutory provisions concerning benefits in kind which are to be found in ITEPA 2003, Part 3, are discussed below, paras **[8.56–8.62]**.]
255 [The position has now been altered by various special statutory provisions; see generally below, for the taxation of benefits, some of which may be inconvertible, received by employees receiving employment income of £8,500 or more a year and 'directors' within the meaning of the special provisions.]

what is reasonable for his own consumption, no tax charge is made in respect of them. Nor is tax charged on cash payments which coal miners receive in lieu of their former perquisite of free coal. [256] The idea seems to be that perquisites of this kind are primarily intended for the consumption of the recipient and his family and though they are of a nature that is convertible, the general understanding is that they are for personal enjoyment. They are therefore analogous to the inconvertible benefit. Since however, the concession depends upon the volume of goods not being larger than would be needed for personal requirements, it does not go far as to make it possible for any one individual to escape anything beyond a very small amount of tax.[257]

210. On the other hand a taxable benefit arises whenever an employer discharges a pecuniary liability of an employee that he has not incurred in the course of performing the duties of his employment. Usual instances are the payment of the rent of a dwelling-house where its occupation is not part of the employment[258] or the provision of a season ticket for travel from home to work.[259] Sometimes children's school fees[260] or holiday expenses are provided. This rule cuts across the distinction between convertible and inconvertible benefits, since the payment of a particular bill for a man gives him no option between personal enjoyment and realisation. But any different rule would be contrary to commonsense; and, presumably, the same difficulties of valuation do not occur as those that tend to defeat the assessment of the ordinary inconvertible benefit. However, liability is not attached to an employee's occupation of a house if the occupation is incidental to the duties of his employment, as it would be in the case of a lodge-keeper or level-crossing keeper or a colliery manager required to live in the neighbourhood of the mine.[261]

211. What we have said is sufficient to illustrate the very great difficulty of applying any logically consistent treatment to this subject. Theoretically, all benefits in kind received in the course of employment and attributable to it are a form of remuneration and should rank as taxable income, since otherwise one taxpayer's income is not equitably balanced against another's.[262] **[8.44]**

(a) *Is it a benefit in kind?*

In the not uncommon situation where an employee agrees to take a lower salary in return for some benefit, one difficulty is in ascertaining whether this amounts to a benefit in kind at all. **[8.45]**

256 [See ITEPA 2003, s 306.]

257 [The stricter regime relating to benefits in kind which has come into force since 1955, and which continues to be strengthened, has rendered many previously untaxed benefits subject to tax.]

258 [See now ITEPA 2003, Pt 3 Ch 5.]

259 [This is now taxable under ITEPA 2003, ss 82–88 in relation to all employees.]

260 [Now see ITTOIA 2005, s 776, which provides for an exemption for scholarship income, and ITEPA 2003, s 215, which provides that the exemption only applies to the holder of the scholarship; this does not exempt, say, the parent director or employee in receipt of employment income of £8,500 or more a year.]

261 [See ITEPA 2003, s 99.]

262 [This view was put into practice for directors and employees receiving emoluments of £8,500 or more a year by FA 1976, ss 60–72; see now ITEPA 2003, Pt 3 and below, para **[8.56]**. See also the views of the Colwyn Commission, Report of the Royal Commission on the Income Tax Cmd 615 (1920), paras 101 and 102.]

Heaton v Bell [1970] AC 728 (HL) (see below, para [8.48])

The taxpayer agreed to participate in a car loan scheme initiated by his employers. In return for the use of a car, he was to receive an amended lower wage. Two questions were considered: (1) whether the wage was reduced or whether there was merely a deduction from his gross wage, the gross wage remaining taxable; and (2) whether the benefit of the car-loan scheme was a taxable perquisite and, if so, what was the value. With respect to the first question, it was held, with Lord Reid dissenting, that it was a deduction and the gross wage was taxable; with respect to the second, with Lord Hodson and Lord Upjohn dissenting, that in any event, the benefit was a taxable perquisite.

> LORD REID [dissenting]: . . . My Lords, the question of general importance in this case relates to the proper method of taxing perquisites. The respondent is a craftsman. His employers introduced a scheme under which they provided private cars for certain classes of their employees at moderate cost to them. A man who took advantage of the scheme, which was optional, could use the car to travel to and from his work but he was under no obligation to do so; and he could use the car otherwise in any way he chose provided that he drove it himself. We are not concerned with the effect of this scheme on the tax position of the employers. The respondent is assessed to income tax under Schedule E, and the question which the Special Commissioners had to determine was whether sums of £2 10s. per week and later of £2 18s. per week "being the amount of car loan scheme adjustments" were correctly included in computing the amount of his emoluments. The commissioners held that "the use of the car is not in our view money's worth" and that therefore these sums were not part of the respondent's emoluments. Their decision was reversed by Ungoed-Thomas J. but restored by the Court of Appeal.
>
> The first question to be decided is the true construction of the agreement made between the respondent and his employers when he came into the scheme. This agreement is not embodied in any document and its terms must be inferred from what the parties said and did. The appellant says that there was no variation of the existing wage and that the respondent merely authorised his employers to deduct from that wage the weekly sum which he had to pay them for the use of the car which they provided. If that is right then no question as to perquisites arises. It is well settled that a taxpayer's liability to tax on his emoluments is not diminished by the fact that he has authorised his employer to make a deduction from his wages or salary before paying it to him and to apply the part deducted in an agreed manner.[263] What he chooses to do with the wage or salary to which he is entitled is of no moment.
>
> But the respondent says that that is not what the parties agreed. He says that he agreed to accept a reduced wage and that as a counterpart his employers agreed to give him the use of a car. If that is right then he became entitled to two things – first the reduced wage and secondly the use of the car. Then the question arises whether the use of the car was a perquisite within the meaning of the Income Tax Acts so that he had to pay tax in respect of it . . . **[8.46]**

Although the majority held that the gross wage, before deduction, was taxable, it was not strictly necessary to consider whether, had this not been so, participation in the scheme was a taxable 'perquisite', but their Lordships did so in any event.[264]

See also *Machon v McLoughlin*,[265] where the taxpayer, who was a male attendant at an asylum, received a weekly salary subject to fixed deductions,

263 [But now see the payroll deduction scheme in favour of charities, ITEPA 2003, ss 713–715.]
264 See below, para **[8.48]**.
265 (1926) 11 TC 83.

before payment, for board and lodging and for laundry. His contention that he should only be assessable on the net amount of his salary was rejected by Rowlatt J, who said:

> 'If a person is paid a wage with some advantage thrown in, you cannot add the advantage to the wage for the purpose of taxation unless that advantage can be turned into money. That is one proposition. But when you have a person paid a wage with the necessity – the contractual necessity if you like – to expend that wage in a particular way, then he must pay tax upon the gross wage, and no question of alienability or inalienability arises . . .'[266] **[8.47]**

(b) Money or money's worth – is the benefit convertible?

Heaton v Bell (HL) (above, para [8.46])

The House of Lords held by a majority of 3-2 that the benefit of membership of the car-loan scheme was a taxable perquisite.

> LORD MORRIS OF BORTH-Y-GEST:. . .How, then should the well-established principles be applied if it be assumed that since 1961 the respondent was employed on the terms that his wage was a reduced one but that he was to have the free use of a car? In my view, his free use of a car was a perquisite which represented money's worth and was taxable. It is true that his right to use the car could not be assigned (just as the option in *Abbott v. Philbin*[267] could not be transferred) but the right could be converted into money. The option in *Abbott v. Philbin* could be exercised and the shares acquired by its exercise could then be sold. It was recognised that by such process the option was by its nature capable of being turned into money. In the present case the respondent's right to use the car could be converted into money or was capable of being turned into money by a much simpler process. The respondent could at any time (subject only to giving two weeks' notice) and without making any new contract say to his employers that he relinquished in their favour his right to use the car and in exchange could require that an ascertained sum of money should be paid to him. His employers would be bound to accept the use of the car which was all that the respondent had a right to. They would then be bound to pay him a sum which (on the basis now being considered) was equal to the amount by which he had agreed that his wage was to be reduced. His employers, for their part, could at any time (subject only to giving two weeks' notice) require him to give up his right to use the car and require him to accept a sum of money in exchange. At all times and at any time since 1954 the respondent was in a position to decide whether he would choose to have from his employers a particular and ascertained sum of money and no car or whether he would choose not to have that particular and ascertained sum of money but to have a car. The fact that two weeks' notice of change of will was needed does not, in my view, alter the fact that the perquisite represented money's worth.
>
> At any time since 1961 the respondent, after giving notice, could have had money rather than the use of a car. . .
>
> LORD UPJOHN [dissenting]**:. . .** So is this perquisite a taxable perquisite? Of course you can sensibly value it at £2 13s. 6d. per week, but that plainly is not the test; you must be able (and I care not what expression is used, for we are not now construing an Act of Parliament) to turn it into money.
>
> Ungoed-Thomas J. was of opinion that as the respondent could terminate the car loan scheme so far as he was concerned by giving 14 days' notice he could convert the perquisite into money by receiving higher wages thereafter.

266 (1926) 11 TC 83 at 89. The judgment of Rowlatt J was upheld by the Court of Appeal. It has to be asked whether the outcome would have been the same had the taxpayer been entitled to a smaller salary and 'free' board and lodging. But see now ITEPA 2003, Pt 3 Ch 5, and below, para **[8.56]**.

267 [1961] AC 352; [below, para **[8.50]**].

My Lords, powerful reasons were advanced by the judges of the Court of Appeal for disagreeing with and overruling that reasoning. I agree with them. The respondent could not turn the perquisite, which was no more than the personal use of the car, into money or anything which could be equated to money; all he could do would be to give up his perquisite and obtain higher wages. In my opinion, this personal unassignable right for use of the car was not equivalent to money while it continued and that, surely, must be the test ... **[8.48]**

With the exception of those who are lower paid, employees and office-holders are taxed additionally under the benefits code where a car is made available to him or his family or household by reason of his employment.[268] **[8.49]**

Abbott v Philbin [1961] AC 352 (HL)

The taxpayer was secretary to a company. For a small consideration, he was offered an option to purchase shares in the company at the then market price of £3 8s. 6d. per share. About 18 months later he exercised the option, at which time the shares were worth £4 2s. each.

He was assessed on a sum equal to the difference. He contended that any benefit he had received had been conferred at the time he acquired the option, and that any excess in value was not an emolument but represented an appreciation in the value of property (the option) owned by him. His contention was upheld; it was held that the benefit of the option contract was a perquisite which fell to be taxed only in the year in which it was granted.

LORD RADCLIFFE: ... I think it has been generally assumed that this decision[269] does impose a limitation upon the taxability of benefits in kind which are of a personal nature, in that it is not enough to say that they have a value to which there can be assigned a monetary equivalent. If they are by their nature incapable of being turned into money by the recipient they are not taxable, even though they are in any ordinary sense of the word of value to him. It is obvious that this conception raises many attendant uncertainties which are not, so far as I know, cleared up except where some particular class of benefit in kind has offended the eye of the legislature and has been dealt with by special legislation. Must the inconvertibility arise from the nature of the thing itself, or can it be imposed merely by contractual stipulation? Does it matter that the circumstances are such that conversion into money is a practical, though not a theoretical, impossibility; or, on the other hand, that conversion, though forbidden, is the most probable assumption?[270]

I do not think that the decision of this case can go very far, if any distance, to clear up such points as these. I think that the Revenue are right in saying that a line has to be drawn somewhere between convertible and non-convertible benefits and that somehow we have to put a general meaning on the not very precise language used in *Tennant v. Smith*. What I do not think, however, is that a non-assignable option to take up freely assignable shares lies on that side of the line which contains the untaxable benefits in kind. The option, when paid for, was thereafter a contractual right enforceable against the company at any time during the next ten years so long as the holder paid the stipulated price and remained in its service. That right is, in my opinion, analogous for this purpose to any other benefit in the form of land, objects of value or legal rights. It was not incapable of being turned into money or of being turned to pecuniary account within the meaning of these phases in *Tennant v. Smith* merely because the option itself was not assignable. What the option did was to enable the holder at any time, at his choice, to obtain shares from the

268 ITEPA 2003, Pt 3 Ch 6, and s 64(2). For the benefits code generally, see below, paras **[8.56–8.62]**.

269 [*Tennant v Smith* [1982] AC 150.]

270 [See *Heaton v Bell*; cf *Weight v Salmon* (1935) 19 TC 191 (HL), where there was an immediate benefit, directors being permitted to take up at par (£1) shares then worth more than £3.]

company which would themselves be pieces of property or the property rights of value, freely convertible into money. Being in that position he could also at any time, at his choice, sell or raise money on his right to call for the shares, even though he could not put anyone he dealt with actually into his own position as option holder against the company. I think that the conferring of a right of this kind as an incident of service is a profit or perquisite which is taxable as such in the year of receipt, so long as the right itself can fairly be given a monetary value, and it is no more relevant for this purchase whether the option is exercised or not in that year, than it would be if the advantage received were in the form of some tangible form of commercial property... **[8.50]**

See also *Nicoll v Austin*,[271] where the value of the upkeep of the taxpayer's mansion, paid for by his employer company, was held to be of direct monetary benefit to him and, accordingly, taxable; *Richardson v Worrall*,[272] where an employer provided his employee with credit card facilities to obtain petrol for private motoring, and discharged the indebtedness produced by the employee's use of the card. It was held that the discharge of the employee's debt represented money's worth to the employee, and was thus a taxable emolument; and *Brown v Bullock*,[273] where subscriptions to a club paid by an employing Bank on behalf of one of its managers were treated as emoluments.[274] **[8.51]**

(c) The valuation of benefits

Wilkins v Rogerson [1961] Ch 133 (CA)

The company employing the taxpayer, Rogerson, wrote to him stating that it had decided to make a Christmas present of clothing suitable for wearing at the office to all male members of staff. He was instructed to obtain the garments of his own choice up to a total of £15 from a specified branch of Montague Burton, a men's outfitter, and to take the letter with him. The bill was to be sent directly to his employer, and no cash payments would be made to the taxpayer should he select clothes of a total value of less than £15. Burton's had also received a copy of the letter. The bill of £14 15s. for the clothing acquired by the taxpayer from Burton's was sent to his employer.

LORD EVERSHED MR: . . . The claim of the Crown has been that that figure, £14 15s., is to be treated as part of the taxable income of the taxpayer for the tax year in question. It is said that it falls within the terms of paragraph 1 of the Ninth Schedule to the Income Tax Act 1952: "Tax under Schedule E shall be annually charged on every person having or exercising an office or employment of profit mentioned in Schedule E or to whom any annuity, pension or stipend chargeable under that Schedule is payable, in respect of all salaries, fees, wages, perquisites or profits whatsoever therefrom for the year of assessment. . ." It is the Crown's case that the £14 15s. must be treated as a perquisite or profit from the employment for the year of assessment 1955–56.

On behalf of the taxpayer it was said that any perquisite or profit was limited in this case to the value expressed in money of the thing which he got, namely, the clothing. For the purposes of this case, the value of the clothing, treated, of course, as second-hand the

271 (1935) 19 TC 531.
272 [1985] STC 693.
273 [1961] 1 WLR 1095.
274 The issue in the case was whether the manager was entitled to deduct the amount as allowable expenditure. See below, para **[8.64]**.

moment it had been delivered, has been agreed at £5. Let me say at once that this involves no reflection upon Messrs. Montague Burton Ltd., who are not before the court; and it should not, of course, be assumed that goods which they supply are worth only one-third of the price which they charge. But it is, of course, notorious that, apart from purchase tax, the value of clothing is very much reduced the moment it can be called second-hand. In any case, the value is one which has been mutually accepted and agreed, and nothing turns upon it. It may have been agreed at a low figure to discourage any cross-appeal by the taxpayer. If so, it has achieved its purpose, for it is now accepted on his behalf that he is rightly taxed, as the judge in the court below held, upon the money value of what he got.

It seems to me that the taxpayer never acquired any rights against anybody. He received this letter; armed with it, he went to Messrs. Montague Burton's establishment, and Montague Burton expressed themselves as willing to supply him with the clothes he ordered. When the clothes were delivered, then (and then only) the taxpayer got something which was his own. He acquired at that point of time a suit, albeit he had no right against anyone to get the suit. Nor had he, as I conceive, any right against the company, though as a matter of ordinary decency as between master and servant he could no doubt rely upon the company doing what they said they would do. But this was not a case in which he was entitled to call upon the company to pay some sum of money on his behalf, as that phrase is ordinarily understood.

If I have incurred a debt – for example, my debt due for income tax comparable to *Hartland v. Diggins*[275] – and my employer chooses to discharge the debt for me, then it is no doubt true that what I have received in money or money's worth is the equivalent of the debt; and the sum of money is, therefore, properly brought within the scope of the charge. But as I think in this case, and in accordance with Mr. Heyworth Talbot's argument, what the taxpayer got – what the company intended to give him, what the letter to him and Montague Burton said would be done – was a present of a suit. Until he got it, he got nothing; and when he got it, the thing which came in (which was his income expressed in money's worth) was the value of the suit... **[8.52]**

(2) Expense allowances and reimbursements

An expense allowance received by a lower paid employee[276] is not generally taxable since it is presumed to represent a reimbursement of expenditure. This presumption may be rebutted by the Revenue proving the sum to be earnings. Where an employee actually incurs expenditure and is then reimbursed, it appears that the reimbursement will not be taxable if the employee could have deducted the amount spent as an expense of the employment.[277] **[8.53]**

Owen v Pook [1970] AC 244 (HL) (also below, para [8.73])

The taxpayer, a general medical practitioner in practice in Fishguard, also held two part-time appointments as obstetrician and anaesthetist at a hospital in Haverfordwest, 15 miles from Fishguard. These appointments required that he should be on 'stand-by duty' and accessible by telephone at certain specified times to deal with emergency cases. If the hospital telephoned him, he would either give instructions over the telephone and immediately drive to the hospital, or advise

275 [1926] AC 289.

276 For the treatment of expense allowances of those earning over £8,500 and certain directors, see para **[8.56]**, below.

277 For the deduction of expenditure from earnings, see below, paras **[8.64–8.76]**.

treatment over the telephone and await a further report. He was also on call at all times as part of an obstetric 'flying squad' operating all over Pembrokeshire. His responsibility for a patient commenced on receipt of the telephone call.

Under the terms of service of hospital staff, the taxpayer was paid travelling expenses at a fixed rate per mile, limited to a single journey of ten miles, for journeys between Fishguard and the hospital. He paid the cost of the additional five miles himself.

In each of the fiscal years 1962–1963 and 1963–1964 the taxpayer made over 100 journeys to the hospital. The travelling expenses he received were included in his income tax assessment for each of these years. The taxpayer's appeal to the Commissioners that he might deduct the whole cost of travelling between Fishguard and the hospital was allowed. This decision was reversed on appeal to the High Court. The Court of Appeal (Lord Denning MR dissenting) upheld the decision of the High Court. The taxpayer appealed to the House of Lords.

> LORD GUEST: ... Two questions arise: (1) whether the travelling allowances were properly included in the appellant's emoluments for income tax purposes under Schedule E and (2) was the actual cost of the journeys deductible from his emoluments under the relevant rule.[278]
>
> ...The Court of Appeal, certainly the Master of the Rolls, appear to have treated the payments as allowances payable to the appellant whether he incurred the expenses or not. But Edmund Davies L.J. would have decided the case the same way whether the payments were actual reimbursement for expenses incurred or allowances. From their reliance on *Fergusson* v. *Noble*,[279] I take it that the case was treated as one where the payment was truly an allowance and not a reimbursement.
>
> There is, in my view, a distinction between the two cases. If the allowance was, as in *Fergusson* v. *Noble*, a clothing allowance payable whether it was expended or not, I can see the argument that it was an emolument in the sense of a profit or gain and I do not wish to question the authority of that case; but if the payment was merely a reimbursement for actual expenditure, different considerations arise. This case is, in my view distinguishable...
>
> LORD PEARCE: ...There is a further point raised by the appellant in the Court of Appeal. He contends that reimbursements such as that which is here in question do not come within the "emoluments" of an appointment or employment under Schedule E. They therefore never fall to be charged, and it is unnecessary to consider whether they are allowable under rule 7. In my opinion, that contention is correct. "Emoluments" are charged. These are defined as including "all salaries, fees, wages, perquisites and profits whatsoever."
>
> The reimbursements of actual expenses are clearly not intended by "salaries," "fees," "wages" or "profits." It is contended that they are "perquisites." The normal meaning of the word denotes something that benefits a man by going "into his *own* pocket." It would be a wholly misleading description of an office to say that it had very large perquisites merely because the holder had to disburse very large sums out of his own pocket and subsequently received a reimbursement or partial reimbursement of these sums. If a school teacher takes children out for a school treat, paying for them out of his (or her) own pocket, and is later wholly or partially reimbursed by the school, nobody would

278 [This point is further considered below, para **[8.73]**.]

279 (1919) 7 TC 176 (Court of Session). [In that case, the taxpayer, a detective-sergeant in the Glasgow police force, was assessed to tax on £11 paid to him as an allowance for clothing. He was obliged to spend this sum to provide "plain clothes". The payment, which could not be looked upon as a reimbursement of expenditure, was held to accrue to him by reason of his office and, accordingly, assessable to tax under Schedule E. Lord Salvesen expressly did not comment upon whether the taxpayer would have been able to deduct the amount from his income. Had the employer instead bought the clothes for the taxpayer (as in *Wilkins v Rogerson*, above, para **[8.52]**), or reimbursed him for money already expended upon the clothes, the approach, if not the result, taken by the court would have been different in each case. Lord Donovan distinguished *Fergusson v Noble* from the case under discussion on the ground that in that case there was a 'benefit or advantage' to the taxpayer.]

describe him (or her)) as enjoying a perquisite. In my view, "perquisite" has a known normal meaning, namely, a personal advantage, which would not apply a mere reimbursement of necessary disbursements. There is nothing in the section to give it a different meaning. Indeed, the other words of the section confirm the view that some element of personal profit is intended...

LORD WILBERFORCE: ... I agree, therefore, with the judgment of Lord Denning M.R.[280] and would allow the appeal. I should add that, if I had not reached this conclusion, I should have difficulty in seeing how the appellant could succeed, on his alternative point, in establishing that reimbursement of a non-deductible expense is something other than an emolument.

LORD PEARSON: ... The other question in the appeal is whether the travelling allowance which the appellant receives from the hospital authorities constitutes an "emolument" of his employment. I would arrive at the answer in this way. Suppose that A, B and C are employed each at a salary of £500 per annum, and in the first year each has to pay entirely out of his own pocket the expenses of travelling between his home and his place of work. Then, in the second year the employer reimburses to A the cost of his season ticket or gives him an allowance of (say) 8d. per mile for coming to work and returning home by car. A is better off financially by the amount of the reimbursement or allowance. He is better off than he himself was in the first year, and better off than B and C who still have to pay entirely out of their own pockets the expenses of travelling between their homes and their places of work. As A has effectively a better income than B and C, he ought to pay more income tax than they do. The reimbursement or car allowance is a sum of money. In my opinion, it is a perquisite, a profit, an emolument.

There is a quite different position when the employee incurs an expense in performing the duties of his employment – e.g. making a journey from head office to branch office and back to head office, or buying stamps and stationery for the firm – and has it reimbursed to him. In such a transaction there is no benefit – no profit or gain – to the employee. He does not receive any emolument ... **[8.54]**

However, whilst the approach taken by both Lord Wilberforce and Lord Pearson (who dissented from the actual decision, holding that the expenditure incurred by the taxpayer was not an allowable deduction and found the case indistinguishable from *Ricketts v Colquhoun*,[281] which equates the question of whether an allowance paid to reimburse an employee for an expense constitutes earnings to that of whether the expense is an allowable deduction), *ought* to be the correct approach, this is not always the one that is taken–see the note on this case by JGM in [1969] BTR 190 and *Donnelly v Williamson*.[282] In that case, the High Court held that an allowance received by a school teacher in respect of travel to attend out-of-school activities, did not form part of her earnings and was not taxable. Since attendance at these activities was voluntary and unpaid, and thus not part of the teacher's contract of employment, the sum received would not have been deductible as an expense of the employment.[283] However, taking a different approach, Walton J said that the simple question was 'whether the allowance here in question was intended as a genuine estimate of the cost to [the taxpayer] of undertaking the journeys she did in fact undertake, or whether, on the other hand, it included an element of bounty'.[284] **[8.55]**

280 [In the Court of Appeal [1968] 2 WLR 591; [1968] 1 All ER 261. This judgment, a dissenting one, was that the expenditure incurred by Dr Owen was an allowable deduction. It was on this ground that Lord Wilberforce found for the taxpayer.]
281 [1926] AC 1, discussed below, para **[8.74]**.
282 [1982] STC 88.
283 See below, para **[8.64]**.
284 [1982] STC 88, 97.

C. *Amounts treated as earnings*[285] *– the benefits code*

The benefits code charges to tax both specific benefits[286] and a category of residual benefits.[287] Specific benefits comprise expenses payments,[288] vouchers and credit tokens,[289] living accommodation,[290] cars, vans and related benefits (ie, fuel)[291] and beneficial loans.[292] The provisions dealing with residual benefits are, in effect, sweeping-up provisions that are intended to bring within the tax net all employment-related benefits apart from those that are expressly excluded.[293]

A person who earns less than £8,500 per annum and who is not a director for the purposes of the benefits code[294] is excluded from the benefits code *except* in relation to vouchers and credit tokens and living accommodation.[295]

A person who falls within the benefits code will be taxable in relation to expenses payments, be they in the form of an allowance or reimbursement for expenditure incurred (unlike someone who earns less than £8,500[296]), but he may seek to deduct them as expenses of the employment under ITEPA 2003, Part 5.[297]

Where the specific benefits are concerned, the relevant provisions include a formula for assessing the taxable amount. For residual benefits, it is provided that the 'cash equivalent' of the benefit is the amount that is to be treated as earnings.[298] The 'cash equivalent' is defined as the 'cost of the benefit less any part of that cost made good by the employee' to the person providing the benefit.[299] The cost of providing the benefit is:

> 'the expense incurred in or in connection with provision of the benefit (including a proper proportion of any expense relating partly to provision of the benefit and partly to other matters.'[300] **[8.56]**

Final Report of the Royal Commission on the Taxation of Profits and Income Cmd 9474 (1955)

213. All that has been said above must be read subject to the effect of the special legislation introduced in 1948 by Part IV of the Finance Act of that year.[301] Speaking

285 'Earnings' also embrace 'any amount which counts as employment income': ITEPA 2003, s 7(2)(c). This covers share-related income, as well as income which is not earnings and not share-related. The latter includes payments in connection with the termination of an employment, above, paras **[8.36]**.
286 ITEPA 2003, Pt 3, Chs 2-7.
287 *Ibid*, s 201.
288 *Ibid*, Pt 3, Ch 3.
289 *Ibid*, Pt 3, Ch 4
290 *Ibid*, Pt 3, Ch 5.
291 *Ibid*, Pt 3, Ch 6.
292 *Ibid*, Pt 3, Ch 7.
293 *Ibid*, s 202. It should be noted that the specific benefits are excluded from the residual charge by this provision.
294 A director of a company is not a director for the purposes of the benefits code if he has no material interest in the company *and* either he is a full-time working director or the company is non-profit making or is established for charitable purposes only: ITEPA 2003, s 216(3).
295 ITEPA 2003, s 216 (1)–(4).
296 See above, para **[8.53]**.
297 See below, paras **[8.64–8.76]**.
298 ITEPA 2003, s 203(1).
299 *Ibid*, s 203(2).
300 *Ibid*, s 204.
301 [Expanded and recast by FA 1976, ss 60-72; formerly ICTA 1988, Pt V, Ch II, now ITEPA 2003, Part 3.]

generally the persons to whom the legislation applies are directors of trading companies and employees whose gross remuneration (salary plus expenses payments and benefits in kind) amounts to £2,000[302] per annum. It makes every benefit in kind, convertible or inconvertible, chargeable to tax as part of the remuneration of the director or employee who has received it, except for certain limited services which are specified in the Act. Thus, neither director nor employee is chargeable with (*a*) accommodation, supplies and services used wholly for business purposes on the business premises, or (*b*) meals taken in canteens where meals are provided for the staff generally: and an employee, but not a director,[303] receives a further exemption in respect of living accommodation provided on the employer's premises,[304] if the employee is required to live there for the purposes of his duties. But, these exceptions apart, all benefits are brought in, even though some of them would not be taxable under the general law: the provision of a motor car, free accommodation and entertainments, free travel, personal services, the expenses of foreign travel. The Act directs that the measure of liability is to be the expense which the company or employer has been put to in providing the benefit in question.

224. An employee who has expenses to meet in the performance of his duties may have those expenses met in one of several ways. He may have a gross salary out of which his employer requires him to meet them. His problem, then, is to get those expenses allowed against his gross salary for the purpose of determining his taxable income.[305] Or he may incur the expenses on the understanding that the charges will be met by the employer, or that, if he pays them in the first instance, the employer will reimburse him. In those cases, his problem is not a tax one, since neither the moneys paid nor the moneys reimbursed can form any part of his taxable income, unless they are in reality, contrary to what they appear, a provision of personal benefit to him, instead of a payment of expenses necessary to his work.[306] Lastly, the employer may provide the employee with a round sum to cover his expenses of the year, thus eliminating the necessity of any detailed accounting between them.

225. So far as the general law goes, an expense allowance is not treated as taxable income of the recipient if it is no more than a reasonable estimate of the expenses which he would have to incur in the performance of his duties.[307] Theoretically this must be so, since it would be aimless first to add the allowance to the remuneration and then to deduct an equivalent amount as permissible expenses under rule 9. The Board do not treat an expense allowance as necessarily constituting taxable income even if it is intended to cover some expenses which are not of a nature to qualify as deductible expenses under the rule. If this practice is right[308] it creates a curious no-man's land between taxable income and deductible expenses. In any event the uncertainty of the frontier line contributes another reason for regarding the expense allowance system, though in itself a reasonable and, indeed, unavoidable business arrangement, as one that invites special precautions at a time of high taxation of personal incomes.

302 [The specified earnings limit was laid down in FA 1948, s 41(3). It has been increased since that time, but the current figure of £8,500 (ITEPA 2003, s 217) has remained constant since 1979; see above, n 238.]
303 [But now see ITEPA 2003, s 100, which exempts all employees where the accommodation is provided as a result of a possible security threat.]
304 [That the accommodation should be on the employer's premises is not now a requirement of ITEPA 2003, s 90.]
305 [This problem is discussed below, para **[8.64]**.]
306 [See ITEPA 2003, s 70 and *Owen v Pook;* above, para **[8.54]**.]
307 [But see ITEPA 2003, s 70 and *Fergusson v Noble;* above, n 279.]
308 [Cf the remarks of Lord Wilberforce and Lord Pearson in *Owen v Pook;* above, para **[8.54]**.]

226. It is obvious that a payment by way of expense allowance or in reimbursement of expenses could be used to cover more than those expenses which would be deductible under rule 9. If such a payment really amounted to a concealed personal benefit to the recipient the law would treat the quantum of benefit as part of his taxable income. But in the nature of things it would be very difficult for the Revenue to challenge any but the most obvious cases of disguised remuneration or to make good their challenge before appeal Commissioners.[309] The purpose of the special legislation of 1948 was to reverse the position to the extent that the onus of showing that any payment made in respect of expenses covers no more than deductible expenses is placed upon the recipient instead of the onus being placed upon the Revenue to show that the allowance in fact covered a quantum of personal benefit.

227. The method by which this was brought about was to declare that, for directors and employees affected, all sums "paid in respect of expenses" should be treated as part of the assessable income (Income Tax Act 1952, s.160)[310]: and to leave the recipient free to make good such deductions from that income as he could show to be represented by money expended, wholly, exclusively and necessarily in performing the duties of the office or employment. He is not put by this under any rule different from that which governs the expenses of all income assessable under Schedule E. What he loses is the possibility of escaping the full rigour of the rule by becoming the recipient of a payment in respect of expenses without being called upon to itemise and prove them as complying with the terms of rule 9.[311] **[8.57]**

See also the views expressed about FA 1948, Part IV in paras 181 and 182 of the Memorandum of Dissent, Final Report of the Royal Commission on the Taxation of Profits and Income, G Woodcock, H L Bullock and N Kaldor, Cmd 9474 (1955). **[8.58]**

Rendell v Went [1964] 1 WLR 650 (HL)

While driving on company business the appellant taxpayer, who was a full-time company director, struck and killed a pedestrian. Having been advised by the company's solicitors that, if convicted, the taxpayer might be imprisoned, and that the company might be involved in liability, and knowing that the absence of the taxpayer would have had a deleterious effect on the company's business, the chairman instructed the company's solicitor to spare no reasonable expense in the taxpayer's defence. This was accepted by the taxpayer, who was ultimately acquitted. The company paid £641 for his defence.

LORD REID: . . . The appellant was then assessed to income tax for the year 1958-59 in the sum of £3,919 in respect of his emoluments as director. This sum included the sum of £641 spent by the company on his defence. The question in this appeal is whether that sum ought to have been included in the assessment.

. . . The facts make it quite clear that the company did incur expense in the provision of a legal defence for their director, the appellant. And it appears to me to be equally clear

309 [See *Perrons v Spackman* [1981] 1 WLR 1411 and *Donnelly v Williamson* 54 TC 636.]

310 [Now see ITEPA 2003, s 70.]

311 [But see the effect upon his status as an employee earning £8,500 or more a year under ITEPA 2003, s 70. This matter was discussed by Standing Committee E when considering Finance Bill 1976 cl 51 (formerly FA 1976, s 60), now ITEPA 2003, s 70. See 22 June 1976, Hansard HC, Session 1975–1976, vol VI, Standing Committee E, col 1006.]

that the provision of that defence as a benefit within the meaning of this subsection.[312] It was argued that the expense had been incurred solely for the purpose of protecting the interests of the company. That may be so. But it cannot be doubted that in fact the provision of his defence was a benefit to him: if it had not been provided by the company he would have had to pay for his own defence or take the risk that lack of a proper defence might lead to his being convicted and sent to prison. No one suggests that he could have obtained free legal aid. And I can find nothing in the Act to support an argument that a benefit in fact provided by the company ceases to be a benefit within the meaning of the section if it is proved that the company's sole reason, motive or purpose was to protect itself and was not to favour its director.

The main argument for the appellant was that, although he had received a benefit, it was not worth £641 to him and that that sum should be apportioned. I could understand a case being made for apportionment if the expenditure had been for two objects, only one of which was of benefit to the director. But here there was only one object – to prevent conviction of the appellant. The company's reason for trying to achieve that object may have been different from the appellant's. The company did not want to be deprived of his services, while he wanted to avoid going to prison. But the whole of the money was spent for the purpose of avoiding that.

It is found as a fact that the appellant would not have spent so much on his own defence: he mentioned a sum of £60. But then he would not have got the same benefit. His defence would not have been prepared in the way it was and he would not have been defended by experienced counsel. There is nothing to suggest that the £641 was extravagantly spent or that the benefit which he actually received could have been got for less. This is not a case of the company spending without the director's knowledge a large sum to procure a benefit which he did not want, and I do not intend to consider how such a case ought to be dealt with. The appellant knew and accepted what was being done on his behalf though he may not have realised how much it was costing.

Where there is in fact a benefit and, therefore, a perquisite the Act provides that the measure of the perquisite shall be the expense incurred by the company in providing it. Whether there can be circumstances in which it would be possible to depart from that rule in a case where the money was wholly spent to provide the benefit is a matter which it is unnecessary to consider. I can see nothing in the facts of this case to justify any reduction of the sum in which the appellant has been assessed, and accordingly I would dismiss this appeal. **[8.59]**

For another case on the question of apportionment, see *Westcott v Bryan*[313] and R S Nock 'Company Houses' [1969] BTR 253. **[8.60]**

Pepper v Hart [1993] AC 593 (HL) (see above, para [3.28])

The taxpayers were masters at an independent school, where each had one or more sons under a concessionary fees scheme, whereby 20 per cent of the normal school fees were paid in respect of each child. The issue to be decided was whether FA 1976, s 63(1) (referring to the 'cost of the benefit to the employer)[314] was concerned only with the marginal cost, that is, any additional direct expense attributable to each boy, or the average cost, calculated by reference to a proportion of the running expenses of the school. Since it was accepted that the fees actually paid more than covered any direct additional expense resulting from

312 [Income Tax Act 1952, s 161(1), repealed and replaced by FA 1976, ss 60–72, now ITEPA 2003, s 201.]
313 [1969] Ch 324.
314 This later became ICTA 1988, s 156(2), and see now ITEPA 2003, s 204.

the presence of the boys in the school, it followed that the taxpayers could be in receipt of a benefit only if the 'cost' to the employer referred to the 'average' cost. Taking into account statements made by the then Financial Secretary to the Treasury during Standing Committee debates on the Finance Bill 1976 by referring to Hansard for the very first time, the House of Lords held that the cost to the employer was the marginal, ie, additional cost.

> LORD BROWNE-WILKINSON: ... [*Having decided that reference to parliamentary materials could be permitted where:*
>
> (*a*) *Legislation is ambiguous or obscure, or leads to absurdity;*
>
> (*b*) *The material relied upon consists of one or more statements by a Minister or other promoter of the Bill together if necessary with such other parliamentary material as is necessary to understand such statements and their effect;*
>
> (*c*) *The statements relied upon are clear.*
>
> *and that this particular case fell within these rules, his Lordship proceeded to discuss what the outcome would be if reference to Hansard were to be permissible...*]
>
> In my judgment there can be no doubt that, if parliamentary privilege does not prohibit references to Hansard, the parliamentary history shows that Parliament passed the legislation on the basis that the effect of sec. 61[315] and 63[316] of the 1976 Act was to assess in-house benefits, and particularly concessionary education for teachers' children, on the marginal cost to the employer and not on the average cost. Since the words of sec. 63 are perfectly capable of bearing that meaning, in my judgment that is the meaning they should be given.
>
> Therefore if reference to Hansard is permissible, I would allow the appeal.
>
> [*His Lordship then went on to consider what was the true construction of the provision without reference to Hansard...*]
>
> To apply sec. 63(2)[317] it is first necessary to identify "the benefit". It has throughout been common ground that the benefit in this case to each taxpayer is that "his son is allowed to participate in all the facilities afforded by the school to boys who are educated there". These facilities are exactly the same as those afforded to every boy in the school, whether his parents are paying the full or concessionary fees. Therefore the relevant question is "what is the expense incurred in or in connection with providing those facilities". On the literal meaning of the words, the expense to the school of providing those facilities is exactly the same for each boy in the school i.e. a proportion of the total cost of running the school.
>
> Even if it could be said that, because the school would have incurred the basic expense of running the school in any event, such expense was not incurred "in" providing the facilities for the taxpayer's child; on the literal meaning of the words such expense was in any event incurred "in connection with" the provision of such facilities. The words "in connection with" have the widest connotation and I cannot see how they are to be restricted in the absence of some context permitting the restriction.
>
> The strongest argument in favour of the taxpayers is the anomaly which would arise if the employer's business were running at a loss or was subsidised by endowment: as I have explained, in such a case the adoption of the literal meaning of the statutory words would lead to a result whereby the taxpayer is assessed at an amount greater than that charged by the employer to the public for the same service. The Crown have no answer to this anomaly as such. But there are other anomalies which arise if the taxpayer's argument is correct. For example if, unlike the present case, the school could have been filled with boys paying the full fee, the school would have lost the fee income from the places occupied by the children of the taxpayers for whom only the concessionary fee was

315 [See now ITEPA 2003, s 201.]

316 [ITEPA 2003, s 204.]

317 [ICTA 1988, s 63(2) provided that 'the cost of a benefit is the amount of any expense incurred in or in connection with its provision, and includes a proper proportion of any expense relating partly to the benefit and partly to other matters'. See now ITEPA 2003, s 204, which is couched in almost identical terms.]

payable. Without deciding the point, it seems to me arguable that, on the taxpayer's argument, such loss or part of it would be an expense incurred by the school in providing the concessionary places. If so the amount on which the taxpayer would be assessed to tax would vary from year to year depending upon the success of the school in attracting applicants. To my mind, such a variation on a year by year basis by reference to an extraneous factor would be a most anomalous result, and would involve great difficulties in quantifying the cost to the employer.

In the circumstances, if I could detect from the statute any statutory purpose or intention pointing to one construction rather than the other, I would certainly adopt it. But the statute yields no hint. The basic problem is this. What is taxable is the benefit to the employee and one would have expected the quantum of that benefit to be assessed by reference to the value of the benefit to the employee. But the statutory formula does not seek to value the benefit to the employee as such, but requires the quantum of the benefit to be fixed by reference to the cost to the employer in providing it. Given this dislocation between the benefit which is assessable to tax and the basis on which its value is to be assessed it is impossible to gain any guidance in the statute as to the parliamentary intention. In the circumstances there is in my judgment no option but to give effect to the literal meaning of the words as did the Court of Appeal. In the result, the Revenue's argument should succeed and the appeal should be dismissed.

[*Having concluded that the outcome of the case would differ according to whether the Court could look at parliamentary material, his Lordship went on to hold that:*]

...this House should look at Hansard and give effect to the parliamentary intention it discloses in deciding the appeal....

...it would not in my view be right to withhold from the taxpayers a decision to which, in law, they are entitled. **[8.61]**

Other in-house benefits of a similar nature would include airline travel by airline employees at a nominal charge where there are empty seats on the aeroplane.

HM Treasury have the power to exempt minor benefits from a charge to tax,[318] and HMRC staff have been encouraged to treat benefits involving small amounts 'with a sense of proportion', so that they will not be assessable to either income tax or NICs.[319] **[8.62]**

D. *Exempt income*

ITEPA 2003 contains a number of provisions exempting certain employment income and earnings from a charge to tax. The bulk of these[320] are to be found in Pt 4 of the Act, some of which except income from liability under particular provisions (such as the benefits code) whilst not preventing liability from arising under some other provision (for example, mileage allowances,[321] work-related training[322] and removal-related expenses[323]), and others which prevent liability from arising at all.[324] **[8.63]**

318 ITEPA 2003, s. 210. For exemptions generally, see below, para **[8.63]**.
319 See *Working Together* Inland Revenue, September 2003, Issue 14, at p 9.
320 Note, for example, the exemption from the charge under ITEPA 2003, s 403 set out in ss 405–414.
321 ITEPA 2003, s 229.
322 *Ibid*, s 250.
323 *Ibid*, s 271.
324 These exemptions are listed in ITEPA 2003, s 228(2) and include small gifts from third parties, long service awards and annual parties and functions.

4. Allowable expenditure

Rules allowing for the deductibility of expenditure by an employee are to be found in ITEPA 2003, Pt 5. The overriding principles are that, as a general rule, deductions may be made from any earnings of the employment, but not from earnings of any other employment,[325] and that they may not exceed earnings and thus cannot be used to create a loss.[326] The detailed rules are divided into those covering general expenses, and those concerned with travelling expenses. Where an employee is left to bear an expense from his wage or salary, the simple question to be asked is whether he can deduct the amount of that expense from his earnings. Alternatively, where the *employer* pays the expense, the question then is whether that payment is a benefit in kind and thus treated as earnings.[327] Further, it will be recalled that, where an employer pays an allowance to an employee earning less than £8,500, the amount paid is presumed to represent actual expenditure and will not constitute earnings; where, however, such an employee is reimbursed for expenditure actually made by him, the correct approach appears to be that the reimbursement will not constitute earnings if he could have deducted the amount spent as an expense of the employment.[328] In comparison, for those earning over £8,500, or who are 'directors' for the purposes of ITEPA 2003, Part 3, the amount of an expenses allowance or reimbursement of expenditure will be treated as earnings,[329] and it will then be left to the employee to seek to deduct that same amount as an expense of the employment under the rules described below.

Although the rules for deductibility of expenditure under ITEPA 2003 bear a close resemblance to those in ITTOIA 2005, which provide for the deductibility of expenditure incurred in the course of a trade, profession or vocation,[330] it would appear to be more difficult for an employee to deduct expenses than it is for a trader etc. **[8.64]**

A. *Expenses not connected with travelling*

An expense, other than one incurred in travelling, is deductible if–

'(a) the employee is obliged to incur and pay it as holder of the employment, and

(b) the amount is incurred wholly, exclusively and necessarily in the performance of the duties of the employment.'[331]

It can be seen that there are three essential requirements that must be satisfied if an item of expenditure is to be deductible. *First*, the expenditure must be incurred *in the performance of* the duties and not in respect of some act preparatory to the actual work itself. *Secondly*, it must be 'necessarily' incurred in the performance of the duties, rather than arising because of some personal choice of the taxpayer.[332] *Thirdly*, the expense must be incurred 'wholly and exclusively' in the performance of the duties. **[8.65]**

325 ITEPA 2003, s 328(1). To this there are exceptions: see s 328(2)–(5).
326 *Ibid*, s 329(1).
327 As in *Rendell v Went* [1964] 1 WLR 650 and above, para **[8.59]**.
328 Above, para **[8.53]**.
329 ITEPA 2003, s 72.
330 See below, para **[10.23]**.
331 ITEPA 2003, s 336(1).
332 See *Ricketts v Colquhoun* [1926] AC 1.

Fitzpatrick (No 2) v IRC; Smith v Abbott [1994] 1 WLR 306 (HL) (see above, para [3.9])

In a series of appeals, the House of Lords held that an allowance paid to journalists by their employer to cover the costs incurred by them in the purchase of newspapers and periodicals was not deductible since the reading of these materials was done, not in the performance of their duties as journalists but, rather, in order to carry out their duties more efficiently.

LORD TEMPLEMAN: . . . The conditions necessary to be fulfilled in order for expenses of an employee to qualify for deduction under section 189 of the Act of 1970[333] or its predecessors have been judicially considered in the past but not in relation to journalists.

In *Simpson v Tate*[334] a medical officer of health joined certain medical and scientific societies in order that by means of their meetings and published transactions he might be aware of all recent advances in sanitary science and keep himself up to date on all medical questions affecting public health. Rowlatt J. said, at p. 219:

> "The respondent qualified himself for his office before he was appointed to it, and he has very properly endeavoured to continue qualifying by joining certain professional and scientific societies, so that by attending their meetings and procuring their publications he may keep abreast of the highest developments and knowledge of the day. He seeks to deduct from his assessable income the subscriptions paid by him to these societies as money expended necessarily in the performance of the duties of the office. When one looks into the matter closely, however, one sees that these are not moneys expended in the performance of his official duties. He does not incur these expenses in conducting professional inquiries or get the journals in order to read them to the patients. If he did, the case would be altogether different. He incurs these expenses in qualifying himself for continuing to hold his office, just as before being appointed to the office he qualified himself for obtaining it . . . In my view the principle is that the holder of a public office is not entitled . . . to deduct any expenses which he incurs for the purpose of keeping himself fit for performing the duties of the office, such as subscriptions to professional societies, the cost of professional literature and other outgoings of that sort. If deductions of that kind were allowed in one case every professional office holder would claim to be entitled to deduct the payments made by him to every scientific society to which he happened to belong and the price which he paid for every professional publication, and there would be no end to it."

Similarly in the present case it seems to me that a journalist does not purchase and read newspapers in the performance of his duties but for the purpose of ensuring that he will carry out his duties efficiently. If deductions of this kind were allowed in one case every journalist or other similar employee would claim to be entitled to deduct the payment made by him for every newspaper and periodical which he chose to purchase "and there would be no end to it." A sports reporter is employed to report sport, not to read newspapers, a photographer is employed to produce pictures for his newspaper not to study the pictures of others. An editor is employed to select, draft and arrange items in his newspaper, not to read other newspapers. A journalist who reads newspapers does so in order to be able to perform his duties to the highest possible standard but he does not read "in performance of his duties." These were the reasons given by Lord Hope and Lord Cullen for upholding the Scottish commissioners in *Fitzpatrick v. Inland Revenue Commissioners (No. 2)*[335]. I am unable to agree with the contrary conclusion reached by Lord McCluskey and emphatically unable to approve the attempt by Lord McCluskey, at p. 440, to express the words of section 189 in his own terms.

In *Ricketts v Colquhoun*[336] the Recorder of Portsmouth was not allowed the expense of

333 [Now ITEPA 2003, s 336.]
334 [1925] 2 KB 214.
335 [1992] STC 406.
336 [1926] AC 1.

travelling from his home in London to his court in Portsmouth. Travelling expenses fall into a separate category because each employee chooses where he will live and cannot establish that every employee must incur the same expenses. Lord Blanesburgh said, at p. 7:

> "the language of the rule points to the expenses with which it is concerned being only those which each and every occupant of the particular office is necessarily obliged to incur in the performance of its duties – to expenses imposed upon each holder ex necessitate of his office, and to such expenses only . . . the terms employed are strictly, and, I cannot doubt, purposely, not personal but objective: . . ."

In the present case every journalist is free to choose the method by which he will keep himself up to date and efficient. This may or may not involve reading one newspaper or any particular number of newspapers.

In *Nolder v Walters*[337] an airline pilot was not allowed to deduct the cost of transport between his home and the aerodrome or the cost of the telephone at his home. Rowlatt J. said, at p. 387:

> "In the performance of the duties' means in doing the work of the office, in doing the things which it is his duty to do while doing the work of the office. A man who holds an office or employment has, equally necessarily, to do other things incidentally, and spend money incidentally, because he has the office. He has to get to the place of employment, for one thing . . . Incidentally, he is obliged to do that, but it is not in doing the work of the office, which begins when he arrives, and sets to work to perform his duties."

In the present case the work of each journalist began when he arrived at the office or when he went out on location to obtain information or other material designed to be incorporated in his newspaper.

A recorder and an airline pilot must travel from home in order to work; a journalist must read in order to work well. But in both cases, it seems to me, travelling to work and reading are not activities carried out in the performance of the work but activities which are a necessary preliminary to or preparation for performing the work.

In *Blackwell v Mills*[338] a student assistant in the research laboratory of a company was required, as a condition of his employment, to attend classes in preparation for the final examination for the degree of Bachelor of Science. He was allowed time off to attend classes for that purpose and claimed to deduct for income tax purposes the expenses he incurred in travelling to and from the classes and in the purchase of text books. Macnaghten J. said, at p. 470:

> "It was a condition of Mr. Mills's employment that he should attend the evening classes. Mr. Honeyman contended that, since the subject-matter of the evening classes was not unconnected with the duties that Mr. Mills had to perform, he should be regarded as performing the duties of his office when he was attending the Chelsea Polytechnic. In my opinion any such view is inadmissible. The duties of his employment were as a student assistant in the research laboratories of the General Electric Company. It seems to me impossible to say that, when he was listening to the lecturer at the Chelsea Polytechnic, he was performing the duties of a student assistant at the laboratories of the company."

In the present case there was some dispute as to whether a journalist was required as a condition of his employment to read newspapers and periodicals of his choice. But it appears from *Blackwell v. Mills*[339] that this dispute is not relevant. The duties of a sports reporter were to report sport. Adapting the words of Macnaghten J. it seems to me impossible to say that when the sports reporter was reading newspapers in the quiet of his home he was performing the duties of a sports reporter either at the offices of the newspaper or on location.

337 (1930) 15 TC 380.
338 (1945) 26 TC 468.
339 *Ibid.*

In *Lomax v Newton*,[340] Vaisey J. said[341]:

> "'the provisions of rule 9 of Schedule E' – now section 189(1) of the Act of 1970 – "are notoriously rigid, narrow and restricted in their operation. In order to satisfy the terms of the rule it must be shown that the expenditure incurred was not only necessarily, but wholly and exclusively incurred in the performance of the relevant official duties ... An expenditure may be ' necessary' for the holder of an office without being necessary to him in the performance of the duties of that office; it may be necessary in the performance of those duties without being exclusively referable to those duties; it may perhaps be both necessarily and exclusively, but still not wholly so referable. The words are indeed stringent and exacting; compliance with each and every one of them is obligatory if the benefit of the rule is to be claimed successfully."

In that case a regimental officer was not allowed to deduct his annual mess subscription although he was obliged to be a member of the mess and would no doubt have been transferred or even cashiered if he failed to pay. An officer in the Territorial Army was not allowed his mess subscriptions or his share of mess expenditure on guests. The officer was also not allowed the cost of attending social functions given by warrant officers and other ranks. Vaisey J. said, at p. 1127:

> "I agree that participation in the social life of the battalion was part of the social duties of the respondent, but was it any part of his official duties? Was the respondent at the sergeants' dance in the proper sense of the expression 'on duty?' I think not. I am quite unable to see how this item can be brought within the rule. I apply to it descriptions from the contentions of the Crown as set out in the case, and say that they are expenses incurred from tradition and custom, accepted voluntarily by the officers of the unit and containing elements of personal choice and benefit, and therefore not within the rule."

Similarly in the present case the journalist is not on duty when he is reading at home and his expenditure on newspapers contains elements of personal choice and benefit. Indeed one of the journalists gave evidence that he was a "compulsive" buyer of newspapers.

In *Humbles v Brooks*[342] the headmaster required to teach history was not allowed the expense of attending a series of weekend lectures on history. Ungoed-Thomas J. citing the authorities said, at p. 502:

> "'In the performance of the said duties' means in the course of their performance ... It means 'in doing the work of the office, in doing the things which it is his duty to do while doing the work of the office' ... It does not include qualifying initially to perform the duties of the office, or even keeping qualified to perform them ... it does not mean adding to the taxpayer's usefulness in performing his duties. The requirement of the employer that the expenditure shall be incurred does not, of itself, bring the expense within the rule, nor does the absence of such a requirement exclude it from the application of the rule ..."

and the judge accepted, at p. 503, that the headmaster:

> "attended the course to improve his background knowledge of the subject ... he gleaned useful information from the lectures ... he felt the course was essential to keep himself up to date; ... to provide him with material which he reproduced in the history lessons."

All these advantages were claimed by the journalists in the present case plus the claim that reading newspapers provided ideas and inspiration. This advantage however is no different in quality from the other advantages claimed.

In *Brown v Bullock*[343] a bank manager who was instructed by his employers to foster local contacts and for that purpose to join a club was not allowed as an expense in the performance of his duties as a bank manager the entrance fee and annual subscriptions to the club which were paid by his employers. In approving the decision of Vaisey J. in *Lomax*

340 [1953] 1 WLR 1123.
341 *Ibid.*, at 1125.
342 (1962) 40 TC 500.
343 [1961] 1 WLR 1095.

v Newton[344] Lord Evershed M.R. said that the language of the statute is of a somewhat rigid character the adverb "necessarily" added to the phrase "in the performance" of his duties clearly narrows very much the scope of any expenditure which can fairly be deductible. Donovan L.J. said, at p. 1102:

> "The test is not simply whether the employer imposes the expense, but primarily whether the duties do, in the sense that irrespective of what the employer may prescribe, the duties themselves involve the particular outlay."

It does not matter therefore whether in the present case the journalists were contractually bound to their employers to expend money in the purchase of other newspapers and magazines or whether they did so voluntarily. Whether or not a journalist thinks it is necessary to read one or more newspaper and periodical his duty is in the production of his employer's newspaper and he is not carrying out that duty when he is reading other newspapers.

Elwood v Utitz[345] was a case in which travelling expenses from one place of work to another were held to be deductible in contrast to travel expenses from home to a single place of work. *Pook v Owen*[346] is a similar case. The question in the present case is whether the journalist was reading in order to qualify himself to work to the satisfaction of himself and his employer or whether he was reading in the performance of his work. *Taylor v Provan* [347] was another case concerned with travelling expenses. Lord Salmon, at p. 226, distinguished between expenses which were deductible because they were incurred "in the performance of the duties" and expenses which were not deductible because they were incurred "in order to enable the duties to be performed." Applying this distinction a journalist does not read in the performance of his duties but in order to enable his duties to be performed.

The reasons for the strictness of the rule governing deductible expenses are not hard to find. If a journalist or other employee were allowed to deduct expenses incurred by him in his spare time in improving his usefulness to his employer, the imposition of income tax would be distorted and the amount of the expenses claimed by an individual would depend entirely on his own choice. In the present case for example the Scottish appeals and the English appeals are test cases. The numbers of members of the National Union of Journalists have in the past exceeded 30,000. No doubt every journalist is prepared to give evidence sincerely and honestly that he considers it is necessary to purchase the newspapers and magazines which he chooses to read and up to the amount for which he receives an allowance. If each spend £1,000 a year the total deduction for 30,000 journalists will be £30,000,000 a year. There may be a large number of journalists who would not spend this amount but the principle of the decision in the present case does not apply only to journalists; the ramifications of the decision in their favour would be enormous. **[8.66]**

It is also the case that the expenditure must be 'necessarily incurred'. This is illustrated by this case, *Simpson v Tate* [348] and *Lupton v Potts.*[349] See also *Humbles v Brooks*[350] and *Lomax v Newton,*[351] both referred to in the above case. In *Lomax v Newton,* Vaisey J observed that an 'expenditure may be 'necessary' for the holder of an office without being necessary to him in the performance of the duties of that office; it may be necessary in the performance of those duties

344 [1953] 1 WLR 1123.
345 (1965) 42 TC 482.
346 [1970] AC 244; [see above, para **[8.54]**, and below, para **[8.73]**.]
347 [1975] AC 194.
348 [1925] 2 KB 214.
349 [1969] 1 WLR 1749.
350 (1962) 40 TC 500.
351 [1953] 1 WLR 1123.

without being exclusively referable to those duties; it may perhaps be both necessarily and exclusively, but not wholly so referable.'[352]

Fitzpatrick also demonstrates that it is not enough for the employer to require his employee to incur certain expenses. See also *Bolam v Barlow*[353] and *Brown v Bullock*,[354] where Donovan LJ said that the 'test is not whether the employer imposes the expense but whether the duties do, in the sense that, irrespective of what the employer may prescribe, the duties cannot be performed without incurring the particular outlay.'[355] **[8.67]**

Ward v Dunn [1979] STC 178 (Ch D)

The General Commissioners had allowed the taxpayer's claim for a greater special allowance for wear and tear on his clothing than the £20 which was allowed by the Inland Revenue as an extra statutory concession,[356] even though it was not strictly justified in law. The Crown appealed to the Chancery Division against the Commissioners' decision.

> WALTON J: . . . The short answer in law to Mr. Dunn's claim, whatever may be thought about the justice of the matter, is that none of the money which he is claiming is "wholly" expended in the performance of his duties as an assistant surveyor because the clothes which he wears when he visits sites "are the clothes which he ordinarily wears and are not clothes bought specifically for his visits to such sites." That is a finding by the General Commissioners and it has not in any way been challenged. That being so, it follows of necessity that when Mr. Dunn purchases a suit he purchases it, maybe partly with a view to going round the sites but, at any rate, partly with a view to wearing it in the ordinary course as one wears clothing for comfort and for covering one's nakedness. Similarly, when he has clothing cleaned it is cleaned, doubtless partly as a result of what happens on the construction sites, but also so that he may wear clean clothing and not dirty clothing. Similarly, when it is repaired as a result of damage which it has sustained when he has visited sites, it is repaired so that he may wear clothes which hang together, not clothes which are in rags. The matter would be very different indeed if the clothes which he wore when visiting the sites were clothes which he wore only when visiting those sites. I can sympathise very much with him when he says that that really, in his station of life, is not a practical proposition. He can hardly change into a boiler suit or a pair of jeans, or something like that. He has a position to maintain, and therefore it is necessary that he wears respectable clothing when he is actually going round these sites. So be it; but the mere fact that that clothing is his ordinary clothing makes it, in my view, completely impossible for it to be said that the money which he is now claiming is money which is "wholly" expended by him in the performance of his duties. . . **[8.68]**

See also *Woodcock v Commission of Inland Revenue*[357] and *Hillyer v Leeke*;[358] compare the deductibility of clothing expenditure from trading income under ITTOIA 2005 and *Mallalieu v Drummond*.[359] **[8.69]**

352 *Ibid* at 1125.
353 (1949) 32 TC 136.
354 [1961] 1 WLR 1095.
355 *Ibid* at 1102.
356 The relevant concession, ESC A1, has now been enacted in ITEPA 2003, s 367.
357 [1977] STC 405.
358 [1976] STC 490.
359 [1983] 2 AC 861; below, para **[10.32]**.

B. *Travelling expenses*

The rules allowing for deduction of travelling expenses were changed for the tax year 1998–99 and subsequent years,[360] the old ones having been in place for over 140 years and failing to reflect modern working practices.

A deduction from earnings may be made in respect of travel expenses if the employee is obliged to incur and pay them as holder of the employment *and* either the expenses are necessarily incurred on travelling in the performance of the duties of the employment[361] or they are attributable to the employee's necessary attendance at any place in the performance of the duties of that employment.[362]

Whilst the new rules allow for the deduction of travelling expenses by site-based employees, that is, employees with no normal place of work, as well as for those employees with a normal place of work who travel directly from home to a temporary place of work, it remains the case that there can be no deduction for the expense of 'ordinary commuting',[363] defined as travel between the home and a permanent workplace or a place that is not a workplace and the workplace.[364] This is because the expense of 'ordinary commuting' is incurred *before* the work has started and not, therefore, 'in the performance' of the duties of the employment.[365] **[8.70]**

Employee Travel & Subsistence: A Consultative Document Inland Revenue, 1996

1. INTRODUCTION

1.1 Under the Schedule E expenses rule, a deduction for tax is, in general terms, available for travel expenses – but only if they are necessarily incurred by the employee in the performance of his or her duties. This long standing test has been strictly interpreted by the Courts.

1.2 A key feature of the tax treatment of expenditure on travel is that no deduction is available for the costs of travelling between an employee's home and normal place of work. The Courts have held that such travel is undertaken to put the employee in a position to perform his or her duties, rather than in the performance of those duties. So there is no deduction under the terms of the existing legislation. The proposals in this consultative document do not alter that basic rule. The proposed changes address two particular issues where the current rules can cause difficulties – travel to and from work by 'site-based employees' and the treatment of, what is known as, 'triangular travel'.

1.3 <u>Site-based employees</u> have no permanent place of work. Typically, they spend a period working in one place and then move on to work somewhere else. Each site at which they work is, for the time they are there, their normal place of work. In general, therefore, they get no deduction for any of the costs of travel between home and each of the sites where they work, nor for the costs of subsistence while they are there. Many see this as unduly harsh.

360 See now ITEPA 2003, ss 337–342.
361 *Ibid*, s 337(1).
362 *Ibid*, s 338(1).
363 *Ibid*, s 383(2).
364 *Ibid*, s 338(3). For the meaning of 'workplace' and 'ordinary workplace', see ITEPA 2003, s 339.
365 *Ricketts v Colquhoun* [1926] AC 1. This case was discussed by Lord Guest in *Owen v Pook* [1970] AC 244, below, para **[8.73]**, and by Lord Reid in *Taylor v Provan* [1975] AC 194, below, para **[8.74]**.

1.4 Triangular travel occurs where an employee with a normal place of work travels not between home and that normal place of work but directly between home and a temporary workplace. The Revenue's approach to the costs of such journeys is intended to give relief for the business element of the journey, without generally including the costs of home to work travel. Although this approach is more generous than a strict interpretation of the law might require, it is often criticised because of the administrative burden it puts on employers and is generally viewed as being inequitable…

2.9 Travel from 'Home' to 'Normal Place of Work'

2.9.1 The Courts have established as a clear general principle that the cost of an employee's travel between home and a normal place of work is not deductible. Such expenditure merely puts the employee in a position to perform the duties of the job. It is not incurred in actually doing the job. Furthermore, the journey depends on where the employee lives. The expense is not an expense of a journey that every holder of the job would have to undertake…

2.11 Travel between Places of Work

2.11.1 Where someone has two employments, the duties of which are at different places, the cost of travelling between them is not usually deductible.

2.11.2 Where, however, an employee is required by his duties to travel between two places of work in the same employment, the travel may be necessary and in the performance of those duties – with a deduction available for the expense incurred. For a place to be a place of work, the employee should be able to show that he is required to perform substantive duties there…

3.1 Aims

3.1.1 The main aims underlying the proposals contained in the draft legislation are:

- to give relief for travel expenses incurred by site-based employees as a result of their employment and
- to make more equitable and less complex the tax treatment of triangular travel.

To enhance clarity and certainty, the draft legislation incorporates those aspects of the present treatment of travel expenses which are based upon case law and long standing concessionary practice. It is emphasised, however, that this is not intended to tighten the rules but to make them easier to understand and apply…

3.2 Site-based employees

3.2.1 The tax treatment of travel between home and work generally follows from the law which says that only travel which is objectively needed in actually doing the job is allowable. A useful test of this is whether or not anyone doing the job would need to undertake that particular journey. Different people living in different places would have different home to work travel. That is a product, not of the job, but of where they live.

3.2.2 The working pattern of many site-based employees, with the place where they normally work changing frequently, may be such that travel between home and work is more a product of the nature of their employment than of where they live. Even so, under current rules, no relief is available for the home to work travel of the site-based employee.

3.2.3 Under the proposals in this consultative document, the rules on the deductibility of travel expenses would be changed to allow relief for travel by site-based employees. To achieve this, new rules would allow a deduction for the costs of travel to or from any place where attendance at that place is in the performance of the duties of a person's employment. To maintain the status quo for ordinary travel between home and an employee's normal place of work, there would be an exclusion from relief for the costs of 'normal commuting'.

3.3 Triangular travel

3.3.1 The issue here is that these journeys are, to an extent, the product of where someone lives in relation to their normal place of work. Logically, relief should be available for part of the cost of the journey or, more precisely, the full cost of the business part of the journey. However, any system which involves calculating partial relief carries with it a significant compliance cost. Until now, the Revenue's approach has been the pragmatic solution of the 'lesser of' rule ... Relief is calculated on the basis of the travel costs incurred or the costs that would have been incurred if the journey to the temporary place of work had started and finished at the normal place of work, whichever is the smaller.

3.3.2 There are various drawbacks to the 'lesser of' rule. Arguably, the approach is inequitable because, depending on the arrangements made, some travellers profit from the rule while others cannot obtain full relief for the out of pocket expense they actually incur. Those whose costs of normal commuting are incurred on a journey by journey basis, most notably car drivers, can benefit significantly from the existing rules. **[8.71]**

For an overview of the modernised travelling expenses rules, see John Whiting [1998] BTR 425.

[8.72]

Owen v Pook (HL) (above, para [8.54])

LORD GUEST: ... In *Ricketts v. Colquhoun*[366] there was only one place of employment, Portsmouth. It was not suggested that any duties were performed in London. In the present case there is a finding of fact that Dr. Owen's duties commenced at the moment he was first contacted by the hospital authorities. This is further emphasised by the finding that his responsibility for a patient began as soon as he received a telephone call and that he sometimes advised treatment by telephone. It is noteworthy that under section 19(b) 3(iv) of his terms and conditions of service the hospital is referred to as "where his principal duties lie." There were thus two places where his duty is performed, the hospital and his telephone in his consulting room. If he was performing his duties at both places, then it is difficult to see why, on the journey between two places, he was not equally performing his duties. Indeed Mr. Heyworth Talbot did not contend to the contrary. It follows that he had to get from his consulting room to the hospital by car to treat the emergency. The travelling expenses were, in my view, necessarily incurred in the performance of the duties of his office...

LORD WILBERFORCE: ... What is required is proof, to the satisfaction of the fact finding commissioners, that the taxpayer, in a real sense, in respect of the office or employment in question, had two places of work, and that the expenses were incurred in travelling from one to the other in the performance of his duties ... **[8.73]**

366 [*Ibid.*]

Taylor v Provan [1975] AC 194 (HL)

The taxpayer, a Canadian citizen who was a resident in Canada and the Bahamas, had special skills which were needed by an English brewery company, of which he was made a director. He worked only on special assignments connected with his skills, 'as a kind of business recreation', and received no remuneration from the English company. He did most of the work on the special assignments in either Canada or the Bahamas, but made frequent trips to England, for which he was paid his expenses. He was assessed to income tax on his expenses, and appealed against these assessments on the ground that the expenses were not emoluments, or if they were, the expenses were deductible. The House of Lords held unanimously that the expenses were emoluments, and by a majority of 3:2 that the expenses were deductible.

LORD REID: ... Two questions arose (1) whether these sums were emoluments within the scope of Schedule E and (2) if they were, the deductions allowable under paragraph 7 of Schedule 9 of the Income Tax Act 1952.[367]

I have no doubt that these sums were emoluments. It was argued that they were not paid to the appellant as a director because they were paid under special assignments independent of his directorships. I can see no grounds for splitting up his duties in that way. He was made a director with a special assignment. There was one appointment not two. Section 160 of the Act of 1952[368] provides that any sum paid to a director in respect of expenses shall be treated as a perquisite of the office and included in the emoluments thereof assessable to income tax.

The substantial question in the case is whether these expenses of travelling are a permissible deduction. If so, then the whole of the sum assessed to tax is deductible and the appeal succeeds. This depends entirely on the proper construction of paragraph 7 of Schedule 9[369].

... The case for the revenue is that the appellant was not "necessarily obliged" to incur these travelling expenses because if he had so chosen he could have resided during these five years in England and then there would have been no need to cross the Atlantic. To that the appellant replies that the terms of his office or employment were that he was to perform his duties so far as he could in Canada or the Bahamas and only to visit the United Kingdom when necessary. Then the revenue say that the test is not what the parties had agreed, however reasonable their agreement might be, but what his work required. Here they say that all his work could equally well have been done if he had resided throughout in England. There is no finding to that effect but I assume that that is so.

I can understand a distinction between what the parties' contract requires and what the work requires when the office has an independent existence so that if this man had not been appointed someone else would have been. But here the office or employment was created for the appellant because of his special qualifications and there is nothing to suggest that if he had not been available anyone else would or could have been appointed for the very special work. The appellant clearly would not have agreed to reside in England. So I do not see how in any reasonable sense it can be said that his travelling was unnecessary if this peculiar work was to be done ...

... At first sight it might seem a simple matter to determine whether an officer or employee was necessarily obliged to incur certain travelling expenses. The first question would be whether it was necessary to make the journeys in respect of which the claim to deduct expenses is made. But everyone is agreed that it is not enough to show that on the facts as they existed the man's duties could not have been performed if he had not made the journeys. Something more is needed. But what? That can only be discovered by a careful examination of two decisions of this House. *Ricketts v. Colquhoun*[370] and *Pook v.*

367 [Now ITEPA 2003, s 337(1).]
368 [This was the forerunner to what is now ITEPA 2003, s 70.]
369 [Now ITEPA 2003, s 337(1).]
370 [1926] AC 1.

Owen.[371] I do not think that the interpretation of these two decisions is materially assisted by a consideration of other reported cases and I propose to confine my attention to them.

Up to a point the facts in these two cases were similar. Both concerned part-time offices or employments. In the first a barrister practising in London was appointed Recorder of Portsmouth and on at least four occasions in each year he travelled from London to Portsmouth to perform his official duties there. In the second a doctor practising in Fishguard was given an appointment in a hospital at Haverfordwest and he made frequent journeys from Fishguard to Haverfordwest to perform his duties there. But the barrister was held not to have necessarily incurred his travelling expenses, whereas the doctor was held to have necessarily incurred his travelling expenses.

In *Ricketts*' case[372] the findings of fact of the commissioners were very short, containing nothing material beyond what I have already stated. Reasons were given in only two speeches in this House – those delivered by Viscount Cave L.C. and Lord Blanesburgh. The speech of Lord Blanesburgh has generally been regarded as best expressing the ratio of the decision. He said[373]:

> "...the language of the rule points to the expenses with which it is concerned being only those which each and every occupant of the particular office is necessarily obliged to incur in the performance of its duties – to expenses imposed on each holder ex necessitate of his office, and to such expenses only."

Then, having pointed out that the terms of the rule are not personal but objective, he continued:

> "... the deductible expenses do not extend to those which the holder has to incur mainly and, it may be, only because of circumstances in relation to his office which are personal to himself or are the result of his own volition."

Mr. Ricketts had no finding to show either that he had to reside at a distance from Portsmouth or that no one could have been appointed to the office who could reside in Portsmouth. So it was true to say on the facts found in the case that his continuing to reside in London was "the result of his own volition."

Lord Cave's speech was on the same lines. He put the matter rather differently in one passage[374]:

> "they must be expenses which the holder of an office is necessarily obliged to incur – that is to say, obliged by the very fact that he holds the office and has to perform its duties – and they must be incurred in – that is, in the course of – the performance of those duties. The expenses in question in this case do not appear to me to satisfy either test."

Then apparently explaining what he meant by "in the course of," he said that the expenses were incurred because he travelled to Portsmouth before he could begin to perform his duties and travelled home after concluding them.

I have considerable doubt whether Lord Cave's second test is not too rigid. He does not refer to the fact that the rule also authorises the deduction of the expenses "of keeping and maintaining a horse to enable him to perform" the duties of the office.[375] The holder of the office would keep his horse at home, so he would use it to get from his home to the various places where his duties had to be performed. So this part of the rule must mean to enable the holder of the office to get from his home to the place where his duties are to be performed as well as to enable him to get from one place to another in the course of performing his duties. There is no suggestion of a distinction between travelling from his home to the place of work and travelling between places of work. He can deduct the whole cost of keeping his horse – not merely part of it.

Lord Cave recognises that the holder of an office may have to travel if his duties have to be performed in several places in succession. I would doubt whether such travelling is

371 [1970] AC 244; [above, para **[8.54]** and para **[8.73]**].
372 [1926] AC 1.
373 *Ibid.*, at p. 7.
374 *Ibid.*, at p. 4.
375 [This was removed by FA 1997, s 62.]

always "in the course of" the performance of his duties. If a part-time officer has to work at A today and B a week hence he is not on duty meanwhile and can travel whichever day he chooses. He is entitled to deduct the expense of travelling from A to B but it seems to me unreal to say that during the hours he is travelling he is on duty. He is travelling not in the course of performing his duties but to enable him to perform his next duty when the time comes.

In *Pook v. Owen*[376] the findings of the commissioners were also comparatively short. In addition to the facts which I have mentioned they found that there was a scarcity in the area of persons duly qualified to do the work and they found facts with regard to the nature of the work which enabled the majority in this House to hold that Dr. Owen had two places of work: some of his work had to be done at his home in Fishguard and some at the hospital in Haverfordwest. The question whether he had two places of work was the main question at issue.

But I do not see how consistently with the main ratio in *Ricketts'* case[377] that could in itself be sufficient to justify the decision. And no one suggested that the House was reaching a decision inconsistent with *Ricketts*. *Ricketts* decided that if the place where a man resides is his personal choice he cannot claim with regard to expenses made necessary by that personal choice. If the holder of an office or employment has to do part of his work at home the place where he resides is generally still his personal choice. If he could do his home work equally well wherever he lived then I do not see how the mere fact that his home is also a place of work could justify a departure from the *Ricketts* ratio.

I do not find it easy to discover the ratio decidendi of *Pook's* case. But that does not diminish the authority of the decision. I am sure that the majority did not intend to decide that in all cases where the employee's contract requires him to work at home he is entitled to deduct travelling expenses between his home and his other place of work. Plainly that would open the door widely for evasion of the rule. There must be something more.

I think that the distinguishing fact in *Pook's* case was that there was part-time employment and that it was impossible for the employer to fill the post otherwise than by appointing a man with commitments which he would not give up. It was therefore necessary that whoever was appointed should incur travelling expenses. It was theoretically possible for Dr. Owen to give up his practice and go to live in Haverfordwest. His employer would not have objected. The nearer to the hospital Dr. Owen lived the better. But the majority disregarded that theoretical possibility and had regard to the realities of the situation. I do not think that there was any departure from the ratio in *Ricketts'* case in deciding in favour of Dr. Owen. He contracted on the basis that he would continue to live at Fishguard and be paid expenses of travelling. He would not have contracted on any other basis. And it was impossible to find an appointee who was free to avoid incurring travelling expenses. I find nothing in *Ricketts* which necessarily excludes such a case.

Turning then to the present case, I think that it is covered by *Pook's* case. It was not enough that the appellant contracted to do most of his work in Canada, and would not have taken the employment otherwise. It was impossible for the companies which contracted with him to get the work done by anyone else. That I regard as the essential feature. That made it necessary that these travelling expenses should be incurred, and that is what is required to satisfy the rule.

I would allow this appeal.

LORD WILBERFORCE [dissenting]: . . . [*Having referred to paragraph 7 of Schedule 9 to the Income Tax Act 1952*[378]*:*]

The relevant word for the purpose of this case is "necessarily." It is a word which has a long history of interpretation and application. It does not mean what the ordinary taxpayer might think it should mean. To do any job, it is necessary to get there: but it is settled law that expenses of travelling to work cannot be deducted against the

376 [1970] AC 244; [above, para **[8.54]** and para **[8.73]**].
377 [1926] AC 1.
378 [Now ITEPA 2003, s 337(1).]

emoluments of the employment. It is only if the job requires a man to travel that his expenses of that travel can be deducted, ie. if he is travelling on his work, as distinct from travelling to his work. The most obvious category of jobs of this kind is that of itinerant jobs, such as commercial traveller. It is as a variant upon this that the concept of two places of work has been introduced: if a man has to travel from one place of work to another place of work, he may deduct the travelling expenses of his travel, because he is travelling on his work, but not those of travelling from either place of work to his home or vice versa. But for this doctrine to apply, he must be required by the nature of the job itself to do the work of the job in two places: the mere fact that he may choose to do part of it in a place separate from that where the job is objectively located is not enough. The case of *Pook v. Owen*[379] brought out this distinction. The basis of the decision of the majority in that case (the minority holding the opposite) was that the nature of the office, or employment, of part-time anaesthetist and obstetrician required the doctor to work partly at his surgery and partly at the hospital. This was what the general commissioners found and the finding was accepted in this House. The words which I used in that case,[380] and which have been invoked on the present appeal, presuppose, as the context would show, that the matter must be viewed objectively and were intended to provide a test whether the office or employment in question so regarded was such as to require that its duties be performed in two places.

The question then, in this case, is whether the element of "necessity" in the objective sense existed. Necessity from the personal circumstances of the taxpayer is not enough. Necessity for the employer to agree to Mr. Taylor's terms if it was to get his services, even if proved, which it certainly was not, is not enough – still less is a demonstration either that Mr. Taylor was the best, or only, man for the job, or that to obtain his services was beneficial to the company. This sort of consideration, even if proved, is irrelevant to the question whether Mr. Taylor should be taxed. The only necessity which is relevant is an objective necessity arising from the nature of the job itself in the performance of its duties. **[8.74]**

Kirkwood v Evans [2002] 1 WLR 1794 (Ch D)

The taxpayer civil servant joined his employer's homeworking scheme, making a journey one day each week to his employer's office in Leeds from his home in King's Lynn, the expense of which he sought to deduct under ICTA 1988, s 198(1).[381]

PATTEN J: . . .

8. I turn first to the 1997/98 year of assessment. In its unamended form s.198(1) lays down as an essential requirement that the employee should be "necessarily obliged" to incur the travel expenses in the performance of the duties of his employment. This is in contrast to the position under Schedule D[382] which merely requires that the expenditure should have been wholly and exclusively laid out or expended for the purposes of the trade, profession or vocation in question: see ICTA 1988 s.74.[383]
9. The strictness of the test under Schedule E was recognised by the House of Lords in the case of *Ricketts v Colquhoun*[384] which was concerned with a claim by a barrister residing and practising in London to deduct from the amount of the emoluments of his office as Recorder of Portsmouth the cost of travelling to and from Portsmouth and the hotel expenses incurred whilst staying there. There was no doubt that these expenses had to be incurred in order for the taxpayer to carry out his duties as Recorder. Living and working, as he did, in London he had to travel and stay there as

379 [1970] AC 244; [above, para **[8.54]** and para **[8.73]**].
380 [1970] AC 244 at 262.
381 The taxpayer's claim was for the tax years 1996–97, 1997–98 and 1998–99. For the tax year 1998–99, s 198(1) was amended following an Inland Revenue consultation (above, para **[8.71]**). See now ITEPA 2003, ss 337, 338.
382 [Trading income.]
383 See now ITTOIA 2005, s 34(1); below, para **[10.23]**.
384 [1926] AC 1.

and when he performed those duties. But that was not sufficient to satisfy the condition that the expenses should have been necessarily incurred in the performance of the duties of his office as Recorder. In his speech (at p.4) Viscount Cave LC put the matter in this way:

> "In order that they may be deductible under this rule from an assessment under Sch.E, they must be expenses which the holder of an office is necessarily obliged to incur – that is to say, obliged by the very fact that he holds the office and has to perform its duties – and they must be incurred in – that is, in the course of – the performance of those duties.
>
> The expenses in question in this case do not appear to me to satisfy either test. They are incurred not because the appellant holds the office of Recorder of Portsmouth, but because, living and practising away from Portsmouth, he must travel to that place before he can begin to perform his duties as Recorder and, having concluded those duties, desires to return home. They are incurred, not in the course of performing his duties, but partly before he enters upon them, and partly after he has fulfilled them. No doubt the rule contemplates that the holder of an office may have to travel in the performance of his duties, and there are offices of which the duties have to be performed in several places in succession, so that the holder of them must necessarily travel from one place to another. That was no doubt the case of the minister whose expenses were in question in the case of *Jardine v Gillespie*.[385] But it rarely, if ever, happens that a Recorder is in that position, and there is no suggestion that any such necessity exists in the case of the present appellant."

10. The essence of this reasoning is that what qualifies as a necessary expense falls to be determined not by reference to the circumstances of the particular individual who holds the office or employment under consideration but rather by reference to the dictates and scope of the office or employment itself. This principle has been qualified in more recent times by the decisions of the House of Lords in *Pook v Owen*[386] and *Taylor v Provan*[387] in both of which the taxpayer was held to be entitled to claim as allowable expenses the cost of travelling between his home and place of work. In *Pook v Owen* the taxpayer was a general practitioner who also held part time appointments as an obstetrician and anaesthetist at a hospital some 15 miles from his home and surgery. The evidence was that he was on standby duty under these appointments at certain times in order to deal with emergencies and was required to be accessible at home by telephone. His responsibility for a patient began on receipt of a call and he travelled from home to the hospital as part of those duties.

11. In *Taylor v Provan* the taxpayer was a Canadian citizen resident in Canada who was appointed as a director of various English brewery companies with the object of expanding the group by mergers and acquisitions. Most of his duties were performed in Canada but as part of his work he was required to travel to the UK. By a majority of 3 to 2 the costs of his air travel were held to be a deductible expense. The majority speeches go out of their way to stress that the decisions in *Pook v Owen* and *Taylor v Provan* are not to be regarded as diluting the strictness of the test laid down by the House in *Ricketts v Colquhoun. ... [Patten J referred to that part of Lord Reid's judgment that is extracted above,* para **[8.74]**.*]* ...

    In his dissenting speech Lord Wilberforce[388] also stressed the limited nature of the exception created by *Pook v Owen ...[Patten J cited the extract set out above,* para **[8.73]***]* ...

12. I mean no disrespect to Mr. Evans when I say that he was obviously not uniquely qualified for the work he did and he accepted that in argument. The highest that he can put his case is that he was under the terms of the Homeworking agreement with the CAS required to visit the office in Leeds to deliver and collect work and to update the information needed for his work. On the authorities this is not enough to make the travelling expenses ones which are necessarily incurred in the

385 (1906) 5 TC 263.
386 [1970] AC 244; [above, para **[8.54]** and para **[8.73]**].
387 [1975] AC 194; [above, para **[8.74]**].
388 Ibid at 215; [above, para **[8.74]**].

performance of those duties. Even accepting that the terms of his contract (whilst the Homeworking agreement subsisted) required him to work four days in King's Lynn and one in Leeds his choice to live in King's Lynn rather than Leeds was historical and is unconnected with any term of his employment. The necessity of travelling to Leeds is dictated by his choice of the place where he lives and not by nature and the terms of the job itself.

13. In paragraph 10(b) of the case stated the reasoning and decision of the General Commissioners on this point is set out in the following terms:

 "b) Having found as a fact that the Respondent had two places of work, one his home in King's Lynn and the other at his employer's office in Leeds, the Commissioners determined that the Respondent was obliged in respect of the performance of his work duties to travel from his King's Lynn office to Leeds and therefore the expense of so doing was necessary within the meaning of Section 198 of the Act, as was the expense relating to heating and lighting his King's Lynn office."

 It seems to me that the Commissioners considered that the mere fact that Mr. Evans had two places of work (one being his home) and was required to travel between them was sufficient to bring the expenses involved within the provisions of s.198(1). For the reasons set out in the speech of Lord Reid in *Taylor v Provan* this is not correct as a matter of law. Unless it could be shown either that Mr. Evans was uniquely qualified to do that job or that objectively the job could only be done by working at home in King's Lynn (as opposed to anywhere else) and at the office in Leeds the expenses cannot be said to have been necessarily incurred in the performance of Mr. Evans' duties. The Crown's appeal will therefore be allowed in respect of the travel expenses which relate to the year 1997/8.

14. In relation to the year 1998/9 there is no change in the pattern or terms of the employment which affects its fiscal treatment. The only new factor is the amendment of the legislation so as to broaden the scope of s.198(1). In order to be able to claim the costs of travel as a deductible expense they must satisfy the definition of "qualifying travelling expenses" in s.198(1)(a). Section 198(1)(A) which contains the definition of "qualifying travelling expenses" preserves as one of the two tests for determining whether an expense is allowable the condition that the sums in question should be necessarily expended in travelling in the performance of the duties of the office or employment: see s.198(1A)(a).[389] This is the same test as existed for travelling expenses under s.198(1) in its unamended form and is to be applied in accordance with the decisions of the House of Lords in *Ricketts v Colquhoun* and *Taylor v Provan*. The new provision is s.198(1A)(b).[390] To come within this sub-section the travel expenses must still be incurred in the performance of the duties of the office or employment, must be attributable to the necessary attendance of the employee at any place in the performance of those duties and must not be excluded by the definitions of ordinary commuting or private travel which are set out in Schedule 12A.

15. If one reads s.198(1A)(b)(i) for the moment it would appear to cover travel expenses to and from a place of work regardless of the point of departure. The concept of "necessary attendance" at a place in the performance of the duties of an office or employment would cover travel by most employees to their usual place of employment or to any other place which they are required to visit as part of that employment. But the provisions of Schedule 12A indicate that the scope of s.198(1A)(b) is far more limited than that. The definition of "ordinary commuting" in paragraph 2 of Schedule 12A excludes travel between an employee's home or some other place which is not a workplace and the employee's "permanent workplace". The definition of "permanent workplace" in paragraph 4 would therefore exclude the costs of travelling to work in most if not all cases. What however it will allow the employee to claim are the costs of travelling from home to a "temporary workplace" as defined or from one workplace to another workplace provided that

389 [See now ITEPA 2003, s 337(1).]
390 [See now ITEPA 2003, s 338(1).]

attendance at the destination workplace is necessary for the performance of the employee's duties. Travel of this second kind was probably an allowable expense under s.198(1) in its unamended form at least in relation to certain kinds of itinerant employment but the costs of travelling from home directly to a temporary workplace would probably have fallen foul of the decision in *Ricketts v Colquhoun* that the choice of location of one's home was a matter of personal choice and not a necessity of the office or employment. That objection is no longer available to the Revenue provided that the employee or office holder needs to attend the temporary workplace in order to perform his duties and the workplace is truly a temporary one. To avoid the costs of regular commuting being reclaimed simply because the employment itself is of limited duration special provisions have been included in paragraphs 4 and 5. The effect of these provisions is to exclude travel to a workplace during the course of a limited or fixed term of employment if the place is one at which the duties of the employee are performed to a significant extent: see para 5(2). Commuting to and from work at a temporary job is therefore ordinary commuting because the locus in quo is a "permanent workplace" within paragraph 4 and not a temporary one. Having regard to the provisions of paragraph 5 the definition of a "temporary workplace" is intended to encompass places of work which require the employee's attendance for a limited or temporary purpose within a course of employment (whether of limited duration or otherwise).

16. I have set out these new provisions in some detail in order to show how limited their scope is. But the Crown's appeal in relation to Mr. Evans' travel expenses for 1998/9 turns in the end on a very short point. The travel in question was between his home in King's Lynn and the CAS office in Leeds. The fact that his home was also a "workplace" does not prevent it from being his home. Sub-paragraphs 2(1)(a) and (b) are alternatives. They do not both have to be satisfied for the definition of "ordinary commuting" to apply. The taxpayer cannot therefore succeed in his claim to deduct the cost of travelling to and from Leeds under s.198(1A)(b) unless the office in Leeds is a "temporary workplace" within the meaning of Schedule 12A, paragraph 4. Although the General Commissioners appear to have concluded that Leeds was not a "permanent workplace" Mr. Evans conceded before me that this finding was incorrect. In my judgment he was right to do so. The terms of the Homeworking scheme which he agreed required him to attend the office in Leeds on one day per week. This attendance was both regular and was not "for the purpose of performing a task of limited duration or for some other temporary purpose". Although only one day a week his attendance at Leeds on that day was a permanent and continuing part of his duties as an employee. It subsisted for the entire length of his employment. His travel to and from Leeds did therefore in my judgment amount to "ordinary commuting" within the meaning of s.198(1A)(b)(ii). **[8.75]**

See also *Parikh v Sleeman*,[391] where the taxpayer, a general practitioner, ran his own practice from his home, and was also employed as a clinical officer under three contracts with three different hospitals, each of which paid him for the time expended in his travelling from his home or surgery to each hospital. He claimed a deduction for the cost of travelling from his home or surgery to the hospitals. Vinelott J held that this was not travelling in the performance of his duties, and could not be deducted under what is now ITEPA 2003, s 337.

Where an employer pays or reimburses an employee for expenses incidental to an overnight stay at a place in the UK or elsewhere, and the costs of the journey to that place are deductible under ITEPA 2003, ss 337–342, then those expenses are exempt from tax.[392]

391 [1988] STC 580.
392 ITEPA 2003, ss 240, 241. The maximum amount permitted per night is £5 for the UK and £10 elsewhere.

As to whether expenditure may be apportioned, see *Woodcock v Commission of Inland Revenue*,[393] where Walton J found that the very words used in the statute, 'wholly, exclusively and necessarily', did not allow for an apportionment of expenditure. A similar decision was reached in *Hillyer v Leeke*,[394] where a computer engineer was required to wear a suit for his work, which was often dirty. The engineer bought two suits, which he used only for work. His claim for the cost of one of them was rejected, with Goulding J confirming Walton J's view that expenses of this kind are not severable. See, however, the observations on the interpretation of ICTA 1988, s 198(1) (now ITEPA 2003, ss. 336-342) made by Vinelott J. in *Perrons v Spackman*.[395] This case concerned a car allowance, consisting of a lump sum and mileage allowance paid to a local authority rent officer. The mileage allowance contained a significant contribution towards the cost of putting the taxpayer's car on the road. The lump sum and the mileage allowance, less the actual cost of using the car on official journeys, were taxable as an emolument. The entire cost of running the car was not held to be an expense necessarily incurred in the performance of his duties. Vinelott J accepted that travelling expenses can be apportioned between private use and use for the performance of the duties of the employment, but that apportionment may be concessionary for other types of expenses. This is contrary to the views of both Walton and Goulding JJ.

Contrast the treatment of travelling expenses incurred by a person carrying on a trade, profession or vocation. Under ITTOIA 2005, s 34, 'no deduction is allowed for–(a) expenses not incurred wholly and exclusively for the purposes of the trade ...'.[396] See below, para **[10.31]** for a full explanation of this provision. **[8.76]**

393 [1977] STC 405.
394 [1976] STC 490.
395 [1981] 1 WLR 1411.
396 The provisions apply equally to professions and vocations: ITTOIA 2005, s 32.

9 Trade, Profession or Vocation

1. Introduction

Section 5 of the Income Tax (Trading and Other Income) Act 2005 ('ITTOIA 2005') charges to income tax 'the profits of a trade, profession or vocation'.[1]

If the trading profits arise to a UK resident, then they are chargeable 'wherever the trade is carried on';[2] if they arise to a non-UK resident, then they are chargeable if they arise 'from a trade carried on wholly in the United Kingdom'.[3] These rules apply to 'professions' and 'vocations' in the same way that they apply to 'trades'.[4]

In order to decide, therefore, whether a particular person is chargeable to income tax under ITTOIA 2005, s 5 it is necessary for that person to satisfy three conditions. First, a 'profit' must have 'arisen' to him. Secondly, he must be carrying on a 'trade, profession or vocation' and, thirdly, the profit must be 'derived' from the trade, profession or vocation.[5] If, in a particular case, all three conditions are satisfied, then income tax is chargeable 'on the full amount of the profits of the tax year'.[6]

Although the question of whether a person is carrying on a trade is one of fact, the concept of a 'trade' is partly defined in statute and partly in case law and, in certain situations, statute deems certain activities to constitute a trade. The definition of a 'trade' can be difficult to apply in certain cases, and, in order to decide whether a person is carrying on a trade, reference is made to six so-called 'badges of trade'. There also exist case law definitions of 'profession' and 'vocation'. **[9.1]**

2. A question of fact, not law

Whether a person is carrying on a trade is a question of fact, rather than one of law.[7] **[9.2]**

1 Formerly ICTA 1988, s 18(1).
2 See ITTOIA 2005, s 6(1) (formerly ICTA 1988, s 18(1), Schedule D, para (a)(ii)).
3 *Ibid*, s 6(2) (formerly ICTA 1988, s 18(1), Schedule D, para (a) (iii)).
4 *Ibid*, s 6(3) (formerly ICTA 1988, s 18(1), Schedule D, paras (a)(ii) and (a) (iii)).
5 Since s 5 refers to the 'profits *of* a trade', etc. [emphasis added].
6 See ITTOIA 2005, s 7(1).
7 As to which, see, eg, Timothy Endicott 'Questions of Law' (1998) 114 LQR 292–321.

***Erichsen v Last* (1881) 8 QBD 414 (CA); below, para [10.3]**

> SIR GEORGE JESSEL MR: . . . There is not, I think, any principle of law which lays down what carrying on a trade is. There are a multitude of things which together make up the carrying on of a trade, but I know no one distinguishing incident, for it is a compound fact made up of a variety of things . . . **[9.3]**

Responsibility for determining the question is therefore a matter for, as the case may be, the General Commissioners or Special Commissioners.[8] As Tiley says:

> "... it is for the Commissioners not only to determine the primary facts, such as what transactions were carried out, when, by whom and with what purpose, but also to conclude that the transaction was or was not a trade as defined.[9] Although this conclusion is an inference it is usually treated as one of fact."[10]

Two main consequences flow from the factual nature of whether a person is trading or not. First, since, under TMA 1970, ss 56 and 56A, an appeal lies to a higher court only on a point of law, the Commissioners' finding on the question of fact is conclusive. However, this is subject to the principle in *Edwards (Inspector of Taxes) v. Bairstow and Harrison*, ' . . . it may be', said Lord Radcliffe in that case, 'that the facts found are such that no person acting judicially and properly instructed as to the relevant law could have come to the determination under appeal'.[11] 'The court', continued his Lordship, 'must intervene ... [since] [i]t has no option but to assume that there has been some misconception of the law and that this has been responsible for the determination. So there . . . has been an error in point of law'.[12]

Secondly, it is important, when reading cases on whether or not a trade has been carried on, to assess their value as precedent. Cases where the court reluctantly holds that there are facts to justify the Commissioners' finding but states that it would itself have drawn a different conclusion from that drawn by the Commissioners are of very little use.[13] Very valuable, however, are cases where, holding that the facts point in the direction of only one conclusion, the Court has reversed the Commissioners' finding.[14] **[9.3a]**

3. Definitions

There is no definition of the words 'profession' or 'vocation' in either ITTOIA 2005 or ICTA 1988, although the latter contains a partial definition of 'trade'. It is therefore necessary to look to case law for definitions of each of these terms. **[9.4]**

8 See Chapter 3.
9 See *Jones v. Leeming* [1930] AC 415; *Hillerns and Fowler v. Murray* (1932) 17 TC 77.
10 See John Tiley, *Revenue Law* (5th edn., 2005), p. 346.
11 [1956] AC 14, 36; see Chapter 3, above, para **[3.15]**.
12 *Ibid.*
13 See *Pilkington v. Randall* (1966) 42 TC 662; *IRC v Reinhold* (1953) 34 TC 389; *Jenkinson v Freedland* (1961) 39 TC 636; *Iswera v IRC* [1965] 1 WLR 663; *Page v Pogson* (1954) 35 TC 545; *Lucy and Sunderland Ltd v Hunt* (1961) 40 TC 132.
14 See *Dunn Trust v Williams*, above; *Edwards v Bairstow and Harrison* [1956] AC 14, see above, para **[3.15]** and below, para **[9.19]**; *Eames v Stepnell Properties Ltd* [1967] 1 WLR 593; *Snell v Rosser, Thomas & Co Ltd* [1968] 1 WLR 295; *Taylor v Good* [1974] 1 WLR 556; *Kirkham v Williams* [1991] 1 WLR 863; and *Vodafone Cellular Ltd v Shaw* [1997] STC 734 (see Chapter 10, below, para **[10.30]**).

A. *Trade*

The Income Tax (Trading and Other Income) Act 2005 incorporates by reference the inclusive definition of a 'trade' in ICTA 1988, s 832(1):[15]

> '(1) In the Tax Acts, except in so far as the context otherwise requires- . . .
> "trade" includes every trade, manufacture, adventure or concern in the nature of trade . . .'

Fletcher Moulton LJ, in *Liverpool and London and Globe Insurance Company v Bennett* [1912] 2 KB 41 at 55, said that the words 'in the nature of trade' should be read as only qualifying the word 'concern'. However, the expression 'adventure in the nature of [a] trade' is in common use and, in *Johnston v Heath* [1970] 1 WLR 1567 at 1574, Goff J stated that Fletcher Moulton LJ's view was inconsistent with the House of Lords' decision in *Edwards (Inspector of Taxes) v Bairstow and Harrison*, above. **[9.5]**

Ransom v Higgs [1974] 1 WLR 1594 (HL)[16]

LORD WILBERFORCE: . . . Trade has for centuries been, and still is part of the national way of life: everyone is supposed to know what "trade" means: so Parliament, which wrote it into the Law of Income Tax in 1799, has wisely abstained from defining it and has left it to the courts to say what it does or does not include.

Trade is infinitely varied; so we often find applied to it the cliché that its categories are not closed. Of course they are not: but this does not mean that the concept of trade is without limits so that any activity which yields an advantage, however indirect, can be brought within the net of tax. Some systems tax in general terms all profits or income arising from personal exertion; some also tax the produce of any profit making enterprise; but English law does not do this. It names the commonest and most recognisable forms of personal exertions or enterprises in Schedules D and E of the Code[17] and, apart from special provisions which are not invoked here, each case must be brought within one of them.

"Trade" cannot be precisely defined, but certain characteristics can be identified which trade normally has . . .

Trade involves, normally, the exchange of goods, or of services, for reward, not of all services, since some qualify as a profession, or employment, or vocation, but there must be something which the trade offers to provide by way of business. Trade, moreover, presupposes a customer (to this too there may be exceptions, but such is the norm), or, as it may be expressed, trade must be bilateral – you must trade with someone. The "mutuality" cases are based in part at least upon this principle, and it was the existence of it that made *Sharkey v. Wernher*[18] an interesting problem . . . **[9.6]**

Simmons (as Liquidator of Lionel Simmons Properties Ltd) v IRC [1980] 1 WLR 1196 (HL)

LORD WILBERFORCE: . . . Trading requires an intention to trade: normally the question to be asked is whether this intention existed at the time of the acquisition of the asset. Was it acquired with the intention of disposing of it at a profit, or was it acquired as a permanent investment?[19] Often it is necessary to ask further questions: a permanent investment may be sold in order to acquire another investment thought to be more

15 See ITTOIA 2005, s 885(1) and Sch 4, Pt 2.
16 See also *British Olympic Association v Winter* [1995] STC (SCD) 85.
17 [Schedule D is still applicable for corporation tax purposes (see Chapter 7).]
18 [1956] AC 58 [see Chapter 10, para **[10.37]**.].
19 [This passage was referred to by Etherton J in *Re Loquitar* [2003] EWHC 999 (Ch), [2003] STC 1394.]

> satisfactory; that does not involve an operation of trade, whether the first investment is sold at a profit or at a loss. Intentions may be changed. What was first an investment may be put into the trading stock – and, I suppose, vice versa. If findings of this kind are to be made precision is required, since a shift of an asset from one category to another will involve changes in the company's accounts, and, possibly, a liability to tax: see *Sharkey v. Wernher*.[20]
>
> What I think is not possible is for an asset to be both trading stock and permanent investment at the same time, nor for it to possess an indeterminate status – neither trading stock nor permanent asset. It must be one or the other, even though, and this seems to me legitimate and intelligible, the company, in whatever character it acquires the asset, may reserve an intention to change its character. To do so would, in fact, amount to little more than making explicit what is necessarily implicit in all commercial operations, namely that situations are open to review. **[9.7]**

Lord Wilberforce's reference, in *Ransom v Higgs*, above, to 'the mutuality cases' is to the concept of 'mutual trading'. This is where people form an association, whether incorporated (eg a mutual company)[21] or unincorporated (eg a members' club), and make contributions jointly to a fund for their mutual benefit. If the fund is in surplus, the surplus is not subject to income tax.[22] This may either be because it is generally not possible to trade with oneself (see *Ransom v Higgs*, above) or because the surplus is not a profit:[23] **[9.8]**

New York Life Insurance Company v Styles (1889) 14 App Cas 381 (HL)

The insurance company's membership consisted solely of participating policy holders. The generality of the membership was entitled to any surplus of income over expenditure. The House of Lords held that the surplus was not taxable.

> LORD WATSON: ... When a number of individuals agree to contribute funds for a common purpose, such as the payment of annuities, or of capital sums, to some or all of them, on the occurrence of events certain or uncertain, and stipulate that their contributions, so far as not required for that purpose, shall be repaid to them, I cannot conceive why they should be regarded as traders, or why contributions returned to them should be regarded as profits ... **[9.9]**

A person may be carrying on activities that neither fall within the scope of his trade nor amount to trading in their own right.[24] It is also possible that a person may be carrying on two or more separate trades[25] or that he may be carrying on a particular trade that includes a number of activities.[26]

20 [1956] AC 58 [see Chapter 10, para **[10.37]**].

21 Eg the BBC (see *BBC v Johns* (1964) 41 TC 471).

22 The profits attributable to the trade of a members' club with non-members are, however, taxable (see *Carlisle and Silloth Golf Club v Smith* [1913] 3 KB 75). See also Robert Burgess 'The Mutuality Principle' [1976] BTR 361.

23 See also ITTOIA 2005, s 104, which contains an anti-avoidance provision designed to tax any surplus on a return of assets where the contributor had originally obtained a deduction in calculating his own trading profits.

24 See *Dunn Trust Ltd v Williams* (1950) 31 TC 477; *West v Phillips* (1958) 38 TC 203.

25 See *Hawes v Gardiner* (1957) 37 TC 671; *Lewis Emanuel and Son Ltd v White* (1965) 42 TC 369. The question of whether a person is expanding an existing trade or starting a new one may be relevant in relation to trading loss relief (see *Howden Boiler and Armaments Co Ltd v Stewart* (1924) 9 TC 205 and *Cannon Industries Ltd v Edwards* [1966] 1 WLR 580).

26 See *Gloucester Railway Carriage and Wagon Co Ltd v IRC* [1925] AC 469; *Spiers and Son Ltd v Ogden* (1932) 17 TC 117.

Finally, the fact that a trade is either illegal (see, eg, *Hayes v Duggan* [1929] 1 IR 406; *Minister of Finance v Smith* [1927] AC 193) or is carried on by means of contracts unenforceable for illegality (see, eg, *IRC v Aken* [1990] STC 497, 506 (Parker LJ)) should not prevent the profits arising from it from being taxable (see, generally, Mary Mulholland and Roger Cockfield, 'The Implications of Illegal Trading' [1995] BTR 572–580). **[9.10]**

B. Profession

The meaning of 'profession', the existence of which, like 'trade', is a question mainly of fact (see *Currie v IRC* [1921] 2 KB 332), was considered by Scrutton LJ in the following case: **[9.11]**

IRC v Maxse [1919] 1 KB 647 (CA)

> SCRUTTON LJ: . . . The next question is what is a "profession"? I am very reluctant finally to propound a comprehensive definition. A set of facts not present to the mind of the judicial propounder, and not raised in the case before him, may immediately arise to confound his proposition. But it seems to me as at present advised that a "profession" in the present use of language involves the idea of an occupation requiring either purely intellectual skill, or of manual skill, controlled, as in painting and sculpture, or surgery, by the intellectual skill of the operator, as distinguished from an occupation which is substantially the production or sale or arrangements for the production or sale of commodities. The line of demarcation may vary from time to time. The word "profession" used to be confined to the three learned professions, the Church, Medicine, and Law. It has now, I think, a wider meaning. It appears to me clear that a journalist whose contributions have any literary form, as distinguished from a reporter, exercises a "profession"; and that the editor of a periodical comes in the same category. It seems to me equally clear that the proprietor of a newspaper or periodical, controlling the printing, publishing and advertising, but not responsible for the selection of the literary or artistic contents, does not exercise a "profession" but a trade or business other than a profession . . . **[9.12]**

It seems, moreover, that the world's oldest profession, namely prostitution, is actually a trade (see *IRC v Aken,* above). **[9.13]**

C. Vocation

The term 'vocation' was considered in the following case. **[9.14]**

Partridge v Mallandaine (1886) 18 QBD 276 (QBD)

The appellant, a bookmaker, was held to be carrying on a vocation.

> DENMAN J: . . . But the word "vocation" is analogous to "calling", a word of wide signification, meaning the way in which a person passes his life . . .
>
> HAWKINS J: . . . "Vocation" and "calling" are synonymous terms, and if anyone were asked what was the calling of the appellants, the answer would be that they were professional bookmakers. What that means is well known, and is fully described in the case. Mere betting is not illegal. It is perfectly lawful for a man to bet if he likes. He may, however, have a difficulty in getting the amount of the bets from dishonest persons who make bets and will not pay. The appellants, in fact, make considerable profits, and I cannot see why they should not be taxed as those made in any other profession or calling. **[9.15]**

Habitual gambling is not, however, treated as a vocation; see *Graham v Green (Inspector of Taxes)* [1925] 2 KB 37 at 42, where Rowlatt J said:

> '... I do not think that he [the habitual gambler] could be said to organise his effort in the same way as a bookmaker organises his, for I do not think the subject matter from his point of view is susceptible of it ... I think all you can say of that man [ie the habitual gambler], in the fair use of the English language, is that he is addicted to betting.' **[9.16]**

4. The 'badges of trade'

In addition to the definitions of a trade set out above, there are the six so-called 'badges of trade' contained in the 1955 Final Report of the Royal Commission on the Taxation of Profits and Income (1955, Cmnd. 9474). The six badges of trade are derived from the Commission's analysis of the case-law extracted below, and they are used to determine whether a business activity is a trade, or an adventure in the nature of trade. They are used often, although not universally.[27]

Before capital gains tax ('CGT') was introduced in 1965, the question of whether a person was carrying on a trade could determine whether tax was chargeable at all. Even after the introduction of CGT, the fact that there was for many years a difference in the rates of income tax and CGT meant that the distinction could still be very important. Although FA 1988 removed the disparity between rates of tax, recent changes to CGT, in particular the introduction of taper relief[28] and the Enterprise Investment Scheme ('EIS'), have again emphasised the importance of the distinction between the two taxes. **[9.17]**

Final Report of the Royal Commission on the Taxation of Profits and Income (Cmd 9474 (1955))

116 ... each case must be decided according to its own circumstances. The general line of enquiry that has been favoured by appeal Commissioners and encouraged by the Courts is to see whether a transaction that is said to have given rise to a taxable profit bears any of the "badges of trade." This seems to us the right line, and it has the advantage that it bases itself on objective tests of what is a trading adventure instead of concerning itself directly with the unravelling of motive. At the same time we have noticed that there has been some lack of uniformity in the treatment of different cases according to the tribunals before which they have been brought. This seems to us unfortunate and, for the sake of clarity, we have drawn up and set out below a summary of what we regard as the major relevant considerations that bear upon the identification of these "badges of trade."

(1) *The subject matter of the realisation.* While almost any form of property can be acquired to be dealt in, those forms of property, such as commodities or manufactured articles, which are normally the subject of trading are only very exceptionally the subject of investment. Again property which does not yield to its owner an income or personal enjoyment merely by virtue of its ownership is more likely to have been acquired with the object of a deal than property that does.

27 See, eg, Tiley, above, para 19.3; *Marson v Morton* [1986] 1 WLR 1343.
28 See Chapter 20, para **[20.45]**.

(2) *The length of the period of ownership.* Generally speaking, property meant to be dealt in is realised within a short time after acquisition. But there are many exceptions from this as a universal rule.

(3) *The frequency or number of similar transactions by the same person.* If realisations of the same sort of property occur in succession over a period of years or there are several such realisations at about the same date a presumption arises that there has been dealing in respect of each.

(4) *Supplementary work on or in connection with the property realised.* If the property is worked up in any way during the ownership so as to bring it into a more marketable condition; or if any special exertions are made to find or attract purchasers, such as the opening of an office or large-scale advertising, there is some evidence of dealing. For when there is an organised effort to obtain profit there is a source of taxable income. But if nothing at all is done, the suggestion tends the other way.

(5) *The circumstances that are responsible for the realisation.* There may be some explanation, such as a sudden emergency or opportunity calling for ready money, that negatives the idea that any plan of dealing prompted the original purchase.

(6) *Motive.* There are cases in which the purpose of the transaction of purchase and sale is clearly discernible. Motive is never irrelevant in any of these cases. What is desirable is that it should be realised clearly that it can be inferred from surrounding circumstances in the absence of direct evidence of the seller's intentions and even, if necessary, in the face of his own evidence ... **[9.18]**

Edwards (Inspector of Taxes) v Bairstow and Harrison [1956] AC 14 (HL); above, para [3.15]

LORD RADCLIFFE: ... This seems to be, inescapably, a commercial deal in secondhand plant.[29] What detail does it lack that prevents it from being an adventure in the nature of trade, or what element is present in it that makes it capable of being aptly described as anything else? Well, to judge by the respondents' contentions as recited in the case, there were some circumstances lacking in this deal of which the presence has been regarded as of importance in other cases. I do not think that this line of argument is ever very conclusive; but, in any event, it breaks down completely on the facts that are found. It is said that there was no organisation for the purposes of the transaction. But in fact there was organisation, as much of it as the transaction required. It is true that the plant was not advertised for sale, though advertisements asking for plant were answered by the respondents. But why should they incur the cost of advertising if they judged that they could achieve the sale of the plant without it? It is said that no work had been done on the maturing of the asset to be sold. But such replacement and renovation as were needed were in fact carried out, and I can see no reason why a dealer should do more work in making his plant saleable than the purposes of sale require. It is said that neither of the respondents had any special skill from his normal activities which placed him in an advantageous position for the purposes of this transaction. It may be so, though one of them was the employee of a spinning firm. In any case the members of a commercial community do not need much instruction in the principles and possibility of dealing, and I think that, given the opportunity, the existence or non-existence of special skill is of no significance whatever. It is said, finally, that the purchase and sale of plant lent itself to capital, rather than commercial, transactions. I am not sure that I understand what this is intended to mean. If it means that at the relevant period there was no market for

29 [See Chapter 10, para **[10.66]**.]

secondhand plant in which deals could take place, there is no finding to that effect and all the facts that are recited seem to be against the contention. If it means anything else, it is merely an attempt to describe the conclusion which the respondents would wish to see arrived at on the whole case.

There remains the fact which was avowedly the original ground of the commissioners' decision – "this was an isolated case." But, as we know, that circumstance does not prevent a transaction which bears the badges of trade from being in truth an adventure in the nature of trade. The true question in such cases is whether the operations constitute an adventure of that kind, not whether they by themselves or they in conjunction with other operations, constitute the operator as a person who carries on a trade. Dealing is, I think, essentially a trading adventure, and the respondents' operations were nothing but a deal or deals in plant and machinery . . . **[9.19]**

A. *'The subject matter of the realisation'*

Rutledge v IRC (1929) 14 TC 490 (CS)

THE LORD PRESIDENT (CLYDE): . . . The Appellant is a business man with many interests; he lends money, he is connected with film business, and he deals in real property. He happened to be in Berlin in connection with one of these interests a few years ago, and while there had the opportunity of making a purchase of a very large quantity of toilet paper from a bankrupt German firm for £1,000. He had the paper sent over to this country and endeavoured to market it. He ultimately found a purchaser for the whole quantity at the price of £12,000. He has now been assessed to Income Tax and Excess Profits Duty on the profit of about £11,000 which thus arose or accrued to him.

The question in the case is whether the profits thus assessed are, or are not, profits of an "adventure . . . in the nature of trade" within the meaning of section 237 of the Income Tax Act 1918.

An adventure it certainly was; for the Appellant made himself liable for the purchase of this vast quantity of toilet paper obviously for no other conceivable purpose than that of re-selling it at a profit; and that is just what he did. The element of adventure accordingly entered into the purchase from the first. It has been said, not without justice, that mere intention is not enough to invest a transaction with the character of trade. But, on the question whether the Appellant entered into an adventure or speculation, the circumstances of the purchase, and also the purchaser's object or intention in making it, do enter, and that directly, into the solution of the question. An adventure, then, the Appellant's speculation certainly was, and a most successful adventure.

The question remains whether the adventure was one "in the nature of trade." The Appellant's contention is that it could not be such, because it is essential to the idea of trade that there should be a continuous series of trading operations; and an observation made in the course of my opinion in *Inland Revenue v. Livingston*[30] was founded on, according to which "a single transaction falls as far short of constituting a dealer's trade, as the appearance of a single swallow does of making a summer. The trade of a dealer necessarily consists of a course of dealing, either actually engaged in or at any rate contemplated and intended to continue." But the question here is not whether the Appellant's isolated speculation in toilet paper was a trade, but whether it was an "adventure . . . in the nature of trade"; and in the opinion referred to I said that, in my opinion, "the profits of an isolated venture . . . may be taxable under Schedule D provided the venture is 'in the nature of trade.'" I see no reason to alter that opinion. It is no doubt true that the question whether a particular adventure is "in the nature of trade" or not must depend on its character and circumstances, but if – as in the present case – the purchase is made for no purpose except that of re-sale at a profit, then there seems little difficulty in arriving at the conclusion that the deal was "in the nature of trade," though it may be wholly insufficient to constitute by itself a trade.

30 (1927) 11 TC 538.

... Reverting to the facts of the present case, it seems to me to be quite plain (1) that the Appellant, in buying the large stock of toilet paper, entered upon a commercial adventure or speculation; (2) that this adventure or speculation was carried through in exactly the same way as any regular trader or dealer would carry through any of the adventures or speculations in which it is his regular business to engage; and therefore (3) that the purchase and re-sale of the toilet paper was an "adventure ... in the nature of trade" within the meaning of the Income Tax Act 1918. If that is right the appeal cannot succeed.

LORD SANDS: ... The nature and quantity of the subject dealt with exclude the suggestion that it could have been disposed of otherwise than as a trade transaction. Neither the purchaser nor any purchaser from him was likely to require such a quantity for his private use ... **[9.20]**

Cooke v Haddock (1960) 39 TC 64 (ChD)

A solicitor bought, and subsequently resold, a piece of land. When he was assessed to income tax under what was then Schedule D, Case I,[31] he claimed that he had bought the land as a long-term investment. It was held that the assessment was correctly made on the basis of the transaction being a trading one.

PENNYCUICK J: ... There are a number of facts in the present case which justify the finding of the Commissioners. In particular, (i) the land was ripe for building subject to the necessary licences being obtained; (ii) the land was unsuitable for occupation by the Appellant or for retention as an income-producing investment by the Appellant; (iii) the Appellant obtained planning permission for the development of the estate (although this was to safeguard himself against the threat of compulsory purchase and not with a view to developing the estate himself); (iv) the Appellant sold parts of the land piecemeal; and (v) the Appellant has been concerned in companies and in a partnership firm engaged in dealings in land. I think all these elements have been referred to in other reported decisions on this particular question as to what constitutes the carrying on of a trade of a dealer in land. It seems to me that those circumstances amply warrant the conclusion to which the Special Commissioners came. **[9.21]**

Land and shares, both being capable of producing an income and therefore being particularly suitable to acquire as investments, have traditionally produced difficult cases in this area: see *Simmons v IRC*, above, and *Taylor v Good* [1974] 1 WLR 556.[32] In *Marson v Morton* [1986] 1 WLR 1343, the property sold was land and Sir Nicolas Browne-Wilkinson V-C held that the Commissioners were correct in holding that Mr Morton and his brothers, who were all shareholders in a family potato-trading company, did not make a trading profit when they re-sold land originally bought by them in 1977 with the benefit of planning permission. His Lordship emphasised the very unusual nature of the facts, since the brothers did not themselves intend to develop the land. He went on:

"The subject matter was land with planning permission, which is an item of property which I would have thought was neutral, namely it could have been bought for investment purposes. On the other hand, it is of course manifestly a commodity which is dealt with by way of property deals [ie trading transactions]. It is not to my mind the same as whisky [see *Cape Brandy Syndicate v. IRC* (1921) 12 TC 358, below] or toilet paper, in relation to which profit is incapable of being realised other than by a quick sale ... I can see no reason why ... the mere fact that land is not income-producing should not be decisive, or even virtually decisive, on the question whether it was bought as an investment (see [1986] 1 WLR 1343, 1349G-H and 1350D)."

31 Still applicable for corporation tax purposes (see Chapter 7).
32 See under sub-heading F below.

It should therefore be possible, on this reasoning, for a seller to contend, even when land is not bought to rent out, that the profit realised is not a trading profit.

However, where the relevant subject matter is not such as to produce an income and not the kind of property that one might keep for personal use or enjoyment, it will be extremely difficult to argue that any profit realised on its sale is not a trading profit (see, eg, *Wisdom v Chamberlain* [1969] 1 All ER 332, below). **[9.22]**

B. 'The length of the period of ownership'

Wisdom v Chamberlain [1969] 1 All ER 332 (CA)

Norman Wisdom, the comedian, wanted 'a nest-egg' for the future, because '...after all a comedian's life does not go on for ever and he needs something for his declining years ...'.[33] In 1961, therefore, he purchased £200,000 in silver bullion, as a hedge against a devaluation in the pound sterling. He sold the bullion little more than a year later and made a profit of £48,000, which the Court of Appeal held to be a profit from an adventure in the nature of trade.

> HARMAN LJ: ... In the first place it seems to me that, supposing it was a hedge against devaluation, it was nevertheless a transaction entered into on a short-term basis for the purpose of making a profit out of the purchase and sale of a commodity, and if that is not an adventure in the nature of a trade I do not really know what is. The whole object of the transaction was to make a profit. It was expected that there would be devaluation, and the reason for wanting to make a profit was that there would be a loss on devaluation, but that does not make any difference, it seems to me, to the fact that the motive and object of the whole transaction was to buy on a short-term basis a commodity with a view to its re-sale at a profit. That, as it seems to me, is an adventure in the nature of trade ... **[9.23]**

It will be material to a finding that the transaction was a trading transaction that the taxpayer entered into a contract to sell certain land before he had bought it (see *Johnston v Heath* [1970] 1 WLR 1567). **[9.24]**

C. 'The frequency or number of similar transactions by the same person'

Pickford v Quirke (1927) 13 TC 251 (CA)

Syndicates were formed to buy companies which owned cotton-mills. They would liquidate a company once it had been bought and sell its property to anyone who was willing to buy it. Although the membership of the syndicates varied, the taxpayer in this case had taken part in four such transactions. The Court of Appeal held that, although each transaction was not an adventure in the nature of trade in itself, the fact that the taxpayer had taken part in four such transactions meant that he was carrying on a trade, and the profits on the four sales were taxable under what was then Schedule D, Case I.[34]

> LORD HANWORTH MR: ... It must be remembered that under the interpretation clause trade "includes every trade, manufacture, adventure or concern in the nature of

33 [1969] 1 All ER 332 at 334 (Harman LJ).
34 See Chapter 7 (still applicable for corporation tax purposes).

> trade." When, however, you come to look at four successive transactions, you may hold that what was, considered separately and apart, a transaction to which the words "trade or concern in the nature of trade" could not be applied, yet when you have that transaction repeated, not once or twice but three times, at least, you may draw a completely different inference from those incidents taken together. That is what the Commissioners have done ... **[9.25]**

See also *Burrell, Webber and Others v Davis* (1958) 38 TC 307 (the effect of three 'inexperienced adventurers' joining in with two others who had already taken part in similar transactions); *Leach v Pogson* (1962) 40 TC 585 (the effect of subsequent transactions on an initial isolated transaction – taxpayer had sold 30 driving school businesses). **[9.26]**

Martin v Lowry [1927] AC 312 (HL)

In June 1919, Mr Martin, who did not generally buy and sell aircraft linen,[35] purchased 45 million yards of it, ie the whole of the Government's surplus stock after the First World War, from the relevant Government department. On failing to dispose of it in one bulk sale, he rented an office in High Holborn from July 1919 until March 1920, and set up a large and skilled organisation for disposing of it in smaller quantities. He made a profit on the sales of over £1.5 million. The House of Lords held that Mr Martin had set up a trading organisation and that the profit was therefore taxable under Schedule D, Case I.[36]

> VISCOUNT CAVE LC: ... My Lords, the Commissioners have found as a fact that he did carry on a trade, and they set out in the case ample material upon which they could come to that conclusion. Indeed, having regard to the methods adopted for the resale of the linen, to the number of operations into which the appellant entered, and to the time occupied by the resale, I do not myself see how they could have come to any other conclusion ... **[9.27]**

D. *'Supplementary work on or in connection with the property realised'*

Cape Brandy Syndicate v IRC (1921) 12 TC 358

Three people, who were wine-traders, formed a syndicate to buy 3,000 casks of a particular kind of brandy. They blended it with another kind of brandy, recasked it, and sold it to customers at a significant profit, from July 1916 to September 1917. Rowlatt J did not interfere with the General Commissioners' finding that the profit on the transactions was a trading profit.[37]

> ROWLATT J: ... It is quite clear that these gentlemen did far more than simply buy an article which they thought was going cheap, and re-sell it. They bought it with a view to transport it, with a view to modify its character by skilful manipulation, by blending with a view to alter, not only the amounts by which it would be sold as a man might split up an estate, but by altering the character in the way it was done up so that it could be sold in smaller quantities. They employed experts – and were experts themselves – to dispose of it over a long period of time. When I say over a long period of time I mean by sales which began at once but which extended over some period of time. They did not buy it and put

35 The case dates from the time when aeroplanes were built on wooden or metal frames, across which linen was stretched and doped or varnished, in order to form the fuselage, wings, and tail.

36 See Chapter 7 (still applicable for corporation tax purposes).

37 Neither did the Court of Appeal (see [1921] 2 KB 403).

> it away, they never intended to buy it and put it away and keep it. They bought it to turn over at once obviously and to turn over advantageously by means of the operations which I have indicated. Now under those circumstances the Commissioners have held that they did carry on a trade, and I think it is a question of fact, and I do not think, by telling me all the evidence, that the Commissioners can make me, or indeed give me authority – because they cannot give me any authority if I do not possess it by law – to determine the question of fact. I think that it is a question of fact, and a question of degree which generally is a question of fact. I need not say any more than that. I am not prepared to say that there was no evidence before the Commissioners. I think it is just one of those cases where there was evidence. I can conceive people deciding the other way. I do not say which way I should decide myself. But I certainly think there were materials upon which they could find as they did ... **[9.28]**

See *IRC v Livingston* (1927) 11 TC 538 (profit on sale of steam drifter converted from cargo vessel held to be a trading profit);[38] *Jenkinson v Freedland* (1961) 39 TC 636 (profit on sale of two stills[39] to the taxpayer's own company, the stills having been treated by a process which the taxpayer had himself invented, held not to be a trading profit). See also *Hudson v Wrightson* (1934) 26 TC 55. **[9.29]**

E. 'The circumstances that were responsible for the realisation'

The Hudson's Bay Company v Stevens (1909) 5 TC 424 (CA)

The Company had, over a period of years, sold a significant amount of land that it had acquired in part consideration for the surrender of its Charter. The Court of Appeal held that the profits on the sales were not trading profits because the sales themselves were not trading transactions.

> Sir HH COZENS-HARDY MR: ... The real question is whether this money can be regarded as profits or gains derived by the Company from carrying on a trade or business. In my opinion it cannot. The Company are doing no more than an ordinary landowner does who is minded to sell from time to time, as purchases offer, portions suitable for building of an estate which has devolved upon him from his ancestors. I am unable to attach any weight to the circumstance that large sales are made every year. This is not a case where land is from time to time purchased with a view to resale; the Company are only getting rid by sale as fast as they reasonably can of land which they acquired as part of a consideration for the surrender of their Charter ... **[9.30]**

It seems to be less likely that a court would hold there to be a trading transaction on a sale in a case where the property in question was originally acquired other than by purchase (see *Balgownie Land Trust Ltd v IRC* (1929) 14 TC 684; *McClelland v Commissioner of Taxation of the Commonwealth of Australia* [1971] 1 WLR 191).

Where a person is compelled to sell by circumstances beyond his or her control, any profit will tend not to be a trading profit. In *West v Phillips* (1958) 38 TC 203, a builder had made a profit on the sale of a large number of houses originally built to hold as an investment. He successfully argued that

38 The case is referred to in Lord Clyde's judgment in *Rutledge v IRC*, above, para **[9.20]**.
39 Ie pieces of distillation equipment.

he had been forced to make the sale by Government rent control and rising rates of taxation. In the circumstances, therefore, the profit on the sale of the houses was not derived from the builder's trade and thus did not fall within Schedule D, Case I (see Chapter 10). **[9.31]**

Cohan's Executors v IRC (1924) 12 TC 602 (CA)

When living, the deceased had been a partner in a shipping brokers' firm and had entered into a shipbuilding contract. After his death, his executors completed the contract and sold the ship. In these circumstances, the Court of Appeal held that the executors were only carrying out their duty to realise the deceased's assets and were not therefore carrying on the deceased's trade.

> POLLOCK MR: ... I think it is clear that the Commissioners in the Case did find that the deceased carried on a trade or business within the meaning of the words used in the Finance Act of 1915, and perhaps one may say, although it is not in one's province to do so, that I should certainly agree with them in that finding. But it is quite a different question as to whether or not after his death that business, which had been carried on by him, now in the relevant period was carried on by his executors. The executors would have the duty of getting in the estate, of winding up the deceased's affairs and concluding his business, and they would necessarily have to deal with the business situation created by the testator in his lifetime; and the fact that the Commissioners have found that the testator was carrying on a business clearly indicates that the executors were presented with a business being carried on at that time which they had to handle in a business-like way for the purpose of the realisation of the estate. **[9.32]**

But see also *Weisberg's Executrices v IRC* (1933) 17 TC 696; *Hillerns and Fowler v Murray* (1932) 17 TC 77, 92 (Romer LJ).

A similar issue arises where, instead of allowing a partnership to continue, the executors of a deceased partner insist on realising the deceased's share in the partnership assets. If there is clear evidence that the executors insisted on realising the deceased's share and did not consent to the trade being continued, then a profit on sale will be treated as a realisation rather than as a trading transaction (see *Marshall's Executors v Joly* (1936) 20 TC 256 (mere realisation) but see also *Newbarn's Syndicate v Hay* (1939) 22 TC 461 (continuing trade)).

Liquidators, since their duty is similar to that of personal representatives, face a similar problem: *IRC v The 'Old Bushmills' Distillery Co. Ltd* (1927) 12 TC 1148; *IRC v Burrell* [1924] 2 KB 52; *IRC v Oban Distillery Co. Ltd* (1932) 18 TC 33; *Wilson Box (Foreign Rights) Ltd v Brice* [1936] 3 All ER 728; *Baker v Cook* (1937) 21 TC 337; *IRC v Toll Property Co. Ltd* (1952) 34 TC 13; *John Mills (Production) Ltd v Mathias* (1964) 44 TC 441.

Depending on the facts of the case, a trader's disposal of trading stock after retirement may be a trading transaction: see *IRC v Nelson* (1939) 22 TC 716 (one sale of whole stock 12 days after deciding to retire was not a trading transaction); *J and R O'Kane Ltd v IRC* (1922) 12 TC 303 (many small sales of stock in period of almost two years after decision to retire). **[9.33]**

F. 'Motive'

Kirkham v Williams [1991] 1 WLR 863

The appellant, who carried on a trade mainly as a general dealer and demolition contractor, sold a four-bedroom house that he had built on land called 'Havannah

Mills'. He had acquired the land five years previously with the principal purpose of using it for office and storage space. The General Commissioners held that the profit of £90,000 that arose on the sale of the property was a trading profit. The CA reversed this finding, invoking the principle in *Edwards (Inspector of Taxes) v Bairstow and Harrison* (above, para **[3.15]**).

> NOURSE LJ: . . . Viewing the primary facts found by the commissioners and the inferences which they could properly draw from them in the light least favourable to the taxpayer, I would state the position thus. The taxpayer acquired Havannah Mills in order to provide the office and storage space which he needed for his business as a result of the difficulties he had had with the local authority over storage at his mother's address. He also intended to develop and sell the site as a whole if he could obtain planning permission to do so and if and when he had been able to provide himself with suitable office and storage space elsewhere, an event which would not occur in the immediate future and might not occur for some time . . .
>
> It was established by the decision of this court in *Taylor v. Good* [1974] 1 WLR 556[40] that where a taxpayer, not being a dealer in land, acquires a property, enhances its value and disposes of it at a profit, there is no adventure in the nature of trade unless he had the intention of so disposing of it at the time of its acquisition ... [*his Lordship quoted the extract from Simmons v. IRC extracted above at para* **[9.7]**], 'a passage which both sides accept as a correct statement of the law'; *Iswera v. IRC* [1965] 1 WLR 663; and the decision of the CA in *Ensign Tankers (Leasing) Ltd v. Stokes* [1991] 1 WLR 341][41]
>
> These [latter] two authorities show that the first question to be answered is whether the transaction is equivocal or unequivocal. If it has all the characteristics of trading, that is to say, if it is unequivocal, then, in the words of Lord Reid in *Iswera v. Inland Revenue Commissioners* [1965] 1 WLR 663, 668:
>
> > "[the taxpayer's] purpose or object alone cannot prevail over what he in fact does. But if his acts are equivocal his purpose or object may be a very material factor when weighing the total effect of all the circumstances."
>
> Similarly, if an equivocal transaction is entered into for two different purposes, both must be taken into account when weighing the total effect of all the circumstances . . .
>
> The taxpayer's acquisition of Havannah Mills was an equivocal transaction. If viewed on its own, it does not tell you whether the property acquired was trading stock or a capital asset of the taxpayer's business. It might have been either. So account must be taken of the two purposes which the commissioners have attributed to the taxpayer, in the one case by express finding and in the other by presumed inference . . . In my judgment no body of commissioners acting judicially and properly instructed as to the relevant law could have come to the conclusion that the property was acquired as trading stock. On that view of the matter the assessment must be discharged . . . **[9.34]**

The intention to make a profit is only one of a range of factors relevant to deciding whether a particular activity amounts to trading (see also *Waylee Investment Ltd v Commissioner of Inland Revenue* [1990] STC 780; *Kirkby v Hughes* [1993] STC 76). Although there is some authority to suggest that activities that must of necessity produce a loss cannot be trading activities (see *Religious Tract and Book Society of Scotland v Forbes* (1896) 3 TC 415), the fact that there is no profit motive does not prevent an activity from constituting a trade.[42]

For the significance of motive in the context of the trustees of a pension scheme, see *Clarke (Inspector of Taxes) v British Telecom Pension Scheme Trustees* [2000] STC 222 (CA) (noted by Roger Kerridge at [2000] BTR 397). **[9.35]**

40 [A significant case, since it involved a reversal of the Commissioners' finding (see above, n 14).]

41 [*Ensign Tankers* was decided, subsequently, in the House of Lords (see [1992] 1 AC 655).]

42 See also *Re Duty on the Estate of the Incorporated Council of Law Reporting for England and Wales* (1888) 22 QBD 279; *Mersey Docks and Harbour Board v Lucas* (1883) 8 App Cas 891.

5. Statutory trades

ITTOIA 2005 deems certain activities to be trades. These include farming and market gardening;[43] the commercial occupation of land other than woodlands[44] and the profits of quarries, mines and similar businesses.[45] **[9.36]**

43 See ITTOIA 2005, s 9 (formerly ICTA 1988, s 53(1) and (2)).
44 Ibid, s 10 (formerly ICTA 1988, ss 53(3) and (4)). The commercial occupation of woodlands is not a trade (see ITTOIA 2005, s 11 (formerly ICTA 1988, ss 53(3) and 53(4)).
45 Ibid, s 12.

10 Trading Income

1. Introduction

Where it is ascertained that a person's activities constitute a trade, profession or vocation, income tax is charged on the full amount of the profits that arise from it.[1] Put simply, any amount of income remaining after deductible expenses have been subtracted from trading receipts is the trading profit for the basis period. This chapter considers, initially, the idea of 'profits' in the related contexts of tax and accounting, and, thereafter, examines the conditions that must be satisfied for a particular receipt to be included in the calculation of a person's trading receipts or for expenditure to be deductible. It also considers the treatment of trading losses, and, in outline, the availability of capital allowances. **[10.1]**

2. The relevance of accounting practice in calculating trading income

Whilst there are some important differences between the treatment of profits for tax purposes and the role played by generally accepted accounting practice ('GAAP') in calculating them,[2] ITTOIA 2005, s 25, which provides that '[t]he profits of a trade must be calculated in accordance with generally accepted accounting practice [GAAP]', and its counterpart for corporation tax purposes,[3] have brought accounting practice and tax law much closer together than used to be the case. For sole traders, GAAP means 'UK generally accepted accounting practice', which requires the trader's accounts 'to give a true and fair view'.[4] Although trading profits must be calculated in accordance with UK GAAP, this is 'subject to any adjustment required or authorised by law in calculating profits for income tax purposes'. **[10.2]**

Erichsen v Last (1881) 8 QBD 414 (CA); above, para [9.3]

> SIR GEORGE JESSEL MR: . . . The next point is the question of profits. Now what is profit? It is, as I understand, the difference between the price received on a sale and the cost price of what is sold . . . **[10.3]**

1 ITTOIA 2005, s 7. Corporation tax is charged on the 'annual profits of the trade, profession or vocation': ICTA 1988, s 18.
2 Eg, the accounting practice concept of 'depreciation', as against the concept of capital allowances in tax law (see *Barclays Mercantile Business Finance v Mawson* [2005] STC 1 at 3). See, generally, Peter Holgate, *Accounting Principles for Lawyers* (2006).
3 FA 1998, s 42; see Chapter 18, below, para **[18.12]**.
4 See ITA 2007, ss 997(2) and (6). (See FA 2004, s 50(4) for corporation tax.)

Gresham Life Assurance Society v Styles [1892] AC 309 (HL)

The society carried on the business of granting annuities in return for payments of lump sums. The House of Lords held that, when calculating its profits, the society was entitled to deduct sums paid to discharge the annuity contracts.

> LORD HALSBURY LC: . . . Profits and gains must be ascertained on ordinary principles of commercial trading, and I cannot think that the framers of the Act could be guilty of such confusion of thought as to assume that the cost of the article sold to the trader which he in turn makes his profit by selling was not to be taken into account before you arrived at what was intended to be the taxable profit . . . **[10.4]**

Sun Insurance Office v Clark [1912] AC 443 (HL)

> VISCOUNT HALDANE: . . . It is plain that the question of what is or is not profit or gain must primarily be one of fact to be ascertained by the tests applied in ordinary business. Questions of law can only arise when . . . some express statutory direction applies and excludes ordinary commercial practice, or where, by reason of its being impracticable to ascertain the facts sufficiently, some presumption has to be invoked to fill the gap. **[10.5]**

As seen above, the notion that it is necessary in computing the profits or losses of a trade to begin with 'what accountancy . . . [prescribes], and then see whether any rule of law . . . [contradicts] it'[5] is now to be found in ITTOIA 2005, s 25, which is the rewritten version of FA 1998, s 42 (a provision that continues to apply for corporation tax purposes). However, as is evident from the following extracts, there was support for this approach which predates these provisions. **[10.6]**

Report of the Committee on the Taxation of Trading Profits (Cmd 8189 (1951))

133. It is important to set out at the beginning what we understand to be the present general state of the law as to the computation of business profits for tax purposes. For the majority of businesses the main rules governing the computation of taxable profits are either the Rule applicable to Case I or the Rule applicable to Case II, together with the Rules applicable to both Cases I and II of Schedule D, although scattered here and there over the many Acts of Parliament dealing with Income Tax are other rules relating to items of a more or less special nature. Each of the first two main Rules expresses the taxable profit as being "the full amount of the balance of the profits . . .", so that in order to compute that balance a profit and loss account[6] is necessary. It is at this stage that questions arise as to what particular items qualify for inclusion in either side of the account or fall to be excluded from it altogether.

134. Except in relation to a comparatively few special items, however, the Income Tax Acts themselves contain no rules which lay down affirmatively what

5 See John Tiley *Revenue Law* (5th edn., 2005), p 393.

6 ['Profit and loss account' is 'the UK term for the statement that summarizes the difference between the revenue and expenses of a period' (see Christopher Nobes *The Penguin Dictionary of Accounting* (2nd edn, 2006), p 237).]

sums are to be treated as receipts and what as expenses in the compilation of such an account. In the main the Acts merely set out various classes of expenses which cannot be included, or the maximum extent to which a particular kind of expense is to be allowed. It has therefore been for the Courts to lay down the general principle to be observed.

135. The decision of the House of Lords in the case of *Usher's Wiltshire Brewery Ltd.* v. *Bruce*[7] can be taken as the one which first expressed that general principle in definite terms. As a result of this case and of decisions in subsequent cases we think it can now be taken as settled that the profits or losses of a business for tax purposes are to be computed in accordance with established commercial accountancy principles as they apply to the particular business in question, subject nevertheless to a number of qualifications ... **[10.7]**

Odeon Associated Theatres Ltd v Jones [1971] 1 WLR 442 (ChD)

PENNYCUICK V-C: ... The effect of the principles laid down in *Usher's Wiltshire Brewery Ltd.* v. *Bruce*[8] and other cases, including those in which the expression "ordinary principles of commercial accountancy" is used is this: first one must ascertain the profits of the trade in accordance with ordinary principles of commercial accountancy. That, of course, involves bringing in as items of expenditure such items as would be treated as proper items of expenditure in a revenue account made up in accordance with the ordinary principles of commercial accountancy. Secondly, one must adjust this account by reference to the express prohibitions contained in the relevant statute, those being now contained in section 137 of the Income Tax Act 1952.[9] That is to say, an item of expenditure, even if it would be allowed as a deduction in accordance with the ordinary principles of commercial accountancy, must be struck out if it falls within any of those statutory prohibitions. I believe that to be the true principle upon which the profit of the taxpayers' trade must be ascertained for the present purpose.

I ought to say a few words by way of explanation of the time-honoured expression "ordinary principles of commercial accountancy". The concern of the court in this connection is to ascertain the true profit of the taxpayer. That and nothing else, apart from express statutory adjustments, is the subject of taxation in respect of a trade. In so ascertaining the true profit of a trade the court applies the correct principles of the prevailing system of commercial accountancy. I use the word "correct" deliberately. In order to ascertain what are the true principles it has recourse to the evidence of accountants. That evidence is conclusive on the practice of accountants in the sense of the principles on which accountants act in practice. That is a question of pure fact, but the court itself has to make a final decision as to whether that practice corresponds to the correct principles of commercial accountancy. No doubt in the vast proportion of cases the court will agree with the accountants but it will not necessarily do so. Again there may be a divergency of view between the accountants, or there may be alternative principles, none of which can be said to be incorrect, or, of course, there may be no accountancy evidence at all. The cases illustrate these various points. At the end of the day the court must determine what is the correct principle of commercial accountancy to be applied. Having done so, it will ascertain the true profit of the trade according to that principle, and the profit so ascertained is the subject of taxation. The expression "ordinary principles of commercial accountancy" is, as I understand it, employed to denote what is involved in this composite process. Properly understood it presents no difficulty, and I would not be at all disposed to attempt any alternative label ... **[10.8]**

7 [1915] A.C. 433.
8 ... [*Ibid.*]
9 [See ITTOIA 2005, s 34(1) (formerly ICTA 1988, s 74).]

Gallagher v Jones (Inspector of Taxes) [1993] STC 537 (CA); below, para [10.59]

The issue was whether so-called 'front-loaded lease rentals' should be spread over the useful life of certain assets, as the Crown argued, or whether, as the taxpayer argued, they should be deductible in the accounting period in which they had been incurred. The Crown's argument invoked the principles of *Odeon Associated Theatres Ltd v Jones* and *Sun Insurance Office v Clark* in that since SSAP 21, 'Accounting for leases and hire purchase contracts',[10] read with SSAP 2, 'Accounting policies', embodied the relevant ordinary commercial practice, there was no room for any contrary judge-made rule of law[11] to the effect that expenditure was deductible in the period in which it was incurred. The Court of Appeal accepted the Inland Revenue's argument and, in doing so, held that no judge-made rule could override the application of the generally accepted rule of commercial accountancy for which the Crown had contended.

> SIR THOMAS BINGHAM MR: . . . The object is to determine, as accurately as possible, the profits or losses of the taxpayers' businesses for the accounting periods in question. Subject to any express or implied statutory rule, of which there is none here, the ordinary way to ascertain the profits or losses of a business is to apply accepted principles of commercial accountancy. That is the very purpose for which such principles are formulated. As has often been pointed out, such principles are not static: they may be modified, refined and elaborated over time as circumstances change and accounting insights sharpen. But so long as such principles remain current and generally accepted they provide the surest answer to the question which the legislation requires to be answered. As Pennycuick V-C pointed out in *Odeon Associated Theatres Ltd v Jones (Inspector of Taxes)*,[12] different considerations arise where there is no accounting evidence or where there are two or more principles either or any of which is generally accepted. But those considerations do not apply here.
>
> The authorities do not persuade me that there is any rule of law such as that for which the taxpayers contend and the judge found. Indeed, given the plain language of the legislation,[13] I find it hard to understand how any judge-made rule could override the application of a generally accepted rule of commercial accountancy which (a) applied to the situation in question, (b) was not one of two or more rules applicable to the situation in question and (c) was not shown to be inconsistent with the true facts or otherwise inapt to determine the true profits or losses of the business. I need not pursue this speculation, however, since I do not understand it to be challenged that the principles embodied in SSAPs 2 and 21 meet these three conditions and I find no judge-made rule which could require these principles to be displaced.
>
> It would be extraordinary, given the statutory provisions recited above,[14] if these taxpayers could claim to be taxed on the basis of accounts which, according to the uncontradicted evidence of an eminent accountant, accepted by the Special Commissioner, give a completely misleading picture of their trading results. I am satisfied that the Crown is correct in submitting that they cannot.[15] **[10.9]**

10 Reproduced in Ian Barlow and David Milne (eds) *Tax Statutes and Statutory Instruments 2005–2006* (5 vols, Kingston-upon-Thames, 2005) vol. 1C, pp. 11,350–11,351.
11 [See the judgment of Harman J at [1993] STC 199.]
12 [1971] 1 WLR 442.
13 [ie ICTA 1988, ss 1(1), 18(1), (2) and 60 (1).]
14 [Ibid.]
15 [See also *Johnston (Inspector of Taxes) v. Britannia Airways* [1994] STC 763 in which the court was faced with evidence of several accounting principles either or any of which was generally accepted.]

Judith Freedman 'Ordinary Principles of Commercial Accounting – Clear Guidance or a Mystery Tour?' [1993] BTR 468, 477–478

... *Gallagher* v. *Jones* has not produced a final balance of the relationship between legal principles of tax law and accountancy practice. The arguments for the taxpayer were too stark and left important issues unexplored. There was no detailed analysis of the rights obtained as a result of the payments under the lease and thus no discussion of whether they were, in law, prepayments or payments for rights acquired in the period in question. If they were prepayments, it was accepted that they might not be wholly deductible in the period in which the liability to pay them was incurred but it does not follow from that that the formula in SSAP 21 should apply. There are alternative methods which both reflect proper accountancy practice and may fit better with an analysis of the transaction for tax purposes.

These issues were not investigated because of the weight given to SSAP 21. To accept a standard without investigation of its objectives and effects is, it is submitted, an abdication of responsibility by the court. Under any interpretation of the position, it is the court which must determine what is the correct principle of commercial accountancy to be applied.[16] "Correct" here must mean "correct" within the tax context. A refusal to examine the detail of a standard renders such determination impossible. The attitude of the Court of Appeal in *Gallagher* must be contrasted with that of the Privy Council in *Anaconda*[17] where Viscount Simonds made it clear it was not questioned that LIFO might be appropriate for corporate purposes but

> "the evidence of expert witnesses that the LIFO method is generally acceptable, and, in this case, the most appropriate method of accountancy, is not conclusive of the question that the court has to decide ... The question remains whether it conforms to the prescription of the Income Tax Act."

Of course, the court in *Gallagher* was not assisted by the way the case was argued but it could have placed more weight on the facts and insisted on further discussion and explanation of the SSAP and the alternative accounting treatment referred to by Mr. Miller.

The rule which emerges from *Gallagher* v. *Jones* is that a judge-made rule will not override a generally accepted rule of commercial accountancy which (a) applies to the situation in question (b) is not one of two or more rules applicable to the situation and (c) is not shown to be inconsistent with the true facts or otherwise inapt to determine the true profits or losses of the business. In itself, this formulation has little meaning but should not preclude discussion. Accounting standards are not equivalent to legislation and so it will often be possible to bring evidence of the existence of alternative rules (as it would have been in this case). The concepts of the "true" facts and "true" profits, as argued above, are subjective in nature. In most cases there will be room for argument about the facts and estimates on which the accounting treatment is based (as it would have been here). The real barrier to sensible development of the law on determination of profits will be if the courts assume that an SSAP or FRS by definition precludes alternative rules and is always apt to determine the profits of a business for tax purposes. If this course is followed, taxpayers may have a number of shocks to absorb as the ASB continues with its work.

16 *Odeon Associated Theatres Ltd.* v. *Jones* [1971] 1 W.L.R. 442.
17 ... [ie *Minister of National Revenue v Anaconda American Brass Ltd* [1956] 1 All ER 20.]

... there must be great uncertainty, following the Court of Appeal's decision in *Gallagher,* as to just how far the Courts will be prepared to follow the developing accounting standards. Much is likely to depend on the quality of the accounting evidence and we can expect to see some complex accounting discussions before the Commissioners once taxpayers and their advisers appreciate just how important it is in these cases to guide the courts through an examination of the implications of accounting standards rather than allowing them to be accepted as the final word for tax purposes. **[10.10]**

Revenue and Customs Commissioners v William Grant & Sons Distillers Ltd; Small (Inspector of Taxes) v Mars UK Ltd [2007] UKHL 15, [2007] STC 680

Depreciation has never been an allowable deduction in calculating trading profits (see below, para **[10.63]**). Where fixed assets used in making goods have been depreciated for accounting purposes, the amount of the depreciation must therefore be added back in calculating trading profits for tax purposes. These conjoined appeals involved William Grant, a whisky manufacturer, and Mars, a manufacturer of pet food. The companies argued that the amount to be added back was limited to the depreciation of fixed assets used in producing the goods sold during the year, and did not therefore include carried forward depreciation on fixed assets used in producing unsold stock. However, the Revenue argued that both types of depreciation should be added back. The companies relied on the GAAP contained in SSAP 12, 'Accounting for depreciation' (later superseded by FRS 15, 'Tangible fixed assets') and in SSAP 9, 'Stocks and long-term contracts'. The Revenue relied on a fundamental accounting principle that, so it said, required the carried forward depreciation also to be treated as incurred in the year. The House of Lords rejected the Revenue's argument.

LORD HOFFMANN: ... Submissions that accounts must comply with fundamental principles of accounting additional to the best practice of accountants as embodied in the accounting standards have been made in other cases. But they have always been rejected. In the *Odeon Associated Theatres* case [1971] 2 All ER 407 at 414, [1971] 1 WLR 442 at 454 Sir John Pennycuick V-C described the argument as 'entirely novel'. It was rejected by the Court of Appeal in *Gallagher v Jones (Inspector of Taxes)* [1993] STC 537, [1994] Ch 107. In this case, it takes the form of saying that profits *must* be ascertained by taking all the revenue received during the year, deducting all the costs (including depreciation) incurred during the year and making an adjustment for the difference between opening and closing stocks, treating an increase in stock value as if it was revenue. That is certainly one way of computing profits and there are dicta in earlier cases which show that half a century ago and more, judges and accountants thought it was the normal and obvious way of computing profits. It may have been the only practical method when record-keeping was not sufficiently sophisticated to enable one to make a meaningful attribution of costs in one year to sales in some future year. It is not, however, the philosophy of SSAP 9, which permits the cost of unsold stock to be carried over into future years and set against future sales. In this exercise, relevant depreciation is simply another cost....

LORD HOPE OF CRAIGHEAD: ... In *Gallagher*'s case [1993] STC 537 at 558, [1994] Ch 107 at 137, Nolan LJ referred to the general rule that trading expenditure on revenue account is deductible in the year in which it is incurred. Nobody disputes that there is such a rule. But a rule expressed in such broad terms is susceptible to modification as accounting principles are developed and modified and, as Sir Thomas Bingham MR put it in *Gallagher*'s case [1993] STC 537 at 555, [1994] Ch 107 at 134, 'accounting insights sharpen'. Is there a more fundamental rule of law to which, for tax purposes, these accounting principles must be subordinated? I do not think that it has been shown that there is any such rule.... **[10.11]**

Lord Hoffmann also remarked that he thought that the result reached by the House of Lords was the 'plain and obvious' one (see [2007] UKHL 15; [2007] STC 680 at [13]). To appreciate why the Revenue ran the argument that it did, see Jason Collins and Dennis Dixon, 'Open and Shut Case? *William Grant* and *Mars' The Tax Journal*, 9 April 2007, pp 6–8. For further implications of the decision, see, too, Maurice Parry-Wingfield, 'Depreciation in Stock: Where Next?', *The Tax Journal*, 28 May 2007, pp 13–15, and John Whiting, 'Tax and Accounting' [2006] BTR 267, 277–279. Towards the end of his speech, Lord Hoffmann approved 'the lucid dissenting opinion of Lord Reed' (see [2007] UKHL 15, [2007] STC 680 at [26]) which was delivered when *William Grant* was in the Court of Session (see *Inland Revenue Commissioners v William Grant & Sons Distillers Ltd* [2005] CSIH 63, [2006] STC 69).

With regard to 'ordinary principles of commercial accounting', or GAAP, and to the role of evidence on the correct accounting principles for determining profits, see also Robert Burgess, 'Revenue Law and Accountancy Practice' [1972] BTR 308; J R Edwards 'Tax Treatment of Capital Expenditure and the Measurement of Accounting Profit' [1976] BTR 300; Judith Freedman 'Profit and Prophets – Law and Accountancy Practice on the Timing of Receipts Recognition' [1987] BTR 61 and 104; Judith Freedman 'Defining Taxable Profit in a Changing Accounting Environment' [1995] BTR 434; Geoffrey Whittington 'Tax Policy and Accounting Standards' [1995] BTR 452; Adam Broke Accounting Standards and Taxable Profit: An Accountant's View' [1995] BTR 457; Patricia McCourt and George Radcliffe '*Les Relations Fiscalité-Comptabilité* in France: A Model For Europe? [1995] BTR 461.

Against this background, it might be wondered why the law does not simply align accounting profits and taxable profits. The arguments for and against alignment are summarised in the following extract. **[10.12]**

Judith Freedman 'Aligning Taxable Profits and Accounting Profits: Accounting standards, legislators and judges' (2004) 2 eJournal of Tax Research 71

Arguments for alignment of taxable profits and accounting profits

The case for alignment is simple and prima facie attractive. It is based on the view that alignment would bring simplicity, cut compliance costs and reduce avoidance. The argument runs as follows. Companies must all make up commercial accounts following accounting standards so why not use these for tax purposes also? This simplification would save compliance costs, since only one set of accounts would be needed. It would also help to increase transparency and prevent avoidance. Since most companies, at least quoted companies, want to keep their commercial profits high, they would not wish to enter into tax schemes that reduce these profits if the same figure had to be used for both purposes. Transactions should be entered into for commercial and not for tax reasons and consistency in the accounts might help to achieve this.[18] Both those setting accounting standards and the tax authorities are

18 This seems to be the assumption of the UK Government in their consultation papers on Corporation Tax Reform, supporting alignment: Inland Revenue and H.M. Treasury (2002) *Reform of Corporation Tax* (London); Inland Revenue and H.M. Treasury (2003) Reform *of Corporation Tax*, London.

aiming at the same figure – the 'true' economic profit.[19] The tax authorities should be able to tax the same profit as is enjoyed by the owners. There is no need to have two sets of rules and no justification for it. At an international level, the expert work done to harmonise accounting standards could be utilised in the tax field without having to duplicate effort. Accountants have expertise in defining profit that lawyers do not have and this should be recognised.

Arguments for divergence of accounting and taxable profits

The counter arguments are less immediately obvious but are nevertheless well known. It is argued here that they are stronger than the arguments for alignment. This view is based on the differing objectives of calculating taxable profits on the one hand and presenting financial accounts on the other and the need to keep each system true to its objectives and robust against any pollution by considerations more relevant to the other system.

Alignment is only helpful if it simplifies the process of preparing accounts, thus reducing compliance costs. Major simplification may not be possible because in practice complete alignment is neither achievable nor desirable. Commercial accounts and tax accounts have different objectives. Tax must raise revenue and do so equitably and efficiently as between taxpayers. This points to reasonably objective rules that take account of taxable capacity and administrative efficiency. Tax avoidance opportunities must be blocked. Financial accounts must give relevant and reliable information and prevent businesses from hiding the substance of their position. In each case these objectives are perfectly valid, but the functions performed by the accounts for these two purposes may dictate some differences although there will be a central core of similarity. In addition to the above objectives of a tax system, governments wish to use the tax system to provide economic incentives and disincentives. Whilst many economists would argue against such a use of taxation, it appears to be inevitable and universal, making complete alignment an illusory goal.

Accountants would agree that there is no one true profit figure but that a range of figures is necessary to paint a picture of what is happening in a company.[20] The application of accounting standards requires the use of discretion. Commercial accounts cater for many stakeholders, although primarily for the shareholders. What are needed for this purpose are forward looking figures involving judgment and valuations. The single figure in the accounts will often be backed up or explained by notes and further figures. International accounting standards do not give the profit and loss account primacy but the balance sheet. In fact, the profit and loss account looks set to disappear altogether.[21] Tax, on the other hand, is historical: that is it must be based on an artificial period already completed and is concerned with the profit or loss in that limited period. It may be possible to carry losses or other allowances forwards and back from one period to another, but essentially each period is taken in isolation because taxation is an artificial structure and needs to operate in this way to be manageable. The tax system must arrive at one figure on which to base an assessment.

19 This assumes an ideal of a comprehensive income tax, rarely achieved in practice but accepted as a goal in most tax literature (the Haig-Simons model: R.M. Haig (1921) *The Federal Income Tax*, New York: Columbia University Press; H.C. Simons (1938) Personal Income Taxation, Chicago University of Chicago Press). [See Chapter 6, above, para **[6.3]**.]

20 W.T. Baxter, Correspondence, [1978] *British Tax Review* 67.

21 See . . . [Allister Wilson 'Financial Reporting and taxation: marriage is out of the question' [2001] BTR 86].

In addition, to operate fairly and efficiently, it is often argued that a tax system must recognise ability to pay and subject the taxpayer to tax when it is most convenient to pay the tax.[22] These concepts are sometimes linked to the realisation principle, since without liquid assets there is an obvious difficulty in paying taxes. Whilst in a perfect market this problem of liquidity might be met by borrowing by the taxpayer against unrealised profits, in practice financing taxes in this way not only creates transaction costs but can also be risky as the value of the security for the borrowing may fall. For this reason, the realisation principle seems more important for tax purposes than it is for accounting purposes, particularly as we move towards fair value accounting.[23] The volatility inherent in fair value accounting reflects volatility in the market and so, arguably,[24] should be reflected in the commercial accounts. It is less clear, both from the point of view of the taxpayer and the government, that it is sensible to tax on the basis of volatile accounts.

Generally, the different objectives of tax and financial accounts make it desirable that the rules for each one are not unduly influenced by the rules for the other. At present international accounting standard setters pay little regard to tax implications and would be unlikely to take kindly to the suggestions that they needed to add tax to the list of considerations and pressure they must take on board already.[25] Commercial accounting considerations could be distorted by tax pressures. This is not to say that tax and financial accounting should operate in isolation from each other and some mutual awareness and cross referencing will no doubt be valuable, but there should be clear differences, although these do need to be made explicit and based on some established principles. **[10.13]**

3. Receipts

For a receipt to be included by a trader in the computation of his trading profits in the relevant period (the 'period of account'),[26] it must be derived from the trade and must be an income receipt, not a capital one.[27] **[10.14]**

A. *'Derived from the trade'*

Whilst it is generally clear which of a trader's receipts are derived from his trade, some receipts present analytical difficulties.[28] **[10.15]**

22 For example, Adam Smith's Canons of Taxation, Adam Smith, *The Nature & Causes of the Wealth of Nations*, Book V, Chap. 11, Part II "Of Taxes", paras. 1–7.

23 In an interesting unpublished paper presented to the NYU School of Law Colloquium on Tax Policy and Public Finance (Spring 2004, Number 12), 'An Economic Analysis of the Realization Rule', Deborah Schenk argues that the justifications for the realization rule are not as persuasive as has been thought, but even she agrees that there are valuation and political difficulties in taxing paper gains, making it difficult to abandon realization as a basis for taxation.

24 This is not uncontroversial in relation to commercial accounting either. There is strong resistance to IAS 39 in Europe for this reason, spearheaded by French banks: Roger Murray and Larissa Clark (2003) 'IAS 39, cash flow hedges and tax' 8 *Financial Instruments Tax and Accounting Review* 1; Andrew Parker (2003) 'Compliance costs soar for new IAS rules' *Financial Times* November 24th.

25 Wilson, ... above; ... [Christopher Nobes *A Conceptual Framework for the Taxable Income of Businesses, and How to Apply it under the IFRS* (2003, ACCA, London)], p.38.

26 See ITTOIA 2005, s 198(1): 'The general rule is that the basis period for a tax year is the period of 12 months ending with the accounting date in that tax year.'

27 ITTOIA 2005, s 96; see Chapter 6, above, para **[6.9]**.

28 See, eg, *Davies v The Shell Company of China Ltd* (1951) 32 TC 133.

Higgs v Olivier [1952] Ch 311 (CA)

Laurence Olivier, the famous twentieth century actor, received £15,000 from the production company of his film of Shakespeare's *Henry V*, not to act in, produce or direct another film for anyone else, for a period of 18 months from the date of the agreement. The Court of Appeal held that, rather than being derived from his profession,[29] the sum in question was compensation for *not* carrying out that profession. Unlike the actor's other professional income, this particular receipt did not, therefore, fall to be taxed under Schedule D, Case II.[30]

> LORD EVERSHED MR: . . . I think Sir Frank Soskice was disposed to agree that, if a trader, or a professional man, for a money consideration covenanted to give up his trade or profession for the rest of his life, then it would be difficult to say that the money received was "profits or gains accruing or arising from his trade or profession." On the other hand, it is not difficult to see that a restriction of a very limited or partial character might less easily be taken out of the ambit of the taxing provision. One example in the argument was that of an actor who covenanted for a limited period not to act for one particular company out of a large number. I myself gave the example of an actor who covenanted for a limited period not to act under his own or well-known stage name. But between the two extremes there is a large area, and for myself I am disposed to think that within that area it may well be a matter of degree. In so far as it is a matter of degree it would be, I think, a question of fact.
>
> In this case the Special Commissioners concluded that the £15,000 was not within the taxing provisions I have quoted. "We found it impossible to say that the sum of £15,000 under the deed came to the taxpayer as part of the income from his vocation. On the contrary, it came to him for refraining from carrying on his vocation, and in our opinion was a capital receipt." I agree that in questions of this kind which involve a consideration of the true import and scope of the trading provisions, it is not possible to say that the whole matter is one of fact. It is, I think, a question of mixed law and fact. But I think that, if I am right in saying that in such a case as this it may well be a matter of degree, then so long as it does not appear that the Special Commissioners have misapprehended the effect of the taxing provisions their decision should not be disturbed . . .[31] **[10.16]**

In 1952, the receipt, therefore, escaped taxation. Presently, such an amount might be subject to capital gains tax ('CGT'), possibly as a receipt on a disposal of goodwill, or possibly as a receipt on the surrender of a right, or a receipt in return for refraining from exercising a right.[32] **[10.16a]**

Murray v Goodhews [1978] 1 WLR 499 (CA)

The taxpayer company received ex gratia payments from a brewery company, after the latter terminated a number of tenancy agreements. It was held that the payments were not derived from the taxpayer company's trade.

> BUCKLEY LJ: . . . This is an appeal from a decision of Walton J. of February 20, 1976, when he dismissed an appeal from a decision of the special commissioners, who had held that certain sums paid by Watney Combe Reid & Co. Ltd. (whom I shall call "Watney") to the taxpayer company amounting to £35,823 in the year 1970 and £45,828 in the year 1971 were not trading receipts to be taken into account in the computation of the taxpayer company's profits from its trade, chargeable to corporation tax. The decision below is reported in [1976] 2 All E.R. 296, where the case stated is set out in full. All the relevant facts are there to be found and I need not repeat them.

29 See Chapter 9.
30 See Chapter 7.
31 [See Chapter 3, above, para **[3.5]**.]
32 See Chapter 20.

I would, however, draw attention to the following findings of fact, which seem to me to be crucial. First . . . the commissioners found as a fact that when Mr. Wallace, representing Watney, visited the taxpayer company's board of directors to explain Watney's change of policy, he mentioned that there would be an ex gratia payment, but said nothing about the amount or basis of calculation. Secondly . . . the commissioners found as a fact that apart from the letters referred to in that paragraph and set out elsewhere in the case, there was no correspondence between the two companies, nor was there any bargaining or negotiation. Thirdly. . . the commissioners found as a fact that the amounts of the payments had no connection with the profits earned or barrelage taken by any house; nor was it (which I take to mean the calculation of those amounts) linked with future trading relations between Watney and the taxpayer company.

The question which has to be determined, I think, is whether the sums in issue fall within the description of annual profits or gains arising or accruing to the taxpayer company from their trade . . . or, to put it more precisely in relation to the present case, whether they are receipts which should be taken into account in ascertaining the profits or gains of the taxpayer company's trade for the two years of receipt.

The leases of public houses which Watney determined were terminated by notices in the ordinary course and the taxpayer company had no legal basis for claiming any compensation. There is one possible exception to that, but it is of comparatively small extent and it is not necessary for me to go into that question. The payments made by Watney were entirely voluntary. This feature, however, provides no conclusive answer to the question whether they should be regarded for the relevant purpose as arising or accruing from the taxpayer company's trade so as to be proper to be brought into account in ascertaining the profits or gains of that trade.

. . . Every case of a voluntary payment – and we are only concerned with cases of that kind in the present appeal – must be considered on its own facts to ascertain the nature of the receipt in the recipient's hands. All relevant circumstances must be taken into account. These may include the purpose for which the payer makes the payment, or the terms, if any, upon which it is made, as for example in the *Falkirk* case,[33] where the payment was made for the purpose of its being applied in the recipient's business in the future; or it may be made by way of voluntarily supplementing the price paid for goods or services provided by the taxpayer in the course of his trade or business in the past, as in the *Squatting Investment Co.* case[34] and *Severne* v. *Dadswell*[35] and *McGowan* v. *Brown*;[36] or the payment may be merely in the nature of a testimonial, or a solatium, which, although it recognises the value of past services, is not paid specifically in respect of any of those services, or of expected future services, by the taxpayer to the payer, as in the *Chibbett* case,[37] the *Carnaby Harrower* case[38] and *Simpson* v. *Reynolds*.[39] I stress that it is the character of the receipt in the recipient's hands that is significant; the motive of the payer is only significant so far as it bears, if at all, upon that character.

Mr. Vinelott emphasised that a business relationship continued, and still continues, between Watney and the taxpayer company in relation to other public houses than those of which the tenancies were determined. He contended that the payments were made, inter alia, to maintain goodwill between the two companies. I do not think that the finding of fact in paragraph 5(11) of the case stated goes so far as this. The commissioners found that the payments were made to maintain Watney's own name, goodwill and image in the trade and that the calculation of them was not linked with any future trading relations between Watney and the taxpayer company. The commissioners also found in the same paragraph that the amounts paid were not connected with the profits earned, or beer sold, through any house, which contradicts any suggestion which might be made that the payments were in the nature of compensation for lost profits, or at the very least tends to do so.

33 *IRC* v. *Falkirk Ice Rink Ltd* [1975] S.T.C. 434.
34 *Taxation Commissioner of the Commonwealth of Australia* v. *Squatting Investment Co Ltd* [1954] A.C. 182.
35 [1954] 1 W.L.R. 1204.
36 [1977] 1 W.L.R. 1403.
37 *Chibbett* v. *Joseph Robinson & Sons* (1924) 9 T.C. 48.
38 *Walker* v. *Carnaby, Harrower, Barham & Pykett* [1970] 1 W.L.R. 276.
39 [1975] 1 W.L.R. 617.

It seems to me that upon the findings of fact made by the commissioners, and particularly those to which I specifically drew attention at the beginning of this judgment, the commissioners were fully justified in holding, as in effect I think they did, that the sums now in question were not receipts of the taxpayer company arising or accruing from the taxpayer company's trade or business, and on that ground I would dismiss this appeal ... **[10.17]**

B. Income, not capital

In order to be trading income, the particular receipt must be an income receipt, not a capital one. Since income tax is concerned with income, receipts of a capital nature do not enter into the computation of profits, although they may arise from a transaction which falls within the scope of CGT.[40] **[10.18]**

Glenboig Union Fireclay Co Ltd v IRC (1922) 12 TC 427

The appellants received compensation from the Caledonian Railway Company for the exercise of the statutory power of the railway company to require the appellants not to 'work' particular deposits of fireclay underneath the railway line. The House of Lords held that the compensation was a capital receipt in return for the sterilisation of an asset.

LORD BUCKMASTER: ... The Finance (No. 2) Act of 1915 imposed a duty, known as the Excess Profits Duty, to be levied and paid upon profits arising from trade or business. The method provided for assessment was by comparing the profit in the particular business for the period known as the accounting period with the average pre-war standard of profit, determined by taking the average of any two of the three pre-war trade years, the difference between the two being liable to duty which was imposed at the rate of 50 per cent.

The appellant company here, The Glenboig Union Fireclay Company Limited, in making their return for the purpose of this Statute, included as one of the two pre-war years the year that ended August 31, 1913, and into the accounts of that year they brought as items of profit a sum of £15,316 received from the Caledonian Railway Company on April 9, 1913, and a further sum of £4,500 received from the same Company on August 29, 1913. The question that is raised upon this appeal is whether or no the Company are entitled to increase the amount of their pre-war profits by these two sums and thereby reduce the amount of the Excess Profits Duty payable under the Statute. There is no question whatever about the bona fides of the Appellant's case in this case. Both those sums had been included in their balance sheet as profit for the year 1913, and upon them they had paid Income Tax without demur.

The circumstances in which those moneys were paid may be shortly stated. The Appellants, the Glenboig Union Fireclay Company, carry on business as manufacturers of fireclay goods and as merchants of raw fireclay. Part of their property consisted of mining rights over certain beds of fireclay at Gartverrie, Glenboig, and in the course of working these fields they were at the end of 1907 approaching the line of the Caledonian Railway, and due notice was given on January 25, 1908, to the Railway Company of the intended extension of their working. The Railway Company, being apprehensive as to the result, required the Fireclay Company to desist from working. A dispute arose as to whether or no the fireclay in question was a mineral and litigation ensued, during which the Railway Company were able to obtain against the Fireclay Company interdicts which operated for two periods, one from February 29, 1908, to April 15, 1910, and the second from November 12, 1910, to April 28, 1911, when the interdict was finally recalled. Upon the

40 See Chapter 20.

recall of the interdict the Railway Company accordingly became liable to pay the Fireclay Company the damages that had been caused to them by the order, and the sum of £4,500, to which I have made reference, was the sum that was paid under that head. The Railway Company now proceeded to treat with the Fireclay Company for the purpose of preventing any further working of this fireclay adjacent to their railway, and arbitration proceedings ensued for the purpose of determining what sum the Railway Company were bound to pay for this privilege, and ultimately the sum of £15,316 was fixed as the sum payable by the Railway Company, and this was accordingly paid on April 9, 1913.

[The parties reached an agreement in relation to the £4,500.]

... It therefore only remains to consider whether the sum of £15,316 was properly included as a profit in the Appellants' balance sheet for the year ending August 31, 1913. The argument in support of its inclusion can only be well founded if the sum be regarded as profits, or a sum in the nature of profits, earned in the course of their trade or business. I am quite unable to see that the sum represents anything of the kind. It is said, and it is not disputed, that the amount in fact was assessed by considering that the fireclay to which it related could only be worked for some two-and-a-half years before it would be exhausted, and it is consequently urged that the amount therefore represents nothing but the actual profit for two and a half years received in one lump sum. I regard that argument as fallacious. In truth the sum of money is the sum paid to prevent the Fireclay Company obtaining the full benefit of the capital value of that part of the mines which they are prevented from working by the Railway Company. It appears to me to make no difference whether it be regarded as a sale of the asset out and out, or whether it be treated merely as a means of preventing the acquisition of profit that would otherwise be gained. In either case the capital asset of the Company to that extent has been sterilised and destroyed, and it is respect of that action that the sum of £15,316 was paid. It is unsound to consider the fact that the measure, adopted for the purpose of seeing what the total amount should be, was based on considering what are the profits that would have been earned. That, no doubt, is a perfectly exact and accurate way of determining the compensation, for it is now well settled that the compensation payable in such circumstances is the full value of the minerals that are to be left unworked, less the cost of working, and that is, of course, the profit that would be obtained were they in fact worked. But there is no relation between the measure that is used for the purpose of calculating a particular result and the quality of the figure that is arrived at by means of the application of that test. I am unable to regard this sum of money as anything but capital money, and I think, therefore, it was erroneously entered in the balance sheet ending August 31, 1913, as a profit on the part of the Fireclay Company ... **[10.19]**

Compensation received in respect of loss or sterilisation of *trading stock* will be a receipt of an income sum: see *Gliksten & Sons Ltd v Green* [1929] AC 381 and *Burmah SS Co Ltd v IRC* (1930) 16 TC 67. **[10.20]**

Van Den Berghs Ltd v Clark [1935] AC 431 (HL)

The appellants, who were margarine manufacturers, had entered into an agreement with a competing Dutch company, to restrict competition between them, share profits, etc. A dispute then arose and, ultimately, the Dutch company paid the appellants £450,000 as 'damages' in consideration of the termination of the agreement. The House of Lords held that the receipt was in respect of the cancellation of a capital asset and, as such, was not to be treated as a trading receipt for the purposes of calculating the appellants' trading profits.

LORD MACMILLAN: ... the problem of discriminating between an income receipt and a capital receipt and between an income disbursement and a capital disbursement is one which in recent years has frequently engaged your Lordships' attention. In general, the distinction is well recognised and easily applied, but from time to time cases arise where the item lies on the borderline and the task of assigning it to income or to capital becomes one of much refinement, as the decisions show. The Income Tax Acts nowhere define "income" any more than they define "capital"; they describe sources of income and prescribe methods of computing income, but what constitutes income they discreetly refrain from saying. Nor do they define "profits or gains"; while as for "trade", the "interpretation" section[41] only informs us, with a fine disregard of logic, that it "includes every trade, manufacture, adventure or concern in the nature of trade". Consequently, it is to the decided cases that one must go in search of light. While each case is found to turn upon its own facts, and no infallible criterion emerges, nevertheless the decisions are useful as illustrations and as affording indications of the kind of considerations which may relevantly be borne in mind in approaching the problem.

The reported cases fall into two categories, those in which the subject is found claiming that an item of receipt ought not to be included in computing his profits, and those in which the subject is found claiming that an item of disbursement ought to be included among the admissible deductions in computing his profits. In the former case the Crown is found maintaining that the item is an item of income; in the latter, that it is a capital item. Consequently the argumentative position alternates according as it is an item of receipt or an item of disbursement that is in question, and the taxpayer and the Crown are found alternately arguing for the restriction or the expansion of the conception of income.

I propose to refer first to the case of *British Insulated and Helsby Cables Ltd* v. *Atherton*.[42] This case has been generally recognised as the leading modern authority on the subject, though I fear that Romer L.J. was unduly optimistic when he said that it "placed beyond the realms of controversy" the law applicable to the matter: *Anglo-Persian Oil Co.* v. *Dale*.[43] The facts were that the appellant company claimed to deduct in the computation of its trade profits a sum which it had provided to form the nucleus of a pension fund for its employees. The Crown argued that the sum ought to be debited to capital on the ground that it "was not in its nature recurrent but was made once for all" and that it was a case of the "provision of a capital sum which will for ever after relieve the company from making any further payment whatsoever". This argument prevailed. The Lord Chancellor (Viscount Cave) found in the decisions "considerable authority" for the view which he recommended to the House to adopt – namely, that "when an expenditure is made, not only once and for all, but with a view to bringing into existence an asset or an advantage for the enduring benefit of a trade . . . there is very good reason (in the absence of special circumstances leading to an opposite conclusion) for treating such an expenditure as properly attributable not to revenue but to capital". Lord Atkinson indicated that the word "asset" ought not to be confined to "something material" and, in further elucidation of the principle, Romer L.J. has added that the advantage paid for need not be "of a positive character" and may consist in the getting rid of an item of fixed capital that is of an onerous character: *Anglo-Persian Oil Co.* v. *Dale*.

. . . If the numerous decisions are examined and classified, they will be found to exhibit a satisfactory measure of consistency with Lord Cave's principle of discrimination. Certain of them relate to excess profits duty and not to income tax, but for the present purpose this distinction is immaterial. A sum provided to establish a pension fund for employees, as has already been seen, is a capital disbursement: *British Insulated and Helsby Cables Ltd.* v. *Atherton*; so is a sum paid by a coal merchant for the acquisition of the right to a number of current contracts to supply coal: *John Smith & Son* v. *Moore*[44]; so is a payment by a colliery company as the price of being allowed to surrender unprofitable seams included in its leasehold: *Mallet* v. *Staveley Coal & Iron Co.*[45] Similarly, a sum received by a fireclay company as compensation for leaving unworked the fireclay under a railway was held to be a capital receipt: *Glenboig Union Fireclay Co.* v. *Commissioners of Inland Revenue*.[46]

On the other hand, a sum awarded by the War Compensation Court to a company carrying on the business of brewers and wine and spirit merchants in respect of the compulsory taking over of its stock of rum by the Admiralty was held to be a trade or

41 Income Tax Act 1918, s. 237. [See now ICTA 1988, s 832(1).]
42 [1926] A.C. 205.
43 [1932] 1 K.B. 124 at 145.
44 [1921] 2 A.C. 13.
45 [1928] 2 K.B. 405.
46 (1922) 12 T.C. 427.

income receipt: *Commissioners of Inland Revenue* v. *Newcastle Breweries Ltd.*;[47] so was a sum paid to a shipbuilding company for the cancellation of a contract to build a ship: *Short Brothers Ltd.* v. *Commissioners of Inland Revenue*;[48] so was a lump sum payment received by a quarry company in lieu of four annual payments in consideration of which the company had relieved a customer of his contract to purchase a quantity of chalk yearly for ten years and build a wharf at which it could be loaded: *Commissioners of Inland Revenue* v. *Northfleet Coal and Ballast Co.*;[49] so was a sum recovered from insurers by a timber company in respect of the destruction by fire of their stock of timber: *J Gliksten & Sons* v. *Green*.[50] Conversely, where a company paid a sum as the price of getting rid of a life director, whose presence on the board was regarded as detrimental to the profitable conduct of the company's business, the payment was held to be an income disbursement: *Mitchell* v. *RW Noble Ltd*,[51] so was the payment made in the case of the *Anglo-Persian Oil. Co.* v. *Dale* in order to disembarrass the company of an onerous agency agreement. There are further instances in the reports, but I have quoted enough for the purposes of illustration.

With the guidance thus afforded I now address myself to the question whether the £450,000 received by the appellants in the circumstances already narrated can properly be described as an item of profit arising or accruing to them from the carrying on of their trade, which ought to be credited as an income receipt. It is important to bear in mind at the outset that the trade of the appellants is to manufacture and deal in margarine, for the nature of a receipt may vary according to the nature of the trade in connection with which it arises. The price of the sale of a factory is ordinarily a capital receipt, but it may be an income receipt in the case of a person whose business it is to buy and sell factories.

. . . Now what were the appellants giving up? They gave up their whole rights under the agreements for thirteen years ahead. These agreements are called in the case stated "pooling agreements", but that is a very inadequate description of them, for they did much more than merely embody a system of pooling and sharing profits. If the appellants were merely receiving in one sum down the aggregate of profits which they would otherwise have received over a series of years the lump sum might be regarded as of the same nature as the ingredients of which it was composed. But even if a payment is measured by annual receipts, it is not necessarily itself an item of income. As Lord Buckmaster pointed out in the case of the *Glenboig Union Fireclay Co.* v. *Commissioners of Inland Revenue*: "there is no relation between the measure that is used for the purpose of calculating a particular result and the quality of the figure that is arrived at by means of the test".

The three agreements which the appellants consented to cancel were not ordinary commercial contracts made in the course of carrying on their trade; they were not contracts for the disposal of their products, or for the engagement of agents or other employees necessary for the conduct their business; nor were they merely agreements as to how the trading profits when earned should be distributed as between the contracting parties. On the contrary the cancelled agreements related to the whole structure of the appellants' profit-making apparatus. They regulated the appellants' activities, defined what they might and what they might not do, and affected the whole conduct of their business. I have difficulty in seeing how money laid out to secure, or money received for the cancellation of, so fundamental an organisation of a trader's activities can be regarded as an income disbursement or an income receipt. Mr Hills very properly warned your Lordships against being misled as to the legal character of the payment by its magnitude, for magnitude is a relative term and we are dealing with companies which think in millions. But the magnitude of a transaction is not an entirely irrelevant consideration. The legal distinction between a repair and a renewal may be influenced by the expense involved. In the present case, however, it is not the largeness of the sum that is important but the nature of the asset that was surrendered. In my opinion that asset, the congeries of rights which the appellants enjoyed under the agreements and which for a price they surrendered, was a capital asset.

47 (1927) 12 T.C. 927.
48 (1927) 12 T.C. 955.
49 (1927) 12 T.C. 1102.
50 [1929] A.C. 381.
51 [1927] 1 K.B. 719.

I have not overlooked the criterion afforded by the economists' differentiation between fixed and circulating capital which Lord Haldane invoked in *John Smith & Son v. Moore*[52] and on which the Court of Appeal relied in the present case, but I confess that I have not found it very helpful. Circulating capital is capital which is turned over and in the process of being turned over yields profit or loss. Fixed capital is not involved directly in that process, and remains unaffected by it. If this is to be the test, I fail to see how the appellants could be said to have been engaged in turning over the asset which the agreements in question constituted. The agreements formed the fixed framework within which their circulating capital operated; they were not incidental to the working of their profit-making machine but were essential parts of the mechanism itself. They provided the means of making profits, but they themselves did not yield profits. The profits of the appellants arose from manufacturing and dealing in margarine ... **[10.21]**

However, it does not follow from this that all receipts of compensation for the cancellation of contracts are capital ones. It depends on all the circumstances of the case: see *Kelsall Parsons & Co v IRC* (1938) 21 TC 608; *Bush, Beach & Gent Ltd v Road* (1939) 22 TC 519; *Barr Crombie & Co Ltd v IRC* (1945) 26 TC 406. See also *Sabine v Lookers Ltd* (1958) 38 TC 120 (compensation for the variation of the terms of a contract).

[10.22]

4. Expenditure

Tax is charged under Part 2 of ITTOIA 2005 on 'trading profits', not trading income *per se.* Trading profits are found by deducting allowable expenditure from taxable receipts. Just as receipts must satisfy certain conditions to be trading receipts, so also must expenses satisfy certain conditions to enter into the computation of the profits of the trade. The expense, which must not be specifically disallowed by law, must be of a revenue, not a capital, nature, and it must be 'wholly and exclusively' incurred for the purposes of the trade. **[10.23]**

Usher's Wiltshire Brewery Ltd v Bruce [1915] AC 433

The appellants let premises to tied tenants. Although the tenants were obliged to repair the premises, the appellants bore the costs of repairs, insurance, rates, etc. The House of Lords held that, in computing the appellants' profits, this expenditure was deductible.

LORD SUMNER: ... If a subject engaged in a trade were taxed simply upon "the full amount of the balance of the profits or gains of such trade",[53] there can be no doubt that, upon the facts found in this special case, he would be entitled to deduct all the items which are now in debate before arriving at the sum to be charged. To do otherwise would neither be to arrive at a balance between two sets of figures, a credit and a debit set, which balance is the profit of the trade, nor to ascertain the profits of the trade, for trade incomings are not profits of the trade till trade outgoings have been paid or allowed for and deducted.

Rule 1 of the first Case of Sched. D does not, however, leave matters to the taking of a commercial account simpliciter; it provides that the duty shall be "assessed, charged, and paid without other deduction than is hereinafter allowed", and this must mean, though it

52 [1921] 2 A.C. 13.
53 [See ITTOIA 2005, s 7(1) (formerly ICTA 1988, s 60).]

is not strictly expressed, "without other deductions in the computation of the sum on which the duty is charged". Sect. 159[54] states it thus: "in the computation of duty to be made under this Act in any of the cases before mentioned . . . it shall not be lawful to make any other deductions therefrom than such as are expressly enumerated in this Act", and here "therefrom" is not from the duty but from the sum, whatever it be, that has to be ascertained before duty can be charged on it. Virtually both provisions mean that in computing the sum which, when ascertained, is to be charged with duty, only the enumerated deductions shall be lawfully allowable.

The paradox of it is that there are no allowable deductions expressly enumerated at all, and there is in words no deduction allowed at all, unless indirectly by the words in rule 3 of the First Case, namely, repairs "beyond the sum usually expended for such purposes according to an average of three years"; loss "not connected with or arising out of such trade"; debts, "except bad debts proved", and average loss "beyond the actual amount of loss after adjustment", and by the words in rule 1 applicable to both the first two cases, namely, expenses "not being money wholly and exclusively laid out or expended for the purposes of such trade"; and rent, "except such a part thereof (ie of the premises) as may be used for purposes of such trade".

The effect of this structure, I think, is this, that the direction to compute the full amount of the balance of the profits must be read as subject to certain allowances and to certain prohibitions of deductions, but that a deduction, if there be such, which is neither within the terms of the prohibition nor such that the expressed allowance must be taken as the exclusive definition of its area, is to be made or not to be made according as it is or is not, on the facts of the case, a proper debit item to be charged against incomings of the trade when computing the balance of profits of it . . . **[10.24]**

A. *Deduction disallowed by statute*

The list of deductions disallowed by statute is long and fairly intricate. It was formerly contained in ICTA 1988, s 74(1)(a), which has been rewritten by ITTOIA 2005, Pt 2, Ch 4 for income tax purposes.[55] Deductions which are not allowed include most (but not all) 'expenses incurred in providing entertainment or gifts in connection with the trade' (see ITTOIA 2005, s 45(1)); 'royalties or other sums paid for the use of patents' (see ITTOIA 2005, s 51); and 'expenses incurred ... in making a payment if the making of the payment constitutes a criminal offence . . .' (see ITTOIA 2005, s 55). **[10.25]**

B. *Expenditure must be of a revenue nature*

ITTOIA 2005, s 33 provides that, '[I]n calculating the profits of a trade, no deduction is allowed for items of a capital nature' (see *Revenue and Customs Commissioners v William Grant & Sons Distillers Ltd; Small (Inspector of Taxes) v Mars UK Ltd* [2007] UKHL 15, [2007] STC 680 at [3] (Lord Hoffmann), in relation to depreciation). The distinction between expenditure of a capital, on the one hand, and of an income (or revenue) nature, on the other, is one of law.

There are a number of different tests in the case law: **[10.26]**

54 [See ITTOIA 2005, Pt 2, Ch 4 (formerly ICTA 1988, s 74(1)).]
55 Section 74(1)(a) remains pertinent for corporation tax purposes.

(1) The 'asset or advantage for the enduring benefit of . . . [the] trade' test

British Insulated and Helsby Cables Ltd v Atherton [1926] AC 205 (HL)

VISCOUNT CAVE LC: . . . but when an expenditure is made, not only once and for all, but with a view to bringing into existence an asset or an advantage for the enduring benefit of a trade, I think that there is very good reason (in the absence of special circumstances leading to an opposite conclusion) for treating such an expenditure as properly attributable not to revenue but to capital . . . **[10.27]**

(2) The 'identifiable asset' test

Pitt v Castle Hill Warehousing Co Ltd [1974] 1 WLR 1624 (ChD)

MEGARRY J.: . . . in determining whether expenditure is incurred on revenue account or on capital account one must consider at least three elements. First, what is the nature of the payment? Is there a single non-recurrent lump sum, paid once for all, on the one hand, or are there to be current payments, made, for example, for periods commensurate with those payments? Second, what is to be obtained by the payment? Is it some asset with lasting or enduring qualities, or is it merely ephemeral, or, indeed, something which cannot be described as an asset, whether tangible or intangible? Third, in what manner is what is obtained to be used, or relied on or enjoyed? Will it have a quality of recurrence which will point to an income nature, as by providing a flow of orders for goods, or will it bear a static aspect which points to a capital nature? In considering all these elements, and in looking at the case as a whole, it is the practical and business point of view that counts for more than the juristic classification of the legal rights employed or exhausted in the process . . . **[10.28]**

Tucker v Granada Motorway Services Ltd [1979] 1 WLR 683 (HL)

LORD WILBERFORCE: . . . My Lords, the question in this case is whether a sum of £122,220 paid by the appellant in order to secure a reduction in rent paid by it under a lease is deductible in computing its profits for corporation tax purposes. Although this states the essence of the problem, it is probably desirable to clothe it with some particulars.

The lease in question was granted by the Minister of Transport in 1965 and was of a service area near a motorway. The term was 50 years. The rent payable consisted of two elements: there was a fixed rent of £15,000 per annum, and there was an additional rent of a variable character. The additional rent varied in proportion to the appellant's gross takings from business conducted at the area. It was provided that, in calculating the variable element, the appellant should be entitled to exclude petrol duty but no such exclusion was allowed as to tobacco duty. The lease was expressly made non-assignable.

The appellant company soon realised that the part of the variable rent calculated by reference to tobacco duty (which of course could be raised unilaterally by the Government) exceeded the gross profit margin on sales of tobacco. So it entered into negotiation with a view to having the amount of tobacco duty excluded from gross takings. It was appreciated that some payment would have to be made in order to secure this concession, and negotiations proceeded on the line of taking a number of years' purchase of the tobacco duty element in the additional rent. After some hard bargaining, agreement was reached on a basis representing six years'purchase, described as a lump sum, which produced the figure of £122,220.

...So how is this £122,220 to be regarded? On the one hand the payment was designed to enable the appellant to earn more profits: from this point of view it might be thought that the payment should have a revenue character.

On the other hand, the payment produced a modification in the lease, which could be regarded as an identifiable asset, making the lease less disadvantageous: from this point of view it might be thought that the payment should be regarded as a capital payment.

It is common in cases which raise the question whether a payment is to be treated as a revenue or as a capital payment for indicia to point different ways. In the end the courts can do little better than form an opinion which way the balance lies. There are a number of tests which have been stated in reported cases which it is useful to apply, but we have been warned more than once not to seek automatically to apply to one case words or formulae which have been found useful in another: see *Commissioner of Taxes v. Nchanga Consolidated Copper Mines Ltd.*[56] Nevertheless reported cases are the best tools that we have, even if they may sometimes be blunt instruments.

I think that the key to the present case is to be found in those cases which have sought to identify an asset. In them it seems reasonably logical to start with the assumption that money spent on the acquisition of the asset should be regarded as capital expenditure. Extensions from this are, first, to regard money spent on getting rid of a disadvantageous asset as capital expenditure and, secondly, to regard money spent on improving the asset, or making it more advantageous, as capital expenditure. In the latter type of case it will have to be considered whether the expenditure has the result stated or whether it should be regarded as expenditure on maintenance or upkeep, and some cases may pose difficult problems.

It is in this connection that so many discussions start from the well-known phrase of Viscount Cave L.C. in *British Insulated and Helsby Cables Ltd. v. Atherton*[57]: "... when an expenditure is made, not only once and for all, but with a view to bringing into existence an asset or an advantage for the enduring benefit of a trade ..." These words were regarded as having quasi-statutory force until, in a later case, it was revealed that they might cover an advance more of a revenue character. So Rowlatt J. in *Anglo-Persian Oil Co. Ltd. v. Dale*,[58] explained the phrase as meaning:

> "... a benefit which endures, in the way that fixed capital endures; not a benefit that endures in the sense that for a good number of years it relieves you of a revenue payment. It means a thing which endures in the way that fixed capital endures. It is not always an actual asset, but it endures in the way that getting rid of a lease or getting rid of onerous capital assets ... endures."

So here we obtain an indication that, while the fact that the benefit obtained was enduring, in the sense that it might last for over 40 years, is not sufficient to make the payment a capital payment, a payment to get rid of a lease might be so sufficient. What then if the payment is to get rid of a disadvantage in a lease?

We obtain further guidance from *Mallett v. Staveley Coal and Iron Co. Ltd.*[59] In that case there were two payments one to persuade the landlord under a mining lease to accept a surrender of it – and so to free the lessee from possible liabilities; the other to persuade the landlord to modify a (different) lease. Of the latter, Sargant L.J. used these words:[60]

> "It is a payment made for the purpose of modifying the conditions of an existing asset so as to make the resultant term more advantageous or less disadvantageous for the enduring benefit of the trade."

These words – as words – admirably fit the present case, but we must beware of the formula trap. He was speaking there of a modification which involved the release of a

56 [1964] A.C. 948.
57 [1926] A.C. 205 at 213. [See above, para **[10.27]**.]
58 (1931) 16 T.C. 253 at 262.
59 [1928] 2 K.B. 405.
60 *Ibid.* at 420–421.

parcel of land from the lease – something in other words within the classic case of disposal of an asset. Nevertheless we are asymptotically approaching the present case.

Other instances are provided by cases concerned with petrol filling stations: *Strick* v. *Regent Oil Co. Ltd.*[61] and *B.P. Australia Ltd.* v. *Commissioner of Taxation of the Commonwealth of Australia.*[62] The test there accepted and applied was whether a capital asset could be identified for which the relevant payments were made.

I pass to the other side of the narrow, dividing line. Nearest to this line is the case in this House of *Inland Revenue Commissioners* v. *Carron Co.*[63] There the expenditure was incurred in order to procure a modification to the company's charter in such a way as to enable it to trade more properly and to facilitate day to day operations. This House held that the payment had a revenue character. Unless indeed it could be said that the charter was a capital asset, it is difficult to see what other decision could have been given. In the course of my opinion I used these words:[64]

> "... the disposition of a source of liability may be equivalent to the acquisition of a source of profit – an extension perhaps, but not an exception, to the principle that in some sense or other an asset of a capital nature, tangible or intangible, positive or negative, must be shown to be acquired. If this is correct – and until a case arises which constitutes a true exception I shall continue to think that it is – the present expenditure cannot be brought within the capital class."

With due caution against using these words as if they were statutory, I adhere to them. They were, of course, directed to excluding cases where no capital asset could be "seen" or identified, which was that case; I had not intended to narrow the conception of capital payments to the case of the acquisition of an asset. Clearly expenditure on a capital asset may fall within the principle.

Finally I come to *Anglo-Persian Oil Co. Ltd.* v. *Dale*[65] – the sheet anchor of the appellant's argument. The payment there was in order to free the company from a long term agency agreement which had become onerous to the company. Now there may not be much commercial difference between a payment of this kind and a payment to get rid of an onerous lease. But since the courts have accepted and worked the "identifiable asset" test, the decision was no doubt right in law. The test may be to some extent arbitrary, but it provides a means which the courts can understand for distinguishing capital and income expenditure and I think that we would be wise to maintain it.

My Lords, I shall refrain from analysing further examples of cases either way. The recent decisions, *Pitt* v. *Castle Hill Warehousing Co. Ltd.*[66] and *ECC Quarries Ltd.* v. *Watkis*[67] ... fully support the identifiable asset test. So it remains to decide the present case. For myself I cannot doubt where it lies: it is a case of once and for all expenditure on a capital asset designed to make it more advantageous. It is true that the lease was non-assignable, so it had no balance sheet value before or after the modification. But it was none the less an asset and a valuable one for the appellant's trade, and, if an asset, was a capital asset. It appears to me to be impossible to divorce the payment from the lease and to regard it as simply a payment intended to increase the appellant's share of the profits. That it may have done, but the parties chose to do it through the medium of a lease, just as in the petrol filling stations cases, the object of increasing gallonage sales was effected through a lease. Nor in my opinion can the payment be regarded as payment of rent – that would be to confuse the measure, or basis of calculation of the payment with its nature. I agree therefore with both courts below in regarding the payment as of a capital nature ... **[10.29]**

61 [1966] A.C. 295.
62 [1966] A.C. 224.
63 (1968) 45 T.C. 18.
64 *Ibid.* at 75.
65 [1932] 1 K.B. 124.
66 [1974] 1 W.L.R. 1624. [See above, para **[10.28]**.]
67 [1977] 1 W.L.R. 1386.

Vodafone Cellular Ltd v Shaw [1997] STC 734 (CA); below, para [10.33]

The taxpayer company, part of a group of companies, claimed to deduct the sterling equivalent of $30 million, which it had paid for the cancellation of an agreement with a US company. The Special Commissioners and the High Court both held that the payment was a revenue and not a capital payment, but that it was not made wholly and exclusively for the purposes of the taxpayer company's trade. The taxpayer company appealed against the ruling that the payment was not made wholly and exclusively for the purposes of its trade (see below, para **[10.33]**), and the Crown cross-appealed against the ruling that the payment was of a revenue nature.

MILLETT LJ:

The facts

In 1982 the Racal Electronics Group (Racal) was intent on establishing a cellular mobile telephone network in the United Kingdom. In order to obtain the necessary manufacturing licences and technology it decided to enter into a joint venture with an American company Millicom Inc (Millicom). The taxpayer company was formed as a joint venture company for this purpose, Racal holding 80% of the shares and Millicom 15%. The remaining 5% were held by a financial institution. These shareholdings did not reflect the parties' original intentions, but nothing turns on this. In due course Millicom granted five royalty-free licences to the taxpayer company to manufacture its products and incorporate them into equipment for use in the United Kingdom. The licences were conditional on the taxpayer company obtaining an operating licence for the system from the Department of Trade and Industry.

In the event the Department of Trade and Industry insisted that the operation of the network and the sale of apparatus and service to subscribers must be undertaken by different companies. Accordingly the taxpayer company formed two wholly-owned subsidiaries, one to operate the network and one to sell the apparatus and service; and the operating licence was granted to the company which was to be responsible for operating the network.

On 29 June 1983 the taxpayer company entered into two agreements with Millicom. By one (the share agreement) Millicom was granted its shareholding in the taxpayer company and agreed to supply the initial know-how and technical support for a sum of £2m. By the other (the fee agreement) Millicom confirmed the grant of the manufacturing licences to the taxpayer company. This was necessary because the operating licence had been granted to a subsidiary and not to the taxpayer company itself. In addition Millicom agreed to supply the taxpayer company from time to time at its request with future know-how. In return the taxpayer company agreed to pay an annual fee equal to 10% of its consolidated pre-tax profits for 15 years with provision for losses to be carried forward.

The network was duly established. Afterwards it transpired that Millicom's know-how was not needed. Alternative technology was obtainable more cheaply elsewhere. The fee agreement became a liability. The taxpayer company approached Millicom and asked it to agree to bring the arrangements to an end. This was effected on 29 December 1986 by two further agreements. By one the taxpayer company's ultimate parent company acquired Millicom's shares in the taxpayer company in exchange for an issue of new shares in itself. By the other, called the fee cancellation agreement, the taxpayer company agreed to pay Millicom $30m for the extinguishment of its liability under the fee agreement. In addition the taxpayer company released Millicom from its liability under the fee agreement to supply future know-how, but not from its liability under the five licences, three of which continued in being.

The taxpayer company and its subsidiaries had not earned any profits by the time of the fee cancellation agreement, and accordingly the annual payments provided for by the fee agreement had not yet become payable. It was always intended that the benefit of the fee agreement would be made available to the subsidiaries, and the Special Commissioners found that it was in fact made available to them as there was no other way (at least at first) in which the subsidiaries could operate; moreover, this was the only way in which the benefit of Millicom's expertise could be put to use. They found that there was no formal agreement between the taxpayer company and its subsidiaries for the taxpayer company to be reimbursed for the benefit of the fee agreement; but that when the arrangements were entered into in 1983 it was contemplated that the subsidiaries would be charged with the fees paid to Millicom in the same way that they were charged for management and other services supplied to them by the taxpayer company.... .

Was the payment a capital or revenue payment?

Whether a payment is a capital or a revenue payment is a question of law (see *Regent Oil Co Ltd v Strick (Inspector of Taxes)*[68] per Lord Reid, *IRC v Carron Co*[69] per Lord Wilberforce, *Tucker (Inspector of Taxes) v Granada Motorway Services Ltd*[70] per Lord Wilberforce and *Beauchamp (Inspector of Taxes) v F W Woolworth plc*[71] per Lord Templeman).

There is no single test or infallible criterion for distinguishing between capital and revenue payments (see *Van den Berghs Ltd v Clark (Inspector of Taxes)*[72] per Lord Macmillan, *Comr of Income Tax v Nchanga Consolidated Copper Mine Ltd*[73] per Lord Radcliffe and *Regent Oil Co Ltd v Strick (Inspector of Taxes)*[74] per Lord Reid). On the contrary, there are many factors which tend in one direction or the other, some of which are more relevant in some situations and some in others. Some factors are particularly relevant when the question arises on an acquisition and others are of particular relevance when the question arises on a disposal, as it does in the present case.

Two matters are of particular importance: the nature of the payment, and the nature of the advantage obtained by the payment. The fact that the payment is a lump sum payment is relevant but not determinative. In a case such as the present, where the payment is made in order to get rid of a liability, a useful starting point is to inquire into the nature of the liability which is brought to an end by the payment. Where a lump sum payment is made in order to commute or extinguish a contractual obligation to make recurring revenue payments then the payment is prima facie a revenue payment.

In *Hancock (Surveyor of Taxes) v General Reversionary and Investment Co Ltd*[75] the payment of a lump sum in order to commute an annual pension was held to be an income payment because it merely anticipated payments which if not commuted would have been income payments. In such a case the lump sum might be regarded as of the same nature as the ingredients of which it was composed (see *Van den Berghs Ltd v Clark (Inspector of Taxes)*[76] per Lord Macmillan).

In *Anglo-Persian Oil Co Ltd v Dale (Inspector of Taxes)*[77] the payment of a lump sum in order to secure the cancellation of an agency agreement which was onerous to the principal and would otherwise have endured for a further ten years was held to be a revenue payment. Lawrence LJ said –

> "... neither enlarged the area of its operations, nor improved its goodwill, nor embarked upon a new enterprise; it merely effected a change in its business methods and internal organisation, leaving its fixed capital untouched."[78]

But the principle that a payment made in order to commute or discharge a liability to make recurring revenue payments is itself a revenue payment is subject to an important qualification. If the liability to make recurring revenue payments is reduced or brought to an end by the modification or disposal of an identifiable capital asset, then any payment made for the modification or disposal is itself a capital payment.

68 [1966] AC 295 at 313.
69 (1986) 45 TC 18 at 73.
70 [1979] 1 WLR 683 at 688; [see above, para **[10.29]**.]
71 [1990] 1 AC 478 at 492.
72 [1935] AC 431 at 438; [see above, para **[10.21]**].
73 [1964] AC 948 at 959.
74 [1966] AC 295 at 313.
75 [1919] 1 KB 25.
76 [1935] AC 431 at 442.
77 [1932] 1 KB 124.
78 *Ibid.*, at 141.

In *Tucker (Inspector of Taxes) v Granada Motorway Services Ltd*[79] Lord Wilberforce explained that the assumption that money spent on the acquisition of an asset should be regarded as capital expenditure has been extended in two ways. First, money spent on getting rid of a disadvantageous asset is normally regarded as capital, and secondly money spent on improving the asset or making it more advantageous is also normally so regarded. *Mallett (Inspector of Taxes) v Staveley Coal and Iron Co Ltd*[80] a reverse premium paid by a tenant to a landlord to accept the surrender of a mining lease was held to be a capital payment. In that case the payment was made to dispose of a capital asset. In *Tucker (Inspector of Taxes) v Granada Motorway Services Ltd* a payment made to commute part of the rent payable under a lease was also held to be capital. The payment was not made in order to get rid of a disadvantageous asset, but it was made in order to render the asset less disadvantageous. The lease itself was non-assignable and so had no balance sheet value, but it was nevertheless a balance sheet item, that is to say a capital asset the value of which (if it had had any) would have appeared in the balance sheet. It followed that a payment made to make the lease more advantageous was a capital payment even though the object in making the payment was to increase the taxpayer company's profits by reducing its revenue expenditure.

In the present case the payment in question was made to get rid of the liability to pay annual fees under the fee agreement. The Crown submits that the fee agreement was a capital asset. I do not accept this submission. The fee agreement was certainly not a balance sheet item, and in my opinion it was no more a capital asset than was the agency agreement in *Anglo-Persian Oil Co Ltd v Dale (Inspector of Taxes)*.

It is obvious that not every contract under which a liability to make revenue payments arises is a capital asset for this purpose, or the general principle that payments to get rid of revenue liabilities are revenue payments would be entirely subsumed in the exception. It is only where such a contract is one the cancellation of which would effectively destroy or cripple the whole structure of the taxpayer company's profit-making apparatus that it falls to be treated exceptionally as a capital asset. This was the case in *Van den Berghs Ltd v Clark (Inspector of Taxes)* where the taxpayer company received a capital sum for the cancellation of the contracts which comprised the whole or virtually the whole of the taxpayer company's business. Lord Macmillan said:[81]

> "The three agreements which the appellants consented to cancel were not ordinary commercial contracts made in the course of carrying on their trade; they were not contracts for the disposal of their products or for the engagement of agents or other employees necessary for the conduct of their business; nor were they merely agreements as to how their trading profits when earned should be distributed as between the contracting parties. On the contrary, the cancelled agreements related to the whole structure of the appellants' profit-making apparatus. They regulated the appellants' activities, defined what they might and what they might not do, and affected the whole conduct of their business. I have difficulty in seeing how money laid out to secure, or money received for the cancellation of, so fundamental an organisation of a trader's activities can be regarded as an income disbursement or an income receipt."

In *Barr Crombie & Co Ltd v IRC*[82] a payment by way of compensation for the loss of a management contract which was fundamental to the taxpayer company's business and which represented more than 88% of its profit-earning capacity was held to be a capital payment. This was because the contract represented virtually the taxpayer company's only asset, and when it was abandoned practically nothing remained of its former business.

These and other such cases are in a category of their own. They are not cases where the payment was made or received in order to remove an expense of carrying on the business, but where it was received for the loss or disposal of the greater part of the business.

79 [1979] 1 WLR 683 at 686; [see above, para **[10.29]**].
80 [1928] 2 KB 405.
81 [1935] AC 431 at 442.
82 26 TC 406.

The Crown submits that the fee agreement was (or at least was originally thought to be) fundamental to the taxpayer company's business. It formed an integral and essential part of the arrangements made to establish the business of the taxpayer company and its subsidiaries in 1983. Without the know-how to be supplied by Millicom the telephone network could not be operated successfully. The business was in the forefront of high technology, and technological know-how is central to such a business.

In my judgment the submission fails on two grounds. In the first place, the question whether a payment is capital or income must depend on the circumstances at the time when the payment is made. In the present case this requires the fee agreement to be considered in the light of the circumstances in 1986. By then it was certainly not regarded as central to the business, but as a liability. In the second place, while it was admittedly not a contract for the disposal of the taxpayer company's products, the fee agreement was in my opinion an ordinary commercial contract made in the course of trade for the acquisition of future intangible material believed to be necessary for the carrying on of the trade.

Just as the agency agreement in *Anglo-Persian Oil Co Ltd v Dale (Inspector of Taxes)* was an ordinary commercial contract and not a capital asset (see *Tucker (Inspector of Taxes) v Granada Motorway Services Ltd*[83] , per Lord Fraser) so too was the fee agreement in the present case whether it is considered as in 1983 or as in 1986. Just as in the one case the taxpayer company could choose to carry on its business itself or through outside agents, so in the present case the taxpayer company could obtain the necessary know-how by buying it in or by establishing its own research department. It chose to buy it in. The initial know-how was admittedly a capital asset, and the payment by which it was obtained was admittedly a capital payment. We are not concerned with that. We are concerned solely with the agreement by which the taxpayer company obtained the supply of future know-how, which was an agreement for future services and a very different thing.

In the course of the Crown's submissions we were referred to *S Ltd v O'Sullivan*[84]. The case is instructive, for it bears a superficial resemblance to the present. The question was whether annual payments for the acquisition of know-how were capital or revenue payments. The case is not of direct relevance to anything which we have to decide, for it is conceded by the Crown in the present case that if the annual payments under the fee agreement had ever become payable they would have been revenue payments. In *S Ltd v O'Sullivan* by contrast they were held to be payments of capital. But there were three significant features in that case. First, the payments were expressed to be instalments of capital; secondly, they were payable for present as well as future know-how; and thirdly the taxpayer company obtained the benefit of an agreement by the other party that it would not disclose the information to any other person carrying on business in Ireland. These three features of the case were sufficient to render the payments capital payments. None of them is present in the instant case.

It is now settled that a trade advantage is not a capital asset unless it is for the enduring advantage of the trade and that by this is meant enduring in the way that fixed capital endures (see *Anglo-Persian Oil Co Ltd v Dale (Inspector of Taxes)*[85] per Romer LJ). High technology, particularly in modern times, is quickly obsolete. Expenditure to acquire future know-how is paid to obtain a service; it is not made to acquire an enduring asset, but a commodity which is turned over or exploited in the course of trade at a comparatively early date. It appears to me to have the characteristics of circulating rather than fixed capital and to represent an ordinary operating cost.

The principles derived from the foregoing survey of the authorities are sufficient to satisfy me that the fee agreement was not a capital asset, that it was a liability but only because it was likely to entail a heavy drain on the annual income of the taxpayer company, and that by cancelling it the taxpayer company did not obtain an enduring benefit for its trade in the sense in which that expression is used in this context. It obtained a reduction of its annual revenue expenditure but nothing more. It follows in my opinion that the payment of $30m by which it obtained that reduction was a revenue payment. **[10.30]**

83 [1979] 1 WLR 683 at 695; [see above, para **[10.29]**].
84 [1972] 2 ITR 602.
85 [1932] 1 KB 124 at 146.

The effect of this test is to 'block' the deductibility of repair costs on the acquisition of an asset which is in such bad condition that the repairs are necessary in order to make the asset viable. In *Law Shipping Co. Ltd v IRC* (1924) 12 TC 621, the Court of Session determined that the purchaser of a ship was not allowed to deduct the costs of £51,558 incurred in enabling it to obtain its certificate of seaworthiness. Lord Cullen said:

> It is, in substance, the equivalent of an addition to the price. If the ship had not been in need of the repairs in question when bought, the Appellants would, presumably, have had to pay a correspondingly larger price (see (1924) 12 TC 621, 628). **[10.30a]**

C. *The 'wholly and exclusively' test*

ITTOIA 2005, s 34(1) provides that '[I]n calculating the profits of a trade, no deduction is allowed for – (a) expenses not incurred wholly and exclusively for the purposes of the trade . . .'. However, '[I]f an expense is incurred for more than one purpose, this section does not prohibit a deduction for any identifiable part or identifiable proportion of the expense which is incurred wholly and exclusively for the purposes of the trade'. **[10.31]**

Mallalieu v Drummond (Inspector of Taxes) [1983] AC 861 (HL)

LORD BRIGHTMAN: . . . the immediate issue in this appeal concerns the right of a female barrister, in computing the profits of her profession, to deduct the cost of upkeep of a wardrobe of clothes of a design and colour suitable to be worn under her gown during court appearances. But during the course of the argument this issue was found to resolve itself into a far more general and fundamental question: whether any person carrying on a trade, profession or vocation on his own account is entitled to a similar deduction if he chooses to set apart clothes, underclothes and footwear for use only at his place of work, and when proceeding to and from his place of work.

. . . The effect of para (*a*)[86] is to exclude, as a deduction, the money spent by the taxpayer unless she can establish that such money was spent exclusively for the purposes of her profession. The words in the paragraph "expended *for the purposes* of the trade, profession or vocation" mean in my opinion "expended *to serve the purposes* of the trade, profession or vocation"; or as elaborated by Lord Davey in *Strong & Co of Romsey Ltd v Woodifield (Surveyor of Taxes)*[87] "for the purpose of enabling a person to carry on and earn profits in the trade etc."[88] The particular words emphasised do not refer to "the purposes" of the taxpayer as some of the cases appear to suggest: as an example see the report of this case [1983] 1 WLR 252 at 256.[89] They refer to "the purposes" of the business which is a different concept although the "purposes" (ie the intentions or objects) of the taxpayer are fundamental to the application of the paragraph.

The effect of the word "exclusively" is to preclude a deduction if it appears that the expenditure was not only to serve the purposes of the trade, profession or vocation of the taxpayer but also to serve some other purposes. Such other purposes, if found to exist, will usually be the private purposes of the taxpayer: see for example *Prince v Mapp*.[90]

To ascertain whether the money was expended to serve the purposes of the taxpayer's business it is necessary to discover the taxpayer's "object" in making the expenditure: see *Morgan v Tate & Lyle Ltd*[91]. As the taxpayer's "object" in making the expenditure has to be

86 [ICTA 1970, s.130(a); now ITTOIA 2005, s.34(1).]
87 [1906] AC 448 at 453.
88 [On the one-time significance of which, see Whiting [2006] BTR 267–281, 269.]
89 [In the Court of Appeal.]
90 [1970] 2 WLR 260.
91 [1955] AC 21 at 37 and 47.

found, it inevitably follows that (save in obvious cases which speak for themselves) the commissioners need to look into the taxpayer's mind at the moment when the expenditure is made. After events are irrelevant to the application of s 130 except as a reflection of the taxpayer's state of mind at the time of the expenditure.

If it appears that the object of the taxpayer at the time of the expenditure was to serve two purposes, the purposes of his business and other purposes, it is immaterial to the application of s 130(*a*) that the business purposes are the predominant purposes intended to be served.

The object of the taxpayer in making the expenditure must be distinguished from the effect of the expenditure. An expenditure may be made exclusively to serve the purposes of the business, but it may have a private advantage. The existence of that private advantage does not necessarily preclude the exclusivity of the business purposes. For example a medical consultant has a friend in the South of France who is also his patient. He flies to the South of France for a week, staying in the home of his friend and attending professionally on him. He seeks to recover the cost of his air fare. The question of fact will be whether the journey was undertaken solely to serve the purposes of the medical practice. This will be judged in the light of the taxpayer's object in making the journey. The question will be answered by considering whether the stay in the South of France was a reason, however subordinate, for undertaking the journey, or was not a reason but only the effect. If a week's stay on the Riviera was not an object of the consultant, if the consultant's only object was to attend on his patient, his stay on the Riviera was an unavoidable effect of the expenditure on the journey and the expenditure lies outside the prohibition in s 130.

There is no dispute between the parties as to the true meaning of s 130(*a*), and it is common ground that the principles which I have outlined are those which fall to be applied. The appeal before your Lordships is basically concerned with the distinction between object and effect. The inspector of taxes disallowed the deduction claimed by the taxpayer, with the result that she appealed to the General Commissioners against the assessment made on her. The General Commissioners who had themselves been in practice at the Bar, confirmed the assessment subject to a small adjustment on which there was agreement. The taxpayer successfully appealed to the High Court, and the decision of the Chancery judge was upheld on appeal. The inspector of taxes now appeals to this House with the leave of your Lordships.

The primary facts found by the commissioners are contained in para 4 of the printed case and para 8 of the decision, and are set out in full in the report at first instance.[92] The clothes which the taxpayer maintained for professional purposes were, broadly speaking, worn by her only in connection with her work. That is to say, she travelled in them to her chambers or directly to court, wore them throughout the day and changed out of them when she arrived home at the end of her working day. There were odd occasions on which the taxpayer might find it convenient to remain in her working clothes after her work was done. But no point is taken by the Crown in relation to such occasions nor is any point taken that the clothes were worn not only at work but also when travelling to and from work.

The critical findings of fact as set out in paras 4 and 8 of the case are these:

> "4.—(c) . . . The rules for guidance[93] are . . . normally complied with and it would have been virtually impossible for a lady barrister to practise unless she complied with the rules laid down . . .
>
> "(f) At all material times the taxpayer had a private wardrobe of clothes and shoes which was amply sufficient to keep her clothed and shod in comfort and decency, without having to resort to any of the disputed items. She would not have purchased any of the disputed items had it not been for the requirement of her profession that she should comply with the Notes for Guidance when appearing in court.

92 [1981] 1 WLR 908 at 912, 915.

93 ['Notes for Guidance on Dress in Court' (approved by the Bar Council and with the assent of the Lord Chief Justice).]

> "(j) ... She bought such items only because she would not have been permitted to appear in court if she did not wear, when in court, them or other clothes like them. Similarly the preservation of warmth and decency was not a consideration which crossed her mind when she bought the disputed items.
>
> "(k) The white blouses and black clothing bought by the taxpayer were items of ordinary civilian clothing readily available for purchase by anyone at many clothing stores.
>
> "(8). We consider that the evidence shows that when she bought the clothes she bought them to wear in court and that she would not have bought them but for the exigencies of her profession."

On the basis of those findings of fact the commissioners had to draw an inference and decide whether or not the taxpayer had expended money on her professional wardrobe exclusively to serve the purposes of her business, or alternatively to serve both the purposes of her business and her own private purposes. The inference drawn by the commissioners and the determination reached by them are contained in the second part of paragraph 9 of their written decision, which reads as follows:

> "We consider, in the present case, that when [the taxpayer] laid out money on clothes for wearing in court her purpose in making that expenditure was to enable her to earn profits in her profession and also to enable her to be properly clothed during the time she was on her way to chambers or to court and while she was thereafter engaged in her professional activity, and in the other circumstances indicated in para 2. We do not consider that the fact that her sole motive in choosing the particular clothes was to satisfy the requirements of her profession or that if she had been free to do so she would have worn clothes of a different style on such occasions altered the purpose of the expenditure which remained the purpose of purchasing clothes that would keep her warm and clad during the part of the day when she was pursuing her career as well as the purpose of helping her to earn profits in that career. We think, therefore, that the expenditure had a dual purpose, one professional and one non-professional ..."

The commissioners accordingly concluded that the taxpayer had two objects in making the expenditure, to serve the purposes of her business, and to serve her own purposes by enabling her properly to be clothed. Since there is no appeal from the commissioners on a question of fact, the only question before your Lordships is whether the findings of primary fact were such as to entitle them to draw that inference.

... I return to the question for your Lordships' decision whether there was evidence which entitled the commissioners to reach the conclusion that the object of the taxpayer in spending this money was exclusively to serve the purposes of her profession, or was also to serve her private purposes of providing apparel with which to clothe herself. Slade J felt driven to answer the question in favour of the taxpayer because he felt constrained by the commissioners' finding that, in effect, the only object present in the mind of the taxpayer was the requirements of her profession. The conscious motive of the taxpayer was decisive. The reasoning of the Court of Appeal was the same. What was present in the taxpayer's mind at the time of the expenditure concluded the case.

My Lords, I find myself totally unable to accept this narrow approach. Of course the taxpayer thought only of the requirements of her profession when she first bought (as a capital expense) her wardrobe of subdued clothing and, no doubt, as and when she replaced items or sent them to the launderers or the cleaners she would, if asked, have repeated that she was maintaining her wardrobe because of those requirements. It is the natural way that anyone incurring such expenditure would think and speak. But she needed clothes to travel to work and clothes to wear at work, and I think it is inescapable that one object, though not a conscious motive, was the provision of the clothing that she needed as a human being. I reject the notion that the object of a taxpayer is inevitably limited to the particular conscious motive in mind at the moment of expenditure. Of course the motive of which the taxpayer is conscious is of vital significance, but it is not inevitably the only object which the commissioners are entitled to find to exist. In my opinion the commissioners were not only entitled to reach the conclusion that the taxpayer's object was both to serve the purposes of her profession and also to serve her personal purposes, but I myself would have found it impossible to reach any other conclusion.

It was inevitable in this sort of case that analogies would be canvassed; for example, the self-employed nurse who equips herself with what is conveniently called a nurse's uniform. Such cases are matters of fact and degree. In the case of the nurse, I am disposed to think, without inviting your Lordships to decide, that the material and design of the uniform may be dictated by the practical requirements of the art of nursing and the maintenance of hygiene. There may be other cases where it is essential that the self-employed person should provide himself with and maintain a particular design of clothing in order to obtain any engagements at all in the business that he conducts. An example is the self-employed waiter, mentioned by Kerr LJ, who needs to wear "tails". In his case the "tails" are an essential part of the equipment of his trade, and it clearly would be open to the commissioners to allow the expense of their upkeep on the basis that the money was spent exclusively to serve the purposes of the business. I do not think that the decision which I urge on your Lordships should raise any problems in the "uniform" type of case that was so much discussed in argument. As I have said, it is a matter of degree.

. . . So, my Lords, I respectfully differ from the conclusion reached by Slade J and by the members of the Court of Appeal. I would allow this appeal. **[10.32]**

Vodafone Cellular Ltd v Shaw, above, para [10.30]

Was the payment made wholly and exclusively for the purposes of the taxpayer company's trade?

Whether a payment is made exclusively for the purpose of the taxpayer company's trade or partly for that purpose and partly for another is a question of fact for the commissioners. The court can interfere only if the commissioners have made an error of law in reaching their conclusion. The principles on which the court acts are to be found in the speech of Lord Radcliffe in *Edwards (Inspector of Taxes) v Bairstow*[94] and are too well known to repeat. It is sufficient to say that the court will interfere where the true and only reasonable conclusion from the facts found by the commissioners contradicts the determination.

In the case of an individual taxpayer, the other purpose is usually a private purpose of his own. In a case like the present, where the taxpayer company is a company forming part of a group, the other purpose is likely to be the purpose of the trade of one or more of the other companies in the group. But the same principles apply. The trade of a parent company is for tax purposes distinct from the trade of its subsidiary. The two companies are separate taxable persons, and the trade or business of one is not the same as the trade or business of the other, however closely it may affect it (see *Odhams Press Ltd v Cook (Inspector of Taxes)*[95]).

The leading modern cases on the application of the exclusively test are *Mallalieu v Drummond (Inspector of Taxes)*[96] and *MacKinlay (Inspector of Taxes) v Arthur Young McClelland Moores & Co* [1989][97]. From these cases the following propositions may be derived. (1) The words for the purposes of the trade mean to serve the purposes of the trade. They do not mean for the purposes of the taxpayer but for the purposes of the trade, which is a different concept. A fortiori they do not mean for the benefit of the taxpayer. (2) To ascertain whether the payment was made for the purposes of the taxpayer's trade it is necessary to discover his object in making the payment. Save in obvious cases which speak for themselves, this involves an inquiry into the taxpayer's subjective intentions at the time

94 [1956] AC 14; [see Chapter 3, above, para **[3.15]**].
95 (1938) 23 TC 233 at 254, 257.
96 [1983] 2 AC 861; [see above, para **[10.32]**].
97 [1990] 2 AC 239.

of the payment. (3) The object of the taxpayer in making the payment must be distinguished from the effect of the payment. A payment may be made exclusively for the purposes of the trade even though it also secures a private benefit. This will be the case if the securing of the private benefit was not the object of the payment but merely a consequential and incidental effect of the payment. (4) Although the taxpayer's subjective intentions are determinative, these are not limited to the conscious motives which were in his mind at the time of the payment. Some consequences are so inevitably and inextricably involved in the payment that unless merely incidental they must be taken to be a purpose for which the payment was made.

To these propositions I would add one more. The question does not involve an inquiry of the taxpayer whether he consciously intended to obtain a trade or personal advantage by the payment. The primary inquiry is to ascertain what was the particular object of the taxpayer in making the payment. Once that is ascertained, its characterisation as a trade or private purpose is in my opinion a matter for the commissioners, not for the taxpayer. Thus in *Mallalieu v Drummond (Inspector of Taxes)* the primary question was not whether Miss Mallalieu intended her expenditure on clothes to serve exclusively a professional purpose or partly a professional and partly a private purpose, but whether it was intended not only to enable her to comply with the requirements of the Bar Council when appearing as a barrister in court but also to preserve warmth and decency.

Similarly, in my opinion, the present case does not involve an inquiry whether the directors who resolved to enter into the fee cancellation agreement consciously intended to obtain a benefit thereby for one company rather than another. The primary inquiry is to ascertain the particular object which the directors sought to achieve by it. Once that is ascertained the characterisation of that object as serving the purposes of the trade of one particular company or another is not a finding of primary fact, but a conclusion based upon the primary facts.

. . . The critical findings of fact *[by the Special Commissioners]* are to be found in paras 12.30 and 12.34–36 of their decision (at 388, 389). These read as follows:

> "12.30. However, we find, on the basis of the oral and documentary evidence before us, that the directors of the taxpayer company regarded the taxpayer company with its two subsidiaries as one functioning trading entity as far as its relationship with Millicom was concerned . . .
>
> 12.34. We accept that the evidence was that, in reaching a decision to cancel the fee agreement, the directors of the taxpayer company gave no conscious thought to the position of the two subsidiaries but that, in itself, requires some explanation. It does not appear that the boards of directors of the subsidiaries were consulted about the cancellation even though they may have had a view about the continuing value of the agreements with Millicom. In our view, the reason was as we have stated, namely, that the directors of the taxpayer company regarded the taxpayer company with its two subsidiaries as one functioning entity as far as the relationship with Millicom was concerned.
>
> 12.35. In our view, on a true construction of the arrangements, the purpose of the directors of the taxpayer company, in agreeing to make the cancellation payment, was *to benefit the trading position of the whole group*, which comprised the taxpayer company and the two subsidiaries. The interests of all three were considered together when the decision was made [emphasis added].
>
> 12.36. *Accordingly*, we find that the payment was not made wholly and exclusively for the purposes of the trade carried on by the taxpayer company [emphasis added]."

The reasoning of the Special Commissioners appears to be as follows. (1) The directors gave no conscious thought to the position of the two subsidiaries because they regarded the taxpayer company and its subsidiaries as forming a single trading entity. (2) Their purpose in making the payment was to benefit the trading position of that entity. (3) The entity in question in fact consisted of three separate companies. (4) Therefore their purpose was to benefit all three companies. Now there is a logical fallacy here, for step (4) does not follow. This is easily demonstrated, for if the trading entity included a fourth company which could not possibly derive any benefit from the transaction, the reasoning above would lead to the absurd conclusion that the directors intended to benefit it also. But what follows from the fact that the directors intended to benefit the trading entity and gave no conscious thought to the position of the individual companies is not that they intended to benefit all the companies of which the entity was composed, but that they did not consciously set out to benefit any particular one of them.

The judge fell into the same error. He said (at 397) that once the trade was regarded as a collective one, then the benefit obtained by the removal of the burden on that trade was an inescapable purpose of such removal (sic).

The reasoning of the Special Commissioners also contains two errors of law. It confuses the purposes of the taxpayer company's trade with benefit to the taxpayer company (ie the purpose of the payment with its effect); and it seeks to answer the question "which company were the directors intending to benefit?" instead of "what was the particular object which the directors were seeking to achieve?".

Fortunately para 12.35 of the decision contains the answer to this last question. The purpose of the directors in obtaining the cancellation of the fee agreement was to benefit the trading position of the whole group. Now that could be achieved only and simply by the cancellation of the taxpayer company's liability to Millicom. The consequential release of the subsidiaries from their obligation to reimburse the taxpayer company (even assuming, contrary to the fact, that this would have been necessary) would not affect the trading position of the group at all. The elimination of inter-company indebtedness does not affect the consolidated group accounts, which is where the trading position of the group is reflected.

In my judgment the case is a simple one. The directors' purpose is self-evident: it was to rid the group of a trading liability owed to a third party. The liability in question was a liability of the taxpayer company alone: ergo the directors' intention, whether articulated or not, was exclusively to serve the purposes of the taxpayer company's trade. The elimination of the liability to Millicom would make it unnecessary to put in hand whatever arrangements there might be within the group to enable the taxpayer company to finance the liability. But this was merely a consequential and incidental effect of the elimination of the liability; it cannot possibly have been its purpose. It was, after all, not even necessary to cancel the fee agreement in order to release the subsidiaries from the obligation to reimburse the taxpayer company. That was within the power of the taxpayer company at any time, and did not require Millicom's consent or the expenditure of $30m.

In my judgment the true and only reasonable conclusion from the facts found by the Special Commissioners contradicts their determination.

Conclusion

I would allow the taxpayer company's appeal and dismiss the Crown's cross-appeal.

[10.33]

McKnight v Sheppard [1999] 1 WLR 1333 (HL)

The taxpayer, a stockbroker, sought to deduct the cost of legal expenses incurred in defending himself before the disciplinary committee of the Stock Exchange against charges that included gross misconduct. The House of Lords held that such expenses were wholly and exclusively expended for the purposes of his trade.

LORD HOFFMANN:...The commissioner found that the taxpayer was a sole trader and that expulsion or a period of suspension would have destroyed his trade. He found that his exclusive purpose in laying out the legal costs was the preservation of his trade. The well-known case of *Morgan (Inspector of Taxes) v Tate & Lyle Ltd*[98] is authority for the

98 [1955] AC 21 at 35.

proposition that money spent for the purpose of preserving the trade from destruction can properly be treated as wholly and exclusively expended for the purposes of the trade within the meaning of s 130(a). The commissioner so found.

My Lords, on an appeal from the Special Commissioner by way of case stated, the only question, as Nourse LJ pointed out in the Court of Appeal, is whether, on the facts as the commissioner found them, this conclusion was open to him as a matter of law (see *Edwards (Inspector of Taxes) v Bairstow*[99]). Mr Grabiner QC, who appeared for the Crown, advanced two arguments as to why it was not.

First, he said that the facts found by the commissioner led inescapably to the conclusion that the taxpayer had two purposes in paying the legal expenses. One was the preservation of his business and the other was the preservation of his personal reputation. It followed that he had a dual purpose and the trade purpose thus lacked the necessary exclusivity (see *Mallalieu v Drummond (Inspector of Taxes)*[100]).

I do not think that the commissioner's careful findings of fact lend support to this criticism. He recorded the taxpayer[101] as saying in evidence that he "did not care about his personal reputation". While accepting the taxpayer as an honest witness nine years after the event, he did not accept that this correctly reflected his attitude at the time. He said that the taxpayer would have had to be "extraordinarily thick-skinned not to have experienced feelings of personal distress" at the effect of the charges upon himself and his family. But he went on to make the following important finding:

> 'However, the fact that I do not accept that the taxpayer was wholly unconcerned with his personal reputation does not necessarily mean that his purpose in laying out the legal costs was not exclusively concerned with preserving his trade. Purpose and effect are not the same (see *Mallalieu v Drummond (Inspector of Taxes)*[102] per Lord Brightman).'

The special commissioner is here saying that although he does not accept that the taxpayer was unconcerned about the advantages which a successful defence would have for his personal reputation, he does accept that this was not the purpose for which the money was spent. The reference to Lord Brightman's speech in *Mallalieu v Drummond (Inspector of Taxes)*[103] is illuminating. The relevant passage is as follows:

> "The object of the taxpayer in making the expenditure must be distinguished from the effect of the expenditure. An expenditure may be made exclusively to serve the purposes of the business, but it may have a private advantage. The existence of that private advantage does not necessarily preclude the exclusivity of the business purpose. For example a medical consultant has a friend in the South of France who is also his patient. He flies to the South of France for a week, staying in the home of his friend and attending professionally on him. He seeks to recover the cost of his air fare. The question of fact will be whether the journey was undertaken solely to serve the purposes of the medical practice. This will be judged in the light of the taxpayer's object in making the journey. The question will be answered by considering whether the stay in the South of France was *a* reason, however subordinate, for undertaking the journey, or was not a reason but only the effect. If a week's stay on the Riviera was not an object of the consultant, if the consultant's only object was to attend on his patient, his stay on the Riviera was an unavoidable effect of the expenditure on the journey and the expenditure lies outside the prohibition in s 130."

If Lord Brightman's consultant had said that he had given no thought at all to the pleasures of sitting on the terrace with his friend and a bottle of Côtes de Provence, his evidence might well not have been credited. But that would not be inconsistent with a finding that the only object of the journey was to attend upon his patient and that personal pleasures,

99 [1956] AC 14; [see Chapter 3, above, para **[3.15]**].
100 [1983] 2 AC 861; [see above, para **[10.32]**].
101 [1996] STC 627 at 636.
102 [1983] 2 AC 861 at 870–871.
103 *Ibid.*

however welcome, were only the effects of a journey made for an exclusively professional purpose. This is the distinction which the special commissioner was making and in my opinion there is no inconsistency between his conclusion of law and his findings of fact.

Mr Grabiner's second point was that the words "for the purposes of the trade" meant that the expenditure must be "in furtherance of the relevant commercial activity". There must be a sufficient connection with the earning of profits in the trade. This was not a case like *Morgan (Inspector of Taxes) v Tate & Lyle Ltd*[104] in which the taxpayer was defending his business against an external threat. This expenditure resulted from the taxpayer's own misconduct, that is to say, from behaviour outside the proper scope of his trade. Mr Grabiner referred to *IRC v Alexander von Glehn & Co Ltd*[105] in which the Court of Appeal disallowed the deduction of a penalty imposed upon a company during the 1914–18 war under the Customs (War Powers) Act 1915 for exporting goods without taking all reasonable care to secure that the ultimate destination should not be enemy territory. Lord Sterndale MR said that although the incurring of the penalty was connected with the trade, in the sense that it would not have happened unless the trade had been carried on, it was not for the purposes of the trade but because of a wrongful act on the part of the company.

I have no doubt that their decision was correct. But the Court of Appeal were curiously inarticulate about why the fine was not money expended for the purposes of the trade. Lord Sterndale MR said: "It is perhaps a little difficult to put the distinction into very exact language" but the payment was not a "loss connected with the business, but . . . a fine imposed upon the company personally."[106] Warrington LJ said[107] that the payment was not a loss "connected with or arising out of the trade" because it was a sum which "the persons conducting the trade have had to pay because in conducting it they have so acted as to render themselves liable to this penalty." Scrutton LJ said[108] that the obvious answer to the question whether a trader could deduct penalties imposed for carrying on the trade in an unlawful manner was: "Of course he cannot" but said that he did not find it easy to explain the reasons. He cited some well-known dicta about the criteria for allowable deductions and went on to say[109]:

> ". . . were these penalties an expenditure necessary to earn the profits? Were they paid for the purpose of earning the profits? The answer seems to me to be obvious, that they were not; they were unfortunate incidents which followed after the profits had been earned."

To say that the payments "followed after the profits had been earned" is only another way of saying that they could not be deducted in the calculation of profits. It restates the question rather than explaining the answer. *Von Glehn*'s case was not a case like *Smith's Potato Estates Ltd v Bolland (Inspector of Taxes)*[110] in which it would have involved an illogical circularity to treat the expenditure as a trade expense. In that case, the taxpayer claimed to deduct the legal costs of contesting an assessment to tax. The dispute was about the computation of the taxpayer's profits. It assumed that those profits were ascertainable, one way or another, at the time when the dispute arose. The costs of the dispute could not therefore have been an element in the computation. They were logically as well as temporally subsequent to the profits having been earned.

But there would have been no similar illogicality in treating the penalty in *von Glehn's* case as a trading expense. It was, as the Court of Appeal accepted, incurred in the course of the company's trade. There must therefore have been something in the nature of the expense which prevented it from being deductible. I think with great respect that the Court of Appeal had difficulty in identifying exactly what this was because they were

104 [1955] AC 21.
105 [1920] 2 KB 553.
106 [*Ibid*, at 566.]
107 *Ibid.*, at 569.
108 *Ibid.*, at 571.
109 *Ibid.*, at 572.
110 [1948] AC 508.

looking in the wrong place. They hoped to find the answer in the broad general principles of what counts as an allowable deduction. But the reason in my opinion is much more specific and relates to the particular character of a fine or penalty. Its purpose is to punish the taxpayer and a court may easily conclude that the legislative policy would be diluted if the taxpayer were allowed to share the burden with the rest of the community by a deduction for the purposes of tax. This, I think, is what Lord Sterndale meant when he said that the fine was imposed "upon the company personally."

By parity of reasoning, I think that the commissioner and the judge were quite right in not allowing the fines to be deducted.[111] It does not follow, however, that the costs were not deductible. Once it is appreciated that, in a case like this, non-deductibility depends upon the nature of the expenditure and the specific policy of the rule under which it became payable, it can be seen that the relevant considerations may be quite different. This explains the divergent answers given by the courts in the various cases on fines, penalties, damages and costs to which your Lordships were referred. So, for example, in *Herald and Weekly Times Ltd v Federal Comr of Taxation*[112] the High Court of Australia decided that damages for defamation payable by a newspaper company were a deductible expense. This seems to me correct: as Gavan Duffy CJ and Dixon J said in their joint judgment[113] such claims against a newspaper are a "regular and almost unavoidable incident of publishing it" and the damages are compensatory rather than punitive. There would seem no reason of policy why a rule which allows recovery of damages by plaintiffs defamed in the course of carrying on the business should prohibit deduction of those damages as an expense. In *von Glehn's* case,[114] Scrutton LJ expressed some anxiety lest the broad principles he thought he was applying should exclude the deductibility of civil damages for negligence. But the relevant principles are in fact a great deal more specific and can accommodate both *von Glehn* and *Herald and Weekly Times Ltd v Federal Comr of Taxation* without inconsistency.

The question is then whether there is any reason of policy which prohibits the deduction of legal expenses incurred as a result of penal or disciplinary proceedings arising out of the conduct of the business. In *von Glehn* there was also a claim to deduct the incidental legal expenses associated with the penalty. No separate argument was addressed to this question and it was assumed to be governed by the decision on the deductibility of the penalty itself. But I do not think that this is right. The issues are different. What would have been the position if the allegations had proved to be groundless and the taxpayer had been acquitted? It would have seemed unfair not to allow any deduction for the taxpayer's legal expenses. In principle, however, the purpose of the payment will be the same whether the taxpayer's defence turns out to be successful or not. Can there be a distinction between the costs of a successful and an unsuccessful defence? It might be argued that, as a matter of policy, the unsuccessful defendant should have to bear his legal costs personally in the same way as the penalty itself. But I think there would be great difficulties about giving effect to such a rule. It might not be easy to tell which costs had been expended successfully and which unsuccessfully. The taxpayer may, as in this case, have been convicted on some counts and acquitted on others. He may have had substantial success in mitigation of the penalty. More important, it is fundamental that everyone, guilty or not guilty, should be entitled to defend themselves. I do not see that any clear policy would be infringed by allowing the deduction of the legal expenses incurred in resisting the disciplinary proceedings. On the contrary, I think that non-deductibility would be in effect an additional fine or penalty for which the regulatory scheme does not provide. The commissioner was therefore right to treat the case as governed by the general principle in *Morgan (Inspector of Taxes) v Tate & Lyle Ltd.*[115] **[10.34]**

111 [The taxpayer had initially also sought to deduct the fine that he had incurred. Both the Special Commissioner and the High Court rejected his claim, and he did not appeal to the Court of Appeal on this issue.]

112 (1932) 48 CLR 113.

113 *Ibid.*, at 119.

114 [[1920] 2 KB 553.]

115 [1955] AC 21.

It has been suggested by John Tiley that the decision in *Sheppard* depended crucially on the finding of fact made by the Special Commissioner. Thus, 'Had the commissioner found that concern for personal reputation had been a purpose and not an effect, it is unlikely that the appeal by S[heppard] would have succeeded. Why decency and clothing should be subconscious purposes in *Mallalieu v Drummond*, while personal reputation was here only an effect is unclear; this lack of clarity is institutionalised by treating it as a matter of fact.' (*Revenue Law* (5th edn, 2005), p 393).

See also, generally, Roger Kerridge 'Deductibility of Expenses for Schedule D Income Tax – The "All or Nothing" Rule' [1986] BTR 36, and John Ward '"All or Nothing": More Than Nothing at All' [1987] BTR 141. **[10.35]**

5. Valuation of trading stock

When trading stock (or 'stock-in-trade') is sold, the relevant figure for tax purposes is generally the amount received on the sale. However, there are at least three situations where, when no amount – or an amount less than their market value – has been received, it is necessary to include as a trading receipt an amount representing the market value of the stock. These are: the so-called 'rule' in *Sharkey v Wernher*,[116] valuations of trading stock and work in progress at the end of a year of assessment and transfer-pricing. **[10.36]**

A. *The 'rule' in Sharkey v Wernher*

Sharkey v Wernher [1956] AC 58 (HL)

Lady Zia Wernher, who was the taxpayer's wife,[117] transferred five horses from her stud farm to her racing stables. The cost of breeding the horses was debited from her stud farm accounts. The Inland Revenue contended that, on transfer, the horses' market value should be entered in the accounts. The House of Lords upheld the Inland Revenue's argument.

> VISCOUNT SIMONDS: ... The problem, therefore, in all its simplicity, is whether a person, carrying on the trade of farming or, I suppose, any other trade, who disposes of part of his stock-in-trade not by way of sale in the course of trade but for his own use, enjoyment, or recreation, must bring into his trading account for income tax purposes the market value of that stock-in-trade at the time of such disposition.
>
> ... An attempt has been made to justify the notional receipt of a sum equal to the cost of production by treating such a receipt as the equivalent of an expenditure which in the event proved not to have been for the purpose of trade, since the article was not disposed of in the way of trade. But this is pure fiction. Up to the very moment of disposition (in this case the transfer of a horse from stud farm to racing stable) the article was part of the trader's stock-in-trade and the cost of its production was properly treated as part of his expenditure for income tax purposes. I see no justification for an ex post facto adjustment of account which in effect adds to a fictional receipt a false attribution of expenditure.
>
> This is, however, the position with which we are faced. Your Lordships may not think it necessary to express any opinion on the question whether, if the Crown is not right in requiring market value to be brought into account in the present case, it is nevertheless

116 [1956] AC 58.

117 Prior to the 1990/1991 tax year, the taxable income of a married woman was aggregated with that of her husband (see Chapter 14, below, para **[14.2]**).

entitled to require the cost of production to be brought in. This is said to be of no importance in this case, though it might well be of great importance in other cases. I cannot refrain from calling attention to what must be fundamental to the solution of the question. For I cannot escape from the obvious fact that it must be determined whether and why a trader, who elects to throw his stock-in-trade into the sea or dispose of it any other way than by way of sale in the course of trade, is chargeable with any notional receipt in respect of it, before it is asked with how much he should be charged.

It is, as I have said, a surprising thing that this question should remain in doubt. For unless, indeed, farming is a trade which in this respect differs from other trades, the same problem arises whether the owner of a stud farm diverts the produce of his farm to his own enjoyment or a diamond merchant, neglecting profitable sales, uses his choicest jewels for the adornment of his wife, or a caterer provides lavish entertainment for a daughter's wedding breakfast. Are the horses, the jewels, the cakes and ale to be treated for the purpose of income tax as disposed of for nothing or for their market value or for the cost of their production?

It is convenient at this stage to refer to case of *Watson Brothers* v. *Hornby*,[118] which I have already mentioned. In that case the taxpayers, who were the appellants in the appeal, carried on a business of poultry dealers and breeders of poultry at a hatchery belonging to them which was conceded to be an enterprise chargeable as a trade under Case I of Schedule D of the Income Tax Act 1918. The business of the hatchery was to produce and sell day-old chicks. They also carried on farming activities which were conceded to be, for income tax purposes, a separate enterprise from the hatchery business and, as the law then stood, were an income tax source chargeable under Schedule B of the Income Tax Act 1918. Most of the produce of the hatchery was sold, but a substantial number of day-old chicks were from time to time transferred to the farm and became part of the stock of poultry of the farm. The question in the appeal was whether, in computing the profits of the hatchery business, the day-old chicks transferred to the farm should be brought in at cost or market value. The market value was at the material times much below cost, viz 4d as against 7d per chick. It was contended for the taxpayers that market price and for the Crown that cost of production should be adopted as the appropriate figure in the accounts. It was decided by Macnaghten J that the taxpayers' contention was right, and they were accordingly chargeable upon the footing that as traders in respect of their hatchery business they received 4d only per chick. This decision, which your Lordships were told has ever since been adopted as the basis of assessment by the Revenue in similar cases, involves two things, first, that the taxpayer may in certain circumstances be subject to a sort of dichotomy for income tax purposes and be regarded as selling to himself in one capacity what he has produced in another, and, secondly, that he is regarded as selling what he sells at market price. It is a decision upon which the appellant relies in the present case, and which, as I have said, Vaisey J. regarded as an authority binding him. The learned judge also derived some assistance from *Inland Revenue Commissioners* v. *William Ransom and Son Ltd*,[119] in which it was at least recognised that for tax purposes two parts of an enterprise carried on by a taxpayer should be treated as distinct. But it was not, I think, an issue in that case at what price goods should be determined to be transferred from one part of the enterprise to the other.

. . . For I repeat that I see no valid distinction between a trader crediting himself with a price (market value) which produces a profit or with a price (production cost) which strikes a balance or reduces his loss. Yet it is the basis equally of the judgment of Macnaghten J. in *Watson Brothers* v. *Hornby*[120] and of the observations of Lord Greene in the *Laycock*[121] and the *Briton Ferry*[122] cases that something has to be brought into account where the legislature recognises a sort of artificial dichotomy and a taxpayer is regarded as carrying on more than one taxable activity. And so also, as I have more than once pointed out, in this case it is conceded by the taxpayer that some figure must appear in

118 (1942) 24 T.C. 506.
119 [1918] 2 K.B. 709.
120 (1942) 24 T.C. 506.
121 [1939] 2 K.B. 1.
122 [1940] 1 K.B. 463.

the stud farm account as a receipt in respect of the transferred horses, though Lady Zia in her capacity as transferee did not carry on a taxable activity. In the same way, it would, I suppose, be claimed that, if Lady Zia were to transfer or re-transfer a horse from her racing establishment to a stud farm, some figure would have to appear in the stud farm accounts in respect of that horse, though it cost her nothing to make the transfer: if it were not so and she subsequently sold the transferred horse and the proceeds of sale were treated as receipts of the stud farm, she could justly complain that she had been charged with a fictitious profit.

. . . How far is this principle, which is implicit in the judgments that I have cited and in the admission upon which this case has proceeded, supportable in law? That it conflicts with the proposition taken in its broader sense, that a man cannot trade with himself is, I think, obvious. Yet it seems to me that it is a necessary qualification of the broad proposition. For, if there are commodities which are the subject of a man's trade but may also be the subject of his use and enjoyment, I do not know how his account as a trader can properly be made up so as to ascertain his annual profits and gains unless his trading account is credited with a receipt in respect of those goods which he has diverted to his own use and enjoyment. I think, therefore, that the admission was rightly made that some sum must be brought into the stud farm account as a receipt though nothing was received and so far at least the taxpayer must be regarded as having traded with himself. But still the question remains, what is that sum to be? I suppose that in the generality of cases in which the question arises in a farming or any other business, e.g. where the farmer supplies his own house with milk, or a market gardener with vegetables, an arbitrary or conventional sum is agreed. The House was not given any information as to the prevailing practice. Now the question precisely arises. In answering it I am not influenced by the fact that a change in the law has made the farmer liable to tax under Schedule D instead of under Schedule B, nor does section 10 of the Finance Act 1941, affect my mind beyond the fact that it emphasises the artificial dichotomy which the scheme of income tax law in many cases imposes. But it appears to me that, when it has been admitted or determined that an article forms part of the stock-in-trade of the trader and that upon his parting with it so that it no longer forms part of his stock-in-trade some sum must appear and his trading account as having been received or in respect of it, the only logical way to treat it is to regard it as having been disposed of by way of trade. If so, I see no reason for ascribing to it any other sum than that which he would normally have received for it in the due course of trade, that is to say, the market value. As I have already indicated, there seems to me to be no justification for the only alternative that has been suggested, namely, the cost of production. The unreality of this alternative would be plain to the taxpayer, if, as might well happen, if a very large service fee had been paid so that the cost of production was high and the market value did not equal it.

In my opinion, therefore, the judgment of the Court of Appeal was wrong and should be reversed, and the judgment of Vaisey J. restored. **[10.37]**

Lord Oaksey dissented from this opinion on the ground that it was contrary to the principle that the 'profits and gains' taxed are actual commercial profits and not mere benefits and to the further principle that a man cannot trade (in the sense in which the word 'trade' is used for income tax purposes) with himself.

Further, as seen below, the Court of Appeal determined, subsequently, that the rule in *Sharkey v Wernher* did not apply to a person carrying on a profession. **[10.38]**

Mason v Innes [1967] Ch 1079 (CA)

LORD DENNING MR: . . . Mr. Hammond Innes is a writer of distinction who has for many years carried on the profession of an author. He has written many novels and travel books. He has kept his accounts on a cash basis and has submitted these to the Revenue for tax purposes. On the one side, he has included his receipts from royalties and so forth. On the other side, he has included the expenses of his travels overseas to gather material; the expenses of his study at home; and a small salary to his wife for her work for him.

In this case we are concerned with one particular novel which he wrote called The Doomed Oasis. It was based on material which he gathered in the Persian Gulf in 1953. He started to write it in September 1958, and worked on it up till 1959. He charged all the expenses in his accounts for those years. In 1960 he was about to publish it. But he felt he would like to do something to support his father, who had retired on modest resources. So Mr. Hammond Innes decided to transfer the copyright in the book The Doomed Oasis to his father as a gift. By an assignment made on April 4, 1960, he assigned to his father, "in consideration of natural love and affection," the copyright, performing rights and all other rights in The Doomed Oasis.

The question arises whether he is liable to tax on the value of those rights in The Doomed Oasis. If he had sold the rights at that time in 1960 their market value would have been £15,425. The Crown say that that sum ought to be brought into his accounts and that he should be taxed on it, although he did not receive a penny for the rights because he had given them away. I may add that Mr. Hammond Innes had also before publication assigned rights in two others of his novels, one to his mother and the other to his mother-in-law. So a like question may arise there.

I start with the elementary principle of income tax law that a man cannot be taxed on profits that he might have, but has not, made: *Sharkey* v. *Wernher*.[123] At first sight that elementary principle seems to cover this case. Mr. Hammond Innes not receive anything from The Doomed Oasis.

But in the case of a trader there is exception to that principle. I take for simplicity the trade of a grocer. He makes out his accounts on an "earnings basis."[124] He brings in the value of his stock-in-trade at the beginning and end of the year: he brings in his purchases and sales; the debts owed by him and to him; and so arrives at his profit or loss. If such a trader appropriates to himself part of his stock-in-trade, such as tins of beans, and uses them for his own purposes, he must bring them into his accounts at their market value. A trader who supplies himself is accountable for the market value. That is established by *Sharkey* v. *Wernher* itself. Now, suppose that such a trader does not supply himself with tins of beans, but gives them away to a friend or relative. Again he has to bring them in at their market value. That was established by *Petrotim Securities Ltd* v. *Ayres*.[125]

Mr. Monroe, on behalf of the Revenue, contends that that exception is not confined to traders. It extends, he says, to professional men, such as authors, artists, barristers, and many others. These professional men do not keep accounts on an "earnings basis." They keep them on a "cash basis,"[126] by which I mean that on one side of the account they enter the actual money they expend and on the other side the actual money they receive. They have no stock-in-trade to bring into the accounts. They do not bring in debts owing by or to them, nor work and progress. They enter only expenses on the one side and receipts on the other. Mr. Monroe contended that liability to tax does not and should not depend on the way in which a man keeps his accounts. There is no difference in principle, he says, between a trader and a professional man. And he stated his proposition quite generally in this way: The appropriation of an asset, which has been produced in the ordinary course of a trade or profession to the trader's or professional man's own purposes, amounts to a realisation of that asset or the receipt of its value, and he must bring it into account.

123 [1956] A.C. 58. [See above, para **[10.37]**.]

124 [This refers to the utilisation of the so-called 'accrual basis of accounting', instead of the 'cash basis of accounting'. 'The accrual basis of accounting requires the non-cash effects of transactions and other events to be reflected, as far as is possible, in the financial statements for the accounting period in which they occur, and not, for example, in the period in which any cash involved is received or paid.']

125 [1964] 1 W.L.R. 190.

126 [Following the introduction of what is now, for income tax purposes, s 25(1), ITTOIA 2005 (see above, para **[10.2]**), the cash basis is not, in general, acceptable for tax purposes. Exceptionally, however, the cash basis is permitted for barristers and advocates in the first seven years of practice (see ITTOIA 2005, s 160). See also David Hole, 'Withdrawal of the Cash Basis – Sections 42 to 46 and Schedules 6 and 7' [1998] BTR 405.]

I cannot accept Mr. Monroe's proposition. Suppose an artist paints a picture of his mother and gives it to her. He does not receive a penny for it. Is he to pay tax on the value of it? It is unthinkable. Suppose he paints a picture which he does not like when he's finished it and destroys it. Is he liable to pay tax on the value of it? Clearly not. These instances – and they could be extended endlessly – show that the proposition in *Sharkey v. Wernher* does not apply to professional men. It is confined to the case of traders who keep stock-in-trade and whose accounts are, or should be, kept on an earnings basis, whereas a professional man comes within the general principle that, when nothing is received, there is nothing to be brought into account.

I hold that Mr. Hammond Innes is not chargeable with tax on gifts which he makes of copyright in his books. I think that Goff J. and the Commissioners came to a right decision. I would dismiss this appeal. **[10.39]**

For a criticism of *Sharkey v Wernher* and a clear explanation of why the rule should not apply to those who carry on a profession, see D C Potter 'Reflections on *Sharkey v Wernher*' [1964] BTR 438. **[10.40]**

Roger Kerridge 'The Rule in Sharkey v. Wernher – Time for a Reappraisal?' [2005] BTR 287, 293–298

The facts of Sharkey v Wernher

It may be a good idea to pause here to note that the facts in *Sharkey v Wernher* were not quite as at first they appear. This may explain why the Revenue were so keen to stop Lady Zia from doing things the way she wanted to do them. The reality is that the Revenue were probably right to challenge her; what was wrong was the form of the challenge. When the facts of *Sharkey v Wernher* are recounted, it is said that Lady Zia owned a stud farm, that some of the horses bred in the stud farm were sold to third parties, others were transferred to Lady Zia's own racing stables. It will be vaguely assumed, by most of those who read this, that the stud farm was a profit-making enterprise and that only a relatively small percentage of the horses bred there were transferred to the racing stables. The impression given is that this is similar to the case of the grocer who takes the occasional jar of marmalade from the shelf in his shop to flavour his breakfast toast. Whether the marmalade is withdrawn from stock at cost or at market value is not going to have any significant effect on profitability. It will obviously not be decisive in deciding whether the business is profit-making or loss-making. And, it may be assumed, the same will be true in the case of Lady Zia's withdrawing of the horses. But this would be wrong. In *Sharkey v Wernher* entering the horses at market value, rather than at cost, meant that Lady Zia made a profit rather than a loss. Or, it might be better to express this the other way round. If Lady Zia had been permitted to enter the horses she had removed into the racing stables at cost, she would have ended up making an overall loss on the stud farm, but if she had been obliged to enter them at market value, she would have ended up making a significant profit. This is not the same as the grocer who, from time to time, takes a jar of marmalade from the shelf. It is not the same as the antique dealer, who removes the occasional piece of furniture. It is not the same as Viscount Simonds's diamond merchant who adorns his wife with his choicest jewels – it is in a completely different category.

The calculations in *Sharkey v Wernher* are not set out in the reports of the case in a form which makes them easy to follow, but, for the year of assessment

1949/50, the Revenue sought to assess Lady Zia to tax on an estimated profit of £5,000; this was on the basis that the horses she had transferred from the stud farm to the racing stables had been transferred at open market value. The difference between the open market value and the figure for cost had been about £9,000.[127] So, if the cost figure had been substituted for the open market value, the £5,000 profit would have turned into a £4,000 loss.[128] The figures seem to show three things. First, that most of the horses produced by the stud farm were transferred to the racing stables; secondly, that these were horses which could have been sold on the open market for a substantial profit; and thirdly, that the horses which remained and which were sold to third parties were sold at a substantial loss. This is like the case of someone who claims to be a grocer but who consumes most of his stock, all his best stock, himself and who maintains a shop only so that he can sell rotting and loss-making produce to the general public. It is hardly surprising that the Revenue were not too keen to let the taxpayer get away with it. But inventing the rule, or principle, in *Sharkey v Wernher*, to prevent Lady Zia from presenting things the way she wanted to was to go about things in the wrong way. The correct way was to deny her permission to chalk up "losses" on the stud farm transactions which did not involve transfers to her racing stables. If one were to disregard all transactions involving horses transferred from the stud farm to the racing stables, the remaining stud farm transactions throw up figures which appear to bear no resemblance whatsoever to anything which can legitimately be called "trading"...

How far was the rule to be carried?

Once it is suggested that a taxpayer is going to be taxed on profits he could have made, rather than the profits he did make, where should the line be drawn? Why should a trader not be taxed on the profits which he could have made, but neglected to make, when he took an odd day off because he felt a bit jaded? Why should he not be liable for the profits foregone when he went on a too-long summer holiday, or when he went on an ordinary holiday? Not everyone has holidays. And why should there be a special rule for traders? All self-employed taxpayers could be included. And then, why stop with the self-employed? Employees who work shorter hours than they are capable of working, or who take early retirement, or who fail to seek out the best paid employments are all "neglecting profitable opportunities". Why stop at sales? On this basis, any university teacher of tax law should be taxed on what he or she could earn as a lawyer in private practice.[129]

The idea of taxing people on what they could earn, rather than what they do earn, may have deserved further investigation, but there was no attempt to do so in *Sharkey v Wernher*...

127 (1955) 36 TC 275 at 290. The cost figure for the horses transferred to Lady Zia's racing stables was £1,800, their market value was £10,600.

128 To take account of inflation, the figures in the case need to be multiplied by about fifteen to give their modern equivalents. The £5,000 profit would be £75,000, while the £4,000 loss would be £60,000.

129 Though the fact that university teachers do not have holidays means that different applications of any extended rule in *Sharkey v Wernher* would apply to them in different ways. This all goes to show, if it is not immediately apparent, how hopelessly impracticable it would be even to consider extending the rule.

The position immediately after Sharkey v Wernher

Almost immediately after the decision in *Sharkey v Wernher*, the Revenue published a Statement of Practice[130] which became, in due course, SP A32, which remains in force today. This Statement of Practice reads as follows[131]:

> "A32 Goods taken by traders for personal consumption
> The case of *Sharkey v Wernher* (1955) 36 TC 275, establishes the principle that where a trader takes stock from his business for private use or enjoyment or disposes of stock otherwise than by sale in the normal course of trade, the transfer should be dealt with for taxation purposes as if it were a sale at market value. Inspectors have been authorised to take a reasonably broad view in applying this principle.

The decision is not considered to apply to –

(a) services rendered to the trader personally or to his household which should be dealt with in accordance with [*ICTA 1988 74(1)(b)*];[132]

(b) the value of meals provided for the proprietors of hotels, boarding houses, restaurants etc and members of their families which should also be dealt with on the basis that [*ICTA 1988* s *74(1)(b)*] applies;

(c) expenditure incurred by a trader on the construction of an asset which is to be used as a fixed asset in the trade."

It is not clear what "Inspectors have been authorised to take a reasonably broad view in applying this principle" is supposed to mean, but the part of the Statement which says that the decision is "not considered to apply to" situations (a), (b) and (c) should explain how the Revenue understood the decision to operate. Situation (c) is not important, because it is concerned with capital expenditure; but situations (a) and (b) restrict the application of the rule. Situation (b) seems to be an almost direct refutation of Viscount Simonds's example of the caterer. Situation (a) is not clear, but at its widest, it would appear to cover all services. Although the Revenue may not have realised it, the Revenue rule for situations (a) and (b) appears, in substance, to be the rule contended for by Lady Zia. The effect of calling section 74(1)(b) to aid is to disallow the expenditure, which has the same effect, in substance, as entering the cost figure in the accounts.

Apart from this Revenue Statement of Practice, nobody, at the time *Sharkey v Wernher* was decided, appears to have wanted to discuss the issues raised by the case.[133]

There were now two ways to proceed. One was to say that the decision of the majority in the House of Lords was wrong, that a trader could not trade with himself, that the earlier cases (with the possible exception of *Watson v Hornby*) had been rightly decided, and that there should be no question of attempting to tax

130 This Statement of Practice was first published in Accountants' Journal in January 1957. The writer understands (from enquiries made of the Revenue) that it was first issued as a Statement and it was not until later that it became a Statement of Practice. There now seems to be no record of when it changed its status, but nothing turns on this.

131 The only alterations over a period of fifty years will have been that the references to the current income tax consolidations will have needed to be updated.

132 [Note the point made in ITTOIA 2005, EN III, p 13: 'Section 74(1)(b) is not rewritten for income tax purposes because the deductions which it prohibits are covered by section 34 which rewrites the general prohibition on deductions not "wholly and exclusively laid out for the purposes of the trade, profession or vocation" in section 74(1)(a) of ICTA. And because it applies only to individuals, there is no need to preserve section 74(1)(b) of ICTA. It is therefore omitted.']

133 H. C. Edey, in an article in the first volume of this journal ([1956] BTR 23) did refer (at 34–36) to *Sharkey v Wernher* in the context of a discussion of the rules for valuing stock in trade, but there was no space for an analysis of the underlying problem.

potential, as opposed to actual, profits. The other was to say that the majority were right, and that the limits of the rule would now have to be considered; its extent could be tested by a process of piecemeal expansion. In 1964, D.C. Potter wrote a case note on *Sharkey v Wernher* for this Review.[134] He made it as clear as a practising member of the bar could that he thought that the case had been wrongly decided.[135] But it is highly probable that his reason for writing the case note at this point was that he had advance knowledge that the Revenue were about to attempt to extend the scope of the rule. The case the Revenue chose[136] for the start of their attempted expansion, was that of a well-known author who had given away a copyright . . .

Reconciling Sharkey v Wernher *and* Mason v Innes

Can *Sharkey v Wernher* and *Mason v Innes* be reconciled? The judges in *Mason v Innes* were bound by the House of Lords' decision in *Sharkey v Wernher* and so had, at least, to appear to distinguish it. They made no great effort. Their energies were directed to ensuring that the rule in *Sharkey v Wernher* was taken no further.

There were, and are, four ways in which *Sharkey* and *Mason* can be distinguished. There are passages in the judgments in the two cases which could justify any of them, though none of the four is compelling:

(i) The simplest way of distinguishing *Sharkey v Wernher* from *Mason v Innes* is to say that *Sharkey v Wernher* is confined to those who make their profits from buying and selling things (traders), together with those who provide nonprofessional services (tradespersons): the two groups who have, until the Rewrite takes effect,[137] been taxed together under Schedule D Case I. *Mason v Innes* covers those who provide professional services, those traditionally taxed under Schedule D Case II: or

(ii) *Sharkey v Wernher* could be confined to those who make their profits from buying and selling things (traders), as contrasted with those who provide services, whether professional or non-professional. This differs from (i), in that it puts self-employed carpenters, plumbers, etc, on the *Mason v Innes* side of the line; or

(iii) *Mason v Innes* could be confined to persons taxable on a "cash basis"; or

(iv) *Sharkey v Wernher* could be confined to the (very rare) type of case where the taxpayer concedes that a credit figure has to be entered. Lady Zia conceded that a figure had to be entered, Hammond Innes did not.

If none of these four ways of reconciling the two cases works, one of the cases, at least, must have been wrongly decided.

Looking at the four possible ways of reconciling the two cases, it is suggested that (iv) is the one which makes the least sense. It is true that both Viscount Simonds[138] and Lord Radcliffe[139] in *Sharkey* used the fact that Lady Zia had entered a credit figure in her accounts as a justification for substituting another figure. Hammond

134 [1964] BTR 438.

135 "But for the fact that the case was decided in the House of Lords . . . , the present writer would be tempted to assert that it was wrongly decided."

136 The Revenue always have a potential advantage, in that they choose which cases to take to appeal; they choose whether or not to fight. They will fight cases they expect to win, and, among those, the ones which are likely to set the precedents they would like to see set. If they think that a particular case is likely to be lost, or that the precedent would not favour them, they can simply choose not to dispute matters with the particular taxpayer.

137 [ITTOIA 2005 came into force on 6 April 2005 and applies in the 2005/2006 tax year onwards (see ITTOIA 2005, s 883(1)).]

138 36 TC 275 at 296.

139 36 TC 275 at 306.

Innes did not make the same mistake. But if the rule in *Sharkey v Wernher* were to be restricted in its application to those who choose to enter something in their accounts, it would soon apply to nobody at all.

Version (iii) is the reconciliation which would have best suited the Revenue – it would have restricted the application of *Mason v Innes* to a very small group of cases and left *Sharkey v Wernher* covering almost the whole of Schedule D. Some parts of some of the judgments in *Mason v Innes* could have been called in aid to support this approach.[140] But had the Revenue wanted to confine the application of *Mason v Innes* to taxpayers who were taxable on a cash basis, it would not have been hard for them to have found a test case. All they needed was a solicitor, taxable on the earnings basis, who had drafted his own will in the office. But, just as they chose not to appeal the decision of the Court of Appeal in *Mason v Innes*, so they chose not to bring such a test case. Their failure to do so meant that they were not going to suggest that (iii) was a realistic possibility.

That leaves (i) and (ii) – either *Sharkey v Wernher* is restricted to Schedule D Case I, or it is restricted to those who sell things, not covering those who provide services. Or, maybe, there is some sort of double restriction.

Two extreme rules

[I]t may be best to pause and to note the central problem involved in attempting to draw a line between *Sharkey v Wernher* and *Mason v Innes*. What is odd is how little attention has been paid to the fact that the rules applied in the two cases are both extreme rules – one harsh, the other generous. Neither case takes the middle course . . . **[10.41]**

B. End-of-year valuations

The points at issue here are well-expressed by Tiley: 'The value of trading stock unsold at the end of one period is entered into the account of that period as a receipt and into the account of the next period as an expense; it is thus sold from one year to the next. The figure entered is cost or market value – whichever is the lower.'[141] Equally, 'where the trader is a manufacturer [or a professional person with unfinished contracts] and there is work in progress at the end of the accounting period, the value of that work in progress must be brought into account'.[142] This latter is easier to state, in certain cases, than to apply. **[10.42]**

(1) Trading stock

***Commissioners of Inland Revenue v Cock, Russell & Co Ltd* (1949) 65 TLR 725 (KBD)**

The taxpayer company valued all except two items at cost, when it was valuing its stock of wine. The two exceptional items were valued at market value, which was less than cost. It was held that the company was entitled to do this.

140 See, in particular, Lord Denning M.R. (1966) 44 TC 326 at 339.
141 See Tiley, n 5 above, p 474, referring to *Whimster & Co v IRC* (1926) 12 TC 813.
142 Ibid, p 476.

CROOM-JOHNSON J: . . .there is nothing to be found anywhere in the statutes which indicates how the valuation is to be made. There is no authority which has been called to my attention which indicates that there is any legal principle which is applicable to this, other than the general principle about applying ordinary commercial principles. I cite as a convenient statement about that, and for no other purpose, the observations of Lord Porter in the case of *Absalom* v. *Talbot*[143]: "What has to he ascertained are the profits and gains of the business or, as the wording originally stood, the balance of profits and gains – a difference in language which does not affect the meaning of the provision. In order to ascertain that balance, one has to determine what sums are to be credited and what debited in the annual accounts. No directions are given in the Income Tax Acts as to how those profits are to be ascertained, and in default of direction they must, I think, be arrived at on ordinary commercial principles, subject to such provisions of the Income Tax Acts as require a departure from such ordinary principles". I think in these circumstances that it is impossible for me to say that the General Commissioners have failed to have regard to any principle of law which is applicable other than that principle. It is impossible for me to say that they have misdirected themselves. On the contrary, they appear to have directed themselves accurately and properly. They have accepted the evidence which was before them which, as I have said, was all one way and which I think is overwhelming on this particular point. Profits for Income Tax purposes – and Income Tax principles have to be applied to this computation – are to be computed as a business man employing sound principles commercial accountancy would compute them, subject only to any statutory modification of such principles. I cannot imagine anything which is more clearly a question of fact than what is the value of stock-in-trade at a particular time. I can see nothing to indicate the General Commissioners have gone wrong about it; on the contrary, I think they have gone right. There is no justification, so far as I can see, for a departure now from what admittedly has been the long-continued practice of the Commissioners of Inland Revenue and their officials. **[10.43]**

BSC Footwear Ltd v Ridgway (Inspector of Taxes) (1971) 47 TC 495 (HL)

LORD PEARSON: . . . The Appellants' system is this. They fix from time to time a 'mark-up', which is to be the average difference between their wholesale buying prices and their retail selling prices. Any goods held in stock are carried in the Appellants' books, and taken into the stock valuation for the profit and loss account, at a figure equal to the retail selling price less the mark-up. So long as the retail selling price of the goods remains unaltered, that figure of the retail selling price less the mark-up is approximately equal to the cost of the goods – the actual price at which they were bought wholesale. So far the valuation is approximately at cost and thus accords with the usual formula . . . [*'cost or market value, whichever is the lower'*] But if the goods remain unsold for too long (as they may do for instance in the event of a change of fashion or unexpected weather conditions) and the retail selling price has to be marked down, then the Appellants, instead of retraining the goods in their books at cost price, write them down to a figure equal to the reduced retail selling price less the mark-up. The mark-up is a percentage of the retail selling price. For convenience of illustration the mark-up has in the course of argument been assumed to be 33⅓ per cent., though the Appellants' mark-up would normally be somewhat higher. Then goods bought at 100 units of price would have initially a retail selling price of 150. But if the goods remained unsold for too long and consequently the retail selling price was reduced to 100, the goods would be written down to 66⅔ in the Appellants' books.

The question is whether the Appellants' system of stock valuation is acceptable for tax purposes. As it had been accepted by the Inland Revenue for many years up to 1959, it is now for the Crown to justify their rejection of it for 1959 and subsequent years. In order to do this, I think the Crown must show that the system is likely to produce stock valuations which are seriously and substantially incorrect and thereby to cause a

143 26 TC 166, at 197.

distortion of the assessment of the profits and gains for the year. If that is the effect of the system the Appellants cannot succeed with either of their two alternative contentions, namely, (a) that their system is a permissible application of the usual formula – cost or market value, whichever is the lower, or (b) that their system is a permissible substitute for the usual formula. The usual formula has been lucidly analysed and explained by Salmon L.J. in the Court of Appeal.[144] It is not disputed that even in the case of a retailer's stocks it is right to enter them in the books at cost in the first instance and not to add anything for merely anticipated profits. Nevertheless, the valuation at cost is a very cautious valuation, because normally the retailer expects to sell most of the goods at much higher prices and they are really worth more to him than he has paid for them. Initial valuation at cost is in such cases an under-valuation that is permitted and required by the usual formula. No doubt there are good reasons for it. On the other hand, the usual formula permits and requires a reduction of the valuation when the market value of the goods falls below their original cost. That is a further element of cautious valuation. One has to consider at what point a fall in prevailing prices justifies writing down goods in stock to a figure below their cost price. When the usual formula is applied, how is market value to be ascertained? Is the market which has to be envisaged a wholesale market in which the trader might buy similar goods, or is it the retail market in which he intends to sell his goods? It seems to me the correct principle is that goods should not be written down below cost price unless there really is a loss actual or prospective. So long as the fall in prevailing prices is only such as to reduce the prospective profit the initial valuation at cost should be retained. **[10.44]**

(2) Work in progress

Duple Motor Bodies Ltd v IRC (1961) 39 TC 537 (HL)

VISCOUNT SIMONDS: ... The question at issue between the parties was as to the correct method of ascertaining the cost of work in progress in order to determine the full amount of the profits or gains of the Company's trade, and I will state at once the question as formulated in the Case Stated. It was:

> "whether, on the evidence and in view of our findings ..., our decision that the on-cost method should be applied in arriving at the cost of work in progress for the purpose of computing the Company's Case I profits was erroneous in law".

... [I]t is proper to say – it is, indeed, implicit in what I have said – that it is common ground that some value must be attributed to work in progress and that, in ascertaining that value, two considerations must be borne in mind: first, that the ordinary principles of commercial accounting must, as far as practicable, be observed and, secondly, that the law relating to Income Tax must not be violated (see *Whimster & Co. v. Commissioners of Inland Revenue*)[145]: that is to say, by one means or another the full amount of the profits or gains of the trade must be determined.

... My Lords, I think that ... the prevailing consideration must be that the taxpayer should not be put to any risk of being charged with a higher amount of profit than can be determined with reasonable certainty. He may concede that stock-in-trade and work in progress must, for tax purposes, be regarded as a receipt. Upon that professional accountants appear to be universally agreed, though it might not be at once obvious to the layman. But this concession should not be pressed beyond the point at which the profession is widely, if not universally, agreed; and I should, therefore, if I had to choose (which I have not) between two vaguely defined methods, choose the direct cost method as the less likely to violate the taxing Statute. I should be supported in this choice by the

144 [1970] 2 W.L.R. 888, at 894–5.
145 1926 S.C. 20; 12 TC 813.

reflection that, if the cost is put at too low a figure, the error will be made good to the advantage of the Crown in the following year.

Another consideration that weighs with me is this. I recognise the force of the contention that if the cost of work in progress cannot be ascertained with accuracy, at least the attempt should be made to be as accurate as possible. But against this I put at least two powerful considerations. The first is that it is undesirable to indulge in what is no better than guesswork, though it may be described as an intelligent estimate; and it appeared to me that a large part of the suggested apportionment of overheads to stock-in-trade and work in progress was the wildest guesswork. It may be from the commercial point of view a desirable practice, but it is a very different thing to impose it upon a trader whether he wants it or not. It is not only unreliable for the purpose of ascertaining the year's profit, it is also an elaborate and costly practice if carried to its logical conclusion. And I see no reason why, once embarked on, it should not be carried to its logical conclusion. There appears to me to be no distinction, except perhaps of convenience, between the many varieties of cost which the exponents of one on-cost system or another advocate.

A second and more powerful reason, which the case under appeal illustrates, is that an attempt to get as nearly as possible an accurate estimate of cost may, if it means the consistent application of a theory of costing, lead to what from the taxing point of view is an absurd conclusion. That is not too strong a word. For here, as was well pointed out by Lord Evershed, M.R., and Pearce, L.J., the value of the work in progress at the end of the relevant year was £2,000 less than at its beginning if the direct cost method is adopted, whereas according to the on-cost method it was not £2,000 less but £14,000 more. This difference is due to little else than the fact that the overheads had to be distributed among a smaller number of articles so that each of them bore a greater proportion of such costs. An idle and unprofitable year thus increases for tax purposes the value of the work that has been, or is in course of being, done. Counsel for the Crown did not shrink from this conclusion and accepted my suggestion that, if owing to a prolonged strike little work was produced, the weight of all the overheads would have to be thrown upon that little. The only course then open to the trader would be to take market value as the test. This, I have pointed out, is an invitation that may be accepted.

My Lords, in my opinion this is fundamentally wrong. Stock-in-trade and work in progress are brought into account because, fictitiously but as a matter of plain common sense, they are treated as a receipt of the year's trading. The words "receipt" and "realised profit" were often on Counsel's lips in regard to them. My Lords, I would say, nevertheless, that it is something remote indeed from common sense to say that for taxing or any other purpose an inflated value is to be given to stock-in-trade or work in progress because a slump in trade has reduced the articles between which overhead costs can be apportioned. The asset, regarded as a receipt, is not more valuable, nor is a greater profit realised.

For the reasons that I have given I reject the so-called on-cost method as a method which can be imposed on the taxpayer ... **[10.45]**

C. *Transfer pricing*

ICTA 1988, s 770A and Sch 28AA contain measures to counter the practice of 'transfer pricing', which occurs where there is a sale at under-value or over-value between persons one of whom has been 'directly or indirectly participating in the management, control or capital of the other'.[146] Broadly, such provisions enable HMRC to substitute the market value of the item sold for the 'actual provision' made by the parties.[147] Since April 2004, the provisions have applied to domestic, as well as to cross-border,

146 ICTA 1988, Sch 28AA, para 1(1).
147 Ibid, Sch 28AA, para 1(2).

transactions,[148] although they do not apply to 'small and medium-sized enterprises'.[149] **[10.46]**

6. Timing

It is necessary to know to which basis period trading receipts or deductible expenses may be attributed. As Lloyd J has said:[150]

> 'In relation to almost any business which is carried on over more than one accounting period, questions arise as to whether particular items, whether of receipt or of expenditure, should be attributed to one period rather than another. One of the functions of the principles of commercial accounting is to help towards answers to these questions which are consistent, which reflect the commercial reality and which are readily understandable by a reasonably well-informed reader of a particular set of accounts.' **[10.47]**

A. *Trading receipts*

Receipts must not be anticipated when calculating trading profits.[151] **[10.48]**

J P Hall & Co Ltd v IRC (1921) 12 TC 382 (CA)

In March 1914, the taxpayer company contracted to supply electric motors 'complete with control gear'. Deliveries were to take place between July 1914 and September 1915, and the motors to be paid for within a month of delivery. Because of the 1914–1918 war, the final delivery of the control gear, on which the company made a profit of £1,064, was delayed until July 1916. The Court of Appeal held that the company earned the profit, not when the contract was made, but when the gear was in fact delivered.

> LORD STERNDALE MR: . . . [T]he short and simple answer to this, in my mind, is that these profits were neither ascertained nor made at the time that these two contracts were concluded. There are any number of contingencies that might have happened, by which the profit would not have turned out what it appeared on the face of it when the contracts were made. Any number of complications might have occurred that might have caused quite a different result to have accrued from these two contracts. I think that the Respondents[152] did what was right in the way they carried these profits into their account: it is the ordinary commercial way of making up accounts, and the other would be the wrong way, because the other would be carrying into the accounts as profits of one year the estimated profits which would accrue in subsequent years that might perhaps never be made at all. . . .
>
> ATKIN LJ: I agree. The proposition put forward by the Respondents in this case seems to me so very unsound that I am really left in doubt as to whether I have fully appreciated it, but, as I understand it, it appears to me to be quite wrong. The profits for Excess Profits

148 ICTA 1988, Sch 28AA, para 5.
149 *Ibid*, Sch 28AA, para 5B.
150 *Herbert Smith v Honour* [1999] STC 173 at 189.
151 See FRS 12, 'Provisions, contingent liabilities and contingent assets' reproduced in Ian Barlow and David Milne (eds) *Tax Statutes and Statutory Instruments 2005–2006* (5 vols, Kingston-upon-Thames, 2005), vol 1C, pp 11,406–11,425. More generally, this is in accordance with the concept of 'prudence' in accounting, which 'implies being cautious in the valuation of assets or the measurement of profit. It means . . . anticipating losses but never anticipating profits' (see Nobes, n 6 above, p 241).
152 [ie the Inland Revenue.]

Duty[153] are to be assessed on the same basis as profits for Income Tax purposes, and the word "profits" for Income Tax purposes is to be understood in accordance with the words of Lord Halsbury in *Gresham Life Assurance Society* v. *Styles*,[154] "in its natural and proper sense, in a sense which no commercial man would misunderstand," and he says "that profits and gains must be ascertained on ordinary principles of commercial trading." I need not say anything more after what has been said by the Master of the Rolls. It seems to me that no person here trying to ascertain these profits on the principles of ordinary commercial trading would dream of including profits in his yearly balance-sheet, which would not be made until the goods had actually been delivered in respect of some contract which was to run over a period of at least two years, and possibly more. To my mind the procedure of the Company was the ordinary commercial procedure in taking the profits that they made as and when the goods were delivered. Anything else, it appears to me, would be quite contrary to commercial procedure, and would not be profits in the natural and proper sense. I think, therefore, this appeal should be allowed. **[10.49]**

Willingale v International Commercial Bank Ltd [1978] AC 834 (HL)

The bank was in the business of discounting and purchasing bills of exchange. Its profit and loss account, which had been produced in accordance with accounting practice then used by clearing banks for recording bills of exchange, included on the credit side at the end of each year a fraction of the profit which the bank expected to make if the bills were held until maturity. The House of Lords (Lords Diplock and Russell of Killowen dissenting) held that this expected profit should not be included in the calculation of the bank's trading profits for corporation tax purposes.

LORD KEITH OF KINKEL: . . . The argument for the appellant started from the statement of Lord Haldane in *Sun Insurance Office* v. *Clark (Surveyor of Taxes)*[155]: [*His Lordship quoted the passage extracted above, para* **[10.5]**.]

It was accepted that, in the words of Lord Reid in *B.S.C. Footwear Ltd* v. *Ridgway*[156]:

> "The application of the principles of commercial accounting is, however, subject to one well established though non-statutory principle. Neither profit nor loss may be anticipated."

But it was contended that the bringing in on the credit side of a profit and loss account of a present debt payable in the future does not offend that principle, that the difference between the amount paid for a bill of exchange and the amount payable on maturity was a debt of that nature and that, sound principles of commercial accountancy having led in the present case to the bringing in of a particular part of that difference in each year before maturity, there was no good reason why the result should not be applicable for tax purposes. Reliance was placed on *Newcastle Breweries Ltd.* v. *Commissioners of Inland Revenue*,[157] *John Cronk & Sons Ltd.* v. *Harrison*,[158] *Gardner, Mountain and D'Ambrumenil Ltd.* v. *Commissioners of Inland Revenue*[159] and *Southern Railway of Peru, Ltd.* v. *Owen*.[160]

That group of cases establish that it may be right in principle to bring into credit in a particular accounting year something which will not be received until a later year, and likewise to bring into debit an expenditure which will not require to be made until a future year, and further that it may be correct to strike the appropriate credit or debit by a

153 [The case involved excess profits duty, a wartime tax, but nothing turns on this for present purposes.]
154 3 TC 155, at pp. 158 and 189.
155 [1912] AC 443 at 455.
156 [1972] AC 544 at 552; [above, para **[10.44]**].
157 [(1927) 12 TC 927.]
158 [1937] AC 185.
159 [(1947) 29 TC 69.]
160 [1957] AC 334.

process of estimation or of discounting. The principle which justifies this is that the receipt has been earned by services rendered or goods supplied in the earlier year, or that the liability for the expenditure arises from some transaction in the earlier year, and it is not a necessary objection to the inclusion in the account of the receipt or expenditure in question that it is uncertain, deferred or contingent. Whether or not the credit or debit should be included was said by Lord Radcliffe in the *Southern Railway of Peru Ltd* case[161] to turn on the answer to the practical question, how much more will the trader have to pay out or be able to get in than his current accounts of the year are recording, and later on he said:

> "But, whatever the legal analysis, I think that for liabilities as for debts their proper treatment in annual statements of profit depends not on the legal form but on the trader's answers to two separate questions. The first is – Have I adequately stated my profits for the year if I do not include some figure in respect of these obligations? The second is – Do the circumstances of the case, which include the techniques of established accounting practice, make it possible to supply a figure reliable enough for the purpose?"

Cases suitable for the application of these principles may in many instances be identified without difficulty. In my opinion the present case is not one of these, having regard to the nature of the transactions which form the relevant part of the Respondent Bank's business. In each case a sum of money is paid out by the Bank in a particular year and in return for it the Bank receives a bill of exchange, a chose in action. The bill obliges the issuer to pay the Bank a larger sum at the expiration of a number of years. The situation presents some analogy to the purchase by a trader of goods, which he expects later to sell at a profit, so that one might have expected to see the Bank in the year of purchase enter the cost of the bill in its profit and loss accounts as a debit, in subsequent years to enter as a debit the cost or market value of the bill whichever was the less, and in the year of maturity to enter as a credit the face value of the bill, whether or not it was actually paid in that year. But here the cost of the bill does not enter the profit and loss account; it goes in the balance sheet. It is only the difference between the cost and the maturity value of the bill which ever finds its way into the profit and loss account in annual fractions over the period to maturity. There can be no doubt that from the beginning the issuer of the bill is under a present obligation to pay the Bank a sum certain on a particular future date. So there is attraction in the view that under the principles to which I have referred the Bank, since it has by the transaction received in return for its payment the present right to receive a larger payment at a future date, should bring into its profit and loss account on the credit side the value of that right, suitably discounted, the payment out being likewise brought in on the debit side. But that again is not what was done, nor is it suggested that it should have been done. Nor has the amount of profit expected been brought at a valuation or at a discount. The reason why accounts prepared in the manner adopted by the Respondent Bank shows a true and fair view of its profits over the years is that, in order to have funds available for its bills at exchange transactions, the Bank borrows money at interest. The interest payable each year goes into the debit side of the profit and loss account and it is with the object of showing what benefit there is to counterbalance these payments that a fractional part of the discount on the bills is taken into the account on the credit side in each year. But it is not accurate to say that the interest payments are earning these fractional parts of the discount. The borrowing transactions and the bill of exchange transactions are separate and distinct from each other. It is the bill of exchange transactions on which attention must for present purposes be concentrated. The substance as well as the form of these transactions are such, in my opinion, that the Respondent Bank is by them acquiring assets which in the future it expects to realise at a profit. It is not reasonably to be regarded as rendering services to the issuers of the bills for which the latter there and then become liable to pay. The Case Stated speaks of the Respondent Bank making a profit when the bills reach maturity, and I think that is in accordance with the plain common sense of the matter. What goes into the profit and loss account each year is a fractional part of what it is hoped the profit will

161 *Ibid.*, at 357.

ultimately be, although it is found in the Case Stated that the amount of the profit is not ascertainable, due to a number of circumstances, until the bill is sold or reaches maturity. So I am of opinion that the assessment of the Respondent Bank to corporation tax on the basis of accounts made up in this way does contravene the rule that a profit may not be taxed until it is realised. . .

LORD RUSSELL OF KILLOWEN [*dissenting*]: My Lords, I approach the problem in this case in three stages.

First: suppose a transaction in which A (by way of his trade) advances to B a sum of money to be repaid at the expiration of three years with simple interest thereon at a rate per cent per annum, the obligation to pay the interest being, however, postponed to the date for repayment of the loan. The question arises whether the interest is to be brought into computation of A's trading profits for tax purposes in each of the three years of its accrual, or not until on the date fixed for payment of principal when three years' interest becomes payable. I defer the answer to that question.

Second: the answer to the first question cannot be different if the interest payable is compound rather than simple. This seems to me to be clear. Compound interest accrues annually no less than simple interest.

Third: what is the essential nature of the transaction selected by my noble and learned friend, Lord Fraser of Tullybelton, from page 48 of the Record? The Bank provides finance of £63.10, against a promise by the acceptor of the bill to pay £100 at the expiration of six years. The difference between the two sums (referred to by a convenient label as discount) can on analysis only be attributable to interest on the finance provided at eight per cent per annum for each of the six years compounded with yearly rests. It is not commercially realistic to regard the make-up of the "discount" as anything else, as a figure plucked from the sky. (The straight line treatment in the Bank's accounts of £6.15 annually is a convenient simplification; strictly to represent the discount in terms of accrual of compound interest at eight per cent per annum would involve figures varying from approximately £5.05 in the first year to approximately £7.41 in the sixth.)

Accordingly in my opinion the problem in this case is thrown back to that which I have described as the first stage plus the indistinguishable difference of the second stage; for I see no essential distinction between that and the third stage.

. . . The argument for the Crown is that, the accounts of the Bank being based on sound commercial accounting practice, as they are, they are to be accepted for tax purposes as showing the profits of the trade year by year, unless they are in conflict with some requirement or principle of tax law. The Bank accepts this, but contends that this conflict exists, inasmuch as there is conflict with the principle that for tax purposes there must be no anticipation of profits. For this principle the Bank appealed to the statements of Lord Reid and Lord Morris of Borth-y-Gest referred to by my noble and learned friend Lord Fraser of Tullybelton.[162] At the same time the Bank firmly disclaimed any attempt to depart from the principle of taxation law that profits "earned" in a particular year are for tax purposes profits or gains arising or accruing to the trader in that year; and also disclaimed any assertion of liability to tax only on a cash receipts basis.

Accordingly the answer to the question posed by me at the outset of my opinion (the first stage) depends on what is meant by "anticipation of profit", what is meant by "earnings". Neither is a word of universal application in the same sense in all circumstances. In that sense they are imprecise, and cannot be an instant solution to every problem. Nevertheless the question may be posed at that first stage: is a profit earned in year 1 though payment of the amount is deferred by reason of the terms of the commercial transaction until year 3? In my opinion it is so earned, and the treatment of it as a profit of that year is not a relevant (and forbidden) anticipation of profit. In the example given at the outset of this opinion (the first stage) it is I consider correct to say that in year 1 the finance afforded, or loan, earned in that year interest at X per cent. At the end of that year time had passed on the basis of which the lender had become entitled to a sum of X per cent on the amount of his loan, and nothing could deprive him of the fruits of that entitlement save default of the borrower which would require ultimate adjustment for a bad debt in the ordinary way. I can well understand a ban on anticipation

162 [ie in *BSC Footwear v Ridgway* [1971] 2 All ER 534 at 536, 542.]

> of profits for tax purposes when, for example, a trader buys goods with a view to future sale on a virtually certain rising market; if they are stock in trade there are of course special rules, but, if they be not, there is no time-plus-annual-interest element in the appreciation in value as there is in the case of the chose in action considered at the first stage of this opinion. It follows from what I have said that in my opinion the compound interest which is the content of the "discount" on a bill is not anticipated by being brought in as an annual profit or gain in respect of its periods of accrual. This applies equally whether the bill or note was acquired from the original acceptor or by subsequent purchase; the reason is that the difference between the face value of the bill and the cost of acquisition inevitably represents as a commercial matter compound interest. A money lender in the case of a loan on what I have called an original bill would be hard put to it to deny that.
>
> These, my Lords, I believe to be, though doubtless not so well expressed, the reasons which led Stamp LJ to dissent in his judgment, and I agree with him.
>
> The burden of the argument for the Bank was that the difference between the cost of a bill and the amount due on maturity is not interest; the bill is one chose in action providing for one sum due on maturity and can show no profit until maturity or earlier sale; consequently to treat any part of the difference (discount) as a profit or gain arising or accruing in any fiscal period before one of those events is anticipation of profit not permitted by principles of tax law. But, if my analysis of the essential make-up of the "discount" is correct, that contention is not correct.
>
> Now it is true that the accounting method of the Bank does not with precision reflect the attribution of the compound interest composition of the discount, because of the adoption for convenience and simplicity of the straight line method. But it is common ground that that method is commercially acceptable, and it does not seem to me to conflict with any principle of tax law . . . **[10.50]**

See Jill Pagan 'Measurement of Commercial Profit for Tax Purposes (or what *Willingale* was really about' [1992] BTR 75. Tiley points out that 'FRS 12 [see, para **10.54** below] does not dictate [the decision of the majority] . . . which was probably wrong in 1977 and is certainly wrong now'. Whiting comments (see [2006] BTR 267–281, 272):

> The decision in *Willingale* was in many ways on rather a narrow point on specialised circumstances, but it undoubtedly gave a further twist to the developing arguments about tax and accounting interaction. ICB was a specialist organisation and, were it to be a normal trading bank, the spreading rule would undoubtedly have been correct. However, it regarded the bills as medium-term capital assets and thus tax should only be charged on realisation.

See further, Judith Freedman 'Profit and Prophets – Law and Accountancy Practice on the Timing of Receipts Recognition' [1987] BTR 104, 113–115 and [1987] BTR 61–79. **[10.51]**

B. *Trading expenses*

The problems raised by expenditure can be divided into two categories:[163] liabilities which are uncertain and payments which can be attributed to more than one basis period ('spreading'). **[10.52]**

163 See Tiley, n 5 above, pp 463–467.

(1) Uncertain liabilities

Whether an uncertain liability counts as a trading expense for the purpose of calculating trading profits, depends on whether or not GAAP[164] requires it to be recognised as a 'provision'[165] in the taxpayer's financial statements or merely to be noted as a 'contingent liability'.

The relevant UK GAAP is contained in FRS 12,[166] which requires the recognition of a provision for items that fall within the detailed three-part definition set out below. However, contingent liabilities, the definition of which is also set out below, need only be noted in the financial statements. If a provision is required, the amount of the provision is deductible as a trading expense in calculating trading profits for income tax purposes. **[10.53]**

FRS 12, '*Provisions, contingent liabilities and contingent assets*', reproduced in Ian Barlow and David Milne (eds) *Tax Statutes and Statutory Instruments 2005–2006* (5 vols, 2005) vol 1C, pp 11,406–11,425.

Definitions

Contingent liability

(a) A possible obligation that arises from past events and whose existence will be confirmed only by the occurrence of one or more uncertain future events not wholly within the entity's control; or

(b) a present obligation that arises from past events but is not recognised because:
  (i) it is not probable that a transfer of economic benefits will be required to settle the obligation; or
  (ii) the amount of the obligation cannot be measured with sufficient reliability…

Provision

A liability of uncertain timing or amount.

RECOGNITION

Provisions

14. A provision should be recognised when:
  (a) an entity has a present obligation (legal or constructive) as a result of a past event;

164 Ie UK or International GAAP. References in this text are to UK GAAP, as being more suitable for a discussion of income tax. When reading the material in conjunction with Chapter 18, however, it will be necessary to refer to the IAS equivalents of the UK GAAP documents to which reference is made.

165 As Nobes points out, the term 'provision' has two distinct meanings. It can mean 'an allowance (or impairment or value adjustment) against the value of an asset', such as a provision for bad debts or depreciation, but this is *not* the sense in which the term is used here (see Nobes, n 6, above, pp 240–241).

166 The equivalent international GAAP appears in IAS 37 (see Chapter 18, below, para **[18.12]**).

(b) it is probable that a transfer of economic benefits will be required to settle the obligation; and

(c) a reliable estimate can be made of the amount of the obligation.

If these conditions are not met, no provision should be recognised…

Contingent liabilities

27. An entity should not recognise a contingent liability. **[10.54]**

As John Tiley has stated, 'FRS 12 is a change in accounting practice, and certain cases in which evidence of old accounting practices led the courts to allow a deduction would now be decided differently'.[167] Some, however, would not. **[10.55]**

Owen (Inspector of Taxes) v Southern Railway of Peru Ltd [1957] AC 334 (HL)

Peruvian legislation obliged a UK company to pay compensation to employees when their employment ended. The company claimed as a trading expense the compensation which it calculated would ultimately be due to each employee. The House of Lords held that, since this future liability had not been calculated by reference to factors such as proper discounting, the deduction was not permissible. Nonetheless, their Lordships left open the possibility that, if the liability had been properly discounted, the Company's argument would have prevailed.

LORD RADCLIFFE: … It is true that the Company carries on business from one year to another, but it is not charged on the average of its annual profits. Tax rates and allowances themselves vary and, apart from that, to charge tax on a profit unduly accelerated or unduly deferred is, in my opinion, no more respectable an achievement than to admit that the annual accounts of business do in some cases require the introduction of estimates or valuations if a true statement of profit is to be secured.

Another method is that which the Appellant is seeking to establish with regard to its assessments for the four years 1947–50. I will say at once that what it aims at (I do not say, what it achieves) appears to me to be a more accurate assessment of true annual profit than that which could be provided by the other method. When I am told, then, that its adoption is banned by some established principle of law, to which your Lordships are bound to give effect, I feel that I must enquire closely what that principle of law is and upon what understanding of accountancy practice the principle is said to be based. For the overriding principle of law is still, I believe, as it was stated by Lord Haldane in *Sun Insurance Office* v *Clark*[168]:

[His Lordship quoted the passage extracted above, para **[10.5]**.]

…And our task is not made any easier by the knowledge that, though the law with its system of precedents may sometimes seem to stand still (I hope that it does not), it is quite certain that the techniques and practices of commercial accountancy are very far from static.

… But there is no difficulty if we accept the main argument of the Crown. That argument is that, quite simply, there is a rule of law which forbids the introduction of any provision for future payments in or payments out, if the right to receive them or the liability to make them is in legal terms contingent at the closing of the relevant year. The rule, it seems, is absolute and must be adhered to whatever the current principles or practices of commercial accountancy may require as a method of ascertaining the year's profits. And this is the argument which hitherto has prevailed in the High Court and the

167 See Tiley, n 5 above, p 464.
168 [1912] AC 443 at 455.

> Court of Appeal. Now, in my opinion, there is no such rule of law governing the ascertainment of annual profits. Where does it come from? Not from anything to be found in the Income Tax Acts, which, indeed, by the well-known rule limiting the exclusion of debts, show a different and, as I think, a more realistic approach to the problem. Not from any decided authority which is binding on your Lordships. On the contrary, there are two decisions of this House which negative the existence of any such rule of law.
>
> ... But, whatever the legal analysis, I think that, for liabilities as for debts, their proper treatment in annual statements of profit depends not upon the legal form but upon the trader's answers to two separate questions. The first is: Have I adequately stated my profits for the year if I do not include some figure in respect of these obligations? The second is: Do the circumstances of the case, which include the techniques of established accounting practice, make it possible to supply a figure reliable enough for the purpose? **[10.56]**

Although the result in *Owen (Inspector of Taxes) v Southern Railway of Peru* would probably be the same today, the possibility left open by their Lordships would now have to satisfy FRS 12, para 14(c).

More recent cases, which nonetheless preceded the publication of FRS 12 in 1998, might now be decided differently. These include *Johnston v Britannia Airways Ltd*[169] and *Herbert Smith v Honour*.[170] For an analysis of *Johnston v Britannia Airways Ltd*, see David Oliver, 'Provision for Overhaul Costs: *Johnston v Britannia Airways Ltd*' [1995] BTR 502. **[10.57]**

(2) 'Spreading'

Where payments are attributable to more than one year, the question is the opposite of that regarding contingent liability. It is whether a payment which has been made may be treated as a deduction, or as a payment that must be spread forward. **[10.58]**

Gallagher v Jones (Inspector of Taxes); above, para [10.9]

For the facts, see above, para **[10.9]**. The following extract is concerned with the question of whether SSAP 21 could be displaced by any rule of law.

> SIR THOMAS BINGHAM MR: ...It is said that the Crown's treatment of the hire payments contravenes the general principle of income tax law that neither profit nor loss should be anticipated, in effect by anticipating profits. The principle itself, squarely based on the statutory provisions, is not in doubt. But the accounting principles relied on by the Crown are designed to give effect to the rule of non-anticipation, and it is said (in my view rightly) that the taxpayers' treatment has the effect of anticipating a loss. Unless the principles in SSAPs 2 and 21 are suspect, which in my view they are not, this argument cannot prevail.
>
> It is then said that the Crown's treatment of the hire payments is contrary to the true nature and effect in law of what are admitted to be genuine lease agreements entered into by the taxpayers. I do not accept that this is so. The thrust of the Crown's case is not to challenge the genuineness of the agreements, or treat them as having some effect other than their actual effect, but to subject the agreements as they stand to the appropriate accounting treatment so as to ascertain their true financial effect. This is what the legislation requires.

169 [1994] STC 763.
170 [1999] STC 173.

SIR CHRISTOPHER SLADE: . . .If each of the taxpayers had prepared and submitted his accounts for the first accounting period of his business in accordance with the ordinary principles of commercial accounting, the trading losses incurred by him in that period, as recorded, would have been far smaller than those which were in fact recorded. On the other hand, he would have been able to rely on far larger deductions for the purpose of ascertaining his trading profits or losses for tax purposes in respect of subsequent periods. This might well have been advantageous to him if the rate of tax for the year of assessment 1986–87 had been lower, instead of higher, than in the immediately succeeding years. Nevertheless, if he had chosen to prepare his accounts for the first accounting period in that conventional manner and with those consequences, I cannot conceive that the Crown would have been so bold as to submit that he should have rewritten his accounts on the basis that there should have been treated as a deduction of the full amount of the rents which fell due to be paid in the first accounting period. Nor can I conceive that this submission would have succeeded if it had been advanced, bearing in mind that such a method of accounting, as the Special Commissioner found, not only conflicted with the ordinary principles of commercial accounting but also gave a completely misleading picture of the trading results.

There is no finding as to the motives of the taxpayers in following the course which they did. I do not think these motives are relevant and I intend no criticism of anyone. Nevertheless, it seems to me that the submissions of each of the taxpayers in effect involve the proposition that it was open to him at his option to adjust the figures representing the trading loss of his business for tax purposes for the relevant accounting period by choosing retrospectively to adopt a method of presenting his accounts to the Revenue quite different from that which would be applied under any ordinary accountancy practice.

I recognise that it is possible that SSAP 21 may not represent the only form in which the accounts could have been properly presented. The authorities cited to us demonstrate that there may be at least two alternative methods of dealing with a particular problem in the preparation of trading accounts, both of which are acceptable according to the current ordinary practice of commercial accounting. It appears from the Special Commissioner's decision that while it was Mr Miller's opinion [ie the opinion of the Crown's expert accounting witness] that the taxpayers' accounts should have been prepared in accordance with SSAP 21, in his oral evidence he recognised that there was another method which could have been adopted, namely "by treating rental payments as prepaid expenditure and writing off such expenditure as it is used up". Significantly, however, the taxpayers themselves called no evidence as to normal accounting practice and there was no evidence whatever to suggest that, on any footing, such practice would have supported the particular method of preparation of his accounts adopted by each of them in the present cases.

Thus, in my judgment it would have been open to each of the taxpayers to present his trading accounts for tax purposes in the manner in which they were presented only if there was some rule of law, statutory or judge-made, which both entitled and obliged him to do so. No such statutory rule has been relied on. Though other ancillary submissions were advanced, Mr Bretten QC's [ie counsel for the taxpayers] forcefully presented argument for the taxpayers was primarily based on the proposition that, according to the decided cases such as *Vallambrosa Rubber Co Ltd v Farmer (Surveyor of Taxes)* (1910) 5 TC 529, "expenditure lies where it falls"; this he explained as meaning that expenditure must be a proper deduction for the purposes of computing the profit for the period in respect of which or in relation to which it is made. For the reasons given in the judgments of Sir Thomas Bingham MR and Nolan LJ, I do not think that on the facts of the present case this argument, or Mr Bretten's ancillary submissions, are sustainable.

In conclusion, I would stress that the reason why the courts rightly attach so much importance to accepted principles of commercial accounting in this context is, of course, that these principles will normally afford the surest means of ascertaining the *true* profits or losses of a trader, as the case may be. **[10.59]**

7. Loss relief

When deductible expenditure exceeds the trading receipts for a basis period, the trader has no trading profits, and the figure to be entered for that basis period in his income tax calculation is nil. The 'trade loss'[171] – the negative amount by which deductible expenditure exceeds trading receipts for the basis period – is capable, however, of being used to reduce other income. Trade loss rules specify the categories of income from which losses may be deducted, as well as the periods for which the deductions can be made.

ITTOIA 2005, s 26, provides that '[t]he same rules apply for income tax purposes in calculating losses of a trade as apply in calculating profits'. ITTOIA 2005, s 34 provides that '[i]n calculating the profits of a trade, no deduction is allowed for ... losses not connected with or arising out of the trade'.[172]

Income Tax Act 2007,[173] has the effect of changing the presentation, although not the overall substance, of the trade loss rules for income tax purposes (but not for corporation tax).

Depending on the circumstances, if individuals make a trade loss, they can deduct that loss as:

(1) '**Trade loss relief against general income**', ie, in calculating ... [their] unrelieved total income[174] ... for the [trade] loss-making year, ... for the previous tax year, or ... for both tax years'.[175]

(2) '**Early trade losses relief**, ie, 'in calculating ... [their] unrelieved total income for the 3 tax years before the one in which the loss is made'.[176]

(3) '**Carry-forward trade loss relief**', ie, 'in calculating ... [their] unrelieved total income for subsequent tax years'.[177]

(4) '**Incorporation loss relief**',[178] ie, if they have transferred a trade to a company with carried-forward losses, in calculating their subsequent income from the company, in whatever form it may be derived (eg interest, salary or dividends).[179]

(5) '**Terminal trade loss relief**', ie, if they have made a terminal loss in a trade which they had ceased to carry on, 'in calculating ... [their] unrelieved total income for the final tax year and the 3 previous tax years'.[180]

171 This is the term used in ITA 2007.

172 See *FA and AB Ltd v Lupton (Inspector of Taxes)* [1971] 3 All ER 948 at 953 (Lord Morris of Borth-y-Gest).

173 See ITA 2007, Pt 4, Ch 2 ('Trade Losses').

174 This is the amount left after a person's 'income tax liability' has been calculated under the steps set out in ITA 2007, s 23.

175 ITA 2007, s 64(2). It is also possible, if a person has insufficient, or indeed no, unrelieved total income, for the taxpayer to deduct the loss from chargeable gains (see ITA 2007, s 71, and TCGA 1992, ss 261B and 261C, as inserted by ITA 2007, Sch 1, Pt 2, which rewrite and amend slightly FA 1991, s 72).

176 *Ibid*, s 72(2).

177 *Ibid*, s 83(2).

178 This term is not used in ITA 2007.

179 ITA 2007, s 86.

180 *Ibid*, s 89. Note also the existence of 'post-cessation trade relief', which is designed to apply to the situation where individuals have to make a payment in connection with a business they ceased to carry on within the last seven years – this is again deductible in calculating unrelieved total income (see ITA 2007, s 96).

Each possibility is subject to detailed conditions,[181] which are designed to prevent these reliefs from being used inappropriately. Among these is the rule that trade loss relief against general income is not available 'unless the trade is commercial',[182] thus preventing the artificial generation of losses.

The substance of the loss relief provisions is the result of a long history of incremental change. The following extract is indicative of factors that have influenced the framing of some of those provisions. **[10.60]**

Report of the Committee on the Taxation of Trading Profits (Cmd 8189 (1951))

79. We have come to the conclusion that there is no sufficient reason for restricting the period within which business losses can be carried forward, and we accordingly recommend that **the owner of a business should be allowed to carry forward business losses and set them against subsequent profits from the business without time limit.**[183]

80. A number of our witnesses represented that the owner of a business should be allowed to carry back a loss and set it against earlier profits and thus obtain repayment of tax paid on those earlier profits. Objections of principle can be raised to this suggestion. It would introduce a novel proposition into the Income Tax if tax admittedly due for a particular year and correctly representing the taxpayer's capacity to pay for that year could be reclaimed by reference to circumstances arising in a later year. But whatever the theoretical merits or demerits of the proposal may be, we are of opinion that it must be rejected on practical grounds. In the case of a company there could be no justification for giving relief from tax on the profits of an earlier year where those profits had been distributed to shareholders in the form of a dividend. To meet this objection it might be suggested that the relief should be confined to tax on profits which had not been distributed by the company. Complicated provisions would, however, be necessary to determine out of what profits particular distributions came; in any event the test of distribution is one which could not be applied to a partnership and even less to a "one-man" business. Further, any proposal which involved the reopening of past years' liability is, in our view, exposed to very serious practical objections because of the additional work which it would cause both to the Inland Revenue and to the taxpayer and his advisers. We therefore reject the suggestion that there should be any general power to carry losses backwards.

81. This general conclusion is subject to one reservation. Cases arise where a business incurs a large loss in its last year and unless the taxpayer has a substantial income from other sources for that year he is, under the existing law, unable to obtain any relief. Particular hardship may arise where the loss can be regarded as in some sense artificial, e.g. where it arises because he is entitled for the last year to a substantial balancing allowance on the disposal of plant and machinery, industrial buildings, etc.[184] The existing law recognises this problem in the special case of mines, oil wells, etc.; Section 27(3) of the Income Tax Act, 1945, enables the annual allowances

181 See ITA 2007, Pt 4, Ch 2. The ICTA 1988 provisions are discussed in detail Tiley, n 5 above, pp 383–388, and Natalie Lee (gen ed) *Revenue Law – Principles and Practice* (24th edn, 2006), ch 11.

182 *Ibid*, s 66. See also David Stopforth 'Creating Anti-Avoidance Legislation – A Look Behind the Scenes' [1999] BTR 106–113, in which the background to this requirement, originally introduced in 1960, is considered.

183 [Emphasis in original.]

184 [See below, para **[10.65]**.]

for capital expenditure on mining works, etc., to be recomputed for the last six years of the life of a mine or foreign concession. We think that the principle underlying this provision merits more general application and we recommend that **there should be a provision under which the owner of a business may carry back a loss incurred in the last year of business and set it against the assessments on that business for the three preceding years.**[185] **[10.61]**

The treatment of corporate trading losses, which may, as will be seen, additionally involve EU law questions, is considered in Chapter 18 (see paras **[18.12]**). **[10.62]**

8. Capital allowances

A. *Nature and scope*

As already seen, capital expenditure, as a general rule, cannot be deducted from trading receipts for tax purposes.[186] Moreover, whereas traders will, for accounting purposes, make some deduction for the depreciation in value of capital assets, they cannot do so for tax purposes: see *Re Addie & Sons* (1875) 1 TC 1. Nonetheless, they may be entitled to a measure of tax relief for expenditure on certain types of capital asset. This relief is given through the system of capital allowances, provided for by the Capital Allowances Act 2001 (CAA 2001).[187]

The system is designed to provide an allowance, in each period of account, for a fraction of the original cost of certain types of asset used in the business. **[10.63]**

***Barclays Mercantile Business Finance Ltd v Mawson (Inspector of Taxes)* [2004] UKHL 51, [2005] STC 1 (HL); above, para [5.13]**

For the facts of this case, see Chapter 5, above, para **[5.13]**.

LORD NICHOLLS OF BIRKENHEAD [*delivering the opinion of the Appellate Committee*]:

A trader computing his profits or losses [i.e. for accounting purposes] will ordinarily make some deduction for depreciation in the value of the machinery or plant which he uses. Otherwise the computation will take no account of the need for the eventual replacement of wasting assets and the true profits will be overstated. But the computation required by Sch D (whether for the purpose of income or corporation tax)[188] has always excluded such a deduction. Parliament therefore makes separate provision for depreciation by means of capital allowances against what would

185 [Emphasis in original.]

186 See above, para **[10.26]**.

187 This Act was the first 'Rewrite' Act. It received the Royal Assent on 22 March 2001, and has applied for income tax purposes for chargeable periods ending after 5 April 2001 and for corporation tax to those ending after 31 March 2001. Morse and Williams in *Davies* point out that brevity may not be the soul of simplicity. The predecessor to CAA 2001, CAA 1990, had 165 sections when enacted; CAA 2001 has over 620! (See, Geoffrey Morse and David Williams (eds) *Davies: Principles of Tax Law* (5th edn, 2004), p 121).

188 [But see now Chapter 7, above, para **[7.1]**.]

otherwise be taxable income. In addition, generous initial or first-year allowances, exceeding actual depreciation, are sometimes provided as a positive incentive to investment in new plant. **[10.64]**

However, as intimated above, capital allowances are not a wholesale exception to the rule that capital expenditure cannot be deducted from trading receipts. They cover expenditure on certain types of asset only, and in different ways. Of the assets covered, consideration will be given only to plant and machinery and industrial buildings.[189]

Plant and machinery allowances are available to a trader who incurs capital expenditure on the acquisition of plant or machinery for the purposes of the trade,[190] whereas industrial buildings allowances are available to traders engaged in processing, manufacturing or storing goods, who incur capital expenditure 'on the construction of a building or structure'.[191]

There are three different types of allowance:

(i) **Writing down allowances**. These are the most common way in which relief is provided for expenditure on each of plant and machinery and industrial buildings. They allow the trader to deduct a relatively small percentage (eg 4%[192] or 25%[193]) from trading receipts in each chargeable period.[194] In relation to plant and machinery, the writing down allowance is made on a reducing balance basis;[195] for industrial buildings it is made on a straight line basis.[196]

(ii) **First year allowances** (or **'initial allowances'**). These are restricted to expenditure on plant and machinery and industrial buildings in specific circumstances. They allow the trader to deduct from trading receipts a larger percentage,[197] or possibly the whole,[198] of the cost of an asset in the 'chargeable period'[199] of its acquisition.[200]

(iii) **Balancing allowances**. These apply to each of the above categories of asset. Thus, when assets are sold or destroyed, or the trade comes to an end,[201] the trader is allowed to deduct from his trading receipts any

189 Other expenditure which is capable of qualifying for capital allowances is: expenditure on agricultural buildings (CAA 2001, Pt 4); flat conversions (CAA 2001, Pt 4A); mineral extraction (CAA 2001, Pt 5); research and development (CAA 2001, Pt 6); know-how (CAA 2001, Pt 7); patents (CAA 2001, Pt 8); dredging (CAA 2001, Pt 9) and assured tenancies (CAA 2001, Pt 10).

190 See CAA 2001, s 11.

191 *Ibid*, s 271.

192 *Ibid*, s 310(1)(b) (industrial buildings not within enterprise zones).

193 *Ibid*, s 56 (plant and machinery).

194 *Ibid*, s 247(a) (plant and machinery) and s 352(1)(a) (industrial buildings).

195 *Ibid*. For the accounting significance of this expression, see Nobes, n 6 above, p 252: '. . . the annual charge reduces over the years of an asset's life. A fixed percentage depreciation is charged each year on the cost (first year) or the undepreciated cost (subsequent years).'

196 *Ibid*, s 310(1). Again, for this expression's significance in accounting terms, see Nobes, n 6 above, p 286: '[t]his method charges equal annual instalments against profit over the useful life of the asset'.

197 Eg medium-sized enterprises are entitled to initial allowances of 40% for expenditure on plant and machinery (see CAA 2001, s 52). Small-sized enterprises qualify for first-year allowances for plant and machinery of 50% (see FA 2006, s 30).

198 Eg for 'expenditure on energy-saving plant or machinery' (see CAA 2001, s 52) and for expenditure on industrial or commercial buildings in enterprise zones (see CAA 2001, ss 305–308).

199 See CAA 2001, s 6.

200 *Ibid*, s 247.

201 *Ibid*, s 61 (plant and machinery), s 315 (industrial buildings).

expenditure for which relief has not yet been given.[202] The deduction is reduced by the amount of any sale or insurance proceeds.[203]

In the case of industrial buildings, the effect of sale, destruction or discontinuance may be to produce a significant one-off balancing allowance. Plant and machinery allowances, however, are calculated by reference to 'pooled' expenditure.[204] This means that, unless the trade is discontinued in a period when the 'available qualifying expenditure'[205] in the pool is greater than the total of 'disposal receipts'[206] for the same period, there will be no balancing allowance.[207]

A balancing allowance may be transformed, in certain circumstances, into a 'balancing charge'. This may be referred to as a 'clawback' of allowances. In the case of pooled plant and machinery, there may be a balancing charge where 'before the permanent discontinuance of the ... [trade] ... several assets in the pool were sold in the course of business at prices which compared favourably with the rate of depreciation assumed in the WDAs *[writing down allowances]* already claimed'.[208] In relation to an industrial building, 'a balancing charge is made if the proceeds from the balancing event [ie sale destruction or discontinuance][209] are more than the residue, if any, of qualifying expenditure[210] immediately before the event'[211]; whilst a balancing allowance is treated as a deductible expense of the trade, a balancing charge is treated as a taxable receipt.[212] **[10.65]**

B. *Plant and machinery*

Before 1994, the definition of 'plant and machinery' was a matter of case law. 'Machinery' did not present problems of interpretation, but the notion of 'plant' was the subject of a range of tortuously-reasoned decisions.

CAA 2001, ss 21–24, which date back to FA 1994, now offer a partial definition of 'plant' in that ss 21, 22 and 24 provide that 'expenditure on the provision of plant and machinery does not include expenditure on the provision' of certain capital assets. Thus, an asset cannot be 'plant' if it is a 'building',[213] a 'structure' or any works involving the alteration of land'[214] or the 'acquisition of an interest in land'.[215] CAA 2001, s 21, defines a building as including items both actually incorporated in a building and those normally so incorporated,[216] together with assets such as walls, doors, floors and ceilings, etc,[217] each of which are on 'List A' in s 21. Similarly, s 22 provides a

202 See CAA 2001, s 56(7) (plant and machinery), s 318(2) and (3) (industrial buildings).
203 *Ibid*, s 61 (plant and machinery), ss 316 and 318(3)(b) (industrial buildings).
204 *Ibid*, Pt 2, Ch 5.
205 *Ibid*, ss 57–59.
206 *Ibid*, s 60.
207 See Natalie Lee (gen ed), n 190 above, para [48.59] (Andrew Farley), referring to CAA 2001, s 56(7).
208 *Ibid*.
209 See CAA 2001, s 315.
210 *Ibid*, s 313.
211 *Ibid*, s 318(4).
212 *Ibid*, s 247(1)(b) (plant and machinery) and s 352(1)(b) (industrial buildings).
213 *Ibid*, s 21.
214 *Ibid*, s 22.
215 *Ibid*, s 24.
216 *Ibid*, s 21(3).
217 *Ibid*, s 21(3)(c).

list ('List B') of structures that do not qualify as plant, including, bridges, tunnels, roads, railways and dikes.

However, the items in 'List C', in CAA 2001, s 23, are specifically withdrawn from the definition of a building, structure or land, with the result that whether they count as 'plant' must be decided in the light of the case law. The items in List C include electrical systems, lifts and 'decorative assets provided for the enjoyment of the public in hotel, restaurant or similar trades'.[218]

The principal cases concerned with the meaning of 'plant' were reviewed and rationalised by Hoffmann J in the following extract. **[10.66]**

Wimpy International Ltd v Warland (Inspector of Taxes) [1988] STC 149 (ChD)

HOFFMANN J. . . . The boundaries of the concept of "plant" have been mapped in some detail by a long series of cases. I feel some diffidence in undertaking another survey of the authorities when the House of Lords have considered the topic twice within the past five years. But I do not think that it is possible to do justice to the reasoning of the Special Commissioners or to explain what might otherwise appear to be private language or confusion of thought without examining the earlier cases which have shaped the way in which they expressed themselves.

The celebrated pioneer cartographer was Lindley LJ, who gave the following description of the territory in *Yarmouth v France*[219]:

> " . . . in its ordinary sense, it includes whatever apparatus is used by a businessman for carrying on his business, not his stock-in-trade which he buys or makes for sale; but all goods and chattels, fixed or moveable, live or dead, which he keeps for permanent employment in his business . . ."

It is important to notice the various discriminations which are stated or implied in this description. First, it excludes anything which is not used for carrying on the business. Secondly, it excludes stock-in-trade both expressly and because, although used for the purposes of the business, its use lacks permanence. Thirdly, it excludes things which are not "apparatus . . . goods and chattels, fixed or moveable, live or dead" or not employed *in* the business. This excludes the premises or place in or upon which the business is conducted.

Before going any further I must say something about the third distinction and the way in which the courts in subsequent cases have refined the boundary between plant and premises. The words "apparatus . . . goods and chattels, fixed or moveable, live or dead" might suggest that the distinction turns upon whether the item is a chattel or fixture on the one hand or a building or structure on the other. This was the view of the minority in the House of Lords in *IRC v Barclay, Curle & Co Ltd.*[220] But the majority held that even a building or a structure (in that case a dry dock) could be plant if it was more appropriate to describe it as apparatus for carrying on the business or employed in the business than as the premises or place in or upon which the business was conducted. By this test a swimming pool used in connection with the operation of a caravan park has been held to be plant, in *Cooke (Inspector of Taxes) v Beach Station Caravans Ltd,*[221] while conversely, in *Benson (Inspector of Taxes) v Yard Arm Club Ltd,*[222] a ship used as a floating restaurant, although a chattel, was held not to be plant because it was the place in which the business was conducted: see Lord Lowry in *IRC v Scottish Newcastle Breweries Ltd.*[223]

218 *Ibid*, s 23(4).
219 (1887) 19 QBD 647 at 658.
220 [1969] 1 WLR 675.
221 [1974] 1 WLR 1398.
222 [1979] 1 WLR 347.
223 [1982] 1 WLR 322 at 333.

It will be seen, therefore, that although the three distinctions in *Yarmouth v France* each involves a test which can be called functional, they are subtly different from each other. If the item is neither stock-in-trade nor the premises upon which the business is conducted, the only question is whether it is used for carrying on the business. I shall call this the "business use" test. However, under the second distinction, an article which passes the "business use" test is excluded if such use is as stock-in-trade. And under the third distinction, an item used in carrying on the business is excluded if such use is as the premises or place upon which the business is conducted. The fact that an item may pass the "business use" test but fail what I may call the "premises" test is central to this case.

The seeds of confusion were sown in the judgment of Uthwatt J in *J Lyons & Co Ltd v A-G.*[224] That was a claim under the War Damage Act 1943 for £ 3.5s.2d in respect of 20 electric lamps with their sockets and cords, destroyed by enemy action in a tea-shop in Ilford. The Act gave compensation for damage to "land", which was defined to include buildings and "plant". The owners did not contend that the lamps were part of the building, but claimed that they were plant. It will therefore be seen that there was no question of the "premises" test (if the lamps had been part of the premises, they would have qualified for compensation anyway) and no question of their being stock-in-trade. The only issue was whether they were used in carrying on the business. The judge formulated this question in the following terms[225]:

> "Are the lamps and fitments properly to be regarded as part of the setting in which the business is carried on or as part of the apparatus used for carrying on the business?"

He decided that the lamps were " . . . part of the general setting in which the business is carried on" because they were not specific to the business. Their presence was, he said,

> "not dictated by the nature of the particular trade there carried on or by the fact that it is for the trade purposes that the building is used".

The contrast between "plant" and "setting", while perfectly intelligible in the context of that case, was not, as things have turned out, the happiest choice of words. Uthwatt J was using "setting" to refer to things which were upon the premises but were neither a part of the premises nor used in carrying on the business. However, as Pennycuick J later pointed out in *Jarrold (Inspector of Taxes) v John Good & Sons Ltd*,[226] the "setting" in which a business is conducted can as a matter of ordinary language include the plant used to carry it on. Secondly, a contrast between "plant" and "setting" is not the most precise tool for applying the "business use" test when the provision of what most people would call a "setting" is, as in restaurants and hotels, an important part of the way in which the business is conducted: see the *Scottish & Newcastle Breweries* case. Thirdly, and for present purposes most significantly, the "setting" would normally include the premises themselves. These are also excluded from the concept of plant, but not for the same reason as the lamps in *J Lyons & Co Ltd v A-G*. It is not because the premises are not sufficiently specific to the business but simply because they are the premises. No matter how "purpose-built" the premises may be, they are not plant if they constitute the premises or place upon which the business is conducted: see *St John's School (Mountford & Another) v Ward (Inspector of Taxes)*.[227] The plant/setting dichotomy therefore conceals an ambiguity. Describing an item as "setting" rather than "plant" may mean that, however specifically adapted for the purposes of the trade, it is nevertheless part of the premises upon which the business is conducted. Or it may mean, as Uthwatt J meant, that the item is neither part of the premises nor used in carrying on the business.

This case is mainly about the application of what I have called the "premises" test to additions and improvements to restaurants for the purpose of making them more attractive to customers. In that respect it is unlike the *Scottish & Newcastle Breweries* case which was mainly about the application of the "business use" test to items which were

224 [1944] Ch 281.
225 *Ibid.*, at 287.
226 [1962] 1 WLR 1101 at 1108.
227 [1975] STC 7.

plainly not part of the premises. The items in dispute in that case were wall decor, plaques, tapestries, murals (which were in fact detachable), pictures and metal sculptures used to decorate hotels. All of these were held to be chattels or trade fixtures and not integral parts of the premises. The Crown refused them capital allowances as plant on the ground that they formed part of the "setting", which in one sense, and probably the most obvious sense, they certainly did. But the House of Lords held that they nevertheless passed the "business use" test because they were used to please and attract customers, and therefore were for the promotion of the trade.

... the items in dispute in this appeal ... consist principally of improvements such as tiling on floors and walls, glass shop fronts, raised and mezzanine floors, staircases and false ceilings. Counsel for the taxpayer companies says that all these items were installed to improve the ambience of the restaurants and to attract customers. Their function is the same as that of the items found to be plant in the *Scottish & Newcastle Breweries* case. Therefore, they are plant.

In general terms I accept counsel's premises but his conclusion is, in my judgment, fallacious. It assumes that the "business use" test is the sole criterion for deciding what is plant and ignores the "premises" test altogether. In the *Scottish & Newcastle Breweries* case, however, Lord Lowry made it clear that the "premises" test also applies. In response to a submission that the House was giving too liberal an interpretation to the "business use" test, he said[228]:

> "Moreover, the test accepted in this case by the commissioners and affirmed by the Inner House draws a line which can be held without trouble: something which becomes part of the premises, instead of merely embellishing them, is not plant, except in the rare case where the premises are themselves plant, like the dry dock in *Barclay Curle* or the grain silo in *Schofield (Inspector of Taxes) v R & H Hall.*"[229]

See also the distinction[230] between wallpaper and mural paintings and the decorations and ornaments which were in issue in the case.

I take Lord Lowry to be saying that even if an embellishment for the purposes of trade passes the "business use" test, it still has to pass the "premises" test and something which "becomes part of the premises" fails that test unless the premises are themselves plant. Counsel for the taxpayer companies submitted that this passage was a *dictum* contrary to previous authority. In my respectful opinion, it correctly reflects an essential feature of the concept of "plant" as it has been understood since *Yarmouth v France*. In another passage[231] Lord Lowry distinguished, in the context of an hotel, between "a beautiful or unusual or historic building, attractive views, gardens, shrubberies and waterfalls" on the one hand and "ornaments, the equipment used by the staff and the glasses, china, cutlery, table linen, and the tables and chairs used by the customers" on the other. Both categories of items could be used, he said, for "the creation of the right atmosphere" but the former category is excluded as plant by the "premises" test.

A further application of this principle is provided by the judgment of Templeman J, affirmed by the Court of Appeal, in *St John's School (Mountford & Another) v Ward (Inspector of Taxes)*. This case concerned buildings for a gymnasium and laboratory erected for use at a school. The judge dealt separately with the benches and sinks installed in the laboratory. He upheld the finding of the commissioners that they were not entitled to capital allowances as plant on two grounds. One was that there was no evidence upon which the commissioners could have apportioned part of the total cost of the building to the benches and sinks. With that I am not concerned. The other was that they were "integral parts of the building". No one could have suggested that the benches and sinks were not used in carrying on the business of the school. They were rejected as plant only because they were part of the premises.

Counsel for the taxpayer companies said that there was no trace in the authorities of any distinction between the "business use" test and the "premises" test. The cases assume

228 [1982] 1 WLR 322 at 332.
229 (1974) 49 TC 514.
230 [1982] 1 WLR 322 at 331.
231 *Ibid.*

the existence of a single test. I agree that the existence of different criteria is implicit rather than explicit in the cases and that a reading of some judgments divorced from the context provided by the nature of the issue in each case might suggest that there is one question – is it plant or not-plant? – rather than a series of differentiated questions: Is it used for the purposes of the business at all? Is it used as apparatus or as premises-in-which? Is it used as stock-in-trade? But the actual decisions in their context do in my judgment, support the distinctions I have tried to make. Lord Diplock once remarked :

> "... the law is nearly always most obscure in those fields in which judges say the principle is plain, but the difficulty lies in its application to particular facts."[232]

I venture to suggest that in this corner of the law, obscurity is caused by the talismanic use of terms like "setting" or "embellishment" out of their original context and in a way which disguises the fact that not only is the question one of fact and degree but that there is ambiguity as to what the question is.

How does one apply the "premises" test to items which were not incorporated as part of the original building but have been added by way of subsequent improvement? Lord Lowry, as we have seen, said that the question was whether something had "become part of the premises", and Templeman J spoke of "integral parts of the building". The question is not, I think, the same as whether it has become part of the realty for the purposes of the law of real property or a fixture for the purposes of the law of landlord and tenant. In *Yarmouth v France*, Lindley LJ contemplated that fixed chattels might be plant. In the *Scottish & Newcastle Breweries* case the House of Lords approved a decision of the commissioners that a fixed but not easily removable metal sculpture was not "part of the permanent structure of the hotel" and therefore qualified as plant.

Adopting the words of Lord Lowry, the question seems to me to be whether it would be more appropriate to describe the item as having become part of the premises than as having retained a separate identity. This is a question of fact and degree, to which some of the relevant considerations will be: whether the item appears visually to retain a separate identity, the degree of permanence with which it has been attached, the incompleteness of the structure without it and the extent to which it was intended to be permanent or whether it was likely to be replaced within a relatively short period. Counsel for the taxpayer companies submitted in reply that if, contrary to his submission, this was the proper test, those considerations constituted a series of separate hurdles which had to be overcome before an item could be regarded as a part of the premises. It had to have been attached with the intention of being a permanent fixture, it must have been actually and irremovably fixed and it must not be a mere ornament or embellishment. I do not agree. In my judgment, these matters are factors to be taken into account in answering the question posed by Lord Lowry.

Counsel for the taxpayer companies, in a passionate plea for fiscal justice, said that plant was something which attracted capital allowances and that it was unreasonable that there should be no allowances for items which were likely to be scrapped within five to ten years when the restaurant was refurbished and were depreciated at the appropriate rate in the company's commercial accounts. I do not think that the commissioners failed to take into account the expected life of the improvements when deciding whether or not it was appropriate to regard them as having become part of the premises. But once they had concluded that they were part of the premises, their short expectation of life could not make them plant. I think that this is what they meant when they said that the evidence of the commercial necessity for frequent refurbishment "does not help us to determine whether the expenditure was on 'plant' as explained in the authorities". The premises in which the trade is conducted do not become plant because they are disposable.

In an alternative submission, counsel for the taxpayer companies tried in effect to reintroduce the "business use" test as the criterion for deciding whether or not an addition or improvement should be regarded as being plant or part of the premises. He said that the test was functional: if the improvement served a business purpose such as attracting customers, it was plant; otherwise, it was mere setting and part of the premises.

232 *Ilkiw v Samuels* [1963] 1 WLR 991 at 1004.

This argument is, in my view, equally fallacious. I accept that the test for whether a whole building or structure is premises depends upon its function, although as I have pointed out this functional test is different from the "business use" test favoured by counsel for the taxpayer companies. It is not simply whether the structure is used for a business purpose but whether it is used as plant rather than as premises. But once it has been decided that the building or structure is premises and not plant, the functional test is in my judgment exhausted. Additions or improvements to premises are excluded by the "premises" test not by virtue of the separate functions of items which *ex hypothesi* have lost their separate identity but simply because they have become part of the premises . . . **[10.67]**

C. *Industrial buildings*

In contrast to plant and machinery, industrial buildings are given an exhaustive statutory definition in CAA 2001, s 274. Broadly, an industrial building is one used for processing, manufacturing or storing goods.[233] However, in certain, tightly defined, circumstances, the definition is extended to buildings such as offices and hotels.[234]

Whether a building is used for processing goods depends on whether it is used for '[a] trade consisting of subjecting goods or materials to a process',[235] whereas, whether a building is used for storing goods depends, among other things, on whether the goods are 'to be subjected, in the course of a trade, to a process'.[236] Each of these formulations reflect, and slightly expand, the wording of the relevant predecessor legislation to CAA 2001, namely the Capital Allowances Acts 1968 and 1990. In addition, CAA 2001, s 276, provides that each of these formulations 'apply in relation to part of a trade . . . as they apply in relation to a trade . . .'. **[10.68]**

Bestway Holdings Ltd v Luff (Inspector of Taxes) [1998] STC 357 (ChD)

The parent company of a wholesale cash-and-carry supermarket group, which supplied retailers with merchandise such as groceries, wine and household goods, argued that its premises qualified as industrial buildings. It argued that its trade involved 'the storage of goods', because goods were stored prior to sale on its premise, and were subjected to sorting, checking, unpacking, repacking, labelling and freezing ie actions which constituted 'subjecting goods, in the course of a trade, to a process'.

LIGHTMAN J: . . .

IV. Storage

Bestway contends that the buildings or at least parts of them qualify for capital allowances on the ground that they are used for storage purposes within the meaning of s 7(1)(f) of the 1968 Act.[237]

The commissioners rejected this contention. The relevant part of their decision[238] reads as follows:

233 See CAA 2001, ss 271–285.
234 Ibid, s 271.
235 Ibid, s 274(1).
236 Ibid.
237 [See now CAA 2001, s 274(1).]
238 [[1997] STC (SCD) 87 at 93.]

> " ... we must ask ourselves whether the trade carried on by the Bestway Group involves the storage of goods or materials.
>
> We are inclined to the view that any storage which takes place at Bestway's premises is insufficient to satisfy the provisions of the statute. It is clear from the evidence that Cash & Carry relies on speedy disposal of its stock. Stock levels are carefully managed to the extent that they are run down towards the end of the accounting year, 'in order to improve the appearance of the balance sheet' ... In our view goods are not stored at Bestway's premises. The items on the upper shelves of the tall racks which are not immediately available for purchase by customers and the items held in the general storage areas ... are merely back-up stock held at a minimum level in order to ensure that an adequate supply is available for purchase by customers.
>
> We find as a fact that 'storage' within the meaning attributed to it by s 7(1)(f) does not take place within Bestway's premises.
>
> We hold to this view even in relation to the contents of the bonded warehouse, where once again, we find that there is a speedy turnover of stock."

The critical issue is the meaning of the words "a trade which consists in the storage" of the goods and materials specified in s 7(1)(f) (the specified goods).

... The buildings are plainly used for the trade of a wholesale supermarket which is a use which does not qualify for capital allowances. But if part of that trade consists in the trade of the storage of the specified goods in the buildings or parts of them, Bestway can none the less qualify for the allowances claimed. The first issue is accordingly whether what is done at the buildings constitutes "storage" within the meaning of s 7. Only if this question is answered in the affirmative does the second question arise, namely whether the storage is of the specified goods.

Mr Goy QC for Bestway submits that "storage" is an ordinary English word with the meaning of "keeping in reserve for future use or disposal" and that this meaning should be attributed to the word as it appears in s 7(1)(f); and if this is done, it covers the use of the areas of the buildings where any of the specified goods are kept, or at any rate any of the specified goods other than those immediately available to purchasers. Mr Brennan for the inspector submits that, in the context of this legislation and having regard to the character of the specified goods, what is required is a form of warehousing, and not merely the storage which any wholesaler wants for his goods (citing *Copol*).[239]

I have found this question difficult, but at the end of the day I have concluded that the commissioners' decision cannot be challenged and indeed is correct. The authorities make clear that there may be "storage" where goods are kept or held for a limited period and indeed for shorter periods than the six to eight week period during which Bestway's goods are in the buildings. In *Saxone*[240] the shoes were held to be stored in a warehouse though they remained there for 10 to 13 weeks or less. In *Crusabridge Investments Ltd v Casings International Ltd*[241] a building was held to qualify: (a) under s 7(1)(f)(ii) because tyres were "stored" though often for no more than seven days awaiting removal for processing (ie remoulding) by remoulders; and (b) under s 7(1)(f)(iii) because the processed (ie remoulded) tyres still owned by the remoulder were stored there pending delivery to a purchaser. But the length of time during which goods are kept or held can only be one, and not the decisive factor or the factor of first importance, in determining whether they are stored: the determining factor must be the purpose for which the goods are kept or held. If goods are delivered for safe keeping to a depository (eg a bank providing a safe deposit), so long as the goods remain in the possession of the depository they may be described as "stored"; but this would not be the apt description of goods handed over in the course of his business to a repairer or pawnbroker.

In this case what is critical is the nature of the enterprise intended to be carried on and actually carried on by Bestway at the buildings and the role played by the stock in that enterprise. For a building is only used for storage if the purpose of keeping goods there is their storage as an end in itself: there is no such use for storage if the goods are kept there

239 [ie *Copol Clothing Ltd v Hindmarch (Inspector of Taxes)* [1984] STC 33 (CA).]
240 [*Saxone Lilley & Skinner (Holdings) Ltd v IRC* (1967) 44 TC 122.]
241 (1979) 54 TC 246.

for some other purpose (see *Kay v Burrows*[242]). All the stock in the present case is kept in the buildings, not for storage, but for sale. No goods are reserved or withheld for future use: they are all likewise available for sale and intended to be sold as soon as the turnover allows. For practical reasons only part of the stock can be made physically available for self-service by customers; but that does not alter the fact that the back-up stock is intended to be made immediately available as soon as required to meet demand. In short, as it seems to me, "storage" in s 7(1)(f) means keeping in storage as a purpose and end in itself, and does not extend to such storage as is merely a necessary and transitory incident of the conduct of the business of a wholesale supermarket. The goods enter the buildings upon their final journey to the customers. The six to eight weeks of stock at any time in the buildings may be likened to stock on an extension to the open shelves or on a conveyor belt to the open shelves. Far from being kept in reserve, the stock is in the process or in course of being made available to purchasers at the buildings.

It is submitted by Bestway that this conclusion is inconsistent with the decision in *Crusabridge*. The decision in *Crusabridge* may be explained on its own facts, namely that there was in that case a finding that the collection and storage of tyres was "an essential part" of the business.[243] But in any event I do not think that that decision should stand in the way of what is clearly the correct answer in this case.

V. Subjection to a process

Bestway contends that the buildings or part of them have been in use "for the purposes of a trade or of part of a trade which consists in the subjection of goods or materials to any process" within the meaning of s 7(1)(e) of the 1968 Act. . . .

The decision whether Bestway is entitled to allowances requires consideration of two distinct questions: (a) whether the use of the building or parts of the buildings for the six specified operations constitutes use for the purposes of "part" of Bestway's trade within the meaning of s 7(2); and (b) if so, whether the use for such part of Bestway's trade consists in the subjection of the specified goods to a process. Bestway can only succeed if both questions are answered in the affirmative . . .

(a) *Subjection to process*

The question raised is what is sufficient to constitute use of a building (or part of a building) for the purposes of a trade (or part of a trade) consisting in the subjection of goods or materials to a process. . . . What Bestway did before the commissioners was to identify six limited operations undertaken by it in the course of its trade of a wholesale supermarket, to characterise these operations as processes and to assert that part of its trade consists in those processes. This assertion required the commissioners to examine and evaluate those operations and reach a judgment whether this characterisation and assertion were correct. This they did with the advantage of seeing the witnesses and of a view of two of the buildings and the activities conducted there. Having received from experienced counsel guidance as to the law and the citation of the relevant authorities, they reached the considered conclusion that the answer was in the negative.

The questions before me are whether the commissioners could reach the conclusions of fact which they did and whether those conclusions of fact are in law capable of supporting their decision. I am satisfied that the answer to both questions is in the affirmative. I can find in their reasoning no error of law. Bestway complain of their reference in their reasoning to the activities as "mere preliminaries to sale" as indicating that they held the erroneous view in law that an activity cannot constitute a "subjection to a process" if it is a preliminary to sale. I do not read this reference as indicating anything of the sort. Indeed I find it difficult to believe that the commissioners could have fallen into any such error since the passage in the Lord President (Clyde's) speech in *Kilmarnock*[244] at 680 (a case cited to them), which establishes that this proposition is not correct, must very much have been in their minds. I read the reference to "mere" preliminaries as reflecting their judgment that, fairly and properly viewed, the activities in question were limited, mundane and of no substantial significance and that they could not properly be

242 [1931] AC 454.
243 (1979) 54 TC 246 at 248-249.
244 [ie *Kilmarnock Equitable Co-operative Society Ltd v IRC* (1966) 42 TC 675 at 680.]

> elevated to the status of processing goods or materials. They decided that as a matter of language (but properly informed by the authorities cited to them) the carrying on of these activities did not amount to the use of the buildings or part of them for the purpose of the subjection of goods or materials to a process within the meaning of the section. This is a view they were entitled to take. Intuitively this view has much to recommend it. Indeed in my judgment to recognise the activities in the buildings in this case (as claimed by Bestway) as use of the buildings for the subjection of goods or materials to a process is totally unreal and to extend the availability of the capital allowances far beyond what the legislature can conceivably have intended . . .[245] **[10.69]**

For a commentary on this case, see David Salter [1999] BTR 189. See also *Revenue and Customs Commissioners v Maco Door and Window Hardware (UK) Ltd* [2007] EWCA Civ 545, as yet unreported. **[10.70]**

D. *Prospective reforms*

Following the 2007 Budget, industrial buildings allowances are to be phased out over a period of four years (see Budget Notes 02 and 07 and FA 2007, s 35 – although more draft legislation is to follow). The justification for their gradual abolition was that they were 'poorly targeted' and 'their abolition would help fund a reduction in the large companies' corporation tax rate' (see Martin Wilson 'Budget 2007 – Capital Allowances' *The Tax Journal* 9 April 2007, pp 11–12).

There is also to be a consultation on the detail of two major alterations to writing down allowances on plant and machinery, to take effect from April 2008: (1) the reduction of the allowance from 25% to 20% in relation to 'movable plant and non-integral fixtures', and (2), in relation to fixtures, the reduction of the allowance from 25% to 10%.

Finance Act 2007, s 36, 'extends for one further year the increase from 40 per cent to 50 per cent in the rate of first-year capital allowances for spending by small businesses on most plant and machinery'.[246]

The above, together with other changes of detail, are helpfully described in Wilson's article referenced above, which also includes a worked example of the effect of the abolition of industrial buildings allowances. **[10.71]**

245 See also the Lightman J's observations in this case about the meaning of 'part of a trade', [1998] STC 357, 383–385.

246 FB 2007, EN, cl 36.

11 Savings Income: Interest and Annual Payments

Until 6 April 2005, Schedule D Case III charged to tax:

(a) any interest of money, whether yearly or otherwise, or any annuity or other annual payment;
(b) all discounts; and
(c) income from securities payable out of the public revenue.[1]

These provisions have been abolished for income tax purposes,[2] and replaced by the Tax Law Rewrite provisions in the Income Tax (Trading and Other Income) Tax Act 2005 (ITTOIA 2005). Whilst the rewritten provisions are not meant to change the substance of the law, they do alter the form considerably. **[11.1]**

1. The charge to tax

ITTOIA 2005, Pt 4 imposes a charge to tax on 'savings and investment income', which includes interest.[3] Pt 5, Ch 7 of the Act provides for a charge on 'miscellaneous income', which covers a wide range of receipts and includes annual payments not otherwise charged to tax.[4] However, Pt 6, Ch 8 exempts most annual payments from the charge, with only a tiny residual category remaining within the tax net.[5] The interest, annuity or annual payment must be paid pursuant to some legal obligation[6] and voluntary gifts, although they may be annual, are not within the charge.[7] Consequently, it may

1 ICTA 1988, s 18(3).
2 They remain in place for the purposes of corporation tax.
3 ITTOIA 2005, s 365(1)(a). The charge under s 365(1) also applies to: (i) dividends from UK resident and non-UK resident companies; (ii) stock dividends from UK resident companies; (iii) release of loan to participator in close company; (iv) purchased life annuity payments; (v) profits from deeply discounted securities; (vi) gains from contracts for life insurance; (vii) distributions from unauthorised unit trusts; (viii) transactions in deposits; (ix) disposals of futures and options involving guaranteed returns; and (x) sales of foreign dividend. See Chapter 7, para **[7.36]**, above.
4 ITTOIA 2005, s 683(1). See Chapter 7, para **[7.39]**, above. Part 5 also covers: (i) receipts from intellectual property; (ii) films and sound recordings as non-trade businesses; (iii) telecommunication rights as non-trading income; (iv) income from settlements (see Chapter 15, below); (v) beneficiaries' income from estates in administration (see Chapter 15); and (vi) income not otherwise charged to tax (see Chapter 13).
5 See below, para **[11.11]**.
6 *Ridge Securities Ltd v IRC* [1964] 1 WLR 479, and see also *Drummond v Collins* [1915] AC 1011; below, para **[16.19]**.
7 *Peters' Executors v IRC* [1941] 2 All ER 620. As to payments to a beneficiary, under a discretionary trust, see *Drummond v Collins* below, para **[16.19]**; see below, para **[11.11]** for the provisions in FA 1988, ss 36–40, which introduced a new regime for the taxation of annual payments; many such payments are tax free in the hands of the payee.

be said that, for income to be chargeable under these provisions, it must have a 'source'; the 'source' being the property or interest out of which the payment is charged or reserved, by virtue of any deed or will or otherwise, or the personal debt or obligation which supports it. Further, tax is charged on the income arising to the taxpayer and, consequently, if the payment is not made at all, there is no liability to tax.[8] **[11.2]**

Girvan v Orange Personal Communication Services Ltd [1998] STC 567 (Ch D)

By agreement between the taxpayer and its bank, interest on deposit accounts was compounded quarterly and was not to be paid until a specified date or, if earlier, when the accounts were closed. The accounts were closed and the interest paid, prior to the specified date. Both the Revenue and the taxpayer agreed that the interest payable was 'income arising' to the taxpayer, but the Revenue argued that each quarterly instalment of interest due on each of the deposit accounts should be treated as 'income arising' in respect of the accounting year in which the quarter fell. In contrast, the taxpayer contended that the interest should be treated as 'income arising' in respect of the accounting period in which the accounts were closed and the interest actually paid. The court found in favour of the taxpayer.

NEUBERGER J: . . . First, as a matter of ordinary language, and putting on one side for the moment the substantial number of authorities on the point, it appears to me that, from Orange's point of view, the interest was not 'income' which 'arose' until it was actually paid over to Orange in December 1992. Following the arrangements agreed in mid-1990, Orange had no right to receive any interest until January 1993, unless it . . . . closed the relevant deposit account . . .

It is true to say that the interest was accruing, and indeed was being compounded on a quarterly basis, but it was being retained by the bank. To my mind, therefore, while it may have been a debt which was accruing, and could be called by Orange at any time on notice, it was not, as a matter of ordinary language, income, until it was paid.

. . . In my judgment, payment of money into a person's bank account (although it may be said to involve nothing more than an entry into the bank's computer records) would be regarded in the commercial world as payment, in a way that payment into an account set up by the bank in its own name for internal accounting purposes would not. As was said by Scott J in *Parkside Leasing Ltd v Smith (HMIT)* [1985] BTC 25 at p. 29:

> 'To regard the payment of money into the payee's bank account as equivalent to the payment of money to the payee is one thing. It reflects the part that banking arrangements play in the manner in which people arrange their financial affairs. Money credited to a person's bank account in accordance with his instructions must, in common sense and in law, be regarded as money thereby received by that person. The money is thereby placed at the disposal of that person.'

Of course, the question of what constitutes 'income arising' in the context of taxation legislation is by no means free of authority. It appears to me that the conclusion I have reached as a matter of ordinary language is supported by authority. In *St Lucia Usines and Estates Co Ltd v Colonial Treasurer of St Lucia* [1924] AC 508, Lord Wrenbury, giving the judgment of the Privy Council in relation to an ordinance which rendered interest liable to tax if it was 'income arising and accruing' in the relevant year said this at p. 512:

> 'The words "income arising or accruing" are not equivalent to the words "Debts arising or accruing". To give them that meaning is to ignore the word "income". The

8 *Woodhouse v IRC* (1936) 20 TC 673. Where payment is made to the taxpayer by cheque, the sum is received when it is credited to his account (see *Parkside Leasing Ltd v Smith* [1985] 1 WLR 310).

> words mean "money arising or accruing by way of income". There must be a coming in to satisfy the word "income".'

> I find this short passage helpful. In the first place, it does seem to support the simple proposition that there is no 'income' liable to tax unless some money has 'come in'. Secondly, it distinguishes between income and debt: so long as the interest in the present case was accruing and not called by Orange, it appears to me to be an accruing debt, which . . . is the antithesis of income in the sense that, so long as the debt is wholly unpaid, there is no income, and once it is wholly paid, the payment is income, and the debt is no more. . . . **[11.3]**

A. *Interest of money*

(1) The meaning of interest

Although the term' interest' is not statutorily defined[9], it has been described as 'payment by time for the use of money'.[10] From case law, four further elements emerge, namely: (i) there must be a debt to be repaid; (ii) the use of the word 'interest' is not conclusive; (iii) the payment must not be excessive; and (iv) the payment must be one of income and not capital; dependent upon the circumstances, the payment of a premium may amount to interest. **[11.4]**

Re Euro Hotel (Belgravia) Ltd [1975] 3 All ER 1075 (Ch D)

(The facts are immaterial for present purposes)

> MEGARRY J: . . . The word "interest" has a wide and flexible meaning. It has, quite rightly, not been suggested that the language used by the parties to an instrument in describing payments to be made under it can bind the Inland Revenue, or affect the operation of a statute. The question must always be one of the true nature of the payment. The language, of course, is important, for the words used may mould or affect the nature of the obligation; but one must always return to a consideration of what, given that language, the payments made under the obligation truly are: are they "interest of money" within the meaning of the statute?
>
> The relevant sense of the word "interest" as given in the Shorter Oxford English Dictionary[11] is "Money paid for the use of money lent (the *principal*), or for forbearance of a debt, according to a fixed ratio *(rate per cent.)*." A similar idea is conveyed by the language used in certain authorities. In *Bond v. Barrow Haematite Steel Co.,*[12] a case on company law, Farwell J. said "Interest is compensation for delay in payment," and he said that the term could not accurately be applied to a share of the profits of trading, though it could be used as "an inaccurate mode of expressing the measure of the share of those profits." In *Bennett v. Ogston,*[13] an income tax case on the expression with which I am concerned, "interest of money," Rowlatt J. said that "interest" was "payment by time for the use of money." *Re Morris*[14] was also concerned with "interest of money," but I do not think it helps much here. The main point was that a liability for compound interest on a loan remained a

9 See Y Beer 'The Credit Price: Income or Capital' [1986] BTR 271. For the circumstances where interest is charged to tax, see ITTOIA 2005, s 369.

10 *Bennett v Ogston* (1930) 15 TC 374 at 379.

11 3rd Ed. (1944), p. 1026.

12 [1902] 1 Ch. 353 at 363.

13 (1930) 15 TC 374 at 379.

14 [1922] 1 Ch. 126.

liability to pay "interest of money even after the instalment in question had been added to the capital for the purpose of computing the next instalment of interest."

The Canadian case of *Reference Re Saskatchewan Farm Security Act 1944, Section 6*[15] is on a subject far removed from the present, but it is of value for some words that Rand and Kellock JJ. uttered in the Supreme Court of Canada. Rand J. said[16]:

> "Interest is, in general terms, the return or consideration or compensation for the use or retention by one person of a sum of money, belonging to, in a colloquial sense, or owed to, another."

The learned judge added:

> ". . .the definition, as well as the obligation, assumes that interest is referable to a principal in money or an obligation to pay money. Without that relational structure in fact and whatever the basis of calculating or determining the amount, no obligation to pay money or property can be deemed an obligation to pay interest."

Kellock J. said[17]:

> "There can be no such thing as interest on principal which is non-existent."

To these authorities, which were duly put before me, I would add a passage from the speech of Lord Wright in *Riches v. Westminster Bank Ltd.*,[18] a case concerned with "interest of money" in the taxing Acts. He said:

> ". . .the essence of interest is that it is a payment which becomes due because the creditor has not had his money at the due date. It may be regarded either as representing the profit he might have made if he had had the use of the money, or, conversely the loss he suffered because he had not that use. The general idea is that he is entitled to compensation for the deprivation."

It seems to me that running through the cases there is the concept that as a general rule two requirements must be satisfied for a payment to amount to interest, and *a fortiori* to amount to "interest of money." First, there must be a sum of money by reference to which the payment which is said to be interest is to be ascertained. A payment cannot be "interest of money" unless there is the requisite "money" for the payment to be said to be "interest of." . . . Second, those sums of money must be sums that are due to the person entitled to the alleged interest; and it is this latter requirement that is mainly in issue before me. I do not, of course, say that in every case these two requirements are exhaustive, or that they are inescapable. Thus I do not see why payments should not be "interest of money" if A lends money to B and stipulates that the interest should be paid not to him but to X: yet for the ordinary case I think that they suffice. **[11.5]**

Ridge Securities Ltd v IRC [1964] 1 WLR 479 (Ch D)

Pursuant to an agreement between the plaintiffs and the borrowers, debentures were issued with the express intention that the plaintiffs would obtain a repayment of tax on the payments of 'interest' which the borrowers covenanted to pay, rather than to satisfy the financial requirements of the borrowers. It was held that the payments were not payments of interest.

> PENNYCUICK J:. . .The rate of interest may be low or high, but it seems to me impossible to treat as having the quality of interest a sum greater than the principal advanced and payable a few days after the advance. The net interest on the Ridge Investments debenture, namely £88,134, is less than the amount of the advance, viz., £123,000, and the interval between the issue of the debenture and payment of interest extended over two

15 [1947] 3 D.L.R. 689.
16 *Ibid.*, at 703.
17 *Ibid.*, at 707.
18 [1947] 1 All ER 469 at 472, [1947] AC 390 at 400, 28 Tax Cas 159 at 189.

months. Here, too, however, the ratio of interest to principal is such that it seems to me impossible to attribute to the payment the character of interest. There was of course in each case a continuing liability for payments calculated in the same manner, but the existence of this continuing liability does not, I think, alter the character of the payments.

I have been reminded of *Inland Revenue Commissioners v Duke of Westminster*[19] but here the description "interest" is, I think, merely a label which inaccurately describes the transaction as it appears upon the terms of the instrument read in the light of surrounding circumstances. The distinction is neatly drawn by Lord Simon in *Inland Revenue Commissioners v Wesleyan and General Assurance Society*,[20] where he says[21]:

> "It may be well to repeat two propositions which are well established in the application of the law relating to income tax. First, the name given to a transaction by the parties concerned does not necessarily decide the nature of the transaction. To call a payment a loan if it is really an annuity does not assist the tax payer, any more than to call an item a capital payment would prevent it from being regarded as an income payment if that is its true nature. The question always is what is the real character of the payment, not what the parties call it." . . . **[11.6]**

Lomax v Peter Dixon and Sons Ltd [1943] 1 KB 671 (CA)

An English company had advanced a large sum to its Finnish subsidiary. In consideration the Finnish company issued notes to the English company on the following terms:

(1) The value of the notes was greater than the loan made (ie the issue was at a discount).
(2) The repayment of the notes (phased over a number of years) would attract a premium of 20 per cent, if the profits of the Finnish company allowed.
(3) The notes were interest bearing.

The issue was whether the discount and the premium on the notes were income (and thus taxable) or capital payments. Reversing the judge at first instance, the Court of Appeal held that they were both capital payments.

> SIR WILFRID GREENE MR: . . . It may be convenient to sum up my conclusions in a few propositions. (1.) Where a loan is made at or above such a reasonable commercial rate of interest as is applicable to a reasonably sound security there is no presumption that a "discount" at which the loan is made or a premium at which it is payable is in the nature of interest. (2.) The true nature of the "discount" or the premium (as the case may be) is to be ascertained from all the circumstances of the case, and, apart from any matter of law which may bear on the question (such as the interpretation of the contract), will fall to be determined as a matter of fact by commissioners. (3.) In deciding the true nature of the "discount" or premium in so far as it is not conclusively determined by the contract, the following matters together with any other relevant circumstances are important to be considered, namely, the term of the loan, the rate of interest expressly stipulated for, the nature of the capital risk, and the extent to which, if at all, the parties expressly took or may reasonably be supposed to have taken the capital risk into account in fixing the terms of the contract. In this summary I have purposely confined myself to a case such as the present where a reasonable commercial rate of interest is charged. Where no interest is payable as such, different considerations will, of course, apply. In such a case, a "discount" will normally, if not always, be a discount chargeable under para. (b) of r. 1 to case III.[22] Similarly, a "premium" will normally, if not always, be interest, but it is not necessary or desirable to do more than to point out the distinction between such cases and the case

19 [1936] AC 1. [See para **[5.3]**, above].
20 64 TLR 173; [1948] 1 All ER 555.
21 64 TLR 173 at p. 174.
22 [Now ITTOIA 2005, s 381 (and ICTA 1988, s 18(3) for corporation tax purposes).]

of a contract similar to that which we are considering. For these reasons I am of opinion that the Special Commissioners came to the right conclusion and that their decision ought to be restored. **[11.7]**

See also *Chevron Petroleum (UK) Ltd v BP Petroleum Development Ltd* [1981] STC 689 and *Davies v Premier Investment Co Ltd* [1945] 2 All ER 681. **[11.8]**

(2) Deduction of tax at source

Interest paid by building societies and deposit takers is paid net of lower rate income tax (20%); those recipients who do not pay income tax may submit a claim to recover the tax paid.[23] In a limited number only of other interest payments, tax at the lower rate must be deducted[24] but, for these provisions to operate, generally, the interest must be 'yearly'. This will be the case where it is stated that the loan will last for a year or longer, or where the loan is expected to last, or is capable of lasting, for that time. Whether or not interest is yearly will depend upon the intention of the parties. **[11.9]**

Cairns v MacDiarmid [1983] STC 178 (CA)

Under a tax avoidance scheme that was widely-used at the time,[25] the taxpayer borrowed from his employer the sum of £37,740 for two years at 13.25% payable in advance (amounting to £5,000.55 per annum), to enable a bonus payment of £5,000 (otherwise assessable to income tax under what was then Schedule E) to attract income tax relief.[26] The taxpayer paid £5,000 to his employer, allegedly as a payment of interest, and his remaining liability under the loan was taken over by another company (controlled by the taxpayer's employer) in return for the payment of £32,740 to that company by the taxpayer, thereby relieving him of any further obligations under the loan. The Court of Appeal rejected the claim that the payment of £5,000 was in the nature of annual interest.

SIR JOHN DONALDSON MR: ... It is well settled that the difference between what is annual and what is short interest depends upon the intention of the parties. Thus interest payable on a mortgage providing for repayment of the money after six months, or indeed a shorter period, will still be annual interest if calculated at a yearly rate and if the intention of the parties is that it may have to be paid from year to year (*Bebb v. Bunny* (1854) 1 K. & J. 216 and *Corinthian Securities Ltd. v. Cato* (1969) 46 T.C. 93). I would

23 ITA 2007, Pt 15, Ch 2. Deduction at source is applied to payments of interest on 'relevant investments' within ITA 2007, s 856 by any building society and any 'deposit-taker' falling within ITA 2007, s 853. 'Relevant investments' include deposits held by any person for the benefit of UK resident individuals or deposits where the person entitled to the interest receives it in the capacity of personal representative. Excluded from the term are those held for companies, associations and charities, and deposits with a nominal value never falling below £50,000.

24 Deduction is made in accordance with ITA 2007, Pt 15, Ch 3; the circumstances which give rise to deduction of tax in respect of interest payments chargeable under ITTOIA 2005, s. 369 comprise interest paid: (i) either by a company or local authority otherwise than in a fiduciary or representative capacity (for eg, debenture interest); (ii) by or on behalf of a partnership of which a company is a member; (iii) by any person to another person whose usual place of abode is outside the UK. Even where the payment satisfies these criteria, the interest must be paid gross if it falls within the exceptions set out in ITA 2007, ss 876–888.

25 FA 1976, s 38 put a statutory end to the scheme.

26 Under FA 1972, s 75, annual interest chargeable under Schedule D, Case III could be set off against other income of the taxpayer in computing the income tax payable.

personally wish to avoid the use of the term "investment" as providing any sort of test in the context of whether interest is annual interest, notwithstanding its use in the latter case, because it is possible to have a short term and indeed a very short term investment, e.g. overnight deposits, and such an investment does not involve any annual interest, regardless of whether the interest is calculated at an annual rate. On the facts found by the Commissioners, the loan to [*the taxpayer*] was never intended to last for more than a few days, albeit he was entitled to postpone repayment for two years. In fact, as was always intended, his liability was discharged within the week, not by repayment but by novation. The payment of £5,000 was not therefore annual interest. It may, although this is immaterial, have been interest because, whilst the payment of £5,000 to secure a loan of £37,740 for less than a week is "grotesque" (*Ridge Securities Ltd. v. I.R. Commrs.* (1963) 44 T.C. 373), there is nothing grotesque about a payment of £5,000 to secure the right to have the use of £37,740 for a year with the ability to transfer that right to a third party for a consideration of £5,000, as in fact occurred under the novation agreement (Payment of £32,740 to discharge future liability of £37,740). **[11.10]**

B. *Annual payments*

Historically, because of the basic and higher rate tax relief enjoyed by a payer on the making of annual payments (such as covenants), they were used increasingly over the years for tax avoidance purposes.[27] These advantages were gradually eroded by anti-avoidance legislation designed to prevent income tax advantages being obtained by the use of short-term covenants,[28] revocable settlements, assignments of income to the unmarried infant child of the settler and covenants to trustees who fail to distribute income.[29] This attack on the use of annual payments to gain tax advantages culminated in 1988 with provisions that took most annual payments by individuals outside of the tax net altogether.[30] The result is that the payer now remains liable to tax on the income regardless of the obligation to pay it to someone else. Despite further legislation that removed two more categories of annual payment from the tax net[31], it remains important to identify a certain sum of money as an annual payment because, if it is, it cannot fall within any other head of charge and be classified, for example, as trading or earned income; it will simply remain outside of the tax net. The factors that identify an annual payment are:

(a) the quality of recurrence; and
(b) it is pure income profit in the hands of the recipient. **[11.11]**

Whitworth Park Coal Co Ltd v IRC [1961] AC 31 (HL)

The appellants, an investment company which prior to nationalization, had been a coal mining company, received certain payments from the Ministry of Fuel and Power as a form of interim compensation. The payments were held to be subject to direct assessment under the former Schedule D, Case III.

27 See, for example, *IRC v Duke of Westminster* [1936] AC 1; above, para **[5.3]**.
28 Short-term covenants were defined as covenants not capable of lasting for more than six years, or three years in the case of covenants to charities.
29 Now to be found in ITTOIA 2005, Pt 5, Ch 5: see Chapter 16.
30 FA 1988, s 36, now ITTOIA 2005, s 727(1).
31 By virtue of FA 1999, generally, relief for maintenance payments under a court order or agreement made prior to 15 March 1988 was withdrawn from 6 April 2000; see Chapter 14. Covenanted payments to charity were removed from the charge by FA 2000, s. 39 and were incorporated into the 'Gift Aid' rules (see now ITA 2007, Pt 8, Ch 2).

VISCOUNT SIMONDS: ... "Annual payment" must, it is said, be read in its context and must in some way resemble or be ejusdem generis with interest or annuities, but these payments are *sui generis*. That argument appears to me to be no more than a play on words. One must look at the true nature of the payments. It is well recognised that many payments which in the ordinary sense of the words might well be called annual payments do not come within Case III. One limitation is that Case III only applies to payments received as pure profit income[32]; that is, because no deductions are permitted under Case III. And further, the payments must recur or at least be of a recurring character. I think that the payments in this case comply with both requirements ... **[11.12]**

(1) Quality of recurrence

Moss' Empires Ltd v IRC [1937] AC 785 (HL)

The appellants entered into a guarantee to pay to another company each year for five years a sum of an amount sufficient to bring the recipient company's yearly profits up to a stated sum in order to enable a dividend to be paid on certain preference shares. The amounts paid varied each year. The House of Lords held that the payments were "annual payments," despite being contingent and variable in character, and were the chargeable income of the recipient company under Case III. Consequently, the appellants were entitled to deduct the payments from their own profits.

LORD MAUGHAM: ... The sole difficulty in the case, as I see it, is the question whether sums paid under the agreement of January 31, 1928, were annual payments within the language of rule 21 of the General Rules of the Income Tax Act 1918.[33] The sentence runs: "Upon payment of any interest of money, annuity or other annual payment, etc.;" and the charging section is to be found in Schedule D, 1 (b), taken with the words of rule. 1 applicable to Case III of that Schedule[34] as stated by his Lordship.

It is, I think, to be noted that we are not concerned here with the case of annual profits or gains arising from a trade, as to which the decision in *Martin v. Lowry*[35] would be decisive to show that in that context "annual" means "in any one year." In rule 21 "annual" must be taken to have, like interest on money or an annuity, the quality of being recurrent or being capable of recurrence. The payments we are concerned with were to continue for five years, subject to their being required to make up the guaranteed annual dividend, and were plainly payments intended to supplement so far as necessary the income of the recipients during each of the years in question. In these circumstances I am of opinion that they had the necessary quality of recurrence ... **[11.13]**

Note that annual payments which varied in amount were also covenanted in *IRC v Black* [1940] 4 All ER 445; and *IRC v Wolfson* [1949] 1 All ER 865. See also *Drummond v Collins* [1915] AC 1011, where child beneficiaries with a contingent interest under a discretionary trust received maintenance payments from the trustees. These payments were held not to be 'voluntary in any relevant sense' (per Lord Loreburn at 1017). Compare with *British Commonwealth International Newsfilm Agency Ltd v Mahany* [1963] 1 All ER 88. **[11.14]**

32 [Below, para **[11.15]**].
33 [Now ITA 2007, Pt 15, Ch 6.]
34 [See now ITTOIA 2005, P 5, Ch 7.]
35 [1927] AC 312; [above, para **[9.27]**].

(2) Pure income profit

Annual payments must be in the nature of a 'pure income profit' in the hands of the recipient; in particular, it is necessary to distinguish annual payments from trading receipts. With the exception of payments made for bona fide commercial reasons in connection with the individual's trade, profession or vocation,[36] and payments for non-taxable consideration[37] (when the amounts payable are not included in the income of the payer and may be deducted by him in computing his total income[38]), the former, if made by individuals, are now exempt from income tax (with the result that they are made out of the taxed income of the payer); the latter merely enter into the computation of the recipient's *profits* (and are not deductible by the payer as such, though they may, of course, be deductible for some other reason, eg as a proper expense of the payer's own trade[39]). In order for a payment to be one of pure profit, the recipient must not have incurred allowable expenditure in return for the payment. **[11.15]**

Re Hanbury Decd (1939) 38 TC 588 (CA)

In proceedings in connection with a settlement, an executor was awarded a sum of money in respect of the remainderman's use and enjoyment, for a period of years, of certain mining plant. It was held that the payment was not pure income profit in the hands of the recipient but merely an element in ascertaining profit. Thus, it was not within the former Schedule D, Case III[40] and tax was not deductible from the payment.

> SIR WILFRID GREENE MR: . . . There are two classes of annual payments which fall to be considered for Income Tax purposes. There is, first of all, that class of annual payment which the Acts regard and treat as being pure income profit of the recipient undiminished by any deduction. Payments of interest, payments of annuities, to take the ordinary simple case, are payments which are regarded as part of the income of the recipient, and the payer is entitled in estimating his total income to treat those payments as payments which go out of his income altogether. The class of annual payment which falls within that category is quite a limited one. In the other class there stand a number of payments, none the less annual, the very quality and nature of which make it impossible to treat them as part of the pure profit income of the recipient, the proper way of treating them being to treat them as an element to be taken into account in discovering what the profits of the recipient are. This matter was dealt with in a very well-known passage in the judgment of Scrutton L.J. in *Earl Howe v. Commissioners of Inland Revenue*,[41] which, if I may say so, I have always found particularly illuminating on questions of this kind. The type of example he gives is that of a yearly payment made, for instance, to the proprietor of a garage for the hire of a motor car. Nobody would suggest that on making that payment the hirer would be entitled to deduct tax, and yet it is annual payment, the reason being that the very nature of that payment itself, having regard to the circumstances in which it is made, necessarily makes the sums paid in the hands of a recipient an element only in the ascertainment of his profits. . . .
>
> Some light on the nature of a payment may, I think, also be ascertained by looking at it from the point of view of the payer. If the owner of a business has for the purpose of carrying on that business hired chattels under an agreement under which he is liable to

36 ITTOIA 2005, s 728; ICTA 1988, s 347A(2)(c).
37 ITTOIA 2005, s 729; ICTA 1988, s 125(1).
38 See below, para **[11.22]**.
39 See Chapter 10.
40 Now ITTOIA 2005, Pt 5, Ch 5.
41 [1919] 2 KB 336.

make annual payments, I should have thought it was beyond the possibility of doubt that the sum which he so paid was a sum which merely came into computation in ascertaining the profits of his trade. In the present case, upon the assumption that I make throughout, that this is a payment with which Income Tax is concerned, so far as regards the payers the position that they are in is that they have paid a sum of money for the use of chattels which they have used in a profit-making business. That seems to me to stamp that payment so far as the payer is concerned with a particular quality. From the point of view of the recipient, his position may be summarised. Being the owner of chattels the use and enjoyment of which has been had by the Respondents against payment, is he bound to submit to having the sum he so receives treated as pure income profit in relation to which as between himself and the Revenue he would be entitled to no item of deduction at all on the other side of his profits account, or is it a sum in respect of which he is liable to direct assessment and upon such assessment would be entitled to put forward such claim, if any, as he may have on the other side of the account? It seems to me that the nature of the payment brings it within the second class quite clearly. The matter, I think, can be tested in this way. If the Appellant had been carrying on a business of letting out plant for reward, the receipt which he obtains under the present circumstances would have been an item to be taken into account in ascertaining the profits of that business for the purpose of assessment under Case I of Schedule D. Nobody could suggest in such a case, it seems to me, that this payment would be a thing which must be segregated from the receipts of his business and subjected to some special treatment. If that be right – and I have no doubt that it is right – it appears to me to show the quality of this payment to be such that by its nature it is merely an element in the ascertainment of profits and is not a pure profit to be taken by itself.... **[11.16]**

IRC v National Book League [1957] Ch 488 (CA)

LORD EVERSHED MR:...The National Book League is a company limited by guarantee which was formed in the year 1925. It was not disputed that since September 1951, the league has been a body established for charitable purposes only. The question on the appeal arises in relation to some 2,000 or more deeds of covenant in a common and well-recognised form entered into by persons who were members – I have emphasised that word for reasons which will later appear – of the league whereby the covenantors covenanted to pay for a period of seven years, if they so long lived, such a sum as after deduction of income tax would leave the net figures of either one guinea or 10s. 6d. The National Book League sought to recover the amount of tax which had been deducted from the notional gross sums named in the deeds of covenant pursuant to section 447(1)(b) of the Income Tax Act 1952[42] [*which his Lordship read*].

It is the contention of the National Book League that the gross sums in question are the annual sums within the comprehension of Case III or section 123, and that the league is entitled, according to the terms of paragraph (b) of section 471(1),[43] to recover the tax which has been deducted by the covenantors.

I confess I have found the case somewhat troublesome, not least because of the conclusions to which the extremes of the argument on either side might appear to lead. It was, for example, on the one side observed by Mr. Cross that, if the argument for the league were sustained, it might be possible for a charity which, in accordance with well-known practice, may require each year to augment its funds or increase public interest by holding a dance, to invite well-disposed persons to enter into deeds of covenant for seven years for a figure in return for which they would be supplied with dance tickets for the charity dance in each of the following seven years. In such a case I do not myself feel much doubt that the substance of the matter would be an arrangement for buying in advance dance tickets for charity dances by means of a covenanted payment of that kind. That being the substance of the matter, it would be difficult to see, as it seems to me, how it could be brought within Case III and entitle the charity to recover tax.

42 [Now to be found in ITA 2007, Pt 10.]
43 [This should refer to s 447(1)(b) of the 1952 Act, now ITA 2007, Ch 10].

On the other side and at the other extreme, the instance was taken of well-known charities, of which the National Art-Collections Fund may be taken as an example. In such cases, as is well known, the donors, the covenantors in favour of such charities, get certain privileges. They may be allowed the use of certain reading rooms; they may be given the privilege of attending private exhibitions in private houses or elsewhere; and to many I do not doubt these privileges are by no means negligible. But although that case, again is not before us, it seems to me, as at present advised, that it would altogether offend good sense and good law to say that the sums covenanted in such cases were not gifts to the charity in question, that they were not pure income profit, to use Lord Greene M.R.'s phrase, in the hands of the charity. But the present case (and this is, of course, a truism applicable in all cases) must turn upon its own special facts; and the facts in the present case are special in a marked degree. The question, therefore, as I see it, turns first upon this. Looking at the substance and reality of the matter, can it be said that those who entered into these covenants have paid the sums covenanted without conditions or counter stipulations; and, on the whole, I have come to the conclusion that they cannot so say. It seems to me that against the special background of this case, and, having regard to the terms of the letter, there was here, in a real sense, a condition or counter stipulation on the part of the league against which the covenant was entered into. I must guard myself against saying that whenever one finds a covenantor in favour of a charity getting allowed to him certain privileges, it therefore follows that such a covenantor no longer can say that he has paid without conditions or counter stipulations. If the test be, as I venture to think it is, whether in all the circumstances, and looking once more at the substance and reality of the matter, these covenantors can be treated as donors of the covenanted sums to the charity, I have come to the conclusion that the answer must be in the negative, subject to the point to which I will now come as to the extent of the conditions or counter stipulations. The aspect of the matter, with which I have so far dealt, does not appear, as I follow the case stated and the judgment of Vaisey J., to have taken at all a prominent part in the argument before the matter was debated in this court. The matter seems rather to have been dealt with before the Special Commissioners and before the judge solely upon the question whether the privileges which the covenantor members admittedly obtained were of so illusory and negligible a character as to be properly disregarded on the principle of *de minimis non curat lex*.

The question whether particular advantages or promises can be dismissed on the principle of *de minimis non curat lex* must, I think, be a matter for the lawyer rather than for him who has to find facts, and, on the facts as they are here presented, I am unable to see any proper justification for the conclusion which the Special Commissioners upon this point reached. Particularly, I refer to the fact that the covenantors, I think, did get at the very least a clear promise from which the league could not draw back without gross breach of faith and, as I am inclined to think, without also a breach of contract, that they would continue to have advantages of membership at a lower subscription rate than other persons, and that they would be immune from the possibility of increase of subscription rates during the whole period of the covenant. It seems to me impossible to dismiss that matter as being trifling and illusory, and to disregard it on the principle of *de minimis non curat lex*. I am, therefore, upon this point unable to accept the argument of Mr. Brennan that it is a pure question of fact upon the conclusion of the Special Commissioners must be found. Upon that matter I agree entirely with the conclusion of Vaisey J. to which, indeed, I cannot usefully add anything.

Taking that view, and also concluding, as I do, that in the circumstances of this case the league failed to establish that the sums paid under the covenants can be regarded, to use again Lord Greene M.R.'s phrase, as pure income profit within Case III of Schedule D, and such as to entitle under section 447[44] the league to recover the tax, I would dismiss the appeal. **[11.17]**

This decision was followed in *Taw and Torridge Festival Society Ltd v. IRC* (1959) 38 TC 603, where subscriptions by covenant to a charity carried with it the privilege of admission to concerts and other performances at reduced rates. For Gift Aid purposes, there are limits on benefits which a donor may receive

44 [Now ITA 2007, Ch 10].

in return for his donation.[45] These restrictions do not apply where a payment made to a charity carries with it the right of admission for the purpose of viewing property preserved, maintained, kept or created by the charity in relation to its charitable work, provided that the right to make such gifts is available to members of the public.[46] In order to prevent charities reclassifying admission charges as donations so that they may benefit from Gift Aid, if a visitor makes a donation to charity in order to view property falling within one of the exceptions, Gift Aid will only apply (a) where a right of admission given in return for a gift is valid for a period of at least one year at all times that the general public can gain admission;[47] or (b) a member of the public could purchase the same right of admission and the gift must be at least 10% more than the amount that any member of the public would have to pay to gain the same right of admission.[48] **[11.17a]**

(3) Capital or income?[49]

Those annual payments that remain subject to charge[50] must, necessarily, be of an income nature; instalments of a capital sum, not being income at all, are not taxable.[51] Some payments may consist, in part, of a payment of capital and, in part, of interest on that capital, in which case only the interest portion of the payment is taxable.[52] Special rules relate to purchased life annuities.[53] **[11.18]**

IRC v Mallaby-Deeley [1938] 4 All ER 818 (CA)

SIR WILFRID GREENE MR: ... It seems to me that the cases to which we have been referred, and, indeed, the principle of the thing, must depend upon there being a real existing capital sum, not necessarily pre-existing but existing in the sense that it represents some kind of capital obligation. If you had a case where a man merely made up his mind that he would like a covenantee to have a certain sum of money more than he had got at present, and then effectuated that intention by entering into a covenant to make annual payments, the sum which he thought of, which in no real sense would be a sum at all, would be no more than the motive for entering into the covenant to make the annual payments. On the other hand, if there is a real liability to pay a capital sum, either pre-existing or then assumed, that the capital sum has got a real existence, and, if the method adopted of paying it is a payment by instalments, the character of these instalments is settled by the nature of the capital sum to which they are related. If there is no pre-existing capital sum, but the covenant is to pay a capital sum by instalments, the same result will follow.

45 ITA 2007 ss 418, 419.

46 ITA 2007 ss 420(4)(5). Particular purposes of viewing are set out in s 420(5) and the property that may be viewed comprise (i) buildings; (ii) grounds or other land; (iii) plants; (iv) animals; (v) works of art (but not performances); (vi) artifacts; and (vii) property of a scientific nature (s 420(6)).

47 ITA 2007 s 420(7).

48 *Ibid*, s 420(8).

49 See Y Beer 'The Credit Price Income or Capital' [1986] BTR 271.

50 See above, para **[11.11]**.

51 It is necessary to have regard to the character of the payments in the hands of the recipient. Payments made out of a capital fund may nevertheless take on the character of income and be taxable in the hands of the recipient, see *Brodie's Will Trustees v IRC* (1933) 17 TC 432; *Williamson v Ough* [1936] AC 384; *Cunard's Trustees v IRC* [1946] 1 All ER 159; and *Stevenson v Wishart* (below, para **[16.26]**).

52 See *Re Euro Hotel (Belgravia) Ltd* [1975] 3 All ER 1975 above, para **[11.5]** and *Lomax v Peter Dixon and Sons Ltd* [1943] 1 KB 671 above, para **[11.7]**.

53 ITTOIA 2005, ss 717, 719. These provisions permit the amount of any annuity payment which falls within its scope to be divided into an income and capital amount.

Proceeding upon that basis, the position, at the date when the deed of March 10, 1930, was executed, was that Sir Harry was under an obligation to pay a capital sum, or what was left of a capital sum, of £28,000 by certain annual instalments. That obligation he got rid of, substituting for it the obligation under the deed. It seems to me that, putting all those circumstances together, what he was doing under the deed of March 10, 1930, was liquidating a capital obligation of his own, an obligation which, it is true, was only to be carried out by instalment payments, but which, nevertheless, was of a capital nature, and he was liquidating that obligation by a series of instalments differing in amounts and times from those which were referred to in the pre-existing document. On that basis, it seems to me that the case is one where it is not possible to say of the payments made under this document that they are of an income mature. They are given the character of capital. That character is stamped upon them by the circumstances that they are the means of liquidating a capital obligation, and it is quite wrong to say that you must look at the documents alone, and disregard the other elements in the legal relationship between the parties and the legal results which the transaction achieved ... **[11.19]**

IRC v Church Commissioners for England [1977] AC 329 (HL)

The taxpayers, a charity, sold their reversions on certain properties to the leaseholder, Land Securities Investment Trust Ltd, in consideration for rentcharges of £96,000 per annum for ten years. This sum represented the annual rental income plus an amount, which, if invested, would produce at the end of the ten-year period, an amount equivalent to the annual rental income. Under the Income Tax Act 1952, s 177 standard rate income tax was deducted by the leaseholder on paying the rentcharge,[54] and the taxpayers, being a charity attempted to reclaim the tax so deducted from the Revenue under what is now ITA 2007, Pt 10. The Special Commissioners held that they could do so as the rentcharges were entirely of an income nature. The House of Lords agreeing with the lower courts, found in favour of the charity.

LORD WILBERFORCE: ... On general logical grounds and perhaps on considerations of an economic character, there may be much to be said for a rule which recognizes the existence of an interest element in all deferred capital payments – I think that Cross J. was attracted by this kind of argument in *Vestey v Inland Revenue Commissioners*.[55] But illogical or not (and the consequences of rejecting the dichotomy might introduce other illogicalities) it is too clearly and firmly rooted in the income tax law to be displaced except, in selected cases, by legislation. And it has been, if not without difficulty, at least with fair consistency, applied by the courts. I shall not go through the long list of cases in which the courts have considered the problem of "income" or "capital" in relation to terminable payments. But leaving aside *Foley v. Fletcher*[56] which was decided on demurrer, *Inland Revenue Commissioners v. Ramsay*[57] *Inland Revenue Commissioners v. British Salmson Aero Engines Ltd.*[58] *Mallaby-Deeley v. Inland Revenue Commissioners*[59] and *Southern-Smith v. Clancy*[60] all rest upon the basis that there are two alternatives, instalments of capital, or production of an annual payment, and that the task of the court is to find which it is. That this basis is a solid one is borne out by the fact that most of these decisions, as well as that in *Inland Revenue Commissioners v. Wesleyan & General Assurance Society*,[61] bear the authority, or contain the judgment of, Lord Greene – a hallmark of gold.

54 Rentcharges no longer fall within the term 'annual payments' for income tax purposes, and are now taxable under ITTOIA 2005, Pt 3 Ch 2 as income arising from a property business. For deduction of tax at source, see below, para **[11.22]**.
55 [1962] Ch 861.
56 (1858) 3 H & N 769.
57 (1935) 20 TC 79
58 [1938] 2 KB 482.
59 (1938) 23 TC 153; [above, para **[11.19]**].
60 [1941] 1 KB 276.
61 [1946] 2 All ER 749.

I cannot, therefore, for these reasons accept that the revenue's proposition[62] either represents, or ought to represent, the existing law, and I now must consider their alternative argument.

This argument involved the proposition that, even though it may be impermissible to predicate, in general, that payments of a purchase price, spread over a number of years, contain a capital element and an interest element, this "dissection," as it has come to be called, is permissible where the true legal character of the bargain, or the transaction, calls for it. Dissection is, at least as a plain case, permissible if the parties who are buying and selling a capital asset, having agreed upon a price, then make provision for payment of that price by instalments, the amount of which is so calculated and shown to be so calculated as to include an interest element. Whether there are other possible cases of dissection, *i.e.*, apart from the case where a lump purchase price has been agreed upon, may be a debatable area.

There is no doubt, in my opinion, that the plain case is recognized by authority: *Scobie v. Secretary of State for India.*[63] There was an agreed purchase price for the railway but the Secretary of State had an option, instead of paying the lump sum, of making payment by an annuity spread over a long period, "the interest used in calculating the annuity being determined" as prescribed. There was no difficulty whatever in deciding that, under the bargain between the parties, there was a (taxable) interest element and a capital element, and the fact that the word "annuity" was used did not prevent the capital element being recognized and consequently not taxed.

This case has never been doubted or qualified; if it has not been much followed, that is because it is seldom that the case for dissection is so clear as it was there. There is not much light to be derived from *East Indian Railway Co. v. Secretary of State for India*[64] which seems to have followed *Scoble's* case. *Goole Corporation v. Aire & Calder Navigation Trustees*[65] was one where dissection was allowed on the basis that there was a pre-existing capital sum: but *Scoble's* case does not seem to have been cited. *Perrin v. Dickson*[66] again followed *Scoble's* case on a consideration of the true nature of the bargain, *i.e.*, as one for the capital sums carrying interest. *Vestey v. Inland Revenue Commissioners*[67] is much more directly relevant, and is the decision on which the revenue chiefly relies. The agreement in that case was for the sale of shares for £5,500,000, to be paid without interest by 125 yearly instalments of £44,000. On the face of it – a face with some cosmetic reconstruction – this was a case of a principal sum payable over a period of years, within Lord Greene's first category, and not admitting of dissection. However, evidence was given and admitted (i) that the value of the shares at the time of transfer was approximately £2 million and (ii) that on an actuarial basis, the annual sum payable over 125 years equivalent to a present value of £2 million and taking interest at 2 per cent. was £43,670. On this, Cross J. felt able to decide that the case was for dissection of each annual payment between capital and income. This case represents, so far, the high water mark of dissection cases and the revenue seeks to apply it here. I would, for myself, accept this decision as correct, even though I would be unable to follow those portions of the judgment in which the learned judge appears to favour a general rule of dissection wherever there is a deferred payment of a purchase price. And on that basis I will consider whether on the same principle the revenue can succeed in the present case.

[*His Lordship then considered whether Megarry J. at first instance was correct in admitting certain extrinsic evidence outside the contract between Land Securities and the Church Commissioners, and decided that the evidence was admissible*]

The evidence in question consists of correspondence, file notes and inter-office memoranda relating to the negotiations between the Church Commissioners and Land

62 [That wherever a capital asset is transferred in consideration of a series of cash receipts of fixed amounts over a fixed period, the cash receipts are partly income and partly capital in the hands of the recipient].
63 [1903] AC 299.
64 [1905] 2 KB 413.
65 [1942] 2 All ER 276.
66 [1930] 1 KB 107.
67 [1962] Ch 861.

Securities before the agreement of January 5, 1960, and of a series of findings made by the special commissioners after hearing the evidence of the secretary to the Church Commissioners. The significance of this evidence from the point of view of the revenue was that it introduced a figure of £720,000 which, they claimed, represented the "purchase price" and upon which, taking an assumed rate of interest of 5½ per cent, the commissioners could obtain an income of £40,000 in perpetuity if they were paid rentcharges totalling £96,000 for 10 years. Therefore, the revenue claimed the present case was indistinguishable from *Vestey v. Inland Revenue Commissioners*[68] and was within the *Scoble* principle [*Scoble v. Secretary of State for India*].

I was impressed by this argument and it came near to convincing me, but the conclusion I have come to, on reflection, is that the case is on the other side of a narrow line.

The essential feature of the negotiations and of the bargain, as shown by the documents, was that Land Securities did not wish, on any account, to pay a lump sum for the properties. This is so found in terms. The Church Commissioners, on their side, wished to maintain their existing income by rentcharges for a longer period. The figure of £720,000 was not an agreed purchase price, or even an agreed valuation. It was, as I understand it, simply a checking figure in the calculations, worked out on the basis of 18 years' purchase (corresponding to 5½ per cent.) of the existing rents of £40,000. The bargain was always thought of in income terms, and was concluded on income terms, and there is nothing in the documents which gives to the transaction, or to any element in it, a capital character. The resemblance to the facts of *Vestey v. Inland Revenue Commissioners* (itself a borderline case), though at first sight striking, is, in the end, more superficial than real, and the essential "*true*" character found to exist in *Vestey v. Inland Revenue Commissioners* is missing here. A fortiori, the present case differs from the clear factual situation in *Scoble v. Secretary of State for India.*[69]

In the end, the decision in the present case rests upon a narrow point but I find that it does not come within a dissection principle. I agree with both courts below and I would dismiss the appeal. **[11.20]**

In *IRC v Land Securities Investment Trust Ltd* [1969] 1 WLR 604 it was held that, so far as the leaseholder, Land Securities, was concerned, the payment of the rentcharge to the Church Commissioners was a payment of capital. See J G M 'Annual Payments or Instalments of Capital' [1965] BTR 328; and R S Nock 'Form or Substance?' [1969] BTR 256. See also A Sumption *Vestey v Inland Revenue Commissioners* [1980] BTR 4. **[11.21]**

2. Transfers of income

Historically, one of the key characteristics of annual payments was the way in which tax was collected. Basic rate tax was not directly assessed on the recipient, but was deducted and collected at source from the payer.[70] The payer was then permitted to deduct that sum from the amount to be paid to the payee, meaning that, generally, the payee would receive a net sum together with a credit for the basic rate income tax deducted at source. Accordingly, this system drew a distinction between the person on whom the burden of tax actually fell, and the person from whom it was actually collected. The payer was looked upon as having alienated that part of his income that represented the annual payment. This resulted in such payments being deductible in computing the total income of the payer, with the burden of both basic and

68 [1962] Ch 861.
69 [1903] AC 299.
70 ICTA 1988, ss 3, 348, 349.

higher rate tax falling on the payee, but with the possibility of the payee recouping basic rate tax if he was not liable to pay income tax. As a consequence, annual payments played an important part in tax planning since they provided a tax-efficient way of transferring income from one taxpayer to another, usually from a higher rate taxpayer to one who paid no income tax, such as a charity. However, the income tax benefits were gradually eroded by provisions that, *first*, restricted the circumstances in which such benefits could be obtained through the transfer of income in this way[71] and, *secondly*, that sought to restrict relief to basic rate tax only in the vast majority of cases. Finally, by provisions enacted over a number of years, the majority of annual payments by individuals were removed from the tax system altogether,[72] meaning that the annual payment does not, for tax purposes, form part of the income of the recipient or any other person and remains that of the payer.[73]

Further, structural changes have now been made to the machinery of tax collection by the Tax Law Rewrite team, who had highlighted various difficulties with the scheme, not least the fact that the concepts of alienation that underpinned the machinery and of deduction at source did not rest easily with a system that no longer assesses different sources of income, but which looks instead to total income (see Chapter 6). The result is that where the payer of an annual payment not otherwise charged to tax (ITTOIA 2005, Pt 5, s 683), either makes the payment to an individual for genuine commercial reasons in connection with that individual's trade, profession or vocation, or it is a payment within ITTOIA 2005, s 729, there is a duty upon the payer to deduct from it in all cases a sum representing income tax at the basic rate in force for the tax year in which it is made.[74] The sum deducted is then collected as part of the payer's self-assessment return. Provided that the payment is not deductible in calculating the payer's income from his trade, profession or vocation, relief for the payment is then given by way of a deduction equal to the gross amount of the payment in computing the payer's net income.[75] It follows that relief is dependent upon the payer having taxable income that is sufficient to cover the payment. The recipient of an annual payment falling under ITTOIA 2005, s 683, will have income under s 683 equivalent to the gross value of the payment and not simply the sum that is actually received, and will be given a tax credit equal to the basic rate income tax deducted from the payment by the payer. Accordingly, the recipient may be entitled to reclaim that tax, for example, if there are unused personal allowances, or the tax may exactly discharge his tax liability, or he may be liable to extra income tax at the higher rate.

Payments to charity are now governed by the Gift Aid scheme,[76] and the only relief afforded in respect of maintenance payments, namely that the payer's tax liability on his total income is reduced by a percentage (10% for 2007-08) of a specified amount or, if lower, the actual amount of the maintenance payment, is restricted to where one or both parties to the marriage were aged 65 or over on or before 5 April 2000.[77] **[11.22]**

71 These provisions are now to be found in ITTOIA 2005, Pt 5, Ch 5. See above, para **[11.11]** and Chapter 16.

72 By FA 1988, s 36 (now ITTOIA 2005, s 727(1)), FA 1999, s 31 and FA 2000, s 41.

73 ICTA 1988, s 347A(1)(b), inserted by FA 1988, s 36 (1) (now ITA 2007, s 900(1)).

74 ITA 2007, s 900.

75 ITA 2007, s 448 Deduction is Step 2 of the tax calculation (ITA 2007, s 23, and see Chapter 14).

76 See above, para **[11.17a]**.

77 See Chapter 14.

12 Property Income

1. The charge under ITTOIA 2005, Part 3 and Schedule A

The rules relating to the taxation of income from land, which are now to be found in the rewritten provisions of ITTOIA 2005, Pt 3 and, for corporation tax purposes, in Schedule A,[1] have been the subject of much change over a number of years; indeed the history of the taxation of land in the UK has been described as 'long and tangled'.[2] The charge to tax is on the profits of a property business carried on for generating income from land.[3] Whether or not this is the most efficient way of taxing property income is arguable. **[12.1]**

John Tiley 'Aspects of Schedule A' in John Tiley (ed) *Studies in the History of Tax Law* (2004) pp 81–97

Schedule A was part of the original schedular tax system introduced in 1803,[4] which, as Dr Avery Jones shows . . ., meant that, thanks to the effectiveness of the system of deduction at source, there was no need for the taxpayer to make a general statement of income (the main objective of these changes being to counter evasion).[5] Schedule A remained part of the UK tax system until 1963 and so its last full legislative enactment is to be found in the Income Tax Act of 1952. After 1803 it reappeared with some changes in 1805 and more changes in 1806 when it was streamlined by having the relief for repairs

1 For a discussion of the categories of income under the Schedular system and under the rewritten provisions, see Chapter 7.

2 Geoffrey Morse and David Williams *Davies: Principles of Tax Law* (5th edn, 2004) p 97.

3 ITTOIA 2005, s 264; s 266 defines the term 'generating income from land'; see below, para **[12.9]**.

4 43 Geo III chapter 122, substantially re-enacted as 45 Geo 3 c. 49 (1805) and 46 Geo 3 c. 65 (1806). [. . .] on the genesis of the legislation from 1799 to 1806 see A. Farnsworth Addington: Author of the Modern Income Tax Stevens London, 1951 and Piroska Soos: The Origins of Taxation at Source International Bureau of Fiscal Documentation, 1998. These two works contain references to much contemporary material especially the Exposition of the 1803 Act and "A Guide to the Property Act 1806' both published by Joyce Gold, Shoe Lane. It appears that no copy of the latter (1806) book exists in the United Kingdom; however there is a copy in the library of Congress Washington DC 1806 and I am very grateful to Dave Hartnett, Head of Revenue Policy and Deputy Chairman, Board of Inland Revenue for enabling me to see a copy of this work.

5 For a comparison of Pitt's scheme of 1799 and Addington's of 1803 see Farnsworth op cit chapter 3.

removed;[6] it reappeared in this form in 1842.[7] There were few changes until the end of the nineteenth century and the start of the twentieth. It duly appears in the consolidations of 1918[8] and 1952.[9] It was accepted as sound doctrine by the Royal Commission of 1920, which nonetheless recommended some changes eventually made by FA 1926, and by the Royal Commission of 1955. It was repealed by FA 1963.[10]

The Schedule A currently in force in the UK[11] began life as Schedule D Case VIII[12] by that same FA 1963 and was restored as Schedule A in the 1970 consolidation. This taxes profits from the ownership of land – actual profits not notional profits and so not imputed income. By contrast, the original Schedule A did tax imputed income – as one now puts it. More correctly, it charged tax on the annual value of land in the United Kingdom; the current concept of annual value is to be found in TA 1988 s. 837.[13]

... Our original Schedule A had three subdivisions called rules (with numbers) rather than Cases.[14] Rule I, which has just been outlined, was the general rule and applied to all lands tenements, hereditaments or heritage capable of actual occupation.

...

The annual rental value used for the old Schedule A Rule I differs from what is now taxed under the current (post 1963) Schedule A in two principal ways. First, its relationship to any actual rent depended on the reliability (ie accuracy and contemporaneity) of the valuation and the reaction of the Revenue if receipts fell below the annual value. If the valuation process failed to keep up with current values, as happened in a particularly serious way after 1936, one could get a situation in which the annual value fell far below not just the value for which the property could have been left [*sic*] but also the amounts for which the property was actually let. This "excess rents" problem gave rise to the leading schedular system case of *Fry v Salisbury House Estates Ltd*,[15] in which the House of Lords refused to allow the Revenue to tax these receipts either under Schedule A or Schedule D Cases I or VI.[16] Secondly, Schedule A taxed the owner-occupier who received no rent at all. So a person owning and occupying land had to pay tax on the annual value – this profit arose from ownership and therefore came under Schedule A. If it was a home, tax was paid under Schedule A and that was that. If the land was used for a trade or profession, tax was due under Schedule A on the land in addition to tax under Schedule D on any business profits – the Schedule A value was taxed under Schedule A and so did not form part of the Schedule D income. If there was a net loss under Schedule A, as computed under Schedule A rules, the excess could not

6 45 Geo 3 c. 49 (1805) and 46 Geo 3 c. 65 (1806). The earlier allowance for repairs of property was a general one and limited to a fraction of the annual value. The deduction for children was discontinued at the same time. £60 exemption reduced to £50 and restricted to earned income (or income from professions trades and offices); for arguments over the restriction see Farnsworth op cit.

7 5 and 6 Vict c. 35 opening paragraphs; the detailed rules are in ss. 60–88.

8 ITA 1918, First Schedule.

9 ITA 1952 ss. 82 et seq.

10 FA 1963, ss. 14; consequent changes and the introduction of Schedule D, Case VIII were effected by ss. 15–32.

11 [Prior to ITTOIA 2005].

12 Schedule D Case VII was the short term capital gains tax introduced by FA 1962 ss. 10 et seq.

13 [Now repealed as unnecessary.]

14 This tripartite division dates from the 1805 Act.

15 [1930] AC 432, 15 TC 266.

16 [Schedule D Case I charged to tax income from a trade; Case VI caught income that was intended to fall within the tax net, but which did not fall within any other Schedule.]

be used against D profits [*sic*].[17] An owner occupier who was also a farmer was originally taxed under Schedule B rather than, as now, under Schedule D on the farming profits but was still liable to pay tax under Schedule A as well.

The burden of the charge under Schedule A fell on the person in occupation – whether or not the owner. If L, a landlord, owns land and leases it to T, the tenant, it was generally T who was liable to tax under Schedule A in the first place[18] and this was collected by direct assessment on T. However, . . ., T, on paying the rent to L, was allowed to deduct the amount of tax he has [*sic*] paid under Schedule A from the rent paid to L. In this way the burden is shifted from T to L.

. . . *Bring back Schedule A?*

It appears to be some time since there was a systematic official look at the taxation of housing and it is perhaps worth mentioning three current problems: a) rising prices b) rising rents and c) rising repair costs – recent newspaper reports suggest that repairs are not being carried out or not carried out well enough and that the quality of the housing stock is going down. The right to buy council houses has enabled people to buy their own homes but as anyone who has recently employed builders will know not necessarily to have enough money to maintain them; Cambridge man with his electric drill and a TV programme is not necessarily good for the housing stock.[19] The state welfare system does not seem to be interested in helping with repair costs. A systematic look should look at all these points especially the interaction with the welfare system we call social security.

Such a review might involve looking again at the old Schedule A. The absence of an old fashioned Schedule A charge is often cited as prime [*sic*] example of discrimination in the continuing discrepancy between the treatment of investment in housing and investment in shares. One may however question how far this is true. Traditionally, we look at three questions a) relief for interest on loans received b) taxation of income derived and c) taxation of capital gains. Trying to answer this traditional question shows how difficult life has become.

Taking shares first: a) there is no relief for interest on loans to buy shares[20] – although there was before 1969; b) there is a tax on dividends (Schedule F) c) there is CGT to pay on a disposal. However today and for some years now, neither b) nor c) is true if the shares are held in a PEP or ISA – with the important qualification that there is no relief for capital losses either. Moreover, if the shares are not held in such a privileged intermediary, the annual exemption may enable the gains to escape tax, an exemption which can be the more valuable with the device known as "bed and spousing" under which the shares are sold by one spouse and a similar investment is made by the other spouse so that the first spouse realises the gain or loss as required.

With housing the answers depend on whether the property is to be let or occupied. If it is for letting there is interest relief against the rent,[21] taxation of the rent under Schedule A and taxation of the gain under capital gains tax. The gain may attract tapering relief but normally as a non-business asset – unless it is furnished holiday accommodation.[22] The long-life nature of the asset means that the annual

17 ITA 1952 s. 136, formerly Schedule D Cases I and II Rule 5; against such a background some of the apparently curious rules in TA 1988 s. 74 make more sense.
18 The list of situations in ITA 1952 s. 175 in which the lessor is liable applies to the excess rents charged under D [sic] Case VI and not the general Schedule A liability.
19 Cambridge man with his electric drill may also strain the notion of improvement embedded in TCGA 1992, s. 38(1)(b).
20 [But see ITA 2007, Pt 8, Ch 1.]
21 TA 1988 s. 21A superseding relief as a charge on income under TA 1988 s. 355 (1)(b) by FA 1995 s. 42(1).
22 TCGA 1992, ss. 2A and 241; [see Chapter 20, below, para **[20.45]**.]

exemption will be of relatively little use here. Property cannot be held through a PEP or a [*sic*] ISA – nor as part of a personal pension scheme.

It has been suggested that one way of dealing with high prices is to tax capital gains, i.e. to remove the exemption.[23] This rather half baked idea ignores the fact that much of the recent surge in demand has been due to the buy-to-rent movement – where there is no exemption. Its introduction, presumably only with prospective effect, might have a significant effect on the tax take – and a one-off bonanza for valuers – but, as we all know tax rules have monetary effects, sometimes unpredictably so. How quickly would the extra tax be built into the price asked; to what extent would it reduce the price but increase the costs of housing?[24] Other tax systems have been wary about taxing such gains. Taxing owner occupied housing on its gains would lead to lock in of a very literal sort. So the US used to have a rollover relief rule (s 1034) supplemented by a once in a lifetime exemption of a fixed amount of gain (s 122). It has now moved to our exemption system (new s 122 since 1997).[25]

Bringing back the old Schedule A is, in theory at least, another option. An overnight reintroduction would have a dramatic effect on the price of houses, giving rise to further negative equity problems for those who have bought recently and abolishing those retirement nest-eggs older purchasers are expecting. This is not compatible with a government wish to encourage people to be self reliant in retirement. Moreover while it would reduce the price of housing, it would not reduce the actual costs of buying – what had previously been payable to the bank as interest might well be paid to the government in tax. In principle it is to be preferred it [*sic*] to a major change in stamp duty rates even though high rates are the norm in several continental European countries. This is because the stamp duty only arises when there is a transaction and transactions may be the result of chance or mischance. A periodic charge like the Schedule A income tax avoids these issues.

One can come to like the idea of the old Schedule A and to admire its thinking and its balance. One can like the idea of getting rid of those rules about lease premiums as well as the idea of equity between owner and renter. At a more adventurous level one can like its defiance of the idea that income is everything. However its reintroduction is a political non-starter and one know [*sic*] that given the chance everyone would vote against it out of that acute self-interest which grips us all. **[12.2]**

For a further, and brief, consideration of the history of land taxation, see Geoffrey Morse and David Williams *Davies: Principles of Tax Law* (5th edn, 2004) pp 97–99. The question of whether the 'notional income' derived from the enjoyment of land by an owner-occupier should be taxed is aired in the Final Report of the Royal Commission on the Taxation of Profits and Income (1955, Cmd. 9474) ch 28, particularly paras 826–827. **[12.3]**

A. *Property income is not trading income*

Although the income of a property business is now treated for computation purposes in a similar way to the income of a trade under ITTOIA 2005, Pt 2,

23 [For a discussion of the capital gains tax exemption for private residences, see Chapter 20, below, para **[20.53]**.]

24 On capitalisation of tax effects, see Kay and King *The British Tax System* (5th edn) p. 10.

25 On US, see J M Burke and M K Friel *Understanding Federal Income Taxation* chapter 6.

it is not trading income[26] and it remains unearned.[27] Accordingly, with the exception of income arising from the letting of furnished holiday accommodation,[28] it cannot give rise to pension entitlement, nor to capital gains tax business reliefs (see Chapter 20, below, para **[20.59]**). **[12.4]**

John Durnford 'The Distinction Between Income from Business and Income from Property, and the Concept of Carrying on Business'(1991) 39 Can Tax Jo 1131, 1139–1140

The evidence . . . is all too clear that the courts have failed to help us determine the dividing line between business income and property income where the income does not fall clearly within the one category or the other. Couzin has aptly pointed out that since business income results from the application of both capital and labour, and since capital is property, there is a blending of the two sources.[29] Consequently, the mere fact that property is involved does not prevent the income from being from business; it all depends on which of the two elements of business and property predominates in a given situation.

To conclude, in the words of Krishna:

> "Since most businesses use property to generate income, it is not particularly helpful to ask whether the income is derived from the *use* of property. The critical question is: does the income flow *from* property or *from* business?"[30]

Richardson put it as follows:

> "The basic assumption is that all income is earned or produced in one sense or another, from "property." Property income attains the quality of business income where the evidence is that the profits generated derive from the active exploitation of property in a commercial and businesslike manner.[31] **[12.5]**

Durnford's examination of the distinction between property income and trading income is in the Canadian context. Although, in that jurisdiction, the term 'trade' has a narrower meaning than the term 'business',[32] for the purpose of the extract, 'trade' may be substituted for 'business'. **[12.6]**

26 See below, para **[12.9]**.
27 Note, however, the special rules that apply with respect to income from furnished holiday lettings: see below, para **[12.19]**.
28 See below, para **[12.19]**.
29 Robert Couzin, 'Business and Property Income' in *Current Developments in Measuring Business Income for Tax Purposes* 1981 Corporate Management Tax Conference (Toronto: Canadian Tax Foundation, 1982, 41–71 at 42–45).
30 Vern Krishna, *The Fundamentals of Canadian Income Tax*, 3d ed. (Toronto: Carswell, 1989) paragraph 461, at 231.
31 Elinore J. Richardson, 'Holding Real Estate for the Production of Income' in *Income Tax Aspects of Real Estate Transaction* 1983 Corporate Management Tax Conference (Toronto: Canadian Tax Foundation, 1983) 1–58 at 5. . . A case in which rental income was classified as business income is *R v Canadian-American Loan & Investment Corporation* [1974] CTC 101 . . . (the rentals were received in consideration of services rendered in connection with the storage of boats in a marina).
32 See Couzin, n 29, above, at p 43.

Webb v Conelee Properties Ltd [1982] STC 913 (Ch D)

WARNER J: So I turn to the question whether, on the facts found by the Commissioners, it was open to them to decide that the activities of the company constituted a trade. On that question I was referred to a number of authorities: namely, in chronological order, *Rotunda Hospital, Dublin v. Coman*,[33] *Fry v. Salisbury House Estates Ltd*,[34] *Sywell Aerodrome Ltd. V. Croft*,[35] *Jennings v. Middlesbrough Corporation*,[36] and *Gittos v. Barclay*.[37] It was I think common ground between Counsel that those authorities establish that the owner of land may carry on activities on the land that may go beyond the mere exploitation of his proprietary rights in the land and which constitute a trade. Where it is shown that there have been such activities, it is a matter of fact and degree whether they are sufficient to amount to the carrying on of a trade.

Mr. Carnwath, who appears for the Inspector of Taxes, submits that, in the present case, it does not appear from the Case Stated that the Respondent company carried on on its properties any activity, such as the provision of services or of equipment, capable of constituting a trade. I think he is right.

Looking again at para. 10 of the Case Stated, I find that in the first sentence the Commissioners state that

> "the Respondent company was not an investment company within the meaning of s.304(5) of Income and Corporation Taxes Act 1970[38] but a trading company trading in the letting of properties producing a rental of £32,487 in the *[relevant]* period . . . There is no such trade known to tax legislation as "the letting of properties producing a rental."

That is precisely what is taxed under Schedule A,[39] and it cannot constitute a trade taxable under Case I of Schedule D.[40] Then the Commissioners go on: "This consisted" – that is to say, the trade of letting properties producing a rental – "in the acquisition of properties, the finding of licensees, the granting of licences to occupy the properties, and the disposal of properties from time to time." Those words, it seems to me, simply describe the activities of someone exploiting proprietary rights in land. The next sentence is: "The whole activity of the Respondent company required a greater degree of personal involvement and active management by those managing the company than would normally be associated with those managing an investment company." It seems to me, however, that Mr. Carnwath was right when he said that mere management activity was not an activity that was capable of giving rise to the existence of a trade, and that the degree or amount of that activity made no difference so long as it was only management.

Lastly, the Commissioners say: "We considered that the Respondent company's practice of granting licences to occupiers of properties instead of exclusive possession under leases or tenancy agreements bore this out." Had the matter been free from authority, I would have had little or no hesitation in saying that it could not make any difference whether the owner of land exploited his proprietary rights in that land by granting leases or by granting licences; but there is a very helpful passage in the judgment of Lord Greene M.R. in the *Sywell Aerodrome*[41] case, to which Mr. Carnwath drew my attention.

> "If in the present case the land had been demised to the Brooklands Company with appropriate restrictions on user and a power reserved to the Company to grant

33 7 TC 517.
34 15 TC 266 [and above, para **[7.15]**].
35 24 TC 126.
36 34 TC 447.
37 55 TC 633.
38 [Now ICTA 1988, s 130.]
39 [Now ITTOIA 2005, Pt 3.]
40 [*Ibid*, Pt 2.]
41 24 TC 126 at 139.

> licences to others to bring their aircraft to ground upon the land, there could, since the *Salisbury House*[42] case, have been no question but that the Schedule A assessments covered the profits derived from the lease. But it is suggested that the case is different because here the Brookland Company so far as the land is concerned are merely licensees. Does this make any difference? On principle I cannot see that it does. When the owner of land grants a licence to another to come upon his land he is exercising his rights of property just as much as when he is granting a lease. It is by virtue of his proprietary rights that he has power to grant the licence and this is equally true be he freeholder or leaseholder. The fact that a licensee carries on a trade on the strength of his licence has nothing in the world to do with the owner who grants the licence. It does not convert him for tax purposes into a person carrying on a trade. The fact that the land is peculiarly suitable for carrying on the trade whether under lease or a licence will, or should in the long run, be reflected in the annual value for tax purposes.[43] If, for instance, a person owns a piece of land contiguous to a racecourse where there is great demand for parking accommodation, the existence of the demand should in theory be reflected sooner or later in an increased assessment for Schedule A. But I cannot see on what principle the profit which the person in question makes from granting temporary licences to park motor cars on the land can be said not to be covered by the Schedule A assessment, but to fall under Case I or Case VI of Schedule D. If, on the other hand, more is done than the mere granting of licences, for example, if the cars are washed or repairs effected, the profits realised by those activities will clearly fall outside Schedule A. I cannot find in any one of the Company's activities anything but the exercise and exploitation of its rights of property. If the grant of one licence is merely an exercise of such rights I cannot see that the grant of half-a-dozen licences bears a different character."
>
> That seems to me exactly to cover the present case. I cannot in this case find in any one of the company's activities anything but the exercise and exploitation of its rights of property. **[12.7]**

See also *Griffiths v. Jackson*,[44] where, in relation to the business of letting furnished flats and rooms, Vinelott J stated:

> 'It is not too easy to see why in the modern world a business consisting of the exploitation of the right of property in land should be treated differently from a business consisting of the exploitation of other assets. However, the principle is now too deeply embedded in the law to be altered except by legislation.'

The position with respect to furnished lettings has now changed, so that all lettings of property, including furnished lettings where the rent includes the use of furniture, are within the ITTOIA, Pt 3 charge.[45] The particular case of furnished holiday lettings is discussed below, para **[12.19]**. **[12.8]**

B. *Scope of the rules*

(1) 'Other receipts'

The charge to tax under ITTOIA 2005, Pt 2 is on the profits of a taxpayer's property business, which consists of 'every business which the person carries

42 15 TC 266 [and above, para **[7.15]**].
43 [The former Schedule A charged tax on the annual value of the land that was being exploited for income purposes.]
44 (1983) TC 583.
45 ITTOIA 2005, s 308.

on for generating income from land . . .'[46] 'Generating income from land' means 'exploiting an estate, interest or right in or over land as a source of rents or other receipts'.[47] The most common type of income within this charge is undoubtedly the profit derived from the business of letting property, but other payments are also caught. For example, capital payments made by a tenant to his landlord on the grant of a lease, known as lease premiums are treated as payments of rent (see below, para **[12.12]**). Further, the legislation itself expressly provides for the taxation of profits arising from income receipts other than rent, but without specifying the exact nature of these 'other receipts.' **[12.9]**

Lowe v JW Ashmore Ltd [1971] Ch 545 (Ch D)

MEGARRY J: . . . The case arises out of the taking of turf from the Company's farm by two other companies (which I shall call "the contractors") from fields chosen by them, at a price of £75 per acre, during the two years ended March 31, 1965, under informal oral contracts. A letter from one of the contractors dated September 3, 1964, to which I shall later refer more fully, referred to "two inch thick turf," and the case has been argued on the footing that this was what was taken. The Company had done only normal farming work prior to the removal of the turf, and it was removed by the contractors without any supervision by the Company. After the turf had gone the Company ploughed the land and drilled it with corn. The turf was taken once and for all, says the Case, and the Company was not producing turf for resale. The initiative for the sale of the turf came not from the Company but from the contractors: the Company had no thoughts of selling the turf until approached by the contractors. The Company was then in difficulties about obtaining labour for its dairy herd, but the Company's immediate reason for the sale was to obtain more capital. Eventually the Company might have ploughed the land . . .

Put in the shortest possible way, the question is whether or not the sums received are free from liability for income tax as being sums of a capital nature resulting from a partial realisation of the freehold, or whether they are liable to income tax in the sense that they fall to be taken into account in computing the farming profits, or, in the case of the Case VIII[48] assessment, as income from property. The General Commissioners decided the case in favour of the Company in these words:

> "We, the Commissioners who heard the appeals, on the facts of this particular case upheld the contention of the Respondent on the grounds that the turf in question formed part of the freehold and accordingly that the sums received from the contractors were of a capital nature which were not assessable."

From that decision the Crown now appeals . . .

I now turn to Case VIII. This arises under the Finance Act 1963, s. 15.[49] By virtue of ss. 14 and 20, this provision in effect replaced the Income Tax Act 1952, s. 179, as from April 6, 1964, and so applied to the first year. The Finance Act 1963, s. 15(1), provides that Schedule D tax is to be charged

> "on the annual profits or gains arising in respect of any such rents or receipts as follow, that is to say – (*a*) rents under leases of land in the United Kingdom; (*b*) rentcharges, ground annuals and feu duties, and any other annual payments reserved in respect of, or charged on or issuing out of, such land; (*c*) other receipts arising to a person from,

46 ITTOIA 2005, s 264 (for a UK property business) and s 265 (for an overseas property business).
47 *Ibid*, s 266 (1).
48 [Case VIII, Schedule D was the predecessor to a former Schedule A, which taxed the annual profits and gains derived from certain rents and other receipts arising from the ownership of land or an interest in the land.]
49 [This was succeeded by ICTA 1988, s 15 relating to Schedule A, now replaced by ITTOIA 2005, Pt 3.]

> or by virtue of, his ownership of an estate or interest in or right over such land or any incorporeal hereditament or incorporeal heritable subject in the United Kingdom . . ."

The words "other receipts arising to a person from, or by virtue of, his ownership of an estate or interest in or right over . . . land" in s. 15(1)(c) are wide, general and devoid of authority. Mr. Templeman's submission *[Mr. Templeman appeared for the Crown]* that these words covered the sale of turves in this case fell under two heads: first, the wide and general nature of the language, and second, the indications provided by the Finance Act 1963, s. 28(3).[50] Under the first head, he says that the payments were undoubted receipts from the sale of turves and these plainly came to the Company from or by virtue of its ownership of the fee simple in the farm (which I infer was the interest bought). It was only by virtue of the Company's ownership of that estate in the farm that the Company was able to authorise the contractors to take what they paid for. Mr Walton's reply was that it was absurd to say that these words applied to what was a sale of part of the ownership, for the language of the subsection implied that the ownership was being retained.

. . . In the absence of any explicit finding of fact on the point, I refuse to infer that the intention of the parties was to carry through any such transaction, particularly as there are alternative ways of giving effect to what they agreed which avoids these extravagances. In particular, I am quite unable to see why contractors who merely want the turves should wish to have a fee simple in anything, least of all in the air space which the turves left behind them, or why the Company should desire to sell the turves in a way that would leave much of their land in perpetuity beneath an alien pall.

There is, however, a further point. Mr. Templeman referred me to Halsbury's Laws of England,[51] where a *profit a prendre* is defined as "a right to take something off the land of another person."

. . . As for the definition of a profit as a right to take something off the land of another, it is clear that this indeed it is. But the converse does not hold: not all such rights are profits. To be a profit the right must be a right to take part of the land or the creatures on it; what is taken must, when taken, be susceptible of ownership; and the right must be created by a transaction capable of creating an interest in land. A profit in the soil giving the right to take sand, gravel and so on is a well-known form of profit, and so is a profit of turbary, giving the right to dig and take turf or peat for fuel. Either form may exist as appurtenant or, at all events when limited to a defined quantity, in gross. In this case the right to take the turf seems to me to be aptly described as being, or being in the nature of, a *profit a prendre* in gross. However, the agreement recorded in the letter of 3rd September provided for the turf to be removed by the end of March 1965, so that the right granted was for a limited period. This, coupled with the informality of the transaction, gives ground for inferring that there was no intention to create any interest in the land at all, but merely to create a contractual obligation and right to enter the land, sever the turf and keep it, being thus a form of contract for the sale of goods: see, for instance *Kursell v. Timber Operators and Contractors Ltd.*[52] which concerned Latvian timber. From Mr. Templeman's point of view it does not matter much whether the correct classification is *profit a prendre* or sale of goods; his concern is that there should be no estate or interest in the unsevered turf. I think that it is clear that the evidence adduced does not begin to support any contention that the contractors owned in equity any estate or interest in the unsevered turf greater than at most an equitable *profit a prendre*. It accordingly does not need to be resolved whether the right is correctly classified as a profit or as a contract to enter, sever and take, and so I do not resolve it.

Before I turn to certain authorities, I must deal with Mr. Templeman's second submission under this head, based on the indications provided by the Finance Act 1963, s. 28(3).[53] This reads as follows:

> "Profits or gains in any year of assessment from payments for any easement over or right to use any land made to the person who occupies the land shall not be excluded

50 [See below, pp. 409–410.]
51 (3rd edn, 1955), Vol. 12. [See now (4th edn, 1975) vol 14.]
52 [1927] 1 KB 298.
53 [Later ICTA 1988, s 15(3), repealed by FA 1988, Sch 14, Pt V.]

> from the charge to tax under Case VIII by reason only that he is chargeable with respect to the land under Schedule B,[54] but shall be treated for purposes of Case VIII as limited to the amount (if any) by which they exceed the assessable value of the land or, as the case may be, by which they exceed such proportion of that value as corresponds to the proportion of the year for which he occupies the land."

This subsection makes it plain, Mr. Templeman says, that "profits or gains arising . . . from payments for any easement over or right to use any land made to the person who occupies the land" are assumed to fall within Case VIII, so that this explains, to some extent the words of s. 15(1)(*c*) with which this case is concerned. Mr. Walton, on the other hand, says that as s. 28(3) was concerned only with woodlands under Schedule B, it throws little light on s. 15(1)(*c*). That, however, does not seem to me to meet the point that the assumption made by s. 28(3) supports Mr. Templeman's contention. Mr. Walton also contended that the *ejusdem generis* principle applied, so that "other receipts" in s. 15(1)(c) meant other receipts of the same kind as the rents, rentcharges, ground annuals and feu duties in s. 15(1)(*a*) and (*b*), the genus being repetitive payments. This contention, however, seems to ignore the wording of the latter part of s. 15(1)(*b*). That paragraph, as I have already mentioned, refers to "rentcharges, ground annuals and feu duties, and any other annual payments reserved in respect of, or charged on or issuing out of, such land." The words "any other annual payments" seem to me both to attract and to exhaust the *ejusdem generis* principle of construction, so that the words "other receipts" with which s. 15(1)(*c*) begins accordingly mean receipts other than those previously specified or *ejusdem generis* with them.

The expression "profits or gains arising . . . from payments for any easement over or right to use any land made to the person who occupies the land" formerly appeared verbatim in the Income Tax Act 1952, s. 179, and before that in the Finance Act 1948, s. 31(1). The authorities on these provisions show that "the right to use any land" was construed as including all *profits a prendre*. At first sight it is somewhat surprising that the words "right to use any land" should embrace every *profit a prendre*, for some of such rights allow part of the land to be removed. The right to "use" something hardly seems to permit the destruction or removal of part of that something, as in the case of a profit of turbary or a profit in the soil. In such cases it might be contended that more is involved than the mere use of land. Other profits leave the land intact, as in the familiar profit of pasture, where the beasts merely take by their mouths the grass that grows on the land, or rights of sporting, whereunder game is taken. However, in *Smethurst v. Davy*[55] the Court of Appeal applied what had been said by the House of Lords in *Russell v. Scott*[56] and held that the digging of sand and gravel was a "right to use land" within the Finance Act 1948, s. 31(1). In the words of Lord Evershed MR, at page 606, it was "neither sensible nor practicable" to divide *profits a prendre* into two categories. In effect, profits which did not involve the removal of any of the land, and so could readily be held to be comprehended within the phrase "right to use land," were treated as drawing with them into the grasp of the phrase other profits which, since they allowed the removal of part of the land, less readily fell within the word "use." In this way, on Mr. Templeman's argument, the right to remove the turves is a "right to use land," and s. 28(3) shows that this is within the wide language of s. 15(1)(*c*).

. . . In my judgment, the payments that the Company received from the contractors for the turf were, after allowing for expenses, within the words "annual profits or gains arising in respect of any such . . . receipts as follow, that is to say . . . receipts arising to a person from, or by virtue of, his ownership of an estate or interest in or right over such land," that is, land in the United Kingdom. This seems to me to be wide and relatively simple language and I do not find the attempt to cut down its meaning at all persuasive. In particular, I think

54 [The taxation of woodlands under Schedule B was abolished in 1988. In order to prevent the claiming of losses, woodlands occupied on a commercial basis are not taxed either as property income under ITTOIA 2005, Pt 3 nor under ITTOIA 2005, Pt 2 (trading income). Note, however, that profits arising from the trees themselves are taxable under Pt 2, with relief being given for any losses.]

55 (1957) 37 TC 593.

56 [1948] AC 422.

that s. 28(3) indicates that easements and rights to use land fall within s. 15(1). In a difficult case, involving complex questions of law, and without the aid of all the authorities put before me, I think the Commissioners have erred in law and have reached a conclusion not supported by the evidence. I accordingly allow the appeal both on Case I and Case VIII. . . **[12.10]**

The issue in this case remains relevant today despite the change to the taxation of property income, since receipts other than rents currently include 'payments in respect of the exercise of any . . . right *[other than a licence for the occupation or use of land]* over land'.[57] See also *McClure v Petre,*[58] where a sum was paid in compensation for the reduction in the value of land after soil excavated during the construction of a motorway had been tipped on it under a licence granted by the taxpayer. Browne-Wilkinson V-C held this sum to be a capital receipt. John Tiley gives as examples of 'other receipts' 'licence fees for advertisements hoardings, parking fees and service charges which are not reserved as rent, provided they are not in respect of services constituting a trade'.[59] **[12.11]**

(2) Lease premiums

Rents and other like payments are payments of an income nature. On the other hand, a premium is a capital 'sum paid by the tenant to the landlord in consideration of the grant of the lease.'[60] Prior to the introduction in 1965 of capital gains tax, a landlord could have avoided paying income tax under the former Schedule A by taking a premium instead of rent from a tenant, with no possibility of a capital gains tax charge either. In the case of a lease for a short term, the effect of a lease at a low premium (or none at all) and a high rent is really no different from that of a lease at a high premium and a correspondingly reduced rent. In consequence, provisions were introduced in 1963[61] whereby a premium granted under a short lease[62] was to be treated, in part, as rent. **[12.12]**

Final Report of the Royal Commission on the Taxation of Profits and Income Cmd 9474 (1955)

Nature of the problem

851. Over the years there has been considerable controversy regarding the appropriate tax treatment of a premium paid in order to secure a lease of property. The payer acquires an asset of limited life but receives no tax relief in respect of it. A man who lets property at a premium forgoes the whole or part of the rent he might otherwise have received over the term of the lease, and the premium which he receives instead is normally treated as a capital receipt not subject to taxation. It has long been asked whether a lessee should not receive some relief for his wasting

57 ITTOIA 2005, s 266(3)(b).
58 [1988] STC 749.
59 John Tiley *Revenue Law* (5th edn, 2005), p 537.
60 *Clarke v United Real (Moorgate) Ltd* [1988] STC 273 at 299 (per Walton J).
61 Now ITTOIA 2005, s 277.
62 For these purposes, a short lease is one granted for a period not exceeding 50 years.

asset and it is also a question whether a lessor should be required to include his receipt in his taxable income...

865. One line of approach is to enquire: What is the real nature of a premium? For if it is rent in advance, as it is sometimes called, there would be a strong theoretical argument for making the recipient of the premium liable to an equivalent share of the tax on the income of the land and for giving a corresponding measure of relief to the payer.

866. We do not think it possible to assert that a premium can be categorised as rent in advance. If paid in respect of a very short term of lease, it is no doubt practically indistinguishable from rent: if paid in respect of a long term, it has no natural equivalence with rent: and if afforded in kind not in money, as in the case of buildings or improvements to buildings, it is not like rent at all. And even if a premium for the grant of a lease could be treated as rent in advance, it would be a great deal more difficult to say that a sum paid to purchase the assignment of a lease is rent. Therefore we consider that a premium is best treated as a sum of money paid upon a sale, the thing bought being the beneficial right or part of the beneficial right of occupation for the period of years in question. From this point of view the transaction differs in degree, but not in substance, from the purchase and sale for freehold, which is the right of beneficial occupation in perpetuity. **[12.13]**

The Report states the problem, and concludes that lease premiums should continue to be treated as being of a capital nature. However, at that time, income tax on land was related to the annual value of land; when, later, the charge related instead to the profits from land or to the actual rental income, there could be no further justification for the Report's conclusion. In contrast, a gain accruing on the *assignment*, as opposed to the *grant* of a lease is assessable to capital gains tax rather than income tax.

More recently, Lightman J in *Hurlingham Estates Ltd v Wilde & Partners* echoed the sentiments of the Law Commission and Scottish Law Commission (see extract, below) in drawing attention to the complexity of the provisions relating to the taxation of lease premiums by speaking of the 'concealed trap for the unwary'.[63] **[12.14]**

Report of the Law Commission and the Scottish Law Commission, *Taxation of Income and Gains Derived from Land* Cmnd 4654 (1971)

18. A premium for the grant of a lease exceeding 50 years is regarded for tax purposes as a wholly capital payment and receipt; but a premium paid for a lease of any lesser duration is treated as containing a rental element, and this element is taxable under Schedule A[64] as if it were rent payable in the year of grant (section 80).[65] Certain other sums are treated as premiums for this purpose ...

20. These provisions are by no means simple and it was represented to us that if Capital Gains Tax had existed in 1963 they might never have been enacted. We think, however, that it would be going too far to abolish the taxation of premiums

63 [1997] STC 627 at 634. The claimant in this case sought damages against the defendant firm of solicitors for failing to advise that a transaction structured by them would give rise to a charge to tax under these provisions.

64 This refers to the former Schedule A.

65 Now ITTOIA 2005, ss 276–279.

(as income) altogether: a premium for a very short lease is not sensibly distinguishable from rent in advance and should be taxed as such at income tax rates.

21. An alternative method of taxing premiums would be to provide that those for terms not exceeding X years wholly constitute payments of rent chargeable under Schedule A (thus excluding any charge to Capital Gains Tax); premiums for longer terms being treated as wholly capital, outside the scope of Schedule A.

22. This alternative method would seriously affect the revenue yield if X were pitched too short, and it would be hard on the taxpayer if it were too long . . .there is no doubt that a change in the law in favour of this alternative method would represent a considerable simplification and *we RECOMMEND it*. Because of the conflicting considerations, we do not make any positive recommendations as to the term which we have called X, but if the change is to win general acceptance we think that X would have to lie in the 7–10 years range. **[12.15]**

These recommendations have never been adopted, and the charge continues to be on a proportion of the premium, rather than on the whole amount, where the lease upon which it is taken does not exceed 50 years.

C. *Exceptions to the charge*

The occupation of land is specifically excluded from the property income charge by ITTOIA 2005, s 267. This means that an occupier of land is not charged to tax under ITTOIA 2005, Pt 3 on the value of that occupation; it is the *generation of income* from the land that forms the basis of the charge.[66] Despite this move away from taxing the mere occupation of land for the purpose of ITTOIA 2005, Pt 3, it has emerged in a different context. **[12.16]**

Geoffrey Morse and David Williams *Davies: Principles of Tax Law* (5th edn, 2004), p 107

An occupation tax returns?

Schedule 15 to the Finance Act 2004 contains provisions that bring back a form of income tax on the occupation of property as an anti-avoidance measure. A practice developed of seeking to avoid inheritance tax by an older person passing his or her ownership of the family home (and often its contents) to younger members of the family, subject to a right to continue living in it. Schedule 15 seeks to impose income tax on the taxable amount that accrues from the continuing benefit to the donor of such a transfer. Where the property was transferred since March 1986, the donor becomes, under Schedule 15, liable to income tax on the rental value of the property. In other words, the donor is assumed for income tax purposes to be

66 Profits may nevertheless arise from the occupation of land, which are taxed under another source. For example, in *Jaggers v Ellis* [1996] STC 440, a case concerning the former Schedule B, which taxed the occupation of woodlands, the Special Commissioners held that the profits from Christmas tree operations were taxable under the former Schedule D, Case I (trading income), since the source of the profits was the planting and cultivation of Christmas trees and not the occupation of the woodland *per se*.

receiving the value of the rent that would be paid to live in the house. This is a clear echo of the old Schedule B,[67] which was in its heyday a tax on the value of occupying property, based on the rental value. **[12.17]**

The profits and gains arising from farming and market gardening,[68] mines and quarries,[69] mineral rent and royalties,[70] and miscellaneous income receipts from, for example, wayleaves or tolls, which are received after deduction of basic rate income tax,[71] are also specifically excluded from the property income charge under s 267.

Although the letting of overseas property[72] is treated as a separate trade, rental income accruing to UK residents from land situated outside of the UK is within the Pt 3 charge,[73] and the profits are computed in the same way as those arising from UK property. **[12.18]**

D. *Furnished holiday lettings*

The commercial letting of furnished holiday accommodation is treated as a property business rather than as a trade, with the profits assessable under ITTOIA 2005, Pt 3.[74] However, certain benefits that are normally only enjoyed in respect of trading profits also apply to the profits from furnished holiday lettings.[75] Thus, in addition to the income being treated as earned income, which is relevant income for pension purposes,[76] the rules, which 'may be seen as recognition of the artificial nature of the division between property income and trading income',[77] also allow for the following: loss relief as for trades,[78] capital allowances,[79] CGT rollover relief,[80] CGT relief for business assets,[81] relief for pre-trading expenditure.[82] Moreover, expenditure is deductible as if the letting were a trade.[83]

The conditions that must be satisfied for a letting to qualify as a 'furnished holiday letting' prevent a second (or indeed third etc.) home from being dressed up as a commercial enterprise in order to attract the above reliefs. **[12.19]**

John Tiley *Revenue Law* (5th edn, 2005) p 543

Stringent conditions must be satisfied before a letting is treated as a furnished holiday letting. The property must be in the UK, the letting must be on a commercial

67 Schedule B was a charge on the occupation of woodlands; see n. 53.
68 The activities of farming and market gardening are treated as the carrying on of a trade: ITTOIA 2005, s 9.
69 These are charged to tax as trading profits under ITTOIA 2005, s 12.
70 These are taxed half as income of a trade and half as capital; see ITTOIA 2005, s 340.
71 See ITTOIA 2005, s 335.
72 Not within the charge to tax under the former Schedule A.
73 ITTOIA 2005, s 265.
74 ITTOIA 2005, Pt 6.
75 ITTOIA 2005, s 322(2).
76 ITTOIA 2005, ss 322(2), 328.
77 John Tiley, n 58 at p 543.
78 ITTOIA 2005, ss 322(2), 327 and see Chapter 10, above, para **[10.60]**.
79 See Chapter 10, above, paras **[10.63]–[10.71]**.
80 See Chapter 20, below, para **[20.59]**.
81 See Chapter 20, below, para **[20.59]**.
82 See Chapter 10, above, para **[10.23]**.
83 ICTA 1988, s 503(5), and see Chapter 10, above, para **[10.23]**.

basis and with a view to the realisation of profit, the tenant must be entitled to the use of the furniture and the property must be qualifying holiday accommodation.[84] The property must be available for letting to the general public during the season and available for not less than 140 days, it must be let for at least 70 days and, for a period of at least seven months, it must not normally be in the same occupation for continuous periods exceeding 31 days. Where these conditions are fulfilled in relation to one property but not another, the taxpayer may elect to have the properties averaged.[85] Thus, if property 1 is let for 80 days and property 2 for 68 days, an averaging election will make both properties let for 74 days, so that both will qualify. **[12.20]**

E. Permissible expenditure

The profits of a property business are calculated in the same way as the profits of a trade,[86] and depend, broadly, on generally accepted accounting practice. Accordingly, the trading income principles discussed in Chapter 10 apply equally to property income. Under these principles, items of expenditure incurred wholly and exclusively for the purposes of a property business are deductible provided they are of an income nature and not prohibited by statute.[87] In practice, this means that costs incurred in maintaining, repairing, insuring or managing a property and payments made by the taxpayer in the form of rates, rent to a superior landlord and similar payments are deductible. **[12.21]**

Report of the Law Commission and the Scottish Law Commission *Taxation of Income and Gains derived from Land* Cmnd 4654 (1971)

31. It is not unusual for difficulties to arise in connection with the deduction of expenditure in respect of deferred repairs to property which has been recently acquired. The problem is of a general nature, and is by no means limited to the field of Schedule A: indeed, the principal authorities relate to the computation of trading profits under Schedule D. The leading case of *Law Shipping Co. Ltd. v. IRC*[88] has generally been taken to establish the proposition that a purchaser may not deduct expenditure incurred to make good dilapidations referable to the period of the previous ownership. This is supported on two grounds: first, that such expenditure is not sufficiently related to the earning of the purchaser's profits from which the deduction is sought; and, secondly, that although expenditure on repairs is prima facie of a revenue nature, in such circumstances it should be treated as an outgoing on capital account as an addition to the purchase price of the asset. So far as Schedule A is concerned, it seems that statutory force has been given to this view – section 72(2)(*b*).[89]

84 ITTOIA ss. 323–325.
85 ITTOIA s. 326.
86 *Ibid*, s 272.
87 *Ibid*, Pt 2, Ch 5 contains the rules allowing for the deductibility of trading expenses. See Chapter 10, above, para **[10.23]**.
88 1924 SC 74; 12 TC 621.
89 [The successor provision, ICTA 1988, s 25 was repealed by FA 1998, s 165 when the basis for the taxation of land changed to a 'property income business' and with the consequent adoption, for computation purposes, of the rules for trading income.]

32. In the recent case of *Odeon Associated Theatres Ltd. v. Jones,*[90] however, Pennycuick V.-C. held that certain deferred repairs referable to the pre-acquisition period were deductible in computing the purchaser's trading profits. In that case the nature of the repairs was not such that they had to be carried out before the assets were commercially viable in the purchaser's hands and the *Law Shipping* case was distinguished on that ground, and on the ground that in the earlier case there had been no evidence of accountancy practice. **[12.22]**

The Law Shipping Co Ltd v IRC (1924) 12 TC 621 (CS)

THE LORD PRESIDENT (CLYDE): ... In December 1919, the Appellants bought for £97,000 a ship, built in 1906, which was at the time of the purchase ready to sail with freight booked. The periodical survey of the ship was then considerably overdue; indeed, for the purposes of the voyage about to commence, exemption from survey had had to be obtained. When the ship returned from the voyage she underwent survey, and the purchaser had to expend a sum of £51,558 on repairs (in addition to certain further expenditure of an admittedly capital nature).

The assessment appealed against is for Excess Profits Duty and is made in terms of section 47 of the Finance Act 1916, which specially deals with the case of ships changing hands by purchase. Accordingly, the pre-war profits are calculated with reference to the profits arising from the use of the ship by the purchasers' predecessors during the pre-war trade years.

As required by section 40 of the Finance (No. 2) Act 1915, the *purchasers' own profits* during the accounting period fall to be determined on the same principles as those upon which the profits and gains of their business would be determined for the purpose of Income Tax, subject to the modification contained in Part I of the Fourth Schedule to the said Act. By paragraph 3 of Part I it is enacted: "Deductions for wear and tear, or for any expenditure of a capital nature for renewals, or for the development of the trade or business ... shall not be allowed except such as may be allowed under the Income Tax Acts ..."

The whole question in the case is as to the admissibility of the above mentioned repair account of £51,558 as a deduction in the determination of the purchasers' profits; and it will be seen from the foregoing narrative that that question really turns on the Income Tax Act 1918, and particularly Rule 3 of Cases I and II of Schedule D of that Act.

The expense laid out in keeping a ship, which is employed in trade, in proper repair is certainly an expense necessary for the purposes of the trade. It is made for the purpose of earning the profits of the trade. Repairs may be executed as the occasion for them occurs; or, if they are such as brook delay, they may be postponed to a convenient season: but, in either case, they truly constitute a constantly recurring incident of that continuous employment of the ship which makes them necessary. They are therefore an admissible deduction in computing profits, and, as is admitted in the case, if the ship had not been sold, the purchasers' predecessors would have been entitled to deduct the whole of the £51,558 in returning their profits for Income Tax. Accumulated arrears for repairs are, in short, none the less repairs necessary to earn profits, although they have been allowed to accumulate.

In the present case, however, the accumulation of repairs, represented by the expenditure of £51,558 required to overtake them, was an accumulation which extended partly over a period during which the ship was employed, not in the purchasers' trade, but in that of the purchasers' predecessors. And the question relates to the computation of the *purchasers' profits only*.

The purchasers started their trade with a ship already in need of extensive repairs. The need was not so clamant as to make it impossible to employ her (as she stood at the time

90 [1971] 1 WLR 442, [1971] 2 All ER 407. The decision was affirmed by the Court of Appeal [1972] 2 WLR 331.

of the purchase) in the voyage she was then about to commence. So much is clear from the fact that she was allowed exemption from survey for the purposes of that voyage. But, while, some portion of the repairs executed after her return was no doubt attributable to her employment in the purchasers' trade between the date of their purchase and the return of the ship – and while such portion was therefore necessary to the earning of profits by them in that and subsequent voyages – it seems plain that a large portion of them was attributable solely to her employment by the purchasers' predecessors, in whose profits the purchasers had no interest whatever. The admissibility of deduction of the latter thus appears to be negatived by the terms of Rule 3(a) of Cases I and II.

It is obvious that a ship, on which repairs have been allowed to accumulate, is a less valuable capital asset with which to start business than a ship which has been regularly kept in repair. And it is a fair inference that the sellers would have demanded and obtained a higher price than they actually did, but for the immediate necessity of repairs to which the ship was subject when they put her in the market. The additional gains they had made by postponing repairs were thus counter-balanced by the diminished value of the ship on realisation; but it is not relevant to the question of the extent of the purchasers' assessibility to Income Tax on their own profits, that the Revenue may have gained by the inflation of the profits of their predecessors consequent on the postponement of repairs which – if regularly made – would have diminished them.

Again, when the purchasers started trade with the ship, the capital they required was not limited to the price paid to acquire her, but included the cost of the arrears of repairs which their predecessors had allowed to accumulate; because, while their own trading with her would – in ordinary course – provide a revenue out of which the repairs incidental to such trading would be met, it would be unreasonable and abnormal – in any commercial sense – to saddle such trading with the burden of arrears of repairs incidental to the trading of their predecessors from which the purchasers derived no benefit. If the purchasers had "succeeded to the trade" of their predecessors within the meaning of Rule 11 of Cases I and II of Schedule D, the case would have been otherwise; but this view of the purchasers' relation to the sellers is excluded by the case of *Watson Bros. v. Lothian*[91] mentioned in the Case.

The Commissioners have allowed deduction of £12,000 (out of the £51,558) as being in their view of the facts applicable to the period during which the purchasers were owners of the ship, and to the extent of the £12,000 thus allowed I think the Company is entitled to deduction, but not to the extent of the whole £51,558. **[12.23]**

Odeon Associated Theatres Ltd v Jones [1972] 2 WLR 331 (CA); above, para [10.8]

The taxpayer company bought a number of cinemas, some of which, at the time of purchase, were fairly run down because the previous owners had been unable to spend sufficient money on keeping them in repair owing to restrictions in place during the war years. Despite this, at the time of acquisition, the cinemas were effective profit-earning assets, and the price paid by the taxpayer had not been reduced by reason of the lack of repair. During a nine-year period following acquisition, the taxpayer spent considerable sums of money on the cinemas, including expenditure on deferred repairs and renewals charged to its accounts as revenue. The issue was whether such expenditure was income, and thus deductible, or capital.

BUCKLEY LJ:... First, all the disputed expenditure was of a kind which, if the theatres had remained in the ownership of the owners from whom they were acquired by the taxpayer company and the expenditure had been incurred by those owners, would have been deductible as revenue expenditure. Secondly, the amount of dilapidation which occurred

91 (1902) 4 T.C. 441.

before the acquisition by the taxpayer company of a theatre (in the case stated called "deferred repairs") did not in any case significantly affect the price paid by the taxpayer company for the theatre. Thirdly, the deferred repairs were not for the most part such as to require immediate remedy, and there was no question of danger to the public or of any theatre having to be closed for repairs. Fourthly, all cinema theatre owners were in a like position of being unable, on account of wartime restrictions, to carry out any but the most urgent repairs, redecorations or refurnishing of their theatres; there was no competition in this respect: this state of affairs continued until the early 1950s.

The cost of acquiring or creating the physical capital asset for use in a trade or business is clearly capital expenditure. The cost of improving such an asset by adding to it or modifying it may well be capital expenditure. On the other hand, the cost of works of recurrent repair or maintenance of such an asset attributable to wear and tear occurring in the course of use of the asset in his trade or business by the person carrying out the works is revenue expenditure, and so constitutes a proper debit item in the profit and loss account of the business. Whether, where there has been a change of ownership, the cost of works of repair or maintenance attributable to wear and tear which occurred before the change of ownership should be regarded as revenue expenditure or capital expenditure is a question the answer to which must, in my opinion, depend on the particular facts of each case. The Solicitor-General has argued that any repair must improve the article repaired and, avoiding undue cynicism, I think that proposition must be accepted. He says further that if the state of the article, when repaired, is better that its state was when it was acquired by the person carrying out the repairs, the cost of the repairs should pro tanto be regarded as capital expenditure. A tradesman, for example, who acquires a dilapidated shop in which to carry on his business, and, either before he commences business or as soon thereafter as he can afford to do so, puts the shop into a state of repair and decoration suitable for his business, has incurred the cost not only of acquiring the shop but also of repairing and decorating it in a suitable manner in order to provide himself with a capital asset of a character which he regards as appropriate to his business. The whole of this expenditure, it is said, is capital expenditure because it constitutes the cost of acquiring such a capital asset as the trader requires for the purpose of his business. The argument is an attractive one, but should not, in my opinion, be accepted without careful consideration.

The Solicitor-General contends that the expenditure on deferred repairs was what he described as "a once and for all jacking-up of the value of the principal asset," and so was non-recurrent expenditure by the taxpayer company for the enduring benefit of its trade. He says that the fact that the prices paid for theatres took no account of the circumstances that at the dates of purchase repairs had already been deferred is of no importance. He contends that the cost of doing the deferred repairs was an additional cost to the taxpayer company of acquiring the capital assets, that is, the theatres. Such expenditure, he says, should be regarded as capital expenditure. As Lord Reid observed in *Strick v. Regent Oil Co. Ltd.*[92]

> "The question *[whether a particular outlay can be set against income or must be regarded as a capital outlay]* is ultimately a question of law for the court, but it is a question which must be answered in light of all the circumstances which it is reasonable to take into account, and the weight which must be given to a particular circumstance in a particular case must depend rather on common sense than on strict application of any single legal principle."

In answering that question of law, it is right that the court should pay regard to ordinary principles of commercial accounting so far as applicable. Accountants are, after all, the persons best qualified by training and practical experience to suggest answers to the many difficult problems that can arise in this field. Nevertheless the question remains ultimately a question of law.

No one, I think, would dispute that the cost of ordinary current repairs in the normal course of maintenance of a fixed capital asset employed in a business is revenue expenditure. Such cost arises out of the wear and tear of the asset in the course of

92 [1966] AC 295 at 313.

earning the profits of the business and so is a proper debit to be set against the revenue of the business in its profit and loss account. I would myself think that, save in exceptional circumstances, this is true even in the case of the first repairs in the normal course of maintenance of an asset acquired in a part worn condition. A tradesman who acquires a shop, the outside painting of which was last done two years before his purchase, will have to repaint the shop earlier than if it had been redecorated immediately before acquisition, but this, I think, is something which, as a commercial matter, he will take into account in considering the prospective profitability of the shop during the early years of his ownership. In other words, he will regard it as a revenue expense. He will not say to himself: "When I have to repaint the outside of the shop perhaps three years hence, only three-fifths of the cost will be chargeable against revenue in my profit and loss account: the balance will be a capital investment in my business."

The *Law Shipping* case is, in my view, more nearly analogous to the case of a trader who has bought a capital asset which at the date of acquisition was not in working order and has to put it into working order before being able to use it in his business. When the Law Shipping Co. bought the ship they knew that in order to be able to use her in their business beyond the one voyage they would need to spend not only the purchase price of the ship but also the cost of the necessary repairs. The facts of the present case are quite different. **[12.24]**

These two decisions concern the deductibility of expenditure in calculating trading profits for the purpose of the former Case I of Schedule D (now ITTOIA 2005, Pt 2), which issue is discussed in Chapter 10.[93] However, the cases are of special importance to the problem of deductibility of expenditure on repairs. *Odeon Associated Theatres* is considered by G S A Wheatcroft 'The Law Shipping Rule Eroded' [1972] BTR 51. As to the relevance of accounting evidence, see Chapter 10, above, para **[10.2]**. See also P F Smith 'Repair or Renewal' [1982] BTR 360. **[12.25]**

2. Rent-a-room relief

Rent-a-room relief is given under ITTOIA 2005, Ch 7, and is thus distinct from the property income provisions discussed above. **[12.26]**

Natalie Lee (gen ed) *Revenue Law: Principles and Practice* (24th edn, 2006) pp 291–292

Designed as a tax incentive to encourage owner-occupiers and tenants who have a spare room in their home to let it out, gross annual rents not exceeding £4,250 are exempt from income tax. The following conditions must be satisfied:

(1) relief is available to *individuals* on a letting of *furnished* accommodation;
(2) the individual does not derive any taxable income other than rent-a-room receipts from a relevant trade, letting or agreement;
(3) the letting must be the individual's '*only or main residence*' in the '*basis period*' (ie in the current year: letting for office accommodation does not qualify);
(4) the gross income limit of £4,250 will be halved if more than one person lets rooms in the same house. A husband and wife may so arrange matters that the income is either wholly the wife's or wholly the husband's;[94]

93 See above, paras **[10.23]–[10.35]**.

94 [The reference to husband and wife now includes civil partners: the Civil Partnership Act 2004, which came into force on 5 December 2005.]

(5) the individual can elect for this exemption not to apply (he may wish to do so, for instance, in order to claim loss relief for the relevant period);
(6) if gross annual receipts exceed £4,250, the individual can choose either to pay tax in the normal way (on gross receipts less actual expenses) or, alternatively, on gross receipts less £4,250, (this is termed 'the alternative basis'). An election must be made on or before the first anniversary of the 31 January next following the year of assessment for which it is made (or such later date as the Board may allow) if the alternative basis is to apply. Such election remains in force until withdrawn. **[12.27]**

HMRC Property and Income Manual 4002: *Rent-a-room: letting as office accommodation*

There have been some suggestions in the professional press that relief could be available where a residence, or part of a residence, is used as an office or for other trade or business purposes (other than the business of providing furnished living accommodation) and sums are paid in respect of that use. We take the view that such claims are inadmissible since:

- the words of the legislation, in our opinion, do not permit such claims, and
- the legislation was never intended to give relief in such circumstances.

Where a room is used exclusively as an office or as other trade or business premises, it is no longer occupied or intended to be occupied as a separate residence – one of the conditions for rent-a-room relief. As such, it is no longer, for rent-a-room purposes, part of the 'residence' because F2A92/SCH10/PARA7 permits the identification of parts of buildings which are occupied or intended to be occupied as a residence.

Rent-a-room relief can only apply where 'relevant sums' accrue in respect of the use of 'furnished accommodation' in a 'qualifying residence'. The Act does not define 'accommodation' which should therefore take its everyday meaning. The dictionary meaning of 'accommodation' is 'lodgings' or 'a place to live' and in our opinion, the normal unqualified meaning of 'accommodation' is 'living accommodation'. Consequently, even if an entire residence, or part of a residence, is used as trade or business premises and payments are made in respect of that use, we take the view that rent-a-room relief will not be due. The payments will not have been made in respect of the use of living accommodation as such.

The Standing Committee debate in Parliament on rent-a-room indicates that the context in which rent-a-room was being considered was that of providing additional residential accommodation and not office or business accommodation. We do not think that the legislation is ambiguous or obscure. However, should Commissioners, for example, consider that it is, then following the decision in the case of *Pepper v Hart* [1992] 65 TC 421 it may be possible for them to refer to relevant Parliamentary material. This material supports our interpretation that lettings other than furnished residential lettings are excluded from rent-a-room relief.

The foregoing does not apply to genuine lodgers such as students who are provided with study facilities in their lodgings. In such cases, we would not want to deny relief where a lodger living in the home is provided with a desk, or the use of a room with a desk, which he or she uses for work or study. **[12.28]**

3. Capturing development gains: transactions in land

The Income Tax Act 2007, Pt 13, Ch 3 contains anti-avoidance provisions, which have the effect of charging to income tax under ITTOIA 2005, Pt 2 gains of a capital nature arising on the disposal of land in certain circumstances. These circumstances are:

(a) where land, or property deriving its value from land, is acquired with the sole or main object of realising a gain from disposing of the land; or
(b) where land is held as trading stock; or
(c) where land is developed with the sole or main object of realising a gain from disposing of the land when developed.[95]

The gain need not be made by the person acquiring, holding or developing the land; it will also be caught by Pt 13, Ch 3 if it is obtained by any connected person, or any person who is concerned in any arrangement or scheme under which the gain is obtained by any indirect method, or by a series of transactions.[96]

Once entitled 'Artificial Transactions in Land', the provision does not in fact require the transaction to be artificial, and a tax avoidance motive is not a precondition to liability. **[12.29]**

Page v Lowther [1983] STC 799

Trustees were the freehold owners of land in London, including four large houses and a strip of land that formed a site suitable for redevelopment. They granted a 99-year lease to developers, who, when the new dwellings had been constructed, then granted underleases each at a premium partly payable to the trustees and partly to the developers. The total of premiums received by the trustees amounted to some £1.2m. The Court of Appeal held that the grant of the lease by the trustees to the developers was an arrangement within the term 'scheme or arrangement', and that the absence of a common purpose to avoid tax was immaterial.

> SLADE LJ: . . . I myself feel no doubt that, even having full regard to the side note *[to the relevant section]* and s. 488(1),[97] the lease of 1971 was an "arrangement" within the meaning of s. 488(2), entered into between the trustees and *[the developer]*. The trustees' task on this appeal in this context would have been much easier if s. 488 had specifically provided that a condition for the application of s. 488(2)(ii)[98] should be that the main object, or one of the main objects, of the scheme or arrangement in question was for the avoidance or reduction of liability to tax. Significantly and in contrast, the immediate preceding section, s. 487(1),[99] does contain an express provision rendering as a condition precedent to the operation of the section the existence of an object, or a main object, of such a nature.
>
> Mr Taylor *[Counsel for the taxpayer]*, however, in my opinion clearly correctly, did not feel able to submit that section 488(1), or indeed the side note, goes so far as actually to

95 ITA 2007, s 756(3).
96 *Ibid*, s 757.
97 [ICTA 1970. See now, ITA 2007, s 752(1).]
98 [See now ITA 2007, ss 752(2), 756(3).]
99 [This provision was designed to catch schemes whereby high-earning individuals such as actors, film directors and others sold a company having the exclusive rights to their services to a public company in exchange for either loan stock or shares of the public company. The idea was to avoid income tax and surtax on future earnings (at the time, up to 91.25%), and be chargeable instead to capital gains tax at a (then) maximum rate of 30% on any increase in the value of his holding of the public company. For a modern-day approach to this type of problem; see Chapter 8.

> impose any such condition precedent to the application of s. 488, additional to those conditions set out in the second sub-section. According to the wording of s. 488(5),[100] any number of transactions are capable of being regarded as constituting a single arrangement or scheme if a common purpose can be discerned in them. This sub-section does not state, and, in my opinion, it cannot be implied, that the common purpose must be that of avoiding tax. It is quite enough if the common purpose is that of enabling a gain to be realised by a person who is a party to the arrangement, as in the present case. The wording of s. 488(2)[101] does not permit the presence or absence of the motive of avoiding tax to be a relevant consideration. **[12.30]**

ITA 2007, Pt 13, Ch 3 does not apply to a capital gain made by an individual on a disposal of his principal private residence where this is exempt from capital gains tax,[102] or which would be exempt from capital gains tax but for the fact that the property was acquired with the intention of making a gain on its disposal.[103] **[12.31]**

4. Real estate investment trusts

The rise in the price of property in recent years has made it impossible for many individuals to invest in property directly. As an alternative, they may purchase shares in a property company, which invests its combined shareholders' funds in a professionally managed portfolio of properties. In such a case, the shareholders enjoy the profits of the business in the form of dividends. However, after the company's profits have been assessed to corporation tax, and the dividend has been charged to income tax in the hands of the shareholder, an individual is generally at a fiscal disadvantage by investing in property through a company rather than owning a property directly.

The effect of the new real estate investment trusts (REITs) legislation,[104] which took effect from 1 January 2007, and which was introduced 'to widen the number of investors in the residential and commercial property markets',[105] is to levy a zero tax charge on a company's profits from its property rental business,[106] including capital profits made on the sale of properties.[107] This ensures that virtually all of the profits[108] are to be distributed by way of dividends to its shareholders, resulting in fiscal neutrality between owning a property directly and owning shares in a company operating a rental business, with tax on the rental income and dividends[109] respectively being charged at the individual's marginal rate of income tax. **[12.32]**

100 [See now ITA 2007, ss 756(5), 757(3).]
101 [ITA 2007, s 757(3).]
102 Taxation of Capital Gains Act 1992, s 222; see below, para **[20.53]**.
103 TCGA 1992, s 223(3).
104 Introduced by FA 2006, ss 103–145; see now ITA 2007, ss 973, 974 for income tax purposes.
105 *Hansard*, HC Debs, vol 440, col 608 (5 December 2005).
106 FA 2006, s 119(1).
107 *Ibid*, s 123(d).
108 A minimum of 90% of profits must be distributed to the shareholders: FA 2006, s 107(8).
109 In the case of pension funds and charities, distributions may be made gross: Real Estate Investment Trusts (Assessment and Recovery of Tax Regulations 2006, SI 2006/2867, regs 7(3)(b) and (d) respectively.

13 Income Not Otherwise Charged: ITTOIA 2005, Part 5, Chapter 8 (Schedule D, Case VI)

1. Introduction

Prior to the enactment of ITTOIA 2005, which, as seen above, abolished the schedular system for income tax purposes[1], Schedule D, Case VI fulfilled a dual function. First, it was 'the residual Case in the residual Schedule'[2] which charged 'annual profits or gains' not otherwise charged,[3] and, secondly, it charged those receipts specifically directed to be charged under Schedule D, Case VI.[4] However, according to the Explanatory Notes to ITTOIA 2005, one of the features of that Act is that it 'unpacks the Schedule D Case VI charge in the source legislation to provide separate provisions for the various specific charges (routed through Case VI in the source legislation) and a pure sweep-up provision for both United Kingdom and foreign income not otherwise charged to tax while preserving the Case VI loss relief regime'.[5]

Reference is made in other Chapters to provisions introduced by ITTOIA 2005 'for the various specific charges (routed through Case VI in the source legislation)', see, for example, ITTOIA 2005, s 242 which relates to the taxation of post-cessation receipts from a trade.[6]

This Chapter is concerned with the 'pure sweep-up provision' in ITTOIA 2005, s 687. It provides that 'income tax is charged under this Chapter [8] on income from any source that is not charged to income tax under or as a result of any other provision of this Act or any other Act'.[7] The imposition of the charge on 'income' not otherwise charged rather than on 'annual profits or gains' is intended to denote simply a change of terminology rather than substance (see the extract from the Explanatory Notes set out below). Further, the reference to 'income from *any* source' not otherwise charged intimates that the territorial scope of ITTOIA 2005, s 687 may extend beyond UK sources of income.[8] Indeed, ITTOIA 2005, s 577(1) provides that, in this regard, income arising to a UK resident is chargeable to income tax whether or not it is from a source in the UK.[9] In circumstances where ITTOIA 2005,

1 See, Chapter 7, above, para **[7.1]**.
2 See John Tiley *Revenue Law* (5th edn, 2005), p 595.
3 See ICTA 1988, s 18(3).
4 Schedule D, Case VI still applies for corporation tax purposes.
5 See ITTOIA 2005, I EN, p 13, para 19.
6 See Chapter 10, above.
7 Its residual character is confirmed by the priority given to other provisions in ITTOIA 2005, s 575.
8 The sweeping-up function of Schedule D, Case VI applied to income derived from a source in the UK, because Schedule D, Case V acted as the residual charging provision in respect of 'income from possessions out of the UK'.
9 The pre-existing sweep-up functions of Schedule D, Cases V and VI have been brought together in ITTOIA 2005, s 687; see ITTOIA 2005, II EN, paras 1182–1186.

s 687 applies, income tax is charged on the full amount of the income arising in the tax year.[10]

Broadly, ITTOIA 2005, s 687 is 'meant to cope with uncertain circumstances and isolated instances'[11], and, in this respect, it is indistinguishable from Schedule D, Case VI when it was used as a sweeping-up provision in cases concerned with the imposition of a charge to income tax on a receipt or receipts of a taxpayer. Thus, the extracts from the following cases, which involved the applicability or otherwise of Schedule D, Case VI in cases concerning the taxation of individuals, are significant for the application of ITTOIA 2005, s 687. **[13.1]**

2. The meaning of income (annual profits or gains)

Explanatory Notes to the Income Tax (Trading and Other Income) Act 2005, Volume II (London, 2005)

1187. The charge under this Chapter [8] is restricted to amounts that are "income" on first principles. That is, they are "annual profits or gains" under section 18(1) of ICTA, as that phrase has been interpreted by case law, and are not profits or gains of a capital nature...

1190. ...Case law does not indicate a difference, in the context of section 18 of ICTA, in the meaning of "annual profits and gains" and "income". The choice of term appears to be dictated (although not consistently) by the degree to which a calculation of profit or loss is relevant to the calculation of the income charged.

1191. The section [687] uses *income* rather than *(annual) profits or gains*. There is nothing known which is "income" within the usual meaning of the term and therefore caught by this section but which would not be caught under Schedule D Cases V or VI. **[13.2]**

Ryall v Hoare [1923] 2 KB 447 (KBD)

ROWLATT J:... In these two cases the question for decision is whether two directors of a limited company who received sums by way of commission for guaranteeing the company's overdraft with its bankers are liable to be assessed to income tax under the Sixth Case of Sch. D[12] in respect of those commissions. The Special Commissioners for Income Tax have discharged the assessment, and from their decision the Crown appeals.

The facts are that the company, which was in want of money at the time, asked the directors to give a personal guarantee to the company's bankers in consideration of an increase from £5,000 to £10,000 in the company's overdraft. The directors, although unwilling to do this, ultimately consented. The transaction was not one in which the directors were interested as a matter of business, and one of them, who is a solicitor, declares that he never previously entered upon such a transaction and in all probability would never again do so. Therefore, although the circumstances are that they are men of affairs and that the company is engaged in business, in view of the facts found by the Special Commissioners and included in the case stated I must treat the case as if a person

10 See ITTOIA 2005, s 688.

11 See Tax Law Rewrite, *Draft Income Tax (Trading and Other Income) Bill*, Volume 1 (March, 2004), para 3244.

12 [See now ITTOIA 2005, s 687.]

> who was not connected with business at all received a commission from another person also not connected with business, in return for the favour of guaranteeing his account at a bank. In these circumstances are these commissions received as "annual profits or gains" under Case 6?[13] Two kinds of emolument may be excluded from Case 6. First, anything in the nature of capital accretion is excluded as being outside the scope and meaning of confirmed by the usage of a century. For this reason, a casual profit made on an isolated purchase and sale, unless merged with similar transactions in the carrying on of a trade or business is not liable to tax. "Profits or gains" in Case 6 refer to the interest or fruit as opposed to the principal or root of the tree. The second class of cases to be excluded consists of gifts and receipts, whether the emolument is from a gift inter vivos, or by will, or from finding an article of value, or from winning a bet. All these cases must be ruled out because they are not profits or gains at all.[14] Without giving an exhaustive definition, therefore, we may say that where an emolument accrues by virtue of service rendered whether by way of action or permission, such emoluments are included in "Profits or gains". Assuming then that these commissions constitute "profits or gains", the further question for consideration is whether they are "annual" profits or gains. The word "annual" may mean "annually recurring", as applied to the seasons of the year, or "recurring over a long period of years": or it may mean "lasting only for one year", as we speak of certain flowers as annuals which must be sown afresh every year: or, as in the case of interest on a sum of money, it may mean "calculated with reference to a year". In the present case the transaction did last for a year and was renewed for another year, although it did not so continue of its own accord, but by agreement between the parties. I do not think that any of those meanings are applicable to the word "annual" as used in Case 6...The word "annual" here can only mean "calculated in any one year", and "annual profits or gains" means "profits or gains in any one year or in any year as the succession of years comes round"...
>
> The case raises the whole question of "casual profits"... I need only mention the case of casual authorship, as where a person who is neither a journalist nor an author by profession is called in by a firm of publishers to write a single book or a single article for reward. There again the amount which it is sought to tax is an instance of casual profits, but is liable to tax under Case 6 in the same way... as the commissions paid to the directors who gave the guarantee in the present case. **[13.3]**

For other examples of the taxation of 'casual profits', see *Lyons v Cowcher* (1926) 10 TC 438 (payment of an underwriting commission), *Sherwin v Barnes* (1931) 16 TC 278 (bonus paid to guarantor of an overdraft), and *Wilson v Mannooch* (1937) 21 TC 178 (sums received for arranging loans for the purchase of property). **[13.3a]**

3. Income or capital?

As seen above, for a profit or gain to be taxable under ITTOIA 2005, s 687 it must be income in nature; a capital profit derived from an isolated transaction is not taxable under the section. **[13.4]**

Jones v Leeming [1930] AC 415 (HL)

The taxpayer was a member of a syndicate of four individuals who made a net profit by acquiring options on two rubber estates (apparently without payment), and then

13 [Now 'income' under ITTOIA 2005, s 687.]
14 [The same position pertains in respect of 'income' taxable under ITTOIA 2005, s 687.]

transferring these options to a company. The General Commissioners made a finding of fact that this did not constitute a 'concern in the nature of trade'. The issue to be determined by the House of Lords was whether, in view of this finding, the profit could, nevertheless, be regarded as in the nature of income and taxable under Schedule D, Case VI.

LORD THANKERTON: . . . I agree with the view taken in both the Courts below that that finding [*by the General Commissioners*] was a finding in fact which excludes the application of Case I. of Schedule D.[15]

There remains Case VI., which brings into charge "any annual profits or gains not falling under any of the foregoing Cases and not charged by virtue of any other Schedule".[16]

It is now settled that annual profits and gains taxable under Schedule D may be satisfied by profits falling within the year of charge and accruing during a period of less than a year: see *Martin v. Lowry*[17], in which the opinion of Rowlatt J. on this point in *Ryall v. Hoare*[18] was approved. In that case Rowlatt J. said: "The word 'annual' here can only mean 'calculated in any one year', and 'annual profits or gains' mean 'profits or gains in any one year or in any year as the succession of years comes round.'" While this is so, the isolated nature of a transaction, as opposed to a series of transactions of the same kind, will have a material bearing not only on the question as to whether it was a "trade, adventure or concern in the nature of trade", but also as to whether the profit arising therefrom was an accretion of capital or "profits or gains" within the meaning of the Income Tax Act [*1918*], which connotes the idea of revenue or income.

In the present case two options for the purchase of real estate were acquired and disposed of within two months; the estates themselves were not taken up or dealt with in any way. This was a simple case of purchase and sale, once the Commissioners had decided that the transaction was not a concern in the nature of trade. I agree with Lawrence L.J. when he says[19]: "I have the greatest difficulty in seeing how an isolated transaction of this kind, if it be not an adventure in the nature of trade, can be a transaction ejusdem generis with such an adventure and therefore fall within Case VI. All the elements which would go to make such a transaction an adventure in the nature of trade, in my opinion would be required to make it a transaction ejusdem generis with such an adventure. It seems to me that in the case of an isolated transaction of purchase and re-sale of property there is really no middle course open. It is either an adventure in the nature of trade, or else it is simply a case of sale and re-sale of property." . . .

VISCOUNT DUNEDIN: . . . The limitations of the words "profits or gains" were pointed out by Blackburn J. long ago in the case of *Attorney-General v. Black*[20] when he said that profits and gains in Case VI. must mean profits and gains ejusdem generis with the profits and gains specified in the preceding five Cases. And then there came the memorable and often quoted words of Lord Macnaghten in the *London County Council* case[21], when he begged to remind people "that income tax is a tax on income". The only question, therefore, here was – Was there in any sense income? It is quite true that, as counsel for the Crown said, the word "annual" does not mean something that recurs every year, but none the less the receipt must be of the nature of income. Lawrence L.J. put the matter very succinctly when he said[22]: "It seems to me that in the case of an isolated transaction of the purchase and re-sale of property, there is really no middle course open. It is either an adventure in the nature of trade, or else it is simply a case of sale and re-sale of property". It was sought to assail this dictum by quoting *Cooper v. Stubbs*[23], where there was a finding, as here, that no trade had been carried on and yet the tax was imposed. But

15 [See now ITTOIA 2005, s 5.]
16 [ITTOIA 2005, s 687. Section 687 refers to 'income' rather than 'annual profits or gains'.]
17 [1927] AC 312.
18 [1923] 2 KB 447, 455; [see above, paras **[6.18]**, **[13.3]**.]
19 [1930] 1 KB 279, 301.
20 (1871) LR 6 Ex 308, 309.
21 [1901] AC 26, 35; [see above, para **[7.13]**.]
22 [1930] I KB 279, 301.
23 [1925] 2 KB 753.

the answer is simple, the whole point of *Cooper v. Stubbs* was that the transaction was not an isolated transaction. Warrington L.J. says that the transactions extended over a considerable period of years, and Atkin L.J. says that an annual profit or gain must be something which is of the nature of revenue or income, and he points out that the transaction in that case had been going on for eight years running... **[13.5]**

A distinction may be drawn between the return from a purchase and re-sale of property and that derived from the use or exploitation of property subsequent to its acquisition. In *Leader v Counsel* [1942] 1 KB 364, Lawrence J held that receipts derived from the *user* of an asset were income in nature and taxable under Schedule D, Case VI (receipts from the disposal of nomination rights in a stallion which was part owned by the taxpayer). **[13.6]**

4. Sale of an asset (capital) or performance of services (income)?

In some cases it may be difficult to determine whether a receipt is in respect of the sale of an asset, and, is of a capital nature, or is in respect of the performance of services, and chargeable as a revenue receipt. In the latter respect, it has been established that a receipt derived from an 'adventure in the nature of a profession' may be charged to tax under Schedule D, Case VI,[24] and such receipt would now fall, for income tax purposes, within ITTOIA 2005, s 687. **[13.7]**

Hobbs v Hussey [1942] 1 KB 491 (KBD)

LAWRENCE J:...In this case the commissioners have held that the appellant, a solicitor's clerk, who has never carried on the profession of an author, is assessable under case VI. of sch. D[25] in respect of a sum of money received from the People newspaper for the serial rights in his life story.

It was contended for the appellant that the transaction was a sale of the copyright of the series of articles and, therefore, resulted in the realisation of capital and was not a revenue receipt, and the case of *Earl Haig's Trustees v. Inland Revenue Commissioners*[26] was relied on. The Solicitor-General, while not admitting that *Earl Haig's Trustees v. Inland Revenue Commissioners* was rightly decided argued that it is distinguishable and that it was settled by *Ryall v. Hoare*[27] so far as courts of first instance are concerned, that profits from a single article by a person who is not an author are assessable under case VI. of sch. D.[28] He also submitted that the true question in such cases is whether the transaction in question is really a sale of property or the performance of services, that the present transaction falls into the latter category, and that profits therefrom are therefore of a revenue nature.

In my opinion, the test suggested is correct. Any sale of property where no concern in the nature of trade is carried on must result in the realisation of capital: compare *Ryall v. Hoare*, per Rowlatt J.: and it is also true, in my opinion, that the performance of services, although they may involve some subsidiary sale of property (e.g. dentures sold by a

24 See, for example, *Ryall v Hoare* [1923] 2 KB 447; see above, paras **[6.18]**, **[13.3]**.
25 [See now ITTOIA 2005, s 687.]
26 1939 SC 676. [It is surprising that the receipt in that case was found to be capital in nature bearing in mind that there was no outright sale of the subject matter, ie diaries, which was retained by the trustees.]
27 [1923] 2 KB 447; [see above, paras **[6.18]**, **[13.3]**.]
28 [See now, ITTOIA 2005, s 687.]

dentist) are in their essence of a revenue nature since they are the fruit of the individual's capacity which may be regarded in a sense as his capital but are not the capital itself. Does then the fact that the present transaction involved the sale of the copyright in the appellant's series of articles constitute the profits therefrom capital, or is such sale merely subsidiary to what was in essence a performance of services by the appellant? In my opinion, the true nature of the transaction was the performance of services. The appellant did not part with his notes or diaries or his reminiscences. He could re-publish the very articles themselves so long as they were not in serial form, and, on the whole, I am of the opinion that the profits he received were of a revenue nature and not the realisation of capital. In the case of *Earl Haig's Trustees* the facts were totally different. The trustees possessed diaries of unique importance and great value, and the view of the Court of Session was that these diaries were capital assets and that the trustees had realised some part of such assets. The court had not to consider the profits received by the author of the book, nor could it be said that from the point of view of the trustees the sale was subsidiary to the performance of services by them.

In any event, in view of the decision in *Ryall v. Hoare* approved, as it was, by the Court of Appeal in *Martin v. Lowry*[29] and adhered to by Rowlatt J. in *Sherwin v. Barnes*[30], I consider that I ought to follow the dicta of Rowlatt J. which are directly in point and were approved by the Court of Appeal. The appeal will, therefore, be dismissed, with costs... **[13.8]**

The case of *Earl Haig's Trustees* was also distinguished by the Court of Appeal in *Alloway v Phillips* [1980] 1 WLR 888 where the wife of one of the men convicted of participating in the Great Train Robbery in the 1960s agreed to tell her story to a journalist from an English newspaper, who visited her at her home in Canada. Subsequently, a series of articles was published in England by the newspaper. A large sum of money was then paid by the newspaper to the wife's London agents. This sum was held by the Court of Appeal to be taxable under Schedule D, Case VI, as the wife had acquired property in the UK (a chose in action entitled her to receive the agreed sum), and the payment was received as income arising from this property. See also *Housden v Marshall* (1958) 38 TC 233 (payments made by a newspaper to a jockey for access to his reminiscences and related documents held to be taxable under Schedule D, Case VI). **[13.9]**

Scott v Ricketts [1967] 1 WLR 828 (CA)

During a redevelopment of property, the taxpayer, an auctioneer and estate agent, took part in complicated negotiations relating to various building sites. He claimed that he had acquired an 'interest' in one of the sites. One of the developers bought out his 'interest' for £39,000. The Inland Revenue claimed that this sum was taxable either under Schedule D, Case I or II as income from the taxpayer's profession, or, alternatively, under Schedule D, Case VI. These claims were rejected by the Special Commissioners, who held that the sum was a gratuitous payment of a non-revenue nature. On appeal to the Chancery Division (Cross J), it was held that the sum was taxable under Case VI. The taxpayer appealed.

LORD DENNING MR: ... The one point is whether this £39,000 is chargeable under Case VI. That Case is a "sweeping up" provision.[31] It catches "annual profits or gains" which have not been caught by the other provisions.[32] It is difficult to construe and we have to go by the decided cases.

29 [1926] 1 KB 550.
30 (1931) 16 TC 278.
31 [See now, ITTOIA 2005, s 687.]
32 [As seen above, s 687 of ITTOIA 2005 refers to 'income' rather than 'annual profits or gains'.]

In *Ryall v. Hoare*[33] Rowlatt J. staked out the guide-lines: and there have been other cases following it. Some things are clear. "Annual" profits does not mean profits which are made year by year. It is satisfied by profits made in one year only. "Profits and gains" include remuneration for work done, services rendered or facilities provided. They do not include gratuitous payments which are given for nothing in return. Nor do they include profits in the nature of capital gains. So they do not include gains made on purchase and sale of an asset. Such gains (except for recent legislation[34]) are only taxable if the transaction was an adventure in the nature of trade.

The crux of the present case is that Mr. Ricketts had no legal ground to be paid anything. All he had – to use the judge's words – was a moral claim or a nuisance value. Ravenseft [*the developer*] paid him £39,000 in order that he should not feel aggrieved, and to get rid of any possible claim. If they had paid this sum over to him as a gratuitous payment, it would not have come within Case VI. But because it was "dressed up" as a contract – to use the judge's own words – he has held that it is caught by Case VI. I do not think that is right. Take the case where a man has a good legal claim which he agrees to forgo in return for a sum of money, such as a claim for personal injuries which is compromised by payment of a lump sum. That is not an annual profit or gain within Case VI. It is the sale of an asset – namely, his legal claim – for a price. Next, suppose that the man has a claim which he believes to be good but which is in fact unfounded – and he agrees to forgo it in return for a sum of money. It might be a claim for personal injuries when he has no evidence of negligence. It is not strictly an "asset", because it would not stand up in the courts. But the compromise is binding. The payment has the same quality as if the claim were well founded. It is not an annual profit or gain within Case VI. Finally, take a man who has a moral claim but knows that he has no legal claim. He tries it on so as to see if the defendants will pay him something. They agree to buy him out so as to save the cost of fighting it. It seems to me that the payment for tax purposes has the same quality as that in a compromise. It is not an annual profit or gain within Case VI.

The judge seems to have thought that, as the payment was made under a contract, that was enough to bring it within Case VI. I cannot agree with him. It must be a contract for services or facilities provided, or something of that kind.

The present case is rather like *Leeming v. Jones*.[35] If the sum was taxable at all, it was taxable as part of the profits of Mr. Ricketts' trade or profession. Once that is negatived, it becomes simply a sum received in compromise of a disputed claim: whether legal or moral makes no difference.

I think that this case does not fall within Case VI. I would allow the appeal and restore the decision of the commissioners. **[13.10]**

This case is problematic. A gratuitous payment which is made, for example, in respect of services already rendered, and not in pursuance of any contract is not normally regarded as 'income': see *Dickinson v Abel* [1969] 1 WLR 295, and *Bloom v Kinder* (1958) 38 TC 77. On the other hand, if there is an enforceable contract for services, a payment made under that contract is assessable to income tax: see *Brocklesby v Merricks* (1934) 18 TC 576, and *Bradbury v Arnold* (1957) 37 TC 665. Consequently, it is questionable whether a payment made in respect of a contract for services can be portrayed, not as income in nature, but as a capital payment (to extinguish a contractual right), and, as such, avoid income tax. It might be argued, however, that *Scott v Ricketts* can be explained on the basis that the sum of £39,000 was not paid under a contract, because Mr Ricketts' moral claim/'interest' to which this payment related did not constitute sufficient consideration. **[13.11]**

33 [1923] 2 KB 447; [see above, paras **[6.18]** and **[13.3]**.]
34 [Ie the Capital Gains Tax Act 1965.]
35 [1930] AC 415; [see above, para **[7.9]**.]

14 The Individual and the Family

The previous chapters have been concerned with the different types and sources of taxable income. It is now necessary to consider the persons and entities in respect of whom that income is assessed. The basic taxpaying unit is the individual to whom the income belongs, although it may be expanded in certain circumstances to comprise the married couple,[1] and the couple or family for tax credit purposes.[2] Further persons or groups of persons may constitute an entity for the purposes of assessment and payment of tax, in particular the executors or administrators of an estate,[3] the trustees of a settlement,[4] and the members of a partnership.[5] Moreover, a company constitutes a taxable entity in its own right and is liable to corporation tax.[6] **[14.1]**

1. The tax unit

In the past, the 'problem of the tax unit was to decide how households should be taxed relative to individuals'.[7] As Tiley points out, however, 'the question whether the tax system should look to the family unit is separate from the question of whether that unit should be based on the legal status of marriage'.[8] It is thus not surprising that, since the tax year 1972–73, when the unearned income of an unmarried infant who was not in regular employment, ceased to be treated as income of its parent or parents,[9] discussion focused on the changing role of women and a recognition of the right of married women to be treated differently from 'infants and lunatics', with whom, for legal purposes, they had always been associated. Prior to the tax year 1990–91, a married woman's income chargeable to income tax was deemed to be that of her husband for income tax purposes and, accordingly, both their incomes were aggregated, with the husband bearing the

1 Where one spouse reached the age of 65 on or before 5 April 2000, a married couple's allowance is available, and is enhanced for those aged 75 and over. From 5 December 2005, the term 'married couple' includes a same sex couple who have entered into a civil partnership; see Civil Partnership Act 2004, FA 2005, s 103 and below, para **[14.2]**.
2 Chapter 15.
3 Chapter 16.
4 *Ibid.*
5 Chapter 17.
6 Chapter 18.
7 Kay and King *The British Tax System* (4th edn, 1986).
8 John Tiley *Revenue Law* (5th edn, 2005).
9 FA 1971, s 16. The income of an unmarried infant will continue to be treated as that of its parent where it arises under a settlement made by a parent: ITTOIA 2005, s 629; see below, para **[16.32]**.

responsibility for the income tax return and payment of tax. This system resulted in the possibility of a married couple paying more income tax than an unmarried couple with equivalent income,[10] and a total lack of privacy for the married woman in her financial affairs.

Under the system of independent taxation introduced in 1990, such aggregation of incomes ceased,[11] married women are now taxpayers in their own right, and both husbands and wives have their own personal allowances.[12] At that time, the existence of marriage was recognised and rewarded by an additional married couple's allowance, which initially went to the husband, with any unused portion capable of being transferred to the wife. However, since 1997, there has been a sea change in the impact of taxation on the family unit, with emphasis being placed on the reduction in child poverty rather than on the promotion of marriage. To this end, there was introduced in 2000 the children's tax credit, paid for by the abolition in 1999 of the married couple's allowance and other reliefs available for children.[13] The children's tax credit was itself abolished in 2003, and replaced by the new Child Tax Credit,[14] which was intended to integrate for the first time all income-related support for children, be they social security benefits or tax reliefs. The introduction of the Child Tax Credit was accompanied by the Working Tax Credit,[15] the aim of which was to make work pay, and encourage those who had been unemployed and in receipt of benefits to return to the workforce. This measure was also directed at reducing child poverty within the household. Importantly, the new tax credits are administered by HMRC, and operate through the tax system. However, their introduction provides an assault to the notion of individual taxation, since eligibility depends upon the income of the couple, which, in a sense, means a return to the pre-1990–01 era with all its attendant problems. Nevertheless, the Chancellor of the Exchequer, the Right Honourable Gordon Brown MP took the opportunity to confirm the Government's commitment to independent taxation by saying:

> 'In all our reforms we will honour the important principles of independent taxation: that we will never allow the wife or partner to be regarded as the chattel as was the case until the late 1980s; everyone should be treated equally in the tax system and everyone should have the right to their own personal allowance whatever their household status.'[16]

The Civil Partnership Act 2004, which came into force on 5 December 2005, creates a new legal status of civil partner, giving same-sex couples in the UK the opportunity of acquiring a legal status for their relationship, and gaining rights and responsibilities that mirror those available to a married couple. Although the Act itself does not provide for taxation measures, the Finance

10 Although a married couple could elect to have the wife's earned income taxed separately, with the wife receiving the equivalent of a single person's allowance, any of her unearned income was aggregated with that of her husband, thus raising, in some cases, the husband's marginal rate of tax.

11 FA 1988, s 32.

12 ICTA 1988, s 257 (substituted by FA 1988, s 33 with effect from 1990–91); see now ITA 2007, s 35.

13 ICTA 1988, s 257AA, inserted by FA 1999, s 30; see below, para **[15.4]**. The married couple's allowance remains for persons who had reached the age of 65 on or before 5 April 2000; see above, n 1.

14 See Chapter 15, para **[15.12]**, below.

15 See Chapter 15, para **[15.12]**, below.

16 The Right Honorable Gordon Brown MP, Chancellor of the Exchequer, in a speech given at the Institute for Fiscal Studies, May 1999. Speech: CX 270599, available at www.hm-treasury.gov.uk

Act 2005 enables the Treasury to make regulations providing similar treatment for civil partners and civil partnerships as is given to married persons and marriage.[17] In practice, this means that from 5 December 2005, tax charges and reliefs, in addition to the various anti-avoidance rules, will apply to married couples and civil partners alike. Most significantly, this will enable property passing on the death of one civil partner to the other to enjoy the benefit of the Inheritance Tax 'spouse exemption'.[18] Cohabiting heterosexual couples will remain as individuals for all tax purposes except for tax credits, and will not, for example, be able to take advantage of the spouse exemption for inheritance tax purposes. **[14.2]**

The Structure and Reform of Direct Taxation Report of a Committee chaired by Professor J E Meade (1978) p 377

[Chapter 18]

The Tax Unit

CONFLICTING CRITERIA FOR THE CHOICE OF TAX UNIT

There are a number of different criteria concerning the tax treatment of married couples, each of which would find its enthusiastic supporters but many of which are not in fact compatible with each other. As a result the treatment of the tax unit must inevitably be a matter of compromise between a number of conflicting considerations. The following is a list of some of the most important of these criteria:

1. The decision to marry or not to marry should not be affected by tax considerations.
2. Families with the same joint resources should be taxed equally.
3. The incentive for a member of the family to earn should not be blunted by tax considerations which depend upon the economics of other members of the family.
4. Economic and financial arrangements within the family (e.g. as regards the ownership of property) should not be dominated by sophisticated tax considerations.
5. The tax system should be fair between families which *rely* upon earnings and families which enjoy investment income.
6. Two persons living together and sharing household expenditures can live more cheaply and therefore have a greater taxable capacity than two single persons living separately.
7. The choice of tax unit should not be excessively costly in loss of tax revenue.
8. The arrangements involved should be reasonably simple for the taxpayer to understand and for the tax authorities to administer.[19] **[14.3]**

17 FA 2005, s 103. The main regulations are to be found in the Tax and Civil Partnership Regulations 2005 (SI 2005/3229). See also the Tax and Civil Partnership (No. 2) Regulations 2005 (SI 2005/3230) and the Civil Partnership Act 2004 (Tax Credits, etc.) (Consequential Amendments) Order 2005 (SI 2005/2919).
18 Inheritance Tax Act 1984, s 18; see Chapter 21, n 3, below.
19 Compare Adam Smith's Canons of Taxation; [see above, para **[1.2]**.]

For further literature, see also the Royal Commission on the Taxation of Profits and Income: Second Report, 1953 Cmd 9105 paras 113–126, and the Reservation by Messrs Woodcock et al, paras 23–25; and the Report of the Royal Commission on Taxation; Carter Commission, Canada 1966 Vol 1: Objectives, and Vol 3: Taxation of Income (A) Individuals and Families, (D) The Family Unit. See also Cedric Sandford, 'Carter Twenty Years On' [1987] BTR 148. **[14.3a]**

Budget Speech by the Chancellor of the Exchequer, The Right Honourable Nigel Lawson MP, *Hansard*, HC, vol 129, col 999, 15 March 1988

The Taxation of Marriage

My first reform concerns the taxation of marriage. The present system for the taxation of married couples goes back 180 years. It taxes the income of a married woman as if it belonged to her husband. Quite simply, that is no longer acceptable. This is a matter on which there has already been extensive consultation. The time has come to take action.

I therefore propose a major reform of personal taxation, with two objectives. First, to give married women the same privacy and independence in their tax affairs as everyone else. And second, to bring to an end the ways in which the tax system can penalise marriage. I have decided to introduce, at the earliest practicable date, April 1990, a completely new system of independent taxation. Under the new system, a husband and wife will be taxed independently, on income of all kinds. All taxpayers, male or female, married or single, will be entitled to the same personal allowance, which will be available against all income, whether from earnings, pensions or savings.

In addition, there will be a married couple's allowance, equal to the difference under the present system between the married man's allowance and the single allowance. This new allowance will go in the first instance to the husband, so that his tax threshold does not fall. But if he does not have enough income to use it in full, he will be able to transfer any unused portion to his wife, to set against her income. This ensures that the tax system will continue to recognise marriage, as it should do. At the same time, from 1990 married women will pay their own tax, on the basis of their own income, and have their own tax return, when one is necessary.

There will, of course, be nothing to stop married women from asking their husbands to handle their tax affairs, or vice versa, as before; and many will no doubt do so. But what matters is that, for the first time ever, married women will have the right to complete independence and privacy so far as tax is concerned. In the same way, a husband and wife will be taxed independently on any capital gains they may have, with an annual exemption each, instead of one between them, as now. But transfers of capital between husband and wife will continue to be entirely free of any liability to tax.

As I have said, the new system will come into force in 1990. This is much sooner than would have been possible for most of the alternatives that have been canvassed. The necessary legislation will be contained in this year's Finance Bill. The cost of this historic reform, which for the first time ever gives a fair deal to married women, will be a little over £2 billion in 1990–91.

I mentioned a few moments ago the tax penalties on marriage. It is clearly wrong that some couples should find themselves paying more tax, simply because they are married. I propose to put that right. Independent taxation by itself will remove the most common penalty – the taxation of a married woman's income at her husband's marginal rate. But there are other tax penalties on marriage, and I propose to abolish all of them. These changes need not await the introduction of Independent Taxation. **[14.4]**

The question of the most appropriate method of taxing married couples is discussed in a number of articles, in particular by H G S Plunkett 'The Taxation of Married Women' [1957] BTR 134, 248, 337; G S A Wheatcroft 'Earned Income of a Married Woman' [1959] BTR 309; G C Hockley 'Taxation and the Employment of Married Women' [1967] BTR 171; G P Marshall and A J Walsh 'Marital Status and Variations in Income Tax Burdens' [1970] BTR 236; N A Barr 'The Taxation of Married Women's Incomes' [1980] BTR 398 and 478; J A Kay and C Sandler 'The Taxation of Husband and Wife: A View of the Debate in the Green Paper' (1982) 3(3) Fiscal Studies 173; R W Blundell, C Meghir, E Symons, and I Walker 'On the Reform of the Taxation of Husband and Wife: Are Incentives Important?' (1984) 5(4) Fiscal Studies 1; N S Spencer 'Taxation of Husband and Wife: Lessons from Europe' (1986) 7(3) Fiscal Studies 83; C N Morris and G K Stark 'The Reform of Personal Taxation' IFS Commentary (1986); J Freedman, E Hammond, J Masson and N Morris 'Property and Marriage: An Integrated Approach' IFS Report No 29; B Robinson and G Stark 'The Tax Treatment of Marriage: what has the Chancellor really achieved?' (1988) 9(2) Fiscal Studies 48; R Kerridge 'Taxation and Marriage' [1988] CLJ 77; and 'Tax, Marriage and the 1988 Budget' [1988] CLJ 477; J Tiley 'Tax, Marriage and the Family' [2006] CLJ 289. **[14.5]**

Speech given at the Institute for Fiscal Studies by the Chancellor of the Exchequer, the Right Honorable Gordon Brown, May 1999

Our aim is not just to deliver high and stable levels of growth and employment today but for the future. We must recognize that our economy can never reach its full potential unless everyone in our country has the opportunity to develop their talents to the full.

Children are, rightly, the responsibility of the families in which they grow up. But they are more than this – invest in our children and we invest in the future of our country.

We say – indeed we all agree – that every child should have the best possible start in life. And this Government sees it as a national goal. This is why Tony Blair has said we will abolish child poverty over 20 years.

It is not enough to tackle absolute poverty and simply prevent destitution.

We should do more. It is not fair that children should be disadvantaged from the start of their lives because of who their parents are, what school they go to and where they live.

Ensuring each child has a good start in life takes more than just money but cannot be done without money. We must ensure that children grow up in surroundings which enable their needs to be met.

So Government must play its part by using its system of child support to tackle the disadvantages that come from low incomes and poor parental support.

The truth about Britain today is that millions of children are born into poverty.

The facts of child poverty in Britain in 1997 are that: over four million children – more than a third of all children – live in low income families. And very many of them will remain poor for a large part of their childhood – up to a quarter of all children are persistently in low income families. **[14.6]**

The Modernisation of Britain's Tax and Benefit System. Tax Credits: reforming financial support for families, Report No 11, March 2005[20]

3.1 The Government's aim is to promote a fair and inclusive society where everyone shares in rising national prosperity and no one is held back from achieving their potential through disadvantage or lack of opportunity.

3.2 The Government believes that for those who can, work provides the best form of security and independence. This belief lies at the heart of the Government's reforms of the tax and benefit system. People of working age have the responsibility to work if they are able to and the right to expect a tax and benefit system that supports them in moving into work. Employment opportunity for all, the modern definition of full employment, is essential to reducing the risk that children grow up in poverty and to ensuring that those of working age today can provide for their own security in retirement.

3.3 However, employment opportunity for all is not sufficient in itself. It is vital that the most vulnerable and disadvantaged also share in rising prosperity. The tax and benefit system should provide guaranteed support for adults of working age who cannot work due to a health condition or disability, and for pensioners to underpin their security and independence in retirement. And it should help ensure that every child, irrespective of their parents' circumstances, has the best possible start in life.

3.4 The system of financial support in 1997 often failed to meet these requirements. The key to understanding its weaknesses lies in the complete separation of payments made to government through income tax and national insurance contributions and support from government through the benefits system.

3.5 Most working-age households pay income tax and national insurance contributions (NICs) for most of their working lives. At various times, they also receive financial support from government, for example through Child Benefit. And of course almost all households receive state financial support in retirement. So as their children grow up this means that at different points in their life-cycle households may be:

- net contributors to the Exchequer, when their tax liability exceeds the financial support they receive from the state; or
- net beneficiaries from the Exchequer, when the financial support received exceeds their tax liability; or
- neither net contributors to the Exchequer nor net beneficiaries from it, when the two cancel out.

3.6 Before the Government's reforms, the system for assessing and collecting income tax liabilities was quite separate from the system for providing financial support for families and disadvantaged or vulnerable groups. This separation between the tax and social security systems tended to obscure the fundamental financial relationships between government and individuals or families over their life-cycles and to label people as either "taxpayers" or "claimants". The stigma potentially attached to claiming benefits – even in-work benefits – was one of the factors thought to explain the low take up.

20 [For a detailed discussion of tax credits, see Chapter 15.]

3.7 Support through the social security system often involved complex and burdensome means-testing. The tax system, which has been based on the principle of independent taxation since 1990, was less intrusive. But it could not easily take account of different household circumstances, and joint incomes, or make payments to households. This made it a very ineffective means of targeting support on families, particularly for increasing numbers of people who were choosing to combine work with care for their children.

3.8 It is possible to use the income tax system to improve work incentives for the low paid, but the range of options is limited. Special tax allowances can provide a degree of targeting but they cannot reach those on the lowest incomes because they cannot reduce an individual's income below zero. [14.7]

R Probert (ed) *Family Life and the Law: Under One Roof* (Ashgate, 2007) (David Salter)

. . . in recent years, there have been two significant developments that impinge on the notion of independent/separate taxation within the family and which are addressed in the latter part of this chapter: first, the introduction of tax credits and, secondly, the on-going litigation in *Jones v Garnett (Inspector of Taxes)* [2005] EWCA Civ 1553 (*Jones v Garnett*). The former are representative of a policy shift away from the preoccupations which led to the introduction of independent/separate taxation within the family and towards a recognition of the impact of tax on the family (especially in relation to child poverty). Broadly, they provide income-related financial support to families through the tax system. However, they do not sit comfortably with independent/separate taxation, because the entitlement to tax credits, currently in the guise of the working tax credit and the child tax credit, is determined in the case of a couple (regardless of whether they are married, civil partners or cohabitants) by reference to the income of the couple. The case of *Jones v Garnett*, which is awaiting final determination by the House of Lords, raises a myriad of issues (see Robson 2005; Loutzenhiser 2005 and 2006), but, for present purposes, it is important in the following respect. It draws attention to the fact that the notion of independent/separate taxation for income tax purposes may not be absolute in that there are instances, notwithstanding independent/separate taxation, in which a familial connection (in that case husband and wife, but also in other instances, for example, parent and child), may have a bearing on the liability to tax, especially where individuals to use Tiley's phrase are perceived to be 'taking undue advantage of the tax rules' (Tiley 2006, 290). [14.8]

Civil Partnership: a framework for the legal recognition of same sex couples, Consultative document, Women and Equality Unit, Department of Trade and Industry, June 2003

1. Introduction

1.1 For a same-sex couple, the denial of the opportunity to have their relationship recognized provides a number of day-to-day challenges when they attempt to organize their joint lives.

1.2 Civil partnership registration would be an important equality measure for same-sex couples in England and Wales who are unable to marry each other. It would provide for the legal recognition of same-sex partners and give legitimacy to those in, or wishing to enter into, interdependent, same-sex couple relationships that are intended to be permanent. Registration would provide a framework whereby same-sex couples could acknowledge their mutual responsibilities, manage their financial arrangements and achieve recognition as each other's partner. Committed same-sex relationships would be recognized and registered partners would gain rights and responsibilities which would reflect the significance of the roles they play in each other's lives. This in turn would encourage more stable family life.

1.3 It is a matter of public record that the Government has no plans to introduce same-sex marriage. This consultation document is about a civil partnership registration scheme.

1.4 We have considered the position of opposite-sex couples, many of whom now choose to cohabit instead of marrying, and other people who live together in a close supportive household environment. The Government believes that these situations are significantly different from that of same-sex couples who wish to formalize their relationships but currently are unable to do so. **[14.9]**

Holland v IRC [2002] STC 43 (SCD); see above, para [4.30]

The appellant and her partner had lived together as husband and wife for thirty-one years before his demise. She claimed that the property which passed to her on his death should be exempt from inheritance tax under the Inheritance Tax Act 1984, s. 18 on the basis that the word spouse in that section should not be restricted to those who were legally married, but should also include those who had lived together as husband and wife. This claim was refused by the Inland Revenue.

THE SPECIAL COMMISSIONERS (STEPHEN OLIVER QC and DR NUALA BRYCE):
40. We are confirmed in our view that the word spouse in section 18 means a person who is legally married as this is consistent with the other provisions of the 1984 Act and with the provisions of the tax code generally. We accept the argument of Mr Tidmarsh that the 1984 Act is a taxing statute which cannot be considered outside the context of all other taxing statutes which together form a tax code. The tax code recognises the legal obligations of married persons to contribute to one another's maintenance.

41. Other examples of special provisions relating only to married persons are found in the 1984 Act itself. In considering the 1984 Act it is relevant that it taxes not only transfers of value on death but also transfers of value made within seven years of death. Again, some of the provisions of the 1984 Act are advantageous for married persons and others are not. In each case certainty is required so that at any time it is possible to say that a person comes within the provisions or not. For example, section 11 provides that a disposition is not a transfer of value if it is made by one party to a marriage in favour of the other and is for the maintenance of the other. Section 30 applies to conditionally exempt transfers and contains special provisions relating to transfers where the transferor and his spouse are beneficially entitled to the property. Section 48 applies to excluded property and provides that, in general, a reversionary interest is excluded property but not if it is one to which either the settlor or his spouse has been beneficially entitled. Section 161 contains the related property provisions and provides that property

is related to property comprised in a person's estate if it is comprised in the estate of his spouse. Section 203 is a corollary to section 18 and provides that in certain circumstances a spouse who receives a transfer becomes liable for the tax on another transfer made by the other spouse. The Finance Act 1986 also contains provisions relating to inheritance tax. Section 102A applies to a disposal of an interest in land by way of gift with reservation and applies if either the donor or his spouse enjoys a significant right or interest in the land. Some of these provisions provide advantages for spouses (for example, section 18) but others do not.

42. A number of examples of the special treatment for spouses in the income tax legislation appear in the 1988 Act. Section 257A gives a special personal allowance for some married couples. Section 304 contains special provisions for transfers of shares between husband and wife in connection with the business expansion scheme. Section 347B contains provisions about maintenance payments by one of the parties to a marriage to the other. Section 660A contains provisions about the income arising under a settlement where the settlor retains an interest and contains special provisions about the spouse of the settlor. Some of these provisions favour married couples (for example, sections 267A and 347B) but others do not (for example, section 660A). The same theme of special treatment for spouses has been carried through to capital gains tax, which was first introduced in 1965 and where the provisions are now found in the 1992 Act. Section 58 provides that there is no capital gains tax on transfers between husband and wife (which is an advantage for married couples) but section 222(6) provides that a husband and wife can have relief on the disposal of only one residence whereas an unmarried couple could have relief on the disposal of two (which is a disadvantage for married couples).

43. As both the 1992 Act and the 1984 Act concern capital taxes there is a coherence of provisions. For example, section 58 of the 1992 Act, which exempts from capital gains tax transfers between husband and wife, is mirrored by section 18 of the 1984 Act which exempts from inheritance tax such transfers during life or on death.

44. The fact that the whole of the taxing statutes form an inter-connected code, and that there are many provisions which are specific to married persons, confirms our view that when Parliament used the word spouse in section 18 of the 1984 Act it intended to mean only married persons and not persons living together as husband and wife.

45. Finally, of course, the intention of Parliament, that the word spouse in section 18 means a person who is legally married, appears unequivocally from the Official Report of 5 February 1975 ... **[14.10]**

The appellant also argued that a wider interpretation of the word 'spouse' was required by s 3(1) of the Human Rights Act 1998 so as to give effect to the rights in art 14 of the Convention read with art 8 and/or art 1 of the First Protocol and to remove discrimination on the grounds of status. The Commissioners held (obiter, since the Act had not come into force at the time of the death of the appellant's partner) that it was permissible for Parliament to legislate for different tax provisions to apply to married persons, since this reflected the fact that marriage is accompanied by mutual rights and obligations between the spouses relating to maintenance both during their lives and after their deaths.[21] As a heterosexual couple, they had a choice as to whether to marry or not and, having decided against, they had to accept the fiscal consequences. **[14.11]**

21 See below, paras **[4.25]**–**[4.33]**.

2. The structure of personal taxation

The unified system of taxation came into existence in 1973–74,[22] and forms the basis of the existing structure of personal taxation. The Income Tax Act 2007, which came into force on 6 April 2007, rewrites the jumble of rules that previously existed in respect of an individual's tax computation. A key feature of this rewritten legislation is the tax calculation, which sets out how amounts liable to income tax and those eligible for relief are combined to compute a person's income tax liability.[23] The new Act has abolished the concept of 'charges on income',[24] with a deduction now being given for allowable payments. By virtue of ITA 2007, s 23, the individual's total income[25] is determined by adding together the various components upon which the taxpayer is charged to income tax (Step 1), and deducting from that amount any reliefs (Step 2) to determine 'net income'. Any personal allowances[26] to which the taxpayer may be entitled are then deducted from the net income (Step 3). Progressively increasing rates of tax are applied to the resulting sum (Step 4). For the tax year 2007–08, the lower (or starting) rate is 10%, the basic rate, which is applied to a broad band of taxable income, is 22%, and the higher rate is 40%. The tax is calculated by adding together the amounts of tax calculated at Step 4 (Step 5); from this amount are deducted any *reductions* to which the taxpayer may be entitled (Step 6)[27] and, finally, any amounts of tax for which the taxpayer may be liable for the tax year (eg, under the gift aid provisions[28]) are added on (Step 7). The result is the taxpayer's liability to income tax.

Historically, the tax system was far more progressive than it now is[29] and, in addition, for the tax years 1973–74 to 1983–84 an additional rate of tax, the investment income surcharge[30], was imposed on investment income. This was abolished for 1984–85 and subsequent tax years.[31] **[14.12]**

22 FA 1971, ss 32–39, Schs 6 and 7. Previously, up to 1972–73, a different system applied, under which there were two taxes on income, namely, income tax and surtax. Income tax was levied at the *standard rate*, with a complex set of reliefs for earned income and personal allowances, which were given in terms of tax. Income in excess of a certain amount suffered surtax, for which there was also the earned income relief, as well as a special earnings allowance. This system was complicated, both in terms of computation and of administration, as surtax was assessed and collected by a different office from income tax. It was also based on, and discriminated against, investment income, and produced an uneven graduation of rates. It was thus ripe for reform, which was discussed in the White Paper 'Reform of Personal Direct Taxation' 1971, Cmnd 4653. The reformed system was called 'Unified' because it combined income tax and surtax in the new system of basic and higher rates of tax. See now ITA 2007, s 6.

23 ITA 2007, s 23.

24 If a payment was made by a taxpayer under an obligation (for example, an annual payment made for bona fide commercial reasons: see Chapter 11), the obligation to pay (the charge on income) rendered the payment as no longer that of the payer but that of the recipient. Accordingly, such a payment was deducted from the payer's income in calculating his tax liability.

25 See below, para **[14.21]**.

26 See below, para **[14.32]**.

27 See below, para **[14.29]**.

28 See below, para **[14.29]**.

29 See below, para **[14.34]**.

30 FA 1971, s 32(1).

31 FA 1984, s 17(2) and Sch 7.

A. *Income which is free of tax*

Some types of income are not subject to income tax under the Taxing Acts. Such income is free of tax, and includes child benefit and certain social security benefits,[32] war widows' pensions,[33] various forms of income specially exempted by ITEPA 2003[34] and by ITTOIA 2005,[35] and the income of charities used wholly for charitable purposes.[36] The first £30,000 of a statutory redundancy payment (and of a non-statutory redundancy payment that is genuine) is also free of tax.[37] **[14.13]**

B. *Tax free savings*

It is commonly believed that investment is for both the personal and the common good, and that, accordingly, it should be encouraged through fiscal policy. However, whether measures that encourage efficient ways of saving actually result in an increased rate of saving is debatable. Various savings incentive measures that exempt income and, in some cases, also capital gains from tax have been introduced in the UK over the years, and include the following:

(a) Individual Savings Accounts (ISAs). Like TESSAs and PEPs (see below) before them, the intention on their introduction was to provide a favoured environment for savings, and to permit individuals over the age of 18 and resident or ordinarily resident in the UK to hold various investments free of income tax (and also capital gains tax)[38]. Accounts, which are administered by a manager, may comprise cash, life insurance and stocks and shares. The maximum sum that can be invested each year by an individual in an ISA is £7,000, of which no more than £3,000[39] may go in cash. A husband and wife are each entitled to a full allowance. There is no 'lock in' period for investments, so that withdrawals can be made at any time without forfeiting tax relief.

(b) Personal Equity Plans (PEPs). PEPs were introduced in 1987 to allow individuals over the age of 18 to invest, through a manager, directly in UK companies, although the scheme was later widened to include investment through unit trusts, in bonds and in gilt-edged securities

32 See ITEPA 2003, s 677 for a list of social security benefits which are wholly exempt from income tax. These include the attendance allowance, back to work bonus, bereavement payment, child benefit, child's special allowance, council tax benefit, disability living allowance, guardian's allowance, housing benefit, industrial injury benefits, pensioner's Christmas bonus, social fund benefits, severe disablement allowance, and state maternity allowance. The child tax credit, working tax credit and state pension credit are also non-taxable. ITEPA, s 665 exempts income support payments except when received in particular circumstances.

33 ITEPA 2003, s 639.

34 Including certain pensions and other specified allowances, awards and gratuities paid to members of the armed forces (ITEPA 2003, Pt 9, Ch 17).

35 See ITTOIA 2005, Pt 6. Exempt income includes interest on certain types of damages for personal injury (ITTOIA 2005, s 751), housing grants (ITTOIA 2005, s 769), scholarship income paid to a full-time student at school, college or university (ITTOIA 2005, s 776) and interest on certain sorts of Government investments (ITTOIA 2005, Pt 6, Ch 2).

36 ICTA 1988, s 505.

37 ITEPA 2003, ss 309(3), 403; see Chapter 8, para **[8.36]**, above.

38 Until 5 April 2004, investors received payment of a 10% tax credit in respect of dividends on UK equities: FA 1998, s 76.

39 These limits are to be increased to £7,200 and £3,600 respectively from 6 April 2007.

and, from 1991, securities quoted on a recognised stock exchange in any member state of the European Community.[40] Since April 2001, PEPs can hold listed shares from any recognised Stock Exchange in the world. Although, since 6 April 1999, there can be no subscription to new PEPs or subscription of new money to existing ones, existing PEPs, which may continue to be held outside an ISA, still enjoy the available tax reliefs. The maximum annual investment in a PEP was £9,000,[41] rather more than the current ISAs. No income tax is charged on the income arising from the investments (and no CGT arises on either a disposal or switch of investments).

(c) Tax Exempt Special Savings Accounts (TESSAs). TESSAs, which were introduced in 1990,[42] enabled adult individuals[43] to open an account with either a bank or a building society, in which interest earned on the cash sum deposited was free from income tax provided that the savings were left in that account for five years. The maximum permitted savings over the five-year period was £9,000. As with PEPs, no new TESSAs could be made after 5 April 1999,[44] and all such accounts have now expired. On expiry, the capital (but not the interest) could be transferred to a TESSA only ISA, without affecting the amount that can be subscribed for the new account.

These schemes were, and are, aimed mainly at the smaller investor who, typically, began investing in the 1980s on the privatisation of the various utilities. That, of course, does not mean that those with larger sums to invest will not also take advantage of these incentives. However, for the more serious investor, there are additional measures which give some relief from income tax. These include the enterprise investment scheme (EIS)[45] and venture capital trusts (VCTs)[46]. Both of these incentives were introduced to assist the growth of small businesses by helping them to overcome the difficulty of raising equity finance. Under the EIS, income tax relief is given for the cost of eligible shares in, and issued by, a qualifying company, defined as being unquoted and carrying on one or more qualifying trades.[47] The minimum amount that can be subscribed in any one year is £500,[48] with a maximum of £400,000,[49] and relief is given at the lower rate of 20 per cent.[50] Individual investors are exempt from income tax on dividends received from eligible shares in a VCT,[51] and are also entitled to relief at 40 per cent[52] for investment in new ordinary shares

40 Inland Revenue Press Release, 19 March 1991 (1991) *Simon's Tax Intelligence* 300.
41 The limit for investment in a single company PEP was £3,000, whilst up to £6,000 could be invested more generally.
42 FA 1990, s 28.
43 A husband and wife are each individuals for these purposes.
44 ICTA 1988, s 326A(3), as amended by FA 1998, s 78.
45 See FA 1994, s137 and Sch 15 as amended by FA 1995 reviving ICTA 1988, ss 289–312 as further amended by FA 1998. For shares issued on or after 5 April 2007, see ITA 2007, Pt 5.
46 ITTOIA 2005, Pt 6, Ch 5 replacing ICTA 1988, Sch 15B.
47 ICTA 1988, s 293. For shares issued on or after 5 April 2007, see ITA 2007, Pt 5, Ch 4. For the definition of a qualifying trade, see ICTA 1988, s 297 and, for shares issued on or after 5 April 2007, see ITA 2007, ss 189, 192–198).
48 ICTA 1988, s 290(1); for shares issued on or after 5 April 2007, see ITA 2007, s 157(2).
49 ICTA 1988, s 290(2); for shares issued on or after 5 April 2007, see ITA 2007, s 158(2).
50 ICTA 1988, s 289A(2); for shares issued on or after 5 April 2007, the relief is given at the savings rate (of 20%): see ITA 2007, s 158(2).
51 ITTOIA 2005, s 709.
52 For the tax years 2004–05 and 2005–06 only. For 2006–07 and subsequent tax years, relief is at 20%.

in a VCT.[53] EIS and VCT relief is given by way of a reduction at Step 6 of the income tax calculation[54] after any reduction for married couples and civil partners,[55] but before any other reductions.[56] **[14.14]**

Mark Robson 'Taxation and Household Survey: Reflections on the OECD Report'[57] (1995) 16(1) Fiscal Studies 38

There is no clear evidence that the level of taxation along with other factors affecting the rate of return, *does* affect the aggregate level of saving. Some studies claim to find a positive relationship, but some a negative one; the most influential have concluded that there is no discernible effect. At first, this might seem surprising: certainly cuts in capital income taxes among many OECD Member governments in the 1980s were at least partly motivated by a concern to increase the saving rate. However, such policies could be justified on alternative grounds. In a number of countries (but most notably the UK and the US), it was argued that resources were likely to be more efficiently used in the private sector than in the public sector. On this argument, even if the level of national saving did not increase, reducing taxes so as to leave greater post-tax income in the hands of households would lead to a better allocation of resources. Because of conflicting objectives, there can be no uniform prescription for the taxation of saving, which will reflect political judgements on horizontal equity, taking into account social security systems, benefits, public expenditure and the role of the state generally.

The report stresses the importance of tax neutrality, deviations from which should be clearly justified by reference to some overriding policy objective . . .

If special tax measures are introduced to encourage saving in particular assets, they must be carefully targeted if their effect is not simply to increase government budget deficits. A prior question should be why saving in those assets by particular groups is considered insufficient. For example, if it is because of perceived risk, and the tax measures do not result in effective sharing of that risk, then the motivation for using those measures is unclear.

One way of reconciling conflicting objectives is to offer tax-free or low, flat-rate schemes up to a limit per person by type of asset, even though enforcement of the limit may be difficult. Several countries have introduced such schemes for direct investment in equities, and some for saving in bank deposits or for a wide class of, but not all, savings assets. But there seems to be no consensus on how and at what level the threshold under such schemes should be set. **[14.15]**

C. *National insurance contributions*

National insurance benefits are funded by a system of compulsory contributions (NICs), paid by employees, employers and self-employed people. NICs are charged on earnings from employment and self-employment only. In comparison, income tax is charged on an individual's total income (see below, para **[14.21]**), which includes savings and

53 This relief is limited to investments of up to £200,000 in any tax year, and requires the shares to be retained for five years.
54 See above, para **[14.12]**.
55 See below, para **[14.32]**.
56 ITA 2007, s 26.
57 *Taxation and Household Survey*, OECD (November 1994).

investment income, state and occupational pensions as well as earnings replacement benefits. Moreover, anyone resident in the UK and others with income in the UK are liable to pay income tax, whereas only individuals over the age of 16 and under state pension age working in the UK are liable to pay NICs. **[14.16]**

Andrew Dilnot and Steven Webb 'Reforming National Insurance Contributions: A Progress Report' (1989) 10(2) Fiscal Studies 38

II. Development to 1985

The system of National Insurance benefits and contributions from which the current structures have grown was introduced in 1948. Although not precisely that which Sir William Beveridge had proposed in the Beveridge report (Beveridge *(1942)),* it was very close to his suggestions. The basic characteristic of the contribution was that it had the form of a lump sum tax, unrelated to income, except insofar as it was to be paid only by those with incomes above a lower floor.

> 'The second fundamental principle of the scheme is that the compulsory contribution required of each insured person or his employer is at a flat rate, irrespective of his means. All insured persons, rich or poor, will pay the same contributions for the same security...'

This was what Beveridge meant by the contributory principle.

It did not last. As benefits were increased more quickly than Beveridge had forecast with no increase in Treasury contribution from general tax revenue, the level of contribution had to be steadily increased. As the level of contribution was raised, it came to bear more and more heavily on those on low incomes. By 1960, further increases in the flat rate contribution were felt to be unacceptable, and an element of graduation was introduced, with a flat rate contribution and a contribution related to earnings being charged. In 1975 the explicitly flat rate contribution was abolished, and an entirely earnings related system introduced for the great bulk of the contributing population. In the years which followed, the rate of contributions tended to rise: in 1975 the standard class I employee rate was 5.5 per cent., the employer rate 8.5 per cent.; by 1985 these rates were 9 per cent. and 10.45 per cent. respectively.

Throughout this period, and indeed even now, reference is made to the contributory principle. It should be clear from Beveridge's description of the contributory principle that if any such concept can still be said to exist, it is very different to that which he had in mind. This is perhaps most clearly seen by comparing the relationship between contributions and benefits in 1948 and 1985. Then, as now, entitlement to the basic National Insurance benefits depended solely on the number of contributions which had been made, and not at all on their level.

In 1948 total contributions per week were £0.454, the single person's pension £1.30. Thus contributions were 35 per cent. of the weekly value of pension, regardless of earnings. In 1985, the single retirement pension was £38.30. At the lower earnings limit of £35.50, total contributions due were £6.91, 19 per cent. of the pension. At the ceiling of £265 per week, total contributions due were £51.54, 144 per cent. of the pension. In 1948, it was possible to describe a relationship between contributions and benefits. By 1985 such a relationship did not exist.

III. The 1985 Reform

1989 was not the first time that Mr Lawson produced a surprise reform of the structure of National Insurance contributions, having done the same in 1985. It seems from his 1985 Budget speech that there were two objectives. The first aim was to remove disincentives caused by the sudden jump in liability as contributions became due at the lower earnings limit (LEL), for both employee and employer. The second aim was to reduce the burden on low paid employees and their employers. These two aims were clearly linked.

The problem of incentives was caused by the way in which contributions were charged. At earnings below the LEL no NICs were due, at earnings £0.01 above the LEL NICs of 9 per cent. of all earnings were due from the employee and 10.45 per cent. of all earnings from the employer. This structure meant that earning a little more than the LEL could lead to a substantial fall in net income for the employee, and a substantial increase in costs for the employer. It is clear that there was bunching immediately below the LEL, reflecting the costs to both employee and employer of earnings in excess of this level.

The 1985 reform changed the structure of both employees' and employers' contributions. The jump in contributions of the LEL was reduced from 9 per cent. to 5 per cent., at the cost of introducing two further jumps for the employee and three for the employer. To pay for these reductions, the ceiling was abolished for employers' contributions.

The great bulk of employees were unaffected. The jump in contributions at £43.00 per week was reduced from 9 per cent. of £43.00 to 5 per cent. of £43.00. However, at £75.00 the rate of contribution rose from 5 per cent. of all earnings to 7 per cent. of all earnings, and at £115 from 7 per cent. of all earnings to 9 per cent. of all earnings. The system is the same for employers up to earnings of £165.00 at which there is a further jump, to a rate of 10.45 per cent. of all earnings. For employers there is no ceiling, so contributions continue to rise beyond £325 per week. Gains are concentrated in families with gross incomes of between £50 and £ 150.[58] The gains at higher income levels are the result of second earners, typically married women.

The 1985 reform reduced disincentives of the LEL, but introduced several new jumps in liability. At the same time, it did reduce the burden of NICs on low paid employees and their employers. It was a step in the right direction, but by no means a solution.

IV. The 1989 Reforms

Despite the 1985 reforms, problems still existed in the NI system. Perhaps the most significant was that although the jump in liability at the LEL had been reduced, further jumps in liability were introduced.

It is fairly clear that bunching still existed below the LEL, and there is some (less clear) evidence of bunching at both higher thresholds. It was this problem which Mr Lawson aimed to tackle in his 1989 Budget.

Under the new system all employees will pay contributions of 2 per cent. of £43.00 once their earnings exceed this level, and 9 per cent. of the excess of their earnings over £43.00 until earnings reach £325. The clearest way of thinking of this

58 The data on which this is based is reflated to 1989 levels, and the reform is based on the levels of the LEL, thresholds and ceiling of April 1989.

system is as a single rate of tax of 9 per cent. with an allowance of £43, plus a charge of 86p (2 per cent. of £43) for entering the system.

It is clear that whereas the gains from the 1985 reform were concentrated at low earnings, the gains from the 1989 reform increase with earnings at first, and are then fairly evenly spread. This mirrors the fact that those on earnings of less than £115 per week had effectively already received in 1985 some of the benefit now given to those with earnings at that level.

There have been some suggestions that much of the benefit of the reduction in NIC liability for the low paid will be offset by corresponding reductions in receipt of means-tested benefits such as Family Credit and Housing Benefit. While it is true that for anyone in receipt of Family Credit or Housing Benefit reductions in NIC will be partially offset by reductions in benefit, relatively few of the low paid are actually recipients of such benefits.

The great majority of the low paid are women and most of the women below the LEL are married, and therefore likely to be second earners.

V. Assessment

The 1989 reform of the National Insurance system was far more expensive than that of 1985, and as it affects employees, more extensive. The continued existence of a charge for entering the NI system is untidy, but the charge of £0.86 is at least now much smaller. The removal of the jumps in liability at higher earnings is also welcome, as is the tacit move to a system with an allowance and a single rate.

The most important failing in the reform is the lack of change in the structure of employers' contributions. The jump in liability at £43.00 is not reduced, and the jumps at £75.00, £115.00 and £165.00 continue to exist.

In his Budget speech in 1989, Mr Lawson said of the structure including the jumps in liability 'This is not a real problem as far as employers' contributions are concerned'. This seems a surprising statement. If it costs an employer £42.50 to pay someone £42.50, and £45.68 to pay someone £43.50, it seems very unlikely that an employer would offer a job at £43.00. A similar argument holds immediately above the thresholds of £75, £115 and £165. Since it is employers who determine the wages and hours offered, at least in the first instance, their preferences must surely affect the distribution of earnings. Bunching of employees below the threshold corresponding to £165 in 1989 would be convincing evidence that employers were affected in this way, since there is no corresponding jump in employees' liability at this earnings level . . .

The 1989 reform of employees' NICs is a major change, and a beneficial one. It would be churlish not to applaud Mr Lawson and his officials. Nonetheless, more is still needed. The existence of a charge for entry to the National Insurance system is an irritating hangover from a long lost ideal. The failure to increase the NI ceiling leaves us with a system with lower average and marginal direct tax rates for many individuals earning £25,000 than for those earning £15,000. Finally, there was no mention of imposing NICs on benefits in kind.

But by far the most serious omission was a reform of the employers' structure to match that of the employees. Such a reform would no doubt this year have been prohibitively expensive, but must be made before the worst distortions caused by the NI system can be said to have been removed. **[14.17]**

Report of the Social Security Committee, HC 56–II 1999–2000

The history of National Insurance

The system devised by Beveridge

23. The contributory principle was central to William Beveridge's plan for a comprehensive social security system after the Second World War. He described his Plan for Social Security as: "first and foremost a plan of insurance – of giving in return for contributions benefits up to subsistence levels, as of right and without means test, so that individuals may build freely upon it."[59] The quotation summarises the key features of Beveridge's plan. His overall concern was to prevent poverty through provision of a subsistence income, rather than the creation of a system which replaced wage levels. The idea was that flat rate benefits would provide a floor, on which the contributor could build. Beveridge's view was that "the State in organising security should not stifle incentive, opportunity, responsibility; in establishing a national minimum it should leave room and encouragement for voluntary action by each individual to provide more than that minimum for himself and his family."[60] Contributory benefits were to be something better and more worth having than means-tested "national assistance", which he felt should be "less desirable than insurance benefits; otherwise the insured person gets nothing for their contributions."[61] Beveridge expected that national assistance would be a minor part of the social security system, necessary mainly during a period of transition to cater for older people who would not qualify for contributory retirement pension: "the scope of assistance will be narrowed from the beginning and will diminish throughout the transition period for pensions. The scheme of social insurance is designed of itself when in full operation to guarantee the income needed for subsistence in all normal cases."[62]

24. Beveridge's plan was never fully realised. Political pressures meant that, at the outset, the Government decided to pay out the full retirement pension, before the 20 years had elapsed which were needed for the National Insurance Fund to mature. Benefits were paid out of contributions collected. As a result, rather than acting as a funded insurance scheme as Beveridge intended, NI operated on a 'pay-as-you-go' basis with the cost of current benefits being borne by current contributions paid. From the start, benefit rates were also lower than the subsistence rates envisaged by Beveridge. In 1954 the Government accepted the recommendations of the Phillips Committee that it should abandon any long-term aim of raising retirement pensions to subsistence level on the ground that it would present an unduly heavy burden on the Exchequer. As a result, National Insurance benefits have never achieved the comprehensive coverage envisaged by Beveridge, being supplemented in many cases by means-tested benefits and contingency-based benefits.

Economic and social changes

25. Economic and social changes have also undermined the assumptions on which National Insurance was based. There have been substantial changes in the labour

59 *Social Insurance and Allied Services*, Cm. 6406, HMSO, 1942. para. 10.
60 *Ibid.*, para. 9.
61 *Ibid.*, para. 369.
62 *Ibid.*, para. 23.

market. As the DSS commented: "Generally speaking, the National Insurance system was geared to a world in which men had full-time regular working patterns, with only brief spells out of work, and the overwhelming majority of women did not take paid employment, but were expected to rely on pensions built up on their husband's contributions."[63] Today that world has gone. Full-time, largely male, jobs in large scale manufacturing have been replaced with more 'flexible', often part-time, jobs primarily in new service industries, employing many women. In the 1950s, just over half of all jobs were in manufacturing, compared to around one in five today. In the 1950s less than five per cent of workers worked part-time; today part-time workers account for 25 per cent of the workforce. Self-employment has also increased, from 8 per cent in 1978 to 12 per cent recently. Professor Alcock pointed out that the decline in manufacturing had been a major cause of the massive increase in unemployment in Britain which put enormous pressure on the National Insurance scheme. The result of these changes has been that more and more people are failing to qualify for National Insurance benefits, due to unemployment, intermittent work records, or low pay.

26. The growth in part-time, often low-paid, employment has focussed attention on the exclusion from National Insurance protection of workers who earn below the Lower Earnings Limit (currently £67 a week). There are currently around 2.45 million workers earning below the Lower Earnings Limit. The Low Pay Unit pointed out that developments in the labour market mean this figure is likely to remain, if not increase. Four out of five of those earning below the Lower Earnings Limit are women and this kind of low paid work is much more likely to be long term for them than for men. Ninety-five per cent of women earning below the Lower Earnings Limit are part-time workers, the majority over 25 and with young children.[64]

27. Beveridge's National Insurance scheme assumed that women out of the labour market and caring for children would be supported by their husbands. In fact, the last three decades have seen a rise in separation and divorce and a growth in the number of parents bringing up children alone. Many of these lone parents do not qualify for National Insurance benefits, and have therefore been dependent on means-tested benefits. DSS expenditure on Supplementary Benefit and its successor Income Support grew from £1 billion in 1980–81 to £4 billion in 1998–99.

28. Disability Alliance drew attention to the fact that "over the last 20–30 years the whole pattern of life for disabled people has changed as the old institutions and psychiatric hospitals have closed down and disabled people have moved to independent living in the community. [There are now] longer life expectancies and better survival rates for people with severe disabilities." Many of such people have, at best, limited work records. The increasingly competitive labour market also meant that people in poor health found it difficult to enter the market. Invalidity Benefit caseloads grew steadily until 1995 reaching 1.8 million, due mainly to people remaining on benefits longer, rather than a higher number of new claims. These changes increased the need for carers, many of whom found their own ability to work and pay National Insurance contributions reduced as a result. The lack of an insurance benefit specifically for carers means that even those who have previously worked and paid contributions do not qualify for National Insurance help.

29. Finally, an aging population has put pressure on pensions. The Secretary of State reminded us that: "[Beveridge] wrote his report at a time when the average

63 In evidence to this committee.

64 *Low Pay and the National Insurance System: A Statistical Picture,* McKnight, Elias and Wilson, Equal Opportunities Commission, 1998.

life expectancy of a man after retirement was one year.[65] People are now living for 20 or 30 years in retirement."

Government policies towards National Insurance

30. The policies of successive governments since Beveridge have also had a substantial effect on the structure and coverage of the National Insurance scheme. The changes can be characterised as an expansion of the system during the 1960s and 1970s, followed by contraction in the 1980s and 1990s. During the 1960s and 1970s, the limits of flat rate benefits were recognised by the gradual introduction of earnings-related benefits into both short-term benefits, and most importantly, long-term benefits through the establishment of the State Earnings Related Pension scheme (SERPS). The plight of carers was recognised in two ways. Home Responsibilities protection made it easier for people with caring responsibilities to qualify for Retirement Pension, and, in 1975, a non-contributory, non means-tested benefit, Invalid Care Allowance, was introduced. The 1970s also saw the development of the system of credits, bringing more people into the National Insurance scheme without monetary contributions. A number of other non-contributory, non means-tested benefits were also introduced in the 1970s, aimed at people with long-term illness or disabilities with poor or non-existent contribution records. Non-contributory Invalidity Benefit (which ultimately became Severe Disablement Allowance) was an earnings-replacement benefit aimed at people unable to work and ineligible for contribution-based Invalidity Benefit (which later became Incapacity Benefit) due to a lack of contributions. Disabled people with care and mobility needs were offered Attendance Allowance and Mobility Allowance.

31. However, from 1980 onwards, the National Insurance system was cut back. Mr Field observed, "Recently, there has been much talk about modernising welfare to take account of the changes in family composition and labour markets. In fact, most of the changes affecting welfare in the last twenty years have been government cuts, not societal changes." The 1980 Social Security (No. 2) Act reduced children's allowances paid with benefits (later abolished completely); removed the earnings link for the uprating of pensions; abolished earnings-related supplements on short-term benefits; and introduced an abatement of Unemployment Benefit to take account of occupational pensions. Other changes during the same decade included substantial reductions in the value of SERPS, the transfer of payment of Sickness Benefit and Maternity Allowance to employers (with reimbursement from the State, later reduced and eventually largely discontinued in the case of Statutory Sick Pay); and a series of measures to tighten eligibility for and reduce entitlement to, Unemployment Benefit. Two major reductions in contributory benefits took place in the mid-1990s. In 1995, Invalidity Benefit was replaced with Incapacity Benefit, which tightened the medical test for eligibility whilst cutting the age-related additional allowance for most claimants; abolishing the earnings-related supplement; and making the benefit taxable. In 1996, Unemployment Benefit, paid for 12 months, was replaced with Jobseeker's Allowance, payable for only 6 months.

32. Our survey of the history of National Insurance since Beveridge has led us to conclude that the National Insurance scheme has been undermined, both directly as a result of successive governments' policies and indirectly as a result of economic and social change.

65 The average age a male born in 1942 in England and Wales could expect to live to, if the 1942 mortality rates were to prevail throughout his life was 62.1 years. (Source: Government Actuary's Department)

National Insurance: the current debate

33. Many of the contributors to this inquiry were agreed that the National Insurance scheme is in serious trouble. Professor Ruth Lister commented, "On current trends... the future for the contributory principle and for the social insurance scheme in the UK must look bleak." Growing numbers are excluded from National Insurance, and, while benefits have reduced significantly in value, National Insurance contribution rates have risen from 6.5 per cent in 1979 to ten per cent today. Mr Field warned of the potential for resentment among people who contribute, when greater rewards go to those who do not:

> " there is an inherent instability in a system which is asking people to contribute and then actually rewarding people, who do not contribute or cannot contribute, with more money than those who have contributed, and you can only get away with that in a world where the electorate is either very trusting or not very concerned."

34. Far from withering away as Beveridge had intended, means-tested benefits now represent a large and growing proportion of benefit expenditure. At the start of the post-war welfare state, just over 60 per cent of social security expenditure went on contributory benefits; and 13 per cent went on means-tested benefits.[66] Today, contributory benefits make up around 47 per cent of spending, and means-tested benefits have grown to 33 per cent of the total. The considerable growth in means-tested benefits is due partly to the failure of increasing numbers of people to qualify for National Insurance benefits at all, and also the necessity for many of those who do qualify, to claim means-tested benefits to 'top-up' the low level of their contributory benefit to give them a basic amount to live on. It is also due to the gradual introduction, since the late 1960s, of new means-tested benefits. Rate rebates were introduced in 1967 and rent rebates in 1972. Rent deregulation and higher council tax levels caused rapid increases in (renamed) Housing and Council Tax Benefits, which contributed to an additional £10 billion on these two benefits between 1980–81 and 1998–99. Family Income Supplement (later re-named Family Credit) was introduced in 1971 as a means-tested top-up for families in low-paid employment. Between 1979 and 1999, the proportion of benefits which families received which were means-tested rose from 19 per cent to 52 per cent.

35. There are conflicting signals regarding the present Government's attitude towards National Insurance. On the one hand, a series of measures has eroded the contributory system still further, reducing both access to benefits and the amounts payable. The Welfare Reform and Pensions Act 1999 tightened the eligibility conditions for Incapacity Benefit, and introduced an abatement of Incapacity Benefit to take account of occupational pensions – effectively introducing a means-tested element. Widows' Pension, including a SERPS element for older widows, was payable to widows aged 45 and over without dependants. It was abolished and replaced by Bereavement Allowance, paid for six months to both widows and widowers, without a SERPS component.

36. On the other hand, the Government has sought to reform the structure of National Insurance contributions in a way which reduces the financial burden on low-paid workers, whilst ensuring that they continue to qualify for contributory benefits. Coupled with the raising of the Upper Earnings Limit in two successive years by more than price inflation, the system is now less regressive in its effects. The Chancellor has also brought into the contributory system an estimated 16,000 women who earn over £30 per week but less than the Lower Earnings Limit, who

66 Non means-tested benefits represented just over a quarter of benefit expenditure at that time, and is now about a fifth of all benefit expenditure, according to the evidence of the DSS.

will have access to contributory Maternity Allowance. A further 11,000 women who are self-employed, will also benefit from enhanced access to Maternity Allowance.

37. Professor Lister's pessimistic conclusion was that, "Although there is not a completely consistent pattern emerging from the individual benefit reviews, on balance the net effect is likely to be a further diminution of the role played by contributory benefits in the social security system."

38. The Secretary of State for Social Security has argued, "Today the important difference in social security is not whether they are insurance based or means tested, but whether or not they provide enough help to get people back to work and improve their lives."[67] The question we sought to answer was: is the contributory principle and the benefits to which it gives rise worth fighting for? Do the values which underpin National Insurance stand up against current social, political and economic realities? **[14.18]**

The Modernisation of Britain's Tax and Benefit System, No 2. Work Incentives Report by Martin Taylor, HM Treasury, March 1998

2.02 If an employee earns over the lower earnings limit (£64 a week in 1998–99), he or she pays NICs at a rate of 2 per cent on earnings up to the lower earnings limit (LEL) and 10 per cent on earnings over the LEL subject to a cap at the upper earnings limit (UEL) of £485 a week. Employees contracted out of the state earnings related pension scheme (SERPS) receive a rebate of 1.6 per cent on earnings between the LEL and UEL, ie a reduction in the rate of national insurance they pay ...

2.04 Entitlement to some benefits is based on earnings on which employee NICs have been paid. These benefits include basic state Retirement Pension, SERPS, Jobseeker's Allowance, Incapacity Benefit and Statutory Maternity Pay. Typically they use "earnings factors", which relate benefit entitlement to the length of time when pay is above the LEL. For example, entitlement to Statutory Maternity Pay turns on average weekly earnings being at or above the LEL for eight weeks.

2.05 Employees pay a uniform rate of NICs on all earnings for employees earning above the LEL. The rate paid depends on the earnings of the employee as set out below:

- £64–£110 3%
- £110–£155 5%
- £155–£210 7%
- £210 and over 10%

For those contracted out of SERPS, employers receive a 3 per cent rebate on earnings between the LEL and UEL.

2.06 With employer NICs, entry into each new band triggers the application of the higher rate to all earnings (unlike income tax where the tax rate only applies to income in excess of any threshold). The result is that for employers there are steps not just at the LEL, but at the three other thresholds ...

2.07 The current national insurance system imposes a burden on the low paid and distorts the labour market – there is clear evidence of bunching of employees below the LEL.

67 *The Guardian* 16 May 1999.

2.08 NICs place a greater burden on the low-paid than income tax in that they become payable on much lower earnings. A married employee only begins to pay more income tax than NICs at earning of £165 a week.

2.09 In addition, there are a number of steps in the system where a small increase in earnings can result in a significant increase in NICs. The step at the LEL has the greatest impact, since the employee will incur a NIC charge of £1.28 per week in 1998–99 and the employer a charge of £1.92 per week, resulting in a combined 5 per cent charge on earnings of £64 a week. The employer also faces the administrative burden of having to calculate and account for NICs.

2.10 As a result of the entry fee at the LEL, low paid individuals face high marginal tax rates. This is one of the few remaining causes of marginal rates in excess of 100 per cent. The minimum wage may very well mean this is not an issue for full-time workers. But it will remain an issue in attracting people into flexible work – for example, women with children looking for work fitting their childcare opportunities.

2.11 Moreover there is a lack of alignment between the income tax system and the national insurance system. The main areas of difference are:

- base of charge. Income tax is paid on total income including savings and investment income, state and occupational pensions and earnings replacement benefits. NICs are paid only on earnings from employment and self-employment and excludes many taxable benefits in kind.
- reliefs and rebates. The income tax system has a wide range of allowances and reliefs, whereas no reliefs can be set against earnings for NICs. NICs are, however rebated for both employer and employee, where the employee is contracted out of SERPS.[68]
- period of assessment. PAYE may be deducted each time an employee is paid but the employee's final income tax is based on total taxable income from all sources for the tax year. NICs are calculated fully and finally for each pay period on the basis of earnings in that pay period.
- structure of charge. Particularly with the 10p rate income tax would be a progressive tax charged at graduated rates above the personal allowance. NICs are charged as above.

2.12 There is a strong case for reforming the structure of NICs so as to improve work incentives, cut red tape and encourage job creation.

2.13 Some employers and representative bodies have in the past argued that NICs should be completely merged with income tax. This would save them the work of separately recording and accounting for two sorts of NICs as well as tax. This is an understandable suggestion, particularly for small employers who face relatively high unit costs for operating PAYE and NICs. However, full integration of employee NICs would require a substantially higher, basic rate of income tax. This could have very large redistributional effects, particularly if this higher rate were applied to other sources of income, such as pensions. Abolishing employer NICs would leave a large gap of £27 billion in government revenue, which would need to be filled. This would be equivalent to, for example, a rise in the rate of corporation tax to over 50 per cent. Full integration would also mean a complete redefinition of the contributory principle for short term benefits and for pensions. It seems more worthwhile to focus on changes which would reduce the disincentives in the NICs system without raising such major policy questions...

68 State earnings related pension scheme.

2.31 I recommend:

- Increasing the LEL to the level of the income tax personal allowance for employer NICs and (subject to ensuring people do not face unacceptable losses of benefit entitlement) employee NICs;
- Abolishing the "entry fee" and "steps" for both employee and employer NICs;
- Progressive alignment of the NICs legislation with income tax, and bringing NICs operational and policy functions into the Inland Revenue;
- Abolishing the Class 2 charge for the self-employed, increasing the Class 4 rate and aligning LPL and the LEL;
- Considering the extension of NICs to all taxable benefits in kind (for practical reasons, by extending the current tax-aligned Class 1A employer-only charge). **[14.19]**

John Tiley *Revenue Law* (5th edn, 2005) pp 166–167

NICs are important because they affect the tax burden on the employer, the employee and sometimes the self-employed.[69] For employees, the normal rate in 2005–06 is 11% of earnings between the 'primary threshold' set at £94 a week (£4,888, p.a.)[70] and the upper earnings limit, set at £630 a week (£32,760 p.a.).[71] There is a further charge at 1% on sums above £630 a week.[72] The rate of employer's NICs for 2005–06 is 12.8% on all earnings over £94 a week (£4,888 p.a.).[73] These rates are reduced for both employer and employee if the employee is contracted out of the state earnings related pension scheme, by 1%[74] for money purchase schemes and 3.5%[75] for salary related ones. The employer's threshold is now tied to the value of the personal allowance in TA 1988, s.257[76]; the employee's threshold was similarly tied in 2001.

The sums raised are large. The IFS Green Budget 2005 Table 6.2 shows this as 6.6% of national income and makes the contrast with income tax (11.3%) and VAT (6.2%).[77]

Confusingly, there is also the 'lower earnings limit' which is £82 a week for 2005–06. This figure is not relevant for NIC purposes but is the minimum which must be reached if the year is to count for contribution purposes and so give entitlement to contributory benefits. The government is considering moving from years of contribution to years of residence.

These rates represent a considerable rationalization on what had previously been in force. Earlier systems had been progressive in that the tax rate rose as income rose. However, at first these applied the new rate not just to the 'slice' above the critical threshold figure, but also to all earnings. This system, known as the 'slab' system, meant that the marginal effects of £1 of extra income could be to cause a very severe tax burden. It is no wonder, therefore, that it was not in the interests of either employer or employee to raise wages in certain situations unless by a very great amount – hence, the bunching of wage rates at certain levels. NICs provided the last example of the UK's use of the slab system; the slab system was also used for super tax from 1911–1926 and for estate duty until 1968.

69 See IFS Green Budget 2004, ch 4.
70 [For 2007–08, the primary threshold is set at £100 a week.]
71 [For 2007–08, the upper earnings limit is set at £670 a week.]
72 [For 2007–08, the further charge of 1% is on sums above £670 a week.]
73 [For 2007–08, the employer's rate of 12.8% is in earnings of over £100 a week.]
74 [1.6% for 2007–08.]
75 [3.7% for 2007–08.]
76 [See now ITA 2007, s 35.]
77 For a chart showing changes since 1997 see IFS Green Budget Table 2005, Table 7.1.

'Poverty traps', 'unemployment traps' or, more generally, the 'surtax on the poor', have been addressed in stages. Before the Social Security Act 1986 came into force, the reduction in benefits combined with the start of income tax and NICs led to the net rate of 'tax' exceeding 100%. This was because the social security claw back rules were applied to gross income, ie, before income tax or NICs. After the Social Security Act 1986 the amount of the benefit was related to income net of tax and NICs.[78] Despite this, the rates remain much higher than the top rate of income tax (40%). Writing in 1993 Hills suggested that while the 1986 reforms largely removed the problem of people losing more than 100% of any extra income, and so ending up worse off, substantially more people faced rates above 70%. These figures applied to families in work; those out of work and receiving income support could still lose 100% of additional part-time earnings.[79] Further work was carried out by Nigel Lawson in 1989,[80] but it fell to Gordon Brown to complete the process by aligning the earnings threshold for NICs to that of personal relief for income tax, paid for by an extra charge on employer's contributions for higher paid.[81] The introduction of tax credits, beginning with the working families' tax credit, has been another major reform, but the proud boast that the credit will help many relatively well-off families means a major extension of people facing high marginal effective rates of tax[82] . . .

NICs are not charged on the same basis as ordinary income.[83] They apply to ITEPA earnings and, sometimes, ITTOIA Part 2 profits. Class 1A rates apply to all benefits in kind taxable under ITEPA; however, this is usually a charge on the employer and not on the employee.[84] **[14.20]**

The National Insurance Contributions Act 2006 provides for a power to make regulations, retrospective in effect, in respect of NICs avoidance involving employee remuneration. It also provides for a power to extend to NICs the anti-avoidance disclosure rules contained in the Finance Act 2004, Part 7. Such measures must surely lay to rest any residual argument that NICs are not income tax by another name. **[14.20a]**

3. Net income

It is necessary to determine the net income of the individual in order to establish:

(i) the individual's entitlement to personal reliefs.[85] There are two aspects to this; first, personal reliefs available to the individual in one tax year can only be deducted from his or her net income for that year. Personal reliefs cannot be brought forward or carried back for use in other tax years. Secondly, age relief[86] is reduced if the claimant's net income exceeds the statutory limit;[87]

78 See Cmnd. 9691.
79 Hills, *The future of Welfare* (1993) 25, who pointed out that in 1992–93 1.9m unemployed non-pensioners were receiving income support and in this position.
80 For assessment, see Dilnot and Webb, (1989) 10(2) *Fiscal Studies* 38 [above, para **[14.17]**.]
81 Report No. 3, paras 2.15 *et seq.*
82 Written Answer (see Hansard, 23 May 2000).
83 See Sandler, *Harmonising the Fringes of National Insurance and Income Tax* (IFS Commentary 36).
84 See generally Tiley and Collison, *UK Tax Guide*, Pt IX.
85 Personal reliefs are given only to individuals resident in the UK and those non-residents to whom ICTA 1988, s 278 applies; see para **[14.32]**, below.
86 Available for those aged 65 and over: see ITA 2007, ss 36(1), 37(1).
87 ITA 2007, ss 36 (2), 37(2).

(ii) whether, and to what extent, the higher rate of tax applies;
(iii) whether the individual has reliefs or allowances[88] which may be set against income which has suffered tax and is thereby entitled to a repayment of tax.

For income tax purposes, net income is determined by ascertaining a taxpayer's total income,[89] which is an aggregate of all the amounts of the taxpayer's income under the various taxing statutes (ie, under ITEPA 2003, ITTOIA 2005 and ITA 2007), including such income as may already have suffered tax at source, for the tax year, and by deducting from this aggregate any reliefs to which the taxpayer may be entitled.[90] **[14.21]**

A. *Receipts*

A sum which, though due, is not paid in a year of assessment, is not part of the individual's total income for that year. **[14.22]**

Parkside Leasing Ltd v Smith [1985] 1 WLR 310 (Ch D)

Upon the cessation of the taxpayer company's business as a haulage contractor due to the compulsory purchase of its premises, it received, on 9 April 1979, a cheque for compensation plus interest. This cheque was presented on 11 April, and cleared a few days later. On 10 April 1979, the taxpayer company commenced a new trade and incurred allowable losses, which it claimed could be used to offset the interest paid by means of the cheque. The Crown contended that the interest was received by the company on the date it received the cheque (9 April), when it was not trading, and thus had no allowable losses.

> SCOTT J.: . . . I must, accordingly, decide whether the taxpayers company's liability to tax under Case III of Schedule D in respect of the interest comprised in the cheque which it received on April 9, arose when the cheque was received or on some subsequent date. If I decide in favour of some subsequent date it does not matter in the present case what that subsequent date may be. For the taxpayer company's purposes any date subsequent to April 9, 1979 will do.
>
> Under section 109(1) of the Income and Corporation Taxes Act 1970[91] tax is chargeable under Case III of Schedule D in respect of "any interest of money." It is well established that for liability to tax to be incurred under Case III receipt of interest is necessary and that receivability of interest is not enough.
>
> . . .The question is whether and when the taxpayer has received the interest. Actual receipt in the sense that, at least, the money is at his disposal is required. But, as it seems to me, receipt of a cheque is merely a first step in the process that may lead to actual receipt, in the sense I have mentioned, of the proceeds. Mr. Carnwath suggested that since in the present case the cheque was drawn on the Bank of England it was, in a commercial sense, as good as cash. As a comment that may be justified, but I do not think that can be the right approach. The question whether receipt of a cheque is receipt of money for the purposes of Case III cannot, in my view, depend on the financial substance of the drawer of the cheque, nor on the financial soundness of the bank on which the cheque is drawn; otherwise complicated investigations might be necessary in order to decide what should

88 Ie allowances in excess of those used to offset income which has not suffered tax at source.
89 ITA 2007, s 23 (Step 1).
90 *Ibid*, s 23 (Step 2).
91 [Now ITTOIA 2005, s 365(1)(a).]

be a simple question of fact, namely, whether the taxpayer has received the money and, if so, when . . .

. . . In my opinion, liability under Case III of Schedule D requires actual payment. Delivery of a cheque may, no doubt, for some purposes be regarded as a conditional payment. But it is not, in my view, such a payment as allows the receipt of the cheque to be regarded as the receipt of the proceeds. It is the receipt of the proceeds, whether as cash or by the crediting of the sum to an account of the payee, that places the proceeds at the disposal of the payee and, in my judgment, attracts the liability to tax under Case III of Schedule D. In my judgment, therefore, the taxpayer company's liability to tax did not arise on April 9, 1979 when it received the cheque comprising the interest, and accordingly I allow the appeal. **[14.23]**

Girvan v Orange Personal Communications Services Ltd [1998] STC 567 (Ch D) (above, para [11.3])

The effect of a renegotiated agreement between the taxpayer and its bank was that interest on deposit accounts was to be compounded quarterly and not paid until January 1993 or, if earlier, when demanded by Orange or when the accounts were closed. The Revenue argued that each quarterly instalment of interest due on each of the deposit accounts should be treated as 'income arising' in respect of the accounting year in which that quarter fell. The taxpayer submitted that, while it was undoubtedly the case that the income did 'arise' to it, it should not be considered to have done so until the accounting period during which the whole of the interest payable was actually paid. The court preferred the argument of the taxpayer.

NEUBERGER J.: . . . Of course, the question as to what constitutes 'income arising' in the context of taxation legislation is by no means free of authority. It appears to me that the conclusion I have reached as a matter of ordinary language is supported by authority. In *St Lucia Usines and Estates Co Ltd v Colonial Treasurer of St Lucia* [1924] AC 508, Lord Wrenbury, giving the judgment of the Privy Council in relation to an ordinance which rendered interest liable to tax if it was 'income arising and accruing' in the relevant year said this at p. 512:

> 'The words "income arising or accruing" are not equivalent to the words "Debts arising or accruing". To give them that meaning is to ignore the word "income! The words mean "money arising or accruing by way of income". There must be a coming in to satisfy the word "income".'

I find this short passage helpful. In the first place, it does seem to me to support the simple proposition that there is no 'income' liable to tax unless some money has 'come in'. Secondly, it distinguishes between income and debt: so long as the interest in the present case was accruing and not called by Orange, it appears to me to be an accruing debt, which, as Mr. David Goldberg QC, who appears on behalf of Orange, contended, is the antithesis of income in the sense that, so long as the debt is wholly unpaid, there is no income, and once it is wholly paid, the payment is income, and the debt is no more. Thirdly, in so far as the words that qualify 'income' are relevant, that case could be said to have been stronger than the present from the Revenue's point of view, because of the words 'or accruing' after the word 'arising'.

To much the same effect, in *Leigh v IR Commrs* (1927) 11 TC 590, Rowlatt J said at p. 595:

> 'Now one must, I think, remember this, that receivalibility without receipt for the purpose of Income Tax is nothing at all. There is no Income Tax or Super-tax upon a good debt or upon the value of a moderate debt. I am not speaking, of course, of mercantile accounts where these things are brought in, or anything of that sort; but there is no such thing as Income Tax upon a debt until it is paid.'

Those observations were cited with approval in *Dewar v IRCommrs* (1935) 19 TC 561 at p. 576–577. I appreciate that in *Dunmore v McGowan* (HMIT) (1978) 52 TC 307 at p. 316,

Stamp LJ (with whom the other members of the Court of Appeal agreed) said that 'the doctrine that "receivalibility without receipt is nothing" is a doctrine which can be pressed too far'. However, that was in a case where the taxpayer was arguing that payment of interest by the bank into an account at the bank, set up by agreement between the taxpayer and the bank, for the taxpayer's own benefit, was not 'income arising' when it was paid, because the account was charged to the bank to support a guarantee given by the taxpayer to the bank. Despite the fact that, because of the existence of the charge, the taxpayer could not do what he liked with the interest, on the date that the interest was paid into the account 'every penny of that interest inured to the [*taxpayer's*] benefit in any event; it swelled the assets of the [*taxpayer*] on that day', see at p. 315 from the judgment of Brightman J, which Stamp LJ fully endorsed, at p. 316. In the present case, the interest may have been 'accruing' until 18 December 1992, but I do not think one can say that 'every penny of that interest inured' to Orange's benefit until it was paid on that day. Stamp LJ at p. 317 put it in his own words in this way:

> 'The interest was received or "got" when it was credited to the deposit account, an account of money which was at all times owed by the bank to the taxpayer, albeit charged in support of the guarantee.'

It appears to me that that observation also supports Orange's contention in the present case. Following the initial agreement in correspondence between Orange and the bank, no interest was credited to any account in the name of Orange, or in favour of Orange. Furthermore, while Orange had the right at any time to 'get' the interest, either by asking for it or by closing the deposit account, it would not, as a matter of ordinary language, 'get' the interest until it asked for it or closed the account or until January 1993. **[14.24]**

See also *IRC v Hamilton-Russell's Executors* [1943] 1 All ER 474; *Spens v IRC* [1970] 1 WLR 1173; *MacPherson v Bond* [1985] 1 WLR 1157, and Chapter 15 generally.

A considerable limitation is placed upon the principle stated above in that, if there is actual 'income' it is part of the total income of the person entitled to it, without the need for actual payment. Actual receipt is also unnecessary in the computation of profits of a trade, etc where the 'earnings' basis is used to draw up accounts (see Chapter 10, above).

See J Tiley 'Receivability and Receipt: The Problem of Timing under Income Tax Legislation' [1982] BTR *23*, and 'More on Receivability and Receipt' [1986] BTR 152. See also J Freedman 'Profit and Prophets – Law and Accounting Practice on the Timing of Receipts – Recognition Under the Earnings Basis (Schedule D, Cases I and II)' [1987] BTR 61 and 104. **[14.25]**

B. Income received after deduction of tax

Income may be received gross (for example, trading income), or after deduction of tax at source. Thus:

> 'Income from which a deduction in respect of income tax is to be made (or treated as made) at the basic or savings rate in force for a tax year is treated as income of that tax year.'[92]

In this case, this net sum must be grossed up for the purpose of ascertaining a taxpayer's total income. **[14.26]**

92 ITA 2007, s 31(1).

Natalie Lee (gen ed) *Revenue Law, Principles and Practice* (25th edn, 2007) paras [7.22]–[7.25]

2. Income received after deduction of tax

a) General

Some income is received and enters the income calculation gross: ie without having suffered any tax. The tax on that income is collected by self-assessment when the tax return is submitted. For certain types of income, however, tax is deducted at source. In such cases, the payer of the income is obliged to act as a tax collector by deducting from the payment an amount of tax and paying it to HMRC. If the recipient is not liable to income tax (or is only liable at the lower rate), he will be able to obtain a repayment from HMRC of the tax deducted. If, however, he is liable to the higher rate tax, a further tax payment will be necessary. These payments are made (and repayments given) through the self-assessment system. For UK dividend income, a tax credit is available (although it is not refundable) which satisfies the tax payer's lower or basic rate liability.

Accordingly, any sum received after deduction of tax (or with a tax credit, in the case of UK dividend income) is normally grossed up to discover the sum from which the tax was deducted (or deemed deducted). The resulting (gross) figure must be entered in the recipient taxpayer's calculation of total income to find his tax liability. The tax that has already been paid on this income is credited against his tax bill.

b) Savings income

Dividends and other company distributions are paid with a tax credit of 10% and are treated as forming the top slice of the individual's income. The credit was treated as satisfying the taxpayer's starting or basic rate liability so that no further tax was charged unless the taxpayer suffers tax at the higher rate (ITA 2007 ss 13–14 and ITTOIA 2005 s 397). This treatment also applies to interest and other savings income which is paid with a tax deduction at the savings rate of 20%. The tax deducted also satisfies the taxpayer's starting and basic rate liability so that no further tax is charged unless the taxpayer suffers tax at the higher rate (ITA 2007 s 12). Tax must also be deducted in a number of other cases such as annual payments, rents paid to foreign landlords and some annuities and patent royalties (ITA 2007 Part 15) . . .

c) Illustrations

The main examples of income received after deduction of tax at source are:

(1) trust income received by a beneficiary after deduction of tax;
(2) earnings and pensions from which tax is deducted under the PAYE system;
(3) some annuities and certain other annual payments from which basic rate tax is deducted;
(4) income arising from deposit accounts, received after deduction of tax at 20%.

d) Irrecoverable tax credits

Certain forms of income are treated as though they have already suffered income tax when received but that tax is irrecoverable. The main examples are:

(1) UK dividend income: tax at 10% is treated as having been paid but no further liability arises if the individual is liable at the basic rate. The higher rate of tax on such income is 32.5%.
(2) Stock dividends: TA 1988 s 249. Tax of 10% is treated as paid.
(3) Loans to participators which are waived: TA 1988 s 421. Tax of 10% treated as paid.

An individual receiving a stock dividend of £90 is therefore treated as if tax of £10 had been paid on income of £100. If he does not pay income tax there is no refund of this sum: if he is a basic rate taxpayer the tax credit satisfies his basic rate tax liability in full: if he is a higher rate taxpayer further tax of £22.50 will be payable (being a liability of £32.50 on the income of £100 less the £10 credit) leaving the individual with £67.50. **[14.27]**

C. *Interest paid by building societies and banks*

Interest paid by building societies and banks were once subject to tax at a reduced rate (known as the 'composite rate'), and investors were treated as having suffered basic rate income tax, although the tax deemed to have been deducted was not refundable. This system was abolished with effect from 6 April 1991, and was replaced by one that involves the interest being paid net of lower rate income tax (20%), with those who do not pay tax being able to claim recovery of the tax deducted.[93] **[14.28]**

D. *Deductible reliefs*

An individual is permitted to deduct certain allowable payments from his total income (Step 2 in the income tax calculation) and before personal reliefs, to ascertain his or her 'net income.' These payments are set out in ITA 2007, s 24 and include relief for annual payments[94] and patent royalties.[95] The extent of the relief depends upon there being sufficient total income available; any amount of relief that is not absorbed cannot be carried forward to future tax years.[96]

As far as certain annual payments are concerned (see Chapter 11), tax is collected at source from the payer, whilst the burden of the tax rests with the recipient. A sum representing income tax at the basic rate must be deducted by the payer from the payment,[97] and income tax equivalent to that sum will be collected through the payer's self-assessment return under ITA 2007, Pt 15, Ch 6. Relief for such payments, provided for by ITA 2007, s 448, is given by way of deduction from total income at Step 2 in the income calculation. For his part, the recipient of the annual payment will receive a sum net of tax together with a credit for the basic rate tax that has been deducted at source and paid to HMRC on his behalf. The recipient will enter the grossed-up amount of the payment in establishing his total income. Accordingly, he may be liable to higher rate tax in

93 ITA 2007, ss 851,855.
94 These are annual payments falling within ITTOIA 2005, s 683.
95 ITA 2007, Pt 8, Ch 4. Relief is also given at this stage for trading losses (ITA 2007, ss 64, 72, 83, 89 and 96), share loss (ITA 2007, s 72) and interest payments (ITA 2007, Pt 8, Ch 1), to name but a few.
96 *Ibid*, s 25(4).
97 *Ibid*, s 900.

respect of the payment or, if he is not liable to pay income tax (because his income is below the taxable threshold), he will be entitled to repayment by HMRC of the basic rate already paid on his behalf.

Historically, annual payments played an important roll in tax planning, particularly through the use of both charitable and non-charitable covenants, although these opportunities were subject to various anti-avoidance settlement provisions,[98] the effect of which was to deem the payment to belong to the taxpayer for all income tax purposes, thus restricting the payment's deductibility in the computation of his total income. However, in this context, these provisions were reduced in importance from 1988 onwards[99], at which time most annual payments entered into on or after 15 March 1988 were excluded from the tax system altogether. Annual payments which fall within ITTOIA 2005, s 727(1) cannot be deducted by the payer, and are not part of the income of the payee. All annual payments made by an individual and entered into on or after 15 March 1988, which would otherwise have been taxed under the former Schedule D, Case III (see para **[11.11]**, above), come within s 727(1), except those payments specifically excluded by s. 727(2) (and see ITA 2007, ss 900(1), 901(2)). These exceptions comprise payments made for *bona fide* commercial reasons in connection with the payer's trade, profession or vocation (such as partnership retirement annuities)[100] and payments for non-taxable consideration.[101] The former rules will apply to these excluded payments; see para **[11.15]**, above. Payments of interest are also excluded under ITA 2007, s 899(5)), but are subject to deduction under different rules.[102] Covenanted payments to charity, once an exception within what is now ITA 2007, ss 900(1), 901(2), were removed from the scope of the former Schedule D Case III to Gift Aid,[103] but are taxed in a like way to the exceptional cases. Subject to a minor exception, maintenance payments have been entirely removed from the tax system:[104] see para **[11.11]**, below.

Once relief has been deducted from total income, the sum remaining is the taxpayer's 'net income', from which personal allowances may then be deducted at Step 3 (see below). Relief by way of a reduction in the amount of tax payable attributable to investments in the enterprise investment scheme,[105] venture capital trusts,[106] and allowances attracting relief at 10% is given at Step 6. **[14.29]**

98 Now to be found in ITTOIA 2005, Pt 5, Ch 5, comprising s 629 (payments of income to or for the benefit of the settlor's own unmarried infant child to be treated as the income of the settler) and ss 624–628 (if, during the life of the settler, any property subject to a settlement, or any 'derived property' can become payable to, or for the benefit of, the settlor or spouse of the settlor, the income of the settlement is treated as the settlor's own income for all income tax purposes).

99 See FA 1988, s 36, inserting ss 347A and 347B; ITTOIA 2005, s 727(1).

100 ITTOIA 2005, s 728; ITA 2007, s 900(1), 901(2).

101 *Ibid*, s 729; ITA 2007, s 900(1), 901(2).

102 ITA 2007, Pt 15, Ch 3. Types of loan included are those used to acquire an interest in a close company, a partnership or a co-operative, loans to purchase plant or machinery or a life annuity, and a loan to a personal representative to pay inheritance tax.

103 *Ibid*, Pt 8, Ch 2.

104 *Ibid*, Pt 8, Ch 5.

105 ICTA 1988, ss 289–312; for shares issued on or after 5 April 2007, see ITA 2007, Pt 5, Ch 4.

106 ITA 2007, Pt 6, Ch 2.

IRC v Frere [1965] AC 402 (HL)

VISCOUNT RADCLIFFE: . . . This system of charging tax at source and then setting up machinery for distributing the burden of that tax between the source holder and the person who was regarded, pro tanto, as the real owner of the source was evolved for the purpose of income tax, which was assessed and collected under the various Schedules, item by item. The problem of exempting those with income below a statutory minimum was that which first raised in a practical form the question what was a person's total income from all sources (as we should now call it) or, to use the words of section 168 of the Act of 1842, what was the "aggregate annual amount of his income, estimated according to the several rules and directions of this Act." It was section 164 of that Act which, as I read it, laid down explicitly the range of matters that were to be taken into account in determining whether or not a person had an aggregate income within the exemption. He was to deliver to the assessor a notice of his claim, together with a declaration "setting forth therein all the particular sources from whence the income of such claimant shall arise, and the particular amount arising from each source, and also every sum of annual interest or other annual payment reserved or charged thereon, whereby the income shall or may be diminished . . . ." On the basis of a claim made out in this way, if not objected to by the inspector or surveyor, the commissioners were authorized to "allow such claim of exemption." Nothing, I agree, is ever plain when one comes to deal with the income tax code, but I would, with respect, have thought it reasonably clear that, when the makers of the Act of 1842 wished to prescribe what was to be taken as the "aggregate annual amount" of a man's income for the purposes of their Act, they allowed the amount to be reduced by the sum of any annual interest payable out of his income but not by the sum of any interest that did not qualify as "annual." If you like to put it that way, they thought that annual interest and other annual payments "diminished" the income or that the amount required to pay them was not the payer's income at all: they do not seem to have thought of other kinds of payment as having this effect. **[14.30]**

Proska E Soos 'Taxation at the Source and Withholding in England, 1512–1640' [1995] BTR 49

The principle of taxation at the source occupies a special place in the history of the British income tax and is recognised as one of the primary causes of its success. The first comprehensive tax on income was introduced in England in 1799 as a temporary war measure to raise revenue for the hostilities with France. The tax was levied by means of a direct assessment on recipients of income, based on general returns of total income from all sources which taxpayers were required to make. This form of assessment led to widespread abuse and the tax was a failure. The tax was repealed in 1802, but revived in 1803 when hostilities resumed. The principle of taxation at the source was introduced in the income tax of 1803 in an effort to reduce the frauds that had marked the first income tax. Under this principle, the tax was assessed, wherever possible, on the source of income rather than its destination, and the **source** was permitted to recover the tax by deducting it when distributing the income. The tax was thus collected from persons not directly interested in its payment, and evasion was reduced because the tax was deducted before the income reached the ultimate proprietor. The United Kingdom Inland Revenue explained the principle of taxation at the source in the income tax of 1803:

"The abuses to which this [*the 1799 income tax*] mode of assessment on total income was open led the framers of the Income Tax Act of 1803 to make their approaches to the taxpayer in a less direct but more certain fashion. Instead of looking in the first place at the taxpayer, they looked at the source of income, classified incomes according to their kind under the Schedules . . ., and levied the tax so far as they could at the point where the income first emerged and became visible, leaving the first possessors of the income to deduct a proportion of the tax when distributing any part of the income among those

> who had charges upon it. So entered into our Income Tax system the great principle of taxation at the source, a principle which has lasted . . . to the present day, and has proved of such central importance in Income Tax administration . . ."[107]

Taxation at the source proved effective, nearly doubling the tax yield, and became a permanent feature of the British income tax. Since then taxation at the source, also commonly referred to as "deduction at the source", has been universally acclaimed. The Royal Commission on the Income Tax of 1920 considered it "the only sure safeguard against evasion of duty",[108] and the Inland Revenue described it as the principle which "remains the great buttress of Income Tax stability and efficiency".[109] Historians too have acknowledged the effectiveness of taxation at the source. One called it a principle of "dramatic efficiency and durability",[110] and another regarded it as "perhaps the chief cause of the great success of the English income tax".[111]

Much has been written about taxation at the source, and its application in the income tax of 1803 is well known. Less well known are the origins of taxation at the source. Most historians now agree that Henry Addington, Prime Minister and Chancellor of the Exchequer in 1803, should be credited for applying taxation at the source to the income tax in 1803.[112] Some historians have implied that taxation at the source originated in 1803,[113] but others have traced it back to earlier taxes, notably the land tax in 1688[114] or 1692[115] or the monthly assessment in 1657. **[14.31]**

For some earlier cases on the deduction of income tax from interest and other annual payments, see *Earl Howe v IRC* [1919] 2 KB 336; *Re Hanbury, decd* (1939) 38 TC 588; and *Ang v Parrish* [1980] 1 WLR 940. **[14.31a]**

4. Personal allowances and reliefs

In determining an individual's liability to income tax, certain personal allowances, once quite numerous and now severely reduced in number may be deducted from net income. These allowances, which may be claimed only by an 'individual',[116] are based on the individual's personal circumstances

107 *Royal Commission on the Income Tax: First Instalment of the Minutes of Evidence with Appendices*, Cmd. 288–1 (1919, London, His Majesty's Stationery Office ("HMSO")), Appendix No. 7(g); Board of Inland Revenue, "Historical Note on Taxation at the Source", para.1.

108 *Report of the Royal Commission on the Income Tax*, para. 156, Cmd. 615 (1920, London, HMSO).

109 *Royal Commission on the Income Tax: First Instalment of the Minutes of Evidence with Appendices*, *supra* n.90, Appendix No.1: Board of Inland Revenue, "Brief History of the Income Tax", para. 3.

110 Sabine, BEV, *A Short History of Taxation* (1980, London, Butterworths), p. 118.

111 Seligman, Edwin RA, *The Income Tax* (2nd ed., 1914, New York, The Macmillan Co.), p. 216.

112 See, *e.g.* Seligman, [n 111] at pp. 89–91; Freemantle, A.F., *England in the Nineteenth Century 1801–1805* (1929, reprinted in 1978, London, George Allen & Unwin Ltd), p. 366; Hope-Jones, Arthur, *Income Tax in the Napoleonic Wars* (1939, Cambridge, Cambridge Univ. Press), pp. 20–22; Farnsworth, A., *Addington: Author of the Modern Income Tax* (1951), London, Stevens & Sons Ltd), pp. 40–61, 125–127; Ziegler, Philip, *Addington: A Life of Henry Addington, First Viscount Sidmouth* (1965, London, Collins), pp. 189–191; Sabine, B.E.V., *A History of Income Tax* (1966, London, George Allen & Unwin Ltd), pp. 35–37.

113 See, *e.g.* Seligman, [n 111] at pp. 90–91, 98; Hope-Jones, [n 112] at pp. 20–22.

114 Phillips, William, "A New Light on Addington's Income Tax" [1967] B.T.R. pp. 271, 276–279. See also Sabine, *A Short History of Taxation*, [n 110] at p. 118 and Sabine, "Tax Deduction at Source: It Started with a War," *Taxation Practitioner*, August 1994, p. 8.

115 See, *e.g.* Farnsworth, [n 112] at pp. 46–47; Ziegler, [n 112] at p. 190. These historians gave the date of the original land tax as 1692; according to Phillips ([n 114] at pp. 275–276), the original land tax was in 1688.

116 ITA 2007, s 23 (Step 3). They cannot be claimed by personal representatives, trustees, or by a company. A child, however young, has its own personal allowance.

rather than on the type of income concerned. Personal allowances that once existed, but which have been abolished include the married couple's allowance for those aged below 65 on 5 April 2000,[117] the additional personal allowance (given, in effect, to relieve the financial position of 'one-parent' families) and the widow's bereavement allowance.[118] These allowances were replaced by the children's tax credit, which took effect from April 2001, and which was itself replaced by the child tax credit in April 2003. Both of these measures were part of the Government's weaponry in reducing child poverty.[119]

In the event that personal allowances exceed an individual's total income in any one year, the surplus cannot be carried forward to later years, and thus must remain unused. The personal reliefs and allowances (available for 2007–08) comprise (i) the personal allowance;[120] (ii) the personal allowance for those aged between 65 and 74;[121] (iii) the personal allowance for those aged 75 and over;[122] (iv) the married couple's allowance for those who married before 5 December 2005, where either spouse was born before 6 April, 1935;[123] (v) the married couple's allowance for those who married or who entered into a civil partnership on or after 5 December 2005, where either spouse or civil partner was born before 6 April, 1935;[124] and (vi) blind person's relief.[125] The allowance in (ii)–(v) is reduced if the individual's income exceeds the given income limit (£20,100 for 2007–08[126]). With reference to marriages entered into prior to 5 December 2005, the allowance is given automatically to the husband;[127] for post-5 December 2005 marriages or civil partnerships, it is allocated to the individual with the higher income.[128] Those who were married prior to that date may elect to opt into the new scheme if they wish to do so.[129] In any event, either the couple may make a joint election to have the whole of the specified amount (£2,440 for 2007–08) allocated to the individual's spouse or civil partner,[130] or the individual's spouse or civil partner may elect to receive one-half of the specified amount.[131] Moreover, notice may be given by an individual whose income is insufficient to absorb the relief that the individual's spouse or partner should be entitled to an income tax reduction calculated by reference to the unused part of the allowance.[132] Historically, all personal reliefs were given by way of a deduction from an individual's total income but, from 1994–95 onwards, the married couple's allowance has been given by reducing the tax payable by a percentage of that allowance (10% for 1999–2000 and subsequent years).[133]

117 This was removed for the tax year 2000–01 and subsequent years.
118 see FA 1999, s 34.
119 See, in particular, Budget Speech, 21 March, 2000, *Hansard*, HC, Vol 346, col 865.
120 ITA 2007, s 35.
121 *Ibid*, s 36.
122 *Ibid*, s 37.
123 *Ibid*, s 45. The allowance is greater for those aged 75 and over.
124 *Ibid*, s 46. The allowance is greater for those aged 75 and over.
125 *Ibid*, s 38.
126 *Ibid*, s 36(2), 37(2).
127 *Ibid*, s 45(1).
128 *Ibid*, s 46(2)(e).
129 *Ibid*, s 44.
130 *Ibid*, s 48.
131 *Ibid*, s 47.
132 *Ibid*, s 51.
133 *Ibid*, s 23 (Step 6 of the tax calculation).

For an historical review of personal reliefs, see *The Taxation of Husband and Wife* (HMSO, 1980, Cmnd. 8093), *The Reform of Personal Taxation* (HMSO, 1986, Cmnd 7956) and *Independent Taxation of Husband and Wife* (Inland Revenue Press Release, 15 March 1988). **[14.32]**

Budget Speech: The Chancellor of the Exchequer, The Right Honourable Gordon Brown MP, *Hansard*, HC, vol 327, col 182, 9 March 1999

. . . What is today called the married couple's allowance is in fact neither restricted to marriage, nor restricted to couples, nor is it strictly an allowance. It is in fact a tax credit paid at the same flat rate to married couples, single parents and unmarried parents living together.

Far from recognising marriage it is now so confused that it can even be paid at twice the rate in the year of separation or divorce. A married couple's allowance that can pay more for separation or divorce cannot be said to uphold the institution of marriage.

The last Government called the married couple's allowance an anomaly and reduced it from 40 per cent to 15 per cent, cutting its value in half.

If we were now to restrict the married couple's allowance to married couples only, as some propose, we would unfairly exclude, for example, widows with children, and wives who have been deserted and left to bring up their children alone.

So we will replace the married couple's allowance with a new family tax cut that will increase the amount that goes to help families with children. This children's tax credit will give more – not less – help to families at the time they need it most, when they have their children and when their children are growing up.

Today's pensioner couples will retain the married couple's allowance. And couples without children or whose children have grown up will benefit from other changes I will shortly announce.

The married couple's allowance is now worth 190 pounds to married couples. The children's tax credit, the tax cut for families, to be introduced from April 2001, will be worth 416 pounds, and as a result the typical family with children will be over 200 pounds a year better off.

This tax cut for families represents the first recognition in the tax system for over 20 years of the extra costs of bringing up children. **[14.33]**

5. Progressive taxation

Income tax is chargeable on a progressive basis, that is to say, as the income of the individual increases, so the *proportion* of that income which is payable as tax also increases. Under the present system, this is achieved by imposing income tax at the starting rate on the first band of the taxpayer's *taxable income*, at the basic rate on the next band, and the remainder at the higher rate.[134] Progressive taxation must be distinguished from proportional taxation, which takes the same proportion of an individual's income

134 For the tax year 2007–08, the starting rate is set at 10% for taxable income up to £2,230, the basic rate at 22% on income over £2,230 and up to £34,600 and the higher rate at 40% on income above £34,600. Taxable income is net income (Step 2 in the income etax calculation) less personal allowances (Step 3) .

irrespective of the amount of that income, and regressive taxation, which takes an increasing proportion of income as that income decreases. Until 1999,[135] there was no 'starting' or 'lower' rate, but simply a wide basic rate band. The introduction in 1999 of a starting rate was part of the Government's policy of 'making work pay'; other measures included the national minimum wage and the introduction of the Working Families' Tax Credit.[136] In the past, the basic rate band has been followed by a number of narrower bands of taxable income, each of which was taxed at a progressively *higher rate* of tax.[137] From 1988–89, a single higher rate band of 40 per cent was imposed, and this band has no limit. Given a fairly wide basic rate band and a single higher rate band, it is arguable that the UK system of income tax is far from being progressive. **[14.34]**

Royal Commission on the Taxation of Profits and Income, Second Report, 1953 Cmd 9105

PROGRESSIVE TAXATION

101. The system of personal taxation is progressive. The effective rate of tax upon the income of the individual taxpayer, the amount of tax that he pays divided by the amount of his total income, increases as the income increases. By this means the burden of tax is so distributed that the owner of the larger income contributes a larger proportion of it in tax than the owner of the smaller income. But the tax burden is adjusted not only by variation of rate but also by the grant of allowances in respect of (1) certain categories of personal circumstances that affect taxpaying capacity of individual taxpayers and (2) a differentiation between earned income on the one hand and investment income on the other.[138] Before we could come to any conclusion about the extent to which the present distribution is satisfactory, we found it necessary to establish a point of view about the basis upon which the principle of progressive taxation rests.

102. It is plain that progression is not the only possible scheme of tax distribution. It is possible for tax to be levied in such a way that each taxpayer is assessed for an equal amount, whatever the size of his income; taxes have often been levied in such a form that tax is proportional to income; nor do these alternatives exhaust the possibilities. The United Kingdom income tax, as first levied in 1799, was in its main lines (apart, that is, from certain exemptions for small incomes) a proportional tax; it did not begin to acquire a generally progressive character until the year 1907. Today the progressive character of the tax is taken for granted; to return to the old proportional tax would be quite impracticable. It is, however, necessary for our purposes to consider the grounds upon which this great change in opinion can be

135 With the exception of tax years 1978–79 and 1979–80, when a reduced rate of 25% was applied to a narrow band of income before the application of the wide basic rate band to the next slice of income. The starting rate of 10% was introduced by FA 1999, s 22. It is to be abolished for 2008–09 and subsequent tax years.

136 See Chapter 15, below, para **[15.4]**.

137 In 1987–88, and for some years previously, the higher rates started at 40% and increased by 5% for each band until the highest rate of 60% was reached.

138 [Investment income was formerly taxed more heavily than earned income by an additional rate of tax (either 15% or 10%) which was imposed by FA 1971, s 32(3) on investment income over a certain limit. This investment income surcharge was abolished from 1984–85 onwards (FA 1984, Sch 7), but an additional rate of tax still applies to the income of discretionary trusts; see below, para **[16.13]**.]

justified, since it would be insufficient for us to rest our treatment upon the mere historical fact that the change has occurred. We are called upon to judge the scheme of progressive taxation as it now stands, and we must accordingly have some basis for our judgment.

103. The case for progressive taxation has often been argued upon the basis of the following propositions. The aim of government, in taxation as in other matters, is to promote the greatest happiness of the governed. All payment of taxes being in some measure a sacrifice by the taxpayer of the means of happiness, taxation ought to be so adjusted between the payers as to cause as little sacrifice in the aggregate as possible. In general, and in the absence of special needs, there is a presumption that to take £1 from a man with a large income will cause less sacrifice than to take the same sum from a man whose income is smaller. Taxation should therefore be laid predominantly upon the wealthy, and a progressive income tax is justified as a means of bringing about this result. **[14.35]**

The argument for progressive taxation is one of respectable antiquity; thus Adam Smith stated: 'It is not very unreasonable that the rich should contribute to the public expense not only in proportion to their revenue, but in something more than proportion' (The *Wealth of Nations,* Book V, Chapter II). There is a considerable volume of literature on the principle of progressive taxation; see, in particular, A R Prest and N A Barr *Public Finance* (6th edn, 1979) Chapter 4 and W J Blum and H Kalven, Jr *The Uneasy Case for Progressive Taxation* (Chicago, 1953). See also Tiley (ed) *Butterworth's UK Tax Guide 1986–87,* Policy Supplement, ch 1, which contains many useful references to the USA literature on this subject. See also the Report of the Royal Commission on Taxation (Carter Commission) Canada, 1966, vol 1: Objectives. This aspect of the proposals of the Carter Commission is considered by G C Hockley 'Fiscal Reform' [1969] BTR 81. **[14.36]**

6. Indexation for inflation

Where inflation causes both prices and wages to rise, a progressive system of income tax with previously determined tax rate bands will bring in more tax revenue than would have been the case before the inflation occurred. As the monetary value of income increases, more and more income will either be taxed at the higher rates, or enter the basic rate tax band for the first time. This effect, known as *fiscal drag,* is enhanced if the level of personal allowances and reliefs remain unchanged. However, the rise in income is not an increase in its real value, and as the amount of tax paid increases, the actual value in real terms of what remains is reduced. Thus in a progressive tax system, inflation can cause post-tax income to fall unless the effects of inflation are taken into account in the design of the tax system.[139] **[14.37]**

139 Sir Geoffrey Howe commented thus on what he considered to be insufficient increases in personal allowances proposed by the Labour Government in the 1977 Budget: 'The amendments that we are now discussing do not go far enough to restore the position that existed in 1973. They would not remedy the damage that has been done by inflation in imposing on these people *(skilled workers)* tax increases that Parliament has not authorised but that have been increased by the stealthy process of inflation.' Debate on the Finance Bill, May 10, 1977. Parliamentary Debates: Commons, 1976–77, Vol 931, Col 1160.

***The Structure and Reform of Direct Taxation*, Report of a Committee chaired by Professor J E Meade (1978) pp 99, 115–118**

[Chapter 6]

Indexation for Inflation

THE CASE FOR INDEXATION

In any modern developed economy transactions take place through the medium of money, values are expressed in monetary terms, and – like all other transactions – tax bases are measured and taxes are levied in monetary forms and expressed in monetary values. No intolerable problems arise as a result provided that the general level of money prices – i.e. the real value of the monetary unit in terms of goods and services in general – is reasonably constant. But when the general level of prices is rapidly inflated (and in particular when the future rates of inflation are difficult to predict) very important inefficiencies and inequities can result. The resulting distortions to the tax system are only a part, though an important part, of this process. In the introduction to their Final Report in 1955, the Royal Commission on the Taxation of Profits and Income[140] emphasised this point in the following way: "One point upon which we must make our position clear is the question of monetary inflation. It lies at the base of our whole subject and it directly affects several of the topics with which we deal. We have taken it as our general premise that there will not be any marked decrease or increase in the purchasing power of money in the United Kingdom. It would be absurd to assume a complete stability of purchasing power in the future, nor do we need to do so for any recommendations that we make. Nor again do we require to assume that there will be no sudden and temporary variations. But if we could not take it as our premise that stability in purchasing power is the normal thing to be expected, we think that our review would be beating the air, for there would be lacking a condition that is a necessary assumption upon which to build either a satisfactory tax structure or a satisfactory distribution of the total burden of tax."

The monetary unit in the United Kingdom has in fact lost half its real purchasing power in the five years since 1972.[141] With the rates of monetary inflation that have recently been experienced in all modern developed economies, and in a particularly marked degree in the United Kingdom, it is no longer sensible to consider the tax structure on the Radcliffe Commission's assumption of a basic constancy of the general level of prices. A reasonable tax structure must be considered in real terms and not in monetary terms, and this implies adjustment of the monetary value of any tax base in such a way as to measure the real value of the tax base...

Average earnings

... In the absence of any bracket indexation there is the phenomenon of "fiscal drag," namely that when money incomes per head go up then, with a progressive tax system, the proportion of the total national income which is levied in direct taxes automatically goes up. This occurs because, with a general rise in money incomes per head, taxpayers automatically move from lower to higher income brackets and

140 [Royal Commission on Taxation of Income and Profits (Chairman. Lord Radcliffe), Cmd 9474, HMSO, 1955.]
141 [The Meade Report was published in 1978.]

thus, with a progressive scale of taxes, from lower to higher tax rates. But money incomes per head may rise either because money prices have risen or else because real output per head has risen. Fiscal drag may be due to either of these phenomena, which we will call *monetary fiscal drag* and *real fiscal drag* respectively.

The use of an index of the prices of finished products (such as the price of the gross domestic product) will remove monetary fiscal drag; but it will not remove real fiscal drag. If money income per head goes up because real income per head has gone up, there will be no adjustment of tax brackets if prices have remained constant.

But using an index of average earnings will remove both monetary and real fiscal drag. Tax brackets will be adjusted when earnings per head go up whether this is due to a rise in real output per head or in the monetary price of an unchanged output per head. There are two reasons why such a result may be welcomed:

1. If real output is growing because of increased productivity, it may be considered better to have a tax system which, in the absence of planned changes in the tax schedule, shares the gain more or less equally between the private and the public sectors of the economy (which will be the result of tax brackets which are indexed on average earnings) rather than a tax system which automatically raises the proportion of resources which accrue to the government in taxes.
2. As we have already argued, there may be social reasons for thinking of many of the brackets (e.g. the value of the tax threshold for low wage earners or the value of social security payments) in relative terms, *i.e.* as properly bearing a certain relationship to average earnings.

Average earnings are likely to move very much in line with money incomes per head of the population. The correspondence may not be exact because the proportion of the national product which goes not to earnings but to profits or other investment income may change, although with the very high proportion of the national income which now goes to earnings any discrepancy due to this cause is likely to be of minor significance. There is, however, another and much more important reason for a discrepancy, namely variations in the level of employment. If unemployment rises and total output is reduced, the value of output per head of the population will fall even if the value of output per person employed remains unchanged.

This phenomenon presents an important argument for using an index such as average earnings rather than an alternative index of money income per head, such as the value of the total national income (e.g. of the gross domestic product) divided by the total population. In times of recession in the level of real output and employment the latter index would have a perverse destabilising effect. When real output and employment fall, it is desirable to reduce rather than to raise the average level of taxes in order on Keynesian principles to maintain total effective demand. If, however, in times of trade recession the fall in the value of real output per head of the population were used as the index for the adjustment of tax brackets, the money value of social benefits, of tax thresholds and of other tax brackets would be reduced, a higher proportion of incomes would be levied in tax, and effective demand would be reduced. The use of an index of average earnings of persons in employment avoids this destabilising effect. **[14.38]**

During the passage of the 1977 Finance Bill, two members of the Labour Government (Audrey Wise and Geoff Rooker) introduced the so-called 'Rooker-Wise Amendment', which resulted in FA 1977, s 22(2) and (3).[142] This

142 Now repealed.

index-linked those personal reliefs in ICTA 1970, ss 8 and 14[143] to the increase in the retail price index for the previous year, subject to the Opposition's amendment permitting a smaller increase to be substituted by Parliament. The current position is set out in ITA 2007, s 57. The index used is the general index of retail prices (for all items) published by the Office of National Statistics.[144] Indexation occurs automatically; the words 'unless Parliament otherwise determines' that were found in the previous legislation[145] are omitted from TA 2007 because it is always open to a Finance Act to disapply the provision and thus it was decided that no express provision to that effect was needed. Parliament frequently does 'otherwise determine – see, for example, FA 1983, s 4(1); FA 1985, s 36(1); FA 1986, s16(2); FA 1987, s 20(4); FA 1988, s 25(2); FA 2002, s 28 (personal allowance for those aged under 65; FA 2004, s 24 (personal allowance for those aged 65 or more); and FA 2005, s 9 (personal allowance for those aged 65 or more).

See A Alter 'Different Techniques for Adjusting Taxable Income under Inflationary Conditions' [1986] BTR 347, and Ian Roxan 'Influence of Inflation' in *The Notion of Income from Capital* (eds Peter Essers and Arie Rijkers), EATLP Tax Series, Volume 1 (IBFD, 2005), 223.

For the indexation of capital gains, see Chapter 20, below, para **[20.44]**.

[14.39]

7. Financial provision for the family

The tax system once had a part to play in securing financial provision for members of the family in a variety of situations including separation and divorce, where elderly or incapacitated relatives[146] were unable to support themselves financially, and on the occasion of a 'child' of the family embarking upon higher education. Generally, such provision could be made by way either of capital settlements, which are, and always have been, subject to restrictive anti-avoidance measures,[147] or by payments out of income. Voluntary payments out of income have always fallen outside of the income tax system, being viewed as a gift in the recipient's hands and made by the payer out of income that had already suffered tax.[148] Payments under deeds of covenant could, subject to anti-avoidance measures, secure significant tax advantages for the payer but, from March 1988, most such payments were removed from the tax net altogether,[149] along with maintenance payments on separation and divorce, subject to a limited exception. Since 5 April 2000, relief in respect of maintenance payments has been even further restricted. The result is that where neither party to the marriage was aged 65 or over on or before 5 April 2000, there is no tax relief whatever on maintenance payments, even those entered into prior to 15 March 1988. This means that the payments will be made out of the taxed income of the payer, and will be tax free in the hands of the recipient. However, where one or both of the parties to a marriage or civil partnership was aged 65 or over on or before 5

143 The personal allowance and additional relief in respect of children (now abolished).
144 ITA 2007, s 989.
145 ICTA 1988, ss 1(4) and 257(9).
146 See also Inheritance Tax Act 1984, s 89.
147 See below, Chapter 16 especially para **[16.32]**.
148 There may, however, be inheritance tax consequences: see Inheritance Tax Act 1984, ss 11, 12, 18–22.
149 See now ITTOIA 2005, s 727(1). See, also, para **[14.29]**, above.

April 2000, although the maintenance payment (which must be a 'qualifying maintenance payment[150]) is made out of the taxed income of the payer, made gross to the recipient and is received by the recipient free of tax, some modest measure of tax relief is afforded to the payer in that his tax liability is reduced by a percentage (10% for 2007–08) of a specified amount (£2,440) or, if lower, the actual amount of maintenance paid (Step 6 in the income tax calculation: see para **[14.12]**, above).[151] This relief is only available in the case of payments to a former or separated spouse or civil partner; it is not available where maintenance payments are made directly to a child. If payments in respect of a child are to be made, the court order (which, for these purposes, includes an assessment of maintenance by the Child Support Agency) or agreement under which they are made must specify that they are being made to the other parent for the maintenance of the child. If the former recipient spouse or civil partner subsequently enters another marriage or civil partnership, the payer is precluded from obtaining relief, even if that second marriage or civil partnership has itself come to an end. **[14.40]**

Norris v Edgson [2000] STC 494 (Ch D)

The taxpayer and his wife divorced two years after the birth of their daughter, and the wife remarried. After his wife's second divorce, the taxpayer was assessed by the Child Support Agency to pay maintenance to his former wife for the benefit of their daughter. He argued unsuccessfully that he was entitled to relief under ICTA 1988, s 347B(1)[152] on the basis that, although his wife had remarried, on her second divorce the situation reverted to what it was after the first divorce, namely that there was no existing remarriage.

150 ITA 2007, s 454. Under this provision, a payment is a 'qualifying maintenance payment' if conditions A-E are met –

'(2) Condition A is that the payment is a periodical payment made by–
  (a) one of the parties to a marriage or civil partnership (including a marriage or civil partnership which has been dissolved or annulled) to or for the benefit of the other party and for the maintenance of the other party, or
  (b) one parent of a child to the child's other parent for the maintenance of the child by the other parent or by one person to another for the maintenance by the other of a relevant child of theirs.

(3) Condition B is that –
  (a) in a case falling within subsection (2)(a), either of the parties to the marriage or civil partnership was born before 6 April 1935, and
  (b) in a case falling within subsection (2)(b), either the person who made the payment, or the person to whom it is made, was born before that date.

(4) Condition C is that the payment is made –
  (a) is made under an order made by a court in a member State, or
  (b) under a written agreement the law applicable to which is the law of a member State or of a part of a member State,

(5) Condition D is that the payment is due at a time when –
  (a) in a case falling within subsection (2)(a) –
    (i) the two parties are not a married couple, or civil partners of each other, living together ..., and
    (ii) the party to whom or for whose benefit the payment is made has not entered into a new marriage or a new civil partnership, and
    (iii) in a case falling within subsection (2)(b)(ii), the person making the payment and the person to whom the payment is made are not living together.

(6) Condition E is that relief from tax in respect of the payment is not available to the person making it under any provision of the Income Tax Acts other than section 453.'

151 ITA 2007, s 453. If the payer's income tax liability is insufficient to offset the whole of the reduction, relief is given by reducing the liability to nil; no repayment of tax can be claimed.

152 Now ITA 2007, s. 453.

PARK J:...To a degree I can understand why the general commissioners were sympathetic to Mr Edgson. I am sympathetic myself. The reason is that, whereas I can see a logic and policy behind saying that a former husband should not be entitled to tax relief at a time when his former wife (the mother of his child) is married to someone else, that same logic and policy seems to me to have ceased to apply once the remarriage to a second husband has come to an end.

In this case Mr Edgson's adviser, Mr Henderson, who has helpfully assisted him before me and who appeared on his behalf before the general commissioners, is recorded as having said to the commissioners that, because Mrs Edgson had not remarried after the second divorce, the situation was identical to that which existed after the first divorce and before her remarriage. I entirely agree with that. From the policy point of view it seems to me that if Parliament thought it right for someone in Mr Edgson's position to be entitled to tax relief after his divorce and before his wife's remarriage, Parliament, if it had addressed the matter more fully, would have taken the same view of the position at a subsequent stage when Mrs Edgson, even though she had been remarried for a time in the meantime, was single again with no present husband to whom she could look for family support of herself and her daughter.

Unfortunately ... the wording of the statute is unambiguous. The question is whether Mrs Edgson 'has' or 'has not' remarried. The question is not whether she 'is' or 'is not' currently remarried. One might take the view, and indeed for myself I do take the view, that if Parliament had thought the matter through comprehensively it would have been quite likely to adopt a different wording under which Mr Edgson would have qualified for relief. However, I do not believe that there is any principle of statutory construction on which I can disregard the plain meaning of what has been enacted and substitute for it a different effect and interpretation which, try as I may, I cannot extract from the statutory words. **[14.41]**

Billingham v John [1998] STC 120 (Ch D)

Subsequent to their divorce, the taxpayer entered into an agreement with his wife (Cynthia) to pay maintenance to their daughter (Christina). He then made payments directly to his wife, who had care and control of the daughter. The Revenue denied the taxpayer relief under ICTA 1988, s 347B[153] on the basis that, under the terms of the agreement, the payment was not made for the benefit and maintenance of his wife, and nor was it made to his wife for the maintenance of their daughter; under the terms of the deed, the payment was to be made to the daughter herself. The Revenue were successful in their appeal from the General Commissioners.

RIMER J:... It is agreed that the taxpayer can make the claimed deduction in respect of his payments to Cynthia only if they were 'qualifying maintenance payments' for the purposes of s. 347B(1). For the Crown, Mr Brennan submits that they were not. His point is that they could have so qualified only if they were paid to Cynthia under an agreement which in terms provided for them to be paid to her for Christina's maintenance. Only then would the payment be made–

> '... under a written agreement ... by one of the parties to a marriage (including a marriage which has been dissolved ...) ... to the other party for the maintenance by the other party of any child of the family'

so as to satisfy the combined requirements of s. 347B(1). As it is, although by cl. 3 the taxpayer covenanted with Cynthia to make maintenance payments for Christina, he covenanted to make them to Christina, not to Cynthia, so that any payments made in discharge of that obligation became Christina's own property. Even assuming that the making of the payments to Cynthia as Christina's parent would have discharged the taxpayer's cl. 3 obligation, the payments so made were not payments to Cynthia for the maintenance of Christina; they were payments to Cynthia of money which was Christina's

153 Ibid.

own property. Alternatively, if the payments so made are to be regarded as having become Cynthia's own property for the purpose of swelling her income so as to assist her with Christina's maintenance, then the payments cannot be regarded as having been made under the agreement . . . at all. Either way, the payments to Cynthia cannot be regarded as qualifying maintenance payments.

The general commissioners' contrary reasoning could not have been expressed more shortly, but it can probably be elaborated as follows, as was essentially the argument which Mr John, who appeared in person, advanced in support of the commissioners' decision.

First, the payments were made 'under a written agreement' for the purpose of s. 347B(1)(a). Although the agreement provided for the payments to be made to Christina, that was not a practicable proposition because at her age she could neither have given a good receipt for them nor have been expected to apply them towards her maintenance. So it was sensible to make them to Cynthia for her to apply them in maintaining Christina, but this did not mean that they were not made 'under' the agreement for the purposes of s. 347B(1)(a): if they were not so made, to what else could they have been referable? Secondly, the payments were made by one of the parties to the relevant, but dissolved, marriage for the purposes of s. 347B(1)(b). Thirdly, they were made 'to the other party for the maintenance by the other party' of Christina for the purposes of s. 347B(1)(b)(ii), and the subsection does not require the written agreement under which the payments are made to specify that they must be made to such other party. Thus, the reasoning runs, the requirements of the subsection were all satisfied.

Such reasoning has a superficial attraction to it, but I consider that it is incorrect and that Mr Brennan's argument is to be preferred. I regard it as fatal to the taxpayer's argument that cl. 3 did not provide expressly that the payments had to be made to Cynthia for the maintenance of Christina, since I agree with Mr Brennan that only if it had done so could it be said that the payments made to Cynthia were qualifying maintenance payments within s. 347B(1) interpreted as a whole. The point is that payments covenanted to be made to a former spouse for the maintenance of a child of the family become the property of the former spouse, not of the child (compare *Stevens (HMIT) v Tirard* [1940] 1 KB 204), and have tax consequences different from payments covenanted to be made to the child. Section 347B(1)(b)(ii) shows that s. 347B is concerned with payments of this nature made under a written agreement, not with payments to the child made under such an agreement. Payments which satisfy the requirements of s. 347B(1) entitle the paying party to claim certain deductions in computing his total income. He has no such right in respect of maintenance payments which he covenants, as here, to pay the child. **[14.42]**

15 Tax Credits

1. Introduction

During his first term in government, the then Prime Minister, the Right Honourable Tony Blair, pledged that the Government's 'historic aim will be for ours to be the first generation to end child poverty'.[1] This sentiment was reiterated by the Chancellor of the Exchequer, the Right Honourable Gordon Brown, who pledged to halve child poverty by 2010 and 'abolish it in our generation'.[2] As a first step, the Department for Work and Pensions and HM Treasury had a joint Public Service Agreement target for the number of children in poverty in 2004–05 to be 25% lower than its 1998–99 level.[3] To this end, a review of child poverty was undertaken in 2004 to assess the effectiveness of the Government's current strategy.[4] It should be noted that a tax credits policy is but one small part of that strategy.

The aim of giving 'working families with children a better deal'[5] was, and continues to be, part of a wider strategy of making work pay.[6] The problem that had existed prior to recent reforms can be summed up in terms of the 'unemployment trap' and the 'poverty trap'.[7] The unemployment trap arises when the difference between in and out of work incomes is too small to provide an incentive for those currently out of work to take a job. The poverty trap discourages those entering work, or those already in work, from working longer hours, or moving to a better paid job because higher in-work income is offset by reduced in-work support and higher tax and National Insurance Contributions (NICs), resulting in high marginal tax rates. In a calculation made by the Meade Committee in its report, *The Structure and Reform of Direct Taxation* (IFS, 1978 at p 84), a marginal tax rate as high as 137% was produced. Part and parcel of the problem was the child poverty inherent in the poverty trap. This was recognised by the Chancellor of the Exchequer, who said:

1 Beveridge speech, Toynbee Hall, March 1999.

2 In his speech to delegates at the Labour Party's 2001 spring conference, *The Times*, 17 February 2001. The date for eradication is set at 2020.

3 Using a poverty line of 60% of median income.

4 *Child Poverty Review*, HM Treasury, July 2004, and see below para **[15.2]**.

5 *Your Guide to Working Families Tax Credit*, Inland Revenue, August 2000.

6 Part of this strategy, outlined in *New Ambitions for our country: A New Contract for Welfare* (1998) Department of Social Security, Cm 3805, also included reforms to National Insurance, the 10% starting rate of income tax and a reduction to 22% of the basic rate of income tax. All of this was underpinned by the National Minimum Wage.

7 The problems derived from the coincidence of levels of income used to delineate the tax threshold and to determine eligibility for means-tested or income-related benefits are discussed in A Dilnot and S Webb *The 1988 Social Security Reforms* (1988) 9(3) Fiscal Studies 26. For further discussion of the poverty trap, see A Dilnot and G Stark *The Poverty Trap, Tax Cuts and the Reform of Social Security* (1986) 7(1) Fiscal Studies 1.

'Family life is the foundation of society, and our first principle in society's support for the family is that the interests of children must be paramount ... For the last third of this century families with children have been losers in the tax system. Their tax burden has risen by nearly 20 per cent under successive governments ...'[8] **[15.1]**

HM Treasury *Child Poverty Review* (2004)

Background to the Review

1.1 The Government wants all children to have the best possible start in life, both for the sake of a happy childhood and to enable them to achieve their full potential in adult life. The Government wants to ensure that every child has the opportunity to achieve the good outcomes that some children may take for granted: economic well-being; enjoying and achieving; being healthy; staying safe; and making a positive contribution.[9]

1.2 The human rights of children and the standards to which governments must aspire in realizing these rights are articulated in the United Nations Convention on the Rights of the Child. The UK's second periodic report on the Convention, published in 1999, made it clear that the Government is committed to implementing changes which will be of direct benefit to children and which fully accord with the principles of the Convention.[10]

1.3 The Government's strategy for achieving equal opportunities for poor children and thus eradicating child poverty was outlined in 2001 and involves:[11]

- ensuring decent family incomes, with work for those who can and support for those who cannot;
- supporting parents in their parenting role;
- delivering high quality public services to break cycles of deprivation and
- harnessing the power and expertise of the voluntary and community sectors.

The review builds on the progress to date and on plans that have already been agreed.

1.4 In the late 1960s the UK suffered higher child poverty than nearly all other industrialized nations.

Over a period of 20 years, the proportion of children living in relative low-income households had more than doubled. In 1997, the Government set out the case for tackling division and inequality in society and the need for strong families and communities. It underlined the importance of providing employment opportunities for those who can work as part of a modern welfare state.

1.5 A growing body of evidence highlighted the extent of child poverty in the UK, the deterioration in levels of child poverty, the UK's poor performance on

8 Budget Speech, 9 March 1999.

9 These are the five outcomes in *Every child matters*, Department of Education and Skills, September 2003.

10 Committee on the rights of the Child, Consideration of reports submitted by states parties under Article 44 of the Convention. Periodic reports of States parties in 1998, United Kingdom of Great Britain and Northern Ireland, September 1999. CRC/C/83/Add.

11 *Tackling child poverty: giving every child the best possible start in life*, HM Treasury, December 2001.

child poverty compared to other major developed countries and the resultant harm to individuals, communities and society.[12]

1.6 In response to this, in 1999 the Prime Minister pledged to eradicate child poverty within a generation. The 2000 Spending Review included a Public Service Agreement (PSA) target to *make substantial progress towards eradicating child poverty by reducing the number of children in poverty by at least a quarter by 2004*, held jointly by HM Treasury and the Department of Social Security.

1.7 The 2002 Spending Review consolidated these ambitions as a shared HM Treasury and Department of Work and Pensions (DWP) PSA target: *to reduce the number of children in low-income households by at least a quarter by 2004–05, as a contribution to the broader target of halving child poverty by 2010 and eradicating it by 2020*. In addition, other 2002 PSA targets were formulated to contribute to the long-term goal of eradicating child poverty, for example tackling health inequalities, reducing teenage pregnancy and setting child development targets within the Sure Start programme. **[15.2]**

2004–05 has been and gone and, sadly, the forecasts[13] that suggested the Government's first target would be met have been proved wrong. However, the view has been expressed that this has more to do with the way in which the forecasting is done rather than with any governmental failure.[14] Moreover, there has undoubtedly been *a* decline in child poverty, and it has been said:

> 'The government can take much credit for this fall in child poverty, both through its decisions to increase substantially the amount of cash transfers made to families with children and through welfare-to-work and other policies that have helped parents in previously workless families to find work and therefore increase their incomes.'[15] **[15.3]**

2. Working families' tax credit and children's tax credit

Facing the challenge of making work pay, the Chancellor promised in his Pre-Budget Report of November 1997 the greatest reform of the tax and benefits system for a generation.[16] It should be noted at this point that proposals for a system of tax credits had been discussed as long ago as 1972.[17] The then

12 These points were summarized in *Tackling child poverty: giving every child the best possible start in life*, HM Treasury, December 2001.

13 See, for example, the forecasts in H Sutherland, T Sefton and D Piachaud *Poverty in Britain: The Impact of Government Policy since 1997* (York, Joseph Rowntree Foundation, 2003); M Brewer *Will the Government Hit Its Child Poverty Target in 2004–05?*, Briefing Note no 47 (London, Institute for Fiscal Studies, 2004); and M Brewer, A Goodman and A Shephard *Poverty and Inequality in Britain: 2005* Commentary no 99 (London, Institute for Fiscal Studies, 2005).

14 M Brewer, A Goodman, J Shaw and L Sibieta *Poverty and Inequality in Britain: 2006.* Commentary no 101 (London, Institute for Fiscal Studies, 2006).

15 Ibid at p 44.

16 This sentiment was repeated in the Chancellor's 2005 Budget Speech, when he said that the 'Government's policies to modernize the tax and benefit system constitute the most fundamental programme of welfare reform since the 1940s'. It was in the 1940s that Sir William Beveridge put forward his great plan (*Social Insurance and Allied Services*, Cm 6406, HMSO, 1942), upon which, until very recently, the social security system in the United Kingdom has been broadly based.

17 *Proposals for a Tax Credit System* (1972) Cm 5116.

Conservative Government stated that its aim was to 'seek a way to simplify and reform the whole system of personal tax collection and, at the same time, to improve the system of income support for poor people'. The Green Paper itself envisaged that it would take five years to put the proposals into effect, but the Conservative Government did not have that time, since it was defeated in the general Election in 1974. The incoming Labour Government did not pursue the matter, having shown no previous interest in the question of the integration of the tax and benefits systems. What is interesting, however, is that there was no real consultation on the matter of tax credits when New Labour took office in 1997 and committed itself to them, and no discussion of alternative measures such as a negative income tax or the increase in personal allowances. It was only in 2005, once tax credits had become fully embedded in the tax system, that the Treasury argued publicly why those alternatives would not work.[18]

The key element advanced by the Government in 1998 in its Green Paper on welfare reform[19] was that work was the best route out of poverty. Accordingly, the principle that emerged was that the new welfare state should help and encourage people of working age to work where they are capable of doing so and free them from dependence on the state.[20] Along with other measures such as the national minimum wage, and a programme that sought to give the necessary training to those looking for employment, the first step taken towards the Government's ultimate goal was the introduction of the Working Families' Tax Credit (WFTC).[21] This measure emerged from a government-commissioned report on work incentives,[22] and was hailed as 'an important step towards the greater integration of the tax and benefit system.'[23] Importantly, it was administered by the Inland Revenue alongside income tax.

To qualify for WFTC families, including married couples, unmarried heterosexual couples living together and lone parents, had to have one or more children living with them,[24] and they (or in the case of couples, at least one of them) had to work at least 16 hours per week.[25] WFTC consisted of a basic tax credit for each family, a 30-hour tax credit where one earner worked at least 30 hours per week, a tax credit in respect of each child in the family and a child care credit of up to 70 per cent of eligible child care costs up to

18 See *The Modernisation of Britain's Tax and Benefit System, No 11:Tax Credits: reforming financial support for Families* (HM Treasury, 2005), at para **[15.6]**, below.
19 *New Ambitions for our country: A New Contract for Welfare* (Department of Social Security, 1998, Cm 3805).
20 Ibid at ch 2, para 13. It was reported (*The Times*, 28 February 2000) that the Chancellor had made it very clear that the onus of finding employment should be entirely upon the unemployed. A Treasury official commented: 'Help for the unemployed will be more business, not more benefit offices.' Measures to enable older unemployed people to start their own businesses as well as improved tax breaks for businesses were included in FA 2000. Helping businesses has remained a theme throughout successive Finance Acts since that time.
21 This replaced Family Credit in October 1999. The Disabled Person's Tax Credit (DPTC) was introduced at the same time as WFTC but, as it was a specifically targeted tax credit, will not be discussed in detail in this chapter.
22 HM Treasury *The Modernisation of Britain's Tax and Benefit System – Work Incentives: A Report by Martin Taylor*, Report No 2, 1998.
23 Ibid at para 1.04.
24 A claimant or the claimant's partner had to be responsible for at least one child who was either under the age of 16, or who was aged between 16 and 19 and in full-time education up to 'A' level or equivalent standard.
25 Two further conditions required that they were resident in the UK and entitled to work here, and that they had either no capital or capital of less than £8,000.

maximum costs of £100 per week for one child and £150 per week for two or more children.

Running parallel to WFTC, was the children's tax credit, introduced by the Finance Act 1999,[26] and which was given in the form of a tax allowance for the tax years 2001–02 and 2002–03, with relief being given as a reduction in respect of income tax liability at the rate of 10 per cent. This was, in effect, a temporary measure that sought to replace the married couple's allowance,[27] and was given in respect of the taxpayer's own legitimate or legitimated issue under the age of 16, or of any child or children under that age maintained by the taxpayer for any part of thc year of assessment. Only one allowance was available to a taxpayer regardless of the number of qualifying children. Where the claimant was a higher-rate taxpayer, relief was gradually withdrawn at the rate of £2 for every £3 of his income, and the provisions that required the 'higher-earning' partner to claim the relief in preference to the 'lower-earner' meant that claimants were unable to transfer the credit to their partners to prevent the claw-back. **[15.4]**

HM Treasury, The Modernisation of Britain's Tax and Benefit System, No 2: Work Incentives – A Report by Martin Taylor (1998)

Why work incentives?

1.17 Three major disadvantages arise from having large numbers of people outside the labour force. Aside from the cost to the public purse (and some items of the social security budget are increasing irrespective of the cyclical position of the economy), long periods out of work reduce the chances of future employment for many, entrenching low self-esteem and – since the phenomenon is widespread – entrenching the view that it is acceptable for able-bodied people to live off the state. I believe these psychological factors are significant. And of course the shortfall in the level of national output implied by below-par participation in the labour force affects the economy's potential. This factor is likely to become more significant over the next two decades, given present demographic trends.

1.18 These issues affect groups well beyond the registered unemployed. Indeed, attempts to tackle the problem are likely to lead to increases in the published unemployment figures as economically inactive people pass through the unemployment register on their way back to work. I urge the Government not to be deterred by this presentationally awkward statistical effect from taking the necessary action, which I see as essentially taking four forms:

- making work more financially attractive to the non-employed;
- making it easier for the non-employed to take work by environmental changes (for example better childcare for lone parents, improved training and guidelines);
- requiring those who can work to participate in the labour market (for example by tightening the qualification rules for benefits);
- increasing the availability of work at the lower end of the labour market;

26 Section 30(1), (5).

27 Abolished in 2000. As with the children's tax credit, the married couple's allowance had been given as a reduction in respect of income tax liability at the rate of 10%.

1.19 I do not believe that the number of fundamentally unemployable people is as large as some argue. But I have particularly borne in mind the large number of people whose labour is not sufficiently well rewarded to allow them to support their families in an acceptable way. It seems to me far better that these people should be working, and receiving in-work benefits to top up their net pay, than that they should be idle.

Moreover, once in work there is greater likelihood that they will remain there. In general, therefore, I regard the expansion of relatively low-paying jobs as beneficial. . . .

. . . A Tax Credit for Working Families

3.01 For much of the century the roles of income tax and social security have been perceived to be different. According to the traditional model, the main purpose of income tax is to raise revenue. Its unit of assessment is the individual, and its structure pays little regard to individual or family circumstances. By contrast, the main purpose of social security is to help those in financial need. Its unit of assessment is the household, and it is administered by a separate department from the Inland Revenue: the Department of Social Security. Although this apparent division of functions is useful for some purposes, there is no reason why both systems should not contribute to the same objectives, providing the means to improve work incentives and relieve poverty.

3.02 The Task Force's remit was to examine the interaction of these two systems. . . .

3.03 This chapter looks at the case for greater integration of the tax and benefit systems. . . .

. . . Criticisms of the existing system

3.04 The existing tax and benefit systems perform most of their functions effectively. But there are a number of criticisms of their effect on work incentives and the incomes of the low paid. In particular it has been argued that:

- in-work support is not sufficient to make worthwhile – the unemployment trap – or provide adequate incomes for the low paid;
- the high rate of withdrawal of benefits as incomes rise deters the low paid from seeking to increase their earnings – the poverty trap;
- the impact of in-work benefits is blunted by
  - reluctance to take up entitlements because of the need to claim and the hassle and stigma involved;
  - insufficient recognition of the costs associated with work, in particular childcare;
  - concerns about the disruption to income and resulting cash-flow difficulties while benefit entitlements are re-assessed;
  - uncertainty about the level of in-work income.

The case for greater integration

3.05 There are a number of arguments in favour of greater tax and benefit integration.

3.06 It would simplify and streamline the tax and benefit system, making it easier for the taxpayer and benefit recipient to understand and for the government to administer. A working family can be paying income tax and making national insurance contributions, as well as receiving Family Credit. Housing Benefit, Council Tax Benefit and Child Benefit: administered by several agencies. As well as making the system more transparent for the recipient – in the case of in-work benefits, putting into starker relief the rewards of work over welfare – greater integration has the potential to unlock administrative savings both for the Government and the individual.

3.07 It would reduce the stigma associated with means-tested benefits and could therefore increase take-up. Although the less well-off are more likely to take up their entitlements to means tested benefits than they were 20 years ago, take-up still falls well short of universal benefits, such as Child Benefit, or personal income tax allowances. Around 70 per cent of those entitled to Family Credit claim it, while take-up of Housing Benefit by those in work is lower still.

3.08 It would ensure greater acceptability to both the claimants and taxpayers. . . .

3.09 It could improve work incentives for those caught in the poverty trap. The interaction of Family Credit, Housing Benefit and Council Tax Benefit can give rise to marginal rates of 98 per cent. Ending penal marginal rates would clearly be right and equitable. [15.5]

HM Treasury, The Modernisation of Britain's Tax and Benefit System, No 11: Tax Credits: reforming financial support for Families (2005)

3.8 It is possible to use the income tax system to improve work incentives for the low paid, but the range of options is limited. Special tax allowances can provide a degree of targeting but they cannot reach those on the lowest incomes because they cannot reduce an individual's tax liability below zero.

3.9 It is often suggested that increasing the personal allowance is a good way of providing support for low-income working people. However, tax credits provide a number of advantages over increasing the personal allowance . . .

3.10 Whereas tax credits can make payments to households, increasing the personal allowance can only reduce a household's tax bill to zero. Tax credits mean that a family with two children and a full-time earner on £15,500[28] a year, around half male mean earnings, is receiving a net tax payment of £2,200 a year. If tax credits were abolished, and the money used to increase the personal allowance, this family would instead find itself making a net tax payment to the Exchequer of around £900[29] a year. In addition:

- tax credits can tailor support according to family circumstances – providing more support to families with more children or those who care for disabled children, while increases in the personal allowance benefit all taxpayers irrespective of their circumstances; and
- tax credits can provide the same financial support irrespective of the household's marginal rate of tax, while increasing the personal allowance provides greater benefit to those with higher marginal tax rates – so a higher rate tax payer would gain four times as much from an increase in the personal allowance as a starting rate taxpayer whose marginal tax rate is 10 pence in the pound.

28 This figure is based upon the appropriate tax credit rates for the tax year 2004–05.
29 This figure is based upon the appropriate tax rates and thresholds and rate of personal allowance for 2004–05.

3.11 With tax credits, the support people receive from the tax system is not limited by the amount of tax they are liable for. Instead, they can receive tax credit payments from the Inland Revenue even where they would get no benefit from an increase in the personal allowance. All single earner households pay no tax on their first £4,895[30] of income. For a two child family, Child Benefit[31] cancels out their income tax until they earn £21,200.[32] Increasing the personal allowance by £500 would raise the point at which this family's income tax liability was cancelled out by Child Benefit to £13,200, an increase of £500, but putting the same money into the Child Tax Credit[33] would raise the point at which they start to pay net income tax to £22,500, an increase of around £1,300. So tax credits help more people to pay no net tax. The result is while the net tax rate for a single earner family with two children on half male earnings rose by 4 percentage points between the introduction of Child Benefit in 1977–78 and 1997 ... between 1997 and 2004–05 their net tax rate has fallen by around 23 percentage points and living standards have risen by 34 per cent.

3.12 Probably the most comprehensive approach to addressing these issues would be to design an entirely new tax and benefit system which delivered government financial support as payable tax credits, and paid credits to non-taxpayers in the same way as it pays tax refunds to taxpayers. In broad terms, a fully integrated tax and benefit system of this kind would assess the family's overall tax position by taking account of its joint income, and its entitlements to state support (e.g. for children or a disabled worker). Financial support would therefore be delivered through the tax system – either by reductions in the family's tax bill or through payments of "negative tax". Such "negative income tax" systems have been the subject of extended debate in the economics literature.[34]

3.13 In a system of this kind the tax burden effectively borne by a family is measured by:

- its **net tax liability** after taking account of its tax credit entitlements; and
- its **net (average) tax rate** which expresses that burden as a rate[35].

3.14 Both the values of the family's net tax liability and effective tax rate in a particular tax year could be positive, zero or negative, depending on the balance between tax liabilities and tax credits for the family in that year.

3.15 The main advantages of the pure negative income tax approach to tax benefit integration are that it would:

- enable the government to target support through the tax system to give help to those who need it, cutting out the requirement to contact different agencies, and fill in different forms, to claim support and pay tax;
- produce a single annual assessment of liabilities and entitlements, and a single overall net tax bill, with a single flow of payments to or from the government;

30 The single person's allowance for 2004–05.

31 A non-means tested benefit paid in respect of all children.

32 See above, note 28.

33 [See below, para **[15.8]**].

34 *The Negative Income Tax and the Evolution of U.S. Welfare Policy*, Moffitt, Journal of Economic Perspectives 2003 provides a useful summary. Precursors to the concept of a negative income tax can be traced back as far as the Speenhamland system which operated in parts of England in the early part of the 19th century.

35 The definition of tax liability and the tax rate would depend on whether NICs were included. For some purposes it would be appropriate to include NICs but in other cases it may not be because they finance pension entitlements and health services via the National Insurance Fund and are therefore distinct from general taxation.

- make more transparent the financial relationship between the government and the individual or the family; and
- by fully integrating state support into the income tax system, eliminate any stigma attached to claiming benefits. This would help maximize take up of support by those entitled to it.

3.16 But the purist approach to tax-benefit integration would also have important disadvantages, because it would entail:

- abandoning the government's commitment to the important principle of independent taxation[36];
- substantial and potentially very disruptive changes to the income tax and social security systems and payment and collection mechanisms;
- the risk of undermining the government's approach of matching rights and responsibilities which requires the unemployed to seek work; and
- (assuming an acceptable level of guaranteed income out of work) the potential for very high marginal rates of tax rates or large costs to the Exchequer.

3.17 Whatever the balance of theoretical advantage in moving to a fully integrated system of negative taxation, it would undermine some of the key principles in the current system and the risks involved in the implementation of such systems are clearly very large[37]. Instead the Government has embarked on a fundamental programme to modernize the tax-benefit system – the most significant since the Beveridge reforms of the 1940s – but it has also introduced reforms in carefully planned stages, to minimize risks. [15.6]

Natalie Lee 'The Working Families' Tax Credit: an integration of the tax and benefit systems?' [2000] JSSL 159

A general assessment of WFTC

It is undoubtedly the case that the WFTC has the potential to play an important role in raising the level of family income of low paid workers. It should be noted though, that its benefit is not limited to families with only low to moderate earnings.[38] Thus, for the tax year 2000–01, a family with a joint earned income of £42,000 (where the wife's income for 16 hours per week work is £3,000 and the husband's income from a full-time job is £39,000), with two children aged 13 and 15 and childcare costs of £150 per week, will be entitled to 70 pence per week credit. The income of this family can hardly be called "moderate" for tax purposes since the husband will be paying higher rate tax on his income. That aside, there do exist further and substantial concerns about the new system. Of the greatest importance is the fact

36 Chancellor of the Exchequer's speech at the Institute of Fiscal Studies, May 1999. Available at www.hm-treasury.gov.uk

37 It is interesting to note that although a Negative Income Tax system was the subject of extensive consideration in the United States in the late 1960s and early 1970s it was not implemented. Instead the Earned Income Tax Credit (EITC) was introduced in 1975; the EITC subsequently provided a model for the Working Families' Tax Credit. Similarly, "Proposals for a tax credit system" in the UK (October 1972, Cmnd 5116) gave rise only to Child Benefit.

38 The Revenue itself stated that the WFTC will be payable "to many working families on low to middle incomes." *Proposals for a new system of tax credits for people in work from October 1999*, Inland Revenue, 1998. See also Cockfield, R., *Benefit As You Earn?* (1998) Tolley's Practical NIC Service Vol. 7, No.10, 73 at p. 74.

that it is now becoming apparent that the whole scheme has been introduced too quickly and without the necessary careful considerations commensurate to a reform of this kind. Indeed, it will be recalled that it was to have taken five years to implement the proposed Tax Credit Scheme of 1972. In comparison, WFTC came into operation only nineteen months after its announcement in the Budget Speech of 1998. It may well be that, in its haste for implementation, the Government has brought about a major defect in the scheme for, despite the fact that the WFTC is administered by the Inland Revenue alongside income tax, it would appear that two entirely separate systems remain in operation. This defect has been revealed implicitly by the Low Incomes Tax Reform Group (LITRG) of the Chartered Institute of Taxation.[39] From a general point of view, LITRG is concerned that, rather than having developed a tailor-made approach to a brand new scheme, the Revenue is using the same computer and business processes and the same basic forms that were used in respect of the former social security benefits. It stated:

> "Opportunities seem to have been missed over the past 18 months to create the necessary structure for the completely new approach and philosophy for the new Credits (*the statement refers to both the WFTC and the Disabled Person's Tax Credit*) as promised by Ministers. This was undoubtedly needed since the former benefits had already given cause for concern: a sample check of Family Credits estimated that at least 50% of claims were likely to be incorrect; . . . . . . Revenue staff as ever will no doubt do their best to cope, but what is the likely impact on claimants, the vast majority of whom will not be professionally represented?"[40]

That criticism has even more force when it is noted that a significant number of the claimants will not have previous experience in dealing with the Inland Revenue whilst, by the same token, the Revenue will have little experience in dealing with those particular type of claimants. Indeed, during the 1998 Budget debate, the point was made that the "Inland Revenue does not know anything about children."[41]

This is further exacerbated by the fact that the training of staff has been late.[42]

More particularly, LITRG is concerned that definitions within the new scheme have not been aligned with those used for income tax, with the result that claimants have to cope, in effect, with two separate systems. A similar issue arises in the case of the self-employed, who are required to complete a number of very long and complicated forms, without the benefit of the type of guidance given for tax returns. There is a further requirement imposed upon the self-employed to produce two different figures of taxable profits in respect of their business, one for income tax purposes and the other for the purposes of WFTC.[43] It has been estimated that the inter-action of the two systems can result in a significant loss of credit, resulting, in effect, to a marginal rate of at least 100 per cent, or a claw-back in the amount awarded, resulting in a marginal rate of 55 per cent.[44] . . . .

39 The Chartered Institute of Taxation, Press Release, 4 October 1999.

40 *Ibid.*

41 HC, 23 March 1998; Vol. 309. c. 67. This, of course, mirrors the position of married women prior to the introduction of independent taxation in April 1990.

42 LITRG also pointed out that a Code of Practice still had to be announced but, in February 2000, four months after the introduction of the WFTC, a leaflet detailing customer service standards was in fact published by the Inland Revenue.

43 Expenditure on business equipment is an allowable deduction for income tax purposes, but not for WFTC. The losses of a business in earlier years may be carried forward to reduce the profits of the same business for a later year for income tax purposes, but not for WFTC purposes. Special reliefs available for income tax purposes to help with the start-up of a business cannot be claimed for WFTC. Personal savings are ignored for income tax purposes but are taken into account in calculating entitlement to WFTC.

44 *Government not joining up with the self employed*, Chartered Institute of Taxation (Low Income Tax Reform Group), Press Release, January 2000.

The WFTC and Family Credit

It has been stated that, although it is very much more generous than family credit, "in its structure, WFTC is conceptually in many ways no different to family credit".[45] Indeed, Wikeley correctly points out that this generosity could have been provided by family credit within the existing benefits structure. And, whilst the Institute For Fiscal Studies (IFS) have stated that the "WFTC is an extremely well targeted form of redistribution, directing extra money to low paid families in work with children,"[46] it also points out that family credit had much the same effect, evidenced by the relatively large take up of the benefit.[47] Thus, although from October 1999 WFTC will be administered by the Inland Revenue, rather than the Benefits Agency, through its centralised Tax Credit Offices in Preston and Belfast, it remains very similar to family credit. Both family credit and the WFTC provide for in-work benefits, although a greater number of people will be eligible for the WFTC. Both family credit and the WFTC are payable for six months at a flat rate regardless of changes in circumstances. This, of course, does not rest easily with the cumulative nature of the income tax structure.[48] Both family credit and the WFTC had/have an effect on marginal tax rates. The IFS estimates, however, that whilst the WFTC will bring about a reduction in the number of those with marginal rates above 70 per cent, there will be an increase in the numbers facing higher marginal rates through the increase in the number of recipients of in-work support.[49]

In spite of those remarkable similarities, the operation of the WFTC does effect two far-reaching changes. The first is that it has brought about a "fundamental change in the nature of individual income tax" in that not only does income tax now represent a payment *from* taxpayer to tax collector, but also a payment from the Inland Revenue *to* the individual.[50] To this extent, income tax can be negative, with individuals *receiving* payments, as well as positive, with individuals *making* payments. Secondly, unlike family credit, the WFTC is paid through the pay packet (frequently, then, to the man) rather than as a cash payment direct to the parent who takes responsibility for caring for the children. The fear is that the benefit, unlike family credit, may, in fact, never reach the children, with the original problem of child poverty remaining.

WFTC and integration

It has already been demonstrated through examples that, in spite of the introduction of the WFTC, in a number of ways the new system continues to represent the operation of two entirely separate systems, albeit under the umbrella of one agency, namely the Inland Revenue. The question is, however, whether those examples reveal an inherent defect in a scheme that was meant to represent a move towards integration....

... It is clear that the WFTC fails to satisfy the criteria for full integration since, although it provides a minimum income for those in work, it has by

45 N Wikeley, in *Income-Related Benefits: the Legislation 1999 Supplement* (1999), p. 130. See also D Williams, *Current Law Statutes Annotated*, p. 10–6.

46 *Family Credit and the Working Families' Tax Credit*, The Institute For Fiscal Studies, Briefing Note 3/99.

47 It is estimated that, shortly before the introduction of the WFTC, family credit was received by 3 per. cent of the population. This figure is based upon the Family Credit Statistical Tables that were published by the Department of Social Security.

48 [See below, para **[15.13]**].

49 A Dilnot and J McCrae, *Family Credit and Working Families' Tax Credit*, IFS Briefing Note 3/99) at pp. 14–15.

50 Williams, D., *Current Law Statutes Annotated*, at p. 10–3.

definition no effect on those who are out of work for whatever reason. Moreover, it does not, and was never intended to, replace *all* existing cash benefits and *all* income tax reliefs. A number of important benefits, administered by the Benefits Agency, continue to operate. These include out-of-work benefits, housing benefit and council tax benefit. Similarly, although both the married couple's allowance and mortgage interest relief have now been abolished, other income tax reliefs continue to exist. These include the individual personal allowance and, from April 2001, the children's tax credit,[51] . . . The main difficulty that has already been demonstrated is that administratively, there still appear to be two systems in operation. The plight of the self-employed has already been considered. Moreover, and crucially, the WFTC, like it predecessor, Family Credit, is assessed on the income of the household; in contrast, income tax is based on the principle of independence and, with the abolition of the married couple's allowance, ignores the family altogether. A direct result of this is that, for the purposes of WFTC, the existence of a second parent is taken into account, but only for the purposes of limiting the credit to higher income families. It is very possible that some of these two-parent families have lower equivalised incomes than one-parent families who receive the credit in full.[52] The distinction has further repercussions at two levels, the lower level and the substantive level. The lower level is concerned with the question of privacy. One of the main reasons for the introduction of independent taxation was to allow privacy in respect of financial matters between married couples. It has to be said that this was more perceived than real whilst the married couple's allowance was still operating.[53] However, with its abolition, those who do not claim for the WFTC will be able to enjoy a state of privacy, whilst this important principle will be lost to those who do. The result is that not everyone is being treated "according to the same ground rules." At the substantive level, it demonstrates that the Government continues to regard the nature of tax and benefits as essentially different. This is borne out by the fact that assessment for "beneficiaries" is *prospective*, with a consideration of what the needs of the family *will* be, and an award of WFTC at a flat rate lasting for twenty six weeks to enable the system to be responsive to an applicant's change in circumstances. Assessment for income tax is, by contrast, *retrospective*, income fluctuations throughout the year determining how much tax will ultimately be paid at the end of the year. This distinction is fatal to the notion of integration. **[15.7]**

3. The new tax credits

A. General

It was quite clear that the Government's commitment to abolish child poverty could not be achieved through WFTC and related measures alone. By its very name, it can be deduced that the credit was aimed at working families with

51 The children's tax credit will be given in the form of a tax allowance, £4,160 for the tax year 2001–02, which relief will be given as a reduction in respect of income tax liability at the rate of 10%.

52 The gap between the tax system and the benefit system will be perpetuated when the children's tax credit comes into effect in April 2001, since the means-testing formula will only take account of the second parent for the purpose of limiting the credit.

53 Since 1993–94, a couple were able to decide how to allocate the married couple's allowance; in order to do this, there had to be a flow of financial information between the couple.

children. However, there is a clear link between households with no working adult and child poverty.[54] By the same token, it has to be noted that certain working households without children may be living in poverty. What was required was a continued incentive to work, the surest way out of poverty according to the Government, whilst ensuring that those workless households with children should not be penalised.

Taking those matters on board, two new tax credits were introduced by the Tax Credits Act 2002. The Working Tax Credit (WTC) and the Child Tax Credit (CTC) built upon the framework provided by WFTC and the children's tax credit (which the new credits replaced) but, in so far as there are no capital limits acting as a bar to eligibility, the new tax credits differ fundamentally from WFTC and all other social security benefits. Their aim is to 'separate the support for working adults in a household from support for children'[55] in order both that children may be properly supported, without stigma, within households out of work as well as in working households, and that those who are low-paid receive more financial help whether or not they have children.[56] CTC, intended to provide 'a seamless system of financial support for children',[57] integrating for the first time all income-related support for children,[58] contains the child elements of WFTC, Disabled Person's Tax Credit (DPTC), Income Support and the Income-based Jobseeker's allowance. WTC, intended to provide 'a single, visible instrument underpinned by the National Minimum Wage, to make work pay'[59] contains the adult elements of WFTC and DPTC and the childcare element of WFTC (because it is necessarily associated with work). **[15.8]**

HM Treasury, The Modernisation of Britain's Tax and Benefit System: Tackling Poverty and Making Work Pay – Tax Credits for the 21st Century, (Report No 6, March 2000)

2 SUPPORTING CHILDREN THROUGH AN INTEGRATED CHILD CREDIT

Next phase of reform

2.20 The reforms to date have gone a long way to achieving the Government's aims. They have established the principle that work must pay and be

54 *A League Table of Child Poverty in Rich Nations* (UNICEF, June 2000). The report estimated that a child who lived in a household with no working adult was approximately four times as likely to grow up in poverty than a child in a household with at least one working adult.

55 *New Tax Credits: supporting families, making work pay and tackling poverty*, Consultation Document, Inland Revenue, July 2001 at p 47. See also HM Treasury, *The Modernisation of Britain's Tax and Benefit System – The Child and Working Tax Credits*, Report No 10, April 2002, at p 3, para 2.2.

56 During the passage of the Tax Credits Bill through Parliament, it was estimated that a further 400,000 people without children on low incomes would benefit through WTC. See *Hansard*, HC Debs, Vol 376, col 600 (10 December 2001).

57 HM Treasury *The Modernisation of Britain's Tax and Benefit System: Tackling Poverty and Making Work Pay – Tax Credits for the 21st Century*, Report No 6, March 2000, para 1.5.

58 *The Modernisation of Britain's Tax and Benefit System – The Child and Working Tax Credits*, Report No 10, April 2002, para 2.2.

59 HM Treasury *The Modernisation of Britain's Tax and Benefit System: Tackling Poverty and Making Work Pay – Tax Credits for the 21st Century*, Report No 6, March 2000, para 1.5.

supported through the wage packet, and have improved support for all families with children, targeting extra resources on those most in need based on family circumstances.

2.21 However, the pace and scale of reform has been constrained by the tax and benefit structures and administrative systems which were already in place when the Government was elected. For example, the Working Families' Tax Credit is based on Family Credit, a social security benefit, and the Children's Tax Credit on the Married Couple's and related allowances. But as the Government begins to plan the next generation of tax credits there is much greater scope for creating a radically new system.

2.22 Using one system to achieve two objects – in the case of the Working Families' Tax Credit, better work incentives and increased family support – can give rise to tensions. At the same time, using several different instruments to contribute towards a single goal – increased family support in Income Support, the Working Families' Tax Credit and the Children's Tax Credit can mean duplication of effort.

2.23 In the next phase of reform the Government has announced its intention to:

- create an employment tax credit to be paid through the wage packet based on the adult allowance in the Working Families' Tax Credit and Disabled Person's Tax Credit; and
- bring together the different strands of support for children in the Working Families' Tax Credit, in Income Support and in the Children's Tax Credit to create an integrated and seamless system of financial support for children.

2.24 An employment tax credit, paid through the wage packet to employees, will continue to make work pay for families on low incomes. It will also build on the Disabled Person's Tax Credit and the 50+ Employment Credit to extend in-work support to low income households without children. . . .

2.25 An integrated child credit will create a seamless mechanism for channelling support to children as part of the Government's commitment to abolish child poverty. This will continue the process of reform begun with the introduction of the Working Families' Tax Credit and the Children's Tax Credit by providing:

- **a more transparent system of support for children**, helping parents understand what they can expect to receive, and facilitating public debate about the appropriate level of support in the context of the government's commitment to abolish child poverty within a generation;
- **a portable and secure income bridge spanning welfare and work**, to improve work incentives. Survey evidence suggests that the financial disruption associated with moving off benefits into employment often discourages parents from making the transition into work. It would therefore go a step further than the minimum income guarantee delivered by the Working Families' Tax Credit;
- **a common framework for assessment and payment**, where all families will be part of the same system, rather than dealing with low-income families through the benefits system while giving tax allowances to the better off. Awards would be assessed on the joint income of the couples;
- **a system where all support for children is paid to the main carer**, in line with universal Child Benefit;
- **efficiency gains** for Government and reduced hassle for parents, moving away from a system where support for children is delivered through four different mechanisms. . . .

2.29 ...The new credits will be administered and delivered by the Inland Revenue. This represents a further important step towards tax and benefit integration. It will recognize the fact that the Inland Revenue already collect income information on three quarters of the integrated child credit caseload, over 3.5 million families.

...

3 SUPPORTING WORK THROUGH AN EMPLOYMENT TAX CREDIT

3.1 By increasing employment opportunities for all, the government is tackling worklessness – the most important cause of deprivation and poverty. Central to this strategy are policies to make work pay.

3.2 The Working Families' Tax Credit and the national Minimum Wage have for the first time guaranteed a minimum income for families in work. In the new system, an integrated child credit will provide the financial support for children, and would be complemented by an employment tax credit through the wage packet to ensure that families are better off in work than on benefit.

3.3 ...There is a strong case for extending the principle of more targeted support to working-age households without children, through an employment tax credit to make work pay.

...

Possible parameters of an employment tax credit

3.20

- The older age-group – those over 45 or 50 – face some of the most acute work incentive problems. Their wage on re-entry to work is often low relative to what they earned in their previous job. The wages of older workers have also declined relative to those received by other workers. The employment credit component of the New Deal 50plus is an important new work incentive, giving extra financial support for a year for people who find work after six months or more on benefit. It does not however provide permanent support, not does it help those already in work but with little or no opportunity to increase their incomes.
- For the younger age group, low pay is more likely to be transitory and less likely to be associated with low household income and poverty. Policies such as training. Education and the New Deal may be more effective at tackling the underlying causes of low pay.
- Part-time employment, not just low wages, is a factor in working poverty households without children.
- Couples without children are more likely to be in low-income households than single adults without children. Because benefits for couples are higher than for singles, couples are also more likely to find that when one of them gets a job, it does not pay very much more than benefit. **[15.9]**

Inland Revenue, New Tax Credits: Supporting families, making work pay and tackling poverty, (July 2001)

9. The primary aims of the next phase of reform are
   - to separate the support for adults in a family from support for the children, so as to provide a clearer focus:

  - on making work pay for those in low-income households, including those without children, through the employment tax credit; and
  - on tackling child poverty and providing financial support for families with children, through the integrated child credit and Child Benefit;
- to provide a common framework for assessing entitlement to income tax credits, based more closely on the rules and definitions of income on which people's tax bills are based. As a principle, this follows naturally from the fact that tax credits form an integral part of the income tax system. But this approach also:
  - has the practical advantage of helping people to understand more clearly how their tax credit entitlements and tax liabilities are assessed and the extent of their household's net contribution to the Exchequer;
  - helps further to integrate the tax and benefits systems and to bridge the divide between work and welfare;
  - allows information gathered for income tax purposes to be used more effectively than at present in claiming tax credit entitlements; and
- to rationalize administration by making one department, the Inland Revenue, responsible for administering all aspects of the government's financial support for children, as well as for income tax credits generally. . . .

10. Achieving these objectives will make the system more accessible to users and easier for both claimants and commentators to understand – thus helping to promote higher take-up and to encourage a more informed debate about the level of support the Government should seek to provide through each tax credit. At the same time, the closer links with existing income tax systems will make it easier to cross-check the information on which tax credit awards are based, as a safeguard against abuse.

The role of tax credits

11. What individuals pay in income tax depends, broadly, on their income in the tax year. Their tax bill is based on the principles of independent taxation – that each person should be taxed on their own income and have their own tax allowance and rate bands. None of that will change on the introduction of the new tax credits.
12. Tax credits provide a way for the tax system to recognize a family or household's circumstances and responsibilities in the tax year. Depending on the tax credit in question, they will be paid direct or through the wage packet to a member of the household. New tax credits are 'payable', so that families can benefit from them fully, whether or not the amount they are entitled to exceeds the tax and National Insurance contributions that the individual adults within the family would be due to pay. So, although tax credits are not always an immediate deduction from people's tax and National Insurance contributions, the effect is to reduce or wipe out the household's or family's tax and National Insurance bill or to provide them with a net payment. That is:
    - where the amount of tax credit due to a family is less than the tax and National Insurance contributions they would be due to pay as individuals, the tax credit serves to reduce the overall contribution they have to make to the Exchequer; and
    - where it is equal to or greater than their tax and National Insurance contributions as individuals, they have in practice no net contribution to make – instead, they may be making a withdrawal.

13. As a family's circumstances change over time, they may find their net position in relation to the Exchequer changing. The likelihood of making net withdrawals from the Exchequer is greater, other things being equal, the lower the family's income.

Entitlement based on family income

14. *Tackling Poverty and Making Work Pay* emphasized that a key objective of the new system was to target support to families on the basis of need. That means that entitlement to tax credits must take account of family, rather than individual, circumstances and that the amount of tax credit awarded should reflect both:
    - the specific needs of the family – so that the credits should include additional payments that take into account the number of people in it and any special needs they have. For example, the new integrated child credit will make extra payments for a child with a disability; and
    - the income available to meet those needs – that means that, in families headed by spouses or partners who both have incomes, we need to take account of them both.
15. This principle also leads to the conclusion that new tax credit awards should be made to the family or household rather than to an individual, although different types of payment may be made to different individuals within it. So, for example, although the family will apply for the integrated child credit, it will be paid to the main carer within the family. This contrasts with the current situation where
    - out-of-work benefits like Income Support or Income-based Jobseeker's Allowance are claimed by and paid to an individual applicant, on behalf of a household which may include the spouse or partner of the applicant and, where relevant, dependent children;
    - in-work tax credits – Working Families Tax Credit and Disabled Person's Tax Credit – are claimed by an individual applicant on behalf of the family;
    - the Children's Tax Credit is claimed by an individual taxpayer. But in the case of a married couple, or a couple living together as husband and wife, there is only one credit between them. It may do to either of them or be shared if neither of them is a higher rate taxpayer. But if either, or both, of them, is a higher rate taxpayer, the person with the higher income must claim; and
    - Child Benefit is paid to the individual who is the person responsible for a particular child.
16. For the purpose of new tax credits, what we mean by a 'family' or 'household' is:
    - an individual; or
    - a married couple; or
    - a man and a woman who are living together as though they were married. . . .

2. Support for families with children

Outline

19. The new integrated child tax credit is intended to create a single system of support designed to:
    - provide a continuing stream of income for families with children, irrespective of whether the adults in the family are in work, and which can be relied on by families who move into work;

- pay support for children to the main carer, in line with Child Benefit;
- remove the stigma attached to claiming the traditional forms of support for the poorest families, by creating one system of income-related support for all families with children; and
- enable families to access financial support from one system, even as their income rises or circumstances change.

20. There will be no work conditions attached to the integrated child credit. It will be assessed on the basis of the household income and built on the foundations of universal Child Benefit, which will continue to be paid to all families.
21. The effect of the new credit will be to extend eligibility for financial support to some groups who are currently excluded from all but Child Benefit – because, for example, they are not in work or have no taxable income, but neither are they eligible for Income Support or income-based Jobseeker's Allowance. The main groups to benefit from this extension will be students and student nurses. . . .

3. Support for low-income household in work

Outline

34. In October 1999, the introduction of Working Families' Tax Credit provided targeted support specifically for working families who previously faced particularly poor financial incentives to work. Alongside Working Families' Tax Credit, the government introduced the Disabled Person's Tax Credit to help make work pay for people with a disability. The two credits established the government's principle of providing help through the tax system and strengthened the link with work by payment through the wage packet.
35. The next stage of reform of in-work support is to build on the foundations of the existing payable tax credits with the introduction of an employment tax credit from 2003, which will extend the principle of the Working Families' Tax Credit and the Disabled Person's Tax Credit to those without children. The employment tax credit will be geared to tackling persistent in-work poverty and making work pay more than welfare, by targeting extra financial help to low-income households. It will be a flexible vehicle for providing support to particular groups according to their circumstances and it will continue the link with work established by Working Families' Tax Credit and Disabled Person's Tax Credit by being paid through the wage packet to the employee.
36. The employment tax credit for families with children or people with disabilities replicates the support provided by Working Families' Tax Credit or Disabled Person's Tax Credit. But while the unemployment trap has historically been of particular concern for families with children, those without children can also face poor work incentives. And there are a significant number of working people without children living in poverty. The employment tax credit will be used to extend help to those households, in addition to households with dependent children and working people with disabilities. In extending support, we are also looking to build on the targeted help provided through the Employment Credit in the New Deal 50+ for people aged 50 or more returning to work. **[15.10]**

By virtue of amendments made by the Civil Partnership Act 2004,[60] tax credits may now be claimed jointly by a couple. This is defined as a man and a woman

60 Section 254(1) and Sch 24, para 144, amending the Tax Credits Act 2002, s 3(3)(a).

who are married, or two people of the same sex who are civil partners of each other and not separated, or a man and a woman, or two people of the same sex, living together as if they were married or civil partners. **[15.11]**

B. Child Tax Credit and Working Tax Credit[61]

There are three elements to CTC, namely: (i) a family element in recognition of the responsibilities of caring for children[62]; (ii) an individual element for each child within the family; and (iii) an extra family element for families who have one or more children under the age of 12 months, continuing until the youngest child's first birthday. An extra credit is available for each child with a disability. Unlike WTC, there is no additional second adult element that distinguishes between couples and lone parents; CTC is independent of the status of the adults in the family or the number of parents in or out of work. If there is a couple, the calculation of the credit is based on the joint income of the couple. CTC, along with the childcare element of WTC, is paid directly to the main carer. A claim for CTC may be made in respect of a child or children of a family irrespective of whether one or both of the adults are working. The support will continue until 1 September following the child's 16th birthday or, for those who continue in full-time secondary education or who are undertaking approved training not provided by virtue of any employment or office, until the young person's 20th birthday.[63]

As far as WTC is concerned, the legislation provides, in effect, for three categories of claimant. The first comprises couples with children and workers with a disability, the second, lone parents and the third, workers with no children and no disability. WTC is divided into four main elements, namely, (i) a basic element in respect of all persons entitled to the credit; (ii) an element in respect of persons being a couple (whether married or not) or a lone parent in recognition of their additional needs; (iii) a 30-hour element giving extra credit to a person who, or persons who between them, work for more than 30 hours per week, thus providing an incentive to increase hours towards full-time work; and (iv) a childcare element providing support for working people who incur childcare costs. There are additional elements to help those who may be particularly disadvantaged by their personal circumstances in the work market, for example, disabled workers[64] and those aged 50 and over who are returning to work after a period of unemployment.[65] Apart from the childcare element, which is paid to the main carer, WTC is paid directly by HMRC to the self-employed and, until 2006, to employees by their employers through the pay packet.[66] For couples, it is paid to the partner engaged in remunerative work; if both partners work at least 16 hours per week, they can themselves decide which

61 For a detailed guide to the child tax credit and the working tax credit, see Natalie Lee 'The New Tax Credits' [2003] 1 JSSL 7 and *Revenue Law – Principles and Practice* (24th edn, 2006) ch 51.

62 This broadly replicates the children's tax credit.

63 Tax Credits Act 2002, s 8(3); The Child Tax Credit Regulations 2002 (SI 2002/2007), reg 5 as amended by The Child Tax Credit (Amendment) Regulations 2006 (SI 2006/222).

64 *Ibid*, s 11(3).

65 *Ibid*, s 11(5); The Working Tax Credit (Entitlement and Maximum Rate) Regulations 2002 (SI 2002/2005), reg 3.

66 WTC has been paid direct from HMRC to new employee claimants since 7 November 2005, and to all other employee claimants since 1 April 2006 (The Tax Credit (Payment by Employers, etc.) (Amendment) Regulations 2005 (SI 2005/2200).

of them should receive the payments, in default of which HMRC has the power to make the decision. **[15.12]**

C. The operation of tax credits

Unlike WFTC, which was based on the benefits system, and was paid as a six-month fixed award regardless of a change either in income or in family circumstances (apart from the birth of a new child), WTC and CTC are designed to be responsive to such changes. An award of tax credits runs for a period of twelve months, and takes account of an individual or family's current circumstances (for example, for CTC, how many children they have, and for WTC, how many hours they work and the amount of eligible childcare costs), and of their gross income before income tax and National Insurance Contributions. Broadly speaking, income is defined for tax credit purposes as it is for tax purposes. The award is actually made on the basis of the claimant's previous year's gross income. If there is no change in either the circumstances[67] or the income[68] of the claimant during the year for which the claim is made, then an award will run at the same level for the entire tax year. If, however, changes in either circumstances or income do occur, and HMRC receives notification of such changes, the tax credits are revised accordingly, subject to a disregard of income below a given threshold.[69] There is a requirement to notify HMRC within one month of certain changes, including a cessation of, or a significant reduction in, childcare costs.[70] Other changes in circumstances and of income require no formal notification and, in the event that no notification is made, these changes will be picked up by HMRC at the end of the tax year, when claimants are asked by way of a final notice to confirm their income and circumstances for the year just ended.[71] However, failure to notify HMRC of such changes may lead to an underpayment or overpayment of tax credits. Since most claimants are likely to notify HMRC immediately of any changes that are likely to cause an increase in the amount of tax credits they receive, underpayments are not seen to be much of a problem. In the event that there is an underpayment, HMRC will, until April 2007, make a single payment of any outstanding credits owed at any time during the year.[72] From that date, any underpayment will only be refunded after the award has been finalised at the end of the tax year. Of greater concern is where a claimant has been overpaid, for example, because his income during the year for which the award is made is much greater than in

67 Generally, a change in circumstances does not bring an award to an end (Tax Credits Act 2002, s 5(2) (4)). However, an award will come to an end prior to the end of the tax year if eligibility for the credit ceases (because, for example, there is no longer a child or young person in the family). Moreover, an award will last only until either a couple who have made a joint claim separate, or a single person who has made a claim becomes part of a couple. In these circumstances, a new claim has to be made (Tax Credits Act 2002, s 3(4)).

68 Prior to 6 April 2006, changes in income of up to £2,500 were disregarded (Tax Credits (Income Thresholds and Determination of Rates) Regulations 2002 (SI 2002/2008), reg 5). From 6 April 2006, the disregarded amount is £25,000 (Tax Credits Up-rating Regulations 2006 (SI 2006/963) reg 4).

69 Tax Credits Act 2002, s 7(3)(a)(b) and the Tax Credits (Income Thresholds and Determination of Rates) Regulations 2002 (SI 2002/2008), reg 5.

70 Tax Credits Act 2002, s 6(3); Tax Credit (Claims and Notification) Regulations 2002 (SI 2002/2014), reg 21, as amended by the Tax Credit (Claims and Notification) (Amendment) Regulations 2006 (SI 2006/2689).

71 *Ibid*, s 17.

72 *Ibid*, s 30.

the previous year. Wherever possible, this overpayment will be collected by reducing the claimant's tax credit payments for the following year, although this has meant that, as a result, some families have been left with no tax credit award at all in the following year. To alleviate this problem, from November 2006, tax credit payments are reduced by a maximum of 25% only, and not the full 100%. If there is no entitlement to tax credits in that following year, a claimant may well be asked to repay the amount of the overpayment within 30 days of notice being given by HMRC. A decision by HMRC to collect the overpayment is not subject to appeal. **[15.13]**

D. An assessment of tax credits

Although the 'new' tax credits were meant both to reduce child poverty and encourage people to work, the very fact that CTC may be claimed irrespective of work suggests that the second aim may not be achievable. The question for the future, therefore, will be how to reduce child poverty successfully without weakening work incentives.[73] A more immediate concern is the "loss" to the tax credit system of some £1.74 billion through a combination of overpayments, errors (both by claimants and HMRC) and fraud.[74] As far as overpayments are concerned, it became clear that large numbers of tax credit claimants had been required to repay overpayments, leaving many in dire financial straits. Whilst some of the overpayments came about through faults on the part of HMRC, others arose due to the design of the system itself. The problem, then, is partly an inherent one, and the only way of alleviating it, without changing the entire structure of the scheme, was by increasing the amount of income that is to be disregarded when income from the current year exceeds the income of the previous year.[75] In the case of error and fraud, HMRC have set out their strategy for tackling these problems,[76] although it remains to be seen whether the proposed measures will be successful. These problems have attracted criticism from many different bodies and organisations, and threaten to undermine the stability of the tax credit system as a whole. **[15.14]**

Mike Brewer, Tom Clark and Michael Myck *Credit Where It's Due? An Assessment of the New Tax Credits* (IFS, 2001)

5. So will the tax credits work?

The introduction of the integrated child credit and the employment tax credit from 2003 will represent a major reform of the tax and benefit system, and certainly one of the largest attempted by this government.

73 For a discussion of this issue, see Stuart Adam, Mike Brewer and Andrew Shephard *The poverty trade-off: Work incentives and income redistribution in Britain* (Joseph Rowntree Foundation, 2006).

74 This figure is in respect of the tax year 2003–04. See *Child and Working Tax Credits: Error and Fraud Statistics 2003–04* (HM Revenue & Customs, 2006). It has been noted that, despite this unacceptably high level of loss, HMRC was not expected to set targets for its reduction for the future until Spring 2007, when it will have been able to calculate error rates for 2004–05: Committee of Public Accounts 23rd Report Session 2006–07 *Tax Credits* (3 May 2007) HC 487.

75 The Tax Credits Up-rating Regulations 2006, amending the Tax Credits (Income Thresholds and Determination of Rates Regulations 2002 (SI 2002/2008), reg. 5, and see above, para **[15.13]** and n 68.

76 *Tackling Error and Fraud in the Child and Working Tax Credits* (HM Revenue & Customs, 2006).

The high-level aims of the credits are simple enough. The integrated child credit is intended to simplify and streamline existing financial support to families with children, surely a laudable goal. The employment tax credit, though, extends financial support to a new group: full-time working families without children. The first stated aim here is to reduce poverty. But poverty amongst families without children is concentrated amongst those not working full time and amongst the young, and neither of these groups will be eligible for the new credit. The immediate impact on poverty must therefore be small.

The government also hopes that the employment tax credit will improve the financial reward to work for people without children and so encourage non-working individuals and part-time employees to work full time. In practice, though, these groups do not face particularly poor financial work incentives at present. It is perhaps the case that non-financial factors are preventing non-working people without children from working full time, and so it might be more efficient to tackle these factors directly. Furthermore, under our assumptions, the employment tax credit will do little to help those who face the worst work incentives (those receiving housing benefit), and it will also reduce the incentive to work for potential second earners in couples without children receiving employment tax credit.

The new credits will be operated by the Inland Revenue. This move should help ensure that they really will operate very differently from existing means-tested benefits. The intention is that the new credits will be easier to understand and administer, and less intrusive for claimants. One of the ways the government has compromised on simplicity and predictability for families whose composition or income changes significantly during a year. Many families will find themselves in this position. The need for claimants to monitor annual income, average hours of work and, if appropriate, childcare costs will lead to a less certain and more complicated system for some families, with the associated risk of non-compliance.

The government has not stated how many families might receive the new credits, nor how much they would cost, nor allowed for them in the public finances. Given this, we have had to make some assumptions .... On our assumptions, around 1.1 million better-off families with children will lose, but 3.3 million low-income families with children will be better off.

The employment tax credit could go to around 400,000 families without children ... However, these figures are very sensitive to the restrictions on eligibility. The reforms to the way that changes in circumstances are treated mean, though, that these snapshot calculations underestimate how many families will be treated differently under the new regime compared with the current system. In particular, low-income families with children who experience a drop in earnings may find themselves temporarily worse off than under current rules.

The effect of the reforms on the work incentives of families with children is complicated and something that deserves greater attention. In general, the cash gain from working will increase for those parents currently out of work. But those in work could see either increases or decreases in their marginal deduction rates. The most important reason for these changes is the decision to base the credits on gross income rather than net income, particularly for potential second earners in couples receiving WFTC.

The aggregate impact of both reforms on labour supply is also complicated. Some people may well be induced to enter work but – like the introduction of WFTC – the extension of the employment tax credit to those without children may mean some people in couples decide not to work, because the credit gives their family extra income and increases the marginal deduction rate they face. **[15.15]**

Inland Revenue: Tax Credits and deleted tax cases House of Commons Committee of Public Accounts, Fifth Report of Session 2005–06

1 Administration, complexity and public understanding

1. The Government replaced the Working Families and Disabled Person's Tax credits with the Child Tax Credit and Working Tax Credit (New Tax Credits) in April 2003. Some 5.7 million families received New Tax Credits during 2003–04 at a cost of approximately £16 billion. Of these, several hundreds of thousand claimants were overpaid New Tax Credits mainly because of the inherent design of the scheme, but also because of software errors.
2. The design of the system inevitably results in overpayments to many claimants. The Inland Revenue (the Department) makes provisional Tax Credit awards based on a claimant's income for an earlier year. The final award is assessed on actual income for the year. Tax Credit entitlement is reduced by 37p for every additional £1 of annual income over certain limits. Incomes tend to increase from year to year, so that the final award is often lower than the provisional award. Except where caused by error, the extent of overpayments reflected claimants' improved economic circumstances. Software errors in the New Tax Credits system have resulted in overpayments of £174 million to 540,000 of the overall 1.8 million claimants overpaid.
3. The Department usually seeks recovery of overpayment from future Tax Credit awards in order to ensure that people get no more than they are entitled to. If repayment would cause the claimant hardship, the Department may waive all or part of an overpayment of Tax Credits, or allow more time to pay. But the Tax Credit IT system could not stop the recovery of overpayments while the staff considered hardship cases. The Department planned to start to change the system in the autumn of 2005 to prevent this automatic recovery of overpayments in some circumstances.
4. The Department has written off amounts where the individual overpayment was £300 or less, and has sought recovery of amounts above £300. The Department writes off overpayments over £300 only where it considers that it was reasonable for a claimant to believe that their Tax Credit award was correct. It wrote off £37 million in 2003–04 and expected to write off similar amounts of overpayments in 2004–05. The Department established the £300 threshold by reference to the costs of recovery. The Department is doing more work to improve its understanding of the administrative cost structure to see whether it should revise the write off limit.
5. Members of Parliament and organizations such as the Citizens Advice Bureau have been inundated with complaints from claimants who have found the New Tax Credits scheme complex and who are unsure how much they are due. The situation has been exacerbated by departmental staff who have advised people to contact their Member of Parliament so that their case would be considered more quickly. The Department considers it debateable whether they were typical of the wider story, but without being able to demonstrate that they were not.
6. It believed that it needed to go through two or three annual cycles before making a judgment as to whether the system had met the expectations of Parliament.
7. New Tax Credits have also proved complex and costly to administer. In 2003–04, the Department employed around 7,300 staff on New Tax Credits work and the full administrative cost was £403 million. . . .

Conclusions and recommendations

1. **The operation of Tax Credits has proved unsatisfactory for a significant minority of claimants who were disadvantaged and who cannot understand how much they are due or why in so many cases such large overpayments have been made.** The Department does not have sufficient information about the claimant population to enable it to provide a good service to the public and avoid disruption to its own main business of tax administration. The Department should review the information provided to claimants to enable them to understand their Tax Credit awards, and should develop as a matter of urgency the operational information needed to manage the Department's relationship with claimants and the effects upon them.
2. **Members of Parliament have been inundated with distressing complaints from constituents whose lives have been affected by the Department's management of Tax Credits.** The Department has also received a large volume of complaints about Tax Credits, as have the Citizens Advice Bureaux. The current appeals and complaints procedures do not include any independent process, however, and the Department remains the final arbiter.
3. **The scale of overpayments being recovered from claimants is much higher than envisaged when the Tax Credit scheme was designed.** Tax Credit initial awards are provisional and the final award for the year in question is often significantly reduced because the claimant's pay has increased by more than £2,500, which is disregarded. This leads to recovery of the overpayment. The Department published figures in June 2005[77] showing that some 1.8 million (33%) of claimants had been overpaid in respect of 2003–04. The Department should review and report each year on the effect on claimants of the inbuilt overpayment and recovery of substantial sums of money so that Parliament can judge whether the consequences for claimants are compatible with its intentions in passing the legislation.
4. **The Department cannot show whether error rates attributable to claimant error and fraud have halved as it predicted in December 2003.** The Department undertook to report on this issue by July 2005, by which time over £30 billion would have been spent on New Tax Credits. That report should quantify and analyse in detail the estimated overpayments due to fraud and error; set out targets for reducing overpayments and plans for achieving them; and show the performance indicators used by the Department to manage Tax Credits. . . .
5. **The problems in administering Tax Credits have entailed some impairment of the Inland Revenue's reputation for accuracy, fairness and proper handling of taxpayer affairs**. The Department's effectiveness in managing the tax system depends on maintaining public confidence in its administrative competence. It needs to demonstrate and convince taxpayers that it has resolved the problems caused by Tax Credits; caught up on the backlog of other work; and maintained its capacity for timely, fair and accurate processing of taxpayers' affairs. **[15.16]**

77 HM Revenue and Customs: Tax Credits finalised awards 2003–04 (1 June 2005).

Committee of Public Accounts 23rd Report Session 2006–07 *Tax Credits* (3 May 2007) HC 487

Conclusion and recommendations

3. **Tax credits suffer from the highest rates of error and fraud in central government, undermining HMRC's reputation for accuracy, fairness and proper handling of taxpayer's affairs.** In 2005, the Committee concluded that the Department's effectiveness in managing the tax system depended on maintaining public confidence in its administrative competence. Yet the department neither produces routine estimates for error and fraud nor sets targets for reducing levels. It needs to demonstrate to taxpayers that it maintains its capacity for the proper handling of their tax affairs by setting targets for reducing the level of error and fraud and producing routine estimates to validate its performance against the targets. **[15.17]**

Note that reports from the Parliamentary Ombudsman,[78] Citizens Advice,[79] One Parent Families[80] and the Child Poverty Action Group[81] all reached similar conclusions. See also Chapter 7 of the IFS Green Budget (Mike Brewer, IFS, January, 2006) for an analysis of the tax credits failures. **[15.18]**

78 *Tax credits: Putting things right*, Parliamentary Ombudsman, 3rd Report, Session 2005–06.
79 *Money with your name on it?*, Citizens Advice, June 2005.
80 *The New Tax Credits System: Knowledge and Awareness Among Recipients*, One Parent Families, February 2005.
81 *First Steps To Reform Tax Credits*, Child Poverty Action Group, October 2005.

16 Trust and Estate Income

Chapter 14 concerned the individual and the family, and discussed the calculation of income tax liability for the individual. Although ITA 2007, s 23 provides for the calculation of 'a person's income tax liability for a tax year', the deduction from total income of reliefs and allowances in Steps 2 and 3 of the income tax calculation is limited to 'individuals'.[1] Further, only the individual is liable to higher rate income tax.[2] However, for the purposes of income tax, it is recognised that other taxable persons or bodies do exist, having income upon which they are assessable. These persons and bodies include, in particular, the trustees of a settlement, the administrators or executors of the estate of a deceased person, partnerships and, for the purposes also of corporation tax, companies.[3] **[16.1]**

1. The income of trusts

A. *Introduction*

Following the publication of a series of discussion papers in December 2003, a subsequent consultation document in August 2004 and a further discussion paper in March 2005, provisions were included in the Finance Acts of 2004, 2005 and 2006 aimed at 'trust modernisation' for income (and capital gains) tax purposes.[4] As well as simplifying the tax regime for UK trusts, the main thrust behind the proposals and the new provisions was to move towards a more 'tax neutral' system, in which the amount of income (or capital gains) tax chargeable should not vary to any great extent depending on whether the property upon which it arises is held under a trust or directly by an individual. In achieving this goal, the Government sought to strike a balance between a system that does not provide artificial incentives to set up a trust, and one that avoids artificial obstacles to the use of trusts where significant non-tax benefits could be gained. Reform began with the Finance Act 2004, which increased the trust rate (see para **[16.13]**, below) to bring it in line with the higher rate of income tax. In order to mitigate the possible harsh effects of this measure

1 A company may have 'charges on income', deductible from profits in ascertaining liability to corporation tax. Moreover, trustees may be entitled to a tax *reduction*, which they may deduct at Step 6 in their tax calculation. One such reduction is that provided for by FA 2005, s 26 in the case of trusts with vulnerable beneficiaries. See below, para **[16.26]**.

2 [ITA 2007, ss 10, 11.]

3 The position of partnerships and companies are considered below in Chapters 17 and 18 respectively.

4 Many of the income tax provisions have now been rewritten, and are to be found in ITA 2007.

on smaller trusts and trusts with vulnerable beneficiaries, a standard rate band was introduced for all trusts that pay tax at the trust rate or the dividend trust rate,[5] and a new regime for trusts with vulnerable beneficiaries (see p 516, below). The latest stage in the process of reform, provided for in the Finance Act 2006 and aimed at reducing the burden of administering the taxation of trusts, is an attempt to bring the main trust-related definitions for tax on income and chargeable gains into line with each other.[6]

Assessment to tax in respect of the income of trusts, and the liability to pay income tax, differs according to whether: (i) the beneficiary has a vested interest in the income; (ii) the income accrues directly to the beneficiary; (iii) the trust is a discretionary or other similar trust, in which case, the income is the income of the trust, but not that of any individual; and (iv) the beneficiary falls within the definition of a 'vulnerable' person. **[16.2]**

Inland Revenue, Modernising The Tax System For Trusts (December 2003)

Overview of the Proposals

Government Objectives

4. The Government recognises the important role trusts play in society. As far as possible it wants a tax system for trusts that does not provide artificial incentives to set up a trust but, equally, avoids artificial obstacles to using trusts where they would bring significant non-tax benefits. The Government does not want a system that enables people to use trusts to avoid tax but, equally, as far as possible it does not want the tax system to penalise beneficiaries where a trust is imposed upon them by statute, such as the laws of intestacy. Neither does it want to penalise beneficiaries where a trust exists to protect the vulnerable, such as a disabled person. The Government is not attracted to changing legislation for the sake of change, so would prefer to build on what we have rather than start again from nothing. The Government wants to reduce the compliance burden on small trusts and believes that any new measures should:
    - Be fair.
    - Support the competitiveness of the UK economy.
    - Be clear and easy to operate.
5. Taking all this together implies a tax system that is broadly similar to what we already have but improves upon it. It should remove distortions and unnecessary burdens when trusts are not being used to avoid tax. As far as possible we should aim to tax the person benefiting from the trust where that person can be identified. So the principles to aim for are:

5 FA 2005, s 14, introduced a standard rate band of £500. From 6 April 2006, this amount is increased to £1,000: see FA 2006, Sch13, para 4(b). See now, ITA 2007, s 491.

6 See now, ITA 2007, s 466, which defines settled property as any property held in trust other than property held by a person as nominee, bare trustee for a person absolutely entitled, an infant or disabled person (Taxation of Capital Gains Act (TCGA) 1992, s 60(1). References in the CGT legislation to a settlement, the meaning of which is determined by case law, are construed as references to settled property. 'This measure effectively aligns what is treated as a settlement for the general purposes of income tax and tax on chargeable gains': Natalie Lee (gen ed) *Revenue Law* (24th edn, 2006) [25.2] (Sarah Laing). For the definitions of 'settlor', see ITA 2007, s 467.

- The tax system should be as simple and easy to understand as possible.
- Complying with tax obligations should be straightforward.
- Where a beneficiary receives income or benefits from a trust they should be taxed as if they receive them direct.
- Where a settlor retains an "interest" in a trust they should be treated as if they still owned the assets.
- Where the income of assets cannot readily be identified with settlors or beneficiaries, tax should be levied on the trustees.
- Trustees with little income and no gains should not have to complete Self Assessment (SA) returns every year.
- Trusts set up to protect the vulnerable should receive special treatment.
- Anti-avoidance legislation is appropriate for those who use trusts to avoid tax. **[16.3]**

B. *Basic definitions*

(1) Settlement

Although there is no statutory definition of the term 'settlement' itself, 'settled property' is defined as property held in trust other than property held by one person as nominee for another, or as a trustee for another who, but for being an infant or under some disability, would be absolutely entitled against the trustee,[7] this definition being common to both income and capital gains tax.[8] **[16.4]**

(2) The settlor

The definition of the term 'settlor' is all embracing, and the provisions[9] are virtually identical to their capital gains tax counterparts.[10] A person is a settlor in relation to a settlement if the settlement was made, or is treated as having been made, by that person. A person is treated as having made a settlement if he has made or directly or indirectly entered into it, if he has provided, or undertaken to provide, property directly or indirectly for the purposes of the settlement, or if the settlement arose on his death and any of the settled property is, or is derived from, property of which he was competent to dispose immediately before his death. **[16.5]**

(3) The trustees

The trustees of a settlement are for income tax purposes to be treated as a single person, meaning that the trustees are distinct from the persons who may from time to time be trustees of the settlement.[11] This definition is modelled on the existing capital gains tax provisions.[12] **[16.6]**

7 ITA 2007, s 466.
8 See TCGA 1992, s 68, inserted by FA 2006, Sch 12, para 1(1); see below, para **[20.26]**.
9 ITA 2007, s 467.
10 TCGA 1992, s 68A, inserted by FA 2006, Sch 12, para 1(2).
11 ITA 2007, s 474.
12 See Taxation of Capital Gains Act 1992, s 69(1).

C. *Taxation of trust income*

(1) Basic rate income tax

As a general rule, the trustees are directly assessed on income received by them,[13] and are liable to income tax at the basic rate under the appropriate statutory provision.[14] This, of course, does not apply to income from which tax has been deducted at source,[15] where the tax deducted (10% for dividend income and 20% for other savings income) will satisfy the trustees' liability to pay tax at the basic rate. In the event that the income accrues directly to the beneficiary, it is that beneficiary, rather than the trustee, who is liable to income tax.[16]

Since trustees are *persons* but not *individuals*, they are not liable to higher rate tax on the trust income accruing,[17] and nor are they entitled to deduct reliefs or personal allowances in respect of that income.[18]

Expenses incurred by the trustees in the administration of the fund are not deductible in computing their basic rate liability and, accordingly, are paid out of taxed income.[19]

The trustees are also liable to capital gains tax in respect of chargeable gains from disposals of settled property.[20] **[16.7]**

Williams v Singer [1921] AC 65, 36 TLR 661 (HL)

Trustees resident in the United Kingdom held shares in a foreign company on behalf of a beneficiary resident and domiciled abroad. The dividends were paid directly to that beneficiary and were never received in this country. The House of Lords held that the trustees could not be assessed upon income which had not come into their hands.

VISCOUNT CAVE: . . . My Lords, the question raised in these appeals is whether income from foreign investments which is received abroad by a person not domiciled in this country is chargeable with income tax under the Income Tax Acts by reason of the fact that the investments stand in the names of trustees who are domiciled here. As the point raised in both cases is the same, the appeals have been heard together.

In *Williams v. Singer* the respondents are the trustees of a settlement under which the Princesse de Polignac is the beneficial tenant for life in possession. The settlement is in

13 The normal self-assessment rules apply to trustees.

14 See *Trusts, Settlements and Estates Manual (TSEM)* para 3610, which indicates that the basis for taxing trustees under ITTOIA 2005, s 271 (which encompasses the former Schedules A and D) is that although they are not beneficially entitled to the income, the charge is on 'persons receiving or entitled to' (the income). Similarly, as far as dividends are concerned, under ITTOIA 2005, s 385, a tax credit is available to a person 'receiving' a distribution who pays tax at the appropriate rate, with the amount of tax credit reflecting that fact.

15 Such as dividends and other savings income. See Chapter 14.

16 *Williams v Singer* [1921] 1 AC 65; see below, para **[16.8]**.

17 ITA 2007, s 11. Trustees may, in certain circumstances, be liable for the special trust rate, which currently stands at 40%; see para **[16.13]**, below.

18 *Ibid*, s 23, provides for the 'calculation of a *person's* income tax liability for a tax year'; Steps 2 and 3 in that calculation allow for the respective deduction of reliefs and allowances, but only in respect of '*individuals*'. They may be entitled to make a deduction in respect of a 'reduction,' such as that available for trusts with vulnerable beneficiaries under FA 2005, s 26. Naturally, a trustee may claim allowances in respect of any of his *own* income derived from the trust: *Dale v IRC* [1954] AC 11.

19 Such expenses *are* deductible in computing the amount of income chargeable to the special trust rate: see below, para **[16.13]**.

20 See Chapter 19, para **[20.29]**, below.

English form, and the trustees are all domiciled and resident in the United Kingdom; but the Princess (who is a widow) is a French subject by marriage, and is domiciled and resident abroad. The settled fund, so far as it comes into question in these proceedings, consists of certain foreign investments of considerable value, and under orders signed by the trustees the whole income from these investments is paid to the account of the Princess at a bank in New York, no part thereof being remitted to this country.

. . .It is obvious that, having regard to the proviso to the above section, the Princesse de Polignac and Mrs. Munthe,[21] who are domiciled abroad, could not have been assessed to income tax in respect of the foreign income above referred to. But the revenue authorities contend that they are entitled to levy tax upon that income by means of assessments upon the trustees, who are domiciled in this country. If this contention is upheld, the trustees will of course be entitled to retain the tax so paid out of the trust income payable to the beneficial life tenants, who will thus have to bear the burden of the tax from which the proviso appears to relieve them; but the appellants contend that this is the effect of the statutes. The question to be determined is whether they have that effect.

. . . Indeed, I understood Mr. Cunliffe to go so far as to say that, when funds are vested in trustees, the revenue authorities are entitled to look to those trustees for the tax, and are neither bound nor entitled to look beyond the legal ownership.

My Lords, I think it clear that such a proposition cannot be maintained. It is contrary to the express words of s.42 of the Income Tax Act, 1842[22] which provides that no trustee who shall have authorised the receipt of the profits arising from trust property by the person entitled thereto, and who shall have made a return of the name and residence of such person in manner required by the Act, shall be required to do any other act for the purpose of assessing such person. And, apart from this provision, a decision that in the case of trust property the trustee alone is to be looked to would lead to strange results. If the legal ownership alone is to be considered, a beneficial owner in moderate circumstances may lose his right to exemption or abatement by reason of the fact that he has wealthy trustees, or a wealthy beneficiary may escape supertax by appointing a number of trustees in less affluent circumstances. Indeed, if the Act is to be construed as counsel for the appellants suggests, a beneficiary domiciled in this country may altogether avoid the tax on his foreign income spent abroad by the simple expedient of appointing one or more foreign trustees. Accordingly I put this contention aside.

On the other hand, I do not think it would be correct to say that, whenever property is held in trust the person liable to be taxed is the beneficiary and not the trustee. Sect. 41 of the Income Tax Act, 1842 renders the trustee, guardian or other person who has the control of the property of an infant, married woman, or lunatic chargeable to income tax in the place of such infant, married woman, or lunatic; and the same section declares that any person not resident in Great Britain shall be chargeable in the name of his trustee or agent having the receipt of any profits or gains.

. . .The fact is that if the Income Tax Acts are examined, it will be found that the person charged with the tax is neither the trustee nor the beneficiary as such, but the person in actual receipt and control of the income which it is sought to reach. The object of the Acts is to secure for the State a proportion of the profits chargeable, and this end is attained (speaking generally) by the simple and effective expedient of taxing the profits where they are found. If the beneficiary receives them he is liable to be assessed upon them. If the trustee receives and controls them, he is primarily so liable. If they are under the control of a guardian or committee for a person not sui juris or of an agent or receiver for persons resident abroad, they are taxed in his hands. But in cases where a trustee or agent is made chargeable with the tax the statutes recognise the fact that he is a trustee or agent for others and he is taxed on behalf of and as representing his beneficiaries or principals.

. . .Applying the above conclusions to the present case, it follows in my opinion, first, that the respondent trustees, who have directed the trust income to be paid to the

21 The beneficiary in the other case considered, *Paul v Royal Exchange Assurance*, where the facts were similar.

22 [See now TMA 1970, s 72.]

beneficial tenants for life and themselves receive no part of it, are not assessable to tax in respect of such income ... **[16.8]**

See also *Kelly v Rogers* [1935] 2 KB 446. **[16.9]**

Reid's Trustees v IRC (1929) 14 TC 512 (CS)

LORD PRESIDENT (CLYDE): ... My own opinion – for what it is worth in view of the two cases above referred to[23] – is that trustees are the proper persons to be assessed in all cases in which the income of the trust estate received by them, or to which they are entitled, is not tax-deducted at source; and that – in the case of income of the trust estate which is tax-deducted at source – they could not be heard to ask repayment of the tax on the plea that the income did not arise or accrue to them but to others, whether such others were income-beneficiaries or capital-beneficiaries. There is nothing inconsistent with the Income Tax Acts in recognising and respecting the distinction between property owned by a person as trustee and property owned by him in his own right. The result of the two cases, as regards Schedule D at least, is, I think, no more than this – that, while Rule 1 of the Miscellaneous Rules applicable to that Schedule cannot now be regarded as making trustees, who receive or are entitled to income, assessable and liable *prima instantia* for the tax in all cases, it nevertheless has that effect in a great many.

The conclusion on the whole matter seems to be that trustees, albeit only the representatives of ulterior beneficial interests are assessable generally in respect of the trust income under Rule 1 of the Miscellaneous Rules applicable to Schedule D; but that just because they represent those beneficial interests – they may have a good answer to a particular assessment, as regards some share or part of the income assessed, on the ground that such share or part arises or accrues *beneficially* to *a cestui que trust* in whose hands it is not liable to Income Tax, e.g. a foreigner under Case V, Rules 1 and 3. The fact that most trust income is subject to deduction of Income Tax at the source has probably obscured the specialty which attaches to the representative character of trustees as payers of Income Tax; but if the proposition now maintained for the trustees is a sound one it is incomprehensible that it should never have been advanced with regard to the very large sums of trust income which do not, and never can, reach the hands of an income-beneficiary ... **[16.10]**

Aikin v MacDonald's Trustees (1894) 3 TC 306 Court of Exchequer (Scotland)

Trustees in Scotland received remittances of income from trust properties abroad and distributed the net income, after deducting the expenses of management, among the beneficiaries. It was held that the trustees were assessable upon the full amount of income received by them, without deduction of expenses.[24]

LORD PRESIDENT (ROBERTSON): ... My Lords, the Appellants are testamentary trustees, and in that capacity they are part proprietors of certain estates in India. In the year ending April 5th, 1894, there was remitted to the Appellants from India, as the proceeds of those properties, a sum of £1,684. 2s. 2d., and that was a sum of money which came home net. That sum came into the hands of the Appellants free for them to spend or distribute according to the rights of their beneficiaries. They now propose to deduct certain expenses incurred in this country in connexion with the management of the trust. Now my Lords, it is for them to point to the section of the statutes which entitles them

23 *Williams v. Singer* [1921] 1 AC 65; above, para **[16.8]** and *Baker v. Archer-Shee* [1927] AC 844.

24 Compare the treatment of expenses for the purpose of the rate applicable to trusts (below, para **[16.13]**).

to make such a deduction. I think they have entirely failed. It seems to me that all the authorised deductions and charges occur at an earlier stage than that at which these expenses have been incurred. When the net sum was placed in the hands of the trustees, it had passed through all the vicissitudes which entitled anyone to make deductions. It had come home, and was in their hands for them to apply to their uses. The fact that their uses are trust uses does not seem to me to make any difference in the present question, and the fact that this is a trust for the children of a person deceased again does not make any difference, as is shown by the fact that the trustees themselves are going to pay income tax upon this sum, and merely question the right of the Government to refuse the deduction in question. It seems to me that the expenses which are authorised to be deducted are expenses excluded by the terms of the present claim, because the words of the present claim are quite explicit that these expenses have been incurred in this country in connection with the management of the trust, and they are not expenses at all specifically relating to the investment in question, except in this sense, that the income of the investment in question constitutes the bulk of the trust estate. I am of opinion that the determination of the Commissioners is wrong and should be reversed. **[16.11]**

Where, however, a beneficiary is entitled to and assessed upon trust income, the income of the beneficiary is that part of the trust income to which he is entitled, arrived at *after* the deduction of prior charges, *including* management expenses: *Murray v IRC* (1926) 11 TC 133; *Macfarlane v IRC* (1929) 14 TC 532. **[16.12]**

(2) The special rates for the trustees' income: the trust rate and the dividend trust rate

Because the trustee is liable to basic rate tax only, the temptation for a settlor would be to create a trust, with the income arising being taxed at the basic rate, lower than the individual beneficiary's top rate of 40%, and then accumulated. In order to prevent this type of tax avoidance, the trustees may be liable to the rate applicable to trusts where the income arising to them is –

(a) accumulated or discretionary income in so far as it must be accumulated or payable at the discretion of the trustees or any other person, and includes cases where the trustees have (or any other person has) any discretion over one or more of: (i) whether, or the extent to which, the income is to be accumulated; (ii) the persons to whom the income is to be paid; and (iii) how much of the income is to be paid to any person; and

(b) not income arising under a trust established for charitable purposes only; and

(c) not the income (i) of any person other than the trustees; (ii) from property held for the purposes of a fund to which ICTA 1088, s 615(3) applies (superannuation funds relating to undertakings outside the UK), but which is not held as a member of a property investment limited liability partnership; or (iii) from service charges held on trust by a relevant housing body as defined in ICTA 2007, s 480(5).[25]

It should be noted that the special trust rates are levied on trust *income*, and thus capital sums deemed to be income for tax purposes[26] are not subject to it and suffer tax at the basic rate only.

25 Paragraphs (a)–(c) derive from ITA 2007, ss 479 and 480 (formerly ICTA 1988, s 686).

26 Such as lease premiums under ITTOIA 2005, ss 277ff.

Although not deductible against the trustees' liability to basic rate tax, expenses that are properly chargeable to income by statute or case law[27] may be deducted in determining the amount chargeable at the rate applicable to trusts.[28]

For the tax year 2004–05 and subsequent years, the trust rate is 40%,[29] thus equating it with the higher rate of tax for individuals and removing any advantages that could previously have been gained by using trusts that fell within ss 479 and 480. This measure was introduced with the express purpose of moving towards a system that would be more 'tax neutral', in its treatment of income held under a trust and income held directly by an individual.[30] For 2006–07 and subsequent years, the first £1,000 of income taxable at the special trust rates is taxed instead at either the basic, lower or dividend ordinary rate, depending upon its source.[31] **[16.13]**

IRC v Berrill [1981] 1 WLR 1449 (Ch D)

Trustees held the income arising from some settled shares on protective trusts for the beneficiary until he reached the age of forty five, subject to a power to accumulate the whole or any part of the trust income. Thereafter, the capital was to be held for him absolutely.

VINELOTT J: . . . Sections 16, 17 and 18 of the Finance Act 1973[32] form part – a subsidiary part – of one of the revolutionary changes that have transformed the tax system of the United Kingdom since 1965. Until 1871 the system of taxation in the United Kingdom was unusual in combining a high standard rate of tax with a substantial allowance on earned income up to a given limit. This high, and in the case of the vast majority of taxpayers entitled to earned income relief, misleadingly high, standard rate was coupled with additional tax – surtax – which was payable as a deferred instalment of income tax in the year following the year of assessment in which income was brought into charge to tax at the standard rate. In 1971 a new unified system of taxation was introduced although it did not replace the old system until the year of assessment 1973–74. Under the new unified system tax is charged at a basic rate which in broad terms corresponds to the old rate on earned income reduced by the earned income allowance. Where an individual's total income exceeds a specified figure additional rate tax is charged at 15 per cent. on so much of that income as consists of investment income, which is defined as income which is not earned income. The additional rate tax, in broad terms, restores the old standard rate tax on income other than earned income. Higher rate tax at graduated rates is then charged on an individual's total income in excess of a specified figure. That graduated tax replaces surtax, but, unlike surtax, it is payable in respect of the year of assessment in which income is charged to basic and additional rate tax. Apart from section 16, this new scheme of taxation would have conferred a fortuitous benefit on trust income, necessarily investment income, which did not form part of a beneficiary's income when it arose to the trustees, and which was either accumulated pursuant to some trust or power or simply retained pending the exercise by the trustees of a discretionary trust or power. The trustees would, of course, bear basic rate tax, by deduction or assessment, on the income arising to them but not additional or higher rate taxes, which are chargeable on the total income to which a person is beneficially entitled.

27 For example, the cost of preparing trust accounts.
28 ITA 2007, s 464.
29 *Ibid*, s 9(1). Prior to 6 April 2004, the rate applicable to trusts was 34%. The dividend trust rate was also increased from 25% to 32.5% (ITA 2007, s 9(2)).
30 *Modernising the Tax System for Trusts*, Inland Revenue, 17 December 2003.
31 ITA 2007, s 491. The new rate band applies after deduction of permitted trust management expenses (ITA 2007, s 484(3)).
32 [See now ITA 2007, ss 479, 493.]

Looked at in the context of this statutory scheme it is to my mind quite clear that section 16 must have been intended to impose additional rate tax on income which would otherwise not have attracted additional rate tax when it arose to the trustees as part of the total income of a beneficiary, subject, of course, to . . . specific exceptions . . . I can see no difficulty in reading section 16(2)(a) in this sense. The words "income . . . which is payable at the discretion of the trustees" are, I think, as easily applied to income which trustees have power to withhold from a beneficiary entitled in default of the exercise of the power as to income which they have power to apply or which they are bound to apply pursuant to a mandatory discretionary trust. It is true that the words in parenthesis "whether or not the trustees have power to accumulate it" do not fit naturally the case where the discretion consists of a power to withhold income by accumulating it. . . . But that inelegance of expression does not afford a ground from departing from what appears to me to be the plain intention of the legislature. **[16.14]**

Carver v Duncan [1985] AC 1082 (H L)

Trustees sought to deduct annual premiums paid under policies of assurance and endowment policies and fees paid to investment advisers from income liable to the additional rate. It was held by the House of Lords, with Lord Diplock dissenting, that these were capital expenses and were not deductible from income notwithstanding that the trust instruments authorised payment of these expenses out of income.

LORD TEMPLEMAN: . . . In the present appeals, the appellant trustees of the Paul settlement paid the annual premiums on assurance policies effected by the trustees in order to obtain policy moneys corresponding to the amount of capital transfer tax payable out of the trust fund in the event of the death of the settlor before 20 November 1979. The appellant trustees of the Devonshire settlement paid the annual premiums on endowment policies assigned to the trustees and on other endowment policies effected by the trustees. All these premiums were paid by the Paul settlement trustees and the Devonshire settlement trustees for the benefit of the whole of their respective trust funds because the capital of the trust will be augmented by the policy moneys which will be received if and when the policies mature, and the income of the trust will be increased as and when such augmentation of capital takes place, but not before that event takes place. . .

. . . The Devonshire settlement trustees also paid annual fees to a firm of investment advisers to keep under review and to advise changes in investments comprised in the trust fund. This was a recurrent charge but not an ordinary outgoing and was incurred for the benefit of the estate as a whole because the advice of the investment advisers will affect the future value of the capital of the trust fund and the future level of income arising from that capital. . .

. . . In accordance with the authorities and in accordance with principle, the premiums paid by the Paul and Devonshire settlement trustees in respect of capital transfer tax protection and on endowment policies and the fees paid to investment advisers were capital expenses and not income expenses.

A settlor may authorise or direct his trustees to pay income expenses out of capital or to pay capital expenses out of income.

[After considering the relevant clauses in each settlement Lord Templeman continued]

. . . In the result, the premiums and fees which constitute capital expenses have nevertheless been lawfully paid out of income. Now although a settlor may provide that capital expenses shall or may be paid out of income, the settlor cannot alter the nature of those expenses. The exercise of an express power or duty to pay capital expenses out of income, has the effect of taking income away from the income beneficiaries and bestowing it on the capital beneficiaries, so that capital is augmented. Premiums on an endowment policy remain a capital expense, although pursuant to an express power for that purpose, the sums paid in discharge of those premiums are taken from income. If the income of a trust fund is only sufficient to pay the premiums on a ten-year endowment policy, and income is directed by the settlor to be applied in payment of those premiums, the income beneficiaries are wholly deprived of any income during the ten-year period and capital is augmented. This only means that a capital expense is paid out of income because the settlor has so provided. Similarly, a settlor cannot alter the nature of an income expense by authorising or directing the trustees to pay that expense out of capital. A direction that rates of £1,000 per annum, payable in respect of a trust property settled on a tenant for life shall be paid out of capital, has the effect of taking £1,000 of capital away from the capital beneficiaries and bestowing that sum on the tenant for life. This only means that an income expense is paid out of capital because the settlor has so provided.

Income tax has been judicially pronounced to be a tax on income. In arriving at the amount of income liable to income tax, Parliament may expressly provide that certain income expenses may be deducted. The legislature may go further and expressly provide that certain capital allowances may be deducted for tax purposes. Fiscal legislation of that kind does not convert capital expenditure into an income expense. If the legislature provides for capital expenditure to be deducted for income tax purposes, the legislature does not increase or reduce the income of the taxpayer but reduces the amount of the income of the taxpayer which is liable to tax.

The Paul settlement and the Devonshire settlement created accumulation and discretionary trusts. The appellant trustees concede that section 16(2)(a)[33] applies and that additional rate income tax is chargeable on the income of the settlements under section 16(1).[34]

In my opinion, section 16(2)(d)[35] allows deduction of expenses *properly* chargeable to income, that is to say, income expenses. The words in brackets are explanatory and are placed in brackets because they are merely explanatory; they remove any possible ambiguity in the expression "properly chargeable" by emphasising that expenses which are deductible are those which would be chargeable to income in the absence of any express provisions of the trust. The natural construction of section 16(2)(d)[36] seems to me to authorise the deduction of income applied in defraying income expenses but not income applied in defraying capital expenses. This construction is consistent with trust law, consistent with income tax law and consistent also with common sense. Section 16(2)(a)[37] imposed additional rate tax on the income applied in augmenting capital pursuant to an express provision of the trust authorising the accumulation of income. Section 16(2)(d)[38] cannot have been intended to exempt from additional rate tax the income applied in augmenting capital pursuant to an express provision of the trust authorising the payment of capital expenses out of income ... **[16.15]**

When, in the exercise of a discretion, the trustees make a payment to a beneficiary, and that payment is the income of the beneficiary, or is treated as the income of the settlor, the trustees are required to gross up the payment at the rate applicable to trusts (i.e., 40 per cent), and are then assessable to tax at the special trust rates on that gross amount.[39] The trustees' liability can, however, be reduced by various payments, including the tax already paid under ITA 2007, sections 479 and 491, and any recoverable tax credits.[40] **[16.16]**

33 [Now ITA 2007, s 479(1).]
34 [Now ITA 2007, s 479(2)–(4)).]
35 [Now ITA 2007, s 484.]
36 [Ibid.]
37 [Now ITA 2007, s 479(1).]
38 [Now ITA 2007, s 484.]
39 ITA 2007, s 494.
40 *Ibid*, ss 497, 498. The 10% tax credit in respect of dividends is irrecoverable, and only the difference between the trust dividend rate of 32.5% and the ordinary dividend rate of 10% will be available for credit against the s 494 liability: s 498(2)).

D. Taxation of beneficiaries

It has already been seen that income of the trust is generally assessed to income tax in the hands of the trustees. Where a beneficiary is entitled to the income, or part of the income, of the trust, or receives income through, eg, the exercise of a discretion by the trustees, such income, duly grossed up, forms part of that beneficiary's total income for the year in question. The beneficiary may then be liable to income tax at the higher rate or, depending on the circumstances, may be entitled to set personal allowances against it and reclaim all or some of the tax already deducted (apart from the irrecoverable tax credit on company distributions). The income that a beneficiary receives from the trust is unearned even if it arises from a trade run by the trustees[41] but, if the beneficiary is entitled to the income *as it arises*, then he may be taxed according to the rules of the statutory provision appropriate to that source of income.[42] **[16.17]**

(1) Income of the beneficiary

For income to be liable to income tax in the hands of the beneficiary, there must be income which the beneficiary has received or is entitled to receive.[43] A beneficiary is entitled to trust income if the trustees are under a duty to pay the income to the beneficiary who, at that time, is absolutely entitled to it (or who is entitled to have it applied at his direction[44]). **[16.18]**

Drummond v Collins [1915] AC 1011 (HL)

Income received by a person resident in the United Kingdom, who was an object of a foreign discretionary trust, formed part of his total income for income tax and surtax purposes.

> EARL LOREBURN: . . . My Lords, in this case an American gentleman left by his will a large sum of money to trustees upon trusts which tied up his property with a view to its accumulation for a long time, and created a somewhat complicated series of interests. We have in my opinion no concern with the ultimate destination of these funds. We are concerned only with one provision. The will authorized and indeed required the trustees in America to exercise their discretion as to providing money for the maintenance of the testator's grandchildren, who are now minors. In pursuance of this authority the trustees exercised their discretion and remitted to the appellant, the mother of these children, certain sums of money for their maintenance, and the Court of Appeal by a majority has held that these sums are chargeable with income tax because the lady and the children reside in England, and the money was received in England.
>
> . . . It is abundantly clear that the present case falls within the letter of the Act. These sums were derived from remittances from America payable in Great Britain or from money or value received in Great Britain and arising from property that has not been imported into Great Britain. They also come within the words of Sch. D as profits or gains accruing from property to a person residing in the United Kingdom.

41 *Fry v Shiel's Trustees* (1914) 6 TC 583.
42 See *Baker v Archer-Shee* [1927] AC 844.
43 *Dewar v IRC* [1935] 2 KB 351; and see *Woodhouse v IRC* (1936) 20 TC 673; *IRC v Henderson's Executors* (1931) 16 TC 282. See also John Tiley 'Receivability and Receipt: The Problem of Timing under Income Tax Legislation' [1982] BTR 23 and 'More on Receivability and Receipt' [1986] BTR 152.
44 *Tollemarche v IRC* (1926) 11 TC 277; *Miller v IRC* [1930] AC 222.

It was argued, however, that these allowances sent from America are not "income" of the children, because they were voluntary payments by the trustees. I do not assent to the proposition that a voluntary payment can never be charged, but it is enough to say that these were not voluntary payments in any relevant sense. They were payments made in fulfilment of a testamentary disposition for the benefit of the children in the exercise of a discretion conferred by the will. They were the children's income in fact...

LORD WRENBURY: The gifts are each one of them in favour of the children, but the dates for payment to the children are fixed with reference to the exercise by the trustees of their discretion or the ages from time to time of the children. At the time with which your Lordships have to do there could be no payment except by exercise of the discretion vested in the trustees, but so soon as their discretion is exercised in favour of the child the resulting payment seems to me upon the language of the will to be a payment of income to which the child is entitled by virtue of the gift made by the testator. I cannot see any ground upon which such income is not subject to income tax.

My Lords, let me, however, assume that the above reasoning is not correct, and that the interest of the infants is contingent, that is to say, that the income is income of the child in one contingency and income of another (the person entitled under the gift over) in another contingency – that the money which is paid for the benefit of the child is not income of the child rendered payable by the action of the trustees, but is income which but for the action of the trustees would have been income of someone else (the person entitled under the gift over) which only comes to the child because the trustees under the provisions of the will divert it from that other person and make it available for the child. It remains, however, that in this case directly the trustees exercise their discretion in favour of the child the interests of the child ceases to be contingent and becomes vested ... **[16.19]**

Stanley v IRC [1944] KB 255 (CA)

The appellant was the life-tenant of a trust fund, the income of which, apart from certain payments for the maintenance of the appellant, was accumulated during his minority. The Revenue claimed to assess the appellant to surtax[45] on the accumulated income. The Court of Appeal held that the effect of the Trustee Act 1925, s 31(2) was to prevent the income from being that of the appellant during the years in question.[46]

LORD GREENE M.R.: ... Some highly technical arguments were addressed to us on the question what precise interest in surplus income an infant having a vested interest enjoys during his infancy in view of these provisions. This, no doubt, is a relevant question, but the fundamental question remains, namely, is that interest such as to make the surplus income of the infant for the purposes of surtax? It was said on behalf of the Crown that the infant has a vested interest in the surplus income as it accrues and that there is nothing in the section that deprives him of that interest during infancy – all that the section does is to divest him of his title to the accumulations of surplus income if he dies before attaining his majority. In other words, it was said, he has a vested interest in the accumulations which is defeasible in the event of his dying under twenty-one and, therefore, the surplus income is, during minority, income of the infant and as such is assessable year by year. It is necessary at this point to call attention to a distinction which apparently was not appreciated by the Special Commissioners. The expression "defeasible interest in income" may be used in two senses. In the case of an adult he receives and enjoys the income until the defeasance takes place. Until that event occurs the income is his income and he is assessable accordingly, but the same expression (if it be the correct one to use in

45 Surtax was replaced, with effect from 1973–74, by the current system of 'higher rates'.
46 Where the income is not the income of any person other than the trustees, the rate applicable to trusts will now apply: see para **[16.13]**, above.

reference to surplus income in such a case as the present) means, in the case of an infant in the situation of the appellant, something quite different. The infant does not during infancy enjoy the surplus income. It is not his in any real sense. The title to it is held in suspense to await the event, and if he dies under twenty-one his interest in it (whether or not it be truly described as a vested interest) is destroyed. He is, in fact, for all practical purposes in precisely the same position as if his interest in surplus income were contingent. If he attains twenty-one he takes the accumulations, if he dies under twenty-one he does not . . . **[16.20]**

Cornwell v Barry (1955) 36 TC 268 (Ch D)

Property was settled upon discretionary trusts for the benefit of a number of possible objects but, during the relevant period, there was in fact only one person within the discretion. Part of the trust income was applied by the appellant for the benefit of that object, the remainder being accumulated. A claim on behalf of the beneficiary for repayment of the tax paid on the trust income was unsuccessful, the Court holding that, as the beneficiary was not entitled to the income of the fund, that income could not be regarded as his income for the purposes of relief.

HARMAN J.: . . . The question at issue can be stated tersely: Was the income of this fund in the years in question the infant's income? If it was, he *is* entitled, through his Trustee, to get the usual personal relief against the tax suffered. If, however, it could not be said to be his income, he is not a person who can get that relief.

. . . It follows that the problem here is to decide whether this income, year by year, which was paid by the covenantor, became indefeasibly the income of the infant. He was, as I say, at all times the only object of the covenant. There was no other infant during the eight years of its duration, and it is said, there being no one else, the income was always all his notwithstanding that it was not applied for his benefit, and that if he had died during the duration of the covenant his estate would have become entitled to the accrued instalments up to the date of the death.

. . . Now, says Mr. Monroe, the trust applies "as and when moneys are received," and you should read it in this way: "The Trustee shall hold the moneys upon trust as and when received for all or any one or more of the children," and so on. I quite agree that that is a sensible way of reading it. It means that the trust applies to each half-yearly instalment of the covenanted sums as they reach the Trustee's hands, and that is the trust you would expect to find. So, directly he receives £75, that is, a half-yearly instalment, the Trustee holds it on trust. For whom?

> " . . . for all or any one or more of the children now living or born during the said period."

In other words, any child of the son either in existence when the deed is made or coming into existence during the eight years thereafter is an object of the trust. Mr. Monroe says that, so long as there is only one child who fulfils any of those qualifications, he is entitled to the whole income as and when received, and it is indefeasibly his. In my judgment, that would be an entirely mistaken view of this wording. The Trustee is to look not only at the child in existence but any child who may come into existence, and during the eight years he is not bound, as I see it, to make any application of the money at all. He would if he were a reasonable man, but he is not bound to. It is quite true that the trust is for the absolute use and benefit of these children, but it is in such shares and in such manner as the Trustee thinks fit. Consequently, he has the eight years in which to make up his mind. He may during that time divide it into shares or give it all to one or other of the objects of the trust, and even if at any time during the eight years there were no object of the trust, he would still, in my view, have to hold the money in case, before the end of the period, an object should come into being.

Consequently, though it may well be, and I think is, the fact that Michael being in existence had got a vested interest in this money, it was an interest which was liable to be divested if another object of the trust came into existence during the eight years. It is not until the end of this time that you could say: The class is closed; the object is achieved; and

> the money, if there be any unapplied, vests absolutely in any of the persons who were objects of the trust, and whether then dead or then living matters not . . . **[16.21]**

Where a beneficiary *is* absolutely entitled, accumulated income forms part of his total income: *IRC v Hamilton-Russell's Executors* [1943] 1 All ER 474. **[16.22]**

IRC v Blackwell [1924] 2 KB 351 (KBD); affirmed [1926] 1 KB 389 (CA)

Income accumulated during the minority of an infant was not his income. When the accumulations were subsequently paid to him, they were received as capital and he was not assessable to surtax in respect thereof.

> ROWLATT J.: . . . In this case the testator by his will disposed of property in two ways. There was a specific devise of certain real estate, as to which a question arises whether the eldest son, who is the boy in respect of whose resources this case arises, took a vested interest or only a contingent interest in that property. As regards the rest and residue of the testator's property, both real and personal, there is no doubt that all the children took a vested interest.
>
> The first point which Mr. Latter makes is that it does not matter whether the interest which the eldest son takes under the will is vested or contingent, because, even assuming that this specific bequest is vested in the eldest son, just as the shares in the residue are vested in all, the children under the other part of the will, still, inasmuch as there is a trust to accumulate a fund during the infancy of the eldest son, subject to a power to the trustees to apply such sum as they think proper for his maintenance, the part of the income which is accumulated is not the income of the minor. It is a very important point, but I have come to the conclusion that he is right. It is perfectly true to say, as Mr. Harman did, that in a case of that kind the income must come to the infant in the end if the interest which he takes is a vested interest: but in my judgment it will not come to him as income; it will come to him in the future in the form of capital. The trustees are directed to accumulate the surplus income, and they are bound to comply with that direction and to accumulate it. It is income which is held in trust for him in the sense that he will ultimately receive it, but it is not in trust for him in the sense that the trustees have to pay the income to him year by year while he is an infant. All the minor can get while he is an infant is such amount as the trustees allow for his maintenance. I think that view of the case is supported by what was said in *Inland Revenue Commissioners v. Wemyss.*[47] In my judgment it is fallacious to look into the future and say: This fund that is being accumulated is for his benefit and he will get it all. What you have to do is to ask, whether the surplus income that is accumulated is the annual profits and gains of the year of this infant now? I do not think it is. I think this case is quite different from a case where the infant has the right to the money now but where the money remains in the hands of his trustees not because of any directions in the will which directed it to be accumulated, but because he is an infant and cannot receive the money and give a receipt for it, and it therefore remains in the hands of his trustees, being invested but lying ready for him waiting for the time when the infant can give a good receipt for it. I think that case is quite different. In that case the income would be the income of the infant now, although he could not touch it and could not give a receipt for it. But where the will expressly provides that the surplus income shall be accumulated and only allows the trustees to spend what they think proper on the minor's maintenance it seems to me that it is not the income of the minor yet . . . **[16.23]**

47 (1924) 8 TC 551.

See, however, the doubts expressed by Rowlatt J in *Gascoigne v IRC* [1927] 1 KB 594 about his decision in *IRC v Blackwell*, above. **[16.24]**

(2) Capital or income

It has been seen that income in the hands of the trustees may be received as capital by the beneficiary. Equally, payments from capital may be received as income,[48] and assessed as such in the hands of the beneficiary. **[16.25]**

Stevenson v Wishart [1987] 1 WLR 1204 (CA)

In exercise of a power of appointment over the capital of a discretionary trust, trustees appointed various sums over a number of years to a particular beneficiary. These sums were applied in paying medical and nursing expenses incurred by the beneficiary. It was contended, inter alia, by the Revenue that in view of the recurrent nature of the sums appointed and the purpose for which they were applied, namely the maintenance and support of the beneficiary, such sums should be treated as income in the hands of the beneficiary. The Court of Appeal held that the sums were received as capital by the beneficiary.

FOX L J.: . . . There is no doubt that payments of capital out of a trust may constitute income in the recipient's hands, despite their capital origin. Thus, in *Brodie's Trustees v. Inland Revenue Commissioners*,[49] the trustees of a will held property on trust to pay the income to the testator's widow for life with a provision that if, in any year, the income did not amount to £4,000, the trustees were to raise and pay to her out of capital such a sum as added to the income would make £4,000 – "my intention being," the testator stated in the will "that the income payable to my wife during her life shall in no case be less than £4,000 a year." The income was, in fact, below £4,000 in certain years, and the trustee duly raised sums out of capital in augmentation of the income. Finlay J. held that the sums so raised out of capital were taxable as income in the hands of the widow. He said[50]:

> "But, I think, the governing consideration is this, the question being, was the sum received as income, one has to consider what was the source from which it was received and what were the circumstances in which it was received. If the capital belonged to the person receiving the sums – if he or she was beneficially entitled not only to the income but to the capital – then I should think that, when the payments were made, they ought to be regarded, and would be regarded, as payments out of capital, but where there is a right to the income, but the capital belongs to somebody else, then, if the payments out of capital are made and made in such a form that they come into the hands of the beneficiaries as income, it seems to me that they are income and not the less income, because the source from which they came was – in the hands, not of the person receiving them, but in the hands of somebody else – capital."

As Finlay J. pointed out, on the same page, the provisions of the will in that case were exceedingly strong. The testator was expressly directing the provision out of his estate of an annuity of £4,000 a year.

In *Jackson's Trustees v. Inland Revenue Commissioners*,[51] the trustees of a will were directed to hold the residuary estate on trust to raise out of the capital of the trust fund and pay to each of his four daughters on January 1 in each year during the life of his widow so long as they were living the sum of £250 and subject thereto to pay the income of the trust

48 See, for example, *Brodie's Will Trustees v IRC* (1933) 17 TC 432 and *Cunard's Trustees v IRC* [1946] 1 All ER 159.
49 (1933) 17 TC 432.
50 *Ibid.*, at 439.
51 (1942) 25 TC 13.

fund to the widow until remarriage. Wrottesley J. held that the effect of the will was simply to direct the payment of an annuity to each of the daughters. He regarded the payment as "ordinary income, an ordinary annuity," and not the less so because it was paid out of capital.

In *Cunard's Trustees v Inland Revenue Commissioners*,[52] the testator directed that his residuary estate be held on trust during his sister's life to pay out of the income thereof all rates, taxes and other outgoings of a freehold property (which he had devised to the trustees to permit his sister to live there) and subject thereto to pay or apply the remainder of the income of the residuary estate for the benefit of his sister during her life. The will further provided by clause 10(b) that[53]

> "If in any year the income of my residuary estate shall not be sufficient to enable my sister to live at The Grove in the same degree of comfort as she now lives there with me then I empower my trustees to apply such portion of the capital of my residuary estate by way of addition to the income as they shall . . . think fit . . ."

The trustees raised and paid to the sister various sums out of capital in the years 1937–1940 inclusive. These were held to be taxable as income. Lord Greene M.R. said[54]:

> "That the payments were 'income' in Miss McPheeters' hands is, in my opinion, beyond dispute, and the fact that they were made out of capital is irrelevant. The payments were to be made 'by way of addition to the income' in order to enable Miss McPheeters to live in the same degree of comfort as before. The testatrix was in fact providing for a defined standard of life for her sister, that provision being made in part out of income and in part (at the discretion of the trustees) out of capital. The purpose was an income purpose and nothing else. A similar point was decided by Finlay J. in *Brodie's Trustees v. Inland Revenue Commissioners*,[55] which was, in my opinion, correctly decided. In that case, the trustees were bound to make payments out of capital as required and had not merely a discretion, as in the present case. But that is immaterial on the question whether the payments ought to be regarded as being of an income character."

In the *Brodie* and *Cunard* cases the payments out of capital were in augmentation of an income interest, and their nature as income was determined accordingly. *Lindus and Hortin v. Inland Revenue Commissioners*,[56] and *Milne's Executors v. Inland Revenue Commissioners*,[57] are also, I think, cases of that sort. The *Jackson* case was, on the construction of the will, simply a gift out of the residuary estate of an annuity during joint lives. In the present case, the payments were not in augmentation of an income interest and there is no express gift of an annuity. The decisions to which I have referred do not, therefore, govern this case.

Whilst it is the law that the fact that payments are made out of capital does not prevent the payments being income in the hands of the recipient, the fact that payments made out of capital are either periodic or for personal maintenance, or both, does not necessarily mean that they are income in the hands of the recipient. I take the following examples.

(1) Property is held on trust for a beneficiary absolutely upon attaining the age of 30. If the trustees in exercise of the statutory power of advancement under section 32 of the Trustee Act 1925, instead of making a single advance of a substantial amount make regular annual payments of the capital to the beneficiary because they do not want him to have too much capital too quickly, it seems to me that the payments are capital payments, and nothing else. The beneficiary is contingently entitled to the whole capital, and he is simply getting it in advance of the vesting date. That, I think, is an example of the sort of case that Finlay J. had in mind in *Brodie*,[58] where he refers to cases where the capital "belonged" to the beneficiary.

52 [1946] 1 All ER 159.
53 *Ibid.*, at 162.
54 *Ibid.*, at 163.
55 (1933) 17 TC 432.
56 (1933) 17 TC 442.
57 (1956) 37 TC 10.
58 (1933) 17 TC 442.

(2) If, under the trusts set out in (1) above, the trustees make regular advances of capital to the beneficiary for the purposes of his education or personal maintenance, the advances in my view retain the nature of capital. He is still simply getting capital, which is contingently his, in advance of the vesting date. The fact that he needs it for education or maintenance or both does not alter its nature as capital.

(3) Suppose next a case where the beneficiary is simply an object of a power to appoint capital. That, in substance, is this case, because although Mrs. Henwood had, as one of the beneficiaries as defined in the settlement, a contingent interest in unappointed capital if she was living at the expiration of the trust period, her age made it most unlikely that she would survive. In such a case, if the trustees made a single appointment of, say, £40,000 to Mrs. Henwood because she was without adequate income for her maintenance, I see no basis for saying that the sum would be other than capital in Mrs. Henwood's hands. Nor do I think that the argument would be any stronger if the appointment was repeated for a second year. There are no indications of "income" at all.

In the present case the Crown contended that, taking the size, recurrence and purpose of the payments, they take the character of income. It was said in the words of Finlay J. in *Brodie's* case,[59] that "one has to look at the reality of the thing." Reliance is also placed on the statement of Lord Greene M.R. in *Cunard's Trustees v. Inland Revenue Commissioners*[60] that "The purpose was an income purpose and nothing else."

In dealing with the case it is, I think, necessary to bear in mind throughout that the trustees were disposing of capital under a power to appoint capital. Mrs. Henwood was, it is true, an object of certain trusts of income in the settlement, but the trustees were not exercising or purporting to exercise such powers. Applying the test of the "reality" of the matter, the position was this. Mrs. Henwood was a woman of very advanced age who needed nursing home care. That was exceedingly expensive. It seems to me quite unreal to regard it as an ordinary income expense. Certainly it involved day-to-day maintenance expenditure, but it was expenditure on such a scale that it cannot be regarded as normal. It was emergency expenditure of very substantial amounts which would be quite outside normal income resources. Between 10 May 1978 and 14 April 1980, the payments amounted to £90,000. That was the sort of expenditure which, if it is to be met at all, is in practice met either from the patient's own capital, or from family capital. That receives some emphasis in the present case from the fact that when Mrs. Henwood's flat, which was her only asset of any consequence, was sold in August 1980, the proceeds were used to pay her nursing home expenses until her death in January 1981. In short, the obvious source to meet such expenditure was capital.

In my opinion Lord Greene M.R's words in *Cunard's* case "The purpose was an income purpose and nothing else" have no application to the present case. The words have to be read in their context. Lord Greene M.R. had, only a few lines previously, referred to the fact that the payments were to be made "by way of addition to the income," which was the wording of the will. It seems to me that the "income purpose" in *Cunard's* case was primarily identified by these words. There is no similar provision here. The result, in my opinion, is that there is nothing in the present case which indicates that the payments were of an income nature except their recurrence. I do not think that is sufficient. The trustees were disposing of capital in exercise of a power over capital. They did not create a recurring interest in property. If, in exercise of a power over capital, they chose to make at their discretion regular payments of capital to deal with the special problems of Mrs. Henwood's last years rather than release a single sum to her of a large amount, that does not seem to me to create an income interest. Their power was to appoint capital. What they appointed remained capital. The result, in my view, is that the payments were wholly

59 17 TC 432 at 439–440.
60 [1946] 1 All ER 159 at 163.

of a capital nature ... I should mention that on no view of the case is it suggested that these payments escape taxation. If they were capital, they were liable to capital transfer tax, and indeed we were informed that the trustees had paid capital transfer tax of some £17,500 on that basis.

In my opinion Knox J. came to the correct conclusion. I would dismiss the appeal. **[16.26]**

The current practice of HMRC appears to be to treat advances or appointments out of trust capital as capital in the recipient beneficiary's hands. This will be the case *unless* the payments are intended to augment income,[61] if the trust instrument contains a provision authorising the use of capital to maintain a beneficiary in the same degree of comfort as had been the case in the past[62] or if the capital payment in question really amounts to an annuity.[63] **[16.27]**

2. Trusts with vulnerable beneficiaries

The raison d'être for having trusts for the benefit of disabled persons and minors who have lost one or both parents is to enable the trustees to pay out income for the benefit of such beneficiaries as and when it is needed; the likelihood is that these beneficiaries may be in no position themselves to handle the whole of the income arising in a year. However, the result is that, without further provision, the retained income would suffer income tax at the trust rate, now standing at 40%, and the dividend trust rate at 32.5%, this could be highly detrimental to the operation of these important trusts. This position was acknowledged by the Government, and legislation was introduced[64] providing for special tax treatment for 'qualifying' trusts with 'vulnerable' beneficiaries. The effect of these provisions is to bring the trustees' income tax liability[65] into line with what the beneficiary's liability would have been if he had received the income directly. **[16.28]**

Inland Revenue *Modernising The Tax System For Trusts* (December 2003)

Trusts for the vulnerable

22. ... the Government wants to ensure certain classes of vulnerable beneficiary pay less tax. Some trusts for these groups have to accumulate income and will therefore be liable to income tax at the RAT. **[16.29]**

61 As in *Brodie's Will Trustees v IRC* (1933) 17 TC 432.
62 As in *Cunard's Trustees v IRC* [1946] 1 All ER 159.
63 *Jackson's Trustees v IRC* (1942) 25 TC 13.
64 FA 2005. The effect of the new provisions is backdated to 6 April 2004.
65 Similar provisions apply for chargeable gains; see below, para **[20.29]**.

Inland Revenue, REV BN 10: *Modernising the Tax System for Trusts*, A Consultation Document (August 2004)

OUTLINE OF NEW REGIME

Election system

1.2 The proposal is that trustees of trusts established for the most vulnerable should be able to elect to be taxed on the basis of the vulnerable beneficiary's individual circumstances, for both income tax and CGT. This election would be available to two categories of trusts: those set up for the benefit of individuals who have a disability, and those set up for minor children on the death of a parent.

1.3 The election would be made jointly by the trustee and the beneficiary and would be irrevocable. A compelling argument in favour of irrevocability ... is that vulnerability is not something you can pick and choose. The ability to opt in and out of this regime would not sit well with vulnerability being a lasting state or condition. For a minor child who has lost a parent the vulnerability is due both to the individual's age and the loss of parental support. For such vulnerable children the proposal is that the benefits of this regime should be available up to the date the child reaches the age of eighteen.

1.4 In those cases where the beneficiary is unable to elect on their own behalf the election will have to be made by their parent, guardian or appropriate legal representative. It is important that the beneficiary or his representative is party to the election to ensure that an irrevocable election affecting someone's tax position is not made by a third party. The fact that the system will depend on communication between the trustees and the vulnerable individual is a further pointer to a joint election.

1.5 For trusts for the disabled, the proposal is to use the definition in section 89 of the Inheritance Tax Act 1984. A disabled person will be someone who, when the property was transferred into the trust, was:

> "(a) *incapable, by reason of mental disorder within the meaning of the Mental Health Act 1983 of administering his property and managing his affairs, or*
>
> (b) *in receipt of an attendance allowance under section 64 of the Social Security Contributions and Benefits Act 1992 or section 64 of the Social Security Contributions and Benefits (Northern Ireland) Act 1992, or*
>
> (c) *in receipt of a disability living allowance under section 71 of the Social Security Contributions and Benefits Act 1992 or section 71 of the Social Security Contributions and Benefits (Northern Ireland) Act 1992 by virtue of entitlement to the care component at the highest or middle rate.*"

We recognise that a beneficiary may qualify under the basic tests but have been moved into care for medical reasons. It is proposed that in such cases the trust will still qualify as a trust for a disabled person.

1.6 Trusts for minors would be able to qualify as trusts for the most vulnerable where the trust was set up either under the rules of intestacy or under the terms of the parent's will..... However, such trusts will only qualify where the terms of the trust deed give an unconditional entitlement to any assets in the trust at the age of 18.

1.7 The election system would be available for trusts where either there is more than one vulnerable beneficiary or a mixture of vulnerable and non-vulnerable beneficiaries. The key condition in such cases is that the property for each individual who is a vulnerable beneficiary should be ring-fenced during that individual's lifetime from that of any other beneficiary. Without this

> ring-fencing there is a risk that the benefits of the new regime could be available to non-vulnerable beneficiaries. There will have to be adequate safeguards in place to prevent this. **[16.30]**

These proposals have been incorporated in FA 2005.[66] **[16.31]**

3. Income of the settlor – the anti-avoidance provisions

Prior to the recent changes made to the special trust rates,[67] the manner of taxing the income of trusts and of beneficiaries suggested two main methods of reducing the impact of taxation. One of these was to ensure that the income of the trust belonged to no individual (ie the settlor had completely divested himself of any interest in the trust, and no beneficiary was entitled absolutely to all or any part of the income, as in a discretionary trust). The trustees would then have been taxed on the trust income at the trust rate which, at the then rate of 34% (and 25% for dividend income), was lower than the higher rate of tax possibly faced by a beneficiary. The trustees might have accumulated the post-tax income, and later extracted it in the form of capital distributions to the beneficiaries, or they may have distributed the income to those beneficiaries who paid income tax at the basic rate only (in which case no further tax would have been due from the beneficiary) or to beneficiaries with excess personal allowances when a repayment of tax[68] may have been made to such beneficiaries. Such advantages that did exist have effectively been removed by equating the rate applicable to trusts with the higher rate of income tax. The second advantageous method of minimising tax was (and, in some circumstances, continues to be) by transferring income from a higher rate taxpayer to one who pays tax at basic rate, such as a wealthy grandfather transferring income bearing assets to trustees for the benefit of his grandchildren.

Tax avoidance of this latter kind is not necessarily undesirable (indeed, the voluntary transfer of income from the rich to the less rich may be socially desirable)[69] but, were certain restrictions not imposed upon the use of trusts to reduce tax, avoidance would be both attractive and simple, by:

(i) splitting income among the members of the settlor's own family, for whom he already might be responsible, in particular, the children of the settlor, thereby reducing tax liability while retaining the same disposable wealth within the family unit; or

(ii) disposing of income in other directions, or providing for its accumulation, while still retaining power to enjoy the income by parting with the income for a limited period only, by means of a power to revoke the settlement, by reserving a beneficial interest or by continuing to derive a benefit in some other manner.

66 See ss 23–45.

67 See para **[16.13]**, above.

68 Apart from the irrecoverable tax credit in respect of the 10% deducted at source in respect of dividend income. See para **[14.27]**, above.

69 See Chapter 1, para **[1.3]**, above.

To prevent this type of avoidance, the legislation contains a number of provisions[70] whereby, for income tax purposes, the income under certain types of settlement is deemed to be the income of the settlor,[71] thus nullifying, in whole or in part, any potential tax advantage. The charge to tax is imposed by ITTOIA 2005, s 619 and covers rules which apply where:

(i) the unmarried minor children of the settlor receive a benefit from the settlement;[72]

(ii) the settlor or his spouse or civil partner has retained an interest in the settlement or where the settlor transfers income not capital;[73]

(iii) the settlor or his spouse, civil partner or minor child have received a capital payment or benefit from the settlement.[74]

Critical to the provisions is the term 'settlement', which includes any 'disposition, trust, covenant, agreement, arrangement or transfer of assets'.[75] Much criticism has recently been levelled at the Revenue for seeking to apply these provisions[76] to the setting up of a corporate structure, which they argued (unsuccessfully before the Court of Appeal) was an 'arrangement' within the meaning of the legislation.[77] Importantly, a transaction can be a settlement only if it contains an element of bounty.[78] The exception for outright[79] gifts between spouses and civil partners,[80] allowing a higher rate spouse or civil partner to transfer income-producing assets to the other to ensure that the personal allowance and basic rate band of the other are fully utilised, can only

70 ITTOIA 2005, Pt 5, Ch 5. Whilst these provisions (formerly found in ICTA 1988, ss 660–682A) have been the subject of the tax law rewrite, only relatively minor changes have been made to the former provisions, which were themselves substantially recast with effect from April 1995. These provisions are widely drawn and are *not* mutually exclusive, so that a provision in a settlement may fall within the scope of more than one of the rules: see *Gillies v IRC* (1928) 14 TC 329. As already seen (Chapter 11, para **[11.22]** and Chapter 14, para **[14.10]**), these provisions may also apply to certain *income* settlements. This section is primarily concerned with these provisions in the context of capital settlements.

71 It should also be remembered that, in the case of an *ineffective* disposition, there will be a resulting trust in favour of the disposer, so that the income under the disposition will be his in any event: see *Aked v Shaw* (1947) 28 TC 286. As to a partial failure of a trust, see *Vandervell v IRC* [1967] 2 AC 291; *Watson v Holland* [1985] 1 All ER 290.

72 ITTOIA 2005, s 629.

73 *Ibid*, ss 624–628.

74 *Ibid*, ss 633–643.

75 *Ibid*, s 620. This wording is the same as that found in the former ICTA 1988, s 660(1).

76 Specifically, what is now ITTOIA 2005, ss 624–628 (formerly ICTA 1988, s 660A).

77 *Jones v Garnett* [2005] EWCA Civ 1553, overturning the decision Park J at [2005] EWHC 849 (Ch) and of the Special Commissioners at [2004] SpC 432, [2005] STC (SCD) 9. See para **[16.34]**, below. In the High Court, Park J upheld the Revenue view that the acquisition by each of the husband and wife of one of the two issued shares in a company, with dividends being paid to both in spite of the fact that the husband did the lion's share of the work, is an arrangement. The Court of Appeal disagreed (see para **[16.34]**, below). The Revenue appeal to the House of Lords was heard at the beginning of June 2007, but no judgment had been delivered by the date of submission of the manuscript for this book.

78 A commercial transaction devoid of any element of bounty is not a settlement, see *IRC v Levy* (1982) 56 TC 68. For a discussion of 'bounty', see *Jones v Garnett* [2005] EWCA Civ 1553 and para **[16.34]**, below.

79 A gift is not an outright gift if: (i) it does not carry the right to the whole of the income from the property given; (ii) it is wholly or substantially a right to income; (iii) it is subject to conditions; or (iv) the property given, or any income or property derived from it, is, or might be, paid to or for the benefit of the donor. For a discussion of this provision, see *Young v Pearce* [1996] STC 743, below at para **[16.36]**, and *Jones v Garnett*, at para **[16.34]**, below.

80 ITTOIA 2005, s 626.

apply where, in addition to being outright, the gift is irrevocable, unconditional and of matching proportions of income and capital.

The general characteristics of the anti-avoidance provisions are identified in the following extract from the judgment of Lord Wilberforce in *IRC v Plummer*,[81] whilst the particular issue of the application of the settlement provisions to a commercial arrangement and the limiting factor of bounty are highlighted in the judgment of Sir Andrew Morritt, Chancellor of the High Court, in *Jones v Garnett*.[82] Subsequent extracts from *Jones v Garnett* and *Young v Pearce*[83] are concerned with the exception for outright gifts to spouses or civil partners. **[16.32]**

IRC v Plummer [1980] AC 896 (HL)

LORD WILBERFORCE: . . . it seems to me to be clear that it is not possible to read into the definition *[of settlement]* an exception in favour of commercial transactions whether with or without the epithet "ordinary" or "bona fide." To do so would be legislation not interpretation: if Parliament had intended such an exception it could and must have expressed it.

But it still becomes necessary to inquire what is the scope of the words "settlement" and "settlor" and of the words which are included in "settlement" in the context in which they appear. If it appears, on the one hand, that a completely literal reading of the relevant words would so widely extend the reach of the section that no agreement of whatever character fell outside it, but that, on the other hand, a legislative purpose can be discerned, of a more limited character, which Parliament can reasonably be supposed to have intended, and that the words used fairly admit of such a meaning as to give effect to that purpose, it would be legitimate, indeed necessary, for the courts to adopt such a meaning.

Part XVI of the Act of 1970, which includes sections 434 to 459 is headed "Settlements."[84] It includes a number of provisions which have been enacted at different times, the general effect of which is to cause income of which a person has disposed in various ways to be treated, in spite of the disposition, as the income of the disposer. These had been successively enacted in the Finance Acts 1922, 1936, 1938, 1946, inter alia, with increasing severity. Chapter I of Part XVI is headed "Dispositions for short periods": exempting dispositions for valuable and sufficient consideration, it treats dispositions of income for a period which cannot exceed six years as the income of the disponer.[85] Chapter II deals with settlements on children[86] – the general purpose being to prevent (i.e. to tax if they are made) dispositions the effect of which is to spread income among the children of a settlor? This chapter has its own definition of "settlement" as "any disposition, trust, covenant, agreement, arrangement or transfer of assets" (section 444(2)).[87] Chapter III deals with revocable settlements, settlements in which a settlor retains an interest and capital payments made to a settlor or his spouse, the effect of which is to tax income from which a settlor, or his wife, may benefit as the settlor's

81 [1980] AC 896. The effect of this decision was reversed by *Moodie v IRC* [1993] STC 188 on the application of the principle enunciated in *Ramsay (WT) Ltd v IRC* [1982] AC 300 and *Furniss v Dawson* [1984] AC 474; see paras **[5.7]** and **[5.9]**, above.

82 [2005] EWCA Civ 1553.

83 [1996] STC 743.

84 [See now ITTOIA 2005, Pt 5, Ch 5. For a consideration of these provisions in relation to *income* settlements, see Chapter 11, para **[11.22]**, and Chapter 14, para **[14.40]**.]

85 [Such payments entered into on or after 15 March 1988 are now excluded from the tax system altogether: FA 1988, s 36, inserting ss 347A and 347B; ITTOIA 2005, s 727(1), and see above, Chapter 14, para **[14.40]**.]

86 [See now ITTOIA 2005, s 629. The term 'children' refers to infant, unmarried children.]

87 [Repealed by FA 1995, s 162 and Sch 29, Pt VIII(8). The current definition of settlement in ITTOIA 2005, s. 620 includes 'any disposition, trust, covenant, agreement, arrangement or transfer of assets (except that it does not include a charitable loan arrangement)'.]

income.[88] The definition of "settlement" (section 454(3))[89] is that which I have quoted as applicable in the present case. Lastly Chapter IV, headed "Surtax liability[90] of settlors in certain cases" contains (briefly) a broad sweeping-up provision for taxing any income of a settlement except income from property of which the settlor has divested himself absolutely by the settlement.[91] The definition of "settlement" (section 459) is that which I have quoted.[92]

My Lords, it can, I think, fairly be seen that all of these provisions, in Part XVI, have a common character. They are designed to bring within the net of taxation dispositions of various kinds, in favour of a settlor's spouse, or children, or of charities, cases, in popular terminology, in which a taxpayer gives away a portion of his income, or of his assets, to such persons, or for such periods, or subject to such conditions, that Parliament considers it right to continue to treat such income, or income of the assets, as still the settlor's income. These sections, in other words, though drafted in wide, and increasingly wider language, are nevertheless dealing with a limited field – one far narrower than the field of the totality of dispositions, or arrangements, or agreements, which a man may make in the course of his life. Is there then any common description which can be applied to this?

The courts which, inevitably, have had to face this problem, have selected the element of "bounty" as a necessary common characteristic of all the "settlements" which Parliament has in mind. The decisions are tentative, but all point in this direction ... **[16.33]**

Jones v Garnett [2005] EWCA Civ 1553, [2006] 1 WLR 1123 (CA)

A husband and wife each owned one of the two issued shares of a company (Arctic Systems Ltd), the only business of which was the supply of consultancy services provided by the husband alone. He was the sole director, and his wife provided some administrative services. Both received modest salaries from the company, although substantial dividends were paid equally to both husband and wife in certain years. Bearing in mind the modest services provided by the wife, the Revenue was of the view that there was an 'arrangement'; that the dividends were in lieu of a greater salary for the husband so that the income could be taxed at the lower rate applicable to the wife rather than to the higher rate of the husband, and thus were to be treated as the income of the husband as settlor under ICTA 1988, s 660A (now ITTOIA 2005, s 624(1)). The High Court took the view that the corporate structure created by the taxpayer had been an arrangement falling clearly within the meaning of the legislation, with the taxpayer husband as settlor, and that consequently the dividends paid to his wife had to be treated as his income for income tax purposes. Reversing this decision, the Court of Appeal, held that there was no settlement.

THE CHANCELLOR (SIR ANDREW MORRITT): ...

The decided cases ...

19. Although the decision of the House of Lords in *IRC v Plummer* established conclusively that the relevant test was "element of bounty" rather than "commercial transaction" it was not suggested that any of the previously decided cases in which the latter test had been applied was wrongly decided. Accordingly the examples of the application of the statutory definition which the previously

88 [See now ITTOIA 2005, s 625.]
89 [Now ITTOIA 2005, s 620.]
90 [This refers to 'excess liability', which is the difference between the settlor's higher rate of income tax and the basic rate. This provision was repealed by FA 1995, s 162 and Sch 29, Pt VIII(8).]
91 [See now ITTOIA 2005, ss 624–628.]
92 [See now ITTOIA 2005, s 620.]

decided cases provide remain relevant even though some of the dicta may require reinterpretation. It is to those cases, in so far as we were referred to them, that I now turn.

20. The first is *Copeman v Coleman*[93]. In that case a company had been formed to take over the taxpayer's business in which the shares were held equally between him and his wife. Some three years later the company created a class of preference shares of £200 each carrying a fixed preferential dividend, the right to vote if such dividend were in arrear for three years or more and the right in a winding up to a return of capital paid up. Some of the shares were taken up by his children on which they paid £10 per share. Dividends substantially in excess of the amounts paid up were then declared and the taxpayer, on behalf of his children claimed repayment of the tax paid in respect of the dividend to the extent of that child's personal allowance. That claim was rejected by the Special Commissioners and by Lawrence J on appeal. He said:

> "In my opinion, it is impossible to come to any other conclusion but that this was not a bona fide commercial transaction, and it appears to me that there was a disposition within the meaning of the definition or an arrangement in the nature of a disposition within [*that meaning*]."

That conclusion was evidently justified by the benefit or bounty obtained by the taxpayer's children by means of the dividend on the partly paid up preference shares.

21. In *CIR v Payne*[94] the taxpayer covenanted to pay an annual sum to a company controlled by him for his life or until it was wound up. He claimed to deduct the amount of the covenant in the computation of his total income for surtax purposes. The Revenue refused his claim on the ground that the arrangement constituted a revocable settlement so that the income arising from the property comprised in it was to be deemed to be his. The contentions of the Revenue were upheld by both Lawrence J and the Court of Appeal. Sir Wilfrid Greene MR noted that:

> "The covenant had, apparently, no business purpose whatsoever. It was linked up with the rest of the scheme, the essential parts of which were that [the taxpayer] should put himself in such a relationship to the company that he could entirely control it by means of his voting power."

22. He concluded that there was a settlement within the definition. He said:

> "It appears to me that the whole of what was done must be looked at; and when that is done, the true view, in my judgment, is that Mr. Walter Payne deliberately placed himself into a certain relationship to the company as part of one definite scheme, the essential heads of which could have been put down in numbered paragraphs on half a sheet of notepaper. Those were the things which it was essential that Mr. Payne should do if he wished to bring about the result desired. He did it by a combination of obtaining the control of the company, entering into the covenant, and then dealing with the company in such a way as to achieve his object. Now, if a deliberate scheme, perfectly clear cut, of that description is not an "arrangement" within the meaning of the definition clause, I have difficulty myself in seeing what useful purpose was achieved by the Legislature in putting that word into the definition at all. I am clearly of opinion that, by placing himself into these relationships with the company, Mr. Walter Payne was engaged in making an "arrangement" within the meaning of that clause."

In this case too there was obviously the requisite element of bounty in that the company gave no consideration for the annual payments.

93 (1939) 22 TC 594.
94 (1940) 23 TC 610.

23. The decision in *Crossland v Hawkins*[95] lies at the heart of the argument in this case. Jack Hawkins, a well known film actor, agreed with a newly formed company for a period of three years to render his services as that company might determine at a salary of £50 per week. The shares in the company were transferred by the subscribers to the Memorandum of Association to his wife and his accountant. His father in law set up a £100 settlement for the benefit of Jack Hawkins' children of which his wife and accountant were the trustees. They used the trust fund in subscribing for the remaining 98 shares in the company. Jack Hawkins appeared in a film for which the company was paid £25,000. The company paid a dividend which was applied by the trustees for the benefit of the children. Jack Hawkins then applied on behalf of his children for a repayment of tax to give effect to their personal allowances. The repayment claim was rejected on the grounds that the whole arrangement constituted a settlement of which Jack Hawkins was a settlor because he had provided the funds for it. Jack Hawkins' appeal against that rejection was allowed by the General Commissioners and Danckwerts J but dismissed by the Court of Appeal.

24. On the argument that as the settlement executed by Jack Hawkins father in law had not been contemplated at the outset it could not be included in any arrangement Donovan LJ said:

> "I will accept for the moment the proposition that the family settlement which followed was not decided upon at the outset; but what is important, I think, is that the eventual enjoyment by some individual or individuals of the money which had escaped surtax must have been in contemplation at the outset. Otherwise, as I say, the scheme had no rational purpose."

He repeated this conclusion later and added:

> "But, even were it otherwise, I think that there is sufficient unity about the whole matter to justify it being called an "arrangement" for this purpose, because, as I have said, the ultimate object is to secure for somebody money free from what would otherwise be the burden, or the full burden of surtax. Merely because the final step to secure this objective is left unresolved at the outset and decided upon later does not seem to me to rob the scheme of the necessary unity to justify it being called an "arrangement"."

25. Pearce LJ reached the same conclusion. He said:

> "The mere fact that he [Jack Hawkins] did not concern himself with some of the steps in the legal machinery involved does not make it any the less his arrangement within the [section]. A man does not avoid the incidence of [the section] by merely being absent from, and leaving to his solicitors and accountants, certain parts of the legal machinery, if he is aware of the proposals for an "arrangement" or a settlement and actively forwards them by personally carrying out and assisting in the vital parts in which his performance and co-operation are necessary."

Upjohn LJ agreed with both judgments. There can be no doubt that the test of an element of bounty was satisfied in that case too.

26. To the same effect was the decision of the House of Lords in *Mills v Commissioners of Inland Revenue*[96]. In that case John Mills, the father of Hayley a child actress, was concerned to protect her and her income from the Revenue amongst others. He formed a company (S) and settled the shares on Hayley contingently on attaining the age of 25. Hayley entered into a service agreement with S for five years at a salary of £400 per year. The following year S and Hayley entered into a contract with a film company to render Hayley's exclusive services for five years for annual sums ranging from $30,000 to $75,000. The resultant profits of S were paid by way

95 (1960) 39 TC 493.
96 (1974) 49 TC 367.

of dividend to the trustees of the settlement who accumulated them. Hayley was assessed to surtax on the basis that the overall arrangement was a settlement of which she was a settlor and that she was liable to be assessed on the dividend income accruing to the trustees. The Revenue's contention was upheld by the Special Commissioners and Goulding J.

27. The Court of Appeal, Orr LJ dissenting, took a different view. But the order of the Court of Appeal discharging the assessments was, in turn, reversed by the House of Lords. Viscount Dilhorne, with whom Lords Reid, Morris of Borth-y-Gest, Hodson and Salmon agreed, considered that the Special Commissioners were clearly right to have concluded that the incorporation of S, the issue of the shares, the making of the settlement, the making of the service agreement were all acts done in furtherance of an integrated scheme planned solely for the benefit of Hayley which was an "arrangement" and therefore a settlement to which the relevant section applied. He then considered whether Hayley had provided funds for the purpose of that settlement so as to be a settlor in respect of it. After referring to *Crossland v Hawkins*[97] he concluded that she had. He said:

> "Similarly, in this case it is, to my mind, taking too narrow a view of the arrangement to conclude that the funds which went to the trustees by way of dividends were just provided by [S]. To do so means shutting one's eyes to the fact that the source of the dividends was money paid for [Hayley's] work, and money which but for the arrangement would have been received by her. In my opinion she must be held to have provided funds for the purposes of the "settlement"."

28. In *Butler v Wildin*[98] Vinelott J was concerned with a case in which two brothers had acquired a shell company of which they were appointed the sole directors. By 19th September 1980 the 100 issued shares were held as to 19 each by their four infant children. Such shares had been acquired by the children with their own money. Two later born children also acquired 19 shares therein with their own money from their respective fathers and others so that the brothers had no shares in the company. The company developed a site by building offices with the use of loans from a bank repayment of which was guaranteed by the brothers and let the offices. The company declared a dividend and the brothers, on behalf of their children, made repayment claims in relation to the tax credits attributable to those dividends. Such claims were rejected on the grounds that there was a settlement in consequence of which the dividends were deemed to be the income of the brothers and not of their children. Such a contention was rejected by the Special Commissioners on appeal but accepted by Vinelott J.

29. Vinelott J considered that the time at which the existence or otherwise of the settlement was to be judged was when the company was acquired and the shares allotted. He added (p.678):

> "At that date a potentially profitable venture had been identified and, as will be seen, from that date the brothers did everything that needed to be done to ensure that the opportunity was exploited by the company."

30. He concluded (p.683) that:

> "It is in my judgment plain beyond question that each brother was a party to an arrangement within the definition of a settlement and that the dividends paid to the four older children were paid to them "by virtue or in consequence of" that arrangement. The brothers together arranged for shares in the company to be allotted to the four older children; and they arranged for the negotiations with British Rail to be opened, for the agreement with British Rail to be entered into and for the site to be developed by the company. The steps they took were throughout directed to achieving the end that was in fact achieved, namely of

97 (1960) 39 TC 493.
98 (1988) 61 TC 666.

ensuring that the company and so indirectly the four older children (to the extent of their respective shareholdings) took the benefit of the development of the site at no cost or risk to themselves."

31. Later, after referring to *Copeman v Coleman*[99] and *Chinn v Hochstrasser*[100] he continued (p.684):

"In deciding whether an arrangement is within or without the classes of cases caught by s.437 the starting point must be to identify the arrangement. The question then is whether taken as a whole it did contain the requisite element of bounty. To that question again there can in the instant case be only one answer. The children contributed nothing except the trifling sums which I must assume were paid on the allotment of the shares. They were exposed to no risk."

32. Finally I should refer to *Young v Pearce*[101]. In that case a company created a special class of preference share which were allotted to the wives of the then two shareholders and directors. Substantial preference dividends were paid to the wives but the husbands were assessed in respect of them under the predecessor of s.660A(1).[102] It was conceded that the issue of the preference shares to the wives involved an element of bounty on the part of their husbands. Accordingly Sir John Vinelott, following the decision of Lawrence J in *Copeman v Coleman*, concluded that the creation of the preference shares, the application by each wife and the allotment of the same constituted an arrangement or disposition within the definition of settlement. The wives contended that the subsection was disapplied by the forerunner of s.660A(6).[103] The judge rejected that submission on the ground that the preference share was "wholly or substantially a right to income".

...Conclusions on the existence of a Settlement

70. Before the de-aggregation for tax purposes of the income of a married woman from that of her husband effected in 1990 this case could not have arisen because the income of Mrs Jones would have been aggregated with that of Mr Jones whether or not there was a settlement. It is also somewhat remarkable that this case could not have arisen after 1990 if Mr and Mrs Jones had lived together without being married. The provisions of s.660A(2)[104] may appear anachronistic but they were not amended in 1989 or subsequently[105] and must be given full effect. But that consideration does not, I think, require the court to ignore the increasing tendency for married couples to be involved in the business of each other on a commercial non-bounteous basis. Such involvement may take the form of a partnership or a company in which each own shares. Though one spouse may generate the income of the firm or company, the services of the other may be just as commercially important in providing the essential administrative, accounting, support and backup services.

71. The key word in the statutory definition of settlement is "arrangement". The ordinary meaning of that word is very extensive. It is defined in the Shorter Oxford English Dictionary as "a structure or combination of things for a purpose" and in the New Shorter Oxford English Dictionary as "a number of objects arranged or combined in a particular way".

72. In the context of this case it must be possible to identify income arising from the arrangement and the property comprised in the arrangement for otherwise the terms of s.660A(1)[106] cannot be satisfied. In addition the arrangement must contain

99 (1939) 22 TC 594.
100 [1981] AC 533.
101 (1996) 70 TC 331; see below, para **[16.36]**.
102 [See now ITTOIA 2005, s 624(1).]
103 [See now ITTOIA 2005, s 626.]
104 [See now ITTOIA 2005, s 625.]
105 [The rewritten provisions have not amended this anachronism.]
106 [See now ITTOIA 2005, s 624(1).]

an element of bounty. In that context it is necessary fully to heed the warning of Lord Roskill in *Chinn v Hochstrasser*[107] which I have quoted in paragraph 18 above. The pointers to the existence of bounty have been variously described as "a taxpayer gives away a portion of his income, or of his assets", "a flavour of donation" or "the recipient benefits without any assumption by him of any correlative obligation".

73. In this case there can be no doubt but that the arrangement was or included the acquisition by Mrs Jones of her share in the Company. Equally there can be no doubt that that acquisition on its own was for full value in the context of a joint business venture to which both parties made substantial and valuable contributions. If the arrangement is confined to such acquisition then I would agree with counsel for Mr Jones that it cannot constitute a settlement for the purposes of s.660G(1).[108]

74. I would accept, as Dr Brice[109] did, that the arrangement also included the corporate set-up whereunder Mr Jones held the other share and was the sole director. Thus he controlled the Company both at board and, through the chairman's casting vote, shareholder level. This seems to me to be the necessary consequence of cases such as *CIR v Payne*[110]. Such a corporate set-up gave him the ability to confer benefit, but, of itself, did not do so. Accordingly, in my view, this addition makes no difference because the corporate set-up was no more 'bounteous' than the acquisition by Mrs Jones of her share.

75. The 'bounty' on which the Revenue necessarily rely is that provided subsequently and in fact by the combination of the demand and charge-out rate for the services of Mr Jones, the salary in fact paid to Mr Jones, the other commitments of the Company and the dividend subsequently declared and paid by the Company to Mrs Jones. All these additional elements depended on the will of Mr Jones or wholly extraneous factors. He did not commit himself to working for the Company at any particular rate of salary or at all. His charge-out rate necessarily depended on the demand for his services and the going market rate. Whether any and if so what profits were made depended not only on the difference between Mr Jones' charge-out rate and salary but the level of the Company's overheads and other commitments. If the Company made profits whether to declare any and if so what dividend was a matter for Mr Jones as the sole director and controlling shareholder.

76. For my part, I do not think that these elements can be included in the 'arrangement'. They did not form any part of a structure of things or combination of objects; their uncertainty and fluidity is the converse of an arrangement. It is not that they were not legally enforceable, they were not settled at all. No doubt Mr and Mrs Jones hoped for the best but it cannot be said that they had arranged it. Without these elements there was no element of bounty and no settlement within the statutory definition.

77. In my view all the previous cases are distinguishable on one ground or another. In *Crossland v Hawkins*[111] and *Mills v Commissioners of Inland Revenue*[112] Jack Hawkins and Hayley Mills had committed themselves to working for the company at a salary substantially less than the going rate for their services. The agreements by which they did so were part of the arrangement and the source of the bounty. The arrangement of which the agreements formed part had a 'unity' and probability which in this case is lacking. The beneficiaries under the actual settlements made in those cases contributed nothing.

78. In *Butler v Wildin*[113] Vinelott J appears to have considered that acquisition of the shares by the brothers' children, the agreement with British Rail and the

107 [1981] AC 533, 555.
108 [See now ITTOIA 2005, s 620.]
109 [One of the two Special Commissioners who first heard the case.]
110 (1940) 23 TC 610.
111 (1960) 39 TC 493.
112 (1974) 49 TC 367.
113 (1988) 61 TC 666.

development of the land were all part of one arrangement. The children contributed nothing, by contrast they were presented with a profitable development opportunity at no risk to themselves.

79. In *Copeman v Coleman*[114] the company paid a tax free preferential dividend of four times the amount paid up on the issue of the preference shares two weeks before the dividend was declared. The creation and issue of the preference shares and the declaration and payment of the dividend were plainly all part of a single arrangement in which there was both unity and bounty.

80. In *CIR v Payne*[115] the corporate structure of the company which was the beneficiary under the covenant was necessarily part of the arrangement for the creation of the covenant. The covenant had no business purpose whatever. The element of bounty was clear. Similarly in *Young v Pearce*[116] the creation and allotment of the preference shares were clearly parts of an arrangement and the element of bounty was conceded.

81. Thus, save for the expectation to which Ms Powell[117] referred in paragraph 118 of her decision, . . . I am in substantial agreement with her as to the composition of the arrangement in this case and the lack of any element of bounty therein. By contrast I respectfully disagree with both Dr Brice and Park J.

82. In paragraph 47 of her decision . . . Dr Brice concluded that the relevant arrangement included

> "the payment of the modest salaries, and the declaration by the appellant of the dividends".

Later in the same passage she found that

> "the purpose of the arrangements in this appeal was to reduce tax because the appellant understood that dividends paid to his wife would reduce the tax payable by him".

In paragraph 50, quoted in paragraph 41 above she said

> "The ultimate object was to reduce the tax burden of the appellant."

83. In the absence of any service agreement between the Company and Mr Jones I am unable to accept that the payment of modest salaries to Mr Jones was any part of the arrangement. Similarly the declaration of the dividends was not arranged in advance; it was dependent on the trading fortunes of the Company. Further, as counsel for Mr Jones submitted, and, as I accept, the fact that the structure being set up might lend itself in the future to some tax mitigation is irrelevant to the existence of an element of bounty, see per Pennycuick J in *Bulmer v IRC*[118], and per Lords Wilberforce and Fraser of Tullybelton in *IRC v Plummer*[119].

84. . . . Dr Brice found that Mr Jones "was worse off after them" [the arrangements] and effectively gave away part of the profits of the company earned as a result of his work for the company. It can now be seen with the benefit of hindsight that that occurred but it could not be predicated in 1992 that it would happen. And, in so far as it did, the efforts of Mrs Jones must have contributed to the success of the Company.

85. Park J agreed with the determination of Dr Brice and disagreed with that of Ms Powell. He gave three reasons. The first . . . is that if a structure is created with the intention to provide bounty then that is sufficient to provide the requisite element of bounty. But this assumes that the satisfaction of all the conditions necessary for that intention to be fulfilled are part of the arrangement. For the reasons I have already given I do not think that they were.

114 (1939) 22 TC 594.
115 (1940) 23 TC 610.
116 (1996) 70 TC 331.
117 [The other Special Commissioner who first heard the case.]
118 [1967] 1 Ch 145, 166D.
119 [1980] AC 896, 913 E–F and 928 C–E.

86. The second reason ... is much the same as the first. No doubt the acquisition by Mrs Jones of her share would enable her to receive dividends in the future. But it did not follow that Mrs Jones would receive any dividend; nor, if she did, that each and every dividend received by her constituted an element of bounty. That would all depend on the future trading of the Company and the contribution made by Mrs Jones. The structure did not guarantee any profits. The fact that a profit and a dividend may result is not in my view enough, nor do I think it is contemplated by the decided cases. On a more pedantic note the definition of arrangement contained in the Shorter Oxford English Dictionary, quoted in paragraph 71 above refers to the "purpose" of the structure or combination without including such purpose in the "things" so constructed or combined.

87. The third reason given by Park J ... is much the same as the second. If, as I would hold, the intention is not a part of the arrangement then it matters not that no one can compel its achievement. Intention alone cannot be an arrangement or part of an arrangement though it may provide the requisite element of bounty.

88. ... Park J suggests that it would have made no difference to the result in *Crossland v Hawkins*[120] if there had been no service agreement, but merely an expectation that Jack Hawkins would work for the company at a modest salary. I do not agree. The service agreement was an integral part of the arrangement. In its absence it could not have been predicated when the arrangement was made that there would be any profits or dividends. In any event there is the further distinction that the children contributed nothing to the venture but Mrs Jones did.

89. For all these reasons I conclude that there was no settlement as defined in this case. Consequently s.660A(1)[121] could not apply to the dividend received by Mrs Jones and the assessment under appeal should be discharged.

Having reached the conclusion that there was no settlement, Sir Andrew Morritt did not have to address the second issue before the court, namely, whether the effect of the transaction was an outright gift and thus excluded from the operation of what is now ITTOIA 2005, s 264(1), but he did so in any event:

Submissions and conclusion on the proper interpretation and application of s.660A(6)[122]

90. I have set out the terms of the subsection in paragraph 7 above. The two issues are

(a) whether, if there is a settlement because there is an element of bounty, there is

> "an outright gift by one spouse to the other of property from which the income arises"

and

(b) whether "the property given is wholly or substantially a right to income".

Dr Brice and Park J answered question (b) in the affirmative. Park J answered question (a) in the negative. Logically, as Park J noted, question (a) comes first. Accordingly I shall deal with it first.

91. In paragraph 44 of his judgment Park J said

> "In my judgment that which constituted the "settlement" here was not an "outright gift" at all. The "settlement" was an arrangement which included the following elements: the acquisition by Mrs. Jones of one share in Arctic Systems Limited for £1; Mr. Jones serving the company as an employee; an expectation that he would draw only a modest salary; and an intention that profits would be paid out as dividends. There was far more comprised in that arrangement than

120 (1960) 39 TC 493.
121 [Now ITTOIA 2005, s 624(1).]
122 [See now ITTOIA 2005, s 246.]

> would be covered by the expression "an outright gift". Indeed, the arrangement did not even include an element which could, even taken in isolation, be regarded as an outright gift. Mr. Jones did not give to Mrs. Jones her share. On the findings of the Special Commissioners she purchased it from the company formation agents, and paid for it with her own money. The money was, of course, only £1, but it remains the case that she got her share because she bought it, not because her husband gave it to her."

92. Counsel for Mr Jones submits that the judge was wrong to think that the subject matter of the relevant gift is determined by the nature of the arrangement. He suggests that if there is any element of bounty then it gives rise to the conclusion that Mrs Jones did not pay enough for her share so that, to that extent, there was an outright gift to the extent of the undervalue.

93. The problem with this argument is that it assumes that Mr Jones is right in his submissions as to what constituted the arrangement and whether there was any bounty. If he is wrong, and it is only in that event that the point arises, then I agree with both the reasoning and conclusion of Park J. It is true that the subsection is apt to give rise to a number of anomalies but that does not affect its construction and application in this respect.

94. Question (b) was dealt with by Dr Brice . . . In essence she equated Mrs Jones' one ordinary share in this case with the preference shares in *Young v Pearce*[123]. She concluded,

> ". .it is my view that, in this appeal the property given to Mrs Jones was wholly or substantially a right to income because her share only entitled her to a dividend if the appellant, who was the sole director, decided to distribute profits in any year. As a result of s 660A(6)(b)[124] the gift was not an outright gift for the purposes of that section."

95. . . . Park J said

> "Dr. Brice. . . . . said that, if one has to look through the share to what was really given, it was the income stream in the form of the annual dividends paid on the shares. I can see the force of that analysis. Personally, I would conclude that the reasons why subsection (6) does not apply are those which I have explained in the previous few paragraphs. But alternatively, or in addition, I would adopt Dr. Brice's reason, based on the words "substantially a right to income" in sub-paragraph (b) of the subsection."

96. This is disputed by counsel for Mr Jones. He contends that if the sub-section otherwise applies then it is not excluded by paragraph (6)(b).[125] He suggests that the property given is the share held by Mrs Jones, that as an item of property it has exactly the same rights as the share held by Mr Jones and those rights are more than just a right to income. Counsel for the Revenue accepts that normally an ordinary share would not fall within this paragraph. He submits that in this case it does because of the nature of the arrangement and the fact that the only right of substance in this case is the right to the income stream constituted by the dividends paid out of the profits derived from the services of Mr Jones.

97. On this point, if it arose, I would accept the submissions for Mr Jones. Each share carries a right to share in dividends duly declared. In addition each share carries the right to share in the distribution of assets in the event of a members' winding up and the right to vote at general meetings of the Company. The rights attaching to the ordinary shares in the Company are unaffected by the alleged arrangement. Nor in my view are they qualified by the common condition that the declaration of

123 (1966) 70 TC 331.
124 [See now ITTOIA 2005, s 626(3).]
125 [Ibid.]

a dividend depends on the existence of available profits or reserves and the exercise of a power conferred on persons other than the holder of the share.

Of particular interest, from a more general perspective of the settlement provisions, is the judgment of Carnwath LJ in the same case.

CARNWATH LJ:

105. First, the history of these provisions creates its own difficulties. The court's task is not of statutory interpretation in the conventional sense, but of the interpretation of a "judicial gloss" on a statute; and the term fixed upon by our predecessors – "bounty" – is neither precise nor particularly familiar.

106. Secondly, most of the authorities pre-dated the introduction by the 1988 Act of separate taxation for spouses. The specific references to spouses in section 660A show that arrangements between spouses are potentially within its scope, but the legislative purpose is not easy to discern. Like Park J, and the Chancellor, I find it odd that in this context spouses are still treated by section 660A(2)[126] as sharing the same interest, notwithstanding their separate treatment for other income tax purposes.

107. Equally curious is the fact that the exception created by subsection (6)[127] is confined to "outright gifts". In argument there was discussion of how the section would apply to differing types of "outright" transfer between husband and wife of an income-bearing asset, such as a rented property. We considered three forms of transfer: a sale at market value, a sale at an under-value, and a gift. There was common ground as to the treatment of the first and last: the first is outside the settlement provisions because there is no "bounty"; the last is exempted by subsection (6) as an "outright gift". But what of the second? Mr Baldry, for the Revenue, said that this also would be exempted by subsection (6). Applying a "purposive" construction, as I understood him, any outright transfer of a bounteous nature could be regarded as "gift", to the extent of the bounty. It is unnecessary to decide whether this is right; at first blush it seems more like playing with language than interpreting it.

108. The lack of a clearly ascertainable legislative purpose underlines the need for caution in extending the concept of settlement beyond the scope of existing jurisprudence. The Revenue's position in this case seems to me a significant extension. For the first time, they seek to apply the concept to what has been found to be a normal commercial transaction between two adults, to which each is making a substantial commercial contribution, albeit not of the same economic value. Such a difference, by itself, is not enough to my mind to take the arrangement into the realm of "bounty", as it has been understood in the existing cases. If the legislature wishes such an arrangement to be brought within a special regime for tax purposes, clearer language is necessary to achieve it. **[16.34]**

The Revenue's *Guide to the Settlements Legislation for Small Business Advisers,*[128] is now in conflict with the decision of the Court of Appeal in *Jones v. Garnett.* HMRC, however, have stated that they will not revise this guidance until the case has been finally resolved following their appeal to the House of Lords. **[16.35]**

126 [See now ITTOIA 2005, s 625.]
127 [Ibid, s 626.]
128 November 2004, www.hmrc.gov.uk/trusts.

Young v Pearce [1996] STC 743 (Ch D)

The spouses of two directors who ran a tooling company were allocated preference shares in the company by special resolution. In the subsequent three years, they received dividends amounting to more than 30% of the net profits of the company. They had no voting rights and, apart from the preferential rights to the dividends, their only other entitlement was to repayment of the sums subscribed for the preference shares in a liquidation of the company. The High Court, having decided that the allocation of the preference shares constituted an 'arrangement' amounting to a settlement within the wide definition of the relevant provision,[129] concluded further that, although the allotment of the preference shares did amount to an outright gift to the spouses, it was property which was 'wholly or substantially a right to income', and thus the dividends were caught by the settlement anti-avoidance provisions.

> SIR JOHN VINELOTT: ... If the creation and allotment of the preference shares constituted a settlement, the subject matter of which was the preference shares allotted to the wife of each of the taxpayers, it must follow that the allotment of the preference shares taken by each wife was an outright gift from which income (the dividends paid on the preference shares) arose. It was not subject to conditions, and it cannot be said that the property might 'become, in any circumstances whatsoever, payable to or applicable for the benefit of the settlor/spouse within s. 685(4B).[130] The gift of the preference shares was a gift which carried the right to the whole of that income, that is, the income which arose from the preference shares within subs. (4A)(a).[131] Was the 'property given' – the preference shares – 'wholly or substantially a right to income'?[132] It seems to me that the answer to that question must be in the affirmative. The preference shares entitled the holders to a preferential dividend if the taxpayers (the only directors and the holders of all the ordinary shares) determined to distribute the whole or part of the profits arising in any given year. Apart from that right to income, the only rights conferred on the preference shareholders were the right to repayment of the nominal sum paid on the allotment of the shares and the right to attend and be heard, but not to vote at, general meetings of the company. As a matter of strict legal principle, the preference shares were assets distinct from the income derived from them, but in reality they could never have been realized. The income was dependent upon the taxpayers determining to distribute part of the profits of the company. **[16.36]**

4. Estate income

Income received during the administration period by personal representatives,[133] suffers the equivalent of basic or lower rate income tax in their hands,[134] either by deduction at source in respect of savings income[135] and dividends,[136] or by direct assessment in respect of profits from a trade, rents and royalties. Distributions of income made to legatees and

129 ICTA 1988, s 681(4); [see now ITTOIA 2005, ss 620.]
130 [See now ITTOIA 2005, s 625(1).]
131 [See now ITTOIA 2005, s 626(2).]
132 [If it is, then the exception for outright gifts between spouses cannot apply; see now ITTOIA 2005, s 626(3).]
133 The term 'personal representative' includes an executor and an administrator.
134 Personal representatives are not liable to the rate applicable to trusts: see ITA 2007, ss 463, 483.
135 Savings income comes with a tax credit of 20%.
136 Whilst dividends suffer tax at source at the rate of 10%, the tax credit is irrecoverable.

beneficiaries are paid net, after deduction by the personal representatives of administration expenses chargeable against income.[137] A recipient must gross up the income received as part of his total income for the year of receipt either to ascertain whether he has any excess liability or to obtain a repayment of tax. **[16.37]**

137 For the entitlement of a beneficiary in respect of an estate during the course of administration, see ICTA 1988, ss 695–702, and for the nature of the entitlement, see *IRC v Hawley* [1928] 1 KB 578; *Re Morley's Estate* [1937] 1 Ch 491.

17 Partnerships and Limited Liability Partnerships

1. Introduction

The concept of a partnership, or 'firm',[1] has a long history in English law,[2] and is governed by the Partnership Act 1890 (PA 1890). Limited liability partnerships (LLPs), by contrast, date from, and are governed by, the Limited Liability Partnership Act 2000 (LLPA 2000).[3]

Partners are liable for all obligations and debts of the partnership while they are members of it.[4] Subject to exceptions, however, members of LLPs are liable only for the capital that they have contributed and the sum that they have agreed to contribute if and when the LLP is wound up.[5] A partnership has no legal personality separate from its members; an LLP does, however, have a legal personality separate from its members.[6] Each partner in a partnership is an agent for the other(s); members of LLPs are agents for the LLP.[7]

Despite these differences, the direct tax treatment of partnerships and LLPs is very similar.[8] The Income Tax (Trading and Other Income) Act 2005 ('ITTOIA 2005'), s 863(1), provides that '[f]or income tax purposes, 'if a limited liability partnership carries on a trade, profession or business with a view to profit . . . all the activities of the limited liability partnership are treated as carried on in partnership by its members (and not by the limited liability partnership as such) . . .'.[9] Thus, as Tiley says: ' . . . profits are taxed as accruing to the partner and will be subject to income tax . . . and will attract corporation tax only in the case of a corporate partner.'[10] In relation to a 'traditional' partnership, ITTOIA 2005, s 852, provides that: '[f]or each tax year in which a firm carries on a trade (the "actual trade"), each partner's share of the firm's trading profits or losses is treated . . . as profits or losses of

1 Economists may use the term 'firm' to apply to corporations. In strict legal usage, however, the term refers to a partnership (see Partnership Act 1890, s 4).
2 See Law Commission, *Partnership Law* (Law Com No 283, Cm 6015) (London, 2003).
3 This came into force on 6 April 2001. There is also a third, much older, concept than a limited liability partnership, ie the limited partnership, which is not discussed in the present volume (see the Limited Partnerships Act 1907).
4 See PA 1890, s 9.
5 See LLPA 2000, s 1.
6 See LLPA, s 1(2).
7 LLPA 2000, s 6.
8 See ITTOIA 2005, ss 846–862 for partnerships and 863, for LLPs. Differences in the tax treatment of partnerships and LLPs arise in relation to non profit-making LLPs and LLPs which are in liquidation (see Natalie Lee (gen ed) *Revenue Law – Principles and Practice* (24th edn, 2006) para **[45.9]**).
9 The corporation tax equivalent (where an LLP member is a company) appears in ICTA 1988, s 118ZA, inserted in ICTA 1988 by LLPA 2000, s 10(1).
10 See John Tiley *Revenue Law* (5th edn, 2005) p 848.

a trade carried on by the partner alone (the "notional trade").' Thus, again as Tiley says, 'these rules mean that partners are individually liable for tax on their own shares of the profits and that the taxable share is related to the actual share and not the profit-sharing ratio in force in a subsequent year'.[11]

Although relief for trading losses may be restricted for LLP members in certain circumstances,[12] such losses are generally apportioned on the same basis as trading profits.[13]

> 'Thus, where a partnership produces a loss, the loss is apportioned among the partners and each individual partner may choose to make whatever claim is appropriate for his individual circumstances. ... [For example], partner A may wish to set his share of the trading loss against his investment income; partner B may choose to carry forward his loss against trading profits of a later year.'[14]

Generally, the law on capital allowances applies for partnerships[15] and LLPs as for sole traders and companies.

The capital gains tax[16] treatment of members of LLPs is covered by TCGA 1992, s 59A, which brings their CGT treatment into line with that of partners in a partnership.[17] In essence: '[w]here an asset is disposed of by a partnership to an outside party each of the partners will be treated as disposing of his fractional share of the asset. In computing gains or losses the proceeds of disposal will be allocated between the partners in the ratio of their share in asset surpluses at the time of disposal.'[18] **[17.1]**

2. Partnerships

Questions have arisen both as to the existence of a partnership, and also, whether or not a particular individual is a member of the partnership. **[17.2]**

A. *Whether or not a partnership exists*

Dickenson v Gross **(1927) 11 TC 614 (KBD)**

Although a partnership deed was entered into by the appellant and his three sons, under which the appellant was to lease farmland to the partnership, and providing for the allocation of profits and the preparation of accounts, nothing was ever done in pursuance of the deed.

> ROWLATT J: ... The partnership deed here, of course, was a deed perfectly good according to its tenor; and if it had been what really governed the relations of the parties it would have effected the object of those who entered into it or purported to enter into it, because it would have produced another legal position to which a tax attached differently from the legal position which existed before. As I pointed out in the case Mr. Bremner [*counsel for the* taxpayer] cited to mean as has been often pointed out before – people can arrange their affairs, if they do really arrange them, so as to produce a state of facts in which the taxation is different, and it is no answer – it is perfectly immaterial – to

11 Ibid, p 382.
12 See ITA 2007, s 104. (See also Tiley, n 10 above, p 389.)
13 See ITTOIA 2005, s 849.
14 See Tiley, n 10 above, p 389.
15 But see CAA 2001, Pt 2, Ch 20, especially s 264 ('Partnership using property of a partner').
16 See Chapter 20.
17 See TCGA 1992, s 59.
18 See SP D12 *Partnerships*, 7 October 2002, para 2.

say that they have done it for that purpose. But in this case the facts show that in very many ways the deed was simply set on one side and disregarded, and when you find the deed is disregarded, and also that it was entered into for the purpose of obtaining relief from taxation one is apt, perhaps naturally and quite properly upon the question of fact, to pay a little more attention to those circumstances and those points in which it was disregarded. Now Mr. Bremner , I think, has very truly said that if these young men had come forward and pointed to this deed and said: "Here, Father, you have signed this deed; kindly carry it out", he would have been in a very great difficulty, as King Lear was, in getting out of it, and they probably would have held him to it; and if they had held him to it the Commissioners would have had no justification for finding as they have. But they did not. On the contrary they let the deed slide and proceeded in the ordinary patriarchal way which everybody who is the least familiar with the habits of the countryside, as I have no doubt these three Commissioners were, knows very well.

Now what the Commissioners have done is that they have found that there was no partnership in fact. Mr. Bremner says that looks as if they were splitting some hair and saying there was no partnership in fact, although there was a partnership in law. I do not think that is the way to look at the finding at all. A partnership, of course, is a legal position and a legal result, but like every other legal position it depends on facts, and what the Commissioners are saying here is: "The facts are not those from which a legal partnership results, because although there was the deed they are not acting on it; it is not governing their transactions; they are not paying the slightest attention to it. They are going on just as before." They have not used the word "fictitious," and they have not used the word "sham," but I think they have put it even more clearly. They say: "The facts here were not a partnership although there was a bit of paper in the drawer, which if the facts had been according to it, would have shown there was a partnership."

Then Mr. Bremner says there is some dolus lurking in the phrase that "for Income Tax purposes there was no partnership," as if meaning to say: "You may say there is a partnership, but for Income Tax purposes it will not do, because it is meant to evade Income Tax." I do not think it means that at all. That is not what they are saying at all. What they are saying is this: "There is not any partnership in fact, and there cannot be any partnership for the special purposes of Income Tax when there is no real partnership." That is what they are saying. Many people think there can be. They think by putting a bit of paper in the drawer they can make an Income Tax partnership, and they go on treating the undertaking as though it were still the sole uncontrolled property of the one person, the father, instead of a partnership. I do not think there is any doubt. I do not think the Commissioners could have found otherwise, if I may say so, but I think they clearly have found in a way which makes the position quite right, and the appeal must be dismissed with costs. **[17.3]**

Saywell v Pope (1979) 53 TC 40

SLADE J: . . . I take it to be clear that, when persons enter into a written partnership agreement and state therein that they are to be partners as from some date prior to the date of execution of the agreement, or, as in the present case, that the partnership commenced on a date prior to the date of such execution, such a statement cannot in law operate retrospectively. If it takes the latter form and if it is an accurate statement of fact, it may faithfully reflect the past position. If, however, it is an inaccurate statement of fact, it cannot alter such position with retrospective effect. It may well bind all the parties, as between themselves, to take their accounts and to assume all other obligations on the footing that they have been partners from the stated date. It cannot, however, operate actually to make them partners from the stated date, if they were not in truth partners. If authority for these propositions is needed, it is to be found in the judgment of Rowlatt J. in *Waddington v. O'Callaghan.*[19] I might add that, as is illustrated by the decision of Rowlatt J. in *Dickenson v. Gross* the execution of a partnership deed will not even operate to create a partnership from the date of the deed in a case where the extrinsic evidence clearly

19 (1931) 16 TC 187 at 197.

shows that there is no partnership in fact. As Lord President Clyde said in *Commissioners of Inland Revenue* v. *Williamson*;[20] 'You do not constitute or create or prove a partnership by saying that there is one.' . . . **[17.4]**

B. Who the members of the partnership are

CIR v Lebus' Executors (1946) 27 TC 136 (CA)

The Inland Revenue had assessed the widow of a deceased partner in a firm on her entitlement, under her husband's will, to receive a share of the profits of the partnership for her lifetime. She had, in fact, received very little of the sums due to her. The Court of Appeal held that she was not a member of the firm and, until the money had been paid over to the executors for her benefit, it was not part of her taxable income.

LORD GREENE MR: . . . I think the most convenient way of approaching the question we have to decide is to examine briefly but, I hope, adequately, the arguments presented on behalf of the Crown who are the Appellants here. Their first proposition is this. Mrs. Lebus is the beneficial owner of, or is beneficially entitled to, one-fourth of the profits of the business. That, as I may venture to point out, without, I hope, any disrespect, is a question-begging phrase. If it means she is entitled to some specific existing identifiable fruit of the business in any given year, that is one thing; if, on the other hand, all it means is that she, through the medium of the will trustees, is entitled to call upon the partners to hand her one-fourth of the profits of any year, that is a totally different thing. Unless those two meanings are kept quite distinct confusion is likely to arise. To say that a person is the owner of something is a phrase which is no doubt convenient but often vague. A man may be said to own the credit balance in his banking account, but, from the legal point of view, that is an entirely incorrect expression. Similarly, in the present case, if to say that Mrs. Lebus owns a share of profits means nothing more than that she is entitled to call upon the partners to pay her a share of profits, that is a totally different conception from the implication which appears to me to be inherent in the argument of the Crown – that she, in some way, has a proprietary interest in something identifiable of which it can be predicated that she has received it.

The argument proceeds somewhat in this way. It is said that where partners carry on business and make profits they are assessable to Income Tax in respect of those profits, whether they take them out of the business and divide them or whether they do not. For example, a partnership has had a very profitable year. The whole of its property may be so locked up in its assets that it is quite impossible in that year to get any money out to pay to the partners their shares, or the whole of their shares, of the profits. That is a thing which commonly happens. But, in assessing a partnership in respect of the profits of its business, what you do is to take the account as between the Revenue and the partners, and say: "In this year the partners have made so much profit, it belongs to those partners, and the fact that they cannot pay themselves out in cash has nothing in the world to do with it, for the very simple reason that the partners own the entirety of the assets, and they have themselves realised these profits in the sense that the profits have resulted in an accretion to the value of their assets which belongs to the partners. For Income Tax purposes it is their profit on taking the proper Income Tax account." In the case of partners that is perfectly clear. The fact that the profits are not released and paid over in cash to the partners has nothing to do with it from the Income Tax point of view. From the Income Tax point of view they have made profits and are taxable.[21]

Now, says the Crown: "That is really what is happening here. The three partners have made profits and they are taxable even though they did not draw those profits out of the business." Similarly, the Crown says: "Mrs. Lebus has made some profits and it makes no difference whether she draws the profits out of the business or does not." But there is all

20 (1928) 14 TC 335 at 340.
21 [See *IRC v Blott* [1920] 1 KB 114 at 131 (Rowlatt J) and Chapter 6.]

the difference in the world between the two cases, because Mrs. Lebus is not a partner, and the assets of the partnership do not belong to her. It is therefore impossible to say as against her what can be said as against the partners that she has in the accretion to the value of the partnership assets realised a profit in the Income Tax sense. She has not realised a profit unless and until the profit is paid to her. It is a complete confusion, with great respect to the argument, to put her in the same position as if she had been a partner.

The Crown endeavoured to get out of the difficulty by saying that in some sense – I hope I am not putting it inaccurately – the partners carried on the business as trustees for her. It is said that they are trustees for her of one-quarter share of the profits of the business. What does that mean? If it means that she is beneficially interested in the business and its assets, that is one thing; but, with all respect, it is quite untrue. She is not. If, on the other hand, all it means is that she is entitled to call for one-quarter share of the profits and receive it, it means something totally different. If it means only the latter, then I cannot myself see how she can be said to have received any income, unless and until she has received her share of the profits. The Crown puts her, in substance, in exactly the same position as if she had been a partner for these purposes. The argument failed to realise why it is that a partner who has not received his share of profits nevertheless is liable to taxation in respect of those profits. It is because he is a joint owner of the business and its assets. As soon as the accounts show a profit the partnership has made a profit for income tax purposes. On the other hand, a person who is only entitled to payment by the partners of a share of the profits has no proprietary interest in anything whatsoever unless and until it is paid over.... **[17.5]**

C. *Special features of carrying on business in partnership*

A partner's share of the partnership profits is not deductible in calculating the profits of the partnership, since it is an allocation of profit. The wages of employees of the partnership are, however, deductible, on general principles,[22] as an expense of the partnership. Problems can arise in relation to salaried partners. **[17.6]**

MacKinlay (Inspector of Taxes) v Arthur Young McClelland Moores & Co [1989] STC 898 (HL)

LORD OLIVER OF AYLMERTON. My Lords, this appeal raises what, in the end, is a very short point, namely, the deductibility for the purposes of income tax payable under Sch D Case II of what may be conveniently described as "relocation expenses" paid out of partnership funds to two of the partners.

Schedule D, the provisions of which are to be found in s 108 of the Income and Corporation Taxes Act 1970 (the 1970 Act),[23] charges to tax (inter alia) –

> "... (*a*) the annual profits or gains arising or accruing ... (ii) to any person residing in the United Kingdom from any trade, profession or vocation, whether carried on in the United Kingdom or elsewhere."

Section 109 of the 1970 Act provides that tax under Sch D is to be charged under seven different cases to which individual provisions are applicable, Case II being "tax in respect of any profession or vocation not contained in any other Schedule".[24] Annual profits of a profession may be broadly and colloquially defined as the income earned by the professional activity after deducting the expenses incurred in earning it, ascertained in accordance with ordinary accountancy principles, but s 130 of the 1970 Act contains provisions restricting the types of expenditure which may be treated as deductions from

22 See Chapter 10, above, paras **[10.23–10.35]**.
23 [Now ITTOIA 2005, ss 5, 6; see Chapter 10.]
24 [For a comparison with the approach of ITTOIA 2005, see Chapter 9, above, para **[9.1]**]

annual income including the profits for computing the profits for tax purposes.[25] It provides that:

> "Subject to the provisions of the Tax Acts, in computing the amount of the profits or gains to be charged under Case I or Case II of Schedule D, no sum shall be deducted in respect of – (*a*) any disbursements or expenses, not being money wholly and exclusively laid out or expended for the purposes of the trade, profession or vocation, . . ."

There is a wealth of authority regarding the application of this formula to individual items of expenditure of various kinds, but whilst the cases may be helpful as illustrations or analogues, the question in each case is the simple question of whether the facts are capable of fitting and do fit the formula. There is no very difficult issue of construction involved, for it is not in doubt that the words [*sic*] "exclusively" is used in its ordinary and natural sense. The difficulties, such as they are, lie not in the words "wholly and exclusively" but in ascertaining whether a particular expenditure is, as a matter of fact, laid out "for" and only for the purposes of the trade or profession.

Before turning to the facts of the instant case, I ought, perhaps, to say a word about the position, both generally and in relation to income tax of partners in a firm. A partner working in the business or undertaking of the partnership is in a very different position from an employee. He has no contract of employment for he is, with his partners, an owner of the undertaking in which he is engaged and he is entitled, with his partners, to an undivided share in all the assets of the undertaking. In receiving any money or property out of the partnership funds or assets, he is to an extent receiving not only his own property but also the property of his co-partners. Every such receipt must, therefore, be brought into account in computing his share of the profits or assets. Equally, of course, any expenditure which he incurs out of his own pocket on behalf of the partnership in the proper performance of his duties as a partner will be brought into account against his co-partners in such computation. If, with the agreement of his partners, he pays himself a "salary", this merely means that he receives an additional part of the profits before they fall to be divided between the partners in the appropriate proportions. But the "salary" remains part of the profits.

So far as concerns the assessment of partnership profits to tax, I do not think that I can improve on the analysis in the instant case of Vinelott J (see [1986] STC 491 at 504–505) which I will both quote and adopt:

> "There are, in effect, three stages. First, the profits of the firm for an appropriate basis period must be ascertained. What has to be ascertained is the profits of the firm and not of the individual partners. That is not, I think, stated anywhere in the Income Tax Acts, but it follows necessarily from the fact that there is only one business and not a number of different businesses carried on by each of the partners. The income of the firm for the year is then treated as divided between the partners who were partners during the year to which the claim relates – the year of assessment in one of the many senses of that word: see the proviso to s 26 of the Income and Corporation Taxes Act 1970.[26] That is the second stage. The tax payable is then calculated according to the circumstances of each partner – that is, after taking into account on the one hand any personal allowances, reliefs or deductions to which he is entitled and any higher rate of tax for which he is liable. The Acts do not provide for the way in which personal allowances, reliefs and deductions are to be apportioned between the partnership income and other income. I understand that in practice they are deducted from the share of the partnership income if that was the partner's main source of income. When the tax exigible in respect of each share of the partnership income has been ascertained the total tax payable is calculated. Section 152 (formerly rule 10 of the Rules applicable to Cases I and II of Sch D) provides that the total sum so calculated is to be treated as 'one sum . . . separate and distinct from any other tax chargeable on

25 [Now ITTOIA 2005, s 34; see Chapter 10, above, para **[10.31]**.]
26 [Subsequently consolidated as ICTA 1988, s 277 but now repealed by ITA 2007, s 1031 and Sch 3.]

> those persons . . . and a joint assessment shall be made in the partnership name'.[27] That is the third stage."

The question in the instant case is whether, at the first stage, moneys paid out of the partnership assets to a partner in order to indemnify him against expenses incurred by him out of his own pocket otherwise than on behalf of the partnership or in the course of acting in the partnership business can be deducted at the first stage as being a payment any personal benefit from which is purely incidental or ancillary to the purposes of the firm considered as an entity separate from the recipient.

The relevant facts can be very shortly stated. The respondent firm in which there were at the material time 95 partners, is a well-known firm of chartered accountants with offices in various parts of the United Kingdom. It is impracticable, for obvious reasons, to hold regular partners' meetings and the administration of the partnership is conducted by an executive committee of eight partners under the chairmanship of the senior partner. In order to deploy both partners and staff to the best advantage, it becomes necessary from time to time for the executive committee to request individual partners or members of the staff to move from one part of the country to another and the possibility that he may be required to move is accepted by each partner as part of the firm's policy. To make this more acceptable, the executive committee has adopted a policy which, though not written into the partnership deed, is accepted by all the partners, of paying to a partner acceding to a request to move in the firm's interest a sum of relocation expenses which is equal to the aggregate of estate agents' charges, surveyors' fees, legal costs and disbursements, furniture removal charges and reasonable expenses for travel and subsistence for a maximum of three months whilst looking for a new house. In addition, there is paid a disturbance allowance of £1,000 in the case of a partner and £700 in the case of an employee by way of compensation for the incidental costs of moving such as relaying carpets or refitting curtains. In practice, both partners and employees have moved when requested and no doubt their willingness to do so has been influenced to a greater or lesser degree by the policy which I have described.

The instant appeal concerns two sums of £5,466.25 and £3,122.15 respectively paid out of the partnership funds by way of relocation expenses to two partners, Mr Wilson and Mr Cooper, during the accounting period 1981–82. In the case of Mr Wilson, he had been engaged in working in the firm's London office and was asked to and did move to Southampton in order to open and take charge of their new office in that city. It is not in dispute that he moved to Southampton only because he was asked to and that he would have preferred to stay in London. In the case of Mr Cooper, he was asked to and did, albeit reluctantly, move from Newcastle, where he lived and was working, to Bristol. The Special Commissioners found as a fact and this is not disputed that he would not have agreed to move had his partners not have agreed, in accordance with the firm's policy, to contribute to his removal expenses. The firm having claimed to deduct these two sums as allowable expenses in the computation of its taxable profits for the year, the claim was disallowed by the inspector. The firm appealed to the commissioners who, on 21 January 1985, allowed the appeal, holding that the payment had one purpose and one purpose only, namely, the furtherance of the interests of the partnership practice and were accordingly wholly and exclusively laid out for the purposes of the profession. In, reaching this conclusion it is evident that the commissioners were paying regard to two and only two considerations, that is to say, the conscious motives of Mr Wilson and Mr Cooper in agreeing to move and the motives of the partners (as represented by the executive committee) in requesting them to do so and agreeing to contribute to the cost in accordance with the established policy. They moved, the commissioners held, purely for business reasons and derived no personal benefit from the move, which in fact eventually turned out in each case to be financially disadvantageous. Likewise the executive

27 [Subsequently consolidated as ICTA 1988, s 111, and then rewritten in, and partly repealed by, ITTOIA 2005, ss 847–856. 'Under self-assessment there are no longer partnership assessments (and individual partners are required to include their share of partnership profits in their own tax return) but a partnership return is still required to enable the calculation of the partnership profits to be dealt with centrally (TMA 1970, ss 12AA)' (see Lee, n 8 above, para **[44.2]**).]

committee, in paying the expenses, was motivated solely by the consideration that it would be for the benefit of the partnership practice to have these two partners working at (and therefore living near) the offices at Southampton and Bristol respectively.

Now it is plain that in so holding the commissioners were regarding the firm as being, as it were, an entity quite separate from the two individual partners whose initial personal expenditure was being reimbursed and looking not at all at the immediate purpose which that expenditure served – namely, the establishment of personal residences for themselves and their families – but solely at the advantages which the firm would derive from having these partners residing in their new locations. The real, indeed the only question, in this appeal is whether that was a permissible way in which to test whether the expenditure was laid out not merely as something from which the partnership was intended to and did derive a benefit but exclusively for the purposes of the partnership practice.

The inspector having appealed to the High Court, Vinelott J, in a judgment of admirable clarity, reversed the commissioners' decision and allowed the appeal. It was not, he observed, seriously open to question that if Mr Wilson and Mr Cooper had each been sole traders (if such a description is permissible in the case of chartered accountants) and had moved their respective residences in order to enhance the interests of their respective professional practices, the expenditure incurred in finding a new home and moving to it could not qualify as expenditure incurred solely for the purposes of the practices so as to permit its deduction in the computation of their professional profits as sole traders. In searching for, acquiring and moving to new residences, whatever their motives, they could not possibly be said to be acting as accountants in the course of professional practice. They would be simply individual citizens establishing private residences in places convenient to them and, as Vinelott J observed, the expenditure would be indistinguishable from that incurred by Mr Mason in *Mason v Tyson (Inspector of Taxes)* [1980] STC 284, in repairing and redecorating a flat above his office so that he could, if he wished, work late. In order to justify treating expenditure by an individual partner on a different footing, it was necessary, in effect, to ignore any benefit deriving from the original outlay made by him as an individual and to treat as the relevant purpose only the motive of the executive committee in making the reimbursement out of the partnership funds, from which of course the firm as such derived no benefit beyond that of securing the performance of the individual partner's services in the most convenient area. Thus the firm's case rested before your Lordships on the proposition that, in its relationship to individual partners, the firm can be treated as a separate legal entity in exactly the same way as if the relationship were that of employer and employee. This indeed seems to have been the basis of the judgment of the Court of Appeal (see [1988] STC 116), which reversed Vinelott J and restored the decision of the commissioners. Slade LJ (at 127) stated the question for determination thus:

> "Ultimately, the issue in the present case must be whether the commissioners' findings of primary fact entitled them to draw the inference that *the firm's* object in making the relevant expenditure was wholly and exclusively to serve the purposes of its business."

The ratio of the Court of Appeal's decision is encapsulated in a passage in which, after contrasting the position of the individual sole trader, Slade LJ continued (at 127–128):

> "In the second case, where the payer and the beneficiary are not the same, it is clearly possible . . . to evaluate the objects of the payer in incurring the expenditure separately and distinctly from those of the beneficiary. Where the payer is a partnership, whether or not the recipient is one of the partners, I think that, save in a case where the nature of the expenditure speaks for itself, a proper application of s 130(*a*) requires the Revenue to ascertain the purpose of the expenditure at least primarily by what was referred to in argument as 'the collective purpose' of the partnership in incurring it. True it is that under the general law a partnership has no legal personality of its own distinct from that of the individual partners who compose it (see for example *Income Tax Comrs for London (City) v Gibbs* [1942] AC 402 at 413, per Viscount Simon LC). Nevertheless, in my judgment, the authorities show that, for the purpose of computing the profits of a firm liable to income tax under Case II of Sch D, even if not for other purposes of the Taxes Acts, a partnership is regarded as an entity distinct from its

> members (see for example *Heastie (Inspector of Taxes) v Veitch & Co* [1934] 1 KB 535, 18 TC 305, *Watson and Everitt v Blunden (Inspector of Taxes)* (1933) 18 TC 402 and *Padmore v IRC* [1987] STC 36 at 45, per Peter Gibson J). While the intentions and motives of individual partners may well be relevant in this context, in my judgment s 130 must correspondingly contemplate that ultimately it is the collective purpose of this notionally distinct entity which has to be ascertained."

Now there is, if I may say so respectfully, a confusion here. It is perfectly true that in *Heastie (Inspector of Taxes) v Veitch & Co* [1934] 1 KB 535 at 547, 18 TC 305 at 319, Romer LJ remarked that by r 10 of the Rules applicable to Cases I and II (now contained in s 152 of the 1970 Act) a partnership is treated for the purposes of Sch D taxation as a separate entity from the individual partners composing the firm – that is at stage three of Vinelott J's analysis – but there is nothing in that decision nor in the other cases cited by Slade LJ to justify a conclusion that it can permissibly be so treated at stage one of the analysis in relation to sums which have been received by a partner from the partnership funds in his capacity as a partner. All that *Heastie's* case established was that sums received by a partner in a quite different capacity, for instance, as the landlord of premises let to the partnership or for goods supplied from an independent trade carried on by a partner, are not to be regarded as non-deductible expenses simply because they are received by a person who is also a partner in the firm. But we are not concerned here with sums coming to the hands of Mr Wilson and Mr Cooper as a result of some wholly collateral bargain between them and the firm of Arthur Young and Co. What they received, they received as partners in the firm. The fact that they were partners and were going to continue to act as such was indeed the very justification for the receipt.

My Lords, for my part I am unable to accept that the purpose of "the partnership", considered as if it has a separate legal identity, and the purpose of the individual partners for whose benefit the payment enured can be segregated in this way. I cannot, with respect to the Court of Appeal, resist the conclusion that they allowed themselves to be confused and led astray by a number of extraneous factors which do not, as a matter of analysis have any legal significance. In the first place, they appear to have been influenced by the sheer size of the partnership in the instant case and to have considered that a large partnership falls in some way to be treated differently from a small partnership, so that an element of personal benefit may fall to be taken into account in the case of a small firm but ignored in the case of a large firm (see Slade LJ [1988] STC 116 at 128). It is true that Slade LJ rests this distinction on the ground of the greater ease with which an inference of a confusion of private and collective motive may be drawn in the case of the smaller firm – presumably on the footing that in a large firm a great many of the partners will not, in practice, know anything about the payment and therefore cannot be said to be affected by the purpose of the recipient. But there can surely be no difference in principle. Partners are partners, however numerous; and mere numbers cannot in itself justify an attribution of a "collective purpose" unjustified in the case of a small partnership.

Secondly, I cannot help feeling that some confusion has been caused simply by the mechanics by which the payments concerned in the instant case were effected. They were resolved on by the executive committee and paid out of partnership funds on the orders of the executive committee by way of reimbursement of an expenditure which the two partners had incurred out of their own pockets. Factually this makes it easier to regard the reimbursement and the expenditure reimbursed as quite separate transactions and to have regard only to the motives of the executive committee in sanctioning the reimbursement – a reflection indeed of counsel for the firm's submissions to your Lordships. The purpose of the payment, he submits, was not to pay for the partners' removal expenses. It was to nullify the disadvantage which the partners suffered as a result of having paid those expenses themselves and the only motive for nullifying that disadvantage was to secure their concurrence in moving in the interests of the partnership. Attractively as this submission was put, I find myself quite unable to accept this way of looking at the transactions. Indeed, on this analysis the reimbursement, at the instance of the other partners, of the costs of a chauffeur-driven car to transport the senior partner to and from work in order to increase his efficiency as a working member of the firm or of the cost of a holiday in Switzerland to convalesce after an illness would qualify as deductible expenditure so long as it could be established that the "collective purpose" of the sanctioning partners was to further the partnership business. There is no warrant in statute or authority for this concept of collective purpose and I do not, for my part, find it acceptable as a matter of analysis. It can make not the slightest difference whether a partner incurs an expenditure out of his own pocket and recovers it from the partnership funds or whether he draws the money required directly from the partnership funds in the first instance – for example, where he is enabled to draw cheques on the partnership bank account – and his partners, either expressly or by implication, agree that he need not bring the money drawn into account in ascertaining his share of the profits. There is in either case only one relevant expenditure and it is the purpose of that outlay which has to be regarded.

A third factor which, I think, has led to some confusion at any rate in the minds of the commissioners, is the initial unwillingness of Mr Wilson and Mr Cooper to move. I do not, for my part, see how this can possibly be a relevant consideration in ascertaining whether the costs of moving were exclusively for the purposes of the partnership profession. The expenditure serves the same purpose whether the partner concerned wants to move, is merely willing to move or moves with evident reluctance.

Finally, I think that a good deal of the confusion was caused in the Court of Appeal, as indeed it was before your Lordships, by an appeal to the position of an employee as providing a useful analogy. Superficially, the analogy is attractive, as indeed is the suggestion that "the reality" of the situation renders absurd any distinction between, for instance, a senior employee and a junior partner. But, with respect, the distinction is not only legal but real. An employee has no interest in the property or profits of the firm and anything paid to him by way of additional remuneration for acting as an employee and to secure his continued loyalty to the firm cannot easily fail to be deductible as an expenditure exclusively for the purpose of the firm's business. There are, of course, limits to this – for instance, the firm cannot pay the employee's PAYE tax for him and claim to deduct it as an expense (see *Bamford (Inspector of Taxes) v ATA Advertising Ltd* [1972] 1 WLR 1261, 48 TC 359).[28] But, in general, money laid out in order to secure the continued loyal service of the workforce is referable solely to the business or profession in which that workforce is employed and is accordingly deductible. The purpose to which the employee chooses to devote what he receives does not enter into the picture and one is not concerned to inquire into the connection between that purpose and the business in which the employee is employed. A partner, on the other hand, whether he be senior or junior is in a quite different position. What he receives out of the partnership funds falls to be brought into account in ascertaining his share of the profits of the firm except in so far as he can demonstrate that it represents a payment to him in reimbursement of sums expended by him on partnership purposes in the carrying on of the partnership business or practice – the example was given in the course of argument of the partner travelling to and staying in Edinburgh on the business of the firm – or a payment entirely collateral made to him otherwise than in his capacity as a partner (as in *Heastie*). It may be that in relation to a particular receipt by a partner of partnership moneys not falling under either of the above heads, his co-partners are agreeable to his retaining it without bringing it into account so that to that extent the divisible profits at the end of the year are notionally reduced by the amount retained; but this cannot alter the fact that what is retained is part of the profits which would otherwise be divisible. What is taxable is the actual not the notional profit and what has to be demonstrated if a deduction is to be allowed for tax purposes in respect of moneys paid to a partner is that it was paid exclusively for the purposes of the partnership business.

However attractive, therefore, the employer-employee analogy may seem at first sight, it is not one from which, on analysis, I feel that I can derive any assistance. One is, accordingly, brought back, first, last and all the time to the question whether an expenditure on a partner's removing expenses can be said to be laid out not just partly but exclusively for the purposes of the partnership business. That cannot, in my judgment, be answered simply by ascertaining what was the motive with which the move was undertaken. It is inescapable as it seems to me, that the expenditure, motivated no doubt by the fact of moving house, which in turn was motivated by the desire to put the partner

28 [See Chapter 10, above, paras **[10.23]**–**[10.35]**.]

concerned in a better position to further the interests of the firm, was an expenditure serving and necessarily and inherently intended to serve the personal interests of the partner in establishing his private residence for himself and his family and it cannot be said to be exclusively for the purposes of the partnership practice.

Your Lordships have been referred to what may be regarded as a seminal decision of this House in *Mallalieu v Drummond (Inspector of Taxes)* [1983] STC 665, [1983] 2 AC 861[29] and much argument has been addressed to the question whether the purpose of the particular payment falls to be ascertained objectively or by reference only to the subjective intention of the payer. For my part, I think that the difficulties suggested here are more illusory than real. The question in each case is what was the object to be served by the disbursement or expense? As was pointed out by Lord Brightman in *Mallalieu's* case, this cannot be answered simply by evidence of what the payer says that he intended to achieve. Some results are so inevitably and inextricably involved in particular activities they cannot but be said to be a purpose of the activity. Miss Mallalieu's restrained and sober garb inevitably served and cannot but have been intended to serve the purpose of preserving warmth and decency and her purpose in buying cannot but have been, in part at least, to serve that purpose whether she consciously thought about it or not. So here the payment of estate agents' fees, conveyancing costs and so on, and the provision of carpets and curtains cannot but have been intended to serve the purpose of establishing a comfortable private home for the partner concerned even though his motive in establishing a home in that particular place was to assist him in furthering the partnership interests. Nobody could say with any colour of conviction that in purchasing new curtains he or his wife was acting on partnership business. In my judgment once one escapes from what I regard as the fallacy of confusing the purpose of the expenditure with the motives of the members of the executive committee (and, inferentially, of the other partners) in resolving to reimburse the expenditure, the case presents very little difficulty and is, indeed, a much clearer and easier case than *Mallalieu*. For my part, I entertain no doubt that the decision of Vinelott J was correct and I would allow this appeal. **[17.7]**

3. Limited liability partnerships[30]

While the LLP Bill was making its way through Parliament in 2000, questions were raised about the taxation implications of transferring a business from a partnership to an LLP, and also of transferring the business of an LLP to other entities. **[17.8]**

Hansard HC Standing Committee F, 13 and 15 June 2000, cols 3 and 48–53

Limited Liability Partnership Bill *[Lords]*

Mr. Gibb: . . .As we said on Second Reading, the Opposition welcome the Bill. It started life under the previous Administration in response to the real concerns expressed by the accountancy and legal professions about the unwarranted and unacceptable personal exposure to liabilities that can result from the business activities of partnerships . . .

29 [See Chapter 10, above, para **[10.32]**.]

30 There has been no rush to establish LLPs; only 17,499 LLPs were registered as at 31 March 2006.

Clause 10

INCOME TAX AND CHARGEABLE GAINS

Mr. Gibb: I have just one issue, with which the Minister [*Dr Howells*] should be able to deal swiftly and cleanly. It relates to the conversion of a partnership into an llp [*i.e. an LLP*]. My understanding is that that will not give rise to a tax charge. Will he confirm that that is correct?

Will the Minister also confirm that the reason for that is that, as llps are effectively transparent for tax purposes, on conversion there will simply be a transfer from one identical partnership to another, for tax purposes, which will not trigger a tax charge under existing tax rules? That is not spelt out specifically in the Bill. If that is not the case, will he inform the Committee of the correct interpretation?

Mr. Burnett: I have one or two points on taxation. The first is a plea. Over the past 15 years, steps have been taken by business to persuade successive Governments of the merits of easing the capital gains tax problems associated with disincorporation. In the past, the Department of Trade and Industry – the Minister's Department – has been anxious to facilitate that.

A number of limited companies might wish to disincorporate and become limited liability partnerships. For some, especially those with large inbuilt gains, that will present a problem. Will the Minister have a word with his colleagues in the Treasury, to see whether they can devise a system that would enable disincorporation to happen more easily than it does now? That would be in the interests of a flexible economy and of the better running of business in Britain.[31]

Secondly, I take it that all interest on loans taken out to acquire an interest in an llp will be allowable, for tax purposes, against the total income of an individual. Will the Minister confirm that? Presumably, the same will apply to such loans taken out to purchase an interest in an existing partnership that is converted into a limited liability partnership.

Thirdly, the Minister will recall that in 1998 – when I think his Parliamentary Private Secretary, the hon. Member for Halton (Mr. Twigg), was on the Standing Committee on the Finance Bill-changes were made in partnership taxation, and a phasing out of the cash basis of accounting was introduced for partnerships, especially solicitors' partnerships.[32] The hon. Member for Bognor Regis and Littlehampton [*Mr. Gibb*] was also on that Committee, and he might remember my having to declare an interest because my then firm was operating on the cash basis of assessment, and the original rules that were promoted by the Inland Revenue were punitive, to say the least. They are rather better now. There has been a phasing in from the cash to the earnings basis over a period of eight years. Will that phasing in continue for professional firms that convert into a limited liability partnership?

Fourthly, will the Minister tell the Committee whether transparency for capital gains tax will be lost if an llp ceases to carry on any trade or business? I hope that that transparency will continue to the end of the winding up process, provided that it is not done for tax avoidance purposes.

Fifthly, capital gains tax rollover relief is causing some uncertainty to business.[33] I understand that the Government have accepted that they were unreasonable to recapture gains that an llp member had rolled into an asset outside the llp, and which were unconnected with his membership. Will the Minister confirm that the Government do not intend that gains be recaptured when the llp ceases to be transparent on the cessation of its business?

Mr. Stephen O'Brien: It is important to look down the track in the context of taxation. Several llps may wish, in due course, to convert to limited companies or plcs. Some

31 'Disincorporation' has always presented problems in UK tax law and the issue is still unresolved (see David Wainman, *Company Structures: Tax, Accounting and Company Law* (2nd edn, 1999), p. 3; [also Tiley, n 10 above, pp 839–841, referring to a 1987 joint Inland Revenue/Department of Trade and Industry discussion document on the subject)].

32 [The cash basis was replaced by the earnings basis.]

33 [For consideration of roll-over relief in respect of business assets, see Chapter 20, below, para [**20.59**].]

professional partnerships have already become plcs. Many are in the headhunter profession, not least because of the huge international extent of their business. It is highly likely that llps will be used as a staging point in the development of such firms. What thought has been given to the ease of conversion from an llp to private or public limited company status, and what taxation consequences may flow from that?

Dr. Howells *[The Minister for Competition and Consumer Affairs]*: I must ask the hon. Gentleman to repeat that question, because it is more usual to be asked whether there will be tax implications in converting from a limited company to an llp.

Mr. O'Brien: I shall clarify my point. We have carefully examined conversion from a limited company or unincorporated business to an llp, and the clause addresses many of the taxation issues involved in that. However, I am concerned to look forward, as we create a new corporate beast, to see how it is likely to develop commercially given the speed of international commerce, especially within professional partnerships. I suspect that it will be used as a staging point by companies that want to become public limited companies for greater access to funding and capital over time. The headhunting profession has shown the way in that regard.

The clause does not make it clear how taxation is likely to be affected by conversion from an llp to limited company status. That is the other side of the coin to a matter that has been reasonably well covered.

The Minister for Competition and Consumer Affairs: . . . The hon. Member for Bognor Regis and Littlehampton [*Mr. Gibb*] asked two questions that revolved around transparency on conversion between limited liability partnerships and ordinary partnerships. I can confirm both his points.

The hon. Member for Torridge and West Devon [*Mr. Burnett*] asked about disincorporation. The provisions allow partnerships to become limited liability partnerships without any tax charge arising. In the jargon, the conversion is tax-neutral. I think that he also asked about companies becoming limited liability partnerships. The Bill provides that limited liability partnerships will be taxed in the same way as ordinary partnerships. A company does not enjoy tax neutrality if it becomes a partnership, and the Bill reflects that treatment.

The hon. Gentleman's other questions, are linked. The phasing out of the cash basis will be covered in an article in the Inland Revenue bulletin. The transitional period for phasing out the cash basis will continue. Interest on loans taken out to buy interests in limited liability partnerships is allowable against total income, subject to the clear limits set out in the clause.

The hon. Gentleman asked about transparency if a limited liability partnership ceases to carry on trade or business. In that case, it becomes a body corporate and is taxed as such, by corporation tax instead of income tax. During an orderly winding up, as opposed to liquidation, it is likely that a business will continue, so the transparency will remain.

The hon. Member for Eddisbury [*Mr. O'Brien*] turned the question on its head by asking about limited liability partnerships that convert to limited companies. The position is the same as for a partnership that becomes a company, which means no tax neutrality.[34]

The hon. Member for Torridge and West Devon asked about liquidation and rollover relief for business assets. That is highly technical stuff. If the Committee bears with me, I shall try to answer the question.

Proposed new section 59A of the Taxation of Chargeable Gains Act 1992 applies only when the limited liability partnership is carrying on a business. In liquidation, the limited liability partnership ceases to carry on a business, and the assets are in the hands of the liquidator. When the limited liability partnership goes into liquidation, it will be taxed under normal corporate rules. The liquidator will be taxed on disposal of limited liability partnership assets by reference to the original acquisition cost and date of the asset by the limited liability partnership. The limited liability partnership members each have only one asset, which is their interest in the limited liability partnership. They will be taxed as

34 [This is a puzzling answer, since TCGA 1992, s 162 is capable of applying to partnerships that incorporate, just as it is applicable to sole traders who incorporate. See HMRC Capital Gains Manual CG65757 – 'Transfer of a business to a company: partnerships'.]

individuals on any gain or loss that arises on the disposal of that interest during liquidation.

We were asked to confirm that a limited liability partnership member who realises a limited liability partnership asset on the sale of a business and acquires an asset in another business will not be charged on that gain. We can confirm that rollover relief will be available in the usual way. . .

Mr. Burnett: . . . The Minister answered my question on rollover relief. I believe that he said that if the qualifying rules for rollover relief had applied to an asset that a limited liability partnership owned and that was sold and reinvested in another business, the rollover relief would not be clawed back if the other business continued to function and the limited liability partnership was wound up.

The Government should explain how the tax provisions impact on existing limited partnerships under the Limited Partnerships Act 1907, the provisions of which are to some extent carried over to limited liability partnerships that carry on trades. The rules for 1907 limited partnerships mean that they can have loss relief on the amount of capital that the partner contributes and on the amount of undrawn profits. As there is some confusion in business and in the professional world, I hope that the Minister will confirm that the Government intend to allow limited liability partnerships that carry on trades to benefit from loss relief on the capital contributed and on undrawn profits.

Dr. Howells: I can confirm that the limits set out in new section 118ZC of the Income and Corporation Taxes Act 1988 mean that, subject to the terms of the membership agreement, relief will be available in respect of any capital that the member has subscribed, plus any undrawn profit and any further amounts that the member has undertaken to contribute if the limited liability partnership is wound up. It is important to bear in mind that existing Taxes Acts provisions were designed for limited partnerships under the 1907 Act; in particular, a limited partner's capital is registered, as are any changes in the amount, and certainly does include undrawn capital or amounts committed in the event of winding up. By contrast, a limited liability partnership member's capital can be provided for in the membership agreement. It follows that if the agreement provides that sums of members' undrawn share of profit stand as capital, those sums will count with the members' capital towards the amount of loss relief that can be claimed against their other income. **[17.9]**

For further details, see Natalie Lee (gen ed) *Revenue Law – Principles and Practice* (24th edn, 2006) paras [45.18]–[45.19] (Colin Ives). More generally, see Judith Freedman and Vanessa Finch 'The Limited Liability Partnership: Pick and Mix or Mix-Up?' [2002] Journal of Business Law 475–512, and Judith Freedman 'Limited Liability Partnerships in the United Kingdom – Do they have a role, for small firms?' [2001] 26 Journal of Corporation Law 897. **[17.10]**

18 Companies

1. Introduction

Corporation tax was introduced in the UK in 1965.[1] An outline of its current main characteristics follows the examination in the next section of this Chapter of various approaches that may inform the taxation of companies and, as will be seen, shareholders.

The third section of this Chapter focuses on certain issues which have arisen in relation to the taxation of companies in the context of the EC Treaty and as a result of rulings of the European Court of Justice (ECJ) on matters pertaining to aspects of the corporate tax regimes of individual member states. **[18.1]**

2. Approaches to the taxation of companies

The taxation of companies is an issue with which most jurisdictions must grapple and, yet, there is no universally accepted approach. In devising a tax system, it is common for each jurisdiction to reconcile the recognition of a company as a legal person (and, hence, a potential taxable entity liable to tax on its profits) with the concomitant shareholder interests in that company; interests that, economically, may be made manifest in the income provided by the payment of a dividend by the company (usually, payable out of profits), realised on a return of capital or reflected in the capital value of the shares. Traditionally, the manner in which that reconciliation is undertaken is influenced, as the following extract shows, by the extent to which, if at all, personal and corporate taxes are integrated. **[18.2]**

Sijbren Cnossen 'What Kind of Corporation Tax?' in Cedric Sandford (ed) *Key Issues in Tax Reform* (1993) 40, 41–42

Figure 3.1 presents the various forms of corporation tax that can be distinguished depending on whether and to what extent they are integrated with the income tax of shareholders. At one extreme, the corporation is regarded as an entity entirely

1 Before 1965, companies were liable to pay a combination of income tax, profits tax and, in certain circumstances, surtax (see, eg, G S A Wheatcroft *The Law of Income Tax, Surtax and Profits Tax* (1962) ch 12).

separate from its shareholders and taxed as such (classical system).[2] At the other extreme, the corporation is viewed as a pass-through, a conduit, of all corporate source income of shareholders – distributed as well as undistributed earnings. The corporation tax, if retained, serves solely as a prepayment for the income tax, just like a wage withholding scheme.

Figure 3.1

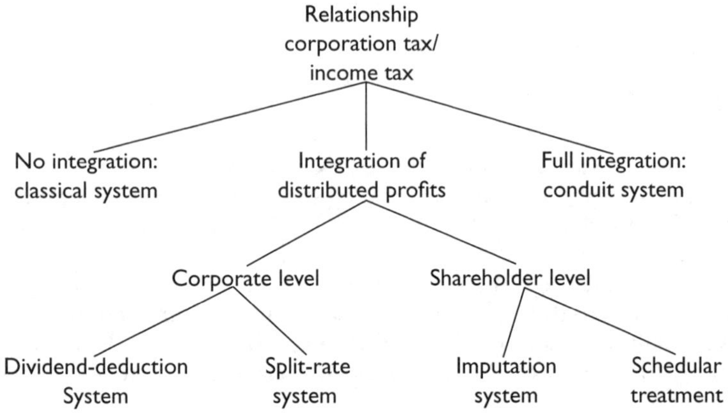

In practice, the integration of the corporation tax with the income tax of shareholders is limited to distributed profits (dividends). This form of partial integration, often referred to as dividend relief, can be achieved at either corporate level or at shareholder level. The most obvious method of dividend relief at the corporate level is to permit a deduction for dividends from taxable profits, as is commonly done for interest. This is called the dividend-deduction system. Another approach that can achieve the same result is the split-rate system, under which a lower rate of tax is levied on distributed profits. At shareholder level, dividend relief may be achieved systematically under the imputation system, which permits shareholders a full or partial credit for the corporation tax that can be imputed to the dividends received by them. Alternatively, dividend relief may be provided by taxing dividend income on a schedular basis, e.g. by applying a separate flat tax to it or by allowing shareholders a tax credit against their income tax without regard to the underlying corporation tax . . .

The concern over the appropriate form of corporation tax arises because, under the classical system, corporate source income is taxed twice if it is distributed: once at corporate level and again at shareholder level. In the tax literature, this phenomenon is referred to as the "economic double taxation of dividends."[3] The existence of a separate corporation tax means that dividends will be "overtaxed"

2 The label "classical system" was introduced by Van den Tempel . . . [A J van den Tempel *Corporation Tax and Individual Income Tax in the European Communities* (1970)]. It should be noted, however, that, contrary to what the terminology suggests, the imputation system. . .is of older date. In the 19th century, some German states already had some form of imputation and in 1922 it was incorporated as the withholding method in the Model Income Tax Ordinance of the United Kingdom, which was introduced in many colonies. For the classic treatment of the separate entity system, see Goode . . . [R Goode *The Corporation Income Tax* (1951)].

3 The classic treatment of the double-taxation issue is McLure . . . [C E McLure Jr *Must Corporate Income Be Taxed Twice?* (1979)].

compared to other capital income, such as interest. The label is pejorative, however, in the sense that retained corporate source income may be "undertaxed" if the rate of corporation tax is lower than the rate of income tax at which dividends would be taxed at shareholder level under full imputation. In the latter case, the separate corporation tax may be said to be biased in favour of retained profits. In a broader (and more correct) view, the real issue is not that dividend income is taxed twice or that the separate corporation tax exhibits a tax bias, but that corporate source income, distributed as well as retained earnings, is not taxed in accordance with the marginal income tax rates of shareholders... **[18.3]**

Experience has shown that jurisdictions have tended to opt either for the classical system (no integration) or for one of the variants of partial integration. However, the symmetry and transparency offered by the full integration of personal and corporate taxes suggest that it is an 'extreme' (to use Cnossen's word) which should not necessarily be disregarded. Indeed, in its 1966 report, the (Canadian) Royal Commission on Taxation, the Carter Commission, recommended a full integration system.[4] In this respect, the Commission opined that the corporate form was simply a convenient device through which individuals held property for conducting business activities and that, consequently, it followed that personal and corporate tax should be fully integrated. The mechanics of its proposed integrated system required, inter alia, that tax would be collected from companies at a single rate, but that full credit would be given to shareholders for tax paid both on dividends and on retained profits allocated to them. **[18.4]**

Report of the Royal Commission on Taxation (Carter Commission, Canada, 1966)

Volume 1: Introduction

INTEGRATION OF PERSONAL AND CORPORATION INCOME TAXES

It is frequently argued that shareholders should not be given credit for underlying corporation taxes because corporations pass such taxes on, typically by charging higher prices for what they sell, sometimes by paying less for what they buy. We accept that this is often true, but do not think it is a valid objection to the full credit to shareholders.

Corporation taxes are "passed on" in two ways: through immediate increases in prices or reductions in costs that quickly restore the after-tax rate of return to corporate assets; through gradual increases in product prices (relative to what they otherwise would be) resulting from reduced capital spending and hence output. In the former case the corporation tax is a crude and inequitable tax on wealth, because the tax is borne by those who happen to hold the "wrong" shares at the time the tax is imposed. These shareholders bear the tax because it is capitalised in lower share prices.

Consumers are worse off in either case. Either their real purchasing power is reduced because prices are higher or wages are lower or there are fewer goods and services available.

4 Report of the Royal Commission on Taxation (Carter Commission, Canada, 1966).

The important issue is, of course, what would happen if full credit was allowed for corporation taxes now. Here again there are two possibilities. The tax reduction on corporate source income could be quickly passed on to consumers through lower prices or passed on to workers through higher wages. The tax reduction could be capitalised in higher share prices. Only when the corporation was completely insulated from the competition provided by the entry of new firms attracted by the higher after-tax rate of return to shareholders would the full amount of the tax reduction likely be capitalised in the price of the shares. Few corporations have such a monopoly position. Probably the rise in share prices would be relatively small. If the tax reduction was not shifted quickly through lower prices, the higher after-tax rate of return to shareholders would stimulate capital spending, increased output and lower product prices and hence push down after-tax rates of return toward earlier levels. This process of adjustment would take a substantial period of time.

Consumers would benefit from the corporation tax credit if the tax reduction was passed on in lower prices or brought about increased output or both. Consumers generally would not benefit from the corporation tax credit if the tax reduction was simply reflected in higher share prices without any increase in capital expenditures and output.

We are confident that the instances of full capitalisation of the tax reduction without favourable price and output effects would be the exception rather than the rule. To deny the tax reduction because the shareholders of a few corporations would obtain windfall share gains would be to cut off our collective noses to spite our collective faces. We would be denying ourselves greater output from the economy generally to ensure that the few did not get what they did not deserve. There are other methods for dealing with corporations that have massive and persistent monopoly power. To design a tax system to suit the exceptional case would be to lose all perspective.

Another advantage of the integration of corporation and shareholder taxes and the full taxation of property gains would be the prevention of tax avoidance. Under this system profits of all kinds and from all sources would be taxable in the same manner. Accordingly, there would be relatively little incentive to arrange transactions in such a way as to change the form of payment. The basic inconsistencies in our law which have resulted in widespread "surplus-stripping" and other abuses would be eliminated. This result is, in our view, further evidence of the fundamental soundness of the system we propose.

Volume III: Taxation of Income. Chapter 7

THE INCOME OF ORGANISATIONS AS A TAX BASE

Intermediaries such as corporations and trusts should not be regarded as entities with tax-paying capacity. It should be recognised that the taxes they pay are borne by people, and accordingly there should be integration of the taxes on resident individuals and families with the taxes imposed on intermediaries. This can be achieved by providing a refundable tax credit to resident shareholders for the income taxes collected from organisations.

Volume IV: Taxation of Income (Part B). Chapter 19

1. Taxes can be collected from organisations such as corporations but the burden is ultimately on people – customers, employees, suppliers or shareholders – whose power to consume is reduced by the tax on the organisation. Corporations have the rights and obligations of persons under

the law; management often makes corporate decisions without consulting the shareholders. These are valid but irrelevant propositions in considering who bears the corporation tax.

2. Equality and neutrality could best be achieved under a tax system where there were no taxes on organisations, and all individuals and families selling and holding interests in organisations were taxed on the realised and accrued net gains derived from these sales and holdings. The net gains from selling and holding interests in organisations would be treated in the same way as other kinds of net gains, and the net gains, from selling and holding interests in all kinds of organisations would be taxed identically.
3. Unfortunately this ideal system cannot be recommended for two reasons:
   (a) At the present time, valuation problems preclude the annual taxation of accrued net gains. In the absence of accrual taxation, and if there was no tax on the income of corporations, some individuals could postpone their personal income taxes on the income they wished to save.
   (b) If the Canadian corporate source income of non-residents were taxed at lower rates than are now in effect, it would reduce the net benefit Canada derives from foreign direct investment in Canada. Because of existing tax treaties and the retaliation that would follow if these treaties were ignored, it would not be feasible to tax this income at the present level except by a corporation income tax like the tax now imposed at a rate of approximately 50 per cent.
4. Retaining the corporation income tax at a rate of approximately 50 per cent., but providing full integration of this tax with the personal income tax of residents, would solve the deferment problem, would maintain the net benefit from foreign direct investment in Canada and would achieve the greatest possible equity and neutrality.[5]

THE PROPOSED INTEGRATION SYSTEM

5. The basic features of the full integration system we recommend are as follows:
   (a) The income of corporations should be subject to tax at a flat rate of 50 per cent.
   (b) The income of individuals and families should be subject to progressive rates of tax with a top marginal rate of 50 per cent.
   (c) The corporation should be allowed to allocate after-tax corporate income to shareholders without having to pay cash dividends.
   (d) The tax base of the resident shareholder should include the corporate income paid or allocated to him, grossed-up for the corporation tax paid.
   (e) The resident shareholder should receive credit against his personal tax liability for the full amount of the corporation tax on after-tax corporate income paid or allocated to him, with a refund of the corporation tax if the credit exceeded the liability.
   (f) Realised gains and losses on corporate shares should be included in income and taxed at full progressive rates.
   (g) The cost basis of shares should be increased when the corporation allocated retained corporate earnings to shareholders and thereby created "allocated surplus," so that share gains resulting from the retention of earnings that had been taxed to the shareholder would not be taxed again to the shareholder when realised.

5 In particular, the proposed system would be neutral as between retained and distributed profits.

(h) When dividends were paid out of allocated surplus they should not be included in the shareholder's income but should be deducted from his cost basis for the shares, because such dividends would represent a realisation of funds already included in income and previously added to the cost basis of the shares.

(i) A corporation with a small number of shareholders which met specified conditions should be entitled to elect to be taxed as a partnership in order to avoid the payment by the corporation of tax at 50 per cent. and the claiming by the shareholders of refunds equal to the difference between that tax and tax calculated at their personal rates.[6] **[18.5]**

Consideration has also been given to the taxation of companies in circumstances in which tax is charged not on *income* but on *expenditure*.[7] In this respect, as the following extract shows, it is possible to envisage a company *expenditure* tax which operates alongside a conventional income tax on individuals and one that operates as part of a general *expenditure tax* on companies and individuals. **[18.6]**

Green Paper *Corporation Tax* (Cmnd 8456 (1982))

A TAX ON DISTRIBUTED PROFITS OR A COMPANY "EXPENDITURE TAX"

7.24 It has often been suggested that the tax should be charged only on distributed profits and that what happens inside the company should not come into the tax at all. In effect a ring fence would be erected around the company: so long as funds were kept inside that ring fence no tax would be charged, but the moment they crossed this ring fence and became personal or institutional income they would be charged to tax. The effect of this would be that full tax relief would be given for all capital expenditure, whether on buildings, plant and machinery or stocks, and for increased working capital. But relief would also be given on profits earned but neither distributed nor invested in the business – i.e. simply accumulated as financial assets.

7.25 The arguments in favour of such a system stem from its apparent extreme simplicity and the smaller influence of taxation on business decisions. It would, of course, mean that the whole of the existing mainstream corporation tax – at present amounting to some £m3,000 – would be lost and this would raise the very considerable problem of just how it was to be recouped if the charge on companies was to be confined to distributions. The other major objection lies in the fact that companies would be allowed to accumulate financial assets tax free. This not only poses considerable problems in itself but would greatly exacerbate the problem of policing distributions.

7.26 Interestingly, the Meade Committee arrived at very similar proposals but through a very different route. They started with the concept that tax should be charged not on *income* but on *expenditure*. Very broadly, individuals would be taxed by reference to the amount they spent in a year but would be entitled to exclude from expenditure any new saving in specified types of asset, including investment in

6 [For an assessment of the impact of this Report, see Cedric Sandford 'Carter Twenty Years On' [1987] BTR 148.]

7 For consideration of various tax bases, see Chapter 6, below, para **[6.7]**.

company shares and unincorporated businesses. In practice, to avoid making the taxpayer keep a precise record of all his expenditure, the tax charge would be based on the receipts of the individual during the tax year (from employment income, dividends, sales of shares, etc.) with deductions being given for the specified categories of saving.

7.27. Under such a system, savings which the individual invested in "business assets" would be excluded from the tax charge. For a company, the equivalent of such savings is the use of funds within the business (e.g. the retention and reinvestment of profits). Therefore applying this approach to companies, the Meade Committee put forward two possible schemes of taxation.[8] The first is to charge tax on the total receipts of the company from the sale of goods and services (including sales of capital assets but excluding financial transactions) after deducting the total purchase of such goods and services (again including purchases of capital assets). This is what the Meade Committee termed the "R" base. In effect, one would look at trading receipts (excluding investment income and interest received) plus realisations of capital assets, and give a full deduction for trading costs (excluding interest paid) plus capital investment. The second scheme – the "S" base – would charge tax on dividends paid to shareholders plus any reduction in share capital and any acquisition of shares in other companies, after deducting any increase in share capital, any dividends received, and any disposals of shares in other companies. In effect, as long as funds were "saved" within the business, they would not be taxed: if they were "spent" outside the business (for instance, paid out as dividends) they would be taxed. It will be seen that the base is in some ways close to a tax on distributed profits only.[9]

"R" base

7.28 The main difference between the "R" and the "S" bases is that the former would take no account of financial transactions. This would mean that no deduction would be given for interest paid by the company (and correspondingly no tax would be due on interest received). As the Meade Committee recognised, this could have major repercussions for the way industry was financed. The highly-geared company could, at the extreme, find itself having to pay tax out of monies which, because of its interest payments, it did not have in hand. Moreover, the "R" base would provide no obvious means of taxing companies whose business consisted, in whole or in part, of financial transactions. In fact, such a company could find that it had a negative tax base: its net receipts from borrowing and lending on money would be outside the tax computation, but the "R" base would allow a deduction for the cost of its expenditure on goods and services – pay, office accommodation, machinery and so on.

7.29 In order not to take time on these technical problems – and to focus discussion on the main and very important issues of principle – the rest of this section concentrates primarily on the expenditure tax on the "S" base. Again, for the sake of simplicity, it concentrates on the effects of a fully-fledged tax. In practice, if it were wished to reach that objective, progress might be made towards it by stages in successive years.

8 "The Structure and Reform of Direct Taxation" (Report of Committee chaired by Professor J E Meade) IFS/Allen and Unwin 1978, Chapter 12.

9 A third variant would be to adjust the "R" base to take account of financial transactions – interest payments, changes in creditors and debtors, and so on. As the Meade Committee Report explains, this is the tax-inclusive equivalent of the "S" base and in substance is identical to that base.

"S" base

7.30 Under the "S" base there would be no tax on company profits as such, so long as they were retained within the company. Instead, tax would be charged broadly on any funds which the company paid out to its shareholders in excess of the funds raised from them. For this purpose, there would be no distinction between items of an income and of a capital nature – dividends, reductions of share capital, liquidation and so on. Thus, in a year when a company raised money by way of a rights issue, it would be able to deduct the amount so raised from the dividends paid out and would pay tax only on any balance of dividends not set off. The company tax base would thus be defined not in terms of profit or income but rather in terms of the net take-out from the company sector. In addition, companies would pay tax on any acquisitions of shares in other companies and a deduction would be allowed for disposals of such shares.

7.31 The present corporation tax system already has some features of a tax of this kind, in particular the 100% capital allowance for expenditure on plant and machinery.[10] The "S" base would extend this allowance to all expenditure on buildings, plant, stock, monetary working capital and other assets in which the company invested.

7.32 There would be no imputation. The company would pay corporation tax on its net "flow of funds" and the shareholder would pay tax as a quite separate and additional matter on his personal expenditure, net of savings. In this connection, it is important to recognise that the Meade Committee saw a company expenditure tax as an integral part of a whole system of taxation based on expenditure, not on income. There are obvious and very considerable problems if one part of the system – e.g. that relating to companies – were put on an "expenditure" basis while other parts – e.g. that relating to individuals – were left on an income basis....

7.34 Payments by individual companies would, of course, vary quite sharply from year to year, and their tax base would commonly be negative in the year of a major share issue. On average, it is estimated that to raise the same amount of corporation tax revenue as in the recent past, the rate of the "S" base tax would need to be equivalent to something in the region of 200 per cent[11] of the cash dividend – or perhaps nearer 300 per cent[12] on an ex-post basis (that is, allowing for companies rearranging their affairs to reduce their tax bills) as companies shifted from equity dividends to more tax-efficient forms of return on capital – such as royalties and directors' remuneration.

7.35 The distribution of the tax between sectors would vary substantially from one year to another. On the whole, there would be a major shift in the burden from low to high distributors. At present this would mean a shift from financial companies to industrial and commercial companies and those operating overseas.

7.36 The main advantages of a corporation expenditure tax, as an integral part of a general expenditure tax covering companies and individuals alike, are seen as:

a. By definition, it would equalise the pre-tax and the post-tax return to the investor, thus encouraging capital to flow where the commercial (pre-tax) return is highest.
b. In particular, it would avoid distortion of investment decisions which (it is argued) follows from the present complex set of reliefs for specific savings and investments of various kinds.

10 [For the present position with regard to the availability of capital allowances for expenditure on plant and machinery, see the Capital Allowances Act 2001, Pt 2; see also Chapter 10, above, para **[10.66]**.]

11 On a tax-exclusive basis.

12 On a tax-exclusive basis. [In the original text, this is the same footnote reference as the previous one.]

c. The simplification that would follow from being able to dispense with all the present complex rules for computing company profits and capital gains and, in particular, for providing adjustments for the costs of inflation.[13]

7.37 Other questions that would need to be considered if a corporation expenditure tax were contemplated – as the Meade Report envisaged – as part of a move towards a general expenditure tax on companies and individuals alike, include:

a. How would companies react, if they paid tax on a basis which was radically divorced from what they – or their auditors – commonly regard as "profit"?
b. How, in particular, would dividends and the financial structure of companies generally react to the four to six-fold increase in the rate of tax on distributed profits, that would be necessary to maintain the present yield of revenue?
c. How far would the simplicity of the system stand up to pressures of the kind which have in practice led to the present complicated system of taxation on profits? Would neutrality itself be accepted permanently as an overriding objective?
d. What would be the effect of the tax on dissavings? For example, to what extent would, in particular, an "R" base tax include a "pro-cyclical" effect (reinforcing the peaks and troughs of the economic cycle) of the kind which recently caused the "clawback" problem under the previous scheme of stock relief?
e. How would UK companies, in an increasingly integrated trading world, be affected by paying tax on a basis radically different from that applying to their overseas competitors? What would be the implications for UK tax on foreign operations by UK companies? What would be the implications . . . if overseas countries did not give double taxation relief for expenditure tax paid by foreign-owned companies trading in the United Kingdom?

7.38 The previous paragraphs have touched on some important issues arising on the proposal to introduce a corporation expenditure tax as part of a general expenditure tax on companies and individuals alike; and this is what the Meade Committee envisaged. Very different and major practical considerations would arise, if one were considering a corporation expenditure tax in isolation, whilst retaining a conventional income tax on individuals.

7.39 On the face of it, formidable economic and commercial distortions could arise, if:

a. a company with surplus income (whether trading profits or investment income) could build up investments free of tax (whether in the form of trading assets, or financial assets, such as bank deposits or securities), whereas by contrast
b. the unincorporated trader or individual investor who wished to make similar savings (whether for the working capital of his business, or more generally to provide for his old age or his children) would have to find the money out of income taxed at the top marginal rate of income tax of up to 75%.

7.40 By the same token, distortions in the opposite direction could arise, if individuals were able to finance consumption out of borrowings or dissavings free of tax, whilst company distributions – whether "income" or "capital" – were heavily taxed.

13 Under the expenditure tax a full and immediate deduction would be given for expenditure, broadly speaking in currency of the same value as that in which it was incurred, and there would be no tax on income derived from the business's assets if it was retained within the company. Hence, the need for inflation adjustments would not arise. . . .

7.41 The fundamental problem would be that of unfair competition and of equity generally between incorporated (in particular, closely held) businesses[14] and investors on the one hand, and unincorporated businesses and investors on the other hand.[15] However, serious problems would also arise from the scope for businesses and investors to move readily from one tax regime to the other. To take only the most simple example, a man could build up his savings free of tax in a company; sell that company (notably to a foreigner or an exempt fund); and use the sale proceeds to finance consumption free of tax as an individual.

7.42 For the reasons outlined in the previous four paragraphs, it is clear that there would be severe difficulties in substituting a company expenditure tax for corporation tax while retaining an income tax system for individuals. As the Meade Committee Report itself envisaged, the case for a company expenditure tax has to be considered in the context of changing the tax system generally from income tax to expenditure tax principles. The discussion of such a development ranges well beyond the compass of the present Green Paper.[16] **[18.7]**

A further departure from the established approaches of taxing companies identified by Cnossen is provided by the allowance for corporate equity system (ACE). Under such a system, the notion of which was first mooted in 1984,[17] a company's taxable profits may be calculated under any current schedule, but it would also be given an allowance representative of the 'opportunity cost of equity finance'. Such allowance comprises the value of funds put into the company by shareholders (including the company's equity capital) multiplied by a nominal rate of interest that reflects a normal market rate of return on, for example, medium term government bonds. **[18.8]**

Michael Devereux and Harold Freeman 'A General Neutral Profits Tax' (1991) 12(3) Fiscal Studies 1, 4–6

...The tax proposed here, which we have called the "Allowance for Corporate Equity" ("ACE") system, retains the neutrality properties of the annual pure profits base, but avoids most of its practical difficulties. Taxable profits could be calculated as under any current schedule, but companies would be given an allowance, reflecting the opportunity cost of equity finance. This new allowance would be reached by adding up the historical value of the funds put into the company by shareholders, and multiplying this figure by an appropriate nominal interest rate. The precise calculation of shareholders' funds for tax purposes is shown in Table 1.

14 [See below, para **[18.9]**.]

15 [In the original, there is a cross-reference to paras of the green paper not extracted in the present volume.]

16 [The Green Paper was part of a drive by the Conservative Government (elected in 1979) to modernise the UK tax system (see Nigel Lawson *The View from No. 11: Memoirs of a Tory Radical* (1992) p 17): 'We [NL and Arthur, later Lord, Cockfield] looked into the theoretically attractive idea of a wholesale switch from an income tax to an expenditure tax system, and had a long session with Professor James Meade, its foremost exponent, but (in my view rightly) shrank from the upheaval and practical problems that would have been involved' (see also, ibid, 344–345).]

17 See Robin Boadway and Neil Bruce 'A General Proposition on the Design of a Neutral Business Tax' (1984) 24 Journal of Public Economics 231–239.

TABLE 1

Calculating Shareholders' Funds

Shareholders' funds for this period *equals*:

Shareholders' funds in the previous period

Plus	total taxable profits (net of the equity allowance)
	The equity allowance
	Dividends received
	Net new equity issues
Less	Tax payable[18]
	Dividends paid
	Net new acquisitions of shares in other companies

Although this sounds rather a long way from the complex valuation and indexation procedures of an annual pure profits base, in present value terms the two bases are identical. This result comes from two crucial properties of the ACE. First, with the equity allowance in place, the tax base becomes very flexible; we can use any schedule of depreciation allowances without altering the present value of tax payments. This implies that the ACE is equivalent in present value terms to an annual pure profits base, and that, therefore, it too is neutral.

The key to these rather surprising results is that shareholders' funds for tax purposes are calculated using *taxable profits*, as shown in Table 1. If an item of accrued profit is not included in this year's taxable profit (for example, if it is an undeclared and unrealised capital gain), then it will not contribute to the shareholders' funds carried forward to the next period.

This principle ensures that, as long as the notional rate of interest used by the tax system is equal to the discount rate of the company[19] and there are perfect capital markets, then the company (and its shareholders) should be indifferent between declaring or not declaring extra taxable profit; higher taxable profits, and higher tax, now will yield higher tax allowances in the future due to the increase in shareholders' funds.

Intuitively, this is because the company can borrow at the notional rate of interest to offset any higher tax payable now (keeping new investment and hence the level of the capital stock unchanged). Repayments on the borrowing will be offset exactly by reduced tax payments in the future. Alternatively, if changes in the tax paid by the company are reflected in dividends paid, then shareholders can borrow or lend to exactly offset the different profile of distributions . . .

This does *not* mean that the present value of all tax payments is zero; if this were the case, it would be simpler to abolish the tax. It would be the case if gross taxable profits were included in shareholders' funds. In fact, however, it is taxable profits *net of tax* which are included in shareholders' funds. Intuitively, in order to maintain the company at the size it would have been in the absence of tax, the company needs to raise more finance (equal to the tax payment). While this new finance (from whatever source) receives a relief corresponding to normal profit, any economic rent earned on assets purchased with such finance will yield a tax liability with a positive present value.

18 Alternatively, we could include tax *paid*. However, using tax payable reduces the benefits that companies may derive from delayed payment of tax.

19 The choice of interest rate is the only decision that cannot be avoided, except by moving to a flow-of-funds base. . . .

Turning to inflation, the ACE can, if desired, be framed entirely in nominal terms, with no provisions for indexation. The nominal interest rate includes both the real cost of finance and some compensation to the lender for the fall in the real value of the principal. It therefore appears that the ACE is too generous. However, in a totally unindexed system, the full nominal capital gain on any asset will be liable for tax. Since the book value of funds put into the company and the book value of assets must be equal, this overpayment of relief will be exactly balanced by an overpayment of tax. If the asset does not happen to be realised in any one year, there will be some mismatch in the timing of payments, but as we have argued above, there will be an exact offset in present value terms.[20]

The implication of this analysis is that, once the basic principle of the ACE is accepted, the rest of the tax base should be *irrelevant* to the company, at least in present value terms. In principle the system could give any set of capital allowances, including, of course, the present set or those used by accountants.[21]

The two well-established neutral bases are clearly special cases of the ACE. The annual pure profits base is the case where the schedule of capital allowances corresponds exactly to true economic depreciation, and where all values are indexed. The flow-of-funds base is the case where investment attracts a 100 per cent initial allowance; since all assets are written off immediately, shareholders' funds for tax purposes, and therefore the value of the equity allowance, will always be zero.[22] **[18.9]**

An ACE system was utilised in Croatia in the latter half of the 1990s; for an assessment of the operation of that system, see Michael Keen and John King 'The Croatian Profit Tax: An ACE in Practice' (2002) 23(3) Fiscal Studies 401. **[18.10]**

3. The United Kingdom's approach to the taxation of companies

A. *Outline of corporation tax*

Presently, the relevant legislation appears in the Income and Corporation Taxes Act 1988 (ICTA 1988), although this has been much expanded and amended by later Finance Acts.[23] There will eventually be a new, clearer, version of the legislation, as a result of the work of the Tax Law Rewrite project.

20 The nominal interest rate is $r(1 + \pi) + \pi$, where $r(1 + \pi)$ is the real cost of finance in current prices and π is the rate of inflation. In the presence of inflation, the ACE therefore overestimates costs by £ π for £1 of shareholders' funds (or debt). An asset then bought with the £1 is taxed on the nominal rise in its value, i.e. on $g(1 + \pi) + \pi$, where $g(1 + \pi)$ is the real gain in current prices, an overestimate of income of £ π. The overestimates of relief and taxable profit exactly cancel out.

21 Since the tax base is neutral, this suggests that there is no scope for the use of more generous capital allowances to promote investment. However, this need not be the case; governments can specifically support investment in particular assets by giving allowances that do not reduce shareholders' funds for tax purposes.

22 [See also IFS Commentary No 26 *Equity for Companies: A Corporation Tax for the 1990s: A Report of the IFS Capital Taxes Group* (1991).]

23 However, the legislation on capital allowances appears in CAA 2001, which deals with both income tax and corporation tax (see below).

Consistently with both international law and the approach of other member countries of the Organisation for Economic Co-operation and Development (the 'OECD'),[24] the basis of liability to corporation tax is 'residence'.[25] Irrespective of where a UK resident company's[26] profits arise, it is liable to pay corporation tax,[27] although this 'worldwide profits rule' is currently the subject of an extended consultation.[28] A non-UK resident company is only liable to pay the tax on profits 'attributable' to a 'permanent establishment' in the UK.[29] 'Profits' are defined to comprise both income and chargeable gains.[30] Corporation tax rates are fixed for financial years but charged 'by reference to' a company's accounting periods.[31] The main rate for the 2007 financial year is 30%, but there is a small companies' rate of 20% for profits up to £300,000,[32] and marginal relief on profits between £300,000 and £1,500,000.[33]

A basic rule of UK corporation tax is that dividends are not deductible in 'computing income', since they are themselves applications of profit.[34] Loan interest, by contrast, is deductible, but only in accordance with the rules of the special accounting-based code on 'loan relationships'.[35]

When a shareholder receives a dividend or other distribution from a company, he is taxed on the gross amount, ie on the dividend plus a 10% tax credit.[36] The 'dividend ordinary rate' of 10% covers the income tax liability of lower and basic rate taxpayers, but higher rate taxpayers are liable to pay the 'dividend upper rate', which is 32.5%.[37]

The tax credit is the system's attempt to avoid 'economic double taxation' ie where the same income is taxed more than once. **[18.11]**

B. *Trading profits*

The income component in a company's taxable profits is calculated in accordance with income tax principles.[38] As already seen, the Income Tax

24 See Organisation for Economic Co-operation and Development *Taxing Profits in a Global Economy: Domestic and International Issues*, p 36.
25 See David W Williams *EC Tax Law* (1998) p 16.
26 See ICTA 1988, s 832, which includes unincorporated associations, but not partnerships; also *Blackpool Marton Rotary Club v Martin* [1990] STC 1; on corporate residence, see Chapter 19, below, para **[19.22]**, and *Wood v Holden (Inspector of Taxes)* [2006] STC 443; below, para **[19.25]**. Special rules, designed to ensure the neutral tax treatment of the 'European Company' (see Council Regulation EC/2157/01), are contained in F(No 2)A 2005, ss 51–65.
27 See ICTA 1988, ss 6 and 8.
28 See HM Treasury and HM Revenue and Customs, *Taxation of the foreign profits of companies: a discussion document: June 2007* (available from www.hmrc.gov.uk).
29 See ICTA 1988, ss 11(1), (2).
30 *Ibid*, s 6(4)(a).
31 *Ibid*, s 8(3).
32 See *R v Inland Revenue Commissioners, ex p Newfields Developments Ltd* [2001] UKHL, [2001] STC 901; *Gascoines Group Ltd v Inspector of Taxes and related appeals* [2004] EWHC 640 (Ch), [2004] STC 844; *Revenue and Customs Commissioners v Salaried Persons Postal Loans Ltd* [2006] EWHC 763 (Ch), [2006] STC 1315.
33 See FA 2007, s 3 (also FA 2006, s 25).
34 See ICTA 1988, ss 208 and 337A(1)(a); also *Mersey Docks and Harbour Board v Lucas* (1883) 8 App Cas 891 and *Pondicherry Railway Co Ltd v Madras Commissioner of Income Tax* (1931) 10 ATC 365.
35 See FA 1996, ss 80–105; Sch 8–15.
36 See ICTA 1988, s 231 and ITTOIA 2005, ss 384 and 385. There was once an obligation on the company to pay advance corporation tax ('ACT') on distributions, but this has not applied since April 1999.
37 See ICTA 1988, ss 1A(1A)(a) and 1B), and ITA 2007, ss 8 and 13.
38 *Ibid*, s 9(1).

(Trading and Other Income) Act 2005 (ITTOIA 2005) does not apply for corporation tax purposes[39] and, although there is an ongoing consultation to move to a 'global' system,[40] corporation tax is still charged under Schedules A and D, with trading income falling under Schedule D, Case I.[41]

Finance Act 1998, s 42, is the corporation tax counterpart of ITTOIA 2005, s 25.[42] Section 42 provides that, '[f]or the purposes of Case I or II of Schedule D the profits of a trade, profession or vocation must be computed in accordance with generally accepted accounting practice, subject to any adjustment required or authorised by law in computing profits for those purposes'. For companies, the relevant 'generally accepted accounting practice' (GAAP)[43] depends on whether the company has chosen to prepare its accounts in accordance with UK GAAP or with International Accounting Standards (IASs).[44] Companies whose securities are traded on specified markets, including the London Stock Exchange, have no choice, however. They must prepare their accounts in accordance with IASs adopted by the European Commission.[45] The reference to 'generally accepted accounting practice' in s 42 is, therefore, to UK GAAP or to IASs, whichever is the applicable accounting practice.[46]

There are detailed provisions, carefully restricted, relating to relief for trading losses.[47] Trading losses can be 'carried forward', ie 'set off for the purposes of corporation tax against any trading income from the trade in succeeding accounting periods'.[48] In relation to the carry forward of trading losses, there is a provision which allows such losses to be set against 'any interest or dividends on investments' of subsequent accounting periods,[49] provided that the interest or dividends 'would fall to be taken into account as trading receipts ... but for the fact that they have been subjected to tax under other provisions'.[50] Trading losses can also be 'set off ... against profits (of whatever description) [of the "accounting period in which the loss is incurred"] ... and the period of twelve months immediately preceding the accounting period in which the loss is incurred.'[51] **[18.12]**

Nuclear Electric plc v Bradley (Inspector of Taxes) [1996] STC 405 (HL)

Nuclear Electric, which carried on the trade of generating and supplying electricity, had put money aside to cover the cost of possible future nuclear decommissioning

39 See ICTA 1988, s 9(2A).
40 By introducing the idea of a company's 'operating business' (see Inland Revenue, *Corporation Tax Reform: Technical Note, December 2004* (2004) pp 9–19).
41 See ICTA 1988, s 18.
42 See Chapter 10, above, para **[10.2]**.
43 See Chapter 10, above, para **[10.2]**.
44 See CA 1985, ss 226(2) and 227(3).
45 *Ibid*, s 227(2) (see European Parliament and Council Regulation EC/1606/02, art 4); also Stephen Mayson, Derek French and Christopher Ryan *Company Law* (22nd edn., 2005) pp 282–286.
46 See FA 2004, s 50(1).
47 See ICTA 1988, ss 393 and 393A.
48 *Ibid*, s 393(1).
49 *Ibid*, s 393(8).
50 *Ibid*.
51 See ICTA 1988, ss 393A(1) and 393A(2).

liabilities. The House of Lords rejected the argument that income generated by the fund could be treated as trading income under ICTA 1988, s 393(8).

LORD JAUNCEY OF TULLICHETTLE (*delivering the opinion of the Appellate Committee*)... The effect of these two subsections [i.e. ICTA 1988, s. 393(1) and 393(8)] in the circumstances predicated is that investment income which would have been treated as trading income in the computation of the annual profits or gains arising from the taxpayer's trade for the purposes of Case I of Sch D but for the fact that it has suffered tax under some other provision is to be treated as trading income for the purposes of Case I.

When does investment income amount to a trading receipt of the taxpayer? The statute provides no guidance on the matter beyond impliedly recognising that it can sometimes do so. Such few authorities as are relevant have refused to lay down any hard and fast rule or draw any distinct line for determining the matter. Thus in *Liverpool and London and Globe Insurance Co v Bennett* (*Surveyor of Taxes*) [1913] AC 610 at 620, 6 TC 327 at 379 Earl Loreburn said: "I know of no formula which can discriminate in all circumstances what are and what are not profits of a trade." It must at the end of the day always be a question of fact. In *Bennett* the taxpayer was a United Kingdom-based insurance company which carried on business both at home and abroad. In certain foreign countries it was required by law to deposit sums of money with the relevant governments and to invest them according to local law. It also invested certain other sums derived from accumulated profits of the business in the country in question and received the interest on all these investments abroad. As this interest was not remitted to the United Kingdom it was only taxable if it was a trading profit for the purposes of Case I of Sch D. The Special Commissioners (see [1911] 2 KB 577, 6 TC 327) found that the investments in question were made in the carrying on of, and were part of, its business transactions and that the interest therefrom was taxable under Case I. In relation to the compulsory deposits Hamilton J (see [1911] 2 KB 577 at 593, 6 TC 327 at 362) quoted with approval the following dictum of Wright J in an earlier case (see *Norwich Union Fire Insurance Co v Magee* (*Surveyor of Taxes*) (1896) 3 TC 457 at 460):

> "If there is a trade which cannot be carried on without making investments abroad, the interest arising on the investments necessarily made for the purposes of the trade is, as it seems to me, part of the gains of that trade."

Hamilton J observed in relation to the voluntary investments (see [1911] 2 KB 577 at 594, 6 TC 327 at 363):

> "And I think it is clear that the investments which this fire insurance company voluntarily makes abroad are made not merely for investment's sake, but for the sake of having a fund readily realisable abroad to meet the liabilities of their business if need should be."

The Court of Appeal (see [1912] KB 41, 6 TC 327) affirmed Hamilton J, and Buckley LJ (see [1912] 2 KB 41 at 60, 6 TC 327 at 374) posed the question as being "whether the interest and dividends are profits of the business as fruit derived from a fund employed and risked in the business." This House (see [1913] AC 610, 6 TC 327) dismissed the taxpayer's appeal. Earl Loreburn (see [1913] AC 610 at 619, 6 TC 327 at 378) cited Buckley LJ's above-quoted text with approval. Lord Mersey said (see [1913] AC 610 at 621, 6 TC 327 at 380):

> "These temporary investments are also required for the formation of the reserve fund, a fund created to attract customers and to serve as a stand-by in the event of sudden claims being made upon the insurers in respect of losses. It is, according to my view, impossible to say that such investments do not form part of this company's insurance business, or that the returns flowing from them do not form part of its profits."

Lord Parker of Waddington, after stating (see [1913] AC 610 at 622, 6 TC 327 at 380) that the compulsory investments constituted a security to the policy-holders should the taxpayer fail to satisfy their claims, concluded (see [1913] AC 610 at 623, 6 TC 327 at 381) that they were made for the purpose of and were "at risk" in the company's business. He went on to observe that the voluntary investments were easily realisable and "at any time available for the purposes" of the taxpayer's business. The words "employed and risked" used by Buckley LJ have been quoted on many occasions but I doubt the utility of the word "risked" as a word of general application. If it is intended to mean that the investments are at risk because they are available to satisfy the claims of the general creditors that does not advance the matter since all assets of the taxpayer for whatever purposes they may be held are similarly available. If it is intended to mean that the fund is used for the purpose of the taxpayer's business it adds nothing to the word "employed". It seems probable that Buckley LJ used the word because the funds of an insurance company are necessarily at risk of claims by policy-holders immediately the policies are effected. I do not therefore think it necessary to go further than consider whether funds are employed in the business whereby any income therefrom arises from the trade for the purposes of Case I of Sch D. What appears clearly from the speeches of Lord Mersey and Lord Parker of Waddington is the importance which they attached to the fact that the investment funds were available at any time during the relevant years of assessment to meet the requirements of the taxpayer's business.

In *IRC v Butterley Co Ltd* [1957] AC 32 at 61, 36 TC 411 at 452 Lord Radcliffe, in the context of profits tax, said:

> "I do not think it possible to say that a company cannot own beneficially assets which do not belong to any trade or business which it conducts or that it cannot receive income beneficially which nevertheless is not income of such a trade or business."

Finally in *Bank Line Ltd v IRC* [1974] STC 342, 1974 SC 166 the Court of Session held that a fund set aside by a ship-owning company to replace some years hence obsolete ships was not to be treated as trading income for the purposes of the statutory predecessor of s 393 of the 1988 Act (s 58 of the Finance Act 1965). The Lord President (Emslie) after referring at some length to *Liverpool and London and Globe Insurance Co v Bennett* said (see [1974] STC 342 at 355–356, 1974 SC 166 at 178):

> "In my opinion, further, if I am correct in holding that what must be demonstrated by the taxpayer company here is the active current employment and risking of the ship replacement fund in its trade of owning and operating ships in each of the relevant accounting periods, the taxpayer company has failed to do so. This reserve fund was a fund laid aside to be employed and risked in the future, and although the taxpayer company may be right in saying that it had a present and continuing purpose in maintaining this fund, I am quite unable to accept that they accordingly 'employed and risked' it in its business in the relevant periods."

Lord Cameron said (see [1974] STC 342 at 358, 1974 SC 166 at 180):

> "The investments of which the interest and dividends are in question were made with a particular purpose in view, replacement of capital assets and not for the current requirements of the trade carried on by the taxpayer company with the ships owned and operated by them."

He further observed (see [1974] STC 342 at 359, 1974 SC 166 at 181–182):

> "The receipts in question are not the receipts of such trading – on the contrary they are receipts from the investment of sums which have been withdrawn from trade and dedicated to and drawn on for the replacement of capital assets. No doubt they are receipts from the investment of sums set aside out of the profits of trading in previous years and that by providing such a replacement fund the taxpayer company made the continued carrying on of the trade possible, but there is in my opinion a material difference between such investments and the investment of funds which are or can be at call to meet the current demands of the trading activity carried on by the company."

Lord Avonside said (see [1974] STC 342 at 366, 1974 SC 166 at 189):

> "Income becomes a trading receipt when it arises from capital activity employed and at risk in the business, capital which is employed in the business because it is required for its support or, perhaps, to attract customers looking to the credit of the business. Trading income is 'the fruit' of the capital employed in the business in a present and active sense."

Like Lord Cameron he also pointed out that the fund, far from being employed in the business, had been created by withdrawing money from it.

All the judges in that case looked at the current use of the capital of the fund during the relevant accounting periods and concluded in the light of the findings of the Special Commissioners that it was not employed in the business of the ship-owners. Mr Aaronson for the taxpayer did not seek to challenge the decision but argued that it was distinguishable because in this case there was in the year of assessment an accrued liability to pay the back-end costs albeit at a future date, whereas in the *Bank Line* case there was no such current obligation on the taxpayer to replace its ships. The answer to this submission may be shortly stated. Although NE [*Nuclear Electric*] had incurred a liability to make future payment it was no more obliged to set up a fund to meet this liability than were the shipowners. However, having done so, NE during the year of assessment neither used the fund for this purpose nor employed it in any other way in the business of generating electricity. The fact that in future years it might invest the fund in plant producing revenue and hence trading receipts cannot alter the character of its current use. It is the year of assessment that has to be looked at. I can therefore see no grounds for distinguishing the *Bank Line* case which I consider to have been correctly decided.

Whether income from investments held by a business is trading income must ultimately depend upon the nature of the business and the purpose for which the fund is held. At one end of the scale are insurance companies and banks part of whose business is the making and holding of investments to meet current liabilities. It has been suggested that tour operators might fall into this category but without a good deal more information I do not feel able to express an opinion on this matter. At the other end of the scale are businesses of which the making and holding of investments form no part. In between these two ends there will no doubt fall other types of businesses whose position is not so clear. However in this case it is absolutely clear that the business of NE was to produce and supply electricity. The making of investments was neither an integral nor any part of its business. Furthermore the investments which it did make were in no sense employed in the business of producing electricity during the year of assessment. It follows that wherever the line may be drawn the income from NE's investment cannot be treated as trading income.

In this case we are dealing with a very large sum of money intended to be invested for a long period. Therefore in reaching the conclusion that this fund was not employed in NE's business I would not wish to be taken as suggesting that sums held by a trader in an interest-bearing account to meet current or short-term trading liabilities should be similarly considered.

For the foregoing reasons I consider that the Court of Appeal arrived at the correct conclusion and that the appeal must be dismissed. **[18.13]**

The Capital Allowances Act 2001 applies to certain capital expenditure incurred by companies and individuals (for the nature and availability of capital allowances in respect of such expenditure, see Chapter 10, para **[10.63]**). The possibility which was raised in a recent consultation document of abolishing the system of capital allowances and 'moving wholly to a regime based on accounts depreciation'[52] seems to have been abandoned.[53] **[18.14]**

C. *Chargeable gains of companies*

Chargeable gains form part of a company's taxable profits. Broadly, the capital gains tax rules applicable to the chargeable gains of individuals[54] apply to

52 See HM Treasury and Inland Revenue *Reform of Corporation Tax: A consultative document* (August 2002) p 14.
53 See Inland Revenue, *Technical Note*, n 40 above, p 6.
54 See Chapter 20, below, paras **[20.14]–[20.25]**.

chargeable gains made by companies. However, companies are not entitled to an annual exemption and the indexation allowance, rather than taper relief, is used to deal with inflationary gains.[55] Graeme Macdonald and David Martin have advocated that, before corporation tax legislation is rewritten, 'significant simplification and rationalisation' should be undertaken. **[18.15]**

Graeme Macdonald and David Martin 'Taxing Corporate Capital Gains: Proposals for Reform' [2005] BTR 628, 629

One of the characteristics of capital gains tax is that the charge only arises on the disposal of an asset; that is, when the gain is realised. Whereas accounting traditionally used realisation as a criterion for recognising profit with the aim of protecting creditors and investors by limiting distributions to those of realised profits, it no longer does so. The purpose of the test was to achieve an acceptable level of certainty in the measure of profits before permitting the distribution of dividend, and, for our purpose, tax. However, accounting now admits gains and losses on the revaluation of assets into the computation of profit in the interest of providing more relevant information to the users of accounts, even though that information is not necessarily certain. Thus, if realisation is to be retained as a criterion for taxing gains, there will regularly be a difference between the accounting and tax measures of profit, though the difference will be one of timing rather than ultimate recognition.

There are problems associated with taxing realised gains only. Economists are concerned with the consequential lock-in effect which creates an incentive to postpone the realisation of a gain because the tax cost is thereby postponed. The concern is that a more optimal purchase of assets could be forgone on account of this tax saving, so making the economy work less efficiently. As a response to this concern rollover relief allows gains to be postponed if they are reinvested in certain classes of asset.[56]

Tax administrators are also concerned with the lock-in effect in that it potentially enables taxpayers to cherry-pick losses whilst postponing the realisation of gains. The response is to introduce rules limiting the set off in such circumstances in order to protect tax revenues.

Notwithstanding these difficulties we consider that generally realisation should remain a criterion for recognising taxable gains.[57] In summary, the inclusion of changes in value is considered inappropriate for assets that are held for use in the business because the basis of valuation does not accord with the fundamental concept of income. If the future flow of benefits to the business holding the asset is not expected to change, notwithstanding that the asset value has increased, it is difficult to see that the change should be recognised as profit for tax purposes. Further, in many cases, roll-over relief would eliminate a gain even if there were a disposal. On the other hand it is recognised that financial assets traded in an active market do represent a store of distribution potential of which the market gives objective evidence. We would thus accept that revaluations of such assets included in the accounts could also be included in the tax base, although it has to be recognised that this would lead to pressure for a

55 *Ibid.*
56 [See TCGA 1992, ss. 152–154; also Tiley, *Revenue Law* (5th edn, 2005) pp 770–776, and see Chapter 20, below, para **[20.59]**.]
57 . . . [See Graeme MacDonald and David Martin, *Tax and Accounting: a Response to the 2003 Consultation Document on Corporation Tax Reform* (2004), paras 3.11–3.20.]

carry back of losses against previously taxed, unrealised gains with consequential volatility of tax revenues. **[18.16]**

D. *Close companies*

'Closely-held' companies presented tax avoidance opportunities where income tax rates were high and corporation tax rates relatively low. Anti-avoidance provisions are still contained in ICTA 1988, ss 414–422. But their practical importance is now somewhat limited.[58] **[18.17]**

Geoffrey Morse and David Williams (eds) *Davies: Principles of Tax Law* (5th edn, 2004) pp 222–223

Lurking in sections 414 to 422 of the 1988 Act are the remaining legislative "ruins" of a once-great Revenue weapon for use in tax collection: the provisions aimed at breaking open close companies. . . . [*which*] deemed dividends to occur, deemed loans to be dividends, and so on. . . .

In practice, the sections are of limited importance for two very different reasons. The first is that in the modern "global" economy, companies move out of range by the simple process of decamping to an offshore jurisdiction. The second is that the tax burden is now much lower. **[18.18]**

E. *Groups of companies*

Every company is a legal person.[59] For corporation tax purposes, however, and, subject to the satisfaction of stringent conditions, it is possible for one company in a group to 'surrender' any trading losses to another company in the group, by way of 'group relief'.[60] The compatibility (or otherwise) of aspects of the group relief provisions with the EC Treaty has recently been the subject of litigation in the European Court of Justice (ECJ).[61] **[18.19]**

F. *Anti-avoidance*

Corporation tax legislation contains numerous and complex statutory anti-avoidance provisions. Some of these, such as the transfer pricing provisions referred to in Chapter 10,[62] and the controlled foreign company ('CFC') provisions,[63] are an incident of most OECD tax systems. Others, such as those

58 It is conceivable that they might be problematic in the context of, for example, informal transactions involving small family companies (see, e.g., Natalie Lee (gen ed), *Revenue Law – Principles and Practice* (24th edn, 2006), Example 41.12). Most non-quoted companies are 'close' according to the definition in ICTA 1988, s 414 (see David Wainman, *Company Structures: Tax, Accounting and Company Law* (2nd edn, 1999) p 159n).

59 See *Adams v Cape Industries plc* [1990] Ch 433.

60 See ICTA 1988, ss 402–413, as amended by FA 2006, s 27 (see below, para **[18.24]**); cf the accounting concept of the consolidated income statement (sc consolidated profit and loss account), which is prepared 'on the basis that the group is a single entity' (see Christopher Nobes *The Penguin Dictionary of Accounting* (2nd edn, 2006) p 77.

61 See below, para **[18.23]**.

62 See Chapter 10, above, para **[10.46]**.

63 See ICTA 1988, ss 747–756; also Tiley, n 55 above, ch 62.

relating to transactions in land in ITA 2007, Pt 13, Ch 3,[64] or, the recently introduced and targeted anti-avoidance rules of FA 2006 on capital losses,[65] have a more 'domestic' character. **[18.20]**

4. Corporation tax in its European setting[66]

A. *The present situation*

Since the UK joined the European Community in 1973, EC law has been increasingly influential in the development of many areas of UK law, and in some respects the law of taxation has not been immune from that influence. Thus, for example, Chapter 2 of the EC Treaty, which is entitled 'tax provisions', provides in art 93 (ex 99) explicitly for 'the harmonisation of legislation concerning turnover taxes, excise duties and other forms of indirect taxation to the extent that such harmonisation is necessary...', and the Sixth VAT Directive (Directive (EEC) 77/388), which was adopted in 1977, accordingly, sets out the structure of the common system of value added tax that member states are required to follow. No equivalent article provides for the harmonisation of direct taxes, and, hence, in the context of this Chapter, corporation tax. Nevertheless, whilst member states have been reluctant to countenance a common European corporate tax system, various Directives pertaining to the taxation of groups of companies operating within member states have been approved.[67] The influence of EC law in relation to corporate tax has also been evident in cases heard by the ECJ in which the court has been required to adjudicate upon the compatibility (or otherwise) of specific legislative provisions with the EC Treaty and the fundamental freedoms which it enshrines. In this respect, a substantial body of case law has been established.[68] The following extract embodies the reflections of the High Court judge who has been, perhaps, most closely involved in recent litigation which has explored the impact of EC law on UK statutory provisions concerning the taxation of companies and dividends. **[18.21]**

64 See Tiley, n 55 above, pp 1061–1065. See also Chapter 12, above, para **[12.29]**.

65 See FA 2006, ss 69–72.

66 See Ben JM Terra and Peter J Wattel, *European Tax Law* (4th edn, 2005) chs 4, 9, 10 and 13, and, generally, Frans Vanistendael, *EU Freedoms and Taxation* (2006). See also the useful early analyses in Paul Farmer and Richard Lyal *EC Tax Law* (1994) chs 11–16 and in David Williams, n 25 above, *passim.*

67 See the Parent–Subsidiary Directive (Council Directive (90/435/EEC), the Merger Directive (Council Directive (90/434/EEC)), and the Interest and Royalty Directive (Council Directive (2003/49/EC)). In each instance, authority was derived from art 94 (ex 100) which enables the Council of Ministers to 'issue directives for the approximation of such laws, regulations or administrative provisions of the Member States as directly affect the establishment or functioning of the common market'.

68 See (some of which are discussed in the extracts below) Case C-264/96 *Imperial Chemical Industries plc v Kenneth Hall Colmer (HM Inspector of Taxes)* [1998] 3 CMLR 293 (see now ICTA 1988, ss 403D, 403E, inserted by FA 2000, s 97, Sch 27); Case C-397/98 *Metallgesellschaft Ltd v CIR and A-G* [2001] ECR I-1727; Case C-446/03 *Marks and Spencer plc v Halsey (Inspector of Taxes)* [2006] EWHC 811, [2006] 1 CMLR 18, [2006] STC 1235 (Park J); [2007] EWCA Civ 117, as yet unreported; Case C-196/04 *Cadbury Schweppes plc v Inland Revenue Commissioners* [2006] STC 1908; Case C-446/04 *Test Claimants in the FII Group Litigation v IRC* [2007] 1 CMLR 35; Case C-374/04 *Test Claimants in Class IV of the ACT Group Litigation v IRC* [2007] 1 CMLR 36; and Case C-524/04 *Test Claimants in the Thin Cap Group Litigation v IRC* [2007] 2 CMLR 31. This list does not include considerations of EC law issues by the HL, nor those corporate income tax cases referred to the ECJ by the courts of other EU member states.

Sir Andrew Park 'A Judge's Tale: Corporation Tax and Community Law' [2006] BTR 322, 323–325

It took quite some time for the possible implications of Community law upon the direct tax systems of Member States to be appreciated. VAT was of course a different matter, but for the direct taxes there was nothing comparable to the Sixth Directive and other VAT directives. No Community law instrument prescribes what the structure of the direct tax systems in the Member States has to be. However, the Court of Justice of the European Communities (the ECJ) has frequently said that, although direct taxation is a matter for the Member States, they must nevertheless exercise their direct taxation powers consistently with Community law. The ECJ proceeds on the basis that they must not structure their taxes so as to infringe basic principles of Community law. Consistently with that approach the court has effectively struck down various rules of national tax systems which it considered to be inconsistent with that law.

In the context of corporation tax a particularly important principle is the freedom of establishment. The relevant Articles of the EC Treaty are now Articles 43 and 48. At an earlier time those Articles were the same in content but differently numbered as 52 and 58. Article 43 is expressed in terms which confer protection in one Member State on nationals of other Member States, but Article 48 requires the same principles to be applied to companies formed in other Member States and having their registered office, central administration or principal place of business in such other Member States. Articles 43 and 48 provide that restrictions on the freedom of establishment in the territory of a Member State of nationals or companies of other Member States are prohibited. It is clear from the jurisprudence of the ECJ that the prohibition applies, not just to national provisions which impose direct restrictions on what a person may or may not do, but also to provisions which may have the practical effect of hindering or discouraging nationals or companies of one Member State from establishing themselves, or establishing companies (like subsidiaries, relevantly for this article), in other Member States.

In my earlier capacity as a barrister specialising in revenue law I did not have much to do with the impact of Community law on the direct taxes, but I encountered the subject in connection with a book called *Practitioners' Handbook of EC Law* that was published in 1998 by the Bar Council, Trenton Publishing and the Bar European Group. Although the book was not published until 1998 two other barristers and I had written in 1996 a chapter about taxation and Community law. We referred to the small number of cases which by then had involved issues of Community law and the taxation of companies. One of them was *Halliburton Services BV v Staatsecretaris von* [*sic*] *Financien*,[69] about a Netherlands tax rule whereby Dutch tax arose on a property transaction between the Dutch and German subsidiaries of the same parent company but would not have arisen if both subsidiaries had been Dutch. The rule was held to have infringed the then Articles 52 and 58. We commented:

> 'It is a cast-iron certainty that more cases along these lines will arise, and that rules of UK tax law will be challenged. The UK tax system provides reliefs of various sorts for intra-group transactions where the group members are UK-resident companies. (Transfers of assets without capital gains tax; dividends without paying advance corporation tax; group relief surrenders of tax losses; and many others.) In general these reliefs do not apply between a UK group-member and a non-resident member. If the non-resident is based in another member state the UK tax rule might be challenged by analogy with the *Halliburton* decision (supra). Indeed, some challenges are known already to be in the pipeline, including *ICI v Colmer*, in which the House of Lords has referred certain questions to the ECJ. This is an important area, and major developments over the next few years are expected.'

69 Case C-1/93; [1994] STC 655.

It was not a difficult prediction to make, but it has certainly turned out to be accurate.

ICI v Colmer[70] did indeed go to the ECJ, and the court decided that certain aspects of the UK corporation tax rules for consortium relief were contrary to Community law.

The next major development, still before I was personally involved, was the challenge mounted by several groups to the rules whereby a UK subsidiary of a parent company resident in another Member State (or, for that matter, resident in any State other than the UK) had to pay advance corporation tax (ACT) if it paid a dividend to the parent, whereas a UK subsidiary of a UK parent could make an election for dividends to be paid as group income, and therefore did not have to pay ACT.[71] Questions of the compatibility of that position with Community law were referred to the ECJ by Neuberger J. in 1998 in cases brought by companies in two German-owned groups, the Metallgesellschaft group and the Hoechst group. The ECJ conjoined the two cases, and (as readers of this *Review* will undoubtedly know) decided in March 2001 that it was contrary to Community law for the UK statute to deny the right to make a group income election where the parent company was resident in another Member State.[72] Further, UK subsidiaries which had in the past paid ACT where they ought lawfully to have had the right to pay dividends as group income were in principle entitled to restitution or compensation. The ECJ's role is solely to answer questions of Community law placed before it by national courts. It does not itself decide the cases in relation to which the national courts refer the questions. Accordingly, the consequences of the ECJ's decision fell to be determined in proceedings brought in the UK courts.

So the *Metallgesellschaft* and *Hoechst* cases reverted to the UK courts, where there were in addition many other cases awaiting the outcome in the ECJ. It was soon after that stage that I became personally involved . . .[73] **[18.22]**

Marks and Spencer plc v Halsey (Inspector of Taxes) [2006] Ch 184 (ECJ)

Marks and Spencer, a UK company, had once had French, Belgian and German subsidiaries. The subsidiaries had been unsuccessful and had sustained significant trading losses. The French subsidiary had been sold off and the German and Belgian subsidiaries had stopped trading. The company argued that, under ICTA 1988 ss 402 and 403, it was entitled to set its losses from the subsidiaries against its own profits for corporation tax purposes.[74] The UK government argued that such 'group relief' was available only where the subsidiaries were either 'economically active' or resident in the UK.

70 Case C-264/96; [1998] STC 874. The report of the House of Lords decision which includes the reference of questions to the ECJ is at [1996] STC 352. For further proceedings in the House of Lords after the decision of the ECJ see [1999] STC 1089.

71 [See ICTA 1988, ss 247 and 248, which were repealed by FA 2001.]

72 *Metallgesellschaft Ltd v IRC* and *Hoechst AG v IRC*, conjoined cases C-397/98 and C-410/98; the ECJ judgment is reported, among other places, at [2001] STC 452. . . .

73 Sir Andrew Park, prior to his retirement in 2006, acted as the management judge for the various GLO cases (i.e. the 'ACT GLO', the 'loss relief GLO', the 'thin cap GLO', the 'CFC and EU dividends GLO', the 'FII GLO', and the 'FIDS GLO') which are concerned with challenges to UK corporation tax provisions on the ground that they are incompatible with EC law; see Chapter 3, above, para **[3.1]**.

74 See above, para **[18.19]**.

13 December 2005. THE COURT [OF JUSTICE OF THE EUROPEAN COMMUNITIES] (GRAND CHAMBER) delivered the following judgment in Luxembourg...

27 By its first question, the High Court seeks essentially to ascertain whether articles 43 and 48 EC preclude provisions of a member state which prevent a resident parent company from deducting from its taxable profits losses incurred in another member state by a subsidiary established in that member state although they allow it to deduct losses incurred by a resident subsidiary.

28 In other words, the question is whether such provisions constitute a restriction on freedom of establishment, contrary to articles 43 and 48 EC.

29 In that regard, it must be borne in mind that, according to settled case law, although direct taxation falls within their competence, member states must none the less exercise that competence consistently with Community law: see, in particular, *Metallgesellschaft Ltd v Inland Revenue Comrs* (Joined Cases C-397 and 410/98) [2001] Ch 620, 656, para 37 and the case law there cited.

30 Freedom of establishment, which article 43 EC grants to Community nationals and which includes the right to take up and pursue activities as self-employed persons and to set up and manage undertakings, under the conditions laid down for its own nationals by the law of the member state where such establishment is effected, entails, in accordance with article 48 EC, for companies or firms formed in accordance with the law of a member state and having their registered office, central administration or principal place of business within the European Community, the right to exercise their activity in the member state concerned through a subsidiary, a branch or an agency: see, in particular, *Cie de Saint-Gobain, Zweigniederlassung Deutschland v Finanzamt Aachen-Innenstadt* (Case C-307/97) [1999] ECR I-6161, 6195, para 35.

31 Even though, according to their wording, the provisions concerning freedom of establishment are directed to ensuring that foreign nationals and companies are treated in the host member state in the same way as nationals of that state, they also prohibit the member state of origin from hindering the establishment in another member state of one of its nationals or of a company incorporated under its legislation: see, in particular, *Imperial Chemical Industries plc v Colmer* (Case C-264/96) [1999] 1 WLR 108, 125, para 21.

32 Group relief such as that at issue in the main proceedings constitutes a tax advantage for the companies concerned. By speeding up the relief of the losses of the loss-making companies by allowing them to be set off immediately against the profits of other group companies, such relief confers a cash advantage on the group.

33 The exclusion of such an advantage in respect of the losses incurred by a subsidiary established in another member state which does not conduct any trading activities in the parent company's member state is of such a kind as to hinder the exercise by that parent company of its freedom of establishment, by deterring it from setting up subsidiaries in other member states.

34 It thus constitutes a restriction on freedom of establishment within the meaning of articles 43 and 48, EC, in that it applies different treatment for tax purposes to losses incurred by a resident subsidiary and losses incurred by a non-resident subsidiary.

35 Such a restriction is permissible only if it pursues a legitimate objective compatible with the Treaty and is justified by imperative reasons in the public interest. It is further necessary, in such a case, that its application be appropriate to ensuring the attainment of the objective thus pursued and not go beyond what is necessary to attain it: see, to that effect, *Futura Participations SA v Administration des Contributions* (Case C-250/95) [1997] ECR I-2471, 2500, para 26, and *De Lasteyrie du Saillant v Ministère de l'Economie, des Finances et de l'Industrie* (Case C-9/02) [2004] ECR I-2409, 2453, para 49.

36 The United Kingdom and the other member states which submitted observations in the present proceedings claim that, from the aspect of a group relief system such as that at issue in the main proceedings, resident subsidiaries and non-resident subsidiaries are not in comparable tax situations. In accordance with the principle of territoriality applicable both in international law and in Community law, the member state in which the parent company is established has no tax jurisdiction over non-resident subsidiaries. As regards the latter, tax competence belongs in principle, in accordance with the usual allocation of competence in such matters, to the states on whose territory they are established and carry out commercial activities.

37 In that regard, it must be noted that, in tax law, the taxpayers' residence may constitute a factor that might justify national rules involving different treatment for resident and non-resident taxpayers. However, residence is not always a proper factor for distinction. In effect, acceptance of the proposition that the member state in which a company seeks to establish itself may freely apply to it a different treatment solely by reason of the fact that its seat is situated in another member state would deprive article 43 EC of all meaning: see *Commission of the European Communities v French Republic* (Case 270/83) [1986] ECR 273, 304, para 18.

38 In each specific situation, it is necessary to consider whether the fact that a tax advantage is available solely to resident taxpayers is based on relevant objective elements apt to justify the difference in treatment.

39 In a situation such as that in the proceedings before the national court, it must be accepted that by taxing resident companies on their worldwide profits and non-resident companies solely on the profits from their activities in that state, the parent company's member state is acting in accordance with the principle of territoriality enshrined in international tax law and recognised by Community law: see, in particular, the *Futura Participations* case [1997] ECR I-2471, 2499, para 22.

40 However, the fact that it does not tax the profits of the non-resident subsidiaries of a parent company established on its territory does not in itself justify restricting group relief to losses incurred by resident companies.

41 In order to ascertain whether such a restriction is justified, it is necessary to consider what the consequences would be if an advantage such as that at issue in the main proceedings were to be extended unconditionally.

42 On that point, the United Kingdom and the other member states which submitted observations put forward three factors to justify the restriction.

43 First, in tax matters profits and losses are two sides of the same coin and must be treated symmetrically in the same tax system in order to protect a balanced allocation of the power to impose taxes between the different member states concerned. Secondly, if the losses were taken into consideration in the parent company's member state, they might well be taken into account twice. Thirdly, and last, if the losses were not taken into account in the member state in which the subsidiary was established, there would be a risk of tax avoidance.

44 As regards the first justification, it must be borne in mind that reduction in tax revenue cannot be regarded as an overriding reason in the public interest which may be relied on to justify a measure which is in principle contrary to a fundamental freedom: see, in particular, *Proceedings brought by Manninen* (Case C-319/02) [2005] Ch 236, 259, para 49 and the case law there cited.

45 None the less, as the United Kingdom rightly observes, the preservation of the allocation of the power to impose taxes between member states might make it necessary to apply to the economic activities of companies established in one of those states only the tax rules of that state in respect both of profits and losses.

46 In effect, to give companies the option to have their losses taken into account in the member state in which they were established or in another member state would significantly jeopardise a balanced allocation of the power to impose taxes between member states, as the taxable basis would be increased in the first state and reduced in the second to the extent of the losses transferred.

47 As regards the second justification, relating to the danger that losses would be used twice, it must be accepted that member states must be able to prevent that from occurring.

48 Such a danger does in fact exist if group relief is extended to the losses of non-resident subsidiaries. It is avoided by a rule which precludes relief in respect of those losses.

49 As regards the last, the third, justification, relating to the risk of tax avoidance, it must be accepted that the possibility of transferring the losses incurred by a non-resident company to a resident company entails the risk that, within a group of companies, losses will be transferred to companies established in the member states which apply the highest rates of taxation and in which the tax value of the losses is therefore the highest.

50 To exclude group relief for losses incurred by non-resident subsidiaries prevents such practices, which may be inspired by the realisation that the rates of taxation applied in the various member states vary significantly.

51 In the light of those three justifications, taken together, it must be observed that restrictive provisions such as those at issue in the main proceedings pursue legitimate objectives which are compatible with the Treaty and constitute overriding reasons in the public interest, and that they are apt to ensure the attainment of those objectives.

52 That analysis is not affected by the indications, set out in the second part of the first question, relating to the arrangements applicable in the United Kingdom to the profits and losses of a foreign subsidiary of a company established in that member state, and to the dividends distributed to a company established in that state by a subsidiary established in another member state.

53 None the less, the court must ascertain whether the restrictive measure goes beyond what is necessary to attain the objectives pursued.

54 The claimant and the commission contended that measures less restrictive than a general exclusion from group relief might be envisaged. By way of example, they referred to the possibility of making relief conditional on the foreign subsidiary's having taken full advantage of the possibilities available in its member state of residence of having the losses taken into account. They also referred to the possibility that group relief might be made conditional on the subsequent profits of the non-resident subsidiary being incorporated in the taxable profits of the company which benefited from group relief up to an amount equal to the losses previously set off.

55 In that regard, the court considers that the restrictive measure at issue in the main proceedings goes beyond what is necessary to attain the essential part of the objectives pursued where (i) the non-resident subsidiary has exhausted the possibilities available in its state of residence of having the losses taken into account for the accounting period concerned by the claim for relief and also for previous accounting periods, if necessary by transferring those losses to a third party or by offsetting the losses against the profits made by the subsidiary in previous periods, and (ii) there is no possibility for the foreign subsidiary's losses to be taken into account in its state of residence for future periods either by the subsidiary itself or by a third party, in particular where the subsidiary has been sold to that third party.

56 Where, in one member state, the resident parent company demonstrates to the tax authorities that those conditions are fulfilled, it is contrary to articles 43 EC and 48 EC to preclude the possibility for the parent company to deduct from its taxable profits in that member state the losses incurred by its non-resident subsidiary.

57 It is also important, in that context, to make clear that member states are free to adopt or to maintain in force rules having the specific purpose of precluding from a tax benefit wholly artificial arrangements whose purpose is to circumvent or escape national tax law: see, to that effect, *Imperial Chemical Industries plc v Colmer* (Case C-264/96) [1999] 1 WLR 108, 126, para 26, and *De Lasteyrie du Saillant v Ministère de l'Economie, des Finances et de l'Industrie* (Case C-9/02) [2004] ECR I-2409, 2454, para 50.

58 Furthermore, insofar as it may be possible to identify other, less restrictive measures, such measures in any event require harmonisation rules adopted by the Community legislature.

59 Accordingly, the answer to the first question must be that, as Community law now stands, articles 43 EC and 48 EC do not preclude provisions of a member state which generally prevent a resident parent company from deducting from its taxable profits losses incurred in another member state by a subsidiary established in that member state although they allow it to deduct losses incurred by a resident subsidiary. However, it is contrary to articles 43 EC and 48 EC to prevent the resident parent company from doing so where the non-resident subsidiary has exhausted the possibilities available in its state of residence of having the losses taken into account for the accounting period concerned by the claim for relief and also for previous accounting periods and where there are no possibilities for those losses to be taken into account in its state of residence for future periods either by the subsidiary itself or by a third party, in particular where the subsidiary has been sold to that third party. **[18.23]**

The decision has resulted in changes to the relevant provisions of ICTA 1988.[75] Meanwhile, Park J, following the referral of the case for determination by the UK domestic courts, held that the ECJ's decision means that whilst, in general terms, the residence requirement in the group relief provisions is valid, it is inapplicable where the non-UK resident subsidiary had exhausted all means of relieving the loss in its state of residence.[76] On that basis, the claim in relation to the French subsidiary failed, since the losses had been used by Galeries Lafayette, the company that bought it. The learned judge referred the cases of the Belgian and German subsidiaries to the Special Commissioners for determination. Although Park J's decision was affirmed by the Court of Appeal on 20 February 2007 [2007] EWCA Civ 117 (Chadwick, Tuckey and Jacob LJJ), it is understood that HMRC proposes to appeal to the House of Lords.[77] **[18.24]**

Stephen Bond 'Taxation of multinationals and the ECJ' in Robert Chote, Carl Emmerson, Andrew Leicester and David Miles (eds) *The IFS Green Budget: January 2007* (2007) 178, 179–181

... Landmark legal cases at the ECJ over the last decade have ruled that important elements of the national corporate income taxes of several member states were inconsistent with EU law. This has led to significant tax reforms in a number of EU countries, affecting areas such as the personal taxation of dividends received by shareholders from companies, and anti-avoidance rules that limit the ability of multinational firms to shift their taxable income between countries with different corporate tax rates.

10.3 Controlled Foreign Companies rules

The impact of the ECJ on UK anti-avoidance rules of this kind continued during 2006 with the ruling in a case brought by Cadbury Schweppes concerning the application of UK Controlled Foreign Companies (CFC) rules.[78]

Overseas subsidiaries of UK companies are not normally subject to UK corporation tax. Dividends received by UK parent companies from their overseas subsidiaries are normally subject to UK corporation tax, with credit given for foreign corporate income taxes that have been paid on the underlying profits by the overseas subsidiaries.[79] Companies with subsidiaries in countries with lower corporate tax rates than the UK and that retain profits in those subsidiaries for long periods can thus normally benefit from a significant deferral of taxation at the higher UK rate, compared with a situation in which the same profits are earned (and taxed immediately) in the UK.

The UK, in common with many other countries, applies CFC rules to limit the extent to which parent companies can benefit from this deferral of taxation. For subsidiaries that are located in countries with significantly lower corporate tax

75 See FA 2006, s 27 and Sch 1.

76 See *Marks and Spencer plc v Halsey (Inspector of Taxes)* [2006] EWHC 811 (Ch), [2006] STC 1235.

77 See Chris Morgan and Jonathan Bridges, 'EU Group Relief: The Court of Appeal's decision in *M&S*', *The Tax Journal*, 26 February 2007, pp 4–5.

78 Case C-196/04. [See Case C-196/04, *Cadbury Schweppes plc and another v Inland Revenue Commissioners* [2006] STC 1908. The CFC rules appear in ICTA 1988, ss 747–756 and Sch 24–26 (see **[18.20]** above).]

79 [...]

rates than the UK and that do not meet one of several conditions designed to distinguish between tax avoidance and normal commercial practices, the profits of those subsidiaries may be apportioned back to the UK and taxed as income of the parent company, as if they had been distributed as dividends, whether they are actually distributed as dividends or not.

Many EU countries have their own form of CFC or similar anti-avoidance rules, and their application against subsidiaries located in "tax havens" outside the EU is not subject to EU law. The UK government sought to apply its CFC rules against two subsidiaries of Cadbury Schweppes located in Ireland that did not meet the UK tests for normal commercial entities. At the relevant time, Ireland was an EU member state with a corporation tax rate of 10%, compared with 33% in the UK.[80] The legality of this application of UK CFC rules was challenged by Cadbury Schweppes on several grounds. In a ruling on 13 September 2006, the ECJ judged that the UK CFC legislation breached the Treaty right to freedom of establishment in the Cadbury Schweppes case. However, the ruling indicates that CFC rules could in principle be used against subsidiaries located in other EU member states, if these are 'wholly artificial arrangements aimed solely at escaping national tax normally due'.[81] National courts may determine whether particular subsidiaries conduct genuine business activities (even if these are partly tax-motivated) or are 'wholly artificial arrangements'.

The December 2006 Pre-Budget Report announced changes to UK CFC legislation in order to comply with this ECJ ruling. In effect, this weakens the conditions that subsidiaries located in EU member states must meet in order to be treated as normal commercial entities and not subjected to CFC rules. This change does not directly affect the use of CFC rules against subsidiaries located outside the EU. In the longer term, however, this may allow UK (and other EU) multinational companies to make more effective use of tax havens, by structuring their ownership of subsidiaries in non-EU tax havens to take advantage of EU member states that have relatively weak CFC regimes. This would mean moving profits from a non-EU tax haven to an EU country with weaker CFC rules than the UK, before bringing them into the UK or using them to finance other activities in the multinational group. **[18.25]**

B. Visions of the future

In the light of developments such as those summarised above, various commentators have recently advanced proposals for the harmonisation, or at least the co-ordination, of European corporate taxes.[82] The European Commission has also set up a working group to investigate a 'common consolidated corporate tax base' (CCCTB), progress reports on which were published in April 2006[83] and May 2007.[84] **[18.26]**

80 The current rates are 12.5% in Ireland and 30% in the UK.
81 [...].
82 See Stephen Bond, Lucy Chennells et al *Corporate Tax Harmonisation in Europe: A Guide to the Debate* (2000). Although, it should not be assumed that this is a novel exercise because proposals for corporate tax harmonisation have been put forward from the earliest days of the European Community, see, for example, *The EEC Reports on Tax Harmonisation* (EEC Commission, 1963) and AJ van den Tempel *Corporation Tax and Individual Income Tax in the EC* (EEC Commission, 1970).
83 See Press Release IP/06/448 (5 April 2006).
84 See Press Release IP/07/593 (2 May 2007).

Malcolm Gammie 'Corporate Taxation in Europe – Paths to a Solution' [2001] BTR 233, 244–246

3.3 Options for convergence

... It may be impossible within any realistic time frame to achieve anything that approximates to a common European corporate tax system. It would be wrong to conclude, however, that there is no scope for convergence of corporate tax systems within the community, or that the single market will not eventually dictate that outcome.

... It is possible to contemplate diversity at the outset but the growing integration of the single market will increasingly impose constraints on the tax systems that Member States can maintain. At the same time, the question is whether any, and if so what agreement Member States can reach to accelerate the convergence that the single market will demand, to a point where a common European corporate tax system or EUCIT [*European corporate income tax*] may seem more realistic options.

3.3.1 Optimal common base taxation

One proposal is that Member States could seek to agree an optional common tax base. The idea that underlies this approach is that Member States should agree and adopt a common base but allow businesses to choose whether to use the common base in every Member State or to continue to use the existing 15 domestic tax systems.[85]

It is unclear, however, why Member States should find it easier to agree a common basis for computing taxable profits under this proposal or why having agreed a common measure of profit, they should allow European business the tax planning opportunities inherent in choosing between domestic corporate taxes and the common base.[86] The effect of such a choice would be likely to detract from the objective of achieving a common system as each Member State would have the incentive to ensure that its corporate tax system was more favourable than the common base, to establish a direct claim on corporate tax revenues rather than securing them through a shared tax base with other Member States.

It may well be appropriate to limit any common European corporation tax system to larger companies and to allow Member States to maintain separate systems taxing the profits of small and medium sized enterprises. This would reflect that [*sic*] it may be more appropriate to approximate the taxation of SMEs with personal sector taxation and that for unincorporated businesses rather than with the taxation of European multinationals. This would not be optional in the sense of allowing enterprises the freedom to choose between domestic tax systems and a European corporate tax system. Each system would apply without option to defined categories of business.

85 Among those who have suggested this approach is Assonime, an organisation representing Italian business. This option has also been considered by the European federation of business organisations, UNICE.

86 There are inevitably similar tax planning opportunities under the Home State Taxation system (see 3.3.2 below), which would require Member States to adopt adequate anti-avoidance measures (e.g. to prevent a change in the Home State solely for tax planning reasons). The justification for these aspects of HST, stated in general terms, is that HST assumes that Member States are otherwise unable to agree a common basis for computing profits and that it is the scope for business to choose between different Home State regimes that imposes a market led convergence in corporate tax systems under agreed parameters.

3.3.2 Home State Taxation

The other proposal for convergence is Home State Taxation ("HST").[87] This was the outcome of my work in 1998 at Leiden University[88] and was thereafter taken forward by the Stockholm Group.[89] The essential feature of this proposal is that a company based in the UK (its "Home State") and all its European branches and subsidiaries should be taxed throughout the Community under UK rules. Correspondingly, a company whose Home State (or that of its parent company) is Germany would be taxed under German rules; and so on. In effect, each State would recognise the profit computation rules used by other States, subject to some generally agreed parameters that would ensure a basic similarity without requiring complete uniformity. Member States could modify their rules within those parameters but not to stray outside them.

I propose in this article to do no more than to outline the basic idea that underlies the HST system.[90] The proposal is predicated on the basis that . . . it is not feasible for Member States to agree within a reasonable time frame or in one step a common base for measuring corporate profits. Instead, the HST system . . . [allows] every European company to adopt a single tax regime (that of its or its parent's Home State). It is important to appreciate, however, that the HST system is not advanced as *the* ideal solution for Europe. Instead it is seen as a path to convergence over time without the need for agreement at the outset on every aspect of a common European corporate tax system.

One feature on which the HST system does require initial agreement is a common formula to divide profits.[91] Subject to that, however, to the extent that HST involves mutual recognition of different profit computation rules, it overcomes the objection that there is no one correct method of computation. A market driven process would "select" the tax base that best suits the EU, without requiring tax policy-makers (whose choices may [*sic*] driven by non-optimal considerations) to select ex ante the "optimal tax base"... **[18.27]**

In a communication of January 2006, the European Commission proposed a voluntary system of HST for Small and Medium Enterprises. The Commission's press release summarised the proposal as follows:

> 'The European Commission has adopted a Communication that presents a possible solution to the compliance costs and other company tax difficulties that Small and Medium enterprises (SMEs) face when doing business across borders. The Commission suggests that Member States allow SMEs to compute their company tax profits according to the tax rules of the home state of the parent company or head office. An SME wishing to establish a subsidiary or branch in another Member State would as a result be able to use tax rules and file tax returns in a country with

87 See *Tax Policy in the EU: Priorities for the years ahead,* Communication from the Commission to the Council, the European Parliament and the Economic and Social Committee, Brussels, May 23, 2001, COM(2001) 260 Final at 17.

88 Gammie, "Taxation Issues for the European Company", [1998–3] EC Tax Review, pp. 159–170.

89 Lodin and Gammie, "The Taxation of the European Company", (1999) European Taxation, Volume 39, No 8, pp. 286–294. See now Lodin and Gammie, *Home State Taxation*, IBFD (Amsterdam), 2001.

90 For further detail, see the material previously cited.

91 The proposal is that a value added formula should be used but this would not rule out the adoption [sic] other formulae, such as the two or three factor formulae used in Canada and the US. HST might well be easier to implement if the formula were used to divide *tax revenues* rather than taxable profits. This would, however, necessitate some agreement on a corporate tax rate or on a range of corporate tax rates.

> which it is familiar. The 'Home State Taxation' system would be voluntary for both Member States and companies and would run for a five-year pilot phase. The Commission's 2004 European Tax Survey (see IP/04/1091) showed that cross-border activity leads to higher company tax and VAT compliance costs for companies and that costs are proportionately higher for SMEs than for large companies . . .'[92]

It remains to be seen to what extent, if at all, consensus can be achieved between member states at Community level as to the future development of corporation tax. Undoubtedly, the ECJ will continue to deliver rulings that will materially affect aspects of the corporation tax regimes of individual member states. **[18.28]**

92 The summary in the Press Release of 10 January 2006 (IP/06/11), reproduced at [2006] STI 171–177.

19 Domicile and Residence

1. Introduction

The general scheme of the UK tax system is to tax all income arising in the UK, no matter to whom it belongs, and to tax all residents in the UK, regardless of where their income arises. The residence of the taxpayer is consequently of fundamental importance.[1] In some cases, the taxpayer is only liable if he is not only resident but also 'ordinarily' resident[2] in the UK, or, in other instances, domiciled in the UK. **[19.1]**

Final Report of the Royal Commission on the Taxation of Profits and Income (Cmd 9474 (1955)); below, para [19.7]

Residence, Ordinary Residence, Domicile

The Three Conceptions

279. There are three conceptions which have an effective bearing upon the taxability of a person's overseas income – residence, ordinary residence, domicile. Each presupposes a certain relation to be subsisting between the person concerned and the United Kingdom or another country in the year in which the question of taxing his income arises, and since each requires a different set of facts to support it any one relation can subsist without the others. Thus, a man can be resident in the United Kingdom without being either ordinarily resident or domiciled there: or ordinarily resident there while domiciled in another country.

RESIDENCE

280. The most important of the three conceptions is that of residence. For upon the test whether a man is resident in a particular year will depend the question whether he is to be taxed in respect of that part of it which arises in the United Kingdom. Secondly, personal allowances and reliefs are not available in full to an

1 See First Report of the Royal Commission on the Taxation of Profits and Income, Cmd 8761 (1953), para 8. See also the OECD Model Tax Convention on Income and on Capital, paras 4 and 5: and J F Avery Jones 'Dual Residence of Individuals: The Meaning of the Expressions in the OECD Model Convention' [1981] BTR 15, 104.

2 But liability to capital gains tax depends upon the taxpayer being *either* resident *or* ordinarily resident in the United Kingdom, TCGA 1992, s 2(1).

"individual who is not resident in the United Kingdom."[3] Thirdly, the question of residence is material for some more limited purposes, such as the establishment of title to certain of the double taxation reliefs. **[19.2]**

For some purposes it is not necessary to establish that an individual is both resident and ordinarily resident; a finding that an individual is either resident or ordinarily resident will suffice for liability to tax to arise.[4] For other purposes, an individual must be resident and ordinarily resident for liability to tax to arise.[5] Occasionally, ordinary residence alone will be sufficient to found an individual's liability to tax.[6] Where an individual is resident but not ordinarily resident in the UK he will be chargeable on the remittance basis in respect of foreign income derived from specified sources outside the UK.[7] Similarly, where the duties of an employment are performed wholly outside the UK, an individual who is resident but not ordinarily resident in the UK will be chargeable only on the remittance basis[8], whereas an individual who is neither resident nor ordinarily resident in the UK will not be liable to tax on employment income for duties performed outside the UK.

With regard to domicile,[9] a UK resident, who is not domiciled in the UK, will be taxed on the remittance basis in respect of foreign income derived from those sources specified in ITTOIA 2005, s 830(2).[10] An individual, resident or ordinarily resident but not domiciled in the UK, who makes a capital gain on the disposal of an asset situated outside the UK will be liable to tax on that gain on the remittance basis.[11] The remittance basis will also apply to overseas earnings derived from an employment where all the duties are performed by a UK resident outside the UK, where the taxpayer does not have a UK domicile, and the employer is not UK resident.[12] The domicile of the settlor and the beneficiary of a trust is pertinent to the attribution of trust gains for capital gains tax purposes where the trustees are neither resident nor ordinarily resident in the UK.[13] Inheritance tax is chargeable on all UK

3 See ITA 2007, s 56.
4 For example, in relation to CGT, where a charge to tax arises if the individual is either resident or ordinarily resident in the UK, see TCGA 1992, s 2(1).
5 For example, in relation to the taxation of the general earnings of an employee in accordance with the provisions of ITEPA 2003, ss 21–24.
6 See, for example, ITA 2007, Pt 13 (Tax Avoidance), Ch 2 (Transfer of Assets Abroad), ss 714–751.
7 The 'relevant foreign income' includes, for example, trade profits, profits of property income, overseas property income, dividends from non-UK resident companies, estate income and certain annual payments – see ITTOIA 2005, s 830(1) and (2).
8 See ITEPA 2003, s 26.
9 See the leading texts on private international law, such as Dicey and Morris *The Conflict of Laws* (13th edn, 2000); Cheshire and North *Private International Law* (13th edn, 1999); and Adrian Briggs *The Conflict of Laws* (2002). For a discussion of possible reforms to the law of domicile, see the Law Commission (Working Paper No 88) and the Scottish Law Commission (Consultative Memorandum No 63). See also the Inland Revenue's comments on domicile expressed in the Consultative Document entitled *Residence in the United Kingdom* (1988), below, para **[19.20]**; J J Fawcett 'Law Commission (Working Paper No 88): The Law of Domicile' [1986] MLR 225; P B Carter 'Domicile: The Case for Radical Reform in the U.K.' [1987] ICLQ 713; Dennis Sheridan 'Private International Law: The Law of Domicile: Observations on the Joint Report' [1989] BTR 230; Susan Green 'Domicile and Revenue Law: The Continuing Need for Reform' [1991] BTR 21; and Timothy Lyons 'Reform of the Law of Domicile' [1993] BTR 42.
10 See n 7.
11 See TCGA 1992, s12.
12 See ITEPA 2003, ss 22 and 23(2).
13 See TCGA 1992, ss 86 and 87.

property, and on the worldwide property of an individual domiciled in the UK.[14] An extended definition of domicile is provided for this purpose.[15]

A summary of the residence and domicile rules produced recently by HM Treasury and the Inland Revenue follows. **[19.3]**

HM Treasury and the Inland Revenue: Reviewing the residence and domicile rules as they affect the taxation of individuals: a background paper (April 2003); see below, paras [19.9] and [19.21]

A Summary of the Residence and Domicile Rules

UK Status			Income Tax on Employment	Income Tax on Savings Income	Capital Gains Tax	Inheritance Tax
Resident	**Ordinarily Resident**	**Domiciled**				
√	√	√	Worldwide (1)	Worldwide (2)	Worldwide	Worldwide
√	√	X	Worldwide (1)(3)	Worldwide (2)(4)	Worldwide (4)	UK
√	X	√	Worldwide (5)	Worldwide (2)(6)	Worldwide	Worldwide
√	X	X	Worldwide (5)	Worldwide (2)(4)	Worldwide (4)	UK
X	√	√	Duties performed in the UK	UK Source (7)	Worldwide	Worldwide
X	√	X	Duties performed in the UK	UK Source (7)	Worldwide (4)	UK
X	X	√	Duties performed in the UK	UK Source	None (8)	Worldwide

For Income Tax and Capital Gains Tax all sources are taxed on the full amount of the income or gain arising except:

(1) Foreign Earnings Deduction of 100 per cent may apply – this only applies to seafarers.
(2) Special rules apply for foreign pensions in certain circumstances.
(3) Where an individual is non-domiciled and works for a non-resident company, earnings from employment wholly outside the UK are taxed on the Remittance Basis.
(4) Foreign sources taxed on the Remittance Basis.
(5) Income from duties of employment performed overseas taxed on Remittance Basis.
(6) Commonwealth and Irish citizens taxed on the Remittance Basis for all foreign sources (except Irish sources).
(7) Taxable on UK source income and FOTRAs.
(8) Gains on the disposal of assets used or held etc. for the purposes of a trade carried on in the UK by a branch or agency are chargeable.

[19.4]

2. Residence of individuals

The meaning of residence of an individual for tax purposes is not equated with physical presence. **[19.5]**

14 For consideration of Inheritance Tax, see Chapter 21 below.
15 See IHTA 1984, s 267.

Denzil Davies *Booth: Residence, Domicile and UK Taxation* (9th edn, 2004) p 21

If 'residing' means no more than 'is really there', 'residence' becomes a mere synonym for 'physical presence' and that ... is what Parliament sought to avoid. Presence is an attribute which is far too easily acquired or shed for it to serve as an adequate determinant of chargeability to tax, and residence was chosen to fill that role because of its ability to provide a more enduring territorial link. Residence can play the part assigned to it, however, only if it carries the *first* of the two senses which Rowlatt J has indicated it may bear [i.e. an individual is regarded as 'residing' where he has attributed to himself a quality which makes him describable in that way with reference to a place][16] and, accordingly, the judiciary has consistently held that, in the context of fiscal legislation, 'residence' is to be regarded only 'as signifying an attribute of the person.'[17] **[19.6]**

It is well established that the determination of the residence of an individual is primarily a question of fact.[18] Various factors are considered to be relevant for determining whether or not an individual can be regarded as resident.[19] In a given case, it may also be necessary to decide when that individual becomes[20], or ceases to be, resident.[21] **[19.6a]**

Final Report of the Royal Commission on the Taxation of Profits and Income (Cmd 9474 (1955)); above, para [19.2]

Residence and Ordinary Residence

289. Neither of these conceptions is defined by statute, but "ordinary residence" has been treated in legal decisions as the equivalent of "habitual residence." The two conceptions interact upon each other, sometimes being indistinguishable and sometimes in conflict. Thus, the great majority of persons living in the United Kingdom are both resident and ordinarily resident. On the other hand, a person who comes here from overseas may well be resident without being or having yet become ordinarily resident: so may a person who comes back after an extended period of absence. **[19.7]**

16 [*Levene v IRC* (1928) 13 TC 486 at 492; see below, para **[19.14]**.]
17 *Pickles v. Foulsham* (1923) 9 TC 261, 274 (Rowlatt J).
18 See *Levene v IRC* (1928) 13 TC 486; *IRC v Lysaght* [1928] AC 234, below para **[19.13]**; and *Reed v Clark* [1986] Ch. 1, below para **[19.10]**.
19 These are referred to collectively as "the badges of connection" and are considered under four heads, namely personal connections – substantial presence in the UK, historical connections – ordinary presence in earlier years, continuing connections – regular visits to the UK, and fixed connections – accommodation in the UK in Abimbola A. Olowofoyeku, 'Where is my Home? Reflections on the Law of Residence', [2003] BTR 306.
20 See, for example, *Back v Whitlock* [1932] 1 KB 747.
21 For instances where an individual may cease to be resident, see HM Treasury and the Inland Revenue, *Reviewing the residence and domicile rules as they affect the taxation of individuals: a background* paper, (April, 2003), para 2.5, below para **[19.9]**.

Inland Revenue: IR20 – Residents and non-residents: Liability to tax in the United Kingdom (December, 1999)

Residence and ordinary residence

1.1 The terms '**residence**' and '**ordinary residence**' are not defined by the Taxes Acts. The guidelines to their meaning in this Chapter and in Chapters 2 (residence status of those leaving the UK) and 3 (those coming to the UK) are largely based on rulings of the Courts. This booklet sets out the main factors that are taken into account, but we can only make a decision on your residence status on the facts in your particular case.

As mentioned in paragraph 1.4, even if you are resident (or ordinarily resident) in the UK under these rules, the terms of a double taxation agreement with another country might affect your final tax position if, for example, you are resident in both that country and the UK.

Residence

1.2 To be regarded as **resident** in the UK you must normally be physically present in the country at some time in the tax year.[22] You will always be resident if you are here for **183 days** or more in the tax year. **There are no exceptions to this.** You count the total number of days you spend in the UK – it does not matter if you come and go several times during the year or if you are here for one stay of 183 days or more. If you are here for less than 183 days, you may still be treated as resident for the year under other tests.[23]

The normal rule is that days of arrival in and departure from the UK are **ignored** in counting the days spent in the UK, in all the various cases where calculations have to be made to determine your residence status . . . (This rule is not relevant to the concessionary split year treatment . . . where a person coming to or leaving the UK part way through a tax year is resident from the date of arrival or to the date of departure.)

Ordinary residence

1.3 If you are resident in the UK year after year, you are treated as ordinarily resident here. You may be resident but not ordinarily resident in the UK for a tax year if, for example, you normally live outside the UK but are in this country for 183 days or more in the year. Or you may be ordinarily resident but not resident for a tax year if, for example, you usually live in the UK during that year.

Residence in both the UK and another country

1.4 It is possible to be resident (or ordinarily resident) in both the UK and some other country (or countries) at the same time. If you are resident (or ordinarily resident) in another country, this does not mean that you cannot

22 [But note the arguments advanced by the Inland Revenue in *Reed v Clark* [1986] Ch 1; below, para **[19.10]**.]

23 [For examples of instances in which an individual may be treated as resident under 'other tests', see HM Treasury and the Inland Revenue *Reviewing the residence and domicile rules as they affect the taxation of individuals: a background paper* (April 2003) para 2.4, below para **[19.9]**.]

also be resident (or ordinarily resident) in the UK. Where, however, you are resident both in the UK and a country with which the UK has a **double taxation agreement**, there may be special provisions in the agreement for treating you as a resident of only one of the countries for the purposes of the agreement . . .

Leaving or coming to the UK part way through a tax year

1.5 Strictly, you are taxed as a UK resident for the whole tax year if you are resident here for any part of it. But, if you leave or come to the UK part way through a tax year, the year may, by concession (extra-statutory concession A11), be split. Where this applies, your tax liabilities on income, which are affected by tax residence will be calculated on the basis of the period of your actual residence here during the year. . . This has the same effect as splitting the tax year into resident and non-resident periods. **[19.8]**

HM Treasury and Inland Revenue: Reviewing the residence and domicile rules as they affect the taxation of individuals: a background paper (April 2003); see above, paras [19.4] and below [19.21]

Residence

2.3 The residence basis of taxation defines the individuals who have a liability for tax in the UK. Non-residents are not generally liable to income or capital gains tax, except on income arising in the UK. They may, however, pay VAT and excise duties, and usually pay national insurance contributions on work they do in the UK for a UK employer. Individuals who are, or become, non-resident in the UK may well, of course, be resident and subject to tax in another country. The terms 'resident', 'ordinarily resident' and 'domiciled' are also used for other purposes in income and capital gains tax – for example, the residence, ordinary residence and domicile of a settlor may be material in determining the residence of trustees in particular circumstances . . .

2.4 The circumstances in which individuals are treated as UK resident for tax purposes include the following:

- they spend 183 days or more here in any tax year or more than 90 days on average over a period of up to 4 years;
- they come to the UK intending to live here permanently or for at least three years;
- they come to the UK for a purpose (for example employment) that will mean that they remain here for at least two years (whether or not, in a particular year, they spend 183 days here); and
- they usually live in the UK and go abroad for short periods, for example on business trips.

2.5 People who have been treated as tax resident may lose that status:

- if they leave the UK permanently, or to live abroad for at least three years, and their return visits since leaving are less than 183 days in any tax year, and average less than 91 days per tax year over the period of absence; or
- if they leave the country to take up full time employment abroad and their absence covers a complete tax year, and their return visits do not exceed those set out immediately above.

For the purposes of various day counting tests, days of arrival and departure are not normally taken into account. **[19.9]**

Reed v Clark [1986] Ch 1 (ChD)

During the 1960s, Dave Clark, the taxpayer, had been the leader of a successful band ('The Dave Clark Five'). He retained the copyrights to many of his former band's recordings. In 1977, he agreed to sell certain recording rights to Polydor Ltd for $500,000, but before doing so he took professional advice with a view to mitigating the tax that might be payable by him on the payment of this sum to him by the company. Broadly, he was advised that, in the relevant tax year, he should cease to be resident in the UK (this was to be achieved by his absence from the UK throughout this tax year) and become resident (on the basis of UK tax law) in the USA. In addition, in order to satisfy USA tax law, he was advised that he should receive the payment from Polydor Ltd. prior to 1 January 1978. The taxpayer acted in accordance with this advice. He remained out of the UK for the whole of the relevant tax year, took steps with a view to securing residence and ordinary residence in the USA under UK tax law, and arranged for the payment to be made to him on 19 December 1977. Notwithstanding these arrangements, the taxpayer was assessed to income tax on the payment. The Special Commissioners allowed his appeal and discharged the assessment. The Crown appealed.

NICHOLLS J: ... The taxpayer is a British subject born in London of English parents and domiciled in England. For all years before 1978–79 he was resident and ordinarily resident in the United Kingdom. Before entering into the Polydor agreement, the taxpayer was advised that as he wished in any event to go to the U.S.A. for a protracted period during the year of assessment 1978–79, it would be possible, on the basis of the tax law and practice then in force in the United Kingdom and the U.S.A. for him to avoid tax completely in both countries on the Polydor payment of U.S. $450,000 provided that (a) he did not set foot in the United Kingdom during the year of assessment 1978–79 and became resident (on United Kingdom tax rules) in the U.S.A. for that year, and (b) he received the whole payment prior to 1 January 1978 (to satisfy a requirement of United States tax law). He was also advised that it was desirable, although not essential, that he should have no place of abode available for his use in the United Kingdom during the year of assessment 1978–79. Accordingly, the taxpayer procured that Polydor paid the sum of U.S. $500,000 on 19 December 1977 and he left England and travelled to Los Angeles on 3 April 1978. He did not set foot in England again until 2 May 1979...

...When the taxpayer left the United Kingdom on 3 April 1978 he did so with the firm intention of living in Los Angeles throughout the year of assessment 1978–79. At the time of his departure and throughout his stay in North America it was his firm intention to return to the United Kingdom to reside here shortly after the end of that year. The taxpayer is unmarried. Before he went to America he considered his home to be at a house in Southgate, London which he had bought and given to his parents in 1964. He lived there with his father (until his death in 1976), his mother and a nephew. He also had the use of a leasehold flat in Mayfair which belonged to his company, where he slept when business prevented him from returning home. He instructed a firm of estate agents to sublet the Mayfair flat from the beginning of April 1978 to the end of April 1979, but they were unable to do so and it was unoccupied while he was away. Since his return the taxpayer has had the use of the flat as before, and his home remains at Southgate. While the taxpayer was in America his business interests in the United Kingdom were looked after by his secretary and his accountant, with whom he was in contact by telephone. After his return from the U.S.A. on 2 May 1979 the taxpayer continued to carry on the same profession as before without any cessation. In each of the two years of assessment preceding the year 1978–79 and in each of the three years of assessment following the year 1978–79 the taxpayer spent between 35 and 81 days in North America, and in the year 1982–83 the total rose to 122 days, engaged in work connected with the American market, most of which had to be done in America. For all the years after 1978–79 the taxpayer has been resident and ordinarily resident in the United Kingdom.

The legislation and the commissioners' decision

Next I should refer to the relevant statutory provisions. So far as material to the present case, section 108 of the Income and Corporation Taxes Act 1970 imposes a charge to tax under Schedule D in the following terms:

> "1. Tax under this Schedule shall be charged in respect of – (a) the annual profits or gains arising or accruing – (i) to any person residing in the United Kingdom from any kind of property whatever, whether situated in the United Kingdom or elsewhere, and (ii) to any person residing in the United Kingdom from any trade, profession or vocation, whether carried on in the United Kingdom or elsewhere..."[24]

With that section must be read section 49[25], which appears under the chapter heading "Residence":

> "Every British subject or citizen of the Republic of Ireland shall, if his ordinary residence has been in the United Kingdom be assessed and charged to income tax notwithstanding that at the time the assessment or charge is made he may have left the United Kingdom, if he has so left the United Kingdom for the purpose only of occasional residence abroad, and shall be charged as a person actually residing in the United Kingdom upon the whole amount of his profits and gains, whether they arise from property in the United Kingdom or elsewhere."

For the taxpayer it was conceded that if he was resident in the United Kingdom for 1978–79 he was ordinarily so resident...

...Before the special commissioners, as before me, the Crown mounted a two-pronged attack. The first prong was that, although the taxpayer spent the whole of the relevant year of assessment abroad, nevertheless he was a person residing in the United Kingdom for that year, and as such he was caught by section 108. The commissioners rejected this. The other prong was section 49. The commissioners rejected this argument also, on the ground that the taxpayer did not leave this country for California "for the purpose only of occasional residence abroad." Their conclusion was:

> "[*The taxpayer's*] journey to America on 3 April 1978 was not made as a matter of 'passing opportunity'. His business activities had previously taken him, and still take him, to America every year for varying periods. In April 1978 he had work ahead of him which could occupy him for 12 months in America and did so occupy him, as we have found. On that visit he established himself in a way which would make him resident, and ordinarily resident, there under United Kingdom tax rules. Finally, he was out of this country for the whole tax year which, if not wholly decisive of the question, must be a factor of great importance in the context of an annual tax. Those factors combine, in our opinion, to prevent him from being assessed under section 49 for the year 1978–79."

24 [These provisions were re-enacted subsequently as ICTA 1988, s 18 (1)(a)(i) and (ii) respectively. In respect of the former, see now ITTOIA 2005, ss 269(2), 579(1), 609(1) and 641(1), and in respect of the latter, see now ITTOIA 2005, s 6 (1) and (3).]

25 [See now, ITA 2007, s 829 which provides in respect 'individuals temporarily abroad' as follows:

'(1) This section applies if –
  (a) an individual has left the United Kingdom for the purpose only of occasional residence abroad, and
  (b) at the time of leaving the individual was both UK resident and ordinarily UK resident.

(2) Treat the individual as UK resident for the purpose of determining the individual's liability for income tax for any tax year during the whole or a part of which the individual remains outside the United Kingdom for the purpose only of occasional residence abroad.']

The first point

I turn first to the Crown' argument based on section 108 alone, that is, without regard to section 49. It is now well settled that where a person resides is essentially a question of fact and degree: see, for example, passages in the speeches of Lord Buckmaster and Lord Warrington in *Inland Revenue Commissioners v. Lysaght.*[26] It is also well settled that when commissioners have made findings of fact, their decision is not open to review provided (a) they had before them evidence from which such findings could properly be made and (b) they did not misdirect themselves in law: see Viscount Sumner in *Lysaght's* case.[27]

The Crown's contention was that in the present case the commissioners misdirected themselves in law. A notable feature of the case is that the taxpayer did not set foot in the United Kingdom on any occasion during the tax year 1978–79. In one part of their decision the commissioners stated that, from speeches in *Lysaght's* case and *Levene v. Inland Revenue Commissioners*[28] they drew the conclusion that to be resident in this country for a tax year a person must live here for part of that year, though not necessarily in his own place of abode. The Crown attacked that conclusion as wrong in law, and submitted that this error vitiated the commissioners' findings concerning residence. . .As to case law I was referred to the master mariner's case of *Rogers v. Inland Revenue*[29]. In that case Mr. Rogers was out of Britain for the whole year from April 1878 April 187, in command of a ship on a voyage to the East Indies. He owned a house in Fife where his wife and children lived. In deciding that Mr. Rogers was resident in Great Britain for that year, the Court of Exchequer in Scotland regarded the case as covered by the Court of Exchequer in Scotland in *In re Young*[30], where the taxpayer was a sea captain who had been absent from his family house in Glasgow on voyages abroad for about three-quarters of the year of assessment. The Lord President, Lord Inglis, said that every sailor has a residence on land, Mr. Rogers' residence was in Great Britain, and the fact that Mr. Rogers had been absent during the whole year was of no consequence but a mere accident arising because the exigencies of his business had happened to carry him away for a longer time than usual during the particular voyage. Rogers' case was referred to with apparent approval by Viscount Cave L.C. in *Levene's* case[31], and by Viscount Sumner in *Lysaght's* case.[32]

I was also referred to *Turnbull v. Foster*[33]. There Mr. Turnbull had carried on business for 40 years as a merchant in Madras, where beside his business premises he had a residence in which he usually resided. His wife lived with their children in the United Kingdom, where Mr. Turnbull visited them for a period nearly every year. During the material year Mr. Turnbull was not in the United Kingdom at all, but his wife and eldest daughter were with him in India. The other children lived in the house owned by the wife in Edinburgh. The Court of Exchequer in Scotland held that Mr. Turnbull was not resident in this country during that year. The judgments emphasised that Mr. Turnbull's usual residence, or his "usual place of residence", was in Madras. But neither the Lord Justice-Clerk nor Lord Moncrieff ruled out the possibility that a man who had never been in the country during the year of assessment might nevertheless reside here. Lord MacDonald, said[34] "that would require a pretty strong case indeed." Lord Moncrieff said[35]:

> "During the year of assessment, that is to say ending 5 April 1903, this gentleman was not residing in this country at all. I do not think that that fact taken by itself would be by any means conclusive, because if he had been travelling, or had been a mariner and had been absent the whole of the year, I do not think that would have prevented him from having a residence in this country."

26 [1928] AC 234, 247 & 249.
27 [1928] AC 234, 243; see below, para **[19.13]**.
28 [1928] AC 217; see above, para **[19.6]** and below para **[19.14]**.
29 (1879) 1 TC 225.
30 (1875) 1 TC 57.
31 [1928] AC 217, 223.
32 [1928] AC 234, 244.
33 (1904) 6 TC 206.
34 (1904) 6 TC 206, 209.
35 (1904) 6 TC 206, 210.

In their decision in the present case the commissioners said that, assuming the merchant seamen's cases to have been decided correctly, they constituted an exception to the general rule, probably confined to wanderers with no other place of residence than the base from which they started and to which they would return. Counsel for the Crown criticised this as irrational, because it involved the proposition that a person's absence from the United Kingdom without establishing another place of abode does not terminate his residence in the United Kingdom but that if a person is absent from this country and he does establish another place of abode that does terminate his United Kingdom residence.

On this part of the case the primary submission of counsel for the taxpayer can be summarised as follows. The question to be answered was whether the taxpayer was a person residing in the United Kingdom in the 1978–79 year of assessment. That question was to be answered in the affirmative if he so resided for any part of that year. As Viscount Sumner observed in *Lysaght's* case[36], "resident" indicates a quality of the person charged and is not descriptive of his property: to ask where a person has his residence is often a convenient form of inquiry but only as leading to the question, "then where is he resident himself?" Thus, it was submitted, whilst a person may have more than one residence, in the sense of place of abode, at the same time, and whilst a person may reside in two or more places at different times in one year of assessment, and thus for tax purposes he may reside in more than one country in one year of assessment, he cannot reside in two or more places at one and the same time. Residence requires physical presence. Thus, the argument continued since the Crown accepted that the taxpayer was present, save for his brief visit to Toronto, in the United Sates throughout the year of assessment, and that he resided there throughout the whole year, he could not have resided in the United Kingdom at all in that year. Alternatively, it was submitted that since the commissioners found that the taxpayer was a person who throughout the complete tax year had established his home and place of business in another country and had not visited the United Kingdom at all, they were right to conclude that the exception to the general rule did not apply in this case.

The taxpayer's primary submission is not without its attraction as applied to the facts of the present case. There are, however, dicta which on their ace point in the opposite direction. For example, in *Lysaght's* case Viscount Sumner commented, at p. 245, that in ordinary speech although a man may be the occupier of two houses he is thought of as only resident in the one he lives in at the time in question, but that for income tax purposes such a meaning is misleading. Again, in *Thomson v. Bensted*[37], The Lord Justice-Clerk, Scott-Dickson, said that even if for eight months of the year in question Mr. Thomson resided in West Africa where he actually was and where his place of employment was, that would not preclude him from being also held to reside during those eight months where his wife and family lived in the house in Scotland which he had provided for them as a place of residence.

In my view the correct approach to this case is as follows. The key word "residing" is not defined by the statute. It is now so well settled as to be trite law that in the income tax Acts that word has no special or technical meaning but bears its natural and ordinary meaning in common use in the English Language. On this probably the most frequently quoted passage is from the speech of Viscount Cave L.C. in *Levene's* case[38], where he said:

> "The word 'reside' is a familiar English word and is defined in the *Oxford English Dictionary* as meaning 'to dwell permanently or for a considerable time, to have one's settled or usual abode, to live in or at a particular place'. No doubt this definition must for present purposes be taken subject to any modification which may result from the terms of the Income Tax Act and Schedules; but, subject to that observation, it may be accepted as an accurate indication of the meaning of the word 'reside'."

Thus the task of the fact-finding tribunal in the present case was to consider and weigh all the evidence and then, giving the word "residing" its natural and ordinary meaning, reach

36 [1928] AC 234, 244; below, para **[19.13]**.
37 (1918) 7 TC 137, 145.
38 [1928] AC 217, 222; see below, para **[19.14]**.

a conclusion on the factual question of whether or not the taxpayer was residing in the United Kingdom in the year of assessment. That a taxpayer may reside here although physically absent from this country for the whole year is exemplified by *Roger's* case...

...In the present case the commissioners' formulation of a general rule with an exception for wanderers has made it possible for the Crown to mount its argument that the commissioners erred in law. On reading their decision as a whole, I am not altogether persuaded that this criticism is well-founded, but I do not pause to pursue this further because I do not think that in this case criticism of the commissioners' reasoning leads anywhere, for this reason: I am in no doubt that the true and only reasonable conclusion from the primary facts found by the commissioners was that the taxpayer was not residing in the United Kingdom in the tax year 1978–79. For the whole of that year his home and place of business were in Los Angeles. In my view on the primary facts that conclusion is inescapable.

Section 49[39]

To be within section 49 (i) a person must be a British subject or citizen of the Republic of Ireland (ii) whose ordinary residence has been in the United Kingdom (iii) who has left the United Kingdom at the time the assessment or charge is made (iv) for the purpose only of occasional residence abroad. It was not in dispute that the first three requirements were satisfied in this case. The dispute centred on the fourth requirement and on whether section 49 was a charging provision at all. On this the arguments were wide ranging. Section 49 bears the side note "British subjects etc. temporarily abroad."

[*Nicholls J then decided that the section was a substantive charging section.*]

...I turn next to the contention that section 49 applies only to a temporary absence during the year of assessment and does not apply to an absence extending throughout the whole year...

The approach which I have found most helpful is to start from the contrast which has been commented on more than once, drawn in section 49 itself between ordinary residence and departure abroad for occasional residence. In the section occasional residence is the converse of ordinary residence. This seems to me to conform to the common usage of the phrase "occasional residence": a person's occasional residence is contrasted with his usual, or ordinary, residence. For the meaning of "ordinary residence" one need look no further than the recent decision of the House of Lords in *Reg. v. Barnet London Borough Council, ex parte Nilish Shah.*[40] In that case the issue was the meaning of the phrase "ordinarily resident", in the context of a student's entitlement to receive an educational grant under an Act and regulations excluding a local authority from being under a duty to bestow an award on a person who had not been ordinarily resident in the United Kingdom throughout a specified period of three years. In delivering the leading speech, with which Lord Fraser, Lord Lowry, Lord Roskill and Lord Brandon concurred, Lord Scarman observed[41] that "ordinary residence" was not a term of art in English law and that in *Levene's* case and *Lysaght's* case the House of Lords construed those words in their tax context as bearing their natural and ordinary meaning as words of common usage in the English language. Lord Scarman said:[42]

> "Unless, therefore, it can be shown that the statutory framework or the legal context in which the words are used requires a different meaning, I unhesitatingly subscribe to the view that 'ordinarily resident' refers to a man's abode in a particular place or country which he has adopted voluntarily and for settled purposes as part of the regular order of his life for the time being, whether of short or of long duration."

He added[43] that a settled purpose did not require an intention to stay indefinitely, but that the purpose while settled, might be for a limited period only: "all that is necessary is that

39 [See now ITA 2007, s 829.]
40 [1983] 2 AC 309.
41 *Ibid.*, at 341.
42 *Ibid.*, at 343.
43 *Ibid.*, at 344.

the purpose of living where one does has a sufficient degree of continuity to be properly described as settled."

On that basis it seems to me plain that a British resident's departure abroad for a period of a few weeks or months with the firm intention of returning at the end of the period to live here as before would be likely always to be for the purpose only of occasional residence. At the opposite end of the scale, it seems to me equally plain that the departure of such a resident abroad for a limited period of, say, three years would not necessarily be for the purpose only of "occasional residence" just because from the outset he had a firm intention of returning at the end of the period to live here as before: "not necessarily," because all the circumstances would have to be considered. *Inland Revenue Commissioners v. Combe*[44] is an example of this, where on the facts Captain Combe's business and residential headquarters were permanently in New York throughout the three years. For my part I think this latter conclusion is also true of residence abroad for just over one year in duration. The difference between these examples is one of degree, and there is an area in which different minds may reach different conclusions. In my view a year is a long enough period for a person's purpose of living where he does to be capable of having a sufficient degree of continuity for it to be properly described as settled. Hence, depending on all the circumstances, the foreign country could be the place where for that period he would be ordinarily and not just occasionally resident. I appreciate that this construction may give little scope in practice for the operation of section 49 as an independent charging provision. But having regard to the origin of the section in the earliest days of income tax at the end of the 18th century I do not find this consideration sufficiently compelling to require the language in section 49 to be given some different meaning.

I turn to the facts in the present case. The Crown submitted that the salient features were that the taxpayer, a British subject, had always lived predominantly in the United Kingdom until late in the tax year 1977–78, and that he has always lived predominantly in the United Kingdom from early in the tax year 1979–80. When the taxpayer left on 3 April 1978 he intended to return a little over a year later and in the event he did so. Thus his absence was inherently limited, inherently temporary. It was further submitted that during his absence his established domestic and business arrangements in this country were maintained to such a degree that on his anticipated return his ordinary pattern of life could be resumed, and in the event it was resumed as before, without any significant disruption. Pausing there, I think that all those features may and often will be present in the case of a British subject ordinarily resident here who leaves to take up a job or pursue a training course abroad for one year with the firm intention of returning. The Crown also submitted, and I suspect that this submission reaches nearer to the heart of what the present case is all about, that there was an artificiality and contrivance in the length of the taxpayer's absence and in the timing of his departure and return: the dates had been carefully chosen with United Kingdom income tax in mind, the object being to avoid bringing into charge. . .the Polydor payment of $450,000[45] received in the preceding year.

. . .In this case the position, as I see it, is that when deciding issues of residence, ordinary residence and occasional residence all the reasons, including any desire to avoid a liability to United Kingdom income tax, underlying a person's being in a particular place are part of the overall picture. They are part of the material to be looked at and considered when deciding those issues. The presence of a tax avoidance intention may help to show, for instance, why a person went abroad at all, or at the particular time he did, how long he intended to remain away, or where his home in fact was in the year of assessment. But residence abroad for a carefully chosen limited period of work there, if that is what the facts establish, is no less residence abroad for that period because the major reason for it was the avoidance of tax. Likewise with ordinary residence.

In this case there was a distinct break in the pattern of the taxpayer's life which lasted, as from the outset he intended, for just over a year. He ceased living in London and for that year he lived in or near Los Angeles, mostly in one fixed place of abode, and he

44 (1932) 17 TC 405.

45 [Ie that part of the payment of $500,000 which was attributable to recordings belonging to the taxpayer individually.]

worked from there. For that year Los Angeles was his headquarters. He did not visit this country at all. On the whole I do not think that he can be said to have left the United Kingdom for the purpose only of occasional residence abroad. In my judgment the conclusion of the commissioners on this was correct...

In the result the appeal fails. **[19.10]**

3. Ordinary residence

There is no statutory definition of 'ordinary residence' for tax purposes, and it is not a legal term of art.[46] Consequently, the courts have sought to attribute to these words their natural and ordinary meaning.[47] In this respect, as seen above, 'ordinary residence' has been referred to as 'a man's abode in a particular place or country which he has adopted voluntarily and for settled purposes as part of the regular order of his life'.[48] **[19.11]**

Reid v IRC (1926) 10 TC 673 (CS)

CLYDE LP:...What is meant by saying that a person is "resident" in the United Kingdom?- and when is a person "ordinarily resident" there ? It is obvious that the more general and wide the scope of expressions used in a statute, the more difficult it may become to convict those whose duty it is to interpret it of an error or misdirection in applying it to a given state of facts. It may be possible in such cases to predicate of a particular state of facts that they lie outside the scope of the expressions used, although it may be really an impossible task to define that scope positively and with exact accuracy. The expression "resident in the United Kingdom" and the qualification of that expression implied in the word "ordinarily" so resident are just about as wide and general and difficult to define with positive precision as any that could have been used. The result is to make the question of law become (as it were) so attenuated, and the field occupied by the questions of fact become so enlarged, as to make it difficult to say that a decision arrived at by the Commissioners with respect to a particular state of facts held proved by them, is wrong.

...Take the case of the homeless tramp, who shelters tonight under a bridge, tomorrow in the greenwood and as the unwelcome occupant of a farm outhouse the night after. He wanders in this way all over the United Kingdom. But will anyone say he does not *live* in the United Kingdom? – and will anyone regard it as a misuse of language to say he *resides* in the United Kingdom? In this case there may be no relations with family or friends, no business ties, and none of the ordinary circumstances which create a link between the life of a British subject and the United Kingdom; but, even so, I do not think it could be disputed that he *resides* in the United Kingdom...

Now, the appellant – a lady of independent means – has, partly, on account of consideration of health, been for many years past in the habit of going abroad for the larger portion of the year, and spending only the summer months (say three and a half months) in the United Kingdom. In 1916, owing to the death of a sister, she and her only surviving sister gave up their house in Scotland, and sold their furniture. The surviving sister went to London, and the appellant also removed there, living in various London hotels until July 1919. Since about that time – the war being ended and travelling abroad having become possible – she has reverted to her former mode of life, and has moved about between various places on the Continent of Europe for about eight and a half months of each year, returning to this country for the remaining three and a half months.

46 See above, para **[19.7]**.

47 Thus, the courts have tended to treat 'ordinary residence' and 'habitual residence' as synonymous. See, for example, *Ikimi v Ikimi* [2001] 3 WLR 672, and *Mark v Mark* [2005] 3 WLR 111.

48 *R v Barnet London Borough Council, ex p Shah* [1983] 2 AC 309 at 343 (Lord Scarman discussed in *Reed v Clark* [1986] Ch 1); see above, para **[19.10]**.

This applies to each of the two tax years to which the present appeal relates. The appellant is a British subject, her family ties are with this country; her business matters (including her banking) are conducted here; the address by which she can be found at any time is in this country; and her personal belongings not required when she is travelling are kept in store in London.

It was contended on her behalf that, even if these facts are consistent with her being held to "reside" in the United Kingdom, they are inconsistent with the view that she "ordinarily" so resides. And, here again, the argument was that the meaning of the word "ordinarily" is governed – wholly or mainly – by the test of time or duration. I think it is a test, and an important one; but I think it is only one among many. From the point of view of time, "ordinarily" would stand in contrast to "casually." But the appellant is not a "casual" visitor to her home country; on the contrary she regularly returns to it, and "resides" in it for a part – albeit the smaller part – of every year. I hesitate to give the word "ordinarily" any more precise interpretation than "in the customary course of events," and anyhow, I cannot think that the element of time so predominates in its meaning that, unless the appellant "resided" in the United Kingdom for at least six months and a day, she could not be said "ordinarily" to reside there in the year in question. A more plausible way of presenting the same argument was used by the appellant's counsel, who maintained that the appellant "ordinarily resided" on the Continent rather than in this country, inasmuch as she spent nearly three times as much of her life abroad as here. I am not sure that there is anything impossible in a person "ordinarily residing" in two places, although no doubt he cannot physically be present in more than one place at the same time...[K]eeping in mind the qualities as well as the durability of the relation between a person and the place (here the United Kingdom) in which he "resides," I find myself unable to affirm that the Commissioners were mistaken in law in regarding the circumstances of the appellant's life in the two tax years ended 5th April 1921, as putting her within the category of a person "ordinarily resident" in the United Kingdom. **[19.12]**

IRC v Lysaght [1928] AC 234 (HL)

VISCOUNT SUMNER:...My Lords, the word "ordinarily" may be taken first. The Act on the one hand does not say "usually" or "most of the time" or "exclusively" or "principally" nor does it say on the other hand "occasionally" or "exceptionally" or "now and then," though in various sections it applies to the word "resident," with a full sense of choice, adverbs like "temporarily" and "actually." I think the converse to "ordinarily" is "extraordinarily" and that part of the regular order of a man's life, adopted voluntarily and for purposes, is not "extraordinary." **[19.13]**

Levene v IRC (1927) 13 TC 486 at 493 (KBD); (1927) 13 TC 495 at 496 (CA); (1927) 13 TC 486 at 509 (HL); see also, para [3.13] and below, para [19.18]

ROWLATT J:...Now it seems to me what the phrase "ordinary residence" means is this: I think that "ordinary" does not mean preponderating, I think it means ordinary in the sense that it habitual in the ordinary course of a man's life, and I think a man is ordinarily resident in the United Kingdom when the ordinary course of his life is such that it discloses a residence in the United Kingdom, and it might disclose a residence elsewhere at the same time. Therefore, I think, as has been thought in Scotland that a man can have two ordinary residences not because he commonly is to be found at those places, but because the ordinary course of his life is such that he acquires the attribute of residence at those two places...

LORD HANWORTH MR:...I find it difficult to attach any distinction of meaning to the word "ordinarily" as affecting the term "resident," unless it be to prevent facts which would amount to residence being so estimated, on the ground that they arose from some fortuitous cause, such as illness of the so-called resident or of some person, which demanded his continuance at a place for a special purpose otherwise than in accordance with his usual arrangement and shaping of his movements...

LORD WARRINGTON OF CLYFFE:...I do not attempt to give any definition of the word "resident." In my opinion, it has no technical or special meaning for the purposes of the Income Tax Act. "Ordinarily resident" also seems to me to have no such technical or special meaning. In particular it is in my opinion impossible to restrict its connotation to its duration. A member of this House may well be said to be ordinarily resident in London during the parliamentary session and in the country during the recess. If it has any definite meaning I should say it means according to the way in which a man's life is usually ordered...[49] **[19.14]**

An individual, who comes to the UK and whose home is or has been elsewhere, will normally, as a matter of practice, be regarded by HMRC as ordinarily resident in the UK from the beginning of the tax year in which he has been in the UK for three years. However, such an individual may be treated by HMRC as ordinarily resident in the UK from the date of his arrival in the UK if it is clear when he arrives that either he intends to take up permanent residence in the UK or he intends to come and remain in the UK for three years or more.[50] **[19.15]**

Inland Revenue: Residence in the UK: when ordinary residence is regarded as commencing where the period to be spent here is less than three years (SP 17/91)

1 The Income and Corporation Taxes Acts do not define the term "ordinary residence". The rules for determining the ordinary residence of an individual have been based on decisions of the courts.

2 Where an individual comes to, and remains in, the UK but does not intend to stay for at least three years and accommodation is not bought or acquired on a lease of three years or more, that individual is treated as becoming ordinarily resident from the beginning of the tax year after the third anniversary of arrival.

3 Where any individual comes to the UK and, before the beginning of the tax year after the third anniversary of arrival, either purchases or acquires on a lease of three years or more accommodation for use in the UK or has change of intention concerning the length of stay, ordinary residence will commence –

- from the day of arrival if one of the above events occurs in the tax year of arrival, or
- from the beginning of the tax year in which one of the above events occurs.

49 [For consideration of the cases relating to ordinary residence, see P St J Smart 'Ordinary Resident: Temporary Presence and Prolonged Absence' [1989] ICLQ 175 and J L Wosner 'Ordinary Residence, the Law and Practice [1983] BTR 347.]

50 See Inland Revenue, *IR20 – Residents and non-residents: Liability to tax in the United Kingdom* (December 1999), para 3.1. For criticism of HMRC's practice in relation to ordinary residence of placing reliance on an individual's future intent or expectations, see Denzil Davies *Booth: Residence, Domicile and UK Taxation* (9th edn, 2004), para **[19.6]**. See also *Nessa v Chief Adjudication Officer* [1999] 1 WLR 1937 in which the House of Lords decided that an individual could not be regarded as 'habitually resident in the UK' for the purposes of entitlement to income support under the Income Support (General) Regulations 1987 unless he had in fact taken up residence and lived in the UK for a period which showed that the residence had become, and was likely to continue to be, habitual.

For example, if an individual arrives in the UK in January 1992 and purchases accommodation here in May 1993, ordinary residence commences from 6 April 1993.[51] **[19.16]**

4. Commentary on and criticisms of the present system as it applies to individuals

The following extracts are illustrative of long-standing concerns about the rules for determining the residence and/or domicile of an individual for tax purposes, and, in the latter instances, express the views of the authors of the respective documents as to the criteria/principles that should inform attempts to address those concerns. **[19.17]**

Levene v IRC (1927) 13 TC 486 at 502 (HL); see above, paras [3.13] and [19.14]

VISCOUNT SUMNER:. . .[T]he subject ought to be told, in statutory and plain terms, when he is chargeable and when he is not. The words "resident in the United Kingdom", "ordinarily" or otherwise, and the words "leaving the United Kingdom for the purpose only of occasional residence abroad", simple as they look, guide the subject remarkably little as to the limits within which he must pay and beyond which he is free. This is the more likely to be a subject of grievance and to provoke a sense of injustice when, as is now the case, the facility of communications, the fluid and restless character of social habits, and the pressure of taxation have made these intricate and doubtful questions of residence important and urgent in a manner undreamt of by Mr. Pitt, Mr. Addington or Sir Robert Peel.[52] The Legislature has, however, left the language of the Acts substantially as it was in their days, nor can I confidently say that the decided cases have always illuminated matters. In substance persons are chargeable or exempt, as the case may be, according as they are deemed by this body of Commissioners or that to be resident or the reverse, whatever resident may mean in the particular circumstances of each case. The tribunal thus provided is neither bound by the findings of other similar tribunals in other cases nor is it open to review, so long as it commits no palpable error of law, and the Legislature practically transfers to it the function of imposing taxes on individuals, since it empowers them in terms so general that no one can be certainly advised in advance whether he must pay or can escape payment. The way of taxpayers is hard and the Legislature does not go out of its way to make it any easier. **[19.18]**

Report of the Committee on Codification of Income Tax Law (Cmnd 5.31 (1936))

59. We are fully conscious of the complexities which surround this question [of determining the residence of an individual] and of the advantages which, from the point of view of a taxing authority, lie in the absence of a statutory definition [of residence]. We are, however, of the opinion that the present state of affairs, under which an enquirer can only be told that the question whether he is resident or not

51 For the circumstances in which a short-term visitor to the UK may be regarded as ordinarily resident in the UK, see Inland Revenue, *IR20 – Residents and non-residents: Liability to tax in the United Kingdom* (December, 1999), paras 3.4–3.6.

52 [The founders of the income tax.]

is a question of fact for the Commissioners, but that by the study of the effect of a large body of case law he may be able to make an intelligent forecast of their decision, is intolerable and should not be allowed to continue. **[19.19]**

Inland Revenue: Residence in the United Kingdom

A Consultative Document (1988)

3. Relevant Criteria

3.1 In considering whether any changes should be made to the present system, it is desirable to set out some yardsticks against which the present system and any proposals for change, can be measured.
3.2 In the broad context of residence, so far as practicable, a tax system should, inter alia, satisfy the following criteria:-

(i) **Fairness and Equity** – it should in principle bear less heavily on those whose connection with the United Kingdom is limited, than on those with permanent and substantial connections with this country; and people in similar circumstances should be liable to a similar extent.

(ii) **Neutrality** – it should not needlessly discourage people from coming to live and invest in this country or encourage people already living here to invest abroad or to leave; any incentives provided by the tax system for particular groups of taxpayers or in relation to certain types of income, should be intentional and specifically targeted.

(iii) **Simplicity and Certainty** – the rules for determining liability should be as clear as possible and based on objective tests. The taxpayer should be able to ascertain his position reasonably quickly and easily and should not have to incur undue expenditure in complying with the law. Similarly, the rules ought to be readily applicable by the tax authority with the minimum of administrative cost.

(iv) **Enforceability** – whatever rules are laid down should be capable of being reasonably enforced.

3.3 In practice, it is unlikely that all these criteria can be satisfied – at least to the same degree – but they are all relevant in judging the existing rules and any proposals for changing them.

4. Criticisms of the Existing System

4.1 In recent years, there has been increasing criticism of the difficulties which a taxpayer may have of knowing under the present system exactly what his status is and therefore of determining his liability to United Kingdom tax. The main criticisms have centred on the following areas:

(i) Lack of Statutory Guidance
4.2 There is a lack of statutory guidance on the meaning of the terms which determine liability to UK tax. Statute law dating from 1799 and Court decisions mostly from the period 1880–1940 are generally regarded as of diminishing value in dealing with a very different world in which there is increasing international mobility of labour and capital and communications between countries are both easy and almost instantaneous. It has been suggested that the Inland Revenue booklet on the subject (IR 20) has, in effect, come to fill the gaps in the law, although it is, of course, not intended to be anything more than a general guide to the way in which the law is interpreted and applied: nor indeed could it be anything other than that under the law.

(ii) Complexity

4.3 Over the years, the UK system has become increasingly complicated. With three main determining factors – residence, ordinary residence and domicile – it is possible to have eight different combinations, each giving rise to a different set of liabilities and title to relief. If an individual's nationality and his employer's residence status are also taken into account there are even more combinations. . . This contrasts with the residence rules which apply in other major countries.[53]

(iii) Uneven Impact

4.4 The present rules bear harshly in some instances and generously in others. The existence of accommodation available for someone's use may make him resident for a year even if he is in the United Kingdom for only one day. . . The rule is criticised because it does not take account of the possibility that many visitors to the United Kingdom consider that buying a house or flat meets their requirements better than the alternatives.[54]

4.5 When an individual arrives in or leaves this country, that day is not counted in calculating the time he has spent here in that particular year.[55] This practice is more generous than the law requires particularly for people making a lot of short visits. At the extreme it is possible for an individual to be in the United Kingdom on every day of the year and not be treated as resident so long as he is absent for a few hours on at least half of them. Similarly, an individual could be in the United Kingdom for almost three-quarters of every year for four consecutive years and not be treated as resident here for tax purposes. Not only is the present practice complicated to understand and apply therefore, but the result may often appear arbitrary.

4.6 Where it is necessary to go beyond the counting of the days in order to determine residence, an individual's mode and habits of life over several years may be relevant; much may then depend on his stated intentions. This introduces an element of subjectivity into the determination of his status. It may be necessary for example, to examine a person's activities for a period of years both before and after the year in question. Such an enquiry means that decisions must be provisional and liabilities may remain unsettled for a number of years. This practice in this area can be contrasted with what a judge has recently called the "normal approach of a taxing statute" which he said is to "make the amount of tax assessable by reference to objective criteria."[56]

(iv) Unsuitability of Domicile

4.7 It is said that domicile is unsuitable for defining the scope of liability to an annual tax, since it often requires a consideration of a person's life history and long

53 [For a recent survey of the rules and procedures for determining 'residence' in member states of the Organization for Economic Cooperation and Development (OECD), see HM Treasury and the Inland Revenue *Reviewing the residence and domicile rules as they affect the taxation of individuals: a background paper* (April 2003) ch 3, pp 11–22.]

54 [Subsequently, the importance of the availability of living accommodation has been considerably diminished. See ITA 2007, s 831 which provides that the availability of any living accommodation shall be ignored in determining whether an individual is in the UK for some temporary purpose and not with a view to establishing residence in the UK. See also ITA 2007, s 830 (residence of individuals working abroad).]

55 [For confirmation that this remains the current practice, see Inland Revenue, *IR 20 – Residents and non-residents: Liability to tax in the United Kingdom* (December 1999), para 1.2, see above para **[19.8]**.]

56 *Per* Browne-Wilkinson L.J. in *Varnam v. Deeble* (1985) 58 T.C. 501 at 517.

term intentions. It might be considered appropriate for a tax such as inheritance tax which is charged on the assets a person has acquired over the whole of his life. But even for this purpose the law recognises that, after a long period of years of continuous residence, an individual's connection with this country has become sufficiently close to justify complete worldwide taxation even if he has not become domiciled here.

4.8 Domicile can also be capricious in its effects. An individual's domicile of origin is determined by reference to that of his parents. A person may be domiciled in a country which he has never visited because only one domicile is possible at any one time and a domicile of origin is difficult to shed. Thus, an individual may not be domiciled in this country even if he was born in the United Kingdom, has lived in this country all his life and holds a British passport. But he will be taxed differently from his neighbour who is in all respects the same except that he has a UK domicile.

4.9 The relevance of domicile runs wider than tax; it also affects matters such as marriage and divorce. As the law stands, any changes in the general law of domicile, such as that brought about by the Domicile and Matrimonial Acts 1973, automatically affect taxation. The Law Commission and the Scottish Law Commission[57] have recently reviewed the law of domicile and suggested some changes. They concluded that their recommendations were unlikely to have a significant impact on taxation. But that if justified anxieties did arise, the continued use of domicile for taxation purposes should be reconsidered...

(vi) Defects of the Remittance Basis[58]

4.13 As indicated earlier, some individuals are liable to UK tax on various bases falling between tax on worldwide income and gains, and tax on income gains from a UK source only. Probably the most significant of these is the remittance basis – under which the liability to tax is based on the "sums received in the United Kingdom."[59]

4.14 At present, it is primarily those who are not domiciled in this country who pay tax on the remittance basis...[I]t is also available to certain categories of UK domiciled individuals who are not ordinarily resident in this country.[60] In practice, this basis suffers from three major drawbacks.

4.15 First, the broad definition of remittance in the Taxes Act and the wide interpretation which has been given to it by the Courts make it extremely difficult for a taxpayer to calculate his own liability; effectively, it requires an analysis each year of almost every financial transaction undertaken.

4.16 It may, for example, be necessary to follow income as it arises through a number of different bank accounts to its final destination. The compliance burden on the taxpayer can be substantial. An Inspector of Taxes faces equal difficulty when examining tax returns if he has reason to suspect that the full amount remitted has not been disclosed.

4.17 Second, it encourages the setting up of arrangements overseas – which may be more or less artificial – in order to secure effective exemption on income which is in reality related to a UK employment, and which would otherwise be taxed in full.

57 In Working Paper No. 88 and Consultative Memorandum No. 63: Private International Law: The Law of Domicile (1985).

58 [For provisions relating to the remittance basis, see ITTOIA 2005, Pt 8 (Foreign Income: Special Rules), ss 829–845.]

59 [See now ITTOIA 2005, s 832(1).]

60 [Ibid, ss 831–832.]

4.18 Third, it is easy for the well advised to arrange to bring back money from overseas to meet their expenditure in the United Kingdom without it being regarded under the present law as a "remittance." These arrangements include:

– opening separate accounts for capital and income and remitting only from the capital account; and
– closing an account or selling an income producing asset in one year, and remitting accumulated income in the next when there is no longer a source of income that can be charged to tax.[61]

5. Evaluation of the Existing System

5.1 When set against the criteria outlined in section 3 above, the present system is open to a number of criticisms. These include the lack of:

– equity. . .the availability of the remittance basis for individuals who are not domiciled in this country means that for a particular group of long term residents here, tax on overseas income and gains is effectively a voluntary tax. . .As a result, there are people with the closest possible connections with this country who pay tax only on their UK income. . .
– neutrality. The remittance basis also operates to bias the non-UK domiciled long term resident towards overseas as against domestic investment. An imbalance also results from the ability to avoid a charge to capital gains tax on assets that have accrued in value over a long period while a taxpayer was resident, by their realisation shortly after departure from the United Kingdom for a relatively short term assignment abroad.[62] A similar result can be achieved with certain income receipts.
– simplicity and certainty. The law on residence consists of a complex set of rules attempting to codify ancient case law and sketchy statutes. It can be difficult for a taxpayer to know his status for a particular year and it may take several years before a definitive ruling can be given. A detailed examination of a person's life style and financial affairs may be necessary in which intentions and motives may be relevant.
– enforceability. The remittance basis in its present form is extremely difficult to apply in practice. In terms of enforcing liabilities, however, to the Rules of the Supreme Court have made it easier for writs and bankruptcy petitions to be served on those living outside the United Kingdom. . . **[19.20]**

Notwithstanding the penetrating critique of the fundamental concepts underlying the system that is apparent in the above extract, no radical reform followed.[63] In the event, a further review of the residence and domicile rules as they affect the taxation of individuals was announced by the Chancellor of the Exchequer, the Right Honourable Gordon Brown MP, in 2002. The ensuing Background Paper, *"Reviewing the residence and domicile rules as they affect the taxation of individuals"* (from which extracts are set out earlier in this chapter[64] and below) was written by HM Treasury and the Inland Revenue and published in 2003. Its object was to encourage 'a process of informed debate'

61 [For further observations on the remittance basis, see Chapter 7, below, para **[7.18]**.]
62 [The ability of a taxpayer to avoid a charge to capital gains tax in this way has been restricted by TCGA 1992, s 10A (introduced by FA 1998, s 127), and in accordance with the subsequent amendment of this provision by FA 2005, s 32.]
63 Subsequent measures were directed solely towards rectifying some of the specific shortcomings highlighted in the Consultative Document, see, for example, the provisions referred to in footnotes 54 and 62.
64 See para **[19.4]** and para **[19.9]** above.

based on the principles set out below, which were intended to 'underpin any modernisation'.[65] **[19.20a]**

HM Treasury and the Inland Revenue: Reviewing the residence and domicile rules as they affect the taxation of individuals: a background paper (April, 2003); see above, para [19.9]

KEY PRINCIPLES

Globalisation and the taxation of income

4.1 Globalisation is creating new challenges for governments in many fields of public policy, and forcing them to modernise aspects of policy and practice that have stood for generations. The tax system is no exception.

4.2 Considerable attention has been paid to the implications of globalisation for the taxation of capital markets, and a number of principles and approaches have been developed at the national and international levels in response; for example through the work of the OECD. The globalisation of capital and labour markets also carries implications for personal taxation systems. A number of labour markets are already internationalised, particularly in occupations requiring skills in very scarce supply. This is especially true in the market for entrepreneurs and senior managers, employment closely linked to international financial markets, and in certain occupations linked to international travel and communication. The globalisation of capital markets is also creating opportunities for high-net-worth individuals, with income from a highly diversified portfolio of international assets, to have highly flexible links between the focus of their economic activity and any concept of citizenship or residence. The implications of these trends for the taxation of the income of individuals have typically received less attention.

4.3 It is clear, therefore, that the arrangements for personal taxation need to be assessed against these developments, including:

- the definition of the relevant tax base, and the nature of the tax liability incurred by economic activity which transcends national boundaries;
- arrangements for determining the taxing rights of individual nation states over income earned by internationally mobile individuals, or those with world-wide income; and
- the approach to defining the obligations of individuals to contribute to the public services in the states in which they are resident.

4.4 These considerations need to be reflected in the rules governing the residence and domicile of individuals, which determine the scope of personal income taxes in the UK...

4.5 In determining these parameters, and applying them in the UK's system, Budget 2002 set out the following principles for any new rules; they:

- should be fair;

65 The reasons cited for the perceived inappropriateness of the rules for determining the residence and domicile of an individual for tax purposes, namely that they 'have developed over the past 200 years, are complex and poorly understood, and do not reflect the reality of today's more integrated world' (see, para 1.2) are not noticeably dissimilar to the reservations about the rules for determining residence identified by Viscount Sumner in the 1920s in *Levene v. IRC* (see above, para **[19.18]**).

- should support the competitiveness of the UK economy; and
- should be clear and easy to operate.

Fairness

4.6 It is generally accepted as fair that those with the same characteristics are taxed in the same way. In the context of residence and domicile, the degree of connection of an individual to a country is an important characteristic, which may vary in intensity and over time. It is also generally accepted as fair that those with a long-term connection owe a special obligation to support the social structures of the state. It is therefore necessary for governments to define the degree of long-term connection which is sufficient to generate this special obligation, and to set criteria for determining when that long-term connection is made, severed or suspended; for example, in cases where people with a long-term connection are temporarily absent.

4.7 At any point in time, a person with a long-term connection to one state may be present, or engage in forms of economic activity in other states. The tax system therefore needs to establish conditions under which a presence, or degree of economic activity, in the country is sufficient to give rise to particular obligations to the tax system.

4.8 The rules need to be applied within this to the taxation of employment income, and of savings income and gains. Their application to savings income is inherently more complex, for example because of the greater mobility of savings, which are more likely to arise across international borders; while the taxation of employment activities will usually be linked to the same geographical location as the person earning the income.

Competitiveness

4.9 The Government is committed to ensuring that the tax system supports the competitiveness of the UK economy. An assessment of the residence and domicile rules therefore needs to take into account the economic impact of any change, including the impact on the ability of UK employers to attract employees from overseas.

4.10 It is important that public policy plays a part in facilitating the international integration of labour markets and the spread of entrepreneurship. Migration – at all levels – can help match the supply and demand for skills, and provide a more flexible labour market response to economic cycles. Cross-border labour mobility can also help to encourage the spread of knowledge, innovation and enterprise. The UK economy is well placed to benefit from this global trend, and a range of factors helps to make the UK an attractive place for foreigners to live, and thus create wealth and contribute to a productive and efficient economy. These include the benefits of economic stability, the UK's labour force, the English language, access to EU markets, access to one of the world's largest financial centres, incentives provided by development agencies, our corporation tax regime and tax treaty network. The residence and domicile rules are part of this framework...

4.11 There are a number of economic instruments that can be directed at securing the optimal level of inward migration, and do so in a manner which contributes most to the economy. It is therefore important to establish the principles that should govern the contribution that the tax system can make, and the factors that may limit the extent to which the tax system is an appropriate instrument. Economic incentives operating through the tax system, should:

- minimise the dead-weight cost of supporting those who work here in the absence of tax incentives;

- take into account the full range of other incentives and instruments, and avoid creating incentives through the tax system if other instruments are more efficient;
- ensure that any differences in tax treatment between locals and visitors, and between long and short-term residents, have a clear economic rationale, and are fair and transparent; and
- take into account the arrangements in place in other countries – to ensure that UK firms are not unreasonably disadvantaged relative to their competitors based in other countries, to ensure a reasonable degree of comparability between British people working abroad and foreigners working in the UK, and to limit the extent to which people either "fall between gaps" or face double taxation...

Clarity and enforceability

4.12 Rules should be transparent, non-discriminatory and simple to apply. They should be applied in a consistent manner, and should not impose unnecessary compliance costs. Ideally, they should be based on objective observable characteristics, rather than subjective or uncertain factors. Any differences between the application of the rules to different forms of income need to be clear and objectively justified. The sophistication of international labour and capital markets makes these difficult objectives to achieve. Employers which draw on a range of nationalities for their workforce already face considerable additional burdens in terms of recruitment costs, costs relating to employment law and the work permit system, as well as complications caused by different training and education systems, and the need to mitigate exchange rate risks and costs of travel and relocation when determining pay rates. The complications inherent in the tax treatment of internationally mobile individuals can be a substantial additional burden, which governments should seek to minimise where possible. Complex tax arrangements can also create opportunities for tax avoidance and other means of minimising tax bills. There is therefore a strong case, in principle, for having clear and easy to apply rules as this better enables individuals to comply with their obligation to pay the right amount of tax at the right time to the right country.[66]

Summary and conclusions

4.13 In this context the principles which underpin the review are that the rules:
- should be fair;
- should support the competitiveness of the UK economy;
- should be clear, and easy to operate.

4.14 These principles give rise to a number of questions and issues, which the Government is using as the basis for the review of the residence and domicile rules. The questions that the Government is considering, and would welcome comments from others upon, are whether the current rules:
- successfully identify those with a long-term connection to the UK who have an obligation to help support the UK exchequer on the basis of their world-wide income;
- successfully identify those with a temporary connection to the UK, and ensure an appropriate contribution to the UK exchequer from those individuals;

66 [These principles with the 'relevant criteria' set out in the Inland Revenue Consultation Document, *Residence in the United Kingdom* (1988), see above, para **[19.20]**.]

- provide objective criteria for determining when a long-term or temporary connection is severed, suspended or restored;
- establish an appropriate divide between long-term and temporary connections to the UK;
- play an appropriate role, alongside other policy instruments, in supporting the internationalisation of labour markets, and ensuring the competitiveness of UK firms in the international market for skills, entrepreneurship and expertise;
- ensure that any difference in treatment between UK locals and visitors, and long and short term residents have a clear economic rationale;
- take into account the equivalent arrangements in other countries;
- are transparent, provide clear and unambiguous outcomes, and minimise the compliance burden on individuals and their employers; and
- present minimal opportunities for exploitation or avoidance. **[19.21]**

It remains to be seen whether any steps will be taken (in furtherance of the above key principles espoused in the Background Paper) to bring about fundamental reform of the present system. **[19.21a]**

5. Domicile and residence of corporations

A company is an artificial person. It is a legal entity whose domicile, nationality or residence may have to be determined for tax purposes. The determination of a company's residence is particularly important, because ICTA 1988, s 6 provides for corporation tax to be charged on the profits of a company resident in the UK.[67] Traditionally, the question of whether a company was resident in the UK was a matter for the courts, and a finding to that effect was made where it was established, as a question of fact, that the central management and control of the company was located in the UK. However, since 1988, the central management and control test has been supplanted. The Finance Act 1988, s 66(1) provides that from 15 March 1988 any company incorporated in the UK shall be regarded as resident in the UK regardless of the location of its central management and control.[68] This statutory test takes priority over any other rule of law, subject only to two caveats. First, its operation is restricted by certain exceptions specified in the Finance Act 1988, Sch 7 for companies incorporated before 15 March 1988, and, secondly, it cannot prevail over the provisions of a double taxation agreement.[69] The central management and control test continues to be the test of company residence for those companies not incorporated in the UK.

By comparison, the determination of the domicile and nationality of a

67 In this respect, a company is 'assessed and charged [to corporation tax] for any accounting period . . . on the full amount of the profits arising in the period (whether or not received in or transmitted to the United Kingdom) . . .' (ICTA 1988, s 12(1)); a provision which, thus, precludes the applicability of the remittance basis to companies. Further, it would seem that in relation to the taxation of companies there is no need to make a distinction between resident and ordinarily resident, because the word 'ordinarily' does not add anything to the word 'resident', see *Union Corporation Ltd v IRC* [1953] AC 482.

68 The same presumption applies in respect of Societas Europaea registered in the UK after 31 March 2005. See FA 1988, s 66A (introduced by FA (No 2) 2005, s 60.

69 See FA 1994, s 249 (as amended by FA (No. 2) 2005, s 60(2) in respect of Societas Europaea).

company is rarely a critical factor.[70] A company is regarded as domiciled in its place of incorporation.[71] **[19.22]**

De Beers Consolidated Mines Ltd v Howe [1906] AC 455 (HL)

LORD LOREBURN LC: . . . Now, it is easy to ascertain where an individual resides, but when the inquiry relates to a company, which in a natural sense does not reside anywhere, some artificial test must be applied.

Mr. Cohen propounded a test which had the merits of simplicity and certitude. He maintained that a company resides where it is registered, and nowhere else. If that be so, the appellant must succeed, for it is registered in South Africa.

I cannot adopt Mr. Chen's contention. In applying the conception of residence to a company, we ought, I think, to proceed as nearly as we can upon the analogy of an individual. A company cannot eat or sleep, but it can keep house and do business. We ought, therefore, to see where it really keeps house and does business. An individual may be of foreign nationality, and yet reside in the United Kingdom. So may a company. Otherwise it might have its chief seat of management and its centre of trading in England under the protection of English law, and yet escape the appropriate taxation by the simple expedient being registered abroad and distributing its dividends abroad. The decision of Kelly C.B. and Huddlestone B. in the *Calcutta Jute Mills v. Nicholson*[72] and the *Cesena Sulphur Co. v. Nicholson*[73] now thirty years ago, involved the principle that a company resides for purposes of income tax where its real business is carried on. Those decisions have been acted upon ever since. I regard that as the true rule, and the real business is carried on where the central management and control actually abides. **[19.23]**

Unit Construction Co Ltd v Bullock [1960] AC 351 (HL)

The appellant company made subvention payments to subsidiary companies registered in Kenya. The payments were deductible in computing its taxable profits provided the recipient companies were *resident* in the UK. The memorandum and articles of association of the recipient companies provided for their management to be exercised in Kenya. In fact, such management was conducted from London. The House of Lords held that the recipient companies were resident in the UK.

VISCOUNT SIMONDS: . . . For it has been trite law for two generations or more that a limited company "resides for the purposes of income tax where its real business is carried on," and that its "real business is carried on where the central management and control actually abides." . . . The familiar words that I have cited come from Lord Loreburn's speech in *De Beers Consolidated Mines Ltd. v. Howe.*[74] At that time the possibility of an artificial person such as a limited company residing in two countries at one and the same time had not been fully examined. Twenty years later, in *Swedish Central Railway Co. Ltd. v. Thompson*[75] Rowlatt J. saw no difficulty in such a concept and, indeed, found it easier for a corporation to have two residences than for a natural person and, though in the same case in the Court of Appeal Atkin L.J. (as he then was) said that he felt constrained by authority to come to a different conclusion, and in the House of Lords Lord Atkinson in a powerful

70 For an instance in which domicile is material, see ITA 2007, Pt 13 (Tax Avoidance), Ch 2 (Transfer of Assets Abroad), ss 714–751.
71 See *Gasque v IRC* [1940] 2 KB 80.
72 (1876) 1 TC 83.
73 (1876) 1 TC 88.
74 [1906] AC 455, 458; above, para **[19.24]**.
75 (1923) 9 TC 342, 352.

dissenting speech took the same view, it must now be regarded as clear law that an artificial person may, like a natural person, have more than one residence. . .It is not necessary for me (and I count it my good fortune) on this occasion at any rate to determine in what sense a company may be said to reside not only in that country in which, and in which alone, the central management of its business is exercised, but in another country also. I share to the full the difficulty entertained and expressed by Dixon J. in *Koitaki Para Rubber Estates Ltd. v. Federal Commissioner of Taxation*[76] to which reference was made in the judgement of the Court of Appeal. I leave to others the reconciliation of the *Swedish Central Railway Co.* case,[77] to which I have referred, and *Egyptian Delta Land and Investment Co. Ltd. v. Todd.*[78]

. . .The business is not the less managed in London because it ought to be managed in Kenya. Its residence is determined by the solid facts, not by the terms of its constitution, however imperative. If, indeed, I must disregard the facts as they are, because they are irregular, I find a company without any central management at all. For, though I may disregard the existing facts, I cannot invent facts which do not exist and say that the company's business is managed in Kenya. Yet it is the place of central management, which however much or little weight ought to be given to other factors, essentially determines its residence. I come, therefore, to the conclusion, though truly no precedent can be found for such a case, that it is the actual place of management, not that place in which it ought to be managed, which fixes the residence of a company. If it were not so, the result to the Revenue would be serious enough. In how many cases would a limited company register in a foreign country, prescribe by its articles that its business should be carried on by its directors meeting in that country, and then claim that its residence was in that country though every act of importance was directed from the United Kingdom?. . . **[19.24]**

Wood v Holden [2006] EWCA Civ 26, [2006] 1 WLR 1393 (CA)

CHADWICK LJ:

27. . .In seeking to determine where "central management and control" of a company incorporated outside the United Kingdom lies, it is essential to recognise the distinction between cases where management and control of the company is exercised through its own constitutional organs (the board of directors or the general meeting) and cases where the functions of those constitutional organs are "usurped" – in the sense that management and control is exercised independently of, or without regard to, those constitutional organs. And, in cases which fall within the former class, it is essential to recognise the distinction (in concept, at least) between the role of an "outsider" in proposing, advising and influencing the decisions which the constitutional organs take in fulfilling their functions and the role of an outsider who dictates the decisions which are to be taken. In that context an "outsider" is a person who is not, himself, a participant in the formal process (a board meeting or a general meeting) through which the relevant constitutional organ fulfils its function. **[19.25]**

In *Wood v Holden*, Chadwick LJ also opined [para 43] that management decisions do not cease to be management decisions either because they might have been taken on fuller information or because they were taken in circumstances which might place the director(s) at risk of an allegation of breach of duty. In his Lordship's words: 'Ill-informed or ill-advised decisions taken in the management of the company remain management decisions.'

76 (1940) 64 CLR 15.
77 [1925] AC 495.
78 [1929] AC 1.

In some instances, a 'presence' in the UK may give rise to fiscal obligations. In *Clark v Oceanic Contractors Inc* [1983] STC 35, the House of Lords decided, by a majority, that a non-resident company, which carried on business in the UK through a branch agency, had *sufficient presence* in the UK for a PAYE scheme to be operated for its UK employees (see also, *Agassi v Robinson (Inspector of Taxes)* [2006] 1 WLR 1380, in which the House of Lords considered the materiality of a *tax presence* in the UK to legislation imposing a duty to collect and account for tax to the Inland Revenue). **[19.26]**

Inland Revenue: *Company Residence* (SP 1/90)

PLACE OF 'CENTRAL MANAGEMENT AND CONTROL'

11. In determining whether or not an individual company outside the scope of the incorporation test is resident in the UK, it thus becomes necessary to locate its place of 'central management and control'. The case law concept of central management and control is, in broad terms, directed at the highest level of control of the business of a company. It is to be distinguished from the place where the main operations of a business are to be found, though those two places may often coincide. Moreover, the exercise of control does not necessarily demand any minimum standard of active involvement: it may, in appropriate circumstances, be exercised tacitly through passive oversight.

12. Successive decided cases have emphasised that the place of central management and control is wholly a question of fact. For example, Lord Radcliffe in *Unit Construction* said[79] that 'the question where control and management abide must be treated as one of fact or 'actuality''. . .It follows that factors which together are decisive in one instance may individually carry little weight in another. Nevertheless the decided cases do give some pointers. In particular a series of decisions has attached importance to the place where the company's board of directors meet. There are very many cases in which the board meets in the same country as that in which the business operations take place, and central management and control is clearly located in that one place. In other cases central management and control may be exercised by directors in one country though the actual business operations may, perhaps under the immediate management of local directors, take place elsewhere.

13. But the location of board meetings, although important in the normal case, is not necessarily conclusive. Lord Radcliffe in *Unit Construction* pointed out[80] that the site of the meetings of the directors' board had not been chosen as 'the test' of company residence. In some cases, for example, central management and control is exercised by a single individual. This may happen when a chairman or managing director exercises powers formally conferred by the company's Articles and the other board members are little more than cyphers, or by reason of a dominant shareholding or for some other reason. In those cases the residence of the company is where the controlling individual exercises his powers.

14. In general the place of directors' meetings is significant only insofar as those meetings constitute the medium through which central management and control is exercised. If, for example, the directors of a company were engaged together actively in the UK in the complete running of a business which was wholly in the UK, the company would not be regarded as resident outside the UK merely because

79 (1960) 38 TC 712, 741; [see above.]
80 Ibid., at 738.

the directors held formal board meetings outside the UK. While it is possible to identify extreme situations in which central management and control plainly is, or is not, exercised by directors in formal meetings, the conclusion in any case is wholly one of fact depending on the relative weight to be given to various factors. Any attempt to lay down rigid guidelines would only be misleading.

15. Generally, however, where doubts arise about a particular company's residence status, the Revenue adopt the following approach –

i. They first try to ascertain whether the directors of the company in fact exercise central management and control.

ii. If so, they seek to determine where the directors exercise this central management and control (which is not necessarily where they meet).

iii. In cases where the directors apparently do not exercise central management and control, the Revenue then look to establish where and by whom it is exercised.

CONCLUSION

18. In outlining factors relevant to the application of the case law test, this statement assumes that they exist for genuine commercial reasons. Where, however, as may happen, it appears that a major objective underlying the existence of certain factors is the obtaining of tax benefits from residence or non-residence, the Revenue examines the facts particularly closely in order to see whether there has been an attempt to create the appearance of central management and control in a particular place without the reality.

19. The case law test examined in this Statement is not always easy to apply. The Courts have recognised that there may be difficulties where it is not possible to identify any one country as the seat of central management and control. The principles to apply in those circumstances have not been fully developed in case law. In addition, the last relevant case was decided almost thirty years ago, and there have been many developments in communications since then, which in particular may enable a company to be controlled from a place far distant from where the day-to-day management is carried on. As the Statement makes clear, while the general principle has been laid down by the Courts, its application must depend on the precise facts. **[19.27]**

Different tests may be used in other jurisdictions to determine the residence of a company eg the 'real seat test'. Moreover, the OECD Model Tax Convention on Income and on Capital[81] employs the 'place of effective management' test as a tie-breaker in cases where a company may be regarded as resident in more than one state.[82] **[19.27a]**

81 OECD, Paris (2005).

82 See OECD Model Tax Convention on Income and on Capital, art 4(3). For consideration of whether the phrases 'central management and control' and 'effective place of management' are synonymous, see Philip Owen 'Effective Management' [2001] BTR 289 and 'Can Effective Management be Distinguished from Central Management and Control?' [2003] BTR 296. See also the view of the Inland Revenue on this issue in Statement of Practice (SP 1/90), *Company Residence*, para 22 and in the *Revenue Manuals International Tax Handbook*, para 348.

20 Capital Gains

1. Introduction

Earlier chapters have drawn attention to the importance of the distinction between 'capital' and 'income', and to the significance of this distinction especially in relation to the characterisation of receipts and expenses.[1] This distinction is also material to this chapter, which is concerned with the taxation of capital gains, in that it might be expected that gains or accretions of a non-income nature would normally be excluded from the province of an income tax. As will be seen, however, the taxation of capital gains may be approached in various ways, and may be influenced, in particular, by the meaning attributed to 'income' and, hence, by the extent of the income tax base. **[20.1]**

2. Capital gains and income

The interrelation between capital gains and income raises important conceptual questions. Thus, it is important to establish what constitutes a capital gain and to ascertain whether a capital gain (once defined) should be regarded, for tax purposes, as conceptually distinct from income, or merely as a species of income. As the following extract shows, the resolution of these questions is not straightforward. **[20.2]**

Judith Freedman 'Treatment of Capital Gains and Losses' in Peter Essers and Arie Rijkers (eds) *The Notion of Income from Capital* EATLP International Tax Series, vol 1, IBFD, Amsterdam, 2005, pp 191, 191–195

1. Introduction: concepts of capital gains and income

...The term "capital gain" has different meanings in different tax systems. Ault defines a capital gain generally as a non-recurring gain, which is not part of the normal stream of income involved in a business or investment.[2]

The analogy of the fruit and the tree is often referred to. Although much criticised now for its accuracy, and discredited by economic theory, the analogy does illustrate

1 In particular, Chapters 6 and 10.

2 *H. J. Ault*, Comparative Income Taxation, Kluwer Law International, The Hague, 1997, p.194.

very graphically the broad notion that, whilst income does not encroach on its permanent source, a capital gain does do so.[3] As Lord *Justice Dyson* has pointed out in a recent UK Court of Appeal decision, however, this does sometimes beg the question: what is tree and what is fruit?[4]

To a UK tax lawyer familiar with the source approach to defining the tax base,[5] a capital gain is as conceptually distinct from income as black is from white. They are dealt with under separate tax codes.[6] The strength of the distinction owes much to the importance of this concept in trust law. This does not mean that there is always a clear distinction in practice. The line between a capital gain and income can be difficult to draw and the conversion of income into capital and vice versa in the case of expenditure is, in the UK as elsewhere, a basic method of tax mitigation or avoidance (which of these two descriptions is more accurate depends on the perspective of the analyst). Much case law is concerned with the grey area where the capital/income distinction is far from clear and the fruit and tree analogy breaks down.

The sharper the difference in treatment between capital and income, the greater is the opportunity for arbitrage. Therefore a strong reason for having a tax on capital gains is to prevent avoidance of income tax by conversion of profits into capital gains. The collection costs of a tax on capital gains and losses tend to be high in relation to the tax raised but this relationship does not reveal the amount of tax saved by removing the incentive to recharacterize receipts.[7] Thus those who argue, correctly, that the United Kingdom raises relatively little revenue from the capital gains tax, usually receive the response that these figures do not reveal the potential loss of revenue should capital gains tax be abolished.[8]

Conceptually, the UK approach is in sharp contrast to the *Haig-Simons* concept of a global income tax or net accretion theory, which includes capital gains. . .Proponents of this concept of income aim to tax all accretions to economic power equally and so failure to tax capital gains, which seem to give an individual increased ability to pay, would contravene the principle of horizontal equity. Those who favour this view. . .would also support an accrual basis rather than a realization basis for the taxation of capital gains, although they might accept that this has to be modified for practical reasons.[9]

It is arguable, however, that not all capital gains do have the quality of income. *Wallich* points out that economists often use a national income concept of accounting that reflects capital gains as income only to the extent that they derive from undistributed corporate profits.[10] Other sources, such as gains reflecting a rise

3 *R.Krever* and *N.Brooks*, A Capital Gains Tax for New Zealand, Institute of Policy Studies, Victoria, 1990, p.2.

4 *IRC v. John Lewis Properties plc.* [2003] STC 117.

5 . . .[See *Joachim Lang* 'The influence of tax principles on the taxation of income from capital' in *The Notion of Income from Capital* (as above), Pt A, Ch I, para 41.]

6 Although the capital/revenue distinction has now been removed in some specific areas in the UK.

7 . . .[See *Manfred Rose* 'Economic aspects of taxation of income from capital' in *The Notion of Income from Capital* (as above), Pt A, Ch II.]

8 In 2002–3, the UK Inland Revenue annual receipt from capital gains tax levied on individuals was £1,720 million as compared with £104,264 million from income tax and £29,204 million from corporation tax. The corporation tax figure includes tax on capital gains of companies (Inland Revenue Statistics: www.inlandrevenue.gov.uk).

9 See, for example, *Meade* Committee report, The Structure and Reform of Direct Taxation, The Institute for Fiscal Studies, London, 1978, p. 129.

10 *H. Wallich*, Taxation of Capital Gains in the Light of Recent Economic Developments, National Tax Journal, June 1965. *Muten* disputes the use of net national income as a more realistic measure of the individual's ability to pay than the Hicks definition: *L. Muten*, Capital Gains Tax- Gaining Ground? in *C. Sandford* (ed), More Key Issues in Tax Reform, Fiscal Publications, Bath, 1995.

in the general price level, are not income in a national accounting sense and do not actually represent an improvement in the owner's economic position. *Sandford* also shows that capital gains may arise from different circumstances and believes it is possible to make out a sustainable case that at least some of them do not amount to income.[11]

Sandford's (non-exhaustive) list of circumstances of events giving rise to capital gains is as follows:

- an increase in share values because the retention and reinvestment of profits has increased the real assets of the company;
- a rise in share prices reflecting the constant capitalisation of larger expected income;
- a rise in the value of land because of community development;
- an increase in asset prices from a fall in interest rates; and
- a rise in asset prices reflecting a rise in the general price level.

It can be seen that gains arising in these different circumstances do have differing qualities, judged against the benchmark of net accretion of economic power between two points of time. The most obvious example of a gain that should not be taxable is that of inflation gains. Even this is arguable, however, as those whose assets have risen by the rate of inflation have still fared better than those whose assets have not kept pace with inflation, so relatively the former do have greater economic power.[12] Taxing a capital gain based on capitalisation of large expected income may involve double counting in the national accounting sense, since the higher income will also be taxed in due course,[13] but for the individual holder of the asset there is an immediate gain, at least there is if the asset is disposed of, which may support both capital taxation but also the realization basis. The arguments are not clear-cut.[14] The fact that inflation gains, for example, have a different quality from others is one of the rationales behind the kind of special capital gains tax reliefs used by various countries to take into account inflation, such as indexation of the base cost, tapering relief and reduced rates for capital gains.

Even if, and to the extent that, it is accepted that, other types of capital gains amount to income, it is often perceived that the quality of the income in the hands of the taxpayer affects the ability to pay. This may be seen to relate to the issue of realization: if the capital gain is taxed on an accruals basis there are problems of valuation and liquidity but if a realization basis is used to counteract these problems the result could be unfortunate as there will be fluctuating and "lumpy" receipts, a particular problem in a heavily progressive system. For this reason capital gains are frequently given different treatment from other income.

A strong argument for taxing capital gains is that of vertical equity, since capital gains accrue mainly to the wealthy minority who own capital.[15] Failure to tax such gains only perpetuates existing inequalities. This equity argument must be weighed in the balance against pressure for special reliefs due to the quality of capital gains, the practical difficulties involved in taxing them and the argument that restraint is needed in taxing capital gains in order to encourage entrepreneurship, saving and

11 *C.Evans* and *C.Sandford*, Capital Gains Tax – The Unprincipled Tax?, 1999, BTR 387, citing *C.Sandford*, Taxing Personal Wealth, George Allen & Unwin, London, 1971, pp. 225–227...[See also Manfred Rose 'Economic aspects of taxation of income from capital' in *The Notion of Income from Capital* (as above), Part A, ch II.]

12 *A.R.Ilersic*, The Taxation of Capital Gains, Staples Press, London, 1962.

13 ...[*Wallich*, n 10; Manfred Rose 'Economic aspects of taxation of inçome from capital', in *The Notion of Income from Capital* (as above), Pt A, ch II.]

14 ...[On the issue of double taxation, see the discussions by Claudio Sacchetto and Laura Castaldi, and Daniel Gutmann in *The Notion of Income from Capital* (as above), Pt A, Chs III and IIIA respectively.]

15 ...[*Ilersic*, n 12.]

investment.[16] There must also be a consideration of the other taxes paid by the wealth owners as this argument could lead to double taxation.

The difficulties created by the capital/income divide are of course one argument for having a consumption or expenditure tax rather than an income tax. In theory the distinction between capital and income receipts would disappear completely, although in practice there could be definitional issues in deciding whether certain capital assets were being used for personal consumption. This led the *Meade* Committee in the UK to suggest the retention of a limited capital gains tax for some assets within its expenditure tax proposals.[17] **[20.3]**

For further contrasting views as to the taxation of capital gains, see the 1955 Final Report of the Royal Commission on the Taxation of Profits and Income[18], the Memorandum of Dissent produced by the minority members of this Royal Commission[19], and the 1966 Report of the Royal Commission on Taxation[20]. More broadly, see the examination of the use and suitability of income as the tax base in the Meade Committee Report, The Structure and Reform of Direct Taxation[21]; see also, in this Report, the consideration of the possible treatment of capital gains under an expenditure tax base.[22] **[20.3a]**

3. The taxation of capital gains in the UK

In the UK, the taxation of capital gains has been approached in various ways. Thus, prior to 1962, capital gains were not subject to tax.[23] Thereafter, for a relatively short period of time (1962–1965), 'speculative' or 'short term' gains were treated as income and taxed under Schedule D, Case VII whilst other capital gains remained free of tax. A capital gains tax, which imposed a charge to tax at a flat rate of 30%, was introduced in 1965, but this did not apply, initially, to 'speculative' or 'short term' gains which continued to be taxed as income (and, hence, at income tax rates) until 1971.

Between 1971 and 1988, capital gains were charged to capital gains tax at the flat rate of 30%, and, during this period, an important development was the acknowledgment of the impact of prolonged periods of inflation on capital gains.[24] This led to the introduction of measures, ie the indexation allowance and rebasing,[25] which were intended to negate inflationary gains in the computation of the capital gains to which this rate was to be applied.

16 ...[Kevin Holmes The Concept of Income – A multi-disciplinary analysis (IBFD Publications, Amsterdam, 2001) p 382.]

17 *Meade* Committee report, discussed in *J. Tiley*, Revenue Law, 4th ed., Hart Publishing, Oxford, 2000, p. 604.

18 1955, Cmd 9474, paras 84 and 88–108.

19 *Ibid*, Memorandum of Dissent, paras 34–70.

20 1966, Carter Commission (Canada), vol 1, Introduction.

21 The Institute for Fiscal Studies, London (1978), pp 30–33.

22 *Ibid*, pp 179–180.

23 This does not mean, however, that the taxation of capital gains had not been contemplated, see, for example, the views expressed on this issue in the majority and minority reports of the Royal Commission on the Taxation of Profits and Income (Cmd 9474, 1955) referred to above (see, para **[6.20]**), and see also David Stopforth 'Deliberations Over Taxing Capital Gains – The Position Up to 1955' in John Tiley (ed) *Studies in the History of Tax Law* (Hart Publishing, Oxford, 2004) p 133.

24 For a recent analysis of the impact of inflation on taxation and of measures that may be taken to counteract it, see Ian Roxan 'Influence of inflation' in Peter Essers and Arie Rijkers (eds) *The Notion of Income from Capital* (EATLP International Tax Series, vol I, IBFD, Amsterdam, 2005) p 223.

25 See below, paras **[20.7]** and **[20.44]**.

Since 1988, capital gains have been treated as the top slice of a taxpayer's income for the purpose of computing liability to capital gains tax and they have been charged to tax at income tax rates. Although, the introduction of a taper relief in 1998 (as a substitute for the indexation allowance),[26] under which, eg in the case of a capital gain on the disposal of a business asset which has been owned by a taxpayer for two years, the effective rate of tax is 10%.[27]

The extracts, which comprise the remainder of this section, trace, chronologically, the principal steps referred to in this section's opening paragraphs which have been taken in relation to the taxation of capital gains in the UK, and also reveal the reasons espoused for the taking of those steps by the respective Chancellors of the Exchequer who were responsible for them. **[20.4]**

A. *Taxation of speculative gains*

Budget Speech: The Chancellor of the Exchequer, The Right Honourable Selwyn Lloyd MP, *Hansard*, HC, vol 657, cols 979–980, 9 April 1962

I have not, therefore, come here today to propose a capital gains tax, but to suggest that what may loosely be called speculative gains should be subject to tax.

While the main function of any system of taxation must be to bring in revenue, it must also be designed to produce a feeling of broad equity of treatment between taxpayers. At present, it is pretty widely felt to be inequitable that those who supplement their incomes by speculative gains should escape tax on those gains. I do not think that they should continue to do so; and I tell the Committee frankly that it is on this account, and not merely for yield, that I put forward this proposal.

Certain types of quick gains secured by those not engaging in such operations as a business, are under the present law treated as capital receipts. Although ordinary people find it difficult to distinguish them from income, and they may often be used as income, they are not taxed. Those engaged in certain types of profit-seeking transactions now escape tax altogether – for example, the man who buys stocks and shares not to invest but in the hope of a quick profit, and the man who buys land in the hope of a quick speculative profit through a sale to a genuine developer.

Those who make a business of such transactions are taxed already as traders. Those to whom the new arrangements will apply are those of whom it cannot be established that they are carrying on a business. In my view, however, it is wrong that such people should escape taxation on such activities.

The problem is not a new one. The 1920 Royal Commission advocated action: the Radcliffe Commission said that it needed consideration. I have said repeatedly that I intended to tackle it. I propose to bring such profits within the existing charge under Schedule D of Income Tax by way of a new Case VII.

I have examined various ways of doing this and have come to the conclusion that the appropriate method is by a time test. What I propose is that if assets are acquired and disposed of within a stated period of time – and the period will differ for different kinds of asset – any gain will be taxable under the new Case VII. The periods fixed will be such that the reasonable inference can be drawn that in general the transactions were of an income-seeking nature. What I am asking the

26 The Indexation Allowance is retained for corporation tax purposes.

27 For consideration of this taper relief, see below, para **[20.11]** and para **[20.45]**.

Committee to do is to bring within Schedule D transactions which, some say – wrongly, I am advised – are already within the law. **[20.5]**

B. Introduction of a capital gains tax

Budget Speech: The Chancellor of the Exchequer, The Right Honourable James Callaghan MP, *Hansard*, HC, vol 710, col 245, 6 April 1965

First, I begin with tax reform. The failure to tax capital gains is widely regarded, outside as well as inside the Labour Party, as the greatest blot on our existing system of direct taxation. There is little dispute nowadays that capital gains confer much the same kind of benefit on the recipient as taxed earnings more hardly won. Yet earnings pay tax in full while capital gains go free. This is unfair to the wage and salary earner. It has in the past been one of the barriers to the progress of an effective incomes policy, but now my right hon. Friend the First Secretary of State has carried this policy forward to a point which many did not believe was possible six months ago. This new tax will provide a background of equity and fair play for his work.

Moreover, there is no doubt that the present immunity from tax of capital gains has given a powerful incentive to the skilful manipulator of which he has taken full advantage to avoid tax by various devices which turn what is really taxable income into tax-free capital gains. We shall only make headway against avoidance of this sort when capital gains are also taxed.[28] **[20.6]**

C. Provision for inflationary gains: the indexation allowance and rebasing

Budget Speech: The Chancellor of the Exchequer, The Right Honourable Sir Geoffrey Howe QC, MP, *Hansard*, HC, vol 19, col 755, 9 March 1982

I now come to the incidence of capital gains tax on inflationary gains. This is a matter which has rightly given rise to a great deal of discontent. No one has yet succeeded in finding a solution to this problem. Innumerable proposals for full indexation, for tapering and other ingenious devices have been put forward. None, unfortunately, overcome all the practical difficulties. I cannot, however, allow this injustice to continue. It is intolerable for people to be permanently condemned to pay tax on gains that are apparent but not real – gains that exist only on paper.

I propose, therefore, that as from this April, gains, including those of companies, will, in principle, be calculated after taking account of inflation which occurs after that date. No relief will, however, be given in respect of the first year of ownership. The problem that we seek to solve is one which relates essentially to assets held for a period of years and it would not be appropriate to extend relief to assets bought and sold within a comparatively short period of time. **[20.7]**

28 [See also, David Stopforth 'The Birth of Capital Gains Tax – The Official View' [2005] BTR 584.]

Budget Speech: The Chancellor of the Exchequer, The Right Honourable Nigel Lawson MP, *Hansard*, HC, vol 75, cols 791–792, 19 March 1985

I have decided that the right way to reform capital gains tax is to build on the important change made by my predecessor three years ago when he introduced the 1982 indexation relief. That relief, valuable though it is, and increasingly valuable as it will become, suffers from three serious limitations.

First, indexation does not cover the first 12 months of the ownership of an asset. This provision was introduced to discourage the short-term conversion of income into capital, but it has made the tax much more complicated for the taxpayer. I am now in a position to remedy this defect. . .I now propose to abolish the 12 month rule. So far as most disposals are concerned, this will take effect from 6 April. . .

Second the indexation does not at present extend to losses. I propose to remove this restriction.

Thirdly, the present indexation provision unfairly discriminates against those who acquired their assets prior to 1982. For them the allowance is based not on the 1982 value of the asset but on its original cost. I now propose to remedy this injustice. The indexation allowance will henceforth be based on March 1982 values. Capital gains made prior to 1982 will still not be indexed, of course, but at least all purely inflationary gains made since that date will now be free of tax, irrespective of when the asset was acquired. **[20.8]**

Budget Speech: The Chancellor of the Exchequer, The Right Honourable Nigel Lawson MP, *Hansard*, HC, vol 129, cols 1004–1005, 15 March 1988

Lastly, capital gains tax. Strictly speaking this should not be a tax on the original capital at all. Nor is it, so far as gains which have arisen since 1982 are concerned, thanks to the indexation provisions introduced by my predecessor in 1982 and extended in my 1985 Budget. But for gains that arose before 1982 the tax falls largely on purely paper profits resulting from the rampant inflation of the 1970s. In other words, it bites deeply, and capriciously, into the capital itself.

This has long been recognised as manifestly unjust. Indeed, from the time I first entered the House I have argued that capital gains tax should fall only on real gains and not on paper gains. I have therefore looked hard to see if the indexation provisions could be applied right back to the inception of the tax in 1965. Unfortunately, they cannot. The necessary information is in many cases no longer available.

Accordingly, I have decided to bring the base date for the tax forward from 1965 to 1982. That is to say, for all disposals on or after 6 April, that part of any capital gain which arose before April 1982 will be exempt from tax altogether for individuals and companies alike.

This Budget thus ends once and for all the injustice of taxing purely inflationary gains.

. . .At present, the first £6,000 a year of capital gain is tax free. The relatively high level of this threshold stems from the substantial increase my predecessor made in 1982 explicitly as rough and ready partial compensation for the continued taxation of pre-1982 paper gains. Now that I have taken pre-1982 gains out of tax altogether, I propose to reduce the capital gains tax threshold to £5,000. It should also be borne in mind that, with the introduction of independent taxation in 1990, a husband and wife will each have their own threshold for capital gains tax as well as for income tax. . . **[20.9]**

D. *Taxation of capital gains at income tax rates*

Budget Speech: The Chancellor of the Exchequer, The Right Honourable Nigel Lawson MP, *Hansard*, HC, vol 129, col 1006, 15 March 1988

Rebasing the tax so as to produce a fully indexed system [*see the extract immediately above*] makes it possible to bring the taxation of gains closer to that of income. In principle, there is little economic difference between income and capital gains, and many people effectively have the option of choosing to a significant extent which to receive. And in so far as there is a difference, it is by no means clear why one should be taxed more heavily than the other. Taxing them at different rates distorts investment decisions and inevitably creates a major tax avoidance industry.

Moreover, at present, with capital gains taxed at 30 per cent for everybody, higher rate taxpayers face a lower – sometimes much lower – rate of tax on gains than on investment income, while basic rate taxpayers face a higher rate of tax on gains than on income. This contrast is hard to justify.

I therefore propose a fundamental reform. Subject to the new base date, capital gains will continue to be worked out as now, with the present exemptions and reliefs. But the indexed gain will be taxed at the income tax rate that would apply if it were the taxpayer's marginal slice of income. In other words, I propose in future to apply the same rate of tax to income and capital gains alike . . . **[20.10]**

E. *Withdrawal of the indexation allowance and the introduction of taper relief*

Budget Speech: The Chancellor of the Exchequer, The Right Honourable Gordon Brown MP, *Hansard*, HC, vol 308, col 1101, 17 March 1998

We must do more to increase the quantity and quality of long-term investment. The capital gains tax regime that we inherited rewards the short-term speculator as much as the committed long-term investor. It is time also for a fundamental reform of capital gains tax.

In a low inflation environment a complex system of indexation is no longer necessary. Indexation will continue until April 1998 and will then be frozen. The annual exempt amount will rise in line with prices. Following extensive consultation, I have decided to phase out complex allowances, and instead I will introduce a new structure of capital gains tax which will explicitly reward long-term investment, and which is based on a downward taper and lower tax rates.

The short-term rate of capital gains tax will remain at 40p. For investors holding non-business assets, who invest long-term for 10 years, the rate of capital gains tax will fall from 40p to 24p in the pound. For those who build businesses or stake their own hard-earned money in them, the long-term rate will be reduced even more from 40p to 10p in the pound – the lowest rate ever achieved . . . **[20.11]**

Inland Revenue Press Release, Capital gains tax reform, 17 March 1998

A number of fundamental changes to the structure of capital gains tax are proposed by the Chancellor [*Gordon Brown*] in today's budget.

The reform will help investment through encouraging longer-term holding of assets by reducing the effective rate of capital gains tax on longer-held assets. It will stimulate entrepreneurial activity by rewarding longer-term investment in businesses. Gains on business assets that have been held for ten years or more will be taxed at a rate equivalent to 10% or less.

The changes will lead to simplification of the capital gains tax system by progressively removing indexation, a major complicating factor...[29]

DETAILS

1 For those within the charge to capital gains tax (individuals, trustees and personal representatives, but not companies), indexation will be replaced by a taper which reduces the amount of the chargeable gain the longer an asset has been held. The effective rate of tax for longer-held assets, particularly business assets, will be reduced. This is part of the Government's initiative to encourage longer-term investment and encourage entrepreneurship.

Indexation

2 For gains realised on or after 6 April [*1998*], indexation allowance will be given for periods up to April 1998, but not thereafter. So for an asset held at 6 April 1998 and disposed of after that date, indexation allowance will be computed for the period from the date of acquisition (or the date the expenditure was incurred) to April 1998, but not for the period from April 1998 to the date of disposal. For assets acquired on or after 1 April 1998 no indexation allowance will be allowable in computing the chargeable gain.

Tapering chargeable gains

3 Indexation will be replaced by a taper. The taper will reduce the amount of the chargeable gain according to how long the asset has been held for periods after 5 April 1998. The taper will be more generous for business assets...than for non-business assets... **[20.12]**

The indexation allowance, rebasing and taper relief are considered later in this chapter, see below paras **[20.44]** and **[20.45]**. **[20.13]**

4. Capital gains tax

Capital gains tax is charged on chargeable gains accruing, during a year of assessment, to a person, other than a company, on the disposal of assets.[30] **[20.14]**

29 [Notwithstanding this statement, indexation was (and still is) retained for corporation tax purposes (see Chapter 18 above).]

30 See Taxation of Chargeable Gains Act 1992 (TCGA 1992), s 1. The TCGA, which came into force on 6 April 1992 (see TCGA 1992, s 289(2)), consolidated capital gains tax legislation. Chargeable gains made by companies are liable to corporation tax; see above, para **[18.5]**.

A. *Persons*

Persons chargeable to capital gains tax include individuals, resident or ordinarily resident in the United Kingdom,[31] who are beneficially entitled to the asset disposed of,[32] and those who are entitled in a fiduciary capacity, eg personal representatives and trustees.[33] **[20.15]**

B. *Disposal of assets*

(1) Assets

Apart from a limited number of items (non-chargeable assets) which are expressly exempted from the regime of capital gains tax,[34] all forms of property are assets for capital gains tax purposes whether situated in the United Kingdom or not. Assets specifically include:
(a) options,[35] debts and incorporeal property generally; and
(b) any currency other than sterling; and
(c) any form of property created by the person disposing of it, or otherwise coming to be owned without being acquired.[36] **[20.16]**

O'Brien v Benson's Hosiery (Holdings) Ltd [1980] AC 562 (HL)

The taxpayer company received £50,000 from one of its directors in furtherance of an agreement to release that director from his obligations under his service contract with the company. The taxpayer company was assessed to capital gains tax on the basis that its rights under the service contract were assets and that the release of those rights in return for the capital sum was a disposal of assets under the Finance Act 1965, s 22(3)(c).[37] The House of Lords held that the rights released by the taxpayer company were assets and that the capital sum received by the company in return for their release was chargeable to tax.

31 TCGA 1992, s 2. 'Resident' and 'ordinarily resident' have the same meanings as for income tax, TCGA 1992, s 9(1); see above, Chapter 19.

32 Where two or more persons carry on a trade or business in partnership capital gains tax in respect of chargeable gains accruing to the partners on the disposal of partnership assets is assessed and charged on the partners separately, see TCGA 1992, s 59. See also, in the context of a limited liability partnership carrying on a trade or business with a view to profit, TCGA 1992, s 59A for the treatment of capital gains accruing to the members of such a limited liability partnership on the disposal of any of its assets.

33 Trustees are treated as a single and continuing body, and that body is treated as being resident and ordinarily resident in the UK unless the general administration of the trust is ordinarily carried on outside the UK and the trustees or a majority of them are not resident or not ordinarily resident in the UK, see TCGA 1992, s 69.

34 See, for example, passenger vehicles (TCGA 1992, s 263). Further, a gain on the disposal of certain other assets will, in specified circumstances, not be a chargeable gain, for example, no chargeable gain accrues on the disposal of an asset which is tangible movable property and designated as a wasting asset; see TCGA 1992, s 45. Essentially, tangible movable property means chattels. A wasting asset is defined as an asset which has a predictable life of 50 years or less, see TCGA 1992, s 44.

35 For the treatment of the grant of an option and its exercise for capital gains tax purposes, see TCGA 1992, s 144. See also, *Garner (Inspector of Taxes) v Pounds Shipowners and Shipbreakers Ltd* [2000] STC 420 and *Mansworth (Inspector of Taxes) v Jelley* [2003] STC 53.

36 TCGA 1992, s 21(1). For observations on the construction of the predecessor of this provision, namely s 19(1) of the Capital Gains Tax Act 1979, see *Kirby (Inspector of Taxes) v Thorn EMI plc* [1987] STC 621 at 624–626 (per Nicholls LJ).

37 Now TCGA 1992, s 22(1)(c); see below, para **[20.22]**.

LORD RUSSELL OF KILLOWEN: ... It was contended for the taxpayer that the rights of an employer under a contract of service were not "property" nor an "asset" of the employer, because they cannot be turned to account by transfer or assignment to another. But in my opinion this contention supposes a restricted view of the scheme of the imposition of the capital gains tax which the statutory language does not permit. If, as here, the employer is able to exact from the employee a substantial sum as a term of releasing him from his obligations to serve, the rights of the employer appear to me to bear quite sufficiently the mark of an asset of the employer, something which he can turn to account, notwithstanding that his ability to turn it to account is by a type of disposal limited by the nature of the asset. In this connection I would also refer to the provisions of section 22(3)(*a*)[38] which appear to me apt to cover a case where damages are recovered by an employer from a third party for wrongful procurement of breach by the employee of his contract of service.

Reliance was placed by the taxpayer and the Court of Appeal upon the provisions of section 22(4) and 44(1) of the statute[39] which in certain circumstances introduce the concept of a market value: the contention being that the rights of the employer under the contract of service being non-transferable they could have no market value. In my opinion it is erroneous to deduce from section 22(4), the language of which has no direct application to the present case, a principle of general application for the purposes of capital gains tax that an asset must have a market value. This appears to me to be a preferable answer to the alternative contention of the Crown of analogy with the estate duty cases such as *Inland Revenue Commissioners* v. *Crossman*[40] in which a market value could be found notwithstanding restrictions on transfer of shares in a private company. It appears to me that there is a distinction to be drawn between a case in which the asset has the essential character of transferability but subject to restrictions imposed by the contract contained in the articles of association and the asset in the instant case which lacks that essential character... **[20.17]**

For further examples of the wide meaning of 'asset' for capital gains tax purposes, see *Marren v Ingles* [1980] 1 WLR 983 (chose in action); see below, para **[20.23]** and *Zim Properties v Proctor* [1985] STC 90 (a right of action); see below, para **[20.24]**; *Kirby v Thorn EMI plc* [1987] STC 621 (goodwill). **[20.18]**

(2) Disposal

Disposal is not defined for capital gains tax purposes, but it is accepted that there is a disposal if the ownership of an asset changes, eg by sale or exchange, and whenever the owner divests himself of any rights in or interests over an asset.[41] Further, certain other events are deemed to be within the meaning of disposal. **[20.19]**

(a) Gifts

Turner v Follett 48 TC 614 (CA)

RUSSELL LJ: ...It is necessary first to have a look at the language of the Finance Act 1965, which for the first time introduced what may be conveniently labelled "long-term capital gains tax". That is to be found in Part III of the Act, and s.19(1) provides[42]:

38 [Finance Act 1965. Now TCGA 1992, s 22(1)(a).]
39 [Finance Act 1965. See now TCGA 1992, ss 17 and 272 respectively.]
40 [1937] AC 26.
41 The meaning of the word 'disposal' is not confined to the 'first legal transfer in the ownership of an asset', see *Floor v Davis* [1978] Ch 295 at 312 (per Eveleigh LJ). It is also possible for a *part* disposal of an asset to occur, see TCGA 1992, ss 21(2) and 42; see also, *Watton (Inspector of Taxes) v Tippett* [1997] STC 893 (see below, para **[20.62]**).
42 [See now TCGA 1992, s 1(1).]

> "Tax shall be charged in accordance with this Act in respect of capital gains, that is to say chargeable gains computed in accordance with this Act and accruing to a person on the disposal of assets."

Let me say at once that there is nowhere any precise definition of the word "disposal". If one paused there one could say, I think, with some justification, in Mr. Turner's favour, that it is not readily apparent that that section is ultimately going to bring into charge for capital gains tax any part of a gift. Section 20(1) provides[43]:

> "Subject to any exceptions provided by this Act, a person shall be chargeable to capital gains tax in respect of chargeable gains accruing to him in a year of assessment during any part of which he is resident in the United Kingdom or during which he is ordinarily resident in the United Kingdom."

...Thus far, it does not look very much as if there was going to be any tax on a person who made a present of property and who therefore could not, in the ordinary sense of the word, be said to have made a capital gain. But we then come to s.22. Section 22 starts with a description of the sort of assets the disposal of which is under consideration, and subs. (4) provides this:

> "Subject to the provisions of this Part of this Act, a person's acquisition of an asset and the disposal of it to him shall for the purposes of this Part of this Act be deemed to be for a consideration equal to the market value of the asset...in particular where he acquires it by way of gift."[44] I have left out the irrelevant parts.

At first sight it would seem that that was looking at the matter only from the point of view of the donee in the case of a gift; but, as was pointed out by Mr. Medd, for the Crown, it is in fact apparently looking at it both from the donor's end and the donee's end, because if it was looking at it only from the donee's end it would have been sufficient to say "a person's acquisition of an asset" and to have left out the following words, "and the disposal of it to him." Therefore the argument goes that here is a section which in terms, in the case of a gift, provides that the disposal of the subject-matter, the asset – for example, in this case 300 shares – by Mr. Turner by way of gift shall be deemed to have been a disposal by him to his children for a consideration equal to the market value of the asset. It is by that deeming provision that it is said that, although in the ordinary sense of the words it cannot be said that Mr. Turner had made a capital gain, or indeed made any gain of any kind, nevertheless for the purposes of this Act he is artificially deemed to have disposed of it for (in this case) a total of £2,100.

The matter does not rest on that particular construction of s.22(4), because there are in other parts of the Act indications which appear to be quite plain that a purpose of Parliament in providing for this capital gains tax was to provide for tax on a notional gain accruing to the donor on the occasion of a gift. It is to be observed that on the death of an individual, as the Act was originally passed, though not as since amended, there is deemed to be a disposal of all his assets by him on the date of his death, for capital gains tax purposes, to his personal representatives.[45] That included, as originally enacted, any asset the subject-matter of a *donatio mortis causa*.[46] We then go to s.25, and we find that under s.25(2)[47] a particular type of gift, namely a gift in settlement, whether revocable or irrevocable, is for the purposes of this Act

> "a disposal of the entire property thereby becoming settled property notwithstanding that the donor has some interest as a beneficiary under the settlement and notwithstanding that he is a trustee, or the sole trustee, of the settlement."

43 [See now TCGA 1992, s 2(1); see above, para **[20.15]**.]
44 [See now TCGA 1992, s 17(1). A gift is an example of a species of transaction 'otherwise than by way of a bargain made at arm's length.' For examples of other such transactions which are also treated as made at market value, see TCGA 1992, s 17(1), but note the exceptions in TCGA 1992, s 17(2).]
45 [See now TCGA 1992, s 62(1).]
46 [See now TCGA 1992, s 62(5).]
47 [See now TCGA 1992, s 70. For the treatment of settlements for capital gains tax purposes, see below, para **[20.26]**.]

So there is one type of gift clearly brought within the ambit of the capital gains tax legislation as a disposal. Another example is to be found in an exemption provision in s.27(2)[48], which provides that "A gain accruing to an individual on a disposal by way of gift of an asset the market value of which does not exceed one hundred pounds shall not be a chargeable gain". That again assumes that on the disposal by way of gift of an asset there is a chargeable gain accruing to the individual who happens to be the donor. Otherwise the exemption would not have been required. Section 31 is another exemption provision which shows exemption in connection with a gift. It is dealing with works of art. I need only mention that it provides, in subs. (1) "A gain accruing on the disposal of an asset by way of gift...shall not be a chargeable gain," and then it refers to the special provisions under other Statutes in respect of gifts of works of art and so forth for national purposes.[49]

I should then, I think, next turn to Sch. 6, which provides for computation of capital gains. Paragraph 1 of Part I of that Schedule says: "The provisions of this Schedule shall have effect for computing for the purposes of this Part of this Act the amount of a gain accruing on the disposal of an asset." Then para. 3, dealing with exclusion of short-term gains, provides in sub-para. (2) as follows:

> "A gain accruing on the disposal by way of gift of an asset shall not be a chargeable gain for the purposes of this Part of this Act – (a) if by virtue of provisions of the 1962 Act, which introduced short-term capital gains tax, the donee is treated as if the donor's acquisition of the asset had been his acquisition of it."

– again a reference to gifts as something coming within the scope of the capital gains tax. Then I would turn next to Sch. 7, para. 19, of which the cross-heading is "Gifts: recovery of tax from donee":

> "(1) If in any year of assessment a chargeable gain accrues to any person on the disposal of an asset by way of gift and any amount of capital gains tax assessed on that person for that year of assessment is not paid within twelve months from the date when the tax becomes payable the donee may, by an assessment made no later than two years from the date when the tax becomes payable, be assessed and charged (in the name of the donor) to capital gains tax ... (2) A person paying any amount of tax in pursuance of this paragraph shall be entitled to recover a sum of that amount from the donor."[50]

It is abundantly plain from that language that the donor is considered as being, for the purposes of this Statute, a person to whom a gain accrues when he makes the gift. Indeed, in this particular instance, if Mr. Turner did not pay the capital gains tax which had been assessed on him in respect of these gifts, it follows from the paragraph I have just read out that his children could be assessed for the amount in his name; and if they paid it they would (at least as a technical matter) be entitled to reclaim it from their no doubt indignant father. The only other passage I think need refer to in the Statute is para. 17 of the same Sch. 7, which is concerned with "transactions between connected persons"[51] which I can describe broadly as members of the family. Sub-paragraph (1) provides that the paragraph shall apply "where a person acquires an asset and the person making the disposal is connected with him."[52] Sub-paragraph (2) provides[53]:

> "Without prejudice to the generality of section 22(4) of this Act[54] the person acquiring the asset and the person making the disposal shall be treated as parties to a transaction otherwise than by way of a bargain made at arm's length."

48 [This exemption was abolished with respect to disposals on or after 6 April 1984 by FA 1984, s 63(1).]
49 [See now TCGA 1992, s 258(2)(a) and IHTA 1984, Sch 3.]
50 [See now TCGA 1992, ss 282(1) and 282(2).]
51 [For the meaning of 'connected persons', see TCGA 1992, s 286.]
52 [See now TCGA 1992, s 18(1).]
53 [See now TCGA 1992, s 18(2).]
54 [See now TCGA 1992, s 17(1).]

> This, it is, I think rightly, argued by Mr. Medd, underlines the true construction of s.22(4)[55] as deeming a donor, for the purposes of this Act and for the purposes of this tax, to have disposed of that which he gives away for a consideration equal to the then market value of the asset... **[20.20]**

It may be possible to defer or 'hold-over' a gain otherwise chargeable to capital gains tax which arises on a gift or other disposal made 'otherwise than under a bargain at arm's length' of certain business assets.[56] The claim for this relief must be made by the donor/transferor and the donee/transferee. The effect of the relief is to postpone the incidence of tax until there is a disposal of the asset by the donee/transferee which gives rise to a charge to tax.[57] **[20.21]**

(*b*) *Capital sums derived from assets*

There is a deemed disposal of assets by their owner for capital gains tax purposes 'where any capital sum is derived from assets'. This will be so even though no asset may be acquired by the person paying the capital sum, and applies, in particular, to:

(a) capital sums received by way of compensation for any kind of damage or injury to assets or for the loss, destruction or dissipation of assets or for any depreciation or risk of depreciation of an asset; and

(b) capital sums received under an insurance policy of the risk of any kind of damage or injury to, or the loss or depreciation of, assets; and

(c) capital sums received in return for forfeiture or surrender or rights, or for refraining from exercising rights; and

(d) capital sums received as consideration for use or exploitation of assets.[58] **[20.22]**

Marren (Inspector of Taxes) v Ingles [1980] 1 WLR 983 (HL)

The taxpayer sold shares in a private company in consideration of an immediate payment and a right to a future payment (deferred consideration) to be calculated by reference to the sale price quoted on the first days of dealing in those shares on the Stock Exchange following the flotation of that company. The flotation took place and the taxpayer received a deferred consideration of £2,825 per share. The House of Lords held that the taxpayer's right to receive the further payment after the flotation of the company was incorporeal property (a chose in action), which was disposed of when the deferred consideration was paid.

55 [Ibid.]

56 The business assets in respect of which a claim for hold-over relief may be made include assets used for the purposes of a trade, profession or vocation carried on by the transferor or his personal company, unquoted shares or securities in a trading company, shares or securities in a trading company which is the transferor's personal company, or property which qualifies for IHT agricultural property relief (see TCGA 1992, s 165 and Sch 7, para 1(1).

57 See also TCGA 1992, s 260. This section allows a claim for hold-over relief in respect of a gain which arises on a disposal of *any* asset and where such disposal constitutes an immediately chargeable transfer for the purposes of IHT. For the treatment of *inter vivos* transfers for IHT purposes, see Chapter 21, para **[21.1]**.

58 See TCGA 1992, s 22. Note the interaction between this section and TCGA 1992, s 23.

LORD WILBERFORCE: ...The first question, that concerning section 22(3),[59] involves consideration of the words "notwithstanding that no asset is acquired ...", for the rest of the paragraph gives rise to no difficulty. There was an asset in the form of the obligation (a chose in action) to pay the deferred consideration. The deferred consideration when it was paid, in 1972, was, it is difficult to deny, a capital sum derived from that asset. Section 22(1)(*a*)[60] of the Act expressly provides that incorporeal property, of which a chose in action is an undoubted example, is an asset for the purposes of the tax. I do not think that there is any doubt or problem up to this point. But the question remains whether the taxpayer can succeed in the contention that the words "notwithstanding that no asset is acquired" introduce a condition of a limiting character, with the result if an asset *is acquired* the subsection does not apply. For the purposes of this argument I shall assume that an asset was acquired by the payer of the capital sum (viz. I.C.F.C.), though there is much to be said for the contrary view and indeed the Court of Appeal accepted it. Support for the taxpayer's contention is given by a passage from the judgment of Walton J. in *Inland Revenue Commissioners* v. *Montgomery*,[61] which was followed and applied by Slade J. and which led him to accept the taxpayer's contention. But I regret that I am unable to agree. Section 22(3),[62] after the provision which I have quoted, goes on to provide some examples, to which in particular the subsection is stated to apply.[63]

[*After citing these examples, his Lordship continued*]

Now it is obvious that in some, if not most of these examples there is the possibility that an asset may be acquired by the person paying the capital sum. The clearest of these is (*d*), if the sum is paid for the grant of a licence or a profit: but also under (*b*), if the payer of the sum acquires rights by subrogation, or under (*a*) if after payment of damages the property in respect of which they were paid vests in the payer. The observations of Walton J, in *Inland Revenue Commissions* v. *Montgomery*,[64] do not take account of these possibilities (to which others could be added) and to that extent must be too wide. But apart from this, I cannot read the words in question ("notwithstanding..." etc.) as pointing in the direction desired by the taxpayer. In my understanding they are evidently words not of limitation, but of extension, the purpose of which is to apply the subsection (so as to establish a "disposal") to cases to which it would not otherwise apply and in which a "disposal" would not naturally be thought to exist. In other words they mean, in my opinion, "Whether or not an asset is acquired." With this meaning the examples given under (*a*) to (*d*) easily fit...

LORD FRASER OF TULLYBELTON:..."Asset" is defined in section 22(1)[65] in the widest terms, to mean all forms of property and it has been construed accordingly – see *O'Brien* v. *Benson's Hosiery (Holdings) Ltd.*[66] – by my noble and learned friend Lord Russell of Killowen. It is therefore apt to include the incorporeal right to money's worth which was part of the consideration given for the shareholdings in 1970. The vendors could have disposed of the right at any time after September 15, 1970, by selling it or giving it away and assigning it. If they had done so, there would have been an actual disposal of an asset and the vendors would have been liable for capital gains tax on the amount, if any, by which the price or value of the asset at the date of disposal exceeded its value on September 15, 1970. Of course, if the price or value had been less than the value on September 15, 1970, they would have made a chargeable loss which they could have set off against gains in the same or future fiscal years. So there is nothing unfair in treating it as an asset. In fact, they did not dispose of the right but they held it until it matured on December 5, 1972. If the right was an "asset", then the sum which the vendors received on that date was "derived from" the asset. There was therefore, by virtue of section 22(3),[67] a disposal of the asset,

59 [See now TCGA 1992, s 22(1).]
60 [Now TCGA 1992, s 21(1)(a).]
61 [1975] Ch 266 at 271–272.
62 [See now TCGA 1992, s 22(1).]
63 [See above, para **[20.22]**.]
64 [1975] Ch 266.
65 [See now TCGA 1992, s 21(1).]
66 [1979] 3 WLR 572, 575; [see above, para **[20.17]**].
67 [See now TCGA 1992, s 22(1).]

notwithstanding that no asset was acquired by the "person paying the capital sum", the purchaser. The sum was paid to satisfy or extinguish the right and not as any part of the consideration for the shareholdings: full consideration for them had already been given on September 15, 1970. The capital sum is therefore not in any relevant sense derived from the shareholdings, and the appellant's complaint that he was being assessed to capital gains tax twice over on the price is misconceived. The position is no different in principle from what it would have been if the vendors had received new shares in another company as part of the consideration for the shareholdings and had later disposed of the new shares.

In my opinion, Slade J. was mistaken in treating the receipt of the shareholdings by the purchasers as relevant for the purposes of section 22(3).[68] The reference there to no asset being "acquired by" the person paying the capital sum must be to an asset acquired in exchange for the capital sum, and the shareholdings were not acquired by the purchaser in exchange for the capital sum paid in December 1972. The material question is not whether acquisition of the asset and payment of the capital sum were contemporaneous or not, but whether one was consideration for the other. Moreover Slade J., following a decision of Walton J. in *Inland Revenue Commissioners* v. *Montgomery*,[69] held that the words "notwithstanding that no asset is acquired by the person paying the capital sum" in section 22(3)[70] meant that the application of the subsection was confined to cases where no asset was acquired. I am unable to agree. The ordinary meaning of the word "notwithstanding" according to the *Shorter Oxford English Dictionary* is "despite, in spite of". One might perhaps suggest also "whether or not." It is a word of extension not limitation, and I see no reason to read it here in a limiting sense. The comprehensive provisions of subsections (1) and (2) of section 22[71] may render it not strictly necessary for subsection (3)[72] to apply to cases where an asset is acquired by the person paying the capital sum, but even if there is some overlapping, that is not uncommon in fiscal legislation, in order to avoid leaving a loophole. In my opinion subsection (3)[73] applies whether or not an asset is acquired by the person paying the capital sum. That construction is, if anything, fortified by reference to the examples given in paragraphs (*a*) to (*d*) of subsection (3),[74] some of which are of cases where payment of the capital sum might well attract corresponding assets. Thus, looking at paragraph (*b*), where a capital sum is paid under a policy of insurance the insurers will often acquire by subrogation an asset consisting of the assured's right of action against a wrongdoer. Accordingly, I consider that the decision in *Montgomery* on this point was erroneous... **[20.23]**

Zim Properties Ltd v Proctor (Inspector of Taxes) [1985] STC 90 (ChD)

A conveyancing transaction involving the proposed sale of three properties owned by the taxpayer company fell through. The taxpayer company alleged that the transaction had fallen through because of the negligence of its solicitors, and brought an action in negligence for damages against the solicitors. The action was compromised, and, consequently, the taxpayer company received compensation from the solicitors of £69,000. Warner J held that the compensation was derived from the right to sue the solicitors, and as that right could be turned to account by the negotiation of a compromise yielding a capital sum, it constituted an asset for capital gains tax purposes.

WARNER J:...One way in which counsel for the taxpayer company attacked the decision of the commissioners to the effect that the £69,000 was 'derived' from the taxpayer

68 [Ibid.]
69 [1975] Ch 266 at 271.
70 [See now TCGA 1992, s 22(1).]
71 [See now TCGA 1992, s 21(1) and (2).]
72 [See now TCGA 1992, s 22(1).]
73 [Ibid.]
74 [Finance 1965. See now TCGA 1992, s 22(1); above, para **[20.22]**.]

company's right of action against the firm was this. (He did not put it first, but I think that logically I should deal with it first.) He pointed out that, on the pleadings in the action between the taxpayer company and the firm, the outcome of the trial might have depended on whether the court preferred the evidence of Zimen[75] or that of a partner in the firm. Alternatively, it might have depended on whether the court found as a fact that, if Courtdeals Ltd[76] had been told that the 1960 conveyance was missing, Courtdeals Ltd would none the less have entered into the contract or would have declined to do so. In other words, what the Crown referred to as the taxpayer company's 'right of action' against the firm was in reality no more than a claim which might or might not succeed. Such a claim, unlike an undoubted right, was not a form of property and therefore, having regard to the terms of s 22(1) of the Finance Act 1965,[77] was not an 'asset' for capital gains tax purposes...

Counsel for the Crown submitted that such a claim was a form of property. Alternatively, he submitted that, if it was not a form of property, it was none the less an 'asset' for capital gains tax purposes. He urged on me the undesirability of reaching a conclusion in this case that would make it necessary, in any future like case, for the appellate commissioners to decide, albeit on a balance of probabilities, whether a civil action that had in fact been compromised would or would not, if fought out, have succeeded.

I have, after considerable hesitation, come to the conclusion that counsel for the Crown is entitled to succeed on that point. He is entitled to do so, I think, not on the strength of the various authorities to which he referred me on the scope of the concept of a 'chose in action' in English law or on the strength of what it is desirable or undesirable that appellate commissioners should have to decide, but on the strength of the decision of the House of Lords in *O'Brien (Inspector of Taxes) v Benson's Hosiery (Holdings) Ltd.*[78] True the contractual rights that were there held to constitute an asset for capital gains tax purposes were undisputed. They were not a mere claim. But that formed no part of the ratio decidendi of the case. The ratio decidendi was that those rights were an asset for capital gains tax purposes because they were something that could be turned to account...

...it would in my view be inconsistent with the decision in *O'Brien (Inspector of Taxes) v Benson's Hosiery (Holdings) Ltd*[79] to hold that a right to bring an action to seek to enforce a claim that was not frivolous or vexatious, which right could be turned to account by negotiating a compromise yielding a substantial capital sum, could not be an 'asset' within the meaning of that term in the capital gains tax legislation. I propose, for the sake of convenience, to refer to the right that the taxpayer company had, in that sense, to bring an action against the firm as its 'right to sue' the firm.

So I come to the contention that counsel for the taxpayer company put in the forefront of his case, which was that, in the correct analysis, the assets from which the taxpayer company derived the £69,000 were the properties comprised in the contract of sale. Counsel for the taxpayer company based that contention on the provisions of s 22(2) and (3) of the Finance Act 1965.[80] He submitted that the receipt of the £69,000 should be treated as a part disposal of those properties, either by virtue of the general words of s 22(3),[81] that is to say the words 'there is for the purposes of this Part of this Act a disposal of assets by their owner where any capital sum is derived from assets', or by virtue of s 22(3)(*a*)[82] or by virtue of s 22(3)(*c*).[83]

The argument of counsel for the taxpayer company based on the general words rested on a premise which seems to me correct and which is this. The words 'and this subsection applies in particular to' that introduce the lettered paragraphs in the subsection connote

75 [A director of the taxpayer company.]
76 [The prospective purchaser.]
77 [See now TCGA 1992, s 21(1).]
78 [1979] STC 735 [above, para **[20.17]**].
79 [Ibid.]
80 [See now TCGA 1992, ss 21(2) and 22(1) respectively.]
81 [See now TCGA 1992, s 22(1).]
82 [See now TCGA 1992, s 22(1)(a).]
83 [See now TCGA 1992, s 22(1)(c).]

that those paragraphs describe particular instances of the application of the principle enacted by the general words. From that two consequences follow. The first is that a case cannot come within any of the lettered paragraphs if it cannot come within the general words. The other is that the lettered paragraphs may properly be looked at as aids to the interpretation of the general words. That indeed is what, in effect, Lord Wilberforce and Lord Fraser both said in *Marren (Inspector of Taxes)* v *Ingles*.[84] Of the other three Law Lords, two expressed their agreement with the speech of Lord Wilberforce and one expressed his agreement with the speech of Lord Fraser. The contrary view expressed by Nourse J in *Davenport (Inspector of Taxes)* v *Chilver*[85] must therefore be mistaken – nor did counsel for the Crown seek to uphold it.

From that it follows that a capital sum may be derived from assets within the meaning of the general words of s 22(3)[86] even though those assets may not be the immediate source of that sum. That is not to say that Walton J was wrong in holding in *IRC* v *Montgomery*[87] that the sum received by the trustees from Mr Greene was derived from their rights under the policies. It means no more than that it would be a mistake to interpret Walton J's decision in that case as authority for the proposition that the asset from which a capital sum is derived must always be the asset that constitutes its immediate source. The true view was hinted at by Fox J in *O'Brien (Inspector of Taxes)* v *Benson's Hosiery (Holdings) Ltd* when he referred to 'the reality of the matter'. One has to look in each case for the real (rather than the immediate) source of the capital sum.

On that premise, with which, as I have already indicated, I agree, the argument of counsel of the taxpayer company proceeded as follows. If the properties had been sold, the sale price would have been derived from them. Because the properties were not sold, compensation was received from the firm's insurers for the loss that the taxpayer suffered by reason of there having been no sale of the properties. Thus the compensation was derived from the properties as much as the sale price would have been if the properties had been sold. To hold otherwise would be to transgress the basic rule that capital gains tax is a tax on real gains, not on 'arithmetical differences'. It would also be inconsistent with authorities showing that a right to compensation for loss is not an 'asset' for capital gains tax purposes.

The reference of counsel for the taxpayer company to the basic rule that capital gains tax is a tax on real gains, not on 'arithmetical differences' was of course a reference to the words of Lord Wilberforce in *Aberdeen Construction Group Ltd* v *IRC* where he said[88]

> 'The capital gains tax is of comparatively recent origin. The legislation imposing it, mainly the Finance Act 1965, is necessarily complicated, and the detailed provisions, as they affect this or any other case, must of course be looked at with care. But a guiding principle must underlie any interpretation of the Act, namely, that its purpose is to tax capital gains and to make allowance for capital losses, each of which ought to be arrived at on normal business principles. No doubt anomalies may occur, but in straightforward situations, such as this, the courts should hesitate before accepting results which are paradoxical and contrary to business sense. To paraphrase a famous cliché, the capital gains tax is a tax upon gains: it is not a tax upon arithmetical differences.'

It does not, however, seem to me 'contrary to business sense' to treat the £69,000 received by the taxpayer company in this case as a gain. The fact is that, after its receipt of that sum, the taxpayer company still owned the properties, unaffected and unimpaired by the fate of its contract with Courtdeals Ltd...

...In support of his submission that a right to compensation for loss is not an 'asset' for capital gains tax purposes, counsel for the taxpayer company cited *Davis (Inspector of Taxes)* v *Powell*,[89] *Davenport (Inspector of Taxes)* v *Chilver*[90] and *Drummond (Inspector of Taxes)*

84 [1980] STC 500.
85 [1983] STC 426, 439.
86 [Now TCGA 1992, s 22(1).]
87 [1975] STC 182.
88 [1978] STC 127, 131; see below, para **[20.50]**.]
89 [1977] STC 32.
90 [1983] STC 426.

> v *Austin Brown*[91]. He also pointed out that, as a matter of common sense, it must be accepted that not every right to a payment is an asset for capital gains tax purposes. He gave as examples of rights that it would manifestly be ridiculous to treat as capable of generating capital gains a right to a repayment of tax and a right to the payment of costs at the end of successful litigation. Yet, he said, unless some general rule as he was contending for existed, there would be, at all events since the enactment of s 90 of the Finance Act 1981, no escape from the conclusion that a repayment of tax, of a payment under an award of costs, should be treated as pure capital gain.
>
> I have no difficulty in accepting that not every right to a payment is an 'asset' within the meaning of that term in the capital gains tax legislation. Perhaps the most obvious example of one that is not is the right of a seller of property to payment of its price. The relevant asset, then, is the property itself. What that shows, however to my mind, is no more than that the interpretation of the capital gains tax legislation requires, as does the interpretation of any legislation, the exercise of common sense, rather than just the brute application of verbal formulae. In saying that I am, I think, expressing much the same thought as was expressed by Lord Wilberforce in *Aberdeen Construction Group Ltd* v *IRC*...
>
> ...It really seems to me that, if one is to search 'for the reality of the matter', the reality is that the taxpayer company derived the £69,000 from its right to sue the firm...[92] **[20.24]**

There is also a deemed disposal on the occurrence of the total loss, destruction, dissipation or extinction of an asset whether or not the owner of the asset receives compensation for that loss etc. (see TCGA 1992, s 24(1)); see also TCGA 1992, s 24(2) (asset becoming of negligible value). **[20.25]**

C. *Settlements*[93]

Property is settled when it is held in trust,[94] except, in the following circumstances, when, notwithstanding that there may be a trust of property, the property is deemed not to be settled property:

(i) where assets are held by a person as nominee for another person, or as trustee for another person absolutely entitled as against the trustee; or
(ii) where assets are held on trust for any person who would be absolutely entitled but for being an infant or other person under disability; or
(iii) where assets are held on trust for two or more persons who are or would be, jointly absolutely entitled as against the trustee.

In each of these instances, the property is treated as if it were vested in the person or persons for whom the property is held by the nominee or trustee, the acts of the nominee or trustee are treated as acts of that person or those persons, and the trustee is often referred to as a bare trustee.[95] **[20.26]**

91 [1984] STC 321.
92 See further, Peter Sparkes, 'The Derivation of Capital Sums' [1987] BTR 323, and note also ESC D33 (Capital gains tax on compensation and damages: ZIM PROPERTIES LTD – COMPENSATION AND DAMAGES) which addresses some of the issues arising from *Zim Properties*.
93 The transfer of assets into a settlement is a disposal of those assets even though the transferor has a beneficial interest under the settlement and notwithstanding that he may be a trustee of the settlement, see TCGA 1992, s 70.
94 TCGA 1992, s 68.
95 *Ibid*, s 60(1). Property may cease to be settled property (and the trustee may become a bare trustee) when a person *becomes* absolutely entitled as against the trustee; see below, para **[20.29]**.

Jerome v Kelly (Inspector of Taxes) [2004] STC 887 (HL)

LORD HOFFMANN:. . .the capital gains tax legislation deals with trusts in a practical way. Like most tax legislation, it is concerned with economic reality and efficiency of collection. In the case of bare trusts, such as nominee shareholdings, it ignores the trustee and treats his acts as those of the beneficiary. The latter has the entire economic interest in the assets and is therefore treated as having dealt with them. In the case of more complicated settlements, this system would not work. It might be no easy matter to determine how the economic benefit of the disposal has accrued to the various people with interests (fixed, vested, contingent and so forth) under the settlement. So that tax is charged upon the trustee, who is left to indemnify himself out of the fund.

In both cases, the law avoids taxing the same gain twice. In the case of the bare trust, the mechanism is simple. The law taxes the beneficiary whether he disposes of his beneficial interest or the trustee disposes of the entire property. In both cases there is a simple charge upon the beneficiary. In the case of other trusts, the mechanism is different. The trustee is charged to tax, but because he is only the legal owner, he is entitled to an indemnity out of the fund. The beneficiary's interest is an item of property distinct from the underlying assets but an assignment of that interest is not ordinarily treated as a disposal giving rise to a liability to tax. Otherwise a beneficiary who disposed of his interest would be taxed twice on the same gain; once through the trustee's right of indemnity and once in his own right.

This scheme for dealing with trusts has been part of the architecture of the capital gains tax since it was introduced by the Finance Act 1965. . . **[20.27]**

Stephenson v Barclays Bank Trust Co Ltd [1975] 1 WLR 882 (ChD)

WALTON J:. . .If the concept of a person being beneficially entitled as against a trustee stood alone, there would, I think, be little difficulty in the concept. But it does not stand alone, because in section 22(5) of the Finance Act 1965[96] one finds the additional words "(or for two or more persons who are or would be jointly so entitled)", the "would be" being a reference to infancy or disability. Now it was decided by Foster J. in *Kidson* v. *Macdonald*[97] that the word "jointly" was to be read in the sense of "concurrently, or in common", and was not to be confined to the strict joint tenancy – that is, a tenancy with benefit of survivorship – as known to English conveyancers.[98] While this point is only one in the foothills, as it were, of the argument, Mr. Lawton did not like this decision in any way and submitted thereon, first, that it was a decision relating to a trust for sale of land where the joint tenants were such legally and beneficially, and that there is no reason to suppose that Foster J. would have intended his decision to apply to pure personalty, which constitutes the bulk of the present remaining residuary estate. As a final measure, if necessary, he submitted that that case was wrongly decided.

I reject both these submissions. It appears to me perfectly clear that, although the ratio decidendi of that case arises out of the consideration that the ordinary English conveyancing concept of a joint tenancy in real property is unknown North of the Border, while the same statutory provisions apply indifferently either side of it, nevertheless the decision is a perfectly general one as to the scope of the relevant phrase in section 22(5),[99] and is in no wise confined to real property. The arguments as to the generality of the meaning of "jointly" would have been precisely the same whatever the subject matter of

96 [See now TCGA 1992, s 60.]
97 [1974] Ch 339.
98 [The word 'jointly' does not, however, apply to interests which are successive as the beneficiaries must be concurrently entitled in the same interest, see *Booth v Ellard* [1980] 1 WLR 1443.]
99 [See now TCGA 1992, s 60(1).]

the trust. As regards the soundness of the decision as a whole, although technically I am not strictly bound to follow it, it appears to me that, even if I had thought the decision logically dubious, I ought to follow a decision of Foster J. on a novel point otherwise untouched by authority. But I go much further than that. The reasoning of Foster J. in that case appears to me to be well founded and, were the matter res integra, such as I should have hoped myself to reproduce.

I now turn to a consideration of the phrase "absolutely entitled as against the trustee", which is now of course fairly closely defined in the Finance Act 1969, Schedule 19, paragraph 9.[100] It is therefore defined as meaning that the person concerned

> "has the exclusive right, subject only to satisfying any outstanding charge, lien or other right of the trustees to resort to the asset for payment of duty, taxes, costs or other outgoings, to direct how that asset shall be dealt with."

Now it is trite law that the persons who between them hold the entirety of the beneficial interests in any particular trust fund are as a body entitled to direct the trustees how that trust fund is to be dealt with, and this is obviously the legal territory from which that definition derives. However, in view of the arguments advanced to me by Mr. Lawton, and more particularly that advanced by him on the basis of the decision of Vaisey J. in *In re Brockbank*[101], I think it may be desirable to state what I conceive to be certain elementary principles.

(1) In a case where the persons who between them hold the entirety of the beneficial interests in any particular trust fund are all sui juris and acting together, ("the beneficial interest holders"), they are entitled to direct the trustees how the trust fund may be dealt with. (2) This does not mean, however, that they can at one and the same time override the pre-existing trusts and keep them in existence. Thus, in *In re Brockbank*, itself the beneficial interest holders were entitled to override the pre-existing trusts by, for example, directing the trustees to transfer the trust fund to X and Y, whether X and Y were the trustees of some other trust or not, but they were not entitled to direct the existing trustee to appoint their own nominee as a new trustee of the existing trust. By so doing they would be pursuing inconsistent rights. (3) Nor, I think, are the beneficial interest holders entitled to direct the trustees as to the particular investment they should make of the trust fund. I think this follows for the same reasons as above. Moreover, it appears to me that once the beneficial interest holders have determined to end the trust they are not entitled, unless by agreement, to the further services of the trustees. Those trustees can of course be compelled to hand over the entire trust assets to any person or persons selected by the beneficiaries against a proper discharge, but they cannot be compelled, unless they are in fact willing to comply with the directions, to do anything else with the trust fund which they are not in fact willing to do. (4) Of course, the rights of the beneficial interest holders are always subject to the right of the trustees to be fully protected against such matters as duty, taxes, costs or other outgoings; for example, the rent under a lease which the trustees have properly accepted as part of the trust property.

So much for the rights of the beneficial interest holders collectively. When the situation is that a single person who is sui juris has an absolutely vested beneficial interest in a share of the trust fund, his rights are not, I think, quite as extensive as those of the beneficial interest holders as a body. In general, he is entitled to have transferred to him (subject, of course, always to the same rights of the trustees as I have already mentioned above) an aliquot share of each and every asset of the trust fund which presents no difficulty so far as division is concerned. This will apply to such items as cash, money at the bank or an unsecured loan, Stock Exchange securities and the like. However, as regards land[102], certainly, in all cases, as regards shares in a private company in very special circumstances (see *In re Weiner*)[103] and possibly (although the logic of the addition escapes me) mortgage

100 [Now TCGA 1992, s 60(2). See *Allison v Murray* [1975] 1 WLR 1578.]
101 [1948] Ch 206.
102 [See eg *Crowe v Appleby* [1975] 1 WLR 1539.]
103 [1956] 1 WLR 579.

debts (see *In re Marshall*)[104] the situation is not so simple, and even a person with a vested interest in possession in an aliquot share of the trust fund may have to wait until the land is sold, and so forth, before being able to call upon the trustees as of right to account to him for his share of the assets...[105] **[20.28]**

(1) Disposals by trustees (other than bare trustees)

A charge to capital gains tax may be imposed on gains which arise on either actual or deemed disposals by trustees of assets comprising settled property.[106] The rates at which trustees pay capital gains tax on such gains are set out later in this chapter.[107]

TCGA 1992, s 71 provides that a deemed disposal (which is peculiar to trustees), occurs when a person *becomes* absolutely entitled to settled property as against the trustee *e.g.* where assets are held in trust for a beneficiary contingently on his attaining a particular age, and he attains that age. In such an instance, TCGA 1992, s 71 further provides that the assets to which the person has become absolutely entitled are deemed to have been disposed of by the trustees and immediately reacquired by them as bare trustees for a consideration equal to their market value. When a chargeable gain accrues to the trustees on such a deemed disposal it may be possible for the trustees and the relevant beneficiaries to defer the incidence of capital gains tax by electing to 'hold-over' the gain.[108] A deemed disposal may also occur under TCGA 1992, s 71 when a beneficiary (other than the settlor) becomes absolutely entitled to settled property because of the death of a person who was entitled to an interest in possession. In this instance, provided that the person became entitled to that interest in possession prior to 22 March 2006 or, if on or after that date, the interest was either an immediate post-death interest, a transitional serial interest, a disabled person's interest or (in the event of the person dying being under the age of 18) immediately before the death the interest was held on an 18–25 trust, there is a deemed disposal and reacquisition by the trustees, but no charge to capital gains tax is imposed on any gain that may arise on the disposal.[109] **[20.29]**

104 [1914] 1 Ch 192 at 199, *per* Cozens-Hardy MR.

105 See further, Anthony Sumption, 'Absolutely Entitled as Against the Trustee' [1980] BTR 341.

106 A trustee, who is not resident or ordinarily resident in the UK, will not be liable to capital gains tax where a chargeable gain accruing on the disposal of settled property is attributed either to a settlor or to beneficiaries under TCGA 1992, ss 86 and 87 respectively. When a gain arises on the disposal by a beneficiary of his *beneficial interest* in settled property, the basic rule is that no charge to capital gains tax is imposed (see TCGA 1992, s 76); the rationale for this rule is explained in the above extract from the judgment of Lord Hoffmann in *Jerome v Kelly* (see above, para **[20.27]**). A charge to capital gains tax may be imposed, however, where the gain arises on the disposal by a beneficiary of a *beneficial interest* in a non-resident settlement (see TCGA 1992, s 85); see also the anti-avoidance provisions in TCGA 1992, ss 76(1A), (1B), and (3).

107 See below, para **[20.46]**. Note, however, that, where a settlor has an 'interest' in a settlement, chargeable gains accruing to trustees of a settlement on the disposal of settled property are attributed to the settlor (and taxed at his rates), see TCGA 1992, ss 77–79.

108 See TCGA 1992, s 165 and Sch 7, para 2 as amended by FA 2006, Sch 20, para 32. For the operation of hold-over relief, see above, para **[20.21]**.

109 See TCGA 1992, s 73 as amended by FA 2006, Sch 20, para 31; see also TCGA 1992, s 72 as amended by FA 2006, Sch 20, para 30 (death of a person entitled to an interest in possession in settled property, but the settlement continues). The amendments to ss 71 and 73, bringing with them a new terminology, are in consequence of the substantial changes made to the inheritance taxation of trusts, which are discussed in Chapter 21.

(2) Resettlements

The phrase 'absolutely entitled to settled property as against the trustee' is not confined to absolute *beneficial* entitlement. It may apply, for example, where there has been a transfer of property from one settlement to another. The trustee of the settlement to which the property is transferred then becomes absolutely entitled to that property as against the original trustee. It is a question of fact whether such a resettlement has occurred. **[20.30]**

Hoare Trustees v Gardner (Inspector of Taxes) [1979] Ch 10 (ChD)

BRIGHTMAN J:. . .I will first consider section 25(3)[110] without reference to paragraph 9 of Schedule 19 to the Finance Act 1969[111], which elaborates the meaning of "absolutely entitled as against the trustee". The conception of a person being absolutely entitled to an asset as against the trustee of that asset would not seem to pose great difficulties in most cases. If property is held by T, the trustee, in trust for L for life with remainder to R, R, if living at L's death, would then be absolutely entitled to that property as against T. If R were dead, one would think that R's executor would similarly be absolutely entitled to that property as against T, even if the executor is not beneficially entitled. If R's estate is fully administered and there has been an assent in favour of the trustees of R's will, one would think that the trustees of R's will had become absolutely entitled to the property as against T or as against R's executor, as the case might be. If R, in the lifetime of L, assigned his remainder interest to X, on L's death X would become absolutely entitled to the property as against T. The answer should be the same whether X is a person who became beneficially entitled by virtue of the assignment or whether he is trustee of some new settlement. The absolute entitlement of the propositus as against T, the new trustee, would appear to be reasonably clear in those cases as a matter of simple language. There is no particular reason to equate absolute entitlement with beneficial ownership in such cases, but rather with the ability to give a good discharge.

Section 22(5)[112] shows beyond doubt that, in the Finance Act 1965, "absolutely entitled" is not identically the same as "beneficially entitled", for the subsection is drawn on the footing that an infant who is an absolute beneficial owner of property held in trust does not, apart from specific provision in the subsection, qualify as a person absolutely entitled as against the trustee. Furthermore, if "absolutely entitled" is confined to absolutely entitled in a beneficial sense, then the words "as against the trustee" are meaningless because they add nothing. An absolute beneficial owner of property held in trust is absolutely entitled as against the whole world, and not merely as against his trustee: he cannot have absolute beneficial ownership as against some persons and not others. On the other hand, the words have meaning if the phrase is interpreted as suggested by the Crown. In the example last given, where R assigns to X and X is the trustee of a new settlement, it would be imprecise merely to describe X as absolutely entitled. He could sensibly be described as absolutely entitled as against T, while he could not be described as absolutely entitled as against the beneficiaries under the settlement of which he is the trustee. The description of a person as being "absolutely entitled as against the trustee" carries the implication that the expression is being used in the sense that that person is not necessarily absolutely entitled as against everyone else. . . **[20.31]**

110 [See now TCGA 1992, s 71(1).]
111 [Now TCGA 1992, s 60(2).]
112 [See now TCGA 1992, s 60(1).]

Swires (Inspector of Taxes) v Renton [1991] STC 490 (ChD)

HOFFMANN J:...Section 54(1) of the 1979 Act[113] provides that a disposal of assets comprised in a settlement shall be deemed to have taken place when any person has become absolutely entitled to those assets against the trustees. There is no dispute that by virtue of the appointment there was such a deemed disposal of the assets to which [a named individual] became absolutely entitled. The issue in this appeal is whether there was also a deemed disposal of the appointed fund. This remained vested in the trustees. But the 1979 Act treats the trustees of settled property as a single continuing body of persons distinct from the actual persons who may from time to time be the trustees. It is conceptually possible for persons acting in their capacity as trustees of a new settlement to become absolutely entitled to assets against themselves as trustees of the old settlement. Therefore, the appeal turns on the question whether the assets remain subject to the trusts of the settlement as varied by the appointment or whether the effect of the appointment was to subject them to the trusts of a new settlement.

The decision of the House of Lords in *Roome v Edwards (Inspector of Taxes)*[114], as expressed in the speech of Lord Wilberforce, shows that the question must be answered according to the view which would be taken of the transaction by a person with knowledge of trusts who uses language in a practical and commonsense way. Which description would be considered more appropriate: that new trusts had been grafted onto the old settlement or that a new settlement had been created?

The more recent decision of the Court of Appeal in 1983 in *Bond (Inspector of Taxes) v Pickford*[115] shows that a critical element in deciding how to describe the transaction may be the scope of the power which has been exercised. If that power allows the trustees to define or vary the beneficial interest but not remove the assets from the settlement or delegate their powers and discretions it is difficult to imagine any appointment within the scope of the power which could be construed as the creation of a new settlement. On the other hand, the power may be expressed in terms wide enough to permit the creation of a new settlement, and the question will then be whether this is what the trustees have chosen to do.

The cases show there is no single litmus test for deciding that question. The paradigm case of the creation of a new settlement would involve the segregation of particular assets, the appointment of new trustees, the creation of fresh trusts which exhaust the beneficial interest in the assets and administrative powers which make further reference to the original settlement redundant (see *Hart (Inspector of Taxes) v Briscoe* per Brightman J[116]). The absence of one or more of those features is not necessarily inconsistent with a resettlement. It seems to me that the question is one of construction of the settlement using the approach recommended by Lord Wilberforce and looking at the documents in the light of the surrounding circumstances. Putting the same thing another way, it is a matter of endeavouring to ascertain the intention of the parties...[117] **[20.32]**

D. Chargeable gains

Gains are computed in accordance with the relevant statutory provisions[118], and every gain, except as otherwise expressly provided,[119] is a chargeable gain.[120]

[20.33]

113 [See now TCGA 1992, s 71(1).]
114 [1981] STC 96 at 100.
115 [1983] STC 517.
116 [1978] STC 89 at 105.
117 [For the circumstances in which hold-over relief may be available in respect of a gain which arises on the deemed disposal of settled property on a resettlement, see TCGA 1992, s 165 and Sch 7, para 2; see above, para **[20.29]**.]
118 See, in particular, the chapters in TCGA 1992 specifically relating to the computation of gains, namely TCGA 1992, Pt II, Chs III and IV (ss 35–57).
119 For exemptions and reliefs, see below paras **[20.47]–[20.63]**.
120 In some instances, gains accruing before a particular date may be excluded from the charge to capital gains tax, see TCGA 1992, s 35 and Schs 2 and 3 (rebasing to 1982 and assets held on 6 April 1965).

Harrison v Nairn Williamson Ltd [1978] 1 WLR 145 (CA)

> BUCKLEY LJ:. . .Broadly speaking, the method of computation so provided has the result that the gain which attracts tax is the excess of the proceeds of disposing of an asset over the cost to the taxpayer of the acquisition of the asset, including the cost of any improvements he may have effected to the asset while in his ownership. So that to compute the taxable gain one has to ascertain two factors: the cost to the taxpayer and the receipts of the taxpayer when the asset is disposed of . . . **[20.34]**

Thus a capital gain, on which capital gains tax may be chargeable, is ascertained, normally, by deducting allowable expenditure (see below, para **[20.47]**) from the disposal consideration received on the disposal of the asset. It is possible, however, that the disposal of an asset may give rise to a loss, and, generally, the amount of a loss is computed in the same way as the amount of a gain.[121] For the purposes of capital gains tax, a loss is usually allowable (and, thereby, may be deductible from chargeable gains) if had a gain been made on the disposal of the asset it would have been a chargeable gain.[122] As a rule, an allowable loss must, in the first instance, be deducted from chargeable gains made in the same year of assessment, but, where this is not possible, such a loss may be carried forward and may be allowed, subsequently, as a deduction from chargeable gains made in future years.[123] **[20.35]**

(1) Consideration

Disposal consideration comprises, generally, either of the following:
(a) the proceeds or value received on the disposal of the asset;[124] or
(b) the market value of the asset disposed of.

'Market value' means the price which the asset might reasonably be expected to fetch on a sale in the open market.[125] **[20.36]**

(2) Allowable expenditure

Generally, allowable expenditure may comprise the following three categories of expenditure:[126]
(a) the amount or value of the consideration given by the taxpayer or on his behalf wholly or exclusively for the acquisition of the asset (together with the incidental costs to the taxpayer of acquisition), or if the asset was not acquired, expenditure wholly and exclusively incurred by the taxpayer in providing the asset.[127] **[20.37]**

121 TCGA 1992, s 16(1).
122 *Ibid*, s 16(2).
123 *Ibid*, s 2(2).
124 If a husband and wife are living together a disposal by one to the other is treated as if the consideration were such that neither a gain nor a loss accrues to the disposing spouse: see TCGA 1992, s 58. The same position pertains in relation to disposals between individuals registered as civil partners under the Civil Partnership Act 2004.
125 TCGA 1992, s 272(1), but note the method by which the market value for shares and securities listed in the Stock Exchange Daily Official List is calculated: see TCGA 1992, s 272(3) and *Crabtree v Hinchcliffe* [1972] 2 AC 707. Note also, TCGA 1992, s 19 (deemed consideration in certain cases where assets are disposed of in a series of transactions).
126 See TCGA 1992, s 38, but see also the treatment of allowable expenditure on the part disposal of an asset (TCGA 1992, s 42), and on the disposal of a wasting asset (TCGA 1992, ss 44–47, 240 and Sch 8).
127 See TCGA 1992, s 38(1)(a).

Stanton (Inspector of Taxes) v Drayton Commercial Investment Co Ltd [1983] AC 501 (HL)

LORD FRASER OF TULLYBELTON:...The next step is to ascertain the value of that consideration. The argument for the Crown, which was accepted by Vinelott J., was that "value" in paragraph (4)(1)(*a*) of Schedule 6 to the Finance Act 1965[128] meant "market value" and might be different from the price agreed between the parties. It was said that the value of consideration was something to be determined by reference to an objective standard, and not by reference to the cost of a particular party. I was at first attracted by this argument. But further reflection has convinced me that it is erroneous for two reasons.

First, as a pure matter of construction of paragraph 4(1)(*a*),[129] I see no indication that value is used as meaning market value. The paragraph is part of the general provisions for computing the amount of gain accruing on the disposal of an asset in the ordinary case: see section 22(9) of the Act. It is to be contrasted with section 22(4) of the Act[130] which makes provision for some special cases, including the case where a person acquires an asset "otherwise than by way of a bargain made at arm's length and in particular where he acquires it by way of gift..." Section 22(4) provides that acquisition of such an asset shall be deemed to be for a consideration equal to the "market value" of the asset, and the obvious reason is that no agreed value, arrived at by an arm's length transaction, is available. But in the ordinary case under paragraph 4(1)(*a*)[131] such a value is available – namely the price agreed between the parties. Consequently there is no need to look to the market value, and no need to read in the word "market" before "value" where Parliament has not seen fit to use it. Further, the deduction permitted by paragraph 4(1)(*a*) includes 'the incidental costs *to him* [the taxpayer] of the acquisition'[132] (emphasis added). The words that I have emphasised show that, at least so far as the costs of acquisition are concerned, it is the costs to the particular taxpayer that are relevant, and they are some indication that the value of the consideration given by him is to be calculated on the same basis.

Secondly, *Osborne* v. *Steel Barrel Co. Ltd.*[133] and *Craddock* v. *Zero Finance Co. Ltd*[134], are ample authority for saying, in the words of Lord Wright in the latter case, that the Revenue are not entitled to go behind the agreed consideration in a case where, as in the present case, the transaction is not alleged to be dishonest or otherwise not straightforward... **[20.38]**

The acquisition cost of an asset may not be obvious. See, for example, the acquisition cost to be attributed to the right to deferred consideration in *Marren v Ingles* [1980] 1 WLR 983; above, para **[20.23]**, and to the right to sue (which can be turned to account) in *Zim Properties Ltd v Proctor* [1985] STC 90; see above, para **[20.24]**. Moreover, in some circumstances, there may be a *deemed* acquisition cost, for example, when the rebasing rules apply, see below, para **[20.44]**.

(b) Expenditure wholly and exclusively incurred by the taxpayer or on his behalf for the purpose of enhancing the value of the asset, and expenditure wholly and exclusively incurred by the taxpayer in establishing, preserving or defending title to, or a right over the asset.[135] **[20.39]**

128 [See now TCGA 1992, s 38(1)(a).]
129 [*Ibid.*]
130 [See now TCGA 1992, s 17(1).]
131 [See now TCGA 1992, s 38(1)(a).]
132 [For the meaning of 'incidental costs', see TCGA 1992, s 38(2).]
133 [1942] 1 All ER 634.
134 27 TC 267.
135 See TCGA 1992, s 38(1)(b).

Oram (Inspector of Taxes) v Johnson [1980] 1 WLR 558 (ChD)

WALTON J: ... So I return basically to paragraph 4(1)(*b*)[136] "the amount of any expenditure". It seems to me that, although one does in general terms talk about expenditure of time and expenditure of effort, having regard particularly to the opening words of paragraph 4(1), where the expenditure is to be "a deduction," the primary matter which is thought of by the legislature in sub-sub-paragraph (*b*)[137] is something which is passing out from the person who is making the expenditure. That will most normally and naturally be money, accordingly presenting no problems in calculation; but that will not necessarily be the case. I instance the case (it may be fanciful, but I think it is a possible one and tests the principle) of the taxpayer employing a bricklayer to do some casual bricklaying about the premises, the remuneration for the bricklayer being three bottles of whiskey at the end of the week. It seems to be that that would be expenditure by the taxpayer, because out of his stock he would have to give something away to the person who was laying the bricks, and I do not think that that would present any real problems of valuation or other difficulty.

But when one comes on to his own labour, it does not seem to me that that is really capable of being quantified in this sort of way. It is not something which diminishes his stock of anything by any precisely ascertainable amount; it is something which would have to be estimated. It has been estimated here by taking the very modest sum of £1 an hour, but the fact that the taxpayer has been modest in his demands does not enable one to escape from the crucial crunch, which is how, in a case which was contested and where the amount claimed was something which was larger that was obviously right, one would test it. It seems to me that there would undoubtedly have to be found in the end some machinery for translating into money terms the work put in by the owner of the asset himself, if that was to be allowable. But it seems to me that that does not fall into the ordinary meaning of "the amount of any expenditure wholly and exclusively incurred on the asset by him or on his behalf." The wording, to my mind, just does not fit that sort of situation.

It is perhaps a matter of first impression based on the impression that the word "expenditure" makes on one, but I think that the whole group of words, "expenditure", "expended", "expenses" and so on and so forth, in a revenue context, mean primarily money expenditure and, secondly, expenditure in money's worth – something which diminishes the total assets of the person making the expenditure – and I do not think that one can bring one's own work, however skilful it may be and however much sweat one may expend on it, within the scope of paragraph 4(1)(*b*).[138] **[20.40]**

Chaney v Watkis (Inspector of Taxes) [1986] STC 89 (ChD)

NICHOLLS J:. . .The taxpayer, Mr Michael Chaney, purchased 25 Sydney Road, Teddington (the property) in 1973 for the sum of £2,000. He disposed of the property with vacant possession by a contract dated 12 February 1981 for the sum of £26,000. At the time of purchase the property was occupied by the taxpayer's parents-in-law as protected tenants. They paid the registered rent. The taxpayer spent altogether £1,475 on improvements.

After the death of the taxpayer's father-in-law discussions took place with the taxpayer's mother-in-law, Mrs Elizabeth Williams, and those discussions culminated in an oral agreement between the taxpayer and Mrs Williams that as compensation for her leaving the property he would pay her half the difference between the tenanted value of the property of £7,200 and the actual sale price; that is £9,400. That was the position when the taxpayer exchanged contracts for the sale of the property.

136 [See now TCGA 1992, s 38(1)(b).]
137 [*Ibid.*]
138 [*Ibid.*]

At the date of exchange of contracts the taxpayer resided at Pope's Cottage, Southleigh, Colyton, Devon. Between that date and completion of the contract on 10 March 1981 a subsequent oral agreement was made between the taxpayer and Mrs Williams varying the earlier one, whereby the taxpayer agreed to construct an extension to Pope's Cottage consisting of a sitting room and a bedroom which would be for the exclusive use of Mrs Williams for the rest of her life, in return for which she released the taxpayer from payment of the sum of £9,400. The extension was duly constructed as part of improvements to Pope's Cottage, costing the taxpayer approximately £25,000. Mrs Williams resided with her son-in-law at Pope's Cottage until the sale of that property on 23 February 1984 and she now resides with him at another property elsewhere in Devon pursuant to the terms of an agreement in writing made on 1 November 1983 which recited the previous arrangements and provided that on the disposal of Pope's Cottage similar accommodation would be provided for Mrs Williams. . .

. . .Before me it was common ground, in that I did not understand the Crown to argue to the contrary, that payment of a sum of money by a landlord to a protected tenant to obtain vacant possession of the property and thereby increase the value of the landlord's interest, could be expenditure wholly and exclusively incurred on the asset for the purpose of enhancing the value of the asset within s 32(1)(*b*).[139] Where the arguments before me diverged was on the legal effect of the fact that after the contract of sale was made the taxpayer did not fulfil his obligation to pay £9,400 to Mrs Williams but in lieu assumed an obligation to provide her with rent-free accommodation for life in Pope's Cottage.

The General Commissioners rejected the taxpayer's claim for the sum of £9,400 to be allowed as a deduction on the short ground that that sum had not been paid. Before me the taxpayer's submission that that decision was wrong had, in effect, two limbs: first, that what happened after the contract was made was irrelevant because the relevant time for looking at the matter was when the contract was made; and, secondly, that the fact at that date the taxpayer's obligation to pay £9,400 was outstanding and not yet fulfilled did not prevent that sum being treated as expenditure.

On the first of these two points the taxpayer's argument was, broadly, that the contract dated 12 February 1981, being an unconditional contract for sale, the time of disposal of the property was when that contract was entered into. Reference was made to the familiar provisions of s 27(1) which, so far as material, provides:

> 'Where an asset is disposed of and acquired under a contract the time at which the disposal and acquisition is made is the time the contract is made (and not, if different, the time at which the asset is conveyed or transferred).'[140]

Then, turning to s 32(1)(*b*)[141], one finds that to be deductible the expenditure must be reflected in the state or nature of the asset 'at the time of the disposal.' Thus, putting together these two provisions, what emerges is that events happening after the time of the disposal, namely after the date of the contract, are not material for s 32(1)(*b*)[142] purposes.

The difficulty with this proposition is that it only has to be stated for it to be obvious at once that if this is correct, and the effect of s 32(1)(*b*)[143] is to freeze the position at the date of the contract, some odd results would follow. I give only one example. A taxpayer might have incurred a liability to make payments to a builder for improvements to be carried out by him and then after a contract for sale of the property had been made and before completion the works were abandoned because they were unwanted by the purchaser, so that in the event no payment was made to the builder. That the vendor in such a case should be entitled to deduct the amount of his liability to the builder at the date of the contract would be absurd.

Thus it was not surprising that in the course of the argument counsel for the taxpayer

139 [See now TCGA 1992, s 38(1)(b).]
140 [See now TCGA 1992, s 28(1).]
141 [See now TCGA 1992, s 38(1)(b).]
142 [*Ibid.*]
143 [*Ibid.*]

felt constrained to accept (in my view, rightly) that a construction of s 32(1)(*b*)[144] which precluded regard being had to what happened post-contract and pre-completion in the case of a liability to make a payment existing when the contract was entered into could not be correct. This is in line with the opening words of s 32(1)(*b*)[145], which contain no requirement that the expenditure must have been incurred before the contract was made. The only difficulty is that created by the 'words at the time of the disposal' in the provision which stipulates that one of the attributes needing to be possessed by expenditure before it can lead to an allowable deduction is that it must be 'reflected in the state or nature of the asset at the time of the disposal'. Counsel for the Crown drew attention to the fact that whilst the statutory predecessor to s 32(1) was in the original Act which introduced capital gains tax (see the Finance Act 1965, Sch 6, para 4(1))[146], what is now s 27(1) was not introduced into the capital gains tax legislation until 1971, by para 10 of Sch 10 to the Finance Act 1971.[147] The Crown's contention was that in s 32(1)(*b*)[148], and despite the provisions of s 27(1)[149], 'time of the disposal' means the time of the conveyance.

In view of the measure of agreement ultimately reached between counsel on this point, this is not an appropriate occasion to attempt a definitive exposition of the temporal ambit of s 32(1)(*b*).[150] Suffice to say that in my view the context in which the phrase 'at the time of the disposal' is found in s 32(1)(*b*)[151] compels the conclusion that that phrase does not exclude expenditure which is first reflected in the state or nature of the property after the date of the contract but before completion.

Given, then, that regard is to be had to post-contract events, what one finds in this case is that the debt of £9,400 was never paid. Instead, the taxpayer agreed with Mrs Williams that in lieu of paying that sum he would provide her for life with rent-free accommodation in Pope's Cottage. I can see no reason in principle why the obligation thus undertaken by the taxpayer is not capable of being valued in money terms. It is not suggested that because of the domestic nature of the arrangement there was not a genuine, legally binding contract for provision of the rent-free accommodation. That being so, I would have thought that, equally as if this accommodation arrangement had been made at arm's length with a stranger, a figure, albeit of a very approximate nature, could be placed on this agreement as the measure in lump sum terms of the cost of such an agreement. So I think that incurring this obligation is capable of passing the test enunciated by Walton J in *Oram (Inspector of Taxes)* v Johnson[152] of expenditure in s 32[153] meaning expenditure in money or money's worth . . . **[20.41]**

Emmerson (Inspector of Taxes) v Computer Time International Ltd [1977] 1 WLR 734 (CA)

The taxpayer company went into voluntary liquidation. At that time, it was in arrears of rent with respect to certain leasehold interests to which it was entitled. The Liquidator of the taxpayer company paid the arrears. On the subsequent disposal of the leases, the liquidator sought to deduct those payments from the consideration received.

ORR LJ: . . . The first question in the appear is therefore whether Fox J. was right in assuming that the payments qualified as deductions under paragraph 4(1)(*b*)[154]; Fox J., as I

144 [Ibid.]
145 [Ibid.]
146 [See now TCGA 1992, s 38(1).]
147 [See now TCGA 1992, s 28(1).]
148 [See now TCGA 1992, s 38(1).]
149 [See now TCGA 1992, s 28(1).]
150 [See now TCGA 1992, s 38(1)(b).]
151 [Ibid.]
152 [1980] STC 222 at 226; [see above, para **[20.40]**.]
153 [See now TCGA 1992, s 38.]
154 [See now TCGA 1992, s 38(1)(b).]

> have stated earlier, not having been satisfied that the expenditure fell at all aptly within the words "for the purpose of enhancing the vale of the asset", but taking the view that they might be considered to have been incurred in establishing, preserving or defending the title to, or right over, the assets in question. For my part I do not find it possible to fit within either of these phrases the performance of obligations under a lease which are an incident of the tenant's title. If a tenant, in breach of his covenants, allows premises to fall into disrepair, it is clear that as a result they will be less valuable than they were immediately before; and if he later repairs them their value will be restored; but I consider that it would be a misuse of language to say that in such circumstances the value will have been enhanced; and it would in my view be very surprising if a tenant who could not claim that timely repairs had enhanced the value was able, by deferring the repairs, to make such a claim and bring himself within the paragraph. Similarly as to a payment of rent, if an overdue payment can be said to preserve or defend the lessee's title, I do not see why the same could not be said of a payment made on the due date, and in my judgment the phrase "expenditure wholly and exclusively incurred in establishing, preserving or defending his title to or to a right over the asset" applies to such matters as evicting a squatter or registering a charge over property, but has no application to the performance of a tenant's obligations under a lease . . .[155] **[20.42]**

(c) the incidental costs of making the disposal.[156]

These costs comprise 'fees, commission or remuneration paid for the professional services of any surveyor or valuer, or auctioneer, or accountant, or agent or legal adviser and costs of transfer or conveyance (including stamp duty)' together with the advertising costs incurred in finding a buyer and any reasonable costs for a valuation required for the purposes of computation.[157] **[20.43]**

(3) The indexation allowance and rebasing[158]

As seen above (para **[20.4]**), the Indexation Allowance (IA) was introduced in 1982. It was intended to counteract the effect of inflation on capital gains and, in so doing, to facilitate the taxation 'real' rather than paper gains.[159] However, over the years, the impact of inflation diminished and, in 1998 following a period of low inflation, measures were enacted, which will lead, in time, to the gradual demise of the IA for capital gains tax purposes.[160] Thus,

155 [It is also evident from the judgments in this case that even if the expenditure had been found to be made for any of the purposes specified in FA 1965, Sch 6, para 4(1)(b) (now TCGA 1992, s 38(1)(b)) it would, nevertheless, have not been deductible, because the expenditure incurred ie the payment of arrears of rent was not *capital* expenditure. On the question of 'establishing' title, compare *IRC v Richards' Executors* [1971] 1 WLR 571 (deductibility of valuation costs incurred, inter alia, for the purpose of 'establishing' the title of executors to assets.), and see also *Allison v Murray* [1975] 1 WLR 1578 and *Passant v Jackson* [1986] STC 164.]

156 See TCGA 1992, s 38(1)(c). Such costs may include actual, but not notional, expenditure incurred on a deemed disposal and reacquisition of assets, see TCGA 1992, s 38(4) and *IRC v Chubb's Settlement Trustees* (1971) 47 TC 353.

157 See TCGA 1992, s 38(2). The 'allowable' valuation costs include neither costs associated with negotiating a valuation with HMRC nor costs incurred in appealing against an assessment, see *Administrators of the Estate of Caton (deceased) v Couch (Inspector of Taxes)* [1997] STC 970.

158 See TCGA 1992, ss 53–57.

159 Broadly, therefore, the operation of the IA may lead to the reduction or extinguishment of a capital gain, but it cannot apply to a capital loss; see TCGA 1992, s 53(1) and s 53(2A) respectively.

160 Although, perhaps surprisingly, the indexation allowance was (and is) retained for corporation tax purposes; see Chapter 18 below (para **[18.5]**).

the IA has been withdrawn for the purpose of computing gains made on the disposal of assets acquired on or after 1 April 1998, ie for an asset acquired on or after this date no indexation allowance is allowable in computing a gain which may be made on its disposal.

Further, in those instances where the IA continues to be a factor in the computation of gains for capital gains tax purposes (see the section entitled 'Indexation' in the extract from the Inland Revenue Press Release, Capital gains tax reform, 17 March 1998, above, para **[20.12]**) it remains as a further allowable deduction for the purposes of computation, which comprises the aggregate of the indexed rise in each item of expenditure allowable under TCGA 1992, s 38(1)(a) and (b) (see above, para **[20.43]**), but it is computed only for the period from the date of acquisition of the asset[161] to April 1998.[162] The indexed rise in such items of expenditure is calculated by multiplying each of those items by a decimal determined by the following formula:

$$\frac{RD-RI}{RI}$$

RD = the retail prices index for the 'relevant month' (ie April 1998 for capital gains tax purposes).

RI = the retail prices index for March 1982 or the month in which the expenditure is incurred, whichever is later.[163] **[20.44]**

(4) Taper relief[164]

It has already been seen (above, para **[20.44]**) that the decision in 1998 to curtail the operation of the IA was accompanied by the introduction of its replacement, taper relief (TR).TR was introduced as part of a reform of capital gains tax which was intended to 'explicitly reward long-term investment' and to discourage, implicitly, short term or speculative ventures. The intention to encourage long-term investment is manifest in the manner in which TR is structured and the nature of the relief which it provides. Thus, generally, TR provides relief on gains made on the disposal of a business or a non-business asset[165] where such an asset has been held for a minimum qualifying period.[166] The effect of TR is to reduce the percentage of gain chargeable with reference to the number of years that the asset has been held i.e. to take part of the gain out of the charge to tax.[167] The following table, which is derived from TCGA 1992, s 2A(5), illustrates the modus operandi of TR.

161 Generally, on the disposal by the taxpayer of an asset which he acquired before 1 April 1982, the IA is calculated by reference to the market value of that asset on 31 March 1982. This rebasing is premised on the assumption that on 31 March 1982 the taxpayer sold the asset and immediately re-acquired it at its market value on that date; see TCGA 1992, s 55(1).

162 Hence, no indexation allowance is available for the period from April 1998 to the date of disposal.

163 See TCGA 1992, s 54(1) and s 54(1A).

164 See TCGA 1992, s 2A and Sch A1.

165 For the conditions which determine whether an asset qualifies as a business asset, see, particularly, TCGA 1992, Sch A1, paras 3–6A.

166 For the purposes of taper relief, the period for which an asset is held is gauged, generally, by reference to periods after 5 April 1998; see TCGA 1992, Sch A1, para 2.

167 See TCGA 1992, s 2A(4). It follows that as the purpose of TR is to reduce the gain it cannot create a loss.

Gains on disposal of business assets		Gains on disposal of non-business assets	
Number of whole years in qualifying holding period	Percentage of gain chargeable	Number of whole years in qualifying holding period	Percentage of gain chargeable
1	50	–	–
2 or more	25	–	–
		3	95
		4	90
		5	85
		6	80
		7	75
		8	70
		9	65
		10 or more	60

The table also shows that the fiscal consequences for a taxpayer, who disposes of an asset (business or non-business), which he has held for the specified maximum period, are significant. Thus, for example, a higher rate taxpayer who makes a gain on the disposal of a business asset which he has held for the maximum period, i.e. two or more years, will have an effective rate of tax of 10%, whilst a higher rate taxpayer who makes a gain on the disposal of a non-business asset which he has held for the maximum period, i.e. ten or more years, will have an effective rate of tax of 24%. **[20.45]**

E. The rates of tax

Chargeable capital gains are taxed at the following rates:

Individuals	the appropriate income tax rate applicable to the taxpayer in the year of assessment.[168] In this regard, capital gains are treated as the top slice of the taxpayer's income.
Trustees	'the trust rate' ie 40% for the year of assessment 2007/2008.[169]
Personal Representatives	'the trust rate' ie 40% for the year of assessment 2007/2008.[170]

The rate of corporation tax imposed on the chargeable capital gains of companies is considered in Chapter 18. **[20.46]**

168 See TCGA 1992, s 4(1). See also, Chapter 14, below, para **[14.34]**.

169 See TCGA 1992, s 4(1AA)(a), and ITA 2007, s 9(1), 15 and Pt 9, Chs 3–6. In the latter respect, note, in particular, the provisions of ITA 2007, s 491 which specify circumstances in which, exceptionally, the trust rate may not be applicable. See also, the treatment of chargeable capital gains of a trust in which the settlor or the settlor's spouse retains an interest (see TCGA 1992, ss 77–79), and the treatment of chargeable capital gains of trusts for vulnerable persons (see FA 2005, ss 30 and 31).

170 See TCGA 1992, s 4(1AA)(b) and ITA 2007, s 9(1).

F. *Exemptions and reliefs*

The gain on the disposal of an asset is not chargeable to capital gains tax where either the gain is exempt or the asset from which the gain is derived is exempt. Further, even if a gain is chargeable, reliefs may be available which reduce the tax payable, eg taper relief which reduces 'the percentage of gain chargeable'[171] or postpone its incidence, eg roll-over relief in relation to the replacement of business assets.[172] An annual exemption is also available.[173]

This section is concerned with some of these exemptions and reliefs. **[20.47]**

(1) Debts

A debt is a chargeable asset for capital gains tax purposes.[174] Generally, however, no chargeable (or allowable loss) arises on the disposal of a debt, unless that debt can be regarded as a debt on a security.[175] The word 'debt' is not defined in TCGA 1992, whilst the word 'security' includes 'any loan stock or similar security whether of the Government of the United Kingdom or of any other government, or of any public or local authority in the United Kingdom or elsewhere, or of any company, and whether secured or unsecured'.[176] **[20.48]**

(*a*) *The meaning of debt*

Marren (Inspector of Taxes) v Ingles (HL; see above, para [20.23])

> LORD FRASER OF TULLYBELTON: . . . The meaning of the word debt depends very much on its context. It is capable of including a contingent debt which may never become payable: *Mortimore v Inland Revenue Commissioners.*[177] It is also capable of including a sum of which the amount is not ascertained: *O'Driscoll v Manchester Insurance Committee.*[178] But I agree with Slade J. and with Templeman L.J., both of whom held that the word 'debt' in para 11[179] does not apply to the obligation of the purchaser under this agreement, which was described by Templeman LJ[180] as 'a *possible* liability to pay an *unidentifiable* sum at an *unascertainable* date'. The words to which I have added emphasis bring out the three factors of this obligation which cumulatively prevent its being a debt in the sense of para 11.[181] Further, the reference to a person who "incurs" a debt "whether in sterling or in some other currency" points, in my opinion, towards the debt being definite, or at least

171 See above, para **[20.45]**.
172 See below, para **[20.59]**.
173 The annual exemption for an individual for the year of assessment 2007/2008 is £9,200 (see TCGA 1992, s 3 and the Capital Gains Tax (Annual Exempt Amount) Order 2007). A husband and wife and members of a registered civil partnership are each entitled to a full annual exemption. Personal representatives are entitled to the same annual exemption as an individual in the year of assessment in which the deceased dies and for the next two years of assessment (see TCGA 1992, s 3(7)). Generally, trustees are entitled to half the annual exemption of an individual ie £4,600 for the year of assessment 2007/2008 (see TCGA 1992, s 3(8) and Sch 1, para 2), but note the availability of the full exemption for trustees of trusts for specified types of disability (see TCGA 1992, Sch 1, para 1(1) and 1(6).
174 See TCGA 1992, s 21(1)(a); see above, para **[20.16]**.
175 See TCGA 1992, s 251(1).
176 See TCGA 1992, s 132(3)(b).
177 (1864) 2 H & C 838.
178 [1915] 3 KB 499.
179 [FA 1965, Sch 7, para 11; see now TCGA 1992, s 251.]
180 [1979] 1 WLR 1131, 1147.
181 [FA 1965, Sch 7, para 11; see now TCGA 1992, s 251.]

ascertainable, in amount. Similarly, paragraph 14 of Schedule 6 to the Act of 1965, dealing with consideration payable in instalments which, by paragraph 14(5),[182] is to be brought into account initially with regard to *inter alia* "a risk of any part of the consideration being irrecoverable", seems clearly to be referring to consideration of an ascertained amount. It is appropriate for dealing with a debt which cannot increase in value, but may decrease if it proves to be partly irrecoverable. Both paragraph 11 of Schedule 7[183] and paragraph 14 of Schedule 6[184] are to be contrasted with section 22(3)[185] which applies to an asset which might either rise or fall in value.

Finally, it was suggested that even if the right to receive half of the profits[186] was not a debt at first, it became one which it was quantified and became immediately payable on December 5, 1972. I agree with Slade J. and Templeman L.J. that that cannot be right because it would lead to absurd results. Every obligation that is ultimately discharged by a money payment must be quantified before payment, and on this argument, capital gains tax would always be excluded when a definite price became payable. In my opinion, paragraph 11 of Schedule 7[187] only applies to an obligation which has been a debt from the time it came into existence, or at least from the time when it was acquired by the taxpayer... **[20.49]**

(b) 'Debt on a security'

Aberdeen Construction Group Ltd v IRC [1978] AC 885 (HL)

LORD WILBERFORCE:...The revenue claims that the disposal of this debt is prevented from giving rise to a gain (or a loss) by Schedule 7, paragraph 11(1)[188] which, as between the original debtor and creditor, does so prevent "except in the case of the [sic] debt on a security (as described in paragraph 5 of this Schedule)".[189] Reference to paragraph 5 plunges us at once into a thicket. The relevant sub-paragraph is (3)(*b*)[190] which reads:

> "'security' includes any loan stock or similar security whether of the Government of the United Kingdom or of any other government, or of any public or local authority in the United Kingdom or elsewhere, or of any company, and whether secured or unsecured."

This raises several difficulties. First, the sub-paragraph does not provide a definition except by inclusion, so the question must arise whether the reference in paragraph 11[191] is limited to what is specifically mentioned as included, or to some wider class. Second, if it defines anything, it defines "security" not "debt on a security", and in view of the words "whether secured or unsecured" the latter must include some unsecured debts. As Lord Cameron said in *Cleveleys Investment Trust Co. v. Inland Revenue*,[192] "whatever else it may mean, the phrase 'the debt on a security' is not a synonym for a secured debt". But which unsecured debts come within the exclusion to paragraph 11[193] and which do not is not stated and I find it impossible to discover any principle on which to state a discrimen.

The general subject of company indebtedness, or of loans to companies seems to be one as to which the legislative mind is clouded. The courts have had difficulties over the

182 [See now TCGA 1992, s 48.]
183 [See now TCGA 1992, s 251.]
184 [See now TCGA 1992, s 48.]
185 [See now TCGA 1992, s 22(1).]
186 [Ie the deferred consideration.]
187 [See now TCGA 1992, s 251.]
188 [See now TCGA 1992, s 251(1).]
189 [See now TCGA 1992, s 132.]
190 [See now TCGA 1992, s 132(3)(b).]
191 [See now TCGA 1992, s 251.]
192 1971 SC 233, 244.
193 [See now TCGA 1992, s 251.]

subject of "funded debt" as to which this House felt obliged to differ from the Court of Appeal (*Reed International Ltd.* v. *Inland Revenue Commissioners*).[194] They have had difficulties over "loan capital" and "issue of loan capital" (*Agricultural Mortgage Corporation Ltd.* v. *Inland Revenue Commissioners*).[195] In that case money was borrowed by the company for capital purposes, the purpose being to enable it to make loans to other persons. The members of the court thought that the money borrowed had the character of loan capital. "The money was required for capital purposes: and it was borrowed money": *per* Scarman L.J.[196] But they did not consider that there had been an "issue". The decisions were on different statutes inter se and from the Finance Act 1965 and it is difficult to find any clear common principle underlying them, but taking such guidance as they do provide leads me to think that the basis on which a distinction can be drawn is between a pure unsecured debt as between the original borrower and lender on the one hand and a debt (which may be unsecured) which has, if not a marketable character at least such characteristics as enable it to be dealt in and if necessary converted into shares or other securities. This is indeed lacking in precision but no more can be drawn from the statutory provisions than the draftsmen have put in – and that is both meagre and confusing ... **[20.50]**

WT Ramsay Ltd v IRC; Eilbeck v Rawling (HL; above, para [5.7])

LORD WILBERFORCE: ... The distinction between a debt, and a debt on a security, and the criteria of the difference, have already been the subject of a consideration in the Court of Session in *Cleveleys Investment Trust Co.* v. *Inland Revenue Commissioners*;[197] *Aberdeen Construction Group Ltd.* v. *Inland Revenue Commissioners*,[198] and in this House in the latter case.[199] I think it no overstatement to say that many learned judges have found it baffling, both on the statutory wording and as to the underlying policy ...

... Such positive indications as have been detected are vague and uncertain. It can be seen, however, in my opinion, that the legislature is endeavouring to distinguish between mere debts, which normally (though there are exceptions), do not increase but may decrease in value, and debts with added characteristics such as may enable them to be realised, or dealt with at a profit. But this distinction must still be given effect to through the words used.

Of these, some help is gained from a contrast to be drawn between debts simpliciter, which may arise from trading and a multitude of other situations, commercial or private, and loans, certainly a narrower class, and one which presupposes some kind of contractual structure. In *Aberdeen Construction* I drew the distinction between[200]

> "a pure unsecured debt as between the original borrower and lender on the one hand and a debt (which may be unsecured) which has, if not a marketable character at least such characteristics as enable it to be dealt in and if necessary converted into shares or other securities."

To this I would now make one addition and one qualification...

... I am not convinced that a debt, to qualify as a debt on a security, must necessarily be constituted or evidenced by a document. The existence of a document may be an indicative factor, but absence of one is not fatal ...

... Secondly, on reflection, I doubt the usefulness of a test enabling the debt to be converted into shares or other securities. The definition in paragraph 5(3)(*b*)[201] is, it is true, expressed to be given for the purposes of paragraph 3[202] which is dealing with

194 [1976] AC 336.
195 [1978] 2 WLR 230.
196 [1978] 2 WLR 230, 247.
197 (1971) 47 TC 300.
198 1977 SC 265.
199 [1978] AC 885.
200 [1978] AC 885, 895.
201 [See now TCGA 1992, s 132(3)(b).]
202 [See now TCGA 1992, s 132(3).]

> conversion: but I suspect that it was false logic to suppose that, because of this, "securities" are to be so limited, and in any event I doubt whether the test supposed, if a necessary one, is useful, for even a simple debt can, by a suitable contract, be converted into shares or other securities... **[20.51]**

Further consideration was given to the meaning of 'debt on a security' in *Taylor Clark International Ltd v Lewis (Inspector of Taxes)* [1998] STC 1259. In that case, the Court of Appeal indicated that the fact that a debt was secured was not a sufficient characteristic in itself for a debt to be a 'debt on a security'. In this respect, Peter Gibson LJ opined (at p 1271) that 'Parliament could not have intended that the existence of any security, however inadequate, for any debt, however impermanent, should without more turn the debt into a debt on a security'. **[20.52]**

(2) Private residences[203]

A gain made by an individual is wholly or partly exempt if it is attributable to the disposal of or of an interest in a dwelling house (or a part thereof) which is or has been his only or main residence.[204]

It is important, therefore, to identify and to define the composition of a taxpayer's dwelling house. **[20.53]**

Lewis (Inspector of Taxes) v Lady Rook [1992] STC 171 (CA)

The taxpayer purchased an estate comprising a large house (Newlands), an adjacent coach house and two cottages. The cottages were about 175 metres from the main house. Subsequently, she sold one of the cottages (No 1 Hop Cottages), which had been previously occupied successively by the widow of an employee of the former owner and by the taxpayer's gardener, and claimed relief from capital gains tax on the ground that the resultant gain was attributable to the disposal of part of a dwelling house which was her only or main residence.

> BALCOMBE LJ: ... The Crown maintains that no reasonable tribunal of fact, properly directing itself, could have reached the conclusion that No 1 Hop Cottages (the cottage) and Newlands together formed one dwelling house which was the taxpayer's residence.
>
> It is to be noted that s 101(1)(a)[205] refers to 'a dwelling-house ... which is ... his ... residence'. The Crown would wish to argue from the reference to a dwelling house (in the

203 See TCGA 1992, ss 222–226B.

204 Where the taxpayer makes a gain on the disposal of the dwelling house in which he has resided such gain will normally be exempt from capital gains tax. However, the courts have drawn a distinction between occupation and residence, and for the exemption to be available there must be 'some assumption of permanence, some expectation of continuity to turn mere occupation into residence' (per Millett LJ in *Goodwin v Curtis* [1998] STC 475 at 480). If a taxpayer has two or more residences it is a question of fact as to which comprises the 'only or main residence' for the purposes of the exemption (see *Frost v Feltham* [1981] 1 WLR 452); although, in such circumstances, the taxpayer may opt for one to be treated as his 'only or main residence' – see TCGA 1992, s 222(5) and *Griffin v Craig-Harvey* [1994] STC 54 (see also, W V W Norris 'Still more about residences: Griffin v. Craig-Harvey' [1994] BTR 534). The exemption may also apply to a gain accruing to a trustee on the disposal of a dwelling house which had been occupied as his 'only or main residence' by a beneficiary entitled to occupy it under the terms of the settlement, see TCGA 1992, s 225 and *Sansom v Peay* [1976] 3 All ER 375. See also TCGA 1992, s 225A (availability of the exemption where the residence is held by personal representatives).

205 [Now TCGA 1992, s 222(1)(a).]

singular) that the buildings which form a taxpayer's dwelling house under s 101(1)(a) cannot include buildings apart from the taxpayer's main house which themselves form a separate self-contained dwelling house. Mr Warren, counsel for the Crown, accepted that this argument was not open to him before us because of the decision of this court in *Batey (Inspector of Taxes) v Wakefield*[206], although he reserved the right to argue the point in a higher court.

Since *Batey v Wakefield* is the first of the three reported cases in which a question arose similar to that in the present case, it will be convenient to consider those cases before turning to the arguments in the present case.

In *Batey v Wakefield* the main house (Paddocks) was a four-bedroomed house set in 1.1 acres of land. On a part of that land the taxpayer built a chalet bungalow (Paddocks Lodge) for occupation by a caretaker/gardener. Paddocks Lodge had one main bedroom, its own garage and separate access from the road. It was separated from Paddocks by the width of a tennis court and a little more. It was built behind an established yew hedge. The taxpayer subsequently sold Paddocks Lodge which sale gave rise to a capital gain and the question was whether that gain was exempt from capital gains tax under the provisions of the Finance Act 1965 corresponding to ss 101 and 102 of the 1979 Act [207] The General Commissioners decided that the gain was exempt. The Crown appealed. The appeal was dismissed, both at first instance by Browne-Wilkinson J and by this court (Stephenson, Oliver and Fox LJJ). Browne-Wilkinson J said[208]:

> 'The difference between the two sides depends on whether one stresses the words "a dwelling house", as the Crown suggests, or the words "a residence", as the taxpayer suggests. In the ordinary use of the words, if one looks at a man's residence it includes not only the physical main building in which the living rooms, bedrooms and bathroom are contained, but also the appurtenant buildings such as the garage and buildings of that kind. One is looking at the group of buildings which together constitute the residence. It is true, as the Crown says in this case, that s 29 [*of the Finance Act 1965*] draws a distinction between a dwelling house, which is dealt with by sub-s (1)(a)[209], and the land occupied and enjoyed with residence as its garden or grounds, which is separately dealt with by sub-s (1)(b).[210] Therefore the dwelling house referred to in sub-s (1)(a) does not include the whole of its curtilage. But in my judgment sub-s (1)(a) is including in the dwelling house some other buildings which are appurtenant thereto; for example, the garage, the potting shed and the summer house, which otherwise would not come within s 29 at all . . . In my judgment the commissioners were right in saying that what one has to look at and discover is: what was the residence of the taxpayer? For that purpose, you have to identify the dwelling house which is his residence. That dwelling house may or may not be comprised in one physical building; it may comprise a number of different buildings. His dwelling house and residence consists of all those buildings which are part and parcel of the whole, each part being appurtenant to and occupied for the purposes of the residence. The Crown does not go so far as to maintain that a building separate from the main can never be part of the dwelling house. If that be so, then it seems to me that the commissioners directed themselves rightly in seeing whether the lodge was itself appurtenant to and occupied for the purposes of the building occupied by the taxpayer. On the commissioners' findings, the lodge was built and occupied to provide services and caretaking facilities for the benefit of the main house. The lodge was occupied by the taxpayer through his employee, who was employed for the purpose of promoting the taxpayer's reasonable enjoyment of his own residence. In those circumstances, bearing in mind the fact that the buildings are very closely adjacent, it seems to me proper to find that the lodge was part of the residence of the taxpayer, and accordingly the gain falls within the exemption in s 29(2).'

206 [1981] STC 521.
207 [See now TCGA 1992, ss 222 and 223 respectively.]
208 [1981] STC 521, 576–577.
209 [Now TCGA 1992, s 222(1)(a).]
210 [Now TCGA 1992, s 222(1)(b).]

Fox LJ (with whom the other members of the court agreed) said[211]:

> '. . .what one is looking for is the entity which in fact constitutes the residence of the taxpayer. I can see no difference in principle between a coachman's flat in the stable yard used for the purpose of serving the main house and a bungalow such as Paddocks Lodge, built on the comparatively small area of land held with Paddocks for the purpose of serving Paddocks. It is, it seems to me, a question of degree in each case. The question is what are the true constituents of the residence which is in question? . . . What has to be determined is the identity of the dwelling house. The fact that it comprised separate accommodation in which staff, or children, or guests may be accommodated does not, in my view, determine conclusively that such accommodation is not part of the dwelling house. It may be a factor, but it is no more. It is, as I have indicated, a matter of degree in every case whether a separate building does or does not in truth form part of the residence in question. That question is one for the commissioners to determine.'

The next case in the sequence is *Markey (Inspector of Taxes) v Sanders*.[212] There there was a main house with outbuildings in 12 acres of land. The taxpayer built a detached three-bedroomed bungalow some 130 metres away from the main house and separated from it by a paddock. The bungalow, which was occupied rent-free by staff, had its own garden, and was also screened by trees and separated by a ha-ha from the main house. The issue was whether the main house and bungalow together formed a dwelling house which was the taxpayer's residence. The General Commissioners held that they did. This decision was reversed by Walton J on appeal. He considered *Batey v Wakefield* and said[213]:

> 'The way in which it was put by the Court of Appeal, therefore, was that one had to look to see whether the separate building was one which was "very closely adjacent"; and so I think one can lay down fairly simply the conditions which have to be satisfied before a taxpayer can claim that a building which is not the part of his main residence where he himself normally resides does for the purposes of the Capital Gains Tax Act 1979 fall within that description. The first condition is that the occupation of the building in question must increase the taxpayer's enjoyment of the main house. That is a necessary but clearly not a sufficient condition. The second condition, and again I take this at the moment straight from the Court of Appeal, is that the other building must be "very closely adjacent" to the main building; and, once again, that is a necessary but not sufficient condition.'

Then after rejecting a test based on the words 'curtilage' and 'appurtenant' as used by the judges in *Batey v Wakefield*, he said:[214]

> 'Now I myself would prefer to ask: looking at the group of buildings in question as a whole, is it fairly possible to regard them as a single dwelling house used as the taxpayer's main residence? I prefer to put it that way because the concept of "very closely adjacent" does not of itself indicate that the scale of the buildings must be taken into consideration, which appears to me to be fairly obvious: for what would be "very closely adjacent" were one dealing with the sale of no 7 Paradise Avenue, Hoxton, might very well be quite different from what those words would mean if one were considering the sale of Blenheim Palace. Of course, those are two absurd examples at either end of the scale, but the fact that buildings can vary as much as those two vary indicates quite clearly that "very closely adjacent" is perhaps in itself too imprecise, whereas if one takes the test that I suggest, which I think is fully in line with the spirit of the decision of the Court of Appeal, it becomes very much easier to see what one is really talking about . . . What is said by counsel for the taxpayer, who has taken every conceivable argument on the part of the taxpayer, is that the test of "very closely adjacent" is an elastic test and that it is one which must be left to the commissioners to determine. I entirely agree that it is an elastic test, but merely

211 [1981] STC 521, 524.
212 [1987] STC 256.
213 Ibid., at 263.
214 Ibid., at 263–265.

> because it is an elastic test does not mean that the commissioners are entitled to apply it absolutely regardless of the facts. Following up his way of putting it, there comes a time when the elastic snaps and the court is entitled to say, "You have gone too far". It is no use the commissioners describing in great detail what is clearly recognisable as an elephant and then concluding that it is a giraffe: it just does not work. So it seems to my mind that something has gone wrong here, but I am totally unable to determine precisely what it is. . .Whilst I do not put it in the forefront of my reasons, it does strike me that it would be a very curious circumstance indeed that where a house, including the ground upon which it stands, is allowed (as it were) free of capital gains tax up to one acre (and there has been no determination by the commissioners that any area greater than one acre would be proper in this case, although I understand that the Revenue is prepared to concede that the gardens, which do exceed the one acre, do qualify for relief) a house which is sited well over an acre's worth of land away from the main residence and separated from it by a paddock which is not part of the ground so allowed could nevertheless be part of it. It seems to me that that really is a totally absurd conclusion.'

The last case in the series is *Williams (Inspector of Taxes) v Merrylees.*[215] In that case a lodge some 200 metres from the main house was held by the General Commissioners to be part of a dwelling house which was the taxpayer's residence, being 'within the curtilage of the property of and appurtenant to' the main house. Vinelott J dismissed an appeal by the Crown, although expressing doubts that he would himself have reached the same conclusion. He considered both *Batey v Wakefield* and *Markey v Sanders*. He doubted[216] whether it was possible to spell out of the decision of the Court of Appeal in *Batey v Wakefield* two distinct conditions each of which must be satisfied before a separate building can be considered part of a dwelling house.

I have to say that I do not find the current state of the authorities very satisfactory, and it is hardly surprising that different sets of General Commissioners have reached conclusions which are not always easy to understand.

In these circumstances it is necessary to go back to the words of the statute. What has first to be determined is what in the particular case constitutes the 'dwelling house'. This is an ordinary English word of which the definition in the Shorter Oxford English Dictionary is 'a house occupied as a place of residence'. That dwelling house can, following the decision of this court in *Batey v Wakefield*, consist of more than one building and that even if the other building itself constitutes a separate dwelling house. Nevertheless, I agree with what Vinelott J said in *Williams v Merrylees*[217]:

> 'What one is looking for is an entity which can be sensibly described as being a dwelling house though split up into different buildings performing different functions.'

How, then, can that entity be identified in any given case? First, attention must be focused on the dwelling house which is said to constitute the entity. To seek to identify the taxpayer's residence may lead to confusion because where, as here, the dwelling house forms part of a small estate, it is all too easy to consider the estate as his residence and from that to conclude that all the buildings on the estate are part of his residence. In so far as some of the statements made in *Batey v Wakefield* suggest that one must first identify the residence they must, in my judgment, be considered to have been made per incuriam.

In all the cases to which I have referred there has been an identifiable main house. Where it is contended that some one or more separate buildings are to be treated as part of an entity which, together with the main house, comprises a dwelling house, Mr Warren submitted for the Crown that no building can form part of a dwelling house which includes a main house, unless that building is appurtenant to, and within the curtilage of, the main house.

At first I was inclined to the view that this introduced an unnecessary complication into the test, even though this was the way in which Browne-Wilkinson J approached the problem in *Batey v Wakefield*. On reflection I have come to the conclusion that this is a

215 [1987] STC 445.
216 Ibid., at 453.
217 [1987] STC 445, 454.

helpful approach, since it involves the application of well-recognised legal concepts and may avoid the somewhat surprising findings of fact which were reached in *Markey v Sanders, Williams v Merrylees* and, indeed, in the present case. In *Methuen-Campbell v Walters* Buckley LJ said[218]:

> 'In my judgment, for one corporeal hereditament to fall within the curtilage of another, the former must be so intimately associated with the latter as to lead to the conclusion that the former in truth forms part and parcel of the latter. There can be very few houses that do not have associated with them at least some few square yards of land, constituting a yard or a basement area or passageway or something of the kind, owned and enjoyed with the house, which on a reasonable view could only be regarded as part of the messuage and such small pieces of land would be held to fall within the curtilage of the messuage. This may extend to ancillary buildings, structures or areas such as outhouses, a garage, a driveway, a garden and so forth. How far it is appropriate to regard this identity as parts of one messuage or parcel of land as extending must depend on the character and the circumstances of the items under consideration.'

That passage was cited with approval by all the members of this court in *Dyer v Dorset CC*[219], all of whom emphasised the smallness of the area comprised in the curtilage. This coincides with the close proximity test to which the other cases refer: 'very closely adjacent' (see *Batey v Wakefield* per Browne-Wilkinson J[220], approved in the same case by Fox LJ[221], and adopted by Walton J in *Markey v* Sanders).[222]

This approach also avoids the difficulty to which Walton J referred[223] in the final passage cited from his judgment in *Markey v Sanders*. Since under sub-ss (2) and (3) of s 101 the 'permitted area' of garden and grounds which is exempt from capital gains tax is limited to one acre or such larger area as the commissioners may determine as required for the reasonable enjoyment of the dwelling house as a residence[224], it does seem to me to be remarkable that a separate lodge or cottage which by any reasonable measurement must be outside the permitted area can nevertheless be part of the entity of the dwelling house.

If the commissioners in the present case had applied what in my judgment was the right test: 'Was the cottage within the curtilage of, and appurtenant to, Newlands, so as to be a part of the entity which, together with Newlands, constituted the dwelling house occupied by the taxpayer as her residence?' – I do not see how they could have reached the decision that they did. The fact that the cottage was 175 metres from Newlands, that Newlands was on the northern boundary and the cottage on the southern boundary of the 10.5 acre estate, and that they were separated by a large garden with no intervening buildings other than the greenhouses and tool shed (as is apparent from the commissioners' findings and the plans and photographs which were before us as they were before the commissioners) leads me to the inescapable conclusion that the cottage was not within the curtilage of, and appurtenant to Newlands, and so was not part of the entity which, together with Newlands, constituted the taxpayer's dwelling house... **[20.54]**

Donald Pearce-Crump 'Paddocks Lodge Revisited (or Private Residence Relief Again)' [1993] BTR 12, 13–17

Taken together, the *Batey* and *Lewis* cases establish the test to be applied in ascertaining the composition of a taxpayer's dwelling-house. It can comprise a

218 [1979] QB 525, 543–544.
219 [1989] QB 346.
220 [1980] STC 572, 577.
221 [1981] STC 521, 524.
222 [1987] STC 256, 263.
223 Ibid., at 265.
224 [See now TCGA 1992, s 222(2) and (3).]

number of separate buildings provided they are within the curtilage of and appurtenant to the main building. *Lewis* has completed the jigsaw left unfinished by *Batey* and as such the Court of Appeal's decision is welcome. It confirms yet again that revenue law does not operate in a vacuum but interacts with the other branches of the law. In order to apply section 222(1)[225] from now on, a tax practitioner will require an understanding of those terms which Balcombe L.J. chose as the ingredients for the "entity test". It is the purpose of this paper to describe those ingredients and evaluate the test.

Preliminary Definitions

... three terms require definition, the first two of which are "corporeal hereditaments" and "incorporeal hereditaments". These are the categories into which real property is divided. The former, as *Blackstone*[226] puts it, consist of such real property as affect the senses – as are seen and handled by the body. This includes both the land itself and also the physical objects which are annexed to it and form part of it, such as buildings and other edifices. Incorporeal hereditaments are not the objects of sensation, and are neither seen or handled, but are creatures of the mind and exist only in contemplation. They are rights attached to land, such as easements and profits à prendre.

The third term is "messuage" which may be regarded as synonymous with the word dwelling-house used in the statute...

"Appurtenant to"

The first element of the test is that the separate building be "appurtenant to" the main house. This is the same as saying that it must "appertain to" the main house. The primary sense of these phrases is derived from the primary meaning of the word "appurtenant", which is itself a term of art...

According to its strict meaning, one corporeal hereditament cannot be appurtenant to another. As a matter of law, only an incorporeal hereditament can be appurtenant to a corporeal hereditament. In *Lister v. Pickford*[227] Romilly M.R. put it this way:[228]

> "... it is settled by the earliest authority, repeated without contradiction to the latest, that land cannot be appurtenant to land. The word 'appurtenances' includes all the incorporeal hereditaments attached to the land granted or demised, such as rights of way, of common, of piscary, and the like, but does not include lands in addition to that granted."

However, it has been recognised by the Courts that the context in which the word "appurtenant" is used may cause its technical meaning to yield to a less strict interpretation. This situation was acknowledged as far back as the reign of Queen Mary Tudor in *Hill v. Grange.*[229] An authority of such antiquity deserves quotation.

> "[All four justices] argued to the same intent and agreed unanimously that land could not be appurtenant to a messuage in the true sense of the word appertaining. For a messuage consists of two things, *viz.* the land and the edifice, and before it was built upon it was but land, and then land cannot be appurtenant to land. [However, they also agreed] that the word [appertaining to the messuage] shall here be taken in the sense of usually occupied with the messuage or lying to the messuage, for when appertaining is placed with the said other words, it cannot have its proper signification...for it is commonly used in the sense

225 [TCGA 1992.]
226 *Commentaries.*
227 (1865) 34 Beav. 576. Also see *Buzzard v. Capel* (1828) B. & C. 141, p.150 and *Cuthbert v. Robinson* (1882) 52 L.J. Ch. 230.
228 *Ibid.* p. 580.
229 (1556) 1 Plowd. 164.

of occupied with, or lying to, *ut supra*, and being placed with the said other words it cannot be taken. . .according to the true definition of it."[230]

In *Evans v. Angell*[231] Romilly M.R. said[232] ". . .where the words are not simply 'appurtenances' but 'lands appurtenant' or 'lands appertaining thereto' . . .[they] rest on a totally different footing."

Where these phrases are used and intended then, the primary sense of the words "appurtenant" and "appertaining" is excluded and one corporeal hereditament can be appurtenant to another. This was the situation in *Lewis* for it is clear from Balcombe L.J.'s test that the primary meaning of the word "appurtenant to" was not within his contemplation as he was clearly speaking of buildings being appurtenant to other buildings.

Having established that one building can be appurtenant to another, the question arises as to how one ascertains whether two buildings are in this relationship. In *Evans* Romilly M.R. said[233] that one piece of land would not be appurtenant to a second if the first did not pass under a conveyance of the second without being specifically mentioned. This, too, was the opinion of Eyre C.J. in *Buck d Whalley v. Nurton.*[234] This means that if a building No. 1 is appurtenant to building No. 2 and a person has building No. 2 expressly conveyed to him, then building No. 1 will also pass to him *sub silentio*, because being appurtenant it did not need express mention.

In *Trim v. Sturminster Rural District Council*[235] Slesser L.J. identified the occasion on which this automatic conveyance would occur. His Lordship put it this way[236]:

> ". . .nothing will pass, in the case of a demise, by the word 'appurtenances' which would not equally pass under a conveyance of the principal subject-matter without the addition of the word 'appurtenances'. . . [No] case has been cited to us in which the word 'appurtenances' has ever been extended to include land which does not fall within the curtilage of the yard of the house itself – that is within the parcel of the demise of the house."

In *Methuen-Campbell v. Walters*[237] the Court also concluded that a piece of land is appurtenant to another only if it is within the curtilage of the principal subject-matter. Roskill L.J. said[238]:

> "It seems to be clear that the cases show that the courts have never yet, even when treating 'appurtenances' as apt to cover a corporeal hereditament, gone as far as construing the word as including land which does not itself fall within the curtilage of the house in question."

It is clear therefore that one building will be appurtenant to another if it is confined to and stands within the curtilage of the other. The crux of the problem becomes identifying the curtilage of a building and this takes one to the other limb of Balcombe L.J.'s test.

"*Within the Curtilage of*"

As to what lies within the curtilage of a building is a question of fact depending on the physical features and circumstances of the building. In *Barwick v. Kent County*

230 *Ibid.* p.170.
231 (1858) 26 Beav. 202.
232 *Ibid.* p. 206. This distinction is also made in *Hearn v. Allen* (1672) Cro. Car. 57.
233 [Above, n 231, (1858) 26 Beav 202 at 205.]
234 (1797) 1 Bos & P. 53.
235 [1938] 2 All E.R. 168.
236 *Ibid.* p. 170.
237 [1979] 1 All E.R. 606.
238 *Ibid.* p. 619. Also see Buckley L.J. at *ibid.* p. 620 and p. 621 where His Lordship quotes from *Bettisworth's Case* (1591) 2 Co. Rep. 31b, p. 32a.

Council[239] the Court of Appeal held that the layout of the buildings and their physical separation was crucial. But what does the term mean?

Stroud's Judicial Dictionary[240] quotes Termes de la Ley[241] which ascribes the following meaning: "A garden yard, field or peece of viode ground laying neare and belonging to the messuage." This definition was approved by the Court of Appeal in *Pilbrow v. Vestry of St. Leonards, Shoreditch*[242]. Some authorities however, would exclude the garden from the definition.

Burn's Law Dictionary[243] gives the following: "A courtyard, backside or piece of ground lying near and belonging to a house." For the purposes of the House Tax of 1808 premises were said to "belong to" a dwelling-house if they were adjuncts to it and were used with it for a common purpose, e.g. the stables of an inn. In *Re St. John's Church, Bishop's Hatfield*[244] Newsome, Q.C., the Chancellor of St. Albans Consistory Court, said that "belong" in the context of the above definition means that the curtilage and the house must go together in a physical sense; both the land and house must be occupied together.

The Oxford English Dictionary defines curtilage as "a small court, yard or piece of ground attached to a dwelling-house and forming one enclosure with it."

In the Scottish case of *Caledonian Railway Co. v. Turcan*,[245] Lord Halsbury L.C. approved the *dicta* of Lords Moncrieff and Watson to the effect that ground was curtilage if its purpose was as much part of a house as a room in the house, that is if it was an integral part of the property.

In *Sinclair-Lockhart's Trustees v. Central Land Board*[246] Lord Mackintosh held:

> "Ground which is used for the comfortable enjoyment of a house or other building may be regarded in law as being within the curtilage of that house or building and thereby as an integral part of the same, although it has not been marked off or enclosed in any way."

In *Re St. George's Church, Oakdale*[247] Chancellor Judge Ellison said that curtilage was to be construed as meaning such small area of the churchyard which physically adjoins the church building and is required to serve some purpose of that building in a necessary and useful way, as an integral part of the church.

In *Dyer v. Dorset County Council*[248] the Court held that the curtilage denotes a small area which is part and parcel of the building it contains or is attached to. In that case it was held that a house on a campus but at a distance from the college buildings was not within the curtilage of those buildings.

The concept which is being developed here is one which describes an area of land which surrounds or adjoins a building and the size of which, while depending on the nature of that building is, even so, not very large. Although Termes de la Ley,[249] and the *Turcan*[250] and *Sinclair-Lockhart*[251] cases suggest that the curtilage might comprise an area of some extent (the latter two seeming to imply that the test also depends upon the function and not the physical criteria alone), it is submitted that the weight of the evidence provides the better view that emphasises the smallness of the

239 [1992] E.G.C.S. 12.
240 3rd Edn.
241 1671 Edn.
242 [1895] 1 Q.B. 433 at p. 445.
243 1792 Edn.
244 [1966] 2 All E.R. 403.
245 [1898] A.C. 256.
246 1950 S.L.T. 283.
247 [1975] 2 All.E.R. 870.
248 [1989] Q.B. 346.
249 [1671 edn.]
250 [[1898] AC 256.]
251 [1950 SLT 283.]

curtilage and its immediate proximity to the house. In *Dyer*[252] Nourse L.J. said that the concept has never escaped from the influence of the diminutive suffix. The land comprising the curtilage is identified as being an adjunct to, belonging to, intimately associated with, a building. Both building and curtilage form a closely knit entity. In the *St. George's Church*[253] case the church and curtilage were treated as one and the same – one entity so to speak. The authorities also show that physical criteria are important in determining the extent of the curtilage and not function. In *Methuen-Campbell* Goff L.J. said[254]; "...the evidence as to user ...goes, I think, no further than to show that the paddock is a valuable amenity. It does not make it an appurtenance and it does not show it to be within the curtilage of the house."

In the context of a homestead, therefore, it can be concluded that buildings are appurtenant to a main house if they stand on ground which is in such a relationship with that house. Those buildings are then part of the entity which comprises a taxpayer's dwelling-house for the purpose of the exemption from capital gains tax.

In *Methuen-Campbell* Buckley L.J. said[255]: "In my judgment, for one corporeal hereditament to fall within the curtilage of another, the former must be so intimately associated with the latter so as to lead to the conclusion that the former in truth forms part and parcel of the latter." All such buildings taken together constitute a dwelling-house for the purposes of section 222(1) ... **[20.55]**

The so-called 'entity test' espoused by Balcombe LJ in *Lewis (Inspector of Taxes) v Lady Rook* was applied by Vinelott J in *Honour (Inspector of Taxes) v Norris.*[256] In that case (in relation to facts which were markedly dissimilar to the 'country house cases' epitomised by *Lewis (Inspector of Taxes) v Lady Rook*), it was argued for the taxpayer that several flats in separate buildings situated in a London square comprised together a dwelling house which constituted the taxpayer's 'only or main residence'. In rejecting this contention, Vinelott J said[257] 'the proposition that [the flats] formed part of a single entity which could sensibly be described as a dwelling house split into different buildings and performing different but related functions is an affront to common sense.'[258]

Further, as the above extract from the judgment of Balcombe LJ in *Lewis (Inspector of Taxes) v Lady Rook* indicates, the exemption may also apply to land, which the taxpayer has for his own occupation and enjoyment with his residence as its garden or grounds, up to an area of 0.5 of a hectare or such larger area as in the determination of the Commissioners is required for the reasonable enjoyment of the house (or a part of it) having regard to its size and character.[259] **[20.55a]**

Varty v Lynes [1976] 1 WLR 1091 (ChD)

BRIGHTMAN J: ... The short point at issue is the capital gains tax position where the taxpayer is the owner of a dwelling house and a garden, the dwelling house being his only

252 [[1989] QB 346.]
253 [[1975] 2 All ER 870.]
254 [[1979] 1 All ER 606 at 615]. Also see Buckley L.J. *ibid.* p. 621e.
255 *Ibid.* p. 621.
256 [1992] STC 304.
257 Ibid, p 312.
258 For further commentary, see William Norris, 'Capital Gains Tax – More about Residences' [1993] BTR 24, and 'Capital Gains Tax – More about Residences' [1994] BTR 32.
259 It would appear that the determination of whether a larger area of land is 'required' for the reasonable enjoyment of the dwelling house having regard to its size and character should be made without regard to the convenience or requirements of the owner of the dwelling house, see *Longson v Baker* [2001] STC 6.

residence; he sells off his dwelling house and a small piece of the garden; then, at a later date, he disposes of the remainder of the garden. Is the gain resulting from the disposal of the remainder of the garden a taxable gain?...

...When the matter came before the general commissioners, the taxpayer maintained that section 29 of the Act of 1965[260], to which I will refer in detail in a moment, did not expressly deal with the case of the disposal of a property in two parts, and that the exemption afforded by that section was equally applicable whether the whole of the property was the subject of a single disposal or of two separate disposals....

...Section 29(1)[261] has identified the two items which can qualify for exemption; namely, the dwelling house or what I will shortly describe as "the garden". The word "or" is used, but clearly it is not intended to be disjunctive. Subsection (2)[262] reads:

> "The gain" – that means the gain in respect of the dwelling house or the gain in respect of the garden – "shall not be a chargeable gain if the dwelling house or part of a dwelling house has been the individual's only or main residence throughout the period of ownership, or throughout the period of ownership except for all or any part of the last 12 months of that period".

The qualification for the exemption, which applies to the two items within section 29, is defined accordingly by reference to one only of those items; there is no mention in subsection (2) of the garden. The exception of "all or any part of the last 12 months of that period"[263] may perhaps have been inserted in order to take into account the not uncommon case where a person who is changing his residence buys and enters into occupation of the new residence before he has been able to sell the previous residence.

Section 29(3)[264] deals with apportionment in a case where the dwelling house was the only or main residence for part only of the period of that taxpayer's ownership, leaving aside the 12 months period[265] covered by section 29(2). It reads:

> "Where subsection (2) of this section does not apply a faction of the gain shall not be a chargeable gain, and that fraction shall be – (*a*) the length of the part or parts of the period of ownership during which the dwelling house or the part of the dwelling house was the individual's only or main residence, but inclusive of the last 12 months of the period of ownership in any event,[266] divided by (*b*) the length of the period of ownership."

Section 29(4)[267] contains a further relaxation. I need not read subsection (4) in detail, but paragraph (*a*) allows one to disregard a period of absence not exceeding three years; paragraph (*b*) a period of absence when the taxpayer worked outside the United Kingdom; and paragraph (*c*) a period of absence of up to four years where his employment precluded occupation...[268]

...The point of interpretation is a short one. I think it can be summarised in exactly the way that the taxpayer put it in his contentions before the general commissioners; namely, should the court read the words "land which he has for his own occupation and enjoyment with that residence as its garden or grounds" as meaning land which he has at the date of the disposal or land which he has at any time while owning the residence?

... I accept Mr Davenport's submission that in these circumstances all that the court can do is to look at that wording adopted by the legislature and decide whether or not

260 [See now TCGA 1992, ss 222–226B.]

261 [Now TCGA 1992, s 222(1)–(4).]

262 [See now, TCGA 1992, s 223(1). The period of 12 months has been extended twice. Initially, it was extended to 24 months in relation to disposals after 5 April 1980, and, subsequently, to 36 months in relation to disposals after 18 March 1991. In practice, the first 12 months of ownership is deemed to be a period of owner occupation if occupation was delayed because the house was being built or altered: ESC D49.]

263 [For the subsequent extensions to this period, see n 262.]

264 [See now TCGA 1992, s 223(2).]

265 [For subsequent extensions to this period, see n 262.]

266 [Ibid.]

267 [See now TCGA 1992, s 223(3).]

268 [This provision will only apply if both before and after the relevant period of absence there was a time when the dwelling house was the taxpayer's only or main residence.]

the remainder of the garden in the present case falls or does not fall within the description in section 29(1)(*b*).[269] If it does fall within that description, then it qualifies for exemption under section 29(2)[270]: if it falls outside that description, then it does not. It is no good counting up anomalies on one side and the other and twisting the language in order to produce what may seem to be, on balance, the most sensible result, and the one which perhaps Parliament might have preferred if all the various combinations of circumstances had been fully debated. The words are: "This section applies to a gain accruing to an individual so far as attributable to the disposal of, or of an interest in, ... land which he has for his own occupation and enjoyment with that residence" *i.e.*, a dwelling house or part of a dwelling house which is, or has at any time in his period of ownership been, his only or main residence "as its garden or grounds". The difficulty of relating the expression "land which he has for his own occupation and enjoyment with that residence as its garden or grounds" to any moment except the actual time of disposal is that section 29(1)(*a*)[271] is clearly looking both to the present and the past – "a dwelling house or part of a dwelling house which is, or has at any time in his period of ownership been, his only or main residence" – while by contrast section 29(1)(*b*)[272], as a matter of language, is looking only to the present; namely, "land which he has for his own occupation and enjoyment with that residence as its garden". In the face of that comparative wording, it does not seem to me possible, without doing violence to the language of section 29(1)(*b*)[273], to read it in the manner desired by the taxpayer... **[20.56]**

(3) Tangible movable property

Generally, no chargeable gain accrues on the disposal of an asset which is tangible movable property and which is a wasting asset.[274] Broadly, tangible movable property means chattels and a wasting asset is an asset with a predictable life of 50 years or less.[275]

If there is a disposal of tangible movable property, which is not a wasting asset, any gain is exempt if the consideration does not exceed £6,000.[276] **[20.57]**

(4) Charities

A gain which accrues to a charity on the disposal of an asset which 'is applicable and applied for charitable purposes' is not a chargeable gain.[277] Consequently, if a charity sells an asset and uses the proceeds of sale for its charitable purposes no charge to capital gains tax will arise.

Where a taxpayer makes a gift of an asset to a charity it is treated for capital gains tax purposes as giving rise to neither a gain nor a loss. In the event of a subsequent disposal of the asset by the charity, the charity is deemed to have acquired the property at the acquisition cost of the donor.[278] **[20.58]**

269 [See now TCGA 1992, ss 222(1)(b), 222(2) and 222(3).]
270 [See now TCGA 1992, s 223(1).]
271 [Now TCGA 1992, s 222(1)(a).]
272 [See now TCGA 1992, ss 222(1)(b), 222(2) and 222(3).]
273 [*Ibid.*]
274 See TCGA 1992, s 45.
275 See TCGA 1992, s 44(1).
276 See TCGA 1992, s 262(1). For the position where the value of the consideration exceeds £6,000, see TCGA 1992, s 262(2), and note also the situation where two or more assets which 'have formed part of a set of articles of any description all owned at one time by one person' are disposed of by that person, see TCGA 1992, s 262(4).
277 See TCGA 1992, s 256(1).
278 See TCGA 1992, ss 257(1) and 257(2).

(5) Replacement of business assets[279]

If a liability to pay capital gains tax arose on all disposals of business assets resulting in a chargeable gain the funds available for running the business and for re-investment would be seriously diminished. Consequently, a trader may elect on the disposal of certain assets used for his trade purposes throughout his period of ownership[280] to postpone any liability to capital gains tax by means of roll-over relief.[281]

A trader may make an election when he disposes of a business asset, which falls within specified statutory classes of asset[282], at a gain, and uses the disposal consideration to acquire, within a prescribed period[283], a new asset (which must fall within one of the classes, but need not be of the same class as the asset disposed of). The new asset so acquired must, on the acquisition, be 'taken into use, and used only, for the purposes of the trade.'[284]

If the election is made, the relief postpones any liability to tax and the trader can deduct the gain on the disposal of the old asset from the acquisition cost of the new asset. The liability to tax is postponed until the trader disposes of the new asset.[285] **[20.59]**

Williams v Evans (Inspector of Taxes) [1982] 1 WLR 972 (ChD)

The taxpayers were in partnership and carried on the business of plant hirers and contractors. They sought roll-over relief following the disposal at a gain of various earth moving machines which had been used in the business. The disposal consideration was used to purchase new machines.

> NOURSE J:... Shortly stated the question for decision on all four appeals is whether roll-over relief from capital gains tax is available in respect of moveable machinery or only in respect of fixed machinery...
>
> ... Roll-over relief was introduced as part of the original capital gains tax legislation enacted by the Finance Act 1965, although it was then in a more limited form than is now available. The present provisions are set out in sections 115 to 121 of the Capital Gains Tax Act 1979.[286] Although in the cases of the present appeals the claims for relief were made under the material provisions of the Act of 1965 it is agreed on both sides that I can work, as did the commissioners, from the provisions of the Act of 1979.

279 See TCGA 1992, ss 152–159.

280 If the asset was used for trade purposes for only a part of the trader's period of ownership an apportionment may be made, see TCGA 1992, s 152(7).

281 Roll-over relief may also be available to those conducting certain activities other than trades, see TCGA 1992, s 158. The meaning of 'trade' for the purposes of a roll-over relief claim was considered in *Re Loquitur* [2003] STC 1394, 1406–1414 (per Etherton J).

282 See the extract from the judgment of Nourse J in *Williams v Evans* below.

283 Generally, the new asset must be acquired in the period beginning 12 months before and ending 3 years after the disposal of the old asset, see TCGA 1992, s 152(3). However, this provision also confers power on the HMRC to allow an extended period within which the acquisition of the new asset might take place, and the HMRC has a discretion as to when the power should be exercised. This power cannot be exercised by the General Commissioners, see *Steibelt (Inspector of Taxes) v Paling* [1999] STC 594 and *R (on the application of Barnett) v IRC* [2004] STC 763.

284 See TCGA 1992, s 152(1); see also *Campbell Connolly & Co Ltd v Barnett (Inspector of Taxes)* [1994] STC 50 and *Joseph Carter & Sons Ltd v Baird (Inspector of Taxes)* [1999] STC 120. However, in practice, this requirement may be relaxed, see ESC D24 (*Relief for the replacement of business assets: assets not brought immediately into trading use*).

285 If, subsequently, the trader disposes of this new asset and uses the disposal consideration to acquire another asset, which falls within the specified statutory classes, a further election for roll-over relief may be made.

286 [See now TCGA 1992, ss 152–159.]

The particular provisions with which these cases are concerned are contained in section 118 of the Act of 1979, formerly section 33(6) of the Act of 1965.
...That section is in these terms:

> "The classes of assets for the purposes of section 115(1) above are as follows. Class 1. Assets within heads A and B below. Head A. 1. Any building or part of a building and any permanent or semi-permanent structure in the nature of a building, occupied (as well as used) only for the purposes of the trade. 2. Any land occupied (as well as used) only for the purposes of the trade. Head A has effect subject to section 119 below. Head B. Fixed plant or machinery which does not form part of a building or of a permanent or semi-permanent structure in the nature of a building. Class 2. Ships, aircraft and hovercraft ("hovercraft" having the same meaning as in the Hovercraft Act 1968). Class 3. Goodwill."[287]

The sole question on these appeals is whether adjective "fixed" in head B of class 1 qualifies plant alone or machinery as well as plant. The Crown accepted that although the machines with which this case is concerned could equally well be described as plant or machinery, nevertheless if head B embraces moveable as well as fixed machinery then the relief is available.

The arguments of Mr. Parry, who appeared for the taxpayers, in favour of the view that "fixed" applies only to plant and not to machinery were to the following effect. His argument proceeded primarily on semantic grounds. He said that the word "or", given its ordinary meaning, is a disjunctive word; conversely that "and", given its ordinary meaning, is a conjunctive word. He said that if you intend to apply an adjective to two nouns you must either use the conjunction or you must repeat the adjective. In other words, if the draftsman had intended to apply "fixed" to both plant and machinery he would either have said "fixed plant and machinery" or "fixed plant or fixed machinery". Mr. Parry accepted that it is not utterly wrong to use an adjective to qualify two nouns, but he said that in general you ought to qualify a noun which is intended to be qualified by an adjective in one of the two ways I have mentioned. Mr. Parry then broadened his argument in this way. He said that the clear object of roll-over relief was to enable those who run businesses to retain the proceeds of business assets in the business and to use them within a reasonable period to buy further assets of the same, or now of a different, kind without having to bear the tax which would otherwise be payable. He said, correctly, that there is no suggestion in this case of there having been any tax avoidance. He said that the taxpayers were simply attempting to qualify for a relief which Parliament had manifestly intended to give them in the circumstances in this case. He said that if you bear the purpose of the relief in mind it would be strange and arbitrary to limit it in what he describes as the non-specific way for which the Crown now contends...

...First, it seems to me that if one looks at classes 1 and 2 and at the assets specified in those classes one is driven to the view that Parliament intended to put some limitation on the types of business assets which were to qualify for the relief and, moreover, to adopt a limitation which broadly speaking had the effect of restricting those assets to land or buildings, or to other assets which bear some resemblance to land or buildings. Assuming for the moment that the Crown's argument is correct, fixed plant and fixed machinery do bear some resemblance to land and buildings; so also do ships, aircraft and hovercraft, in the sense that they are chattels of exceptional size and value which are for other purposes in the law treated in much the same way as land. Mr. Carnworth suggested that the three classes in section 118 were intended to be, and are, self-contained. I am not completely certain that that is correct. It seems to me that even on the Crown's view of head B there might be some overlapping between ships, aircraft and hovercraft on the one hand and moveable machinery on the other. I do not therefore attach any great weight to that point. Secondly, if Mr. Parry's argument were correct it seems to be clear that moveable plant would in any event be excluded from head B. As Donovan L.J. said in *Jarrold*

287 [See now TCGA 1992, s 155. The number of classes has increased since the enactment of the Capital Gains Tax Act 1979. Currently, there are eight classes of assets for the purposes of a claim for roll-over relief.]

v. *John Good & Sons Ltd.*,[288] "while most machinery would also, I think, be plant, there is certainly plant which is not machinery." There was some discussion in argument as to what might be described as familiar forms of moveable plant which were not machinery. The best example which emerged was that of office furniture – desks, tables and so forth. I can see no reason for moveable plant of that character being excluded from head B and for small items of machinery, for example drills, being included. Thirdly, I look at the wording of head B as a whole. If it had simply read "fixed plant or machinery" then there might have been more force in Mr. Parry's submissions. As it is, he would have me read words which follow as applying only to machinery. I think that that is a possible reading of head B, but I am bound to say that I do not think it is a very natural one. It seems to me that the more natural reading of the words which begin with the word "which" is that they are intended to govern fixed plant as well as machinery. In other words, head B is referring to fixed plant which does not form part of a building, etc., and to machinery which does not form part of a building, etc. On that footing I think it would be unnatural to read "fixed" as qualifying only plant and not machinery as well, because it would be rather strange, if not actually ridiculous, for the provision to contemplate that moveable machinery might form part of a building. On the other hand, it is perfectly natural for it to contemplate that fixed machinery might form part of a building.

In the circumstances, principally for the three reasons I have mentioned, it seems to me that the only fair construction of head B is that it applies to fixed plant and to fixed machinery, but not to moveable machinery... **[20.60]**

As seen above, roll-over relief relating to the replacement of business assets may have a retrospective element.[289] Thus, the acquisition of the new asset may occur in a period beginning twelve months before the disposal of the old asset, and yet, nevertheless, the consideration for the disposal of the old asset may be applied in paying for the acquisition of the new asset. However, there must be an acquisition of an asset other than the asset disposed of. Consequently, a taxpayer who acquires an asset and then disposes of part of it cannot roll-over a gain arising on the part disposal of the asset into the acquisition cost of the same asset. **[20.61]**

Watton (Inspector of Taxes) v Tippett [1997] STC 893 (CA)

PETER GIBSON LJ:...A taxpayer who disposes of one business asset and acquires another is allowed by the capital gains tax legislation to treat the chargeable gain realised on that disposal as not giving rise to tax but as deductible from, or in the taxation jargon 'rolled-over' into, the allowable expenditure on the acquired asset in the circumstances specified in s 115 of the Capital Gains Tax Act 1979[290] (the 1979 Act)...

It is clear from s 115(3)[291] that the roll-over may have a retrospective element, in that the acquisition of, or of the interest in, the new assets may take place, or an unconditional contract for the acquisition may be entered into, in a period beginning 12 months before the disposal of, or of the interest in, the old assets. It is possible to conceive of circumstances in which the acquisition, or the unconditional contract for the acquisition of the new assets could precede the disposal and yet the consideration for the disposal of the old assets be applied in paying for the acquisition: the acquisition could be for a deferred consideration or the unconditional contract could require the consideration to be paid on completion, and the payment date in either event could follow the disposal. But

288 [1963] 1 WLR 214, 223–224. [For the meaning of 'plant' for the purposes of capital allowances, see Chapter 10, above, para **[10.66]**.]
289 See n 283.
290 [See now TCGA 1992, s 152.]
291 [See now TCGA 1992, s 152(3); see also n 283.]

both Mr Bramwell QC for the taxpayer and Mr Henderson QC for the Crown were at one in urging us not to construe sub-s (1) literally. To treat the word 'applied' as requiring some sort of tracing exercise would drastically limit the scope of roll-over relief, as in most cases it would not be possible to trace the consideration for the disposal of the new assets. Further, to confine the retrospective effect of s 115(3)[292] to the circumstances which I have mentioned would be to deprive the provision of much of its utility. Mr Henderson told us that the purpose of s 115(3)[293] is to remove the need for a precise chronological sequence of disposal and acquisition, given that there may be good business reasons for a period of overlap. For example, the new assets may need to be fitted out while the old assets are still in use, or there may be difficulty in selling the old assets in adverse market conditions. He was prepared to go further than what was recorded by the judge when he said. . .:

> 'It has always been accepted by the Crown that sub-s (1) is satisfied if the old assets, or the proceeds of the old assets, are part of the resources available to the taxpayer when the new assets are acquired.'

Mr Henderson accepted that if the old assets the subject of the disposal are other than the new assets the subject of the acquisition, then it matters not that the new assets were acquired before the old assets or their proceeds were not part of the resources available to the taxpayer.

I readily see the good sense of a policy allowing the taxpayer trader roll-over relief whatever the sequence of acquisition and disposal, but I cannot disguise my unease at the distortion of the language of s 115(1)[294] with its central condition that the consideration obtained for the disposal of the old assets should be 'applied' in acquiring new assets. If the draftsman only had intended that the consideration on the disposal of the old assets should be matched by the cost of the acquisition of the new assets, he could easily have said so. However, in the absence of argument from the Crown on the word 'applied', I will proceed on the assumption common to both sides that there must merely be a disposal by the taxpayer of old assets and the acquisition by him of new assets.

Mr Bramwell relies on para 60777 of the Revenue's Capital Gains Tax Manual where it is stated: 'The taxpayer may choose the old and the new assets to be included in the claim. Each disposal of a qualifying asset gives rise to a separate entitlement to claim roll-over relief.' Mr Bramwell submits that this shows that it is the claim which defines the assets to which the relief applies. He puts the essence of the taxpayer's case in this way: the taxpayer acquired a qualifying asset and within the time limits of the relief he disposed of part of the asset; that gave rise to a chargeable gain; the taxpayer made a claim under s 115 in which he identified the part disposal of as the old asset and the part retained as the new asset. Mr Bramwell supports the reasoning of the commissioner who identified the point of time at which it is appropriate to consider whether there are separate and identifiable 'new assets' and 'old assets' as immediately after, and not before, the part disposal. Accordingly, the commissioner held that there was no difficulty in treating the part disposed of as the old assets and the remainder of the premises as the new assets. That analysis he held to be consistent with the modus operandi of s 115, whereas, he said, the contrary view gave rise to absurdity. He instanced a case where the taxpayer acquired two separate properties from the same vendor for a single unapportioned consideration simultaneously and then within a year disposed of one of them; in such a case it is accepted by the Crown that the claim would have been allowed, and the commissioner asked why as a matter of common sense should it make any difference that the premises in the present case were not divided into separate pieces of property until one part was disposed of.

The judge reached a different conclusion for two reasons. First, he held that, because the taxpayer by selling unit 1A had made a part disposal of unit 1, it could not be said that the consideration arising from the sale was applied in the acquisition of 'other assets'. Second, he held that no quantifiable part of the consideration received for the disposal of

292 [*Ibid.*]
293 [*Ibid.*]
294 [See now TCGA 1992, s 152(1).]

unit 1A could have been 'applied' in the acquisition of the retained part of unit 1, whatever meaning was given to the word 'applied'.

The explanation given by the judge for that second reason is, with all respect to him, a little difficult to follow. He said. . .:

> 'Under s 35 (1) and (2)[295] the cost of the acquisition and enhancement of Unit 1 must be apportioned between Unit 1A and the retained part of Unit 1 for the purpose of ascertaining the amount of the gain realised on the part disposal. However, there is nothing in s 35 which would enable an apportioned part of the consideration for the disposal of Unit 1A to be treated as part of the consideration for the acquisition or enhancement of Unit 1 as a whole.'

But as s 35(1) and (2)[296] make clear, the apportionment was not only for the purpose of ascertaining the amount of the gain realised on the part disposal but also for the purpose of applying Ch II of Pt II of the 1979 Act[297] in relation to the property remaining undisposed of. Further, the consideration for the disposal of unit 1A did not need to be apportioned. The question was whether it was 'applied' in acquiring 'other assets'. Perhaps the essence of the judge's reasoning on this point is to be found in the penultimate sentence of the judgment where he said. . .: 'The insuperable difficulty in the instant case is that Unit 1 was acquired as a single asset and for an unapportioned consideration.'

Mr Bramwell criticised the judge's acceptance of the Crown's technical argument based on the fact of part disposal. He submitted that s 19(2)(a)[298] was merely a drafting device of no substantive effect to save the draftsman writing 'or part disposal' after references to 'disposal' and he pointed out that in s 19(2)(b)[299] the draftsman has referred to a part disposal as a disposal. He said that the part disposal of a whole asset was the whole disposal of the part.

I am unable to accept Mr Bramwell's submissions, attractively though they were put. As Mr Henderson rightly submitted, it is crucial for capital gains tax purposes to identify the asset acquired and disposed of. In 1988 unit 1 was the asset acquired and it was acquired for a single consideration. Unit 1A did not exist as such. It only came into existence as a separate asset, and the remainder of unit 1 only came into existence as a separate asset, when the requisite partitioning was done and unit 1A was disposed of. Only then could s 35[300] operate to deem for the computational purposes of Ch II[301] part of the original consideration for unit 1 to be the acquisition cost of that retained remainder of unit 1.

Section 19(2)[302] has effect for the purposes of the whole of the 1979 Act.[303] The significant part of the subsection is para (b)[304] which defines what is meant by a part disposal of an asset in a way which makes clear that it is the whole asset which is the subject of the part disposal. As the judge pointed out, a part disposal may or may not involve the disposal of a separable part. The grant of an easement, for example, is a part disposal just as much as the disposal of unit 1A was a part disposal of unit 1. What is crucial to the application of s 115(1)[305] is that there must be an acquisition of assets other than the assets disposed of. The part disposal of unit 1 when unit 1A was sold prevents the remainder of unit 1 being 'other assets' acquired by a relevant acquisition so as to constitute 'new assets'. Mr Henderson pointed to the fact that s 115(5)[306] made express provision for part of a building or structure to be treated as if it were a separate asset in the circumstances specified. Mr Bramwell's riposte was that that subsection applied to old assets and has no application to new assets. But the significance of the point is that when

295 [See now TCGA 1992, s 42 (1) and (2).]
296 [*Ibid.*]
297 [See now TCGA 1992 Pt II, Ch III.]
298 [See now TCGA 1992, s 21(2)(a).]
299 [See now TCGA 1992, s 21(2)(b).]
300 [See now TCGA 1992, s 42.]
301 [See now TCGA 1992, Ch III.]
302 [See now TCGA 1992, s 21(2).]
303 [See now TCGA 1992.]
304 [See now TCGA 1992, s 21(2)(b).]
305 [See now TCGA 1992, s 152(1).]
306 [See now TCGA 1992, s 152(6).]

> the draftsman for the purposes of s 115[307] wanted to modify what constituted the relevant asset he did so expressly. There is no relevant modification in the case of a part disposal of an asset.
>
> I see the force of the commissioner's point that if roll-over relief is obtainable when two separate properties are purchased from a vendor at the same time for a single unapportioned consideration and one is sold within the period allowed by s 115[308], as a matter of common sense it should not make any difference if one property only is purchased but part is subsequently disposed of. But the explanation for the different treatment in those two instances lies in the fact that in the commissioner's example two assets were acquired for the single consideration (apportionable under s 43(4) of the Act[309]), whereas in the present case only one asset was acquired and only one asset existed until the part disposal . . .
>
> It is inherently undesirable that the basis on which in practice roll-over relief, a relief of great importance to traders, is allowed or restricted should be so inadequately reflected in the statutory language . . . **[20.62]**

For an interesting observation on a possible consequence of the interaction between roll-over relief relating to the replacement of business assets and taper relief, see Natalie Lee (gen ed) *Revenue Law – Principles and Practice* (24th edn, 2006) pp 499–500. **[20.63]**

307 [See now TCGA 1992, s 152.]
308 [*Ibid.*]
309 [See now TCGA 1992, s 52(4).]

21 Inheritance Tax

1. Introduction

Unlike capital gains tax, which seeks only to charge tax on the gain arising from the disposal of a capital asset, inheritance tax, which is a tax on the transfer of wealth, often from one generation to the next, can truly be described as a tax on capital insofar as it is levied on the *value* of the property transferred either at death or within seven years of death. The existence of such a tax is rooted in equity, for it has been said that 'income by itself is not an adequate measure of taxable capacity. The ownership of wealth, whether it produces income or not, adds to the economic resources of a taxpayer so that the person who has wealth as well as income of a given size necessarily has a greater taxable capacity than one who only has income of that size'.[1] And yet a case for its abolition is not without merit. In addition to the arguments that capital taxes discourage enterprise and saving and that they are relatively costly to administer, there are two further issues that need careful consideration. The first is the fact that, in many cases, wealth subject to inheritance tax may also have suffered both income and capital gains tax in the hands of the testator. Secondly, whereas it has always been believed that gifts and death taxes only adversely affect the really wealthy,[2] many 'ordinary' people are potentially within the inheritance tax net due to a combination of sharply rising house prices and a tax threshold that has failed to keep pace with this rise, whilst the really wealthy are able to avoid the incidence of the tax by giving away much of their wealth more than seven years before death. These arguments were recognised by the last Conservative Government, which pledged to repeal inheritance tax when it could afford to do so. However, that day may never come. Taxes on the passing of property on death, as well as on certain *inter vivos* gifts made within a limited time before death, have provided the Exchequer with a source of revenue for many years.[3] Although in more recent years the revenue arising from taxes on death has formed a declining proportion of total tax receipts,[4] current HMRC statistics

1 Green Paper on the proposed wealth tax, Cmnd 5704 (1974).

2 See, for example, Wheatcroft & Hewson, *Capital Transfer Tax* (London, Sweet & Maxwell, 1975).

3 Probate Duty was imposed on property passing on death in 1694, and Account Duty (on inter vivos gifts made, initially, three months or less before death) in 1881; see below, para **[21.2]**. In 1894 these were replaced by Estate Duty; see below, para **[21.2]**.

4 For the tax years 1908–09, Estate Duty of £18 million provided the Exchequer with 18.75 per cent of total tax receipts; in 1968–69, duty of £382 million accounted for only 5.8 per cent of total Inland Revenue receipts, and for 2004–05, IHT of £2,907 million was a mere 1.7 per cent.

estimate that inheritance tax for 2006–07 is likely to total some £3.56 billion,[5] a significant increase on previous years.

Although inheritance tax bears more than a passing resemblance to estate duty, it is built upon the foundations of capital transfer tax. The replacement of estate duty by capital transfer tax[6] radically changed the taxation of the transfer of capital from a regime under which duty was imposed on property passing on death, and certain inter vivos transfers made within seven years of death, to a system under which all transfers of value[7] were taxable unless they were specifically exempt.[8] Capital transfer tax was a progressive donor based tax,[9] which was charged on the value transferred by a chargeable transfer made by an individual during his lifetime, with death being the occasion of the final transfer. Key features of the tax were the principles of cumulation[10] and grossing-up.[11]

In 1986, two years after the consolidation of the capital transfer tax provisions in the Capital Transfer Tax Act 1984, the Chancellor of the Exchequer announced that important changes were to be made to the tax.[12] The resulting tax was called 'inheritance tax', and the Capital Transfer Tax Act 1984 was amended to become the Inheritance Tax Act 1984.[13] Inheritance

5 Inland Revenue Statistics, July 2006.

6 By FA 1975, capital transfer tax was charged on inter vivos gifts made after 26 March 1974 and on property passing on deaths occurring after 12 March 1975; FA 1975 ss 20(5) and 22(1). There was much opposition to the tax both within Parliament and outside, and the Conservative opposition vowed to repeal it if and when they were returned to office. In fact, the first Conservative Government under Margaret Thatcher took the bite out of CTT (see n 10 below), before eventually metamorphosing it into inheritance tax.

7 Both inter vivos and on death; see now IHTA 1984, ss 1 and 4(1). Transfers of value are defined in s 3, and ss 10–17 list dispositions which are not transfers of value eg, by s 10, dispositions not intended to confer gratuitous benefit.

8 See now IHTA 1984, s 2 and ss 18–29A. The most important of these are transfers between spouses and civil partners (s 18), the annual exemption (s 19), small gifts (s 20), normal expenditure out of income (s 21), gifts in consideration of marriage (s 22), gifts to charities (s 23), and gifts for national purposes or for the public benefit (ss 25 and 26). Conditional exemption may be claimed under ss 30–35A in respect of property which is, inter alia, of national, scientific, historic or artistic interest. There are also certain reliefs which can be claimed on business property and agricultural property (ss 103–124C), as well as relief for transfers made within seven years of death (ss 131–140) and other miscellaneous reliefs; see ss 141–159.

9 Ie the rate of tax was determined by the donor's estate and cumulative total, and the tax was primarily payable by the donor, or paid out of his estate, although provision could be made for the donee to pay the tax.

10 The rate of tax applicable for both inter vivos transfers and transfers on death was based on the donor's cumulative total transfers at the time of the gift. Initially this cumulation was to continue for the life of the donor, but this period was reduced to one of ten years by FA 1981. During the years 1980 to 1985 there was also a reduction in rates and an increase in the nil rate band, as well as expansion of the other rate bands. This made CTT less severe in its impact.

11 The theoretical basis for the principle of grossing-up was that, where the transferor paid the tax, the tax would itself augment the diminution of his estate consequent on the transfer and, accordingly, the tax itself had to be added to the amount or value actually transferred to determine the 'value transferred' for the purpose of applying the appropriate CTT rate. By contrast, if the donee paid the tax, only the net amount was taxed. There was no grossing up at death.

12 Budget Statement, Hansard, HC, vol XXX, col 175, 18 March 1986. This was later given effect by FA 1986, ss 100–107 and 114, and Schs 19, 20 and 23. Although these changes came without warning, the Conservative Government was going some way towards fulfilling the promise it had made, when in opposition, to repeal CTT.

13 FA 1986, s 100.

tax[14] is based on capital transfer tax, but several major changes were made to the structure of the tax.

Although the value of an estate immediately before death continued to attract inheritance tax, the most critical change was the abolition of tax on inter vivos gifts to individuals[15] unless made within seven years of death,[16] when there is a tapered charge.[17] Such gifts are referred to as potentially exempt transfers[18] (PETS) and, whereas with respect to transfers made prior to 22 March 2006, the term included inter vivos gifts into accumulation and maintenance trusts,[19] trusts for the disabled,[20] the inter vivos creation of trusts with an interest in possession, and the termination of interests in possession,[21] for those made on or after 22 March 2006, aside from outright gifts to individuals, it includes only gifts into disabled trusts, and gifts into bereaved minors trusts on the coming to an end of an immediate post-death interest.[22] Like capital transfer tax, inheritance tax continued to be levied on the inter vivos creation of trusts without an interest in possession (albeit at a reduced rate), as well as on several occasions during the continuation of such a trust. By virtue of FA 2006, this harsher regime has been extended to cover post-22 March 2006 interest in possession trusts as well, with the exception of those that give rise to transitional serial interests, immediate post-death interests and disabled persons interests.[23] And while the inheritance tax advantages arising from accumulation and maintenance trusts created on or after 22 March 2006 have now been removed,[24] they have been replaced by provisions, albeit more limited, dealing with trusts for bereaved minors and age 18–25 trusts.[25] Settled property subject to these trusts are generally, but not necessarily wholly, exempt from the harsher regime. For a detailed explanation of these complex settlement provisions, see para **[21.42]**, below.

Further changes from capital transfer tax to inheritance tax included a return to the estate duty concept of tax being chargeable on the donor when he has made an *inter vivos* gift with a reservation of benefit,[26] and the abolition of the progressive rate structure which formerly existed.[27] There are now only two rates: nil for cumulative chargeable transfers up to the upper limit (£300,000 for 2007–08) and 40% for transfers on death above this threshold. The rate for *inter vivos* transfers is half of the death rate.[28]

This chapter deals with three aspects of Inheritance Tax: history and theory; gifts subject to a reservation; and settlements. **[21.1]**

14 This tax belies its name: it is a mutation duty, as was capital transfer tax, not an accessions duty of the type discussed in the Green Paper 'Taxation of Capital on Death: A possible Inheritance Tax in place of Estate Duty' Cmnd 4930 (1972) (see below, para **[21.3]**). For the distinction between mutation and accessions duties, see below, para **[21.2]**.
15 FA 1986, Sch 19, para 1, inserting s 3A into IHTA 1984.
16 IHTA 1984, s 3A(4).
17 *Ibid*, s 7(4).
18 *Ibid*, s 3A(1).
19 *Ibid*, ss 3A (1)(c) and 71.
20 *Ibid*, ss 3A(1)(c) and 89.
21 *Ibid*, s 3A(7).
22 *Ibid*, s 3A (1A)(c), inserted by FA 2006, Sch 20, Pt 3, para 9.
23 *Ibid*, Pt 2, para 4.
24 *Ibid*, Pt 1, para 2.
25 *Ibid*, Pt 1, para 1.
26 FA 1986, s 102 and Sch 20; see below, para **[21.9]**. Under CTT, there had been no need for such a provision, since all lifetime gifts were charged to tax at the time they were made.
27 By the FA 1988, s 136(1), (2).
28 IHTA 1984, s 7(2).

2. History and theory

John Coombes *Capital Transfer Tax* (1977) pp 1–6

Introduction

A. GENERAL

It is fashionable to classify taxes on gifts and on death into two types. First, *mutation duties,* of which Estate Duty and Capital Transfer Tax represent the best-known and most recent English examples, are those which are essentially charged by reference to the property of the *donor* or *deceased.* Where charged on death only they are frequently called *estate taxes.* These are usually charged at progressive rates on the value of the property leaving the donor's or deceased's ownership on the gift or death. They are affected by the financial and other circumstances of the donor or deceased. Thus, the value of gifts earlier made by him may be added to the value now charged to increase the rates on the latter; deductions may be allowed in respect of the debts and other liabilities of the donor or deceased; reliefs may be allowed if the property was used by him in certain types of business; a reduction may be allowed in respect of property which he recently acquired under another disposition attracting the tax, and so on.

Secondly, *acquisition* or *accessions duties or taxes* (called *inheritance taxes* when confined to transfers on death) are those which are charged by reference to the value of the benefit received by the *donee* or *beneficiary,* and whose rates and exemptions are governed by his circumstances rather than by those of the donor. An accessions duty will normally be charged at lower rates on the benefits received by close relatives of the donor or deceased than on benefits taken by strangers. The rates may be affected by the donee's total wealth, or the value of other gifts earlier received by him. Although these features are usually contrasted with those of mutation taxes, in that in their case it is the wealth and circumstances of the donor or deceased which determine the amount of tax, a pure mutation tax, which ignores altogether the position of donees and beneficiaries, is unlikely to be found, except in the case of very simple and undeveloped taxes (see, e.g., Probate Duty, below). In the case of developed mutation taxes accessions elements will be incorporated. For example, there will typically be favourable treatment for such part of an estate or gift as passes to a spouse or widow or which is given to a public or charitable body.

Broadly speaking, mutation taxes are typical of the English and United States tax systems, whilst the countries of Western Europe tend to favour accessions taxes. Both forms may be found in the various Commonwealth countries. It may be said that accessions duties are the more sensible and fairer. In the end a gift or death tax will normally fall upon the donee and reduce his benefit, and it appears more appropriate that his wealth and financial circumstances-those of the *real* taxpayer-should be the determinant of the amount of tax rather than those of the donor. Further it is sometimes argued that accessions duties are better instruments for the redistribution (*i.e.*, equalisation) of wealth within a community. A wealthy testator or donor may be induced to make a large number of relatively small gifts, each of which will be charged at the lower rate(s), rather than a single gift which will because of its size attract the higher rates. Under the mutation system it generally makes little difference (subject to exceptions) since the value treated as passing will attract the higher rates regardless of the beneficiary. As against this it may be claimed in favour of mutation taxes that:

(i) They are easier to administer. There is no need for a separate enquiry into the circumstances of each and every donee or beneficiary;

(ii) They are sufficiently flexible to take some account of the circumstances of the beneficiary (see, e.g., the examples of gifts to spouses and to public bodies mentioned above);
(iii) Acquisition duties will tend towards redistribution of wealth *within families,* but not throughout the whole population;
(iv) Acquisition duties, being easy to avoid by giving to a large number of beneficiaries, will tend to have a lower tax yield.

B. HISTORY OF BRITISH DEATH AND GIFT TAXATION

It is only with the advent of Capital Transfer Tax (C.T.T.) that taxation on death and on *inter vivos* gifts has been integrated within a single system. Two historical strands, one for death duties, the other for gift taxes, must be traced up to this point. These strands are, however, inter-woven, for it was found that taxes on death must, to be effective, claw in gifts made within some period before the death, because otherwise tax was very easily avoided by the simple expedient of giving away the whole of one's property shortly before death.

DEATH DUTIES

1. Probate Duty. Death duties may be said to begin with this duty which was brought into force as long ago as 1694. This simple mutation duty was essentially a stamp duty, and indeed was called Administration Stamp Duty in the case of intestacies. The duty was charged at first at a fixed rate and later at ad valorem rates (*i.e.*, ascending with the value of the property passing) on death. It applied only to personal estate (*i.e.*, excluding real estate). The tax lasted exactly two centuries, being repealed in 1894.

2. Legacy Duty (introduced in 1780) and Succession Duty (introduced in 1853). These dealt with personal estate and land respectively. They were Inheritance Duties and co-existed with the other duties mentioned above and below until 1949.

3. Account Duty. This was a mutation duty brought in by the Customs and Inland Revenue Act 1881 to combat avoidance of Probate Duty by the giving away of property *inter vivos* shortly before death, or by way of *donatio mortis causa.* Originally the period was set at three months, but not surprisingly it was soon lengthened to one year (in 1889). This duty was repealed in 1894.

4. Temporary Estate Duty. This was a very short-lived duty, introduced in 1889. It supplemented Probate, Account and Succession Duties, where the property passing exceeded £10,000. It was repealed in 1894.

5. Estate Duty (1894–1975). This was a mutation duty. It replaced the old Probate and Account Duties, and Temporary Estate Duty. It applied to property passing under a will or intestacy, to gifts made within a period before the death, and to settled property .... It may be mentioned here that the duty originally only applied on the first death in the case of settlements, *i.e.*, on the testator's death if the settlement was created by his will, or on the death of the first life tenant if the settlement was created *inter vivos*. To compensate the Revenue for the loss of duty where a number of life interests were created, a supporting duty called Settlement Estate Duty was levied from 1894 at a low rate (l per cent. and later 2 per cent.) in addition to the Estate Duty on the first death. Settlement Estate Duty became redundant and was repealed when in 1914 Estate Duty on settled property was extended to deaths subsequent to the first death.

6. Capital Gains Tax. This is more appropriately dealt with under Taxes on Gifts, below. It applied on deaths between 1965 and 1971 and its amount was allowed as a credit (*i.e.*, as a deduction) against the value of an estate for Estate Duty purposes.

TAXES ON GIFTS

1. Estate Duty. The Estate Duty charge, as we have seen, extended back from the death to catch any gifts made by the deceased within a period immediately prior to the death. No duty was, therefore, payable if one survived the "gifts period" after completing a gift. The charge on gifts was not separated from the charge on the rest of the estate. The gift was treated as part of the estate for the purpose of finding the rates of tax on both.

2. Capital Gains Tax. This tax, as already mentioned, was introduced in 1965. In addition to taxing true capital profits it charged (and still charges) donors on the notional gain arising on a gift by treating the gift as a disposal of the property for full market value. The difference between acquisition cost (and expenditure on' enhancement of value, plus the incidental expenditure on acquisition and disposal) and the value of the property at the date of the gift is therefore brought into charge. Thus the whole value of the gift is only charged where the donor himself acquired the property without payment and has incurred no allowable expenditure; and a gift whose value is less than the donor's cost cost of acquisition (plus allowable expenditure) is not chargeable to the tax. In practice, the longer an asset is held the greater becomes the potential gain, at least where the type of asset is rising in value, and the complaint is frequently made that the tax operates indiscriminately upon inflationary and real increases in value.[29]....

It may be noted that Capital Gains Tax was preceded in 1962 by a short-term gains charge to Income Tax (under Case VII of Schedule D). This tax was not intended as a true Capital Gains Tax but was designed to catch "speculative" gains. In fact it operated on both speculative and fortuitous gains indiscriminately. This tax was only charged, as the name implies, where the asset in question was held for a short time. Initially the period varied with the type of asset: it was three years for land and six months for shares. After the introduction of Capital Gains Tax the period for short-term gains was amended to one year for all assets, and the taxes ran concurrently until 1971, when the short-term gains charge was repealed and absorbed into Capital Gains Tax. The short-term gains tax did apply to gifts *inter vivos,* but it did not operate on death.[30]

C. SALIENT FEATURES OF ESTATE DUTY

Estate Duty was charged on property treated as "passing" on a death. The treatment of property as passing was fundamentally changed in 1969, and it will suffice for the purpose of this outline to mention the chief heads of charge as from that time.

BASIC HEADS OF CHARGE

Free Estate. The main head of charge was property of which the deceased was at the time of his death competent to dispose. This caught his "free estate'," *i.e.,* property passing under his will or intestacy (including any property which was subjected to a settlement by the terms of the will or under the statutory intestacy rules). The charge also caught (i) property over which the deceased had a general power of appointment, (ii) his interest in joint property (passing to the co-owner(s) by the right of survivorship). In addition, interests in expectancy (interests in

29 [But now see the indexation and re-basing provisions, above, para **[20.44]**.]

30 [Capital Gains Tax was formerly charged at 30% of the chargeable gain, but since the unification of rates of tax on income and capital gains (see FA 1988, s 98) the rate of CGT is equivalent to either the basic rate of income tax, or the higher rate, where the individual pays higher rate tax on his income.]

remainder or reversion under settlements) were regarded as part of a person's free estate. Further, certain property in respect of which the deceased had no right of enjoyment during his lifetime was caught as property of which he was competent to dispose; for example, superannuation benefits due on death to the estate (because of this many superannuation schemes were so framed that all benefits on death should be payable at the discretion of the trustees of the fund); and damages for loss of expectation of life under the Law Reform (Miscellaneous) Provisions Act 1934 (but not damages for loss of dependency under the Fatal Accidents Acts, which are not payable to the deceased's estate but belong to his dependants)

Gifts *Inter Vivos*. The old provisions relating to Account Duty were kept in force and applied to Estate Duty. The statutory period began at one year but was increased to three years in 1909–10, and to five years in 1946, and finally to seven years in 1968. To prevent avoidance by a deceased who gave property away but was allowed by the donor to continue to use and enjoy it, it was provided that the donor must have assumed possession and enjoyment of the property immediately on the gift and henceforward retained the property to the entire exclusion of the donor, or of any benefit to him by contract or otherwise. The requirement was treated as satisfied if the deceased was excluded for the whole of the statutory period before death.

Settled Property. The rules distinguished between fixed and discretionary trusts.

(A) Fixed Trusts

The settled capital was charged to duty on the death where the deceased was beneficially entitled to an interest in possession in the property either at death or in the seven years before death. This rule ensured that duty was attracted (i) when a life tenant died, (ii) on the death of a former life tenant who had disposed of his interest within the seven years before his death. The value of the entire fund was charged (or a share thereof if the life tenant was entitled to part only of the income), not merely the value of the life tenant's interest (which at death would in any event be nil).

(B) Discretionary Trusts

Different rules applied here because these trusts have no beneficiaries entitled to interests in possession. Broadly, duty was charged where the deceased was eligible to benefit under a discretionary trust of income within the seven years before the death and in fact benefited during that time (or during the seven years preceding the cessation of his elegibility, where that occurred earlier than, but within the seven years before, his death). Where the trustees had allocated the entire income of the fund for the material period to the deceased discretionary beneficiary the entire fund was chargeable. Where he had received part only of the income a slice of the capital was charged, corresponding to the fraction of the total trust income which he had received in the material period. If, therefore, his eligibility ceased, say, two years before his death, and in the seven years before the cessation of eligibility he received a third of the trust income, one third of the fund would be chargeable on his death.

Gifts in settlement (*inter vivos* or by will) were not dealt with by the above provisions, but under the ordinary rules for gifts *inter vivos* or free estate respectively. Further, as already mentioned, the interest of a person having an interest in expectancy under a trust-which of course was not an "interest in possession" – was treated as part of his free estate, so that the value of the interest rather than of the trust fund supporting it was chargeable .... **[21.2]**

Taxation of Capital on death: A possible Inheritance Tax in place of Estate Duty (Cmnd 4930 (1972))

1. Since its introduction in 1894, the estate duty has been the principal duty charged on capital on the occasion of death and it has been the sole duty charged since 1949. As the Chancellor of the Exchequer announced in his Budget statement,[31] the Government believe that the time has come for a thorough-going review which should extend to possible alternative forms of death duty. A detailed examination of these alternatives must be carried out before there can be any question of changing and the Government do not intend to reach a decision on such an important matter without a full public discussion of the possibilities. It is the aim of this paper to encourage such discussion and if, in the light of it, the Government decide that the time is ripe for a change they will, in deciding the form of the new tax, wish to take account of views expressed on the suggestions made in this paper. The main alternative to an estate duty of the type that now exists in this country is an inheritance tax.

2. The essential feature of an estate duty as we now have it is that the tax is graduated by reference to the total value of the property passing on a death, so that for an estate of any given size the same tax is payable whether the whole estate passes to one person or is dispersed among a number of beneficiaries. An inheritance tax, on the other hand, would take no account of the total value of an estate but would be charged on the amounts received by individual beneficiaries. In its simplest form the rate of inheritance tax would be determined for each beneficiary by the total amount of the inheritance he had received on the death in question....

3. An inheritance tax might also take account of other circumstances. The burden could for example be varied according to the relationship between the beneficiary and the deceased....

4. Another possibility would be to fix the rate of tax payable by aggregating all bequests received by the beneficiary during a prescribed period of time.

CRITICISMS OF THE ESTATE DUTY

23. Estate duty has come under increasing criticism in recent years partly because of the growing burden which it represents by reason of the effect of inflation on property values,[32] and partly because of its nature as a tax upon the estates of those who die rather than upon the receipts of those who benefit. Taking the latter first, several points of criticism can be identified. First, although its imposition reduces the amount available to individual beneficiaries, the duty payable is not related to the size of the legacies that they receive nor to their taxable capacity. Second, the tax does not lend itself to variation of the burden by reference to the relationship of the deceased to the beneficiary or by reference to some other special circumstance such as the charitable status of the beneficiary. Third, the tax charged on the value of property passing on death does not take account of expenses incurred in the administration of an estate, a significant part of which can, in some circumstances, arise from the determination of liability to the duty itself.[33]

31 [On 21 March 1972.]

32 [But now see Inheritance Tax Act 1984, s 8, which links the thresholds and rate bands for inheritance tax to the retail prices index.]

33 [Cf the position with regard to capital gains tax: *IRC v Richards' Executors* [1971] I WLR 571; above, para **[20.42]**, n 155.]

Part III: An Inheritance Tax

BASIC PRINCIPLES

43. The essential difference between an inheritance tax and an estate duty is that, whereas an estate duty is charged by reference to the value of the property left by the deceased, an inheritance tax is concerned with what the beneficiaries get. It would therefore be charged on the total amount which each beneficiary received on a death by way of inheritance (which might include, as well as absolute bequests, one or more interests in settled property and gifts from the deceased within a prescribed period before death). The tax so charged would be borne by a beneficiary out of his receipts (or by trustees on his behalf) and would be graduated, like the estate duty. But the graduation would take into account, instead of the total value of the property left by the deceased, either the size of a beneficiary's inheritances on any one occasion, or the amount of his inheritances over a specified period, or perhaps other circumstances of the beneficiary. These might include the beneficiary's relationship to the deceased, so that the differentiation for consanguinity could readily be extended beyond surviving spouses to take account of varying degrees of consanguinity. . . .

57. The fundamental question in relation to graduation is whether the principle should be to relate the tax charge to inheritances on any one death or whether to adopt some wider test of a beneficiary's capacity to pay. The simple principle would be to aggregate all inheritances (including gifts *inter vivos* within the relevant period) which any one beneficiary receives on any one death and to ignore any other circumstances of the beneficiary. This would correspond with the general treatment of inheritances in European countries and, simplicity apart, would recognise that receipt of a substantial inheritance tends to be an isolated occurrence in an individual's experience. It would also accord with the general principle that a death duty sets out to tax capital on the occasion of its passing on death. This method is subsequently referred to as a Variant I.

58. On the other hand it can be argued that the tax should take into account wider considerations than the amount which a beneficiary has received on any one occasion. Thus the approach described in paragraph 57 would mean that on a bequest of £20,000 the same rates would be charged on a poor man, who might have received no other significant inheritances during his lifetime, and a rich man who had recently inherited a very large sum indeed.

59. One way sometimes suggested of adjusting the tax burden to the beneficiary's capacity to pay would be to graduate the inheritance tax by reference to the beneficiary's total wealth. Adoption of this principle would, however, mean that on the occasion of every death it would be necessary to obtain returns of the total wealth of each beneficiary. These would have to be verified and valuations made of many types of property. Apart from other considerations, the resulting administrative burden would be quite impossible.[34]

60. An alternative principle would be to relate the tax to the totality of bequests which a beneficiary had received during his lifetime. Theoretically there is something to be said for this approach but administratively it would represent a most formidable task because it would involve keeping a record over a lifetime for every person who might at some time receive an inheritance above a *de minimis* limit that might be prescribed. Moreover it might be objected that a taxpayer receiving an

34 [One possible solution would be to treat 'accretions' (eg gifts and inheritances), or a proportion thereof, as the *income* of the recipient in the year received, as suggested by the Carter Commission in Canada.]

inheritance in his middle or late years could have his tax bill settled by reference to events of long ago which might have no bearing on his present taxable capacity.

61. There would thus be strong objections to aggregation over a lifetime. But the simplest form of inheritance tax (Variant I) would have the unsatisfactory consequence that the tax burden could be artificially reduced if the members of a family in one generation agreed among themselves that each would divide his estate among the members of the family in the next generation. Each member of the next generation would thus get a number of modest inheritances (taxed at a low rate) from his father and his uncles instead of one large inheritance from his father (taxable at a higher rate). This possibility could be prevented by aggregating inheritances over a specified period of years. Such a scheme, which would be more realistic than aggregation over a lifetime, would also have the advantage that, to produce any given yield from the tax, a lower set of rates would be needed than for Variant I. What the period for aggregation should be would be a matter of judgment; it might be as long as ten years but could well be less . . . . This scheme would call for some *de minimis* exemption of small inheritances in order to simplify administration.

62. The purpose of aggregation over a period would be to determine the appropriate rate (or rates) of tax on successive inheritances; there would be no question of revising, on the occasion of a later inheritance, the tax charge on an earlier one. A suitable method of achieving this purpose would proceed by the following stages:

(1) The most recent inheritance would be aggregated with those received earlier within the preceding ten years.

(2) The total of the earlier inheritances would be treated as the bottom slice of the aggregate.

(3) The tax due on the most recent inheritance would be calculated on the balance as the top slice of the aggregate. **[21.3]**

Note that this donee based accessions duty is very different from the Inheritance Tax introduced in 1986. **[21.3a]**

Graham Moffat *Trusts Law: Text and Materials* (4th edn, 2005) pp 368–371

Inheritance tax (IHT)

(a) Introduction: estate duty to inheritance tax – a return journey?

Death duties have a long history in the UK but the last quarter of the twentieth century witnessed particularly sharp changes of direction in this form of capital taxation. Moreover, given the absence of any political consensus on the issue, the longevity of any particular tax structure seems doubtful. It is, therefore, both useful for purposes of comparison and necessary for an understanding of the present and possible future tax treatment of trusts to trace how the present framework of tax law regulating transfers of capital emerged (see Sandford, *Taxing Personal Wealth* (1971) for an informative account of the history of death duties).

From 1894 to 1974 the main, and from 1949 the sole, death duty in the UK was estate duty. Two interlinking features dominated the history of estate duty during this period. These were the ever-increasing nominal burden of estate duty and the growth of avoidance.

From its inception, estate duty incorporated a progressive rate structure, ie the rate of tax increased with the value of the estate. In 1894 the rates varied between 1 and 8 per cent, and in future years the rate schedule consistently grew steeper. By 1914 the maximum rate had risen to 20 per cent, by 1919 to 40 per cent, by 1939 to 60 per cent and by 1949 to 80 per cent. The rates remained broadly at this high level thereafter. Furthermore the nominal burden of the tax after the Second World War was increased by the effects of continuous inflation. Under a progressive rate schedule, if no allowance is made for inflation by changing the rate structure of the tax, the result is to push the same real value of estates into even higher tax brackets. Sandford has estimated, for instance, that an estate valued at £100,000 in 1949 and paying duty at 45 per cent would have been equivalent to an estate valued at £195,000 in 1967, but the rate of duty on the latter would have been 55 per cent. The absence of indexation increased the incentive to take advantage of the numerous loopholes and concessions. Attempts were made to nullify these, for example by extending the length of the period before death within which gifts were made taxable. Also steps were taken in FA 1969 to counter the avoidance potential of discretionary trusts. Consequently, on the death of a beneficiary of a discretionary trust, a proportion of the value of that fund based on the beneficiary's share of the income of the fund in the seven preceding years was attributed to the deceased's estate. The effectiveness of these responses to avoidance is questionable. They did nothing to still the criticisms of estate duty based on grounds both of horizontal equity ('fairness') and vertical equity ('ability to pay') . . .

A range of alternatives was extensively canvassed with opinion divided between the competing merits of inheritance-based or donor-based systems. (Amongst those favouring a donor-based system were Wheatcroft (cd.) *Estate and Gift Taxation* (1965), and Prest, *Public Finance* (1967). Those favouring an inheritance-based system included Meade, *Efficiency, Equality and the Ownership of Property* (1964) and Sandford, Willis and Ironside, *An Accession Tax* (1973).) Eventually in 1974 a Labour government introduced a donor-based lifetime gifts tax with the title 'capital transfer tax' (CCT). The distinguishing characteristic of CTT as compared with estate duty was the extension to include lifetime gifts on a cumulative basis, rather than to those made only within seven years of death. The principle of cumulation is simply that the rate of tax on any gift, or on an estate left at death, is determined by the amount of taxable transfers previously made during the cumulation period. When cumulation is added to a steeply progressive rate schedule the potential for a severely redistributive tax is apparent.

Yet it was soon claimed that CCT was even less effective than estate duty as an attack on inequality of wealth distribution. The reason in the opinion of one sharp critic (Sutherland, 'Capital Transfer Tax: An Obituary' (1981) Fiscal Studies 51) is that 'CTT has become, as estate duty was, a voluntary tax.' This assessment depends on the assumption that wealth-holders would utilize fully the various concessions made available after the introduction of CTT (see Robinson. and Sandford, *Tax Policy-Making in the United Kingdom* (1983) for a detailed account of the policy process involved). Among the more important concessions were:

(i) the granting of business and agricultural property relief so that for tax purposes the value of the property transferred could be reduced by up to 50 per cent (now 100 per cent in some circumstances);
(ii) the increase in the tax threshold greater than that required to keep pace with the rise in the Retail Price Index; and
(iii) the abandonment in 1981 of the principle of lifetime cumulation and the substitution instead of a cumulation period of ten years.

In consequence it was theoretically possible at 1985–6 tax rates for a married couple – transfers of property between spouses generally being 'exempt transfers' – to pass on to heirs over an eleven-year period £334,000 free of CTT. These figures take no account of the possible eligibility of the assets transferred for business or agricultural property relief. When it is appreciated that an individual with sufficient wealth to fund such a transfer would be among the top 1 per cent. of wealth-holders in the UK the limited nature of the revenue raising and redistributed potential of CTT is apparent.

Then in 1986 significant changes to the structure of CTT were introduced. To the chagrin of tax purists the title of the tax was misleadingly altered to inheritance tax (IHT), a name commonly associated with a receipt-based or accessions tax, whereas the result of the changes was in substance a return to a form of estate duty. Indeed the new structure is an unwieldy amalgam of estate duty and CTT rules. The major alteration to CTT is that the tax charge on lifetime gifts between individuals is abolished as is a charge on gifts into certain trusts. But, as with estate duty, you must make sure you live for seven years after making the gift if tax is to be avoided altogether, since gifts made within seven years before the transferor's death are chargeable. At that point, however, IHT breaks with estate duty by retaining the principle of cumulation, albeit in a modified form based on a seven-year cumulation period. Consequently, where a transferor dies within seven years of making a gift, that gift will be brought into the tax net *and* will, in some circumstances, itself be cumulated with certain other transfers made within the seven years previous to that particular gift. One further and important modification concerns the tax rate structure. Unlike the position under estate duty and CTT there is no longer any progressive rate structure. . . .

None of the initial reforms to CTT or subsequent concessions related specifically to transfers of property into trusts or to the problems of taxing trust under a gifts-tax regime. But CCT did introduce a radical scheme for taxing trusts, particularly discretionary trusts. . . . a significant feature of IHT is that it retains many of the CTT rules for charging tax on trust property. **[21.4]**

For comments on the changes made in the Finance Act 1986 see Cedric Sandford 'Mr. Lawson's Inheritance Tax' [1986] BTR 14, and Robert Walker 'The Reform of Capital Transfer Tax-Better the Devil You Know?' [1986] BTR 145. Generally, see J C Dobris 'Marshalling the Arguments in Favour of Abolishing the Capital Transfer Tax' [1984] BTR 363; C Sandford 'Death Duties: Taxing Estates or Inheritances' (1987) 8(4) Fiscal Studies 15; W Goodhart 'Too Good to be True? A Proposal for the Reform of Taxes on Gifts and Inheritances' [1988] BTR 473; and B Robinson 'Reforming the Taxation of Capital Gains, Gifts and Inheritances' (1989) 10(1) Fiscal Studies 32. **[21.5]**

The Structure and Reform of Direct Taxation, Report of a Committee chaired by Professor J E Meade (IFS, 1978) pp 317–318

THREE OBJECTIVES OF CAPITAL TAXES

To what extent do taxes on the transfer of wealth meet the objectives which it is desired to achieve through the taxation of capital? There are three major sets of objectives which people have in mind when they consider this range of capital taxes.

BENEFITS CONFERRED BY WEALTH

The first of these is to recognise that the ownership of wealth confers benefits upon the owner and is therefore a proper subject for tax. . . . Capital produces an income which, unlike earning capacity, does not decline with age and is not gained at the expense of leisure. . . . wealth itself, quite apart from any income which it produces confers independence, security and influence. Moreover, a tax on wealth, as contrasted with a tax on income from wealth, will . . . increase the incentives of the owners of wealth to seek the most productive uses of their capital so as to yield the highest rate of return.

THE DISTRIBUTION OF WEALTH

A second set of objectives is to promote a more equal distribution of the ownership of wealth. High rates of taxation on the holding of wealth will impede the accumulation of large fortunes; high rates of taxation on the transfer of wealth will impede the inheritance of large fortunes. But capital taxes may have the effect not merely of impeding the accumulation or inheritance of large fortunes by surrender of part of them to the state in the form of capital taxes; they may also have the effect – indeed (as we argue below) they may be imposed in a form expressly designed to have that effect – of giving an incentive to owners of wealth to disperse their fortunes more widely by gift or bequest to those with smaller fortunes.

THE DISTINCTION BETWEEN INHERITED AND SAVED WEALTH

Closely connected with this is a third set of objectives, which is very generally in mind when capital taxes are considered, namely a differentiation of the treatment of inherited wealth as contrasted with wealth accumulated out of the owner's own earnings and savings. Inherited wealth is widely considered – and we share the view – to be a proper subject for heavier taxation on grounds both of fairness and of economic incentives. The citizen who by his own effort and enterprise has built up a fortune is considered to deserve better tax treatment than the citizen who, merely as a result of the fortune of birth, owns an equal property; and to tax the former more lightly than the latter will put a smaller obstacle in the way of effort and enterprise. Whereas an annual wealth tax will fall on wealth which results from a man's own effort, enterprise and saving just as much as inherited wealth, taxes on capital transfers may be chosen so as to fall on the inheritance of wealth without falling on the accumulation of wealth. **[21.6]**

Paying for Progress: A new Politics of Tax for Public Spending, The Fabian Commission on Taxation and Citizenship (2000)

12 Taxing Wealth: the reform of inheritance tax

The taxation of wealth

Those on the highest incomes in society should make a larger contribution to social goods through taxation. From a citizenship perspective the growth of income inequality is a serious concern. But there is another aspect of inequality which –

though it tends to receive much less public attention – is equally important. This is the distribution of wealth. The distribution of wealth in the UK is extremely unequal – more unequal, in fact, than distribution of income. And the trend has been increasing in recent years. The Inland Revenue estimates that the wealthiest 10% of the population own 52% of the country's total marketable wealth – an increase from 49% in 1982. Meanwhile the top half of the population own 93% of all marketable wealth, up from 91% in 1982.[35] At the other end of the scale, the proportion of households with no wealth at all is also rising: an estimated 10% of the population today have no savings or capital to fall back on, compared with just 5% twenty years ago.[36]

Moreover this trend is set to continue. The increasing use of share options as a way of paying executive salaries in the private sector, coupled with the growth of more general equity-sharing schemes, will boost personal wealth further. But only a small proportion of the population will share in the rewards. Those missing out will include not just the low paid and the unemployed, but also workers in the public and voluntary sectors where there is no equity to hold. Rising house prices, particularly in the south east of England, are further widening the gap between owner-occupiers and those whose housing is rented. Meanwhile an increasing number of second generation homeowners are now inheriting the houses of their parents, creating a kind of 'wealth windfall'.

Does this matter? Some degree of wealth inequality is inevitable in any market economy. Indeed, the opportunity to accumulate wealth is as valid an incentive to economic performance, for both entrepreneurs and employees, as higher pay. But the gross inequality in wealth distribution exhibited in the UK is a concern because of the effect it has on equality of opportunity.

Wealth conveys considerable advantages. Those with wealth can borrow more than those without, enabling them to enjoy a higher level of consumption. Wealth provides financial security, the comfort of knowing that unemployment or other misfortunes need not bring immediate poverty. It is difficult to set up a business without some starting capital. It is almost impossible to get on the housing ladder without an initial deposit. Parental wealth is linked with children's educational attainment. For all these reasons, lack of capital entrenches the disadvantage of those on low incomes, and the advantages of the well off. If opportunity is to be extended more widely, it is important that wealth is distributed likewise. One source of wealth to which these arguments apply especially strongly is inheritance, which consolidates inequality across generations.

This is clearly all relevant to the tax system. It suggests the idea that wealth as well as income should be taxed. If wealth confers advantages in the same way as income – and indeed may in some cases simply be income in another form – it should not be treated differently by the tax system. And it suggests a particular focus on the taxation of inheritance.

. . . Inheritance Tax

. . . 'Inheritance tax' 'is something of a misnomer . . . since it is levied not on people who inherit, but on the estates of the deceased. In fact it bears virtually no relation to the amount that any individual inherits, either from the estate in question or over a lifetime. It should therefore be called an estate duty (as indeed existed before 1975). Perhaps the most remarkable feature of inheritance tax today is how few

35 Inland Revenue *Inland Revenue Statistics 1999*, Stationery Office, 1999 (provisional 1996 figures).

36 James Banks and Sarah Tanner *Household Saving in the UK*, Institute for Fiscal Studies, 1999.

people pay it. The main reason is that it is only levied above a threshold of £234,000.[37] The vast majority of people leave less than this when they die (though rising house values have brought more into it over recent years). But it is also because, for the very rich, the tax has become largely voluntary. By passing one's wealth during one's lifetime – so long as this is done more than seven years before death – legacies can be completely tax-free. At the same time, a series of reliefs and exemptions, such as for agricultural land, forestry and private businesses, along with the availability of tax-limiting devices such as trusts, provide ample means of avoidance for those with good advisers. The result is that only 3% of estates end up paying inheritance tax.[38] These are mainly the affluent but not very rich: those whose houses bring them above the threshold but who do not have sufficient savings to feel confident about giving them away before they die...

Objections to the current inheritance tax

There are a number of objections to the current structure of inheritance tax. The first is the basic principle. Exempting most inheritance and gifts from taxation runs against the principle of equality of opportunity. Indeed there is something rather odd about a tax system which taxes income earned from hard work and talent relatively heavily (through income tax) while leaving unearned income largely exempt. If anything, the reverse should be the case.

The second objection is to the formal incidence of the tax. An estates tax bears no relation to the ability to pay of those who inherit. All taxes levied on death are really taxes on legatees, since it is they, rather than the deceased, who are deprived of assets they would otherwise have had. (As Winston Churchill said, an estates duty pretends 'to tax the dead instead of the living.'[39]) Levying the tax on the estate means that no account can be taken of the circumstances of the person who inherits....

The third objection is to the exemption of lifetime gifts. This creates an obvious loophole which encourages the wealthy (who can afford to give away their wealth before death) to avoid paying tax. To the recipient, gifts are no less a contribution to unearned income than legacies; the tax system should therefore treat them in exactly the same way.

The seven year rule in the UK inheritance tax goes some way towards closing the loophole, but not very far. And it introduces a rather morbid feature. As one tax expert has put it, the rule 'represents a state-created lottery ... in which a donor is obliged to engage in a gamble with the state on the length of his life. If he survives the statutory period he wins; if not, the state wins and the family loses. Yet the earlier a man dies, the greater his family's need is likely to be'.[40]

...A capital receipts tax

There are thus strong grounds for reform of the current system of inheritance tax. There are a number of ways in which the present inheritance tax could be reformed to address its current defects. One would be simply to scale back some of the reliefs it offers for agricultural and business property, through which much IHT avoidance is conducted. Another would be to introduce a more progressive sliding scale of rates, coupled with a lower starting threshold. A third option would be to shift the

37 For the tax year 1999–2000.
38 Office for National Statistics, *Britain 2000: The Official Handbook*, Stationery Office 1999.
39 Winston Churchill, *Lord Randolph Churchill*, Macmillan, 1960.
40 Cedric Sandford, 'Towards a Real Inheritance Tax', *Accountancy*, January 1988.

tax to a donee rather than a donor basis: ie levied on the recipient of the legacy rather than the person making it.

In the Commission's view, however, a more thoroughgoing reform is possible, which combines all of these and other features. We would propose the introduction of a Capital Receipts Tax. This would tax not just inheritances but all receipts of capital or 'accessions', whether legacy or gift. The model for such a tax is the Capital Acquisitions Tax levied in Ireland. This tax, incorporating inheritance, gift, discretionary trust and probate taxes, was introduced in 1976 and reformed in 1982, and appears to have worked well,[41] **[21.7]**

Ruth Patrick and Michael Jacobs *Wealth's Fair Measure – The Reform of Inheritance Tax* (Fabian Society, 2003)

3. Taxing the recipient

The first principle of reform we propose is the shifting of the point of taxation (ie the person being taxed) from the estate (the donor) to the recipient. As several people noted during our research, taxing estates is particularly convenient for the tax authorities: the number of taxpayers is limited and well-defined, and evasion is difficult. However, there are a number of reasons why we regard a shift to a recipient-based system as desirable.

Reflecting what we are trying to tax

However administratively convenient, . . . death is itself no reason for a tax to be levied. . . . IHT should not be thought of as a tax on the assets of the deceased, or justified by any claims of under-taxation during life. Being levied on estates, it is true that IHT looks like a tax on the hard work of those who have died. But in practice it is a tax on the unearned windfalls of their legatees. The deceased are no longer alive to pay the tax: although levied on estates, IHT is effectively paid by those who receive the legacies – whose inheritances are reduced as a result.

This would be much clearer, however, if the tax were levied on the recipients rather than on the estate. Shifting the point of taxation would make it evident that its purpose is not to double-tax earned income, but to take account of the increase in taxable capacity enjoyed by individuals when they receive unearned windfalls of wealth.

Public attitudes research suggests that changing the point of taxation in this way would make a considerable difference to the public acceptability of IHT. It would reduce the potency of the 'double taxation' argument (if not remove it altogether) and would make the essential fairness of taxing unearned wealth clearer. It would also remove some of the negative associations of IHT as a 'tax on the dead'. . . . the donor-based system used in the US has helped fuel negative public attitudes to estates taxes, where it has been widely castigated as 'punishing success and savers' . . .

41 For a full account of the Irish tax, see J Condon and J Muddiman *Capital Acquisitions Tax*, 12th Edition, The Institute of Taxation in Ireland, 1999. The proposal for an accessions tax for the UK was comprehensively argued as long ago as 1973 in C T Sandford *et al, An Accessions Tax,* Institute for Fiscal Studies, 1973. This has been an invaluable source of the present report.

Fairness to the individual

Changing the point of taxation from donor to recipient has the important advantage that it takes account of the circumstances of the person receiving the inheritance or gift. At present IHT taxes an estate at a single rate however it is divided up between those receiving inheritances. This means that someone receiving an inheritance who has no other capital assets faces exactly the same rate of tax as someone who is already wealthy. Someone who receives their wealth in the form of gifts escapes tax; the same amount as an inheritance is taxed. This is 'horizontally inequitable' even between recipients of unearned wealth transfers, let alone between them and those with earned income.

A recipient-based system is more progressive than an estate tax, since the starting threshold applies to those receiving rather than to the estate as a whole. Under the current, donor-based system, the tax rate paid is the same whatever the size of the inheritance received. Now let us imagine a recipient-based tax with a starting exemption of £100,000 and a tax rate of 40 per cent, and consider an estate of £500,000. If the estate were left to only one person, he or she would pay £160,000 (40 per cent of £400,000). This represents an effective tax rate on the whole legacy of 32 per cent. If on the other hand the estate were left to two people receiving £250,000 each, each would pay only £60,000 (40 per cent of £150,000). This is an effective tax rate of 24 per cent. If the estate were left equally to five people, each receiving £100,000, none would pay anything (tax rate = 0 per cent). Thus the tax rate declines according to the size of the legacy received, an important principle of progressive taxation...

Changing Behaviour

The Fabian Commission on Taxation and Citizenship argued that a recipient-based tax would change the behaviour of those leaving legacies. By giving their money away more widely, donors could effectively reduce the tax burden suffered. This was indeed one of the principal arguments which the Commission used in favour of reform: they saw it as a means to widen the distribution of wealth. Donors would have a financial incentive to divide up their estates between more people, with a particular incentive to leave it to those with no other wealth.

We are now unconvinced by this argument.... people are unlikely to change their estate planning in response to a different kind of IHT regime. Donors tend to bequeath to their immediate families (spouse and children); the size of the family unit is much more important in determining the number of beneficiaries than the law or tax rate...

This is an important conclusion, since it removes the argument that a reform of IHT would in itself lead to a wider distribution of wealth. It does not alter the argument that the wealthy should contribute a greater proportion of the common tax pool than they do currently, or that the tax system should treat people equally however they have come by their funds. But it leaves the argument for wider wealth distribution elsewhere. This must depend on how the revenues from IHT and other taxes are used, particularly how far they can be redistributed to those without wealth ....

Incentives to saving and enterprise

Opponents of any form of IHT argue that taxing bequests creates a disincentive to enterprise and investment. It is claimed that people are put off generating wealth and then saving it because they know that when they die they will be unable to pass it all on to their children or other chosen recipients....

But there is actually very little evidence for this argument. Most lifetime saving is not undertaken for the purpose of bequest, but simply for security and later consumption. The majority of people only begin to think seriously about the size of their legacies when they reach a certain age, at which time most of their saving has been completed, and their savings habits have become ingrained. And if rates of tax do affect some people's incentives, it is not clear how. On the one hand an individual trying to build a target capital sum to bequeath will be required to work and save harder to reach it; on the other, the person weighing effort or sacrifice against reward may be discouraged into working and saving less. Which of these effects will be the stronger will depend on the individual. In fact . . . research in the US suggests that taxing wealth at death has a positive impact on saving and wealth creation.

In terms of our own proposal, which involves only modest tax changes (and which could well involve reductions in the tax rate for certain recipients), we find it hard to believe that the impact will be significant. . .

On the other hand, the incentive effect on recipients does seem fairly clear. Since IHT reduces unearned wealth, it can only increase the incentives to work and save for the recipients. In this sense a higher IHT could be described as a positively pro-enterprise measure: it encourages those who might otherwise rest on the laurels of inheritance to go out and work for their wealth. . .

4. Taxing gifts

The second principle of reform we propose is the taxation of lifetime gifts as well as legacies. This would include gifts of money, artefacts (such as cars and jewellery) and property. Tax would be charged on the market value of the gift. . .

We argue for the assessment of gifts on a cumulative basis. Inheritances and gifts should not be taxed in isolation; rather all wealth transfers to the recipient during their lifetime should be aggregated and the tax rate based on this. . .

Closing the avoidance loophole

At present, lifetime gifts are not taxed if they are given more than seven years before the death of the donor. This creates a simple means of avoidance, particularly for those wealthy enough to give their money away before death. Those with more modest assets are more likely to preserve them in case they are needed as income in old age, or for long term care. Many will only have their home, which cannot be liquidated before death.

The exemption of most lifetime gifts is the principal reason why IHT in its current form, can be described as more or less voluntary for the very wealthy. In turn, this makes the tax effectively regressive over those people to whom it is intended to apply: a higher rate of tax is paid by the less well off than by the very affluent.

The cumulative principle is then required to ensure against 'gift-splitting'. If gifts are not aggregated it would be possible to avoid tax by dividing the sum to be given into a succession of separate gifts over a period, each under the gift threshold. The cumulative principle ensures that all gifts from the same person, and from different donors, are added together, and the tax rate based on the aggregate sum.

Equity

This would in turn ensure horizontal equity. At present people who choose not to make gifts, who are insufficiently secure to do so, whose wealth is in a form which makes giving away part of it difficult, or who are simply unlucky in calculating their date of death, have a greater liability to tax than others with the same size of estate. For the recipients, it means that the person who receives wealth in the form of an inheritance (above the threshold) will be taxed; another individual who receives the same amount in the form of gifts will not . . . **[21.8]**

It was concluded by Dominic Maxwell in '*Fair Dues: Towards a more progressive inheritance tax*', Institute for Public Policy Research (2004), that "a progressive and effective CRT would be a difficult challenge. A whole new category of activity would be taxed, and that the hoped-for benefits in giving behaviour are far from certain." The preferred alternative was to break inheritance tax rates down into different bands. This was favoured because of its simplicity and because it would contribute to what was viewed as a 'fairer, more progressive inheritance tax.' In contrast, '*Inheritance Tax: A New Direction*', Consultation Paper No 3, Conservative Central Office (December 2004), was more concerned with the effect of rising house prices, bringing more estates within the inheritance tax net, and widening still further the gulf between those who have the means to plan to minimise their IHT liability, and those whose only form of real wealth is the house in which they live. The main thrust of this consultation paper was how to reduce the burden of IHT and how to remove the burden on ordinary families. For arguments in favour of the abolition of inheritance tax, see Barry Bracewell-Milnes, *Euthanasia for Death Duties* (2002, Institute of Economic Affairs). **[21.8a]**

3. Gifts subject to a reservation of benefit by the donor

A. *General*

The reservation of benefit rules comprise a series of anti-avoidance measures which seek to prevent donors from making lifetime gifts of assets (and thus free of inheritance tax on surviving seven years from the date of the gift) while continuing to enjoy or benefit from those assets; in other words, a donor is not allowed to have his cake and eat it.[42] The basic rule is to be found in the Finance Act 1986, s102:

'(1) . . . This section applies where, on or after 18th March 1986, an individual disposes of any property by way of gift and either–

(a) possession and enjoyment of the property is not bona fide assumed by the donee at or before the beginning of the relevant period; or
(b) at any time in the relevant period the property is not enjoyed to the entire exclusion, or virtually to the entire exclusion, of the donor and of any benefit to him by contract or otherwise;

and in this section "the relevant period" means a period ending on the date of the donor's death and beginning seven years before that date or, if it is later, on the date of the gift.

(2) If and so long as–

(a) possession and enjoyment of any property is not bona fide assumed as mentioned on subsection (1)(a) above, or
(b) any property is not enjoyed as mentioned in subsection (1)(b) above,

the property is referred to (in relation to the gift and the donor) as property subject to a reservation.'

42 Per Lord Hoffmann in *Ingram v IRC* [2001] AC 293.

If property subject to a reservation exists within seven years of the donor's death, the property in question is treated as property to which he was entitled immediately before his death. Accordingly, the value of the property will be brought into charge at that time, and will be charged to IHT at the donor's death rate. Moreover, if property ceases to be the subject of a reservation, for example, because a donor moves out of property that he had previously given to the donee but in which the donor had remained in possession, he is treated as making a PET which he must survive by seven years to avoid a charge to IHT. **[21.9]**

B. The relevance of estate duty cases

Both the estate duty legislation and the Stamp Duties Act 1920–1940 (as amended) of New South Wales contained very similar provisions to those found in the FA 1986. The question that arises is whether cases decided on these provisions are of any relevance to IHT. **[21.10]**

Barry McCutcheon and Withers LLP *Inheritance Tax* (4th edn, 2005) p 196

II. BACKGROUND: THE ESTATE DUTY CASES

The IHT reservation of benefit provisions are modelled on the estate duty legislation, which contained similar provisions: see the Customs and Inland Revenue Act 1881, s.32(2)(a), the Customs and Inland Revenue Act 1889, s.11(l), the Finance Act 1894, s.2(l)(c) and the Finance (1909–10) Act, s.59(3). The key provision was s.11 (l) of the Customs and Inland Revenue Act 1889 which referred to "property taken under any gift ... of which property bona fide possession and enjoyment shall not have been assumed by the donee immediately upon the gift and thenceforward retained, to the entire exclusion of the donor, or of any benefit to him by contract or otherwise."[43]

Over the years, the Privy Council heard a number of cases on appeal from the High Court of Australia concerning the effect of section 102(2) of the Stamp Duties Act, 1920–1940, as amended, of New South Wales. At the material times, this provision charged duty on:

> " ... any property comprised in any gift made by the deceased at any time ... of which bona fide possession and enjoyment has not been assumed by the donee immediately upon the gift and thenceforth retained to the entire exclusion of the deceased or of any benefit to him of whatsoever kind or in any way whether enforceable at law or in equity or not and whenever the deceased died."

The concluding part of this provision is thus wider than the equivalent estate duty and IHT provisions, but it is thought that nothing in the decided cases turns on this. They have been accepted as authorities on the relevant United Kingdom legislation,[44] and they are treated as such in the following discussion.

43 F.A. 1986, s.102(1), unlike s.11(1) makes no reference to enjoyment and possession of the property being retained by the donee, but, as will be seen, this is not material to the cases concerned with s.11 (I) (or with its Australian equivalent).

44 *Oakes* v. *Commissioner of Stamp Duties of New South Wales* [1954] AC 57 at 71–72; [see below, para **[21.17]**.]

Since the introduction of the IHT reservation of benefit provisions there have been two decided cases – *Ingram v IRC*[45] and *Eversden v IRC*,[46] decided respectively by the House of Lords and the Court of Appeal – which have made it clear that while the Court will be informed by the estate duty cases, the position in any case will have to be determined by reference to the IHT legislation. The estate duty cases, while not decisive, thus remain relevant ... **[21.11]**

C. Determining the subject matter of the gift

Both the estate duty and New South Wales cases draw a distinction between a gift with some benefit reserved (a reservation), and a gift of property from which the donor had carved out a separate interest (a partial gift). The former will fall foul of the reservation of benefit rules, while the latter will not. Thus, a settlor who reserves an interest for himself under the settlement, whether expressly or by operation of law, will be treated as making a partial gift and will not be subject to the reservation of benefit rules. The situation is different where the settlor creates a discretionary trust, of which he is one of the discretionary objects. Because a discretionary object enjoys only limited rights,[47] he cannot be treated as making a partial gift, and his non-exclusion from benefit will mean that the value of the entire fund will be included in his estate. **[21.12]**

Munro v Commissioner of Stamp Duties [1934] AC 61 (PC)

In 1909 the deceased agreed with his children that his business as a grazier should be carried on by them as partners under a partnership at will, whereby he was to be sole manager and each partner was to receive a specified share. Ten years later he transferred a part of the grazing land to each child by way of gift, the property being taken subject to the partnership agreement.

> LORD TOMLIN: . . . It is unnecessary to determine the precise nature of the right of the partnership at the time of the transfers. It was either a tenancy during the term of the partnership or a licence coupled with an interest. In either view what was comprised in the gift was, in the case of each of the gifts to the children and the trustees, the property shorn of the right which belonged to the partnership, and upon this footing it is in their Lordships' opinion plain that the donee in each case assumed bona fide possession and enjoyment of the gift immediately upon the gift and thenceforward retained it to the exclusion of the donor. Further, the benefit which the donor had as a member of the partnership in the right to which the gift was subject was not in their Lordships' opinion a benefit referable in any way to the gift. It was referable to the agreement of 1909 and nothing else, and was not therefore such a benefit as is contemplated by section 102, subsection 2(d).[48]
>
> ... In their Lordships' opinion it is the substance of the transactions which must be ascertained and if when so ascertained the substance does not fall within the words of the statute it cannot be brought within them merely because the forms employed did not give true effect to the substance. It is not always sufficiently appreciated that it is for the taxing authority to bring each case within the taxing Act, and that the subject ought not to be taxed upon refinements or otherwise than by clear words... **[21.13]**

45 [2000] 1 AC 293.
46 [2003] STC 822 .
47 *Gartside v IRC* [1968] AC 553.
48 [Stamp Duties Act (NSW) 1920–1931.]

Commissioner for Stamp Duties of New South Wales v Perpetual Trustee Co Ltd [1943] AC 425 (PC)

The deceased settlor had transferred shares of which he was the owner to Trustees (of whom he was one) in trust for his son.

> LORD RUSSELL OF KILLOWEN: ... For the reasons hereinafter appearing their Lordships are in agreement with the decision of the High Court in this case. In their opinion the property comprised in the gift was the equitable interest in the eight hundred and fifty shares, which was given by the settlor to his son. The disposition of that interest was effected by the creation of a trust, *i.e.* by transferring the legal ownership of the shares to trustees, and declaring such trusts in favour of the son as were co-extensive with the gift which the settlor desired to give. The donee was the recipient of the gift; whether the son alone was the donee (as their Lordships think) or whether the son and the body of trustees together constituted the donee, seems immaterial. The trustees alone were not the donee. They were in no sense the object of the settlor's bounty. Did the donee assume bona fide possession and enjoyment immediately upon the gift? The linking of possession with enjoyment as a composite object which has to be assumed by the donee indicates that the possession and enjoyment contemplated is beneficial possession and enjoyment by the object of the donor's bounty. This question therefore must be answered in the affirmative, because the son was (through the medium of the trustees) immediately put in such bona fide beneficial possession and enjoyment of the property comprised in the gift as the nature of the gift and the circumstances permitted. Did he assume it and henceforth retain it to the entire exclusion of the donor? The answer, their Lordships think, must be in the affirmative, and for two reasons: namely, (1) the settlor had no enjoyment and possession such as is contemplated by the section; and (2) such possession and enjoyment as he had from the fact that the legal ownership of the shares vested in him and his co-trustees as joint tenants, was had by him solely on behalf of the donee. In his capacity as donor he was entirely excluded from possession and enjoyment of what he had given to his son. Did the donee retain possession and enjoyment to the entire exclusion of any benefit to the settlor of whatsoever kind or in any way whatsoever? Clearly, yes. In the interval between the gift and his death, the settlor received no benefit of any kind or in any way from the shares, not did he receive any benefit whatsoever which was in any way attributable to the gift... **[21.14]**

This case is considered further in *Oakes v Commissioner of Stamp Duties of New South Wales* [1954] AC 425 (below, para **[21.17]**). For the effect of the settlor's transactions with trustees see *Commissioners of Stamp Duties of New South Wales v Way* [1952] AC 95. **[21.15]**

St Aubyn v Attorney-General (No 2) [1952] AC 15 (HL)

This case concerned the former charge in connection with the extinguishment of a life interest under FA 1940, s 43 (and s 56 of that Act, relating to 'associated operations' concerning certain companies).[49]

> LORD SIMONDS: ... I apply the provisions of this section to the facts that I have stated. On March 27, 1927, Lord St. Levan had an interest in possession limited to cease on his death in the settled property which on that date had assumed the form of (1) 50,000 ordinary shares of the company and (2) the sum of £750,000 payable in the instalments that I have mentioned and (3) the sum of £100,000 paid or immediately payable by the

49 Although dismissing the claim to duty in respect of the extinguished life interest, the court held that there was a charge to duty under FA 1940, s 46, in so far as the deceased had transferred property to a company from which he had subsequently received benefits.

company. But he had also jointly with Mr. Ponsonby an overriding general power of appointment which could be exercised so as to vest all or any part of the settled property in him absolutely. They so exercised it as to vest in him the properties I have numbered (2) and (3), and, when they had done so, he surrendered his life interest in the ordinary shares. It is agreed that bona fide possession and enjoyment of the shares was assumed immediately thereafter by the persons becoming entitled upon the determination of Lord St. Levan's interest. But was it – and this is the only question – "thenceforth retained to the entire exclusion of [Lord St. Levan] and of any benefit to him by contract or otherwise?"

My Lords, I cannot think that any doubt could be entertained upon this matter but for the use which the Crown seeks to make of certain decisions, particularly *Attorney-General* v. *Worral*[50] and *Grey* v. *Attorney-General*,[51] to which I will refer later. If A, being the owner in fee of an estate in Yorkshire and an estate in Wiltshire, gives outright to B his estate in Yorkshire, it is an irrelevant circumstance that he retains his estate in Wiltshire: equally it is irrelevant, if, being the tenant for life of the two estates, he surrenders his interest in one and retains it in the other: and equally so, if, his interest being not in two geographically separate estates but in land and capital moneys subject to the same settlement, he surrenders his interest in the one form of property and retains it in the other. But let it be supposed that he is neither the owner in fee, nor the tenant for life and nothing more, but that he is tenant for life with an overriding general power of appointment, by virtue of which he can dispose of all or any part of the settled property at his absolute discretion. I cannot doubt that, if he chooses so to exercise the power as to make some part of the settled property his own, it is wholly irrelevant that by a contemporaneous or later transaction he surrenders his life interest in other parts of it. It is true that he has disposed of his life interest in one part of the property and is true that he has enlarged his life interest in the other part of it into an absolute interest, but these two truths do not add up to the proposition that the property in which he has surrendered his interest is not retained by the trustees to the entire exclusion of him and of any benefit to him by contract or otherwise.

... It appears to me, my Lords, that this is nothing but the logical application to a more complex situation of the proposition which I venture to think was self evident, *viz.* that the life tenant of two separate pieces of property can surrender his life interest in one and retain it in the other without duty becoming exigible in respect of the former. The question is what he has given: it may be a life interest in part of the settled property; it may be a part of the income of settled funds and that part may be a fixed sum which is payable in priority or the residue after the prior payment of a fixed sum thereout. I venture to think that much of the argument that was addressed to the House in this case and much of the confusion that has arisen in the past on this admittedly difficult branch of the law have been due to the failure to bear in mind that that of which enjoyment is to be assumed and retained and from which there is to be exclusion of the donor and any benefit to him by contract or otherwise is that which is truly given, a proposition which is obvious enough in the case of two separate estates but more difficult to follow and apply where trusts are declared of a single property which are not completely exhaustive in favour of a donee. It should at least be clear from the judgment of Lord Russell of Killowen that by retaining something which he has never given a donor does not bring himself within the mischief of the section. I venture to repeat in other words what I have already said when dealing with section 43 alone, for its underlying principle is not altered by an alliance with section 56. In the simplest analysis, if A gives to B all his estates in Wiltshire except Blackacre, he does not except Blackacre out of what he has given: he just does not give Blackacre. And if it can be regarded as a "benefit" to him that he does not give but keeps Blackacre, it is a benefit which is in no relevant sense (to use the language of Lord Tomlin) "referable" or (to use that of Lord Russell of Killowen) "attributable" to the gift that he made of the rest of the Wiltshire estate. Applying this principle to the artificial situation created by the statutory hypothesis, I see no reason for saying that that which Lord St. Levan gave was not retained by the donee to the entire exclusion of him and of

50 [1895] I QB 99.
51 [1900] AC 124.

any benefit to him by contract or otherwise. To avoid misunderstanding I must add that different considerations arise where the donor obtains some benefit which is "referable" to the gift or "attributable" to it. Thus, if in the present case there had been a bargain by which in consideration of the surrender of his life interest in part of the settled property Lord St. Levan had been enabled to enlarge his life interest in another part of it, it might be that following *Worrall's* case I should be bound to hold that he had not been excluded from the surrendered part. But as I have already pointed out, here was no bargain of any kind. What Lord St. Levan chose to give he gave, and what to keep he kept. He made no bargain and he was entirely excluded from, and obtained no benefit referable to, that which he gave... **[21.16]**

Oakes v Commissioner of Stamp Duties of New South Wales [1954] AC 57 (PC) (see also below, para [21.29])

The deceased, the owner of certain grazing property, executed a deed poll by which he declared that he held the property on trust for himself and for his four children as tenants-in-common in equal shares. The deed gave him wide powers of management and entitled him to remuneration for work done in managing the property, on which he continued to reside. He managed the property until his death, receiving remuneration and dividing the profits into five shares. The children's shares he applied for their maintenance and education during their respective minorities. Duty was claimed on his death under s 102(2)(d) of the New South Wales Stamp Duties Act 1920–1940.

LORD REID:... The next advantage to the deceased was of quite a different character. The deceased, under the power which he reserved to himself under clause (4)(j) of the deed of trust, took considerable sums as remuneration for his services in managing the trust property. Their Lordships will assume that those sums were reasonable and no more than would have been appropriate remuneration for any other manager. But receiving those sums was clearly an advantage or benefit to the deceased, and the question is whether it was a benefit of such a kind as to come within the section. If a donor reserves to himself a beneficial interest in property and only gives to the donees such beneficial interests as remain after his own reserved interest has been satisfied, it is now well established that such reservation of a beneficial interest does not involve any benefit to the donor within the meaning of the section.[52]

... It follows that if the right to take remuneration could be regarded as a beneficial interest in the property reserved by the deceased when making the deed of trust, then his remuneration would not be a benefit within the scope of the section. But their Lordships cannot regard a right to take remuneration for managing property as a beneficial interest in the property. A trustee is not permitted to take remuneration for services performed by him unless he is authorised to do so: in this case the trustee was authorised to do so because the deceased provided in the deed of trust that he as trustee or the trustee for the time being should be entitled to remuneration as if he were not a trustee. If the deceased had resigned office and another trustee had taken his place it could hardly have been contended that this provision gave to the new trustee a beneficial interest in the trust property, and in their Lordships' judgment the deceased did not reserve to himself a beneficial interest in the property by inserting this provision in the deed of trust. Indeed, the terms of the deed of trust make it clear that the whole beneficial interest in the property passed to the deceased and his children in equal shares, so that the subject-matter of the gift to each child was one-fifth of the whole beneficial interest in the property. Clause 2 declared that the capital and interest of the trust fund should be held

52 [See *Commissioner for Stamp Duties of New South Wales v Perpetual Trustee Co Ltd* [1943] AC 425; above, para **[21.14]**; *St Aubyn v A-G.* [1952] AC 15; above, para **[21.16]**; both relied upon by Lord Reid.]

upon trust for the deceased and his first named children as tenants in common in equal shares, and neither the right of the trustee to take remuneration, nor any other right, power or discretion conferred on the trustee affected the position of the deceased or his children as tenants in common of the whole beneficial interest in the trust property. Any remuneration taken by the deceased or any other trustee must come out of the trust property and must therefore diminish the amount available for division among the tenants in common for their enjoyment.

But the appellant argued that the children had had all the possession and enjoyment to which they were entitled under the deed of trust: they could only possess through the trustee and subject to his rights and powers, and therefore the exercise of his rights by the trustee could not trench on or impair that possession. The appellant founded on another passage in the judgment of Lord Russell in the *Perpetual Trustee Co.* case,[53] when he referred to the donee being "put in such bona fide beneficial possession and enjoyment of the property comprised in the gift as the nature of the gift and the circumstances permitted." It was said that in the present case the nature of the gift to the children and the circumstances never permitted the children to have any greater possession or enjoyment than in fact they had. But to understand what Lord Russell meant by those words it is necessary to quote the preceding passage:

> "In their opinion the property comprised in the gift was the equitable interest in the eight hundred and fifty shares, which was given by the settlor to his son. The disposition of that interest was effected by the creation of a trust, *i.e.* by transferring the legal ownership of the shares to trustees, and declaring such trusts in favour of the son as were co-extensive with the gift which the settlor desired to give. The donee was the recipient of the gift; whether the son alone was the donee (as their Lordships think) or whether the son and the body of trustees together constituted the donee, seems immaterial. The trustees alone were not the donee. They were in no sense the object of the settlor's bounty. Did the donee assume bona fide possession and enjoyment immediately upon the gift? The linking of possession with enjoyment as a composite object which has to be assumed by the donee indicates that the possession and enjoyment contemplated is beneficial possession and enjoyment by the object of the donor's bounty. This question, therefore, must be answered in the affirmative, because the son was (through the medium of the trustees) immediately put in such bona fide beneficial possession and enjoyment of the property comprised in the gift as the nature of the gift and the circumstances permitted."

Lord Russell was there explaining in general terms how the section is to be interpreted when the subject-matter of the gift is an equitable interest. He was not dealing with a case like the present, when the donor received money which, if he had not taken it, would have gone to the donee under the terms of the gift. In the *Perpetual Trustee Co.* case the settlor derived no actual benefit from the shares or their dividends. He might have exercised voting powers in respect of the shares, but did not do so; and he was one of several trustees and they might have used trust money for the maintenance of the son, but did not do so. With the exception of some insurance premiums the whole income was accumulated and the trust fund was paid to the son on his majority. Their Lordships do not read the words on which the appellant founds as modifying or intended to modify the later passage in Lord Russell's judgment which has been quoted above and in which he only refers to reservation by the donor of a beneficial interest in the property.

But, even if there is no authority to support it, the appellant's case requires further examination. The argument is clearly and forcibly stated in the dissenting judgment of Kitto J. in the High Court of Australia where he said[54]:

> "If the property comprised in the gift had consisted of four one-fifths of the fee simple of the trust property (whether legal and equitable or only equitable), and the donees, pursuant to a collateral agreement or otherwise, had allowed the deceased to have the benefits which in fact he enjoyed, the case would have fallen clearly enough within

53 [[1943] AC 425; see above, para **[21.14]**.]
54 (1952) 85 CLR 421.

> section 102(2)(d).[55] But it seems to me that, in order to hold that four-fifths of the fee simple was the property comprised in the gift, one would have to construe the deed, not as a whole, but as if it were divided into two sections, effecting two quite distinct transactions; the first transaction being a disposition in equity of aliquot parts of the fee simple, and the second transaction consisting of a set of provisions operating to exact from the disponees a power for the disponor to derogate from the possession and enjoyment which an undivided share of an equitable fee simple enables the owner of it to have and to keep to himself. I cannot construe the deed in that way. It was a deed poll, and the benefits which the deceased derived in accordance with its provisions were benefits which the donees neither permitted him to derive nor had any power to deny him. They were in the position of impotence, not by their own choice, but because the deceased, in exercise of his right to give exactly what interests he liked and withhold exactly what he liked, had chosen to give them interests so hedged about as not to enable them to exclude him from those benefits. It was for him, when framing his deed, to delimit the interests he was parting with; and he did delimit them, not by any one part of the deed considered by itself, but by the entirety of its provisions. The donees had no voice in deciding to what extent their interests should be subject to rights, powers or privileges retained by the deceased. They got interests which were limited *ab initio,* by the terms of their creation; and the limits were such that the interests were inherently insusceptible of being so possessed and enjoyed as to preclude the deceased from deriving those benefits which in fact he derived."

It is true that the deceased did not exact from his children his power to take benefits and that the benefits which he took were benefits which they neither permitted him to derive nor had any power to deny him. But in their Lordships' judgment the question is not whether the donees permitted the donor to take benefits. It is whether the donor took benefit out of that which was given. If a benefit arises by way of reservation out of interests which were given then no doubt the donees' interests are inherently insusceptible of being so possessed and enjoyed as to preclude the donor from taking that benefit, but the section applies because there is not entire exclusion of the donor or of benefit to him from the interests comprised in the gift. The contrast is between reserving a beneficial interest and only giving such interests as remain on the one hand, and on the other hand reserving power to take benefit out of, or at the expense of, interests which are given, and for reasons already stated their Lordships are of opinion that the present case is within the latter class. **[21.17]**

It appears that HMRC will not apply the *Oakes* case where a settlor is entitled under the relevant trust deed to remuneration for acting as a trustee.[56] **[21.18]**

Ingram v IRC [2000] 1 AC 293 (HL)

Lady Ingram transferred landed property to her solicitor as nominee and, on the following day and pursuant to her directions, he granted her 20-year rent-free leases in different parts of the property. On the following day, the property (subject to the leases) was transferred to trustees, who immediately executed declarations of trust whereby the property settled was held for the benefit of her children and grandchildren to the exclusion of Lady Ingram. Lady Ingram died two years later, failing to survive three years from the date of the gift, which would have entitled her estate to pay a reduced rate of duty.[57] However, the question of whether the

55 [See above, para **[21.11]**, and compare with FA 1986, s 102(1).]
56 *Inheritance Tax Manual* (IHTM) 14394.
57 IHTA 1984, s. 7(4).

reservation of benefit rules applied remained important. If they did not, tax would be payable by reference to the value of the property at the time of the gift;[58] if they did apply, the property would be deemed to form part of Lady Ingram's estate at her death and tax would be payable upon its value at that time. In the intervening period there had been a sharp rise in property prices in south-east England, and the value at death was much higher than it had been at the time of the gift.

In the High Court, Ferris J held that the original grant of the leases had been a nullity: just as a person cannot contract with himself (*Rye v Rye* [1962] AC 496), neither can a nominee contract with his principal in order to create new rights and obligations involving no third party (*Kildrummy (Jersey) Ltd v IRC* [1990] STC 657). Nevertheless, when the trustees took the legal estate as volunteers with knowledge of the interests purportedly granted to Lady Ingram, she acquired at that same time equitable interests equivalent to those that she believed she had at law. Ferris J concluded, however, that no benefit had been reserved; there was no point at which the trustees and beneficiaries had held the property otherwise than subject to the leasehold interests. Lady Ingram never intended to give them the property free from those interests and they were not therefore included in the gift.

The Court of Appeal agreed by a majority that the leases were invalid, but disagreed with the judge's finding that s 102 did not apply. They held that it was conceptually impossible for a lease to come into existence until the lessor had acquired the freehold interest. It followed that the gift must have been the unencumbered freehold interest and the equitable leases must have been a benefit reserved out of them.

The House of Lords found for the taxpayer. Irrespective of the validity of the leases granted, Lady Ingram had not made a gift subject to a reservation since the trustees and beneficiaries never had anything more than the freehold subject to her interests. This decision involved the determination that, in relation to land, the term 'property' in s 102 referred to property in its legal sense, not the physical land itself, with a recognition that any number of interests could co-exist in the land, some of which could be retained, and some given away.

> LORD HOFFMANN: . . . Section 102 has a long history. Provisions in similar terms existed in connection with estate duty (section 2(1)(c) of the Finance Act 1894 (57 & 58 Vict. c. 30)) and before that account duty (section 11(1) of the Customs and Inland Revenue Act 1889 (52 & 53 Vict. c. 7)). There have been similar provisions in Australia. It has been interpreted on a number of occasions by the House of Lords and Privy Council. The theme which runs through all the cases is that although the section does not allow a donor to have his cake and eat it, there is nothing to stop him from carefully dividing up the cake, eating part and having the rest. If the benefits which the donor continues to enjoy are by virtue of property which was never comprised in the gift, he has not reserved any benefit out of the property of which he disposed: see Lord Simonds in *St. Aubyn v. Attorney-General* [1952] A.C. 15, 22–23.
>
> If one applies this proposition to the highly sophisticated English land law, by which various interests, each regarded as separate items of property, can subsist simultaneously in respect of the same land, it is clear that the scope for discrimination in limiting the terms of the gift to exclude interests which the donor wishes to retain is very wide. In particular, the beneficial ownership of land may be divided in terms of time as well as space, so that the right to enjoyment of the land for a limited period, such as for life or a term of years, and the right to enjoy the land after the expiry of that period, can exist simultaneously as property interests in possession and in remainder or reversion. . .
>
> It is a curious feature of the debate in this case that both sides claim that their views reflect the reality and not the mere form of the transaction. But the Revenue's version of reality seems entirely dependent upon the scintilla temporis which must elapse between

58 IHTA 1984, ss. 3, 3A.

the conveyance of the freehold to the donee and the creation of the leasehold interest in favour of the donor. For my part, I do not think that a theory based upon the notion of a scintilla temporis can have a very powerful grasp on reality. (Compare *Abbey National Building Society v. Cann* [1991] 1 A.C. 56, 92–93)...It is true that as a matter of conveyancing, no lease can come into existence until the freehold has been vested in the intended lessor. But section 102 is concerned not with conveyancing but with beneficial interests. It uses words like "enjoyment" and "benefit". In *Attorney-General v. Worrall* [1895] Q.B. 99, 104, a case on a predecessor of section 102, Lord Esher M.R. began his judgment with the words:

> "It has been held that in cases of this kind the court has to determine what the real nature of the transaction was, apart from legal phraseology and the forms of conveyancing."

Before parting with this aspect of the case, I should say something about the more general considerations involved in the application of section 102. Its policy has puzzled people for a long time. For one thing, it is in one sense a penal section. Not only may you not have your cake and eat it, but if you eat more than a few de minimis crumbs of what was given, you are deemed for tax purposes to have eaten the lot. Secondly, a superficial reading of phrases like "beneficial enjoyment of the property" and enjoyment of property "to the entire exclusion ... of the donor" has led to numerous occasions in the past century in which the revenue has put forward the proposition that, as a matter of practical common sense, it simply must be contrary to the policy of the statute for a donor to be able to give away property such as a house and go on enjoying the benefit of the property by continuing to live there. This is the premise upon which the revenue claim the high ground of substance and reality. Mr. Nugee said that for Lady Ingram to have made a potentially exempt transfer and retained the right to stay in the house was simply too good to be true and in the Court of Appeal, Evans L.J. accepted this proposition. But this approach ignores the fact that "property" in section 102 is not something which has physical existence like a house but a specific interest in that property, a legal construct, which can coexist with other interests in the same physical object. Section 102 does not therefore prevent people from deriving benefit from the object in which they have given away an interest. It applies only when they derive the benefit from that interest.... What, then, is the policy of section 102? It requires people to define precisely the interests which they are giving away and the interests, if any, which they are retaining. Once they have given away an interest they may not receive back any benefits from that interest. In *Lang v. Webb*, 13 C.L.R. 503, 513 Isaacs J. suggested that the policy was to avoid the "delay, expense and uncertainty" of requiring the revenue to investigate whether a gift was genuine or pretended. It laid down a rule that if the donor continued to derive any benefit from the property in which an interest had been given, it would be treated as a pretended gift unless the benefit could be shown to be referable to a specific proprietary interest which he had retained. This is probably the most plausible explanation...[59] **[21.19]**

IRC v Eversden [2003] EWCA Civ 668, [2003] STC 822 (CA)

Reserving for herself a five per cent absolute beneficial share, a wife settled the remainder of her interest in her house (Beechwood) upon her husband for life subject to discretionary trusts for a class of beneficiaries including herself. The settlor occupied the property (by virtue of her retained interest as a tenant in common) with her husband until his death, and for a further year thereafter until it was sold by the trustees. A replacement property (the Meadows) and an investment bond were acquired with the proceeds of sale (including the wife's five per cent

59 [In the event of the conclusion that the leaseback did not involve any reservation of benefit, the House of Lords held that it was unnecessary to consider the *Ramsay* principle (see para [**5.7**]).]

share). She was in sole occupation of the Meadows until her death five years later, although she received no benefit from the bond. The Revenue argued that although the gift of the life interest was covered by the spouse exemption,[60] the gift on discretionary trusts was not and, because the settlor was an object of that discretion, she had reserved a benefit. The Court of Appeal decided that the exception in s 102(5) meant that the spouse exemption applied in the case of settled property, even after the initial interest in possession for the donor's spouse had come to an end.

CARNWATH LJ:

13. Turning to the reservation of benefit provisions, it is now common ground that, as decided by Lightman J, the reservation of benefit provisions apply in principle for two separate reasons:
    i) in relation to the Meadows alone, because the settlor actually enjoyed a benefit by virtue of her rent-free sole occupation; and
    ii) in relation to both the Meadows and the Bond, because the settlor was a discretionary object in relation to the entire trust fund.

    Thus, on the death of the settlor, apart from s 102 (5), the property which had been the subject matter of the gift, being "subject to a reservation" as defined, would be treated as part of her estate immediately before her death (s 102 (3)), and accordingly subject to tax by virtue of the deemed transfer of value under s 4. The property actually in the trust at that date, having been derived from the original property, is treated as the subject matter of the gift (1986 Act Sch 20, para (5)).
14. The only issue before us is whether the provisions are displaced by virtue of s 102 (5) (a), taken with IHTA s 18.

Discussion

15. Against this background it is necessary to look in more detail at the effect of s 102 (5). At first sight, it appears reasonably straightforward. The section is displaced "if or, as the case may be, to the extent that" the disposal is an exempt transfer by virtue of various provisions of Part II of the 1984 Act. They are the exemption provisions which I have already outlined, with the exception of ss 19 (annual exemption) and 21 (normal expenditure out of income). The words "if or. . .to the extent that" appear to correspond to the same words as used in the exemption provisions. For example, s 18 provides that a transfer of value is exempt "to the extent that" the value satisfies the provisions of the section. Conversely, s 20 (small gifts) provides that transfers of value are exempt "if" the values do not exceed the stated amount. On a natural reading, therefore, the draftsman has simply imported into section 102(5) the 1984 Act exemptions, subject to the same conditions.
16. In the present case the "disposal of the property by way of gift" was the transfer of the property in 1988. As is common ground that was an exempt transfer, by virtue of s 18. Accordingly, it is outside section 102, and the settlor's estate is not subject to tax in relation to the subject-matter of the gift. On the other hand, although the interest of the husband was limited to his life, he was treated by virtue of s 49 as beneficially entitled to the whole property, and his estate was charged to tax on that basis.
17. This seems the natural reading of the section as applied to this case. However, Mr Ewart for the Revenue has argued that it is an over-simplification, and is inconsistent with Lord Hoffmann's authoritative exposition of the section in *Ingram*, set out above. Mr Ewart submits that, properly understood in the light of *Ingram*, the concept of the disposal of property by way of gift in s 102 cannot be directly equated with that of transfer of value in s 18. There is as he says a "mis-match" between the two which requires some modification to be made to the language of s 18 in order

60 Gifts between spouses (and civil partners) are exempt and the reservation of benefit rules do not apply to such gifts (FA 1986, s 18).

to give effect to Parliament's intention. Following Lord Hoffmann, he submits that the term "property" in section 102, in relation to a house, is not referring to the house as a physical object, but to "a specific interest in that property, a legal construct, which can co-exist with other interests in the same physical object".

18. Thus, he says, the gift of Beechwood in 1988 cannot properly be treated as the transfer of a single property or of the value of that property, but must be analysed as a gift of a number of distinct interests in the property as defined by the settlement. In summary, he divides the transaction into four separate elements:
   i) the husband's life interest;
   ii) the interest of the potential beneficiaries, as a class, under the discretionary trust during the specified period of eighty years;
   iii) the interests of the settlor's daughter and other beneficiaries at the end of the specified period; and
   iv) in default of any such beneficiaries, the resulting trust in favour of the settlor or her estate.

   The "gift" for the purposes of s 102 comprises the first three elements, which are thus potentially within s 102; the fourth, which was an interest retained by the settlor, is outside the scope of s 102 altogether.

19. Following this analysis, he says that s 18, which refers in terms to the different concept of "transfer of value", needs to be adjusted in order to apply it to a gift of property in the sense used by s 102. He proposes the following wording (the words in square brackets indicating the changes from the original):-

   > "[A gift] is an exempt transfer to the extent that [the property which is the subject matter of the gift] becomes comprised in the estate of the transferor's spouse..."

   On his analysis, the only part of the 1988 gift which became part of the spouse's estate was the interest defined by his life, and accordingly it is only "to that extent" that the gift is to be treated as an exempt transfer. Since that interest had ceased to exist by the material date (that is, the death of the settlor), there is no relevant exemption, and nothing to prevent the full application of s 102 to the interests then remaining.

20. In spite of the ingenuity of the argument and its attractive presentation, I find it unconvincing. It involves an unwarranted extension of the reasoning of the House of Lords in *Ingram*, and an unwarranted distortion of the statutory language. It is important to keep in mind the factual background of *Ingram*. In that case the settlor had procured the conveyance of her house and surrounding land to trustees for her children and grandchildren, but before doing so had procured the grant to herself of two leases of different parts of the property for 20 years rent-free. The conveyance to the trustees was subject to those leases. The House of Lords held that the reservation of benefit provision had no application because her enjoyment of the land was derived from her leasehold interest which was not subject of the gift. It was in that context that it was relevant to distinguish between the property as a physical object and the interests in it. Section 102 did not prevent the donor deriving benefit from the physical property, provided that benefit was not derived from the interest which she had given away. That case, in my view, throws no light on the present. Lord Hoffmann was solely concerned to identify the nature of the interest retained by the settlor. He was not considering section 102(5), or the interaction of section 102 with the exemption provisions of the 1984 Act. Nor was it necessary for him to consider the position of successive interests forming part of a gift under a settlement.

21. Mr Ewart also relied on the decision of the Privy Council in *Commissioner for Stamp Duties of New South Wales v Perpetual Trust Company Ltd* [1943] AC 425. This concerned similar reservation of benefit provisions in the New South Wales Stamp Duties Act 1920. Under the settlement in that case the trustees were required to hold certain company shares, to apply the income for the maintenance of the settlor's son during his minority, and to transfer the shares to him absolutely on his attaining the age of 21. It was held that, although the son's interest was contingent upon his attaining 21, the property comprised in the gift was his equitable interest in

the shares; that was assumed by him immediately upon the gift and retained thereafter to the entire exclusion of the settlor; accordingly the shares were not part of the settlor's dutiable estate. In the opinion of their Lordships (see pp 439 – 440, per Lord Russell of Killowen) –

> "The property comprised in the gift was the equitable interest in the 850 shares which was given by the settlor by his son. . .The son was (through the medium of the trustees) immediately put in such bona fide beneficial possession and enjoyment of the property comprised in the gift as the nature of the gift and the circumstances permitted. . ."

Again, in my view, this case does no more than show that in applying the section, one needs to have regard to the nature of the particular gift. It throws no light on the application of s 102(5) of the 1986 Act, nor on the treatment of successive interests under a settlement.

22. In any event, it is impossible to introduce such conceptual subtleties into s 102(5) without distorting the language. Rightly or wrongly (from the purist's point of view), the draftsmen clearly did find it possible to equate a disposal by way of gift with a transfer of value. That is the effect of posing, in the sub-section, the question whether the disposal by way of gift "is an exempt transfer", with specific reference to the provisions of Part II of the 1984 Act all of which are references to "transfers of value". The alleged "mis-match" to which Mr Ewart refers would apply equally to all the provisions listed in s 102(5). No doubt corresponding amendments would be needed to those other provisions, in line with that suggested by Mr Ewart for s 18. In my view such an approach is neither necessary nor within the scope of the Court's powers of interpretation.

23. If further support were needed for this view that the draftsmen of the 1986 Act did not share Mr Ewart's conceptual problems, it may perhaps be found in IHTA s 3A (see above), as inserted by the 1986 Act, dealing with "potentially exempt transfers". Such a transfer is defined as "a transfer of value," subject to certain conditions, "to the extent that it constitutes. . .a gift to another individual. . ." By sub-section (2), a transfer of value is regarded as a gift for these purposes to the extent that either (a) "the value transferred is attributable to property which. . .becomes comprised in the estate of that other individual", or (b) "to the extent that, by virtue of the transfer, the estate of that other individual is increased." Although (b) may be seen as an extension of the normal meaning of "gift", (a) is wholly consistent with the interpretation which I would regard as the natural reading of s 102(5), and shows no difficulty in marrying the two concepts. Although the relationship is not spelt out in s 102(5) in the same detail, it would be surprising if the draftsman was intending to use the term "gift" in a radically different sense in two places in the same Act.

24. I have already referred to the Revenue's concern that this interpretation will undermine the effectiveness of the provisions. Mr Ewart illustrates the problem by the following example:

> "A husband owns property. He settles that property on trusts which give his wife an initial interest in possession for her life or 3 months whichever is the shorter. Thereafter, there are discretionary trusts in favour of a class of beneficiaries which include the husband and wife. If the construction favoured by the Respondents and Lightman J is correct, the husband can continue to enjoy substantial benefits from the property (in the present case Mrs Greenstock had sole occupation of the dwelling-house) without it being part of his estate on death. Schemes such as this are currently being promoted."

25. Mr Thornhill for the Respondents does not dispute that this is a possible effect of his submissions. However he counters it by putting forward potential anomalies which would result from the Revenue's interpretation, in this and other provisions. I do not find it necessary to examine these suggested anomalies in detail. Experience shows that the Court's task of applying a particular statutory provision to a particular set of facts is rarely assisted by considering the hypothetical application of other provisions to other hypothetical sets of facts. I am ready to accept that this

particular battle of anomalies comes out in favour of the Revenue. However the problem if it exists derives from s 49, which treats the acquisition of an interest in possession as equivalent to the acquisition of the property itself. That has the result that, in the present case, the estate of the settlor's husband is taxed on the property, but that of the settlor is not. There is nothing in section 102 to modify that aspect of the scheme of the 1984 Act. If that is of concern to the Revenue, they must look for correction to Parliament, not to the Courts. **[21.20]**

Barry McCutcheon and Withers LLP *Inheritance Tax* (4th edn, 2005) pp 196–212

. . . the estate duty cases drew a distinction, sometimes subtle, between a gift "with strings attached" and a gift of property out of which the donor had carved an interest, the principle being that one did not reserve a benefit out of that which one kept back. . . .

The Nichols case and prior independent transactions

In *Nichols* v. *I.R.C.*[61] the Court of Appeal had to consider the effect of a gift of property by a father to his son and a contemporaneous leaseback, made under a binding equitable obligation, of the property by the son to the father. The lease contained a full repairing covenant by the son. It subsequently proved necessary to adjust the lease somewhat in favour of the father. The Revenue contended that the subject-matter of the gift was the unencumbered property, not the property subject to lease. The Court of Appeal, following the *Earl Grey* case,[62] held that the existence of the covenant was sufficient to support the Revenue's claim for duty . . . .

The need for a prior independent transaction

It will be noted that in the *Munro*[63] case the donor's rights existed over the property before he gave it away, while in the *Nichols* case they arose contemporaneously with the gift

. . . Goff J., while recognising the authority of *Munro*, referred to the need for the existence of what he called a "prior independent transaction", stating that only rights reserved by such a transaction could be enjoyed by the donor without infringing the reservation of benefit provisions. Prior to the House of Lords' decision in *Ingram* the Revenue placed considerable store by Goff J.'s statement. *Ingram* made it clear that there is no such requirement. . . . .

The implications of *Eversden*

. . . *The subject-matter of the gift: the scope of the "carve-out" principle*

The fact that the subject matter of the gift where there is an initial interest in possession – and possibly regardless of the terms of the settlement – is the settled property arguably has important implications concerning the scope of the "carve-out" principle. Before *Ingram* the estate duty carve-out cases tended to be seen as concerned with identifying the subject-matter of the gift. *Ingram* was taken as continuing this approach; Lady Ingram never gave away the lease and therefore did

61 [1975] STC 278; [see below, para **[21.24]**].
62 [1900] AC 124.
63 [[1934] AC 61; see above, para **[21.13]**.]

not reserve a benefit by reason of her continued occupation of the property under the lease. On that basis, the Revenue argued in *Eversden* that *Ingram* and the estate duty cases ... meant that when a donor settled property upon trust the subject matter of the gift was not the settled property but the interests of the beneficiaries under the trust. This appears to have assumed that *Ingram* and the estate duty cases were authority for the proposition that a settlor who enjoys gifted settled property pursuant to a retained interest in it *prima facie* reserves a benefit in respect of it and that this result is to be avoided by regarding him as having made a series of gifts of the unretained equitable interests under the settlement rather than of the settled property *per se*.

The Court of Appeal, echoing the Special Commissioners, by implication rejected this line of argument – in their view *Ingram* (and the *Perpetual Trustee* case) was concerned solely with the nature of the interest retained by the donor in circumstances which were not concerned with the position of successive interests under a settlement.

But where does that leave us: is one test being applied *per Ingram* to determine what the donor retained and another *per Eversden* to determine what he gave away? The authors suggest otherwise and invite the view that *Eversden* is authority for the proposition that the retention by a donor of an equitable interest in settled property which he has disposed of by way of gift is not relevant in determining the subject-matter of the gifted property but is relevant in determing whether his enjoyment of the gifted property infringes the reservation of benefit provisions. In other words, the Revenue's argument in *Eversden* unduly limited the carve-out principle. *Eversden* has, in this respect, reminded us of the full scope of the principle.

It must be said at once that this is not part of the ratio of *Eversden*. But it must also be said that such a view is arguably not inconsistent with *Ingram*; indeed, Lord Hoffmann's statement in *Ingram* ... that the policy behind s.102 was, *per* Isaacs J. in *Lang v Webb*[64] that:

> "It laid down a rule that if the donor continued to derive any benefit from the property in which an interest had been given, it would be treated as a pretended gift *unless the benefit could be shown to be referable to a specific proprietary interest which he had retained* (authors' italics) ..."

is capable of embracing this view.

The approach is now arguably a two tier one. First, one identifies the subject-matter of the gifted property. If, as in *Ingram*, the donor derives no benefit from the gifted property, he clearly does not reserve a benefit in respect of it. But even if the donor enjoys the subject-matter of the gift, the reservation of benefit provisions will not apply if his enjoyment derives from a proprietary interest which he retained over (but the retention of which did not affect the subject-matter of) the gifted property. Strictly, the latter point did not arise in *Ingram*, because in that case Lady Ingram enjoyed the property which she retained; but in the authors' view the ratio in *Ingram* is arguably an application of the wider principle alluded to by Lord Hoffmann, namely, that whether or not a donor reserves a benefit depends not just on the subject-matter of the gift *per se* but rather on the nature of the interests, if any, which the donor has retained in respect of the gifted property. Identifying the subject-matter of the gift is only the first step in a two step process for determining whether or not a gift is caught by the provisions. Adopting this approach allows *Eversden* to sit comfortably with the carve-out principle, at least in relation to settled property involving successive interests. Having said that, there seems to be no reason why it should be limited to applying to such property. **[21.21]**

64 (1912) 13 CLR 503.

D. *Application of the reservation of benefit rules*

(1) Full possession and enjoyment and exclusion from benefit

The subject matter of the gift having been determined, it has then to be asked whether the donee has full possession and enjoyment of the gifted property and, if he has, whether the donor has been excluded from benefiting from it. If the answer to either of these questions is in the negative, then the rules will apply. **[21.22]**

John Tiley *Revenue Law* (5th edn, 2005) pp 1282–1284

Rule (i)

If the gift is to escape IHT on the ground that it was made outside the statutory period, the first essential is that possession or enjoyment must have been assumed by B, the donee, outside the relevant period. In turn, therefore, the gift must have effectively deprived A, the donor, of all rights in the property before that time, a problem to be resolved by looking at the rules relevant to the transfer of the particular type of property involved.

Rule (ii)

Possession and enjoyment must then satisfy rule (ii) which contains two distinct limbs. There must be both (a) the entire, or virtually the entire, exclusion of A, the donor and (b) the entire, or virtually the entire, exclusion of any benefit to A by contract or otherwise.

Limb (a) of rule (ii)

This requires the total exclusion of the donor both in law and in fact. Two cases illustrate the severity of this rule and explain the need for the rules in §69.3.[65] In *Stamp Duties Commr of New South Wales v. Permanent Trustee Co, of New South Wales,*[66] A, the donor, had settled property on B. his daughter, contingently on her attaining the age of 30; A retained no benefit and was entirely excluded. Fourteen years later, shortly before the daughter reached 30, he arranged with the daughter to borrow some of the income of the trust fund. He later died within the relevant period beginning with the date of the loan. The court held that he had not been entirely excluded from the property which was therefore taxed as part of his estate. Thus, the rule may apply not only where B, the donee, is obliged to allow A, the donor, to continue to use the property, but also where there is an "honourable understanding" to this effect and even where there is no such understanding but simply an application of the property for the benefit of the donor at some later time.

Chick v. Stamp Duties Commr[67] is similar. In 1934, a father made an absolute gift of

65 [See below, para **[21.31]**.]
66 [1956] 2 All ER 512, PC.
67 [1958] 2 All ER 623, PC.

grazing land to his son. A year later the son brought the land into a farming partnership with his father and another brother. The partnership was an arm's length arrangement and yet the Privy Council held that the son had not retained possession and enjoyment of the land to the entire exclusion of the donor, so the land was liable to estate duty when the father died some 18 years after the original gift.

Limb (b) of rule (ii)

This requires the property to be enjoyed to the entire exclusion, or virtually the entire exclusion, of any benefit to A, the donor, by contract or otherwise. To fall foul of this rule, however, it is not necessary that the benefit should be reserved out of the property itself; it suffices that it "trenches on" the possession and enjoyment of the property given. Examples include a covenant by B, the donee, to pay A, the donor, an annuity, even though not charged on the property given,[68] and a right to remuneration as a trustee.[69] Where an annuity was charged on the whole of the property given, the whole property given was held to be a gift with reservation; it was immaterial how small a percentage of the property's income was needed for the annuity.[70] However, a covenant for quiet enjoyment given by a lessor to a lessee would not amount to the reservation of a benefit where the lessee had given the freehold interest to the lessor in the first place, since this was, in reality, nothing more than contractual backing for a landlord's obligation not to derogate from her grant.[71]

Another example concerns a family company. If A wishes to make a gift of shares to the next generation, e.g. by a PET, the gift will fail if A takes out a service contract or pension plan with the company as part of the deal. The pension plan will not have this effect if it is "a prior independent transaction".[72]

These points are reinforced by the rule that a benefit obtained by virtue of any associated operations, as defined in IHTA 1984, s.268, of which the disposal by way of gift is one shall be treated as property comprised in the gift.[73]

The meaning of "or otherwise" in the expression "by contract or otherwise" has not been definitively settled by the courts. In *A.-G. v. Seccombe*[74] the court construed the expression *eiusdem generis* with contract so as to require a legally enforceable obligation. This is at best doubtful and the Revenue has indicated that it does not regard it as correct. It follows that there is probably no need for there to be a legally binding obligation – at least provided there is a moral obligation.[75]

In *Seccombe* the donor made a gift of a farm to his great nephew who resided with him and who had taken over the management of the farm the previous year. Until his death the donor continued to reside in the farmhouse and was, from the date of the gift, maintained by the donee. The donor no longer sat at the head of the table, but at the side. There was no enforceable agreement, nor any arrangement, that the donor should continue to reside there. It was held that the donee had assumed possession and enjoyment of the property to the entire exclusion of the donor and of any benefit to him by contract or otherwise. The court said that "or

68 *A.-G. v. Worrall* [1895] 1 QB 99, CA.
69 *Oakes v. Stamp Duties Commr of New South Wales* [1953] 2 All ER 1563, PC.
70 *Earl Grey v. A.-G.* [1900] AC 124, HL.
71 *Ingram v. IRC* [1997] STC 1234, 1247, *per* Nourse L.J. (the matter did not arise in the House of Lords).
72 Potter and Monroe, *Tax Planning*, §§9–06A, 9–06B.
73 FA 1986, Sch. 20, para. 6(1)(c).
74 [1911] 2 KB 688.
75 Potter and Monroe, *Tax Planning*, §3–33.

otherwise" should be construed *eiusdem generis* with contract and so required an enforceable obligation. If it is correct to conclude that the presence or absence of a legal right is irrelevant to the first limb, i.e. in determining whether the donor has been entirely excluded from the property, why should a different rule apply for the second limb? Why did *Seccombe* not fall within the limb (a) of rule (ii) in any case? Today it can hardly be contended that the extensive privileges enjoyed by the donor were such as to amount to his virtual exclusion from the property. **[21.23]**

Nichols v IRC [1975] 2 All ER 120 (CA)

A father gave a mansion house to his son. The son contemporaneously, under a binding equitable obligation, granted a lease of the property to his father. This lease contained a covenant requiring the landlord-son to repair the property.

> GOFF J (delivering the judgment of the court): . . . Having thus reviewed the authorities, we return to the question what was given, and we think that a grant of the fee simple, subject to and with the benefit of a leaseback, where such a grant is made by a person who owns the whole 'freehold free from any lease, is a grant of the whole fee simple with something reserved out of it, and not a gift of a partial interest leaving something in the hands of the grantor which he has not given. It is not like a reversion or remainder expectant on a prior interest. It gives an immediate right to the rent, together with a right to distrain for it, and, if there be a proviso for re-entry, a right to forfeit the lease. Of course, where, as in the *Monroe* case,[76] the lease, or, as it then may have been, a licence coupled with an interest, arises under a prior independent transaction, no question can arise because the donor then gives all he has, but where it is a condition of the gift that a leaseback shall be created, we think that must, on a true analysis, be a reservation of a benefit out of the gift and not something not given at all . . . .
>
> The right to have the mansion house and outbuildings repaired under that covenant did not exist before, and therefore could not be something simply not given. Moreover, it was reserved out of that which was given, since it was a covenant immediately operative and running with the land. In any event, however, being a covenant for the benefit of the donor, at the expense of the donee, and one which he was as a condition of the gift obliged to enter into and for the protection and better enjoyment of the property by the donor, it must in our judgment be a benefit to the donor by contract or otherwise referable to the gift and so within the section.[77] It appears to us to be just as much a benefit taken by the donor out of that which was given as the power to charge remuneration in the *Oakes* case.[78] **[21.24]**

Chick v Commissioner of Stamp Duties [1958] AC 435 (PC)

In 1934 the deceased gave certain grazing lands to his son, without any reservation or condition. Some time later they entered into a partnership agreement whereby the lands belonging to each were to be used by the partnership.

> VISCOUNT SIMONDS: . . .It is not in dispute that the donee assumed bona fide possession and enjoyment of the property upon the gift to the entire exclusion of the deceased or of any such benefit to him as is mentioned in the subsection. The question is whether he also thenceforth retained it and this depends on the impact of the subsection on the facts. Their Lordships have no doubt that the Supreme Court were right in upholding the contention of the respondent.

76 [1934] AC 61; [see above, para **[21.13]**].
77 [Customs and Inland Revenue Act 1889, s 11(1).]
78 [1954] AC 57; [see above, para **[21.17]**, and below, para **[21.29]**].

The respondent took his stand upon the plain words of the section. How, he asked, could it be said that the deceased was entirely excluded from the property, the subject of the gift, or from the possession and enjoyment thereof, when for some seventeen years before his death he had been a member of a partnership, whose right it was to agist their stock upon it, and himself, moreover, was the manager of the partnership business with the power to make final and conclusive decisions upon all matters relating to it.

... It is, however, right to refer to some of the contentions which were advanced on behalf of the appellants. In the first place, it is not disputed that the property was given outright by the deceased to his son. As was said by Dixon CJ. in *Commissioner of Stamp Duties* v. *Owens*[79]: "If ever there was a gift of an estate in fee simple, carrying the fullest right known to the law of exclusive possession and enjoyment, surely this was such a gift." It follows that the decision of this Board in *Munro* v. *Commissioner of Stamp Duties,*[80] on which the appellants relied, has no application to the present case. It must often be a matter of fine distinction what is the subject-matter of a gift. If, as in *Munro's* case, the gift is of a property shorn of certain of the rights which appertain to complete ownership, the donor cannot, merely because he remains in possession and enjoyment of those rights, be said within the meaning of the section not to be excluded from possession and enjoyment of that which he has given. This view of the section, which was reaffirmed in *St. Aubyn* v. *Attorney-General*[81] upon a consideration of a similar section in a British statute, need not be further elaborated. But the question may arise and, having arisen, may lead to a difference of opinion as to what is the subject-matter of the gift. It was, as it appears to their Lordships, for this reason that in *Owen's* case Williams and Taylor JJ. dissented from the majority of the court. In the present case there is no room for any such difference.

Then it was contended that the subsection had no operation because the partnership agreement was an independent commercial transaction for full consideration later than and in no way related to the gift,[82] and was a mode of enjoyment by the donee of his property and an exercise by him of the possession of it. (These are the words of the appellants' second formal reason.) In this reason there are several elements. The partnership agreement was "later" than the gift. This point was not pressed by counsel for the appellants. If possession and enjoyment are "thenceforth" to be retained by the donee, it is clearly irrelevant that there is an interval between the dates when the donor is excluded and ceases to be excluded. Nor is there wanting ample authority which shows that this Is an irrelevant consideration. A recent example is *Commissioner of Stamp Duties of New South Wales* v. *Permanent Trustee Co. of New South Wales (Davies'* case).[83] Next, it was an "independent commercial transaction for full consideration." It is to be assumed that it was an "independent" transaction: there was no evidence to the contrary. But the subsection says nothing about independent transactions. The sole question is one of fact – was the donor excluded? If he was not excluded, it is not relevant to ask why he was not excluded. Equally with regard to the transaction being "commercial" and "for full consideration." Their Lordships see no reason why a gloss should be put upon the plain words of the subsection by excluding from its operation such transactions.

...Then it is said that the transaction was "in no way related to the gift and was a mode of enjoyment by the donee of his property." ... the words "was a mode of enjoyment by the donee of his property." may be linked with the appellants' contention that the subsection was not applicable because (again to cite the formal reason) "neither the partnership agreement nor the use of the property pursuant thereto impaired or detracted from bona fide possession and enjoyment by the donee of the property given." This contention, in their Lordships' opinion, involves a misconception, for which the subsection provides no justification. It may be that the donee can make no better use of the property given to him than, for instance, by leasing it back to the donor. The question still is whether as a fact the donor has been excluded. This appears to be the contention

79 (1953) 88 C.L.R. 67 at 88.
80 [1934] AC 61; [above, para **[21.13]**].
81 [1952] AC 15; [above, para **[21.16]**].
82 [But for estate duty purposes see FA 1959, s 35(2), and for inheritance tax, FA 1986, Sch 20, para 6(1)(a) and below, para **[21.31]**.]
83 [1956] AC 512; [below, para **[21.27]**].

raised in another form that a commercial transaction is not within the subsection. The answer is that the possession and enjoyment by the donee of the property given to him in the manner most advantageous to himself are by no means incompatible with the donor not being excluded from it. It was, however, natural that the appellants should refer to and rely on the case of *Oakes* v. *Commissioner of Stamp Duties of New South Wales*.[84]

... But it was the cited passage on which the appellants relied.[85] Applying it to the facts of this case they said that the partnership agreement and all that was done under it by the deceased may have been beneficial to him, but the benefit or advantage derived by him did not impair or diminish the value of the gift of the property to the donee. On the contrary, it was the method most advantageous to the donee of dealing with the property. It was therefore not a benefit to the donor which brought the subsection' into operation. Their Lordships cannot accept this view. It is in flat contradiction to the law cogently stated by Isaacs J. in *Lang* v. *Web*[86] at an earlier stage in this opinion which has been consistently followed. Where the question is whether the donor has been entirely excluded from the subject-matter of the gift, that is the single fact to be determined. If he has not been so excluded, the eye need look no further to see whether his non-exclusion has been advantageous or otherwise to the donee. **[21.25]**

The effect of this decision was largely reversed for Estate Duty by FA 1959, s 35(2), which was enacted as a result, and provided that subsequent possession or enjoyment of the gifted property by the donor is to be disregarded if for full consideration in money or money's worth. A similar provision in relation to Inheritance Tax is found in FA 1986, Sch. 20, para 6(1)(a); see below, para **[21.31]**. **[21.26]**

Commissioner of Stamp Duties of New South Wales v Permanent Trustee Company of New South Wales [1956] AC 512 (PC)

In 1924 the deceased transferred to the respondent company certain shares and other property upon trust for his daughter. Many years later the daughter authorised her father to draw on her account with the respondent company; he did so on several occasions, using the money withdrawn for his own purposes, and eventually almost entirely depleted the account.

VISCOUNT SIMONDS: ... it appears to their Lordships that the inference is not only open but inevitable that from 1939 onward the testator was (to use the words of the Chief Justice) "master of the income as it was paid over by the trustee." He was, too, in a position to ensure that it was so paid over. His dual authority from his daughter, which enabled him on the one hand to direct the trustee how her money should be disposed of and on the other to deal with it when it reached the bank, placed him in a position of unchallengeable control, unless and until it was revoked. And it was not revoked. In these circumstances the conclusion is irresistible that the daughter, who at material times was the sole beneficiary under the settlement, did not retain bona fide possession and enjoyment of the trust property to the entire exclusion of her father or of any benefit to him. Here it does not seem that any nice question arises whether it was from the subject-matter of the gift that the donor (the testator) was excluded or, alternatively, from any benefit, nor whether' it is necessary that the benefit taken by the donor should impair the possession and enjoyment by the donee of the subject-matter of the gift. For here the design and the result of the arrangement were that the daughter's possession and

84 [1954] AC 57 at 73; [above, para **[21.17]** and below, para **[21.29]**].
85 [1954] AC 57 at 73–74; [quoted below, para **[21.29]**].
86 (1912) 13 CLR 503 at 517.

enjoyment were reduced and impaired precisely by the measure of the testator's use and enjoyment of her income.

It was argued for the respondent that this was not the way in which the whole transaction should be regarded. It was said that when the testator, armed with the authority given by the daughter's letter of December 1, 1938, directed the trustee to pay the trust income to her bank account, he acted in a fiduciary capacity, and that when he drew upon that account for his own purposes, he was not using the trust income but was borrowing from her money which had lost its identity. She chose, it was said, to lend it to him: she might equally well have lent it to a stranger. In the joint judgment of Kitto and Taylor JJ. (in which Webb J. concurred) this is the decisive point. It would, they say, be difficult to resist this conclusion *(i.e.* a conclusion favourable to the appellant) if the testator, when he took moneys out of his daughter's bank account, had taken them free from any obligation of repayment. In that case, though the same relationship of creditor and debtor had been established between the bank and the daughter, the trust income presumably retained its identity so far at least that for the purpose of the section it could not be said that the donee had retained exclusive possession and enjoyment of the subject-matter of the gift. But this does not appear to their Lordships to be a valid distinction. The transaction must be viewed as a whole and, since an integral part of it was that the testator before the account was opened was authorised to draw on it for his own purposes, it is irrelevant whether, when he did draw on it, he was or was not under any obligation to repay. Gift or loan, he for his own advantage used her money, paying no interest for it, and by so much reduced her enjoyment of what was her trust income and nothing else. The obligation to repay affected the quantum of the benefit obtained by him: it did no more .... **[21.27]**

For a similar view that a loan amounts to a 'benefit', see *St Aubyn v A-G* [1952] AC 15 (above, para **[21.16]**) per Lord Radcliffe (at 57): 'A man receives for his own benefit moneys paid to him on an advance by way of loan, not the less because the transaction involves an obligation to repay an equivalent amount at a future date with interest in the meantime.' A comparison with the income tax concept of exclusion of settlor is also instructive, see above, Chapter 16, para **[16.32]**. See also the case of *A-G v Seccombe* [1911] 2 KB 688, where the donee permitted the donor to stay in the gifted house as a guest. This was held not to fail the 'exclusion from enjoyment' hurdle. **[21.28]**

Oakes v Commissioner of Stamp Duties of New South Wales (above, para [21.17])

LORD REID: ...But the statute requires not only exclusion of the donor but also exclusion of any benefit to him, and it was on that matter that the argument turned. It appears from the case that after the children came of age they received payment of their shares of the income; it is not said that that involved any benefit to the deceased. But before they came of age their shares of income were used to pay for their maintenance and education, and it was said that this afforded some relief to the deceased, who would otherwise have had to pay out of his own money. Two arguments were submitted. In the first place it was said that spending the children's money in this way was improper or at least disadvantageous to them, and that this combination of advantage to the donor with disadvantage to the donee brought the case within the statute. Their Lordships do not find any sufficient basis in fact for this argument. There is nothing in the case from which it can be inferred that the deceased acted at all improperly in this matter. At least after 1925 this money could properly be spent on the children's maintenance under statutory powers if that was in the best interests of the children. In the absence of anything to indicate the contrary it must be taken that the deceased acted properly in so applying his children's income, that this was in the best interest of the children, and therefore the children must be held to have had full benefit and enjoyment of their money. The case might have been very different if it had appeared that the deceased had so spent his children's shares of the income from the trust not entirely in their interests but wholly or partly for his own benefit in order to relieve himself from the expense of maintaining his children...

Then it was said that even if the income which accrued to the children was properly spent for their maintenance and they are to be held to have had full benefit and enjoyment of it, yet there was also a benefit to the deceased because if it had not been available he would have had to spend more of his own money. The findings in the case are not very specific, but their Lordships will assume that there was some advantage to the deceased; but that advantage was not at the expense of the children and did not impair or diminish the value of the gift to them or their enjoyment of it. It is possible for a donee, in the full and unrestrained enjoyment of his gift to use or spend it in a way that happens to produce some advantage to the donor without there being any loss or disadvantage to the donee. But, in their Lordships' judgment, any such advantage is not a benefit within the meaning of the section. The point is not strictly covered by authority, but the contrary view would be difficult to reconcile with what was said in the House of Lords in *St. Aubyn's* case.[87]

On the view of the facts of the case which their Lordships have felt bound to adopt, this alleged benefit neither encumbered the enjoyment of the gift nor arose by way of reservation out of that which was given, and their Lordships can find no good reason for holding that it brings this case within the statute.

For similar reasons their Lordships are not able to accept the ground of judgment of the Supreme Court of New South Wales to the effect that the linking together of the one-fifth beneficial interests of the donor and the donees resulted in a benefit or advantage to each share, and that this advantage to the donor brought the case within the section. Even if this linkage was of advantage to the deceased (of which there is no evidence) that advantage did not in any way impair the enjoyment of the gift by the donees or trench upon their rights .... **[21.29]**

(2) Permitted benefits[88]

The reservation of benefits provisions will not apply in certain circumstances. First, there are qualifications to 'rule (ii)', which apply only to that rule and do not affect the necessity in 'rule (i)', which requires full possession and enjoyment of the property by the donor. Secondly, the provisions will not apply where the gift by which the property is disposed of is within a list of exempt transfers. **[21.30]**

John Tiley *Revenue Law* (5th edn, 2005) pp 1284–1286

69.3 Qualifications to Rule (ii)

These qualifications apply to both limbs of rule (ii).

De minimis: *virtually the entire exclusion*

FA 1986, s. 102 requires the entire or "virtually" the entire exclusion of A, the donor; by contrast, entire exclusion was required for estate duty. While these words are obviously apt to cover such matters as social visits paid by A, the donor, to B, the donee, at the property, their precise ambit is inevitably obscure. It is puzzling that the legislation retains the words "entire exclusion" if "virtually entire exclusion" will do.

The Revenue view (see Revenue Interpretation RI 55) is that these words exclude very small benefits, as where a gift of a house is followed by a short visit by

87 [1952] AC 15; [see above, para **[21.16]**].

88 Per Tiley's categorisation.

A to B.[89] RI 55, having cited the *Shorter Oxford English Dictionary*, interprets the words as meaning a benefit to the donor which is insignificant in relation to the gifted property, adding that it is not possible to reduce the test to a single, crisp proposition and that each case is one of fact and degree. It states:

> "Some examples of situations in which we consider that Section 102(1)(b) permits limited benefit to the donor without bringing the GWR provisions into play are given below to illustrate how we apply the de minimis test:

- a house which becomes the donee's residence but where the donor subsequently–
  - stays, in the absence of the donee, for not more than 2 weeks each year, or
  - stays with the donee for less than one month each year;
- social visits, excluding overnight stays made by a donor as a guest of the donee, to a house which he had given away. The extent of the social visits should be no greater than the visits which the donor might be expected to make to the donee's house in the absence of any gift by the donor;
- a temporary stay for some short term purpose in a house the donor had previously given away, for example
  - while the donor convalesces after medical treatment,
  - while the donor looks after a donee convalescing after medical treatment,
  - while the donor's own home is being redecorated;
- visits to a house for domestic reasons, for example baby-sitting by the donor for the donee's children;
- a house together with a library of books which the donor visits less than 5 times in any year to consult or borrow a book;
- a motor car which the donee uses to give occasional (ie. less than 3 times a month) lifts to the donor;
- land which the donor uses to walk his dogs or for horse riding provided this does not restrict the donee's use of the land.

It follows, of course, that if the benefit to the donor is, or becomes, more significant, the GWR provisions are likely to apply. Examples of this include gifts of–

- a house in which the donor then stays most weekends, or for a month or more each year;
- a second home or holiday home which the donor and the donee both then use on an occasional basis;
- a house with a library in which the donor continues to keep his own books, or which the donor uses on a regular basis, for example because it is necessary for his work;
- a motor car which the donee uses every day to take the donor to work."

The Board claims that it does not operate s. 102(1)(b) in such a way that donors are unreasonably prevented from having limited access to property they have given away and that a measure of flexibility is adopted in applying the test.

Land and chattels: full consideration

This was introduced for estate duty as a result of the *Chick* case ... In the case of property which is an interest in land or a chattel, retention or assumption by the donor of actual occupation of the land or actual enjoyment of an incorporeal right

89 Revenue Booklet IHT 1, para. 3.4.

over the land, or actual possession of the chattel is disregarded under FA 1986, Schedule 20, paragraph 6(1)(a) if it is for full consideration in money or money's worth.[90] Thus, where a donor makes a gift of a house to a donee and continues to reside in it under a lease providing for payment of a full rent, presumably the maximum allowed by law, there is no gift with reservation. It must also be noted that this qualification applies only to land and chattels and that the only types of enjoyment ignored are actual occupation and enjoyment. Thus, the rule has no mitigating effect in a situation such as the New South Wales case or trusts of insurance policies. The taxpayer will have to prove that full consideration was given, as where both sides have bargained at arm's length and have been separately advised, and the lease follows normal commercial criteria in force at the time it is negotiated.[91]

This was the subject of elaboration in the following statement in the course of the debate on the 1986 Finance Bill[92]

> "Elderly parents make unconditional gifts of undivided shares in their house to their children and the parents and the children occupy the property as their family home, each owner bearing his or her share of the running costs. In these circumstances, the parents' occupation or enjoyment of the part of the house they have given away is in return for similar enjoyment of the children of the other part of the property. Thus the donor's occupation is for full consideration."

IR 55 states that while the Board takes the view that:

> "such full consideration is required throughout the relevant period – and therefore consider that the rent paid should be reviewed at appropriate intervals to reflect market changes – we do recognise that there is no single value at which consideration can be fixed as 'full'. Rather, we accept that what constitutes full consideration in any case lies within a range of values reflecting normal valuation tolerances, and that any amount within that range can be accepted as satisfying the para. 6(1)(a) test."

Land: unforeseen circumstances

Under EA 1986, Schedule 20, paragraph 6(1)(b) where the property is an interest in land, any occupation by the donor can be ignored if it was unforeseen, was not brought about by the donor to receive the benefit of the rule, occurs when the donor is unable to maintain himself through old age, infirmity or otherwise and it represents a reasonable provision for the care and maintenance of the donor. The donee must also be a relative of the donor or his spouse. **[21.31]**

Barry McCutcheon and Withers LLP *Inheritance Tax* (4th edn, 2005) pp 231–232

Exempt transfers blanket let-out

Section 102(5) provides that the reservation of benefit rules do not apply if, or to the extent that, the property is disposed of by way of a gift which is an exempt transfer under any of the following exemptions:

90 See also Revenue Interpretation RI 55.
91 IHT 1, para. 3.5; this is simply an illustration. See *IRC v Spencer-Nairn* [1991] STC 60, Court of Session.
92 HC Official Report, Finance Act 1986, Standing Committee G, col. 425, 10 June 1986. Emphasis was placed on the fullness of the consideration.

- spouse exemption
- small gifts exemption
- marriage gifts exemption
- charities exemption
- political parties exemption
- housing associations exemption
- national purposes exemption
- maintenance funds for historic buildings exemption
- employee trusts exemption

The annual exemption and the normal expenditure out of income exemption are conspicuous by their absence from this list. A PET will also not come within it. **[21.32]**

E. Closing loopholes

As more taxpayers have sought to circumvent the reservation of benefit rules, particularly in relation to the family home, further provisions have been enacted in an attempt to close any remaining loopholes. **[21.33]**

(1) *Ingram v IRC* and Finance Act 1986, s 102A

Section 102A was inserted by s 104 of the Finance Act 1999, and sought to reverse the effect of *Ingram v IRC*.[93] The Paymaster General said the legislation would 'restore the tax position as it was understood to be prior to the House of Lords' ruling in *Ingram*.'[94] **[21.34]**

***Revenue Law: Principles and Practice* (23rd edn, 2005) p 537**

Unsurprisingly the *Ingram* decision was reversed in respect of gifts of interests in land made after 8 March 1999, but the reversing legislation is narrowly targeted and, it would seem, does not otherwise change the reservation of benefit rules. If the following conditions are met the donor is treated as reserving a benefit in the gifted property with the normal consequences:

(1) There must be a gift of an interest in land (other assets are not included). Note that as with the original legislation the trigger is a gift.

(2) The donor must retain 'a significant right or interest . . . in relation to the land' (in certain circumstances it will be sufficient if this is retained by his spouse) or be a party to a significant arrangement in relation to the land. A right or interest is not 'significant' if the donor pays full consideration for it nor if the interest was obtained at least seven years before the gift (hence it is possible to grant a lease, wait seven years and then gift the freehold interest without falling foul of these rules).

It is not thought that these rules apply where a property is divided (eg lodge/main house) and one is gifted, one retained. **[21.35]**

93 Above at para **[21.19]**.

94 *Hansard*, 15 June 1999. As Barry McCutcheon has pointed out, this 'was a bit rich, as the prevailing body of professional opinion was, to the authors' knowledge, that *Ingram* simply confirmed the existing law' (*Inheritance Tax*, 2005).

Section 102A will not operate if s 102 already does so.[95] **[21.36]**

(2) The *Eversden* case and the Finance Act 1986, s 102(5)(B)

Gifts between spouses are exempt[96] and the reservation of benefit rules do not apply to such gifts.[97] Use was made of the interaction between these two provisions in order to avoid inheritance tax by structuring schemes around a short-lived interest for the donor's spouse. A husband or wife was able to remove the family home, or a portfolio of financial assets, from IHT on both their deaths, while continuing to live in the home or enjoy the financial assets throughout their lifetimes. This was the scenario in *Eversden v IRC*[98] and is now curtailed by legislation. **[21.37]**

Barry McCutcheon and Withers LLP, *Inheritance Tax* (4th edn, 2005) pp 232–233

The Finance Act 2003, s.185 introduced ss.102(5A)–(5C) in order to remove any doubt as to the application of s.102(5) in certain circumstances. The issue in doubt was the effect of s.102(5) where an individual settled property on terms under which his spouse took an interest in possession which interest subsequently terminated leaving the property held upon discretionary trusts under which the settler was capable of benefiting. Did s.102(5) mean that the reservation of benefit rules were incapable of applying on the basis that the initial disposal qualified for the spouse exemption, or were the provisions capable of applying on the basis that the settler had made two gifts – one to his spouse of the interest which he had given her and another of the reversionary interest to the discretionary class? ...

...Sections 102(5A)-(5C) have effect in relation to disposals made on or after 20 June 2003. Section 102(5A) provides that s.102(5)(a) does not apply if or, as the case may be, to the extent that the four conditions are satisfied:

(1) the property becomes settled by virtue of the gift;
(2) by reason of the donor's spouse (who is referred to as "the relevant beneficiary") becoming beneficially entitled to an interest in possession in the settled property, the disposal is or, as the case may be, is to any extent within the spouse exemption because of s.49(1);
(3) sometime after the disposal during the donor's lifetime the relevant beneficiary's interest in possession comes to an end;
(4) on the occasion when the interest in possession comes to an end, the relevant beneficiary does not become entitled to the settled property or to another interest in possession in the settled property.

For this purpose (i) the disposal of an interest is treated as the termination of that interest, and (ii) references to any property or to an interest in any property include references to part of any property or interest.[99]

Section 102(5B) then provides that to the extent that s.102 applies by virtue of s.102(5A), s.102 has effect as if the disposal by way of gift had been made immediately after the beneficiary's interest in possession came to an end. **[21.38]**

95 Finance Act 1986, s 102C(7).
96 IHTA 1984, s 18.
97 FA 1986, s 102(5).
98 [2003] EWCA Civ 668. [2003] STC 822; see above, para **[21.20]**.
99 F.A. 1986, s. 102(5C).

(3) Pre-owned assets

The most recent anti-avoidance measure, introduced by the Finance Act 2004, Sch 15, and to apply from the tax year 2005–06, is the imposition of an annual income tax charge on the value of assets that are still used, or enjoyed, or capable of being enjoyed by a donor. The raison d'être of this self-contained income tax charging provision is to both 'punish' individuals for avoiding the reservation of benefit rules by means not favoured by HMRC, and thus a charge to IHT and to act as a disincentive to others who may be thinking of using such means. It has been noted that the scheme is retroactive rather than retrospective[100] in that it operates with respect to arrangements put into effect on or after 18 March, 1986, but it imposes a charge only on benefits enjoyed since on or after 6 April, 2005. Whilst the rules for establishing the benefit that is chargeable are set out in the Finance Act, Sch 15, the all-important machinery for determining the relevant valuation date and the rate of interest are to be found in regulations.[101] **[21.39]**

Tax Treatment of Pre-Owned Assets, Inland Revenue Consultation, December 2003

General

As part of its wider strategy to protect tax revenues the Government announced on 10 December 2003 that income tax will in future be charged on the benefit people enjoy when they have arranged free continuing use of major capital assets that they once owned. Arrangements like this are often made to get round the IHT gifts with reservation (GWR) rules. Essentially, these rules are intended to stop people from giving their assets away, so that for IHT purposes they are out of their estate when they die, while still continuing to enjoy the practical benefits of owning them during their lifetime.

Who is likely to be affected?

People who continue to enjoy the use of assets (free of charge, or at a below-market rent) they formerly owned (or provided the funds to purchase). **[21.40]**

McCutcheon and Withers LLP *Inheritance Tax* (4th edn, 2005) pp 256–257

Guiding principles

The Regime appears to be based on the following guiding principles:

- value which is subject to IHT should not be subject to the Regime;

100 See, McCutcheon and Withers LLP *Inheritance Tax* (2005), at pp 255–256.

101 The Charge to Income Tax by Reference to Enjoyment of Property Previously Owned Regulations 2005 (SI 2005/724). Although these regulations also include provision to prevent a double charge to income tax and inheritance tax where an election has been made by the taxpayer to disapply the pre-owned assets income tax charge, further regulations will provide similar relief in circumstances where no such election has been made, but where taxpayers have sought instead to dismantle their previous arrangements so that the pre-owned income tax charge is no longer due.

- property and transactions which resulted in IHT not being payable either by reason of qualifying for favoured IHT treatment or by reason of what the Revenue regarded as "acceptable" IHT planning should not be caught by the Regime;
- land, chattels and settled intangible property not subject to IHT and to which no favoured treatment is expressly given by the Regime are within the scope of the Regime.

Unfortunately, the actual provisions do not always give effect to these principles.

Statutory links with IHT

Although the Regime is a freestanding regime, it is intimately linked with IHT in a number of ways:

(a) not only is property comprised in an individual's estate for IHT purposes outside the scope of the Regime, but so is other property not comprised in the individual's estate but from which property which is comprised in his estate derives its value. This prevents the same value being subject both to IHT and to the Regime.

(b) Subject to certain qualifications, property which would fall to be treated as property subject to a reservation in relation to the person chargeable under the Regime is outside the scope of that Regime so that the same property is not subject to both IHT and to the Regime. Furthermore, it is open to a person to opt out of the Regime in relation to property by electing to subject himself to the reservation of benefit rules in relation to that property. He thus has the choice of the lesser of two evils;

(c) The territorial scope of the Regime is framed by reference to the territorial scope of IHT in some respects – there are notable mismatches – and the IHT deemed domicile provisions apply;

(d) Favoured treatment given to posthumous transactions is linked to the IHT favoured treatment given to such transactions so this remains a fruitful area for planning;

(e) Certain reliefs and exemptions are framed by reference to IHT reliefs and exemptions;

(f) Various IHT definitions apply for the purpose of the Regime.

Basic structure

The broad structure of the Regime is to establish a separate charging system for each of three different kinds of property:

- Land
- Chattels
- Intangible property comprised in a settler-interested settlement.[102]

Parallel charging codes

More than one of the charging codes can apply to an arrangement. Assume that X lives in a house owned by a company all the shares in which are owned by a

102 "Chattel" and "intangible property" are defined as follows: (a) "Chattels" means any tangible moveable property (or, in Scotland, corporeal moveable property); "intangible property" means any property other than chattels or interests in land. "Intangible property" is thus a default term in that it applies to all property other than chattels and interests in land; FA 2004, Sch.15, para.1.

discretionary trust of which he is the settlor and under which he can benefit. The Regime is capable of applying to two assets: first, the house in which X lives under the charge on land; secondly, the shares in the company, under the charge on settled intangible property.[103]

Reliefs and exemptions

Certain conditions, which vary according to the type of property concerned, must be satisfied before the Regime can apply to that kind of property. Where land and chattels are concerned these conditions must be satisfied otherwise than by certain transactions called "excluded transactions". Even if the conditions are satisfied, certain exemptions may prevent the Regime from applying. **[21.41]**

4. Settlements

For inheritance tax purposes, the term 'settlement' is defined[104] to include:

> 'any disposition or dispositions of property, whether effected by instrument, by parole or by operation of law, or partly in one way and partly in another, whereby the property is for the time being–
> (a) held in trust for persons in succession or for any person subject to a contingency . . .'

The width of this provision is discussed in *IRC* v *Lloyds Private Banking Ltd*[105] and *Rysaffe Trustee Co (CI) Ltd* v *IRC*[106], below.

Prior to FA 2006, there existed two very different regimes for the taxation of each of two classes of trusts – trusts with an interest in possession and trusts with no interest in possession. Broadly speaking, the latter class comprised discretionary trusts, trusts that in estate duty days had been used with some success to minimise the amount of tax payable. The distinction in taxation between the two (still relevant for certain trusts) is that the charge in respect of an interest in possession trust is based on the fiction that the fund belongs to the person with the interest in possession. In contrast, where other settlements are concerned, instead of attributing the fund to one of the beneficiaries, the settlement itself is the taxable entity. Critical to identifying into which regime a particular trust fell was the definition of "interest in possession", discussed in *Pearson v IRC*[107] and *IRC v Eversden,*[108] below. Following FA 2006, the whole structure for the inheritance taxation of trusts has changed, with most inter vivos interest in possession trusts created on or after 22 March 2006 becoming subject to the harsher regime that formerly applied only to trusts with no interest in possession.[109] However, the term 'interest in possession' remains important *(i)* because trusts with an interest in possession created before 22 March 2006, whether during lifetime or on

103 There are provisions in Sch.15, para.18 to prevent double taxation arising in such a case, but the point to bear in mind is that each situation must be carefully analysed for its consequences under the Regime.
104 By IHTA 1984, s 43. Note that the term 'settlement' is not statutorily defined for the purposes of income tax, although 'settled property' is; see above, para **[16.4]**. See above, para **[20.26]**, for the CGT definition of 'settlement'.
105 [1998] STC 559 (see below, para **[21.56]**).
106 [2003] EWCA 356; [2003] STC 536 (see below, para **[21.57]**.
107 [1981] AC 753; see below, para **[21.52]**.
108 [2003] EWCA Civ 668; [2003] STC 822; see above, para **[21.20]**.
109 See FA 2006, Sch 20.

death, will continue to be subject to the former regime, and *(ii)* it continues to be used in the amended legislation, albeit not in a way that is definitive of whether a trust should be taxed according to one regime or the other. There also existed favoured trusts, namely accumulation and maintenance trusts and trusts for disabled persons. Accumulation and maintenance trusts, which were used to provide for the benefit of minors, were excluded from the harsher regime that applied to trusts with no interest in possession even though a minor had no such interest, provided that the minor would become entitled to the settled property, or to an interest in it, by the age of 25. In other words, this type of trust allowed for all the benefits and flexibility of a discretionary trust, whilst escaping from being taxed as one. Such treatment will no longer be available for trusts created on or after 22 March 2006[110] and, in their stead, are to be found trusts for bereaved minors and age 18–25 trusts.[111] Once again, however, accumulation and maintenance trusts established before 22 March 2006 will remain free of inheritance tax under the former regime until the 18th birthday of the minor concerned. Accordingly, it is necessary to have an appreciation of this type of trust, which is discussed in *Inglewood* v *IRC*.[112]

Since there are a large number of trusts in existence that are subject to the former regime, this chapter will consider both the pre-22 March 2006 rules, as well as those introduced by FA 2006. **[21.42]**

A. *Pre-22 March 2006 rules*

(1) Interest in possession trusts[113]

The life tenant of a trust with an interest in possession is treated as being beneficially entitled to property in which his interest subsists (the 's 49' regime).[114] Inheritance tax is therefore charged on his death as if he had made a transfer of value immediately before his death equivalent to the value of his interest in the capital,[115] if this, together with his other estate and the cumulative transfers made by him in the previous seven years (together with any PETs that thereby become chargeable) exceed the upper limit of the nil rate band, after any available exemptions and reliefs have been given. Inheritance tax is also charged during the lifetime of the life tenant if he disposes of his interest under the trust, or if his interest ceases.[116] In these cases, the transfer would usually have been potentially exempt (the 'PET' regime), and tax will only be charged if the life tenant dies within seven years of the termination or disposal.[117] The transfer of property into an interest in

110 IHTA 1984, s 71(1A), inserted by FA 2006, Sch 20, Pt 1, para 2.
111 FA 2006, Sch 20 Pt 1, para 1.
112 [1983] WLR 366; see below, para **[21.54]**.
113 Pre-22 March 2006 interest in possession trusts will remain subject to this regime unless (i) property is added to the trust on or after 22 March 2006; and (ii) the beneficiary with an interest in possession is changed on or after 6 April 2008 (other than where the interest passes to the spouse on the beneficiary's death) and the new beneficiary is not absolutely entitled.
114 IHTA 1984, s 49(1).
115 Ibid., s 4(1).
116 Ibid., ss 51 and 52. In these cases, and also on death, the life tenant is deemed to have made a notional transfer of value.
117 Ibid., s 54A.

possession trust would also have been a PET[118]; if so, provided the settlor survives for seven years after the transfer, no IHT will be payable on the creation of the settlement with an interest in possession, provided that the anti-avoidance rules are not infringed.[119] **[21.43]**

(2) Trusts with no interest in possession

A trust without an interest in possession is taxed in an entirely different way. The regime for these trusts (the 'relevant property' regime), first introduced by FA 1982, provides for three occasions of charge that apply to trusts of this type. First, tax is charged at the rate appropriate to the settlor on the creation of the trust.[120] Secondly, an exit charge[121] is imposed when property ceases to be 'relevant property'[122] (ie is taken out of the settlement or becomes subject to an interest in possession). Thirdly, a periodic charge is made on the tenth anniversary of the creation of the trust, and every ten years thereafter.[123] Inheritance tax is charged on the 'relevant property' in the trust on the anniversary. The rate of tax is computed in a complicated way,[124] and is based on a number of factors, including the cumulative chargeable transfers made by the settlor in the seven years before the creation of the settlement. It is reduced to 30% of the applicable lifetime rate; since the lifetime rate is 20%, this means that the maximum rate on the ten-year charge is 6%. **[21.44]**

(3) Accumulation and maintenance trusts

Trusts for the benefit of minors are usually classified as having no interest in possession,[125] and special provision is made where the interest does not vest until the beneficiary marries, or attains an age not exceeding 25 years.[126] Such trusts are called 'accumulation and maintenance settlements'. The benefits arising from these trusts are (i) as with other interest in possession trusts, a transfer into an accumulation and maintenance trust would have been a PET; (ii) no charge arises when the beneficiary becomes entitled to the settled property, or to an interest in it[127] before reaching the age of 25 (eg, on becoming entitled to the income at 18) or should the beneficiary die before that age[128]; (iii) where the beneficiary becomes entitled to the income, say, at 18, there is no charge when he becomes entitled to the capital on or before reaching the age of 25.[129] If, on the 6 April 2008, the date for the vesting of capital in respect of an accumulation and maintenance settlement subsisting on 22 March 2006 remains at an age greater than 18, between that age and the

118 See IHTA 1984, s 3A(7) (inserted by F(No 2)A 1987, s 96(1),(3) for transfers of value made after 16 March 1987.
119 See IHTA 1984, ss 54A and B.
120 Such a transfer will not be a PET, but is a chargeable transfer: see IHTA 1984, s 3A(1).
121 IHTA 1984, s 65.
122 *Ibid*, s 58.
123 *Ibid*, ss 61, 64.
124 *Ibid*, s 66.
125 Because the trustees' powers of accumulation are either expressed in the trust instrument, or incorporated into it by the Trustee Act 1925, s 31 (see Inland Revenue Press Release, below para **[21.51]**).
126 IHTA 1984, s 71.
127 *Ibid*, s 71(4)(a).
128 *Ibid*, s 71(4)(b).
129 *Ibid*, s 53(2).

vesting age (which must be no greater than 25), the trust assets will become relevant property on and from 6 April 2008, and the periodic and exit charges will apply. **[21.45]**

B. Post-22 March 2006 rules

The new regime for the inheritance taxation of trusts introduced by FA 2006 abandons, in effect, the classification of trusts into those with, and those without, an interest in possession and, whilst it is not particularly easy to formulate a new classification, a possible one might be to distinguish between those trusts which continue to enjoy PET status, those which are subject to the s 49 regime, those subject to the relevant property regime and trusts for bereaved minors and age 18–25 trusts. **[21.46]**

(1) Creation of trusts that are potentially exempt transfers

An interest in possession trust created on or after 22 March 2006 in favour of a disabled person[130] is the only type of trust that will now give rise to a potentially exempt transfer. **[21.47]**

(2) Trusts subject to the s 49 regime

Trusts subject to the s 49 regime are trusts with an interest in possession where the settled property forms part of the beneficiary's estate, and comprise:[131]

(a) an immediate post-death interest. This is an interest in possession arising immediately on a death on or after 22 March 2006.[132]

(b) a disabled person's interest;[133] or

(c) a transitional serial interest. This includes: (i) an interest in possession arising on or after 22 March 2006 but before 6 April 2008 in immediate succession to an interest in possession that was subsisting prior to 22 March 2006 under a trust created before then; and (ii) an interest in possession to which a surviving spouse or civil partner becomes entitled on the death on or after 6 April 2008 of his or her late spouse or civil partner, where that late spouse or civil partner's interest in possession had been subsisting prior to 22 March 2006 under a trust created before then.[134] **[21.48]**

(3) Relevant property regime

With the exception of trusts for bereaved minors and age 18–25 trusts (see below, para **[21.50]**), all interest in possession trusts (apart from post-death interests, transitional serial interests and trusts in favour of disabled persons) together with trusts with no interest in possession are accorded the same treatment as pre-22 March trusts with no interest in possession (see above, para **[21.44]**). This means that the creation of such a trust will now give rise to

130 See n 133, below, for a definition of a disabled person.

131 IHTA 1984, s 49 (1A), inserted by FA 2006, Sch 20, Pt 2, para 4.

132 *Ibid*, s 49A, inserted by FA 2006, Sch 20. Pt 2, para 5.

133 Generally, a disabled person is someone mentally incapable of managing their affairs, or who is in receipt of, or qualified to receive, an attendance allowance (person of 65 or over), or who is in receipt of, or qualified to receive, disability living allowance with the care component at the highest or middle rate (persons under 65); see IHTA 1984, ss 89, 89A.

134 IHTA 1984, s 49B-E, inserted by FA 2006, Sch 20, Pt 2, para 5.

an immediately chargeable transfer on a value in excess of the nil rate band. As far as interest in possession trusts are concerned, this is a return to the position that existed prior to the changes made by FA 1987. **[21.49]**

(4) Trusts for bereaved minors and age 18–25 trusts

No settlement created on or after 22 March 2006, nor any settlement created before then, where an accumulation and maintenance trust came into possession on or after that date (eg, on the death of a life tenant on or after 22 March 2006) can any longer enjoy the benefits previously afforded to accumulation and maintenance trusts. In their stead there are the bereaved minor and age 18–25 trusts, but it should be noted that these are limited in terms of the inheritance tax advantages they confer. Trusts for bereaved minors, which can be existing trusts or trusts created on or after 22 March 2006, are exempt from the relevant property regime, and can generally be described as trusts established under the will or intestacy of a parent whereby the child will become entitled to the settled property on or before attaining the age of 18.[135] Thus, grandparents wishing to create a favoured trust for their infant grandchildren can no longer do so either in their lifetime or by will, and a parent can only do so on his or her death. And in this latter case, to avoid any charge at all, the vesting date is now 18 rather than 25.

Age 18–25 trusts can also be existing trusts or trusts established on or after 22 March 2006, and include a trust for a bereaved minor established under the will of his parent,[136] under the terms of which the minor will become entitled to an interest in possession before 6 April 2008 (eg, at 18 under Trustee Act 1925, s 31), and to the capital between the ages of 18 and 25 and, in the meantime, the income and capital can only be paid to him or for his benefit.[137] Settled property subject to these trusts will be exempt from the relevant property regime, except that there will be an inheritance tax charge[138] if and when the bereaved minor becomes absolutely entitled to the property after attaining the age of 18.[139] **[21.50]**

Inland Revenue Press Release (12 February 1976)

Capital Transfer Tax-Settled Property – Interest in Possession

The Board of Inland Revenue are aware that doubts have been expressed in the legal press and elsewhere concerning the precise scope of the term "interest in possession" as used in F.A. 1975, Part III,[140] and in particular about its application where an interest in settled property is subject to a discretion or power to accumulate the income of the property or to divert it elsewhere.

The Board therefore feel it appropriate, in view of the importance of the expression in F.A. 1975, Sched. 5,[141] to make known their understanding of the

135 *Ibid*, s 71A, inserted by FA 2006, Sch 20, Pt 1, para 1.
136 This term includes a step-parent; see IHTA 1984, s 71H.
137 IHTA 1984, s 71D-G.
138 If the beneficiary becomes entitled at the age of 25, the maximum rate of charge is 4.2%: IHTA 1984, s 71F.
139 Or if the property is advanced to him or applied for his benefit after he attains the age of 18, or if he dies between the ages of 18 and 25: IHTA 1984, s 71D(6).
140 [Now see IHTA 1984, Pt III.]
141 [*Ibid.*]

meaning of the expression. This is that an interest in possession in settled property exists where the person having the interest has the immediate entitlement (subject to any prior claim by the trustees for expenses or other outgoings properly payable out of income) to any income produced by what property as the income arises; but that a discretion or power, in whatever form, which can be exercised after income arises so as to withhold it from that person negatives the existence of an interest in possession. For this purpose a power to accumulate income is regarded as a power to withhold it, unless any accumulations must be held solely for the person having the interest or his personal representatives. On the other hand the existence of a mere power of revocation or appointment, the exercise of which would determine the interest wholly or in part (but which, so long as it remains unexercised, does not affect the beneficiary's immediate entitlement to income) does not in the Board's view prevent the interest from being an interest in possession. **[21.51]**

Pearson v IRC [1981] AC 253 (HL) reversing [1980] Ch 1 (CA)

The income and capital of a fund were held on trust for the settlor's three daughters (adults at the relevant time) in equal shares on attaining the age of 21, subject to overriding powers exercisable by the trustees to appoint capital and income amongst the beneficiaries, their spouses and issue and to accumulate so much of the income as they thought fit. The trustees, who had regularly exercised their powers to accumulate the income, made an irrevocable appointment of part of the capital to one of the beneficiaries, giving her an interest in possession of the appointed sum. The issue to be decided was whether, on reaching 21, she had already acquired an interest in possession of the fund for, if she did, no CTT would have been chargeable on the appointment;[142] if she had enjoyed no such interest previously, there would have been a charge when the appointed funds passed from a settlement with no interest in possession into an interest in possession settlement.[143]

> VISCOUNT DILHORNE: . . . The meaning to be given to the words "interest in possession in settled property" is . . . of vital importance in ascertaining liability to capital transfer tax.
>
> . . . No attempt is made in the Finance Act 1975 to define "interest in possession" apart from the definition in paragraph 11(10)[144] and the definition for the purpose of applying the Schedule to Scotland. What then should be the next approach to construing those words in the Act? In my view one should first seek to determine the ordinary and natural meaning of those words and then consider whether there is anything in the context in which they are used to lead to the conclusion that the proper interpretation of them involves a departure from the ordinary and natural meaning . . . So the parties agree that for there to be an interest in possession, there must be a present right to the present enjoyment of something, the revenue contending that it must be to the enjoyment of the whole or part of the net income of the settled property.
>
> The difficulty lies in its application to the facts of the present case. It is said by both parties to be one of fundamental importance. Whether or not that is the case, all we have to decide is whether on reaching 21, Fiona and her sisters acquired interests in possession in settled property. In other words had they then a present right of present enjoyment of anything?

142 IHTA 1984, s 53(2). Although this case was decided under the CTT regime, the same principles apply for IHT and for trusts created prior to 22 March 2006. For all but particular trusts created on or after that date, the essential distinction between trusts with an interest in possession and those without no longer exists, since they are all treated as if there was no such interest; see above, para **[21.49]**.

143 IHTA 1984, s 65.

144 [Repealed by FA 1982, Sch 22, Pt VII; see now IHTA 1984, s 59(1).]

As to that, there are, it seems to me, two possible conclusions. The first is that the power of appointment . . . not having been exercised, the three sisters on reaching that age acquired interests in possession defeasible should the trustees decide to exercise their power to accumulate income. They were then entitled absolutely to the capital and income of the trust fund in equal shares subject to the exercise of that power. The second is that they never secured an interest in possession for they never acquired on reaching that age the right to the enjoyment of anything. Their enjoyment of any income from the trust fund depended on the trustees' decision as to the accumulation of income. They would only have a right to any income from the trust fund if the trustees decided it should not be accumulated or if they failed to agree that it should be or if they delayed a decision on this matter for so long that a decision then to accumulate and withhold income from the sisters would have been unreasonable.

As I read their judgments, the courts below took the first view. Reluctant as I am to differ from judges so experienced in the law relating to trusts, I find myself unable to agree with them. Fox J.[145] held that:

> ". . . the interest of a person who is entitled to the income of property subject only to a power in the trustees to accumulate is in possession . . . it is a present interest giving a present right to *whatever income is not accumulated*."[146]

In *Gartside* v. *Inland Revenue Commissioners*[147] an estate duty case, Lord Reid said: " 'In possession' must mean that your interest enables you to claim now whatever may be the subject of the interest. For instance, if it is the current income from a certain fund your claim may yield nothing if there is no income, but your claim is a valid claim, and if there is any income you are entitled to get it. But a right to require trustees to consider whether they will pay you something does not enable you to claim anything. If the trustees do decide to pay you something, you do not get it by reason of having the right to have your case considered: you get it only because the trustees have decided to give it to you."

That case concerned a discretionary trust where payment was made to the beneficiaries at the discretion of the trustees. Here the three sisters' entitlement to income was subject to the trustees' power to accumulate. On reaching 21 they had no valid claim to anything. If there was any income from the settled property, they were not entitled to it. Their right to anything depended on what the trustees did or did not do and the receipt of income by them appears to me to have been just as much at the discretion of the trustees as was the receipt of income by the beneficiaries in the *Gartside* case.

It was recognised by the respondents that if *[the relevant clause in the trust deed]* had created a trust to accumulate subject to which the trust fund was to be held in trust for the three sisters absolutely on their attaining 21 they would not have secured an interest in possession on reaching that age. It makes all the difference, so it was said, that the trustees were not under a duty to accumulate but only had power to do so if they thought fit. I am not able to accept this for in neither case can it in my opinion be said that the sisters on attaining that age secured the right to the present enjoyment of anything.

Fox J.[148] in the course of his judgment distinguished the cases of *Attorney-General* v. *Power*[149] and *Gartside* v. *Inland Revenue Commissioners*[150] from the present case on the ground that in those cases "the beneficiaries got nothing unless the trustees decided to give it to them" whereas in the present case the sisters were "absolutely entitled to income unless the trustees decided to accumulate."

I do not think that that is the case. I do not read the trust deed as providing that. *[The relevant clause]* gives the trustees power to accumulate as they think fit and the sisters' entitlement depends on whether that power is exercised. If it were the case that the deed did so provide, then I would agree that the sisters had a defeasible interest in possession.

145 [1980] Ch 1 at 9.
146 [Emphasis of Viscount Dilhorne.]
147 [1968] AC 553 at 607.
148 [1980] Ch 1 at 14D.
149 [1906] 2 IR 272.
150 [1968] AC 553.

Such an interest may be terminated by the exercise of a power of revocation or of an overriding power of appointment . . . The existence of such a power does not prevent the holding of an interest in possession prior to the exercise of the power and until it is exercised, the holder of the interest has a present right of present enjoyment.

A distinction has in my opinion to be drawn between the exercise of a power to terminate a present right of present enjoyment and the exercise of a power which prevents a present right of present enjoyment arising. If in this case the power of appointment . . . had been exercised before the sisters became 21, it could not be said that they then got an interest in possession.

The revenue, while contending that it made no difference in this case that the sisters' entitlement was subject to a power to accumulate as distinct from being subject to a trust to do so, contended that a distinction was to be drawn between what may be called the administrative and the dispositive powers in a trust deed. It was said that such a distinction was drawn in the Finance Act 1969, section 36(6)(d) where it was enacted that references in the part of the Act dealing with estate duty to the income of any property were to be construed as references to income after deduction of any costs, expenses or fees properly payable out of that income. Section 8(1) of the Perpetuities and Accumulations Act 1964 provides that:

> "The rule against perpetuities shall not operate to invalidate a power conferred on trustees . . . to do any act in the administration (as opposed to the distribution) of any property."

These provisions show that Parliament distinguished between the administration of a trust and the dispositive powers of trustees and in my opinion there is a very real distinction. A life tenant has an interest in possession but his interest only extends to the net income of the property, that is to say, after deduction from the gross income of expenses etc. properly incurred in the management of the trust by the trustees in the exercise of their powers. A dispositive power is a power to dispose of the net income. Sometimes the line between an administrative and a dispositive power may be difficult to draw but that does not mean that there is not a valid distinction. In the present case the revenue contended that the power given . . . to apply income towards the payment of duties, taxes etc. which but for the provisions of the clause would be payable out of or charged upon capital was a dispositive power and that this clause alone would prevent the sisters having an interest in possession on reaching 21. I do not think that this is so. I think *the relevant clause]* falls on the administrative side of the line and merely elucidates the meaning to be given to *[the clause that provided that the trustees should have "all the powers of management and exploitation of an absolute beneficial owner" in respect of any property subject to the trusts]*.

A considerable part of the arguments addressed to us was devoted to consideration of what would have been the position in relation to estate duty. I do not think it necessary to consider those arguments as I do not think that the position in relation to estate duty assists in determining the application of the words "interest in possession" in Schedule 5.[151]

In my opinion the words "interest in possession" in Schedule 5 should be given their ordinary natural meaning which I take to be a present right of present enjoyment and as in my view the sisters on attaining 21 did not obtain that, this appeal should succeed.

LORD RUSSELL OF KILLOWEN (*dissenting*): . . . My noble and learned friend Lord Keith of Kinkel, in forming the opposite opinion, suggests that otherwise a conclusion follows that the interest goes in and out of possession according as the trustees refrain from accumulating or decide to do so, and to the further conclusion that as the trustees did actually accumulate all the income up to the date of the 1976 appointment, the interest was never in possession . . . I consider, with respect, that the conclusions stated above do not follow from the view which I have, supporting the courts below, formed. The fact that an interest in possession is liable to defeasance by *subsequent* exercise of the power does not deny it that description when the benefit of it is thus subsequently taken away . . .

151 [FA 1975; now mainly consolidated in Inheritance Tax Act 1984, Pt III.]

The crucial question, in my opinion, lies in the well known distinction between a trust and a power, a distinction recognised by this House *In re Baden's Deed Trusts*,[152] and there only regretted as a distinction which might lead in a given case to invalidity of the disposition. As I have already indicated this is clearly a case of a mere power to accumulate, as distinct from a trust to accumulate unless and to the extent to which the trustees exercised a power to pay allowances to the sisters or any of them. The sisters were able to say that as income accrued on the £16,000 they were then entitled to that income, subject to the possibility that the trustees might *subsequently divert* it from them by a decision to accumulate it. (Indeed but for the ... power of appointment, and the possibility until the death of the settlor in December 1976 of the birth of further children, they were, notwithstanding the power of accumulation, entitled to claim transfer of the £16,000.) Similar considerations apply to the possibility of the exercise of the *relevant clause]* application of the income for a capital purpose. The case is also distinguishable from the case of a discretionary trust of income among a class – as in *Gartside*.[153]

These considerations persuade me that at the time of the 1976 appointment it is not correct to say that no interest in possession subsisted in the three sisters in the £16,000... **[21.52]**

The House of Lords (Viscount Dilhorne, Lord Keith of Kinkel and Lord Lane, Lord Salmon and Lord Russell of Killowen dissenting) allowed the Revenue's appeal from the decision of the Court of Appeal (Buckley, Bridge and Templeman LJJ) affirming the decision by Fox J.

See also *von Ernst & Cie SA v IRC* [1980] STC 111, *Moore & Osborne v IRC* [1984] STC 23, *Swales v IRC* [1984] STC 413 and *Oakley v IRC* (2005) Sp C 460. For the distinction between administrative and dispositive powers (discussed by Viscount Dilhorne in *Pearson v IRC*, above at para **[21.52]**) see *Miller v IRC* [1987] STC 108 and *Stenhouse's Trustees v Lord Advocate* [1984] STC 195. See also Inland Revenue Statements of Practice E5 to E8: Interests in Possession, and SP 10/79: Power to allow a beneficiary to occupy a dwelling house. **[21.53]**

Inglewood (Lord) v IRC [1983] 1 WLR 366 (CA)

The court had to determine whether a power of appointment included in an accumulation and maintenance settlement affected the relief from CTT granted in respect of such settlements by para 15 of Sch 5 to the Finance Act 1975.[154] Provided that 'one or more persons ... will, on or before attaining a specified age not exceeding 25, become entitled to, or an interest in possession in, the settled property ...',[155] an accumulation and maintenance settlement was relieved from being treated as a settlement with no interest in possession.

FOX LJ: ... Looking at the whole matter more widely it appears to us unlikely that Parliament can have intended that a trust should have the benefit of paragraph 15 if it was subject to a power of revocation which could be exercised for the benefit of other persons at ages exceeding 25. The Finance Act 1975 plainly continued and extended the policy of the Finance Act 1969 of reducing the fiscal advantages enjoyed by discretionary trusts. It did that by imposing the discretionary trust regime. That regime was burdensome

152 [1971] AC 424.
153 [1968] AC 553.
154 Repealed by FA 1982, Sch 22, Pt VII. New provisions for settlements without interests in possession were substituted by FA 1982, Pt IV, Ch II. See now Inheritance Tax Act 1984, ss 58–85. For the provisions for accumulation and maintenance settlements, see IHTA. 1984, s 71, although they are no longer effective for trusts created on or after 22 March 2006; see para **[21.50]**, above.
155 The same words are used in IHTA 1984, s 71(I)(a) (amended for trusts created on or after 22 March 2006) for IHT purposes.

on trusts for persons contingently upon attaining a specified age – which are necessarily very common because it is undesirable to give capital to persons absolutely at too early an age. Paragraph 15 was enacted accordingly. Existing trusts could be converted into paragraph 15 trusts at low rates of tax under the provisions of paragraph 14. Parliament, having decided on assistance for contingent trusts, would, it seems to us, in the context of this legislation, be likely to confine it within fairly strict boundaries. In particular, it seems to us, highly unlikely that the benefit of paragraph 15 was intended to be available to what were, in effect, discretionary trusts, by reason of the existence of wide powers of revocation and reappointment, merely by the device of a primary trust for a person at 25 which could be revoked at any time.

We summarise our view of the matter as follows: (1) Paragraph 15(1)(a) leaves upon us the strong prima facie impression that its provisions are not satisfied by a trust subject to a power of revocation and reappointment under which the beneficiary's interest can be destroyed and reappointed to another person at the absolute discretion of the trustees. The word "will" involves a degree of certainty which is inconsistent with such a power. (2) We accept that the word "will" is capable of bearing such a meaning as that for which the trustees contended but it involves the addition of words which are not in the paragraph and we see no circumstances which compel us to adopt it. Thus: (a) none of the possible events in which a beneficiary might be prevented from attaining a vested interest (death, bankruptcy, etc.) seem to us to be of any weight at all in support of the trustees' construction except the power of advancement. That power is so wholly different in its nature from an unrestricted power of revocation that its acceptance by Parliament must for practical reasons be assumed. (b) Whilst the Crown's construction may involve some anomalies so does the trustees' construction. (3) The legislative framework and purpose of the statute seem to us to be more in accord with the Crown's construction. In the circumstances we think that the judge's decision was correct and that the appeal should be dismissed. **[21.54]**

See also Inland Revenue Statements of Practice: 18 July 1978: Accumulation and Maintenance Settlements: El and E2. **[21.55]**

IRC v Lloyds Private Banking Ltd [1998] STC 559 (Ch D)

A married couple owned their home as beneficial tenants in common in equal shares. Under the terms of the wife's will, it was provided that her husband should live in their home for as long as he wanted, keeping it in good repair and insured and paying all the outgoings, and that her trustee (Lloyds) should make no objection to her husband's residence, would not disturb or restrict it in any way and would not take steps to enforce a sale. On the husband's death, the property was to pass to their daughter. The husband lived in the property until his death. The Revenue argued successfully that the husband had an interest in possession in his wife's share of the property and that, accordingly, the entire value of the property should be included in his estate for IHT purposes.

LIGHTMAN J: . . .The critical question . . . is whether cl.3(1) of the will was dispositive (i.e. made a disposition of an interest in the half share to Mr Evans) or merely laid down administrative directions to the trustee. The Revenue contends that it was dispositive: Lloyds contends that it was not. It is common ground that the words 'On the death of my husband' in cl. 3(2) of the will do not postpone the interest of the daughter until the death of Mr Evans so that, if Mr Evans decided not to live in the property or declined to comply with the conditions contained in cl. 3(1), the half share was held on trust thereafter pending Mr Evan's death for the four children as residuary beneficiaries: the words merely mean 'subject to the foregoing provisions in cl. 3(1)'. Accordingly the only persons with any possible claim to a beneficial interest in the half share must be the daughter and, if and only if cl. 3(1) is not dispositive, the daughter is solely beneficially entitled and as such was, as soon as Mrs Evans died, entitled to bring an end to the trust, to require the half share be vested in her and to treat as totally ineffective the (in those circumstances) purely administrative provisions of cl. 3(1). It would appear improbable that this can have been the intention of Mrs Evans, involving as it does writing out of the will as devoid of legal effect elaborate directions in the will on their face designed to secure that Mr Evans could continue to occupy the property as his home for the rest of his life....

In my view, though the drafting and language of cl. 3(1) of the will is in terms of placing restrictions on Lloyds as trustee, its purpose and effect is to confer upon Mr Evans a life interest in the half share. His own rights as tenant in common were not enough to entitle him to exclusive occupation of the property for the rest of his life: he required for this purpose during this period also the rights attaching to the half share, and it was intended he should enjoy these rights though the draftsman of the will for one reason or another chose not to spell this out. In short cl. 3(1) is dispositive and confers upon Mr Evans a determinable life interest in the half share though it is dressed up as a set of administrative directions. What is decisive however is the substance of the provision and not the clothes or label which it wears. **[21.56]**

Rysaffe Trustee Co (CI) Ltd v IRC [2003] EWCA Civ 356, [2003] STC 536 (CA)

A settlor believed that the inheritance tax liabilities on trust property would be lower with five trusts than with one. Accordingly, he executed five identical settlements (each containing discretionary trusts) in the sums of £10 each, dated on five separate days within a period of about a month. Shares were later added to each trust. The Revenue sought to treat the five settlements as one by invoking the associated operations provisions in IHTA 1984, ss 272 and 268, with the result that the anniversary charge[156] was levied at the rate applicable to the total value of the property in all five settlements. The Court of Appeal was in agreement with Park J that the reference in IHTA 1984, s 43 to the term 'disposition' was not to be extended by IHTA 1984, s 272 to a disposition made by associated operations; that the correct approach in applying IHTA 1984, s 64 was not to invoke the associated operation rule, but to ask what property was comprised in the settlement at the relevant time.

MUMMERY LJ:

12. Section 43(1) expressly contemplates that two questions should be addressed for the purposes of determining the charge to inheritance tax on settled property:
    (a) What is to be taken to be a settlement?
    (b) What property is referred to as property comprised in a settlement or as settled property?
13. Section 43(2) supplies the definition of "settlement" to be applied in answering each of these questions. It should be noted that s 43 does not specifically address a numerical question: what is the number of relevant settlements existing in a particular inheritance tax situation? In the absence of specific statutory provisions the answer to the numerical question is to be found in the general law of trusts.
14. There would appear to be no difficulty in answering each question in Mr Richard Utley's case if the provisions of s 43 are applied in their ordinary and natural sense.
15. As for question (a) in paragraph 12 above, the answer is that each of the five trust deeds executed by Mr Richard Utley is to be taken to be "a settlement" for the purposes of the 1984 Act, because each of them satisfies the definition of "settlement" in s 43(2)(b). It logically follows that there are five settlements.
16. As for question (b) in paragraph 12 above, the answer in respect of each of the five settlements, which satisfy the statutory definition, is that " the property comprised

156 IHTA 1984, s 64.

in a settlement" is 6,900 shares in the Company, and not the totality of 34,500 shares.

CIR Submissions

17. The CIR submit that this simple analysis is flawed, as it ignores the effect of the key concept of a "disposition or dispositions of property" referred to in the opening words of s 43(2). In particular, Park J's approach was wrong, as he failed to give effect to the provision expanding "disposition" to include a "disposition by associated operations." The effect of that provision is to extend the state of affairs relevant for inheritance tax purposes under s 43 beyond what would normally constitute a settlement under the general law of trusts. The CIR contend that this error occurred because, although Park J began by asking the correct question (i.e. *What is a settlement* for the purposes of s 43?), he in fact concluded by answering a different question (*Was there a settlement* for the purposes of s 43?). If he had answered the correct question, he should have held that there was, in the case of each brother, only one settlement for inheritance tax purposes and that it comprised all the shares in the Company settled by that brother.
18. Section 272 of the 1984 Act provides that:
" In this Act, except where the context otherwise requires,-
"disposition" includes a disposition by associated operations;"
19. "Associated operations" are defined by s 268(1) as meaning:
". . . .any two or more operations of any kind, being–
(a) operations which affect the same property, or one of which affects some property and the other or others of which affect property which represents, whether directly or indirectly, that property, or income arising from the property, or any property representing accumulations of any such income, or
(b) any two operations of which one is effected with reference to the other, or with a view to enabling the other to be effected for facilitating its being effected, and any further operation having a like relation to any of those two, and so on,
whether those operations are effected by the same person or different persons and whether or not they are simultaneous; and "operation" includes an omission."
20. Relying on those provisions, the CIR submit that the establishment of the five identical, parallel settlements and the subsequent transfers of the shares to the trustee of each settlement were to be treated as "a disposition or dispositions" creating a single settlement. They were "dispositions by associated operations" within s 268, each of the settlements being an "operation" horizontally linked and associated with four other operations establishing the settlements, and each of the subsequent issues and transfers of the deferred shares in the Company being vertically linked and associated with each settled fund. The result of the composite "disposition or dispositions" of shares to five different funds by "associated operations" was to constitute a single settlement under s 43. That single settlement is a discretionary settlement within s 43 for the purposes of, and subject to, the charge to inheritance tax under s 64. . . .

Conclusion

23. In my judgment, the definition of "disposition" in s 272 so as to include a disposition by "associated operations", as defined in s 268, does not affect the suggested answers in paragraphs 15 and 16 above to the relevant questions arising under s 43. The definition of "settlement" in s 43(2) is supplied for the purpose of determining the two questions raised by s 43(1): first, what is to be taken as a settlement? And, secondly, what property is comprised in a settlement? As already indicated, it is sufficient for the purposes of determining those questions to find that there were undoubtedly "dispositions" of property into five settlements falling within s 43(2)(b). There has never been any dispute that there were "dispositions" of the shares in the Company, whereby they were held on discretionary trusts within the meaning of s 43. Both questions arising under s 43(2) can be determined without asking any

additional questions, such as whether the dispositions were by "associated operations." The identity of the disponer and the disponee under the dispositions and the subject matter of the dispositions are plain. The inclusion of "associated operations" in the statutory description of "disposition" is not intended for cases, such as this, where there is no dispute that there was a "disposition" of property falling within section 43(2). They are intended for cases where there is a dispute as to whether there was a relevant "disposition" at all. The CIR may be entitled to invoke the extended description to catch a case which would not be regarded as a "disposition" of property in its ordinary and natural sense.

24. In this case the CIR are not seeking to use the extended sense of "disposition" to determine what is to be taken as a settlement or what is the property comprised in a settlement. They are seeking to use it for the purpose of determining the different question of counting how many settlements there are in a given case. The provisions do not entitle the CIR, in the absence of clear language, to conduct the exercise of shrinking the number of settlements, which satisfy the definition of a "settlement" in s 43(2), or to aggregate the settled property comprised in each of the separate settlements, so as to treat, for inheritance tax purposes, property subject to discrete settlements as if it were comprised, along with other settled property, in a single settlement.

25. Like Park J, I am unable to accept the CIR's submission as to the correct interpretation and application of s 43 of the 1984 Act. I agree with, and find it impossible to improve upon, the judge's concise and clear statement of his reasoning in para 17 i) –iv) of his excellent judgment:

"i) As a matter of the general law Mr Utley made five settlements, not one.

ii) Section 43 does not change the position: under the terms of section 43, as under the general law, Mr Utley made five settlements, not one. In saying that, I am applying section 43 on the basis that the word "disposition" in it has its ordinary meaning: in the present case the word need not be, and is not, extended to include a disposition by associated operations. (As to whether it would make any difference if it was so extended, see vi) below.

iii) In the case of each of the five settlements, the property comprised within it was within the scope of the ten-yearly IHT charge under section 64 which arose in February or March 1994. There were five charges, calculated on the basis (corresponding to the actual legal position both under the general law and under section 43) that each of the settlements was a separate settlement.

iv) All of the property comprised in the five settlements was within the ten-yearly charge because each settlement was created by a "disposition" in the ordinary sense. In order to bring the property within the charge it was not necessary or appropriate to consider whether the five settlements were created by associated operations." **[21.57]**

Index

[all references are to paragraph number]